ANTIQUE MAP
PRICE RECORD
&
HANDBOOK
FOR 1995

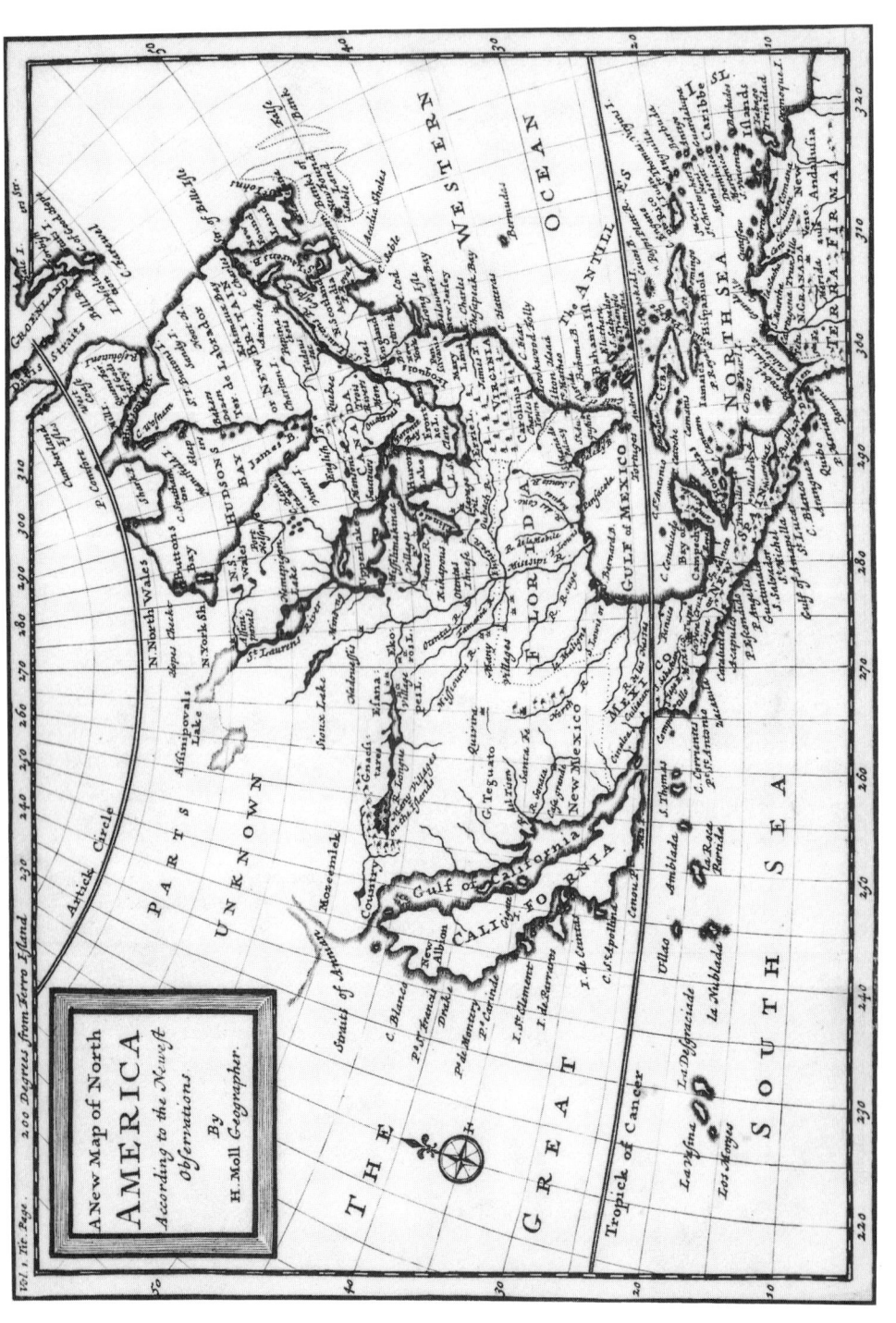

ANTIQUE MAP PRICE RECORD & HANDBOOK FOR 1995

Including SEA CHARTS, CITY VIEWS, CELESTIAL CHARTS and BATTLE PLANS

Compiled and edited
by
Jon K. Rosenthal

Amherst, Massachusetts
Kimmel Publications
1995

Copyright © 1995 by Jon K. Rosenthal. All rights reserved.

Portions of introductory remarks originally copyrighted by David C. Jolly.

Volume 13

ISBN 0-9638100-2-2   ISSN 1070-8421

Library of Congress Catalog Card Number 94-640696

Printed in the United States of America

Volumes 1 and 2 appeared as *Antique Maps, Sea Charts, City Views, Celestial Charts & Battle Plans: Price Guide and Collectors' Handbook* (ISSN 0747-7597)

Volumes 3 through 10 appeared as *Antique Maps, Sea Charts, City Views, Celestial Charts & Battle Plans: Price Record & Handbook* (ISSN 0749-4971)

Volumes 11 and 12 appeared as *Antique Map Price Record & Handbook* (ISSN 1070-8421)

Ordering information appears on Page 370. Requests for information, communications to the editor and all other correspondence should be sent to:

Jon K. Rosenthal
Kimmel Publications
P.O. Box 12
Amherst, Massachusetts 01004, USA

Frontispiece: Herman Moll's map of North America from *The British Empire in America, Containing The History of the Discovery, Settlement, Progress and present State of all the British Colonies, on the Continent and Islands of America.* London, Printed for John Nicholson ... and Richard Parker and Ralph Smith ..., 1708. (Courtesy of Amherst Antiquarian Maps, Amherst, Massachusetts.)

CONTENTS

PREFACE	vi
NEWS AND COMMENTS	1

HOW TO USE THE *PRICE RECORD*
     Standard Form of Map Entries
     Factors Affecting Value
	5

RECOMMENDED REFERENCES	8
BOOK REVIEWS Cumulative Index of Books Reviewed	11
GLOSSARY OF TERMS	20

FOREIGN LANGUAGE DICTIONARIES
     Dutch-English; French-English; German-English;
     Italian-English; Latin-English
	25

DEALERS' CONCERNS: Catalogues Dealer Questionnaire – 41	39

DIRECTORY OF DEALERS
     United States Dealers; Canadian Dealers;
     International Dealers
	42

CUMULATIVE FREQUENCY DISTRIBUTION OF MAP-MAKERS with Sketches of Map-Makers	65

PRICE LISTING
     References Cited – 284
     Abbreviations Used – 287
	101

TITLE INDEX	288
GEOGRAPHICAL INDEX	351
ORDERING INFORMATION; Other Publications	370
CUMULATIVE ERRATA	372
CURRENCY CONVERSION TABLES	373
CATALOGUE CODES	374

PREFACE

This year's edition is the first to be produced entirely without the presence and counsel of the originator, the late David C. Jolly. It follows that the successes and shortcomings are entirely the responsibility of the new editor and publisher. We apologize for the delay in issuing Volume 13. It fell behind the schedule we had intended which was for a release in the spring. We'll try again next year.

Almost 4800 entries are included in this edition of *Antique Map Price Record & Handbook*, up over ten percent from when we took over in 1993. The total series has now reported on over 61,000 antique maps offered for sale. With more information for each entry and the merging of "Sketches of Map-Makers" with the "Cumulative Frequency Distribution of Map-Makers" table this year, the page count has been increased, but not without some sacrifice of introductory material. Much of the early sections of the *Price Record* were repetitive from year to year. We believe that what remains is more current and robust.

We have urged the dealers who are listed in the directory to return a questionnaire (such as appears on Page 41) every two years so that the reader can be reasonably assured that the information is up to date. Those who have complied with our request are so indicated with a [•] before their name. The listing of dealers world-wide not only points to a source of antiquarian maps, but also to a vast reservoir of knowledge and expertise as well.

ACKNOWLEDGMENTS

We are grateful to the many dealers in antiquarian maps who have provided the catalogues that form the basis of the information in *Antique Map Price Record & Handbook*. The data we have extracted from these sources is but a small portion of the wealth of knowledge that these dealers represent. We consult with Thomas Aalund, of Trade Winds Gallery in Mystic, Connecticut in matters of German translation. The Price Record could hardly continue to exist without the patience and assistance of my wife, Bernice Massé Rosenthal, who is virtually the co-editor. The errors and omissions are wholly my responsibility.

Jon K. Rosenthal

WARNING!

Users of this work are warned that typographical errors may be present, and that prices for some items may not reflect the price that would be set by a majority of dealers. The publisher disclaims responsibility for any consequences of such errors and anomalies. Price information is given as an approximate guide to market values, and should be used with caution. An expert should always be consulted before making purchases or sales.

To Bernice
with admiration and love

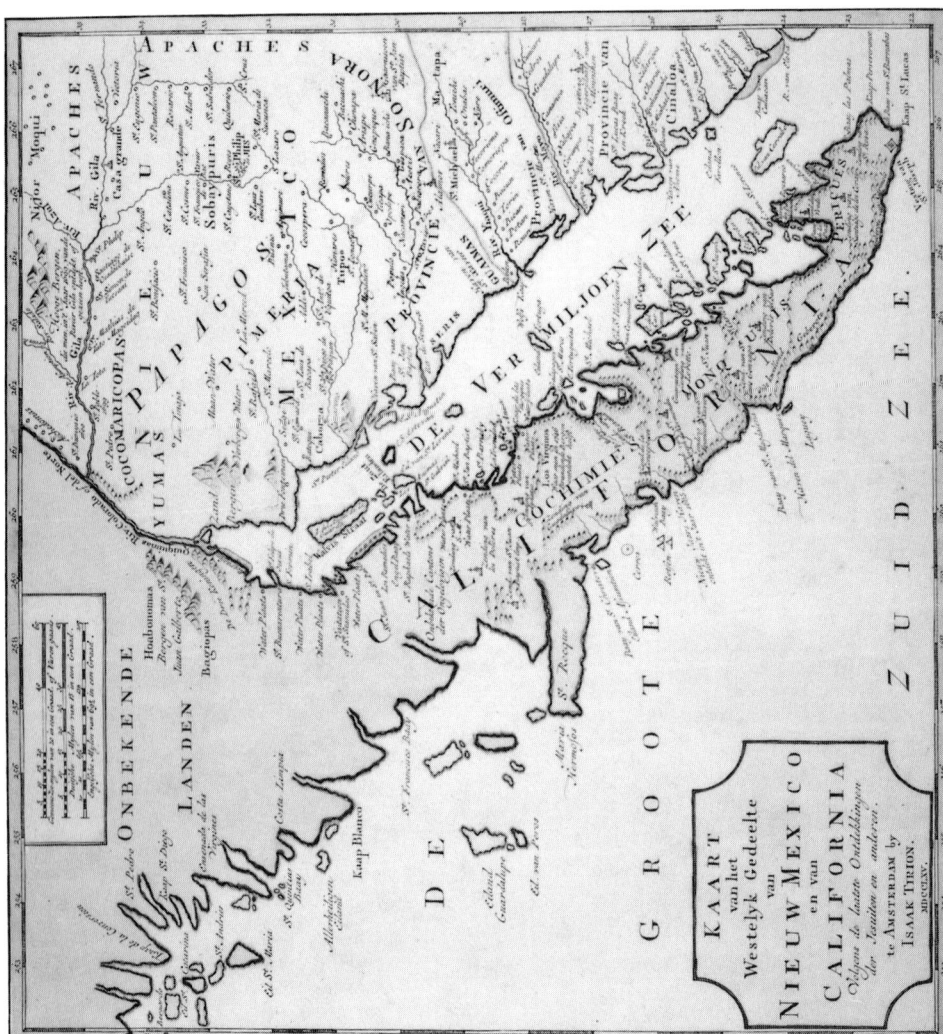

Isaak Tirion's map of present day Southern California and Arizona, with Mexico's Baja and Sonora. As from *Nieuwe en Beknopte Hand-Atlas*, Amsterdam: 1765 [1769]. Reference: Phillips (Atlases) 600, no.102.

With its northern inlets and estuaries shrouded in mist, California might well be taken to be an island, as indeed it is in the frontispiece example by Herman Moll.

It would have been one of the world's largest islands, had not Father Kino determined during his missionary travels in the Baja and the "mainland" interior that California was firmly attached to the continent.

Tirion's map follows Kino's view of California which is correct in concept, but awaits refinement along the Pacific coast.

NEWS and COMMENTS

One reason for the tardy release of Volume 13 is that we have completely converted to commercially available computer software from the very personalized system of gathering and manipulating data that David Jolly had developed over the years. David, borrowing from his M.I.T. experience, took pride in making his computer programs jump precisely through the hoops he had prescribed. The problem was that he was the only one who completely understood them and they were written in an antiquated version of *basic* that served as the channel from his data base to the word processor. We encountered another difficulty when upgrading our computer power while this edition was in "mid-stream". With new equipment and software, there is always a learning period, if only to put to use the brand new features that become available. But the incompatibility of two versions of a backup program from the same well known software company was unexpected. What would seem to have been an easy transfer became a tedious and worrisome task. Our conclusion, not dissimilar to that of others, is that computers exact their own hidden price from those who rely on them.

About This Year's Edition

Sixty-four catalogues from twenty-eight dealers are included in the 1995 *Price* Record. The sampling includes 4,784 entries representing 580 map-makers. Total asking prices are more than $3,350,000 for an average of about $700 per map. There are more maps than last year; the average price is down a bit. What appears to be a proliferation of catalogues is actually a change in form. Some dealers are issuing smaller catalogues more frequently. When we spot a repeated offering of an apparently identical item it is only listed once. If the price has changed, the most recent price is given. More framed items are being offered than previously. These are listed, and so noted, only if it is deemed that the value added by the frame is but a small fraction of the total.

This year, *Cumulative Frequency Distribution of Map-Makers* and *Sketches of Map-Makers* have been combined into a single table. "Sketches" had not been brought up to date since the earlier "David Jolly" days and was seriously out of synch with the expanding list of map-makers that ever appeared in the *Price Record*. In the process, an attempt has been made to identify which map-makers under a particular surname have actually been included in the Price Listing over the years. Sometimes it is not the most prominent individual who is cited.

The *Directory of Dealers* now includes an indication as to whether we have received an updating questionnaire within the last two years and if over half of the business is in antiquarian maps or closely related material. The purpose is to suggest if the information is up to date and whether the antique map component is central to the enterprise. The "over half" threshold may be misleading, however, in the case of a large establishment with a large volume in all areas.

The Accuracy of the Data

The *Price Record* provides tertiary information. It is drawn from dealer's catalogues, which themselves are secondary sources. After three years of publishing the A*ntique Map Price Record*, we have become accustomed to uneven accuracy among catalogues.

We have received mere lists of available maps that may be suitable for marketing purposes, but provide precious little additional information and do not qualify for inclusion in the *Price Record*. We do not guarantee the accuracy of the information provided to us. Where we are near certain of verbatim titles, dates, dimensions, or sources, we will correct information that is obviously erroneous or augment that which is lacking, but this can only be in a small proportion of the entries. With intervention, however, there is always the danger of tampering with an accurate report of an unusual variant which at first glance appears to be in error. When questions arise, however, we suggest you first check the entry with appropriate cartobibliographic sources, if possible, and then with the dealer issuing the catalogue. We make errors, but not many. When you catch them, we will check them and note the error in the next edition.

Another question of primary interest to buyers is "are the prices real?" Our suspicion, confirmed by the occasional specific report, is that they are not far off the mark for the maps that are sold. Many sell at the prices that are quoted; others sell at a modest discount, a common reciprocal courtesy among dealers. In other cases prices may be altered -- lowered or raised -- to better conform to market conditions. Prices may be reduced when a large quantity is sold or to reduce inventory. Some marketing strategies involve high pricing levels with the expectation of making reductions. None of these procedures are alien to examples in other industries such as automobiles or airline services. In our own experience as dealers, we have frowned on discounting as part of the sales technique, simply as a matter of fairness to customers with differing levels of sophistication, personality and aggressiveness. While buyers may wonder if discounts are available, they should take a negative reply with good grace and the realization that pricing policies vary among dealers. Perhaps it is best to think of *the Antique Map Price Record* as the Antique Map <u>Pricing</u> Record.

How's the U.S. Dollar Doing? Does It Matter?

Much press has been given to the weakness of the U.S. dollar in recent months. It is worthwhile looking at the record against other major currencies since 1982 which was the first year cited in the "Currency Conversion Tables" in the *Price Record* The following table gives the number of money units of each in terms of U.S. dollars. A high number is a measure of the dollars strength; declining numbers mean a weakening dollar.

Number per US $	'82	'83	'84	'85	'86	'87	'88	'89	'90	'91	'92	'93	'94	'95
BRITAIN. Pound	0.57	0.65	0.73	0.76	0.64	0.61	0.58	0.64	0.57	0.62	0.52	0.66	0.64	0.63
CANADA. Dollar	1.29	1.23	1.31	1.35	1.37	1.33	1.21	1.19	1.16	1.14	1.20	1.28	1.38	1.37
FRANCE. Franc	6.83	7.63	8.53	9.26	6.94	6.01	6.12	6.63	5.61	6.13	5.11	5.74	5.45	4.84
GERMANY. Mark	2.46	2.54	2.78	3.04	2.17	1.82	1.81	1.95	1.67	1.82	1.52	1.70	1.59	1.38
JAPAN. Yen	255	239	237	248	162	146	133	144	152	138	125	107	98.5	84.9

Three patterns emerge: The first is the case of fluctuation up and down around a central figure as with the British pound and the Canadian dollar. Second is the case of slow, uneven decline in value over the years as exemplified by continental currencies, pronounced in the case of the German mark, but also evident with the French franc. Finally there is the case of inexorable decline in terms of the Japanese yen against which the dollar is at about one-third of its 1982 value.

Exchange rates mean little if there is little trade. Among countries with significant trade in antiquarian maps, a strong currency makes it easy to buy abroad and hard to sell, but adverse exchange rates in a major buying nation can have negative feedback on prices in the selling country.

Nevertheless, since antiques are generally inelastic in supply, especially in the case of older material, demand will be the driving factor in price over the years. Collecting antique maps was never the occupation of a pauper, even when they were cheap. There is no sign that demand is slackening, nor has there been a transient demand spike reflecting a fad, trendiness or a buying frenzy. Perhaps the intellectual nature of antiquarian maps precludes such foolishness. The inelasticity of supply and slow, steady increase in demand should overwhelm exchange rates as a pricing factor in the long run.

Map Societies

This spring we had the pleasure of attending the inaugural meeting of the Boston Map Society which was held in the rooms of the Harvard Map Collection in Pusey Library. A fine exhibition of early maps lined the walls to complement a talk by Robert Karrow of the Newberry Library on "Ortelius and Friends; a Celebration of 16th Century Maps." More than 125 people were in attendance.

Over the years, we have found *map society* gatherings to be an enlightening and even a thrilling experience. One can count on meeting people who have become especially knowledgeable in their areas of interest and are eager to exchange ideas and information. We have assembled a list of North American map societies and their contact people and would be grateful for corrections of further information about similar organizations in the United States or abroad.

- Boston Map Society; David A. Cobb, Harvard Map Collection, Harvard College Library, Cambridge, MA 02138; (617) 495-2417; E-mail: cobb@fas.harvard.edu
- California Map Society; Alfred W. Newman, 1414 Mariposa St., Vallejo, CA 94590; (707) 642-9091
- Chicago Map Society; c/o Robert W. Karrow, Newberry Library, 60 West Walton St., Chicago, IL 60610-3380; (312) 943-9090
- Map Society of Arizona; Jack Mount, sec., Science-Engineering Library, Univ. of Arizona, Tucson 85721; (602) 621-2823, E-mail: mount @ ccit.arizona.edu
- Map Society of British Columbia; P.O. Box 37109, 2930 Lonsdale Ave., North Vancouver, British Columbia, Canada
- Michigan Map Society; P.O. Box 1201, Ann Arbor, MI 48106
- New York Map Society; c/o Map Division, The New York Public Library; Fifth Ave. and 42nd St., New York, NY 10018-2788
- Northern Ohio Map Group; c/o Cleveland Public Library, Map Collection, 325 Superior Ave., Cleveland, OH 44114
- Rocky Mountain Map Society; c/o Wes Brown, 1726 Hudson St., Denver, CO 80220; (303) 333-0568
- Washington Map Society; c/o Robert Highbarger, 7509 Hackamore Drive, Potomac, MD 20854

Symposia, Fairs and Periodicals

The 14th annual IMCoS International Symposium (International Map Collectors' Society) returns to the United States this year to meet in San Francisco from October 8 to 11, 1995, hosted by the California Map Society. The program includes a map fair, auction, lectures, panel discussions and planned visits and tours. For general information, contact Al Newman, '95 IMCos Chair, 1414 Mariposa St., Vallejo, CA 94590; Tel (707) 642) 9091. -- Next year its Riga.

We received the schedule of the Bonnington Fair for 1995, "The Only Monthly Antique Map Fair in the World." For the rest of 1995: August 14, September 11, October 9, November 13, and December 11. The fair is at the Bonnington Hotel, Southampton Row, London. Admission is free. The announcement lists 14 regular exhibitors.

The Annual Miami Map Fair is noteworthy because it appears to be the first ongoing yearly *antiquarian map* fair to be held in the Western Hemisphere. This represents a breakthrough for the map trade which is always a bit of a stranger in either paper, antique or book fairs. The 3rd annual event will be held at Miami's Historical Museum of Southern Florida on February 24 and 25, 1996. Contact Marcia Kanner at (305) 375-1492. With the Florida show, old maps have found a home in the United States.

Cartomania is the quarterly (often combined to semiannual) Newsletter of the Association of Map Memorabilia Collectors based at 8 Amherst Road, Pelham, MA 01002, USA. Dues are $12.50 in the U.S. and Canada ($17 elsewhere). All forms of cartography are addressed, with much coverage of more recent material.

Imago Mundi. The Journal of the International Society for the History of Cartography. Currently a 180 page scholarly journal with new studies or summaries of current information on maps and cartographers. Imago Mundi, 'Meadow Bank', 26 Lucastes Road, West Sussex RH16 1JW, United Kingdom. As of 1994, the current volume and society membership was £30 per year or $60.

The Map Collector. Published quarterly, with articles on early maps and map collecting, auction records, dealer advertisements and classifieds. Map Collector Publications, Ltd., 48 High Street, Tring, Hertfordshire HP23 5BH, England; £30 per year in the U.K., £35 in other countries, $56 per year in the United States.

The *Nurembega News, Newsletter of the Osher Library Associates* announced the opening of the Osher Map Library of the University of Southern Maine, 314 Forest Avenue, Portland ME, 04101-2000, USA. Call (207) 780-4850 for schedule. After the initial event, *The Land of Norembega*, an exhibition *Maine 175* [years] is planned. In October 1996 the library will host the annual meeting of the Society for Historical Discoveries.

Keep an Eye on Your Jollys

We received a call from a long standing subscriber inquiring about the availability of back issues of David Jolly's *Antique Maps, Sea Charts, City Views, Celestial Charts & Battle Plans* ... It seems that some of the earlier editions had been stolen. You may recall his remarks in Volume 11, in which he described the role of the *Price Record and Handbook* in replacing loose maps in their proper volumes following the apprehension of a library stock thief who had used the books as a guide to the crime. David would have been flattered, but dismayed, to have his own work become the object of larceny. Replacement will be difficult, because Volumes 1 through 10 are out of print.

HOW TO USE THE *PRICE RECORD*

Antique Map Price Record & Handbook is composed of six parts:
1. Reference material.
2. Cumulative Frequency Distribution of Map-Makers.
3. Main PRICE LISTING with References cited.
4. Title index to main price listing.
5. Geographical index to main price listing.
6. Currency conversion table and catalogue codes.

The reference material includes recommended references, reviews of recent books, a glossary of terms, brief foreign language dictionaries of Dutch, French, German, Italian and Latin into English, and a directory of dealers. This year, Sketches of Map-Makers has been folded into the Cumulative Frequency Distribution of Map-Makers.

Most readers want to know if an old map of interest to them is listed in the *Price Record*. The first step is to see if any names appear on the map or view. If so, then try under that name in the main **Price Listing**. If not found there, then try the **Title Index**. If still not found, and if there were no entries in the main listing under the names on the map or view, then try the indexed **Cumulative Frequency Distribution of Map-Makers** to see if there were any entries under those names in past years.

Standard Form of Map Entries

The *Price Record* is organized by Map-Makers. Maps attributed to a particular map-maker are all listed under his name in the *Price Listing*. There are a number of special categories for maps not involving personal names or names of private companies. These include governmental entities such as *British Admiralty* or *U.S. Pacific R.R. Survey*, maps printed in non-Roman letters, including East Asian cartography, and various thematic or "catch-all" categories such as *Anonymous or Unknown, Manuscript Maps*; *Local and State Maps* and *Railroad Company Maps* that were previously listed under the individual rail line. Maps from the early editions of Ptolemy's Geography are generally listed under Ptolemy; the later editions by Münster, Gastaldi, Ruscelli and Magini are listed under their names. Maps in Cyrillic characters are normally listed under their transliterated author and titles. A full listing of the thematic categories appear at the start of the Cumulative Frequency Distribution on Page 65. A typical entry follows:

BLAEU
MOLUCCAE INSULAE CELEBERRIMAE [1635] From *Theatre du Monde* .... 38x48cm (15x19") Orig color. Excel. Ref: Koeman Bl 12.   [10] £330 $495

Map-Maker. The name is in boldfaced, large capitals letters. Assigning an item to a particular name is somewhat arbitrary. For example, a map may have been surveyed by Smith, drawn by Jones, engraved by Black, published by White in an atlas edited by Brown, and then reissued in another atlas published by Green. There is no consistent standard for assigning a map to one of these names. The name assignments in this book generally follow custom. For example, maps from atlases published by Ortelius, the Blaeu family or Mathew Carey are usually assigned to Ortelius, Blaeu and Carey rather than to the name of a cartographer that might appear on the map itself.

Title. Given in bold capital letters. This is not always straightforward. Some maps have two titles, more than a single title cartouche, or a title repeated in another language. Maps without a title are supplied with a descriptive title in square brackets [ ]. In other cases a dealer might have paraphrased or abbreviated the title. Diacritical marks such as umlauts and accents are omitted here. Where appropriate, "U" and "V" are given in their intended form, for example, NOUA is transcribed as NOVA.

Date. Given next, in square brackets. Usually the date given in the catalogue. This may be either the date of first appearance or the date of actual publication of the map or both.

Remarks. If present, these follow the date and may include the source of the map and any other brief information of relevance to the map in general.

Dimensions. Size is given to the nearest centimeter – height first and width second – followed, in parentheses, by dimensions rounded to the closest half-inch. Dimensions are usually for the outer neat line, but in some cases may represent the plate mark size, or the paper size. Diameters are expressed as a single figure.

Color. Antique maps come in a variety of color styles. They may be in full color (also called wash color or body color); full color to the primary subject; outline color of the political subdivisions; highlight color for features such as cities; map border color; cartouche color; any combination of the above heightened with gold, and not least -- uncolored. Before the printed color of the mid to late 19th-century, all coloring was by hand.

Condition. A condensed phrasing of the dealer's statement of condition is given. Some dealers say nothing of condition; others issue a blanket statement covering an entire catalogue except as noted. Expansive laudatory comments are omitted. Terms in general use describing condition are reported, – usually ranging from "mint" or "pristine" to "fair" and rarely "poor" – with the caveat that in the antiquarian map trade there is little agreement as to the meaning of the words.

References. Increasingly, dealers are making use of references to direct the reader to a further source of information or an illustration. When given, they are reported.

Catalogue Code. The number in square brackets (just before price) corresponds to the catalogue in which the map was offered for sale. The key can be found at the end of the book.

Price. Given in both pounds and dollars. The conversion rates at mid-year, used in computing the prices, are given at the end of the book. Note, however, that the volatility of relative currency values in the course of a year may significantly affect prices across borders. Although the same item may appear at different prices, it cannot be inferred that one is overpriced, or the other underpriced. Condition is extremely important and may not be adequately described in but a few words.

Factors Affecting Value

Historical importance. Maps which are pivotal in the history of exploration and cartography tend to be in great demand. Particularly sought after are maps that are the first to show some discovery or event. Examples might be maps initially revealing features of the New World or with the first depiction of an important battle. A derivative map of similar appearance, published a few years later, might be worth considerably less.

Region depicted. This factor is probably most important in explaining the wide range in the price of maps from a given source, say an atlas by Ortelius, Blaeu, or Sanson. "World" maps are of global interest; demand is high and prices follow. Collectors in certain countries have developed a fondness for antique maps, particularly of their own regions. Other regions in demand include Bermuda, some of the West Indian islands and, increasingly, Japan and the Far East. Maps of other areas, which may be remote, less affluent or with alternative cultural interests, tend to be less expensive.

The Map-Maker. For similar maps, the maker can strongly influence the price. To take one example, Ortelius and de Jode both produced similar maps at about the same time. However, Ortelius produced far more editions of his atlas, making de Jode maps relatively scarce by comparison. Thus, de Jode maps appear far less frequently on the market; that is, the supply is less. The result is that maps of comparable areas from de Jode's atlas are considerably more expensive than those of Ortelius.

Age. For similar maps, the older map is generally the more valuable. But age as the sole basis of evaluation is risky, since some maps from the 1500s fetch far less than some from the 19th century.

Size. For maps of about equal age and subject matter, larger maps tend to be more valuable. Folio maps of an area will bring considerably more than miniature or pocket versions by the same map-maker. Larger maps allow for more detail and decoration.

Aesthetic qualities. Many buyers intend to frame their maps for display. A map with sea monsters, scrollwork, decorative borders, sailing ships, gargoyles, putti, and the like are more tempting to such buyers, and consequently decorative maps sell for a premium.

Color. Since most decorative maps look better colored, these are the maps in highest demand. Collectors seem to agree that original color commands a premium, but this is where agreement ends. Some prefer the original condition whether with color or without. Others may choose good modern color instead of an uncolored original. Most agree that no coloring is preferable to a bad, unskilled application of modern color, if for no other reason than that the option remains to have color skillfully applied by a knowledgeable artisan in a way that is historically plausible. Some maps were almost never colored, such as Dudley's sea charts and U.S. Coast Survey maps. Knowledgeable collectors might refuse to buy such items if colored. A few collectors even prefer uncolored examples under any circumstances to better appreciate the engraving. While sometimes it may be difficult to guarantee original color, it may be easier to confirm a suspicion of modern color.

Condition. Condition plays a major role in pricing. When a map is extremely rare, condition may be relatively unimportant, since choice may be simply "to have or to have not." With maps in greater supply, condition becomes a discriminating factor. Problems affecting appearance are more serious for a decorative map than for an item primarily of historical value. While very minor flaws, such as tiny spot stains or a slight crease, generally have only a minimal effect on value, more serious problems can cause a substantial disparity in price between copies of the same item. Factors affecting condition include:

Stains. Foreign matter such as ink or coffee can be spilled on a map. Water spills, even of clean water, leave stains by redistributing soluble material in the paper. Browning, caused by oxidation, tends to occur at the centerfold, where paste contacts the paper. It also tends to occur at the edges of atlas maps, where the paper was more exposed to airborne pollutants. Sometimes the entire map browns. Mildew spots, called foxing, also occurs. Stains in the printed area are more serious than stains in the blank margin.

Tears. Many maps eventually develop rips and tears from handling and use. Large folding maps such as those from Moll's *The World Described* ..., tend to develop weaknesses and tears along the fold lines. Maps folding into books are stressed at the corner of the guard holding them into the book. Maps in atlases often develop tears or separations at the centerfold. Tears affecting only the blank margin are considered less serious than tears entering the printed area. Professional restorers can make reversible repairs which are almost invisible. Under no circumstance should repairs be made with non-archival self-adhesive tapes.

Margins. The blank margins of maps may get trimmed over the years. It may be the work of the original binder, a recent framer, or it may be a means of removing flaws from a chipped or torn margin. Trimming reduces value, especially if the margin is less than about one-quarter inch (5 mm.), making it difficult to mat for display. A few maps normally have narrow margins, among them the larger Dutch sea charts.

Creases. This is a minor fault. Folding maps, or maps with centerfolds, will always show traces of the folds, and this does not affect the value. Multiple and repeated hard creasing from mis-folding can be visually intrusive and detracts from value.

Backing. Sometimes maps are pasted or glued to cheap backing, such as cardboard, pressboard, or brown paper. This can substantially reduce value. Paper conservators can often reverse this form of abuse with a minimum of side effects if modern mounting material has not been used. In other cases, maps are professionally backed, with thin tissue or rice paper. This is acceptable when done to reinforce a weak or brittle item, but should not be done on a sound copy.

RECOMMENDED REFERENCES

The *general references* listed below may prove useful and interesting for the novice as well as the seasoned collector. The list is necessarily brief; there are scores, even hundreds, of fine books dealing with antique maps. Next is a list of *specialized references*, arranged alphabetically by category, focusing on particular regions or aspects of antiquarian maps. The list is more suggestive than comprehensive; books can be found on almost any aspect of antique maps. Most of these books were published before the initiation of the *Price Record* reviews in 1985 and have never been the subject of a review in these pages. Many are still in print or are available as used books from map dealers. For additional recently published books, see this year's "Book Reviews" and "Cumulative Index of Books Reviewed".

Dealers are providing much more in the way of documentation in their catalogues. With the proliferation of citations, we have returned to the earlier practice of listing "References Cited" separately. This list follows the "Price Listing" and constitutes an additional reference source.

General References

Bagrow, Leo, *The History of Cartography,* Chicago: Precedent Publishing, Inc., 1985. R.A. Skelton, ed. This is perhaps the most highly regarded book on old maps, although not specifically about collecting. The text is definitive, and the numerous plates, some in color, are of the highest quality.

Brown, Lloyd A., *The Story of Maps,* Boston: Little, Brown & Co., 1949. Reprinted by Dover Books, New York. A readable and scholarly history of map-making.

Imago Mundi. The Journal of the International Society for the History of Cartography, a scholarly periodical with articles on early maps, reports and news. Back issues available. (Imago Mundi, Meadow Bank, 26 Lucastes Road, West Sussex, RH 16 1JW, U.K.; Vol. 45, £30, $60)

Lister, Raymond, *Antique Maps & their Cartographers* London: G. Bell & Sons Ltd., 1970. This is a very fine introductory book for collectors.

Lister, Raymond, *Old Maps & Globes,* London: Bell & Hyman, 1979. An exceptionally fine introductory book. Ample material on early cartography, map-making techniques, and early globes is supplemented with a lengthy dictionary of map-makers and illustrations of about 200 watermarks.

Koeman, I.C., *Atlantes Neerlandici: Bibliography of terrestrial, Maritime and celestial atlases and pilot books, published in the Netherlands up to 1880,* 5 vols. Amsterdam: Theatrum Orbis Terrarum, 1967-71.

Map Collector, The. Published quarterly since 1977. Highly polished and illustrated; *articles* of general and special interest on early maps and map collecting, with news of the field, and dealer advertisements and classifieds. (Map Collector Publications, Ltd., 48 High Street, Tring, Hertfordshire HP23 5BH, U.K.; £29 per year, $51 in the U.S.)

Map Collectors' Series, London: The Map Collectors' Circle. 110 numbered issues in 11 volumes, 1964-1974.

Mickwitz, Ann-Mari, *The A.E. Nordenskiold Collection in the Helsinki University Library: Annotated Catalogue of Maps Made up to 1800.* 3 vols. Includes full collations of atlas maps in the collection and maps from books of travels and voyages which are seldom listed elsewhere. [Vol. 3 reviewed in 1986]

Moreland, C. & D. Bannister, *Antique Maps: A Collector's Handbook,* Oxford: Phaidon/Christies, 1986. A superior reference, with many illustrations and much useful information. [reviewed in 1987]

Nordenskiöld, A.E., *Facsimile-Atlas to the Early History of Cartography,* Stockholm, 1889. Reprinted by Dover Publications, New York. Although somewhat out of date, a useful reference work for those interested in maps of the 15th and 16th centuries. There are almost 200 illustrations of old maps.

Phillips, Philip L., *A List of Geographical Atlases in the Library of Congress*, Vols. I-IV, continued by Clara Egli LeGear, Vols. 5-8. Washington: Government Printing Office, 1909 through 1974. Volumes I through IV reprinted in two volumes at Amsterdam: Theatrum Orbis Terrarum, 1971. An exhaustive listing of the Library's extensive collection of atlases. Many are collated or with a list of maps pertaining to America. May be difficult to use due to complicated indexing, but becomes easier with familiarity.

Skelton, R.A., *Decorative Printed Maps of the 15th to 18th Centuries,* London: Spring Books, 1965. A good reference for collectors of decorative maps. There are 84 plates, some in color.

Tooley, R.V., *Maps and Map-Makers,* New York: Crown Publishers, 1982, revised ed. Perhaps the most useful general purpose book for map collectors. It is always reasonably priced and usually in print. *Buy it!*

Tooley, R.V., *Tooley's Dictionary of Mapmakers* 1979, and *Tooley's Dictionary of Mapmakers, Supplement* 1985, New York: Alan R. Liss, Inc., & Amsterdam: Meridian Publishing Co. These books give information about almost any cartographer likely to be encountered. Recommended for *all* dealers. [reviewed in 1987]

Tooley, R.V., C. Bricker, & G.R. Crone, *Landmarks of Mapmaking,* New York: Thomas Y. Crowell, 1976. Numerous illustrations, including folding color plates, and an informative text make this an excellent book for the collector.

Wallis, H.M. & A.H. Robinson, eds., *Cartographical Innovations: An international handbook of mapping terms to 1900,* Tring: Map Collector Publications, Ltd., 1987. Contains a wealth of information on early mapping, with numerous references for further reading. [reviewed in 1988]

Wilford, J.N., *The Mapmakers,* New York: Alfred A. Knopf, 1981. Very similar to Brown's book, this is essentially a history of cartography, and good background reading for the collector.

Specialized References

AMERICA: Phillips, Philip L., *A List of Maps of America in the Library of Congress Preceded by a List of Works Relating to Cartography*, Washington: Government Printing Office, 1901. This is the starting point in looking up any American map, and is normally found at the right hand of all dealers in American maps.

ANIMALS: George, Wilma, *Animals & Maps,* Berkeley: University of California Press, 1969. A zoologist finds that the animals decorating old maps are not mythical beasts located at random. On the contrary, old maps turn out to be an interesting source of zoological data. This is not an essential book, but it is fun to read.

BRITISH PERIODICALS, 18th CENTURY: Jolly, David C., *Maps in British Periodicals: Part I, major monthlies before 1800* and *Part II, annuals, scientific periodicals & miscellaneous magazines, mostly before 1800* Brookline: David C. Jolly, 1989 & 1990. [reviewed in 1990 & 1991]

CELESTIAL: Warner, D., *The Sky Explored: Celestial Cartography 1500-1800*, New York: Alan R. Liss, Inc. & Amsterdam: Theatrum Orbis Terrarum, 1979. This is the definitive work on early celestial charts and should be obtained by anyone interested in that area of collecting. [reviewed in 1986]

HOLY LAND: Laor, Eran, *Maps of the Holy Land: Cartobibliography of Printed Maps, 1475-1900*, New York: Alan R. Liss, 1986. [reviewed in 1988]

NORTH AMERICA: Schwartz, Seymour I., & Ralph E. Ehrenberg, *The Mapping of America*, New York: Harry N. Abrams, Inc., 1980. A detailed, informative, and well-illustrated work of great value to collectors and dealers.

NORTH AMERICA: Sellers, John R. & Patricia M. van Ee, *Maps and Charts of North America and the West Indies 1750-1789: A guide to the collections in the Library of Congress*, Washington: Library of Congress, 1981. An excellent compilation of maps just before, during and right after the American Revolution.

RAILROADS: Modelski, Andrew M., *Railroad Maps of the United States: A selective annotated bibliography of original 19th-century maps in the Geography and Map Division of the Library of Congress*, Washington: Library of Congress, 1975.

UNITED STATES: Howes, Wright, *U.S.iana [1650-1950] A selective bibliography in which are described 11,620 uncommon and significant books relating to the continental portion of the United States*, revised and enlarged edition, New York: R.R. Bowker, 1962.

U.S. CITY VIEWS: Reps, John W., *Views and Viewmakers of Urban America: Lithographs of towns and cities in the United States and Canada, notes on the artists and publishers, and a union catalog of their work, 1825-1925*, Columbia: University of Missouri Press, 1984. [reviewed in 1985]

U.S. COMMERCIAL CARTOGRAPHY: Ristow, Walter W., *American Maps and Mapmakers: Commercial Cartography in the nineteenth century*, Detroit: Wayne State University Press, 1985. A scholarly treatment of this period. [reviewed in 1986]

U.S. PUBLISHED MAPS: Wheat, James C. & Christian F. Brun, *Maps and Charts Published in America before 1800: A bibliography*, London: Holland Press Ltd., 1985 (Revised 2nd ed.). Lists the 919 maps known in 1978.

U.S. WEST: Wheat, Carl I., *Mapping the Transmississippi West 1540-1861*, Vols. 1-5. San Francisco: Institute of Historical Cartography, 1958-63. The definitive work on maps of the American West.

WORLD: Shirley, Rodney W., *The Mapping of the World: Early printed world maps 1472-1700*, London: Holland Press Cartographica, 1983; 2nd edition, 1993. The definitive listing of early world maps.

See also the "**Cumulative Index of Books Reviewed**" starting on Page 15 and "**References Cited**" on Page 284 following the "Price Listing".

BOOK REVIEWS

We continue to receive the assistance of guest contributors who have helped in the review of books. The commentary remains the full responsibility of the editor, however. Books for review should be sent to Kimmel Publications, P.O. Box 12, Amherst, MA 01004, USA.

The following reviews are arranged alphabetically by author. The trim dimensions give height first. Bindings are characterized as cloth, hard cover (i.e., non-cloth), and paper. Most books can be ordered directly from the publisher. If available, addresses and prices are given. Since prices may change and a shipping charge is likely, it is wise to write or call the publisher for precise ordering information. In North America, most books by North American publishers can be ordered through book stores. Some map dealers also stock reference books as a helpful complement to their trade in antiquarian maps.

Manasek, Francis J. *Uncommon Value: A Rare Book Dealer's World*. Ann Arbor: Arbor Libri Press, 1995. ISBN 1-883817-02-1. 9 x 6 inches. 146 pp. Cloth with dustjacket. (Arbor Libri Press, P.O. Box 7024, Ann Arbor, MI 48107, or G.B. Manasek, Inc., Box 1204, Norwich, VT 05055, $20.00.)

At last, a readable bookseller memoir! The author, an established dealer in rare maps and books, shares some memorable experiences. Unlike the usual bookseller autobiography ("...I sold a book to Mr. X, then I bought a book from Mr. Y, then we had dinner..."), this fast-paced work tells you what it's like on the front lines of the antiquarian trade. The style is personal and many anecdotes enliven the narrative. Mr. Manasek, a keen observer of humanity, has traveled widely and operated shops both in America and England.

Along the way there are almost lyrical passages on the joys of travel, a moment of physical danger, idiosyncratic characters and many useful nuggets. For example, few people realize auction commissions are negotiable. The chapter on hazards of buying and selling at auction -- even with name-brand houses -- gives perspective to a poorly understood subject. Another chapter evaluates book fairs in America and Europe. The author's experience with shops is revealing, particularly his decision to open in London to profit from the American fantasy of England as the land where collectors always buy maps cheaply.

The author has no patience with folly or knavery. While bouquets are offered, the truncheon is brought out for villains. Names and details are changed to protect the guilty, but alert readers will learn about protecting themselves from shady practices.

It has been said no man is a hero to his bookseller, and Mr. Manasek demonstrates why this is so. Collectors will discover that many seemingly casual practices actually frustrate dealers and hamper building a collection.

There are a number of typographical errors, and tighter editing would have helped the flow of ideas. Nevertheless, the book is recommended both as a good read and for illuminating the inner workings of the rare book and map trade

Monmonier, Mark. *Drawing the Line: Tales of Maps and Cartocontroversy*. NY: Henry Holt and Company, 1994. ISBN 0-8050-2581-2. 9 x 6 inches. 351 pp. Numerous text illus.

While maps have the appearance of objectivity, they are in fact subjective documents. Although the information displayed may be scientifically verifiable, the selection of data to include, the emphasis placed on specific items, and the form of the map are all subjective decisions by the cartographer.

Mark Monmonier has written extensively on the uses and misuses of maps. His best know book is *How to Lie with Maps*. In *Drawing the Line* he looks at controversies in which maps become tools for propagandists, or even are the cause of disputes.

He starts with the debate over the Peters-Gall projection, which represents the relative area of land masses at the cost of distorting shapes. Despite Peters' claims that his politically correct projection was new, it actually had been devised in 1855 by one James Gall. It is not known where Peters studied cartography, but he was clearly expert at promotion, and received a great deal of favorable mention in the press, as well as a strong counter-attack from the cartographic establishment. Monmonier provides detailed and even-handed coverage of the debate.

Chapter headings such as "Place-Names, Ethnic Insults, and Ideological Renaming," "The Vinland Map, Columbus, and Italian-American Pride," and "Boundary Litigation and the Map as Evidence" reveal some of the flavor of the book. The history of the infamous Gerrymander map and distortion of electoral districts are covered, as well as where to put waste sites, and dealing with environmental and other hazards. Naturally, there are a number of maps in the text including several quite fascinating maps on the risk of earthquake and volcanic eruption in certain areas. This book is recommended to anyone wanting a better understanding of maps.

Shirley, Rodney W. *The Mapping of the World: Early Printed World Maps 1472 - 1700*. London: New Holland (Publishers) Ltd., 1993. ISBN 1-85368-271-3. 13½ x 10 inches. xlviii, 669 pp. 444 plates, 19 in color. Cloth with dustjacket. (Map Collector Publications, 48 High Street, Tring, Herts., HP23 5BH England. £130 including postage and packing at surface rates.)

This exemplary work was reviewed by David Jolly in 1985, but the appearance of a new edition requires comment. As Jolly wrote, "to criticize such an admirable effort is a bit like complaining that the Great Pyramid is dusty," and this review should be taken in that light.

During the decade since *The Mapping of the World* was first published much new information has come to light, and 182 entries are incorporated in the 19 page *Corrigenda and Addenda* at the beginning of the book. Subsequent material appears to be unaltered from earlier editions, excepting minor typographical changes. Presumably, the publisher decided against a complete rewrite for reasons of economy.

Regrettably, the new material is not incorporated in the index, necessitating additional work by readers wishing to look up a map. Also, the problems noted by Jolly have not been addressed, notably the uncertainty created by a combined rarity/significance table.

Having thus disposed with the picking of nits, this book remains a fine work which is highly recommended. Collectors without a copy should not hesitate to buy it. Because of the substantial cost, the decision is more perplexing for owners of earlier editions. It should be noted that the publisher lacks a North American distributor; consequently, many American map dealers have had difficulty obtaining the book and are not carrying it. The most convenient method of purchasing it is through *The Map Collector* above.

Walter, Lutz (editor). *Japan A Cartographic Vision: European Printed Maps from the Early 16th to the 19th Century*. Munich & New York: Prestel-Verlag, 1994. ISBN 3-7913-1321-5 (English trade edition) and 3-7913-1291-X (German trade edition). 12¼ x 9½ inches. 232 pp. 84 text illus. + 138 plates. (te Neues Publishing Company, 16 West 22nd Street, New York, NY 10010. $75.)

First published in German as a catalog to an exhibition organized for the German East-Asiatic Society in Tokyo on its 120th anniversary, the soft cover catalog (circa $40) was also issued in English and Japanese, and appears to be identical in content to the hard cover book. The soft cover version is not available to the trade, but it may be possible to obtain copies from the Japan Society Gallery in New York City where the exhibition also appeared.

The book opens with eleven well-illustrated essays on various aspects of European mapping of Japan, followed by a section of color plates and a catalog of maps in the exhibition. In addition there is a 4-page bibliography and, of particular interest to collectors, a list attempting to describe all pre-1800 European printed maps of Japan. Entries, which include several quite obscure items, contain short descriptions and note variant states. The book is well organized and production quality is excellent. This work is most welcome as there is a scarcity of English-language material on the mapping of Japan, and it is recommended to all who are interested in the subject.

Wheat, Carl I. *Mapping the Transmississippi West*. Five volumes bound in six: *From the Spanish Entrada to the Louisiana Purchase 1540-1804*, xiii, 264 pp; *From Lewis and Clark to Fremont 1804-1845*, xiii, 281 pp; *The Mexican War to the Boundary Survey 1846-1854*, xiii, 349 pp; *Pacific Railroad Surveys to the Onset of the Civil War 1855-1860*, xiii, 259 pp; *Civil War to the Geological Survey*, xviii, 487 pp in two parts; 376 map reproductions; 12 x 9 inches, cloth. Originally published in San Francisco: The Institute of Historical Cartography, 1957-1963; reprinted by Maurizio Martino Publisher & About Books, 1995. (Martino Fine Books & Publishing, 746 Mansfield City Road, Mansfield, CT. $600, $700 after Sept. 1995)

Carl Wheat's massive treatise is an essential reference for anyone with more than a passing interest in the American West. It is a history as much as a carto-bibliography and this breathes life into adventures that the mapping implies. The Spanish come from the south; then the French from the east; next the English from the north; finally the Americans flood in to populate a continental region. Clearly, it is a Eurocentric approach, for the untold story is of Native Americans who certainly must have had magnificent maps of the mind which, as Wheat suggests, may have been given an ephemeral physical presence with available materials.

The narrative places 1302 maps in the context of each volume's period or theme, with frequent interspersion of the illustrations, many of which fold out. Then comes the "Bibliocartography" with the author, verbatim title, size, source, and additional remarks. Finally, there is an alphabetical index of mapmakers, with a grand listing in the final volume. One could ask for little more, other than a title index.

The pages are reproduced in black and white facsimile, but without the rubric, occasional map coloring and the luxurious wide margins of the original designed by the Grabhorn Press. When placed beside the original, the shortcomings in the reproduction of *half-tone* illustrations are apparent. They appear murky and the eye struggles with the finer lettering and details. This problem is much less pronounced with *line art* which is almost as sharp as the original.

If the reader is not familiar with the Grabhorn edition, he will be overjoyed with this one. The good news is that Carl Wheat's overwhelming *opus magnus* is available with few compromises at less than 20% of the "street price" of the original. The bad news is that it may not last long because "This reprint is strictly limited 350 copies." While this may satisfy the market for a spell, demand is likely to reemerge soon, for the West is a subject that will continue to spark the imagination, curiosity and pride of Americans for generations to come.

Recent releases also noted

American Beginnings: Exploration, Culture and Cartography in the Land of Nurembega. Emerson W. Baker et al, ed. (Lincoln & London: University of Nebraska Press, 1994)

Andrée Stieler Meyer & C.: Bibliographie der Handatlanten. Jürgen Espenhorst. (Schwerte: Pangaea Verlag, 1994)

Battle Maps of the American Civil War. Richard O'Shea *et al.*

Flattening the Earth: Two Thousand Years of Map Projections. John P. Snyder. (Chicago and London: University of Chicago Press, 1993)

Globes from the Western World. Elly Dekker and Peter van der Krogt. (London: Trevor Philip & Son, 1993)

The International Map Collectors' Society - Journal Index 1980-1994. Compiled by Susan Gole. (Susan Gole, editor, 14 Oakford Road, London NW5 1AH)

Monumenta Cartographica Neerlandica IV: Single-Sheet maps and Topographical Prints Published by Willem Jansz Blaeu. Günter Schilder. (Uitgeverij Canaletto, Alphen aan de Rijn, 1993)

The Image of the World: 20 Centuries of World Maps. Paul Whitfield. (London: The British Library, 1994)

Maps Are Territories: Science Is an Atlas. David Turnbull. (Chicago: University of Chicago Press, 1993)

Maps of Southern Africa. Oscar I. Norwich. (Johannesburg: A.D. Doncker & Jonathan Ball, 1993)

Maps in Tudor England. P.D.A. Harvey. (London: The British Library and the Public Record Office, 1993)

Phantom Islands in the Atlantic. Donald S. Johnson

Thomas Holme 1624-1695 Surveyor General of Pennsylvania. Irma Corcoran. (Philadelphia: The American Philosophical Society, 1992)

Virginia Cartography: A Bibliographical Description of P. Lee Phillips 1896. reprint by F.J. Manasek

Voies Oceanes: Cartes Marines et Grande Découvertes. Mireille Pastoureau. (Paris: Bibliothèque Nationale, 1992)

Cumulative Index of Books Reviewed

All books reviewed are listed below, including the current year. The number in square brackets after the title is the year of review.

Akerman, J.R. & D. Buisseret, *Monarchs, Ministers & Maps: A cartographic exhibit at the Newberry Library* [1988]

Allen, P., *The Atlas of Atlases: The map maker's vision of the world* [1993]

Bagrow, L., *A history of cartography of Russia up to 1600* and *A history of Russian cartography up to 1800* [1990]

Bagrow, L. & R.A. Skelton, *History of cartography, 2nd ed.* [1987]

Bellec, F., *Océan des Hommes* [1989]

Beresiner, Y., *British County Maps: Reference and price guide* [1985]

Brandão, A.F., *Dialogues of the Great Things of Brazil* [1988]

Buczek, K., *The History of Polish Cartography from the 15th to the 18th Century* [1985]

Buisseret, D., *Tools of Empire: Ships and maps in the process of westward expansion* [1988]

Cajori, F., *The Chequered Career of Ferdinand Rudolph Hassler* [1989]

Calissano, M, et al., *Architettura Rurale In Valle Stura: Il paesagio agricolo nel Cabreo Spinola di Campofreddo* [1988]

Campbell, T., *The Earliest Printed maps 1472-1500* [1989]

Campbell, T., *Early Maps* [1989]

Cobb, D. & N. Vick, eds., *Early Maps of Terra Sancta: Maps of the Holy Land* [1989]

Cobb, D., *New Hampshire Maps to 1900: An annotated checklist* [1989]

Conzen, M.P., ed., *Chicago Mapmakers: Essays on the rise of the city's map trade* [1986]

Cook, T., *Archival Citations* [1985]

Coppo, P., *Il Portolano* [1988]

Cotter, C., *A History of the Navigator's Sextant* [1989]

Dawson, J., *The Mapmaker's Eye: Nova Scotia through early maps* [1992]

Delano-Smith, C. and E. M. Ingram, *Maps in Bibles 1500 - 1600 An Illustrated Catalogue.* [1994]

Delpar, H., ed., *The Discoverers: An encyclopedia of explorers and exploration* [1989]

Dilke, O.A.W., *Greek and Roman Maps* [1987]

Dörflinger, J., *Österreichische Karten des 18. und zu Beginn des 19. Jahrhunderts unter besonderer Berücksichtigung der Privatkartographie zwischen 1780 und 1820* [1991]

Dreyer-Eimbcke, O., *Die Entdeckung der Erde: Geschichte und Geschichten des kartographischen Abenteuers* [1991]

Dreyer-Eimbcke, O., *Island, Grönland und das nördlich Eismeer im Bild der Kartographie seit dem 10 Jahrhundert* [1990]

Dubreuil, L., *Early Canadian Topographic Map Series: The Geological Survey of Canada 1842-1949* [1992]

Dubreuil, L., *Sectional Maps of Western Canada, 1871-1955: An early Canadian topographic map series* [1992]

Dubreuil, L., *Standard Topographical Maps of Canada, 1904-1908* [1992]

Edwards, A.C. & K.C. Newton, *The Walkers of Hanningfield: Surveyors and mapmakers extraordinary* [1987]

Emlen, R.P., *Shaker Village Views: Illustrated maps and landscape drawings by Shaker artists of the nineteenth century* [1990]

Falk, M.W., *Alaskan Maps: A cartobibliography of Alaska to 1900* [1987]

Farrell, B. & A. Desbarats, *Explorations in the History of Canadian Mapping: A collection of essays* [1992]

Faupel, W.J., *A Brief and True Report of the New Found Land of Virginia: A study of the de Bry engravings* [1990]

Fell, R. T., *Early Maps of South-East Asia* [1993]

Gasset, J., ed., *Cartografia de Catalunya Dels Segles XVII i XVIII* [1989]

Globe, A., *Peter Stent, London Printseller, Circa 1642-1665: Being a catalog raisonné of his engraved prints and books with an historical and bibliographical introduction* [1987]

Goss, J., *Blaeu's The Grand Atlas of the 17th-Century World* [1992]

Goss, J., *The Mapmaker's Art: An Illustrated History of Cartography* [1994]

Graffagnino, J.K., *The Shaping of Vermont from the Wilderness to the Centennial 1749-1877* [1986]

Hadjipaschalis, A., *Cyprus: 2500 years of cartography* [1989]

Hale, E., *The Discovery of the World: Maps of the earth and the cosmos. From the David M. Stewart Collection* [1988]

Harley, J.B., assisted by E. Hanlon & M. Warhus, *Maps and the Columbian Encounter: An Interpretive Guide to the Travelling Exhibition.* [1994]

Harley, J.B. & D. Woodward, *The History of Cartography Volume Two, Book One: Cartography in the Traditional Islamic and South Asian Societies* [1993]

Harris, H.M., *The Asiatic Fathers of America: Book one, The Chinese discovery and colonization of ancient America (2640 B.C. to 2200 B.C.); Book two, the Asiatic kingdoms of America (458 A.D. to 1000 A.D.)* [1988]

Heijden, H.A.M. van der, *The Oldest Maps of the Netherlands: An illustrated and annotated carto-bibliography of the 16th century maps of the XVII provinces* [1988]

Higman, B.W., *Jamaica Surveyed: Plantation maps and plans of the eighteenth and nineteenth centuries* [1990]

Holton, M., *The James W. Macnutt Collection of maps of the Gulf of St. Lawrence with Particular Emphasis on Prince Edward Island* [1991]

Jackson, J., R. Weedle & W. de Ville, *Mapping Texas and the Gulf Coast: The contributions of Saint-Denis, Oliván, and Le Maire* [1991]

Javorski, M., *The Canadian West Discovered: An exhibition of printed maps from the 16th to early 20th centuries* [1985]

Johnson, P., *Celestial Images: Astronomical charts from 1500 to 1900* [1986]

Jolly, D.C., *Maps in British Periodicals: Part I, major monthlies before 1800* [1990]

Jolly, D.C., *Maps in British Periodicals: Part II, annuals, scientific periodicals & miscellaneous magazines mostly before 1800* [1991]

Jolly, D.C., *Maps of America in Periodicals before 1800* [1989]

Jourdin, M.M. du, & M. de la Roncière, *Sea Charts of the Early Explorers, 13th to 17th Century* [1987]

Karrow, R.W. Jr. *Mapmakers of the Sixteenth Century and Their Maps: Bio-Bibliographies of the Cartographers of Abraham Ortelius, 1570.* [1994]

Karamitsanis, A., ed., *From Terra Incognita to the Prairie West: A map exhibit* [1990]

Kaufman, K. (ed.), *The Mapping of the Great Lakes in the Seventeenth Century: Twenty-two Maps from the George S. & Nancy B. Parker Collection: A Portfolio with an Introduction and Commentary by Kevin Kaufman.* [1994]

Kershaw, K.A., *Early Printed Map of Canada I. 1540-1703.* [1994]

King, G.L., *The Printed Maps of Staffordshire 1577-1850* [1990]

Klein, C., *Maps in Eighteenth-Century British Magazines: A checklist* [1990]

Koepp, D.P., ed., *Exploration and Mapping of the American West: Selected essays* [1988]

Konvitz, J., *Cartography in France, 1660-1848: Science, engineering, and statecraft* [1988]

Kroessler, J., *A Guide to Historical Map Resources for Greater New York* [1989]

Krogt, P.C.J. van der, *Advertenties Voor Kaarten, Atlassen, Globes e.d. in Amsterdamse Kranten 1621-1811* [1989]

Krogt, P.C.J. van der, *Old globes in the Netherlands: A catalogue of terrestrial and celestial globes made prior to 1850 and preserved in Dutch collections* [1986]

Lago, L. & C. Rossit, *Pietro Coppo Le "Tabulae" (1524-1526): Una preziosa raccolta cartografica custodita a Pirano. Note e documenti per la storia della cartografia* [1988]

Lanman, J., *Glimpses of History from Old Maps: A collector's view* [1991]

Lanman, J., *On the Origin of Portolan Charts* [1989]

Laor, E., *Maps of the Holy Land: Cartobibliography of printed maps, 1475-1900* [1988]

Larsgaard, M.L., *Map Librarianship: An introduction* [1990]

Lawson, S. & W.J. Faupel, *A Foothold in Florida; The Eye-Witness Account of Four Voyages made by the French to that Region and their attempt at Colonisation 1562-1568.* [1994]

Lemon, D.P., *Theatre of Empire* [1990]

Lépine, Pierre, *Cartes Anciennes: cartes originales ou reproduites.* [1994]

Lépine, P. & J. Berthelette, *Documents Cartographiques Depuis la Découverte de l'Amérique jusqu'à 1820: Inventaire sommaire* [1989]

Luebke, F, F. Kaye & G. Moulton, eds., *Mapping the North American Plains: Essays in the history of cartography* [1989]

Lyons, R., *The Conquest of Mexico by Hernan Cortez 1518-1521* [1988]

Mackal, R.P., *A Living Dinosaur? In search of Mokele-Mbembe* [1991]

Mackower, J., ed., *The Map Catalogue: Every kind of map and chart on earth and even some above it,* 2nd ed. [1991]

Manasek, F.J. *Uncommon Value: A Rare Book Dealer's World* [1995]

Martin, J.C. & R.S. Martin, *Maps of Texas and the Southwest, 1513-1900* [1987]

Martin-Merás, L. & B. Rivera, *Catologo de Cartografía Historica de España del Museo Naval* [1992]

Meinig, D.W., *The Shaping of America, Volume 1: Atlantic America, 1492-1800* [1987]

The Mercator Society, *English Mapping of America 1675-1715* [1989]

Mertz, H., *Pale Ink: Two ancient records of Chinese exploration in America,* 2nd ed. [1988]

Meurer, P.H., *Atlantes Colonienses: Die Kölner Schule der Atlaskartographie 1570-1610* [1990]

Michael, D.M.M., *The Mapping of Monmouthshire: A descriptive catalogue of pre-Victorian maps of the county (now Gwent) from Saxton in 1577 with details of British atlases published during that period* [1991]

Mickwitz, A.M., ed., *The A.E. Nordenskiöld Collection: Annotated catalogue of maps made up to 1800, vol. 3, Books containing maps, loose maps, addenda to vols. 1-2* [1986]

Monmonier, M., *Maps with the News: The development of American journalistic cartography* [1992]

Monmonier, M., *Drawing the Line: Tales of Maps and Controversy* [1995]

Mooney, J., *Maps, Globes, Atlases and Geographies through the Year 1800: The Eleanor Houston and Lawrence M.C. Smith Cartographic Collection at the Smith Cartographic Center, University of Southern Maine* [1992]

Moore, J.N., *The Mapping of Scotland: A guide to the literature of Scottish cartography prior to the Ordnance Survey* [1986]

Moreland, C. & D. Bannister, *Antique Maps: A collector's handbook, 1983 ed.* [1985]

Moreland, C. & D. Bannister, *Antique Maps: A collector's handbook, 1986 ed.* [1987]

Moulton, G.E., ed., *Atlas of the Lewis & Clark Expedition: The journals of the Lewis and Clark Expedition, Volume 1* [1987]

Mueller, G.F., *Bering's Voyages: The reports from Russia* [1988]

National Library of Ireland, *Ireland from Maps* [1985]

Nebenzahl, K., *Atlas of Columbus and the Great Discoverers* [1992]

Nebenzahl, K., *Maps of the Holy Land: Images of Terra Sancta through two millennia* [1988]

Noel, T.J., P.F. Mahoney & R.E. Stevens, *Historical Atlas of Colorado.* [1994]

Norwich, O.I., *Maps of Africa: An illustrated carto-bibliography* [1986]

Pagani, L., (Introduction), *Cosmography: Maps from Ptolemy's Geography* [1993]

Pedley, M. S., *Bel et Utile: The work of the Robert De Vaugondy Family of mapmakers* [1993]

Pennick, N., *Lost Lands and Sunken Cities* [1989]

Popescu-Spineni, Marin, *Rumänien in seinen Geographischen und Kartographischen Quellen* [1992]

Portinaro, P. & F. Knirsch, *The Cartography of North America 1500-1800* [1990]

Potter, J., *Country Life Book of Antique Maps: An introduction to the history of maps and how to appreciate them* [1990]

Public Archives of Canada, *National Map Collection* [1989]

Quaini, M., ed., *Carte e Cartografi in Liguria* [1988]

Quaini, M., *Piante delle Due Riviere della Serenissima Repubblica di Genova Divise ne' Commissariati di Sanita* [1987]

Reinhartz, D. & C.C. Colley, *The Mapping of the American Southwest* [1990]

Reps, J.W., *Views & Viewmakers of Urban America: Lithographs of towns and cities in the United States and Canada, notes on the artists and publishers, and a union catalog of their work, 1825-1925* [1985]

Rey, L., ed., *Unveiling the Arctic* [1987]

Ristow, W., *American Maps & Mapmakers: Commercial cartography in the nineteenth century* [1986]

Schulz, Juergen, *La Cartografia Tra Scienza e Arte: Carte e cartografi nel Rinascimento italiano* [1992]

Sertima, I. van, ed., *African Presence in Early America* [1989]

Shirley, R.W., *Early Printed Maps of the British Isles 1477-1650.* [1994]

Shirley, R.W., *The Mapping of the World: Early printed world maps 1472-1700* [1985; 1995]

Sider, S., A. Andreasian & M. Codding, *Maps, Charts, Globes: Five Centuries of Exploration An Exhibition in Commemoration of the Columbus Quincentenary* [1993]

Simpson, A., *The Mysteries of the "Frenchman's Map" of Williamsburg, Virginia* [1987]

Society for the History of Discoveries, *Terrae Incognitae: The journal of the history of discoveries*, v.18 [1989]

Snyder, G., *Maps of the Heavens* [1985]

Stevens, A.R. & W.M. Holmes, *Historical Atlas of Texas* [1991]

Stommel, H., *Lost Islands: The story of islands that have vanished from nautical charts* [1987]

Suarez, T., *Shedding the Veil: Mapping the European discovery of America and the world based on selected works from the Sidney R. Knafel collection of early maps, atlases, and globes, 1434-1865* [1992]

Taliaferro, H.G., comp., *Cartographic Sources in the Rosenberg Library* [1991]

Tompkins, E., *Newfoundland's Interior Explored* [1990]

Tooley, R.V., *Dictionary of Mapmakers: Supplement* [1987]

Tooley, R.V., *Tooley's Handbook for Map Collectors: The map collector's vade mecum arranged by subjects and personalities alphabetically* [1988]

Van Ermen, E., *The United States in Old maps and Prints* [1992]

Vigeant, L., *Dealer's Thesaurus: 6,000 Ways to Describe Books and Historical Paper.* [1994]

Wallis, H.M. & A.H. Robinson, *Cartographical Innovations: An international handbook of mapping terms to 1900* [1988]

Walsh, J., *Maps Contained in the Publications of the American Bibliography, 1639-1819: An index and checklist* [1990]

Walsperger, A., *Untitled World Map of 1448* [1988]

Walter, L. (ed.), *Japan A Cartographic Vision: European Printed Maps from the Early 16th to the 19th Century* [1995]

Warner, D.J., *The Sky Explored: Celestial cartography, 1500-1800* [1986]

Wheat, C.I. *Mapping the Transmississippi West* (reprint) [1995]

Williams, G. & A. Frost, eds., *Terra Australis to Australia* [1990]

Wolter, J.A., ed., *World Directory of Map Collections, 2nd ed.* [1988]

Wood, D., with J. Fels, *The Power of Maps.* [1994]

Woodward, D., ed., *Art and Cartography: Six historical essays* [1988]

Zögner, L., ed., *Bibliographia Cartographia: International documentation of cartographical literature*, vol. 11 [1986]

Zögner, L., *Von Ptolemaeus bis Humbolt. Kartenschätze der Staatsbibliothek Preußischer Kulterbesitz: Ausstellung zum 125 jährigen Jubiläum der Kartenabteilung* [1986]

GLOSSARY OF TERMS

AGE TONING. A pleasant-sounding synonym for browning. See *browning*.

AQUATINT. A type of etching in which rosin is dusted onto a copper plate. Upon heating, the particles fuse and merge, leaving small portions of the copper still exposed. When treated with acid, a speckled pattern of pits results. Impressions from the plate will approximate a gray tone. Aquatint was occasionally used for maps in the late 18th and early 19th centuries. Henry Pelham's beautiful 1777 map of Boston is perhaps the most noted example.

BACKED. Sometimes a map is pasted or glued onto another material, such as cloth, to make the map more rugged and durable. Many folding maps and many wall maps were backed with cloth when issued. Maps are sometimes backed for conservation purposes, usually with thin tissue. Archival quality paste and backing material should be employed to prevent chemical deterioration of the paper. This protects fragile maps from further damage from handling. Maps should not be backed when there is no good reason to do so.

BAROQUE. A style of decoration developed in late 16th-century Italy characterized by exaggerated form and extravagant ornamentation. Cartouches on maps from this period were often in a baroque style.

BLEACHING. This is sometimes done to remove stains, or lighten browning. Bleaching almost inevitably weakens paper, and should not be done casually, nor should it be done without regard to modern conservation practices. Excessive bleaching gives the paper a ghostly white appearance that experienced collectors avoid.

BORDER. The printed area toward the edges of a map constitutes the border. In some cases, the border may consist of a simple neat line. In other cases the border may be scrollwork, geometrical designs, or even decorative panels with costumed figures or town views. Occasionally, a map may have no border at all. Do not confuse border with margin. See *margin* and *neat lines*.

BROWNING. As the organic material in paper ages, it undergoes a chemical transformation that causes the paper to darken. The early stages of browning may produce a pleasing tone. Extreme browning is often accompanied by embrittlement of the paper. To retard aging, maps should be protected from atmospheric pollutants, contact with cheap paper or cardboard, and from exposure to too much ultraviolet light from sunlight or fluorescent lamps.

CARTA MARINA. A term applied to 16th-century rectangular world maps, usually with rhumb lines.

CARTE à BORDURES, CARTE à FIGURES. A map having decorative panels of costumed figures, views, and the like, at the borders.

CARTOUCH, CARTOUCHE. Information surrounded by a border. Cartouches typically enclose the title, the scale, or the imprint. The cartouche may be a simple rectangle or oval, or may incorporate decorative elements such as scrollwork, botanical elements, gargoyles, costumed figures, appropriate scenery, and so on.

CENTERFOLD. Many old maps have been removed from atlases. Often such maps have a vertical fold down the center. Opening and closing the atlas often results in a weakening of the paper at the centerfold, frequently necessitating repair. Browning tends to occur at the centerfold because the paste used to hold the map in the atlas attacks the paper.

CHAIN MARKS, CHAIN LINES. Part of the visible impression left by the wire grid used in the fabrication of laid paper. The chain marks are the coarsely spaced lines running parallel to the short dimension of the original sheet. They are typically about 1 inch (25 mm.) apart. See also *laid lines* and *laid paper*.

COLORING. Color applied to the map, usually watercolor applied by brush. Coloring generally greatly enhances the appearance of decorative maps, but not all maps were intended to be colored.

COMPASS ROSE. A small starlike device used to indicate direction, often found in combination with radiating rhumb lines. North is usually indicated by a pointer on the compass rose.

COMPOSITE ATLAS. An atlas compiled, often to order, by a mapseller from maps on hand. Maps by different map-makers are often bound together in such atlases.

CONTEMPORARY. Indicates something done at about the time the map was published, for example, contemporary coloring.

DECKLE-EDGED. Used to characterize hand-made paper retaining the original rough edges as produced by the papermaker. Most maps have the deckled edge trimmed off during binding, and deckle-edged maps are considered quite desirable.

DISSECTED. Cut into sections. This is often done with large maps, which are cut into rectangles and pasted to cloth so that they can easily be folded down to the size of a single section for easy carrying and storage.

ENGRAVING. A printing process employing a metal plate on which has been scratched a design. When ink is applied to the plate, and the plate wiped, ink remains behind in the grooves. A dampened sheet of paper is laid onto the plate and under pressure the inked design is transferred.

ETCHING. A printing process similar to engraving, except that the plate is produced by coating it with an acid resistant material upon which the design is scratched. Acid is used to eat away at the scratched areas, creating the grooves to hold the ink for printing.

FOLIO. A folio book is bound from sheets of paper folded one time. A map from such a book is sometimes said to be folio-sized. Typically, the vertical paper dimension of a folio map is greater than about 11 inches (24 cm.). Large folio maps would be about 17 to 22 inches (45 to 55 cm.), and imperial folio greater than about 22 inches (55 cm.)

FOXING. Small, usually brown, spots on the paper caused by mold. Foxing often results from storage in damp conditions.

GORE. A section of a globe printed on paper, intended to be cut out and pasted to the surface of a sphere. Gores are usually shaped like an American football.

IMPRESSION. See discussion at the end of this section.

IMPRINT. Information printed on a map giving some combination of the publisher, place of publication, or date of publication.

INCUNABULA, INCUNABLE. Terms used to describe books printed prior to 1500 A.D., and also to maps printed before that time.

INSET MAP. A smaller map within the border of a larger map.

LAFRERI ATLAS. A term used to describe 16th-century Italian composite atlases of printed maps. These were apparently often made to order, and contents vary from atlas to atlas.

LAFRERI MAP, MAP OF THE LAFRERI SCHOOL. Terms often applied to Italian maps of the 16th-century, particularly those issued separately or in composite atlases.

LAID DOWN. See *backed*.

LAID LINES. Part of the visible impression left by the wire grid used in the fabrication of laid paper. The laid lines are the finely spaced lines running parallel to the long dimension of the original sheet. There are typically 25 lines per inch (10 lines per cm.). See also *chain marks* and *laid paper*.

LAID PAPER. Handmade paper made by depositing cloth fibers suspended in water onto a wire grid. The grid leaves an impression on the paper, which may be seen when looking though the paper at a bright light. Most maps before about 1800 are printed on laid paper. See also *chain marks*, *laid lines*, and *wove paper*.

LEO BELGICUS. A species of map depicting the low countries in the form of a lion.

LINED. See *backed*.

LITHOGRAPHY. A form of printing first used for maps early in the 19th-century. The image is printed from a stone or other material on which ink adheres only to specially treated areas.

LOSS OF (PRINTED) SURFACE. A cataloger's term to describe a map in which a portion of the paper is missing. Sometimes maps lacking printed surface are restored by pasting paper at the missing area on which the design is reproduced in facsimile.

LOXODROMIC LINES. See *rhumb lines*.

MANUSCRIPT. Handwriting. A manuscript map is one drawn by hand. Manuscript notations are handwritten notes on a map.

MARGIN. The blank area outside the border of a map. Do not confuse margin with border.

MEDALLION. A circular or oval region, usually containing a portrait, sometimes used to embellish maps.

MOUNTED. See *backed*.

NEAT LINES. The straight, printed lines bounding the map.

OCTAVO. An octavo book is bound from sheets of paper folded in half three times. A map from such a book is sometimes said to be octavo-sized. Typically the vertical paper dimension of such a map is about 8 to 9 inches (20 to 23 cm.). Abbreviated 8vo.

OFFSETTING. When the surface of a map contacts another surface for many years, as in an atlas, there may be a transfer of printer's ink or color, or a chemical reaction, which faintly reproduces a mirror image of the other surface. Offsetting can even occur from one part of a map to another if the map is folded on itself.

ORIGINAL. An original is a map or view printed from the original plate, block, or stone before it has been retired from commercial use. Sometimes the last user does not destroy the plate or block, and it is later used to make restrikes.

OUTLINE COLOR. Coloring of only the boundaries, borders, or coastlines.

PANELS. Usually rectangular frames around the outside of a map enclosing views, scenes, or figures.

PERIPLUS. A text of sailing directions used in classical times.

PLATE MARK. Impressions made from metal plates often show an indentation of the paper extending to just outside the printed area, made when the paper was crushed by the plate during printing.

POCKET MAP. A map that is intended to be folded so that it can be easily carried in a pocket or purse and referred to in the field. These maps are often issued with covers, a slipcase, and with supplementary information such as an index.

PORTOLANO, PORTOLAN CHART. A manuscript sea chart prepared for the use of mariners from about the 14th through the 16th-centuries.

PRINTER'S CREASE. When a map is printed, a small wrinkle in the paper may be compressed to form a permanent crease.

QUARTO. A quarto book is bound from sheets of paper folded in half twice. A map from such a book is sometimes said to be quarto-sized. Typically the vertical paper dimension of such a map is about 9 to 11 inches (23 to 28 cm.). Abbreviated 4to.

RECTO. The side of the paper on which the image of interest appears. Also, the right-hand page of an open book.

REMARGINED. A remargined print has had paper added to the edges to extend them, protecting the original edges, and improving the appearance.

REPRODUCTION. A copy, usually photographically produced, of an original print. The reproduction may in some cases be difficult to distinguish from the original.

RESTRIKE. A map or view printed from the original plate, block, or stone, after the plate, block, or stone had fallen into disuse. The collector of maps will seldom, if ever, encounter restrikes since few plates or blocks have survived.

RHUMB LINES. Lines criss-crossing old charts at various angles, usually along the directions of the compass points, to help plot courses.

ROCOCO. A style of ornamentation evolving from the baroque in early 18th-century France distinguished by refined use of scrollwork, seashells, foliage and so on. Rococo-style cartouches are often found on maps of the 18th- century.

SEPARATELY PUBLISHED, SEPARATELY ISSUED. A separately published map is one not issued as part of a book or atlas. Sometimes maps usually found in atlases were also separately sold to customers who did not need an entire atlas. Separately issued maps tend to be in poor condition since they were not protected inside a book.

VERSO. The reverse or opposite side of the sheet from the image of interest. Many maps from atlases have text on the verso. Also the left-hand page of an open book.

VOLVELLE. A contrivance with moving parts for making certain astronomical calculations, sometimes made of paper and found in old geographical works.

WALL MAP. A large map, typically four or five feet (1.5 m.) on a side, with a top rail and a roller, designed to be displayed on a wall. Many are very decorative. Because wall maps are easily soiled and damaged, many were discarded, and examples of early wall maps are quite scarce and often in bad condition.

WATERMARK. A design in the paper visible by transmitted light. For handmade paper, the watermark is made with bent wires placed on the rack on which the fibers are deposited to make the paper. Designs vary from simple initials to intricate coats of arms. Watermarks are often helpful in identifying the age of the paper. See *chain marks*.

WOODCUT. An image made by printing from a wooden block on which a mirror image of the design has been carved. Woodcut maps are most often associated with the earliest days of map-making, up to about 1600, but many examples are found well into the 18th-century and later, often as text illustrations.

WOOD ENGRAVING. Similar to a woodcut, but the design is engraved on the end grain, resulting in better detail and a somewhat more uniform appearance. Since the size of exposed end grain is limited by the diameter of the tree trunk, it was usually more economical to cut the design on small squares, which can be glued together for final printing. The joint lines are often visible, for example on the views in *Harper's Weekly.*

WORMING, WORMHOLES, WORM TRACKS. Damage to paper by hungry insect larvae that eat the paper, leaving small holes or tracks.

WOVE PAPER. Machine-made paper deposited during manufacture on a fine wire screen having about the same mesh size as gauze. The impression left by the screen can often be seen by holding the paper to the light. Wove paper came into use around 1800, and is often watermarked with the maker's name.

Terms That Distinguish a Printing or Publication

From a bibliographical standpoint, maps can be difficult to classify because they combine elements of both books and prints. There is particular confusion about the terms *impression*, *plate*, *state*, *issue*, and *edition*. The definitions here follow Lloyd Brown's *Notes on the Care & Cataloging of Old Maps* as closely as possible. Any confusion in the explanation is the fault of the editor, not his. The term *plate* is used below generically as shorthand for *plate, block,* or *stone.*

IMPRESSION. A single copy of a map. For example, if 1,000 copies of a map are printed, there will be, at that time, 1,000 impressions. By this definition, expressions like "second impression" are meaningless, since at this late date, one cannot know the order in which copies were printed. Occasionally, however, it is possible to distinguish between early and late impressions of copper engravings. Copper is soft, and tends to wear. Therefore early impressions tend to be darker, and sometimes faint lettering guidelines used by the engraver are visible on impressions made early in the plate's life.

PLATE. Strictly speaking, the plate is the object from which impressions are made. Sometimes the plate becomes worn or damaged, and is replaced with a second plate. Impressions from the second plate are sometimes referred to as something like "2nd Plate."

STATE. All impressions printed from a given plate, without deliberate alteration of that plate, belong to the same state. If the plate is altered, for example, by adding a new place name or changing the date, impressions from that plate constitute a new state. Some maps have a dozen or more states. States are usually numbered serially. However, "intermediate" states often turn up later. When giving a state number, one should specify who numbered the states, since different authorities often have different numbering. If a new plate was cut, the state numbering may start anew, as in "first state of the second plate."

ISSUE. All impressions printed at one time without alteration of the plate belong to the same issue. Thus, if two impressions are different states, the plate has been altered and they cannot belong to the same issue. However, an unaltered plate might have been used several times over a period years. In that case, the several issues would all be of the same state. Issues can sometimes be distinguished by the watermark, since different paper might have been used for each issue. For maps from atlases, different issues can often be distinguished by the text on the verso.

EDITION. Following Brown, an edition of a map is determined only by the imprint. If the imprint is changed, then there is a new edition. Obviously, since the plate has been changed, a new edition means a new state. However, a new state is not necessarily a new edition, since the imprint may not have been changed.

FOREIGN LANGUAGE DICTIONARIES
Dutch-English

Dutch resembles a cross between English and German. Many variant spellings are found in old Dutch. For example, France has appeared on maps as *Francrijck, Francryck, Frankrijk, Frankryk, Vranckrijck, Vranckryck, Vrancrijck, Vrancryck, Vrankrijk, Vrankryck,* and *Vrankryk,* to mention a few. In some cases, variant spellings are given below. However, users should be aware that many other variants exist. The following letters are often used interchangeably: **(c-ck-k), (d-dt-t), (f-v), (i-ij-y),** and **(s-z)**.

aan *adj* on, at
aangrenzend *adj* adjacent
aardbodem *n* earth, earth's surface
aarde *n* earth
aardkloot *n* earth-sphere
acht *card num* eight
achter *prep* behind
Achter Indie *n* Further India
achtste *ord num* eighth
afbeelding *n* depiction, picture
afteekening *n* depiction
al, alle *adj* all
algemeen *adj* general
als mede as well as
anders *adv* otherwise
Antwerpen *n* Antwerp
baai, bay *n* bay
beginnende, beghijnnende *pres part* beginning
begrepen *adj* included
behalve *prep* except, besides
bekend *adj* known
belegering *n* siege
Beloofde Landt *n* Promised Land
bemagtigd *adj* captured
berg *n* mountain
beschrijving *n* description
bij *prep* by (location)
bocht *n* gulf, bight, bend
boeckverkooper, boekverkoper *n* bookseller
Bretagne *n* Brittany
canaal *n* channel
clippen, klippen *n* rocks, reefs
cust *n* coast
d' *art* the
de *art* the
deel *n* part
derde *adj* third
diepte *n* depth
Donau *n* Danube

door *prep* by (authorship), through
dorp *n* village
drie *card num* three
droogte *n* dryness
Duitsland *n* Germany
duizend *card num* thousand
een *art* an, one
eerst *adj* first
eiland *n* island; also *eijland, eijlandt, eylant*
elf *card num* eleven
elfde *ord num* eleventh
en, ende *conj* and
gaet, gat *n* entrance
gebetert *adj* improved
gebiedt *n* region
gecorrigeert *adj* corrected
gedeelte *n* portion
gedruckt *adj* printed
geheel *adj* whole, entire
gelegen *adj* situated
gelegenheid *n* situation; also *gelegentheijt, gelegentheyt, ghelegentheyt*
gelijk gradige zee kaart plane chart
getrokken *adj* extracted
gezigt, gezicht *n* view
Goud Kust *n* Gold Coast
graadboogh *n* quadrant
graade *n* compass
graafschap *n* county, earldom
's-Gravenhage *n* The Hague
Groenlandt *n* Greenland
groot *adj* great
Groot-Brittannie *n* Great Britain
haar *pron* their; also *hare, heure*
half eilandt *n* peninsula
halfrond *n* hemisphere
haven *n* harbor

heerlijkheid *n* manor, district
heilig *adj* holy
Heilige Land *n* Holy Land
het *art* the
Heylighe Landt *n* Heligoland
Hispangien *n* Spain
hoek *n* angle, corner
honderd *card num* hundred
hoofdstad *n* capital
Ierland(t) *n* Ireland
in *prep* in
in sig begrypende containing; also *in zig begrypende*
inde in the
ingang *n* entrance
inhoudende *adj* containing
inkomen, inkoomen *n* entrance
Ioodtsche Landt *n* Holy (i.e., Jewish) Land
jaar *n* year
kaap *n* cape
kaart *n* map; also *caart, caert, kaert*
kaartje *n* maplet, small map
kaartverkoper *n* mapseller
keizerrijk, keyzerryk *n* empire
klein *adj* small
koningrijk *n* kingdom
kust *n* coast
laatste *adj* latest
landengte *n* isthmus
landschap *n* landscape
landstreek *n* region
langs *prep* along
meer *n* lake
met *prep* with
Middellandsche Meer *n* Mediterranean Sea
mitsgaders *prep* together with
mond, mont *n* mouth
na *prep* after
naar *prep* to, towards**

Dutch-English

naaukeurige, nauwkeurig *adj* accurate
nabijgelegen, nabygelegen *adj* adjacent
neder, neer *adj* lower
Nederland *n* The Netherlands
negen *card num* nine
negende *ord num* ninth
nieuwe *adj* new
noord *adj* north; also *noord, nort*
noordelijk *adj* northern
noordelijkste *adj* northernmost
Noorwegen *n* Norway
oceaan *n* ocean
of, ofte *conj* or
om *prep* round, round about, about
omleggende *adj* surrounding
onder *prep* under
onderkoningschap *n* viceroyalty
ondiepte *n* shoal
ontdekking *n* discovery
ook *adv* also, likewise
oost *adj* east
oostelijcke *adj* eastern
oostelijkste *adj* easternmost
Oostenrijk *n* Austria
op *prep* on, upon, at
opdoeningh *n* discovery
opper *adj* upper
oud *adj* old
over *prep* over, across, beyond
pascaart *n* sea chart; also found with hyphen or space, as *pas-caart* or *pas caart;* also *pascaert, paskaart, paskaert*
plaatsnijder *n* engraver
plaeten, platen *n* banks
platte zee kaart plane chart
plattegrond *n* ground plan, map
Polen *n* Poland
Pruisen *n* Prussia
reede *n* roadstead
reize *n* journey
rievier, rivier *n* river
rijk, ryk *n* kingdom
Rusland *n* Russia

sande plaeten *n* sand banks
schets *n* sketch, outline
schipvaert *n* navigation, seafaring
slick, slijk *n* mire
Soute Eijlanden *n* Cape Verde Islands
Spanje *n* Spain
stad *n* city, town
steeg, steegh *n* alley, lane
straet *n* strait
strekkende *adj* stretching
strom, stroem *n* stream
stuck, stuk *n* part
stuurman *n* helmsman
t' *prep* at, in
't *art* the
Tandt Kust *n* Ivory Coast
te *prep* at, in
tegenvoeters *n* antipodes
tegenwoordig *adv* nowadays
tekening *n* sketch, drawing
tien *card num* ten
tiende *ord num* tenth
tocht, togt *n* journey, expedition
toneel *n* theater, scene
tot *prep* until, to, as far as
tot aan as far as, up to
tusschen, tussen *prep* between, 'twixt
twaalf *card num* twelve
twee *card num* two
tweede *adj* second
uit, uyt *prep* out
uitgegeven *adj* published
van *prep* from, of
vande of the
verbeetert *adj* improved
verdeelt *adj* divided
verdeling *n* division
verdrag *n* treaty, pact
vereenigd, verenegd *adj* united
Verenigde Staten *n* United States
vermaard, vermaerde *adj* famous
vermeerdert *past part* augmented

verthoonende, vertonende *pres part* showing
vertooninghe *n* appearance
vier *card num* four
vierde *adj* fourth
vijf *card num* five
vijfde *ord num* fifth
Vlaanderen *n* Flanders
Vlaemsche *adj* Flemish
Vlaemsche Eijlanden *n* The Azores
vliet *n* brook
vlijt *n* diligence
voerbij *prep* before
volgens *prep* according to
volksplanting *n* colony
voor *prep* for
voornaamste *adj* principal
waar *adj* true
waar *adv* where
waarneming *n* observation
waerachtig *adj* true, accurate
wassende *pres part* increasing
wassende gradige pascaart increasing degree chart, i.e., a Mercator chart
wereld *n* world; also *waereld, wareld, weereld, werreld, werelt*
west *n* west
westelijcke *adj* western
westelijkste *adj* westernmost
wijk *n* district
woestyne, woestijn *n* desert
Yerlandt, Yrlandt *n* Ireland
Ysland, IJsland *n* Iceland
zee *n* sea, ocean
zee kaart sea chart
zeer *adv* very
zes *card num* six
zeste, seste *ord num* seventh
zeven *card num* seven
zevende *ord num* seventh
zijne *pron* its
zuid *n* south; also *zuijd, zuyd, zuyt, zur, suyt*
zuidelijk *adj* southern
zuidelijkste *adj* southernmost
Zwarte Zee *n* Black Sea

French-English

French nouns and adjectives have two genders, masculine and feminine. Adjectives and articles agree in gender with the nouns they modify. Plurals are formed as in English by adding **s**, except for words ending in **-au** or **-eu** which add **x**. Adverbs are usually formed from adjectives by adding **-ment** as in *exactement* (exactly). Verbs are conjugated in a somewhat complex manner. Generally the infinitive ends in **-er** **-ir** **-oir** or **-re**. The third person singular present indicative often ends in **-t** (*il peut*, he can), while the third person plural ends in **-nt** (*ils peuvent*, they can). In the definitions below, adjectives are given in their masculine and feminine forms.

a *v* (he, she, it) has
à *prep* at, in, to
abrégé, -ée *adj* shortened, condensed
académie *n* academy
Acadie *n* Nova Scotia
actuel, -elle *adj* present, current
adjacent, -ente *adj* adjoining, contiguous
aiguille aimantée *n* compass needle
Allemagne *n* Germany
alors *adv* then
Américain, -aine *adj* American
Amérique *n* America
ancien, -enne *adj* ancient, previous
Anglais, -aise *adj* English
Angleterre *n* England
année *n* year
anse *n* cove
Anvers *n* Antwerp
appellé, -ée *adj* called
après *prep* after
aquatique *adj* aquatic
archiduché *n* archduchy
archevesché, archevêché *n* archbishopric, archdiocese
archipel, archipelague *n* archipelago
armée *n* army
arpent *n* land measure of about an acre
Asie *n* asia
assujetti, -ie *adj* attached, subject
au at the, in the, to the, contraction of *à le*
augmenté, -ée *adj* enlarged, augmented
auspices *n* patronage
aujourd'hui *adv* today
aussi *adv* also, likewise
auteur *n* author

autres *adj* other
autrefois *adv* formerly
Autriche *n* Austria
Autrichien, -ienne *adj* Austrian
aux at the, in the, to the, contraction of *à les*
avec *prep* with
baie, baye *n* bay
banc *n* bank
bas, basse *adj* low
blanc, blanche *adj* white, empty
Bohême *n* Bohemia
bois *n* forest
bouche *n* mouth
bourg *n* borough, market town
boussole *n* compass
Brésil *n* Brazil
Bretagne *n* Brittany
Britannique *adj* British
campement *n* encampment
canal *n* channel, canal
cap *n* cape, headland
capitaine *n* captain
carénage *n* careenage
carte *n* map
Catalogne *n* Catalonia
catholique *adj* catholic
ce *pron* this, that
ceci *pron* this
cela *pron* that
célèbre *adj* celebrated
celles *pron* these, those
celui, celle *pron* this, that
cent *card num* hundred
cet, cette *pron* this, that
cercle *n* circle
ces *adj* these
ceux *pron* these, those
chemin *n* path, track, route
chez *prep* at the place of
Chine *n* China
chinois, -oise *adj* Chinese
chrétien, -enne *adj* Christian
cinq *card num* five

cinquième *ord num* fifth
circonvoisin, -e *adj* surrounding
cité *n* city
Cochinchine *n* Cochin China
colonie *n* colony
comme *conj, adv* like, as
composé, -ée *adj* composed, constituted
comprenant *pres part* comprising, covering
comprend *v* comprises, includes, covers
compris *past part* comprised, included
comte *n* count
comté, comtez *n* county
confins *n* confines, borders
connaissance *n* understanding, knowledge
connu, -ue *adj* known
contenant *pres part* containing
contre *prep* against
copié, -ée *adj* copied
Corée *n* Korea
corrigé ée *adj* corrected
cosmographe *n* cosmographer
cosmographie *n* cosmography
cosmographique *adj* cosmographic
côte, coste *n* coast
couronne *n* crown
cours *n* course
croquis *n* sketch
curieux, -euse *adj* curious, strange
dans *prep* in
dauphin, -ine *n* prince(ss)
de *prep* of
débouquement *n* where a river or strait disembogues, or enters, the sea
déclinaisons *n* magnetic variations
découverte *n* discovery

French-English

décrit, -te *past part* described
dédié, -ée *adj* dedicated, inscribed
degré *n* degree
dépost, dépôt *n* depository
depuis *prep* from
dernier, -ère *adj* past, latest
des of the, contraction of *de les*
description *n* description
dessinateur *n* draftsman
dessiné, -ée *adj* drawn, laid out, designed
dessus *prep* upon
destroit, détroit *n* straits
détaillé, -ée *adj* detailed, itemized
deux *card num* two
deuxième *ord num* second
devant *prep* before
dire *v* to say
distinctement *adv* distinctly
distingué, -ée *adj* distinguished
divers *adj* diverse, different, varying
divisé, -ée *adj* divided
dix *card num* ten
dixième *ord num* tenth
Dominique *n* Dominica
dont *rel pron* of which
douze *adj* twelve
douze *card num* twelve
douzième *ord num* twelfth
dressé, -ée *adj* drawn, laid down
du of the, contraction of *de le*
duc *n* duke
duché, duchez *n* duchy
echelle *n* scale
Écosse *n* Scotland
église *n* church
électorat, eslectorat *n* electorate
elle *pron* it, she
elles *pron* they
embouchure *n* river mouth
empereur *n* emperor
empire *n* empire
en *prep* in, at, to
encore *adv* again, more
entier, -ère *adj* entire
entre *prep* between
environs *n* environs
équateur *n* equator
Escosse *n* Scotland

Espagne *n* Spain
espagnol, -ole *adj* Spanish
Espagnols *n* the Spanish
Espérance, Cap de Bonne *n* Cape of Good Hope
esquisse *n* sketch
essai, essay *n* trial, first attempt
est *n* east
est *v* (he, she, it) is
et *conj* and
établissement *n* settlement, establishment
état, estat *n* state
été *past part* been
étendu, -ue, estendu *adj* lying, stretched
étude *n* study, early draft
évangile *n* the Gospel
évêché, éveschez *n* bishopric, see
exactement *adv* exactly
extrait *n* extract
extrémite *n* extrémity, end of the earth
faisant *pres part* making
fait, faite *adj* made, done
faubourg *n* suburbs, outskirts
feu *n* fire
feuille *n* leaf, sheet
fils *n* son
fleuve *n* river
flibustier *n* buccaneer
Floride *n* Florida
fond *n* depth, bottom
fort *n* fort
fort, forte *adj* strong, large
Français, -aise *adj* French
françaises *n* the French
frégate *n* frigate
frère *n* brother
général, -ale *adj* general, universal
Gênes *n* Genoa
Genève *n* Geneva
géographe *n* geographer
géographie *n* geography
géographique *adj* geographical
Georgie *n* Georgia
globe *n* Globe
golfe, golphe *n* gulf, bay
gouvernement *n* government, governance

grand, grande *adj* large, great
gravé, -ée *adj* engraved
Grèce *n* Greece
Grenade *n* Grenada
Groenland *n* Greenland
Gueldre *n* Gelderland
guerre *n* war
habit *n* dress, attire
haut, haute *adj* high
havre *n* harbor
héritier *n* heir
histoire *n* history
historique *adj* historical
horloge *n* clock
huit *card num* eight
huitième *ord num* eighth
hydrographe *n* hydrographer
hydrographie *n* hydrography
hydrographique *adj* hydrographic
illustré, -ée *adj* illustrated
il *pron* he, it
ils *pron* they
impératrice *n* empress
important, -ante *adj* important
imprimé, -ée *adj* printed
inclinaison magnétique *n* magnetic dip
les Indes *n* the Indies
Indien *n* Indian
indiquant *pres part* indicating
inférieur, -ieure *adj* lower
ingénieur *n* engineer
intelligence *n* intelligence, understanding
intérieur, -ieure *adj* interior, inland
intitulé, -ée *adj* entitled
isle, île *n* island
isthme *n* isthmus
itinéraire *n* route
Jamaïque *n* Jamaica
Japon *n* Japan
journal *n* journal, logbook, pl. *journaux*
jusque *prep* up to, as far as
l' *art* the (singular)
la *art* the (singular)
lac *n* lake
laquelle *rel pron* who, which
le *art* the (singular)
lequel *rel pron* who, which

French-English

les *art* the (plural)
lesquels, lesquelles *rel pron* who, which
leur *pron* their, them
levé, -ée *adj* raised, levied
libraire *n* bookseller
lieu *n* place, pl. *lieux*
lieue *n* league, pl. *lieues*
ligne *n* line, one-twelfth inch
limite *n* limit, boundary
limitrophe *adj* adjoining, bordering
Londres *n* London
lors *adv* then
Louisiane *n* Louisiana
lui *pron* him, her
lunaire *adj* lunar
luy *pron* he
maison *n* house
Malouines *n* Falkland Islands
La Manche *n* English Channel
manière *n* manner, behaviour
manuscrit *n* manuscript
mappe *n* map
mappemonde *n* world map
Maragnon *n* Amazon
marine *adj* marine
marine *n* navy
marqué, -ée *adj* marked
marquisat *n* marquisate
meilleur, -eure *adj* better
même *adj* same
mémoire *n* memoire, report
mer *n* sea
Mer Glaciale *n* Arctic Ocean
Mer du Nord *n* Atlantic Ocean
Mer du Sud *n* Pacific Ocean
méridional, -ale *adj* southern
Mexique *n* Mexico
mieux *adv* better
mille *card num* thousand
ministre *n* minister
moderne *adj* modern
moin *adv* less; least (with *definite article*)
monde *n* world, earth, universe
monseigneur *n* title of respect
mont *n* mountain
montagne *n* mountain
montrant *pres part* showing
mouillage *n* anchorage

mouvement *n* movement, motion
navigateur *n* navigator, sailor
neuf *card num* nine
neuf, neuve *adj* new
neuvième *ord num* ninth
nom *n* name
nord *n* north
nouveau, -el, -elle *adj* new
nouvellement *adv* recently
nouvelles *n* news
observations *n* observations
occident *n* west
occidental, -ale *adj* western
océan *n* ocean
océanique *adj* oceanic
on *pron* someone, one, he
ont *v* (they) have
onze *card num* eleven
onzième *ord num* eleventh
opération *n* operation
ordinaire *adj* ordinary, usual
ordre *n* order
oriental, -ale *adj* eastern
ou *conj* or
où *adv, pron* where
ouest *n* west
ouvrage *n* work
païs, pays *n* land, country, nation
palais *n* palace
palatinat *n* palatinate
par *prep* by, at
particulier, -ière *adj* particular, detailed, special
particulièrement *adv* particularly
partie *n* part
pas *adv* not
pas *n* strait
passage *n* passage
Perse *n* Persia
petit, petite *adj* small
peuples *n* peoples
plan *n* plan, draft, urban map
planisphere *n* planisphere
plus *adv* more; most (with *definite article*)
plusieurs *adj, pron* several
point *n* point
politique *adj* political
Pologne *n* Poland

port *n* harbor, seaport
portugais, -aise *adj* Portuguese
possédé, -ée *adj* possessed
possédent *pres part* possessing
possessions *n* possessions
pouce *n* inch
pour *prep* for
premier, -ière *adj* first, foremost
près de near
presenté, -ée *adj* presented, offered
preséntement *adv* for the time being, presently
presque *adv* almost, nearly
presqu'île *n* peninsula
principal, -ale *adj* principal, leading, main
principalement *adv* principally, mainly
principauté *n* principality
pris, prise *adj* taken
privilège *n* permission, copyright
province *n* province, country
publié, -iée *adj* published
quatre *card num* four
quatrième *ord num* fourth
quay *n* quay, wharf
que *conj* that
quelque *adj* some
qui *rel pron* who, which, that
rade *n* roadstead, anchorage
recent, -ente *adj* recent, new
récif *n* reef
reconnu, -ue *adj* recognized
rectifié, -iée *adj* corrected
recueil *n* collection, compendium
redigé, -ée *adj* composed, drafted, edited
reduite *adj* reduced, scaled down
reine *n* queen
relation *n* narrative, account
remarque *n* sailor's landmark, comment
remarqué, -ée *adj* remarked, observed
renommé, -ée *adj* well-known
retour *n* return
revu ue *n* revised
riviere *n* river

29

French-English

rocher *n* rock
roi, roy *n* king
route *n* course, road
royaume *n* kingdom
rue *n* street
Russe *n* Russian
Russie *n* Russia
sa *pron* his, her, its
saint, sainte *adj* holy
sauvage *n* savage
se, s' *reflex pron* himself, herself, themselves
seigneurie *n* manor, domain
selon *prep* according to
sept *card num* seven
septentrional, -ale *adj* northern
septième *ord num* seventh
service *n* assistance, service
servir *v* to assist, to serve
ses *pron* his, her, its
siège *n* siege, seat
situé, -ée *adj* located, situated
six *card num* six
sixième *ord num* sixth
son *pron* his, her, its
sonde *n* sounding

sont *v* (they) are
sortie *n* going out, exit
sous *prep* under
statistique *adj* statistical
successeur *n* successor
sud *n* south
Suède *n* Sweden
Suisse *n* Switzerland
suite *n* continuation
suivant *prep* according to, following
supérieur, -ieure *adj* upper, higher
sur *prep* on, upon, above
tableau *n* picture, view
Tamise *n* Thames
terre *n* land, earth, world
Terre Neuve *n* Newfoundland
terrestre *adj* terrestrial
territoire *n* territory, district
tiré, -ée *adj* extracted, derived
titre *n* title
toise *n* fathom
topographique *adj* topographical

tout, toute *adj* all, whole; pl. **tous, toutes**
traduit, -e *adj* translated
treize *card num* thirteen
très *adv* very
tributaire *n* tributary
trois *card num* three
troisième *ord num* third
trouvé, -ée *adj* found
un, une *card num* one
uni, -ie *adj* united
universel, -elle *adj* universal
usage *n* use, *à la usage de* for the use of
vaisseau *n* vessel, pl. *vaisseaux*
vent *n* wind
vierge *n* virgin
vieux, vieil, vieille *adj* old
ville *n* city, town
Virginie *n* Virginia
voir *v* to see
voisin, -ine *adj* neighboring, nearby
voyage *n* voyage
voyageur *n* traveller
vue *n* view

German-English

This list of words most commonly found on German maps should help decipher most titles and legends. Plurals of nouns usually form by adding **-en**, **-e**, **-er**, or **-eln**, and practically never by adding **-s**. Nouns, pronouns, adjectives, and articles have four cases, these also being indicated by endings. It is usually not necessary to know these endings to get the meaning of a short title or phrase. Vowels with umlauts are sometimes written without umlauts followed by an e. Thus ä becomes **ae**, ö becomes **oe**, ü becomes **ue**. Sometimes ss is writtin as ß. German spelling has mutated over the centuries. Sometimes interchanged are: **(c-z)**, **(ch-k)**, **(dt-t)**, **(f-v)**, and **(i-y)**.

Abbildung *n* illustration
Abriß *n* summary, plan, outline
acht *card num* eight
achte *ord num* eighth
all *adj* all
allgemeine *adj* general
alt *adj* old
am at the (*an dem*)
Amt *n* office
an *prep* at, on, by
ander *adj* other
angrenzend *adj* bordering

ans to the (*an das*)
Armee *n* army
auch *conj* also
auf *prep* on, at, by
aus *prep* from, out of, by
ausführlich *adj* detailed, complete
außer *adj* exterior, outer
Aussicht *n* view, prospect
Bach *n* brook, stream
Bad *n* bath
Bahn *n* road, path

Bai, Bay *n* bay
Bayern *n* Bavari
begreifend *pres part* comprising, containing
Begriff *n* concept, idea
bei, bey *prep* at, with, by
Belagerung *n* siege
Belgien *n* Belgium
benachbart *adj* adjoining, neighboring
Berg *n* mountain, hill
berühmt *adj* famous

German-English

Beschreibung *n* description
bis *prep* as far as (spatial), till (temporal)
Bisthum, Bistum *n* bishopric, diocese
Blatt *n* sheet
Böhmen *n* Bohemia
Brasilien *n* Brazil
Bruch *n* swamp
Bucht *n* bay, inlet, creek
Charte *n* chart
Churfürstenthum *n* electorate
das *art* the
den *art* the
der *art* the
des *art* the
deutsch *adj* German
Deutschland *n* Germany
die *art* the
Dorf *n* village
drei *card num* three
dritte *ord num* third
durch *prep* through, by means of
eigentlich *adj* true, proper
ein *card num* one
ein, eine *art* a, an
Eismeer *n* Polar Sea
elf *card num* eleven
elfte *ord num* eleventh
Elsaß *n* Alsace
Entdeckung *n* discovery
enthaltend *pres part* containing
Entwurf *n* sketch, draft, plan
Erbe *n* heir
Erde *n* earth, world
Eroberung *n* conquest, acquisition
erst *ord num* first
Erzbisthum *n* archbishopric, archdiocese
Erzherzogthum *n* archduchy
Erzstift *n* archbishopric, archdiocese
Etlich *adj* some, several
Eyland, Eiland *n* island
Fluß *n* river, flow
Fortsetzung *n* continuation
Frankreich *n* France
französisch *adj* French
frey, frei *adj* free
fünf *card num* five
fünfte *ord num* fifth

Fürstenthum *n* principality
gantz, ganz *adj* entire
Gasse *n* street, alley
Gebiet *n* district, region
Gebirge *n* mountain range
gegen *prep* towards, opposite to
Gegend *n* region, district
gehörig *prep* belonging to
Gelobte Land *n* Promised Land
gennant *adj* called, named
Geschichte *n* history
Gestalt *n* shape, form, figure
gezeichnet *past part* signed, drawn, designed
Grafschaft *n* count's domain, county
Griechenland *n* Greece
Grönland *n* Greenland
groß *adj* large
Grundriß *n* ground plan, sketch
Guten Hoffnung, das Kap der *n* Cape of Good Hope
Hafen *n* harbor
Haff *n* lagoon
Halbkugel *n* hemisphere
Halbinsel *n* peninsula
Haupt *n* principal; *Haupt-* main
Hauptmannschaft *n* captaincy
Hauptstatt, Hauptstadt *n* capital
heilig *adj* holy
Herrschaft *n* manor, estate, dominion
Herzogthum, Herzogtum *n* dukedom, duchy
heutig *adv* nowadays
Hinterindien *n* Indochina
Hochstift *n* bishopric
hundert *card num* hundred
ihr *pron* its, their
im in the (*in dem*)
in *prep* in
Indien *n* India
ins in the (*in das*)
Insel *n* island
Island *n* Iceland
Jahr *n* year
jenseits *prep* beyond
Kap *n* cape
Karte *n* map, chart
Kaspische Meer *n* Caspian Sea
Keyser *n* emperor

klein *adj* small
Kloster *n* monastery, nunnery
Köln *n* Cologne
König *n* king
Königriech *n* kingdom
Kreis *n* circle, district
Kriegsshauplatz *n* theater of war
Kriegstheater *n* theater of war
Krim, der *n* the Crimea
Kurfürstentum *n* electorate
Küste *n* coast
Lager *n* camp
Land *n* land, country
Landgrafschaft *n* landgraviate
Landkreis *n* district, hinterland
Landschaft *n* landscape, estate, district
Lauf *n* course, route
Litauen *n* Lithuania
Livland *n* Livonia
Lothringen *n* Lorraine
Magalhäesstraße *n* Straits of Magellan
Mähren *n* Moravia
Markgrafschaft *n* margraviate
Markt *n* market, market-town
Maßstab *n* scale
Meer *n* sea, ocean
Meerbusen *n* bay, gulf
Meerenge *n* strait, channel
Meile *n* mile, league
mit *prep* with
Mittag *n* south, noon
Mittelländische Meer *n* Mediterranean Sea
Mitternacht *n* north, midnight
Moldau *n* Moldavia
München *n* Munich
nach *prep* after, according to
Neapel *n* Naples
nebst *prep* besides
neu *adj* new
neuest *adj* newest
neun *card num* nine
neunte *ord num* ninth
nieder *adj* low
die Niederlande *n* the Netherlands
Nörd *n* north
nördlich *adj* northern

German-English

Nördlicher Polarkreis *n* Arctic Circle
Norwegen *n* Norway
ober *adj* upper, higher
oder *conj* or
Ort, Ohrt *n* place, region
Ost *n* east
Österreich *n* Austria
Ostindien *n* East Indies
östlich *adj* eastern
Ostsee *n* Baltic Sea
die Pfalz *n* the Palatinate
Plan *n* plan, map, chart
Platz *n* place
Preußen *n* Prussia
Provinz *n* province
Quell *n* source
Reich *n* empire, kingdom
Reichsstadt *n* imperial city
Reise *n* voyage
richtig *adj* correct
Russland *n* Russia
sampt, samt *prep* together with
Schlesien *n* Silesia
Schloß *n* castle
die Schweiz *n* Switzerland
sechs *card num* six
sechste *ord num* sixth
See *n* lake, sea, ocean
sehr *adv* very
sein *its* its
sieben *card num* seven
siebente *ord num* seventh
so *adv* so, thus
solch *adj* such
sowohl *conj* as well as
Staat *n* state, country
Stadt, Statt *n* city
Stift *n* bishopric
Stille Meer *n* Pacific Ocean
Straße *n* street, strait
Stück *n* part
Süd *n* south
südlich *adj* southern
Südlicher Polarkreis *n* Antarctic Circle
Südsee *n* South Sea
Sund *n* sound, strait
Tafel *n* table, chart
Tag *n* day
tausend *card num* thousand
Theil, Teil *n* part
Tote Meer *n* Dead Sea
Treffen *n* encounter, battle
über *prep* over, above
übrig *adj* remaining
um *prep* about, around
und *conj* and
Ungarn *n* Hungary
Venedig *n* Venice
verbessert *adj* improved
vereinigt *adj* united
Vereinigten Staaten *n* United States
Vestung *n* fortress
vier *card num* four
vierte *ord num* fourth
vom from the, of the (*von dem*)
von *prep* from, of
vor *prep* before, in front of
Vorgebirge *n* promontory, cape, headland, foothills
Vorstellung *n* conception, representation
wahr *adj* true, correct
wahrhaftig *adj* true, genuine
Wald *n* forest
Wasser *n* water
welch *rel pron* which, what, who
Welt *n* world
weltberühmt *adj* world-famous
Welttheil, Weltteil *n* part of the world
Wendekreis des Krebses *n* Tropic of Cancer
Wendekreis des Steinbocks *n* Tropic of Capricorn
Westindien *n* West Indies
wie *adv* how
Wiek *n* bay, cove
Wien *n* Vienna
zehn *card num* ten
zehnte *ord num* tenth
zu *prep* to
zum to the (*zu dem*)
zur to the (*zu der*)
zwei *card num* two
zweite *ord num* second
zwischen *prep* between, among
zwölf *card num* twelve
zwölfte *ord num* twelfth
Zypern *n* Cyprus

Italian-English

A number of early maps have titles in Italian, among them maps by Coronelli, Dudley, Zatta, and publishers of the Lafreri School. Most titles are fairly easy to guess, but the following list of terms may be helpful. Italian nouns and adjectives have two genders, masculine and feminine. Many masculine words end in -o, which changes to -i in the plural. Many feminine words end in -a, which changes to -e in the plural. However, there are exceptions. Nouns ending in -e in the singular become -i in the plural.

For the articles and article-preposition combinations, several forms are given. The form used depends on the gender and starting letter of the following word, but the rules need not be known to translate into English. Occasionally, when a word ends in a vowel, and the following word begins with a vowel, the terminal vowel is often replaced by an apostrophe, as in *dell'America*..

Italian-English

a *prep* to
adiacente *adj* adjacent
ai, agli, alle *prep* to the (pl.)
al, allo, alla *prep* to the (sing.)
alto *adj* high, upper
altrementi *adv* otherwise
altro *adj* other
anticamente *adv* anciently
appresso *prep* near
arcano *n* mystery
atlante *n* atlas
australe *adj* southern
baia *n* bay
banco di sabbia sandbank
basso *adj* low, lower
Belgio *n* Belgium
bocca *n* mouth
boreale *adj* northern
caduta *n* waterfall
canale *n* channel
capitale *n* capital
capo *n* cape
carta *n* map, chart
cento *card num* hundred
che *conj* that
chi *rel pron* who, whom, whose
chiamato *adj* named
Cina *n* China
cinque *card num* five
citta, civita *n* city
coi, cogli, colle *prep* with the, by the (pl.)
col, collo, con lo, colla *prep* with the, by the (sing.)
cominciare *v* to begin
con *prep* with
conosciuto *adj* known
contea *n* county, earldom
contenere *v* to contain
corretto *adj* correct
corso *n* course
cosmografo *n* cosmographer
costa *n* coast
da *prep* from
dai, dagli, dalle *prep* from the, by the (pl.)
dal, dallo, dalla *prep* from the, by the (sing.)
Danimarca *n* Denmark
decimo *ord num* tenth
dei, degli, delle *prep* of the (pl.)
del *prep* of

del, dello, della *prep* of the (sing.)
delineato *adj* drawn
della *prep* of
descritta *adj* described
descrittione, descrizione *n* description
detto *adj* said, called
di *prep* of
dieci *card num* ten
disegno *n* plan, drawing
dodicesimo *ord num* twelfth
dodici *card num* twelve
ducato *n* duchy
due *card num* two
e, ed *conj* and
Egitto *n* Egypt
emisfero *n* hemisphere
entrata *n* entrance
esatto *adj* exact
est *n* east
fatto *adj* done
finire *v* to finish, to end
fino *prep* as far as, until
fiume *n* river
foce *n* mouth
foglio *n* sheet
fortezza *n* fortress
fra *prep* in, between, among
Francia *n* France
Galles *n* Wales
geografia *n* geography
geografico *adj* geographical
geografo *n* geographer
gia *adv* formerly
Giappone *n* Japan
gli *art* the
golfo *n* gulf
grado *n* degree
grande, gran *adj* large
Grecia *n* Greece
hoggidi *adv* nowadays
i *art* the
il *art* the
impero *n* empire
in *prep* in
Inghilterra *n* England
Inglesi *n* Englishmen
intagliata *adj* engraved
intagliatore *n* engraver
intorno *prep* around
Irlanda *n* Ireland

isola *n* island
isoletta *n* islet
istmo *n* isthmus
la *art* the
lago *n* lake
le *art* the
levante *n* east
lo *art* the
Luigiana *n* Louisiana
maestro *adj* main
maestro *n* master
maggiore *adj* greater, major
mappa *n* map
mare *n* sea
meridionale *adj* southern
Messico *n* Mexico
meta *n* half
miglio *n* mile
mille *card num* thousand
minore *adj* lesser, minor
molto *adj* much
mondo *n* world
montagna *n* mountain
monte *n* mount
navigare *v* to navigate, to sail
nei, negli, nelle *prep* in the (pl.)
nel, nello, nella *prep* in the (sing.)
nono *ord num* ninth
nord *n* north
nove *card num* nine
Nuova Zelanda *n* New Zealand
nuovamente *adv* again, newly
nuovo *adj* new
o *conj* or
occidentale *adj* western
Olanda *n* Holland
Olandesi *n* the Dutch
orientale *adj* eastern
osservazione *n* observation, comment
ostro *n* south
ottavo *ord num* eighth
otto *card num* eight
ovest *n* west
ovvero *conj* or
paese *n* country, village
parte *n* part
particolare *adj* particular
penisola *n* peninsula
pianta *n* map
piu *adj* most

Italian-English

polo *n* pole
ponente *n* west
porto *n* harbor, port
Portogallo *n* Portugal
presso *prep* at, by, near, in
primo *ord num* first
principale *adj* principal
privilegio *n* copyright
projezione *n* projection
provincia *n* province, pl. -cie
quarto *ord num* fourth
quattro *card num* four
questo, questa *adj* this
qui *adv* here
quinto *ord num* fifth
rada *n* roadstead
rappresentante *pres part* representing
redatto *adj* written, drawn up
regno *n* kingdom
ridotto *adj* reduced
ritratto *n* image
riviera *n* coast
scoperta *n* discovery, pl. *scoperte*
scoperto *adj* discovered
Scozia *n* Scotland
secca *n* shoal
secondo *ord num* second
secondo *prep* according to
sei *card num* six
selvaggio *n* savage, native
sesto *ord num* sixth
sette *card num* seven
settentrionale *adj* northern
settimo *ord num* seventh
sia *conj* else; *sia...sia,* both...and; *o sia,* or else
sino *prep* as far as, until
sobborgo *n* suburb
sonda *n* sound
Soria *n* Syria
sotto *prep* under
Spagna *n* Spain
Spagnuola *n* Hispaniola
specchio *n* mirror
spiaggia *n* shore, beach
stabilimento *n* establishment
stampa *n* printing press, print
stamperia *n* printing establishment
Stati Uniti United States
stretto *n* straits
su *prep* on
sud *n* south
sui, sugli, sulle *prep* on the (pl.)
sul, sullo, sulla *prep* on the (sing.)
suo *adj* his, her, its
superiore *adj* upper
Svezia *n* Sweden
Svizzera *n* Switzerland
tavola *n* map
terra *n* earth
terzo *ord num* third
tramontana *n* north
tre *card num* three
Turchia *n* Turkey
tutto *adj* all
ultimo *adj* latest
un, uno, una *art* a
undicesimo *ord num* eleventh
undici *card num* eleven
Ungheria *n* Hungary
universale *adj* universal
uno *card num* one
vecchio *adj* old
veduta *n* view
vero *adj* true

Latin-English

The following list of words may help beginners translate Latin titles and legends appearing on maps. The Renaissance Latin used on maps is very similar to classical Latin, although there are vocabulary differences.

One cannot teach Latin in a paragraph. However, as a reminder, Latin is an inflected language. Word endings change to reflect usage. Nouns are declined, and entries below give the nominative (subject) case, followed by the genitive (possessive) ending. Plurals and other cases exist, but are not given here. Adjective entries give the three endings for the masculine, feminine, and neuter nominative case. Verbs appear in the third person singular. The vocabulary below should be sufficient to extract the essence of simple phrases. Bear in mind that adjectives may appear before or after the nouns they modify. Also, the letters **i** and **j** are often used interchangeably. In addition, words such as *sculpsit* and *scripsit* were often used loosely, and may merely indicate some unspecified connection between the person named and the map. Some examples may be helpful:

W. Marshall sculpsit. Literally, W[illiam]. Marshall engraved, or more loosely, engraved by William Marshall.

Americae Nova Tabula. Here *America* has been inflected, and appears in the genitive (possessive) singular. Thus the title is New Map of America.

Hispaniae Novae Descriptio. This is very similar to the above example, but now *Novae* agrees with, and thus modifies, *Hispaniae*. Therefore, the translation is Map of New Spain, and not New Map of Spain, which would have been written as *Hispaniae Nova Descriptio*.

Latin-English

a, ab *prep* from, by
Aberdonia *n* Aberdeen
ac *conj* and, and also
accuratissimus, -a, -um *adj* most accurate
adjacens *pres part* adjoining, connecting
Aestivarum Insulae *n* Bermuda, lit. Islands of Summers, i.e., Sommer's Islands
Africus *n* southwest wind
Albion *n* Britain
Albis Fluvius *n* Elbe River
aliquot *indecl num* some, several
Alostum *n* Aalst
Alsatia *n* Alsace
alter, -era, -erum *adj* other
amplissimus, -a, -um *adj* most glorious, splendid, or esteemed
Amstelodamum, -i *n* Amsterdam
Andegavensis Ducatus *n* Anjou
Andegavum *n* Angers
Andreapolis *n* St. Andrews
Anglia, -ae *n* England
annus, -i *n* year
anthropophagi *n* cannibals
Antverpia *n* Antwerp
Aparctias *n* northwind
Apelliotes *n* eastwind
apud *prep* at the establishment of; usually indicates publisher or printer
aqua, -ae *n* water
Aquilo *n* north by northeast wind
Aquisgranum *n* Aachen
archiducatus, -us *n* archduchy
archiepiscopatus, -us *n* archipiscopate
Archipelagus Meridionalis *n* Cyclades Islands
Archipelagus Septentrionalis *n* Aegean Sea
Argentina *n* Strassburg
Argentoratum *n* Strassburg
Argestes *n* northwest wind
Artesia *n* Artois
atque *conj* and, and also
auctor, -is *n* author, creator; *auctore* usually indicates cartographer or draftsman
Augusta *n* Augsburg
Augusta Perusia *n* Perugia
Augusta Trebocorum *n* Strassburg
Augusta Treverorum *n* Treves
Augusta Trinobantum *n* London
Augusta Vangionum *n* Worms
Augusta Vindelicorum *n* Augsburg
Augustodunum *n* Autun
Aurea Chersonesus *n* Malay Peninsula
Aurelia *n* Orleans
Aurelia Allobrogum *n* Geneva
Auster *n* southwind
australis, -e *adj* southern
Babenberga *n* Bamberg
Barchino *n* Barcelona
Bardum *n* Barth
Batavia *n* Djakarta
Bellovacum *n* Beauvais
Bercheria *n* Berkshire
Biturigum *n* Berry
Bononia *n* Bologna
borealis, -e *adj* northern
Borbetomagus *n* Worms
Boreas *n* north by northeast wind
Borussia *n* Prussia
Borysthenis *n* Dniepr River
Brechiniae Comitatus *n* Brecknockshire
Brema *n* Bremen
Breslanus *n* Breslau, Wroclaw
Britannia *n* Britain, Brittany
Brixia *n* Breschia
Brugae *n* Bruges
Brunopolis *n* Braunschweig
Bruxellae *n* Brussels
Byzantium *n* Istanbul
Cadomum *n* Caen
caelavit *v* (he) engraved
caelestis, -e *adj* celestial
Caesar Augusta *n* Saragossa
Caesarea Insula *n* Jersey
Caesarodunum Turonum *n* Tours
Calatia *n* Ciazzo
Caletensium *n* Calais
Caletum *n* Calais
Cambria *n* Wales
Candia, -ae *n* Crete
Cantabrigiensis Comitatus *n* Cambridge
Cantium *n* Kent
Carinthia *n* Karnten
Cecias *n* northeast wind
centum *card num* hundred
Ceretica *n* Cardigan
Cestria *n* Chester
chalcographus, -i *n* engraver
chersonesus, -i *n* peninsula
chorographica, -ae *n* geography
Cimbrica Chersonesus *n* Jutland
Circius *n* north by northwest wind
cis *prep* on this side of
citra *prep* on this side of
Claudiopolis *n* Cluj
Clivia *n* Cleve
cognitus, -a, -um *adj* known, reconnoitered
Colonia *n* Cologne
Colonia Agrippina *n* Cologne
Colonia Allobrogum *n* Geneva
Colonia Claudia *n* Cologne
Colonia Munatiana *n* Basle
Colonia Ubiorum *n* Cologne
Comensis Lacus *n* Lake Como
comitatus, -us *n* county
compendiosus, -a, -um *adj* abridged
complectens *pres part* embracing, comprising
comprehendens *pres part* including
Conatia *n* Connacht
conatus, -us *n* effort, endeavor; *ex conatibus,* by the efforts of
Condivincum Nannetum *n* Nantes
confinis, -e *adj* adjacent
confinis, -is *n* neighboring region
Constantia *n* Constance
Constantinopolis *n* Istanbul
continens, -entis *adj* adjacent, neighboring
conventus, -us *n* district assigned to a city, association
Corcagia *n* Cork
Cornubia *n* Cornwall
Corus *n* northwest wind
Cracovia *n* Cracow
cum *prep* with
Cumbria *n* Cumberland
Dania *n* Denmark
Darbiensis Comitatus *n* Derbyshire
Daventria *n* Deventer**

35

Latin-English

decem *card num* ten
decimus, -a, -um *ord num* tenth
delineavit *v* (he) sketched; usually indicates cartographer or draftsman
Delphi *n* Delft
Denbigiensis Comitatus *n* Denbigh Shire
descripsit *v* (he) drew, indicates cartographer or draftsman
descriptio, -ionis *n* map, representation, description
Devonia *n* Devonshire
dicio, -ionis *n* dominion, sovereignty; also *ditio, -ionis*
dioecesis, -is *n* district, governor's jurisdiction, diocese
Divio *n* Dijon
divisus, -a, -um *adj* divided, separate
dominium, -ii *n* ownership, property, rule
Dorcestria Comitatus *n* Dorsetshire
Dordracum *n* Dordrecht
Duacum *n* Douay
ducatus, -us *n* duchy, dukedom
Dunelmensis Episcopatus *n* Durham
duo, duae, duo *card num* two
duodecim *card num* twelve
Eblana *n* Dublin
Eboracensis Ducatus *n* Yorkshire
editus, -a, -um *adj* published, produced
Elvetiorum Argentina *n* Strassburg
emendatus, -a, -um *adj* corrected, improved, amended
Enipontius *n* Innsbruck
episcopatus, -us *n* episcopate, bishopric
Erfordia *n* Erfurt
et *conj* and
Euroafricus *n* south by southwest wind
Euroauster *n* south by southeast wind
Euronotus *n* south by southeast wind
Euros *n* southeast wind
Eustadium *n* Eichstadt
ex *prep* from, out of

exactissime *adv* most exactly
exactissimus, -a, -um *adj* most exact
excudebat, excudit, excud., exc. *v* (he) made or struck; usually indicates printer or publisher
exhibens *pres part* displaying
Exonia *n* Exeter
facies *n* shape, appearance, face
Faventia *n* Faenza
Favonius *n* westwind
fecit *v* (he) made, produced, created, or prepared; usually indicates engraver
fere *adv* approximately
finitimus, -a, -um *adj* neighboring
Fionia *n* Funen Island
Firenze *n* Florence
Florentia *n* Florence
florentissimus, -a, -um *adj* most flourishing, prosperous, or eminent
flumen, -inis *n* river
fluvius, -ii *n* river
forma, -ae *n* figure, design, sketch, plan
formis indicates publisher
Forum Iulii *n* Friuli
Forum Livii *n* Forli
fretum, -i *n* strait, channel
Frisia *n* Friesland
Fulgineum *n* Foligno
Gades *n* Cadiz
Gallia, -ae *n* France
Gallovidia *n* Galway
Ganabum *n* Orleans
Gand, Gandavum *n* Ghent
Gebenna *n* Geneva
Geldria *n* Gelderland
Genabum *n* Orleans
geographicus, -a, -um *adj* geographical
Germania Inferior *n* Netherlands
Glascua *n* Glasgow
Glotta *n* Clyde
Graecia *n* Greece
Gratianopolis *n* Grenoble
Gravionarium *n* Bamberg
Hafnia *n* Copenhagen
Haga Comitis *n* The Hague
Hammona *n* Hamburg
Hannonia *n* Hainaut

Hanovia *n* Hanau
Hantonia Comitatus *n* Hampshire
Hassia *n* Hesse
Helenopolis *n* Frankfort on Main
Hellas *n* Greece
Hellespontius *n* northeast wind
Helvetia *n* Switzerland
Herbipolis *n* Wurtzburg
heres, heredis *n* heir, successor
Hibernia, -ae *n* Ireland
Hierosolyma *n* Jerusalem
Hispalis *n* Seville
Hispania *n* Spain
hodie *adv* today, nowadays
hodiernus, -a, -um *adj* present, modern
Holmia *n* Stockholm
Holsatia *n* Holstein
Huntingdonensis Comitatus *n* Huntingdonshire
Illyricum *n* Dalmatia
imago, -inis *n* image, likeness, copy
Imaus Mons *n* Himalayas
impensa, -ae *n* cost, expense; *impensis* usually indicates publisher
impensus, -a, -um *adj* expensive
imperium, -ii *n* empire, dominion
in *prep* in, on, at
incidit, incidebat *v* (he) cut; usually indicates engraver
incola, -ae *n* inhabitant
inferior, -ius *adj* lower
instruavit *v* usually indicates engraver
insula, -ae *n* island
integro, -a, -um *adj* whole, entire
invenit *v* (he) devised; usually indicates cartographer or draftsman
inventor *n* usually indicates cartographer
Islandia *n* Iceland
item *adv* likewise, also, in the same manner
Iuliacensis Ducatus *n* Julich
Iutia *n* Jutland
iuxta, juxta *prep* near
lacus, -us *n* lake

Latin-English

Lancastria Palatinatus *n* Lancashire
Larius Lacus *n* Lake Como
Latium *n* Lazio
Legio *n* Leon
Leida *n* Leyden
Leicestrensis Comitatus *n* Leicestershire
Lemovicense Castrum *n* Limoges
Lemovicum *n* Limousin
Leodium *n* Liege
Leucorea *n* Wittemburg
Libonotus *n* south by southwest wind
Libs, Lips *n* southwest wind
limes, limitis *n* boundary, route
Lipsia *n* Leipzig
litus, litoris *n* coast, beach
locus, -i *n* place, district
Londinum *n* London
Lotharingia *n* Lorraine
Lovanium *n* Louvain
Ludoviciana *n* Louisiana
Lugdunum *n* Lyons
Lugdunum Batavorum *n* Leiden
Lusatia *n* Lausitz
Lusitania *n* Portugal
Lutetia *n* Paris
Lutzenburgum *n* Luxembourg
Mantua Carpetanorum *n* Madrid
mappa, -ae *n* map
marchionatus, -us *n* marquisate
Mare Hyrcanum *n* Caspian Sea
Mare Rubrum *n* Red Sea
mare, -is *n* sea, ocean
Matritum *n* Madrid
Mediolanum *n* Milan
meridionalis, -e *adj* southern
Mervinia Comitatus *n* Merionethshire
milia, -ium *card num* thousand
mille *adj* a thousand
Misnia *n* Meissen
Moguntia *n* Mainz
Moguntiacum *n* Mainz
Momonia *n* Munster
Mona *n* Isle of Man
Monachium *n* Munich
Monasterium *n* Munster
Montensis Ducatus *n* Bergh

Montisferratus *n* Monferrato (Italy)
Monumenthis Ducatus *n* Monmouthshire
mundus, -i *n* the world, the universe, the earth
Mutina *n* Modena
Namurcum *n* Namur
Nannetum *n* Nantes
Nassovia *n* Nassau
Natolia *n* Asia Minor
nec non besides, and also
nec, neque *conj* and besides, and also
Neocomum *n* Neuchatel
neotericus, -a, -um *adj* modern
Nicsia *n* Naxos
nonus, -a, -um *ord num* ninth
Nordovicum *n* Norwich
Norimberga *n* Nuremberg
Northantonensis Comitatus *n* Northamptonshire
Notus *n* southwind
novem *card num* nine
Novesium *n* Neuss
Noviodunum *n* Nevers
Noviomagum *n* Nijmegen
novissimus, -a, -um *adj* newest, most recent
noviter *adv* newly
novus, -a, -um *adj* new
nunc *adv* now, nowadays
ob *prep* because of, against
occidentalis, -e *adj* western
oceanus, -i *n* ocean
octavus, -a, -um *ord num* eighth
octo *card num* eight
officina, -ae *n* workshop, factory, *ex officina -,* from the workshop of, i.e., published or printed by
olim *adv* once, at that time, formerly
oppidum, -i *n* town
ora *n* border, coast
ora maritima *n* seacoast
orbis, -is *n* globe, circle, world, earth, orbit
Orcades *n* Orkneys
orientalis, -e *adj* eastern
Oxonium Comitatus *n* Oxfordshire
pagus *n* village, province

Palatinatus Bavariae *n* Oberpfalz
Palatinatus Rheni *n* Rheinland-Pfalz
Panormum *n* Palermo
Papia *n* Pavia
pars, partis *n* part, region
Parthenope *n* Naples
Parthenopolis *n* Magdeburg
passim *adv* here and there, all over
Patavium *n* Padua
Pedemontana *n* Piedmont
per *prep* through, by
Perusia *n* Perugia
Pictavium *n* Poitiers
pictor, -oris *n* painter
pinxit *v* (he) drew, painted, or decorated
plus, pluris *adj* more
Polonia *n* Poland
Pontus Euxinus *n* Black Sea
praecipuus, -a, -um *adj* excellent, extraordinary, special
praesertim *adv* especially
praeter *conj* besides
praeter *prep* past, beyond
presbiter *n* elder, priest
Presbiter Ioannis *n* Prester John
pretiosus, -a, -um *adj* expensive, valuable, precious
primus, -a, -um *ord num* first
privilegium, -ii *n* private law; *cum privilegio* usually indicates copyright
promissionis *n* promise
proprius, -a, -um *adj* special, individual, particular
prout *conj* as, just as
Provincia *n* Provence
quartus, -a, -um *ord num* fourth
quattuor *card num* four
-que *conj* and, used as a suffix
qui, quae, quod *rel pron* who, which, what, that
quinque *card num* five
quintus, -a, -um *ord num* fifth
Ratisbona *n* Regensburg
recens, -entis *adj* recent
recens, recenter *adv* recently, newly
regio, -ionis *v* line, boundary, region

37

Latin-English

Regiomontium *n* Konigsberg
regnum, -i *n* kingdom, dominion
retectus, -a, -um *adj* discovered, opened, made accessible
Rhedones *n* Rennes
Rhenolandia *n* Rheinland
Rhenus Fluvius *n* Rhine River
Ripen *n* Ribe
Rothomagum *n* Rouen
Rugia *n* Rugen Island
Rupella *n* La Rochelle
Sabaudia *n* Savoy
Sacra Insula, Insula Sacra *n* Holy Island
Salmantica *n* Salamanca
Salopia *n* Shrewsbury
Salopiae Comitatus *n* Shropshire
sanctus, -a, -um *adj* holy
Sarnia Insula *n* Guernsey
Saxonia Inferior *n* Lower Saxony
Saxonia Superior *n* Upper Saxony
Scania *n* Zealand Island
Schedamum *n* Scheidam
scilicet *adv* certainly, naturally
Scio *n* Chios
Sclavonia *n* Slavonia
Scotia, -ae *n* Scotland
scripsit *v* (he) wrote or drew; sometimes indicates lettering engraver
sculpsit, sculp., sc. *v* (he) carved; usually indicates engraver
secundum *prep* according to
secundus, -a, -um *ord num* second
sedes belli *n* seat of war
Senae *n* Siena
septem *card num* seven
Septentrio *n* northwind
septentrionalis, -e *adj* northern
septimus, -a, -um *ord num* seventh
Servia *n* Serbia
seu *conj* or
sex *card num* six
sextus, -a, -um *ord num* sixth
Sinarum Regio *n* China
Sinus Gangeticus *n* Bay of Bengal
situs, -a, -um *adj* situated
situs, -us *n* position, situation, site

sive *conj* or
Somersettensis Comitatus *n* Somersetshire
sophus, -a, -um *adj* wise
Soria *n* Syria
Sorlinges *n* Scillies
stellatus, -a, -um *adj* starry
Stiria *n* Steiermark
subjacens, -entis *adj* near
Subsolanus *n* eastwind
Suecia *n* Sweden
Suevia *n* Sweden
sumptus, -us *n* cost; *sumptibus,* at the cost of; usually indicates publisher
superior, -is *adj* upper, higher
Sylva Ducis *n* Bois-Le-Duc
tabula, -ae *n* map
tam *adv* so, so much, to such an extent
tam ... quam... both ... and ...
Taprobana *n* Ceylon
Taraco *n* Tarragona
Tarvisium *n* Treviso
Taurica Chersonesus *n* Crimea
Taurinum *n* Turin
Terra Sancta *n* Holy Land
terra, -ae *n* the earth, land
terrestris, -e *adj* earthly, terrestrial
tertius, -a, -um *ord num* third
theatrum belli *n* theater of war
Tholosa *n* Toulouse
Thrascias *n* north by northwest wind
Ticinum *n* Pavia
Tigurum *n* Zurich
Toletum *n* Toledo
Tornacum *n* Tournai
totus, -a, -um *adj* all, entire, total; gen. *totius*
tractus, -us *n* district, region
Trajectum *n* Utrecht
Trajectum ad Mosam *n* Utrecht
Trajectum ad Viadrum *n* Frankfort on Oder
trans *prep* across, beyond
Transisulana *n* Overijssel
Trebia *n* Trevi
Trecae *n* Troyes
tres, tria *card num* three
Treveris *n* Treves (Trier)

tribus, -us *n* tribe
Tricasses *n* Troyes
Tridentum *n* Trent
Turcicum Imperium *n* Ottoman Empire
Turonum *n* Tours
Tuscia *n* Tuscany
typus, -i *n* image, figure
Ultonia *n* Ulster
Ultrajectum *n* Utrecht
Ulyssipo *n* Lisbon
undecim *card num* eleven
universalis, -e *adj* universal
unus, -a, -um *card num* one
urbs, urbis *n* city
Ursina *n* Bern
uterque, utraque, utrumque *adj or pron* each, both; gen. *utriusque*
Utinum n Udina
Valesium *n* Valois
Vallisoletum *n* Valladolid
Vectis Insula *n* Isle of Wight
vel *conj* or
Venetia *n* Venice
Venetum *n* Veneto
ventus, -i *n* wind; *ventorum,* of the winds
verissimus, -a, -um *adj* truest
vernacule *adv* in the vernacular
Veromandua *n* Vermandois
Verona *n* Bonn, Verona
verus, -a, -um *adj* true, actual
vetus, -eris *adj* old
Vicentia *n* Vicenza
vicinus, -a, -um *adj* nearby
Vienna *n* Vienne
Vindobona *n* Vienna
Vitemberga *n* Wittemburg
Vormatia *n* Worms
vulgo *adv* commonly, generally, in the vernacular
Vulturnus *n* southeast wind
Wallia *n* Wales
Wetteravia *n* Wetterau
Wigorniensis Comitatus *n* Worcestershire
Wiltonia, Wiltoniensis Comitatus *n* Wiltshire
Zephyrus *n* westwind
Zerbi *n* Djerba Island

DEALERS' CONCERNS: Catalogues

The information in *Antique Map Price Record* is drawn from dealers catalogues. There are several methods of catalogue organization in common use, including:

1. Chronologically, beginning with the earliest item.
2. Alphabetically by map-maker.
3. Geographically, and chronologically within each region.
4. Geographically, and alphabetically by author within each region.

Regardless of which system is used, the following information should be provided for the customer and is highly desirable, if not essential, for inclusion in *Antique Map Price Record*.

MAP-MAKER. There may be some ambiguity in map authorship. One might cite the cartographer, engraver, publisher, or others associated with the map production. Custom generally dictates the choice. For example, maps in Blaeu's atlases are generally attributed to Blaeu, regardless of engraver or cartographer.

TITLE. This is where the sophisticated collector encounters the most difficulty. The title should be given as fully as possible. Strict bibliographical standards dictate copying the exact spelling and punctuation. Some titles are very long, and it is customary in such cases to omit some of the unnecessary verbiage. Ellipses (...) should be used to indicate portions omitted. However, it is best to retain places, dates, and personal names, since these are of most value in identifying the item. For example, a title might be:

> A NEW & ACCURATE CHART OF THE WORLD. DRAWN FROM AUTHENTIC SURVEYS, ASSISTED BY THE MOST APPROVED MODERN MAPS & CHARTS & REGULATED BY ASTRONL. OBSERVATIONS.

A barely acceptable abbreviation might be:

> A NEW & ACCURATE CHART OF THE WORLD ...

Some confusing abbreviations would be:

> A NEW AND ACCURATE CHART OF THE WORLD ...   (& replaced by *and*)
> A NEW & ACCURATE CHART OF THE WORLD ETC.   (*Etc.* not really part of title)
> CHART OF THE WORLD   (Too vague, and no ellipses)
> ... CHART OF THE WORLD ...   (Better, but still too vague and hard to alphabetize)
> THE WORLD   (Much too vague to identify)

For purposes of the *Price Record*, it is well to have the exact beginning of the title since that makes the alphabetical "Title Index" more useful. It is also helpful to have the title set off in some manner – by quotes, underlining, boldface type, or some other method – since it is sometimes hard to tell where the title stops and the description begins. Common problems in title transcription include interchanging 'and' and '&,' or 'etc.' and '&c.,' or substituting 'U.S.' for 'United States'. Map titles can be a confusing mix of lettering styles which may not appear as correct when transcribed. Most dealers just use normal capitalization, or give the title in all capitals. When a map has no title, a descriptive title can be supplied in brackets [ ].

DATE. The date can be somewhat confusing. For example, a map from a 1587 edition of Ortelius could be dated as **1587**. However, the map may have first appeared in the 1570 edition, and last appeared in the 1612 edition. Ideally, one could explicitly state something like **1570 (1587)**. However, it is sometimes not possible for the dealer to determine the exact edition. In such cases, the date of first publication is often used. If one knows the range, but not the exact date, one might give **1570-1612**. Sometimes it is easier to just explain what is known about the date.

DIMENSIONS. The dimensions should be given accurately. Height first, and width second, is the most common system. Dimensions are usually measured to the outside of the border. Sometimes a title or signature appears outside the border. It is preferable to exclude this from the dimensions, but there is no standard system. Dimensions can, of course, be given in inches or metric units (either cm. or mm.) Dimensions in the *Price Record* are rounded to the nearest centimeter and half-inch. Because some customers may want more accurate measurements, it is well to measure small maps to the nearest eighth-inch or millimeter. On larger maps this precision can be difficult, and the nearest quarter-inch or half-centimeter is usually adequate. On huge wall maps, or folding maps, the nearest half-inch or nearest centimeter is about the best attainable.

COLORING. If it is known that coloring is original or "modern", it should be noted. Printed color should be mentioned to distinguish it from the presumption of hand coloring on older maps. When the land areas are wash colored, this is often referred to as *full color*. If the cartouche has been left uncolored on an otherwise fully colored map, it can be specifically mentioned. Outline color usually means that just the boundaries or coastlines are colored.

CONDITION. If the map is in reasonably typical condition for its age, condition is sometimes omitted. It is advisable to mention noticeable flaws. The customer deserves to know the quality of the paper and if there are tears, separations at the centerfold, spotting (foxing), offsetting, stains, narrow margins, and other flaws. Any repairs should be noted.

PRICE. It can (and does) get omitted from time to time. Some dealers provide a separate sheet listing the prices for the items in their catalogue.

Items which are helpful, but not necessary, include item numbers for certainty in ordering, the publisher and place of publication, the work (if any) from which the map was removed, comments about the significance of the map, reference books mentioning the map, and an illustration of the map. Not only should a catalogue offer essential and supplementary information, but it should be easy to read and understand and pleasing to the eye.

There are a few terminology problems, including confusing margin and border. The border is the printed line or design surrounding the map. The margin is the blank area outside the border. The term *marginal* should be avoided, since *marginal staining* could mean either staining in the margins, or minor staining. *Mounted* is also ambiguous, since it often means backed, but could also mean matted.

Lloyd Brown's *Notes on the Care & Cataloguing of Old Maps*, is a good source of information for preparing a catalogue.

Map Dealer Questionnaire

Note to Map Dealers: We urge you to return a photocopy of this form *annually* so that our records and the information about your firm is certain to be current and correct. We are now requiring that a *questionnaire be returned every two years for a listing to be continued*. Volume 13 represents a grace period in which unconfirmed entries are still included. The (•) symbol signifies that a questionnaire has been received within the last two years. Dealers lacking this symbol must submit a completed questionnaire to be listed in next years edition. The reason is to assure our readers that the information we supply is reasonably accurate.

If you were omitted and wish to appear in the "Directory of Dealers" next year, please complete a photocopy of this form and return it to us by our February 29, 1996 deadline. Thank you for your cooperation.

1. Your business name: _____

2. Your personal name: *(optional)* _____

3. Your preferred address: _____

   _____

   _____

4. Telephone number: _____

5. FAX number: _____

6. Check any that apply:

   (a) _____ Do you maintain regular shop hours?

   (b) _____ Do you see customers by appointment only?

   (c) _____ Do you sell by mail order?

   (d) _____ Do you exhibit at fairs?

   (e) _____ Do you issue catalogues or price lists?

   (f) _____ Is your establishment an auction house?

7. If *over 50%* of your business is in Antique Maps, Sea Charts, City Views, Celestial Charts, or Battle Plans, please check here. (it will be noted) _____

8. If you have a cartographic specialty (i.e., American West, sea charts, Africa, etc.), indicate it briefly. If your stock is reasonably general, please note it. Limit your listing to cartographic material. Entries may be edited with regard to relevance and length.

   _____

9. If you are no longer in business or wish to discontinue your listing, check here. _____

Please return a photocopy of this form to:
Kimmel Publications, P.O. Box 12, Amherst, MA 01004, USA.   Fax (413) 256-6291

DIRECTORY OF DEALERS

The dealer listing that follows has been compiled from various sources. What started as a directory of 26 dealers in the first edition in 1983 has expanded to a global directory of over 700 names of individuals or firms trading in antique maps. With growth has come the problem of keeping the listing reasonably current. Some dealers may be retired, no longer active or may have moved. Others might be book, print, or antique dealers who deal only occasionally in maps. One or two dealers in modern maps may have been included. While every attempt is made to keep it reasonably current, there may be some inappropriate entries.

Last year we requested that dealers submit a questionnaire (as on the previous page) every two years in order for a directory listing to be continued. The response from the United States, Canada, Australia, and among prominent dealers in other parts of the world has been heartening. Nevertheless, the current edition incorporates a grace period in which the dealers in the lists assembled by David Jolly prior to 1993 are still included unless there is a specific reason for removal. The [•] symbol indicates that a questionnaire has been returned within the last two years.

We continue to need the cooperation of dealers world wide in assembling the data. Please note our requirement that *dealers return a questionnaire every two years for a listing to be continued.* We urge all dealers in antique maps to take a moment to return a copy of the *Map Dealer Questionnaire* (on the previous page – Page 41) to us by February 29, 1996, for inclusion in the next edition of the *Antique Map Price Record & Handbook*. For your convenience, you may use the publisher's Fax Number, (413) 256-6291.

Apologies are extended to any dealers inadvertently omitted or mistakenly included. Again, dealers who are not yet listed should use the questionnaire. Any errors should be called to the attention of the publisher so that corrections can be made in future editions.

IMPORTANT!

Inclusion of a name should not be regarded as an endorsement by the publisher, nor should omission be regarded as a lack of such endorsement.

Even though some entries do not indicate that an appointment is required, the information is not always complete, and even dealers with shop hours can be preoccupied with some activity such as preparation for a book fair. Therefore it is suggested that you either write or telephone before visiting.

Finally, when writing to dealers for catalogues or quotes, please remember that it is far more efficient for dealer and customer alike to give a detailed description of the desired material. Some dealers charge a small fee for their catalogues, many of which are held to scholarly standards and generously illustrated.

United States Dealers in Alphabetical Order

• denotes dealers who have returned a questionnaire within the last two years
[> ½] dealers indicated that over 50% of business is in antique maps or closely related

• **Acquitania Gallery**, Diane D. Vasica, 158 Carl St., San Francisco, CA 94117. (415) 664-2707, Fax same. by appt., by mail, lists/catalogues. California as an island; San Francisco
  Richard H. Adelson, North Pomfret, VT 05023.
  Alaskan Heritage Bookshop, P.O. Box 22165, Juneau, AK 99802. (907) 586-6748.
  Alaskana Book Shop, 4617 Arctic Blvd., Anchorage, AK 99503. (907) 561-1340. shop hours, by mail. Alaska, mountain climbing, hunting, U.S.G.S.
• **Amherst Antiquarian Maps**, , P.O. Box 12, Amherst, MA 01004. (413) 256-8900, Fax (413) 256-6291. by appt., by mail, fairs/shows. [> ½]
• **Sy Amkraut**, 35 Winding Wood Rd. N., Rye Brook, NY 10573. (914) 939-1509, Fax same. by appt., by mail. [> ½]
  Andover Antiquarian Books / Gallery, 68 Park St., Andover, MA 01810. (617) 475-1645. shop hours.
• **Anian Ltd.**, James V. Walker, 4450 Pinecrest Dr., Eugene, OR 97405. (503) 485-8727 [eves]. by appt., by mail.
  Antipodean Books, D. & C. Lilburne, P.O. Box 189, Cold Spring, NY 10516. (914) 424-3867. Australia.
• **The Antiquarian Shop**, George E. Chamberlain, 4246 N. Scottsdale Rd., Scottsdale, AZ 85251. (602) 947-0535, Fax (602) 947-7815. shop hours, by mail.
  Antique Brokers, 1716 Westheimer, Houston, TX 77098.
• **Antique Map Company**, Richard D. Stout, P.O. Box 1274, Fort Payne, AL 35967. (205) 845-5171. by appt., by mail. Southeast, North America 1600-1860. [> ½]
• **Antique Maps & Collectibles, Ltd.**, Suite 3-C, 7051 W. Commercial Blvd., Tamarac, FL 33319. 800-943-4330, Fax (305) 726-2700. shop hours, by mail, fairs/shows, lists/catalogues.
• **Antique Maps & Prints, Inc.**, Joseph Rubini, 5794 Sunset Dr., South Miami, FL 33143. (305) 665-5070, Fax same. shop hours. General. [> ½]
• **Antique Prints Ltd.**, Robert & Martha Seamans, Rt. 1, Box 156, Central Ave., Ocean View, DE 19970. (302) 539-6702, Fax (302) 539-9507. shop hours, by mail, fairs/shows. Specializing in VA, MD, DE and DC. [> ½]
• **Antiques Americana**, K.C. Owings, Jr., P.O. Box 19, North Abington, MA 02351. (617) 587-6441. by appt., by mail, lists/catalogues. General U.S., Civil War.
• **Antiquities**, 2575 Chantilly Dr. NE, Atlanta, GA 30324. (404) 329-2500, Fax (404) 329-9930. shop hours. [> ½]
  W. Graham Arader III, 435 Jackson St., San Francisco, CA 94111.
• **W. Graham Arader III**, 620 N. Michigan Ave., Chicago, IL 60611. (312) 337-6033, Fax (312) 337-8072. shop hours, by mail, fairs/shows, lists/catalogues. 16th-20th c. prints, maps & Americana.
  W. Graham Arader III, 29 E. 72nd St., New York, NY 10021. (212) 628-3668, Fax (212) 879-8714.
• **W. Graham Arader III**, 1000 Boxwood Court, King of Prussia, PA 19406. (610) 825-6570, Fax (610) 825-2152. shop hours, fairs/shows, lists/catalogues. Maps, celestial charts, city views.
  W. Graham Arader III, 1835 County Line Rd., Villanova, PA 19085. (215) 527-7950.
  W. Graham Arader III, Galleria One, 5015 Westheimer; Suite 2303, Houston, TX 77056. (713) 527-8055.
• **Argonaut Book Shop**, Robert D. Haines, Jr., 786 Sutter St., San Francisco, CA 94109. (415) 474-9067, Fax (415) 474-2537. shop hours, by mail, fairs/shows, lists/catalogues.
• **Argosy Gallery**, 116 E. 59th St., New York, NY 10022. (212) 753-4455, Fax (212) 593-4784. shop hours, by mail.
  Ark-La-Tex Book Company, L.S. Hooper, P.O. Box 564, Shreveport, LA 71102.
  Arkadyan Books & Prints, Gerald Webb, 926 Irving St., San Francisco, CA 94122. (415) 664-6212. shop hours, by mail, fairs/shows, lists/catalogues. California as an island.
• **Richard B. Arkway, Inc.**, 59 E. 54th St., Suite 62, New York, NY 10022. (800) 453-0045, (212) 751-8135, Fax (212) 832-5389. shop hours, by mail, fairs/shows, lists/catalogues.
  Art Source International, 1237 Pearl, Boulder, CO 80302. (303) 444-4080, Fax (303) 444-4298. shop hours, by mail, lists/catalogues. Also: 413 E. Hyman Ave., Aspen, CO 81611; (303) 925-6856.
  Asian Rare Books, Inc., 234 5th Ave., 3rd floor, New York, NY 10001.
• **The Atlas**, P.O. Box 3822, North Providence, RI 02911. (401) 353-1161. by appt., by mail.
  Authentic Antique Maps, Stuart Kaminsky, 3101 State Rd., 580, Safety Harbor, FL 33572.
  Barrister's Gallery, (At Nearing's Antiques), 526 Royal, New Orleans, LA 70130. (504) 525-2767. shop hours, by mail. 19th century, search service for fine items.
  Donald M. Barton, 2336 Magnolia Blvd. West, Seattle, WA 98199. (206) 285-4500. by appt., by mail, lists/catalogues, auction. General, north Pacific & northwest America.

United States Dealers

- **Bay Books, David N. Harbaugh**, 27115 E. Oviatt Road, P.O. Box 40306, Bay Village, OH 44140. [bus.] (216) 892-9191; [res.] (216) 835-5444. shop hours, by appt., by mail, fairs/shows.

  Bayou Books, 1005 Monroe St., Gretna, LA 70053. (504) 368-1171.

  Mary Beth Beal, 3913 N. Claremont Ave., Chicago, IL 60618. (312) 539-0105.

  James K. Beier Co., Suite 109, 2312 N. Grandview Blvd., Waukesha, WI 53188. (414) 549-5985, Fax (414) 549-5701. shop hours, by mail, lists/catalogues, auction. Maps & prints of all areas, specializing in early European, Colonial, Civil War, and Old West newspapers.

- **Bickerstaff's**, Stephen P. Hanly, 3 Ellery Road, Waltham, MA 02154. (617) 899-5504. by mail, fairs/shows, lists/catalogues. 18th & 19th-century American maps; New England.

- **Bill George International**, William G. Smith, 200 E. 66th St. C-1702, New York, NY 10021. (212) 356-1448, eve (212) 688-2693, Fax (212) 356-0955. business hours, by appt., by mail. General; atlases 16-19th c. [> ½]

  The Book Cellar Ltd., 8227 Woodmont Ave., Bethesda, MD 20814.

  Booked Up, 1214 31st St. NW, Washington, DC 20007. (202) 965-3244.

- **The Bookpress**, John Ballinger & John Robert Curtis, Box KP, Williamsburg, VA 23187. (804) 229-1260, Fax (804) 229-0498. shop hours, by mail, fairs/shows, lists/catalogues. Colonial America; Virginia.

  The Bookstall, 570 Sutter St., San Francisco, CA 94102.

  Boxwood Farm, Antique Prints, Richard Procopio & Diane Ihrig, P.O. Box 422, Rockport, ME 04856. (207) 236-8233.

- **Branford Rare Books**, John R. Elliott, P.O. Box 2088, Branford, CT 06405. (203) 483-7477, Fax same. by appt., by mail, fairs/shows.

- **Phyllis Y. Brown**, Antique Prints, Maps & Books, 736 De Mun St., St. Louis, MO 63105-2226. (314) 725-1023. shop hours, by mail, fairs/shows, lists/catalogues.

  Buxbaum Geographics, P.O. Box 465, Wilmington, DE 19899.

  California Book Auctions, Butterfield & Butterfield, Inc., 220 San Bruno Avenue, San Francisco, CA 94103. (415) 861-7500, Fax (415) 861-8951. auction.

- **California Land & Exploration Co.**, Scott Brake, 126 Stanford, Irvine, CA 92715. (714) 854-4440. by appt., by mail, fairs/shows. Globes; CA as "island" maps.

- **Camelot Books**, James A. Kissko, 2403 Hillhouse Rd., Baltimore, MD 21207. (410) 448-1015, Fax same. by appt., by mail, lists/catalogues. America maps & atlases.

- **Cape James Antiquarian Books & Maps, Ltd**, Kevin Moore & Greg Williams, 109 E. Fourth St., Lewes, DE 19958. (302) 645-7224, Fax (302) 227-8847. by appt., by mail, fairs/shows, lists/catalogues. Mid-Atlantic; Southeastern U.S. [> ½]

  Caravan Book Store, Lillian Bernstein, 550 S. Grand Ave., Los Angeles, CA 90071. (213) 626-9944.

  Bernard Conwell Carlitz, 1970 New Rodgers Rd. C-36, Levittown, PA 19056.

- **Thomas Edward Carroll**, P.O. Box 398, Hatfield, MA 01038. (413) 247-9767. by appt., by mail, fairs/shows, lists/catalogues. American Northeast, pre-1800. [> ½]

  Cartographic Arts, Patricia & Luke Vavra, P.O. Box 2202, Petersburg, VA 23804. (804) 861-6770. by appt., by mail, fairs/shows, lists/catalogues.

- **Cartographics of Vermont**, Christopher Watters, P.O. Box 145, East Middlebury, VT 05740. (802) 388-6488, Shop (802) 388-6229. shop hours, by mail, lists/catalogues. 19 c. American wall & pocket maps; atlases, geographies, exploration, guides. [> ½]

- **The Cartophile**, William T. Clinton, 934 Bridle Lane, West Chester, PA 19382-2172. (610) 692-7697. by appt., by mail, fairs/shows. Early American atlases; maps, Americana; books with maps.

- **El Cascajero**, The Old Spanish Book Mine, Anthony Gran, 506 La Guardia Place, New York, NY 10012. (212) 254-0905. by appt., by mail, lists/catalogues.

- **Jo-Ann and Richard Casten Ltd.**, 4 Dodge Lane, Old Field, NY 11733. (516) 689-3018, Fax (516) 689-8909. by appt., by mail, fairs/shows, lists/catalogues. World, North America, Holy Land. Also 101 W. 81st St., New York, NY 10024; (212) 496-5483. [> ½]

- **The Centuries**, Antique Maps and Prints, F.I. Mapes, 517 St. Louis, New Orleans, LA 70130. (504) 568-9491. shop hours, by mail. General. [> ½]

  Chafey's Books & Prints, 3511 Sunnyside Ave., Philadelphia, PA 19129. (215) 843-2499.

- **Chartifacts**, Walter J. Auburn, P.O. Box 8954, Richmond, VA 23225. (804) 272-7120. by appt., by mail, fairs/shows, lists/catalogues. U.S. Coast Survey, U.S. Coast & Geodetic Survey. [> ½]

- **Chartwell Mapsellers**, S.I. Miller, P.O. Box 1207, Huntsville, AL 35807. (205) 536-1521, Fax (205) 534-0533. by appt., by mail, lists/catalogues. Southeast U.S., AL, TN.

- **Chilton's Fine Art & Framing**, Chilton G. Powell, Jr., 4404 Old Shell Rd., Mobile, AL 36608. (205) 343-1736. shop hours, by mail.

- **Dennis Clare**, 818 Duboce Ave., San Francisco, CA 94117. (415) 552-0437. by appt., by mail. Western U.S.

  Taylor Clark Gallery, 2623 Government St., Baton Rouge, LA 70806. (504) 383-4929.

United States Dealers

John P. Coll, 2944 Pine Ave., Berkeley, CA 94705. (415) 845-8475.
- **Collectors Circle Ltd.**, Lili Ramonis, P.O. Box 225, Lemont, IL 60439. (312) 257-5958.
  Compass Rose Gallery, Antique Maps & Prints & Books, 671 Highway 179, Sedona, AZ 86336. (602) 282-7904, Fax (602) 284-1321
  Condy House, 1893, Antiquarian Maps & Prints, 820 N. Madison, Stockton, CA 95202. (209) 465-9951. by appt., by mail, fairs/shows, lists/catalogues. Americas, U.S. West, all pre-1850.
  Country Lane Books, P.O. Box 47, Collinsville, CT 06022.
- **Crone Antique Maps & Prints**, Patricia & Richard Crone, P.O. Box 164, Essex Junction, VT 05453. (802) 878-8539. by appt., by mail, fairs/shows, lists/catalogues. American Revolution, French & Indian Wars. [> ½]
- **Darvill's Rare Print Shop**, Dale Pederson, P.O. Box 47, Eastsound, WA 98245. (206) 376-2351, Fax (206) 376-2391. shop hours, by mail, lists/catalogues.
  Dawson's Book Shop, 535 N. Larchmont Blvd., Los Angeles, CA 90004. (213) 469-2186.
- **C. Dickens**, Fine, Rare & Collectible Books, 3393 Peachtree Rd., N.E., Atlanta, GA 30326. (800) 548-0376, (404) 231-3825, Fax (404) 364-0713. shop hours, by mail.
- **Frank Draskovic**, P.O. Box 803, Monterey Park, CA 91754-0803. (818) 281-9281. by appt., by mail, fairs/shows. North America; Far East Asia.
  Drew's Bookshop, P.O. Box 163, Santa Barbara, CA 93102. (805) 966-3311. shop hours, by mail, lists/catalogues.
  Drumbeat Americana Books, 7701 Shirley Dr. 2 West, St. Louis, MO 63105-2053.
- **Duck Creek Books**, Jim Richards, P.O. Box 203, Caldwell, OH 43724. (614) 732-4856. by appt., by mail, fairs/shows, lists/catalogues. General.
  Andre Dumont, Maps & Books, P.O. Box 10117, Santa Fe, NM 87504. (505) 986-9603, Fax (505) 986-6114. by appt., by mail, fairs/shows, lists/catalogues. Western Americana.
- **V. & J. Duncan**, Antique Maps, Prints & Books, Virginia & John Duncan, 12 E. Taylor St., Savannah, GA 31401. (912) 232-0338, Fax same. shop hours, by mail, fairs/shows. 16th-20th c. maps, prints & Americana. [> ½]
- **Einhorn Associates, Inc.**, Joseph J. Einhorn, 337 Demarest Dr., P.O. Box 973, Orange, CT 06477. (203) 795-5830, Fax same. by appt., by mail, lists/catalogues, auction. [> ½]
- **Emerson Booksellers**, Thomas & Mary Emerson, 420 Fore St., P.O. Box 366, Portland, ME 04112. (207) 874-2665. shop hours, by mail. [> ½]
  Emery's Book Auctions, Duston Rd., Contoocook, NH 03229.
  The Erie Book Store, 717 French St., Erie, PA 16501. (814) 452-3354.
- **Eugene Galleries**, Barbara Fischer, 76 Charles St., Boston, MA 02114. (617) 227-3062. shop hours. General; New England.
  Exnowski Enterprises, Eugene Exnowski, 31512 Reid, Warren, MI 48092. (313) 264-1686. by mail, fairs/shows, lists/catalogues.
  F & I Books, P.O. Box 1900, Santa Monica, CA 90406.
- **Joseph J. Felcone Inc.**, P.O. Box 366, Princeton, NJ 08542. (609) 924-0539, Fax (609) 924-9078. by appt., by mail, fairs/shows, lists/catalogues.
  Clifton F. Ferguson, Antique Maps & Atlases, 4999 Meandering Creek Dr., Belmont, MI 49306. (616) 874-9297.
- **First of Florida Maps**, Ashby M. Moody, 4305 El Prado, Tampa, FL 33629. (813) 839-7098. Florida, 1500's-1840's.
  Richard Fitch, Old Maps, Prints & Books, Dick & Dottie Fitch, 2324 Calle Halcon, Santa Fe, NM 87505. (505) 982-2939, Fax (505) 982-3148. shop hours, by appt., by mail, lists/catalogues. 19th c. development of American West; cartography books. [> ½]
  Fleetstreet Appraisals, Harold Square, 153 Madrone Lane North, Winslow, WA 98110. (206) 842-7488, Fax (206) 842-7489. shop hours.
- **Craig Flinner Gallery**, 505 N. Charles St., Baltimore, MD 21201. (410) 727-1863. shop hours, by mail, fairs/shows.
  Freeman Fine Arts, 1808 Chestnut St., Philadelphia, PA 19103. (215) 563-9275.
- **Freeman-Victorius Framing Shop, Inc.**, Richard B. Freeman, 1413 University Ave., Charlottesville, VA 22903. (804) 296-3456, (804) 293-3342. shop hours.
  Daphne Frost, Antique Maps, Books & Prints, P.O. Box 57, Rancho Palos Verdes, CA 90274.
  GA Maps & Books, Randall A. Detro, 202 Windsor East, Thibodaux, LA 70301. (504) 446-1726. by appt., by mail, lists/catalogues. North America, Mississippi Valley, Southeast U.S., general worldwide travel books & maps.
- **Gallery 515**, M. Sisk & D. McAfee, 515 E. Paces Ferry Rd., N.E, Atlanta, GA 30305. (404) 233-2911, Fax same. shop hours, by mail. General 16-19th century; S.E. USA. [> ½]

45

United States Dealers

Michael Ginsburg Books, Inc., P.O. Box 402, Sharon, MA 02067. (617) 784-8181.
George D. Glazer, 28 East 72nd St., New York, NY 10021. (212) 988-4535, Fax (212) 988-3992. Globes.
Goodspeed's Book Shop, Antique Map & Print Dept., 7 Beacon St., Boston, MA 02108. (617) 523-5970. shop hours, by mail, fairs/shows.
- **Goreham Collectibles**, Dennis B. Goreham, 1539 East, 4070 South, Salt Lake City, UT 84124. (801) 277-5119. by appt., by mail, fairs/shows. General U.S. stock.
- **Grace Galleries, Inc.**, Jacqueline Grace, Box 2488, R.R.5, Brunswick, ME 04011. (207) 729-1329, Fax (207) 729-0385. by appt., by mail, fairs/shows, lists/catalogues.
- **Graton & Graton**, Waldo & Marilyn Graton, P.O. Box 889, Islamorada, FL 33036. (305) 644-9419, Fax same. Also: 1601 Oakwood Ave., Highland Park, IL 60035; (708) 432-4722. by appt., fairs/shows. Pre-1800, Great Lakes, Caribbean. [>½]

William F. Hale Books, 1222 31st St. NW, Washington, DC 20007. (202) 546-2293.
Milton Hammer, Books, 789 N. Ontare Rd., Santa Barbara, CA 93105.
Wendell P. Hammon, 1115 Front, Sacramento, CA 95814. (916) 446-1782.
Hanzel Galleries, 1120 S. Michigan, Chicago, IL 60605. (312) 922-6234.
- **Douglas N. Harding**, Harding Book Shop, Route 1 North, Wells, ME 04090. (207) 646-8785, Fax (207) 646-8862. shop hours, by mail, fairs/shows.
- **Hawkins Maps**, Richard S.D. Hawkins, P.O. Box 931, Farmington, CT 06032-0931. (203) 675-5615. by appt., by mail.

Michael D. Heaston Co., P.O. Box 91147, Austin, TX 78709.
Heinoldt Books, T.H. Heinoldt, Central & Buffalo Aves., South Egg Harbor, NJ 08215. (609) 965-2284.
- **Heirloom Book Store**, Judi & Jim McMeans, 4100 Atlanta Highway, Athens GA 30622. (709) 369-7304. shop hours, by mail, fairs/shows, lists/catalogues.
- **Here Be Dragons**, Ed Curley, P.O. Box 57520, Tucson, AZ 85732. (602) 326-3132. by appt., by mail. General; West, Southwest & Mexico.
- **Heritage Antique Maps**, 551 Christopher Lane, Doylestown, PA 18901. (215) 340-9662, Fax same. by appt., fairs/shows, lists/catalogues. General; Ortelius. [>½]
- **Heritage Map Museum**, James E. Hess, 55 N. Water St., P.O. Box 412, Lititz, PA 17543. (717) 626-5002, Fax (717) 626-8858. shop hours, by appt., by mail, fairs/shows, lists/catalogues.

Robert M. Hicklin Jr.,Inc., 509 E. St. John St., Spartanburg, SC 29302. (803) 583-9847. shop hours, by mail, lists/catalogues. Southeastern North America.
High Latitude, P.O. Box 11254, Bainbridge Island, WA 98110. (206) 842-0202. Voyages & maritime books, seldom individual maps.
High Ridge Books, Inc., P. O. Box 286, Rye, NY 10580. (914) 967-3332, Fax (914) 976-6056.
Jonathan A. Hill, Apt. 10B, 325 West End Ave., New York, NY 10023-8143.
The Historian's Gallery, Robert C. Hill III, 3232 Cobb Parkway, Suite 207, Atlanta, GA 30339. (404) 432-3788 ext 24, Fax (404) 434-0285
- **Historic Urban Plans, Inc.**, Box 276, Ithaca, NY 14850. (607) 272-6277. by appt., by mail, lists/catalogues. Town plans & views; American maps.

Historical Americana, 3405 Woodley Rd. N.W., Washington, DC 20016.
Historical Technology, 6 Mugford St., Marblehead, MA 01945. (617) 631-2275. by appt., by mail, lists/catalogues. Antique instruments, charts, books, globes, orreries.
- **Historicana**, Irvin Ungar, 1200 Edgehill Dr., Burlingame, CA 94010. (415) 343-9578, Fax (415) 579-6014. by appt., by mail, fairs/shows, lists/catalogues. Maps of the Holy Land.

Hobbit Shop, 305 W. South Ave., Westfield, NJ 07090. (201) 654-4115.
The Holmes Book Co., 274 14th St., Oakland, CA 94612. (415) 893-6860.
- **The Holy Land**, Dr. Samuel Halperin, 3041 Normanstone Terr., N.W., Washington, DC 20008. (202) 965-4831, Fax (202) 965-1746. by appt., by mail, fairs/shows. Holy Land maps & views. [>½]

Holy Land Treasures, 1200 Edgehill Dr., Burlingame, CA 94010. (415) 343-9578. by appt., by mail, fairs/shows, lists/catalogues. Holy Land maps, views, prints.
- **Houle Rare Books & Autographs**, 7260 Beverly Blvd., Los Angeles, CA 90036. (213) 937-5858, Fax (213) 937-0091. shop hours, by mail, fairs/shows, lists/catalogues.
- **Murray Hudson Books & Maps**, 109 S. Church St., P.O. Box 163, Halls, TN 38040. (800)-748-9946 [USA], (901) 836-9057, Fax same. shop hours, by mail, fairs/shows, lists/catalogues. Atlases, books with maps, guides, etc. Wall & folding maps, south & western U.S., globes.
- **Indian Ocean Books**, Larry W. Bowman, 458 Middle Turnpike, Storrs, CT 06268. (203) 486-3355, Fax (203) 486-3347. lists/catalogues. Indian Ocean & islands only.

Jeltrup's Books, Thomas & Dorothy Jeltrup, King Cross St., Christiansted, St. Croix, VI 00820.

United States Dealers

The Jenkins Company, P.O. Box 2085, Austin, TX 78768. (512) 444-1616. shop hours, by mail, fairs/shows, lists/catalogues. Maps & books on America.
- **Capt. Kit S. Kapp**, Antiquarian Maps, Box 64, Osprey, FL 34229. (813) 966-4181. by appt., by mail, lists/catalogues. Maps of the Americas. [> ½]
- **Kauai Fine Arts**, Paul & Mona Nicholas, P.O. Box 1079, Lawai, HI 96765. (808) 332-8508, (808) 742-7608, Fax (808) 332-9808. shop hours, by mail, lists/catalogues. Americas, N.W. Coast, Pacific, West Indies. [> ½]

Keith Library & Gallery, 217 W. Front St., Red Bank, NJ 07701. (201) 842-7377.
Robert P. Kipp, 16 Wedgemere Rd., Beverly, MA 01915. (508) 922-6852.
H.P. Kraus, 16 E. 46th St., New York, NY 10017. (212) 687-4808.
Lahaina Printsellers Ltd., 636 Luakini St., Lahaina, Maui, HI 96761.
Maggie Lambeth-Books, Star Rte. 4, P.O. Box 361, Blanco, TX 78606. (512) 833-5252.
- **The Lamp**, W. E. Mayer, Jr., P.O Box 11302, Pittsburgh, PA 15238. (412) 963-0663. by appt., by mail, fairs/shows. General, mostly 19th c.c American; atlases, maps, reference.
- **Latitudes**, Tom Lazor, P.O. Box 66, Essex, CT 06426. (203) 767-3001, Fax (203) 767-7838. shop hours, by mail, fairs/shows, lists/catalogues. Atlases, coast charts, wall maps of North America.c. [> ½]
- **Don Leeper**, 3645 N.W. Glenridge Drive, Corvallis, OR 97330. (503) 758-3242. by mail, fairs/shows, lists/catalogues. [> ½]
- **Edward J. Lefkowicz**, 43 Fort St., P.O. Box 630, Fairhaven, MA 02719. (508) 997-6839, Fax (508) 996-6407. by appt., by mail, lists/catalogues. Nautical books; sea charts.

Harry A. Levinson, Rare Books, P.O. Box 534, Beverly Hills, CA 90213. (213) 276-9311. by appt., by mail, fairs/shows, lists/catalogues.
Librairie Bookshop, 823 Chartres St., New Orleans, LA 70116.
- **Lighthouse Books**, Michael Slicker, 1735 First Avenue North, St. Petersburg, FL 33713. (813) 822-3278. shop hours, by mail, fairs/shows. General; Florida & Caribbean.

Lincoln Rare Books & Globes, P.O. Box 85, Lincoln, MA 01773. (617) 259-8496. by mail, lists/catalogues.
- **Little Hundred Gallery**, Paul L. Whitfield, 1500 East Fourth Street, Charlotte, NC 28204. (704) 372-8322, Fax (704) 372-1954. by appt., by mail, lists/catalogues. Americana.
- **Lombard Antiquarian Maps & Prints**, P.O. Box 281, Cape Elizabeth, ME 04107. (207) 799-1889, Fax (207) 799-9593. by appt., by mail, fairs/shows.
- **Lorson's Books & Prints**, James Lorson, 116 W. Wilshire Ave., Fullerton, CA 92632. (714) 526-2523.
- **Low Country Collectibles Gallery**, George Timmons III, 32 Palmetto Rd., P.O. Box 7084, Hilton Head, SC 29938. (803) 842-8543, Fax same. shop hours, by mail, fairs/shows. General; Southern U.S.

Phyllis Lucas Gallery, 981 2nd Ave., New York, NY 10022. (212) 755-1516.
Lyons Ltd Antique Prints, Charles & Leila Lyons, 2700 Hyde, San Francisco, CA 94109. (415) 441-2202, Fax (415) 441-3124. shop hours, by mail, fairs/shows, lists/catalogues.
George S. MacManus Co., 1317 Irving St., Philadelphia, PA 19107. (215) 735-4465.
- **G.B. Manasek, Inc.**, P.O. Box 1204, Norwich, VT 05055. (802) 649-1722, Fax (802) 649-2256. by appt., by mail, fairs/shows, lists/catalogues. Mostly pre-1800. [> ½]
- **Manning's Books & Prints**, Kathleen Manning, 580 M Crespi Dr., Pacifica, CA 94044. (800) 879-6277; (415) 621-3565, Fax (415) 355-1851. shop hours, by appt., by mail, fairs/shows, lists/catalogues. World; U.S. [> ½]

The Map Bin, 109 39th St., Sea Isle City, NJ 08243.
Map Centre, 2611 University Ave., San Diego, CA 92104. (619) 219-3830.
Map Land, Robert Caruthers, P.O. Box 358, Nevada City, CA 95959. by appt., by mail, lists/catalogues.
- **The Map Store**, Mike McGuire, 5821 Karric Sq. Dr., Dublin, OH 43017. (800) 332-7885, (614) 792-6277, Fax (614) 848-5045. shop hours, by mail, fairs/shows, lists/catalogues.
- **Map World**, Dave Moser, 123-D N. El Camino Real, Encinitas, CA 92024. (619) 942-9642, in CA (800) 246-MAPS, Fax (619) 942-3229. shop hours, by mail, lists/catalogues. Pacific Rim, American West.

Mapquest, J. Scott Smith, P.O. Box 14211, Atlanta, GA 30324.
- **Maps of Antiquity**, Lynn Vigeant, P.O. Box 569, Montclair, NJ 07042. (201) 744-4364. by appt., by mail, lists/catalogues. Also June-Sept: 1022 Route 6A, West Barnstable, MA 02668; (508) 362-7169. shop hrs. [> ½]
- **Maps of the Promised Land**, Howard I. Golden, 305 Madison Ave., 46th Floor, New York, NY 10165. (212) 682-2300, Fax (212) 922-1353. by appt., by mail, lists/catalogues. Holy Land maps; views & books of Israel, 1480-1850.
- **Margolis & Moss**, David Margolis, P.O. Box 2042, Santa Fe, NM 87504. (505) 982-1028, Fax (505) 982-3256. shop hours, by mail, fairs/shows, lists/catalogues.
- **Douglas W. Marshall**, 545 University Pl., Grosse Pointe, MI 48230. (313) 882-6322, Fax (313) 974-7102. by appt., by mail. North America; Great Lakes. [> ½]

United States Dealers

- **Martayan Lan Inc.**, , 48 E. 57th St., New York, NY 10022. (800) 423-3741 [USA], (212) 308-0018, Fax (212) 308-0074. shop hours, by mail, fairs/shows, lists/catalogues. General; early & rare. [> ½]

  McClendon's Trash & Treasure, 1714-16 Westheimer Rd., Houston, TX 77098. (713) 522-7415. shop hours.

  Metsker Maps, P.O. Box 110669, Tacoma, WA 98411.

- **Mickler's Antiquarian Books**, Georgine & Thomas Mickler, P.O. Box 660038, Chuluota, FL 32766-0038. (407) 365-3636. by appt., by mail, fairs/shows, lists/catalogues. Florida material only.

  J.T. Monckton, Ltd., 1050 Gage St., Winnetka, IL 60093. (708) 446-1106, Fax (708) 446-1103.

- **Moon Marine**, Martin M. Cassidy, P.O. Box 846, Cypress, TX 77429. by mail, lists/catalogues. [> ½]

  Musgrave Antique Prints/Maps, Mrs. Helen Musgrave, P.O. Box 4895, Cave Creek, AZ 85331.

- **Kenneth Nebenzahl, Inc.**, Ken & Jossy Nebenzahl, P.O. Box 370, Glencoe, IL 60022. (708) 835-0515, Fax (708) 835-0519. by appt., by mail, fairs/shows. World, America, Asian regions, 19th c. Trans-Mississippi West. [> ½]

  Ken Nesheim, 45 High Meadow Road, Hamden, CT 06517-2131.

  Walter Neuman, F.R.G.S., 10500 Wyton Dr., Westwood, CA 90024.

- **New Albion Island Classics**, Sally A. Lewis, P.O. Box 10517, Oakland, CA 94610. (510) 893-7543, Fax (510) 452-2804. by appt., by mail. General; 17 c. Italy; Insular California. [> ½]

- **New World Maps, Inc.**, Charles R. Neuschafer, 1123 South Broadway, Lantana, FL 33462. (407) 586-8723. by mail, fairs/shows, lists/catalogues. General; American Southeast. [> ½]

  New York Bound Bookshop, Barbara Cohen, 29 E. 11th St., New York, NY 10003.

- **Cheryl M. Newby Inc.**, 5001 N. Kings Hwy. 106, Myrtle Beach, SC 29577. (800) 435-2733, (803) 449-4157, Fax (803) 449-1007. shop hours, by mail, lists/catalogues.

- **Newman's Books & Maps**, Alfred W. Newman, 1414 Mariposa St., Vallejo, CA 94590. (707) 642-9091. by appt., by mail. California maps & prints.

- **Nineteenth Century Prints**, Elisabeth Burdon, 2732 S.E. Woodward St., Portland, OR 97202. (503) 234-3538. by appt., by mail, fairs/shows, lists/catalogues.

  Jeremy Norman & Co. Inc., 720 Market St., San Francisco, CA 94102.

  North Shore Antique Maps & Prints, Bob & Marian Teplin, 339 Woodlyn Dr., Mequon, WI 53092. (414) 241-5704.

- **Northern Map Co.**, Victoria Bates, 11639 Cherokee Circle, Dunnellon, FL 34431-6601. (904) 489-3967, Fax same. by mail, lists/catalogues. General. [> ½]

- **Oak Dale Maps**, Bill Landefeld, 268 Lenape Rd., Kennett Square, PA 19348. (610) 347-2423, Fax same. by appt., by mail. North America, Africa. [> ½]

  The Observatory, Dee Longenbaugh, 235 Second Street, Juneau, AK 99801. (907) 586-9676, Fax same.

- **Oinonen Book Auctions**, Richard E. Oinonen, P.O. Box 470, Sunderland, MA 01375. (413) 665-3253, Fax (413) 665-8790. lists/catalogues, auction.

- **Old Ink**, Jan Hanna, P.O. Box 211, Annandale, VA 22003. (703) 941-8256. by appt., by mail, fairs/shows. General.

- **The Old Map Gallery**, Paul F. Mahoney, 1746 Blake St., Denver, CO 80202. (303) 296-7725, Fax (303) 296-7936. shop hours, by mail, lists/catalogues. [> ½]

- **Old Maps and Prints**, Preston & Petra Figley, P.O. Box 2234, Fort Worth, TX 76113. (817) 923-4535. by appt., by mail, lists/catalogues. North America, Southwest, Texas. [> ½]

- **The Old Print Gallery**, Judith Blakely, James von Ruster, 1220 31st St., N.W., Washington, DC 20007. (202) 965-1818, Fax (202) 965-1869. shop hours, by mail, lists/catalogues. General.

  The Old Print Shop, 150 Lexington Ave., New York, NY 10016. (212) 683-3950.

  Old World Mail Auctions, 671 Highway 179, Sedona, AZ 86336. (602) 284-1361, Fax (602) 284-1321. auction.

  Orientalism, Joseph Snyder, P.O. Box 540, Sharpsburg, MD 21782.

- **Overlee Farm Books**, Martin Torodash, Box 1155, Stockbridge, MA 01262. (413) 637 2277. by appt., by mail, lists/catalogues. Cartographic reference works; atlases.

  Pacific Book House, 435 Atkinson Dr., Honolulu, HI 96814.

- **Pacific Shore Maps**, Richard S. Cloward, 5664 Menorca Dr., San Diego, CA 92124. (619) 571-7487. by mail, lists/catalogues.

- **Ridler Page Rare Maps**, 205 King St., Charleston, SC 29401. (803) 723-1734, Fax same. shop hours, by mail, lists/catalogues. General. [> ½]

- **Pageant Book & Print Shop**, Shirley Solomon, 114 W. Houston St., New York, NY 10012. (212) 674-5296, Fax (212) 674-2609. shop hours, by appt., by mail, fairs/shows, lists/catalogues.

  John G. Panacy, 196 Walnut St., Stoughton, MA 02072. (617) 344-5043.

  Scott Petersen, P.O. Box 384, Kenilworth, IL 60043.

United States Dealers

- **The Philadelphia Print Shop, Ltd.**, Christopher Lane & Donald Cresswell, 8441 Germantown Ave., Philadelphia, PA 19118. (215) 242-4750, Fax (215) 242-6977. shop hours, by appt., by mail, fairs/shows, lists/catalogues. [>½]
  Philips, Son & Neale, Inc., 406 E. 79th St., New York, NY 10021. (212) 570-4851. auction.
  Donald T. Pitcher, P.O. Box 64, North Haven, CT 06473. (203) 239-2660.
- **Gary Pletcher**, 410 Surrey Lane, Bloomsburg, PA 17815. (717) 784-7892. by mail, fairs/shows.
- **The Portsmouth Bookshop**, Brian DiMambro, 110 State Street, Portsmouth, NH 03801. (603) 433-4406, Fax (603) 433-0901. shop hours, by mail.
  The Print Mint Gallery, Betty D. Sobel, 1147 Greenleaf Ave., Wilmette, IL 60091. (312) 256-4140.
- **Ptolemaeus Antiquarian Maps, Charts & Plans**, Bruce F. DeVine, 1243 Rossmoyne Ave., Glendale, CA 91207. (818) 507-1201. by appt., by mail, fairs/shows. Maps, charts & city plans, 16th-19th c.
- **Charles Edwin Puckett**, 3767 Forest Lane, Suite 116-445, Dallas, TX 75244. (214) 351-3242, Fax (214) 351-3018. by appt., by mail, fairs/shows, lists/catalogues. Early World, New World, America, Southwest, Texas. [>½]
- **William Reese Co.**, 409 Temple St., New Haven, CT 06511. (203) 789-8081, Fax (203) 865-7653. by appt., by mail, fairs/shows, lists/catalogues. American West.
  Regency Gallery, Derek Nicholls, 750 N. LaCienega Blvd., Los Angeles, CA 90069. (310) 659-3616, Fax (310) 659-3614. shop hours, by mail, lists/catalogues.
- **Riddell Rare Maps & Prints**, Royd L. Riddell, 2607 Routh Street, Dallas, TX 75201. (214) 953-0601, Fax (214) 823-9394. shop hours, by mail, fairs/shows, lists/catalogues. World, Americana, West, railroad, Geological. [>½]
  Warren H. Ringer, 55 Gay Street, Needham, MA 02192. (617) 444-9430.
- **George Ritzlin**, Maps & Books, 469 Roger Williams Ave., Highland Park, IL 60035. (708) 433-2627, Fax (708) 433-6389. shop hours, by mail, fairs/shows, lists/catalogues. [>½]
- **River Gallery**, Maureen Kahoun, 61 W. Clinton St., Joliet, IL 60431. (815) 749-5996, Fax (708) 349-1038. shop hours, fairs/shows, lists/catalogues. [>½]
- **Cedric L. Robinson, Bookseller**, 597 Palisado Ave., Windsor, CT 06095. (203) 688-2582. by appt., by mail, lists/catalogues. Americana, books, maps, historical photography.
- **Charles Robinson Rare Books**, P.O. Box 57, Pond Rd., Manchester, ME 04351. (207) 622-1885. by appt., by mail, fairs/shows, lists/catalogues, auction.
- **George Robinson**, Old Prints & Maps, 124-D Bent St., Taos, NM 87571. (505) 758-2278, Fax (505) 758-1606. shop hours, by mail, lists/catalogues. [>½]
- **Robert Ross & Co.**, Antiquarian Maps, Prints & Related Books, P.O. Box 8362, Calabasas, CA 91372. (818) 348-7867, Fax same. by appt., by mail, fairs/shows, lists/catalogues. General, 100-400 years old. [>½]
  Rouse's Bookhouse, Rte. 2, Eaton Rapids, MI 48827.
- **Barry Lawrence Ruderman**, Old Historic Maps & Prints, 6141 Soledad Mountain Road, La Jolla, CA 92037. (619) 456-7667, Fax (619) 238-0257. by appt., by mail, fairs/shows, lists/catalogues. American West, Pacific Northwest. [>½]
  Rudisill's Alt Print Haus, J.& B. Rudisill, P.O. Box 199, Worton, MD 21678.
  Robert Ellis Rudolph Corp., 1119 S.W. Park Ave., Portland, OR 97205. (503) 223-7518.
  Rulon-Miller Books, Red Hook, P.O. Box 41, St. Thomas, VI 00802.
  Russell Books & Bindery, P.O. Box 686, Spokane, WA 99210. (509) 534-1959.
  Sadlon's Ltd., Fine Print Gallery, 1207 Fox River Dr., De Pere, WI 54115.
- **Ken Sanders, Books**, P.O. Box 26707, Salt Lake City, UT 84126. (801) 467-1490, Fax (801) 467-1495. by appt., by mail, fairs/shows, lists/catalogues. American West; Utah, the Mormons.
  John Scopazzi, 130 Maiden Lane, San Francisco, CA 94108-5302. (415) 362-5708. shop hours.
  The Scriptorium, 427 N. Canon Dr., Beverly Hills, CA 90213. (213) 275-6060.
  Charles Sessler, Inc., 1308 Walnut St., Philadelphia, PA 19107. (215) 735-8811. shop hours, by mail, lists/catalogues.
  John Sharp, P.O. Box 163, Sebastopol, MS 39359. (601) 625-8162. Maps of Mississippi, U.S., world.
  Sherwood's Gallery, Sherwood P. McCall III, 2618 Briar Ridge, Houston, TX 77057. (713) 974-7780. lists/catalogues. Early maps, Americana, Texana.
  The Shorey Bookstore, 1411 1st Ave. 200, Seattle, WA 98101.
- **Dorothy Sloan, Rare Books**, P.O. Box 49670, Austin, TX 78765. (512) 477-8442, Fax (512) 477-8602. by appt., by mail, lists/catalogues, auction. World, Americana, West, Texas.
  E. Forbes Smiley III, 954 Lexington Ave. 186, New York, NY 10021.
  Walter W. Smith & Son Inc., 51 Pondfield Rd., P.O. Box 66, Bronxville, NY 10708. (914) 337-2794.
- **Solomon's Antique Maps**, Edward Solomon, 820 Lavers Circle, Delray Beach, FL 33444. (407) 274-4545. by mail, lists/catalogues. [>½]

United States Dealers

Sotheby Parke-Bernet, Inc., 980 Madison Ave., New York, NY 10021. (212) 472-3400. auction.

The Jean Spedden Gallery, Ltd., P.O. Box 334, Charleston, SC 29402. (803) 571-0199. 73 Broad St.

- **David R. Spivey**, Books, Old Maps, Fine Art, 825 Westport Road, Kansas City, MO 64111. (816) 753-0520. shop hours, by mail, fairs/shows.
- **Carolyn Staley - Fine Prints**, 313 First Ave. S., Seattle, WA 98104. (206) 621-1888, Fax (206) 325-9047. shop hours, fairs/shows. NW maps & views, Pacific voyages of exploration.
- **Harry L. Stern, Ltd.**, 1 S. Wacker Drive. 2280, Chicago, IL 60606. (312) 372-0388, Fax (312) 346-2917. by appt., by mail, fairs/shows, lists/catalogues.

  Paul Roberts Stoney, Print & Mapseller, P.O. Box "F", Williamsburg, VA 23183. (800) 732-4923; (804) 220-3346 [10-6 EST]. by mail, fairs/shows, lists/catalogues. America, colonial North America.
- **Thomas & Ahngsana Suarez**, Rare Maps & Prints, 181 Sherman Avenue, Hawthorne, NY 10532. (914) 741-6155, Fax (914) 741-6156. by appt., by mail, fairs/shows, lists/catalogues. Early World, America. [>½]
- **Susan Benjamin Rare Prints & Maps**, Benjamin & Susan Caughey, Fig Tree Farms, 13721 W. Telegraph Rd., Santa Paula, CA 93060. (805) 933-3193, Fax same. shop hours, by appt., fairs/shows, lists/catalogues. General 16th-19th cent.
- **Bernard Sussman**, Antique Maps, 565 Sanctuary Dr., Longboat Key, FL 34228. (813) 383-5823. by appt., by mail.
- **Swann Galleries, Inc.**, 104 E. 25th St., New York, NY 10010. (212) 254-4710, Fax (212) 979-1017. auction.

  Sykes & Flanders, P.O. Box 86, Weare, NH 03281.
- **William R. Talbot Fine Art**, 129 W. San Francisco St., P.O. Box 2757, Santa Fe, NM 87504. (505) 982-1559, Fax (505) 820-1044. shop hours, by mail, fairs/shows, lists/catalogues. General 16-19th c.; American West; Texas. [>½]

  Henry G. Taliaferro, 110 W. 80th St., New York, NY 10024. (212) 595-0289.

  Terramedia Books, 19 Homestead Road, Wellesley, MA 02181. (617) 237 6485.
- **Jeffrey Thomas**, Fine & Rare Books, 49 Geary St. 230, San Francisco, CA 94108. (415) 956-3272, Fax (415) 956-2738. shop hours, by appt., by mail, fairs/shows, lists/catalogues. Maps only sold peripherally.

  Tombstone & Western Americana, P.O. Box 7, Tombstone, AZ 85638.
- **Trade Winds Gallery**, Thomas K. Aalund, 20 W. Main St., Mystic, CT 06355. (203) 536-0119. shop hours, by mail, fairs/shows, lists/catalogues. [>½]

  G. H. Tweney, Antiquarian Bookseller, 16660 Marine View Dr., S.W., Seattle, WA 98166. (206) 243-8243. by appt., by mail, fairs/shows, lists/catalogues.
- **Unicorn Bookshop**, James Dawson, Route 50; P.O. Box 154, Trappe, MD 21673. (410) 476-3838. shop hours, by mail. Maryland, Chesapeake Bay.

  Adelhe von Hohenlohe, 1696 Nordentoft Way, Solvang, CA 93463.

  Von Maritime, Inc., Fred von Wiegen, 4928 Kuhio Hwy., Kapaa, Kauai, HI 96746. (808) 822-4999.
- **Washington Square Gallery Ltd.**, Denise DeLaurentis, 229 S. 9th St., Philadelphia, PA 19107. (215) 923-8873, Fax (215) 592-8989. shop hours, by mail, fairs/shows, lists/catalogues.
- **Waverly Auctions Inc.**, Dale A. Sorenson, President, 4931 Cordell Ave, Suite AA, Bethesda, MD 20814. (301) 951-8883, Fax (301) 781-8375. lists/catalogues, auction.

  R. M. Weatherford, Inc., Booksellers, P.O. Box 5, Southworth, WA 98386. (206) 871-3617. by appt., by mail, fairs/shows, lists/catalogues. 6 catalogs/yr.
- **Ann H. Wells**, Rare Tennessee Maps, 117 Prospect Hill, Nashville, TN 37205. (615) 383-2767, Fax same. by appt., by mail. Tennessee.
- **Jerry Wentling Rare Books & Maps**, 386 Navahopi Rd., Sedona, AZ 86336. (602) 282-5433, Fax same. by appt., by mail, lists/catalogues. Western Americana.

  Wildwood Books & Prints, 1972 Wildwood Lane, Anchorage, AK 99503.

  A. A. Wills & Sons Inc., P.O. Box 148, Marshfield Hills, MA 02051.
- **Yellowhouse Gallery**, John H. Sandberg, P.O Box 554, 2902 S. Virginia Dare Trail, Nags Head, NC 27959. (919) 441-6928. shop hours, by mail.. Civil War maps. [>½]
- **Yesterday's Gallery**, Earl M. Manz, P.O. Box 154, East Woodstock, CT 06244. (203) 928-5409. by mail, fairs/shows, lists/catalogues.
- **Yesteryear Book Shop, Inc.**, Frank Walsh & Polly Fraser, 3201 Maple Dr., N.E., Atlanta, GA 30305. (404) 237-0163. shop hours, by mail, fairs/shows, lists/catalogues. Southeastern U.S., 18th & 19th c.
- **Yu Heng Art Co.**, Donald Sheff, 303 East 57th St., New York, NY 10022. (212) 371-7050, Fax (212) 867-8122. by appt. 16th-17th c. World, China, NY, New England, celestials.
- **Samuel Yudkin & Associates**, The Woodner, Rm. A232, 3636 16th St., N.W., Washington, DC 20010. (202) 232-6249. shop hours, by mail, fairs/shows, lists/catalogues, auction.

United States Dealers by State and City

For complete information, see United States dealers in Alphabetical Order above.

ALASKA
Anchorage	Alaskana Book Shop
Anchorage	Wildwood Books & Prints
Juneau	Alaskan Heritage Bookshop
Juneau	The Observatory

ALABAMA
Fort Payne	Antique Map Company
Huntsville	Chartwell Mapsellers
Mobile	Chilton's Fine Art & Framing

ARIZONA
Cave Creek	Musgrave Antique Prints/Maps
Scottsdale	The Antiquarian Shop
Sedona	Jerry Wentling Rare Books / Maps
Sedona	Compass Rose Gallery
Sedona	Old World Mail Auctions
Tombstone	Tombstone & Western Americana
Tucson	Here Be Dragons

CALIFORNIA
Berkeley	John P. Coll
Beverly Hills	Harry A. Levinson, Rare Books
Beverly Hills	The Scriptorium
Burlingame	Historicana
Burlingame	Holy Land Treasures
Calabasas	Robert Ross & Co.
Encinitas	Map World
Fullerton	Lorson's Books & Prints
Glendale	Ptolemaeus Antiquarian Maps
Irvine	California Land & Exploration Co.
La Jolla	Barry Lawrence Ruderman
Los Angeles	Caravan Book Store
Los Angeles	Dawson's Book Shop
Los Angeles	Houle Rare Books & Autographs
Los Angeles	Regency Gallery
Monterey Park	Frank Draskovic
Nevada City	Map Land
Oakland	New Albion Island Classics
Oakland	The Holmes Book Co.
Pacifica	Manning's Books & Prints
Rancho Palos Verdes	Daphne Frost
Sacramento	Wendell P. Hammon
San Diego	Map Centre
San Diego	Pacific Shore Maps
San Francisco	Acquitania Gallery
San Francisco	Argonaut Book Shop
San Francisco	Arkadyan Books & Prints
San Francisco	California Book Auctions
San Francisco	Dennis Clare
San Francisco	Jeffrey Thomas
San Francisco	Jeremy Norman & Co. Inc.
San Francisco	John Scopazzi
San Francisco	Lyons Ltd Antique Prints
San Francisco	The Bookstall
San Francisco	W. Graham Arader III
Santa Barbara	Drew's Bookshop
Santa Barbara	Milton Hammer, Books
Santa Monica	F & I Books
Santa Paula	Susan Benjamin Rare Prints
Solvang	Adelhe von Hohenlohe
Stockton	Condy House, 1893
Vallejo	Newman's Books & Maps
Westwood	Walter Neuman, F.R.G.S.

COLORADO
Boulder	Art Source International
Denver	The Old Map Gallery

CONNECTICUT
Branford	Branford Rare Books
Collinsville	Country Lane Books
E. Woodstock	Yesterday's Gallery
Essex	Latitudes
Farmington	Hawkins Maps
Hamden	Ken Nesheim
Mystic	Trade Winds Gallery
New Haven	William Reese Co.
North Haven	Donald T. Pitcher
Orange	Einhorn Associates, Inc.
Storrs	Indian Ocean Books
Windsor	Cedric L. Robinson, Bookseller

DISTRICT OF COLUMBIA
Washington	Booked Up
Washington	Historical Americana
Washington	Samuel Yudkin & Associates
Washington	The Holy Land
Washington	The Old Print Gallery
Washington	William F. Hale Books

DELAWARE
Lewes	Cape James Antiquarian Books
Ocean View	Antique Prints Ltd.
Wilmington	Buxbaum Geographics

FLORIDA
Chuluota	Mickler's Antiquarian Books
Delray Beach	Solomon's Antique Maps
Dunnellon	Northern Map Co.
Islamorada	Graton & Graton
Lantana	New World Maps, Inc.
Longboat Key	Bernard Sussman, Antique Maps
Osprey	Capt. Kit S. Kapp
St. Petersburg	Lighthouse Books
Safety Harbor	Authentic Antique Maps
South Miami	Antique Maps & Prints, Inc.
Tamarac	Antique Maps & Collectibles, Ltd.
Tampa	First of Florida Maps

51

GEORGIA

Athens	Heirloom Book Store
Atlanta	Antiquities
Atlanta	C. Dickens
Atlanta	Gallery 515
Atlanta	The Historian's Gallery
Atlanta	Mapquest
Atlanta	Yesteryear Book Shop, Inc.
Savannah	V. & J. Duncan

HAWAII

Honolulu	Pacific Book House
Kapaa, Kauai	Von Maritime, Inc.
Lahaina, Maui	Lahaina Printsellers Ltd.
Lawai	Kauai Fine Arts

ILLINOIS

Chicago	Hanzel Galleries
Chicago	Harry L. Stern, Ltd.
Chicago	Mary Beth Beal
Chicago	W. Graham Arader III
Glencoe	Kenneth Nebenzahl, Inc.
Highland Park	George Ritzlin
Joliet	River Gallery
Kenilworth	Scott Petersen
Lemont	Collectors Circle Ltd.
Wilmette	The Print Mint Gallery
Winnetka	J.T. Monckton, Ltd.

LOUISIANA

Baton Rouge	Taylor Clark Gallery
Gretna	Bayou Books
New Orleans	Barrister's Gallery
New Orleans	Librairie Bookshop
New Orleans	The Centuries
Shreveport	Ark-La-Tex Book Company
Thibodaux	GA Maps & Books

MASSACHUSETTS

Amherst	Amherst Antiquarian Maps
Andover	Andover Antiquarian Books
Beverly	Robert P. Kipp
Boston	Eugene Galleries
Boston	Goodspeed's Book Shop
Fairhaven	Edward J. Lefkowicz
Hatfield	Thomas Edward Carroll
Lincoln	Lincoln Rare Books & Globes
Marblehead	Historical Technology
Marshfield Hills	A. A. Wills & Sons Inc.
Needham	Warren H. Ringer
North Abington	Antiques Americana
Sharon	Michael Ginsburg Books, Inc.
Stockbridge	Overlee Farm Books
Stoughton	John G. Panacy
Sunderland	Oinonen Book Auctions
Waltham	Bickerstaff's
Wellesley	Terramedia Books

MARYLAND

Baltimore	Camelot Books
Baltimore	Craig Flinner Gallery
Bethesda	The Book Cellar Ltd.
Bethesda	Waverly Auctions Inc.
Sharpsburg	Orientalism
Trappe	Unicorn Bookshop
Worton	Rudisill's Alt Print Haus

MAINE

Brunswick	Grace Galleries, Inc.
Cape Elizabeth	Lombard Antiquarian
Manchester	Charles Robinson Rare Books
Portland	Emerson Booksellers
Rockport	Boxwood Farm, Antique Prints
Wells	Douglas N. Harding

MICHIGAN

Belmont	Clifton F. Ferguson
Eaton Rapids	Rouse's Bookhouse
Grosse Pointe	Douglas W. Marshall
Warren	Exnowski Enterprises

MISSOURI

Kansas City	David R. Spivey
St. Louis	Drumbeat Americana Books
St. Louis	Elizabeth F. Dunlap
St. Louis	Phyllis Y. Brown

MISSISSIPPI

Sebastopol	John Sharp

NORTH CAROLINA

Charlotte	Little Hundred Gallery
Nags Head	Yellowhouse Gallery

NEW HAMPSHIRE

Contoocook	Emery's Book Auctions
Portsmouth	The Portsmouth Bookshop
Weare	Sykes & Flanders

NEW JERSEY

Montclair	Maps of Antiquity
Princeton	Joseph J. Felcone Inc.
Red Bank	Keith Library & Gallery
Sea Isle City	The Map Bin
South Egg Harb.	Heinoldt Books
Westfield	Hobbit Shop

NEW MEXICO

Santa Fe	Andre Dumont
Santa Fe	Margolis & Moss
Santa Fe	Richard Fitch
Santa Fe	William R. Talbot Fine Art
Taos	George Robinson

NEW YORK

Bronxville	Walter W. Smith & Son Inc.
Cold Spring	Antipodean Books
Hawthorne	Thomas & Ahngsana Suarez
Ithaca	Historic Urban Plans, Inc.
New York	Argosy Gallery
New York	Asian Rare Books, Inc.
New York	Bill George International
New York	E. Forbes Smiley III
New York	El Cascajero
New York	George D. Glazer

New York	H.P. Kraus		**TENNESSEE**	
New York	Henry G. Taliaferro	Halls	Murray Hudson Books & Maps
New York	Jonathan A. Hill	Nashville	Ann H. Wells
New York	Maps of the Promised Land		**TEXAS**	
New York	Martayan Lan Inc.	Austin	Dorothy Sloan, Rare Books
New York	New York Bound Bookshop	Austin	Michael D. Heaston Co.
New York	Pageant Book & Print Shop	Austin	The Jenkins Company
New York	Philips, Son & Neale, Inc.	Blanco	Maggie Lambeth-Books
New York	Phyllis Lucas Gallery	Cypress	Moon Marine
New York	Richard B. Arkway, Inc.	Dallas	Charles Edwin Puckett
New York	Sotheby Parke-Bernet, Inc.	Dallas	Royd L. Riddell
New York	Swann Galleries, Inc.	Fort Worth	Old Maps and Prints
New York	The Old Print Shop	Houston	Antique Brokers
New York	W. Graham Arader III	Houston	McClendon's Trash & Treasure
New York	Yu Heng Art Co.	Houston	Sherwood's Gallery
Old Field	Jo-Ann and Richard Casten Ltd.	Houston	W. Graham Arader III
Rye	High Ridge Books, Inc.		**UTAH**	
Rye Brook	Sy Amkraut	Salt Lake City	Goreham Collectibles
	OHIO	Salt Lake City	Ken Sanders, Books
Bay Village	Bay Books, David N. Harbaugh		**VIRGINIA**	
Caldwell	Duck Creek Books	Annandale	Old Ink
Dublin	The Map Store	Charlottesville	Freeman-Victorius Framing Shop
	OREGON	Petersburg	Cartographic Arts
Corvallis	Don Leeper	Richmond	Chartifacts
Eugene	Anian Ltd.	Williamsburg	Paul Roberts Stoney
Portland	Nineteenth Century Prints	Williamsburg	The Bookpress
Portland	Robert Ellis Rudolph Corp.		**VIRGIN ISLANDS**	
	PENNSYLVANIA	Christiansted	Jeltrup's Books
Bloomsburg	Gary Pletcher	St. Thomas	Rulon-Miller Books
Doylestown	Heritage Antique Maps		**VERMONT**	
Erie	The Erie Book Store	East Middlebury	Cartographics of Vermont
Kennett Square	Oak Dale Maps	Essex Junction	Crone Antique Maps & Prints
King of Prussia	W. Graham Arader III	North Pomfret	Richard H. Adelson
Levittown	Bernard Conwell Carlitz	Norwich	G.B. Manasek, Inc.
Lititz	Heritage Map Museum		**WASHINGTON**	
Philadelphia	Chafey's Books & Prints	Bainbridge Is.	High Latitude
Philadelphia	Charles Sessler, Inc.	Eastsound	Darvill's Rare Print Shop
Philadelphia	Freeman Fine Arts	Seattle	Carolyn Staley - Fine Prints
Philadelphia	George S. MacManus Co.	Seattle	Donald M. Barton
Philadelphia	The Philadelphia Print Shop, Ltd.	Seattle	G. H. Tweney
Philadelphia	Washington Square Gallery Ltd.	Seattle	The Shorey Bookstore
Pittsburgh	The Lamp	Southworth	R. M. Weatherford, Inc.
Villanova	W. Graham Arader III	Spokane	Russell Books & Bindery
West Chester	The Cartophile	Tacoma	Metsker Maps
	RHODE ISLAND	Winslow	Fleetstreet Appraisals
No. Providence	The Atlas		**WISCONSIN**	
	SOUTH CAROLINA	De Pere	Sadlon's Ltd., Fine Print Gallery
Charleston	Ridler Page Rare Maps	Mequon	North Shore Antique Maps / Prints
Charleston	The Jean Spedden Gallery, Ltd.	Waukesha	James K. Beier Co.
Hilton Head	Low Country Collectibles Gallery		
Myrtle Beach	Cheryl M. Newby Inc.		
Spartanburg	Robert M. Hicklin Jr.,Inc.		

Canadian Dealers in Alphabetical Order

• denotes dealers who have returned a questionnaire within the last two years
[> ½] dealers indicated that over 50% of business is in antique maps or closely related

Alexandre Antique Prints, 1543 Bayview Ave., Toronto, Ontario M4G 2B5. (416) 489-6701
• **The Allery**, Catherine L. Clatworthy, 322 1/2 Queen St. West, Toronto, Ontario, M5V 2A2. (416) 593-0853. shop hours, by mail. Canadiana.
Hugh Anson-Cartwright Books, 229 College St., Toronto, Ontario, M5T 1R4.
• **The Antiquarian Print Room**, Caroline Harris, 840 Fort St., 2nd Floor, Victoria, B.C., V8W 1H8. (604) 380-1343, Fax (604) 383-8594. shop hours, by mail, lists/catalogues.
The Astrolabe Gallery, John W. Coles, 91 Sparks St., Ottawa, Ontario, K1P 5A5. (613) 234-2348. shop hours, fairs/shows, auction.
• **Beach Antique Maps & Prints**, Kate & Alec Parley, 3 Firstbrooke Road, Toronto, Ontario, M4E 2L2. (416) 694-8119. shop hours, by mail, lists. Shop: Harbour Front Antique Market, 390 Queens Quay W., Toronto.
John Channell Berry, Rare Books, Maps & Prints, 112 Montréal St., Kingston, Ontario, K7K 3E8. (613) 549-6652.
Canadiana Fine Arts Ltd., 1208 Belavista Crescent S.W., Calgary, Alberta, T2V 2B1. (403) 252-3421. shop hours, by mail. Canadian maps, pre-confederation.
Fulford Gallery, Daniel Fulford, 75 Hinton Ave. North, Ottawa, Ontario, K1Y 0Z7. (613) 722-0440, Fax (613) 722-4528. shop hours, by mail. Decorative maps & prints, Canadiana.
• **Judaica Sales Reg'd**, Isidore Baum, P.O.B. 276 - Youville Station, Montréal, Que., H2P 2VS. (514) 687-0632. by appt., by mail, fairs/shows, lists/catalogues. Maps & print of the Holy Land.
• **Helen R. Kahn, Antiquarian Books**, P.O. Box 323, Victoria Station, Montréal, Que., H3Z 2V8. (514) 844-5344, Fax (514) 499-9274. by appt., by mail, fairs/shows, lists/catalogues.
• **Kershaw Old Maps & Prints**, Ken Kershaw, 442 Wilson St. East, Ancaster, Ontario, L9G 2C3. (905) 648-1991, Fax (905) 304-1037. shop hours, by appt., by mail, fairs/shows, lists/catalogues.
• **D. & E. Lake Ltd.**, 239 King St. East, Toronto, Ontario, M5A 1J9. (416) 863-9930, Fax (416) 863-9443. shop hours, by mail, fairs/shows, lists/catalogues. General.
• **The Loose Page**, Joachim M. Waibel, P.O. Box 91158, West Vancouver, B.C., V7V 3N6. (604) 926-1010, Fax (604) 926-9966. by appt., by mail, lists/catalogues. Maps & books of Middle East & Persia.
The Map Room, 18 Birch Ave., Toronto, Ontario, M4V 1C8. (416) 922-5153, (416) 923-2580. shop hours, by mail, fairs/shows, auction.
Brendan M. Moss, 5637 Wallace St., Vancouver, B.C., V6N 2A1. (604) 662-8171 [Bus.], (604) 261-7108 [Home]. by appt., by mail, fairs/shows, auction. At "Lemagazin," 110-332 Water St. General, emphasis on Pacific NW, voyage/travel, mountaineering.
• **North by West**, 53 Scrivens St., Ottawa, Ontario, K2B 8M6. (613) 828-4115, 384-2346. by mail, fairs/shows, lists/catalogues. Also: 731-C Fort St., Royal Mall, Victoria, B.C. V8W 2C5; shop hours.
• **Ptolémée Plus Antique Maps**, David Chandler, C.P. 344, succ. Cartierville, Montréal, Que., H4K 2J6. (514) 334-7418. by appt., by mail, fairs/shows, lists/catalogues. NE North America emphasis. [> ½]
Russborough, P.O. Box 422, Station R, Toronto, Ontario, M4G 4C3. (416) 425-2457. by appt., by mail, fairs/shows, auction. Emphasis on North America, Canada, Arctic, British Isles.
• **Schooner Books**, John D. Townsend, 5378 Inglis St., Halifax, Nova Scotia, B3H 1J5. (902) 423-8419, Fax same. shop hours, by mail, fairs/shows, lists/catalogues. Canadiana specialty.
Vauxhall Antiques Ltd., 1023 Fort St., Victoria, B.C., .
• **Ronald Whistance-Smith**, Antique Maps & Prints, 14520 84 Ave., Edmonton, Alberta, T5R 3X2. (403) 483-5858. by appt., by mail, fairs/shows. Canada, British Isles, Austria-Hungary. [> ½]
• **Joyce Williams**, Antique Prints & Maps, 346 W. Pender St., Vancouver, B.C., V6B 1T1. (604) 688-7434, Fax (604) 530-3079. shop hours, by mail, fairs/shows, lists/catalogues. General; Western Canada, Arctic.
• **Thomas N. Yarmon**, 8 King St. East, Toronto, Ontario, M5C 1B5. (416) 363-5086, Fax (416) 363-6845. by appt., by mail. [> ½]

International Dealers Alphabetically Within Country

* denotes dealers who have returned a questionnaire within the last two years
[> ½] dealers indicated that over 50% of business is in antique maps or closely related

ARGENTINA

Liberia l'Amateur, Esmeralda 882, Buenos Aires 1007. 312-7635.
Libreria de Antano, P.O. Box 1425, Sanchez de Bustamente 1876, Buenos Aires. 83-7178.
Magallanes Books, Virginia Guller de Santiago, 25 de Mayo 158 Of. 114, Buenos Aires 1002. 54-331102.
Enrique Martinez, Maps & Prints, Elfein 3951 - 6 p.E, CP. 1636. (54) 1 743 3342, Fax same.

AUSTRALIA

Antiquarian Maps & Prints Pty Ltd., Brian Chester, 247 Victoria St., Darlinghurst, Sydney NSW 2010. 331-2745.
Antique Print Room, L. & S. Kissajukian, 130 King William Rd., Goodwood 5034, SA. 08-272-3506.
Bibliophile, Susan Tompkins, 24 Glenmore Rd., Paddington NSW 2021, Sydney. 02-331-3411.
Gowrie Galleries, 316 Oxford St., Woollahra 2025. (612) 387 4581, Fax (612) 389 0640
The Map & Print Collector, Jackie MacDougall, P.O. Box N130, Sydney, NSW 2000. 02-969-7953.
* **Tim McCormick**, 53 Queen St., Woollahra, NSW 2025. 612 363-5383, Fax 612 326-2752. shop hours, by appt., by mail, fairs/shows. Australiana.
Robert Muir, Old & Rare Books, P.O. Box 364, Nedlands 6009 WA. 09-3865842.
Read's Rare Bookshop, Harri Peltola, 62 Charlotte St., Brisbane 4000. 07-2293278.
* **Gaston Renard Fine & Rare Books**, Julien Renard, G.P.O. Box 523588, Melbourne, Victoria 3001. +61 3 417 1044, Fax +61 3 417 3025. shop hours, by mail, fairs/shows, lists/catalogues. Australasia, Polar, voyages & travels.
Rex Map Centres, Jim Bowden, 413 Pacific Highway, Artarmon NSW 2064. 428-3566.
Salamanca Place Gallery, Dick & Carol Bett, 65 Salamanca Pl., Hobart TAS 7000. 002-233320.
* **Spencer Scott Sandilands**, 546 High St., Prahran 3181, Melbourne. (03) 9529 8011, Fax (03) 9521 1754. shop hours, by mail, fairs/shows, lists/catalogues. Southeast Asia; West Pacific. [> ½]
* **Terra Australis Antique Maps & Prints**, Nigel J. Tully, 2/10 Hazelbank Rd., Wollstonecraft, NSW 2065. 02-929-6510. shop hours, by appt., by mail. Australasia, Pacific, Japan.
Trowbridge Prints, S. Marcuson & M. Trowbridge, Old Theatre Ln., Bayview Terr., Claremont, Perth WA 6010. 09-384-4814.
* **Ulimaroa**, Prof. R. Clancy, Box 48, New Lambton, NSW 2305. (W) 049-236 135; (H) 049-296 277, Fax 049-252 169. by appt. Australia. [> ½]
Irene Veasey, 19 Swansea St., Swanbourne, Perth WA 6010. 09-384-5403.
* **Weekend Gallery, The Old Bookroom**, Barbara & Sally Burdon, Belconnen Churches Centre, Belconnen, ACT 2617. (06) 251 5191, Fax (06) 285 1074. shop hours, by mail, fairs/shows.

BAHAMAS

* **Balmain Antiques**, Jonathan C.B. Ramsay, F.R.G.S., C.P.F., 1st Fl., Masonic Bldg., Bay St., P.O. Box N-9562, Nassau. 809-323-7421, Fax same. shop hours, by mail. Bahamas, West Indies, N. Amer.

BARBADOS

* **Antiquaria**, David B. Collins, P.O. Box 1241C, Bridgetown. 809-426-0635, Fax 809-427-6798. shop hours, by mail, lists/catalogues. Barbados & Caribbean.

BELGIUM

Le Cadre d'Art, Evelyne & Stephane Uhoda, 33 rue St. Paul, 4000 Liege. 041-223817.
Antiquariaat Garcia, Jacques & Anne Marie Garcia, Sankt Kathelynestraat 1 & 10, 2800 Mechelen. 015-290985.
Greenhill, L.F.J. Hoppenbrouwers, Wielewaalstraat 7, 2350 Vosselaar. 014-422723.
* **Hermans Elisabeth**, Guffenslaan 50 / 10, B 3500 Hasselt. 011.22.7445, Fax 011.31.6696. shop hours, fairs/shows. [> ½]
Antiquariaat Logenhaghen, Philippe Swolfs, Nieuwe Steenweg 31, 2698 Elversele (Temse). 052-462119.
Librairie van Loock, 51 rue St. Jean, 1000 Brussels. 02-512-74-65.
Librairie Louis Moorthamers, rue Lesbroussart 124, Brussels 1050.
Micheline van der Perre, rue van Moer 6, 1000 Bruxelles. 02-512-1433.
De Renaissance van het Boek, Mme. Moreau-Derryx, Walpoorstraat 7, 9000 Gent. 091-254808.
Antiquariat Sanderus, F. Devroe, Brugsestraat 88, B-8500 Kortrijk. 056-35-25-41.
* **Librairie au Vieux Quartier**, Adrienne Goffin, 30, Rue de la Croix, B-5000 Namur. 32-81-221994, Fax same. shop hours, by mail, lists/catalogues.
Antiquariaat Marc van de Wiele, Sankt Salvatorkoorstraat 3, 8000 Brugge. 050-3366317.

International Dealers

BERMUDA

- **Nicholas Lusher Art & Antiques**, Apartment 11, 8 Mount Wyndham Drive, Hamilton Parish CRO 4. shop hours, by mail, lists/catalogues. Bermuda & American East Coast maps.

Pegasus Print & Map Shop, Robert F.Lee, P.O. Box 1551, Hamilton 5. 809-29-5-2900.

Anthony Pettit, P.O. Box FL 318, Flatts Village. (809) 292 2482, Fax (809) 295 5416.

CHANNEL ISLANDS

Channel Islands Galleries Ltd., Trinity Square, Guernsey, Channel Islands, U.K.. (0481) 723 274.

CYPRUS

Antonios Hadjipanayi, P.O. Box 27, Larnaca. 041-52782.

Andreas G. Pitsillides, Collectors' Centre, 10 Pythonos St., Nicosia-101. 02-444316.

DENMARK

Boghallens Antikvariat, Old Dam, Raadhuspladsen 37, 1585 Kobenhavn-V. 01-118511 ext. 763.

Branners Bibliofile Antikvariat, Maria Bloch, Bredgade 10, Kobenhavn DK-1260. 10-15-91-87.

Harcks Antikvariat, GEC Gad-Norreport, Fiolstraede 34, 1171 Kobenhavn. 01-121344.

Kaabers Antikvariat, Alette & Henning Kaaber, Skindergade 34, 1159 Kobenhavn-K. 01-154177.

Rosenkilde & Bagger A/S, Kron-Prinsens-Gade 3-5, Postboks 2184, DK 1017 Kobenhavn K. 01-15-70-44.

ENGLAND

W.F. & V. Ainsworth, Springfield Cottage, The Green, Skelton, York YO3 6XX. 0904-470339.

- **Alfieri Antique Maps**, Pauline McKenna, Martins, 25 Buttsfield Land, East Hoathly, East Sussex BN8 6EE. 0825-841 073, Fax same. by appt., by mail, fairs/shows, lists/catalogues. British Isles & Europe. Also at Antique Atlas Gallery, 31A High St., East Grinstead, West Sussex.
- **Altea**, Mr. M. De Martini, 34 Wentworth Road, London NW11 0RN. 44-181-455 4132, Fax 44-181-731 9723. by mail, fairs/shows, lists/catalogues.

Angel Antiques, Nigel & Anne Harding, 50 High St., Tring, Herts HP23 5A9. 0296-688424.

Antique Map & Book Shop, H.M. & C.D. Proctor, 32 High St., Puddletown, Dorset DT2 8RU. 030-584-633.

Antique Maps & Prints, 30 St. Mary's St., Stamford, Lincolnshire PE9 2DL.

Anything Illustrated, Louis F. Leopold, 134 WisbechRd., March, Cambridgeshire PE15 8EU. 0354-54735.

Arundel Prints, 59 High St., Arundel, West Sussex. 0903-882522.

Ashworth Maps, Mrs. M. Ashworth, Hazelwood, Holtye, Cowden, Kent TN8 7EC. 034-286710.

- **Ascotiques**, Station Approach, Station Hill, Ascot, Berkshire SL5 7JW. 0344-28124. shop hours.
- **Ash Rare Books**, Laurence Worms, 25 Royal Exchange, London EC3V 3LP. 071-626-2665, Fax 071-623-9052.
- **David Bannister**, 26 Kings Rd., Cheltenham, Glos. GL52 6BG. 0242-514 287, Fax 0242-513 890. by appt., by mail, fairs/shows, lists/catalogues. General. [>½]

Barnsbury Gallery, Judith Lassalle, 24 Thornhill Rd., London N1 1HW. 01-607-7121.

- **Roderick M. Barron**, 21 Bayham Road, Sevenoaks, Kent TN13 3XD. (01732) 742 558, Fax same. by appt., by mail, fairs/shows, lists/catalogues. World, Asia, Far East, Japan. [>½]

Roger Baynton-Williams, 37a High Street, Arundel, W. Sussex BN18 9AG. 0903-882898.

- **D.M. Beach**, Anthony Beach, 52 High St., Salisbury, Wiltshire SP1 2PG. 0722-333 801, Fax 0722-333 720. shop hours, by mail.

Benet Gallery, G.H. Criddle, 19 Kings Parade, Cambridge CB2 1SP. 0223-353783.

Paul Bentley, 8 Baxendale, London N20 0EG. 01-445-9791.

Bernard Gallery, F.B. Poynter, Grange Farm, Brewery Ln., Everton, Doncaster. 0777-817324.

Bloomsbury Rare Books, Arthur Page, 29 Museum St., London WC1A 1LH. 02-636-8206.

Books from India, S. Vidyarthi, 45 Museum St., London WC1A 1LR. 01-405-7226.

- **Thomas J. Booth**, Antique Maps & Prints, 33 Beaconsfield Rd., Claygate, Esher, Surrey KT10 0PN. 0372-462 764, Fax 0372-462 161. by mail, fairs/shows. Also: The Woodward Alden Gallery, 1 High Street, Claygate, Esher.

Bow Windows Bookshop, 128 High St., Lewes, E. Sussex BN7 1XL. 0273-472839.

Les Briggs, 174 Ashbrow Rd., Fartown, Huddersfield, W. Yorkshire HD2 1DU. 0484-546883.

Brobury House Gallery, Eugene Okarma, Brobury, Herefordshire HR3 6BS. 09817-229.

Brown Jack Bookshop, Reg Leete, 78 Main St., Lubenham, Leicestershire. 0858-65787.

Burgess Browning, 25 Blue Ball Yard, St. James St., London SW1A 1ND. 01-491-1811.

- **Clive A. Burden Ltd.**, 26 Sandy Lodge Rd., Moor Park, Rickmansworth, Herts WD3 1LJ. (0) 1923 772387, Fax (0) 1923 896520. shop hours, by appt., by mail, fairs/shows, lists/catalogues. Americana, S.E. Asia, Australia, U.K. [>½]

International Dealers

Gabriel Byrne, 29 Museum St., London WC1 A1LH. 01-636-8206.
Channel Bookshop, David Dawson, 5 Russell St., Dover, Kent CT16 1PX. 0304-213016.
Chantry Bookshop, M.P. Merkel, 11 Higher St., Dartmouth.
Chelsea Rare Books, Leo Bernard, 313 King's Rd., London SW3 5EP. 01-351-0950.
Christie's, 8 King St., St. James, London SW1Y 6QT. (071) 839 9060, Fax (071) 389 2263. auction.
Christie's South Kensington, 85 Old Brompton Rd, London SW7 3JS. (0171) 321 3152. auction.
Clevedon Fine Arts Ltd., The Gallery, Cinema Bldg., Old Church Rd., Clevedon, Avon BS21 7JY. 0272-875862.
Coach House Books, M.K. & J.S. Ellingsworth, 31 Broad St., Pershore, Worcestershire WR10 1AV. 0386-556100.
Coltsfoot Gallery, Edwin Collins, Hatfield, Leominster, Herefordshire HR6 0SF. 056-882-277.
Connoisseur Gallery, Makram Irani, 14/15 Halkin Arcade, Belgravia, London SW1X 8JT. 01-245-6431.
A.J. Coombes, 24 Horsham Rd., Dorking, Suffolk RH4 2JA. 0306-880736.
Michael & Verna Cox, 139 Norwich Rd., Wymondham, Norfolk NR18 0SJ. 0953-605948.
Peter Crowe, 77 Upper St. Giles St., Norwich NR2 1AB. 0603-624800.
Davies Antiques, 40a Kensington Church St., London W8 4BX. 01-937-3379.
Deighton Bell & Co., 13 Trinity St., Cambridge CB4 4LZ. 0223-353939.
Richard Doughty, Wessington Gardens, Woolhope, Herefordshire HR1 4QN. 043-277-292.
Robert Douwma Ltd., 173 New Bond St., 2nd Floor, London W1Y 9PB. 071-495-4001, Fax 071-495-4002.
Ivan R. Deverall, Duval House, The Glen, Cambridge Way, Uckfield, Sussex TN22 2AB. (01825) 762 474. lists/catalogues.
Francis Edwards, The Old Cinema, Castle Street, Hay-on-Wye HR3 5DF. 0497-820071.
Egee Art Consultancy, 9 Chelsea Manor Studio, Flood St., London SW3 5SR. 01-351-6818.
- **W.J. Faupel**, 3 Halsford Lane, East Grinstead, Sussex RH19 1NY. 342-315813, Fax 342-318058. by appt., by mail, fairs/shows, lists/catalogues. Viewing at 31a High St., East Grinstead. Americana & general,. [> ½]
- **Susanna Fisher**, Spencer, Upham, Southampton SO3 1JD. 0489-860 291, Fax 0489-860 638. by appt., by mail, fairs/shows, lists/catalogues. Sea charts.

Foss Street Galleries, Bryan Trevorrow, 17 Foss St., Dartmouth, Devon TQ6 9DR. 080-43-4311.
Fox-Smith Gallery, 11 Alfred St., The Hoe, Plymouth, Devon. 0752-221843.
J.A.L. Franks Ltd., 7 New Oxford St., London WC1A 1BA. (0171) 405 0274, Fax (0171) 430 1259.
The Gallery, The Square, Yarmouth, Isle of Wight PO41 0NS. 0983-760784.
John Garner Fine Arts, 51 High St. E., Uppingham, Leicestershire LE15 9PY. 0572-823607.
George & Dragon Gallery, Denis King, Reepham, Norwich, Norfolk NR10 4JN. 0603-870360.
H.G. Girou, 92 Sterndale Rd., London W14. 01-602-4169.
Great Russell St. Books, Denise Altman, 44 Great Russell St., London WC1B 3PA. 01-637-7635.
Grosvenor Prints, Nigel Talbot, 28 Shelton St., Covent Garden London WC1. 01-836-1979.
- **Garwood & Voigt**, 15 Devonshire Buildings, Bath BA2 4SP. 01225-424074, Fax 01225-482502. by appt., by mail, fairs/shows, lists/catalogues.
- **Geldart Antique Maps and Fine Engravings**, Jon Geldart, 13 Oakwood Rd., Wetherby, W. Yorkshire LS22 4QY. 0937-583 385. by appt., by mail. Yorkshire.
- **The Great Ayton Bookshop**, Madalyn Jones, 47-53 High St., Great Ayton, Cleveland TS9 6NH. 0642-723 358. shop hours, by mail, fairs/shows. N. Yorkshire & Durham.

Mrs. D.M. Green, 7 Tower Grove, Weybridge, Surrey KT13 9LX. 0932-241105.
Anne Hall Prints, 19 Dam St., Lichfield, Staffordshire WS13 6AE. 0543-263263.
J. Clarke Hall Ltd., S.M. Edgecombe, 22 Bride Ln., London EC4Y 8DU. 01-353-5483.
Harrod's, Old Map & Print Dept., Brompton Rd., Knightsbridge, London SW1. 01-730-1234.
Helgato, 2 The Broadway, Friern Barnet Rd., London N11 3DU. 01-361-8326.
Heritage Maps, Apsley House, 39 Wellington Rd., Edgbaston, Birm. B15 2ES. 021-440-2734.
- **F. & J. Hogan**, 31 Tranmere Rd., Edmonton, London N9 9EJ. 081-360 6146. by mail, fairs/shows, lists/catalogues.

R.F.G. Hollett & Son, 6 Finkle St., Sedbergh, Cumbria LA10 5BZ. 0587-20298.
Hollyman & Treacher, M.G. Kadwell, 22 Duke St., Brighton, E. Sussex BN1 1AH. 0273-28007.
- **Mrs. Julia Holmes**, South Garden Cottage, South Harting, near Petersfield, Hampshire GU31 5QJ. 0730-825 040. by appt., by mail, fairs/shows. British Isles.

A. Howard, 26 Brunswick Sq., Hove, E. Sussex BN3 1EJ. 0273-738812.
Hughes & Smeeth Ltd., 1 Gosport St., Lymington, Hampshire SO41 9BG. 0590-76324.
- **Simon Hunter Antique Maps**, 3 Meeting House Lane, Brighton, Sussex BN1 1HB. (01273) 746 983, Fax same. shop hours, by mail, fairs/shows, lists/catalogues. General inexpensive. [> ½]

Stephanie Hoppen Ltd., 17 Walton Street, London SW3. 01-589-3678.
Ingol Maps & Prints, Valerie Kidd, Cantsfield House, 206 Tag Lane, Ingol, Preston PR2 3TX. 0772-724769.

International Dealers

InterCol London, Yasha Beresiner, 43 Templars Crescent, London N3 3QR. (0181) 349 2207, Fax (0181) 346 9539. shop hours, lists/catalogues. And 11 Camden Passage, Islington, London N1. (071-354-2599).
Jarndyce Antiquarian Books, Brian Lake, 46 Great Russell St., Bloomsbury, London WC1. 01-631-4220.
Kamiliya Books, Prints & Maps, Box 395, London W23HF. 01-262-6317.
Barry M. Keene, 12 Thameside, Henly on Thames, Oxfordshire. 0491-577119.
King's Court Galleries, Olde King's Head Ct., High St., Dorking, Surrey RH4 1AR. 0306-881757.
Laura's Bookshop, Laura Crooks, 58 Osmaston Rd., Derby DE1 2HZ. 0332-47094.
J. Lawton Ltd., 1 Boundstone Rd., Wrecclesham, Farnham, Surrey GU10 4TH. 025-125-3615.
Leadenhall Gallery, A. & D.L. Greenaway, 12 Palace St., Canterbury CT1 2D2. 0227-457339.
Warwick Leadlay Gallery, 5 Nelson Road, Greenwich, London SE10 9JB. (0181) 858 0317, Fax (0181) 853 1773. lists/catalogues.
Leafield Maps & Prints, Tony Croft, Cotswald View, Leafield, Oxford OX8 5NY. 099387-357.
G. & R. Leapman, Hollycroft, Common Road, Stanmore, Middlesex HA7 3HX. 01-950-2995.
Andrew Leverton, 19 Barrydene, Oakleigh Rd. North, London N20 9HG. 01-445-2203.
Michael Lewis Gallery, 17 High St., Bruton, Somerset BA10 0AB. 074-981-3557.
Leycester Map Galleries Ltd., Tony Forster, Well House, Arnesby, Leicester LE8 3WJ. 053-758-462.
Kitty Liebreich, 5 Monk's Dr., London W3 0EG. 01-992-5104.
Lion Gallery, R.P. Hepner, 15a Minshull St., Knutsford, Cheshire WA16 6HG. 0565-52915.
London Art, Jane Yule, 127 Portobello Rd., London W11. 01-235-4198.
Norman Lord, Antique City Market, 98 Wood St., London E17 3HX. 01-520-8300.
The Lyver & Boydell Galleries, Paul Breen, 15 Castle Street, Liverpool, Merseyside L2 4SX. 051-236-7524.
Maggs Brothers, 50 Berkeley Sq., London W1X 6EL. 01-493-7160.
- **Magna Gallery**, B. Kentish & M.J. Blant, 41 High St., Oxford OX1 4AP. 0865-245 805. shop hours, by mail. English counties, Oxford topography.
The Map House of London, 54 Beauchamp Pl.,, Knightsbridge, London SW3 1NY. 0171-589 4325, 0171-584 8559, Fax 0171-589 1041. lists/catalogues.
- **Map World, J.T. Sharpe**, 25 Burlington Arcade, Piccadilly, London W1V 9AD. 071-495 5377, Fax same. shop hours.
G. & D. Marrin & Sons, 149 Sandgate Rd., Folkestone, Kent CT20 2DA. 0303-53016.
Peter M. Martin, Antique Maps & Prints, 12 Beech Ave., Radlett WD7 7DE. 09276-7653.
Richard Martin, 23 Stoke Rd., Gosport, Hampshire PO12 1LS. 0705-520642.
Roger Mason, 86A Banbury Rd., Oxford. 0865-59380.
W.B. McCormack Books, 6 Rosemary Ln., Lancaster LA1 1NR. 0524-36405.
David Mizon, Yew Tree Cottage, Little Strickland, Penrith, Cumbria CA10 3EG. 093-16-763.
Patrick & Mary Mullen, Stablings Cottage, Goodwin Rd., Ramsgate, Kent CT11 0JJ. 0843-587283.
- **Maynard & Bradley**, 1 Royal Arcade, Silver St., Leicester LE1 5YW. 0533-532 712. shop hours, by mail, fairs/shows, lists/catalogues. Also 30 Friar Lane, Nottingham; 0602-484 824.
- **P.J. Morris Antique Maps**, 11 The Orchard, Marston Green, W. Midlands B37 7DH. (0121) 779 3718. by mail, lists/catalogues.
- **Avril Noble**, 2 Southampton St., Covent Garden, London WC2E 7HA. 0171-240 1970, Fax same. shop hours, by mail, fairs/shows. General. [> ½]
Richard Nicholson of Chester, 25 Watergate St., Chester CH1 2LB. 0244-26818.
A. Nicolas, 57 Fallow Court Ave., Finchley, London N12 0BE. 01-445-9835.
Northwood Maps Ltd., 71 Nightingale Rd., Rickmansworth, Herts WD3 2BU. 0923-772258.
James of Norwich, Auctions, Lt. Col.D.W. James, 33 Timberhill, Norwich, Norfolk NR1 3LA. 0603-624817.
O'Flynn Antiquarian Booksellers, 35 Micklegate, York YO1 1JH. 0904-641404.
Old Church Galleries, Matti Harrington, 320 Kings Rd., Chelsea, London SW3 5UH. 0171-351 4649, Fax 0171-351 4449.
Old Hall Bookshop & Gallery, A. Proud, Shutta Rd., E. Looe, Cornwall PL13 1BJ. 050-36-3700.
Old Soke Books, Peter Clay, 68 Burghley Rd., Peterborough PE1 2QE. 0733-64147.
Oldfield Antiquarian Maps/Prints, Anne Downes, 34 Northam Rd., Southampton SO3 0PA. 0703-38916.
Orbis Terrarum, Christine Faupel, 3 Parkvedras Terrace, Truro, Cornwall TR1 3DF. 0872-77928.
- **Paul Orssich**, 117 Munster Road, Fulham, London SW6 6DH. 071-736 3869, Fax 071-371 9886. shop hours, by appt., by mail, fairs/shows. Spain; Balearic Islands.
O'Shea Gallery, 89 Lower Sloane St., London SW1W 8DA. 01-730-0081, Fax 071-730-1386.
Jean Pain Gallery, 7 King's Parade, Cambridge CB2 1SJ. 0223-313970.
Patterson & Liddle, 2c Chandos Rd., Redland, Bristol BS6 6PE. 0272-731205.
Penn Barn, Paul Hunnings, By the Pond, Elm Road, Penn, Nr. High Wycombe, Buckinghamshire HP10 8LU. 0494-81-5691.

International Dealers

Pennymead Auctions, David Druett, Scotton, Knaresborough, North Yorkshire HG5 9HN. 0423-865962, Fax 0423-869614.
Periwinkle Press, Anthony Swain, 23 East St., Sittingbourne, Kent. 0795-26242.
Pierpoint Gallery, A.G. Beaver, 10 Church St., Hereford HR1 2LR. 0432-267002.
Rex Poland, 25 South End, Corydon, Surrey. 01-680-5311.
Porter Prints, A.J. Sedgwick, 205 Whitham Rd., Broomhill, Sheffield S10 2SP. 0742-685751.
Premier Print Collections, Grays Antique Market, 58 Davies St., London W1. 01-409-1498.
- **The Print Cellar**, Elizabeth Tremlett, 35 Church St., Ashbourne, Derbyshire DE6 1AE. 0335-342933. shop hours. General; Derby & Staffordshire.

The Print Room, John Cumming, 37 Museum St., London WC1A 1LP. (0171) 430 0159, Fax (0171) 831 2874. lists/catalogues.
Printed Page, Christopher & Jean Wright, 2-3 Bridge St., Winchester SO23 9BH. 0962-54072.
- **Phillips**, Book Department, 101 New Bond St., London W1Y 0AS. 071-629-1824. shop hours. Map sections in monthly auctions.
- **Postaprint**, Taidswood House, Iver Heath, Bucks SL0 0PQ. (+44) 0895.833.720, Fax 0895.834.890. by appt., by mail, fairs/shows, lists/catalogues. U.K. counties; general. [>½]
- **Jonathan Potter Ltd.**, 125 New Bond St., London W1Y 9AF. 0171-491 3520, Fax 0171-491 9754. shop hours, by mail, fairs/shows, lists/catalogues. [>½]

Bernard Quaritch Ltd., 5-8 Lower John St., Golden Square, London W1R 4AU. 01-734-2983.
P.J. Radford, Twytton House, Alfriston, Polegate, E. Sussex BN26 5TD. 0323-870440.
- **T.G. Ramsell**, Elm Farm, Burton, S. Wirral, Cheshire L64 5TQ. 051-336 6655. by appt., by mail. Cheshire, W. England, World, Saxton.

Reg & Philip Remington, 14 Cecil Court, London WC2N 4HE. 01-836-9771.
Pat Richardson, G12/13 Grays Mews Antiques, 1-7 Davies Mews, London W1. 01-629-1533.
Stanley V. Riddell, Old Down House, Swelling Hill, Ropley, Alresford, Hamp. SO24 0DA.
John Roberts Books, 43 Triangle W., Clifton, Bristol BS8 1ES. 0272-28568.
Louise Ross & Co., Mulberry House, 8 Mount Rd., Landsdown, Bath BA15 5PW. 0225-448786.
Sanders of Oxford Ltd., 104 High St., Oxford OX1 4BW. 0865-242590.
G.J. Saville, Foster Clough, Heights Rd., Hebden Bridge, West Yorkshire HX7 5QZ. 0442-882808.
Chas. J. Sawyer, Bookseller, The Bees, Camden Rd., Sevenoaks, Kent TN13 3LZ. 0732-457262.
- **The Schuster Gallery**, Thomas E. Schuster, 14 Maddox St., London W1R 9PL. 071-491 2208, Fax 071-491 9872. shop hours, by mail, fairs/shows. Rare & expensive maps, early town views, panoramas & atlases.

The Selective Eye Gallery, John Blench & Son, 50 Don St., Saint Helier, Jersey. 0534-25281.
Albert F. Sephton, 16 Bloemfontein Ave., Shepherds Bush, London W12 7BL. 01-749-1454.
Settings, Ruth Bowdage, 5 Titchwell Rd., London SW18 3LW. 01-870-2402.
Shropshire Map Exchange, Ian M. Guild, 12 Nantwich Road, Woore, Crewe, Cheshire CW3 95A. 063081-274.
Sotheby's Book Dept., Bloomfield Place, New Bond St., London W1A 2AA. 01-493-8080.
Henry Sotheran, 2 Sackville St., Piccadilly, London W1X 2DP. 071-439-6151, Fax 071-434-2019.
Ken Spelman, B. Miller & T. Fothergill, 70 Micklegate, York YO1 1LF. 0904-24414.
- **Stage Door Prints**, 1 Cecil Ct., London WC2N 4E2. 071-240 1683. shop hours.

Stanton Engravings, J. Trivess & W.H.D. Kennedy, 24 Trenchard Rd., Swindon, Wiltshire SN6 7RZ. 0793-764911.
Harold T. Storey, E.J. Kingswood, 3 Cecil Ct., Charing Cross, London WC2N 4EZ. 01-836-3777.
Stratford Trevers, The Long Room, 45 High St., Broadway, Worcestershire WR12 7DP. 0386-853668.
Studio Bookshop & Gallery, Laurence Oxley, 17 Broad St., Alresford SO24 9AW. 096-273-2188.
Studio 18 Ltd, 23a Beresford St., St. Helier, Jersey. 0534-34920.
Surrey Maps & Prints, Little Gables, StokeClose, Stoke d'Abernon, Cobham, Surrey. 0932-62511.
- **The Swan Gallery**, Simon Lamb, 51 Cheap St., Sherborne, Dorset DT8 3QT. 0935-814 465, Fax 0308-868 195. shop hours, by mail.

K.W. Swift, 3 The Turl, Oxford OX1 3DQ. 0865-240241.
- **Peter Taylor & Son**, History Booksellers, 1, Ganders Ash, Watford, Herts. WD2 7HE. by mail, lists/catalogues.

Taviner's, Auctioneers, Prewett St., Redcliffe, Bristol BS1 6PB. 0272-25996.
Nicola Thomson, Green Hedges Farm, Mark Cross, E. Sussex TN6 3PA. 089-275-325.
Charles W. Traylen, Castle House, 49/50 Quarry St., Guildford, Surrey GU1 3UA. 0483-572424.
W.D. Trivess, Heathfield House, Meonstoke, Southampton SO3 1ND. 0489-877326.
John Trotter, 11 Laurel Way, London N20. 01-445-4293.

International Dealers

- **Thomas Rare Books**, 8/9 Station Road, Lanchester, Co. Durham DH7 0EX. 091-373 3526. shop hours, by mail, fairs/shows, lists/catalogues.
- **Thornburgh Gallery**, Leslie Turner, 17 Nicholas St., York YO1 3EQ. 0904-413 000. by appt., by mail, fairs/shows.

Vandeleur Antiquarian Books, 69 Sheen Lane, London SW14. 01-878-6837.

- **Robert Vaughan Antiqurian Booksellers**, 20 Chapel St, Stratford-upon-Avon, Warwickshire CV37 6EP. 0789-205 312. shop hours, by mail.

Vecta Insula, 62 High St., Ryde PO33 3HJ, Isle of Wight. 0983-64362.
L. Walton, 41 Woodland Road, Levenshulme, Manchester M19 2GW. 061-224-6630.
R.G. Watkins, 9 North Street, Stoke Sub Hamdon, Somerset TA14 6QR. 0935-822891, Fax 0935-825485.
Ian Watson, 31 Dene Ave., Rowland's Gill, Tyne & Wear NE39 1DY. 0207-542883.
Leonora Weaver, 6 Aylestone Dr., Aylestone Hill, Hereford HR1 1HT. 0432-267816.
The Welbeck Gallery, Doreen Spellman, 18 Thayer St., London W1M 5LD. 01-935-4825.
Jenny Wagstaff, Little Gables, Stoke Close, Stoke D'Abernon, Cobham, Surrey KT11 3AE. (01932) 862 511, Fax (01932) 860 886.
Welland Antique Maps & Prints, R.A. Warner, Lawnwood, Little Bytham near Grantham, Lincs. NG33 4PX, (01780) 410 254.
Wendover Enterprises Ltd., G.F.C.Sampson, 34A Chiltern Rd., Wendover, Bucks. HP22 6DA. 0296-624368.
Weston Antique Gallery, Boat Lane, Weston, Nr. Stafford ST18 0HU. 0889-270450.
David Weston Ltd., 44 Duke St., Saint James's, London SW1. 01-839-1051.

- **Edna Whiteson Ltd.**, 66 Belmont Ave., Cockfosters, Hertfordshire EN4 9LA. 081-449 8860, Fax same. by appt., by mail, fairs/shows, lists/catalogues.

Willcocks Antiques, E3 Chenil Galleries, 183 Kings Road, Chelsea, London SW3. 01-352-8653.
M.& B.E. Wilmington, Gilling Garth Cottage, Harmby, Leyburn, N. Yorkshire. 0969-23502.
Winton Publications Ltd., 17 Branksome Towers, Westminster Road, Poole, Dorset BH13 6JJ. 0202-764638.
Witch Ball Prints & Maps, Gina Daniels, 48 Meeting House Ln., Brighton, E. Sussex BN2 1HB. (01273) 26618. shop hours.
Charles Woodruff, Rare Books & Prints, 26 Yeoman's Row, London SW3 2AH. 01-584-0370.
Vivian Wright, Fennelsyke, Raughton Head, Carlisle, Cumbria CA57DU. 069-96-431.
Zeno Booksellers, M.P. Zographos, 6 Denmark St., London WC2H 8LP. 01-836-2522.

FINLAND

Classic Antique Shop Ltd., Christer Pettersson, Kefattie 2c, 02200 Espoo. 3580-0-8038373.
C. Hagelstams Antiquarian Bookshop, Cecil Hagelstram, Frederikinkatu 35, Helsingfors 120. 90-649291.
NordiskaAntikvariska Bokhandeln, Tove Olsoni-Nilsson, N. Magasinsgatan 6, 00130 Helsingfors 13. 62-63-52.

- **Jan Strang**, Antiikki-Kirja, Jatasalmentie 1, FIN-00830 Helsinki. +358-0-611 499, Fax same. shop hours, by mail, fairs/shows, lists/catalogues. Finland, Northern Europe.

FRANCE

Librairie Ancienne - Curiosites, Pierre Sieur, 3 rue del'Universite, 75007 Paris. 42607594.
Librairie Bellanger, M. France Maramraud, 6 Passage Pommeraye, 44000 Nantes. 40890608.
Odile Bienvault, 3 rue Corneille, 37000 Tours. 47610071.
Librairie Brocante du Palais, Foucald Bachelier, 28 rue Jean Jaures, 44000 Nantes. 40484364.
Librairie Dudragne, Patrick Dudragne, 86 rue de Maubeuge, 75010 Paris. 878-50-95.
Librairie Elbe, Jean-Louis Bonvallet, 213 bis boulevard St. Germain, 75007 Paris. 45487797.
La Galerie du Bastion, D.R. Lyon, 2 rue du Bastion, 65000 Menton. 93-358732.
Edwouard Lagnel-Tastemain, 25 boulevard Marechal Leclerc, 14300 Caen. 31861335.

- **Louis Loeb-Larocque**, 36, Rue Le Peletier, 75009 Paris. 48 78 11 18, Fax 45 26 32 83.
- **Rod Lyon**, B.P. 138, 06504 Menion CDX. Fax 33 93 57 87 14. by appt., by mail, lists. Pre-1850 Atlases.

R. Musson, 10 bis quai Cypierre, 45000 Orleans. 38535434.
Librairie des Pyrenees, Jacques Saint-Hilaire, 21 rue Vieille Boucherie, 64100 Bayonne. 59597874.
G. Raffy, Stand 83, Marche Biron, 85 rue des Rosiers, 93400 Saint Ouen. 47703651.
Friedrich Weissert, 22 rue de Savoie, 75006 Paris. 43-29-72-59, Fax 46-34-60-63. shop hours.

International Dealers

GERMANY

Antiquariat Peter Babendererde, Jurgen Babendererde, Grosse Burgstrasse 35, D-2400 Lübeck 1. 0451-70776.
Galerie Boisserée, Walter Schilling, Drususgasse 7-11, D-5000 Köln 1. 0221-237733.
- **F. Doerling GmbH**, Neuer Wall 40, 20354 Hamburg. 49-40-374961-0, Fax 49-40-374961-66. lists/catalogues, auction.

Hans G. Fay Antiquariat, Postfach 1108, D-8907 Thannhausen. 08281-3712.
Jochen Granier, Buch- und Kunstauktionen, Postfach 1640, D-4800 Bielefeld, Welle 9. 0521-67148.
Die Gravüre, Elisabeth Keller, Rüttenscheiderstrasse 56, D-4300 Essen 1. 0201-793182.
Hartung & Karl, Karolinenplatz 5a, D-8000 Munchen 2.
Antiquariat & Kunsthandlung Huste, Buch-und Kunstauktionen, Liebigstrasse 46-48, D-4600 Dortmund 1. 0231-122638.
Peter Hattesen, 239 Flensburg, Holm 76. 25077.
Ruthild Jager, Steinweg 17, D-2120 Luneburg. 04131-42797.
E. & R. Kistner, Rolf Kistner, Weinmarkt 6, D-8500 Nürnberg. 0911-203482.
Hans Horst Koch, Buch- und Kunstantiquariat, Ku'damm 216, D-1000 Berlin 15. 030-882-63-60.
Antiquariat Köhl, Peter H. Köhl, St. Johanner Markt 20, D-6600 Saarbrücken. 0681-399667.
Kunstantiquariat Hans Marcus, Ritterstrasse 10, D-4000 Düsseldorf 1. 0221-325940.
- **Lüder H. Niemeyer**, Simrockallee 34, D-53173 Bonn. 0228-35 12 77. shop hours, by mail, lists/catalogues.

Reiss & Sohn, Adelheidstrasse 2, D-61462 Königstein. 49-6174-1017, Fax 49-6174-1602. auction.
Kunstantiquariat Monika Schmidt, Turkenstrasse 48, D-80799 München. 089/284 223, Fax 089/280 0044.
Antiquariat Hanno Schreyer, Georg Schreyer, Euskirchenerstrasse 57-59, D-5300 Bonn 1. 0228-621059.
Das Bücherkabinett A. & C. Simon, Carlota Simon u. Dr. Maria Conradt, Poststrasse 14-16, D-2000 Hamburg 36. 040-34-32-36-38.
Antiquariat Wolfgang Staschen, Potsdammerstr. 138, D-1000 Berlin 30. 030-262-2075.
Antiquariat Stenderhoff, Theo Hobbeling, Alter Fischmarkt 21, 48143 Münster. (02) 51 447 49, Fax (02) 51 515 26.
Kunstantiquariat Valentien, Heinrich Valentien, Niederwall 14, D-4800 Bielefeld 1. 0521-64420.
- **Venator & Hanstein KG**, im Kunsthaus Lempertz, Cacilienstrasse 48, 50667 Koln. 02 21-257 54 19, Fax 02 21-257 55 26. shop hours, by mail, lists/catalogues, auction.

Rainer G. Voigt, Langerstr 2, D-8000 Munchen 80. 089-470-3066.
- **H. Th. Wenner Antiquariat**, Heger Str. 2-3, 49074 Osnabrück. 05 41-331 03 66, Fax 05 41-20 11 13. shop hours, by mail, lists/catalogues, auction.

Zisska & Kistner, Buch-und Kunstauktionhaus, Unterer Anger 15, D-8000 München 2. 089-263855, Fax 089-269088. auction.

GREECE

Les Amis du Livre, Julia & Augusto Spandonaro, 9 Valaoritou St., GR-106 71 Athens. 361-5562.
Vanghelis Dimakarakos, 6 Normanou St., GR-105 55 Athens. 324-5241.
K.E.B.E., Andreas Nicolas, Odos Sina 44, 10672 Athens. 21-3615548.
George Patriarcheas, 6 Solonos St., GR-106 73 Athens. 361-5320.
Aglaia Sambos, 32 Ploutarchou St., GR-106 76 Athens. 721-6578.
Stavros Stavridis, 18 Panagitsas St., Kifisia, 14562 Athens. 801-7079.

GUADELOUPE

A la Reserche du Passe, Laurent Chassaniol, BP 668, 97169 Pointe-a-Pitre. 908415.

GUATEMALA

Paul F. Glynn, Casa el Carmen, 3A Avenida Norte 8, Antigua. 032-0207.

HONG KONG

The Asian Collector Gallery, Frank Castle, Wilson House, G/F, 19-27 Wyndham St. Central. 5-232181.

ICELAND

Bokavardan, Bragi Kristjonsson, Vatnsstigur 4, Reykjavik. 29720.

INDIA

Maria Brothers Antiquarians, O.C. Sud & Sons, 78 The Mall, Simla HP 171001. 5388.
Phillips Antiques, Habib & Farooq Issa, Indian Mercantile Mansions, Madame Cama Rd., Bombay 400039. 2020564.

International Dealers

IRELAND

Kenny's Bookshop & Gallery, Desmond Kenny, High St., Galway, County Galway. 091-62739.
Neptune Gallery, A. Bonar Law, 41 S. William St., Dublin 2. 01-715021.
James H. White, 43 Monkstown Rd., Monkstown, Dublin. 01-809-127.

ISRAEL

The Collector, Jerusalem Hilton Hotel, P.O. Box 4075, Jerusalem 91040. 972-02-53-38-90.
Larry Freifeld, Books, Prints & Maps, Rehov Bialik 9, Tel Aviv 65241. 03-658497.
M. Pollak Antiquariat, 36 & 42 King George St., Tel Aviv 65298. 03-288613.
Terra Sancta Arts, P.O. Box 10009, Tel Aviv 61100. 02-289630.

ITALY

L'Arca, Roberto Fontanella, Via Mazzini 11, Brescia. 030-295740.
Antiquariato Librario, Bado & Mart, Stefania Bado, Via Tadi 21, Padova. 049-586098.
Uberto Bowinkel, Via Santa Lucia 25, Napoli 80132. 081-417-739.
Giampaolo Buzzanca, Via S. Andrea 5, Padova. 049-651831.
L'Antiquario del Garda, Maruizio Campisi, Via Dal Molin4, 25015 Desenzano BS. 030-9142582.
Garisenda Libri E Stampe, Maria Fiammenghi, Strada Maggiore 14/A, Bologna 40125. 23-18-93.
Studio Bibliografico Kairos srl, Via Tartini 38, 20158 Milano. (02) 39.32.10.54.
Libreria Antiquaria Mediolanum, Luca Pozzi, Via Montebello 30, Milano. 02-653-637.
- **Morbiato Armando**, Via Mazzini 12, 35010 Vigonza (PD). 049-80 96 824. by appt., fairs/shows.
Plinio Nardecchia, Piazza Navona 25, Rome. 06-6569318.
Old Times, Le Stampe Antiche, Cesare Giannelli, Via Campo di Marte, 26, 06100 Perugia. 075/7520 18.
Libreria Antiquaria Perini, Ruth Perini, Via Amatore Sciesa 11, 37122 Verona. (045) 803 0073, Fax same.
Libreria Antiquaria Pregliasco, Arturo Pregliasco, Via Accademia Albertina 3 bis, Torino. 011-877-114.
Libreria Antiquaria Rappaport, E.S. Rappaport Seacombe, Via Sistina 23, Rome 187. 06-483-826.
Libreria Antiquaria Soave, V. & E. Soave, Via Po 48, 10123 Torino. 011-878957.
Valeria Bella Stampe, Via S. Cecilia 2, 20122 Milano. 02-782009.
Vecchia Liberia Modenese, Marcello Broseghini, Viale Storchi 26, Modena 41100. 059-219-452.

JAMAICA

Bolivar Bookshop & Gallery, P.O. Box 413, Kingston 10. 926-8799.

JAPAN

Yushodo Booksellers Ltd., 29 San-ei-cho, Shinijuku-ku, Tokyo 160. 357-1411.

LICHTENSTEIN

Antiquariat Gallus, E. Adelsberger, Postfach 298, FL-9485 Nendeln. 075-3-17-44.

MALTA

- **Paul Bezzina**, Early Maps & Prints, 114 St. Lawrence St., Vittoriosa. 356-665 812. by mail.
Emmanuel L. Muscat, 161 Congress Rd., Mosta. 448791.

The NETHERLANDS

- **J.L. Beijers B.V.**, Achter St. Pieter 140, 3512 HT Utrecht. 030-310958, Fax 030-312061. auction.
- **Antiquariaat Broekema**, P.O. Box 75880, 1070 AW Amsterdam. (020) 662 9510. by appt. [> ½]
- **Cartographica Neerlandica**, Dr. Marcel P.R. van den Broeche, Soestdijkseweg 101, 3721 AA Bilthoven. 31 30 202396, Fax same. by appt., by mail, fairs/shows, lists/catalogues. Ortelius & de Jode.
Kunsthadel Drie Kronen BV, Pep Mensink, Luttik Oudorp 114, 1811 MZ Alkmaar. 072-116311.
S. Emmerling, Nieuwe Zijds Voorburgwal 304, Amsterdam 1012 RV. 020-231476.
Van Gendt Book Auctions BV, 96-8 Keizersgracht, Amsterdam 1015CV.
Greenhill BV, L.F.J. Hoppenbrouwers, Torenwijck V, Ruimzicht 137, 1068 CS Amsterdam. 020-198960.
Gysbers & van Loon, F.R. van Loon, Postbus 396, 6800 AJ Arnhem. 085-424421.
B.M. Israel BV, Boekhandel en Antiquariaat, NZ Voorburgwal 264, 1012 RS Amsterdam. 020-247040.
Nico Israel, 489 Keizersgracht, Amsterdam 1017 DM. 020-22-22-55.
Firma Loose, R. Loose, Papestraat 3, 2513 AV den Haag. 070-64-49-99.
Werner Lowenhardt, DeLairessestraat 40-1, Amsterdam 1071 PB. 020-62-00-89.
Marcus v/h Sothmann, Johannes Marcus, Nieuwezijosvoorburgwal 284, 1012 RT Amsterdam. 020-236920.
A. van der Meer, P.C. Hoofstraat 112, 1071 CD Amsterdam. 020-621936.
't Prentenkabinet, E.M. Hauch, Oostzeedijk 350, 3063 CD Rotterdam. 010-4111793.

International Dealers

- **Paulus Swaen Old Maps & Prints**, Pierre W.A. Joppen, Hofstraat 19, 5664 HS Geldrop. 31-(0) 40 853571, Fax 31(0) 40 854075. shop hours, by mail, fairs/shows, lists/catalogues. 16-18th cent. Maps, atlases, globes, views. [> ½]

Boekhandel J. de Slegte, 48-52 Kalverstraat, 1012 PE Amsterdam. 020-225933.
Speculum Orbis Terrarum, Robert Putman, P.O. Box 70084, 1007 KB Amsterdam. (3120) 664 4795, Fax (3120) 664 0465. lists/catalogues.
Antiquariaat Vorkink-Heeneman, D.J. Vorkink, Beeklaan 327-329, 2562 AJ den Haag. 070-634428.
Jan J. van Waning Galerie, Westersingel 35, 3014 GS Rotterdam. 010-4360198.

NEW CALEDONIA
Galerie Ad Lib, Max Shekleton, BP 362, Noumea. 284040.

NEW ZEALAND
Anah Dunsheath, Antiquarian Booksellers, P.O. Box 4181, Auckland 1. 09-790379.
Neil McKinnon Ltd., P.O. Box 847, Timaru. 368 81931, Fax 368 88068.

NORTHERN IRELAND
Phyllis Arnold Gallery, 24 Dufferin Ave., Bangor, County Down BT20 3AA. 0847-469899.
Emerald Isle Books, J.A. & J.E. Gamble, 539 Antrim Rd., Belfast BT15 3BU. 0232-771798.
Ultonia Maps, David Hogg, Doorus, Liggartown, Strabane, Tyrone. 06626-58515.

NORWAY
Damms Antiqvariat A/S, Claes Nyegaard, Tollbodgaten 25, 157 Oslo 1. 02-410402.

PORTUGAL
R.W. Bremner, Chao dos Arcos, Linho, 2710 Sintra.
Antonio Capucho, Viv. Naria Amelia, Av. Marques Leal, S. Joao do Estoril 2765.
Livraria Historica & Ultramarina, J.C. Silva, Travessa da Queimada, 28 Lisboa 2. 36-85-89.

SCOTLAND
Aberdeen Rare Books, A.J. & P.M. Campbell, Slains House, Collieston, Ellon, Aberdeenshire AB4 9RT. 035-887-275.
Billson of St. Andrews, 15 Greyfriars Garden, St. Andrews, Fife KY16 9HG. (01334) 475063.
Corn Exchange Bookshop, B.R. & E.M.B. Young, 55 King St., Stirling FK8 1DR. 0786-73112.
The Carson Clark Gallery, Scotia Maps-Mapsellers, 173 Canongate, Edinburgh EH8 8BN. 0131-556-4710.
- **Benny Gillies**, 31-33 Victoria St., Kirkpatrick Durham, Castle Douglas, Kirkcudbrightshire DG7 3HQ. 055-665 412. shop hours, by mail, fairs/shows, lists/catalogues. Scotland.

The Inverness Bookshop, Charles Leakey, 10 Bank St., Inverness IV1 1QY. 0463-239947.
John Mathieson Gallery, 48A Frederick St., Edinburgh EH2 1HG. 031-225-6798.
Colin Murdoch, 56 High St., Kingussie, Inverness Shire. 05402-552300.
The Ship's Wheel, A.H. & H.E. Munro, 2 Traill St., Thurso, Caithness. 0847-62485.

SINGAPORE
- **Antiques of the Orient PTE Ltd.**, Julie Yeo, 21 Cuscaden Road 01-02, Ming Arcade, Singapore 1024. 65-733 0830, Fax 65-732 8652. shop hours, by mail, fairs/shows, lists/catalogues. [> ½]

SOUTH AFRICA
Clarke's Bookshop, P.V. Mills & H. Dax, 211 Long St., Capetown 8001. 021-235739.
Gail & Jonathan Schrire, P.O. Box 241, Rondebosch 7700, Capetown.
- **Jeffrey Sharpe**, Rare Books & Maps, Mall of Rosebank, Cradock Ave., Rosebank, Johannesburg. 011-788 0791. shop hours. Also Shop No.1, Victoria & Alfred Hotel, Waterfront, Capetown; 021 25-4641.

Peter Visser Antiques, 117 Long St., Cape Town 8001. 021-237870.

SPAIN
El Asilo del Libro, Antonio Lorenzo, c/. Corretgeria 34, 46001 Valencia. 96-3310060.
Llibreria Antiquaria Catedral, Jose del Rio & Teresa Mercade, Cos del Bou 14-16, 43003 Tarragona. 977-232451.
- **Egyptophilia**, Pierre Farid Kioumgi, Lista de Correos, Deya 07179, Mallorca. 34-71-639 254, Fax same. by appt., by mail, fairs/shows, lists/catalogues. Eygpt, Arabia, Balearic Islands.

Frame SL, Grabados y Mapas Antiguas, General Pardinas 69, Madrid 28006. (91) 411-3362, Fax (91) 564-1520.
Gonzalo Fernandez Pontes, Nunez de Balboa 19, 28004 Madrid. +(34) 1 435 8000, Fax same.

International Dealers
SWEDEN
Aspingtons Antikvariat, Mat Aspington, Västerlånggatan 54, 111 29 Stockholm. 08-201100.
Era Antikvariat, Francesco Bacoccoli, Box 45511, 10430 Stockholm. 08-7581412.
K.M. Flodin & Co., S. Flodin, Vasterlanggatan 37, 11129 Stockholm. 08-204881.
Lundquist & Ohman, Kristinelundsgaten 7, Goteborg S-41137.
Medaco, Rolf Ottoson, Verkstadsvagen 21, 5-14170 Huddinge. 08-468918.
Ronnells Antikvariat AB, Birger Jarlsgaten 32, Stockholm. 08-115411.

SWITZERLAND
Asia House Museum, T.P. Nguyen, 16 Hotel-de-Ville, 1204 Geneve. 022-297190.
Buchantiquariat Benz, Aathalstrasse, 8607 Seegraben. 01-9323022.
La Fiera del Libro, Via Marconi 2, 6900 Lugano. 091-227649.
Finden S.A., Via Volta 1, Chiasso 6830. 091-445687.
Germann, Zeltweg 67, Zurich CH-8032.
Haus der Bücher AG, Baumleingasse 18, Basel CH-4051.
Galerie Kempf, Johannes Kempf, Strehlgasse 19, 8001 Zurich. 01-2213830.
August Laube, Trittligasse 19, 8001 Zurich. 01-2518550.
Karl Mohler, Buch- u. Kunstantiquariat, Rheinsprung 7, Basel 4001. 061-25-98-82.
- **Antik-Pfister, Old Prints, Maps**, Postfach 8129, CH-8050 Zurich. 01-47-62-32.
Rene Simmermacher AG, Postfach 215, 8024 Zurich. 01-2525512.

TAIWAN
- **Bipolar International Corp.**, Oliver Yeh, No.9, Alley 10, Lane 237, Wan Ta Road, 109, Taipei. 2-301 1000, Fax 2-307 7777. by appt., by mail, fairs/shows. Formosa & China only, 1500-1900.

THAILAND
White Lotus Co. Ltd., Diethard Ande, G.O.P. Box 1141, Bangkok 10501. 662-286 1100, Fax 662-213 1175.

TRINIDAD
McLeod's Antiques, Julian Bruce & Odette McLeod, La Seiva & Saddle Road, Maraval, Port of Spain. 629-2224.

TURKEY
- **F. Muhtar Katircioglu**, Karanfil Araligi 14, Levent, 80620 Istanbul. 212-264 1786. by appt., by mail. Constantinople, Anatolia, Ottoman Empire.

WALES
Antiques of Newport, J.M. Duggan, 82 Chepstow Rd., Maindee, Newport, Gwent. 0633-59935.
David Archer, The Pentre, Kerry, Newtown, Powys SY16 4PD. (01686) 670 382. lists/catalogues.
The Corner Shop, E.B. Okarma, 5 St. John's Place, Hay on Wye, Hereford. 0497-820045.
Country Antiques, Richard Bebb, Castle Mill, Kidwelly, Dyfed. 0554-890534.
Olwen Caradoc Evans, Bodvor, The Esplanade, Penmaenmawr, Gwynedd LL34 6LY. 0492-623955.
D.G. & A.S. Evans, 7 the Struet, Brecon, Powys LQ3 7LL. 2714.
Sue Lloyd-Davies, Castle House, 12 Picton Terrace, Carmarthen, Dyfed. 0267-235462.
Mona Antiqua, Karel Lek, 31 Castle St., Beaumaris, Anglesey, Gwynedd. 0248-810203.
David Windsor Gallery, E. Creathorne, 201 High St., Bangor, Gwynedd LL57 1NU. 0248-364639.
- **E. Wyn-Thomas**, "Old Quarry", Miners' Lane, Old Colwyn, Clwyd LL29 9HG. 0492-515 336. by appt., by mail.

CUMULATIVE FREQUENCY DISTRIBUTION OF MAP-MAKERS

This year, the information previously found in "Sketches of Map-Makers" has been greatly augmented and brought into the "cumulative frequency table" so that the map-makers that have appeared in the *Price Record* can more easily be associated with their places and dates. This data remains sketchy and is intended to help in finding the appropriate map-maker. In several cases the entry that appears may not be that of the most prominent map-maker with a particular surname. For broader and more detailed information, readers are referred to Tooley's *Dictionary of Mapmakers* and Moreland and Bannister's *Antique Maps*, both of which have been essential as a check on information provided for the *Price Record* and both of which are highly recommended.

With this added data, the cumulative frequency distribution greatly simplifies a search through all volumes of *Antique Map Price Record* in quest of entries for a particular map maker and helps to direct one toward the greatest concentration of entries.

Total Entries for 1995: 4,784   Different Names and Categories in 1995: 580

Cumulative Entries since 1983: 61,308   Different Names and Categories since 1983: 2235

The table includes several categories which are organized by other than the name of the map-maker. These include maps issued by infrequent publishers and organized by *genre*, manuscript maps and items of unknown attribution. Should the reader not find certain kinds of maps under the name of a mapmaker, comparable items may turn up in one of the following categories:

Anonymous & Unknown	Local & State Maps	Nautical Charts
Armenian Cartography	Local & State *Pocket* Maps	Puzzles & Games
Chinese Cartography	Local & State *Wall* Maps	Railroad Company Maps
Company Maps	Manuscript Maps	Real Estate & Promotional
Japanese Cartography	Military Maps	Spanish-American War
Local & State Gov't Maps	Mining Maps	

	Total	'83	'84	'85	'86	'87	'88	'89	'90	'91	'92	'93	'94	'95
Abert. U.S. Army; mid 1800s. see U.S. categories	1	.	1	.	.	.	.	.	.	.	.	.	.	.
Ackermann Lith. NY; mid 1800s. see U.S. categories	7	.	1	.	2	1	3	.	.	.	.	.	.	.
Adams & Son. USA; late 1800s	1	.	.	.	.	.	.	.	.	.	1	.	.	.
Adrichom. see Van Andrichem														
Ainslie. incl John. Scottish; late 1700s	5	.	1	.	.	.	.	.	2	1	.	.	.	1
Ainsworth, W. Glasgow; late 1800s	1	.	.	.	.	.	.	1	.	.	.	.	.	.
Alabern. Barcelona; mid 1800s	1	.	.	.	1	.	.	.	.	.	.	.	.	.
Alaska	1	.	.	.	.	.	.	1	.	.	.	.	.	.
Albrizzi, Giambatista. Venice; mid 1700s	139	25	9	13	4	24	38	8	7	4	3	2	1	1
Alden. wall maps; USA; mid 1800s	2	.	.	.	.	1	1	.	.	.	.	.	.	.
Alexander. late 1800s	2	.	.	.	.	.	1	.	.	.	.	.	.	1
Allard, Carel (& family). Amsterdam; 1648-1709	53	4	1	8	5	7	4	2	1	4	2	6	4	5
Allardt, G.F. San Francisco; late 1800s	1	.	.	.	.	.	.	.	.	1	.	.	.	.
Allen. various	8	1	.	.	.	.	.	.	.	1	.	6	.	.
Almon, John. London; late 1700s	2	.	1	.	1	.	.	.	.	.	.	.	.	.
Alting, Menso (younger). Amsterdam; early 1700s	2	1	.	.	.	.	.	.	.	.	.	.	.	1
American Antiquarian Society	4	.	.	.	.	.	.	.	.	2	1	1	.	.
American Bank Note Co.	2	.	.	.	.	1	.	.	1	.	.	.	.	.
American Ethnological Society	2	.	.	.	.	.	.	.	.	.	1	.	1	.

Name	Total	'83	'84	'85	'86	'87	'88	'89	'90	'91	'92	'93	'94	'95
American Journal of Science	4	.	.	.	.	.	.	1	.	2	.	1	.	.
American Litho. Co. NY; mid 1800s	3	1	.	.	1	.	.	.	1	.	.	.	.	.
American Philosophical Society	2	.	.	.	.	.	.	.	.	.	.	.	2	.
American Publishing Co. Milwaukee; late 1800s	4	.	1	.	.	.	.	1	1	.	1	.	.	.
American Sunday School Union	1	.	.	.	.	.	.	.	.	.	.	.	1	.
Amman, Jost. Zurich; 1539-91	1	.	.	.	.	.	.	.	.	1	.	.	.	.
Analectic Magazine. Phila; early 1800s	2	.	.	.	.	.	.	.	.	.	2	.	.	.
Anburey, Thomas. London.	3	.	1	.	.	.	2	.	.	.	.	.	.	.
Anderson. various. 1800s	7	.	.	.	.	1	1	1	.	.	4	.	.	.
Andreas, Alfred T. Chicago; late 1800s	23	2	2	2	3	2	1	3	1	.	1	1	3	2
Andrews. various	15	.	5	1	.	.	2	.	1	.	3	.	.	3
Andrews & Dury. England; late 1700s	2	1	.	1	.	.	.	.	.	.	.	.	.	.
Andriveau-Goujon (families) Paris; mid 1800s	18	2	2	1	.	.	2	1	3	.	2	3	2	.
Andrus & Judd. Hartford; early 1800s	3	.	.	.	.	1	.	.	1	.	.	1	.	.
Angelo, Theodore G.N. Danish; early 1800s	1	1	.	.	.	.	.	.	.	.	.	.	.	.
Angelocrator, Daniel. Frankfort; early 1600s	3	.	.	.	1	.	1	.	.	.	.	.	.	1
Annales des Mines. Paris	1	.	.	.	.	1	.	.	.	.	.	.	.	.
Annin & Smith. USA; early 1800s	2	.	.	.	.	.	1	.	.	1	.	.	.	.
Anonymous or Unknown	508	77	59	54	49	69	28	29	37	29	13	22	29	13
Ansart. Paris; mid 1800s	3	.	.	1	.	2	.	.	.	.	.	.	.	.
Anson, George. London; mid 1700s	33	3	4	3	1	2	1	3	2	2	1	3	6	2
Anthony. Providence; early 1800s	1	.	.	.	.	.	.	1	.	.	.	.	.	.
Antoine, Louis. Paris; mid 1800s	3	.	2	.	.	1	.	.	.	.	.	.	.	.
Apianus, Peter. early 1500s; Phillip, mid 1500s. German	36	4	2	2	1	8	3	3	.	5	1	1	3	3
Appleton, D. & Co. NY; late 1800s	41	8	6	9	2	4	1	.	2	4	.	2	.	3
Apthorp. USA; late 1800s	1	.	.	.	.	.	.	.	.	.	.	1	.	.
Aquila, Prospero dell'. Venice; late 1700s	2	1	.	1	.	.	.	.	.	.	.	.	.	.
Aragon, J. mid 1800s	1	.	.	.	.	.	.	.	.	.	.	1	.	.
Arbuckle Bros., Coffee Co. map cards	3	.	.	.	.	.	.	.	.	.	2	.	.	1
Archaeological Americana. early 1800s	1	.	.	.	.	.	.	1	.	.	.	.	.	.
Archer, Joshua. London; mid 1800s	26	.	5	.	.	10	5	1	2	1	.	1	.	1
Arias Montanus, Benedictus. Spain; 1527-98	9	.	.	.	.	.	2	2	.	1	2	.	1	1
Armenian Cartography	1	.	.	.	.	.	.	1	.	.	.	.	.	.
Armstrong. incl Mostyn John. Scottish; late 1800s	3	.	.	3	.	.	.	.	.	.	.	.	.	.
Arrowsmith, Aaron Sr; Jr; John; Samuel. London; early 1800s	361	48	33	45	19	15	41	23	35	17	39	27	11	8
Arrowsmith & Lewis. see Lewis & Arrowsmith, '83-'93	126	2	2	7	9	6	4	7	4	7	9	26	34	9
Artaria & Co. Vienna; early 1800s	3	.	.	.	.	.	.	.	.	.	2	1	.	.
Aschbach. Penna; late 1800s	2	.	.	.	.	.	.	1	.	.	.	1	.	.
Ashby, H. London; late 1700s	3	.	1	.	.	.	.	.	.	.	.	.	1	1
Asher	1	.	.	.	.	.	1	.	.	.	.	.	.	.
Asher & Adams. NY; late 1800s	131	2	11	4	5	7	3	12	6	30	5	15	12	19
Asher & Co. mid 1800s	7	.	.	.	.	2	.	1	1	1	1	.	.	1
Aspin, Jehoshaphat. London; early 1800s	5	2	.	.	.	.	.	.	.	.	.	.	1	2
Astley Magazine	1	.	.	.	.	.	.	.	.	.	.	1	.	.
Atcheson	2	.	.	.	.	.	1	.	.	1	.	.	.	.
Atchison, Topeka & Santa Fe R.R.	1	.	.	.	.	.	1	.	.	.	.	.	.	.
Atlantic Neptune. see Des Barres														
Atlas Maritimus & Commercialis. see Cutler														
Atwater, Caleb. American; early 1800s	1	.	1	.	.	.	.	.	.	.	.	.	.	.
Atwood, J.M. Phila; late 1800s	9	2	1	.	.	1	.	2	1	.	1	.	1	.
Aveline, Antonio. mid 1600s	1	.	.	1	.	.	.	.	.	.	.	.	.	.
Avery, H.M. Cleveland; late 1800s	1	.	.	.	1	.	.	.	.	.	.	.	.	.
Bachelder, John B. USA	1	.	.	.	.	.	.	.	.	.	.	.	1	.
Bachiene, Willem Albert. Amsterdam; late 1700s	44	.	2	8	.	22	3	1	1	1	.	2	.	4
Bachmann. see Magnus	9	.	.	1	.	.	.	2	3	.	.	.	.	3
Bacon. incl C.; G.W. & Co., London.	29	.	.	.	.	2	.	2	3	3	8	6	1	4
Baeck, Elias. Augsburg; 1679-1747	1	.	.	.	.	1	.	.	.	.	.	.	.	.
Baedeker, (Company) Leipzig; late 1800s	14	.	14	.	.	.	.	.	.	.	.	.	.	.
Baffin, William. English; 1584-1622	2	.	.	.	.	.	.	1	.	.	.	.	.	1
Bailey & Hazen. NY	1	.	1	.	.	.	.	.	.	.	.	.	.	.
Bailey, O.H. & Co. urban views	10	.	.	.	1	1	.	2	1	.	.	2	3	.
Bailleul, Gaspard. France; early 1700s	1	.	.	.	.	.	.	1	.	.	.	.	.	.
Baillie, Alexander. Edinburgh; mid 1700s	1	.	.	.	1	.	.	.	.	.	.	.	.	.
Baines, John & Co. early 1800s	1	.	.	.	1	.	.	.	.	.	.	.	.	.
Baker. various	5	.	.	.	.	.	.	2	1	.	1	.	.	1
Baker & Harper. Butte, MT; late 1800s	1	.	.	.	.	.	.	.	.	.	1	.	.	.
Balch. USA; late 1800s	1	.	.	.	.	.	.	.	.	.	.	.	.	1

Name	Total	'83	'84	'85	'86	'87	'88	'89	'90	'91	'92	'93	'94	'95
Baldwin. various	17	2	5	2	2	4	2	.	.	.	.	.	.	.
Baldwin & Cradock. London; early 1800s. see S.D.U.K.	35	3	7	5	5	4	2	2	4	2	.	1	.	.
Baldwin & Thomas. Phila; mid 1800s	1	.	.	.	.	.	.	.	.	.	1	.	.	.
Ballino, Giulio. Italy; mid 1500s	1	.	.	.	.	.	.	.	.	.	1	.	.	.
Ballou, Pictorial Drawing Room Companion	5	.	.	3	.	.	1	1	.	.	.	.	.	.
Bancroft. various; mid 1800s	3	.	.	.	1	.	1	.	.	1	.	.	.	.
Bancroft & Knight. San Francisco; mid 1800s	2	.	.	.	1	1	.	.	.	.	.	.	.	.
Bankes, Thomas. London; late 1700s	8	.	2	.	.	.	.	.	2	1	.	.	.	3
Banks, J.H. & Co. London	1	.	.	.	.	.	.	.	.	.	.	.	1	.
Banvard, J. London; mid 1800s	1	.	.	.	.	1	.	.	.	.	.	.	.	.
Barclay, T. London; late 1800s	6	1	1	.	1	1	.	1	.	.	.	1	.	.
Barcleus	1	.	.	.	1	.	.	.	.	.	.	.	.	.
Bardin, Wm. & J.M. globes; early 1800s	1	.	.	.	.	.	.	.	.	.	.	1	.	.
Barfield, J. London; early 1800s	1	1	.	.	.	.	.	.	.	.	.	.	.	.
Barker, William. Phila; late 1700s	1	1	.	.	.	.	.	.	.	.	.	.	.	.
Barlaeus, Caspar (van Baarle). Amsterdam; mid 1600s	1	.	.	.	.	1	.	.	.	.	.	.	.	.
Barlow. incl J. late 1800s	7	.	.	1	1	2	1	.	.	.	1	1	.	.
Barnes, R.L. Phila	9	.	.	.	1	1	1	.	.	.	1	2	3	.
Barnes & Burr. NY; mid 1800s	9	.	8	.	.	.	.	.	1	.	.	.	.	.
Barrow, Sir John. London; late 1700s	11	.	2	1	1	.	.	2	.	4	.	.	.	1
Bartholomew, George; John; John (II); John George. late 1700s +	65	.	8	.	4	4	1	23	1	5	3	4	4	8
Bartlett. incl W.H. views, mid 1800s; J.R., London, mid 1800s.	18	2	2	4	4	2	2	1	.	.	.	1	.	.
Barton. incl C. Claremont, NH.	2	.	.	.	.	.	.	.	.	1	.	1	.	.
Bartram. Paris; late 1700s	1	.	.	.	.	.	.	.	.	.	.	.	.	.
Basire, James, mid 1700s; (II) early 1800s; (III) mid 1800s. English	7	1	1	3	1	.	.	.	1	.	.	.	.	.
Baskin, Forster & Co. Chicago	1	.	.	.	.	.	.	.	.	.	.	1	.	.
Batelli & Fanfani. Milan; early 1800s	3	.	.	1	.	1	.	.	.	1	.	.	.	.
Baudartius. early 1600s	12	12	.	.	.	.	.	.	.	.	.	.	.	.
Baudin, Admiral. Paris; early 1800s	1	1	.	.	.	.	.	.	.	.	.	.	.	.
Bauerkeller, George. mid 1800s	1	.	.	.	.	.	.	.	.	.	1	.	.	.
Baumgarten, Siegmund Jakob. Halle; mid 1700s	5	.	5	.	.	.	.	.	.	.	.	.	.	.
Bauza, Filipe. early 1800s	1	.	.	.	.	1	.	.	.	.	.	.	.	.
Bayly. London; late 1700s	2	.	.	.	.	1	.	.	.	.	.	1	.	.
Beadle, E.F. Buffalo; mid 1800s	1	.	.	.	.	.	.	1	.	.	.	.	.	.
Beaulieu, Sebastian de Pontault. France; late 1600s	2	.	.	1	.	.	.	1	.	.	.	.	.	.
Beautemps-Beaupre, Charles Francois. Paris	7	.	1	.	.	1	.	.	.	2	2	1	.	.
Beck & Pauli. urban views	2	.	.	.	.	.	.	1	1	.	.	.	.	.
Beechey. English; early 1800s	3	.	.	.	1	.	2	.	.	.	.	.	.	.
Beer, Johan Christoph. 1673-1753	32	.	.	.	.	.	.	1	.	.	.	.	.	31
Beers (various companies). NY; late 1800s	77	1	.	.	1	.	1	.	1	1	20	.	25	26
Beers & Lake	1	.	.	.	.	.	.	.	.	.	1	.	.	.
Beers, Comstock & Cline	4	.	.	.	1	1	1	.	.	.	.	.	.	.
Beers, Ellis & Soule. USA; late 1800s	8	.	.	1	.	.	.	2	1	.	4	.	.	.
Beischlag. early 1800s	1	.	.	.	.	.	.	.	.	.	1	.	.	.
Belcher, Sir Edward. mid 1800s	1	.	.	.	.	.	.	.	.	1	.	.	.	.
Belden	2	.	.	.	.	1	.	.	.	.	1	.	.	.
Beldin. incl H., late 1800s	5	1	2	.	1	1	.	.	.	.	.	.	.	.
Bell, A., Edinburgh; Peter, London; late 1700s; James, Glasgow; early 1800s. see Scot's Magazine	16	1	11	.	.	1	.	.	1	.	.	.	.	2
Bellairs, L. London; mid 1800s	1	.	.	.	.	1	.	.	.	.	.	.	.	.
Bellere, Jean. Antwerp; late 1500s	1	1	.	.	.	.	.	.	.	.	.	.	.	.
Bellin, Jacques Nicolas. Paris	482	220	105	157	.	.	.	.	.	.	.	.	.	.
(large). see Depot de la Marine	217	.	.	.	33	23	35	18	24	15	17	22	11	19
(small). see de Charlevoix; Prevost d'Exiles	1043	.	.	.	178	149	72	58	62	103	101	123	118	79
Bellus, assoc with "Ostreichischer Lorberkranz"	6	.	.	.	.	.	.	.	.	.	.	.	6	.
Benard, Jacques F., Paris, early 1700s; Robert, France, late 1700s	54	13	.	9	.	1	8	3	2	4	7	1	4	2
Benton, Henry. Hartford; mid 1800s	2	.	.	.	.	.	.	.	1	.	.	1	.	.
Berard. mid 1800s	1	.	.	1	.	.	.	.	.	.	.	.	.	.
Berey, Nicolas. France; mid 1600s	1	.	.	.	.	.	1	.	.	.	.	.	.	.
Bergen, Daniel & Gracey. Austin, TX; late 1800s	1	.	.	.	.	.	.	.	.	1	.	.	.	.
Berghaus, H. mid 1800s	6	.	.	.	.	.	.	.	.	.	1	.	1	3
Bernard, Jean Frederic. Amsterdam; mid 1700s	6	1	1	.	.	.	1	.	.	.	1	.	1	1
Bernhardt, L. Stockholm; mid 1800s	1	.	.	.	.	.	.	.	.	1	.	.	.	.
Bero, D. with Pierrugues. Bordeaux; early 1800s	1	.	.	.	.	.	.	.	.	.	.	1	.	.
Berry, William. London; late 1600s	8	1	2	.	.	1	1	.	.	2	1	.	.	.
Bertelli, Fernando. Venice; mid 1500s	9	.	2	2	.	3	.	1	.	.	.	1	.	.
Bertholon, C. late 1700s	5	.	.	.	.	.	.	.	.	.	3	.	1	1

Name	Total	'83	'84	'85	'86	'87	'88	'89	'90	'91	'92	'93	'94	'95
Bertius, Pieter. Amsterdam; early 1600s	212	38	9	29	5	6	48	10	11	9	5	7	25	10
Betts, John. London; mid 1800s	14	1	.	.	.	.	1	1	2	2	.	5	1	1
Bevis, John. London	1	.	.	.	.	.	.	.	.	.	.	.	1	.
Bew, John. late 1700s. see Political Magazine	8	.	.	1	1	6	.	.	.	.	.	.	.	.
Bezzera, P. Milan; mid 1800s	1	.	.	.	.	.	.	1	.	.	.	.	.	.
Bickham, George Jr. London; mid 1700s	4	.	2	.	.	.	.	.	1	.	.	.	1	.
Biddle, Edward C. mid 1800s	1	.	.	.	.	.	.	.	.	.	.	1	.	.
Bidwell, Oliver Beckworth. mid 1800s	1	.	.	.	.	.	.	.	.	.	.	.	.	1
Bien, Julius, litho. NY; mid 1800s	23	1	1	1	1	.	4	1	1	1	2	.	10	.
Bill, Henry. mid 1800s	1	.	.	.	.	.	.	.	.	.	1	.	.	.
Bineteau. mid 1800s	1	.	.	.	.	.	1	.	.	.	.	.	.	.
Bingham, J. London; early 1700s	1	.	.	.	1	.	.	.	.	.	.	.	.	.
Bion, Nicolas. Paris; mid 1700s	2	1	.	.	.	.	.	.	.	.	.	1	.	.
Birga, A., Florentine Edifice Society	1	.	.	.	.	.	.	.	.	.	.	1	.	.
Birkbeck, M. early 1800s	1	.	.	.	.	.	.	.	.	1	.	.	.	.
Blachford, William. London; mid 1800s	4	.	.	.	.	.	1	1	.	2	.	.	.	.
Black, Adam & Charles. Edinburgh; mid 1800s	147	19	14	10	13	10	11	17	9	6	12	9	6	11
Blackie & Son. Glasgow, Edinburgh; mid 1800s	29	10	3	2	.	4	4	1	.	.	2	1	1	1
Blackmore, William. mid 1800s	1	.	.	.	.	.	.	.	.	1	.	.	.	.
Blackwood, W. & Son. Edinburgh, London; mid 1800s	2	.	.	.	.	.	.	.	.	.	1	.	.	1
Blaeu, Willem Jans Zoon, 1571-1638; Joan, 1596-1673; Cornelius, 1610-48; Amsterdam	1381	171	104	188	158	204	119	52	66	47	28	52	138	54
Blair, John. England; late 1700s	15	.	.	1	1	1	1	2	2	5	1	.	.	1
Blanchard, Rufus. Chicago; mid 1800s	9	.	1	3	.	.	.	.	.	3	.	.	2	.
Blankaart, Nicolas. Leyden; mid 1600s	3	3	.	.	.	.	.	.	.	.	.	.	.	.
Blankman, Edgar. Constantia, NY; late 1800s	1	.	.	.	.	.	.	.	.	.	1	.	.	.
Blau, F.G. late 1800s	1	.	.	.	.	.	.	1	.	.	.	.	.	.
Blodget, Lorin. late 1800s	1	.	.	.	.	.	1	.	.	.	.	.	.	.
Blome, Richard. London; late 1600s	89	9	11	6	11	2	5	1	3	9	4	19	3	6
Blondeau, Alexandre. Paris; early 1800s	4	.	1	.	.	2	.	.	.	.	.	1	.	.
Bluhme. mid 1800s	1	.	1	.	.	.	.	.	.	.	.	.	.	.
Blundell, J. London(?); early 1700s	7	3	.	1	.	1	.	.	.	1	.	1	.	.
Blunt, Edmund. Newburyport, MA; mid 1800s	117	.	13	5	10	13	19	19	11	10	2	4	5	6
Boardman, Harvey. mid 1800s	2	.	.	.	.	.	1	1	.	.	.	.	.	.
Bocharti, Samuel. Leyden; late 1600s	1	.	.	.	.	.	.	.	.	.	1	.	.	.
Bock, H. early 1800s	1	.	.	.	.	.	.	.	1	.	.	.	.	.
Bode, Johann Ehlert. Hamburg; 1747-1826	11	.	.	.	.	.	.	.	.	.	.	.	.	11
Bodenehr (family). Augsburg; early 1700-early 1800s	128	26	.	.	6	.	1	1	10	.	69	.	9	6
Bogart & Andrews. late 1800s	1	.	.	.	.	.	1	.	.	.	.	.	.	.
Bohn, Carl Ernst, Hamburg, late 1700s; Casimir, Wash, mid 1800s	10	1	.	.	.	.	3	1	1	.	2	.	1	1
Boileau de Bouillon, Gilles. Flemish; 1525-63	1	.	.	.	.	.	1	.	.	.	.	.	.	.
Boisseau, Jean. Paris; mid 1600s	11	.	.	1	2	2	1	.	.	.	1	1	3	.
Boissevin, Louis. Paris; fl.1652-1658	1	.	.	.	.	.	.	.	.	.	.	1	.	.
Bolton, Solomon. London; late 1700s	9	1	.	.	1	.	.	.	.	.	.	3	2	2
Bond. wall map; mid 1800s	1	.	.	.	.	.	.	.	.	.	1	.	.	.
Bongars, J. early 1600s	1	.	.	.	.	.	.	.	.	.	.	.	.	1
Bonne, Rigobert. Paris; late 1700s	562	44	48	35	38	103	56	21	22	50	38	28	41	38
Bonner, William G. Millegeville, GA	1	.	.	.	.	.	.	1	.	.	.	.	.	.
Bonneville, Benj. L.E. de. USA; 1796-1878	5	.	1	.	.	.	.	.	.	.	.	.	1	3
Booth & Hulbert. mid 1800s	1	.	.	.	.	.	1	.	.	.	.	.	.	.
Borden, Simeon. Boston; mid 1800s	2	.	.	.	.	.	.	.	.	.	1	.	1	.
Bordiga, F. Venice; early 1800s	2	.	1	.	.	.	.	.	1	.	.	.	.	.
Bordone, Benedetto. Padua; 1460-1531	89	.	.	53	2	5	3	4	1	1	5	2	7	6
Borghi, A.B. early 1800s	9	.	.	1	.	.	5	.	.	.	1	.	1	1
Bormeester, Joachim. Amsterdam; late 1600s	1	.	.	.	.	.	.	.	.	.	1	.	.	.
Borthwick, J. London; mid 1800s	1	.	1	.	.	.	.	.	.	.	.	.	.	.
Boschini, Marco. Venice; 1613-78	1	.	.	.	.	.	1	.	.	.	1	.	.	.
Bossi, Luigi. Milan; 1758-1835	1	.	.	.	1	.	.	.	.	.	.	.	.	.
Bossuet, J.B. Amsterdam; early 1700s	7	.	.	.	.	5	2	.	.	.	.	.	.	.
Botero, Giovanni. Italian; late 1500s	10	1	.	1	.	.	.	2	1	3	.	1	.	1
Bouchette, Joseph. London; early 1800s	40	4	1	16	1	4	.	2	1	.	7	2	1	1
Bougainville, Comte Louis Antoine de. France; 1729-1811	2	.	.	.	.	.	.	.	.	.	.	.	1	1
Boulton, Dennis & Co. Toronto; mid 1800s	1	.	.	.	1	.	.	.	.	.	.	.	.	.
Bourgoin. Paris; mid 1700s	4	.	.	1	1	1	.	1	.	.	.	.	.	.
Bourrelier. mid 1800s	1	.	.	.	.	.	.	.	.	.	1	.	.	.
Boutatts, Gaspar. Vienna; late 1600s	1	.	.	1	.	.	.	.	.	.	.	.	.	.

Name	Total	'83	'84	'85	'86	'87	'88	'89	'90	'91	'92	'93	'94	'95
Bowen. various to 1992	462	98	68	89	22	41	42	29	13	34	26	.	.	.
Bowen, Emanuel. London; mid 1700s. see Harris	62	.	.	.	.	.	.	.	.	.	.	31	15	16
Bowen, Thomas. London; late 1700s	14	.	.	.	.	.	.	.	.	.	.	5	6	3
Bowen & Gibson	8	.	.	.	6	.	.	.	1	.	.	.	.	1
Bowen & Kitchin	2	.	.	.	.	2	.	.	.	.	.	.	.	.
Bowles, Thomas, early 1700s; John, mid 1700s; Carington, late 1700s. London	85	14	15	10	7	2	4	2	9	3	6	7	2	4
Bowles, Samuel	1	.	.	.	1	.	.	.	.	.	.	.	.	.
Bowyer, R. early 1800s	2	.	.	.	.	.	.	.	.	.	.	.	.	2
Boydell, John. late 1700s	1	.	.	1	.	.	.	.	.	.	.	.	.	.
Boynton, George W. Boston; mid 1800s	9	.	4	1	.	.	.	.	.	2	.	2	.	.
Bradford, Thomas Gamaliel. Boston; NY; early 1800s	449	19	71	20	23	10	28	35	12	115	31	34	27	24
Bradley, Abraham Jr., American, early 1800s; William.& Co., Phila, late 1800s	102	14	7	1	3	4	9	5	6	7	14	7	13	12
Bradshaw, George. Manchester; 1801-53	3	.	.	.	.	.	.	.	.	.	1	.	.	2
Brandard, E.P. London; late 1800s	1	.	.	1	.	.	.	.	.	.	.	.	.	.
Braun & Hogenberg. late 1500s	667	69	69	34	8	11	87	36	25	34	148	24	34	88
Bretez, Louis. mid 1700s	2	.	.	.	.	.	1	.	.	.	.	.	.	1
Briet, Philip. 1601-68	5	.	.	.	2	1	.	.	.	.	.	.	1	1
Brightly & Kinnersley. Bungay, Suffolk; early 1800s	7	2	1	2	.	1	.	1	.	.	.	.	.	.
Brion, A. Forsley. late 1800s	3	.	.	.	.	.	1	.	1	.	1	.	.	.
Brion de la Tour, Louis. Paris; late 1700s	43	3	4	1	3	6	2	.	5	3	1	4	6	5
British Admiralty. see Admiralty to '93.	675	17	.	7	37	64	62	56	87	51	48	56	66	91 15
British American Land Co., London; early 1800s	1	.	.	.	.	.	.	.	.	1	.	.	.	.
British Government. see Great Britain to '92	8	.	1	.	.	.	.	.	1	1	1	1	.	3
British Magazine	1	.	.	.	.	.	.	.	.	.	1	.	.	.
British Ordnance Survey. see Ordnance Survey, to '92	16	.	.	1	.	.	.	.	.	.	.	6	.	9
Britton & Rey. San Francisco; mid 1800s	3	.	.	.	.	.	1	1	.	.	.	1	.	.
Britton Lith. late 1800s	1	.	.	.	.	.	.	.	1	.	.	.	.	.
Brockhaus, F.A. Germany.	2	.	.	.	.	.	.	.	.	.	.	.	2	.
Bromfield. Sacramento; late 1800s	1	.	.	.	.	.	.	1	.	.	.	.	.	.
Bromley, George & W.S. late 1800s	2	.	.	.	.	1	.	.	.	.	.	.	1	.
Brooke, W.H. American; mid 1800s	2	1	.	.	.	.	1	.	.	.	.	.	.	.
Brookes, Richard. early 1800s	8	.	.	.	5	.	.	.	.	.	.	.	.	3
Brooking, Charles. early 1700s	1	.	.	.	.	.	.	.	.	.	.	.	.	1
Broughton, Capt. A. London; early 1800s	1	.	.	.	.	.	.	.	.	.	.	1	.	.
Brown. may incl T., England, late 1700s	6	.	.	.	.	2	.	1	.	1	.	1	1	.
Brown, T., Edinburgh, late 1700s; Grafton T., San Fran, late 1800s	2	1	.	.	.	.	.	.	.	.	1	.	.	.
Brown & Parsons. Hartford; mid 1800s	3	.	.	.	.	2	.	1	.	.	.	.	.	.
Browne. incl Christopher, London; late 1600s; E., late 1700s; H., early 1800s	11	.	1	4	1	4	.	.	.	.	.	1	.	.
Bruce, James. late 1700s	2	.	.	.	.	.	.	.	.	.	2	.	.	.
Brue, Adrien Hubert. Paris; 1786-1832	86	7	5	5	3	18	2	4	14	12	5	6	3	2
Brunacci	2	.	.	.	.	.	.	.	1	.	.	.	1	.
Brunton, R. Henry. London; late 1800s	1	.	.	.	.	.	.	1	.	.	.	.	.	.
Bryan, W. NY; late 1800s	1	.	.	.	.	.	.	.	.	.	1	.	.	.
Bryant, A. London; early 1800s	7	3	1	1	.	.	1	.	.	.	1	.	.	.
Bryant Union	2	.	.	.	.	.	.	.	.	.	.	.	1	1
Buache, Phillipe. Paris; 1700-73	54	1	8	1	5	2	5	4	2	4	3	4	12	3
Bucelini, mid 1600s	2	.	.	.	.	.	.	.	.	.	.	.	2	.
Buchanan, R. Edinburgh; early 1800s	1	.	.	.	.	.	.	.	.	.	1	.	.	.
Buchon, Jean Alexandre. Paris; 1789-1846	158	13	5	9	17	18	16	15	16	9	13	9	10	8
Buffier. mid 1700s	6	.	3	1	.	.	.	1	.	.	.	1	.	.
Buffon. late 1700s	1	.	.	.	.	.	.	.	.	.	.	.	.	1
Bufford, J.H. Boston; mid 1800s	9	1	1	.	.	1	1	1	1	2	.	.	1	.
Buisson. Paris; late 1700s	1	1	.	.	.	.	.	.	.	.	.	.	.	.
Bullock, William. early 1800s	2	.	.	2	.	.	.	.	.	.	.	.	.	.
Bunney & Gold. early 1800s	2	.	.	.	1	1	.	.	.	.	.	.	.	.
Buno. late 1600s	1	.	.	.	.	.	.	.	.	.	.	.	.	1
Bunting, Heinrich. Hanover; late 1500s	42	2	.	5	5	2	2	4	.	4	.	9	4	5
Burchell. early 1800s	1	.	.	.	.	.	.	.	.	1	.	.	.	.
Burder. London; early 1800s	1	.	.	.	.	.	.	.	.	.	.	.	.	1
Bureau of the Amer. Republics	1	.	.	.	.	.	.	.	.	.	.	1	.	.
Burgess, Daniel & Co. NY; mid 1800s	19	2	7	.	1	3	.	1	.	.	3	1	1	.
Burleigh, litho. urban views. Troy, NY; late 1800s	5	.	.	.	.	.	.	.	.	.	.	1	1	2
Burleigh & Thomson. mid 1700s	1	.	.	1	.	.	.	.	.	.	.	.	.	.
Burney, James. London; early 1800s	5	1	.	1	1	.	1	.	.	1	.	.	.	.

	Total	'83	'84	'85	'86	'87	'88	'89	'90	'91	'92	'93	'94	'95
Burr, David H. NY; early 1800s	217	5	12	12	5	53	10	6	13	7	28	46	6	14
Burriel, Father Andres Marcos. Madrid; mid 1700s	1	1	.	.	.	.	.	.	.	.	.	.	.	.
Burritt, Elijah H. mid 1800s	6	.	.	.	3	.	.	.	.	1	2	.	.	.
Busch, Georg Paul. Germany	1	.	.	.	.	.	.	.	.	.	.	.	1	.
Buschbeck, C. Berlin; late 1800s	1	.	.	.	.	.	.	.	.	1	.	.	.	.
Bushman, John. London; early 1800s	3	.	.	.	.	1	.	.	.	.	2	.	.	.
Bussemacher, Johannes. Cologne; late 1500s. see Quad	.	.	.	.	.	.	.	.	.	.	.	.	.	.
Butler, Samuel. English; early 1800s	9	1	.	1	4	.	.	.	2	.	.	1	.	.
Butterfield, Col. C. early 1800s	1	.	.	.	.	.	1	.	.	.	.	.	.	.
Byrne, P. Dublin; late 1700s	1	.	.	.	.	.	.	.	.	.	.	1	.	.
Byron, Commodore J. 1723-86	1	.	.	1	.	.	.	.	.	.	.	.	.	.
Cadell, Thomas. London; late 1700s	4	1	1	.	.	1	1	.	.	.	.	.	.	.
Cadell & Davies	8	2	.	2	.	1	1	.	.	.	.	.	1	1
Cady & Burgess. NY; mid 1800s	1	.	.	.	.	.	1	.	.	.	.	.	.	.
Caillet. Paris; mid 1800s	1	.	.	.	.	.	1	.	.	.	.	.	.	.
California	2	.	.	1	.	.	1	.	.	.	.	.	.	.
Callot, Jacques. Nancy; early 1600s	2	.	2	.	.	.	.	.	.	.	.	.	.	.
Calmet, Augustin. 1672-1757	9	.	.	3	.	.	.	1	.	.	1	1	.	3
Calvert, lith. Detroit; late 1800s	1	1	.	.	.	.	.	.	.	.	.	.	.	.
Camden, William. English; early 1600s. see Hole, Kip	61	2	16	20	5	.	6	1	.	.	4	1	.	6
Cammermeyer, A. late 1800s	1	.	.	.	.	.	.	.	.	.	1	.	.	.
Cammeyer. early 1800s	1	.	.	.	.	.	.	.	.	1	.	.	.	.
Camocio, Giovanni Francesco. Venice; mid 1500s	43	24	4	11	.	.	1	1	1	.	.	.	.	.
Campanius Holm, Tomas. Stockholm; late 1600s. see Holme, '83	12	1	3	6	1	.	.	1	.	.	.	.	.	.
Canada Southern Rwy. Line	1	.	.	.	.	.	1	.	.	.	.	.	.	.
Canadian Governments. see Canada to '92	12	3	4	1	1	.	.	.	.	1	1	.	1	.
Cantelli da Vignola, Giacomo. Modena; 1643-95	18	.	1	1	.	1	.	1	.	.	.	2	1	11
Canzler, Friedrich. early 1800s	1	.	.	.	.	.	.	.	1	.	.	.	.	.
Capewell & Kimmel. mid 1800s	1	.	.	.	.	.	.	.	.	.	.	.	.	.
Cappelen, J.W. Oslo; mid 1800s	1	.	.	.	.	.	.	.	1	.	.	.	.	.
Capper, Benjamin Pitts. London; early 1800s	10	.	10	.	.	.	.	.	.	.	.	.	.	.
Carey, Mathew [& Son]. Phila; 1760-1839. see Lewis	431	17	50	25	39	11	31	17	43	36	54	40	51	17
Carey & Lea. Phila; early 1800s	293	13	26	9	10	33	61	20	10	29	16	18	20	28
Carey & Warner. early 1800s	2	.	2	.	.	.	.	.	.	.	.	.	.	.
Carez, J. Paris; early 1800s	1	1	.	.	.	.	.	.	.	.	.	.	.	.
Carleton, Osgood. Boston; late 1700s	9	1	.	.	1	.	1	1	1	.	3	.	1	.
Carli, Pazzini. Siena; late 1700s	3	.	.	.	.	1	1	.	.	1	.	.	.	.
Carolus, Frans. Amsterdam; early 1700s	1	1	.	.	.	.	.	.	.	.	.	.	.	.
Caron. Cincinnati; late 1800s	1	.	.	.	.	.	.	.	.	.	1	.	.	.
Carpelan, W.M. Swedish; 1780-1830	1	.	.	.	.	.	.	.	.	.	.	1	.	.
Carr. Newport, RI; late 1800s	1	.	.	.	.	.	.	.	.	.	1	.	.	.
Carrigain, Phillip (NH Sec. of State)	1	.	.	.	.	.	.	.	.	.	.	.	1	.
Carter. incl Hosea B. late 1800s	3	.	.	.	.	.	.	.	.	1	2	.	.	.
Carteret, Philip, R.N. late 1700s	1	.	.	.	.	.	.	.	.	1	.	.	.	.
Cartwright, George W. NY; mid 1800s	2	.	.	.	.	.	.	.	.	.	2	.	.	.
Carver, Capt. Jonathan. London; late 1700s	4	.	2	.	.	.	.	.	.	.	.	.	1	1
Cary, John. London; c.1754-1835	258	30	42	22	59	6	4	12	6	11	18	9	11	28
Case, O.D. Hartford, CT	4	.	1	.	.	.	.	1	1	.	.	.	1	.
Case, Tiffany & Co. mid 1800s	3	.	.	.	.	.	1	.	.	1	.	1	.	.
Cassell. incl W., London; mid 1800s	4	.	.	2	.	1	1	.	.	.	.	.	.	.
Cassell & Galpin. London; mid 1800s	6	.	.	1	.	1	2	1	.	.	.	.	.	1
Cassini, Giovanni Maria. Italy; late 1700s	67	2	2	12	4	1	6	4	13	8	5	5	5	.
Castelli, D. early 1600s	1	.	.	.	.	.	.	.	.	1	.	.	.	.
Castellini. Italy	1	.	.	.	.	.	.	.	.	.	.	.	1	.
Castilla, A. de. Madrid; early 1800s	2	2	.	.	.	.	.	.	.	.	.	.	.	.
Catesby, Mark. English; c.1679-1749	4	.	1	.	.	.	.	1	1	.	.	1	.	.
Catlin, George. American; 1796-1872	4	1	2	.	1	.	.	.	.	.	.	.	.	.
Cavazza, J. Battista. Bologna; mid 1600s	4	.	.	.	.	.	.	1	.	.	2	1	.	.
Cave, Edward. London; 1691-1754	3	.	.	.	.	.	1	1	.	.	.	.	.	1
Cellarius, Andreas. Amsterdam; mid 1600s	83	.	14	10	.	29	1	.	.	1	14	2	11	1
Central Pacific R.R.	2	.	.	.	.	.	1	1	.	.	.	.	.	.
Century Atlas. late 1800s	26	.	.	.	1	2	.	2	1	4	.	12	3	1
Chabert, Joseph Bernard. French; mid 1700s. see De Chabert, '88+	.	.	.	.	.	.	.	.	.	.	.	.	.	.
Chain & Hardy. Denver; late 1800s	1	.	.	.	.	.	.	.	.	1	.	.	.	.
Chambers, William & Robert. Edinburgh; late 1800s	13	.	2	.	.	2	2	3	1	1	2	.	.	.
Chamouin, Jean Baptiste Marie. Paris; early 1800s	6	.	1	.	.	1	.	.	.	.	.	.	2	2
Champlain, Samuel de. [repro, c.1850]	1	.	.	.	.	.	.	.	.	.	1	.	.	.

Name	Total	'83	'84	'85	'86	'87	'88	'89	'90	'91	'92	'93	'94	'95
Chanlaire, Pierre Gregoire. Paris; early 1800s	6	.	3	.	.	.	.	.	.	1	.	.	.	2
Chanlaire & Mentelle. Paris; early 1800s	12	2	.	1	.	.	2	3	.	2	1	.	1	.
Chapin, A.M., Boston; William. NY. mid 1800s	3	1	.	.	.	1	.	.	1	.	.	.	.	.
Chapin & Taylor. mid 1800s	2	.	.	.	.	1	.	.	.	1	.	.	.	.
Chapman. incl John, London, late 1700s; Silas, USA; mid 1800s	19	2	.	.	2	1	6	.	.	1	3	2	2	.
Chapman & Hall. London; mid 1800s. see S.D.U.K.	18	2	4	.	.	8	.	.	.	2	1	1	.	.
Chapman & Silas. USA; mid 1800s	9	.	.	.	3	.	1	.	4	.	.	1	.	.
Chardin, Jean. French; 1643-1713	5	.	.	.	.	5	.	.	.	.	.	.	.	.
Chardon, C. Paris; mid 1800s	1	.	.	.	.	.	.	1	.	.	.	.	.	.
Charles, J. Dublin; early 1800s	2	.	.	.	.	1	1	.	.	.	.	.	.	.
Charlevoix. see De Charlevoix, '87+	.	.	.	.	.	.	.	.	.	.	.	.	.	.
Chase, J. wall maps; US, mid 1800s	4	.	.	.	.	.	.	1	.	.	.	1	.	2
Chastenet-Puisegur, Comte Jacques de. late 1700s	2	.	1	.	.	.	.	1	.	.	.	.	.	.
Chatelain, Henry Abraham. early 1700s	209	14	13	34	11	7	13	23	10	14	23	10	15	22
Chedel, F. Paris	1	.	.	.	.	.	.	.	.	.	.	.	1	.
Chereau le Jeune. mid 1700s	1	.	.	.	.	.	.	.	.	.	.	.	1	.
Chetwind, Philip. late 1600s. see Heylin	14	.	.	1	3	.	1	3	1	1	2	2	.	.
Chevalier, Michel. French; 1806-79	2	.	.	.	.	.	.	.	.	.	.	1	1	.
Chicago & Northwestern Rwy.	2	.	.	.	.	2	.	.	.	.	.	.	.	.
Chicago, Burlington & Quincy R.R.	2	.	.	.	.	2	.	.	.	.	.	.	.	.
Chicago, Rock Island & Pacific Rwy.	2	.	.	.	.	1	.	.	.	.	1	.	.	.
Child, G. London; mid 1700s	11	3	2	.	.	.	.	.	1	.	4	.	.	1
Childs. incl G., mid 1700s; O.W., NY, mid 1800s	1	.	.	.	.	.	.	.	1	.	.	.	.	.
Chinese Cartography	3	.	.	.	.	.	.	.	.	1	.	.	1	1
Chiquet, Jacques. French; early 1700s	25	.	11	.	3	8	.	.	.	1	.	1	.	1
Choris. early 1800s	1	.	.	.	.	.	.	.	.	.	1	.	.	.
Church, A.F., Nova Scotia; late 1800s	2	.	.	.	.	.	.	1	.	1	.	.	.	.
Churchill, Awnsham. London; fl.1681-1728	6	.	.	.	.	.	1	.	.	2	.	.	3	.
Citti, Louis F. Richmond; mid 1800s	1	.	1	.	.	.	.	.	.	.	.	.	.	.
Claesz, Nicolas. Amsterdam; early 1600s	1	.	1	.	.	.	.	.	.	.	.	.	.	.
Clarendon, Edward. history; early 1700s	16	.	.	.	.	16	.	.	.	.	.	.	.	.
Claret de Fleurieu. Paris	1	.	.	.	.	.	.	.	.	.	.	1	.	.
Clark, Matthew, USA, late 1700s; Richard, Phila, mid 1800s	9	.	1	.	.	.	2	2	.	.	1	1	2	.
Clark & Tackabury. mid 1800s	1	.	.	.	.	.	.	.	.	.	1	.	.	.
Clark & Wagner. mid 1800s	1	.	.	.	.	.	.	.	.	.	1	.	.	.
Clarke & Stephenson. mid 1800s	1	.	.	.	.	.	.	1	.	.	.	.	.	.
Clarke Lith. Halifax; mid 1800s	1	.	.	.	.	.	.	1	.	.	.	.	.	.
Clason Map Co. Denver; early 1900s	2	.	.	.	.	.	.	.	.	.	.	.	1	1
Clayton Lith. mid 1800s	1	.	.	.	.	.	.	1	.	.	.	.	.	.
Clemens, E.J. late 1800s	1	.	.	.	.	.	.	.	.	1	.	.	.	.
Clerk, Thomas. Edinburgh; early 1800s	1	.	.	.	.	.	.	.	.	1	.	.	.	.
Cloppenburgh, H. Jan Evertsz. Amsterdam; early 1600s	13	.	.	4	.	2	.	.	.	1	.	1	.	5
Clouet, L'Abbe Jean Baptiste Louis. Paris; late 1700s	19	.	3	1	1	4	1	.	.	2	3	.	2	2
Cluny. late 1700s	2	1	.	1	.	.	.	.	.	.	.	.	.	.
Cluver, Philip. Leyden; early 1600s	161	16	4	41	26	17	5	2	4	8	5	5	11	17
Cobbett, W. early 1800s	2	.	.	.	.	1	.	1	.	.	.	.	.	.
Coccetus, J. early 1700s	1	.	.	.	.	.	.	.	.	.	1	.	.	.
Cochin, Nicolas. Paris; mid 1600s	7	.	6	1	.	.	.	.	.	.	.	.	.	.
Cochrane Co. early 1800s	1	.	.	.	.	1	.	.	.	.	.	.	.	.
Coello, Francisco. Spanish; 1820-98	5	.	.	.	.	.	1	.	1	.	2	.	1	.
Coggins, E.H. Phila; mid 1800s	1	.	.	.	.	.	.	.	.	.	1	.	.	.
Coghlan, Francis. London; mid 1800s	1	.	.	.	.	.	.	1	.	.	.	.	.	.
Colburn, H. London; mid 1800s	6	.	4	1	.	.	.	.	.	1	.	.	.	.
Colby. incl C.G., N.Orleans, mid 1800s; George N., Maine, late 1800s	16	.	.	.	.	.	.	.	.	1	6	1	4	4
Colden, Cadwallader. London; mid 1700s	1	1	.	.	.	.	.	.	.	.	.	.	.	.
Cole, Benjamin. London; early 1700s	18	.	13	.	3	.	.	1	.	.	1	.	.	.
Coles, T. London	1	.	.	.	.	.	.	.	.	.	.	.	1	.
Collin, L. French; early 1800s	1	.	.	.	.	1	.	.	.	.	.	.	.	.
Collins, Grenville. English; fl.1669-98	208	19	9	26	24	13	12	15	49	9	9	8	.	15
Collins, H.G. London; mid 1800s	8	.	.	1	3	1	.	2	1	.	.	.	.	.
Collins, William, [& Son] London, Glasgow, Edinburgh; mid 1800s	5	.	1	3	.	.	.	.	1	.	.	.	.	.
Collins & Clark. wall map; USA; mid 1800s	1	.	.	.	.	.	.	.	.	.	1	.	.	.
Collins & Son. London; late 1800s	1	.	.	.	.	.	.	1	.	.	.	.	.	.
Collot, Victor George Henri. French; early 1800s	11	.	.	.	.	1	.	3	.	4	2	1	.	.
Colnett, Capt. James. London; late 1700s	2	.	1	.	.	.	.	.	.	.	1	.	.	.
Colom, Jacob (father) 1600s; Arnold (son), mid 1600s; Dutch	40	.	.	5	6	8	1	3	3	1	3	2	2	6
Colorado & Red River Land Co., mid 1800s	1	.	.	.	.	.	.	.	.	1	.	.	.	.

Name	Total	'83	'84	'85	'86	'87	'88	'89	'90	'91	'92	'93	'94	'95
Colton, Joseph Hutchins, NY, 1800-93; George Woolworth, NY, 1827-1901	1120	35	43	35	135	79	154	78	120	104	134	97	106	.
(Atlas Maps)	78	.	.	.	.	.	.	.	.	.	.	.	78	.
(Pocket & Wall)	8	.	.	.	.	.	.	.	.	.	.	.	8	.
Columbian Magazine. late 1700s	4	.	.	1	.	2	1	.	.	.	.	.	.	.
Comettant, Oscar. traveler; French; mid 1800s	3	.	.	1	.	.	.	.	1	1	.	.	.	.
Comite Geologique. late 1800s	1	.	.	.	.	.	.	1	.	.	.	.	.	.
Company Maps	5	.	.	.	.	.	.	.	.	.	.	1	2	2
Comstock & Cassidy. Albany; mid 1800s	1	.	.	.	.	.	.	.	.	1	.	.	.	.
Conant, A. NY; mid 1800s	1	.	1	.	.	.	.	.	.	.	.	.	.	.
Condamine. see De La Condamine														
Conder, Thomas. London; late 1700s	27	3	5	1	2	10	2	.	.	1	.	3	.	.
Confederate States of America	3	.	.	.	.	.	.	.	.	.	.	3	.	.
Conkey. late 1800s	1	.	.	.	.	.	.	.	.	.	.	.	.	1
Connecticut	1	.	.	.	.	.	.	1	.	.	.	.	.	.
Conover, A.B., lith. Milwaukee; late 1800s	1	.	.	.	.	.	.	.	.	1	.	.	.	.
Conradi & van der Plaats. late 1700s	1	.	.	.	1	.	.	.	.	.	.	.	.	.
Conservancy, Thomas. English; late 1700s	1	1	.	.	.	.	.	.	.	.	.	.	.	.
Constable, Archibald. London, Edinburgh; early 1800s	6	.	.	.	1	3	.	1	.	.	.	.	.	1
Cook, Capt. James. London; late 1700s. see Hogg	209	4	8	21	25	12	16	13	20	23	5	18	28	16
Cooke. incl C., London, late 1700s; G., London, early 1800s; D.B., USA, mid 1800s; Lt Col Phillips St. G., U.S. Army, 1809-95	11	.	2	2	1	3	.	.	1	1	1	.	.	.
Cooper. incl H., London, early 1800s; John M., USA, mid 1800s	6	.	.	1	.	.	.	1	2	.	2	.	.	.
Copley, Charles. mid 1800s	5	.	.	.	.	.	2	.	1	.	.	1	1	.
Coreal. early 1700s	1	.	.	.	.	.	1	.	.	.	.	.	.	.
Cornelis, Lambert. Dutch; early 1600s	1	.	1	.	.	.	.	.	.	.	.	.	.	.
Cornell. incl Sarah Sophia, mid 1800s	8	.	.	.	.	2	.	2	2	.	.	1	.	1
Coronelli, Vicenzo Maria. Venice; late 1600s	379	26	42	54	28	33	29	25	21	27	16	21	36	21
Cotovicus, J. (also Kootwyck). Dutch; early 1600s	12	.	5	7	.	.	.	.	.	.	.	.	.	.
Count & Hammond. NY; mid 1800s	1	.	1	.	.	.	.	.	.	.	.	.	.	.
Cousen. mid 1800s	1	1	.	.	.	.	.	.	.	.	.	.	.	.
Cousin, Paul. late 1800s	1	.	.	1	.	.	.	.	.	.	.	.	.	.
Covens & Mortier. Amsterdam; early 1700s.	260	14	17	45	35	39	17	15	30	8	8	4	17	11
Cowley. incl John, English; mid 1700s; R., London; late 1700s	25	2	7	11	.	2	2	.	.	.	.	1	.	.
Cowperthwait, H. Phila; mid 1800s	9	1	1	2	.	2	2	.	.	.	.	.	.	.
Cowperthwait, Desilver & Butler. Phila; mid 1800s	3	.	.	.	.	.	.	.	1	2	.	.	.	.
Cox, George. London; mid 1800s. see S.D.U.K.	7	.	2	1	.	.	.	1	1	.	1	1	.	.
Coxe, Rev. William. English; 1747-1828	3	.	1	.	.	.	.	.	1	1	.	.	.	.
Craddock & Joy. early 1800s	2	.	.	.	1	.	.	.	1	.	.	.	.	.
Crafts. incl N.; Henry, mid 1800s	4	.	.	1	.	.	.	.	.	.	.	1	1	.
Cram, George. Chicago; late 1800s	491	9	22	15	27	21	32	68	31	43	74	61	50	38
Cramer, John Anthony. England; early 1800s	1	.	.	.	.	.	.	.	.	.	.	1	.	.
Crantz, David. London; late 1700s	6	.	4	.	.	1	.	.	1	.	.	.	.	.
Craskell & Simpson, Thomas. English; mid 1700s	2	.	.	1	.	.	.	.	.	.	.	.	1	.
Crawford. incl C.G. NY; late 1800s	5	1	2	.	.	1	.	.	1	.	.	.	.	.
Crepy (Chez). Paris; mid 1700s	7	1	.	.	.	.	1	1	3	.	.	.	.	1
Crevecoeur. see De Crevecoeur, post-'87														
Crocker. San Francisco; late 1800s	5	.	.	.	.	1	.	1	1	.	.	2	.	.
Crocker & Brewster. publisher. Boston; early 1800s	1	.	.	.	.	.	.	.	.	.	1	.	.	.
Crofutt. USA; late 1800s	1	.	.	.	.	1	.	.	.	.	.	.	.	.
Croisey. engraver for Bellin (at Depot de la Marine??)	1	.	.	.	.	.	.	.	.	.	.	.	1	.
Crosman & Mallory. view; mid 1800s	2	.	.	.	.	.	.	.	.	.	.	1	1	.
Cross, Joseph. London; mid 1800s	6	1	1	1	.	.	1	.	.	.	.	1	1	.
Cruchley, George Frederick. London; mid 1800s	33	2	6	4	2	2	1	1	3	1	1	7	1	2
Cruikshanks, James. late 1800s	1	.	.	.	.	.	.	.	.	1	.	.	.	.
Cruttwell. gazetteer; London; late 1800s	1	.	.	.	.	.	.	.	.	.	.	1	.	.
Cuccioni. mid 1800s	1	.	.	.	.	.	.	.	.	.	.	1	.	.
Cullen, C. London; late 1700s	1	.	.	.	.	.	1	.	.	.	.	.	.	.
Cummings, Jacob Abbot. Boston; early 1800s	1	.	1	.	.	.	.	.	.	.	.	.	.	.
Cummings & Hilliard. early 1800s	7	.	.	.	.	.	1	1	.	.	.	1	.	4
Currier, Nathaniel. NY; 1813-88	3	.	.	.	.	.	.	1	.	1	.	1	.	.
Currier & Ives. USA; late 1800s	1	.	.	.	.	.	.	.	.	.	.	.	1	.
Curtice & Stateler. St. Paul, MN; late 1800s	1	.	.	.	1	.	.	.	1	.	.	.	.	.
Custodis, David & Raphael. early 1600s	3	.	.	1	.	.	1	.	.	.	.	.	1	.
Cutler, Nathaniel. London; early 1700s	12	1	.	2	1	1	3	2	.	.	1	.	.	.
D'Anville, Jean Baptiste Bourguignon. Paris; mid 1700s. see Santini	118	13	15	5	9	5	3	15	8	5	4	15	11	10
D'Apres de Mannevillette, Jean B.N.D. Paris; late 1700s	144	24	2	2	6	4	31	6	14	13	23	11	.	8

72

Name	Total	'83	'84	'85	'86	'87	'88	'89	'90	'91	'92	'93	'94	'95
D'Entrecasteaux, Joseph Antoine Bruni. Gov. of Mauritius	3	.	.	.	.	.	.	.	.	.	.	.	2	1
D'Expilly, Jean Jos. Georges. French; 1719-93	14	.	.	7	.	4	1	.	.	1	.	.	1	.
Dablon, Claude. French; c.1618-97	1	.	.	.	.	.	1	.	.	.	.	.	.	.
Dahlberg, Count Erik J. Stockholm; 1625-1703	1	.	.	.	.	.	.	.	.	.	.	1	.	.
Daily Graphic. NY; late 1800s	3	.	.	.	.	1	.	1	.	1	.	.	.	.
Dal Re, Marc Antonio. Milan; early 1700s	1	1	.	.	.	.	.	.	.	.	.	.	.	.
Dalrymple, Alexander. London; late 1700s	22	1	3	.	2	.	2	.	1	2	4	2	.	5
Dampier, William. London; early 1700s	15	1	3	1	.	2	1	.	1	1	2	2	1	.
Dana, Charles A. mid 1800s	9	.	.	2	.	.	.	.	3	4	.	.	.	.
Danby, T. early 1800s	1	.	.	.	.	.	.	.	.	.	.	1	.	.
Danckerts (family) Cornelis elder, younger, Hendrik, Justus, etc. Amsterdam; 1600s	142	14	9	64	9	15	9	2	3	1	2	6	4	4
Danckwerth, Caspar, Joachim. mid 1600s	3	.	.	.	.	.	.	.	1	1	1	.	.	.
Danckwerth & Meyer. Husum; mid 1600s	2	.	.	.	.	.	.	.	1	.	1	.	.	.
Danet, Guillaume. Paris; early 1700s	6	.	2	.	1	.	.	.	.	1	.	2	.	.
Dapper, Olivier. Amsterdam; late 1600s. see Montanus; Ogilby	45	7	14	10	1	1	4	.	2	.	3	.	2	1
Darby, William. Penna; 1775-1854	2	.	.	.	.	.	.	.	.	.	.	2	.	.
Darton, William. London; early 1800s	19	1	4	3	.	1	.	.	3	1	.	5	1	.
Darton & Clark. London; mid 1800s	2	.	.	.	.	.	.	.	1	.	1	.	.	.
Darton & Harvey. London; early 1800s	2	.	.	.	.	1	.	.	.	.	.	.	.	1
Dashiell, S.L. USA; early 1800s	3	.	.	.	.	.	1	.	.	.	.	.	.	2
Daumont. publisher, Paris; mid 1700s	3	.	.	.	.	1	.	.	1	.	.	1	.	.
Davenport. various	7	3	.	2	.	.	1	1	.	.	.	.	.	.
Davies, Benjamin Rees. London; early 1800s	3	.	1	1	.	.	.	.	.	.	.	.	.	1
Davison, C. Wright. Minneapolis; late 1800s	3	.	.	.	.	1	1	1	.	.	.	.	.	.
Dawson Bros. Montreal; late 1800s	5	.	1	.	.	.	.	1	.	2	1	.	.	.
Day. incl Charles, Macon, late 1800s	1	.	.	.	1	.	.	.	.	.	.	.	.	.
Day & Haghe. lith. London; mid 1800s	3	.	1	.	.	1	.	.	1	.	.	.	.	.
Day & Sons. lith. English; mid 1800s	5	1	.	4	.	.	.	.	.	.	.	.	.	.
De Aefferden, Don Francisco. Antwerp; 1653-1709	12	.	.	.	.	.	.	.	.	1	2	1	3	5
De Azara, Felix. French traveler; 1746-1821	7	.	.	.	.	.	6	.	1	.	.	.	.	.
De Bar, Alexandre. London; late 1800s	1	.	1	.	.	.	.	.	.	.	.	.	.	.
De Beaurain, Jean Chev. Paris; 1696-1722	4	.	1	1	.	2	.	.	.	.	.	.	.	.
De Belleforest, Francois. France; 1530-83	19	2	6	3	1	.	1	.	.	.	2	1	2	1
De Belleyme, Pierre. Paris; 1747-1819	1	.	.	.	.	.	1	.	.	.	.	.	.	.
De Berey, Nicolas. Paris; mid 1600s	3	1	.	1	.	.	.	.	.	.	1	.	.	.
De Bougainville, Comte Louis Antoine. French; 1729-1811	1	.	.	.	.	.	.	.	.	1	.	.	.	.
De Bouge, Jean Baptiste. Brussels; late 1700s	1	.	1	.	.	.	.	.	.	.	.	.	.	.
De Brahm, W. Gerard. 1717-1799	1	.	.	.	1	.	.	.	.	.	.	.	.	.
De Bruyn, Cornelis. Delft; early 1700s	73	.	58	.	10	2	.	2	.	.	.	1	.	.
De Bry, Theodore. Frankfort; 1528-98	334	38	28	34	41	14	11	18	48	10	20	30	26	16
De Chabert, Joseph Bernard Marquis. Paris; late 1700s. see Chabert, to '86	16	.	3	4	.	1	2	2	1	2	1	.	.	.
De Charlevoix, P.F. Xavier. Paris; 1682-1761. see Bellin. (Charlevoix to '86)	24	5	2	3	3	1	.	1	3	4	2	.	.	.
De Chastellux. late 1700s	4	.	.	.	.	.	.	.	2	.	1	1	.	.
De Crevecoeur, Michel Guillaume (J. Hector) St. Jean. French-American; 1735-1813	17	.	1	.	.	1	1	2	2	.	.	5	5	.
De Fer, Nicolas. Paris; 1646-1730	114	18	19	43	.	9	11	14	.	.	.	.	.	.
(large)	38	.	.	.	.	.	.	.	10	.	5	3	6	5	9
(small)	122	.	.	.	.	.	.	.	15	17	8	8	28	25	21
De Freycinet, Henri-Louis & Louis Claude Desaules, French, early 1800s. see Freycinet, '85	7	.	1	.	6	.	.	.	.	.	.	.	.	.
De Grado, Philip. Spanish; early 1700s	2	1	.	.	.	.	.	.	.	.	.	.	1	.
De Groot, J. Netherlands; late 1700s	2	.	.	.	.	.	.	.	.	.	.	.	1	1
De Herrera, Antonio. Madrid; early 1600s. see Herrera, to '87	58	6	2	5	7	3	2	6	4	6	5	6	3	3
De Hondt, P. publisher Hague; mid 1700s	2	.	.	.	1	.	.	1	.	.	.	.	.	.
De Hooghe, Romain. Amsterdam; late 1600s	1	1	.	.	.	.	.	.	.	.	.	.	.	.
De Huyser, J.C. view; late 1700s	1	.	.	.	.	.	.	.	.	.	.	.	1	.
De Jode, Cornelis, Gerard. Antwerp; late 1500s	76	14	13	11	.	9	12	1	3	6	.	.	2	3	2
De Jorio, Andre. early 1800s	1	.	.	.	.	.	.	.	.	.	.	.	1	.
De l'Isle, Guillaume (1675-1726) & family. Paris; 1700s. see Albrizzi; Buache; Covens & Mortier; Dezauche; Lotter	254	31	14	21	.	9	16	15	7	25	7	10	18	12	59
De la Bastide. late 1700s	1	.	.	.	.	.	.	1	.	.	.	.	.	.
De la Condamine, Charles Marie. Paris; 1701-74. see Condamine, '85	8	.	.	1	.	4	.	.	2	.	1	.	.	.
De la Croix, early 1700s.. see Croix, '91	3	.	.	.	.	.	.	.	.	3	.	.	.	.
De la Feuille (family). Amsterdam; early 1700s. see La Feuille, '84	27	.	2	1	7	9	.	.	1	.	.	1	5	1
De la Hire, Phillippe. French; 1640-1718	1	.	.	.	.	.	.	.	.	.	.	1	.	.
De la Houve, Paul. publisher Paris; early 1600s	1	.	.	.	.	.	.	.	.	.	.	.	.	1

Name	Total	'83	'84	'85	'86	'87	'88	'89	'90	'91	'92	'93	'94	'95
De la Potherie, B. Paris; early 1700s	7	4	.	3	.	.	.	.	.	.	.	.	.	.
De la Rue, Phillipe. French; mid 1600s	14	1	.	2	1	.	1	.	1	.	.	2	1	5
De Laborde, Jean Benjamin. late 1700s	6	.	.	.	.	2	2	.	1	.	.	1	.	.
De Laet, Joannes. Leyden; early 1600s	74	2	17	4	1	2	2	8	5	5	6	5	3	14
De Laporte, Joseph. French; 1713-79	11	.	.	.	.	.	2	2	1	1	.	4	1	.
De Lat, Jan. Deventer; mid 1700s	10	2	.	2	2	1	.	.	1	.	.	1	1	.
De Leth, Hendrik (elder & younger). Amsterdam; mid 1700s	12	.	2	.	2	.	.	1	.	.	2	1	2	2
De Monthuchon, H. Altona; late 1700s	1	.	.	.	.	1	.	.	.	.	.	.	.	.
De Nicolay, Nicholas. Lyons; mid 1500s	2	.	.	.	.	1	1	.	.	.	.	.	.	.
De Pages, Vicomte Pierre Marie Francois. French; 1748-93	1	.	.	.	1	.	.	.	.	.	.	.	.	.
De Pretot, Etienne Andre Phillipe. Paris; 1708-87	5	.	.	.	.	1	.	.	.	.	.	1	.	3
De Ram, Johannes. Amsterdam; 1648-93	2	.	.	.	.	.	.	.	1	.	.	1	.	.
De Rienzi, L.G. Demeuy. Paris; 1789-1843	1	.	1	.	.	.	.	.	.	.	.	.	.	.
De Rossi, Giovanni Battista. Rome; 1576-1656	3	.	2	1	.	.	.	.	.	.	.	.	.	.
De Solis, Hermando. late 1500s	1	.	.	.	.	.	.	1	.	.	.	.	.	.
De Ulloa, Antonio. mid 1700s	2	.	1	.	.	.	.	1	.	.	.	.	.	.
De Vaugondy, Gilles Robert, 1686-1766; Didier Robert, 1723-86; Paris. see Delamarche, Didernt	691	43	78	54	135	50	89	19	51	31	21	27	34	69
De Vou, Johannes. late 1600s	1	.	.	.	.	.	.	.	1	.	.	.	.	.
De Wit, Frederick. Amsterdam; late 1600s	359	30	30	63	36	51	28	9	21	20	8	16	37	10
De Witt, Simeon. New York; 1756-1834	2	.	.	1	.	.	.	.	.	.	1	.	.	.
Dean & Munday. London; mid 1800s	1	.	1	.	.	.	.	.	.	.	.	.	.	.
Dearborn, Nathaniel. Boston; mid 1800s	6	2	.	2	.	1	.	.	.	.	.	.	1	.
Decker, Paul. early 1700s	1	.	.	.	.	.	.	.	1	.	.	.	.	.
Deffenbaugh & Burroughs. late 1800s	1	.	.	.	.	.	.	.	.	.	.	1	.	.
Delagrive, Abbe Jean. Paris; 1689-1757	1	.	.	.	.	.	.	.	.	.	.	.	1	.
Delahaye. incl Guillaume Nicolas. French; 1727-1802.. see De La Haye, '89	2	.	.	.	.	.	1	1	.	.	.	.	.	.
Delamarche, Charles Francois. Paris; late 1700s. see De Vaugondy	71	3	4	4	5	23	5	7	4	3	6	2	4	1
Della Gatta, Francesco. publisher Rome; mid 1500s	2	.	.	.	.	.	.	1	.	.	.	1	.	.
Demarest, Benjamin D. NY; late 1800s	1	.	.	.	.	.	.	.	.	.	.	1	.	.
Dember, G. Albany; mid 1800s	1	.	.	.	.	.	.	.	.	.	.	1	.	.
Den Schryver. Dutch (?); early 1700s	1	1	.	.	.	.	.	.	.	.	.	.	.	.
Denis, Louis. Paris; late 1700s	3	1	.	2	.	.	.	.	.	.	.	.	.	.
Denison, J. Boston; late 1700s	1	1	.	.	.	.	.	.	.	.	.	.	.	.
Denver & Rio Grande R.R.	1	.	.	.	.	.	.	1	.	.	.	.	.	.
Deposito Hidrografico	1	.	1	.	.	.	.	.	.	.	.	.	.	.
Depot de la Marine, French Admiralty. Paris. see Bellin; Vincendon-Dumoulin	289	16	41	17	21	16	15	13	30	19	51	15	8	27
Depot General de la Guerre, Paris	2	.	.	1	.	.	.	.	.	.	.	1	.	.
Derfelden van Hinderstein, Gijsbert Franco. Dutch; 1783-1857	1	.	.	.	.	.	.	1	.	.	.	.	.	.
Deroy. view; French; mid 1800s	1	.	.	.	.	.	.	.	.	.	.	1	.	.
Des Barres, Joseph F.W. London; 1721-1824	188	29	6	3	3	1	3	46	6	20	5	17	17	32
Desbordes, Charles. early 1700s	1	.	.	.	.	.	.	.	1	.	.	.	.	.
Desbruslins, father, son. mid 1700s	2	.	.	1	.	.	.	.	.	.	1	.	.	.
Desgranges. late 1600s	2	.	.	.	.	.	.	2	.	.	.	.	.	.
Desilver, Charles. Phila; mid 1800s	171	5	24	9	9	8	16	9	9	4	36	15	11	.
Desnos, Louis Charles. Paris; late 1700s	38	1	2	2	2	6	5	5	4	2	3	1	3	2
Desobry, Prosper. USA; mid 1800s	1	.	.	.	.	.	1	.	.	.	.	.	.	.
Desoer, F.I. late 1700s	1	.	.	.	.	.	1	.	.	.	.	.	.	.
Dessing, J. Nuremberg; mid 1700s	1	.	.	1	.	.	.	.	.	.	.	.	.	.
Dezauche, J.A. Paris; early 1800s	35	2	3	1	3	1	5	4	7	5	2	.	2	.
Dezoteux. French; late 1700s	5	.	2	.	1	2	.	.	.	.	.	.	.	.
Dheulland, Guillaume. Paris; 1700-70	1	.	.	.	.	.	.	.	.	.	.	1	.	.
Di Arnoldi, Fiamengo Aroldo. Bologna; early 1600s	3	.	.	.	.	.	2	.	.	.	.	1	.	.
Diamond Atlas. USA; mid 1800s	3	.	.	.	.	.	.	3	.	.	.	.	.	.
Dicey, William, with Cluer. London; mid 1700s	1	1	.	.	.	.	.	.	.	.	.	.	.	.
Diderot, Denis. encyclopedist, France; 1813-84. see De Vaugondy	94	.	.	.	1	3	2	13	18	10	20	.	15	12
Didot, publisher, Paris; late 1700s+	7	.	1	.	.	2	.	.	.	3	.	1	.	.
Dien	1	.	.	.	.	.	.	.	.	1	.	.	.	.
Dilly, Charles. London; late 1700s	4	1	.	.	1	.	.	.	.	.	1	.	1	.
Dinsmore. mid 1800s	4	.	.	.	1	.	2	.	1	.	.	.	.	.
Direccion de Hidrografia. Spanish Admiralty	78	2	1	13	10	15	6	6	3	1	2	11	1	7
Disturnell, John. NY; 1801-77	14	.	.	1	1	2	3	.	1	1	2	1	2	.
Dixon, George. London; late 1700s	12	2	5	1	1	.	1	.	.	1	.	.	2	.
Dixson, T. London; early 1800s	1	.	.	.	1	.	.	.	.	.	.	.	.	.
Djurberg, Daniel. Swedish; 1744-1834	2	.	.	.	.	.	.	.	.	.	.	.	.	2
Dobson, Thomas. Phila; late 1700s	1	.	.	.	.	1	.	.	.	.	.	.	.	.
Dobson & Cobbett. Phila; late 1700s	1	.	.	.	.	.	.	.	1	.	.	.	.	.

Name	Total	'83	'84	'85	'86	'87	'88	'89	'90	'91	'92	'93	'94	'95
Dockam, C. Augustine. mid 1800s	1	.	.	.	.	1	.	.	.	.	.	.	.	.
Dodd, Mead. late 1800s	1	.	.	.	.	.	.	.	1	.	.	.	.	.
Dodge, Grenville M., mid 1800s; R.P., mid 1800s	2	.	.	.	.	.	.	1	1	.	.	.	.	.
Dodsley, Robert. London; 1703-64	3	.	1	.	.	.	.	.	.	.	.	.	1	1
Dolendo, Bartholomew. Leyden; early 1600s	1	1	.	.	.	.	.	.	.	.	.	.	.	.
Dollar Weekly Tribune. late 1800s	1	.	.	.	.	.	.	.	1	.	.	.	.	.
Donaldson, Thomas. late 1800s	5	.	1	.	.	.	.	.	.	.	.	.	1	3
Doncker, Hendrik. Amsterdam; late 1600s	48	1	.	2	8	3	3	4	10	4	2	2	2	7
Doppelmayr, Johann Gabriel. Nuremberg; early 1700s	15	3	.	.	1	.	.	.	.	.	.	3	3	5
Dorr, Howland & Co. Worcester, MA; mid 1800s	1	1	.	.	.	.	.	.	.	.	.	.	.	.
Dou, Jan Jansz. Dutch; late 1600s	1	1	.	.	.	.	.	.	.	.	.	.	.	.
Doughty, Samuel. mid 1800s	1	.	.	.	.	.	.	.	.	.	1	.	.	.
Douglas, George. late 1800s	1	.	.	.	.	.	.	1	.	.	.	.	.	.
Dower, John. London; mid 1800s. see Teesdale	51	7	7	3	9	3	2	1	7	4	1	3	1	3
Drake, E.C. London; late 1700s	2	.	.	.	.	1	.	.	.	.	.	.	.	1
Drayton, Michael. poet, London; early 1600s	55	29	.	12	5	.	8	1	.	.	.	.	.	.
Drew, Columbus. USA; late 1800s	2	.	.	.	.	.	.	.	1	.	1	.	.	.
Drinkwater, John. London; early 1800s	1	1	.	.	.	.	.	.	.	.	.	.	.	.
Drioux, Claude Joseph. 1820-98	1	.	.	.	.	.	.	1	.	.	.	.	.	.
Drioux & Leroy. mid 1800s	1	.	.	.	.	.	.	1	.	.	.	.	.	.
Dripps, Matthew. NY; late 1800s	16	.	1	.	2	1	.	.	2	2	1	.	6	1
Drummond, A. mid 1700s	1	.	.	.	.	.	1	.	.	.	.	.	.	.
Du Bocage, incl J.D. Barbie du Bocage, French, 1760-1725	4	.	.	.	.	.	1	1	.	2	.	.	.	.
Du Bosc, Claude. mid 1700s	2	1	.	.	.	.	.	.	.	1	.	.	.	.
Du Four. early 1800s	2	.	.	.	.	.	.	.	1	.	.	1	.	.
Du Halde, Jean Baptiste. Paris; 1674-1743	5	.	.	.	.	.	.	.	.	.	.	.	4	1
Du Pinet. France; mid 1500s	1	.	.	.	.	.	.	1	.	.	.	.	.	.
Du Sauzet, Henri. Amsterdam; early 1700s. see De Sauzet, '85	7	2	2	2	.	1	.	.	.	.	.	.	.	.
Du Val, Pierre. Paris; mid 1600s	122	9	4	10	2	11	18	19	3	11	9	7	9	10
Du Vivier, F. Paris; late 1600s	1	1	.	.	.	.	.	.	.	.	.	.	.	.
Duchetti, Claudio. Rome; late 1500s	4	.	.	2	.	.	.	1	.	.	1	.	.	.
Dudley, Robert. Florence; mid 1600s	246	10	1	15	132	4	9	14	16	20	2	11	6	6
Dufertre, V. late 1800s	1	.	.	.	.	.	.	1	.	.	.	.	.	.
Duflot de Mofras, Eugene. 1810-84. see De Mofras to '88	24	.	12	.	.	4	3	4	1	.	.	.	.	.
Dufour. incl Adolphe Hippolyte. Paris; mid 1800s	63	4	3	5	2	12	5	6	3	10	2	3	3	5
Duluth News Co. late 1800s	1	.	.	.	.	.	.	.	.	.	.	1	.	.
Dumont d'Urville, Jules S. C. French; 1790-1842. see D'Urville, '85	6	.	.	2	.	.	.	.	.	.	2	2	.	.
Duncan, mid 1800s	2	.	1	1	.	.	.	.	.	.	.	.	.	.
Dunn, Samuel. London; late 1700s. see Laurie & Whittle; Sayer	32	1	.	1	2	.	5	2	3	8	5	3	1	1
Duperrey, Louis Isidore. French; 1786-1865	13	.	.	6	1	3	2	.	.	.	.	.	.	1
Dupont-Buisson. late 1700s	1	.	.	.	.	.	.	1	.	.	.	.	.	.
Dupuis. French(?); late 1700s	1	1	.	.	.	.	.	.	.	.	.	.	.	.
Durell, Philip. English; mid 1800s	3	.	.	.	.	1	1	.	.	.	.	1	.	.
Durocher, J. French; 1817-60	1	.	.	.	.	.	.	.	.	.	1	.	.	.
Dury, Andrew. London; fl.1742-78	11	.	2	2	2	.	1	1	1	.	1	.	.	1
Dury & Bell. mid 1700s	1	.	1	.	.	.	.	.	.	.	.	.	.	.
Dusacq & Cie. publisher; France; late 1800s	1	.	.	.	.	.	.	.	1	.	.	.	.	.
Dussieux, Louis Etienne. French; 1815-94	3	.	.	.	.	.	1	1	.	.	.	1	.	.
Dutton. incl Clarence, USA, 1841-1912; E.P., Boston, mid 1800s	9	.	.	.	.	4	1	.	1	1	.	.	1	1
Duval, lith. Phila; mid 1800s. see U.S. categories	9	.	.	.	6	.	.	.	.	1	.	2	.	.
Duvotenay, Thunot. French; 1796-1875	8	.	.	.	1	2	2	1	.	.	.	2	.	.
Dwight, Timothy. early 1800s	2	1	.	1	.	.	.	.	.	.	.	.	.	.
Eastman, Capt. S. USA; mid 1800s	11	.	.	.	.	3	2	.	3	.	.	.	2	1
Ecker. early 1800s	1	.	.	.	.	.	.	.	.	.	1	.	.	.
Eckhoff & Riecker. NY; late 1800s	1	.	.	.	.	.	.	.	.	1	.	.	.	.
Eddy. incl John H., NY, early 1800s; R.H., Boston, mid 1800s	5	.	.	.	.	1	.	1	1	.	.	1	1	.
Edgar, William. mid 1700s	1	.	1	.	.	.	.	.	.	.	.	.	.	.
Edinburgh Magazine. mid 1700s	1	.	.	.	.	.	.	.	.	.	1	.	.	.
Edsall, D.A. NY; late 1800s	3	.	.	.	.	1	1	.	.	1	.	.	.	.
Edwards, Bryan. London; late 1700s	101	9	5	6	5	7	11	10	9	3	19	2	9	6
Ehrenberg, Herman. USA; mid 1800s	1	.	.	.	.	.	.	.	.	1	.	.	.	.
Ehrmann, Theodor Friedrich. Weimar; early 1800s	4	1	.	.	.	.	1	.	.	1	.	1	.	.
Eldridge, George. late 1800s	1	.	.	.	.	.	.	.	.	.	1	.	.	.
Ellicott, Andrew. USA; 1754-1820	3	.	.	.	.	.	.	.	.	.	.	1	1	1
Elliot, A. London; late 1800s	2	.	.	.	.	.	1	.	.	.	.	1	.	.
Elliott Publishing Co. San Francisco; late 1800s	3	.	1	.	.	.	.	.	.	1	1	.	.	.
Ellis, John. London; late 1700s	16	1	12	2	.	.	.	.	.	.	1	.	.	.

Name	Total	'83	'84	'85	'86	'87	'88	'89	'90	'91	'92	'93	'94	'95
Elwe, Jan Barend. Amsterdam; late 1700s	45	1	2	4	18	5	3	1	.	1	.	2	6	2
Ely. mid 1800s	1	1	.	.	.	.	.	.	.	.	.	.	.	.
Emery. view; USA; mid 1800s	1	.	.	.	.	.	.	.	.	.	1	.	.	.
Emmerlich. mid 1800s	1	.	.	.	1	.	.	.	.	.	.	.	.	.
Emmons, Samuel Franklin. USA; 1841-1911	1	.	.	.	.	1	.	.	.	.	.	.	.	.
Emory, Major William Hemsley. American; mid 1800s	2	.	1	.	.	.	.	.	.	.	1	.	.	.
Encyclopaedia Britannica	2	.	.	.	1	.	.	.	.	.	1	.	.	.
Endicott & Co. lith, NY; mid 1800s	6	.	.	1	1	.	.	1	1	1	.	.	1	.
Engelmann Lith., early 1800s	1	.	.	.	.	.	.	.	1	.	.	.	.	.
Engelmann, Graf, Coindet & Co. early 1800s	1	.	.	1	.	.	.	.	.	.	.	.	.	.
English Pilot. see Mount & Page	.	.	.	.	.	.	.	.	.	.	.	.	.	.
Enouy, J. early 1800s	1	.	.	.	.	.	.	.	.	.	1	.	.	.
Ensign. incl T. & E.H., NY, mid 1800s; D.W., Chicago, late 1800s	8	.	.	.	.	.	1	.	2	1	1	2	1	.
Ensign & Bridgman. mid 1800s	1	.	.	.	.	1	.	.	.	.	.	.	.	.
Ensign & Thayer. mid 1800s	24	.	.	6	3	8	.	.	1	2	1	3	.	.
Ensign, Bridgman & Fanning. mid 1800s	15	.	.	4	1	5	.	1	1	1	.	1	1	.
Entick, John. London; mid 1700s	11	1	3	1	2	1	.	?	.	.	1	.	.	.
Eriksson, Jon. late 1700s	1	.	.	.	.	.	.	.	.	1	.	.	.	.
Ertl, Anton Wilhelm. Munich; early 1700s	25	24	.	.	.	.	.	.	.	.	.	1	.	.
Eschinardi, Francisco. Rome; 1623-c.1700.	1	.	.	.	.	.	.	.	.	.	.	1	.	.
Espinosa y Tello, Jose de. traveler, Madrid; 1763-1815	1	.	.	.	.	.	.	.	.	1	.	.	.	.
Esquemeling, Alexandre Oliver. English; late 1600s	20	.	3	5	4	1	1	1	4	.	.	1	.	.
Etablissement Geographique de Bruxelles. mid 1800s	1	.	.	.	.	.	.	.	.	.	.	1	.	.
Ettling, Theodore. London; mid 1800s. see Weekly Dispatch	24	.	4	5	.	3	3	3	1	.	1	2	2	.
Euler. see Von Euler	.	.	.	.	.	.	.	.	.	.	.	.	.	.
Euling, T. London; mid 1800s	1	.	.	.	.	.	1	.	.	.	.	.	.	.
European Magazine. late 1800s	2	.	.	.	.	.	.	.	1	.	.	1	.	.
Evans, John. London; late 1700s	10	2	.	1	.	.	.	1	.	3	2	.	.	1
Everts, L.H. & Co. late 1800s	6	.	.	3	.	1	1	.	1	.	.	.	.	.
Everts & Richards. late 1800s	1	.	.	.	.	.	.	.	.	.	1	.	.	.
Everts & Stewart. late 1800s	4	.	.	.	.	.	.	.	.	4	.	.	.	.
Every Saturday. late 1800s	2	.	1	.	.	.	.	.	.	.	1	.	.	.
Ewen, Daniel. mid 1800s	1	.	.	.	.	.	.	.	.	1	.	.	.	.
Ewing, Thomas. Edinburgh; early 1800s	1	.	.	.	.	.	1	.	.	.	.	.	.	.
Exshaw, John. Dublin; mid 1700s	3	1	.	.	.	1	.	1	.	.	.	.	.	.
Faden, William. London; late 1700s	296	36	27	24	29	23	25	27	23	17	10	20	12	23
Fahlberg, Samuel. Sweden	1	.	.	.	.	.	.	.	.	.	.	1	.	.
Fairbanks, H. San Francisco; late 1800s	1	.	.	.	.	.	.	.	1	.	.	.	.	.
Fairburn, John. London; late 1700s	2	1	.	1	.	.	.	.	.	.	.	.	.	.
Family Times. London; mid 1800s	2	.	.	.	.	.	.	.	.	1	.	1	.	.
Fanning. NY; mid 1800s	1	.	.	.	.	1	.	.	.	.	.	.	.	.
Farmer, John. USA; 1798-1859	5	.	.	.	.	.	1	.	1	1	.	2	.	.
Farmer, Silas & Co. Detroit; late 1800s	4	.	.	1	2	.	1	.	.	.	.	.	.	.
Farnham, Thomas. NY; mid 1800s	2	1	.	.	.	1	.	.	.	.	.	.	.	.
Fassmann. early 1700s	2	1	.	.	.	.	.	.	.	.	.	.	1	.
Faulkner, G. Dublin; mid 1700s	15	.	.	.	15	.	.	.	.	.	.	.	.	.
Faure. early 1700s	1	.	1	.	.	.	.	.	.	.	.	.	.	.
Featherstonhaugh, G. mid 1800s	1	.	.	.	.	.	.	.	.	.	1	.	.	.
Felton, Parker & Barker. USA; mid 1800s	1	.	.	.	.	.	.	1	.	.	.	.	.	.
Fenner, early 1800s	2	.	.	1	1	.	.	.	.	.	.	.	.	.
Fenner, Sears & Co., London; early 1800s. see Hinton et al	43	2	4	.	2	14	5	.	4	7	5	.	.	.
Ferguson. incl James, London, mid 1700s; A.M.& J., late 1800s	3	.	.	.	.	.	.	.	.	.	.	.	.	3
Ferraris. early 1800s	1	.	.	.	.	.	.	.	.	1	.	.	.	.
Fidalgo, Joaquin Francisco. Madrid; early 1800s	8	.	7	.	.	.	1	.	.	.	.	.	.	.
Fielding, John. publisher, London; late 1700s	11	4	1	.	1	.	2	.	2	.	.	1	.	.
Fielding & Walker. late 1700s	1	.	.	.	1	.	.	.	.	.	.	.	.	.
Filloeul. mid 1600s	1	.	.	.	.	.	.	.	.	.	.	1	.	.
Filson, John. American; c.1747-1788	1	.	.	.	.	.	.	.	.	1	.	.	.	.
Finaeus. Orontius, French; 1494-1555	2	.	.	.	.	1	1	.	.	.	.	.	.	.
Findlay, Alexander. London; mid 1800s	16	4	1	1	1	1	1	2	1	1	1	2	.	.
Finley, Anthony. Phila; c.1790-1840	260	22	4	23	10	41	21	11	22	17	16	27	22	24
Finn. view; early 1900s	1	.	.	.	.	.	.	.	.	.	.	1	.	.
Fisher. incl H., London; early 1800s	11	1	.	.	1	2	2	.	1	2	.	1	.	1
Fisher & Son. London; early 1800s	1	.	.	.	.	.	.	.	.	.	.	.	.	1
Fisk. late 1800s	2	.	.	.	.	.	.	.	.	1	1	.	.	.
Fisk & Russell. NY; mid 1800s	3	1	.	.	.	.	2	.	.	.	.	.	.	.
Fisk & See. NY; late 1800s	1	1	.	.	.	.	.	.	.	.	.	.	.	.

Name	Total	'83	'84	'85	'86	'87	'88	'89	'90	'91	'92	'93	'94	'95
Fitch, Asa. Albany; mid 1800s	1	.	.	.	1	.	.	.	.	.	.	.	.	.
Flamm. USA; late 1800s	2	.	.	.	.	.	.	.	.	.	.	2	.	.
Flamsteed, John. 1646-1719	7	.	4	.	.	.	.	3	.	.	.	.	.	.
Fleischmann. early 1700s	1	.	.	.	.	.	.	.	.	.	.	.	.	1
Fleming, S.A. Toronto; late 1800s	1	.	.	1	.	.	.	.	.	.	.	.	.	.
Flemming, Carl. Glogau; mid 1800s	25	.	.	1	7	1	3	4	3	.	.	2	4
Fleurieu. late 1700s	2	1	.	.	.	1	.	.	.	.	.	.	.	.
Flinders, Matthew. English; 1774-1814	1	.	.	.	1	.	.	.	.	.	.	.	.	.
Florianus, Antonius. Venice; mid 1500s	2	.	.	.	.	.	1	1	.	.	.	.	.	.
Florimi, Matteo. Siena; early 1600s	2	.	1	.	.	.	.	.	1	.	.	.	.	.
Flushing & North Side R.R. New York; late 1800s	1	.	.	.	.	.	1	.	.	.	.	.	.	.
Foot, Thomas. London; late 1700s	2	1	1	.	.	.	.	.	.	.	.	.	.	.
Foppen. view; early 1900s	1	.	.	.	.	.	.	.	.	.	.	1	.	.
Forbes, Alexander. history; mid 1800s	1	.	.	.	.	.	.	.	.	.	1	.	.	.
Forbes & Russell. Boston; mid 1800s	1	.	.	.	.	.	1	.	.	.	.	.	.	.
Fores, Samuel W. publisher; London; late 1700s-mid 1800s	1	.	.	.	.	.	.	.	.	.	.	.	.	1
Forlani, Paolo de. Venice; mid 1500s	4	.	.	1	1	1	.	.	1	.	.	.	.	.
Forster. various	4	1	.	.	.	.	.	.	.	1	.	1	.	1
Forster & Maurice, Thomas. Erie, PA; early 1800s	1	.	.	.	1	.	.	.	.	.	.	.	.	.
Foster. various	4	1	.	.	.	1	1	.	.	.	.	.	.	1
Foster Groom. early 1900s	1	.	.	.	.	.	.	.	.	.	.	1	.	.
Foster, John. Boston; 1648-81	1	.	.	.	.	.	.	.	.	.	.	.	.	1
Fostes. Paris; mid 1800s	1	.	.	.	.	.	.	1	.	.	.	.	.	.
Fourdrinier, Peter. London; fl.1720-60	1	.	1	.	.	.	.	.	.	.	.	.	.	.
Fowler, T.M. views, late 1800s	1	.	.	.	.	1	.	.	.	.	.	.	.	.
Fowler & Moyer. views, late 1800s	7	.	.	.	2	1	1	.	.	.	1	.	2	.
Fox, Watson A. Buffalo; mid 1800s	1	.	.	.	.	.	.	1	.	.	.	.	.	.
Frank Leslie's Illustrated Newspaper. mid-late 1800s	20	.	1	2	3	.	1	4	3	1	1	.	1	3
Franklin. incl Benjamin, 1709-90; John (to 1993)	25	5	5	5	.	.	1	.	5	.	2	2	.	.
Franklin (Globes). Troy, NY; late 1800s	1	.	.	.	.	.	.	.	.	.	.	.	1	.
Franklin Mint. mid 1800s	1	.	.	.	.	.	.	.	.	.	1	.	.	.
Franklin, John. English; 1786-1847	6	.	.	.	.	.	.	.	.	.	.	.	4	2
Fraser. incl J., London, late 1700s	2	.	.	.	1	.	.	.	.	1	.	.	.	.
Frazier. early 1700s	1	.	.	1	.	.	.	.	.	.	.	.	.	.
Fremin, A.R. Paris; mid 1800s	5	1	.	1	.	1	.	.	2	.	.	.	.	.
Fremont, John Charles. 1813-90	11	.	.	.	.	4	1	.	1	.	2	1	2
French & Smith. mid 1800s	4	.	.	.	.	.	.	1	.	2	.	1	.	.
French Admiralty. see Depot de la Marine	.	.	.	.	.	.	.	.	.	.	.	.	.	.
French, Wood & Smith. mid 1800s	1	.	.	.	.	.	.	1	.	.	.	.	.	.
Freycinet. see De Freycinet	.	.	.	.	.	.	.	.	.	.	.	.	.	.
Frezier, Amedee Francois. Paris; early 1700s	5	.	4	.	.	1	.	.	.	.	.	.	.	.
Fricx, Eugene Henri. Brussels; early 1700s	5	.	1	2	2	.	.	.	.	.	.	.	.	.
Fried. early 1800s	1	1	.	.	.	.	.	.	.	.	.	.	.	.
Friedenreich, P.C. Copenhagen; mid 1800s	1	.	.	.	.	.	1	.	.	.	.	.	.	.
Friederichs, J. mid 1800s	1	.	.	.	.	.	.	.	.	.	.	1	.	.
Fries, Lorenz. Strassbourg; c.1490-c.1532	24	.	.	.	.	.	.	.	.	.	.	5	7	12
Fritz, Samuel. German; 1656-1725	1	.	.	.	.	1	.	.	.	.	.	.	.	.
Froiseth, B.A.M. late 1800s	2	.	.	.	.	.	.	.	.	1	.	.	.	1
Fullarton, Archibald. Glasgow; Edinburgh; London; mid 1800s	257	48	33	29	15	18	26	13	20	7	16	12	14	6
Fuller, Thomas. English; mid 1600s	87	20	.	40	7	1	.	3	2	.	.	6	1	7
Funcke, David. Nuremberg; early 1700s	1	.	.	.	.	.	.	.	.	.	1	.	.	.
Furne (Cie). publisher; Paris; mid 1800s	5	.	.	.	.	.	1	1	.	1	1	.	1	.
Furst, Paul. Nuremberg; c.1605-1666	1	.	.	.	.	.	.	.	.	.	.	.	.	1
Gage, Isaac. mid 1800s	1	.	.	.	.	.	.	.	.	.	1	.	.	.
Galiani, M. late 1700s	1	.	.	1	.	.	.	.	.	.	.	.	.	.
Galiano & Valdes. voyager; early 1800s	2	.	.	.	.	.	.	.	1	.	1	.	.	.
Galignani. Paris; mid 1800s	2	.	.	.	.	.	.	.	.	.	1	1	.	.
Gall & Inglis. Edinburgh, London; late 1800s	23	1	2	.	.	5	1	3	3	2	1	3	.	2
Galle. incl Philippe, 1537-1612; Cornelis, mid 1600s. Antwerp	14	.	3	1	.	.	.	.	2	5	.	1	2	.
Galluci, Giovanni Paolo. Italy; fl. 1569-97	2	.	.	1	.	.	.	.	.	.	.	.	.	1
Galt & Hoy. NY; late 1800s	3	1	.	.	.	.	.	.	.	1	.	1	.	.
Gamble, Wm. H. engr, Phila; mid 1800s	4	.	.	1	.	2	.	1	.	.	.	.	.	.
Gardiner, C.K. USA; mid 1800s	1	.	.	.	1	.	.	.	.	.	.	.	.	.
Gardner, James Sr. London; mid 1800s	7	6	.	1	.	.	.	.	.	.	.	.	.	.
Garneray. mid 1800s	3	.	.	.	.	.	.	.	.	.	.	.	2	1
Garnier. various; mid 1800s	12	1	.	1	.	4	.	.	1	1	.	1	2	1
Garran, Andrew. late 1800s	7	.	.	.	.	7	.	.	.	.	.	.	.	.

Name	Total	'83	'84	'85	'86	'87	'88	'89	'90	'91	'92	'93	'94	'95
Gaskell, C.A. Chicago; late 1800s	10	.	1	.	1	1	.	1	1	1	.	2	2	.
Gast & Co. USA; late 1800s	1	.	.	.	.	.	.	1	.	.	.	.	.	.
Gastaldi, Giacomo. Venice; mid 1500s. see Ptolemy (1548)	22	.	1	.	.	.	.	.	.	.	.	4	6	11
Gaston, Samuel N. NY; mid 1800s	7	6	.	.	.	1	.	.	.	.	.	.	.	.
Gaston & Johnson. publisher; NY; mid 1800s	2	.	.	.	.	.	.	.	.	.	.	1	.	1
Gaubil, Antoine. 1689-1759	2	.	.	.	.	.	.	.	.	1	1	.	.	.
Gaudy, John. mid 1700s	1	.	.	1	.	.	.	.	.	.	.	.	.	.
Gaultier. Paris; early 1800s	1	.	.	.	.	.	.	.	.	.	.	1	.	.
Gauthey. France; late 1700s	1	.	.	.	.	.	.	.	.	.	.	.	1	.
Gavarrete, Juan. late 1800s	1	.	.	.	.	.	.	1	.	.	.	.	.	.
Gavin, H. mid 1700s	1	.	.	.	.	.	.	1	.	.	.	.	.	.
Gavit, John. printer; Albany; mid 1800s	2	.	.	.	2	.	.	.	.	.	.	.	.	.
Gavit & Duthie. mid 1800s	2	.	.	.	.	.	1	.	.	.	.	1	.	.
Gazzettiere Americano. Coltellini, publisher; Livorno; mid 1700s	116	31	5	18	5	4	9	4	14	6	2	3	13	2
Gebauers, J.J. Halle; mid 1700s	1	.	.	.	.	.	.	.	.	.	.	1	.	.
Geddes, James. Albany, NY; early 1800s	2	1	1	.	.	.	.	.	.	.	.	.	.	.
Geil & Jones. Phila; mid 1800s	1	.	.	.	.	.	.	.	.	.	1	.	.	.
Geil, Leamings & Cathcart. Phila; mid 1800s	1	.	.	1	.	.	.	.	.	.	.	.	.	.
Gell, William. 1777-1836	2	.	.	.	.	.	.	.	.	.	.	.	1	1
Gemellis, John Francis. early 1700s	1	.	.	.	1	.	.	.	.	.	.	.	.	.
Gemma Frisius. Louvain; 1508-55. see Apianus	2	.	.	1	.	.	.	.	.	.	.	.	1	.
Gendron, Pedro. Madrid; mid 1700s	6	.	.	.	5	.	.	.	.	1	.	.	.	.
General Magazine of Arts & Sciences. mid 1700s	11	.	.	.	.	1	.	1	3	2	2	1	.	1
Gensoul, Adrien. publisher San Francisco; mid 1800s	4	.	.	.	.	1	1	.	1	.	.	.	1	.
Gentleman's & London Magazine. mid 1700s	2	.	.	.	.	.	.	.	.	.	.	1	1	.
Gentleman's Magazine. mid 1800s	458	28	27	16	19	31	28	20	136	36	18	31	29	39
Genty. late 1700s	1	.	.	.	.	.	1	.	.	.	.	.	.	.
Gerritz, Hessel. 1581-1632	2	1	.	.	1	.	.	.	.	.	.	.	.	.
Gerstmayr. late 1700s	3	.	2	.	.	1	.	.	.	.	.	.	.	.
Gibbes, Charles Drayton. late 1800s	1	.	.	.	.	1	.	.	.	.	.	.	.	.
Gibson, John. London; mid 1700s. see Gentlemen's Mag.	85	5	6	13	8	13	8	8	8	5	4	4	.	3
Gilbert, James. publisher; London; mid 1800s	4	.	.	.	.	.	2	1	1	.	.	.	.	.
Gill, J.K. Portland, OR; late 1800s	5	.	.	.	.	.	.	2	1	2	.	.	.	.
Gillet, George. USA; 1771-1853	1	.	.	.	1	.	.	.	.	.	.	.	.	.
Gilliam. Phila; mid 1800s	1	.	1	.	.	.	.	.	.	.	.	.	.	.
Gilman, E. Phila; mid 1800s	5	.	1	.	.	2	1	.	.	.	.	.	1	.
Gilpin, William. Phila; mid 1800s	9	.	1	.	.	.	1	2	.	3	.	.	1	1
Gilquin & Dupain; mid 1800s	2	.	.	.	.	1	1	.	.	.	.	.	.	.
Giustiniano. various	4	3	.	.	.	1	.	.	.	.	.	.	.	.
Glazier, Willard. Phila; late 1800s	1	.	1	.	.	.	.	.	.	.	.	.	.	.
Gleason; Pictorial Drawing Room Companion. Boston; mid 1800s	10	1	.	.	2	1	2	1	2	.	1	.	.	.
Goad, Charles. late 1800s	32	.	.	14	1	.	1	.	.	.	9	.	.	7
Goeree, Jan. Amsterdam; early 1700s	5	3	.	2	.	.	.	.	.	.	.	.	.	.
Goering, A. Leipzig; late 1800s	3	.	3	.	.	.	.	.	.	.	.	.	.	.
Goggins, Joseph. late 1800s	1	.	.	1	.	.	.	.	.	.	.	.	.	.
Gold, Joyce. London; early 1800s. see Naval Chronicle	20	4	5	2	2	6	.	1	.	.	.	.	.	.
Goldthwait. incl T.H., Boston, mid 1800s	9	.	.	.	2	1	2	.	1	.	2	.	1	
Goodrich, Samuel Griswold (aka Peter Parley) Boston; 1793-1860	51	6	.	.	2	1	2	.	3	34	2	.	1	.
Goodwin, F. NY; mid 1800s	1	.	.	.	.	.	.	.	.	1	.	.	.	.
Goos, Abraham, c.1590-1643; Pieter, c.1616-75. Amsterdam	164	6	13	15	4	11	58	5	7	13	7	14	4	7
Gordon, P. Dublin; late 1700s; incl T., late 1700s	21	1	3	.	2	.	1	.	3	1	10	.	.	.
Gordon, T. engraver, Gordon's History. see Gordon to '93	1	.	.	.	.	.	.	.	.	.	.	.	1	.
Goschen, G. Leipzig; early 1800s	1	.	.	.	.	.	.	1	.	.	.	.	.	.
Gosse & Pinet. mid 1700s	7	.	.	.	.	7	.	.	.	.	.	.	.	.
Gottfried, aka Johann Philipp Abelin. mid 1600s	5	.	.	.	1	.	.	.	1	.	.	.	3	.
Gould, August. late 1800s	2	.	.	.	.	.	.	1	.	.	1	.	.	.
Gould, Jay. American tycoon; 1836-92	1	.	.	.	.	.	1	.	.	.	.	.	.	.
Gourlay, Robert Fleming. mid 1800s	1	.	.	1	.	.	.	.	.	.	.	.	.	.
Graham's Magazine. mid 1800s	1	.	.	.	.	.	.	.	.	.	.	1	.	.
Grand Magazine. late 1700s	2	.	.	1	.	1	.	.	.	.	.	.	.	.
Grand Magazine of Magazines. mid 1700s	6	.	.	.	.	.	.	2	.	.	.	4	.	.
Grand Magazine of Universal Intelligence. mid 1700s	2	.	.	.	.	.	.	.	2	.	.	.	.	.
Grant, A.A. Chicago; late 1800s	9	.	.	.	.	1	.	.	.	.	.	4	.	4
Graphic, The. late 1800s	4	.	.	2	.	.	.	.	.	.	.	2	.	.
Grattan & Gilbert. London; mid 1800s	5	.	1	.	2	.	.	.	.	.	1	.	.	1
Gratz. early 1800s	3	.	.	.	3	.	.	.	.	.	.	.	.	.
Gravier, Giovanni. mid 1700s	1	.	.	.	.	.	.	.	.	.	.	.	1	.

Name	Total	'83	'84	'85	'86	'87	'88	'89	'90	'91	'92	'93	'94	'95
Gravius, N.T. Amsterdam; mid 1700s	7	.	3	.	.	.	.	.	.	.	.	1	3	.
Gray, Ormando Willis. Phila; late 1800s	257	7	6	5	9	29	19	25	24	16	25	27	43	22
Gray & Johns. mid 1800s	1	.	.	.	.	.	1	.	.	.	.	.	.	.
Greenebaum & Sampson. Chicago; mid 1800s	1	.	.	.	.	1	.	.	.	.	.	.	.	.
Greenhow, Robert. USA; 1800-54	1	.	.	.	.	.	1	.	.	.	.	.	.	.
Greenleaf, Moses, Portland, ME; early 1800s; Jeremiah, Brattleboro, VT; mid 1800s	123	3	2	4	4	1	3	16	7	46	15	8	8	6
Greenwood (various imprints) publisher, London; early 1800s	28	5	20	3	.	.	.	.	.	.	.	.	.	.
Gregory. late 1700s	4	.	.	.	.	.	.	.	1	.	1	.	2	
Grenier. late 1700s	1	.	.	1	.	.	.	.	.	.	.	.	.	.
Gridley, Richard. London; mid 1700s	4	1	1	.	.	2	.	.	.	.	.	.	.	.
Grierson, George. Dublin; mid 1700s	18	.	3	3	2	.	.	2	.	.	1	.	7	
Grigg, John. publisher, Phila; early 1800s	1	.	.	.	1	.	.	.	.	.	.	.	.	.
Grimmel. Russia; mid 1700s	1	.	.	.	.	.	.	.	.	.	.	.	1	
Griswold. New Orleans; mid 1800s	6	.	6	.	.	.	.	.	.	.	.	.	.	.
Grose, Francis. c.1731-91	5	.	.	.	5	.	.	.	.	.	.	.	.	.
Gross. incl Rudolph, Germany, late 1800s	1	.	.	.	.	.	.	.	.	.	.	1	.	.
Grosse. late 1700s	2	.	.	.	.	.	.	2	.	.	.	.	.	.
Grundy, John (Sr & Jr) England; mid 1700s	1	.	.	1	.	.	.	.	.	.	.	.	.	.
Grynaeus, Simon. Basle; 1493-1541	7	.	.	.	2	1	2	.	.	1	.	.	.	1
Gugler Lith. Milwaukee; late 1800s	1	.	.	1	.	.	.	.	.	.	.	.	.	.
Guicciardini, Luigi. Antwerp; late 1500s	46	.	1	1	.	24	1	8	.	.	.	2	.	9
Guilquin & Dupain. Paris; mid 1800s	1	1	.	.	.	.	.	.	.	.	.	.	.	.
Gurney Cab Service. late 1800s	1	.	.	.	1	.	.	.	.	.	.	.	.	.
Gussefeld, Franz Ludwig. Nuremberg; 1744-1807. see Homann	17	1	4	.	2	.	1	1	3	1	1	.	1	2
Gussfield. globe; early 1800s	1	.	.	.	.	.	.	.	.	.	1	.	.	
Guthrie, William. London; late 1700s	32	1	4	1	2	5	5	1	3	2	4	.	3	1
Guthrie & Jones. early 1800s	3	.	.	.	.	.	.	.	.	.	.	.	.	3
Haasis & Lubrecht. late 1800s	3	.	.	.	1	1	.	.	.	.	1	.	.	
Habermann. views; mid 1700s	7	.	3	1	.	3	.	.	.	.	.	.	.	.
Hachette. publisher, Paris; mid 1800s +	3	.	1	.	.	.	.	.	1	.	1	.	.	.
Hacke, Capt. William. voyages, late 1600s	2	.	.	.	.	.	.	.	1	.	.	1	.	.
Hadfield, W. London; mid 1800s	1	.	1	.	.	.	.	.	.	.	.	.	.	.
Haffner, Johann Christoph. publisher; early 1700s	1	.	.	.	.	.	.	.	.	.	1	.	.	.
Hagaman & Markham. Auburn, NY; mid 1800s	1	.	.	.	.	.	.	.	.	1	.	.	.	.
Haines, D. Phila; early 1800s	2	.	.	.	.	.	.	.	.	.	1	1	.	.
Hale, Nathan. Boston; early 1800s	2	.	.	.	.	.	.	.	.	.	.	1	.	1
Hales, John Groves. Boston; 1785-1832	1	.	.	.	.	.	1	.	.	.	.	.	.	.
Haliburton, Thomas C. Nova Scotia; 1796-1865	11	2	1	2	.	.	.	.	.	6	.	.	.	.
Hall. incl Ralph	1	.	.	.	.	.	.	.	.	.	.	.	1	.
Hall. incl William, late 1700s. may incl Sidney	83	7	18	13	9	11	4	9	4	2	1	5	.	.
Hall, Sidney. London; fl.1817-60	6	.	.	.	.	.	.	.	.	.	.	.	3	3
Halley, Edmund. English; 1656-1742	1	.	.	.	.	.	.	.	.	.	1	.	.	.
Halma, Francois. Amsterdam; Leeuwarden; early 1700s	2	.	1	1	.	.	.	.	.	.	.	.	.	.
Hals & Rydstrom. late 1800s	1	.	.	.	.	.	.	.	1	.	.	.	.	.
Hamelmann. late 1500s	2	.	.	.	1	.	.	.	.	.	.	.	1	.
Hamilton, Alexander (of East India Co.) 1688-1723	1	.	.	.	.	.	.	.	.	.	.	.	.	1
Hamilton, Adams & Co. London; early 1800s	2	.	.	.	.	1	.	.	.	.	1	.	.	.
Hammond. publisher; Chicago; late 1800s +	2	.	.	.	.	.	.	.	.	.	1	1	.	.
Handtke, Friedrich H. Glogau; 1815-79	6	.	.	1	1	.	.	.	.	.	.	1	2	1
Hanna, Capt. James. late 1700s	1	.	.	1	.	.	.	.	.	.	.	.	.	.
Hannibal & St. Joseph Short Line. late 1800s	1	.	.	.	.	.	.	.	1	.	.	.	.	.
Hansard & Sons. London; early 1800s	1	.	.	.	.	.	.	.	1	.	.	.	.	.
Happel. early 1700s	1	.	.	.	.	.	.	.	.	.	.	1	.	.
Hardesty, H.H. Richmond, VA; late 1800s	23	.	4	.	.	1	2	.	1	2	.	5	4	4
Hardy, John. London; late 1700s	2	.	.	.	1	.	1	.	.	.	.	.	.	.
Harmon, C.E. Grants Pass, OR; late 1800s	1	.	.	.	.	.	.	.	.	.	1	.	.	.
Harper. incl J.J., NY, early 1800s	17	.	1	.	.	.	.	.	.	14	.	.	1	1
Harper & Bros. publisher, NY; mid 1800s	7	.	1	1	.	.	2	.	1	.	.	.	.	2
Harper Bros. publisher, NY; mid 1800s	6	.	.	.	.	.	.	.	1	.	4	.	1	.
Harper's Weekly. NY; late 1800s	78	.	5	6	4	1	7	16	4	2	8	11	6	8
Harrewyn (family) Brussels; early 1700s	1	.	.	.	.	.	.	.	.	.	1	.	.	.
Harris, John. English; early 1700s. see Bowen, E.	56	5	3	2	4	1	7	5	3	13	4	6	1	2
Harrison. incl John E., London, late 1700s; George, Pitts., mid 1800s	44	3	6	5	2	5	2	.	4	3	.	.	.	14
Harrison & Sons. mid 1800s	1	.	.	.	.	.	.	.	.	.	1	.	.	.
Harrison & Warner. Phila; late 1800s	2	.	.	.	1	.	.	.	.	.	.	1	.	.
Hart. early 1800s	2	.	.	.	.	.	.	.	.	.	2	.	.	.

Name	Total	'83	'84	'85	'86	'87	'88	'89	'90	'91	'92	'93	'94	'95
Hassenstein, Bruno. Berlin; 1839-1902	1	.	.	.	.	.	1	.	.	.	.	.	.	.
Hassler, Ferdinanc Rudolph. U.S.C.S.; 1770-1843	1	.	.	.	.	.	.	.	.	1	.	.	.	.
Haszard, George T. P.E.I.; mid 1800s	1	.	.	.	.	.	.	.	.	1	.	.	.	.
Hatch. lith; NY; mid 1800s	1	.	.	.	.	1	.	.	.	.	.	.	.	.
Hauducoeur, C.P. late 1700s	1	.	.	.	.	.	.	.	.	1	.	.	.	.
Haven, John. USA; mid 1800s	3	.	.	.	.	.	2	.	.	.	.	.	.	1
Hawkes, W. publisher, London; late 1700s	2	.	.	.	.	.	.	.	1	1	.	.	.	.
Hawkins, Alfred. Quebec; mid 1800s	2	.	.	.	.	.	.	1	.	1	.	.	.	.
Hayden, Ferdinand Vandeveer. USA; 1829-1887	5	.	1	.	.	.	.	.	.	.	.	.	4	.
Hayward, John. Hartford; mid 1800s	6	1	1	.	.	1	1	.	.	1	.	.	.	1
Hazard, Willis P. Phila; mid 1800s	1	.	.	.	.	.	.	.	.	.	.	.	.	.
Heaphy, Charles. New Zealand; mid 1800s	3	.	.	.	3	.	.	.	.	.	.	.	.	.
Hearne, Samuel. English; 1740-92	16	5	.	.	3	1	.	.	1	2	.	.	.	4
Heather, William. London; early 1800s	22	1	.	2	2	8	.	1	1	.	2	2	.	3
Hebner, John. London; early 1800s	1	.	.	.	.	1	.	.	.	.	.	.	.	.
Heck, G. mid 1800s	12	.	.	.	.	1	.	.	.	.	.	10	.	1
Heliotype Printing Co. Boston; late 1800s	1	.	.	.	.	.	1	.	.	.	.	.	.	.
Heller, C. mid 1800s	1	.	.	.	.	.	.	.	.	.	.	1	.	.
Ilemback. late 1800s	1	.	.	.	.	1	.	.	.	.	.	.	.	.
Henderson, G. early 1800s; J. mid 1800s	2	.	.	.	.	.	.	.	1	1	.	.	.	.
Henn, Williams & Co. mid 1800s	3	.	.	.	.	.	2	.	.	.	.	.	.	1
Hennepin, Louis de. French; 1640-1701	14	.	3	1	1	1	2	2	2	.	.	1	.	1
Henriol, J.N. Paris; mid 1800s	1	1	.	.	.	.	.	.	.	.	.	.	.	.
Henry, J. mid 1800s	2	.	.	.	.	.	.	.	1	.	.	.	1	.
Hentschell. late 1800s	1	.	.	.	.	.	.	1	.	.	.	.	.	.
Herberstein, Sigismund. Austrian; 1486-1566	3	.	1	.	.	.	.	.	.	.	.	.	2	.
Herbert, William. London; mid 1700s	75	1	.	3	1	2	1	2	.	50	1	12	1	1
Herder, B. Freiburg; mid 1800s	1	.	.	.	.	1	.	.	.	.	.	.	.	.
Heriot, George. traveler, early 1800s	8	.	.	8	.	.	.	.	.	.	.	.	.	.
Herisson, Eustache. Paris; early 1800s	12	1	2	1	1	2	.	.	1	1	1	.	2	.
Hermann Bros. San Jose, CA; late 1800s	1	.	.	.	.	.	.	.	.	.	1	.	.	.
Hermannides, Rutger. mid 1600s	1	.	1	.	.	.	.	.	.	.	.	.	.	.
Hermet. late 1800s	1	.	.	.	.	.	.	.	.	.	.	1	.	.
Herrera. see De Herrera, '88+	.	.	.	.	.	.	.	.	.	.	.	.	.	.
Herrman, Augustine. Bohemian, London; 1621-85	1	.	.	1	.	.	.	.	.	.	.	.	.	.
Hesse, J. view; mid 1800s	1	.	.	.	.	.	.	.	.	.	1	.	.	.
Heubache, E. Chicago; late 1800s	1	.	.	.	.	1	.	.	.	.	.	.	.	.
Hewitt, N.R. London; early 1800s	1	.	.	.	.	.	.	.	.	1	.	.	.	.
Heydt, Johann Wolfgang. German; mid 1700s	2	.	.	1	.	.	.	.	.	.	.	.	.	1
Heylin, Peter. London; 1599-1662	11	.	1	.	.	1	.	.	.	2	1	1	4	.
Heyns, Pieter, 1537-1598; Zacharias (son) 1566-1638; Amst.	2	.	.	.	.	.	.	.	.	.	.	2	.	.
Hickling, C. publisher, Boston; mid 1800s	1	.	.	.	.	.	.	.	1	.	.	.	.	.
Higginson, J.H. NY; mid 1800s	1	.	.	.	.	.	.	.	.	1	.	.	.	.
Hildburghausen Bibliographisches Institut. see Hildburg Institut to '91.	96	2	2	2	4	4	5	.	2	1	.	.	8	66
Hildebrandt. views; mid 1800s	2	.	1	1	.	.	.	.	.	.	.	.	.	.
Hill. incl Samuel, early 1800s; J.W., mid 1800s; H.; H.H. & Co.; H.W.	5	1	1	.	1	1	.	.	.	1	.	.	.	.
Hill, Nathaniel. globes; mid 1700s	1	.	.	.	.	.	.	.	.	1	.	.	.	.
Hilliard d'Auberteuil. late 1700s	1	.	.	.	.	.	.	.	.	.	1	.	.	.
Hilliard, Gray & Co. Boston; early 1800s	1	.	1	.	.	.	.	.	.	.	.	.	.	.
Hills, John. Phila; late 1800s	2	.	.	.	.	.	2	.	.	.	.	.	.	.
Hilton, J. engraver, mid 1700s	2	.	1	.	.	.	.	.	.	.	.	.	1	.
Hind, Henry Youle. Canadian travels; mid 1800s	4	.	.	.	.	.	.	1	.	1	1	.	1	.
Hinrichs, O. Chicago; late 1800s	1	.	.	.	.	.	1	.	.	.	.	.	.	.
Hinshelwood, R. NY; mid 1800s	3	1	.	.	1	.	1	.	.	.	.	.	.	.
Hinton, John. London; mid 1700s. see Fenner, Sears	62	4	4	5	8	18	6	2	.	.	.	4	4	7
Hinton, Simpkin & Marshall, London; early 1800s. see Fenner, Sears	10	2	6	1	.	.	.	.	.	1	.	.	.	.
Hitchcock. incl Edward, USA, mid 1800s; Charles, USA, late 1800s	4	.	.	.	.	1	.	.	.	3	.	.	.	.
Hobbs, J.S. London; mid 1800s	2	.	.	.	.	.	1	.	1	.	.	.	.	.
Hobbs & Wilson. charts, mid 1800s	2	.	.	.	.	2	.	.	.	.	.	.	.	.
Hodges, J. London; mid 1700s	1	1	.	.	.	.	.	.	.	.	.	.	.	.
Hodges & Smith. Dublin; mid 1800s	1	.	.	.	.	.	.	.	.	.	.	1	.	.
Hoen & Co. lith; Baltimore; mid-late 1800s. see U.S. categories	6	.	.	1	.	.	3	.	.	.	1	.	1	.
Hoffman, W. Weimar; early 1800s	2	.	.	.	.	.	.	.	.	.	1	.	.	1
Hogenberg, Frans. Cologne; 1535-90	4	1	2	.	.	.	.	.	.	.	1	.	.	.
Hogg, Alexander. London; late 1700s. see Cook	70	12	6	7	14	8	2	1	2	4	3	7	1	3
Holden's Dollar Magazine. mid 1800s	1	.	.	.	.	.	.	.	.	.	1	.	.	.
Hole, William. fl.1600-46. see Camden	37	15	4	3	.	1	3	1	2	.	.	1	5	2

Name	Total	'83	'84	'85	'86	'87	'88	'89	'90	'91	'92	'93	'94	'95
Hollar, Wenceslaus. Bohemian, London; 1607-77	9	3	.	3	.	.	.	.	.	.	.	1	2	.
Holman, Thomas. printer; NY; mid 1800s	1	.	.	.	.	.	.	.	1	.	.	.	.	.
Holme. early 1700s	1	1	.	.	.	.	.	.	.	.	.	.	.	.
Holmes. incl J.B., NY; late 1800s; W.H., late 1800s	5	.	.	.	4	.	1	.	.	.	.	.	.	.
Holt, Warren. San Francisco; late 1800s	6	.	.	.	1	.	1	.	2	1	1	.	.	.
Holtrop, W. Amsterdam; late 1700s	6	.	.	.	.	5	.	1	.	.	.	.	.	.
Homann & Homann Heirs, Johann Baptist. Nuremberg; 1663-1724. see Doppelmayr; Gussefeld	1064	216	31	74	111	37	31	31	111	92	32	169	54	75
Home Insurance Co., NY: mid 1800s	5	.	.	.	.	.	2	3	.	.	.	.	.	.
Hondius, Jodacus (I), 1563-1612; (II) 1594-1629; Henricus, 1597-1651; Amsterdam (& London). see Jansson, Mercator	579	47	76	78	48	44	76	29	18	14	24	45	58	22
Honter, Jan Coronensis. Kronstadt, Zurich; 1498-1549	40	1	2	31	1	.	1	.	.	.	1	1	2	.
Hood, R.V. London; mid 1800s	3	.	.	.	2	.	.	.	.	1	.	.	.	.
Hooker. early 1800s	2	.	.	.	.	.	2	.	.	.	.	.	.	.
Hooper, Samuel. London; fl.1770-93	2	.	.	.	.	.	1	.	.	1	.	.	.	.
Hooper & Berner. San Francisco; late 1800s	2	.	.	.	.	.	1	1	.	.	.	.	.	.
Hopkins. incl G.M., Phila, late 1800s	8	.	.	.	.	.	.	1	2	1	.	.	1	3
Horatius, Andreas Antonius. Rome; early 1700s	1	1	.	.	.	.	.	.	.	.	.	.	.	.
Hornius, Georg. Dutch; 1620-70	3	1	1	.	.	.	.	1	.	.	.	.	.	.
Horsburgh, Capt. James, R.N. 1762-1836	17	.	.	1	2	3	5	1	1	1	.	.	1	2
Horwood, Richard. English; c.1758-1803	1	.	.	1	.	.	.	.	.	.	.	.	.	.
Hough, E. late 1800s	1	.	.	.	.	.	.	.	.	1	.	.	.	.
Houze, Antoine Philippe. Paris; mid 1800s	7	3	.	2	1	.	.	.	.	.	.	.	.	1
Howe, Henry. USA; mid 1800s	2	.	.	.	.	.	.	.	.	.	.	.	.	2
Howell. incl Reading, late 1700s; Mark, late 1800s	5	.	.	1	.	.	.	1	.	.	1	1	1	.
Howells, William C. Hamilton, OH; mid 1800s	1	.	.	.	.	1	.	.	.	.	.	.	.	.
Howen, A. lith; Baltimore; mid 1800s	1	.	1	.	.	.	.	.	.	.	.	.	.	.
Hoxford & Co. NY; mid 1800s	1	.	.	.	.	.	1	.	.	.	.	.	.	.
Hubbs, Edwin C. late 1800s	1	.	.	.	.	.	.	.	1	.	.	.	.	.
Huber. mid 1800s	1	.	.	.	.	.	.	.	.	1	.	.	.	.
Huberti, Adrien. engraver, views; late 1500s	4	.	4	.	.	.	.	.	.	.	.	.	.	.
Hughes. incl William, London, mid 1800s; Michael, Phila, mid 1800s	9	.	1	1	.	.	.	3	.	.	.	1	3	.
Hulett, J. mid 1700s	3	.	.	2	.	.	.	.	.	.	.	.	1	.
Hulsius, Levinus. Frankfort; late 1500s	15	4	4	1	.	1	.	.	.	1	1	1	.	2
Humboldt. see Von Humboldt, '87+	.	.	.	.	.	.	.	.	.	.	.	.	.	.
Hume & Smollett. London; mid 1800s	1	1	.	.	.	.	.	.	.	.	.	.	.	.
Hunt & Eaton. publisher, USA; late 1800s	10	.	.	.	.	.	.	6	.	3	1	.	.	.
Hunter, William S. Boston; mid 1800s	1	.	.	.	.	1	.	.	.	.	.	.	.	.
Huntington, F.J. NY; mid 1800s	4	.	2	.	.	.	.	.	1	.	.	.	.	1
Huntington & Willard. publisher; Hartford; early 1800s	1	.	.	.	.	.	.	.	.	.	1	.	.	.
Huot, Jean Jacques Nicolas. French; mid 1800s	3	1	.	1	.	.	.	.	.	.	.	.	1	.
Huquier. Paris; mid 1700s	1	.	.	.	.	.	.	1	.	.	.	.	.	.
Hurd, D.H. Boston; late 1800s	1	.	1	.	.	.	.	.	.	.	.	.	.	.
Husson, Pieter. publisher, Hague; 1678-1733	6	.	.	4	1	.	.	.	.	.	.	1	.	.
Hutawa, Edward & Julius. lith; St. Louis; mid 1800s	2	.	.	.	.	.	.	.	1	.	.	.	1	.
Hutchings, John.	1	.	.	.	.	.	.	.	.	1	.	.	.	.
Hutchins, Thomas. USA; 1730-89	4	2	.	.	.	.	.	1	.	.	1	.	.	.
Hutchinson. incl Thomas, London, mid 1700s	2	1	.	.	.	.	1	.	.	.	.	.	.	.
Hyde & Co. USA; late 1800s	7	.	.	.	1	.	2	.	1	.	2	.	1	.
Hydrographical Office. see British Admiralty	.	.	.	.	.	.	.	.	.	.	.	.	.	.
I.C.M.R. c. 1800	1	.	.	.	1	.	.	.	.	.	.	.	.	.
Iliff. late 1800s	1	.	.	.	.	.	.	.	1	.	.	.	.	.
Illman, T. & Sons. mid 1800s	7	4	.	.	.	.	1	.	.	.	.	.	2	.
Illustrated London News. mid 1800s	71	2	1	12	2	11	14	9	2	5	5	2	.	6
Illustrated News. mid 1800s	6	1	.	5	.	.	.	.	.	.	.	.	.	.
Imbert, J. Leopold. Paris; late 1700s	3	.	1	.	.	2	.	.	.	.	.	.	.	.
Imray, James. English; mid 1800s	101	5	.	3	3	13	8	25	3	16	7	9	4	5
Ingersoll, Ernest. late 1800s	1	.	.	.	.	.	.	.	.	.	.	1	.	.
International Survey Co. Chicago.	1	.	.	.	.	.	.	.	.	.	.	.	.	1
Irving, Washington. American author; 1783-1859	4	.	.	.	.	.	.	.	1	.	.	1	1	1
Ivison & Blakeman. Chicago; late 1800s	2	.	2	.	.	.	.	.	.	.	.	.	.	.
Jackson. incl P., early 1800s; Wm. A., NY; M. London; mid 1800s	6	.	1	1	.	.	1	1	.	.	.	1	.	.
Jacobsz, (aka Lootsman) Anthonie, c.1606-50; Jacob, Caspar, mid 1600s; Amsterdam	42	2	5	4	7	3	5	3	.	1	1	.	.	8
Jacottet, E. lith; late 1800s	1	.	.	.	.	.	.	.	.	1	.	.	.	.
Jaeger, Johann Wilhelm Abraham. Frankfurt; 1718-90	4	.	.	.	1	.	.	.	2	.	.	.	1	.

Name	Total	'83	'84	'85	'86	'87	'88	'89	'90	'91	'92	'93	'94	'95
Jaillot, Alexis-Hubert. Paris; 1632-1712. see Mortier	232	19	31	36	25	12	28	15	10	8	9	12	15	12
James, W. London; early 1800s	5	.	1	.	.	.	1	.	.	.	.	3	.	.
Jamieson, Alexander. early 1800s	1	.	.	.	.	.	.	.	.	.	.	1	.	.
Jansson, Jan. Amst.; 1588-1664. see Hondius; Mercator; Valk & Schenk	1041	237	50	97	57	100	88	31	43	30	72	117	63	56
Janvier, Jean. Paris; late 1700s	40	3	5	4	2	2	7	1	3	2	4	1	3	3
Japanese Cartography	19	.	.	4	.	.	.	4	.	3	2	.	4	2
Jarves. mid 1800s	1	.	.	.	1	.	.	.	.	.	.	.	.	.
Jean. publisher, Paris; early 1800s	2	.	.	.	.	.	.	.	1	.	.	1	.	.
Jefferys, Thomas. London; c.1710-71. see Laurie & Whittle; Sayer et al	383	59	26	32	32	22	48	29	22	32	14	20	14	33
Jefferys & Faden. late 1700s	2	.	.	.	.	.	1	.	.	.	.	.	1	.
Jeppe, Frederick. Pretoria; 1833-98	1	.	.	.	.	.	.	.	.	1	.	.	.	.
Jewett, Thomas & Co. USA; mid 1800s	2	.	.	.	.	.	.	.	.	.	1	.	.	.
Johnson. incl A.J. NY; mid 1800s. see variants to '89	517	14	23	10	11	22	49	31	41	72	78	49	47	70
Johnson & Browning. NY; mid 1800s	55	4	2	.	26	.	2	13	8	.	.	.	.	.
Johnson & Ward. NY; mid 1800s	128	26	28	20	8	15	12	19	.	.	.	.	.	.
Johnston. incl W. & A.K., Edinburgh; mid 1800s incl Thomas, Boston; mid 1700s;	282	25	33	18	23	19	17	17	39	6	33	15	19	18
Johnstone. mid 1800s	1	.	.	.	.	.	.	.	1	.	.	.	.	.
Joly, Joseph Romain. 1715-1805	1	.	.	.	.	.	.	.	.	.	.	1	.	.
Joslin. globes; Boston; mid 1800s	2	.	.	.	.	.	.	.	.	.	.	.	.	2
Jourdan & Defrenoy. late 1800s	1	.	.	.	.	.	.	.	.	.	1	.	.	.
Journeaux L'Aine. early 1800s	1	.	.	.	.	.	.	.	.	.	.	1	.	.
Jouvet. publisher, Paris; late 1800s	1	.	.	.	.	.	1	.	.	.	.	.	.	.
Judd. early 1800s	1	1	.	.	.	.	.	.	.	.	.	.	.	.
Julien, Roth-Joseph. Paris; fl.1750-80	2	.	.	.	.	.	.	.	.	.	.	.	1	1
Juta. publisher; Capetown; late 1800s	1	.	.	.	.	.	.	.	.	.	.	.	.	1
Kaempfer, Engelbert. 1651-1716	14	1	.	.	.	.	.	.	.	.	.	1	10	2
Kaerius. see Van den Keere														
Kane, Elisha Kent. Phila; mid 1800s	3	.	1	.	.	.	.	1	.	.	.	1	.	.
Kearfott, J. Baker. late 1800s	3	.	.	.	.	1	.	1	.	1	.	.	.	.
Kearsley, George. publisher, London; late 1700s	2	.	.	2	.	.	.	.	.	.	.	.	.	.
Keefer, Thomas C. Montreal; mid 1800s	3	.	.	.	1	.	.	2	.	.	.	.	.	.
Keeler, William J. Wash; mid 1800s	1	.	.	.	.	.	.	.	.	.	1	.	.	.
Keere. see Van den Keere														
Keily, J., with J.W. Otley. New Jersey	1	.	.	.	.	.	.	.	.	.	.	1	.	.
Keller. various	4	1	.	.	.	.	.	.	.	.	.	1	.	2
Kellogg. lith. Hartford; mid 1800s	2	.	.	.	.	.	.	1	.	1	.	.	.	.
Kelly, Thomas. London; mid 1800s	29	2	4	2	1	7	3	2	3	1	.	3	.	1
Kemble, W. NY; mid 1800s	2	.	.	.	.	.	.	.	.	.	2	.	.	.
Kennard. London; mid 1800s	1	.	.	1	.	.	.	.	.	.	.	.	.	.
Kensett, Thomas. New Haven; early 1800s	4	.	.	.	.	1	.	1	.	.	.	1	1	.
Kepler, Johann. German; 1571-1630	1	.	.	.	.	.	.	.	.	.	.	1	.	.
Kepohoni. Hawaii; mid 1800s	2	.	1	.	.	.	.	.	.	.	.	1	.	.
Keur, Jacob & Hendrik. Dutch; late 1600s	9	.	.	.	.	.	1	.	.	2	2	1	1	1
Key, John R. NY; mid 1800s	1	1	.	.	.	.	.	.	.	.	.	.	.	.
Keyser, Jacob. Amsterdam; early 1700s	6	2	1	1	.	1	.	.	1	.	.	.	.	.
Keystone Publishing Co. Chicago; late 1800s	1	.	1	.	.	.	.	.	.	.	.	.	.	.
Kiepert, Heinrich. Weimar; mid 1800s	8	2	.	.	.	.	.	.	1	.	.	4	.	1
Kilbourn, John. Columbus, OH; early 1800s	1	.	1	.	.	.	.	.	.	.	.	.	.	.
Kilburn. Boston; mid 1800s	1	1	.	.	.	.	.	.	.	.	.	.	.	.
Kilian, George Christophe. Augsburg; 1709-80	5	.	.	.	.	.	.	.	.	.	.	.	5	.
Kimmel & Foster. mid 1800s	1	.	.	.	.	.	.	.	.	.	1	.	.	.
Kincaid, Alexander. late 1700s	3	.	.	.	.	.	1	.	.	.	.	1	.	1
King, Daniel. London; mid 1600s	1	1	.	.	.	.	.	.	.	.	.	.	.	.
Kingman Bros. Chicago; late 1800s	6	.	6	.	.	.	.	.	.	.	.	.	.	.
Kingsbury, Lt. J.P. U.S.Army; mid 1800s	2	.	1	.	.	.	.	.	.	.	.	1	.	.
Kinnersley, E. Bungay, Suffolk; early 1800s	2	.	.	.	.	.	.	1	.	.	1	.	.	.
Kino, Eusebio Francisco. Spanish; 1644-1711	5	1	.	1	.	.	.	1	.	.	.	.	1	1
Kip, William. English; early 1600s. see Camden	31	10	17	2	.	1	.	1	.	.	.	.	.	.
Kircher, Athanasius. Amsterdam; mid 1600s	53	3	7	4	6	2	2	2	3	5	2	1	11	5
Kirkwood, James & Son. publisher, Edinburgh; early 1800s	2	.	.	1	.	1	.	.	.	.	.	.	.	.
Kitchin, Thomas. London; 1718-84	276	35	41	59	24	27	15	15	9	5	9	8	14	15
Klaproth, Heinrich Julius von. traveler; 1783-1835	1	.	.	.	.	.	.	.	.	.	.	1	.	.
Klauprech & Menzel. lith, Cincinnati; mid 1800s	1	.	.	.	.	.	.	.	.	.	1	.	.	.
Kleinknecht, L.V. mid 1800s	6	.	.	.	.	.	.	.	.	2	.	.	4	.
Klinckowstrom, Axel Leonhard. Stockholm; 1775-1837	1	.	.	.	.	.	1	.	.	.	.	.	.	.
Klockhoff, H. late 1800s	2	.	.	.	.	.	1	.	1	.	.	.	.	.

Name	Total	'83	'84	'85	'86	'87	'88	'89	'90	'91	'92	'93	'94	'95
Knapton. mid 1700s	1	.	.	.	.	.	1	.	.	.	.	.	.	.
Knight, Charles. London; mid 1800s. see S.D.U.K.	14	3	.	2	2	1	1	.	3	2	.	.	.	.
Knipe, J.A. mid 1800s	1	.	.	1	.	.	.	.	.	.	.	.	.	.
Knox, James. early 1800s	2	.	.	.	.	.	.	.	.	.	.	1	.	1
Koch, Augustus. late 1800s	1	.	.	.	.	.	.	1	.	.	.	.	.	.
Kohl, A. late 1800s	1	.	.	.	1	.	.	.	.	.	.	.	.	.
Kok, J. Amsterdam; late 1700s	3	.	.	.	2	1	.	.	.	.	.	.	.	.
Kolb, Peter. 1675-1726	3	.	.	3	.	.	.	.	.	.	.	.	.	.
Kolben, P. early 1700s	3	.	.	.	.	.	.	3	.	.	.	.	.	.
Koller, G. early 1700s	2	.	.	.	.	.	1	.	1	.	.	.	.	.
Kootwyck. see Cotovicus														
Krayenhoff, Baron C.T.R. van. French; early 1800s	2	.	2	.	.	.	.	.	.	.	.	.	.	.
Kreffeldt, Mart. Karol. Dutch(?); mid 1500s	1	.	1	.	.	.	.	.	.	.	.	.	.	.
Krevelt, A. van. engraver; Amsterdam; late 1700s	3	.	.	.	.	.	.	1	.	2	.	.	.	.
Kruikius, Nicolas Samuelsz. Delft; 1678-1754	11	.	1	.	.	.	.	.	.	.	10	.	.	.
Kuchel, C.C. San Francisco; mid 1800s	1	.	.	.	.	1	.	.	.	.	.	.	.	.
Kurtz & Allison. late 1800s	1	.	.	.	.	.	.	1	.	.	.	.	.	.
La Harpe, Jean Francis de. 1739-1803	3	.	.	.	.	.	.	.	.	.	.	3	.	.
La Hontan, Baron Louis Armond de. The Hague; London; 1666-1715. see Lahonton, '89	52	3	6	8	4	5	6	4	7	.	1	3	1	4
La Perouse, Comte Jean de. Paris; 1741-1788 aka: Jean Francois de Galoup. see Robinson	132	11	4	3	5	3	8	13	8	14	12	24	8	19
La Pointe. engraver; late 1600s	1	.	1	.	.	.	.	.	.	.	.	.	.	.
La Rochefoucault-Liancourt, Francois A. F. late 1700s	1	.	.	.	.	.	.	.	.	1	.	.	.	.
Labat, J.B. The Hague; early 1700s	7	.	1	2	.	.	.	1	1	1	.	1	.	.
Labelye, Charles. London; mid 1700s	1	.	.	1	.	.	.	.	.	.	.	.	.	.
Lacoste, Charles. Paris; late 1800s	3	1	.	.	.	1	.	.	.	1	.	.	.	.
Ladies Repository. mid 1800s	21	.	6	.	1	.	.	3	3	3	1	4	.	.
Lafitau. mid 1700s	8	.	.	.	.	.	.	.	.	.	.	.	.	8
Lafreri School, Antonio. Rome. see Bertelli; Camocio; Duchetti; Forlani; Gastaldi; Rasciotti; Salamanca; Zaltieri.	11	1	3	1	.	.	.	.	.	.	1	3	1	1
Lake Shore & Michigan Southern Rwy. late 1800s	2	.	.	.	1	1	.	.	.	.	.	.	.	.
Lallemand. Paris; mid 1800s	2	.	.	.	.	.	.	.	.	.	2	.	.	.
Lambert, J. traveler; early 1800s	5	1	.	3	.	.	.	.	.	.	.	1	.	.
Lamy, Bernard	1	.	.	.	.	.	.	.	.	.	.	.	1	.
Lancelot, D. views; London; late 1800s	1	.	.	.	.	.	1	.	.	.	.	.	.	.
Lane, W. London; late 1700s	3	2	.	.	.	.	.	.	1	.	.	.	.	.
Lange. incl Henry, German, 1821-93; view, G.G., mid 1800s	6	.	1	.	.	.	.	.	2	.	.	2	.	1
Lange & Kronfeld. view; mid 1800s	1	.	.	.	.	.	.	.	.	.	.	1	.	.
Langenes, Barent. Amsterdam; late 1500s	15	.	1	1	.	.	1	.	.	1	1	3	3	2
Langhans, Paul. Gotha; late 1800s	1	.	.	.	.	1	.	.	.	.	.	.	.	.
Langley, Edward. London; early 1800s	12	12	.	.	.	.	.	.	.	.	.	.	.	.
Langlois, Hyacinthe. Paris; early 1800s	2	.	1	.	1	.	.	.	.	.	.	.	.	.
Langsdorff. view; Frankfort; early 1800s	2	1	.	1	.	.	.	.	.	.	.	.	.	.
Lapie, Alexandre Emile & Pierre. Paris; early 1800s	65	9	.	2	.	6	7	4	5	4	7	6	10	5
Lapointe, D. Paris; mid 1600s	1	1	.	.	.	.	.	.	.	.	.	.	.	.
Laporte, Joseph de. late 1700s	3	.	.	1	.	.	.	.	.	.	.	.	1	1
Las Cases, Comte Emmanuel M.J.A.D. de (aka LeSage) 1766-1842	2	.	.	.	.	2	.	.	.	.	.	.	.	.
Laso. Madrid; early 1700s	1	.	.	.	.	.	.	.	.	.	.	.	.	1
Lasor a Varea, Alphonsus. Padua; early 1700s	100	.	4	1	2	1	.	3	22	1	42	.	24	.
Lathrop, H.P. New Orleans; mid 1800s	3	.	.	.	.	2	.	1	.	.	.	.	.	.
Latrobe, C.I. London; early 1800s	1	.	.	.	.	.	1	.	.	.	.	.	.	.
Lattre, Jean. Paris; late 1700s	33	.	2	4	.	.	2	1	2	1	2	9	4	.	6
Lauremberg, Johannes Wilhelm. Amsterdam; 1590-1658	8	7	.	.	.	.	.	.	.	.	.	1	.	.
Laurent. incl J., Paris, mid 1800s	6	.	1	.	.	1	1	.	.	.	.	.	2	1
Laurie, John, mid 1700s; Robert, 1755-1836; Richard Holmes, fl.1822-58; London	18	2	.	.	1	2	3	2	.	3	4	.	1	.
Laurie & Whittle, publisher; London; late 1700s + . see Dunn, Jefferys	320	24	15	26	11	47	27	18	17	17	22	37	17	42
Lavoisne, C.V. early 1800s	13	2	.	1	.	.	.	2	.	.	.	2	1	5
Law, John (Louisiana Co.) early 1800s	6	.	1	.	.	.	1	.	.	.	.	2	1	.	1
Lawrence, H.L. lith; NY; mid 1800s	1	.	.	.	1	.	.	.	.	.	.	.	.	.
Lawson, John. London; early 1700s	3	.	1	.	.	.	.	1	.	1	.	.	.	.
Lay. incl John, early 1800s	6	.	.	.	.	.	2	1	.	.	1	.	1	1
Lazius, Wolfgang. Hungarian; 1514-65	1	.	.	.	.	.	.	.	.	.	1	.	.	.
Le Beau. mid 1700s	1	1	.	.	.	.	.	.	.	.	.	.	.	.
Le Bruyn, Cornelis. early 1700s	15	15	.	.	.	.	.	.	.	.	.	.	.	.
Le Clerc. incl Jean, French, 1560-1621	18	.	9	2	.	1	.	2	1	1	.	1	.	.

Name	Total	'83	'84	'85	'86	'87	'88	'89	'90	'91	'92	'93	'94	'95
Le Gentil, G.I.H. French traveler; 1725-92	1	.	.	.	.	.	.	.	1	.	.	.	.	.
Le Maire, Jacque. early 1600s	1	.	.	.	.	.	.	.	.	.	1	.	.	.
Le Maitre. engraver; Paris; early 1800s	2	.	.	.	.	.	1	.	.	.	.	.	1	.
Le Page du Pratz. Paris; mid 1700s	3	1	.	.	1	.	.	.	.	.	1	.	.	.
Le Rouge, George Louis. Paris; fl.1740-80	223	15	22	11	12	38	10	8	13	18	24	11	11	30
Le Sage. pseudonym for Las Casas	6	.	.	.	.	3	.	.	1	.	1	.	1	.
Le Temps. publication; Paris	1	.	.	.	.	.	1	.	.	.	.	.	.	.
Le Vasseur de Beauplan, Guillaume. 1595-1685	1	.	.	.	.	.	.	.	.	.	.	.	.	.
Lea, Philip. London; late 1600s	1	.	1	.	.	.	.	.	.	.	.	.	.	.
Lea & Blanchard. publisher; Phila; mid 1800s	23	2	.	7	8	1	1	2	.	.	.	2	.	.
Lea & Overton. late 1600s	1	.	.	.	.	.	.	.	1	.	.	.	.	.
Leadville Daily Herald. late 1800s	4	.	4	.	.	.	.	.	.	.	.	.	.	.
Legrand. early 1800s	1	.	1	.	.	.	.	.	.	.	.	.	.	.
Leigh, Samuel. London; early 1800s	2	.	.	.	.	.	.	2	.	.	.	.	.	.
Leitch. incl R.P., views, mid 1800s; J & Co., London, late 1800s	12	.	10	.	.	.	.	.	.	.	.	.	1	1
Lejeune, T. mid 1800s	5	.	.	3	.	.	1	.	1	.	.	.	.	.
Lemercier. printer; Paris; mid 1800s	1	.	.	.	.	.	.	.	.	1	.	.	.	.
Lester, John S. Boston; late 1800s	2	1	.	.	.	.	.	.	.	.	1	.	.	.
Letts. publisher; London; late 1800s	1	.	.	.	.	.	.	.	1	.	.	.	.	.
Leval, P. Paris; early 1700s	10	.	.	.	1	.	2	.	2	1	1	2	.	1
Levanto, Francesco Maria. Genoa; mid 1600s	1	1	.	.	.	.	.	.	.	.	.	.	.	.
Levasseur, Victor. Paris; mid 1800s	3	1	1	1	.	.	.	.	.	.	.	.	.	.
Levi. mid-late 1800s	92	8	5	4	6	11	8	8	3	6	10	4	13	6
Lewis & Clark. explorers; USA; early 1800s	1	.	.	.	.	.	.	.	.	.	.	1	.	.
Lewis, Samuel. Phila; late 1700s. see Carey	2	.	.	.	.	.	1	.	1	.	.	.	.	.
Lewis, Samuel & Co. London; mid 1800s	26	7	5	2	3	5	.	.	3	.	1	.	.	.
Liebaux, Jean Baptiste. Paris; late 1600s	9	.	.	.	5	.	2	.	.	.	.	2	.	.
Liefrinck, Mynken. Antwerp; late 1500s	1	1	.	.	.	.	.	.	.	.	.	.	.	.
Ligon, Richard. mid 1600s	1	.	1	.	.	.	.	.	.	.	.	.	.	.
Lincoln & Edmands. mid 1800s	8	.	.	1	.	.	.	3	3	.	1	.	.	.
Lindeman. late 1700s	3	.	.	.	.	.	.	.	.	.	.	.	1	2
Lindner, F.L. early 1800s	1	.	1	.	.	.	.	.	.	.	.	.	.	.
Lindsay & Blakiston. Phila; mid 1800s	2	.	.	.	.	.	.	.	.	.	1	.	1	.
Lindstrom	1	.	.	.	.	.	.	.	.	.	1	.	.	.
Linforth, James. author; mid 1800s	1	.	.	.	.	.	.	.	.	1	.	.	.	.
Link, W.F. NY; late 1700s	2	.	.	1	1	.	.	.	.	.	.	.	.	.
Linschoten. see Van Linschoten, '86+	1	.	.	.	.	.	.	.	.	.	.	.	1	.
Linton. incl H. & W.J., London, late 1800s	.	.	.	.	.	.	.	.	.	.	.	.	.	.
Lippincott. late 1800s	4	.	.	1	.	1	.	.	1	1	.	.	.	.
Lippincott & Grambo. publisher; Phila; mid 1800s	5	.	.	.	.	.	.	.	4	1	.	.	.	.
Lirelli. late 1700s	2	.	.	.	.	.	.	1	.	.	1	.	.	.
Literary Magazine. late 1700s	1	.	.	.	.	.	.	.	.	.	1	.	.	.
Lizars, Daniel. fl.1776-1812; William Home, 1788-1859; Edinburgh	1	.	.	.	.	.	.	.	.	.	1	.	.	.
Lloyd. various, 1800s; may incl H.H.	48	2	6	3	1	2	5	12	4	3	3	4	.	3
Lloyd, H.H. NY; mid 1800s	61	1	.	1	5	10	9	5	7	7	2	7	2	5
Lobeck, Tobias. mid 1700s	7	.	.	.	.	.	.	.	.	.	.	.	7	.
Lobineau, D.G.A. Paris; early 1800s	29	.	.	.	.	.	.	.	.	.	29	.	.	.
Local & State Government	2	.	.	.	.	.	.	.	.	.	.	.	1	1
Local & State Maps - Infrequent Publishers	12	.	.	.	.	.	.	.	.	.	.	4	6	2
Local & State Pocket Maps - Infrequent Publishers	13	.	.	.	.	.	.	.	.	.	.	.	8	5
Local & State Wall Maps - Infrequent Publishers	18	.	.	.	.	.	.	.	.	.	.	18	.	.
Lockman, John. mid 1700s	27	.	.	.	.	.	.	.	.	.	.	.	23	4
Lockwood, Benoni. USA; early 1800s	1	.	.	.	.	.	.	1	.	.	.	.	.	.
Lodge, John. London; late 1700s	1	.	.	.	.	.	.	.	.	.	.	1	.	.
Logan & Hartley. Canada; late 1800s	45	1	6	8	6	9	8	2	.	.	2	.	1	2
Logerot. publisher; Paris; mid 1800s	1	.	.	.	.	.	1	.	.	.	.	.	.	.
Loggan, David. English; late 1600s	6	.	.	.	.	.	.	.	.	.	.	2	3	1
London Benevolent Repository. mid 1800s	2	.	.	2	.	.	.	.	.	.	.	.	.	.
London Gazette. late 1700s	1	.	.	.	.	.	.	.	.	1	.	.	.	.
London Illustrated News. mid 1800s+	5	2	.	.	.	2	1	.	.	.	.	.	.	.
London Journal. mid 1800s	2	.	.	2	.	.	.	.	.	.	.	.	.	.
London Magazine. mid-late 1800s	4	.	.	.	.	4	.	.	.	.	.	.	.	.
London News. mid-late 1800s	279	13	18	28	16	21	17	11	37	24	28	19	23	24
London Printing & Publishing. mid 1800s	21	5	4	10	2	.	.	.	.	.	.	.	.	.
London Steam Boat Co. late 1800s	1	.	.	.	.	.	.	.	.	.	1	.	.	.
London Times. late 1800s+	1	.	.	.	.	.	.	.	.	.	1	.	.	.
Long. incl Maj. S.H., U.S. Army, early 1800s; various others	6	.	.	.	6	.	.	.	.	.	.	.	.	.
	3	.	.	.	.	.	.	2	.	1	.	.	.	.

Name	Total	'83	'84	'85	'86	'87	'88	'89	'90	'91	'92	'93	'94	'95
Longchamps, S.G. French; mid 1700s	2	.	.	.	.	.	1	.	.	.	.	.	.	1
Longman (various companies) publisher; London; early 1800s +	20	2	4	5	1	1	.	1	2	.	.	.	1	3
Longman & Rees. London; early 1800s	1	.	.	.	.	.	1	.	.	.	.	.	.	.
Longworth, D. early 1800s	1	.	.	.	.	.	.	.	.	.	.	1	.	.
Lootsman. see Jacobsz														
Lopez, Tomas. Madrid; 1730-1802	24	2	.	1	.	1	.	4	1	1	2	3	9	.
Lorrain. incl N., Paris, mid 1800s	4	.	.	.	1	.	.	.	.	1	1	1	.	.
Lothian, John. Edinburgh; fl.1825-46	5	.	.	.	1	.	2	.	2	.	.	.	.	.
Lotter, Tobias Conrad, 1717-77; Mathais Albrecht, 1741-1810; Augsburg	322	14	16	29	14	17	10	9	50	8	60	13	22	60
Lottery Magazine. late 1700s	2	.	.	.	.	.	.	.	.	.	.	1	1	.
Lottin, M. French; early 1800s	1	.	.	.	.	.	.	.	.	1	.	.	.	.
Loveringh, Jacobus. publisher; Amsterdam; mid 1700s	1	.	.	.	.	.	.	1	.	.	.	.	.	.
Lowden & Johnson. Sacramento; late 1800s	1	.	.	.	.	.	.	1	.	.	.	.	.	.
Lowizio, George Moritz. Nuremberg; mid 1700s	1	.	1	.	.	.	.	.	.	.	.	.	.	.
Lowry. mid 1800s	5	.	.	1	2	1	.	.	.	.	.	.	.	1
Lubrecht, Charles. mid 1800s	1	.	.	.	.	.	.	.	.	.	1	.	.	.
Lucas, Fielding. Baltimore; 1781-1854	209	6	50	5	4	2	7	19	15	5	32	20	19	25
Luffman. incl John, London, early 1800s; I., NY, early 1800s	30	4	.	17	.	6	.	1	1	.	.	1	.	.
Lufft, Hans. Wittemberg; early 1500s	3	1	.	1	.	1	.	.	.	.	.	.	.	.
Lumsden. mid 1700s	1	.	.	.	.	.	.	.	.	.	.	1	.	.
Luther	1	1	.	.	.	.	.	.	.	.	.	.	.	.
Lutke, Frederic. mid 1800s	1	.	.	.	.	.	.	.	.	.	.	.	.	1
Lyell, Charles. English; mid 1800s	1	.	1	.	.	.	.	.	.	.	.	.	.	.
MacClure & MacDonald. Glasgow; mid 1800s	5	.	1	1	1	.	1	1	.	.	.	.	.	.
MacDonald. mid 1800s	2	.	.	2	.	.	.	.	.	.	.	.	.	.
MacDougall & Southwick. Seattle; late 1800s	1	.	.	.	.	.	.	1	.	.	.	.	.	.
MacGregor, M. London; mid 1800s	2	.	1	.	.	1	.	.	.	.	.	.	.	.
MacKenzie. incl Murdoch, English, late 1700s; Alexander, London, early 1800s; William, London, Edinburgh	50	6	3	5	1	4	7	.	4	3	2	7	.	8
MacKinlay, A. late 1800s	7	.	1	.	.	.	1	.	1	.	3	1	.	.
MacPherson, A. London, early 1800s; D. Phila, early 1800s	5	.	1	.	2	1	.	.	.	.	.	1	.	.
Macrobius, Ambrosius Aurelius Theodosius. Roman; 399-423 (after)	1	.	.	.	.	.	.	.	.	.	.	1	.	.
Madison, James. Virginia; early 1800s	1	.	.	.	.	.	.	1	.	.	.	.	.	.
Maescamp. early 1800s	1	.	.	1	.	.	.	.	.	.	.	.	.	.
Maffeius, Peter. Venice, Cologne; late 1500s	2	.	1	.	.	.	.	1	.	.	.	.	.	.
Maggi, C. editor; Turin; mid 1800s	2	.	1	.	.	1	.	.	.	.	.	.	.	.
Magini, Giovanni Antonio. 1555-1617. see Ptolemy (1596-1621) to '93	37	.	.	.	.	.	.	2	.	.	.	.	21	14
Magnelli. late 1700s	1	.	.	.	.	.	.	.	.	.	.	.	.	1
Magnus, Charles. lith; NY; mid 1800s	45	.	1	4	1	2	3	6	6	3	3	.	14	2
Maire, N. mid 1800s	1	.	.	.	.	.	.	.	.	.	.	1	.	.
Maitland, William. mid 1700s	1	.	.	1	.	.	.	.	.	.	.	.	.	.
Malby, T. England; mid 1800s	1	.	.	.	.	.	.	.	.	.	.	1	.	.
Malham, John. late 1700s	15	.	.	.	.	14	.	.	.	.	.	.	1	.
Mallery & Ward. San Francisco; late 1800s	1	.	.	.	.	.	.	1	.	.	.	.	.	.
Mallet, Alain Manesson. Paris; 1630-1706	560	14	45	83	27	25	72	51	49	18	26	52	46	52
Malte-Brun, Conrad. Danish, Paris; 1775-1826	70	7	4	2	18	3	5	.	23	1	1	1	3	2
Mandrillon, J. late 1700s	1	.	.	.	1	.	.	.	.	.	.	.	.	.
Manouvier, J. New Orleans; mid 1800s	1	.	.	.	.	.	.	.	.	.	.	1	.	.
Mansell, F. engraver; mid 1800s	1	.	.	.	.	.	.	.	.	.	.	1	.	.
Mante, Thomas. London; late 1700s	5	1	1	1	.	.	.	.	.	2	.	.	.	.
Manuscript Maps	23	.	.	.	.	.	.	.	.	.	.	.	11	12
Marchand, Etienne. 1755-93	1	.	.	.	.	.	.	.	.	.	1	.	.	.
Marchenkov, Ivan. Russia; late 1700s	1	.	.	.	.	.	.	.	.	.	.	1	.	.
Marchetti, Pietro Maria. Brescia; late 1500s	3	.	.	.	.	.	.	.	.	.	3	.	.	.
Marcy, Capt. R.B. U.S. Army; mid 1800s	2	.	2	.	.	.	.	.	.	.	.	.	.	.
Mariette, Pierre. 1603-57; (II) 1634-1716; Paris	7	.	1	.	.	.	1	1	.	.	.	1	.	3
Marks, S. NY; early 1800s	1	.	.	.	.	.	1	.	.	.	.	.	.	.
Marlin, J.F. views; mid 1800s	1	.	.	.	.	.	1	.	.	.	.	.	.	.
Marryat. mid 1800s	1	.	.	1	.	.	.	.	.	.	.	.	.	.
Marsh, William S. publisher; Hartford; early 1800s	1	.	.	.	.	.	.	.	.	.	.	1	.	.
Marshall, John. USA; 1755-1835. incl T.C., London; mid 1800s	102	.	2	13	20	14	3	3	6	7	13	2	10	9
Martell, Peter. 1701-61	1	.	1	.	.	.	.	.	.	.	.	.	.	.
Martenet, Simon J. publisher; Baltimore; mid 1800s	2	.	.	.	.	.	.	.	2	.	.	.	.	.
Martin. various	4	.	1	.	.	2	.	1	.	.	.	.	.	.
Martin & Smith. NY; mid 1800s	1	.	.	.	.	.	.	.	.	.	1	.	.	.
Marzolla, Benedetto. Naples; mid 1800s	12	.	1	.	.	.	.	.	.	3	2	2	2	2

Name	Total	'83	'84	'85	'86	'87	'88	'89	'90	'91	'92	'93	'94	'95
Mason. incl C. Allen, Portland OR, late 1800s; L.D.V., late 1800s	2	.	.	.	.	.	.	1	.	1	.	.	.	.
Mason & Dixon. late 1700s	1	.	.	.	.	1	.	.	.	.	.	.	.	.
Maspero, M. Turin; early 1800s	3	1	.	.	1	.	.	.	.	1	.	.	.	.
Mast. USA; late 1800s	1	.	.	.	.	.	.	.	.	.	1	.	.	.
Mast, Crowell. USA; late 1800s	3	.	.	.	.	.	2	.	.	.	.	.	1	.
Mast, Crowell & Kirkpatrick. Phila; late 1800s	12	.	2	.	3	3	.	2	.	1	.	.	1	.
Mather. NY; mid 1800s	3	.	1	.	.	.	.	.	1	.	.	.	1	.
Mathews, Alfred E. late 1800s	3	.	.	2	.	.	.	1	.	.	.	.	.	.
Matthews, Northrup Co. publisher; Buffalo; late 1800s	30	.	3	4	5	1	8	5	1	.	2	.	1	.
Maundressi. late 1600s	2	1	.	1	.	.	.	.	.	.	.	.	.	.
Maurepas. late 1700s	1	.	.	.	.	.	.	.	.	.	.	.	.	.
Mauro, Fra. 1400s	1	.	.	.	.	.	.	.	.	.	.	.	.	1
Maverick, Peter. NY; early 1800s	1	.	.	.	.	.	.	.	.	.	.	1	.	.
Mawman, J. London; early 1800s	10	3	.	1	2	.	.	2	.	2	.	.	.	.
Maximilian of Wied. mid 1800s	1	.	.	.	.	.	.	1	.	.	.	.	.	.
Maxwell Land Grant Co. Denver; late 1800s	1	.	.	.	.	.	.	.	1	.	.	.	.	.
May, B. mid 1800s	1	.	.	.	.	.	.	.	.	1	.	.	.	.
Mayer. incl J. & Co., mid 1800s	3	1	.	1	.	.	.	.	1	.	.	.	.	.
Maynard, London; late 1800s	2	.	.	1	.	.	.	.	.	.	.	.	.	1
McConnell, J.L. Phila; mid 1800s	1	.	.	.	.	.	.	1	.	.	.	.	.	.
McElroy, Son & Brown. Brooklyn; late 1800s	1	.	.	.	.	.	.	.	1	.	.	.	.	.
McGregor. incl J., London, early 1800s	38	.	16	1	.	3	.	14	.	.	3	.	1	.
McIntyre. incl A., Edinburgh, late 1700s; H., USA, mid 1800s	6	2	1	.	.	.	1	.	1	.	.	1	.	.
McLoughlin Bros. late 1800s	1	.	.	.	.	.	.	.	1	.	.	.	.	.
McMillan. late 1800s	2	.	.	.	.	.	.	.	.	.	.	2	.	.
McNally, F. USA; mid 1800s	15	10	.	.	.	.	.	.	3	1	1	.	.	.
Mead, Bradock (aka John Green). mid 1700s	1	.	.	.	.	.	.	.	.	.	.	.	1	.
Meares, John. voyager; late 1700s	26	2	9	4	1	3	2	.	4	.	.	1	.	.
Megarey, Henry I. NY; early 1800s	1	.	1	.	.	.	.	.	.	.	.	.	.	.
Meierus, J. late 1600s	1	.	.	.	.	.	.	.	.	.	1	.	.	.
Meijer, Peter. Amsterdam; late 1700s	4	1	.	.	.	.	.	1	.	1	.	1	.	.
Meisner, Daniel. Bohemian; 1585-1625	41	27	2	.	.	1	.	.	.	.	.	.	11	.
Meissas, Achille Pr. de. Paris; mid 1800s	2	1	.	.	.	1	.	.	.	.	.	.	.	.
Mela, Pomponius. Roman; 1st c.	2	.	.	1	.	.	.	.	.	.	.	.	.	1
Melish, John. Phila; 1771-1822	70	2	14	1	1	4	6	2	8	7	10	5	6	4
Melling, Antoine. views; Paris; early 1800s	3	.	.	.	.	.	3	.	.	.	.	.	.	.
Mendel Lith. Chicago; mid 1800s	1	.	.	.	.	.	.	.	.	1	.	.	.	.
Mendenhall, Edward & C.S. Cincinatti; late 1800s	4	.	.	.	2	.	2	.	.	.	.	.	.	.
Mentelle, Edme. French; 1730-1815	7	.	.	.	.	1	.	.	.	.	4	1	.	1
Menzies. Edinburgh; late 1700s	1	.	.	.	.	.	.	.	.	.	1	.	.	.
Mercator, (family) incl Gerard, Duisburg, 1512-94; Rumold, c.1545-99; (folio). see Hondius; Janson; Ptolemy	623	41	33	26	81	36	45	74	54	9	17	57	55	95
Gerard (II) c.1565-1656. (small). see Purchas	394	60	11	15	44	18	18	69	40	20	22	18	35	24
Merchant, G.W. wall map; Albany, NY.	1	.	.	.	.	.	.	.	.	.	.	1	.	.
Mercurio Peruano. late 1700s	1	.	.	.	.	.	.	.	.	.	.	.	.	.
Merian, Matthaus. Frankfort; 1593-1650	486	250	18	11	56	14	3	9	22	6	45	2	41	9
Merritt & Co., Leonidas. USA; late 1800s	1	.	.	.	.	.	.	.	.	1	.	.	.	.
Merula, Paulus. Leyden; 1588-1607	7	.	.	1	.	.	1	1	.	1	1	.	.	.
Metellus, Natalius Sequanus. Cologne; 1520-97	4	1	1	.	.	.	.	.	.	.	.	1	1	.
Meyer, Joseph. Germany; 1796-1856; incl Hermann J., mid 1800s	144	7	6	4	1	14	17	13	12	7	10	38	11	4
Mialhe. view; late 1800s	1	.	.	.	.	.	.	.	.	.	1	.	.	.
Michault, R. Paris; late 1600s	4	1	.	.	.	.	.	.	.	.	.	.	1	1
Michaux, Francois A. early 1800s	1	.	.	.	.	.	.	1	.	.	.	.	.	.
Michelin, F. NY; mid 1800s	1	.	.	.	.	.	.	.	.	1	.	.	.	.
Michelot, Henri. Paris; early 1700s	3	.	.	.	.	.	.	.	.	.	.	.	2	1
Michigan Central R.R. late 1800s	2	.	.	.	1	.	1	.	.	.	.	.	.	.
Middleton, Charles T. London; late 1700s	21	.	1	1	2	2	3	.	1	4	.	2	2	3
Migeon, J. Paris; late 1800s	11	.	1	1	.	3	1	2	.	2	.	.	1	.
Milbert, J. Paris; mid 1800s	2	.	.	.	1	1	.	.	.	.	.	.	.	.
Miles, Frederick B. & Co. Canada; late 1800s	9	.	.	9	.	.	.	.	.	.	.	.	.	.
Military Maps - Infrequent Publishers	10	.	.	.	.	.	.	.	.	.	.	.	4	6
Millar, Andrew. London, mid 1700s; George H., London, late 1700s	20	2	1	5	1	2	2	3	.	3	1	.	.	.
Miller. incl J. Martin, Chicago, late 1800s	4	1	.	2	.	.	1	.	.	.	.	.	.	.
Mills, Robert. USA; 1781-1855	1	.	.	.	.	.	.	1	.	.	.	.	.	.
Mills & Co. Des Moines; late 1800s	2	.	.	.	.	.	.	1	.	1	.	.	.	.
Milne. mid 1800s	2	.	.	1	.	.	.	.	.	.	.	1	.	.
Milton & Cheadle. mid 1800s	1	.	1	.	.	.	.	.	.	.	.	.	.	.

Name	Total	'83	'84	'85	'86	'87	'88	'89	'90	'91	'92	'93	'94	'95
Mining Maps	6	.	.	.	.	.	.	.	.	.	.	.	4	2
Missouri, State of	1	.	.	1	.	.	.	.	.	.	.	.	.	.
Missouri River, Ft. Scott & Gulf R.R.	1	.	.	.	.	.	1	.	.	.	.	.	.	.
Mitchell, George. Phila; mid 1800s	1	.	.	.	.	.	.	.	.	.	1	.	.	.
Mitchell, John. English, Virginia; mid 1700s. see Le Rouge	12	.	1	.	1	.	1	1	3	1	1	1	2	.
Mitchell, S.A. (Samuel Augustus) Phila; 1792-1868	1062	67	89	80	66	82	127	176	92	127	113	5	22	16
(Atlas Maps 1859 & Earlier)	60	.	.	.	.	.	.	.	.	.	42	6	12	
(Atlas Maps 1860 & Later)	204	.	.	.	.	.	.	.	.	.	.	56	95	53
Moffat, J. Edinburgh; early 1800s	4	1	2	1	.	.	.	.	.	.	.	.	.	.
Mogg, Edward. publisher; London; early 1800s	9	.	1	.	1	.	.	2	1	.	4	.	.	.
Moithey, Maurille Antoine. Paris; 1732-1810	5	.	.	1	1	2	.	.	.	.	.	1	.	.
Molini, Guiseppe. Italy; early 1800s	1	.	.	.	.	.	.	.	.	1	.	.	.	.
Moll, Herman. Dutch, London; fl.1678-1732	249	74	92	83	.	.	.	.	.	.	.	.	.	.
(large). see Thesaurus Geographicus	110	.	.	2	7	5	17	7	8	2	9	16	37	
(small)	349	.	.	39	53	38	24	33	23	28	28	38	45	
Mollhausen, Baldwin. London; mid 1800s	2	1	.	.	.	.	.	.	1	.	.	.	.	.
Molyneux, Emery. fl.1587-1605	1	.	.	.	1	.	.	.	.	.	.	.	.	.
Monaldini, Vananzio. publisher; Rome; mid 1800s	3	.	.	.	.	1	.	.	1	1	.	.	.	.
Monarch Co. publisher; Chicago; late 1800s	19	.	15	.	1	2	1	.	.	.	.	.	.	.
Monath. various. Nuremberg; mid 1700s	4	.	.	.	.	.	.	1	2	.	.	1		
Mondhare, L. publisher; Paris; late 1700s	4	.	.	.	.	.	.	.	1	.	3	.		
Monin, Charles V. French; fl.1830-80	13	.	1	1	4	1	1	1	2	1	1	.		
Monin & Fremin. Paris; mid 1800s	4	.	3	.	.	.	.	1	.	.	.	.	.	.
Monin & Vuillemin. mid 1800s	1	.	.	.	.	.	.	.	1	.	.	.	.	.
Monk, Jacob. Baltimore, Phila; mid 1800s	14	.	2	.	.	3	3	.	3	.	.	2	1	.
Montanus, Arnoldus. Amsterdam; late 1600s. see Dapper, Ogilby	87	7	.	4	2	23	22	5	1	8	.	4	5	6
Monthly Chronologer. mid 1700s	2	1	.	.	.	.	1	.	.	.	.	.	.	.
Monthly Intelligencer. mid 1700s	3	.	.	1	1	.	1	.	.	.	.	.	.	.
Montresor, John. English; late 1700s	10	.	.	.	2	.	2	.	.	.	1	3	2	
Moon. mid 1800s	1	1	.	.	.	.	.	.	.	.	.	.	.	.
Moore, John Hamilton. London; late 1700s	7	2	.	.	.	3	.	1	1	.	.	.	.	.
Morales, Jose Pilar. mid 1800s	2	.	.	.	.	.	1	1	.	.	.	.	.	.
Morden, Robert. London; fl. 1668-1703	452	28	31	58	57	45	8	.	7	10	42	32	26	79	29
Morden & Berry. early 1700s	2	.	1	1	.	.	.	.	.	.	.	.	.	.
Morden & Lea. late 1600s	1	.	.	1	.	.	.	.	.	.	.	.	.	.
Morgan. incl Wm. H., Phila, early 1800s	2	.	1	.	.	.	1	.	.	.	.	.	.	.
Morisot, Claude Bartholomew. Dijon; mid 1600s	1	.	.	.	.	.	.	.	.	.	.	.	1	.
Morrill, George. Boston; late 1800s	1	.	.	.	.	.	.	.	.	1	.	.	.	.
Morris, Lewis. mid 1700s; William (son) early 1800s	53	.	3	2	9	.	8	.	.	.	28	.	3	
Morrison. various	7	.	.	.	.	.	3	1	2	1	.	.	.	.
Morrison & West. early 1800s	2	1	1	.	.	.	.	.	.	.	.	.	.	.
Morse. includes Jediah, Sidney to '92	210	24	37	29	22	20	17	19	11	19	12	.	.	.
Morse, Jedidiah. USA; 1761-1826. see Stockdale	62	.	.	.	.	.	.	.	.	.	.	26	14	22
Morse, Sidney. NY; 1794-1871	11	.	.	.	.	.	.	.	.	.	.	3	5	3
Morse & Breese. NY; mid 1800s	124	4	12	3	7	10	4	5	9	39	5	11	7	8
Morse & Gaston. NY; mid 1800s	20	.	.	.	.	1	6	.	1	1	1	2	7	1
Mortier, Pierre. Amsterdam; 1661-1711. see Jaillot	343	17	104	51	19	14	13	10	10	8	7	7	15	68
Mortimer & Co. Ottawa; late 1800s	1	.	1	.	.	.	.	.	.	.	.	.	.	.
Mosting, Hermann. late 1600s	1	.	.	.	.	.	.	.	.	1	.	.	.	.
Mottram, C. mid 1800s	1	.	.	.	.	.	.	.	.	.	1	.	.	.
Moule, Thomas. London; mid 1800s	7	.	5	.	.	.	1	1	.	.	.	.	.	.
Mount & Page (with various partners) London; 1700s	286	28	16	41	35	50	13	29	15	16	10	8	7	18
Mouzon, Henry. 1741-1807	3	.	.	.	.	.	1	.	.	.	.	1	.	1
Moxon. James (elder & younger); Joseph. London; 1600s	19	2	.	3	.	2	3	1	.	2	1	1	.	4
Mudie, Robert. publisher; London; 1777-1842	1	1	.	.	.	.	.	.	.	.	.	.	.	.
Mueller	10	.	.	10	.	.	.	.	.	.	.	.	.	.
Muller, Johann Ulrich. Ulm, late 1600s;	34	6	10	.	.	3	2	1	.	3	.	.	2	4	3
incl J., Chicago late 1800s; others														
Munson. Cincinnati; mid 1800s	1	.	.	.	.	.	1	.	.	.	.	.	.	.
Munster, Sebastian. Basle; 1489-1552	727	83	28	74	86	65	81	48	24	20	23	47	45	103
Murphy & Co. Baltimore; late 1800s	1	.	1	.	.	.	.	.	.	.	.	.	.	.
Murray. incl John; Hugh, early 1800s	13	3	3	3	.	.	2	.	.	2	.	.	.	.
Murray, Heiss & McLaughlin. Cleveland; late 1800s	1	.	.	.	.	.	.	.	.	.	1	.	.	.
Murray, John. London; early 1800	10	.	1	.	.	1	1	1	.	.	.	4	.	2
Mutlow. London; early 1800s	1	1	.	.	.	.	.	.	.	.	.	.	.	.
Myers, J.F. Halifax; mid 1800s	1	.	1	.	.	.	.	.	.	.	.	.	.	.
Myritius, Joannes. Ingolstadt; late 1500s.. see Mauritius, '87	5	.	.	.	.	1	.	.	.	1	.	1	1	1

Name	Total	'83	'84	'85	'86	'87	'88	'89	'90	'91	'92	'93	'94	'95
Nagel & Weingartner. NY; mid 1800s	1	.	.	.	1	.	.	.	.	.	.	.	.	.
Narborough, John. 1640-88	1	.	.	.	.	1	.	.	.	.	.	.	.	.
National Geographic Society	2	.	1	.	.	.	.	.	.	.	.	1	.	.
National Publishing Co. USA; early 1900s	1	.	.	.	.	.	.	.	.	.	.	.	.	1
National Soc. for Promoting Educ. of the Poor. London; mid 1800s	4	.	.	.	.	.	.	.	.	.	2	.	.	2
National Union Executive Committee. NY; mid 1800s	1	.	.	.	.	.	.	.	1	.	.	.	.	.
Nautical Charts - Infrequent Publishers	1	.	.	.	.	.	.	.	.	.	.	.	1	.
Nautical Magazine. mid 1800s	2	.	.	.	.	.	.	.	2	.	.	.	.	.
Naval Chronicle. London; early 1800s. see Gold	18	.	.	1	.	1	6	.	4	1	1	2	1	1
Neele, (family: engravers & publisher) London; late 1700s+	23	1	5	1	2	2	.	2	4	2	.	.	3	1
Nell, Louis. Denver; late 1800s	6	.	.	.	.	.	3	.	1	1	.	.	1	.
Nelson, V.H. London; mid 1800s	1	.	.	.	.	.	.	.	.	.	.	.	.	1
Neptune Francois. see Depot de la Marine; Jaillot; Mortier	.	.	.	.	.	.	.	.	.	.	.	.	.	.
Neugebauer, Saloman. German; early 1600s	1	.	.	.	.	.	.	.	.	.	.	1	.	.
Nevers, Roderick. Hartford; mid 1800s	1	.	.	.	.	.	.	.	.	.	1	.	.	.
New England Lith. Co.	1	.	.	.	.	.	.	1	.	.	.	.	.	.
New York City Manual. see Shannon; Valentine's Manual. N.Y. Manual, to '92	2	1	.	.	.	.	.	.	.	.	1	.	.	.
New York Herald	30	.	.	.	6	.	17	.	.	.	2	.	3	2
New York Illustrated News	2	.	.	.	.	.	.	.	.	1	.	1	.	.
New York State	6	.	.	.	2	.	.	.	.	1	.	3	.	.
New York State Documentary History. Albany; mid 1800s	6	.	.	.	.	.	.	.	.	.	.	5	.	1
New York Sun	1	.	.	.	.	.	.	.	.	.	1	.	.	.
New York Tribune	2	.	.	.	.	1	.	.	.	.	.	.	.	1
Newbery, Francis John. London; late 1700s	1	.	1	.	.	.	.	.	.	.	.	.	.	.
Newton. late 1600s	1	.	.	.	.	1	.	.	.	.	.	.	.	.
Newton & Berry. globes; London; early 1800s	2	.	.	.	.	.	.	.	.	.	2	.	.	.
Nicholls, Sutton. London; early 1700s	1	1	.	.	.	.	.	.	.	.	.	.	.	.
Nicholson, W.L. US Post Office; late 1800s	6	.	.	.	.	.	.	.	.	.	5	.	.	1
Nicol, G. London; late 1700s	11	3	.	1	1	1	.	.	.	.	.	2	2	1
Nicolosi, Giovanni Battista. Rome; mid 1600s	8	1	4	.	.	.	1	.	.	1	.	.	.	1
Nieuhoff. early 1700s	4	.	.	.	.	.	.	.	.	1	1	2	.	.
Nolin, Jean Baptiste, 1657-1725; (Jr) 1686-1762; Paris	64	4	4	10	2	5	2	5	4	4	4	7	8	5
Noll, E.P. Phila; late 1800s	1	.	.	1	.	.	.	.	.	.	.	.	.	.
Norden, John. English; 1548-c.1625	1	.	1	.	.	.	.	.	.	.	.	.	.	.
Nordenankar, Jan de. Sweden; 1722-1804	1	.	.	.	.	.	.	.	.	1	.	.	.	.
Norie, John William. London; 1772-1843	28	2	.	4	2	5	2	2	2	5	1	2	.	1
Norman, John. USA; late 1700s	2	.	.	.	.	.	.	.	1	.	.	1	.	.
Norris, Geo. E. Brockton, MA; late 1800s	1	.	.	1	.	.	.	.	.	.	.	.	.	.
Norris Peters Co. USA; late 1800s	2	.	.	.	.	.	.	.	.	.	.	1	1	.
Norris, Wellge & Co. Milwaukee; late 1800s	1	.	.	.	1	.	.	.	.	.	.	.	.	.
Northern Pacific R.R.	3	.	.	.	.	.	1	1	.	1	.	.	.	.
Norwood, J.G. USA; mid 1800s	1	.	1	.	.	.	.	.	.	.	.	.	.	.
Nuremberg Chronicle. see Schedel	.	.	.	.	.	.	.	.	.	.	.	.	.	.
Nuttall & Dixon. early 1800s	2	.	.	.	.	.	.	2	.	.	.	.	.	.
Nuttall, Fisher & Dixon. early 1800s	4	1	1	1	.	1	.	.	.	.	.	.	.	.
Nutzhorn. late 1600s	1	1	.	.	.	.	.	.	.	.	.	.	.	.
Oakland Land, Loan & Trust Co. late 1800s	1	.	.	.	.	.	.	.	.	1	.	.	.	.
Oakley, Edward. London; mid 1700s	2	.	.	.	.	.	.	.	.	.	.	.	1	1
Oesfeld, Carl Ludwig von. 1781-1843	1	.	.	.	1	.	.	.	.	.	.	.	.	.
Ogilby, John. London; 1600-1676. see Dapper, Montanus	213	35	23	30	20	8	16	6	10	13	5	11	7	29
Olaus Magnus. Swedish, Rome; 1490-1558	1	.	.	.	.	.	.	.	.	.	1	.	.	.
Oldmixon, John. English; 1673-1742	1	.	.	.	.	.	.	.	.	.	1	.	.	.
Olearius, Adam. German; 1599-1671	1	.	.	1	.	.	.	.	.	.	.	.	.	.
Oliver, John. English; late 1600s	1	.	.	1	.	.	.	.	.	.	.	.	.	.
Oliver & Boyd. Edinburgh; early 1800s	2	.	.	.	.	.	.	1	.	.	1	.	.	.
Olmsted, Frederick Law. USA; 1822-1903	2	.	.	.	.	.	.	.	1	.	.	.	.	1
Olney, Jesse. NY; 1798-1872	21	1	2	1	1	.	.	4	.	2	.	3	3	4
Orr. mid 1800s	1	.	.	.	.	.	.	.	.	.	1	.	.	.
Orr & Smith. London; mid 1800s	2	.	.	.	.	.	.	.	.	.	.	.	.	2
Ortelius, Abraham. Antwerp; 1527-98.	.	.	.	.	.	.	.	.	.	.	.	.	.	.
(folio)	1065	143	99	113	91	122	110	45	26	47	34	44	86	105
(miniature)	240	76	16	13	10	19	18	7	9	6	8	15	27	16
Osborne. England; mid 1800s	1	.	.	1	.	.	.	.	.	.	.	.	.	.
Ottens: Joachim, Reiner & Joshua. Amsterdam; early-mid 1700s	98	14	8	8	.	9	10	17	4	5	.	4	9	4 6
Overton, John, 1640-1713; Henry, fl.1706-64; London	16	1	.	3	1	.	2	2	.	.	.	3	2	2
Overton & Bowles. early 1800s	1	.	.	1	.	.	.	.	.	.	.	.	.	.
Overton & Morden. late 1600s	1	.	.	1	.	.	.	.	.	.	.	.	.	.

Name	Total	'83	'84	'85	'86	'87	'88	'89	'90	'91	'92	'93	'94	'95
Owen. incl David Dale, Wash; mid 1800s	8	1	1	3	1	1	.	.	1	.	.	.	.	.
Owen & Bowen. London; mid 1700s	17	.	9	2	5	.	1	.	.	.	.	.	.	.
Owen's Magazine. mid 1700s	1	.	.	.	1	.	.	.	.	.	.	.	.	.
Oxford Magazine. mid 1700s	1	.	.	1	.	.	.	.	.	.	.	.	.	.
Pacific Coast Atlas. San Francisco; late 1800s	9	.	.	.	2	.	3	2	2	.	.	.	.	.
Packard & Bros. late 1800s	2	.	.	1	.	.	.	.	.	1	.	.	.	.
Padley, James Sanby. English; mid 1800s	1	1	.	.	.	.	.	.	.	.	.	.	.	.
Page. incl H.R., Chicago, late 1800s	11	.	.	.	.	.	1	.	4	1	.	.	2	3
Palairet, Jean. England; 1697-1774	3	.	.	.	.	.	1	1	.	.	1	.	.	.
Palfrey, John Gorham. Boston; 1796-1881	2	1	.	1	.	.	.	.	.	.	.	.	.	.
Pallas. traveller; late 1700s	1	.	.	.	.	.	.	.	.	.	.	.	.	1
Panter-Downes. view; London; mid 1800s	1	.	.	1	.	.	.	.	.	.	.	.	.	.
Paoli, Sebastiano. Rome; early 1700s	1	1	.	.	.	.	.	.	.	.	.	.	.	.
Papen, Augustus. Hannover; mid 1800s	2	2	.	.	.	.	.	.	.	.	.	.	.	.
Parke, Lt. J.G. American; mid 1800s	1	.	1	.	.	.	.	.	.	.	.	.	.	.
Parker, Rev. Samuel. Utica; mid 1800s; incl J.W.; Nathan	11	.	2	2	.	.	2	1	.	.	2	1	1	.
Parley. mid 1800s	1	.	.	.	.	.	.	.	1	.	.	.	.	.
Parr, Richard. London; mid 1700s	1	1	.	.	.	.	.	.	.	.	.	.	.	.
Parry, William Edward. London; early 1800s	20	6	3	7	.	1	1	.	1	.	.	1	.	.
Pate, William & Co. view; NY; late 1800s	1	.	.	.	.	.	.	.	.	1	.	.	.	.
Paulin & Chevalier. publisher; Paris; mid 1800s	1	.	.	.	.	1	.	.	.	.	.	.	.	.
Pawley, G. England; early 1800s	3	.	.	2	.	.	1	.	.	.	.	.	.	.
Payne, John. NY; late 1700s	70	.	2	4	2	.	12	5	3	14	8	10	2	8
Payot, Upham & Co. San Francisco; late 1800s	1	.	.	.	1	.	.	.	.	.	.	.	.	.
Peabody & Co. NY; mid 1800s	1	.	1	.	.	.	.	.	.	.	.	.	.	.
Pease & Niles. early 1800s	1	.	.	.	.	.	.	.	.	.	1	.	.	.
Pease Lith. Albany; mid 1800s.. see N.Y. State Doc. History	12	1	.	1	.	3	3	2	.	2	.	.	.	.
Peck, Jacob. USA; mid 1800s	3	.	.	.	.	.	.	.	1	.	.	1	1	.
Pedemonte. early 1800s	1	.	.	.	.	1	.	.	.	.	.	.	.	.
Peeters, Jacques. Antwerp; 1637-95	30	.	.	.	3	23	2	.	.	.	.	.	1	1
Pelham, C. early 1800s	1	.	1	.	.	.	.	.	.	.	.	.	.	.
Pelton, C. Phila; mid 1800s	2	.	.	.	.	.	.	.	.	.	1	1	.	.
Pendleton, John B. lith; Boston; mid 1800s	2	.	1	.	.	.	.	1	.	.	.	.	.	.
Pennant. late 1700s	1	.	.	.	.	.	.	.	.	.	.	.	.	1
Pennsylvania, State of	2	.	.	.	1	.	.	1	.	.	.	.	.	.
Pennsylvania Historical Society	1	.	.	.	.	.	.	.	.	.	.	1	.	.
Pennsylvania Magazine. late 1700s	12	1	.	1	.	.	.	.	1	.	1	3	2	3
Penny Magazine. London; mid 1800s	1	.	.	.	.	.	1	.	.	.	.	.	.	.
Penny National Atlas. early 1800s	1	.	.	.	.	.	.	.	.	.	1	.	.	.
People's Atlas. Chicago; late 1800s	39	.	.	1	4	3	8	4	4	8	1	4	1	1
Perelle. Paris; late 1600s	3	.	2	.	.	.	.	.	.	.	.	1	.	.
Perkins. mid 1800s	1	1	.	.	.	.	.	.	.	.	.	.	.	.
Perrine, Charles O. Indianapolis; mid 1800s	2	.	.	.	.	.	.	.	1	.	1	.	.	.
Perrot, Aristide Michel. French; 1793-1879	4	.	.	3	.	.	.	.	.	.	.	.	.	1
Perry. early 1800s	1	.	.	.	.	.	.	.	.	.	.	.	.	1
Perry & Spaulding. Boston; late 1800s	2	.	.	.	.	1	.	.	.	1	.	.	.	.
Perthes, Justus. Gotha; mid 1800s	41	1	2	.	2	2	6	7	9	3	.	.	9	.
Petavius	1	.	.	.	.	.	.	.	1	.	.	.	.	.
Petermann, Augustus Herman. Germany; 1822-98	38	1	.	1	1	.	6	3	2	4	.	4	4	12
Petri, Heinrich. Basle; 1508-79. see Munster	1	1	.	.	.	.	.	.	.	.	.	.	.	.
Petrini, Paolo. Naples; late 1600s	48	1	.	6	17	9	10	1	.	.	1	.	3	.
Petroschi, Giovanni. Rome; early 1700s	1	.	.	1	.	.	.	.	.	.	.	.	.	.
Peutinger, Konrad. Nuremberg; 1465-1547. (Peutinger Table)	1	.	.	.	.	.	.	.	.	.	.	1	.	.
Pharus-Verlag. Germany; early 1900s	1	.	.	.	.	.	.	.	.	.	.	1	.	.
Phelan. late 1800s	1	.	.	.	.	.	.	.	.	.	.	1	.	.
Phelipeau, Rene. Paris; late 1700s	7	.	.	.	.	2	.	1	2	1	1	.	.	.
Phelps, Humphrey. publisher; NY; early 1800s	15	.	.	.	2	1	4	1	2	1	2	.	2	.
Phelps & Ensign. publisher; NY; mid 1800s	12	.	.	1	.	1	.	2	.	5	.	1	3	.
Phelps & Watson. mid 1800s	8	.	.	.	.	1	.	2	.	.	3	.	1	1
Philadelphia Publishing House. late 1800s	1	.	.	.	.	.	.	.	.	.	.	1	.	.
Philip. may incl George	126	3	4	3	54	8	29	9	6	2	6	.	.	2
Philip, George. Liverpool, London; mid 1800s	26	.	.	.	.	.	.	.	.	.	.	16	6	4
Philippe. late 1700s	1	1	.	.	.	.	.	.	.	.	.	.	.	.
Phillips. incl Richard, London, 1767-1840	22	14	2	.	.	2	1	.	1	.	1	1	.	.
Phinn, Thomas. Edinburgh; late 1700s	1	.	.	.	1	.	.	.	.	.	.	.	.	.
Piale, Luigi. mid 1800s	1	.	.	.	.	.	.	.	.	.	.	1	.	.
Picart, Hughes. Paris; mid 1600s	2	.	.	.	.	.	.	.	.	1	.	1	.	.

	Total	'83	'84	'85	'86	'87	'88	'89	'90	'91	'92	'93	'94	'95
Picquet. Paris, late 1700s. others	5	.	2	.	.	2	.	.	.	.	.	.	1	.
Pictorial Times. London; mid 1800s	1	.	.	.	.	.	.	.	.	.	1	.	.	.
Pietro. engraver; early 1800s	1	.	.	.	.	.	1	.	.	.	.	.	.	.
Pigafetta, Filippo. Rome; 1533-1603.	3	1	.	.	1	.	.	.	.	.	.	.	.	1
Pigot, James & Co. Liverpool, London; early 1800s	15	.	1	11	.	.	.	.	.	.	.	3	.	.
Pike. incl C.J., USA; mid 1800s	1	.	.	.	.	.	.	.	.	.	.	1	.	.
Pike, Zebulon. USA; 1779-1813	1	.	.	.	.	.	.	.	.	.	.	1	.	.
Pine, John. London; 1690-1756	2	2	.	.	.	.	.	.	.	.	.	.	.	.
Pingeling. mid & late 1700s	2	1	.	.	1	.	.	.	.	.	.	.	.	.
Pinkerton, John. Edinburgh; 1758-1826	89	6	10	9	3	3	7	3	6	4	10	.	5	23
Pinnock. mid 1800s	1	.	.	1	.	.	.	.	.	.	.	.	.	.
Pinnock & Maunder. London; early 1800s	2	.	.	.	.	1	.	1	.	.	.	.	.	.
Piquet. Paris; mid 1800s	3	.	.	.	.	.	.	.	.	.	1	1	.	1
Pitt, Moses. London; late 1600s	41	3	1	8	3	4	3	.	4	2	5	2	2	4
Plancius, Petrus. Amsterdam; 1552-1622	24	2	2	4	1	2	2	1	2	.	1	2	1	4
Platen, Charles G. USA; late 1800s	1	.	.	.	.	.	.	.	.	1	.	.	.	.
Playfair, Dr. James. Edinburgh; early 1800s	4	1	.	.	.	1	1	1	.	.	.	.	.	.
Plon. late 1800s	2	.	.	.	.	.	.	.	.	.	.	.	.	2
Plot, Robert. England; 1640-96	1	.	.	.	1	.	.	.	.	.	.	.	.	.
Pluche. Paris; late 1700s	1	.	1	.	.	.	.	.	.	.	.	.	.	.
Pluth, F. Prague; early 1800s	2	.	.	.	.	1	.	.	1	.	.	.	.	.
Poirson, Jean Baptiste. Paris; 1760-1831	24	2	4	.	.	2	2	2	2	2	.	3	2	3
Political Magazine. London; late 1800s	85	4	32	5	1	1	.	.	7	2	17	8	6	2
Pomarede, Daniel. mid 1700s	1	.	.	1	.	.	.	.	.	.	.	.	.	.
Pomba, Cesar. Turin; mid 1800s	1	.	.	.	.	1	.	.	.	.	.	.	.	.
Pont. may incl Timothy. fl.1579-1610	1	1	.	.	.	.	.	.	.	.	.	.	.	.
Pontanus. early 1600s	3	.	.	.	.	1	.	.	.	.	.	.	.	2
Poole Bros. Chicago; late 1800s	2	.	.	.	.	.	.	1	.	.	.	1	.	.
Poor, Henry V. NY; mid 1800s	1	.	.	.	.	.	1	.	.	.	.	.	.	.
Popple, Henry. London; early 1700s	41	5	4	1	5	5	2	3	4	2	2	4	1	3
Porcacchi, Tomaso. Venice; 1530-85	127	9	14	27	11	.	8	11	12	6	7	8	3	5	6
Porro, Girolamo. Venice; late 1500s	3	1	.	.	.	.	.	.	.	.	.	2	.	.
Port Folio. Phila; early 1800s	1	.	.	.	.	.	1	.	.	.	.	.	.	.
Porter, D. early 1800s	2	.	.	.	.	.	.	.	.	1	.	1	.	.
Portlock, Nathaniel. London; late 1700s	3	.	2	.	.	.	.	.	1	.	.	.	.	.
Postlethwait, Malachy. mid 1700s	3	.	.	.	.	.	.	1	2	.	.	.	.	.
Potherie. early 1700s	3	3	.	.	.	.	.	.	.	.	.	.	.	.
Pouchot, Capt. late 1700s	2	.	.	1	.	.	.	.	.	.	1	.	.	.
Poussin, G. mid 1800s	1	.	.	.	.	.	.	.	1	.	.	.	.	.
Powell, J. USA; late 1800s	3	.	.	.	.	.	1	.	.	.	.	.	1	1
Pozzi. mid 1800s	1	.	.	.	.	.	.	.	.	.	1	.	.	.
Prang, Louis. USA; late 1800s	9	.	.	.	.	1	1	5	1	.	.	.	1	.
Presdee & Edwards. mid 1800s	2	.	.	.	.	.	.	.	2	.	.	.	.	.
Preuss, Charles. USA; 1803-54	2	.	.	.	1	1	.	.	.	.	.	.	.	.
Prevost d'Exiles. Paris; mid 1700s. see Bellin	34	5	2	4	3	1	2	1	5	5	5	1	.	.
Price, Charles. London; fl.1680-1720; incl Wm., Boston; mid 1700s	2	.	1	.	.	.	1	.	.	.	.	.	.	.
Price & Senex, with Maxwell. England; early 1700s	2	.	.	1	1	.	.	.	.	.	.	.	.	.
Prinald. engraver; mid 1700s	1	.	.	.	.	.	.	.	.	.	1	.	.	.
Prior, John. England; late 1700s	1	.	.	1	.	.	.	.	.	.	.	.	.	.
Probst, George Balthasar, mid 1700s; Johann Michael, late 1700s; Augsburg	28	1	.	.	1	1	.	.	.	.	4	1	1	1	18
Propper, George N. USA; mid 1800s	1	.	.	.	.	.	.	.	1	.	.	.	.	.
Proud. London; mid 1700s	1	1	.	.	.	.	.	.	.	.	.	.	.	.
Ptolemy (1478-1508 Rome)	8	.	.	.	.	.	2	1	.	.	.	.	2	3
Ptolemy (1482 Florence)	7	3	.	.	.	.	.	.	.	.	.	.	2	2
Ptolemy (1482-1486 Ulm)	17	2	4	3	2	2	1	2	.	.	1	.	.	.
Ptolemy (1511 Venice)	9	.	1	3	2	.	.	1	.	1	.	.	1	.
Ptolemy (1513-1520 Strassburg). see Waldseemuller	85	2	19	4	7	6	3	6	2	.	4	.	32	.
Ptolemy (1522-1541 Strassburg). see Fries; Waldseemuller	171	11	16	18	30	19	24	19	4	6	6	1	4	13
Ptolemy (1540-1552 Basel). see Munster														
Ptolemy (1548 Venice). see Gastaldi, 94+	85	2	27	21	3	7	3	7	2	1	5	7	.	.
Ptolemy (1561-1599 Venice). see Ruscelli, '94+	333	23	29	69	13	26	17	19	18	16	15	88	.	.
Ptolemy (1578-1730 Mercator)	19	.	2	2	.	.	1	3	.	7	2	1	.	.
Ptolemy (1596-1621 Magini). see Magini, '94+	132	30	37	2	.	16	16	4	3	9	4	11	.	.
Purcell, Joseph. late 1700s	1	.	.	.	.	.	.	.	.	.	.	1	.	.
Purchas, Samuel. London; c.1575-1626. see Hondius, Mercator	20	1	4	3	2	.	1	1	1	1	1	.	.	4
Purdy, John. England; 1773-1843	2	.	.	.	.	1	1	.	.	.	.	.	.	.

Name	Total	'83	'84	'85	'86	'87	'88	'89	'90	'91	'92	'93	'94	'95
Putter, A. de. early 1700s	1	.	.	.	.	.	.	.	.	.	.	.	.	1
Puzzles & Games	6	.	.	.	.	.	.	.	.	.	.	.	6	.
Quad, Matthias. Cologne; 1557-1613	244	48	6	5	20	12	48	8	27	13	7	9	24	17
Quick, A.C. late 1800s	1	.	.	.	.	.	1	.	.	.	.	.	.	.
Radefeld, Carl Christian Franz. German; 1788-1874	34	6	1	.	5	3	.	1	10	1	1	1	4	1
Raignauld, Henry. French; early 1600s	5	.	2	1	.	1	.	1	.	.	.	.	.	.
Railroad Company Maps. see each RR to '92	40	.	.	.	.	.	.	.	.	.	.	15	8	17
Railway News. USA; late 1800s	4	1	.	.	2	.	1	.	.	.	.	.	.	.
Rainaldi, Carlo. early 1600s	1	.	.	1	.	.	.	.	.	.	.	.	.	.
Raleigh, Sir Walter. English; c. 1552-1618. see Hole	.	.	.	.	.	.	.	.	.	.	.	.	.	.
Ramble, Reuben. England; mid 1800s	27	.	.	13	5	.	9	.	.	.	.	.	.	.
Ramsay, D. Charleston; early 1800s	11	2	1	3	2	.	.	.	2	.	.	.	.	1
Ramsey, David. late 1700s	1	.	.	.	.	.	.	.	.	.	1	.	.	.
Ramsey, Milleet & Hudson. Kansas City; late 1800s	2	.	.	.	.	.	.	2	.	.	.	.	.	.
Ramusio, Giovanni Battista. Venice; 1485-1557	113	9	11	17	6	10	10	8	9	5	9	6	5	8
Rand, Avery & Co. late 1800s	2	1	.	.	.	1	.	.	.	.	.	.	.	.
Rand, McNally & Co. publisher; Chicago; 1862-present	446	15	7	44	32	30	51	62	42	48	22	46	47	.
(Atlas Maps)	32	.	.	.	.	.	.	.	.	.	.	.	.	32
(Pocket, Wall & Globes)	14	.	.	.	.	.	.	.	.	.	.	.	.	14
Ranney, Adolphus. NY; mid 1800s	2	.	.	.	.	.	.	.	.	2	.	.	.	.
Ransom & Doolittle. San Francisco; mid 1800s	2	.	.	.	.	1	.	.	1	.	.	.	.	.
Rapin-Thoyras, Paul de. mid 1700s. see Tindal	10	.	.	.	.	.	.	.	.	.	3	.	4	3
Rapkin, J. London; mid 1800s. see Tallis	4	.	.	.	.	1	.	.	.	.	.	1	1	1
Rasciotti, Donato of Brescia. Rome; late 1500s	1	.	.	.	.	.	1	.	.	.	.	.	.	.
Raspe, Gabriel Nikolaus. Nuremberg; 1712-85	7	1	.	.	.	.	.	.	1	2	.	1	1	1
Ratcliff. USA; late 1800s	1	.	.	.	.	.	.	.	.	1	.	.	.	.
Ratelband, Johannes. Amsterdam; 1715-93	15	.	1	1	.	.	.	.	7	1	.	5	.	.
Rathbone, Aaron. early 1600s	1	.	.	.	.	.	.	.	.	.	.	.	.	1
Ratino. view; late 1700s	1	.	.	.	1	.	.	.	.	.	.	.	.	.
Rau, Jacob. NY; late 1800s	1	1	.	.	.	.	.	.	.	.	.	.	.	.
Ravenstein. late 1800s	2	.	.	.	.	.	.	1	.	.	.	1	.	.
Rawlings, T. London; mid 1800s	2	.	1	.	.	.	1	.	.	.	.	.	.	.
Raymond, J. view; London; late 1700s	1	.	.	1	.	.	.	.	.	.	.	.	.	.
Raynal, Guillaume Thomas Francois. 1713-96	13	.	.	.	9	.	.	1	.	2	1	.	.	.
Real Estate & Promotional Maps	13	.	.	.	.	.	.	.	.	.	.	4	4	5
Ream, Robert K. NY; mid 1800s	1	.	.	.	.	.	.	.	.	1	.	.	.	.
Reclus, Jean Jacques Elisee. 1830-1905	1	.	.	.	.	.	.	.	.	.	.	1	.	.
Rector, William. Phila; early 1800s	3	.	.	2	.	.	1	.	.	.	.	.	.	.
Reed. incl John A., Phila; late 1700s; Edwin D., Cinc; mid 1800s	2	1	.	.	.	.	.	1	.	.	.	.	.	.
Reed & Barber. Hartford; mid 1800s	3	.	.	.	.	.	.	2	.	.	1	.	.	.
Reed Parsons Co. USA; mid 1800s	2	.	.	.	.	.	.	.	.	2	.	.	.	.
Reese, George W. Buffalo; mid 1800s	1	.	.	.	.	1	.	.	.	.	.	.	.	.
Regnier & Cie. mid 1800s	1	.	.	.	.	.	.	.	1	.	.	.	.	.
Reichard, Christian Gottlieb Theophil. Weimar; 1752-1828	13	.	3	1	.	2	2	3	.	.	.	1	.	1
Reid, John. USA; late 1700s. incl Alexander, mid 1800s	51	.	.	1	8	16	5	2	2	2	7	7	1	.
Reilly. see Von Reilly, '84+	.	.	.	.	.	.	.	.	.	.	.	.	.	.
Reinecke, Johann Matthais Christoph. Germany; 1768-1818	2	.	.	.	.	.	.	.	.	.	.	2	.	.
Reisch, Gregor. Freiburg, Strassburg; c. 1470-1525	5	.	.	.	.	.	3	1	.	.	.	1	.	.
Reland, Adrien. Amsterdam; early 1700s	6	1	.	.	.	1	1	.	.	.	1	2	.	.
Remond, N. view; mid 1800s	1	.	.	.	1	.	.	.	.	.	.	.	.	.
Remquet, M. Paris; mid 1800s	1	.	.	.	.	1	.	.	.	.	.	.	.	.
Remy, Jules. mid 1800s	1	.	.	.	.	.	.	.	1	.	.	.	.	.
Renard, Louis. Amsterdam; early 1700s	51	7	.	11	1	8	4	1	3	1	3	3	6	3
Rennel	1	.	.	.	.	.	.	.	.	.	.	1	.	.
Rennell, James. English, India; 1742-1830	3	.	.	.	.	.	.	.	.	.	1	2	.	.
Renner, J.C. German; mid 1800s	23	8	1	.	2	.	1	.	8	.	.	.	3	.
Renouard, Antoine Augustin. publisher; Paris; mid 1800s	9	.	.	.	.	.	.	1	6	1	.	.	1	.
Reyland. early 1700s	1	.	.	.	1	.	.	.	.	.	.	.	.	.
Reynolds, James. publ; London; mid 1800s. incl Wm. C., mid 1800s	10	.	.	.	.	.	1	.	.	1	.	1	7	.
Rhode, Johann Christoph. Berlin; 1713-86	2	.	.	.	.	.	1	.	.	.	.	.	1	.
Rice, G. Jay. St. Paul, MN; late 1800s	4	.	.	.	.	.	.	.	.	.	1	1	2	.
Richardson, F. view; Boston; mid 1800s	3	.	.	.	.	.	.	.	1	.	.	2	.	.
Ridge, John. Dublin; mid 1700s	4	.	.	.	.	.	1	1	1	.	.	.	.	.
Riedel. late 1700s	1	1	.	.	.	.	.	.	.	.	.	.	.	.
Riegel, Christopher. Nuremberg; late 1600s	41	.	.	.	.	.	.	.	.	.	40	.	1	.
Ringgold, Cadwaller. USA; 1807-67	2	.	.	.	.	.	.	.	1	1	.	.	.	.

Name	Total	'83	'84	'85	'86	'87	'88	'89	'90	'91	'92	'93	'94	'95
Risdon, Orange. Albany; early 1800s	2	.	.	.	2	.	.	.	.	.	.	.	.	.
Ritch, William G. view; late 1800s	1	.	.	.	1	.	.	.	.	.	.	.	.	.
Rivelanti. Italy.	1	.	.	.	.	.	.	.	.	.	.	.	1	.
Rizzi-Zannoni, Giovanni Antonio. Italian; c.1736-1814. see Zannoni, '87	10	.	.	.	1	.	1	.	.	2	1	1	4
Robbins, O.W. USA; mid 1800s	1	.	.	.	.	.	.	.	1	.	.	.	.	.
Robert, A.G. Paris; mid 1700s	1	.	.	.	.	.	.	1	.	.	.	.	.	.
Robert de Vaugondy. see De Vaugondy	.													
Roberts. various	11	1	1	1	.	1	4	.	1	.	.	1	.	1
Robertson, G.J. Cincinnati; mid 1800s; J., late 1800s	4	1	.	1	.	.	2	.	.	.	.	.	.	.
Robinson. various	129	7	30	10	17	13	11	3	5	17	9	4	1	2
Robinson, Lewis, Vermont; mid 1800s	2	.	.	.	.	.	.	.	.	.	.	.	2	.
Robiquet, Aime. Paris; mid 1800s	3	.	.	.	1	.	.	1	.	.	.	.	1	.
Robson, T. Newcastle; late 1700s	1	1	.	.	.	.	.	.	.	.	.	.	.	.
Robyn, Jacob (Robijn) Amsterdam; late 1600s	6	.	.	3	.	.	.	.	.	.	1	1	1	.
Rocky Mountain News Co. mid 1800s+	1	.	.	.	.	.	.	1	.	.	.	.	.	.
Rocque, Jean, Mary Ann. London; mid 1700s	51	2	6	15	.	1	16	1	1	1	1	1	4	2
Roe Bros. St. John, N.B., Canada; late 1800s	29	.	.	.	.	.	.	.	.	.	29	.	.	.
Rogers. various	6	.	1	1	.	.	2	.	.	2	.	.	.	.
Rogers & Johnston. Edinburgh; mid 1800s	16	.	.	6	.	1	1	3	3	.	2	.	.	.
Rogers, Peet & Co. retailer; NY; late 1800s+	2	1	.	.	.	.	.	1	.	.	.	.	.	.
Roggeveen, Arent, d.1670; Arnold, fl.1675-1700; Amsterdam	1	.	.	.	.	.	.	.	.	.	.	.	1	.
Rollandet, Edward. Denver; late 1800s	3	.	.	.	.	.	.	.	.	.	2	.	1	.
Rollinson. late 1800s	2	1	.	1	.	.	.	.	.	.	.	.	.	.
Rollos, G. London; late 1700s	33	3	5	10	2	2	2	.	1	5	2	1	.	.
Romans, Bernard. London; late 1700s	1	1	.	.	.	.	.	.	.	.	.	.	.	.
Romanus, Adrianus. 1561-1615	1	.	.	.	.	.	.	.	.	.	.	.	.	1
Romolo Bulla, view; late 1800s	1	.	.	.	.	.	.	.	.	.	.	1	.	.
Root, C. view; NY; mid 1800s	1	.	.	.	.	.	.	.	1	.	.	.	.	.
Root & Tinker. view; late 1800s	1	.	.	.	.	.	.	.	.	.	1	.	.	.
Rosaccio, Guiseppe. Italian; c.1530-1620	21	.	.	9	.	.	2	1	2	.	.	.	4	3
Rose. early 1900s	1	.	.	.	.	.	.	.	.	.	.	.	.	1
Ross. various	8	.	1	5	.	.	1	.	.	.	1	.	.	.
Rosselin. Paris. mid 1800s	1	.	.	.	.	.	.	.	.	.	1	.	.	.
Rossi, Giacomo Giovanni. publ; Rome; late 1600s. may incl Luigi	47	3	4	2	3	3	2	1	7	6	.	2	6	8
Rossi, Luigi. Milan; early 1800s	16	.	.	.	.	.	.	.	.	.	.	1	15	.
Rota, Martino. Sebenico; late 1500s	2	.	.	2	.	.	.	.	.	.	.	.	.	.
Rouargue, F. views; Paris; early 1800s	1	1	.	.	.	.	.	.	.	.	.	.	.	.
Roussin. mid 1800s	2	.	.	.	.	.	.	1	.	.	.	1	.	.
Roux, Joseph. Marseilles; late 1700s	37	2	.	22	1	3	.	2	2	1	1	.	2	1
Rowe, Robert. London; 1775-1843	1	.	.	.	.	.	.	.	.	.	1	.	.	.
Royal Geographic Journal. London	4	.	.	.	.	.	.	.	.	3	.	.	.	1
Royal Geographical Society. London	18	1	1	1	.	.	.	.	1	2	.	2	.	10
Royal Magazine. London	9	.	.	.	4	3	1	.	.	.	.	.	.	1
Royce. late 1700s	1	.	.	1	.	.	.	.	.	.	.	.	.	.
Rudolphi. early 1700s	5	5	.	.	.	.	.	.	.	.	.	.	.	.
Ruggles, Edward. USA; early 1800s	2	.	.	.	.	.	.	.	1	.	1	.	.	.
Rughesi, Fausto. Italy; late 1500s	1	.	.	.	.	.	.	.	.	1	.	.	.	.
Ruscelli, Girolamo. Venice; c.1504-66. see Ptolemy (1561-99)	35	.	.	.	.	.	.	.	.	.	.	.	11	24
Russel. late 1700s	1	1	.	.	.	.	.	.	.	.	.	.	.	.
Russell, John. London; late 1700s; incl various	121	10	9	15	15	7	21	5	12	11	3	7	3	3
Russian Government	2	.	.	.	.	.	.	.	.	.	.	.	.	2
Russo, G. Italy; mid 1800s	3	.	.	.	.	.	2	.	1	.	.	.	.	.
Ruysch, Johannes. early 1500s	1	.	.	.	.	.	.	1	.	.	.	.	.	.
S.D.U.K.. see Society for the Diffusion of Useful	.													
Sachse & Co. Baltimore; mid 1800s	1	.	.	.	.	.	1	.	.	.	.	.	.	.
Sackersdorff, Otto.	1	.	.	.	.	.	.	.	.	.	.	1	.	.
Sacrobosco. fl.1220-56 (republished early 1500s)	2	.	.	.	.	.	.	.	.	.	2	.	.	.
St. Aubin Lith. mid 1800s	1	.	.	.	.	.	.	.	1	.	.	.	.	.
St. Louis Republican, late 1800s+	1	.	.	.	.	.	.	.	.	.	.	1	.	.
St. Louis, Iron Mountain, & Southern R.R., late 1800s	1	.	.	.	.	.	.	.	.	.	1	.	.	.
Salamanca. Rome; mid 1500s	1	.	.	.	.	.	.	1	.	.	.	.	.	.
Salmon. geographies; mid 1700s+	9	.	.	.	.	.	.	1	.	1	1	.	1	5
Sampson, Davenport & Co. Boston; late 1800s	1	.	.	.	.	.	.	.	.	.	1	.	.	.
Sanderus. incl Antoine, Flemish, 1586-1654	7	.	.	.	.	.	.	7	.	.	.	.	.	.
Sands, John. publisher; Sydney; late 1800s	24	.	.	.	.	.	.	.	.	.	24	.	.	.
Sandys, George. early 1600s	1	.	.	1	.	.	.	.	.	.	.	.	.	.
Sanford & Everts. Phila; late 1800s	3	.	.	.	.	.	.	.	.	.	2	.	1	.

Name	Total	'83	'84	'85	'86	'87	'88	'89	'90	'91	'92	'93	'94	'95
Sanford & Goodhue. Phila; late 1800s.	1	.	.	.	.	.	.	.	.	1	.	.	.	.
Sanson, Nicolas. Paris; 1600-67. sons: Adrian, Guillaume, Nicolas Fils	138	57	38	43	.	.	.	.	.	.	.	.	.	.
(folio). see Jaillot; Mortier	245	.	.	.	22	23	21	31	13	21	55	12	19	28
(small)	290	.	.	.	106	75	38	11	6	7	7	24	12	4
Santini, P. Venice; late 1700s	86	21	12	11	4	8	4	6	1	10	3	3	2	1
Sanuto, Giulio. engraver; Venice; 1540-80	2	.	.	.	.	.	.	.	.	.	.	1	.	1
Sarony & Co. incl Sarony & Major; & with Knapp; NY; mid 1800s	6	.	.	.	1	1	1	.	2	1	.	.	.	.
Sartine. late 1800s	12	.	.	.	.	2	1	3	.	1	.	1	.	4
Sauer, Martin. early 1800s	1	.	.	.	.	.	.	.	.	.	.	.	.	1
Saunders, H. Atlanta; late 1800s	1	.	.	.	.	.	.	.	1	.	.	.	.	.
Sauthier, Claude Joseph. late 1800s	3	.	.	.	.	.	1	.	.	.	.	.	1	1
Savery, Solomon. Dutch; 1594-1670	1	.	.	.	.	.	.	.	.	.	.	.	.	1
Saxton, Christopher. London; c.1542-1606	88	9	.	27	16	5	3	.	27	.	.	.	.	1
Sayer, Robert. London; 1725-1794. see Jefferys	98	9	3	8	8	6	11	16	3	8	5	8	6	7
Sayer & Bennett. London; late 1700s. see Jefferys	243	13	8	15	15	65	19	16	12	22	12	24	10	12
Sayer & Jefferys. London; late 1700s	1	.	.	.	.	.	.	.	.	.	1	.	.	.
Schaus, William. NY; mid 1800s	2	.	.	.	.	.	.	.	.	.	.	1	.	1
Schedel, Hartmann. Nuremberg; 1440-1514	93	6	3	8	4	5	4	6	3	2	3	2	9	38
Schedler. late 1800s	1	.	.	.	.	.	.	.	.	.	.	.	.	1
Schenk, Pieter, 1645-1715; (Jr) c.1698-1775; Amsterdam	159	12	42	19	10	17	2	.	8	15	2	9	3	10	10
Scherer, Heinrich. Munich; 1628-1704	117	7	22	39	2	1	4	.	1	9	2	15	10	5
Schiller, Julius. Strassburg; early 1600s	3	.	.	.	.	.	.	.	.	.	.	.	.	3
Schleuen. mid 1700s	1	.	.	1	.	.	.	.	.	.	.	.	.	.
Schley, Jacob. mid 1700s. see Van der Schley	.	.	.	.	.	.	.	.	.	.	.	.	.	.
Schlieben, Wilhelm Ernst August. Leipzig; 1781-1839	3	.	.	.	.	.	1	2	.	.	.	.	.	.
Schmidt. incl O.E., Germany; early 1800s	4	2	.	.	.	1	.	1	.	.	.	.	.	.
Schomburgk, Robert Hermann. mid 1800s	5	.	2	1	.	.	.	1	.	.	1	.	.	.
Schonberg. NY; mid 1800s	5	.	1	.	.	.	2	.	.	2	.	.	.	.
Schoolcraft, Henry Rowe. USA; 1793-1864	19	.	1	.	6	1	2	5	1	.	1	2	.	.
Schott, C. NY; late 1800s	1	.	.	.	.	.	1	.	.	.	.	.	.	.
Schouten, Willem Cornelisz. Amsterdam; 1567-1625	6	2	1	.	1	1	.	.	1	.	.	.	.	.
Schrader, Th. St. Louis; mid 1800s	1	.	1	.	.	.	.	.	.	.	.	.	.	.
Schraembl, Franz Anton. Vienna; 1751-1803	17	.	1	.	3	.	1	.	.	1	4	1	3	3
Schreiber. incl Johann Georg. Leipzig; 1676-1750	32	1	.	1	.	.	.	1	3	.	1	1	3	21
Schropp & Co. Berlin; early 1800s	1	.	.	.	.	.	.	.	.	.	1	.	.	.
Schroter. Germany; mid 1700s	3	.	.	.	.	.	.	.	1	.	.	1	1	.
Schwabe, J. Leipzig; mid 1700s	1	.	.	.	.	1	.	.	.	.	.	.	.	.
Science [journal]	1	.	.	.	.	.	.	1	.	.	.	.	.	.
Scobie, Hugh. Toronto; mid 1800s	1	.	1	.	.	.	.	.	.	.	.	.	.	.
Scots Magazine. Edinburgh; mid-late 1700s	20	1	3	.	.	.	3	1	4	1	1	.	3	3
Scott, Joseph. Phila; late 1700s; may incl R.	73	2	13	1	23	1	6	2	1	1	.	14	9	.
Scott, E. late 1700s	1	.	.	.	.	1	.	.	.	.	.	.	.	.
Scull, William. late 1700s	2	.	.	.	.	.	.	.	.	.	.	2	.	.
Scull & Heap. Phila; mid 1700s	5	.	.	1	1	.	1	1	.	.	.	1	.	.
Seale, Richard William. London; mid 1700s	43	5	6	2	3	3	3	3	2	4	1	2	4	5
Seaton, Robert. England; mid 1800s	1	.	.	.	.	.	.	.	.	.	.	.	.	.
Seile, Henry, Anna. London; mid 1600s	6	2	.	1	.	.	.	.	.	1	1	.	.	1
Selden & Johnson. late 1800s	1	.	.	.	.	.	1	.	.	.	.	.	.	.
Seligmann, Joh. Michael. Germany; mid 1700s	5	.	1	.	.	2	.	1	.	.	1	.	.	.
Seller, John. London; late 1600s	127	3	61	8	3	4	10	10	.	3	2	2	16	5
Seller & Price. London; early 1700s	1	.	.	.	.	.	.	.	.	.	.	.	.	1
Sellwood Real Estate Co. Portland; late 1800s	1	.	.	.	.	.	.	.	1	.	.	.	.	.
Senex, John. London; early 1700s	191	4	13	11	45	30	26	16	8	6	4	10	7	11
Serres. early 1800s	1	1	.	.	.	.	.	.	.	.	.	.	.	.
Seutter, George Matthaus, 1678-1757; (younger) 1729-60; Albrecht Karl, 1722-62; Augsburg	345	34	16	16	16	41	15	52	24	19	32	13	31	36
Seyfart. battle plans, c.1763	3	.	.	.	.	.	.	.	.	.	.	.	3	.
Shaffner, T. NY; mid 1800s	2	.	.	.	.	.	.	.	2	.	.	.	.	.
Shannon, Joseph. NYC Manual; late 1800s. see New York City Manual	4	.	.	.	.	.	1	3	.	.	.	.	.	.
Sharp, England; mid 1800s	3	.	.	.	.	.	.	.	.	.	.	1	.	2
Sharpe, J. mid 1800s	2	.	.	.	.	.	.	.	.	1	.	1	.	.
Shattuck, USA; early 1800s	1	.	.	.	.	.	1	.	.	.	.	.	.	.
Shaw. USA; late 1800s	1	.	.	.	.	.	.	.	1	.	.	.	.	.
Sheafer, P.W. Pottsville, PA; mid 1800s	2	.	.	.	.	.	.	1	.	1	.	.	.	.
Shearer, W.O. Penna; mid 1800s	1	.	.	.	.	.	.	.	.	.	.	1	.	.
Shelton & Kensett. Conn; early 1800s	2	.	.	.	.	.	.	1	.	.	.	1	.	.
Sherman & Smith. NY; mid 1800s	7	.	.	2	.	.	1	1	.	.	.	1	.	1	1

	Total	'83	'84	'85	'86	'87	'88	'89	'90	'91	'92	'93	'94	'95
Sherwood & Jones. London; early 1800s	3	.	.	.	.	.	.	.	2	1	.	.	.	.
Sherwood, Neely & Jones. London; early 1800s	1	.	.	.	.	.	.	.	.	.	.	.	.	1
Shober, Charles. Chicago; late 1800s	2	.	.	.	.	1	.	.	.	.	.	1	.	.
Shober & Carqueville Lith. Chicago; late 1800s	2	.	.	.	.	.	1	.	.	1	.	.	.	.
Shobere, W. publisher; London; mid 1800s	1	.	.	1	.	.	.	.	.	.	.	.	.	.
Sidman, T. London; mid 1800s	1	.	.	.	.	1	.	.	.	.	.	.	.	.
Sidney, J.S. Phila; mid 1800s	1	.	.	.	.	.	.	.	.	.	.	1	.	.
Sifton, Praed. London; mid 1800s	1	.	.	.	.	.	.	.	1	.	.	.	.	.
Silver. incl Thomas, mid 1700s; S.W. & Co., late 1800s; London	3	.	1	.	.	1	.	.	.	.	1	.	.	.
Silvestre, Israel. 1621-91	1	.	1	.	.	.	.	.	.	.	.	.	.	.
Simonin & Hansen. late 1800s	1	.	.	.	.	.	.	.	.	.	1	.	.	.
Simons, Mathew. English; mid 1600s	1	.	1	.	.	.	.	.	.	.	.	.	.	.
Simplot, Alex. views; late 1800s	1	.	.	.	.	.	.	1	.	.	.	.	.	.
Sinclair Lith., Thomas. Phila; mid 1800s	3	.	.	.	2	.	.	.	.	.	.	1	.	.
Skelton, J. early 1800s	1	.	.	1	.	.	.	.	.	.	.	.	.	.
Skinner, A.B. Keene, NH; late 1800s	1	.	.	.	.	.	.	.	1	.	.	.	.	.
Slator, John & Thomas. USA; mid 1800s	1	.	.	.	.	.	.	.	.	.	1	.	.	.
Slatter, H. Oxford; early 1800s	1	1	.	.	.	.	.	.	.	.	.	.	.	.
Smillie. USA; mid 1800s	2	1	.	.	.	1	.	.	.	.	.	.	.	.
Smith. various. incl others separately listed	93	12	13	6	5	9	5	8	21	4	10	.	.	.
Smith, Asa. mid 1800s	5	.	.	.	5	.	.	.	.	.	.	.	.	.
Smith, Charles. London; early 1800s	15	.	.	.	.	.	.	.	.	1	.	10	4	.
Smith, Fern & Co. mid 1800s	1	.	.	.	.	.	.	.	.	1	.	.	.	.
Smith, G.	2	.	.	.	.	.	.	.	.	.	.	.	1	1
Smith, J. Calvin. NY; mid 1800s	3	.	.	.	.	.	.	.	.	.	.	3	.	.
Smith, John. English explorer; 1580-1631	6	.	.	.	.	.	.	.	.	.	.	1	1	1
Smith, Mason & Co. USA; mid 1800s	1	.	.	.	.	.	.	1	.	.	.	.	.	.
Smith, Roswell C. USA; mid 1800s	7	.	.	.	.	.	.	.	.	1	.	1	1	4
Smith, W. H. England; late 1800s	2	.	.	.	.	.	.	.	.	.	.	2	.	.
Smith & Jones. London; late 1700s	1	.	.	.	.	.	.	.	1	.	.	.	.	.
Smollett. England; mid 1700s	2	.	1	.	.	.	1	.	.	.	.	.	.	.
Smyth. various	4	.	3	.	.	1	.	.	.	.	.	.	.	.
Snow & Co. San Francisco; late 1800s	3	.	.	1	.	.	.	.	.	.	.	.	1	1
Snyder & Black Lith. NY; mid 1800s	1	.	.	.	.	1	.	.	.	.	.	.	.	.
Snyder, Van Vechten & Co. late 1800s	2	.	.	.	.	.	.	.	.	.	1	.	1	.
Society for Anti-Gallicians. London; mid 1700s	1	.	.	.	.	.	.	.	.	.	.	1	.	.
Society for the Diffusion of Useful Knowledge. London; 1800s see Baldwin & Cradock; Chapman & Hall; Cox; Knight; Stanford	786	45	25	44	39	34	120	62	41	64	92	84	61	75
Society for the Promotion of Christian Knowledge. London; mid 1800s	2	.	.	1	.	.	.	.	.	1	.	.	.	.
Society for the Propagation of the Gospel. mid 1800s	2	.	.	.	2	.	.	.	.	.	.	.	.	.
Society of Friends. USA; mid 1800s +	1	.	.	.	.	.	.	.	.	.	.	.	1	.
Sohr, Dr. Karl. Glogau; 1844-1901	1	.	.	.	.	.	.	.	.	.	.	.	1	.
Solinus, Caius Julius. late 1400s	7	1	1	.	1	.	1	.	.	.	2	1	.	.
Solis, Hernando de. Spain; early 1600s	1	.	.	.	.	.	.	.	.	.	.	.	1	.
Sotzmann, Daniel H. Germany; 1754-1840	1	.	.	.	.	.	.	.	.	.	.	1	.	.
Soulavie. mid 1800s	1	.	.	.	.	1	.	.	.	.	.	.	.	.
Soules, Francois. Paris; late 1700s	1	1	.	.	.	.	.	.	.	.	.	.	.	.
Souter, J. London; early 1800s	1	.	.	.	.	.	.	.	.	.	.	.	1	.
Southern Pacific Co.	3	.	.	.	1	1	1	.	.	.	.	.	.	.
Spanish Admiralty. see Direccion de Hidrografia	.	.	.	.	.	.	.	.	.	.	.	.	.	.
Spanish-American War - Infrequent Publisher	1	.	.	.	.	.	.	.	.	.	.	.	1	.
Spaulding, J.R. Boston; late 1800s	1	.	.	.	.	.	1	.	.	.	.	.	.	.
Specht, Caspar. Utrecht; early 1700s	1	.	1	.	.	.	.	.	.	.	.	.	.	.
Speed, John. London; 1552-1629	942	70	202	103	166	119	29	9	14	94	15	22	49	50
Speer, Capt. Joseph Smith. London; late 1700s	3	.	1	.	.	.	.	1	.	.	1	.	.	.
Spilsbury, J. London; late 1700s	1	.	.	.	.	.	.	.	.	.	1	.	.	.
Spirinx, Nicolas. Lyons; early 1600s	1	.	.	1	.	.	.	.	.	.	.	.	.	.
Sprange, Jasper. England; late 1700s	1	.	.	1	.	.	.	.	.	.	.	.	.	.
Sproule, G. English; late 1700s	1	.	.	.	.	.	.	.	.	.	.	.	1	.
Stackhouse, Thomas. publisher; London; 1706-84	20	4	.	1	1	3	.	1	1	2	.	2	1	4
Stalker, C. London; late 1800s	1	.	.	.	.	1	.	.	.	.	.	.	.	.
Standard Atlas. Chicago; late 1800s	16	.	.	.	.	.	.	.	.	.	11	.	5	.
Stanford, Edward. London; 1827-1904. see S.D.U.K.	119	3	4	10	3	5	10	6	4	9	11	43	5	6
Stannard & Son. London; late 1800s	1	.	.	.	.	.	.	.	.	.	.	1	.	.
Stansbury, A.J. USA; early 1800s. see U.S.	1	.	.	.	.	1	.	.	.	.	.	.	.	.
Stansby, Keily & Rea. Phila; mid 1800s	1	.	.	.	.	.	.	.	.	.	.	1	.	.
Starckman. engraver; mid 1700s	2	.	.	2	.	.	.	.	.	.	.	.	.	.

Name	Total	'83	'84	'85	'86	'87	'88	'89	'90	'91	'92	'93	'94	'95
Starling, Thomas. London; early 1800s	25	3	.	9	1	.	.	2	1	.	4	1	2	2
Staveley, E. mid 1800s; with Wood, early 1800s	2	1	.	.	.	.	.	.	.	.	1	.	.	.
Stearns & Hitchcock. late 1800s	1	.	.	.	.	.	1	.	.	.	.	.	.	.
Stebbins, Henry S. USA; late 1800s	8	.	.	.	.	1	.	.	.	1	4	2	.	.
Stedman. incl John Gabriel. London; late 1700s	81	4	11	2	7	5	6	.	3	3	14	15	10	1
Steinberger, L. Augsburg; late 1600s	1	.	.	.	.	.	.	.	.	.	.	.	.	1
Stennett, R. London; early 1800s	1	.	.	.	.	.	1	.	.	.	.	.	.	.
Stent, Peter. London; mid 1600s	3	.	1	.	.	.	1	.	.	.	.	1	.	.
Stetter, Johan Jacob. Frankfurt; early 1700s	1	.	.	.	.	.	.	.	1	.	.	.	.	.
Steudner, Johann Philip. Augsburg; late 1600s	1	.	1	.	.	.	.	.	.	.	.	.	.	.
Stevens, Isaac Ingalls. USA; 1818-62	3	.	3	.	.	.	.	.	.	.	.	.	.	.
Stewart, John. London; late 1800s	1	.	.	.	.	1	.	.	.	.	.	.	.	.
Stieler, Adolph. Gotha; 1775-1836 (sucessors used name)	75	.	.	.	8	6	7	7	18	7	3	5	10	4
Stiger & Co.	1	.	.	.	.	.	.	.	.	.	1	.	.	.
Stockdale, John. London; 1739-1814. see Morse, J.	58	7	9	6	6	3	3	2	3	7	1	6	3	2
Stocklein, Joseph. Augsburg; mid 1700s	2	1	.	.	.	.	.	.	.	.	.	1	.	.
Stoddard, S.R. Glens Falls, NY; late 1800s	2	.	.	.	.	.	.	.	1	.	1	.	.	.
Stone, W.J. engraver; USA; early 1800s	1	.	.	.	.	.	.	.	.	.	.	.	.	1
Stone & Pomeroy. Phila; mid 1800s	1	.	.	.	.	.	.	.	.	.	1	.	.	.
Stoner, J.J. views; USA; late 1800s	4	.	.	.	.	.	.	1	.	1	2	.	.	.
Stoopendaal, Daniel. Amsterdam; early 1700s	23	3	.	4	1	1	.	2	1	2	1	4	3	.
Stopius, Nicolaus. mid 1500s	1	.	1	.	.	.	.	.	.	.	.	.	.	.
Stouf. USA; late 1800s	1	.	.	.	.	.	1	.	.	.	.	.	.	.
Stow, John. London; early 1600s	23	.	.	23	.	.	.	.	.	.	.	.	.	.
Strabo. Greek; c.50 B.C.-25 A.D.	1	.	.	.	.	.	.	.	.	.	1	.	.	.
Strada, Famiano. early 1600s.	8	.	.	1	2	2	.	.	.	.	.	1	1	1
Strahan & Cadell. late 1700s	1	.	.	.	.	.	1	.	.	.	.	.	.	.
Stratford. late 1700s	2	.	.	2	.	.	.	.	.	.	.	.	.	.
Streit, Friedrich Wilhelm. Germany; early 1800s	2	.	.	.	.	1	.	1	.	.	.	.	.	.
Striedbeck, Johann. Strassburg; mid 1700s	2	.	1	.	.	.	.	.	.	.	.	1	.	.
Strobridge & Co. Cincinnati; late 1800s	1	.	1	.	.	.	.	.	.	.	.	.	.	.
Strong, Ezra. Hartford; mid 1800s	1	.	.	.	.	.	.	.	.	1	.	.	.	.
Strype, John. London; early 1700s	11	.	.	6	.	.	.	.	.	.	.	5	.	.
Stuart, J.H. & Co. Maine; late 1800s	2	1	.	.	.	.	1	.	.	.	.	.	.	.
Stucchi. Milan; early 1800s	1	.	.	.	.	.	.	.	.	.	1	.	.	.
Studer. mid 1800s	1	.	.	.	.	.	.	1	.	.	.	.	.	.
Studley, R.P. & Co. St. Louis; late 1800s	1	.	.	.	.	.	.	1	.	.	.	.	.	.
Stukeley, William. England; early 1700s	2	.	1	.	.	.	.	.	.	.	.	.	1	.
Stukely	1	.	.	.	.	.	1	.	.	.	.	.	.	.
Stulpnagel. see Von Stulpnagel, '87+	.	.	.	.	.	.	.	.	.	.	.	.	.	.
Stumpf, Johann. Swiss; 1500-76	8	.	.	.	.	.	1	.	5	.	1	1	.	.
Sudlow. London; late 1700s	5	.	2	1	.	1	.	.	.	.	.	.	.	1
Suhr, Peter. German; mid 1800s	2	1	.	.	1	.	.	.	.	.	.	.	.	.
Sumner. incl William, Pitts; early 1800s; H.F., Hartford, mid 1800s	7	.	.	.	1	1	1	1	.	2	.	.	1	.
Swallow, F.G. Boston; mid 1800s	1	.	.	.	.	.	.	1	.	.	.	.	.	.
Swanston, George H. mid 1800s	21	.	.	.	5	2	1	1	1	1	6	1	3	.
Sweden, Government	1	.	.	.	.	.	.	.	1	.	.	.	.	.
Sweet, Homer D.L. NY; late 1800s	1	.	.	.	.	.	.	1	.	.	.	.	.	.
Sweny, M.A. Liverpool; late 1800s	2	.	.	.	.	.	.	1	.	.	1	.	.	.
Swinton, W. late 1800s	43	13	8	8	2	.	5	3	1	3	.	.	.	.
Synd. late 1700s	1	.	1	.	.	.	.	.	.	.	.	.	.	.
Tackabury, George N. Toronto; late 1800s	5	.	.	5	.	.	.	.	.	.	.	.	.	.
Taintor, mid 1800s. incl Taintor Bros.	3	.	.	.	.	.	1	.	1	1	.	.	.	.
Taintor & Merrill, NY; late 1800s. incl Taintor Bros. & Merrill	13	.	.	3	3	1	1	.	1	1	.	3	.	.
Talbot, John. Leeds; early 1800s	4	.	.	1	.	.	.	2	.	.	1	.	.	.
Tallis, John (& various companies) London, Glasgow, Edinburgh; mid 1800s	764	47	155	61	65	64	80	18	11	66	105	15	21	56
Tanner, Henry Schenck. Phila; NY; 1786-1858	327	11	25	13	6	24	27	42	30	29	44	33	26	17
Tardieu, (family) Paris; late 1700s-mid 1800s	80	9	2	4	6	4	9	12	5	8	6	6	6	3
Tarleton, Banastre. London; late 1700s	5	.	1	.	.	.	.	.	2	1	.	1	.	.
Tassin, Nicolas. early 1600s	1	.	1	.	.	.	.	.	.	.	.	.	.	.
Tasso. early 1800s	1	.	.	.	.	.	.	.	.	.	.	.	.	1
Taunton. late 1800s	2	.	.	.	.	.	.	1	.	.	.	1	.	.
Tavernier, Merchior. 1564-1641 (& family); Paris	14	.	2	1	2	1	1	.	.	1	1	1	2	2
Taylor. incl Thomas; various others	16	.	.	8	6	.	.	.	.	.	.	.	.	2
Taylor, David. NY; mid 1800s	1	.	.	.	.	1	.	.	.	.	.	.	.	.
Taylor, Thomas. London; fl.1670-1721	3	.	.	.	1	.	.	.	.	.	.	1	1	.

Name	Total	'83	'84	'85	'86	'87	'88	'89	'90	'91	'92	'93	'94	'95
Taylor & Skinner. late 1700s	5	.	.	.	.	.	.	.	.	.	.	.	4	1
Teesdale, Henry. London; mid 1800s. see Dower	65	10	13	11	3	10	5	2	3	2	2	1	.	3
Tegg, T. publisher; London; early 1800s	11	.	5	.	.	1	1	1	2	.	1	.	.	.
Teubet & Burty. mid 1800s	1	.	.	.	.	.	1	.	.	.	.	.	.	.
Texas, State of	2	.	.	.	.	.	.	.	2	.	.	.	.	.
Texas & Pacific Rwy.	2	.	.	.	.	.	.	1	.	1	.	.	.	.
Thackara & Vallance. USA; late 1700s	1	.	.	.	.	.	.	1	.	.	.	.	.	.
Thacker, W. late 1800s	1	.	.	.	.	.	.	.	.	.	.	1	.	.
Thaxter, S. & Son. Boston; late 1800s	2	.	.	.	.	.	.	1	.	1	.	.	.	.
Thayer. lith; Boston; mid 1800s	10	.	.	.	.	1	2	.	3	3	.	.	1	.
Thayer, Bridgman & Fanning. publisher; NY; mid 1800s	2	.	.	.	.	.	.	1	.	.	1	.	.	.
Thayer, Horace & Co. mid 1800s	1	.	.	.	.	1	.	.	.	.	.	.	.	.
Theakston, S.W. Scarborough; U.K.; late 1800s	1	.	.	.	.	.	1	.	.	.	.	.	.	.
Therbu, L. late 1700s	1	.	.	.	.	.	.	.	.	.	.	.	.	1
Thesaurus Geographicus. see Moll	9	.	.	.	5	4	.	.	.	.	.	.	.	.
Thevenot, Melchisedech. Paris; 1620-92	14	1	.	.	2	1	3	2	.	2	1	.	.	2
Thevet, Andre. French; 1502-90	4	.	.	1	1	.	.	.	1	.	1	.	.	.
Thierry. engraver; Paris; early 1800s	4	1	.	.	.	.	.	3	.	.	.	.	.	.
Thissel, J. Phila; mid 1800s	1	.	.	.	.	.	.	.	.	.	1	.	.	.
Thomas & Andrews. publisher; Boston; late 1700s+	2	.	.	.	.	.	.	.	1	.	.	.	1	.
Thomas, Cowperthwait & Co. Phila; mid 1800s	441	10	51	25	14	5	16	66	71	69	34	19	37	24
Thompson. various	9	.	1	.	.	2	2	.	.	.	.	.	3	1
Thompson & Everts. USA; late 1800s	1	.	.	.	.	.	.	.	.	.	1	.	.	.
Thompson Bros. & Burr. USA; late 1800s	1	1	.	.	.	.	.	.	.	.	.	.	.	.
Thomson, John & Co. Edinburgh; fl.1813-69	453	56	30	71	26	29	23	19	62	22	54	15	18	28
Thornton, John. London, late 1600s; Samuel, early 1700s	21	1	3	3	1	1	1	1	1	3	2	1	2	1
Thrall, Willis. Hartford; early 1800s	3	.	.	.	.	.	.	.	1	.	.	.	1	.
Throop, O.H. USA; mid 1800s	3	.	.	.	.	.	.	.	.	1	1	.	1	.
Tilden, S.D. Hartford; late 1800s	2	.	.	.	.	1	.	.	.	.	.	.	1	.
Tilgmann, F. early 1900s	1	.	.	.	.	.	.	.	.	.	.	1	.	.
Tillotson, & Son. late 1800s	1	.	.	.	.	.	.	.	.	.	.	.	.	1
Tindal, Nicolas. London; 1687-1774	49	7	16	5	2	.	9	4	.	.	.	.	1	5
Tirinus, Jacobus. Antwerp; mid 1600s	3	.	1	1	.	.	.	.	.	.	1	.	.	.
Tirion, Isaak. Amsterdam; mid 1700s. see Albrizzi	276	21	13	14	38	64	11	.	6	32	11	14	12	22	18
Titsingh, Isaac. early 1800s	1	.	.	.	.	.	.	.	.	1	.	.	.	.
Tombleson. London; mid 1800s	1	1	.	.	.	.	.	.	.	.	.	.	.	.
Toms, William Henry. London; mid 1700s	8	.	1	1	1	2	1	.	.	.	1	1	.	.
Topham. London; early 1800s	1	1	.	.	.	.	.	.	.	.	.	.	.	.
Torbett, C.W. London; early 1800s	2	.	2	.	.	.	.	.	.	.	.	.	.	.
Torniello, Augustine. Milan; late 1500s	13	1	1	1	1	1	3	.	.	.	.	.	1	4
Torrente, M. Madrid; early 1800s	1	.	1	.	.	.	.	.	.	.	.	.	.	.
Toudy, H.J. Phila; late 1800s	1	1	.	.	.	.	.	.	.	.	.	.	.	.
Toussaint. Paris; early 1800s	1	.	.	.	.	.	.	.	.	.	.	1	.	.
Town & Country Magazine. London; late 1700s	1	.	.	.	.	.	.	.	.	1	.	.	.	.
Tramezini, Michaelo. Rome; Venice; mid 1500s	3	.	2	1	.	.	.	.	.	.	.	.	.	.
Tremaine, George C. Toronto; mid 1800s	2	.	1	.	1	.	.	.	.	.	.	.	.	.
Treuttel. late 1700s	1	.	.	.	.	.	.	.	.	.	1	.	.	.
Trine & Hills. Colorado; late 1800s	1	.	.	.	.	.	.	.	.	.	.	.	1	.
Troncoso, Diego. Mexico; late 1700s	1	.	.	.	.	.	.	.	.	.	1	.	.	.
Trusler, John. English; late 1700s	17	1	.	.	1	3	.	.	1	1	.	.	10	.
Trutch, J.W. Ottawa; late 1800s	1	.	1	.	.	.	.	.	.	.	.	.	.	.
Truxton, Thomas. late 1700s	1	.	.	.	.	.	.	.	.	.	.	1	.	.
Tschesky, K. Russian; early 1800s	2	.	.	.	.	.	2	.	.	.	.	.	.	.
Tunison, H.C. USA; late 1800s	21	.	1	1	.	.	1	.	.	1	4	3	6	1
Turner. early 1800s	1	1	.	.	.	.	.	.	.	.	.	.	.	.
Tyson, Philip. Wash; mid 1800s	2	.	1	.	.	.	.	.	.	.	.	1	.	.
U.S., United States government (in general)	1183	1	90	36	59	152	130	168	147	138	95	87	47	33
see Ackerman; Bien; Duval; Hoen; Wagner & McGuigan; individual's surnames														
U.S. Coast & Geodetic Survey	23	.	.	.	.	.	.	.	.	.	9	.	4	10
U.S. Coast Survey	801	19	37	14	76	145	60	142	29	116	43	31	53	36
U.S. Election Map Co. San Francisco; late 1800s	1	.	.	.	.	.	.	.	.	.	.	1	.	.
U.S. Exploring Expedition. mid 1800s	29	.	1	4	2	1	2	6	2	2	1	3	3	2
U.S. Geological Survey	50	2	.	.	.	.	.	2	.	.	.	2	7	19	18
U.S. Hydrographic Office	1	.	.	.	.	.	.	.	.	.	.	.	.	1
U.S. Pacific R.R. Survey. mid 1800s	113	.	.	.	.	66	.	6	10	6	5	12	2	6
U.S. State Surveys. see Dept. of Interior, '83	328	11	.	.	.	64	68	32	18	18	41	40	36	
U.S. Union & Confederate Armies, pub 1891-95. see Cowles, '91-'92.	45	.	.	.	.	.	.	.	.	21	6	.	5	13

Name	Total	'83	'84	'85	'86	'87	'88	'89	'90	'91	'92	'93	'94	'95
U.S. War Department	185	2	.	.	.	.	.	.	.	.	.	71	51	61
Ulloa. incl Ulloa & Juan, Spanish, 1716-95	2	.	.	.	.	.	.	.	.	1	1	.	.	.
Union Pacific R.R.	1	.	.	.	.	.	1	.	.	.	.	.	.	.
Universal Magazine. London; mid-late 1700s	91	2	17	10	3	10	8	6	12	4	1	7	1	10
Universal Museum Magazine. London; mid 1800s	5	.	.	1	1	.	1	1	.	.	.	.	1	.
Universal Traveller. mid 1800s	1	.	.	1	.	.	.	.	.	.	.	.	.	.
Vadianus, Joachim. Swiss; 1484-1551	1	.	.	.	.	.	.	.	.	.	.	.	.	1
Valdes, Antonio. late 1700s	1	.	.	.	.	1	.	.	.	.	.	.	.	.
Valdor, Joannes. Liege(?); early 1600s	1	.	1	.	.	.	.	.	.	.	.	.	.	.
Valegio & Diono. Italy; early 1600s	1	.	.	1	.	.	.	.	.	.	.	.	.	.
Valentine's Manual. NY; mid 1800s. see New York City Manual	5	1	1	.	1	.	.	.	.	1	1	.	.	.
Valentyn, Francois. Amsterdam, Dordrecht; early 1700s	26	1	2	2	1	2	1	1	5	.	1	3	5	2
Valeso. late 1500s	3	.	.	3	.	.	.	.	.	.	.	.	.	.
Valk, Gerard, c.1650-1726; Leonard, 1675-1755; Amsterdam	63	14	2	21	3	2	1	2	2	2	.	5	7	2
Valk & Schenk. Amsterdam; early 1700s	51	9	10	11	3	1	1	3	.	1	3	2	5	2
Vallance, J. Phila; 1770-1823	1	.	.	.	1	.	.	.	.	.	.	.	.	.
Van Adrichem, Christian. Cologne; 1533-85	5	.	1	1	.	.	.	.	1	.	.	.	.	2
Van Aelst, Nicolas. c.1527-1613	1	.	.	.	.	.	.	.	.	.	.	.	.	1
Van Alphen, Pieter. publisher; Rotterdam; mid 1600s	1	.	.	.	.	.	1	.	.	.	.	.	.	.
Van Baarsel. engraver; Netherlands; late 1700s	5	.	.	.	.	.	2	.	1	1	1	.	.	.
Van Call, Pieter. early 18002	1	.	.	.	.	1	.	.	.	.	.	.	.	.
Van Campen, Jacob. Amsterdam; mid 1600s	1	.	.	.	.	.	.	.	.	.	.	.	.	1
Van den Hoeye, Rombout. Amsterdam; 1622-71	1	.	1	.	.	.	.	.	.	.	.	.	.	.
Van den Keere, Pieter. Amsterdam; 1571-1646	137	15	32	51	3	1	3	4	.	1	7	5	6	9
Van der Aa, Pieter. Leiden; 1659-1733	258	17	13	24	26	24	20	22	10	13	18	21	20	30
Van der Hagen. engraver; late 1600s	1	.	1	.	.	.	.	.	.	.	.	.	.	.
Van der Schley, Jacob. German; mid 1700s. see Schley, '83	13	6	.	.	.	1	.	.	2	1	.	1	1	1
Van Doetecum, Baptista (& family) Deventer, Haarlem; late 1500s	2	1	1	.	.	.	.	.	.	.	.	.	.	.
Van Geelkerken, Nicolaas. Amsterdam, early 1600s. & others	7	.	.	.	.	2	1	1	1	.	.	1	.	.
Van Harreveldt & Changuion. publisher; late 1700s	2	.	2	.	.	.	.	.	.	.	.	.	.	.
Van Jagen, C. & Jan. Amsterdam; mid 1700s	2	.	.	1	.	1	.	.	.	.	.	.	.	.
Van Keulen, Johannes, 1654-1715; Gerald, 1678-1727; etc; Amst.	299	10	12	21	14	43	33	22	8	17	40	31	29	19
Van Linschoten, Jan Huygen. Amst; 1653-1610. see Linschoten, to '85	80	7	4	10	8	2	3	3	6	9	7	6	6	9
Van Lochom, Michael. Paris; 1601-47	13	3	1	6	.	.	.	.	.	.	3	.	.	.
Van Loon, Herman, Gillis, Johannes. Amsterdam; mid 1600s	11	.	3	.	.	1	.	.	.	.	1	2	2	2
Van Meurs, Jacob. Amsterdam; 1620-80	9	.	.	2	.	.	1	1	1	1	.	1	1	1
Van Schagen, Gerrit Lucaszoon. Amsterdam; 1642-90	2	.	.	.	.	.	.	.	1	.	.	.	.	1
Van Schoel. incl Hendrick, early 1600s	3	.	.	.	.	.	.	.	1	.	1	1	.	.
Van Spilbergen, Joris. Dutch; early 1600s. see Spilbergen, '84	3	.	.	.	.	.	.	2	.	.	.	.	.	1
Van Zouteveen. late 1800s	1	.	.	.	.	.	.	.	.	.	.	.	1	.
Vance, David H. wall maps; NY; early 1800s	1	.	.	.	.	.	.	.	.	.	.	.	.	1
Vancouver, Capt. George. English; 1758-98	35	.	3	4	7	3	4	4	2	.	.	6	.	2
Vandermaelen, Philippe Marie Guillaume. Brussels; 1795-1869	279	10	8	7	98	15	27	16	5	54	4	14	14	7
Varela y Ulloa, Josef. Madrid; late 1700s	2	.	1	.	.	.	.	.	.	1	.	.	.	.
Varin, late 1700s	1	.	.	.	.	.	.	.	.	.	.	.	.	1
Varle, P.C. French(?); early 1800s	3	.	1	.	1	.	1	.	.	.	.	.	.	.
Varte, late 1800s	1	1	.	.	.	.	.	.	.	.	.	.	.	.
Vascellini, G. Milan; late 1700s	1	1	.	.	.	.	.	.	.	.	.	.	.	.
Vaughan, David; mid 1800s	2	.	.	.	.	.	.	.	.	.	.	1	.	1
Vaugondy. see De Vaugondy														
Velten, J. Karlsruhe; early 1800s	5	.	.	.	2	2	.	.	.	.	.	1	.	.
Venegas, Miguel. Madrid; mid 1700s	1	.	.	.	.	.	.	.	.	1	.	.	.	.
Verbiest, Pieter. Antwerp; mid 1600s	1	.	1	.	.	.	.	.	.	.	.	.	.	.
Verdun de la Crenne, Marquis Jean Rene Antoine de. mid 1600s	1	.	.	.	.	1	.	.	.	.	.	.	.	.
Verleger. early 1800s	2	.	.	.	.	.	.	.	2	.	.	.	.	.
Vertue, George. London; 1684-1756	2	.	.	.	.	1	.	1	.	.	.	.	.	.
Viele, Egbert L. USA; late 1800s	1	.	.	.	.	.	.	.	.	.	.	.	.	1
Villalpando, Juan Bautista. Spanish, Rome; 1552-1608	4	.	.	.	.	.	.	.	2	.	1	1	.	.
Villamena, Francesco. early 1600s	1	.	1	.	.	.	.	.	.	.	.	.	.	.
Villedieu. mid 1800s	1	.	.	.	.	.	.	.	.	.	.	1	.	.
Vincendon-Dumoulin, C.A. French; 1811-1858. see Depot de la Marine	6	.	.	.	.	.	.	.	.	.	2	2	2	.
Vincent. various	3	.	.	2	1	.	.	.	.	.	.	.	.	.
Vincent, Brooks, Day & Son. late 1800s	11	.	.	.	.	.	.	.	.	.	11	.	.	.
Virtue, George. publisher; London; mid 1800s	26	.	4	4	2	4	3	2	3	1	1	.	1	1
Virtue, Yorston & Co. mid 1800s	11	.	.	.	.	.	.	11	.	.	.	.	.	.
Visscher, Claes Janszoon, 1587-1652; Nicolas, 1618-1679; Nicolaes Jansz. II, 1649-1702; etc; Amst. see Schenk; Valk & Schenk	400	61	38	42	54	59	33	7	11	12	11	20	22	30

Name	Total	'83	'84	'85	'86	'87	'88	'89	'90	'91	'92	'93	'94	'95
Vivien. incl Louis...de Saint Martin., Paris, 1802-97	26	1	1	.	.	1	.	1	15	2	1	1	.	3
Vliet, Jesper. Milwaukee; mid 1800s	1	.	.	.	.	.	.	.	1	.	.	.	.	.
Volkamer, Johann Christoph. Nuremberg; 1644-1720	1	.	.	.	.	.	.	.	.	.	.	.	.	1
Von Breydenbach, Bernard. traveler; c.1440-97	3	.	.	.	.	.	.	.	.	.	2	.	.	1
Von de Sandrart, Jacob. German; 1630-1708	2	.	.	1	.	.	.	.	.	.	.	.	1	.
Von der Hayden. mid 1700s	1	.	.	.	.	.	1	.	.	.	.	.	.	.
Von Euler, Leonhard. German; 1707-83	18	1	.	.	.	1	.	4	.	.	7	2	1	2
Von Humboldt, Alexander. German; 1769-1859. see Humboldt, '84	14	.	3	.	.	1	4	.	2	3	1	.	.	.
Von Kotzebue, Otto. Russian; 1787-1846	2	.	.	.	.	.	1	.	.	.	.	1	.	.
Von Mechel, Christian. Basle; 1737-1817	1	.	.	.	.	.	1	.	.	.	.	.	.	.
Von Pufendorf, Nuremberg; late 1600s	5	.	.	.	.	1	1	2	.	1	.	.	.	.
Von Reilly, Franz Johann Joseph. Vienna; 1766-1820. see Reilly, '83	92	34	1	3	10	.	.	.	7	.	.	2	32	3
Von Schlieben, Wilhelm Ernst August. Leipzig; 1781-1839	2	.	.	.	.	.	.	.	.	1	.	1	.	.
Von Siebold, Philip Franz Balthasar. German, in Japan; 1796-1866	3	.	.	.	.	.	.	.	.	.	.	.	3	.
Von Spener, Harde. late 1700s	1	.	.	.	.	.	.	1	.	.	.	.	.	.
Von Staehlin, Jacob. German; late 1700s. see Staelin, '83	1	1	.	.	.	.	.	.	.	.	.	.	.	.
Von Stulpnagel. German; 1781-1865. see Stulpnagel, to '86	13	1	.	1	2	.	.	3	.	.	1	.	3	2
Von Zach, Freiherr Anton. Austrian; 1747-1828. see Anton, '86	1	.	.	.	1	.	.	.	.	.	.	.	.	.
Vose, J.W. NY; late 1800s	2	.	.	.	.	.	.	.	.	1	1	.	.	.
Vouillemont, Estienne. late 1600s	2	.	.	.	.	.	.	.	.	1	.	1	.	.
Vrients, Jan Baptista. Antwerp; late 1500s	5	.	3	.	.	.	1	.	.	.	.	1	.	.
Vuillemin, Alexandre A. Paris; mid 1800s	19	1	.	.	.	.	.	1	1	5	4	4	2	1
Wade, W. early 1800s	1	.	.	1	.	.	.	.	.	.	.	.	.	.
Wadsworth, Unwin & Browne. late 1800s	2	.	.	.	.	.	.	.	2	.	.	.	.	.
Waghenaer, Lucas Janszoon. Leiden, Antwerp; 1533-1606	62	24	4	6	6	3	2	2	3	1	4	4	2	1
Wagner, Matthais. Ulm; 1648-94	1	.	.	.	.	.	.	.	.	.	.	.	1	.
Wagner & McGuigan. USA; mid 1800s. see U.S. categories	1	.	1	.	.	.	.	.	.	.	.	.	.	.
Wahl. early 1800s	2	.	.	.	.	.	.	.	2	.	.	.	.	.
Waite, J.F. Chicago; late 1800s	38	.	.	.	3	3	9	6	7	2	.	7	.	1
Wakefield. early 1800s	1	1	.	.	.	.	.	.	.	.	.	.	.	.
Walch, Johann. early 1800s	4	1	1	.	.	.	.	.	.	.	.	1	.	1
Waldseemuller, Martin. Lorraine; 1470-1521	9	.	.	.	.	.	.	.	.	.	.	1	4	4
Wales. late 1700s	2	1	.	.	.	.	.	.	.	.	.	.	.	.
Walker. Samuel Jr., Boston, mid 1800s; may incl J. & C.; & others	59	6	6	6	12	6	3	4	1	3	10	.	.	2
Walker & Miles. Canada; late 1800s	33	.	.	.	3	2	7	13	4	1	1	2	.	.
Walker, George. Boston; late 1800s	14	.	.	.	.	.	.	.	.	.	.	3	9	2
Walker, J. & C. London; fl.1820-95	4	.	.	.	.	.	.	.	.	.	.	.	.	3
Wall, J. Sutton. Harrisburg, PA; late 1800s	1	1	.	.	.	.	.	.	.	.	.	.	.	.
Walling, Henry F. USA; 1825-88	50	.	.	.	1	.	19	.	3	.	6	8	6	7
Walling & Gray. Boston; late 1800s	31	.	1	2	.	1	1	3	.	1	4	15	2	.
Walling, Tackabury & Co. Boston; late 1800s	3	.	1	.	.	.	2	.	.	.	.	.	.	.
Wallis. various. England; early 1800s	14	.	.	.	7	2	.	1	1	.	1	2	.	.
Wallis & Reid. England; early 1800s	17	.	17	.	.	.	.	.	.	.	.	.	.	.
Walsh. various	2	.	.	.	.	.	.	1	.	.	1	.	.	.
Walter, J. London; late 1700s	3	.	.	.	.	.	3	.	.	.	.	.	.	.
Walther, Johann Georg. Frankfort; late 1600s	1	1	.	.	.	.	.	.	.	.	.	.	.	.
Walton, Robert. London; mid 1600s	7	.	.	1	1	1	.	.	1	.	.	2	.	1
Wangersheim, William. Chicago; late 1800s	6	.	2	2	1	.	.	1	.	.	.	.	.	.
Warburton, John. English; early 1700s	4	1	.	3	.	.	.	.	.	.	.	.	.	.
Ward. various	5	3	.	1	.	.	.	.	.	1	.	.	.	.
Warden. early 1800s	2	1	.	.	.	.	.	.	1	.	.	.	.	.
Ware, R. London; mid 1700s	4	.	.	1	.	.	.	1	.	1	.	.	.	1
Warner & Beers. USA; late 1800s	19	.	.	1	1	1	2	2	.	1	1	1	2	7
Warner & Hanna. USA; early 1800s	1	.	.	.	.	.	1	.	.	.	.	.	.	.
Warner & Higgins. USA; mid 1800s.	1	.	.	.	.	.	.	.	.	1	.	.	.	.
Warner, Benjamin. USA; early 1800s	3	.	.	.	.	.	.	.	.	.	1	1	.	1
Warner, Higgins & Beers. USA; mid 1800s	2	.	.	.	2	.	.	.	.	.	.	.	.	.
Warren, William. USA; 1806-79	1	.	.	.	.	.	.	.	.	1	.	.	.	.
Waterlow. London; late 1800s	1	.	.	.	.	1	.	.	.	.	.	.	.	.
Waters & Son. USA; mid 1800s	3	.	.	.	.	.	.	.	.	.	.	.	.	3
Watson, Gaylord. NY; late 1800s	42	.	1	.	6	5	5	5	3	4	3	3	4	3
Watts. view; USA; mid 1800s	1	.	1	.	.	.	.	.	.	.	.	.	.	.
Waud. views; USA; mid 1800s	3	.	.	.	.	1	.	.	1	1	.	.	.	.
Weale, John. London; mid 1800s	2	.	.	.	.	.	.	1	.	.	1	.	.	.
Weaver, H. mid 1800s	1	.	.	.	.	.	.	.	.	.	1	.	.	.
Weber, P. Karlsruhe; mid 1800s	4	1	.	.	.	.	1	.	1	.	1	.	.	.
Webster, J. USA; mid 1800s	1	.	.	.	.	.	.	.	.	.	.	.	1	.

Name	Total	'83	'84	'85	'86	'87	'88	'89	'90	'91	'92	'93	'94	'95
Weed, Parsons. Albany; mid 1800s	2	.	.	.	.	.	2	.	.	.	.	.	.	.
Weekly Dispatch, London; mid 1800s. see Dower, Ettling, Lowry, Weller	53	.	.	7	1	2	9	3	8	5	2	3	4	9
Weekly Herald. mid 1800s	1	.	.	.	.	.	.	.	.	.	1	.	.	.
Weigel, Christoph. Nuremberg; 1654-1725	47	4	4	.	.	6	1	2	8	1	2	1	10	8
Weiland, Carl Ferdinand. Weimar; 1782-1847	7	.	.	.	1	.	.	1	2	.	1	.	.	2
Weimar Geographisches Institut. early-mid 1800s	45	.	5	3	3	.	1	2	3	2	.	22	.	4
Weis, Jean Martin. Strassburg; late 1800s	1	.	.	.	.	.	.	.	.	1	.	.	.	.
Weiss. late 1700s	1	.	.	.	.	.	.	.	.	.	1	.	.	.
Weld, Isaac. traveler; late 1700s	12	.	1	4	1	1	1	.	.	2	.	1	.	1
Weller, Edward. London; late 1800s. see Weekly Dispatch	67	7	11	14	4	4	3	4	1	2	3	4	7	3
Wellge. USA; late 1800s	1	.	.	.	.	.	.	1	.	.	.	.	.	.
Wells, Edward. London, Oxford; 1667-1727. may incl J.	135	22	4	14	25	9	6	9	4	8	7	6	11	10
Wells, J.. incl J., J.G., NY, mid 1800s; J., Chicago, mid 1800s	7	.	.	.	1	.	4	.	2	.	.	.	.	.
Wells & Rowley. Penna; late 1800s	1	.	.	.	1	.	.	.	.	.	.	.	.	.
Werner, W. lith; Leipzig; early 1800s	9	.	2	1	.	.	1	1	2	1	.	.	.	1
Wescoatt, N. USA; mid 1800s	2	.	.	.	.	.	1	.	.	.	.	.	.	1
West Shore. Portland, OR; late 1800s	7	.	1	5	.	.	.	1	.	.	.	.	.	.
Wetstein, R. & G. Amsterdam; early 1700s	2	.	.	.	.	.	.	.	.	1	.	1	.	.
Weygand. early 1800s	2	.	.	.	.	.	.	2	.	.	.	.	.	.
Whitchurch, William. engraver; London; late 1800s	1	.	.	.	.	.	.	.	.	.	.	1	.	.
White, M.W. USA; late 1800s	5	.	.	1	.	.	.	.	.	.	2	.	1	1
White, W. Sheffield; mid 1800s	1	.	.	.	.	.	.	.	.	.	.	.	.	1
Whitefield, E. Whitefield. Chicago; mid 1800s	1	.	.	.	.	.	.	.	.	.	.	1	.	.
Whitelaw, James. Vermont; late 1700s	1	.	.	.	.	.	.	.	.	.	.	.	1	.
Whiting, E. USA; mid 1800s	1	.	.	.	.	.	.	.	.	.	.	.	1	.
Whitney. incl Charles, Boston, mid 1800s; W.H., Phila, late 1800s	6	.	.	.	.	.	.	1	3	.	1	1	.	.
Whitney & Standish. Albany; mid 1800s	1	.	.	.	.	.	.	.	.	.	1	.	.	.
Whittaker, W.B. publisher; London; mid 1800s	1	.	.	.	1	.	.	.	.	.	.	.	.	.
Whymper, F. views; London; late 1800s	4	.	2	1	.	1	.	.	.	.	.	.	.	.
Wiggin, C.P. Pittsburg; mid 1800s	2	.	.	.	.	.	.	.	.	1	.	1	.	.
Wight. England; mid 1700s	1	.	.	.	.	.	.	.	.	1	.	.	.	.
Wightman, Thomas. engraver; Boston; early 1800s	1	.	.	.	.	.	.	.	.	.	.	.	1	.
Wilcocke, S.H. London; early 1800s	2	.	1	.	.	1	.	.	.	.	.	.	.	.
Wild. publisher; Paris; mid 1800s	1	.	1	.	.	.	.	.	.	.	.	.	.	.
Wilgus, A.W. Buffalo; mid 1800s	1	.	.	.	.	.	.	.	.	.	.	1	.	.
Wilkes, J., London, early 1800s; Charles, USA, mid 1800s. see U.S. Exploring Expedition	19	1	8	.	1	1	.	.	1	1	1	1	.	3
Wilkie, G. & T. publisher; England; late 1700s	7	.	.	.	4	1	.	.	.	.	.	.	.	2
Wilkinson, Robert. London; fl.1785-1825	101	6	1	4	2	3	4	5	10	34	9	5	1	17
Will, Joh. Martin. engraver; Augsburg; late 1700s	1	.	.	.	.	.	.	.	.	.	.	.	.	1
Willard, Emma. Hartford; 1787-1870	3	.	.	.	.	.	1	.	.	.	1	.	.	1
Willdey, George. London; early 1700s	16	4	1	5	1	.	1	2	.	.	2	.	.	.
Willemsz, Marcus. Belgium; mid 1600s	1	.	.	1	.	.	.	.	.	.	.	.	.	.
Williams. incl A.; Alexander; B.; E.P.; John; etc.	23	.	2	4	1	4	4	.	2	3	1	.	1	1
Williams, C.S. publisher; Phila; mid 1800s	9	.	.	.	.	.	3	1	3	1	.	1	.	.
Williams, J.David, People's Pictorial Atlas. USA; late 1800s	2	.	.	.	.	.	.	.	.	.	.	.	2	.
Williams, W. incl William, Utica; early 19 c.; W. at NY, Phila; mid 19 c.	10	.	.	.	1	1	2	.	2	.	2	.	1	1
Williamson, Lt. R.S. US Army; mid 1800s. see U.S.	2	.	2	.	.	.	.	.	.	.	.	.	.	.
Willis. view; mid 1800s	1	1	.	.	.	.	.	.	.	.	.	.	.	.
Willmann, Edward. views; mid 1800s	3	1	.	.	.	.	1	.	.	.	1	.	.	.
Willyams, Cooper. late 1700s	1	.	.	.	.	.	.	.	.	.	.	1	.	.
Wilmore, J.A. Richmond; late 1800s	4	.	.	.	.	.	.	.	.	.	.	1	1	1
Wilson. incl Charles. London, mid 1800s	21	2	.	2	1	1	1	4	2	.	3	4	.	1
Wilson, James, Capt. late 1700s	7	.	.	6	.	.	.	.	.	.	.	.	1	.
Winchell. USA; late 1800s	1	.	.	.	.	.	.	.	.	1	.	.	.	.
Winkelmanns Chronik. late 1600s	2	1	.	.	1	.	.	.	.	.	.	.	.	.
Winslow, E.N. Boston; late 1800s	1	1	.	.	.	.	.	.	.	.	.	.	.	.
Winterbotham, William. 1763-1829	10	.	.	2	.	.	1	.	1	1	1	2	.	2
Wislizenus, A. mid 1800s	1	.	.	.	.	.	.	.	.	.	.	1	.	.
Witsen, Nicolaas. Amsterdam; early 1700s	1	1	.	.	.	.	.	.	.	.	.	.	.	.
Witter, Conrad. St. Louis; mid 1800s	1	.	.	.	1	.	.	.	.	.	.	.	.	.
Wolfe, John. publisher; London; late 1500s	6	.	.	.	.	.	.	.	.	.	.	.	5	1
Wolff. incl T., mid 1700s	2	.	1	1	.	.	.	.	.	.	.	.	.	.
Wood. incl Wm, c.1580-1639; also Wm. H., Jersey City, mid 1800s	2	.	.	.	.	.	.	.	.	1	.	1	.	.
Woodbridge, William Channing. Hartford; 1794-1854	10	.	5	.	.	.	.	.	2	.	.	1	1	1
Woodford, E.M. Phila; mid 1800s	3	.	.	.	.	.	.	1	.	2	.	.	.	.
Woodruff, Charles P. NY; late 1800s	1	.	.	.	1	.	.	.	.	.	.	.	.	.

	Total	'83	'84	'85	'86	'87	'88	'89	'90	'91	'92	'93	'94	'95
Woodruff Mining Co. Calif; mid 1800s	1	.	.	.	.	.	.	.	1	.	.	.	.	.
Woodward, Tiernan & Hale. St. Louis; late 1800s	1	.	.	.	.	.	.	.	.	1	.	.	.	.
Woolman & Rose. Phila; late 1800s. see Rose & Woodman, '92	11	.	.	.	.	.	.	.	.	.	10	.	.	1
Wooten, Joseph. Manchester; early 1800s	1	.	.	.	.	.	.	.	.	.	1	.	.	.
Wright. various	6	1	.	.	1	.	1	.	1	1	1	.	.	.
Wyatt. England; early 1800s	1	1	.	.	.	.	.	.	.	.	.	.	.	.
Wyld, James, 1790-1836; (II) 1812-87; John Cooper, 1845-1907; London	295	19	14	26	21	36	32	21	19	22	28	31	9	17
Wytfliet, Cornelis. Louvain; late 1500s	81	6	1	2	9	9	.	3	2	8	10	7	15	9
Yeager, James. engraver; USA; early 1800s	4	.	.	.	.	.	2	1	.	.	1	.	.	.
Young. incl James H. Phila; mid 1800s	12	1	1	.	2	2	2	1	.	.	.	3	.	.
Young & Brownlee. Canada; late 1800s	1	.	.	.	.	.	.	.	.	.	.	1	.	.
Young & Williams. USA; mid 1800s	1	.	.	.	.	.	.	1	.	.	.	.	.	.
Zahn, Johann. Nuremberg; late 1600s	4	1	.	1	.	.	.	.	1	.	1	.	.	.
Zakreski, Alex. San Francisco; mid 1800s	1	.	.	.	1	.	.	.	.	.	.	.	.	.
Zaltieri, Bolognini. Venice; fl.1550-80	1	.	.	.	.	1	.	.	.	.	.	.	.	.
Zatta, Antonio. Venice; fl.1757-97	436	18	44	35	50	62	31	22	41	30	23	15	22	43
Zeese & Co., A. Chicago; late 1800s	3	.	.	.	1	.	.	.	.	2	.	.	.	.
Zell, T. Ellwood. publisher; Phila; late 1800s	2	.	.	.	.	1	.	1	.	.	.	.	.	.
Ziegler, Jacob. Vienna; early 1500s	7	1	2	1	.	.	.	.	1	2	.	.	.	.
Zimmerman, E.F.W. USA; late 1800s	1	.	.	.	.	.	.	.	.	1	.	.	.	.
Zurner, Adam Friedrich. Amsterdam; 1680-1742	5	.	.	1	.	.	1	.	1	.	.	.	1	1

PRICE LISTING

AINSLIE
A CHART OF PART OF SCOTLAND FROM BERWICK UPON TWEED TO SKATERAW HARBOUR IN THE COUNTY OF KINCARDINE ... SURVEYED AND ENGRAVED BY JOHN AINSLIE 1785 [1785] 4 joinable sheets. 57x52cm (22½x20½") Minor edge damage; generally exc. [15] £480 $739

ALBRIZZI
CARTA GEOGRAFICA DEL MESSICO O SIA DELLA NUOVA SPAGNA [c. 1740] From *Atlante Novissimo*. After De L'Isle. 33x43cm (13x16½") B&W. [46] £114 $175

ALEXANDER
[NORTHEASTERN NORTH AMERICA: CANADA & NEW ENGLAND] [1625] Sir Wm. Alexander. 1st printed map with Cape Cod. 25x36cm (10x13½") Sm lower rt border facsimile replacement; else fine. Ref: Schwartz & Ehrenberg pl.54; Kershaw (Canada) #86; Cumming (Exploration) pl.334. [38] £2,921 $4,500

ALLARD
DE HAVEN EN STRAAT VAN GIBRALTER ... [c.1704 - c.1730] Covens & Mortier. 50x59cm (19½x23") Orig OL color. [52] £450 $693

HYBERNIAE ... [c. 1697] From *Atlas Minor*. Amsterdam: Covens & Mortier. 58x51cm (23x19½") Orig old color. Fine. [1] £649 $1,000

HYBERNIAE REGNI IN PROVINCIAS ULTONIAM, CONNACHIAN, LAGENIAM, MOMONIAMQ DIVISI TABULA ACCURATISSIMA ... [1690] 58x51cm (23½x20") Color. [24] £617 $950

RECENTISSIMA NOVI ORBIS SIVE AMERICAE SEPTENTRIONALIS ET MERIDIONALIS TABULA EX OFFICINA CAROLI ALLARD [1700] Insular Calif. 50x58cm (19½x23") Orig full color. Ref: Tooley (Amer) p.127. Leighly pl.XVI. [46] £1,428 $2,200

[SAME TITLE] [c. 1700] [same dimen] Color. Repaired 1½" tear near c'fold; fine. Ref: Tooley (Amer) p.127 #65. [48] £2,207 $3,400

ALTING
SUMMARIA DESCRIPTIO GERMANIAE INFERIORIS ANTIQUAE CIS & ULTRA RHENUM CUM GERMANORUM POSSESSIONE IN BELGICA INFERIORE ... [1697] From *Notitia Germaniae Inferioris*. 32x42cm (12½x16½") [14] £75 $115

ANDREAS
A MAP OF HENNEPIN COUNTY [MN] [1874] From *An Illustrated Historical Atlas ... of Minnesota*. 41x33cm (15½x13") Printed color. Ref: Le Gear (US) 1901. [56] £42 $65

PLAN OF THE CITY OF ST. PAUL AND VICINITY [1874] From *An Illustrated Historical Atlas ... of Minnesota*. With 3 views. 41x66cm (16½x26½") Color. Ref: Le Gear (US) 1901. [56] £52 $80

ANDREWS
ANDREWS' 18 INCH TERRESTRIAL GLOBE [c. 1890] A.H. Andrews & Co., Chicago. Plaster orb over wood, dull paper gores. Brass time scale. Raised without meridian from walnut pedestal; welded iron bracket. Partial separation at equator; sm surface blemishes & water spots. Restorable. [17] £3,895 $6,000

VIRGIN GORDA [ON SHEET WITH] DEAD CHEST [AND] PETER IS. [AND] NORMAN IS., TORTOLA [1861] From [W.S.] *Andrew's Caribbean Sailing Directions*. Spreat, lith for Day & Son, London. Profile views. 20x25cm (8x10") Ref: Sabin 1517. [27] £62 $95

VIRGIN ISLANDS [ON SHEET WITH] GINGER IS. [AND] ROUND IS. PASSAGE [AND] FALLEN CITY [AND] NEVIS [AND] ST. KITTS [AND] MONKEY HILL [1861] From [W.S.] *Andrew's Caribbean Sailing Directions*. Spreat, lith for Day & Son, London. Profile views. 20x30cm (8x11½") [27] £55 $85

ANGELOCRATOR
[BOOK] DOCTRINA DE PONDERIBUS [1628] With maps still in book on Angelocrator's projection of each hemisphere in four quadrants. Map presented twice, also with polar centers, on 3 sheets. 28x53cm (11x21") Exc. Ref: Shirley (W) 320; *Imago Mundi* XI, p.175-6. [2] £7,466 $11,500

ANONYMOUS or UNKNOWN

[COPPER PRINTING PLATE] LA BATAILLE DE ZORNSDORF DONNE SUR LE 25.EME D'AOUT 1758 [n.d.] "Plate II". Frederick the Great's victory over the Russians. English scale bar. 41x54cm (16x21½") [52] £400 $616

[WORLD: MEDIEVAL] [1491 (1555)] Recut of 1475 Lubeck woodcut with additions in Lyon, but corresponds to Paris ed of *Mer des Hystoires*, 1555. Diameter: 30cm (12") Mint. Ref: Shirley (W) 17; see Campbell (Early). [62] £10,712 $16,500

AFBEELDINGE VAN'T ZEER VERMAARDE EILAND GEKS-KOP. ... [c. 1720] Fool's cap map satirizing John Law's Mississippi Bubble, flanked with related engravings. 15x23cm (6x9") on text sheet. Uncol. [57] £195 $300

BYZANTIUM, NUNC CONSTANTINO [late 17th c.] Possibly Coronelli. 13x43cm (5x17") Uncolored. Top margin replaced. [33] £97 $150

CARTE MAGNETIQUE DES DEUX HEMISPHERES [c. 1800 - 1820] 56x99cm (22½x39") Orig color. Few sh tears at horiz & vert folds. [28] £847 $1,305

ISLE DE FRANCE ODER GEGEND UM PARIS [17th c.] 33x41cm (13x16") OL color. [36] £130 $200

KLYN LORETTEN IN NOORD-AMERICA / PETIT LORETTE ETATS UNIS DE LAMERIQUE / LITTLE LORETTO KENTUCKY UNITED STATES OF AMERICA [c. 1815-1820] View; Nerinx, KY. 28x33cm (10½x13") Sl staining; else VG. [39] £1,169 $1,800

NOVA TABULA AMERICA [c. 1720] Follows Allard's "Recentis Novi Orbis", 1700. Insular California. German text verso; large heraldic watermark. 28x33cm (10½x13½") Body color. 2 folds; fine. [55] £649 $1,000

PLAN DE LA VILLE DE JERUSALEM TELLE QU'ELLE EST DESCRITE DANS LES LIVRES DU VIEUX TESTAMENT ... [1765] 36x41cm (13½x16") Color. Possible attribution to E. Bowen. Ref: Laor 1182 [23] £78 $120

PLAN OF THE CITY OF WASHINGTON [1792] In E. Winchester, *An Oration on the Discovery of America ...*, 2nd ed., with appendix. 23x25cm (8½x10") Disbound; some soiling; else VG. Ref: Ristow (A La Carte) pp.136,149. [39] £2,921 $4,500

POURTRAICT ET DESCRIPTION DE LA GRANDE CITE DE TEMISTITAN, OU, TENUCTUTLAN, OU SELON AUCUNS MESSICO, OU MEXICO ... [c. 1550] Woodblock bird's eye perspective on text page from French Cosmography. 13x16cm (5x6") Uncolored. Overall VG. [32] £114 $175

PREMIERE PARTIE DE L'HEMISPHERE CELESTE SEPTENTRIONAL ... [WITH] ... HEMISPHERE CELESTE AUSTRAL ... [c. 1740] Two charts; each about 29x29cm (11x11") Color. [52] £480 $739

THE ABSENT-MINDED BEGGAR [SOUTH AFRICA: TRANSVAAL / ORANGE FREE STATE] [c. 1899] Boer War souvenir handkerchief map; title is Kipling poem honoring enlisted men. 46x46cm (17½x18") Blue ink on white linen. Few stains, worn spots; else VG. [55] £65 $100

ANSON

CARTE DANS LAQUELLE ON VOIT LA ROUTE QUE LE CENTURION A TENU DANS LA VOIAGE AU TOUR DU MONDE [1749] Amsterdam: Joncourt; Lattre, sc. Insular Calif. 23x41cm (9x16") Color. Ref: Sabin 1637. [22] £224 $345

KAART VAN HET KANAAL IN DE FILIPPYNSCHE EILANDEN WAAR DOOR HET GALJOEN VAN MANILLA PASSEERT ... [c. 1750] Dutch ed. 53x42cm (21x16½") Wash color. Repaired tear; else fine. [63] £341 $525

APIANUS

CHARTA COSMOGRAPHICA, CUM VENTORUM PROPRIA NATURA ET OPERATIONE [1544] P. Apianus. 1st ed., 1st state. 22x29cm (8½x11½") Sl repairs, no loss. Ref: Shirley (W) 82, pl.70. [2] £779 $1,200

[SAME TITLE] [1544 / 1553+] Cordiform map from Gemma Frisius overhaul of 1524 Apianus *Cosmographia*. 19x28cm (7½x11") Exc. Ref: Shirley (W) 82; Potter p.50. [62] £974 $1,500

[SAME TITLE] [c. 1553 - 64] From *Cosmographia*. After Gemma Frisius 1540 map; 2nd state. 18x28cm (7½x11") Ref: Shirley (W) 96. [28] £1,402 $2,160

APPLETON

APPLETON'S MAP OF THE SEAT OF WAR NO.2 [1861] Pocket map; folds into printed guards. Added detail from S.S. Cornell school atlas. 33x51cm (12½x20½") Full color. Folds repaired; good. [20] £617 $950

APPLETONS RAILWAY MAP OF THE UNITED STATES AND CANADA ... BY G.F. THOMAS [1871] RR's shown & named to Nebraska. City insets. 64x71cm (25x28") Uncolored. [44] £52 $80

MAP OF FLORIDA [1892] From *Appleton's Atlas of Modern Geography*. Insets: W FL; middle St. John's River. 30x25cm (12x9½") Printed color. [4] £29 $45

ARBUCKLE BROS.

INDIAN TERRITORY [1900] Coffee promotional. 8x13cm (3x5") Lt rubbing. [13] £16 $25

ARCHER
MEXICO & TEXAS [1841] TX Republic outlined. 23x29cm (9x11") Partial OL color. [46] £84 $130
ARIAS MONTANUS
BENEDICT ARIAS MONTANUS SACRAE GEOGRAPHIAE TABULUM EX ANTIQUISSIMORUM CULTOR. FAMILII A MOSE RECENSITIS ... [1571] In Plantin's Polyglot Bible (in Hebrew, Greek, Latin & Syriac). Bound into 1583 Latin section. 31x53cm (12½x20½") B&W. Ref: Shirley (W) 125, pl.107. Schilder 20; Clancy p.54-5. [16] £9,496 $14,627
ARROWSMITH
CHART OF THE WEST INDIES AND SPANISH DOMINIONS IN NORTH AMERICA [1803] Northern two sheets of four: Florida, Gulf Coast, Cuba & Bahamas. 61x189cm (24x74½") Orig wash color. [14] £243 $375
IRELAND [1798] 41x25cm (15½x9½") [24] £39 $60
JUDAH & ISRAEL: ILLUSTRATING THE BOOKS OF KINGS [1817] London: Rivingtons. 25x20cm (10x8") Ref: Laor 51. [23] £23 $35
MAP OF THE EASTERN TOWNSHIPS OF LOWER CANADA, DRAWN PRINCIPALLY FROM ACTUAL SURVEY FOR THE BRITISH AMERICAN LAND COMPANY BY A. WELLS ... [dated 1842] John Arrowsmith. 2nd state. 64x53cm (25½x21½") Orig color. Ref: MCCS 69, 222. [28] £409 $630
NORTH-WEST AFRICA [1834] J. Arrowsmith. 48x60cm (19x23½") Orig OL color. [14] £49 $75
SYRIA [1817] London: A. Constable. 25x20cm (10x8") [23] £26 $40
UPPER CANADA &C. [1842] John Arrowsmith. 64x53cm (25x21") Orig OL color. 2 sh margin tears. Ref: Winearls 91.5. [28] £409 $630
UPPER CANADA &C. [UPPER TITLE]; LOWER CANADA, NEW BRUNSWICK, NOVA SCOTIA ... [LOWER TITLE] [1838] Folding map mounted on linen in sections with orig slipcase. 64x102cm (25x40") Orig color. Ref: MCCS 69, 231-8. [28] £357 $550
ARROWSMITH & LEWIS
BRITISH POSSESSIONS IN AMERICA [1805] From *New and Elegant Atlas*. 20x24cm (7½x9½") OL & wash color. [57] £71 $110
CONNECTICUT [1805] 23x28cm (8½x10½") Uncolored. [44] £65 $100
DELAWARE [1805] 28x23cm (10½x8½") Uncolored. [44] £78 $120
MAINE [1805] Southern part only. 23x28cm (8½x10½") Uncolored. [44] £81 $125
MARYLAND [1805] 23x28cm (8½x10½") Uncolored. [44] £58 $90
MASSACHUSETTS [1805] From *New and Elegant General Atlas*. 23x28cm (8½x10½") Uncolored. Minor repair verso. [44] £52 $80
NEW HAMPSHIRE [1805] 28x23cm (10½x8½") Uncolored. [44] £52 $80
PENNSYLVANIA [1805] 23x28cm (8½x10½") Uncolored. [44] £52 $80
VIRGINIA [1805] 23x28cm (8½x10½") Uncolored. [44] £78 $120
ASHBY
A NEW PLAN OF LONDON WESTMINSTER AND SOUTHWARK ... [1771] For Noorthouck's *History of London*. 43x69cm (16½x27") Wash color. Obtuse tear from lf margin, city unaffected; very nice. Ref: Howgego 157. [1] £227 $350
ASHER & ADAMS
ARKANSAS AND PORTION OF INDIAN TERRITORY [1872] 41x57cm (16x22½") Pastel col. Exc. [36] £49 $75
ASHER & ADAMS' ARIZONA [1874] 5 counties. 58x43cm (23x16½") Soft color. Edge browning; else clean. [12] £78 $120
ASHER & ADAMS' CALIFORNIA & NEVADA NORTHERN PORTION [IN SET WITH] ... SOUTHERN PORTION [1872] 2 maps, each 42x60cm (16½x23½") Pastel color. Evenly browned. [12] £120 $185
ASHER & ADAMS' DAKOTA [1875] 58x41cm (23x16") Color. Uneven age browning. [13] £62 $95
ASHER & ADAMS' UTAH [1873] 43x58cm (16½x22½") Soft color. C'fold & edge repairs, map unaffected. [10] £78 $120
DAKOTA [1873] 58x41cm (23x16") Color. [51] £97 $150
ILLINOIS [1873] 56x41cm (22½x16") Full orig color. [51] £62 $95
KENTUCKY & TENNESSEE [1873] 41x58cm (16x23") Color. VG or better. [29] £19 $30
MICHIGAN [1873] 58x41cm (22½x16½") Full color. [51] £81 $125

MISSOURI [1872] Town hierarchy by typeface. 41x58cm (16½x22½") Full color. [35] £36 $55
MONTANA, EASTERN PORTION [1873] 41x58cm (16x22½") Full color. [51] £81 $125
NEW HAMPSHIRE, VERMONT, MASSACHUSETTS, RHODE ISLAND & CONNECTICUT [1872] 41x56cm (16x22") Color. VG or better. [29] £19 $30
NEW MEXICO [1873] 43x56cm (16½x22½") Full color. [51] £97 $150
ONTARIO [1873] 40x59cm (16x23½") Full color. [51] £62 $95
PENNSYLVANIA & NEW JERSEY [1872] 41x58cm (16x22½") Pastel color. [35] £39 $60
TEXAS WESTERN PORTION [1874] 57x40cm (22x16") Color. Edge browning; else fine. [12] £97 $150
WASHINGTON [1873] 41x58cm (16x22½") Full color. [51] £81 $125
WISCONSIN [1873] 41x56cm (16x22") Color. VG or better. [29] £19 $30
[SAME TITLE] [1873] 41x58cm (16x22½") Full orig color. [51] £81 $125

ASHER & CO.

THE HISTORICAL WAR MAP [1862] Folding map, with 72 pp war synopsis. 61x61cm (24x24") Covers worn; contents good; map laid down on japan paper; refoldable into book but bulky. Ref: Stephenson (CW) 21. [13] £243 $375

ASPIN

ASPINS FAMILIAR TREATISE ON ASTRONOMY TO ACCOMPANY ... URANIA'S MIRROR [1834] J. Aspin. 32 card set showing star positions, with explanation & 4 folding maps in book in modern slipcase. Each card 14x20cm (5½x8") Uncolored. 1 map torn. [52] £650 $1,001
NORTH AND SOUTH AMERICA FOR THE ELUCIDATION OF THE ABBE GAULTIER'S GEOGRAPHICAL GAMES [1826] U.S. inset. 36x43cm (14x17") Color. VG. [45] £58 $90

BACHIENE

AFBEELDING VAN 'T LAND VAN ISRAEL, NAAR DESZELTS ... [1749] Gorincem: Goetzee. 48x38cm (19x15") Color. Ref: Laor 69. [23] £179 $275
AFBEELDING VAN EGYPTE, DE WOESTYNE DER SCHELF-ZEE EN 'T LAND KANAAN ... [1750] Gorincem: Goetzee. Exodus route. 48x38cm (19½x15½") Color. Ref: Laor 68. [23] £162 $250
AFBEELDING VAN T' JOODSCHE LAND TOEN HET AAN DE HEERSCHAPPY DER ROMEINEN ONDERWORFEN ... DER GESCHIEDENIS VAN CHRISTUS [1750] Amsterdam: N. Goetzee. 38x48cm (15x18½") Color. [23] £146 $225
NIEUWE EN NAUKEURIGE KAART DES GEHEELEN AARDBOLEMS, OPGEMAAKT MIT DE ECHSTE BESCHRYVINGEN EN DE BESTE HEEDENDAAGSCHE LAND EN ZEEKAARTEN ... JAARE 1744. DOOR E. BOWEN VERBETERALD DOOR W. BACHIENE [1772] World Mercator projection on Greenwich. 36x46cm (14½x17½") Color. Ref: Phillips (M) 1092 [26] £260 $400

BACHMANN

BIRD'S EYE VIEW OF LOUISIANA, MISSISSIPPI, ALABAMA AND PART OF FLORIDA [1861] Chromolithograph. 48x71cm (18½x28") Color. Repaired 5" tear lf; o/w fine. [47] £974 $1,500
BIRD'S EYE VIEW OF NORTH AND SOUTH CAROLINA AND PART OF GEORGIA [1861] Chromolithograph. 46x71cm (18x28") Color. Rt margin extended; fine. [47] £974 $1,500
BIRD'S EYE VIEW OF TEXAS AND PART OF MEXICO [1861] Chromolithograph. 48x71cm (18½x28") Color. Marginal repairs; good. [47] £1,136 $1,750

BACON

BACON'S GEM POCKET MAP OF LONDON AND SUBURBS [c. 1890] Linen-backed, folds into 12mo wraps; 32 pp index. 46x61cm (18½x23½") Color. Wraps rubbed, spine torn; index loose; map VG. [7] £36 $55
BACON'S NEW LARGE PRINT MAP OF CHINA [c. 1900] G.W. Bacon, London. Pocket map, folded into wraps. Incl Japan. 61x71cm (24x28") Color. Sl soiled & smudged wraps with library codes. Corner fold separations; o/w clean & bright. [7] £39 $60
BACON'S NEW LARGE PRINT MAP OF LONDON [c. 1890] With 56 pp street guide & ads, in pictorial wrapper. 69x94cm (26½x36½") Full color. Little dusty; good. [21] £49 $75
BACON'S NEW MAP OF LONDON AND STRANGER'S GUIDE ... [1869] Ads on verso; 16 p. guide. 58x89cm (22½x35") folding into printed paper covers 6x4". Color. Fold breaks repaired; cover scuffed; overall VG. Ref: Map Collector 65 (Smith, "... Bacon ...") p.10-15. [55] £97 $150

BAFFIN
A DESCRIPTION OF EAST INDIA CONTEYNING THE EMPIRE OF THE GREAT MOGOLL [1625] Wm. Baffin; Reynold Elstracke, sc. 36x28cm (14x11") Uneven margins; else fine. Ref: Tooley (Landmarks) p.141; Potter p.125. [62] £422 $650

BAKER
A PLAN OF THE CITY AND HARBOUR OF MACAO, A COLONY OF THE PORTUGUEZE ... [1796] G.L. Staunton; B. Baker, sc. City plan at 6"/mile. 69x53cm (27½x21") [14] £276 $425

BALCH
FLORIDA [1891] Boston: Balch Bros. 41 counties. 33x23cm (13x9½") Printed color. [4] £16 $25

BANKES
A PERSPECTIVE VIEW OF THE CITY OF DUBLIN FROM PHOENIX PARK [1787] London: C. Cooke. 20x33cm (8x13") Color. [24] £52 $80
VIEW OF BALE PRINCIPAL CITY OF BALE, ONE OF THE CANTONS OF SWITZERLAND [c. 1790] Basel. From Bankes Geography. 13x18cm (4½x7") Uncolored. [57] £26 $40
VIEW OF ZURICH PRINCIPAL CITY OF ZURICH, ONE OF THE CANTONS OF SWITZERLAND [c. 1790] From Bankes Geography. 13x18cm (4½x7") Uncolored. [57] £26 $40

BARROW
GENERAL CHART OF THE COLONY OF THE CAPE OF GOOD HOPE CONSTRUCTED ... DURING THE YEARS 1797 & 1798 ... [c. 1806] Reduced for 1st American ed by A.J. Stansbury. 33x46cm (12½x18½") Orig color. Horiz & vert folds with tears; sides remargined. Ref: cf Norwich 228. [28] £146 $225

BARTHOLOMEW
[ATLAS] LIBRARY REFERENCE ATLAS OF THE WORLD [1890] London & NY: Macmillan. Sm folio; 84 litho color maps; 209 pp index. Ex lib, with marks. Rubbed corners, edges; torn spine, flap loose; contents clean, tight, complete. [7] £97 $150
ARCTIC REGIONS AND BRITISH AMERICA CONTAINING ALL DISCOVERIES IN ARCTIC SEAS UP TO 1853 [c. 1854] Edinburgh: A. & C. Balck. 42x56cm (16½x22") Orig OL color. MS state names added. Lower margin chipped; c'fold split repaired. [28] £162 $250
BARTHOLOMEW'S NEW POCKET MAP OF ENVIRONS OF EDINBURGH REDUCED FROM THE ORDNANCE SURVEY ... [c. 1895] Dissected, mounted on gauze, folding into pictorial 12mo cloth cover. 46x58cm (17½x23") Full color. Cover dust soiled; map VG. [21] £49 $75
ELECTION MAP OF MIDLOTHIAN ... [1880] 2 miles/inch. Folds into 12mo folder. With register of voters for county, 1879-80. 36x48cm (13½x18½") Full color. Cover bit dusty; good. [21] £39 $60
FIELD MAP OF LOTHIANS HUNT [c. 1880] Wm. Blackwood & Sons. Dissected, laid down on linen, folding into faux 12mo morocco cover. Woods & "fox covers" in green. 33x56cm (13x21½") Printed color. Lacks front cover; map fine. [21] £146 $225
IRELAND [1870] Phila: T. Elwood Zell. 41x30cm (16x12") Full printed color. Fine. [21] £16 $25
NORTHUMBERLAND [c. 1890] W.H. Smith & Son's Reduced Ordnance maps for tourists ... Pocket map, laid down on gauze, folded into printed oil cloth wrappers. 48x33cm (18½x13½") OL col. VG. [21] £32 $50
"THE HUB" CYCLING MAP OF ENGLAND AND WALES [1897] London: George Newnes. 86x71cm (34x27½") Printed color. VG. [21] £29 $45

BARTRAM
ESQUISSE DES OPERATIONS DU SIEGE DE CHARLESTON, CAPITALE DE LA CAROLINE MERIDIONALE, EN 1780 [1793] Paris. 35x28cm (14x11") A close margin; good. [14] £338 $520

BEER
AMERICA [1690] From J.C. Beer, *Geographiae Universelle* (copied from Du Val). 10x13cm (4x5") Possible water staining & restoration. [52] £250 $385
ANGLIA [same date, source, dimen & condition] [52] £50 $77
ARABIA [same date, source, dimen & condition] [52] £160 $246
ASIA [same date, source, dimen & condition] [52] £60 $92
CANADA [same date, source, dimen & condition] [52] £160 $246
CANDIA [same date, source, dimen & condition] [52] £65 $100
CHINA [same date, source, dimen & condition] [52] £80 $123

FLORIDA [same date, source, dimen & condition] [52] £220 $339
IAPONIA [same date, source, dimen & condition] [52] £320 $493
INDIA EXTRA GANGEM [same date, source, dimen & condition] [52] £100 $154
INSULA CEILON [same date, source, dimen & condition] [52] £80 $123
INSULA ISLANDIA [same date, source, dimen & condition] [52] £120 $185
INSULAE ANTILLES [same date, source, dimen & condition] [52] £140 $216
INSULAE BRITANNIAE [same date, source, dimen & condition] [52] £60 $92
INSULAE MOLUCCAE [same date, source, dimen & condition] [52] £70 $108
INSULAE PHILIPPINAE [1690] From J.C. Beer, *Geographiae Universelle* (copied from Du Val). 10x13cm (4x5") Possible water staining & restoration. [52] £140 $216
INSULAE SINDAE [same date, source, dimen & condition] [52] £120 $185
INSULAE TERCERAE ALIAS ACORES [same date, source, dimen & condition] [52] £65 $100
IRLANDIA [same date, source, dimen & condition] [52] £60 $92
ITALIAE TABULA [same date, source, dimen & condition] [52] £60 $92
MALTHA [same date, source, dimen & condition] [52] £140 $216
MEXICO SIVE N. HISPANIA [same date, source, dimen & condition] [52] £100 $154
NOVA MEXICO [same date, source, dimen & condition] Insular California. [52] £340 $524
PERSIA [same date, source, dimen & condition] [52] £80 $123
SABAUDIAE [same date, source, dimen & condition] [52] £65 $100
SCOTIA [same date, source, dimen & condition] [52] £60 $92
SICILIA [same date, source, dimen & condition] [52] £70 $108
TERRA ANTARCTICA [same date, source, dimen & condition] [52] £150 $231
TERRA ARCTICA [same date, source, dimen & condition] [52] £120 $185
TYPUS ORBIS TERRARUM [same date, source, dimen & condition] [52] £150 $231
VIRGINIA [same date, source, dimen & condition] [52] £200 $308

BEERS

[NJ] CITY OF PATERSON [1872] From *Atlas of the State of New Jersey*. 23x36cm (8½x14") Col. [35] £39 $60
[NJ] MILLBURN AND SPRINGFIELD [1867] Cadastral map. 48x38cm (19x15") [35] £39 $60
[NJ: MONMOUTH CO.] ATLANTIC [1873] From *Atlas of Monmouth County*. Shows Colts Neck & vicinity. 33x36cm (12½x13½") Full color. Ref: Phillips (A) 2166. [35] £45 $70
[NJ: MONMOUTH CO.] COLTS NECK [ON SHEET WITH] EDINBURG [AND] HOLMDEL [AND] MARLBORO [same date, source, reference] Town centers. 33x28cm (12½x10½") Full color. [35] £32 $50
[NJ: MONMOUTH CO.] EATONTOWN [same date, source, color, reference] 36x53cm (14x20½") [35] £36 $55
[NJ: MONMOUTH CO.] FAIR HAVEN [ON SHEET WITH] NAVESINK [AND] OCEANIC [AND] PARKERVILLE [same date, source, color, reference] 28x36cm (11x14") [35] £32 $50
[NJ: MONMOUTH CO.] FREEHOLD [same date, source, color, reference] 53x36cm (21x13½") [35] £42 $65
[NJ: MONMOUTH CO.] MARLBORO [same date, source, color, reference] 36x28cm (13½x11½") Tattered edges, misfolded; frameable. [35] £26 $40
[NJ: MONMOUTH CO.] PORTIONS OF SHREWSBURY AND OCEAN TWPS [same date, source, color, reference] Shows Ocean Grove, Asbury Park & Shark River. 33x53cm (12½x21") [35] £52 $80
[NJ: MONMOUTH CO.] RARITAN [same date, source, color, reference] 30x41cm (11½x15½") [35] £36 $55
[NJ: MONMOUTH CO.] RED BANK [same date, source, color, reference] 53x61cm (21x24") Tape repair verso. [35] £42 $65
[NJ: MONMOUTH CO.] SEABRIGHT & MONMOUTH BEACH PROPERTY [same date, source, color, reference] 41x30cm (15½x11½") [35] £39 $60
[NJ: MONMOUTH CO.] TOPOGRAPHICAL MAP OF MONMOUTH COUNTY [same date, source, color, reference] 36x56cm (14x21½") [35] £49 $75
[NJ: MONMOUTH CO.] TOWN OF FREEHOLD [same date, source, color, reference] 56x48cm (21½x19") [35] £39 $60
[NJ: MONMOUTH CO.] TURKEY [ON SHEET WITH] FAIRFIELD [AND] WEST [same date, source, color, reference] 36x28cm (14x11") [35] £26 $40
[NJ: MONMOUTH CO.] UPPER FREEHOLD [same date, source, color, reference] 36x30cm (14x12") [35] £39 $60
[NJ: MORRIS CO.] TOPOGRAPHICAL MAP OF MORRIS COUNTY [1872] 36x56cm (14x22") Col. [35] £45 $70

[NJ: WARREN CO.] **BLAIRSTOWN** [1874] From *Atlas of Warren County*. 38x30cm (14½x11½") Full color. Ref: Phillips (A) 2171. [35] £32 $50

[NJ: WARREN CO.] **FRELINGHUYSEN** [same date, source, color, reference] 38x30cm (14½x12") [35] £32 $50

[NJ: WARREN CO.] **HARMONY** [same date, source, reference] 30x38cm (11½x14½") Full color [35] £32 $50

[NJ: WARREN CO.] **HOPE** [same date, source, color, reference] 38x30cm (14½x11½") [35] £36 $55

[NJ: WARREN CO.] **HOPE** [ON SHEET WITH] **TOWNSBURY** [AND] **MARKSBORO** [AND] **JOHNSONBURGH** [same date, source, color, reference] Town centers. 38x30cm (14½x11½") [35] £29 $45

[NJ: WARREN CO.] **OXFORD** [same date, source, color, reference] 38x30cm (14½x11½") [35] £32 $50

[NJ: WARREN CO.] **OXFORD FURNACE** [1874] From *Atlas of Warren County*. 36x81cm (14x32") Full color. Ref: Phillips (A) 2171. [35] £39 $60

[NJ: WARREN CO.] **PART OF PHILLIPSBURGH** [same date, source, color, reference] 38x79cm (14½x31") [35] £32 $50

[NJ: WARREN CO.] **WARREN COUNTY** [same date, source, color, reference] 36x56cm (14x21½") [35] £36 $55

BELL

MAP OF THE SOUTH-WESTERN PORTION OF THE UNITED STATES AND OF SONORA AND CHIHUAHUA TO ILLUSTRATE THE PAPER BY DR. W.A. BELL ... [1870] 33x38cm (13x14½") Sl color. Some weak folds repaired; sm chip lost. [44] £65 $100

NORTH AMERICA [1841] London: Allan Bell. 28x33cm (11x13") Color. VG. [61] £81 $125

BELLIN (Large)   Try *Depot de la Marine*

8EME CARTE PARTICULIERE DES COSTES DE BRETAGNE ... [1770] Loire estuary. Orig pub by Jaillot, 61x84cm (24x32½") Col. Sl dampmarking & creasing at c'fold. Close top & bottom margins. [15] £120 $185

CARTE DE L'ISLE DE FRANCE ... M.DCC.LXIII [1763] 57x88cm (22½x34½") Orig full color. Formerly horiz dissected, now rejoined. [54] £480 $739

CARTE DE L'ISLE SAINT PIERRE DRESSEE AU DEPOST DES CARTES ET PLANS ... PAR LE S. BELLIN INGENIEUR DE LA MARINE ET DU DEPOST MDCCLXIII [1763] 58x91cm (23½x35½") Tears & crease top margin. Ref: MCCS 96, 758. [28] £292 $450

CARTE DES ENTREES DE LA TAMISE ... [1759] SE England. 58x87cm (23x34½") Color. [14] £286 $440

CARTE DU COMTE DE KENT ET DU PAS DE CALAIS ... [1759] Thames to London. 58x86cm (23x34") Faint browning lower margin; short margin tear repaired. [15] £240 $370

CARTE DU COURS DU FLEUVE DE SAINT LAURENT DEPUIS QUEBEC JUSQU'A LA MER EN DEUX FEUILLES ... IRE FEUILLE [IN SET WITH] ... IIME FEUILLE [1761] Several insets. Two sheets, each about 57x85cm (22x33½") [14] £162 $250

CARTE DU COURS DU FLEUVE DE SAINT LAURENT DEPUIS LA MER JUSQU'A QUEBEC EN DOUX FEUILLES DRESSEE AU DEPOST DES CARTES ET PLANS DE LA MARINE ... IE FEUILLE DEPUIS QUEBEC JUSQU'A MATANE ET RIVIERE DES OUTARDES [1761] From *L'Hydrographie Francoise*. 61x89cm (24x35½") Sm rust stain. Ref: Phillips (A) 590; MCCS 96,733. [28] £325 $500

CARTE REDUITE DE L'ISLE DE SAINT CHRISTOPHE ... M.DCC.LVIII [1758-] Nevis inset. 59x88cm (23x34½") Orig color. Orig laid on canvas in 3 sections, now rejoined. [52] £400 $616

CARTE REDUITE DE L'OCEAN SEPTENTRIONALE COMPRIS ENTRE L'ASIE ET L'AMERIQUE [1766] Updating of Mueller 1758. 56x85cm (22x33½") Orig wash color. Margins bit frayed; map fine. Ref: Wagner (NW) 610. [46] £487 $750

CARTE REDUITE DE LA PARTIE SEPTENTRIONALE DE L'ISLE DE TERRE NEUVE DRESSEE AU DEPOST DES CARTES ET PLAN DE LA MARINE ... [1764 - 1767] In *Hydrographie Francoise*. 64x81cm (24½x32") Ref: cf. Phillips (A) 587. [28] £263 $405

CARTE REDUITE DE LA RADE DES DUNES ... [1757 (c. 1770)] Dover to Reculver. 58x43cm (23x16½") Uncolored. [15] £180 $277

CARTE REDUITE DES COSTES OCCIDENTALES D'AFRIQUE ... [1754] Equator to 20 deg. S. 89x55cm (35x21½") Green rhumb lines. Exc. [15] £90 $139

CARTE REDUITE DES DEBOUQUEMENS DE ST. DOMINGUE DRESSEE POUR LE SERVICE DES VAISSEAUX DU ROY PAR ORDRE DE MLE DUE DE CHOISEUL ... [1768] 58x90cm (23x35½") [14] £62 $95

CARTE REDUITE DES MERS DU NORD [1751 (c.1801)] From *Atlas Maritime*. Genoa: Gravier. 54x87cm (21½x34") Modern OL & cartouche color. Close side margins. Ref: Phillips (A) 697,23. [28] £497 $765

CARTE REDUITE DES PARTIES CONNUES DU GLOBE TERRESTRE ... [1755] 54x82cm (21½x32½") Color. [16] £855 $1,316

ESSAY D'UNE CARTE REDUITE CONTENANT LES PARTIES CONNUEES DU GLOBE TERRESTRE ... [1748 (c.1780)] Show Cook's discoveries. 53x71cm (20½x27½") Folds; side margins trimmed to border; sh fold tear; two sm rust spots. Ref: Wagner (NW) 560. [28] £438 $675

PARTIE OCCIDENTALE DE LA NOUVELLE FRANCE OU CANADA ... [c. 1745] 48x61cm (19x24") Date changed in ms to "1755". Uncolored. Exc. Ref: Verner "The Northpart of America" #12; Johnson (Amer Expl) p.195. [2] £1,623 $2,500

PARTIE OCCIDENTALE DE LA NOUVELLE FRANCE OU DU CANADA PAR MR. BELLIN INGENIEUR DU ROY ET DE LA MARINE ... [1755] Nuremberg: Homann Heirs. 46x56cm (17½x22") Orig OL & border color. Sh lower c'fold split repaired; lt margin foxing. Ref: Heidenreich & Dahl p.15-6,20; Karpinski (MI) p.138; MCC 96,684; Trudel p.120-1. [28] £1,169 $1,800

PARTIE ORIENTALE ... NOUVELLE FRANCE [1755] OL color. 48x62cm (18½x24") OL color. Sl crease near c'fold; sl wear outer margin; VG. [60] £633 $975

BELLIN (Small) Try *De Charlevoix, Prevost d'Exiles*

AJACCIO [CORSICA] [1764] From *Petit Atlas Maritime*. 23x18cm (8½x7") [15] £40 $62

BRASILIEN [c. 1757] From Baumgarten's General History of Travels. After D'Anville. 25x33cm (9½x13") B&W. [46] £29 $45

CARTA DELL' ISOLE FILIPPINE DI MR. BELLIN INGEGNERE DELLA MARINA FOGLIO 1.MO [WITH] CARTA DELL' ISOLE FILIPPINE [c. 1760] Italian re-engraving. Two maps: 21x30cm (8x12") and 21x16cm (8½x6") Exc. [62] £114 $175

CARTE DE L'ACCADIE DRESSEE SUR LES MANUSCRITS DU DEPOST DES CARTES ET PLANS DE LA MARINE [1744] Incl P.E.I. 21x32cm (8x12½") OL & wash color. [58] £97 $150

CARTE DE L'EMPIRE DU JAPON POUR SERVIR A L'HISTOIRE GENERALES DES VOYAGES PAR M. BELLIN [1752] 21x31cm (8½x12") Wash color. Exc. [62] £357 $550

[SAME TITLE] [1752 (c.1780)] 23x33cm (9x12½") Uncolored. [45] £195 $300

CARTE DE L'HEMISPHERE AUSTRAL MONTRANT LES ROUTES DES NAVIGATEURS LE PLUS CELEBRES PAR IL CAPTAINE COOK [c. 1780] From Prevost's *Histoire Generale des Voyages*. Appeared only in late editions. 53x53cm (21x21") Uncolored. Folds as issued. [45] £292 $450

CARTE DE L'ISLANDE ... [c. 1780] 33x41cm (12½x15½") Uncolored. [45] £97 $150

CARTE DE L'ISLANDE, POUR SERVIR A LA CONTINUATION DE L'HISTOIRE GENERALE DES VOYAGES [c. 1758] 30x38cm (11½x15") Color. [14] £71 $110

CARTE DE L'ISLE D'ORLEANS ET DU PASSAGE DE LA TRAVERSE DANS LE FLEUVE ST. LAURENT ... [1744] From Charlevoix, *Histoire*. 19x28cm (7½x11") [14] £55 $85

CARTE DE L'ISLE DE LA BARBADE, POUR SERVIR A L'HISTOIRE GENERALE DES VOYAGES [1754 (c.1780)] 20x15cm (8x6") Uncolored. [45] £49 $75

[SAME TITLE] [1777] Amsterdam; A. Krevelt, sc. [same dimen] [14] £39 $60

CARTE DE L'ISLE DE LA GRENADE ... 1758 [c. 1780] In Prevost's *Histoire Generale des Voyages*. 21x17cm (8½x7") Uncolored. [45] £58 $90

CARTE DE L'ISLE DE LA GRENADE POUR SERVIR A L'HISTOIRE GENERALE DES VOYAGES [1758] 21x16cm (8½x6") [14] £32 $50

CARTE DE L'ISLE DE LA GUADELOUPE, POUR SERVIR A L'HISTOIRE GENERALE DES VOYAGES [1758 (c.1780)] 20x33cm (8½x13") Uncolored. [45] £81 $125

CARTE DE L'ISLE DE LA JAMAIQUE ... 1758 [c. 1780] In Prevost's *Histoire Generale des Voyages*. 23x33cm (8½x13") Uncolored. [45] £81 $125

CARTE DE L'ISLE DE LA MARTINIQUE, POUR SERVIR A L'HISTOIRE GENERALE DES VOYAGES [c. 1780] 23x33cm (8½x13") Uncolored. [45] £81 $125

CARTE DE L'ISLE DE PORTSEY, ET HAVRE DE PORTSMOUTH [1764] From *Petit Atlas Maritime*. 20x15cm (8½x6") [15] £60 $92

CARTE DE L'ISLE DE SAINTE LUCIE, POUR SERVIR A L'HISTOIRE GENERALE DES VOYAGES [c. 1780] 23x33cm (8½x13") Uncolored. [45] £81 $125

CARTE DE L'ISLE ST. CHRISTOPHE, POUR SERVIR A L'HISTOIRE GENERALE DES VOYAGES [c. 1780] 23x33cm (8½x13") Uncolored. [45] £81 $125

CARTE DE LA BAYE DE CHESAPEAK ET PAYS VOISINS [1757] 28x38cm (11x15") Uncol. [45] £211 $325

CARTE DE LA BAYE DE HUDSON [c. 1757] 22x30cm (8½x12") Color. [40] £85 $131

CARTE DE LA BAYE DE HUDSON, POUR SERVIR A L'HISTOIRE GENERALE DES VOYAGES [1757 (c.1780)] 23x33cm (9x13") Uncolored. [45] £58 $90

CARTE DE LA BAYE DE L'ORISTAN [1764] From *Petit Atlas Maritime*. 23x18cm (8½x7") [15] £40 $62

CARTE DE LA CAROLINE ET GEORGIE [1757] 19x28cm (7½x11") [14] £120 $185
[SAME TITLE] [1757] 25x33cm (10x13") Uncolored. [45] £179 $275
[SAME TITLE] [1757] 19x28cm (7½x11") Later color. [51] £243 $375
CARTE DE LA FLORIDE, DE LA LOUISIANE ET PAYS VOISINS. POUR SERVIR A L'HISTOIRE GENERALE DES VOYAGES [1757] 22x30cm (9x12") Uncolored. Clean, bright. [11] £146 $225
[SAME TITLE] [1757] 25x33cm (10x13") Modern color. [44] £276 $425
CARTE DE LA INDE AU-DELA DU GANGE COMPRENANT LES ROYAUMES DE SIAM, DE TUNQUIN, PEGU, AVA, ARACAN, &C. [1764] 28x28cm (11x11") Exc. [63] £159 $245
CARTE DE LA NOUVELLE ANGLETERRE, NOUVELLE YORCK ET PENSILVANIE [1757] 20x29cm (8x11½") [14] £120 $185
[SAME TITLE] [same date & dimen] Color. VG. [38] £162 $250
CARTE DE LA NOUVELLE ANGLETERRE, NOUVELLE YORCK ET PENSILVANIE [1757] 28x38cm (11x15") Uncolored except sm red symbols. [45] £162 $250
CARTE DES BAYES, RADES ET PORT DE PLAISANCE DANS L'ISLE DE TERRE NEUVE... [1744] From Charlevoix, *Histoire et Description Generale.* 20x30cm (8½x12") Ref: MCCS 96, 698. [28] £81 $125
CARTE DES ISLES DE JAVA, SUMATRA, BORNEO &C. LES DETROITS DE LA SONDE MALACA ET BANCA GOLPHE DE SIAM &C. [c. 1757] 26x29cm (10x11½") OL & wash color. [58] £107 $165
CARTE DES ISLES PHILIPPINES ... 1RE FEUILLE ... [1752 (c.1780)] In Prevost's *Histoire Generale des Voyages.* Northern islands, based on Spanish Jesuit Fr. Murillo's map. 23x18cm (9x6½") Uncolored. [45] £81 $125
CARTE DES ISLES PHILIPPINES ... 2E. FEUILLE ... [same date, same source] Southern islands, based on Spanish Jesuit Fr. Murillo's map. 23x30cm (8½x12") Uncolored. [45] £81 $125
CARTE DES ISLES SITUEES AU NORD DE ST. DOMINGUE AVEC LES PASSAGES POUR LE RETOUR APPELLES DEBOUQUEMENS 1763 [1764] From *Le Petit Atlas Maritime.* Caicos and Turks Islands. 23x38cm (9x15") Color. Ref: Phillips (A) 3508. [14] £120 $185
CARTE DES LACS DU CANADA DRESSEE SUR LES MANUSCRITS DU DEPOST DES CARTES, PLANS ET JOURNAUX DE LA MARINE ET SUR LE JOURNAL DU R.P. CE CHARLEVOIX ... [1744] From *Historie et Description Generale.* 30x46cm (12x18") Fold tears repaired, minor loss. Ref: Heidenreich & Dahl p.15; Karpinski (MI) 716; Schwartz & Ehrenberg p.162; MCC 96,716. [28] £584 $900
CARTE DES PROVINCES DE CARACAS, COMANA, ET PARIA ... [1756] 19x29cm (7½x11½") [14] £88 $135
CARTE DES PROVINCES DE TABASCO, CHIAPA, VERAPAZ, GUATIMALA, HONDURAS ET YUCATAN [1764] 20x34cm (8x13") OL & wash color. [58] £94 $145
CARTE DU GOLPHE DU MEXIQUE ET DES ISLES DE L'AMERIQUE [1754 (1757)] 27x38cm (11x15") OL & wash color. [58] £130 $200
CARTE DU GOLPHE DU MEXIQUE ET DES ISLES DE L'AMERIQUE POUR SERVIR A L'HISTOIRE GENERALE DES VOYAGES [1754 (c.1780)] 27x38cm (11x15") Uncolored. [45] £162 $250
CARTE DU LAC DE MEXICO ET DE SES ENVIRONS LORS DE LA CONQUESTE DES ESPAGNOLS [1754] 21x15cm (8½x6") [14] £32 $50
CARTE REDUITE DE LA MER DU SUD [1764] In *Le Petit Atlas Maritime.* 21x35cm (8½x14") Color. Ref: Tooley (Australia) 158. [16] £256 $395
CARTE REDUITE DE LA MER DU SUD POUR SERVIR A L'HISTOIRE GENERALE DES VOYAGES [1753] 21x36cm (8½x14") Color. Ref: Tooley (Australia) 158. [16] £328 $505
CARTE REDUITE DES MERS DU NORD [1758] 33x45cm (13x17½") Sm border stain. [14] £71 $110
CARTE REDUITE DES MERS DU NORD, POUR SERVIR A L'HISTOIRE GENERALE DES VOYAGES [1758 (c.1780)] Coastal chart. 32x45cm (12½x17½") Uncolored. Folds as issued. [45] £91 $140
[SAME TITLE] [1776] Dutch ed; Krevelt, sc. 33x44cm (13x17½") Fine. [14] £39 $60
CARTE REDUITE DES PARTIES SEPTENTRIONALES DU GLOBE, SITUEES ENTRE L'ASIE ET L'AMERIQUE ... [c. 1759] 21x34cm (8x13½") Color. [40] £140 $216
CARTE REDUITE DES TERRES AUSTRALES [1753] In Prevost's *Histoire Generale des Voyages.* 20x28cm (8x11") Ref: Tooley (Australia) 156. [16] £1,045 $1,609
CARTE REDUITE DU GLOBE TERRESTRE [1764] In *Le Petit Atlas.* 22x34cm (8½x13½") Orig color. [16] £275 $424
DETROIT DE MAGELLAN [1753] 20x36cm (7½x13½") B&W. Narrow lf margin. [46] £29 $45
FLUSSE DE LA PLATA [c. 1756] From Baumgarten's General History of Travels. Buenos Aires shown. 18x28cm (7½x11") B&W. [46] £26 $40
FORTSETZUNG DER KARTE VON JANDOSTAN ... [1735+] Leipzig. 22x24cm (8½x9½") [14] £26 $40

GUYANA [c. 1757] From Baumgarten's General History of Travels. After D'Anville. 20x30cm (8x12½") B&W. [46] £29 $45
ISLE FORMOSA [1752] 24x29cm (9½x11") Exc. [62] £224 $345
KARTE VON DEM FLUSSE RICHELIEU UND OEM SEE CHAMPLAIN ... [1744] Dutch ed. 30x14cm (12x5½") OL & wash color. [58] £55 $85
KARTE VON DEN EYLANDEN VON JAPON UND DER HALBINSEL COREA [c. 1750] 20x28cm (8x11") OL & wash color. [58] £162 $250
KARTE VON DEN KUSTEN DES FRANZOSISCHEN FLORIDA [1756] From Charlevoix, *Histoire ... de la Nouvelle France* ... Leipzig; German ed. Cape Fear to St. Augustine. 23x15cm (8½x6") Uncol. [45] £114 $175
[SAME TITLE] [1756 (1774)] Cape Fear to St. Augustine. 20x14cm (8x5½") Wash color. Ref: Cumming (SE) 259. [46] £52 $80
KARTE VON DEN KUSTEN VON PERSIEN, GUZARATTE UND MALABAR [1735+] Leipzig. 24x20cm (9½x7½") [14] £26 $40
LE PAYS DES HOTTENTOTS AUX ENVIRONS DU CAP DE BONNE ESPERANCE [c. 1780] Updated & pub by Laporte. 25x36cm (9½x13½") OL color. [58] £84 $130
LOOP VAN DE MARAGON OF DE GROOTE RIVIER DER AMAZONES [1745] From Campbell *Beknopte Histori ... Spaansche Ryk in America*. Dutch ed. 15x38cm (6½x15") B&W. Narrow rt margin. [46] £26 $40
MITTAEGLICHES AMERICA [c. 1757] From Baumgarten's General History of Travels. 20x15cm (7½x5½") B&W. Narrow margins. [46] £26 $40
PARAGUAY [c. 1756] From Baumgarten's General History of Travels. 20x30cm (8x11½") B&W. [46] £29 $45
PETITES ANTILLES OU ISLES DU VENT [1764] From *Petit Atlas Maritime*. Virgin Is. to Antigua. 23x33cm (9x13") Color. [27] £159 $245
PLAN DE LA BAYE DE CHIBOUCTOU NOMMEE PAR LES ANGLOIS HALIFAX 1763 [1764] 24x37cm (9½x14½") Orig color. Ref: Sellers & Van Ee 460. [28] £234 $360
PLAN DE LA BAYE DE PENSACOLA [1744] In Charlevoix' Journal. 20x18cm (7½x7") Uncol. [4] £179 $275
PLAN DE LA NOUVELLE ORLEANS ... [1744] 20x29cm (7½x11") Color. [58] £162 $250
[SAME TITLE] [1749] From Tom.XIV, No.19. 20x29cm (8x11") Fine. [20] £162 $250
PLAN DE LA VILLE DE LOUISBOURG DANS L'ISLE ROYALE [1764] 23x38cm (9½x14½") Orig color. Ref: Sellers & Van Ee 340. [28] £234 $360
PLAN DE LA VILLE DE QUEBEC [1764] 23x38cm (9x14½") Orig color. Ref: Tooley (Amer) p.215; #136, 2nd. Sellers & Van Ee 606. [28] £234 $360
[SAME TITLE] [c. 1765] 19x28cm (7½x11") Color. [40] £150 $231
PLAN DU PORT ET DU CARENAGE DE CARIACOUA SITUE DANS PARIS [1764] In Grenadines. 17x22cm (6½x8½") Orig color. [14] £42 $65
PLAN DU PORT ET VILLE DE CIVITA-VECCHIA [1764] From *Petit Atlas Maritime*. 23x18cm (8½x7") [15] £40 $62
PORT ET VILLE DE PORTO-RICO DANS L'ISLE DE CE NOM [1764] San Juan. 22x32cm (8½x12½") Color. [25] £185 $285
PORTO VECCHIO [CORSICA] [1764] From *Petit Atlas Maritime*. 23x18cm (8½x7") [15] £40 $62
SUITE DU COURS DE FLEUVE DE ST. LAURENT DEPUIS QUEBEC JUSQU'AU LAC ONTARIO POUR SERVIR A L'HISTOIRE GENERALE DES VOYAGES [1757 (c.1780)] 23x33cm (9x13") Uncolored. [45] £81 $125

BENARD   Try *Cook*

CARTE DE L'HEMISPHERE AUSTRAL MONTRANT LES ROUTES DES NAVIGATEURS LES PLUS CELEBRES PAR LE CAPITAINE JACQUES COOK [c. 1778+] Tracks of 3 voyages. 54x52cm (21x20½") Col. [41] £375 $578
L'AMERIQUE MERIDIONALE [c. 1754] From *Histoire Generale des Voyages*. 46x33cm (17½x13") B&W. [46] £36 $55

BERGHAUS

[ATLAS] BERGHAUS' PHYSIKALISCHER ATLAS [1892] Gotha: Perthes. 3rd ed. Folio; 75 double-paged printed color maps on physical and cultural geography. Ex lib, with marks. Rebound; contents shaken, loosening boards; text soiled, maps clean. [7] £192 $295
SPEZIAL KARTE VOM HIMALAYA IN KUMAON, GURHWAL, SIRMUR &C.&C. [1835] 60x84cm (23½x33") In slip-case. Orig color. [53] £240 $370
STROMGEBIETE DER NEUEN WELT [1842] 2 maps: Rivers of N.& S. America. 33x43cm (13x16½") Color. [9] £49 $75

BERNARD
DETROIT DU MAGELLAN [1722] From *Voyages de Francois Coreal aux Indes Occidentales*. Amsterdam: J.F. Bernard. 43x51cm (16½x20½") B&W. Sl browning; trimmed at lf where bound. [46] £42 $65

BERTHOLON
CARTE DE LA NOUVELLE ANGLETERRE, NOUVELLE YORK, NOUVELLE JERSEY, ET PENNSYLVANIE [1799] From *Atlas Moderne Portatif*. 18x23cm (7x9") Uncolored. Bright, fresh. [35] £81 $125

BERTIUS
ANDALUZIA [1602] SW Spain. 10x13cm (3½x5") Full color. [57] £39 $60
ARABIA [1618] 9x12cm (3½x5") Fine [55] £120 $185
CERRO DE POTOSI [1602] View. 8x13cm (3½x5") Full color. [57] £42 $65
CONNATIA [1616] Ireland. 13x15cm (5x5½") B&W. Lt age-toning; repaired wormhole near border; else VG. [55] £65 $100
CORSICA [1602] 8x13cm (3½x5") [57] £49 $75
INDIA ORIEN. [1602] 9x12cm (3½x5") [14] £97 $150
INSULAE CAPITIS VIRIDIS [1606] 10x13cm (3½x5") Color. [57] £42 $65
MEXICANA [1602] With whole Gulf. 9x12cm (3½x5") Full color. [57] £146 $225
NOVA HISPANIA [1616] Bertius / Hondius. 10x13cm (3½x5") Full color. Early hand alteration of caption. [31] £227 $350
VIRGINIA ET NOVA FRANCIA [1616] 10x14cm (3½x5½") Col. Exc. Ref: Cumming (SE) 31. [62] £146 $225

BETTS
[GLOBE] BETTS PORTABLE TERRESTRIAL GLOBE COMPILED FROM THE LATEST AND BEST AUTHORITIES [c. 1895] George Phillips & Son Ltd. 14" globe printed on 7 silk gores mounted over collapsible wire frame. Age-toned silk, stained along seams, tears; polar ribbon collars frayed & rotted; repairable. [7] £211 $325

BIDWELL
MISSIONARY MAP OF CHINA EMBRACING CHIEFLY THE EIGHTEEN PROVINCES FROM THE LATEST AND BEST AUTHORITIES [1850] Wall map, canvas mounted. 168x213cm (66x84") OL color. Top sl water-stained & torn, sides ragged; rods dismounted; fabric tape reinforcing top & bottom; o/w VG. [7] £422 $650

BLACK
[ATLAS] BLACK'S GENERAL ATLAS: A SERIES OF FIFTY-FOUR MAPS ... BY SYDNEY HALL [1841] Folio; some double-page maps, most in OL color. Half leather covers worn but good. Lt to moderate foxing, incl U.S. & Mexico. [5] £454 $700
[ATLAS] THE SCRIBNER-BLACK ATLAS OF THE WORLD [1890] International ed of *General Atlas*; Chas. Scribner, NY; A. & C. Black, Edinburgh. Imperial folio; 55 printed color maps; 87 pp text & index. Ex lib, with marks. Loose front end papers; contents clean, tight, complete; o/w near fine. [7] £162 $250
AGRICULTURAL MAP OF THE COUNTY OF EDINBURGH BY RALPH RICHARDSON, F.R.S.E. [1884 / 1895] In *The County of Edinburgh ... 1878* and later edition. Author's own copy. 8vo, 36 pp, limp printed cloth. 33x48cm (13x19") Full color. VG. [21] £81 $125
BLACK'S ROAD & RAILWAY TRAVELLING MAP OF SCOTLAND [c. 1840] A. & C. Black; S. Hall, sc. Dissected, linen mounted, folding into 12mo cloth covers. 86x64cm (33½x24½") Full color. Fine. [21] £146 $225
GENERAL MAP OF THE UNITED STATES [1860] NE to Rockies & Canada; horizontal AZ-NM split. 41x55cm (16½x21½") Full color. [58] £97 $150
GEORGIA & FLORIDA [1867] S Florida inset. 38x28cm (15x10½") Hand OL & printed color. [4] £32 $50
MEXICO [1841] By S. Hall; Edinburgh: A.& C. Black. Large independent Texas. 25x37cm (10x14½") OL color. [56] £120 $185
[SAME TITLE] [1846] With Texas Republic, Southwest & Calif. 28x38cm (10½x15") OL color. Sl abrasions from tissue; generally good. [44] £130 $200
[SAME TITLE] [1850] Post-Mexican War version; reduced TX, narrow NM. 25x38cm (10x14½") Full color. [56] £120 $185
PALESTINE ACCORDING TO ITS ANCIENT DIVISIONS [1844] Wm. Hughes. 38x25cm (15x10") Col. [23] £23 $35
UNITED STATES, WESTERN STATES - CALIFORNIA, OREGON, UTAH, WASHINGTON, NEW MEXICO, NEBRASKA, KANSAS, INDIAN TERRITORY &C. [1861] By Bartholomew; Edinburgh: A.& C. Black. Horizontal AZ-NM border. 41x56cm (16x22") Printed color. [56] £120 $185

BLACKIE & SON

THE UNITED STATES OF NORTH AMERICA, PACIFIC STATES [c. 1856] 36x28cm (14x10½") OL color.
[45] £58 $90

BLACKWOOD

PROVINCE OF CANADA [c. 1861] 44x56cm (17½x22") OL color. [40] £29 $45

BLAEU

[TITLE PAGE] LE THEATRE DU MONDE OU NOUVEL ATLAS CONTENANT LES CHARTES ET DESCRIPTIONS ... GUILLAUME ET IEAN BLAEU [1643] 38x23cm (15½x9½") Orig color. Lt toned; good. Ref: Koeman Bl19A, fig.12. [50] £487 $750

AETHIOPIA INFERIOR, VEL EXTERIOR ... [1635 - 1662] 38x50cm (15x19½") Orig full color. Fine. Ref: Norwich #154; Tooley (Landmarks) p.167; MCC #47 p.24. [59] £487 $750

[SAME TITLE] [1642] [same dimen] OL color; full cartouche color. VG+. Ref: Tooley (Africa) frontis, p.29; Koeman Bl32A. [33] £325 $500

AETHIOPIA SUPERIOR VEL INTERIOR; VULGO ABISSINORUM SIVE PRESBITERIIOANNIS IMPERIUM [(1640)] 38x49cm (15x19½") Orig color. Sl top margin separation; o/w fine. [30] £390 $600

AFRICAE NOVA DESCRIPTIO [1634 - 1667] Carte a figures. 41x55cm (16x21½") Recent OL & full color. Sh edge splits & 3" lower c'fold separation repaired; lt margin soiling; soiling or plate residue lf in ocean; sh minor abrasion at border; VG-. Ref: Norwich #32; Potter p.114; Goss (Grand Atlas) 59; Tooley (Landmarks) p.174. [59] £1,591 $2,450

ALEMANNIA SIVE SUEVIA SUPERIOR [c. 1650] From *Niewe Atlas*. Dutch ed. 38x51cm (15x19½") Orig color. Minor tear repaired. [46] £130 $200

AMERICAE NOVA TABULA [c. 1640] Willem Blaeu. Carte a figures. 41x56cm (16x22") Orig color. Exc. [62] £3,246 $5,000

BARONIA UDRONE IN COMITATU CATHERLOUGHAE [1648] 38x25cm (15x10") Old col. [24] £114 $175

BRITANNIA PROUT DIVISA FUIT TEMPORIBUS ANGLO-SAXONUM PRAESERTIM DURANTE ILLORUM HEPTARCHIA [1645] Side panels of king's lives. 41x52cm (16½x20½") Orig color, gold highlight. Exc. Ref: Shirley (BI to 1650) #549; Potter p.76-7. [2] £1,558 $2,400

CHILI [1640] 36x48cm (14x19") Full later color. [51] £438 $675

[SAME TITLE] [c. 1649-1662] 36x48cm (14x19") Verso blank. Orig color. Lt browned; margins foxed. Ref: Koeman II Bl 17. [28] £234 $360

CONTADO DI MOLISE ET PRINCIPATO ULTRA [1640] 38x51cm (15x19½") Contemporary color. Age-toned; else fine. [55] £146 $225

DE CUST VAN ENGELANDT TUSSCHEN DE SINGELS EN DE DROOGHTEN VAN WEEMBRUGH [1623 (1643)] From *Zeespiegel*. Selsey to Romney. 25x36cm (10½x14") Color. 2 sm brown spots; splits at outer margin edges. [15] £250 $385

DIOECESIS STAVANGERENSIS, & PARTES ALIQUOT VICINAE ... [1638-] J. Blaeu. 41x50cm (16x19½") Orig OL color. [53] £450 $693

DIOECESIS TRUNDHEMIENSIS PARS AUSTRALIS [1672] J. Blaeu. 42x53cm (16½x20½") Orig color. [53] £260 $400

DUCATUS UPLANDIA [1638-] J. Blaeu. 38x50cm (15x19½") Orig OL color. [53] £400 $616

EUROPA RECENS DESCRIPTA ... [c. 1640] Panels top & sides. 41x53cm (16½x21½") Full orig color. Good. [2] £1,428 $2,200

EXTREMA AMERICAE VERSUS BOREAM, UBI TERRA NOVA NOVA FRANCIA, ADIACENTIAQ. [1655] Only Blaeu map of Canada. 45x56cm (17½x22") Full orig col. Exc. Ref: Goss (Grand Atlas) p.158. [2] £1,233 $1,900

[SAME TITLE] [1662] 45x56cm (18x22") Orig color. Some offsetting. Ref: Koeman I Bl 56; Portinaro & Knirsch pl.81; Potter p.148. [28] £1,461 $2,250

FEZZAE ET MAROCCHI REGNA AFRICAE CELEBERRIMA ... [1640] 38x50cm (15x19½") Orig OL color. Ref: Koeman I Bl 17. [28] £292 $450

FIONIA VULGO FUNEN [c. 1650] From *Niewe Atlas*. Dutch ed. 38x50cm (15x19½") Orig col. [46] £143 $220

GALLOFLANDRIA [same date & source] 38x51cm (15x19½") Orig color. [46] £156 $240

HERESFELDENSIS [same date & source] 38x51cm (15x19½") Orig color. [46] £143 $220

IAPONIA REGNUM [1655] 42x57cm (16½x22½") Orig color. Exc. Ref: Cortazzi pl.63; Campbell (Japan) 21. [62] £1,883 $2,900

IMPERII SINARUM NOVA DESCRIPTIO [1655-] From *Atlas Chinensis*. 46x59cm (18x23") Orig wash color.
[53] £900 $1,386

INDIA QUAE ORIENTALIS DICITUR, ET INSULAE ADIACENTES [1635] 3rd state. 28x41cm (11x16") Orig color. Ref: Tooley (Australia) pl.122; Clancy pp 80-1. [16] £1,519 $2,340

INSULA GADITANA, VULGO ISLA DE CADIZ ... [c. 1662] 38x51cm (15x19½") Orig color. Margins bit spotted. Ref: Koeman I Bl 56. [28] £308 $475

INSULAE AMERICANAE IN OCEANO SEPTENTRIONALI, CUM TERRIS ADIACENTIBUS [(1635) 1640] 38x53cm (15x20½") Orig color. Faint age tone; fine. Ref: Portinaro & Knirsch pp.178-9. [1] £1,039 $1,600

INSULAE BALEARIDES ET PYTIUSAE [c. 1662] 38x49cm (15x19½") Blank verso. Orig OL & cartouche color; heightened in gilt. Ref: Koeman I Bl 56. [28] £380 $585

INSULAE DIVI MARTINI ... [1635] Oleron et Re near Rochelle. 38x53cm (15x21") Col. VG. [55] £195 $300

LA PRINCIPAUTE D'ORANGE ET COMTAT DE VENAISSIN, PAR JAQUES DE CHIEZE ORANGEOIS. 1627. EXCUDIT GUILJELMUS JANSSONIUS CAESIUS [c. 1638-40] 38x51cm (15x20") Orig OL & cartouche color. Sh tears lower margin. Ref: Phillips (A) 3421; Koeman I Bl 17. [28] £221 $340

LALANDIA FALSTRIA ET MONA INSULAE ... [1662-1672] J. Blaeu. 39x52cm (15½x20½") Orig OL color.
[53] £220 $339

MAGNI DUCATUS LITHUANIAE ... [n.d.] 46x53cm (17½x21") OL color. [36] £292 $450

MANSFELDIA [c. 1650] From *Niewe Atlas*. 38x51cm (15x19½") Orig color. [46] £143 $220

MAPPA AESTIVARUM INSULARUM, ALIAS BARMUDAS DICTARUM ... ACCURATE DESCRIPTA [1630] Based on Norwood. 40x53cm (16x21") Full orig col. Exc. Ref: cf. MCCS (Palmer) 19, #8. [2] £1,461 $2,250

MOMONIA HIBERNICE MOUN ET WOUN; ANGLISE MOUNSTER [c. 1654-1665] 43x53cm (16½x20½") Later OL & cartouche col. Bit foxed; margin tears, one into engraving repaired. Ref: Koeman I Bl 48. [28] £380 $585

MONTGOMERIA COMITATUS ET COMITATUS MERVINIA [1645] 38x51cm (15x19½") Color. Framed. Ref: Skelton (County) 28. [55] £292 $450

NOVA BELGICA ET ANGLIA NOVA [1635] 39x50cm (15½x19½") Orig OL col. Exc. [3] £1,883 $2,900

[SAME TITLE] [1635 / ?] 38x51cm (15½x20") Orig color. Exc. Ref: Schwartz & Ehrenberg pl.58; Goss (NA) 28. [38] £1,818 $2,800

[SAME TITLE] [c. 1635] 39x51cm (15x20") Orig color. Mint. [62] £2,077 $3,200

NOVA HISPANIA ET NOVA GALICIA [1635 - 1665] 38x50cm (15x20") OL & full color. VG+. Ref: Goss (Grand Atlas) p.172. [59] £454 $700

[SAME TITLE] [c. 1640-43] [same dimen] Orig OL & cartouche color. Faint dampmark lf margin. Ref: Koeman I Bl 17. [28] £467 $720

NOVA TOTIUS TERRARUM ORBIS GEOGRAPHICA AC HYDROGRAPHICA TABULA [1630] Carte a figures. 41x54cm (16x21½") Orig color. Exc. Ref: Shirley (W) 255, pl.201 (1606) [1] £5,518 $8,500

PASCAARTE VERRTHOONENDE DE MONT VANDE TEEMSE DE RIVIER VAN LONDEN MET ALLE GRONDEN DIEPTEN EN ONDIEPTEN DAER VOOR GELEGEN [1623] From *Zeespiegel*. Thames estuary. 25x36cm (10x14") Color. 2 sm repaired wormholes. [15] £280 $431

PERU [c. 1649 - 1662] 38x49cm (15x19½") Blank verso. Orig color. Few sh tears; browned; lt foxing to margins. Ref: Koeman II Bl 17. [28] £234 $360

REGIONES SUB POLO ARCTICO [(1647)] 41x53cm (16x20½") Early color. One vert crease; o/w fine.
[33] £649 $1,000

[SAME TITLE] [1649] 1st state; no crest or Backer de Cornelis dedication. [same dimen] Orig color. Trace of foxing. Ref: Koeman I Bl 23b [28] £876 $1,350

RUGIA INSULA ... [1631] 38x51cm (15x19½") Color. Lt surface dirt; else VG. [55] £179 $275

TAURICA CHERSONESUS. NOSTRA AETATE PRZECOPSCA ET GAZARA DICITUR [c. 1635-1647] 38x50cm (15x19½") Blank verso. Orig OL color. Lt browned; vert crease near c'fold. [28] £234 $360

VENEZUELA, CUM PARTI AUSTRALI NOVAE ANDALUSIAE [1659] 38x48cm (14½x18½") Some color. Exc. [29] £312 $480

VIRGINIAE PARTIS AUSTRALIS ET FLORIDAE PARTIS ORIENTALIS INTERJACENTIUMQUE REGIONUM NOVA DESCRIPTIO [1640] 38x51cm (15x20") Orig col. Superb. Framed. Ref: Cumming (SE) #41. [51] £1,169 $1,800

[SAME TITLE] [c. 1640] 39x51cm (15x20") Orig color. Exc. [62] £779 $1,200

[SAME TITLE] [1640 - 1662] 38x50cm (15x19½") Probably orig or early OL color. Cleaned; faint show-through; bright. Ref: Cumming (SE) pl.26; Koeman BL 32A & 82; Schwartz & Ehrenberg p.108; Van Ermen #12; Lowery 130 & 152. [59] £974 $1,500

ZEEKAARTE VAN YERLANDT [1623] From *Zeespiegel*. Ireland. 26x36cm (10x14") Orig color. Exc.
[62] £552 $850

BLAIR
PALAESTINAE SIVE TERRAE PROMISSIONIS IN DUODECIM TRIBUS PARTITAE FACIES VETUS [1768] Bayly, sc. 42x57cm (16½x22½") OL color. Ref: Laor 107 [23] £94 $145

BLOME
A MAPP OF THE KINGDOME OF IRELAND BY RIC. BLOME ... [1673] Dedicated to Earl Ric. Boyle. Palmer, sc. 38x38cm (15x15½") Color. Ref: Phillips (A) 8074; cf. Tooley (M&M) p.92. [24] £445 $685

A MAPP OF THE TRAVELS AND VOYAGES OF THE APOSTLES IN THEIR MISSION AND IN PARTICULAR OF SAINT PAUL [1687] 12 apostle figures below. 30x46cm (11½x18") Color. [23] £224 $345

A MAPP OF YE COUNTY OF ESSEX; WITH ITS HUNDREDS ... [1673] 26x32cm (10x12½") Early color. [14] £149 $230

A MAPP OR GENERALL CARTE OF THE WORLD DESIGNED IN TWO PLAINE HEMISPHERS ... [1669] English ed of Sanson's Mappe Monde. 39x52cm (15½x20½") Modern color. Minor splits & fold tears repaired; o/w fine. [14] £974 $1,500

CANAAN COMMONLY CALLED THE HOLY LAND OR THE LAND OF PROMISE BEING YE POSSESSION OF YE ISRAELITES & TRAVELED THROUGH BY OUR LORD ... [1687] Palmer, sc. 27x46cm (10½x18") Color. Ref: Laor 112. [23] £243 $375

GEOGRAPHY [WORLD] [1686] From *The Gentleman's Recreation* ... Concepts of geography diagramed on a sheet with sm double hemi world. 38x24cm (15x9½") Color. Ref: Shirley (W) 479. [16] £199 $307

BLUNT
[CARIBBEAN SEA] [c. 1845] Blueback covering mainland from Yucatan to Orinoco with southern Cuba. Several harbor insets. 91x206cm (36x81") Binding all around. Spotting, more to rt with some weak paper. [15] £275 $424

CAPE POGE AND ADJACENT SHOALS [MA] [1827] From *American Coast Pilot*. Vineyard & upper Cape. 11x18cm (4x7") Color. [57] £19 $30

CHART OF LONG ISLAND SOUND [1822] 18x43cm (7x17") Wash color. [56] £42 $65

PENSACOLA HARBOUR REDUCED FROM THE SURVEYS OF MAJ. KEARNEY [1854] From *American Coast Pilot*, 17th ed. 25x20cm (10x8") Uncolored. Orig folds. [4] £29 $45

PLAN OF PORTLAND HARBOUR [ME] [1827] From *American Coast Pilot*. 18x10cm (7x4") Col. [57] £19 $30

VIRGIN ISLANDS. TORTOLA, VIRGIN GORDA, GINGER ISLAND ... NORMANS I. [1854] From *American Coast Pilot*. Profile views. 13x20cm (5x8") Color. [27] £71 $110

BODE
[AQUARIUS, CAPRICORN] [1801] In *Uranographia*. Celestial chart. 58x79cm (23x31") Color. Minor repairs. [52] £950 $1,463

[CETUS MONSTRUM MARIUM, APPARATUS CHEMICUS] [same date, source, dimen, color & condition] [52] £750 $1,155

[LEO, CANCER, SENTOUS URANIAE] [same date, source, dimen, color & condition] [52] £950 $1,463

[LIBRA, VIRGO] [same date, source, dimen, color & condition] [52] £950 $1,463

[MILKY WAY - CYGNUS, VULTUR ET LYRA, HERCULES] [same date, source, dimen, color & condition] [52] £750 $1,155

[MILKY WAY - PERSEUS, ANDROMEDA] [same date, source, dimen, color & condition] [52] £750 $1,155

[POLE STAR - DRACO, CEPHEUS, URSA MINOR] [same date, source, dimen, color & condition] [52] £750 $1,155

[SAGITTARIUS, SCORPIO] [same date, source, dimen, color & condition] [52] £950 $1,463

[SOUTH POLE STAR - INDUS, ARGO NAVIS] [same date, source, dimen, color & condition] [52] £750 $1,155

[THE GREAT BEAR, URSA MAJOR, LEO MINOR] [same date, source, dimen, color & condition] [52] £750 $1,155

COELUM STELLATUM HEMISPHAERIUM ARIETIS ... [WITH] COELUM STELLATUM HEMISPHAERIUM LIBRAE ... [same date & source] Johann Elert Bode. Celestial hemisphere pair; each about 58x79cm (23x31") Color. Minor repairs. [52] £1,700 $2,618

BODENEHR
CADIZ NACH MALAGA DURCH DIE STRAASSE ODER MEER-ENGE VON GIBRALTAR AUS DEM OCEAN IN DASS MITTELLAENDISCHE MEER [1705] 17x51cm (6½x20") Orig OL color. Exc. [62] £114 $175

CARTA HYDROGRAPHICA ODER ALGEMEINE WELF [c. 1710] 15x23cm (6x9") Color. [16] £418 $644

DER ALTE WELT BEGRIFF ... AFRICA, EUROPA, ASIA ... [1704] Hemisphere. 15x13cm (6x5") OL color. [14] £39 $60
DER ALTE WELT BEGRIFF ... AFRICA, EUROPA, ASIA ... [IN SET WITH] DER NEUEN WELT BEGRIFF .. NORD AMERICA UND SUD AMERICA ... [1704 - 1715] From *Atlas Curieux oder Neuer und Compendieuser Atlas*. Hemispheres; insular Calif. Each 13x15cm (5x5½") Probably orig OL color. Fine-. [59] £227 $350
DER GANTZE WELT KRESS IN SEINEN ZWEY GROSSEN BEGRISSEN ALS DEM NEUREN UND DEM ALTERN ... [1704 - 1715] From *Atlas Curieux oder Neuer und Compendieuser Atlas*. Double hemispheres & polar spheres; insular Calif. 13x15cm (5x5½") Probably orig OL color. Fine-. [59] £162 $250
TOULON BIS MARSILIEN, UND S: TROPEZ [1705] 17x31cm (6½x12") Orig OL col. Exc. [62] £81 $125

BOHN
SUMATRA [1783] Amsterdam; Haarlem: Bohn & Son. 48x58cm (18½x22½") Orig full col. [46] £29 $45

BOLTON
A NEW AND CORRECT MAP OF THE COAST OF AFRICA FROM CAPE BLANCO ... TO THE COAST OF ANGOLA ... 1753 [1766] In Postlethwayt, *Universal Dictionary of Trade and Commerce*. Vignettes; Gold Coast inset. 38x48cm (15x18½") [14] £49 $75
NORTH AMERICA. PERFORMED UNDER THE PATRONAGE OF LOUIS DUKE OF ORLEANS ... BY THE SIEUR D'ANVILLE. GREATLY IMPROVED BY MR. BOLTON ... [1752] In Postlethwayt, *Dictionary of Commerce*. 4 sheets, two about 46x61cm (18x23½") and two narrower. Damp stains upper border areas; sm stains & foxing traces. [28] £438 $675

BONGARS
CIVITAS ACON SIVE PTOLOMAYDA [1611] Acre, Syria. After Sanudo-Vesconte ms map in 14 c. Holy Land treatise. 15x20cm (5½x7½") Exc. [63] £81 $125

BONNE
CANADA [1787-1788] From *Atlas Encyclopedique*. Paris: Bonne & Demarest. 25x36cm (9½x14") Fine. [14] £49 $75
CARTE ... BERRI, NIVERNOIS, LA MARCHE, BOURBONNIS, LIMOSIN ET L'AUVERGNE [1771 - 1783] From *Atlas Moderne* ... Paris: Lattre & Delalain. 30x43cm (12x17") Orig OL col. Ref: Phillips (A) 646. [59] £32 $50
CARTE ... DAUPHINE ET DE PROVENCE [same date, source, dimen, color & reference] [59] £32 $50
CARTE DE L'ENTREE DE NORTON ET DU DETROIT DE BHERING ... [1787-1788] From *Atlas Encyclopedique*. Paris: Bonne & Demarest. 24x35cm (9½x13½") Fine. [14] £58 $90
[SAME TITLE][1788] Cook's voyages, French ed. 23x35cm (9x13½") Grey marking, mostly in margins. [15] £50 $77
CARTE DE L'ISLE DE LA MARTINIQUE ... [1780] 31x20cm (12½x8") 3 worm holes; o/w fine. [14] £19 $30
CARTE DE LA COTE N.O. DE L'AMERIQUE ET DE LA COTE N.E. DE L'ASIE RECONNUES EN 1778 ET 1779 ... [1780] From *Atlas des Toutes les Parties Connues du Monde Terrestre*. 24x35cm (9½x13½") OL color. Fine. Ref: Phillips (A) 652. [49] £107 $165
CARTE DE LA LOUISIANE, ET DE LA FLORIDE [1781] Probably from Abbe Grenet, *Atlas Portatif*. Andre, sc. 32x21cm (12½x8½") Modern wash color. Good. [20] £162 $250
CARTE DES DOUZE TRIBUS D'ISRAEL ... [1771] Paris: Lattre. 31x44cm (12x17½") Color. Ref: Laor 120. [23] £81 $125
CARTE DES INDES EN DECA ET AU DELA DU GANGE ... [1782] 33x23cm (13x8½") Orig OL col. [51] £81 $125
CARTE DES ISLES DE LA SONDE ET DES ISLES MOLUQUES [1780] From Raynal *Atlas de Toutes les Parties...du Globe Terrestre*. 21x31cm (8½x12½") Fine. [14] £49 $75
CARTE DES ISLES DE ST. DOMINQUE ET DE PORTO-RICO [1782] 23x33cm (8½x12½") Orig OL color. [51] £97 $150
CARTE DES ISLES SANDWICH ... [1787 - 1788] From Bonne & Demarest, *Atlas Encyclopedique*. Nearly identical to Henry Roberts 1778-79 "Chart of the Sandwich Islands". 23x34cm (9x13½") Uncol. VG+. [59] £179 $275
CARTE DES REGIONS ET DES LIEUX DONT IL EST PARLE DANS LE NOUVEAU TESTAMENT [1771] Paris: Lattre. Insets: Jerusalem; Judaea. 30x43cm (12x17½") Color. Ref: Laor 121. [23] £94 $145
CARTE DU GOUVERNMENT DE L'ISLE DE FRANCE ET DE CELUI DE L'ORLEANOIS ... [1771 - 1783] From *Atlas Moderne* .... Paris: Lattre & Delalain. 43x30cm (17x12") Orig OL col. Ref: Phillips (A) 646. [59] £32 $50
CARTE ... NORMANDIE AVEC CELUI MAINE ET PERCHE [1771 - 1783] From *Atlas Moderne* .... Paris: Lattre & Delalain. 30x43cm (12x17") Orig OL color. Ref: Phillips (A) 646. [59] £32 $50

ISLE ET BANC DE TERRE NEUVE, ISLE ROYALE ET ISLE ST. JEAN; AVEC L'ACADIE OU LA NOUVELLE ECOSSE ... [c. 1788] 23x34cm (9x13½") Color. [40] £68 $105

ISLES ANTILLES OU DU VENT AVEC LES ISLES SOUS LE VENT [1782] Inset: Curacao, etc. 33x23cm (12½x8½") Orig OL color. [51] £97 $150

L'ANCIEN ET LE NOUVEAU MEXIQUE, AVEC LA FLORIDE ET LA BASSE LOUSIANE. PARTIE OCCIDENTALE [IN SET WITH] ... PARTIE ORIENTALE [c. 1771-1788] From Bonne & Demarest, *Atlas Encyclopedique*. 2 maps (also offered separately at $300 each). 36x23cm (13½x9½") Uncolored. VG+. Ref: Lowery 543 & 675. Phillips (A) 666. [59] £325 $500

L'ANCIEN ET LE NOUVEAU MEXIQUE, AVEC LA FLORIDE ET LA BASSE LOUSIANE [1781] Rio Grande & westward only. 36x23cm (14x9") Margins browned; sharp, clean. [10] £127 $195

L'ANCIEN MONDE ET LE NOUVEAU EN DEUX HEMISPHERES [c. 1780] "Etat Unis" named. 21x41cm (8½x16") B&W. [46] £49 $75

L'ISLE DE TERRE-NEUVE, L'ACADIE OU LA NOUVELLE ECOSSE, L'ISLE ST JEAN ET LA PARTIE ORIENTALE DU CANADA [1780] From Raynal, *Atlas de Toutes les Parties Connues du Globe* ... 21x32cm (8½x12½") [14] £55 $85

[SAME TITLE] [c. 1788] 21x31cm (8½x12") Color. [40] £95 $146

LE NOUVEAU MEXIQUE, AVEC LA PARTIE SEPTENTRIONALE DE L'ANCIEN, OU DE LA NOUVELLE ESPAGNE [1781] Louisiana to Baja. 21x32cm (8½x12½") Uncolored. [10] £127 $195

LES ETATS UNIS DE L'AMERIQUE SEPTENTRIONALE ... [1781] 33x23cm (12½x8½") OL color. Water stain into rt side. [9] £71 $110

LES ETATS UNIS DE L'AMERIQUE SEPTENTRIONALE CONTENANT EN OUTRE LES ISLES ROYALE, DE ST. JEAN E L'ACADIE, AVEC PARTIE DU CANADA, DE LA LOUISIANE ET DE LA FLORIDE [1781] 33x23cm (12½x8½") OL color. Exc. [29] £91 $140

LES ETATS UNIS DE L'AMERIQUE SEPTENTRIONALE, PARTIE OCCIDENTALE ... [1780's] From Bonne & Demarest, *Atlas Encyclopedique*. Andre, sc. Covers Mississippi & tributaries. 34x23cm (13½x9") Uncolored. VG. Ref: Sellers & Van Ee 794. [9] £162 $250

LES ETATS UNIS DE L'AMERIQUE SEPTENTRIONALE, PARTIE ORIENTALE PAR M. BONNE ... [IN SET WITH] ... PARTIE OCCIDENTALE ... [c. 1791] Atlantic to Mississippi River on 2 maps, each 36x25cm (14x10") OL color. Sl fold discoloration, one map; sm spot left; good. [44] £243 $375

LES ISLES PHILIPPINES, CELLE DE FORMOSE, LE SUD DE LA CHINE, LES ROYAUMES DE TUNKIN, DE COCHINCHINE, DE CAMBOGE, DE SIAM, DES LAOS; AVEC PARTIE DE CEUX DE PEGU ET D'AVA [1780] From Raynal *Atlas de Toutes les Parties...du Globe Terrestre*. 21x31cm (8x12½") Fine. [14] £49 $75

MAPPE-MONDE EN DEUX HEMISPHERES, L'ORIENTAL ET L'OCCIDENTAL [1782] 23x33cm (8½x13") Orig OL color. Superb. [51] £146 $225

MAPPE MONDE SUR LE PLAN D'UN MERIDIEN HEMISPHERE ORIENTAL [1787-1788] 23x34cm (9x13½") Color. [16] £109 $168

MAPPE MONDE SUR LE PLAN DE L'EQUATEUR HEMISPHERE MERIDIONALE [1787-1788] 24x35cm (9½x13½") Color. Ref: Tooley (Australia) 231. [16] £109 $168

MAPPE MONDE SUR UN PLAN HORISONTAL ... HEMISPHERE ORIENTAL [IN SET WITH] MAPPE MONDE SUR UN PLAN HORISONTAL ... HEMISPHERE OCCIDENTAL [1787-1788] From *Atlas Encyclopedique*. Paris: Bonne & Demarest. 2 sheets, each 25x36cm (10x14½") Fine. [14] £97 $150

NUBIE ET ABISSINIE [1771] 30x41cm (11½x16½") OL color. [36] £62 $95

[SAME TITLE] [1771 - 1783] From *Atlas Moderne* .... Paris: Lattre & Delalain. 30x43cm (12x17") Orig OL color. Ref: Phillips (A) 646. [59] £26 $40

PARTIE MERIDIONALE DE L'ANCIEN MEXIQUE ... [1772] Incl Central America. 23x33cm (8½x13") Clean. [12] £36 $55

PLANISPHERE SUIVANT LA PROJECTION DE MERCATOR [c. 1780] 21x32cm (8½x12½") Col. [16] £171 $263

SUPPLEMENT POUR LES ISLES ANTILLES EXTRAIT DES CARTES ANGLOISES [1778] Virgin Is. on sheet with 9 sm island plans. 32x21cm (12½x8½") Color. [27] £120 $185

BONNEVILLE

A MAP OF THE SOURCES OF THE COLORADO & BIG SALT LAKE, PLATTE, YELLOW-STONE, MUSCLE-SHELL, MISSOURI; & SALMON & SNAKE RIVERS, BRANCHES OF THE COLUMBIA RIVER [1837] From Washington Irving *The Rocky Mountains* ... Shows topography & river systems. 46x41cm (17½x16") Cleaned, laid on archival paper. Ref: Howes (US) I85. [9] £260 $400

[SAME TITLE] [same date & source] 1st ed. By S. Stiles. 41x41cm (16½x15½") No color. Tear repaired; lower rt margin trimmed; lt browning; good. Encapsulated. [18] £260 $400

MAP OF THE TERRITORY WEST OF THE ROCKY MOUNTAINS [1837] From Washington Irving *The Rocky Mountains* ... 46x41cm (17½x16") Cleaned, laid on archival paper. Ref: Howes (US) I85. Wheat (TM) 424; Wagner-Camp 67:3. [9] £276 $425

BORDONE
[CRETE] [1528 (1534)] From the *Isolario*. 2nd issue. 16x34cm (6½x13½") No c'fold damage; exc. [63] £422 $650

[CYPRUS] [1528-1547] From *Isolario*. 2nd printed map of Cyprus. 25x33cm (10x13") Orig color; sea in blue wash. Ref: Stylianou, 18. [53] £1,200 $1,848

[EUROPE] [1528+] From *Isolario*. With adjacent Africa & Asia. 28x38cm (11x15") Orig wash color. Bound with tab, not sewn; exc. [62] £617 $950

[WEST INDIES: ST. CROIX & ANTIQUA TO DOMINICA] [1534] From *Isolario ... de Tutte l'Isole del Mondo* ... Wood engraving on quarto page. 10x15cm (4x6") Ref: Sabin 6419. [27] £380 $585

IAVA MINORE [1528] From *Isolario*. Sumatra. 8x15cm (3x5½") on full text sheet. Exc. [63] £179 $275

TAVOLA SECONDO MODERNI [ON VERSO] TAVOLA SECONDO TOLOMEO [1528+] From *Isolario*. "Modern" & Ptolemaic England. 14x15 cm (5½x5½") and 23x16cm (9x6"). Fine. Ref: Shirley (BI to 1650) illus #19 & #20. [62] £227 $350

BORGHI
[WESTERN UNITED STATES] [1817] Florentine map of present MT, NE, ND, SD, WY. 22x29cm (8½x11½") Orig OL color. Exc. [62] £192 $295

BOTERO
REGNUM CHINAE [1596] First appeared in *Theatrum ... oder Schawspiegel*. 16x21cm (6½x8½") Exc. [62] £584 $900

BOUCHETTE
TO HIS MOST EXCELLENT MAJESTY KING WILLIAM IVTH THIS MAP OF THE PROVINCES OF LOWER & UPPER CANADA, NOVA SCOTIA, NEW BRUNSWICK, NEWFOUNDLAND, PRICE EDWARD ISLAND WITH A LARGE SECTION OF THE UNITED STATES ... [1831] London: Wyld; 1st ed. 3 sheets mounted on linen in sections. 99x191cm (39x75") 3 engraved colored views mounted on map. [28] £2,045 $3,150

BOUGAINVILLE
A CHART OF RIO DE LA PLATA [1773] English ed. Buenos Aires inset. 30x48cm (12½x19½") OL & wash color. [58] £65 $100

BOWEN, E.
... CHINESE TARTARY ... [SET OF 12 SHEETS] [1741] London: Regis, Jartoux & Fridelli. Autonomous regional sheets of northern China, such as "The Sixth ... Yu-pi Tartars, & Llan Hala ..." Most around 29x47cm (11½x18½") [14] £286 $440

... YE MAP OF TIBET ... [SET OF 9 SHEETS] [1741] London: P. Regis. Autonomous regional sheets, exemplified by "The First Sheet ... west end of ye Great Sandy Deserts about Ha-Mi ..." All around 45x30cm (17½x12") [14] £286 $440

A COMPLETE MAP OF THE SOUTHERN CONTINENT SURVEY'D BY CAPT. ABEL TASMAN [1744] 37x48cm (14½x19") OL color. Ref: Tooley (Australia) 241, pl.12; Clancy illus 136-7. [16] £2,849 $4,388

A MAP OF THE DIVISIONS & SITUATIONS OF THE TRIBES OF THE CANAANITES, MOABITES, AMMONITES, MIDIANITES, EDOMITES, AMALEKITES &C. BEFORE & AT YE TIME OF YE EXODUS OF YE CHILDREN OF ISRAEL, ACCORDING TO THIS HISTORY [1748] 28x28cm (11x11") Color. [23] £62 $95

A MAP OF THE JOURNEY IN THE WILDERNESS, AND OF THE CONQUEST AND PARTITION OF THE LAND OF CANAAN BY THE CHILDREN OF ISRAEL [1746] 30x26cm (12x10½") Color. [23] £71 $110

A NEW & ACCURATE MAP OF ASIA. DRAWN FROM ACTUAL SURVEYS ... BY EMMAN. BOWEN [c. 1747] 35x43cm (14x17") 2 sh tears lower margin; sm stain. [28] £146 $225

A NEW & ACCURATE MAP OF CHINA, DRAWN FROM SURVEYS MADE BY JESUIT MISSIONARIES ... [1762] 34x42cm (13½x16½") Sh fold split joined. [14] £91 $140

A NEW & ACCURATE MAP OF THE PROVINCE OF NORTH & SOUTH CAROLINA, GEORGIA &C. ... [1747] 35x43cm (14x17") Uncolored. Superb. Framed. Ref: Cumming (SE) #263. [51] £763 $1,175

A NEW AND CORRECT MAP OF AFRICA ... [1748] 37x45cm (14½x17½") B&W. Fine. [55] £162 $250

A NEW AND EXACT MAP OF ASIA [1784] 36x45cm (14½x17½") Fold splits joined. [14] £78 $120

A PLAN OF THE CITY OF JERUSALEM ACCORDING TO THE DESCRIPTION IN THE BOOKS OF THE OLD TESTAMENT BUT MORE ESPECIALLY IN THAT OF NEHEMIAH [1760] 40x41cm (16x16") Color. Minor repair. Ref: Laor 1182. [23] £78 $120

AN ACCURATE MAP OF THE EAST INDIES EXHIBITING THE COURSE OF THE EUROPEAN TRADE BOTH ON THE CONTINENT AND ISLANDS ... [c. 1747] 37x45cm (14½x18") OL col. Ref: Fell illus 5. [16] £328 $505

EUROPE [c. 1747] 33x43cm (13x16½") B&W. [46] £52 $80

GALLIA NARBONENSIS LUGDUNENSIS ET AQUITAINA [c. 1740] 20x30cm (8x12") Col. Exc. [29] £42 $65

MOREA ... GREECE ... AND ISLANDS [1747] 23x33cm (9x13") B&W. Fine. [46] £39 $60

THE GALLAPAGOS ISLANDS DISCOVERED AND DISCRIBED BY CAPT. COWLEY IN 1684 [1748] 32x20cm (12½x8") Uncolored. [52] £150 $231

BOWEN, T.

A CORRECT MAP OF THE COUNTRIES SURROUNDING THE GARDEN OF EDEN OR PARADISE WITH THE COURSE OF NOAH'S ARK DURING THE FLOOD, &C. [c. 1770] 28x18cm (11½x7") OL color. Minor spot rt margin; exc. [29] £42 $65

A CORRECT MAP OF THE UNITED STATES OF NORTH AMERICA, INCLUDING THE BRITISH AND SPANISH TERRITORIES, CAREFULLY LAID DOWN AGREEABLE TO THE TREATY OF 1784 BY T. BOWEN, GEOG. [c. 1784] 30x43cm (11½x16½") Uncolored. Ref: Phillips (M) p.865. [36] £162 $250

AN ACCURATE MAP OF THE HOLY LAND WITH THE ADJACENT COUNTRIES [c. 1770] 28x18cm (11½x7") OL color. Minor chips rt margin; exc. [29] £42 $65

BOWEN & GIBSON

NEW YORK AND PENSILVANIA [1758] From *Atlas Minimus* ... 6x10cm (2½x4") OL & wash color. Ref: Phillips (A) 621,41. [57] £65 $100

BOWLES

A DRAUGHT OF FALKLANDS ISLANDS ... [1770] Based on McBride's 1766 chart. 45x69cm (17½x27½") Orig OL color. [52] £420 $647

A MAP OF ROYAL ISLAND OR CAPE BRETON ... [ON SHEET WITH] THE TOWN AND HARBOUR OF LOUISBOURG ... [c.1745 - 1758] T. Bowles, J. Bowles & Son. 50x31cm (19½x12") Uncol. [53] £420 $647

A NEW & CORRECT MAP OF THIRTY MILES ROUND LONDON SHOWING ALL THE TOWNS, VILLAGES, ROADS &C, WITH THE SEAT OF THE NOBILITY & GENTRY ... [c. 1720] Thomas Bowles, London. Index at sides of circular plan. 64x94cm (25x37") Full color. Lt wear at margins; ink facsimile replacement of sl losses; mounted on board; VG. [21] £779 $1,200

BOWLES'S REDUCED NEW POCKET ATLAS OF THE CITIES OF LONDON AND WESTMINSTER, WITH THE BOROUGH OF SOUTHWARK, EXHIBITING THE NEW BUILDINGS TO THE YEAR 1781 [1781] Carrington Bowles. Folding map backed on linen in sections as issued; marbled slipcase. 38x53cm (15x21½") Orig color. Linen fold tear; slipcase worn. Ref: Howgego 168.3. [28] £133 $205

BOWYER

MAP OF THE ISLAND OF ELBA [1815] From R. Bowyer, *An Illustrated Record of Important Events in the Annals of Europe*. With view of Porto Ferrajo & Napoleon portrait. 33x23cm (13½x9") Orig col. Fine. [49] £185 $285

[SAME TITLE] [same date, source, dimen, color] [54] £220 $339

BRADFORD

[ATLAS] A COMPREHENSIVE ATLAS GEOGRAPHICAL, HISTORICAL & COMMERCIAL [1835] T.G. Bradford. Small folio. 77 maps (without Texas map) with orig OL color. Marbled boards, front almost detached; leather spine. Binding worn, bumped; Frontis soiled; few maps foxed; maps overall VG. [34] £552 $850

ALABAMA [1838] 49 counties. 36x29cm (14½x11½") Full color. [56] £88 $135

BOSTON [1838] 30x36cm (11½x14") Full col. Faint water stain one corner; else exc. [56] £65 $100

DISTRICT OF COLUMBIA [1835] With Alexandria & Georgetown. 25x19cm (10x7½") [36] £29 $45

FLORIDA [1835] Inset: West FL. 26x20cm (10x8") Orig OL color. Offsetting; sl marginal foxing; o/w VG. [4] £81 $125

[SAME TITLE] [c. 1835] No panhandle inset. [same dimen] Orig OL & yellow wash color. Sl offsetting; o/w VG. [4] £75 $115

[SAME TITLE] [1838] 20 counties; 2 grants. 36x30cm (14½x12") Full color. [56] £97 $150

[SAME TITLE] [1843] 17 counties. 26x20cm (10x8") OL color. [36] £81 $125

IOWA AND WISCONSIN [1838] Inset: IA to Canada. 36x29cm (14½x11½") Color. [56] £97 $150

LOUISIANA AND PART OF ARKANSAS [1843] From *Comprehensive Atlas*, 3rd ed. 26x20cm (10x8") OL color. [36] £39 $60
MAINE [1838 (1846)] 38x28cm (14½x11½") Orig pastel col. Sl narrow, chipped lower margin. [46] £42 $65
[SAME TITLE] [1843] From *Comprehensive Atlas*. 25x20cm (10x7½") With text page. OL col. [36] £45 $70
MASSACHUSETTS [1838] 29x36cm (11½x14") Full muted color. Some age toning. [51] £97 $150
MEXICO, GUATEMALA AND THE WEST INDIES [1835] 20x25cm (7½x10") Orig OL col. [46] £62 $95
MICHIGAN [1838] Upper Peninsula inset. 36x29cm (14x11½") Faint water stain lower lf. [56] £97 $150
MICHIGAN AND THE GREAT LAKES [1842] Incl WI 20x25cm (8x10") OL color. [58] £97 $150
[SAME TITLE] [1843] From *Comprehensive Atlas*, 3rd ed. [same dimen] OL color. [36] £65 $100
MISSISSIPPI & ALABAMA [same date & source] 20x26cm (8x10") OL color. [36] £36 $55
MISSOURI, ILLINOIS AND IOWA [1835] 25x20cm (10x8") OL color. [61] £55 $85
NEW HAMPSHIRE AND VERMONT [1835] 25x20cm (10x8") Color. [36] £36 $55
NORTH CAROLINA [1838] 28x36cm (11x14") Orig full color. Fine-. Ref: Phillips (A) 1381; Phillips (M) p.618. [59] £97 $150
TEXAS [1838] Texas Republic; Empressario Grants named, counties forming. 36x28cm (14½x11½") With accompanying text. [56] £422 $650
VIRGINIA [1838] 28x38cm (11½x15") Full color. [56] £84 $130
WASHINGTON [ON SHEET WITH] CINCINNATI [AND] LOUISVILLE [AND] NEW ORLEANS [1841] From *A Universal Illustrated Atlas* .... Charles D. Strong; Boston: Bradford & Goodrich. 28x36cm (11½x14½") Full color. VF. [20] £114 $175

BRADLEY   Try *Mitchell, S.A.   (Atlas Maps 1860 & later)*

[ATLAS] BRADLEY'S ATLAS OF THE WORLD FOR COMMERCIAL AND LIBRARY REFERENCE [1889] Phila: Wm. M. Bradley & Co. Folio. Half-leather covers worn; spine taped. 73 (of 75, lacking MN, Dakota) mostly double-page colored maps. Some margin browning; some c'fold tears; generally VG. [5] £438 $675
ARIZONA AND NEW MEXICO [1889] From *Atlas of the World*. 36x56cm (14½x22") Pastel col. [51] £81 $125
CALIFORNIA [1886] Wm. Bradley & Bro., Phila. 56x41cm (22x16½") Color. [51] £97 $150
COLORADO [1886] From *Atlas of the World*. 42x57cm (16½x22½") Pastel color. [51] £62 $95
COUNTY AND TOWNSHIP MAP OF MONTANA, IDAHO AND WYOMING [1884] Phila: S.A. Mitchell. 36x53cm (14x21") Full color. Lower margin & c'fold repairs; fine. [18] £49 $75
[SAME TITLE] [same date, dimen & color] Wm. Bradley & Bro. Lower margin & c'fold repairs; fine. [19] £49 $75
[SAME TITLE] [1887] 38x53cm (14½x21½") Full color. Fine. [18] £39 $60
COUNTY MAP OF FLORIDA [1882 / 1884] S.A. Mitchell derivative; S Florida inset. 28x37cm (11x14½") Orig wash color. [4] £26 $40
LOUISIANA [1889] Wm Bradley & Bro., Phila. 53x44cm (21x17") Color. [51] £62 $95
NEBRASKA [1889] Wm. M. Bradley & Bro. 42x57cm (16½x22½") Full color. [51] £62 $95
NORTHWESTERN AMERICA SHOWING THE TERRITORY CEDED BY RUSSIA TO THE UNITED STATES [1887] Wm. M. Bradley & Bro. 29x36cm (11½x14½") Full color. VG. [19] £39 $60
PLAN OF NEW ORLEANS [c. 1888] Reverse: partial LA. 20x25cm (8x9½") Full color. Good. [20] £32 $50

BRADSHAW

BRADSHAW'S MAP OF GREAT BRITAIN SHOWING THE RAILWAYS [1857] From *Bradshaw's Shareholders' Guide, Railway Manual* ... W.J. Adams; Bradshaw & Blacklock, London / Manchester. Ireland on verso. 89x66cm (34½x26") Uncolored. Good. [21] £81 $125
BRADSHAW'S MAP OF THE RHINE [1873] Basel to Rotterdam in 2 sections. 53x30cm (20½x12½") Some color. [58] £29 $45

BRAUN & HOGENBERG

[FACSIMILE ATLAS] CIVITATES ORBIS TERRARUM [1966] Cleveland: World Publishing Co. 6 folio vols in 3, from Peter von Brachel 1620 ed in University Library, Amsterdam. 546 tipped-in, double page town plans; 6 separate colored plans. Dust jackets, cloth boards. As new; fine. [7] £357 $550
[TITLE PAGE] CIVITATES ORBIS TERRARUM [1572-] Volume I. 36x22cm (14x9") Uncolored. Sm ink spot. [52] £150 $231
ALEXANDRIA [1572-1618] From *Civitates Orbis Terrarum*. 36x48cm (14x19") Orig col. [3] £487 $750
ALGERII ... [1572-1618] From *Civitates Orbis Terrarum*. Folio. Orig color. [3] £487 $750

ANCONA CIVITAS PICENI CELEBERRIMA AD MARE ADRIATICUM POSITA ... [c. 1574] 33x48cm (13½x19") Orig col. Margin tears & c'fold repaired; lower corners restored; margins discolored. [28] £263 $405

ANTIQUAE URBIS ROMAE IMAGO ACCURATISS: [1572-1618] From *Civitates Orbis Terrarum.* 2 folio sheets. Orig color. [3] £1,461 $2,250

ANVERPIA [1572] 34x48cm (13½x18½") Full orig color. Exc. Ref: Koeman B&H 1, #17. [62] £617 $950

[SAME TITLE] [1572-1618] From *Civitates Orbis Terrarum.* Folio. Orig color. [3] £779 $1,200

ARGENTORATUM STRASBURG ... [c. 1572] 36x43cm (13½x17") Old color. Lt margin foxing. Ref: Koeman II B&H 1. [28] £467 $720

AVIGNON [1572-1618] From *Civitates Orbis Terrarum.* Folio. Orig color. [3] £617 $950

[SAME TITLE] [1575] 31x47cm (12x18½") Full orig color. Exc. Ref: Koeman B&H 2, #13; Goss (Euro Cities) pl.5. [62] £438 $675

BARCELONA, BARCINO, QUE VULGO BARCELONA DICITUR [ON SHEET WITH] ECIJA [1572] 44x47cm (17½x18½") Full orig color. Repair at c'fold. Ref: Goss (Euro Cities) pl.6. [62] £357 $550

BERGEN OP ZOOM [1588] From *Civitates....* 38x34cm (15x13") Orig color. [52] £300 $462

BLOYS [FRANCE] [1572-1618] From *Civitates Orbis Terrarum.* Folio. Orig color. [3] £422 $650

BRIGHTSTOWE [1572 - 1617] From *Civitates ....* 33x44cm (13x17") Color. [52] £500 $770

BRUSXELLA, URBS AULICORUM FREQUENTIA, FONTIUM COPIA, MAGNIFICENTIA PRINCIPALIS AULAE ... [1572] 34x48cm (13x18½") Full modern color. Exc. Ref: Goss (Euro Cities) pl.12. [62] £357 $550

BUDA, VULGO OFEN, PRIMA ET REGIA UNGARICI REGNI CIVITAS, AD DANUBIUM SITA; QUAM PTOLEMAEUS CURTAM, VEL, UT ALIIS PERSUASUM EST, SALNUM NOMINAT. FRAN JRE. [1572] 15x47cm (6x18½") Full orig color. Original "missing" lower lf corner as from plate; exc. Ref: Koeman B&H 1. [62] £357 $550

BYZANTIUM, NUNC CONSTANTINOPOLIS [1572-1618] From *Civitates ...* Folio. Orig col. [3] £1,169 $1,800

CAIRUS, QUAE OLIM BABYLON; AEGYPTI MAXIMA URBS [1572] From *Civitates Orbis Terrarum.* 33x48cm (13x19") Color, heightened with gold. Sm repair; else VG. [39] £487 $750

[SAME TITLE] [1572-1618] From *Civitates Orbis Terrarum.* Folio. Orig color. [3] £1,039 $1,600

CALECHUT CELEBERRIMUM INDIAE EMPORIUM [ON SHEET WITH] ORMUS [AND] CANONOR [AND] S. GEORGII [1572] 34x48cm (13½x18½") Full orig color. Exc. [63] £276 $425

CANDIA [ON SHEET WITH] LA CITA DE CORPHU [1572-1618] From *Civitates Orbis Terrarum.* Folio. Orig color. [3] £974 $1,500

[SAME TITLE] [1575] [same source]. Iraklion; Corfu. 38x48cm (14½x19") Full color. Faint printer's crease; exc. [39] £617 $950

CANTEBRIGIA, OPULENTISSIMI ANGLIE REGNI ... [1575] From *Civitates Orbis Terrarum.* 33x45cm (13x17½") Color. VG. Ref: Goss (Euro Cities) pl.15. [39] £617 $950

[SAME TITLE] [1572 - 1617] [same source & dimen] Color. [52] £750 $1,155

[SAME TITLE] [1572-1618] [same source & dimen] Orig color. [3] £552 $850

CESTRIA (VULGO CHESTER) ANGLIAE CIVITAS [1572 - 1617] From *Civitates ....* 33x43cm (13x17") Color. [52] £500 $770

CIVITAS EXONIAE (VULGO EXCESTER) [1572-1618] From *Civitates ...* Folio. Orig color. [3] £617 $950

COLONIAE AGRIPPINA [1572] Cologne. 34x48cm (13½x18½") Full orig color. Exc. Ref: Koeman B&H 1, #38. [62] £617 $950

DOUAY DUACUM CATUACORUM URBS ... [c. 1588] 33x41cm (13x16") Lt foxing side margins. Ref: Koeman II B&H 3. [28] £234 $360

EDENBURGUM, SCOTIAE METROPOLIS [1581] From *Civitates Orbis Terrarum.* 34x45cm (13½x18") Orig color. C'fold repair; lt staining; overall VG. Ref: Goss (Euro Cities) pl.18 [39] £584 $900

[SAME TITLE] [1572 - 1617] [same source same dimen] Color. [52] £750 $1,155

FRIBERGUM MISINAE [1572 - 1617] [same source] 33x46cm (13x18") Orig full col. VG-. [59] £292 $450

GADES AB OCCIDUIS INSULAE PARTIBUS ANNO 1564 [1598] From *Civitates Orbis Terrarum.* Cadiz view with vignettes. 37x49cm (14½x19½") Full later color. Exc. [63] £617 $950

GENUA [ON SHEET WITH] FLORENTIA URBS EST INSIGNIS HETRUARIAE, OLIM FLUENTIA DICTA [1572] About 32x48cm (12½x19") Full orig col. Exc. Ref: Goss (Euro Cities) pl.22; Koeman B&H 1, 44. [62] £909 $1,400

[SAME TITLE] [1572-1618] From *Civitates Orbis Terrarum.* Folio. Orig color. [3] £974 $1,500

GOA FORTISSIMA INDIAE URBS IN CHRISTIANORUM POTESTATEM ANNO SALUTIS 1509 DEVENIT [ON SHEET WITH] DIU [AND] AZAAMURUM [AND] ANFA [1572] 34x47cm (13½x18½") Full orig col.or. Exc. [63] £227 $350

GRANADA 1563 [1572] From *Civitates Orbis Terrarum*. 33x51cm (13x20½") Full orig color. Lt toning; else exc. [39] £487 $750
GRANATA [1598] From *Civitates Orbis Terrarum*. 37x50cm (14½x19½") Full color. Exc. [63] £552 $850
HAEC EST NOBILIS, & FLORENS ILLA NEAPOLIS ... [1572] From *Civitates Orbis Terrarum*. 33x48cm (13x19") Full color. Exc. Ref: Goss (Euro Cities) pl.37. [39] £779 $1,200
HIEROSOLYMA, CLARISSIMA TOTIUS ORIENTIS CIVITAS IUDAEE METROPOLIS [1572] From *Civitates Orbis Terrarum*. 2 aerial views: Biblical period; 16th cent. 34x48cm (13½x19") Full color, heightened with gold. Exc. Ref: Laor 1039. [39] £844 $1,300
IERUSALEM, ET SUBURBIA EIUS, SICUT TEMPORE CHRISTI FLORUIT, CU LOCIS IN QUIB CHRIST PASS ... DESCRIPTA PER CHRISTIANUM ADRICHOM DELPHUM [1588] From *Civitates Orbis Terrarum*. 2 sheets, each 38x48cm (14½x19") Orig color. Fine. Ref: Humphreys p.107. Nebenzahl (Holy Land) pp.90-1. [1] £1,298 $2,000
[SAME TITLE] [1588] 36x48cm (14x19") One of a matched pair. Col. Ref: Laor 1041. [23] £250 $385
JERUSALEM, ET SUBURBIA EIUS SICUT TEMPORE CHRISTI FLORUIT, CUM LOCIS IN QUIBUS CHRISTUS PASSUS ... DESCRIPTA PER CHRISTIANUM ADRICHOM DELPHUM [1588] Two sheets, each about 35x48cm (14x19") Full orig color. Some repair; generally fine. Koeman B&H 4, 58/59. [62] £1,039 $1,600
[SAME TITLE] [1588] Two sheets forming vertical plan, each about 34x48cm (13½x19") Full orig color. Mint. [63] £1,688 $2,600
LE BRIXA [ON SHEET WITH] SETTENIL [1572-1618] From *Civitates* ... Folio. Orig col. [3] £487 $750
[SAME TITLE] [c. 1583] 32x41cm (12½x16") Modern color. Sm wormholes; sh lower c'fold split. Ref: Koeman II B&H 3 & 15. [28] £250 $385
LONDINUM FERACISSIMI ANGLIAE REGNI METROPOLIS [1572 - 1617] From *Civitates* .... 34x49cm (13½x19") Color. [52] £1,850 $2,849
LUTETIA VULGARI NOMINE PARIS, URBS GALLIAE MAXIMA, SEQUANA NAVIGABILI FLUMINE IRRIGATUR ... [1572] From *Civitates Orbis Terrarum*. 36x48cm (13½x19") Early color. Lt toned; else exc. Ref: Goss (Euro Cities) pl.44. [39] £1,169 $1,800
[SAME TITLE] [same date & dimen] Full orig color. Repaired tears, mainly margin; generally fine. Ref: Goss (Euro Cities) pl.22; Koeman B&H 1, #7. [62] £876 $1,350
[SAME TITLE] [1572-1618] [same dimen] Orig color. [3] £2,272 $3,500
MAGNIFICA ILLA CIVITAS VERONA [ON SHEET WITH] COLONIA AUGUSTA VERONA NOVA GALIENIANA VERONA, CELEBERRIMA, AMPLISSIMAQUE CENOMANORUM URBS, PTOLEMAEO [1588] Two views. About 36x47cm (14x18½") Full orig color. Exc. Ref: Koeman B&H 3, #49. [62] £617 $950
MANTUA [1572-1618] From *Civitates Orbis Terrarum*. Folio. Orig color. [3] £617 $950
MARSEILLE [1572-1618] From *Civitates Orbis Terrarum*. Folio. Orig color. [3] £487 $750
MEXICO, REGIA ET CELEBRIS HISPANIAE NOVAE CIVITAS... [ON SHEET WITH] CUSCO, REGNI PERU IN NOVO ORBE CAPUT. [1572] From *Civitates* .... 27x47cm (10½x18½") Color. Exc. [39] £1,298 $2,000
[SAME TITLE] [same date, source & dimen] B&W. [46] £422 $650
MISENA, HERMUNDUROUM URBS [c. 1575] 33x48cm (13x19") Ref: Koeman II B&H 2. [28] £263 $405
MOSCAVW [1572] From *Civitates Orbis Terrarum*. 36x48cm (14x19½") Orig color. [3] £909 $1,400
NEAPOLIS [1572-1618] From *Civitates Orbis Terrarum*. Folio. Orig color. [3] £812 $1,250
NITIDISSIMAE CIVITATIS MECHLINEENSIS ... [1578] 33x46cm (13x18") Old color. C'fold splits; spots of color weak at c'fold. Ref: Koeman II B&H 3. [28] £279 $430
NORDOVICUM ANGLIAE CIVITAS [1572 - 1617] From *Civitates* .... 29x42cm (11½x16½") Orig color. [52] £400 $616
NULLUS IN ORBE LOCUS BAIIS PRAELUCET AMOENIS [1588] From *Civitates Orbis Terrarum*. Naples & Ischia. Elaborate surround; reference key. 34x48cm (13x19") Full orig col. Sm chip replaced upper rt. [63] £276 $425
OENIPONS, SIVE ENIPONTIUS VULGO INSSPRUCK, TIROLENSIS COMITATUS URBS AMPLISSIMA MDLXXV [1575] 34x44cm (13x17") Full orig color. Exc. Ref: Koeman B&H 2, #42. [62] £617 $950
ORLEANS [ON SHEET WITH] BOURGES [1572-1618] From *Civitates* .... Folio. Orig col. [3] £487 $750
OSTIA [ITALY] [1572-1618] From *Civitates Orbis Terrarum*. Folio. Orig color. [3] £487 $750
OXONIUM NOBILE ANGLEI OPPIDUM [ON SHEET WITH] VINDESORIUM CELEBERRIMUM ANGLIAE CASTRUM ... [1575] From *Civitates* .... 36x48cm (14x19") Color. Exc. Ref: Goss (Euro Cities) pl.42. [39] £617 $950
[SAME TITLE] [1572 - 1617] Oxford; Windsor. 36x49cm (14x19½") Uncolored. [52] £600 $924
[SAME TITLE] [1572-1618] From *Civitates Orbis Terrarum*. Folio. Orig color. [3] £1,233 $1,900
PALERMO [1572-1618] From *Civitates Orbis Terrarum*. Folio. Orig color. [3] £503 $775

ROMA [1572] From *Civitates Orbis Terrarum*. 33x48cm (13x19") Orig color. [3] £1,233 $1,900
[SAME TITLE] [same date & dimen] Full orig color. Exc. Ref: Koeman B&H 1, #45; Goss (Euro Cities) pl.46. [62] £941 $1,450
[SAME TITLE] [same date & dimen] From *Civitates* .... Full orig color. Fine. [63] £812 $1,250
[SAME TITLE] [1575] [same source & dimen] Full color. Exc. [39] £779 $1,200
SANTANDER [1575] From *Civitates Orbis Terrarum*. 32x35cm (12½x14") Orig color. [52] £380 $585
[SAME TITLE] [same date, source & dimen] View. Full color. Exc. [63] £373 $575
SEVILLA [1588] 36x48cm (14x19") Full orig color. Ref: Koeman B&H 4, #2; Goss (Euro Cities) pl.50. [62] £487 $750
SEVILLA HISPALIS [1598] 3rd & last view in 38x50cm (15x19½") Full orig color. Exc. [63] £617 $950
SLUSA, TEUTONICAE FLANDRIAE OPP. ADMODUM ELEGANS. [c. 1583] 29x41cm (11½x16") Pinholes upper margin. Ref: Koeman II B&H 4 & 15. [28] £221 $340
SNEECHA, VULGO SNEEK FRISIAE OCCIDENTALIS ... SLOTEN. DOCCUM. YISTA. [c. 1590] 36x41cm (14x16") Modern color. Sm wormholes top margin. Ref: Koeman II B&H 4 & 16. [28] £279 $430
STOCKHOLM / STOCHOLM [1572] From *Civitates Orbis Terrarum*. 2 horiz views. 33x48cm (13x18½") Orig color. [3] £974 $1,500
[SAME TITLE] [1588] [same source & dimen]. Color. Exc. Ref: Goss (Euro Cities) pl. 52. [39] £779 $1,200
TIBURTUM VOLGO TIVOLI [1572-1618] From *Civitates* .... Folio. Orig color. [3] £325 $500
TOLETUM [1598] From *Civitates* .... Bird's-eye view. 37x50cm (14½x19½") Full col. Exc. [63] £974 $1,500
TOPOGRAPHIA INSULAE HUENAE [1586-] From *Civitates* .... Hven, Tycho Brahe's observatory island. 34x48cm (13½x19") Orig color. [52] £520 $801
VENETIA [1572] 34x48cm (13x19") Full orig color. Lower c'fold mended; old stain trace; else fine. Ref: Koeman B&H 1, #43; Goss (Euro Cities) pl.55. [62] £1,169 $1,800
[SAME TITLE] [1572] From *Civitates* .... 33x48cm (13½x19") Orig color. [3] £1,785 $2,750
VIENNA AUSTRIA METROPOLIS, URBS TOTO ORBE NOTISSIMA CELEBRATISSIMAQ, UNICUM HODIE IN ORIENTE CONTRA SAEVISSIMUM TURCAM INVICTUM PROPUGNACVIUM [1572] View. 15x47cm (6x18½") Full orig color. Exc. Ref: Koeman B&H 1. [62] £422 $650
ZURYCH. TIGARUM SIVE TUREGUM, CAESARI, UT PLERIQUE EXISTIMANT, TIGURINUS PAGUS, VULGO ZURYCH [1588] 37x48cm (14½x18½") Full orig color. Exc. Ref: Koeman B&H 3, #44. Goss (Euro Cities) pl.60. [62] £1,039 $1,600

BRETEZ
PLAN DE PARIS ... DESSINE ET GRAVE SOUS LES ORDRES DE MICHEL ETIENNE TURGOT [1739] 20 bound sheets & key sheet; shows every structure. (no dims.) [39] £4,869 $7,500

BRIET
LA DIVISION DE L'OCEAN DU NOUVEAU MONDE [(1648)] Americas; insular Calif. 19x14cm (7½x5½") Uncolored, except pale cartouche wash. Lower rt margin folded; close lf margin; VG. [31] £390 $600

BRION DE LA TOUR
AMERIQUE SEPTENTRIONALE DIVISEE EN SES PRINCIPALES PARTIES, OU SONT DISTINGUES LES UNS DES AUTRES ... [1783] Paris: Desnos. Jaillot substantially revised. 46x64cm (18x25") Orig color. Trace of foxing. [28] £701 $1,080
GUAYANE TERRE FERME, ISLES ANTILLES ET NLLE. ESPAGNE [1790] Text at sides. 28x48cm (11x19") Orig OL color. [14] £65 $100
L'IRLANDE DIVISEE PAR PROVINCES CIVILES ET ECCLESIASTIQUES [1790] From *Geographe Moderne*. Paris: Chez Desnos. Text at sides. 48x28cm (19x11½") Color. [24] £107 $165
LA JUDEE OU PALESTINE DRESSEE POUR L'INTELLIGENCE DE L'HISTOIRE SAINTE [1767] 28x30cm (11x12") Color. Ref: Laor 131. [23] £97 $150
MAPPE-MONDE DRESSE POUR L'ETUDE DE LA GEOGRAPHIE ... [1786] Double hemisphere; "Sea of West". 23x28cm (9½x10½") Color. Fine. [55] £292 $450

BRITISH ADMIRALTY
[ARCTIC REGIONS] [1818 (1829)] Polar projection. HO; watermarked dated 1830. (1835 updated edition offered at same price.) 61x61cm (24x24") Sl chipping; dust soiling one margin; generally good, clean. [15] £800 $1,232
[ATLAS] PILOT CHARTS FOR ATLANTIC OCEAN [1868] 5 charts covering N & S Atlantic, plus "Ice Chart of Southern Ocean". 94x65cm (37x25½") Orig half calf Admiralty binding, good except hinge wormy; contents mint. [14] £617 $950

[ATLAS] QUARTERLY CURRENT CHARTS FOR THE PACIFIC OCEAN [1897] Large folio with 4 charts: Nos. 2957-2960. Cloth wrappers soiled; charts unspoiled. [14] £114 $175

[ATLAS] WIND AND CURRENT CHARTS FOR THE PACIFIC, ATLANTIC AND INDIAN OCEANS [1872] Large folio, cloth wraps; 5 double page & 10 smaller data charts; with Chart No.2640. Wrappers soiled; charts unspoiled. [14] £114 $175

[CANADA: ST. LAWRENCE RIVER. POINT DES MONTS TO QUEBEC ON SET OF 7 SHEETS] SHEET 1. POINT DE MONTS TO BERSIMIS RIVER ... SHEET 7. QUEBEC AND ISLE OF ORLEANS [1837 - 1874] Bayfield, 1827-1834, HO #311-317. Each 46x64cm (18x24½") [15] £500 $770

... PLAN OF THE HARBOUR OF FOWEY LAID DOWN FROM ACTUAL SURVEY BY MR. GEORGE THOMAS ... [1813, c.1826] Thomas, 1811; HO #1813. 76x58cm (30x23") Offsetting. [15] £160 $246

A CHART OF BAFFIN'S BAY, WITH DAVIS & BARROW STRAITS; BY CAPTN. ROSS & LIEUT. PARRY R.N. IN 1818, 19 & 20, AND THE DISCOVERIES OF CAPTN. PARRY IN 1822 AND 23; & CAPTN. LYON IN 1824 [1822 (1824)] 61x46cm (24x18") Upper edge chipped; generally VG. [15] £700 $1,078

A CHART OF PART OF THE COAST OF DEVONSHIRE ... [1826, c.1840] Orig pub by Faden; HO #25. 58x78cm (23x30½") Deckle-edge; fine. [15] £320 $493

A PLAN OF THE ESTABLISHMENT OF CLARENCE IN THE ISLAND OF FERNANDO PO ... [1828] Badgley; Hydrographical Office. 61x94cm (24x37") Sl browning & offsetting; generally exc. [15] £240 $370

A PLAN OF THE PORT AND BAY IN THE ISLAND OF MAHE ... [SEYCHELLES] [1828] 46x58cm (17½x23½") [15] £180 $277

A SURVEY OF PORT EL ROQUE, COAST OF TERRA FIRMA ... [1828] Johns, 1827. 28x41cm (11x16") Sl reduced margins. [15] £200 $308

A SURVEY OF THE KEYS AND SHOALS IN THE MIRA-POR-VOS PASSAGE ... [1828] De Mayne, 1827 30x46cm (12x18") Sl reduced margins, sm loss at blank edge. [15] £180 $277

ABERDEEN HARBOUR [1843 (1857)] Slater, 1833; HO #1446. 48x61cm (19x24") Lt pencil grid over most of chart. Dust soiling; repaired margin tears. [15] £45 $69

ANCHORAGES IN THE NEW HEBRIDES [1894 (1895)] Adm #856. 7 plans. 46x66cm (18x26") [15] £40 $62

ANCHORAGES ON THE EAST COAST OF JURA [1855 (1874)] The Small Isles; farms named. Bedford, 1853; HO #2374. 43x36cm (17x14") [15] £30 $46

ARBROATH [1885] Tizard, 1884; Adm #1445. 38x48cm (15x19") Sh repaired edge tear. [15] £35 $54

BASS STRAIT [1868 (1892)] Stokes, HMS Beagle, 1839-43; Adm #1695. 2 sheets, each 97x66cm (38x25½") Dampmarking; lower edge tears repaired, sm loss at corner. [15] £190 $293

BAY BULLS [NEWFOUNDLAND] [1899] Hughes, 1898; Adm #3046. Inset: Cape Spear. 46x66cm (18x26") [15] £32 $49

BAY OF THE SEVEN ISLANDS [1838, c.1845] Bayfield; HO #1135. 46x60cm (18x23½") Fine. [15] £110 $169

BOON POINT TO PELICAN POINT [ANTIGUA] [1852] Barnett; HO #2066. 64x94cm (24½x37") [15] £300 $462

BRADORE BAY [QUEBEC] [1892] Tooker, 1891; Adm #1137. 46x66cm (18x26") [15] £32 $49

CAMPBELTON LOCH [1892] Adm #1864. 46x64cm (18x25") Surface soiling in margin. [15] £35 $54

CAPE FERRAT TO CAPE CARBON [ALGERIA] [1846] HO #1766. 48x64cm (18½x24½") Lt browning; sm chip lower margin. [15] £55 $85

CARLISLE BAY TO ST. JOHN'S HARBOUR [ANTIGUA] [1852] Barnett, 1848; HO #2099. 64x94cm (24½x37") [15] £300 $462

CHALA POINT TO KWYHOO BAY [KENYA] [1847] Owen, 1824; HO #1811. 64x48cm (25x19") [15] £200 $308

CHANG TAU HARBOUR AND APPROACHES [1898] Moore; Adm #2974. 48x66cm (19½x26") [15] £45 $69

CHART OF THE COAST OF FRANCE FROM BANDUFF TO RIOU ISLE [1826 (1835)] Hydrographical Office. 46x61cm (17½x23½") [15] £70 $108

CHART OF THE SEYCHELLE ISLANDS BY THE OFFICERS OF H.M. SHIPS LEVEN & BARRACOUTA UNDER...CAPT. W.F.W. OWEN R.N. [1828] Watermark dated. 46x64cm (18x24½") Sl reduced margins. [15] £200 $308

CHART OF THE TRACK AND DISCOVERIES OF THE EAST INDIA COMPANY'S CRUIZERS PANTHER & ENDEAVOUR UNDER THE COMMAND OF LIEUT. JOHN McCLUER, 1790, 1791 & 1792 [c. 1828] Dalrymple, 1792; Hydrographic Office. 30x51cm (12x19½") Sl reduced margins, few sm edge chips; o/w exc. [15] £200 $308

CHATEAU BAY [LABRADOR] [1892] Tooker, 1891; Adm #1151. 46x66cm (18x26") [15] £32 $49

CHINA SHEET I SOUTH COAST FROM HAINAN ID. TO MACAO [IN SET WITH] CHINA SHEET II FROM MACAO TO NAMOA [AND] CHINA SHEET III EAST COAST FROM NAMOA TO HAITAN ISLAND [AND] CHINA SHEET IV EAST COAST FROM HAITAN ISLAND TO THE KWESAN ISLANDS [1840] 4 of 5 sheets in 1st series covering Hainan to north of Yangze. HO #1246-9. Each about 46x61cm (18x24") Some narrow margins; lt soiling; generally good. [15] £500 $770

CLAYOQUOT SOUND, VANCOUVER ISLAND [1898] Richards; Adm #1835. 64x97cm (25x38") [15] £40 $62
DORO CHANNEL TO GULF OF SALONIKI [1896 (1900)] Graves, Brock & Spratt, 1838-48; no.426. 64x97cm (25x38") Cancelled library stamps; good. [15] £28 $43
ELLIS BAY IN THE ISLAND OF ANTICOSTI [1828, c.1845] Bayfield, 1828; HO #308. 27x22cm (10½x8½") Fine. [15] £110 $169
ENTRANCE TO SIERRA LEONE RIVER [1900] Purey-Cust, 1899; Adm #3147. Freetown layout. 66x99cm (26x39") [15] £50 $77
ENTRANCE TO THE CHOU-KIANG OR CANTON RIVER FROM THE OUTER ISLANDS TO LINTIN [IN SET WITH] CHOU-KIANG OR CANTON RIVER FROM LINTIN TO THE SECOND BAR [1840] Hong Kong to Canton approach. Ross, 1815; HO #1254 & #1263. Each 48x64cm (18½x24½") Surface soiling, dust marking; 2 large brown marks on outer chart. [15] £700 $1,078
ENTRANCES TO THE SALM AND JOOMBAS RIVERS ON THE WEST COAST OF AFRICA [1831] Boteler, 1828. Orig uncorrected 1830 watermark printing. 28x28cm (11½x11½") Sm loss at margin corner. [15] £75 $116
FALMOUTH AND ENGLISH HARBOURS [ANTIGUA] [1850] Barnett, 1847; HO #2014. 61x46cm (24½x18") Dust marking, brown spotting left margin; o/w VG. [15] £370 $570
GASPAR STRAIT CHIEFLY FROM SURVEYS PUBLISHED BY THE NETHERLANDS GOVERNMENT TO 1800 [1884] Evans. 97x64cm (38x25") Heavy paper; 3 sm spots; clean. [7] £49 $75
GASPE AND MAL BAYS [1838, c.1845] Bayfield, 1832; HO #1163. 59x46cm (23½x18") Fine. [15] £110 $169
GHUBBET SOGHRA [1894] Adm #2161, after Italian gov't plan. 48x66cm (19x26") [15] £35 $54
GUASOPA HARBOUR, KIRIWINA ISLANDS [1896] Arguimbau & Reeves, 1895; Adm #2641. 46x66cm (18x26") [15] £35 $5
GYNFELIN PATCHES, ABERYSTWITH AND NEW-QUAY [1843 (1859)] Sheringham, 1835; HO #1486. Show town & farms. 46x64cm (18x24½") [15] £80 $12
HARTLEPOOL BAY [1847] Slater. Dock area progress; HO #1628. 91x61cm (36x24") Exc. [15] £140 $21
HEAD OF THE GULF OF NAUPLIA [1900] Gedge, 1899; no.1308. 46x66cm (18x26") Cancelled library stamps; good. [15] £28 $4
HELGOLAND [1856 (1874)] Cudlip, 1855; HO #126. 97x64cm (37½x24½") Browning, minor edge tears o/w VG. [15] £80 $12
ILFRACOMBE HARBOUR [1839] Denham; H.O. no.1158. 25x23cm (10x9") Cancelled lib stamp in margin margins reduced, sh edge tears repaired. [15] £60 $9
INDEX TO THE CHARTS OF THE COAST OF CHINA [1840] HO #1262. 64x48cm (25x19") 1841 pencile ship's track. Lt soiling; narrow margins, lower left trimmed to neat line. [15] £140 $21
KINGSTOWN HARBOUR [1843 (1865)] Frazer; HO #1471. 61x48cm (24x18½") Weakened in places browning & surface soiling; appearance good. [15] £45 $6
LAKE ERIE [1864 (1875)] Bayfield; US surveys, 1849; Adm #332. 64x94cm (25x36½") [15] £140 $210
LAKE HURON [1865 (1874)] Bayfield, 1822; USCS, 1856-60; Adm #519. 99x66cm (38½x26") [15] £90 $139
LAKE NYASA [1900] Rhodes & Phillips. 2 sheets: Adm #3134-5. Each 114x66cm (45x26") [15] £90 $139
LAKE ONTARIO AND THE BACK COMMUNICATION WITH LAKE HURON [1838 (1874)] Owen, 1817; HO #1152. 61x94cm (23½x36½") [15] £175 $270
LOUGH REE ON THE RIVER SHANNON [1844 (c. 1900)] Wolfe & Beechey, 1837; HO #1572 89x56cm (35x22") Repaired margin tear, no loss; library stamp lower margin. [15] £100 $154
LUNDY ISLAND [1880 (1893)] Stanley, 1879; Adm #36. 48x64cm (19x25½") Sl crease lower margin & edge chipped. [15] £35 $54
MACQUARIE HARBOUR [TASMANIA] [1845] King, 1819; Evans, 1822; watermark dated, HO #1629. 48x61cm (18½x24") [15] £300 $462
MILFORD HAVEN [1831 (c. 1846)] Denham; HO #38. 48x61cm (19x24½") Deckle-edge. Fine. [15] £120 $185
[SAME TITLE] [1831 (1852)] Carr Light vessel removed. [same dimen] Deckle-edge. Fine. [15] £100 $154
NINETY MILES BEACH TO OTAGO [NEW ZEALAND] [1857 (1872)] Stokes, 1849-511 Adm #2532. 94x64cm (36½x24½") Staining & dust soiling, mostly in margins. [15] £80 $123
NORTH SUNDERLAND HARBOUR [1847] Slater, 1840; HO #1632. 64x48cm (24½x18½") Edges sl browned; generally exc. [15] £120 $185
PART OF THE CHANNEL BETWEEN THE ISLE OF WIGHT AND HAMPSHIRE ... [1808] Mackenzie, 1781; HO #18. 64x97cm (25x37½") Fine [15] £380 $585
PART OF THE NORTH EAST COAST OF AFRICA, IN THE GULPH OF ADEN, FROM CAPE KURRUM TO BURBURRA ... [WITH] A SURVEY OF PORT BURBURRA ON THE NORTH EAST COAST OF AFRICA ... [1828] Row, 1827; H.O. 2 plans, each about 23x28cm (8½x11") [15] £150 $231

PEKOA CHANNEL AND WAWA CHANNEL, ESPIRITU SANTO IS., NEW HEBRIDES [1894] Purey-Cust, 1892; Adm #1487. 64x97cm (25x38") [15] £35 $54

PENANG OR PRINCE OF WALES ISLAND [1840 (1874)] Woore, 1832+; HO #1366. 61x48cm (24½x18½") General soiling; repaired 9" tear, no surface loss. [15] £75 $116

PLAN AND VIEW OF THE ISLAND FERNANDO NORONHA ... [1811 (1828)] Dalrymple, 1781. 30x33cm (11½x13") Sl reduced margins. [15] £100 $154

PLAN OF SPENCER'S BAY ON THE WEST COAST OF AFRICA [1796, 1810] 28x15cm (11½x6") Crease mark; cancelled library stamp in margin. Ref: Kinahan, *By Command of their Lordhips,* 1992. [15] £85 $131

PLAN OF THE AFRICAN ISLANDS FROM THE OBSERVATIONS OF LIEUT CAMPBELL OF H.M. SCHOONER SPITFIRE BY CHAS. SHAKLETON [ON SHEET WITH] PLAN OF THE AFRICAN ISLANDS TAKEN ON BOARD THE FRENCH FRIGATE, LA CHIFFONNE, CAPT. GUIEYSSE [1811 (1816)] Dalrymple, 1805. Printed on verso, "The Harbour of Bahia or St. Salvador on the Coast of Brazil", Hydrographic Office, 1816. 30x23cm (11½x8½") [15] £90 $139

PLAN OF THE INLETS OF FERROL CORUNA AND BETANZOS ... [1823 (1873)] HO #79. 43x56cm (17½x22½") Linen-backed. 2 wormholes; o/w good, clean. [15] £30 $46

PLAN OF THE PORT OF TCHESME IN THE STRAIT OF SCIO ... [1808] 30x28cm (11½x10½") [15] £45 $69

PLANS OF ANCHORAGES IN THE GRECIAN ARCHIPELAGO (PSARA ISLAND, PURNEA BAY LEMNOS, STRATI ISLAND, KASTRO LEMNOS) [1897] Copeland, 1835; no.1891. 46x66cm (18x26") Cancelled library stamps; good. [15] £28 $43

PLANS OF PORTS IN WALES ... [1843 (1859)] Sheringham, 1838; HO #1485. Fishguard, Cardigan & Newport. 48x61cm (18½x24") Color. [15] £110 $169

PORT AU PORT [NEWFOUNDLAND] [1897] Tooker, 1893-5; Adm #422. 64x97cm (25x38") [15] £32 $49

PORTS IBRAHIM AND THEWFIK [SUEZ] [1901] Purey-Cust, 1900; Adm #3214. 66x48cm (26x19") Cancelled library stamp. [15] £45 $69

RIO DE JANEIRO HARBOUR [1858] De Lamare, 1847; Stanley, 1857; HO #541. 95x62cm (37x24½") Few sm edge tears; good, clean. [15] £340 $524

RIVER DULCE IN GUATEMALA [1839] Owen, 1834; HO #1207. 48x61cm (18½x24") [15] £180 $277

RIVER GABOON [1893] Adm #1877. Libreville inset. 64x97cm (25x38") [15] £35 $54

RU RUAG TO GRUINARD BAY INCLUDING LOCH EWE AND GAIRLOCH [1857 (1900)] Adm 2509. 97x64cm (37½x24½") [15] £25 $39

ST. HELENA ISLAND [1846] Barnes, 1816; H.O. no.1771. 46x61cm (18x24") Lt paper for inclusion in publication. Fold lines; edge tear to engraved area. [15] £90 $139

ST. JOHN'S HARBOUR TO BOON POINT [ANTIGUA] [1852] Barnett, 1848; HO #2065. 4 views. 64x94cm (24½x37") Browning & offsetting. [15] £300 $462

ST. MARY'S POOL [1898] Maxwell, 1897; Adm #3014; Steval to Carn Morval Point. 36x28cm (13½x10½") Surface soiling & discoloration. [15] £30 $46

SHEET 1 POINT DE MONTS TO BERSIMIS RIVER [ST. LAWRENCE RIVER] [1837, c.1845] Bayfield, 1827-1834, HO #311. 46x64cm (18x25") Minor edge tears; generally exc. [15] £120 $185

SHEET 3 GREEN ISLAND TO THE PILGRIMS [ST. LAWRENCE RIVER] [1837, c.1845] Bayfield, 1827-1834, HO #313. 46x64cm (18x25") Minor edge tears; generally exc. [15] £120 $185

SOUND OF BARRA [1863 (1874)] Adm #2770. 98x66cm (38½x26") Reduced lower margin; o/w exc. [15] £30 $46

SOUND OF ISLAY [1856 (1901)] Robinson & Bedford, 1852-53; Adm #2481. 97x64cm (38½x25") Upper & lower margins tape marked; repaired tear just to engraving. [15] £25 $39

SOUTH AMERICA WEST COAST SHEET XIV [1840 (1875)] Peru: Independencia Bay to Vegueta. Fitzroy, 1836; HO #1323. 63x47cm (25x18½") Penciled tracks. Callao bookseller's stamp. [15] £60 $92

STRAIT OF SINGAPORE SHEET II [1855 - 1861] Thomson, 1846-54; HO #2403. 48x64cm (19½x25") Linen-backed. Sl worming damage. [15] £380 $585

SUMATRA WEST COAST SHEET II CHINGKUK BAY TO THE STRAIT OF SUNDA [1860 (1906)] Edeling, 1857; Adm #2761. 64x99cm (25½x39½") [15] £35 $54

SURVEY OF FALMOUTH HARBOUR AND THE COAST TO THE MANACLES WITH HELFORD RIVER ... [1808, c.1847] Hurd, 1806; HO #32. 64x97cm (25x37½") Lt blue watercolor mark at text; o/w VG. 15] £200 $308

SURVEY OF LAKE SUPERIOR. BY LIEUT. HENRY W. BAYFIELD, R.N. ASSISTED BY MR. PHILIP ED. COLLINS, MID. [1828 (1872-74)] 3 sheets. Harbor insets. Adm #320a,b,c. Each 91x64cm (35½x24½") [15] £320 $493

SURVEY OF SOUTHAMPTON RIVER THE BRAMBLES AND COWES ROAD WITH THE ADJACENT PARTS ... [1808, c.1850] Mackenzie, 1783; HO #17. 97x64cm (37½x25") Fine. [15] £380 $585

SWANSEA AND NEATH [1839 (c. 1855)] Denham, 1830; HO #1161. 30x43cm (11½x17") Colored dots & flares. Lt dust soiling. [15] £110 $169

THE ENTRANCE TO THE RIVER MIN [1840] Rees, 1832; HO #1250. 46x61cm (18x24") Lt soiling, mainly dust in margins; generally VG. [15] £150 $231

THE FALKLAND ISLANDS [1884 (1891)] Fitzroy, Sullivan & Robinson, 1838-45. 2 sheets, HO #1354a,b, each 91x64cm (36x25") Margin corner chipped; o/w VG. [15] £120 $185

THE GLENAN ISLES AND PENMARK ROCKS WITH THE ADJACENT COAST OF FRANCE FROM PENMARK POINT TO POINT KEABRAS [1817] 64x94cm (24½x37") Sh repair lower fold split; damp mark upper margin. [15] £180 $277

THE HARBOUR AND ROAD OF PERNAMBUCO ... [1817] Recife. Hewett, 1815; Hydrographical Office. "Plan of the Bay of Macaloe ..." in Mozambique, after Dalrymple, printed on verso. 28x23cm (10½x8½") [15] £90 $139

THE HARBOUR OF SANTA MARTA ... [COLOMBIA] [1818, c.1840] Tait, 1816; HO #514. 38x30cm (15x12") [15] £220 $339

THE KAISER WILHELM CANAL [1895 (1899)] Adm #2469. 28x99cm (11x39") Lithographed plan. [15] £48 $74

THE PENINSULA OF KOREA [1840] HO #1258, 1st issue. 61x46cm (24½x18½") Chips in edges. [15] £300 $462

THE PORT OF VERACRUZ, AND ANCHORAGE OF ANTON LIZARDO ... [1825, c.1845] Phillimore, 1824. Inset: Alvarado. 60x79cm (23½x31") Deckle-edged; fine. [15] £200 $308

THE RIVER CONGO ... [1827] Vidal, 1825. 30x46cm (12x18½") [15] £140 $216

THE SCILLY ISLES [1866 (1899)] Williams & Wells, 1860-63; Adm #34. 66x99cm (26x38½") Margin chips, sh edge tears; library stickers lower corners. [15] £45 $69

TIMOR AND SOME NEIGHBOURING ISLANDS ... [1814, c.1826] Flinders, 1803; H.O. 46x64cm (18½x25") Sm brown marks; minor edge damage; repaired tear just into engraving. [15] £300 $462

TOBERMORY HARBOUR [1848 (1876)] Otter, 1847; HO #1836. 61x48cm (24x18½") Repaired margin tear; discoloration edge top margin; o/w good. [15] £50 $77

TOULON AND THE ADJACENT COAST [c. 1845] Smyth, 1833; HO #151. J. & C. Walker, sc. 46x61cm (18x23½") [15] £80 $123

TUBUAI ISLAND [ON SHEET WITH] ANCHORAGES NORTH COAST TUBUAI ISLAND [1898] 2 plans. Adm #2686. 46x66cm (18x26") [15] £40 $62

VANCOUVER ISLAND, HARBOURS IN DISCOVERY PASSAGE, BROUGHTON STRAIT AND GOLETAS CHANNEL [1863 / 1904] Mainly Beaver Harbour. 48x60cm (19x23½") [14] £39 $60

WARNBRO SOUND [ON SHEET WITH] PEEL HARBOUR [1840] Roe, 1839; HO #1266. 36x20cm (13½x8½") Lt browning; minor margin damage, with cancelled library stamp. [15] £320 $493

WATAGHEISTIC SOUND, MARY ISLANDS &C. [CANADA] [1838, c.1845] Bayfield, 1834; HO #1119. 61x46cm (24x18") Fine. [15] £100 $154

WEMBURY BAY AND YEALM RIVER [1885] Stokes, 1861; Adm #95. 48x66cm (19x25½") [15] £45 $69

WEST COAST OF AFRICA SHEET I [THROUGH] SHEET XX [1830-1848] Complete set of 20 deckle-edge sheets, Morocco to Nigeria. All (except one at full size) are half-size Admiralty sheets 48x64cm (18½x25") Some foxing; generally exc. [15] £1,450 $2,233

WEST INDIES, ANGUILLA TO PUERTO RICO SHEWING THE APPROACHES TO THE VIRGIN ISLANDS SURVEYED ... 1848-52. [1868] 66x102cm (26x40½") Lighthouses colored. 2 tears repaired; o/w/ good. [14] £247 $380

WEST INDIES SHEET XI FROM CAYOS RATONES TO SAN JUAN DE NICARAGUA [1844 (1864)] Barnett, 1837; HO #1579. 48x61cm (19x24½") [15] £90 $139

WEST INDIES SHEET XIV FROM BELIZE TO CAPE CATOCHE ... [1839] Watermarked 1841. Owen & Barnett, 1830 & 1837; HO #1204. One of 14 Admiralty charts covering West Indies. 61x48cm (24½x18½") [15] £100 $154

YANG-TSE-KIANG RIVER [1843] Bethune, Kellett & Collinson, 1842; HO #1480. Printed later as "China Sheet 9". 61x94cm (24x37") Linen-backed. Sl Dampmarking lower margin. [15] £190 $293

YARMOUTH AND LOWESTOFT ROADS [1886 (1899)] Adm #1543. 107x66cm (42x26") [15] £35 $54

BRITISH GOVERNMENT

[ATLAS] CYCLONE TRACKS IN THE SOUTH INDIAN OCEAN [1891] HMSO; Meteorological Council. Oblong folio; 45 outline storm tracks, Madagascar to Australia, 1848 to 1885. Wrapper soiled; o/w good. [14] £114 $175

PLAN OF THE CITY OF ABERDEEN [1879] H.M. Post Office, for P.O. directory. 46x56cm (17½x22") No color. Folded, torn; fair. [21] £58 $90

WRECK CHART OF THE BRITISH ISLES FOR 1855 [1856] By48x36cm (18½x13½") Col. [15] £75 $116

BRITISH ORDNANCE SURVEY

COUNTRY AROUND SANDHURST [1888] A.C. Cooke. Morocco cover. 66x97cm (26x37½") Partial printed color. VG. [21] £65 $100

EPPING (GREAT DUNMOW) AND CHELMSFORD (BRAINTREE) [1899 and 1893] Joined & retailed by Edward Stanford. Dissected, linen mounted, folded into cloth slipcase. 71x102cm (28½x40½") No color. Fine. [21] £114 $175

GEOLOGICAL SURVEY OF GREAT BRITAIN. ORDNANCE SURVEY OF SCOTLAND. SHEET 32 [ENVIRONS OF EDINBURGH] [1858] Geological map. 48x64cm (19x24½") Full col. Dust soiled; good. [21] £81 $125

ORDNANCE SURVEY OF SCOTLAND. GEOLOGICAL SURVEY OF GREAT BRITAIN. SHEET 33. HADDINGTONSHIRE [1859] Geological map. Dissected; linen mounted. 53x69cm (21x27") Full color by strata. Bit dust soiling; blind stamp; VG. [21] £97 $150

ORDNANCE SURVEY OF SCOTLAND, GEOLOGICAL SURVEY OF SCOTLAND, SHEET 81 APPLECROSS [1896] 51x66cm (20½x25½") Color. Exc. [29] £58 $90

ORDNANCE SURVEY OF SCOTLAND. SHEET 16. ST. MARY'S LOCK. ETTRICK [1864] Dissected; linen mounted. 53x71cm (21x27½") No color. VG. [21] £81 $125

ORDNANCE SURVEY OF SCOTLAND. SHEET 21. ISLAND OF ARRAN. BUTESHIRE. [1870] Dissected, linen mounted. 53x71cm (21x27½") No color. VG. [21] £78 $120

ORDNANCE SURVEY OF SCOTLAND. SHEET 25. BERWICKSHIRE [1865] Dissected; linen mounted. 53x71cm (21x28") No color. VG. [21] £81 $125

SURREY [1866] London: Letts, Son & Co. Electrotype engraving after 1816 original. In cloth covers. 64x94cm (25½x37½") Color. Fine. [21] £62 $95

BROOKES

THE EASTERN STATES WITH PART OF CANADA [1812] 20x25cm (8x10") Uncol. VG. [45] £39 $60

THE MIDDLE STATES AND WESTERN TERRITORIES OF THE UNITED STATES INCLUDING THE SEAT OF THE WESTERN WAR [1812] NJ to IL. 20x25cm (8x10") Uncol. Trimmed close at rt; VG. [45] £97 $150

THE NORTHWESTERN TERRITORIES OF THE UNITED STATES [1812] 20x25cm (8x10") Uncolored. Top edge sl rough & trimmed close. [45] £156 $240

BROOKING

A PROSPECT OF THE CITY OF DUBLIN FROM THE NORTH [1729] Upper panel of "Map of the City and Suburbs of Dublin ...", London: John Bowles. 20x89cm (7½x34½") B&W. Trimmed to neatline; else VG. [55] £876 $1,350

BRUE

CARTE DE L'AMERIQUE MERIDIONALE [1820] Mounted on silk boards with orig label, folding to about 8x5"; 51x36cm (20½x14½") OL color. Exc. [29] £58 $90

ETATS UNIS [1820] 38x51cm (14½x20") Margin spotting; faint water mark at corner. [13] £243 $375

BUACHE

CARTE DES NOUVELLES DECOUVERTES AU NORD DE LA MER DU SUD, TANT A L'EST DE LA SIBERIE ET DU KAMTCHATKA QU'A L'OUEST DE LA NOUVELLE FRANCE. DRESSEE SUR LES MEMOIRES DE MR. DEL'ISLE ... [1750] 2nd state; Paris: Dezauche. Incl most of North America. 48x66cm (18½x26½") Orig OL color. Crease near outer border. Ref: Tooley (Amer) p.34-5,#105. Cumming (Exploration) p.222-6; Schwartz & Ehrenberg p.157-61. [28] £701 $1,080

CARTE PHYSIQUE DE LA MER DES INDES [1754] 30x35cm (12x14") Orig OL color. [16] £328 $505

MAPPE MONDE L'USAGE DU ROY PAR GUILLAUME DELISLE ... 1720. AUGMENTEE ... [1755] Double hemi. 43x69cm (17½x26½") Color. [26] £1,136 $1,750

BUCHON   *Dimensions sometimes include text around map.*

CARTE DU TERRITOIRE D'ARKANSAS ET DES AUTRES TERRITOIRES DES ETATS-UNIS [1825] Includes Western territories. Text at sides. 38x38cm (14½x15") on 17x22" sheet. [44] £308 $475

CARTE GEOGRAPHIQUE, STATISTIQUE ET HISTORIQUE DE PORTO RICO / PORTO RICO ET ILES VIERGES [1825] 25x42cm (10x16½") on 18x24" sheet with text. Col. Ref: Phillips (A) 1176. [25] £153 $235

CARTE GEOGRAPHIQUE, STATISTIQUE ET HISTORIQUE DE LA FLORIDE [1825] French ed of Carey & Lea; surround of French text on 17x24" sheet. 30x25cm (11½x9½") [4] £127 $195

[SAME TITLE] [1825] On 21x27" sheet with French text; map 29x25cm (11½x9½") Color. [56] £153 $235

CARTE GEOGRAPHIQUE, STATISTIQUE ET HISTORIQUE DES POSSESSIONS RUSSES [1825] Alaska. On sheet 18x25" sheet with French text. 37x43cm (14½x17") Orig full color. Fine. Ref: Falk (AK) #1825; Phillips (A) 1176. [59] £227 $350

CARTE GEOGRAPHIQUE, STATISTIQUE ET HISTORIQUE DU MEXIQUE [1824] On sheet with text surround, with extra text sheet. 33x38cm (12½x15") Color. Lt spots; else VG. [12] £162 $250

CARTE GEOGRAPHIQUE, STATISTIQUE ET HISTORIQUE DU TERRITOIRE D'ARKANSAS ET DES AUTRES TERRITOIRES DES ETATS-UNIS [1825] On sheet 46x61cm (18x24") Orig OL col. Mint. [14] £250 $385

ETATS-UNIS D'AMERIQUE [1825] Based on Melish. 42x53cm (16½x21") Full color. [56] £195 $300

BUFFON

CARTE DES DECLINAISONS ET INCLINAISONS DE L'AIGUILLE AIMANTEE ... L'ANNE [AUSTRALIA & NEW ZEALAND] [1775] From monumental natural history; shows Cook's discoveries. 42x54cm (16½x21½")
[16] £1,045 $1,609

BUNO

IMPERII SINARUM NOVA DESCRIPTIO [1694] Cluver Wolf. 21x26cm (8x10") Weak impression. [14] £39 $60

BUNTING

AFRICA TERTIA PARS TERRAE [1592] From *Itinerarium Saccrae Scripture*, subsequent ed. 26x34cm (10x13½") + title above. Uncolored. Some plate residue; overall VG. Ref: Norwich 17. MCC 29 #141 p.34, pl.X. [59] £422 $650

ASIA SECUNDA PARS TERRAE IN FORMA PEGASI [c. 1750] Asia as Pegasus. Engraved version of 16 c. woodblock. 25x35cm (9½x13½") Uncolored. [54] £800 $1,232

ASIA SECUNDA PARS TERRE IN FORMA PEGASIR [1581] Asia as Pegasus. 25x35cm (9½x14") plus title & text below. Modern color. Side margins replaced, facsimile replacement of sm image loss. [62] £503 $775

DIE EIGENTLICHE UND WARHAFFTIGE GESTALT DER ERDEN UND DES MEERS. COSMOGRAPHIA UNIVERSALIS [1581] 27x36cm (10½x14") B&W. Ref: Shirley (W) 143, pl.120. [16] £1,709 $2,633

REISEN DER KINDER VON ISRAEL AUS EGYPTEN [1581 -] From *Itinerarum Sacrae Scripturae*. 26x36cm (10x14") Uncolored. Ref: Laor 142. [54] £500 $770

BURDER

OLD JERUSALEM [1810] S. Burder, London. 36x43cm (14x17") Color. [23] £153 $235

BURLEIGH

CASTLETON, VT [1889] Pocket bird's eye view; on thin paper, folds into 12mo wraps. "Souvenir of the State Normal School ...", by legend, a graduation present. 43x64cm (16½x25") Sl waterstain; occas fold separation, sm loss at fold corners. Cover sl rubbed, waterstained; generally VG. [6] £503 $775

CHESTER, MASS. [1885] Lith by Beck & Pauli, after L.R. Burleigh. 38x58cm (14½x23") Color. Good. Ref: Reps 1410. [47] £380 $585

BURR

BRAZIL [1836] 38x30cm (15x12") Full color. VG. [61] £42 $65
CHILE AND PATAGONIA [1836] 38x30cm (15x12") Full color. VG. [61] £29 $45
COLOMBIA [1836] 38x30cm (15x12") Full color. VG. [61] £29 $45
DELAWARE AND MARYLAND [1836] 33x40cm (13x16") Full color. VG. [61] £49 $75
KENTUCKY AND TENNESSEE [1836] 30x38cm (12x15") Full color. VG. [61] £49 $75
MAINE [1836] 33x27cm (13x10½") Full color. VG. [61] £62 $95
MAP OF THE UNITED STATES [1855] Burr as "Draftsman U.S. Senate". Lithographed on 2 sheets; Ackerman, NY. Large western territories. 81x124cm (31½x49") Folded as issued; o/w pristine. [11] £487 $750
MASSACHUSETTS, RHODE ISLAND AND CONNECTICUT [1836] 28x33cm (11x12½") Full col. VG. [61] £49 $75
NORTH AND SOUTH CAROLINA [1836] 30x38cm (12x15") Full color. VG. [61] £49 $75
PALESTINE OR THE HOLY LAND OR THE LAND OF CANAAN [1832] 32x27cm (12½x10½") Col. [23] £49 $75
PERU AND BOLIVIA [1836] 38x30cm (15x12") Full color. VG. [61] £29 $45
SOUTH AMERICA [1836] 38x30cm (15x12") Full color. VG. [61] £29 $45
UNITED STATES ... [1833] West to Great Plains. 27x32cm (10½x12½") Full color. Minor margin age spotting. [9] £114 $175
WEST INDIES [1836] 28x33cm (11x12½") Full color. VG. [61] £81 $125

CADELL & DAVIES
PALAESTINA [1797] 20x25cm (8½x10½") Color. [23] £49 $75

CALMET
DESCRIPTION DE L'ANCIENNE JERUSALEM SELON VILLALPAND [c. 1730] From French ed, *Dictionary History ... Sacred Scripture.* Imaginary plan. 31x43cm (12x17") Uncolored. Top margin trimmed; lower c'fold repaired; old lib stamp on back; bright, clear, clean. Ref: Laor 1153. [59] £81 $125
PLAN ET DISTRIBUTION DE LA TERRE DE CHANAAN SUIVANT LE VISION D'EZECHIEL. CHAP.XLVIII, LAQUELLE DISTRIBUTION NE FUT JAMAIS EXECUTEE A LA LETTRE ... [1730] 33x43cm (13x17½") Color. Ref: Laor 163. [23] £84 $130
TABULA TERRAE PROMISSAE AB AUCTORE COMMENTARII JOSUE DELINEATA ET A LIEBAUX GEOGRAPHO INCISA [1726] Venice: S. Coleti. 46x23cm (18x9") Color. Ref: Laor 153. [23] £120 $185

CAMDEN
BEDFORD COMITATUS ... [1610] From *Britannia* .... Kip, sc. 28x33cm (11x13") Color. Lt surface dirt; else fine. Ref: Chubb XIX. [55] £97 $150
CANTIUM QUOD NUNC KENT [1610] From, *Britannia.* Kip, sc. 25x38cm (10x15") Color. Lower lf plate mark strengthened; else VG. Ref: Chubb XIX. [55] £97 $150
CARDIGAN COMITATUS PARS OLIM DIMETARIUM [1603] Kip, sc. 28x30cm (10½x12") Col. Exc. [29] £94 $145
FRUGIFERI AC AMAENI HEREFORDIAE COMITATUS ... [1610] From *Britannia* .... Kip, sc. 28x33cm (11x13") Color. Margin tears to neat line repaired. Ref: Chubb XIX. [55] £97 $150
HIBERNIAE IRELAND, ANGLIS YVERDON BRITANNIS ERIN-INCOLIS. IERNA ORPHEO & ARIST. IRIS DIODORO SICULO ... [1607] From *Britannia.* Wm. Hole signature. 28x33cm (10½x13") Color. [24] £308 $475
HUNTINGTON COMITATUS ... [1610] From Camden, *Britannia.* 28x33cm (11x13") Color. Ref: Chubb XIX. [55] £97 $150

CANTELLI DA VIGNOLA
DALMATIA MARITIMA OCCIDENTALE E DALMATIA MARITIME ORIENTALE DESCRITTA ... [1689] Rome: G.G. Rossi. 2 sheet map, each 56x43cm (22½x17") Faint creases. [28] £409 $630
IL CORSO DEL FIUME RENO DALLE SUE FONTI SINO AL MARE CON TUTTI LI FIUMI, CHE SI SCARICANO IN ESSO TANTO A DESTRA ... [1689] Rome: G.G. Rossi. 2 sheets, each 46x58cm (17½x22½") Lt spotting one sheet. [28] £351 $540
IL REGNO DELLA SERVIA DETTA ALTRIMENTI RASCIA ... [1689] Rome: G.G.Rossi. 41x56cm (16x21½") [28] £204 $315
IL REGNO DI ARAGONA DESCRITTO DA D. NICOLO CANTELLI GEOGRAFO ... [1696] Rome: Domenico de Rossi. 42x55cm (16½x21½") Some overall toning; added side margins for composite atlas; fine. [62] £308 $475
IL REGNO DI CASTIGLIA VECCHIA DESCRITTO DA GIACOMO CANTELLI DA VIGA GEOGRAFO DEL SERENISS SIGR. DUCA DI MODENA ... [1696] Rome: Domenico de Rossi. 43x55cm (17x21½") Some overall toning; top & bottom margins for composite atlas; fine. [62] £308 $475
IL REGNO DI GALICIA DESCRITTA DA GIACOMO DA VIGNOLA GEOGRAFO ... [1696] Rome: Domenico de Rossi. 42x55cm (16½x21½") Some overall toning; added side margins for composite atlas; fine. [62] £308 $475
ISOLE DELL' INDIA CIOE LE MOLUCCHE LE FILIPPINE E DELLA SONDA ... [1688] 45x58cm (17½x23") Orig OL color. Exc. [63] £1,169 $1,800
L'INDIA DI QUA E DI LA DAL GANGE OUE SONO LI STATI DEL G. MOGOL ... [1683] Rome: G.G. Rossi. 43x53cm (16½x20½") Repaired tear lf margin. Ref: cf Gole (Ganges) 27 1.1. [28] £204 $315
LA PRUSSIA DIVISA IN REALE CHE APPARTIENE AL RE DI POLONIA ET IN DUCALE CHE SPETTA ALL'ELETTORE DI BRANDEBURGO ... [1689] Rome: G.G. Rossi. 43x58cm (17x23") Sh vert creases. [28] £204 $315
PARTE MERIDIONALE DELLE COSTE DELLA FRANCIA, CHE SONO POSTE SUL GRANDE OCEANO ... [1691] Rome: G.G. Rossi. 43x58cm (17x23") [28] £204 $315
PARTE OCCIDENTALE DEL GOVERNO GENERALE D'ORLEANS NELLA QUALE SONO COMPRESE LE PROVINCIE PARTICULARI ... [IN SET WITH] ... PARTE ORIENTALE ... [1692] Rome: G.G. Rossi. Each 58x43cm (22½x17") Rt margin of one trimmed to border. [28] £325 $500

CAREY, M.

A MAP OF THE COUNTRIES SITUATE ABOUT THE NORTH POLE AS FAR AS THE 50TH DEGREE OF NORTH LATITUDE [1795] For *Carey's Edition of Guthries Geography Improved*. 26x25cm (10x10") Orig OL color. Offsetting in blank areas. Ref: Wheat & Brun 915. [28] £117 $180

A MAP OF THE DISCOVERIES MADE BY CAPTS. COOK & CLARKE IN THE YEARS 1778 & 1779 BETWEEN THE EASTERN COAST OF ASIA & THE WESTERN COAST OF NORTH AMERICA [1795] 18x28cm (7x11½") OL color. VG. [19] £114 $175

CONNECTICUT FROM THE BEST AUTHORITIES [1795] Doolittle, del & sc. 31x39cm (12x15½") Uncolored. VG. [44] £195 $300

DELAWARE [1805] From *Pocket Atlas*. 19x15cm (7½x6") OL col. Ref: Phillips (A) 1368,11. [57] £65 $100

LOUISIANA [same date, source, dimen & color] Louisiana Purchase. Ref: Phillips (A) 1368,20. [57] £179 $275

[SAME TITLE] [1814] 41x43cm (15½x17½") OL color. Minor foxing; VG. [20] £325 $500

MEXICO OR NEW SPAIN [1814] Incl Southwest. 44x39cm (17x15") OL color. [58] £260 $400

MISSISSIPPI TERRITORY AND GEORGIA [1805] From *American Pocket Atlas*. 15x20cm (6x7½") OL color Ref: Phillips (A) 1368,19. [57] £146 $225

NEW YORK [same date, source, dimen & color] Ref: Phillips (A) 1368,8. [57] £65 $100

NORTH CAROLINA [same date, source, dimen & color] Ref: Phillips (A) 1368,16. [57] £78 $120

OHIO AND N.W. TERRITORY [same date & source] Indiana Terr. delineated. 18x15cm (7x6") OL color Ref: Phillips (A) 1368,12. [57] £159 $245

SCOTLAND WITH THE PRINCIPAL ROADS FROM THE BEST AUTHORITIES [1814] 36x28cm (14½x11") OL color. Minor transferral; fold repair; minor margin browning; VG. [21] £49 $75

THE PROVINCE OF MAINE FROM THE BEST AUTHORITIES BY SAMUEL LEWIS 1794 [1795] For *Carey's American Edition of Guthries Geography* ... 38x25cm (15x10") Some color, possibly later. Exc. [44] £156 $240

THE STATE OF NEW HAMPSHIRE COMPILED CHIEFLY FROM ACTUAL SURVEYS BY SAMUEL LEWIS, 1794 [1795] 46x30cm (18x12") Uncolored. [44] £156 $240

THE STATE OF PENNSYLVANIA. REDUCED WITH PERMISSION FROM READING HOWELLS MAP, BY SAMUEL LEWIS [1795] 31x47cm (12x18½") Uncolored. Minor lower edge repairs; fold repair. Ref: Wheat & Brun (442). [44] £195 $300

THE STATE OF RHODE-ISLAND COMPILED FROM THE SURVEYS AND OBSERVATIONS OF CALEB HARRIS BY HARDING HARRIS [1814] 35x24cm (14x9½") Orig OL color. Faint discoloration at title. [44] £117 $180

[SAME TITLE] [c. 1818] [same dimen] Orig full col. Discoloration & verso tape at lower edge. [44] £130 $200

CAREY & LEA   *Dimensions sometimes include text around map.*

BRITISH POSSESSIONS IN NORTH AMERICA [1823] On sheet with text 46x56cm (17½x22") Color. VG. [61] £146 $225

GEOGRAPHICAL, HISTORICAL AND STATISTICAL MAP OF AMERICA [1823] 2 maps with surround of text: "North America ...", by E. Pagenaud; "South America ..." by J. Aspin & E. Paguenaud. On sheet 46x53cm (17½x21"). [61] £81 $125

GEOGRAPHICAL, STATISTICAL, AND HISTORICAL MAP OF ARKANSA TERRITORY [ABOVE] MAP OF ARKANSAS AND OTHER TERRITORIES OF THE UNITED STATES [1822] Great Plains. 38x38cm (14½x15") on 16½x21" sheet. OL col. Minor browning; o/w bright, crisp. [11] £276 $425

[SAME TITLE] [1822] Mississippi R. to Rockies, by Maj. Stephen H. Long. On 16½x20½" sheet with text; map 37x40cm (14½x16"). Orig OL & wash color. Good. Ref: Wheat (TM) 348. [48] £422 $650

GEOGRAPHICAL, STATISTICAL AND HISTORICAL MAP OF BRAZIL [1823] On sheet with text 46x56cm (17½x22") Color. VG. [61] £62 $95

GEOGRAPHICAL, STATISTICAL AND HISTORICAL MAP OF CHILI [1823] On sheet with text 46x56cm (17½x22") Color. Sl dampstain. [61] £62 $95

GEOGRAPHICAL, STATISTICAL AND HISTORICAL MAP OF CONNECTICUT [1823] Color. VG. 24x29cm (9½x11½") on 17½x22" sheet. Color. VG. [61] £81 $125

GEOGRAPHICAL, STATISTICAL AND HISTORICAL MAP OF CUBA AND THE BAHAMA ISLANDS [1823] On sheet 46x56cm (17½x22") Color. VG. [61] £107 $165

GEOGRAPHICAL, STATISTICAL, AND HISTORICAL MAP OF FLORIDA [1822] 1st ed of earliest published map of Florida Territory. Surround of text on 17x21" sheet. 30x25cm (11½x9½") Orig wash color. [4] £217 $335

[SAME TITLE] [1823] [same dimen] Color. Faintly browned at fold. [35] £146 $225

[SAME TITLE] [1827] 3rd ed. 12 counties. [same dimen] Orig wash color. Map printed askew; sl printer's crease with orig verso reinforcement; o/w exc. [4] £114 $175

GEOGRAPHICAL, STATISTICAL AND HISTORICAL MAP OF JAMAICA [1823] On sheet with text 46x56cm (17½x22") Color. VG. [61] £114 $175

GEOGRAPHICAL, STATISTICAL, AND HISTORICAL MAP OF LOUISIANA [1827] On sheet with text surround 43x53cm (16½x20½") Full color. Sl discoloration at fold; few fox marks; VG. [20] £195 $300

GEOGRAPHICAL, STATISTICAL AND HISTORICAL MAP OF MEXICO [1827] Text on 3 sides. 41x38cm (16½x14½") Color. Reinforced corner. [10] £162 $250

GEOGRAPHICAL, STATISTICAL AND HISTORICAL MAP OF MICHIGAN TERRITORY [1822] 1st separate map of Mich. Terr. 37x27cm (14½x10½") on sheet 17½x22". OL color. VG. Framed. Ref: Karpinski (MI) 91. [61] £484 $745

GEOGRAPHICAL, STATISTICAL AND HISTORICAL MAP OF NEW JERSEY [1823] F. Lucas. Text on 3 sides; on 17x21" sheet 28x23cm (11x9½") Color. Clean. Ref: Phillips (M) p.489. [36] £146 $225

GEOGRAPHICAL, STATISTICAL AND HISTORICAL MAP OF NORTH AMERICA [1827] Text on 3 sides. 38x33cm (14½x13") Color. VG. [10] £146 $225

GEOGRAPHICAL, STATISTICAL AND HISTORICAL MAP OF PENNSYLVANIA [1827] On 17x22" sheet with text, 30x45cm (11½x18") Orig full col. VG-. Ref: Phillips (A) 1177,18; Howes C133. [59] £114 $175

GEOGRAPHICAL, STATISTICAL AND HISTORICAL MAP OF PERU [1823] 35x32cm (13½x12½") on 17½x22" sheet with text. Color. Sl dampstain. [61] £62 $95

GEOGRAPHICAL, STATISTICAL, AND HISTORICAL MAP OF PORTO RICO AND VIRGIN ISLANDS [1822] 43x53cm (16½x21") Text on lower third. Color. Ref: Phillips (A) 1373a. [25] £172 $265

GEOGRAPHICAL, STATISTICAL, AND HISTORICAL MAP OF PORTO RICO AND VIRGIN ISLANDS [1823] On sheet with text 46x56cm (17½x22") Color. VG. [61] £94 $145

GEOGRAPHICAL, STATISTICAL AND HISTORICAL MAP OF ST. DOMINGO [1823] On sheet with text 46x56cm (17½x22") Color. VG. [61] £94 $145

GEOGRAPHICAL, STATISTICAL AND HISTORICAL MAP OF THE LEEWARD ISLANDS [1823] On sheet with text 46x56cm (17½x22") Color. VG. [61] £107 $165

GEOGRAPHICAL, STATISTICAL, AND HISTORICAL MAP OF THE UNITED PROVINCES OF SOUTH AMERICA [1823] 41x31cm (16½x12") on 17½x22" sheet with text. Color. VG. [61] £62 $95

GEOGRAPHICAL, STATISTICAL, AND HISTORICAL MAP OF THE WEST INDIES [1823] On sheet with text 46x56cm (17½x22") Color. VG. [61] £114 $175

GEOGRAPHICAL, STATISTICAL, AND HISTORICAL MAP OF THE WINDWARD ISLANDS [1823] On sheet with text 42x52cm (16½x20½") Color. VG. [61] £94 $145

GEOGRAPHICAL, STATISTICAL AND HISTORICAL MAP OF UPPER AND LOWER CANADA, AND THE OTHER BRITISH POSSESSIONS IN NORTH AMERICA [c. 1823] Text on 3 sides, on sheet 42x52cm (16½x20½") Color. [40] £175 $270

GEOGRAPHICAL, STATISTICAL AND HISTORICAL MAP OF VIRGINIA [1823] 33x47cm (13x18½") on 17½x22" sheet. Color. VG. [61] £81 $125

CARVER

A PLAN OF CAPTAIN CARVER'S TRAVELS IN THE INTERIOR PARTS OF NORTH AMERICA IN 1766 AND 1767 [1781] Western Great Lakes region. 25x36cm (10½x13½") OL color as issued. Sh tear at fold-out repaired; some lt foxing; overall VG. [55] £617 $950

CARY

[ADVERTISEMENT] NEW GLOBES, CELESTIAL AND TERRESTRIAL ... [c. 1810] 14x9cm (5½x3½") Uncolored. [52] £100 $154

[GLOBES] CARY'S NEW TERRESTRIAL ... [AND] CELESTIAL GLOBE ... [1829 and 1816] 12" table-top globe pair 25" high, each on finely tooled mahogany tripod stand with meridian ring. Color. [3] £22,722 $35,000

A NEW CHART OF THE WORLD, ON MERCATOR'S PROJECTION ... [1811] From *Universal Atlas*. 46x52cm (18x20½") Orig wash color. [53] £180 $277

A NEW MAP OF BERKSHIRE ... [1801] Dissected, linen mounted, marbled guards & case. 51x56cm (20x22½") Full color. Fine. [21] £97 $150

A NEW MAP OF CHINESE & INDEPENDENT TARTARY FROM THE LATEST AUTHORITIES [dated 1806] 1st state. 53x61cm (20½x23½") Orig col. Few stains & sh margin tears. Ref: Phillips (A) 714. [28] £162 $250

A NEW MAP OF EGYPT ... [dated 1805] 1st state. 51x58cm (20½x23½") Orig color. Ref: Phillips (A) 714. [28] £175 $270

A NEW MAP OF ENGLAND ... [1811] 51x61cm (20½x23½") Orig color. Margins lt foxed & sh tears. [28] £192 $295

A NEW MAP OF NORTH AMERICA ... [1811] 46x52cm (18x20½") Orig wash color. [53] £200 $308
[SAME TITLE] [same date & dimen] Orig full color. Image fine; overall VG-. Ref: Goss (NA) 72; Wheat (TM) II, #273; Phillips (A) 714,51. [59] £195 $300
A NEW MAP OF NOVA SCOTIA, NEWFOUNDLAND &C. FROM THE LATEST AUTHORITIES ... [1807] 1st state. 53x61cm (20½x24") Orig col. Sh tears upper margin; foxing traces. Ref: Phillips (A) 714. [28] £204 $315
[SAME TITLE] [1811] From *Universal Atlas*. 46x52cm (18x20½") Orig wash color. [53] £140 $216
A NEW MAP OF PART OF THE UNITED STATES OF NORTH AMERICA, CONTAINING NEW YORK, VERMONT, NEW HAMPSHIRE, MASSACHUSETTS ... [1811] From *Universal Atlas*. 46x52cm (18x20½") Orig wash color. [53] £240 $370
A NEW MAP OF PART OF THE UNITED STATES OF NORTH AMERICA, CONTAINING THE CAROLINAS AND GEORGIA, ALSO THE FLORIDAS AND PART OF THE BAHAMA ISLANDS [1811] From *Universal Atlas*. 46x52cm (18x20½") Orig wash color. [53] £260 $400
A NEW MAP OF PART OF THE UNITED STATES OF NORTH AMERICA, EXHIBITING THE WESTERN TERRITORY, KENTUCKY, PENNSYLVANIA, MARYLAND, VIRGINIA, &C ... [1811] From *Universal Atlas*. 46x52cm (18x20½") Orig wash color. [53] £320 $493
A NEW MAP OF POLAND AND THE GRAND DUTCHY OF LITHUANIA SHEWING THEIR DISMEMBERMENTS AND DIVISIONS BETWEEN AUSTRIA, RUSSIA AND PRUSSIA, ACCORDING TO THE CONGRESS OF VIENNA... [1811] From *Universal Atlas*. 46x52cm (18x20½") Orig wash color. [53] £140 $216
[SAME TITLE] [c. 1819] 45x46cm (17½x18") Color. [42] £60 $92
A NEW MAP OF SCOTLAND FROM THE LATEST AUTHORITIES ... [1801 and 1811] Two sheets: different dates & color tone. 53x107cm (21½x42") Full color. Lower sheet corner replaced; fair. [21] £276 $425
A NEW MAP OF SOUTH AMERICA FROM THE LATEST AUTHORITIES ... [dated 1807] 1st state. 2 sheets 53x61cm (20½x23½") Orig color. Margins bit foxed & spotted; sl c'fold creasing one sheet. Ref: Phillips (A) 714. [28] £292 $450
[SAME TITLE] [1814] From *Universal Atlas*. 53x41cm (20½x16") OL color. Lt soiling; sm inkspot; c'fold reinforced; tender edges, sm removable archival tape mends; VG. [7] £94 $145
A NEW MAP OF THE BRITISH ISLES ... [1807] 1st state. 51x58cm (20½x23½") Orig color. Sh tear lower margin. Ref: Phillips (A) 714. [28] £192 $295
A NEW MAP OF THE CIRCLE OF AUSTRIA ... [1801] 1st state. 51x56cm (20x22") Orig OL color. Ref: Phillips (A) 714. [28] £162 $250
A NEW MAP OF THE EAST INDIA ISLES ... [1811] From *Universal Atlas*. 46x52cm (18x20½") Orig wash color. [53] £200 $308
A NEW MAP OF THE KINGDOM OF PORTUGAL [c. 1801] 48x50cm (19x19½") Color. [43] £56 $86
A NEW MAP OF THE UNITED STATES OF AMERICA ... [1811] From *Universal Atlas*. 46x52cm (18x20½") Orig wash color. [53] £240 $370
A NEW MAP OF THE UNITED STATES OF NORTH AMERICA CONTAINING THOSE OF NEW YORK, VERMONT, NEW HAMPSHIRE, MASSACHUSETTS, CONNECTICUT, RHODE ISLAND, PENNSYLVANIA, NEW JERSEY, DELAWARE, MARYLAND AND VIRGINIA FROM THE LATEST AUTHORITIES [c. 1800] 46x52cm (18x20½") Color. Immaculate. [36] £373 $575
A NEW MAP OF THE WEST INDIA ISLES ... [1811] From *Universal Atlas*. 46x52cm (18x20½") Orig wash color. [53] £200 $308
A NEW MAP OF UPPER AND LOWER CANADA FROM THE LATEST AUTHORITIES BY JOHN CARY, ENGRAVER ... [1807] 1st state. 53x61cm (20½x23½") Orig color. Margins stained; creased. Ref: Winearls 35.1; Phillips (A) 714. [28] £409 $630
CARY'S REDUCTION OF HIS LARGE MAP OF ENGLAND AND WALES, WITH PART OF SCOTLAND [1796] Folding map, dissected & mounted on linen, with marbled board slipcase. 91x66cm (36x25½") OL color. VG. [21] £260 $400

CASSELL, PETER & GALPIN
UNITED STATES OF NORTH AMERICA. NORTH WEST SHEET [IDAHO, DAKOTA, NEBRASKA] [c. 1865] 43x30cm (17x12") OL color. Good. [18] £62 $95

CAVE
A GENERAL MAP OF EASTERN AND WESTERN TARTARY, COMMONLY CALLED TARTARY ... [1741] Based on Du Halde; E. Bowen, sc. 38x54cm (15x21½") [14] £292 $450

CELLARIUS
THEORIATRUM SUPERIORUM PLANETARUM [1660 - 1718] Amsterdam: Valk & Schenk. 43x51cm (17x20") Orig color. Ref: Koeman III p.114 & Cel 3. [28] £351 $540

CENTURY ATLAS
MONTANA [1897] 28x38cm (10½x15") Printed color. [11] £32 $50

CHAMOUIN
AMERIQUE MERIDIONALE [c. 1815] Paris: Chamouin. 30x23cm (11½x8½") Orig OL color. [46] £32 $50
ETATS UNIS ET GRANDES ANTILLES [c. 1815] 30x22cm (12x9") Orig OL color. [46] £39 $60

CHANLAIRE
DES SPHERES ARTIFICIELLES [c. 1825] Armillary sphere pair with text. 43x56cm (17x22") Orig & later color. [51] £390 $600
DIVERSITE DES OMBRES [1807] World map inside framed border. (no dims.) Color. [16] £233 $358

CHATELAIN
CARTE CONTENANT LE ROYAUME DU MEXIQUE ET LA FLORIDE, DRESSEZ SUR LES MEILLEURES OBSERVATIONS ... [1719] 40x52cm (16x20½") Uncol. Lt age toning; o/w fine. [32] £422 $650
CARTE DE LA NOUVELLE FRANCE, OU SE VOIT LE COURS DES GRANDES RIVIERES DE S. LAURENS & DE MISSISSIPI AUJOURD'HUI S. LOUIS, AUX ENVIRONS DES QUELLES SE TROUVENT LES ETATS, PAIS, NATIONS, PEUPLES &C DE LA FLORIDE, DE LA LOUISIANE, DE LA VIRGINIE, DE LA MARIE-LANDE, DE LA PENSILVANIE, DU NOUVEAU JERSAY, DE LA NOUVELLE YORCK, DE LA NOUV. ANGLETERRE ... PLUS NOUVEAUX RECUEILLIS POUR L'ETABLISSEMENT DE LA COMPAGNIE FRANCOISE OCCIDENT [1719] After De Fer. 42x49cm (16½x19") Appears separately issued; full trimmed margins. Modern color. Faint sm stain; exc. [14] £876 $1,350
[SAME TITLE] [1719] 51x56cm (19½x21½") Full col. Minor c'fold reinforcement; else exc. [38] £1,428 $2,200
[SAME TITLE] [1719 or later.] From *Atlas Historique*. 42x48cm (16½x19") Uncolored. Trace of c'fold toning; VG+. Ref: Karpinski (MI) XLVIII. [31] £1,006 $1,550
[SAME TITLE] [1732] From, *Atlas Historique*, 2nd ed. By De Fer. 38x48cm (15x18½") Lower margin trimmed, some loss at neat line; sl stain at fold; VG. [20] £1,071 $1,650
[SAME TITLE] [1732] Based on De Fer. 43x51cm (16½x19½") Ref: Heidenreich & Dahl p.14; Karpinski p.133; Koeman II Cha 7; Phillips (A) 548. [28] £1,104 $1,700
CARTE DU CANADA OU DE LA NOUVELLE FRANCE, & DES DECOUVERTES QUI Y ONT ETE FAITES, DRESSEE SUR LES OBSERVATIONS LES PLUS NOUVELLES, & SUR DIVERS MEMOIRES TANT MANUSCRITS QU'IMPRIMEZ [1719] After 1703 De L'Isle, with text panel in place of cartouche. 40x52cm (16x20½") Mint. Ref: Phillips (M) p.189. [14] £338 $520
[SAME TITLE] [same date & dimen] Offsetting; sh lower c'fold split; eradicated lib stamp verso. Ref: Karpinski (MI); Phillips (A) 548; Koeman II Cha 7. [28] £584 $900
CARTE DU ROYAUME DE CONGO DU MONOMOTAPA ET DE LA CAFRERIE ... [1705+] 41x52cm (16x20½") [14] £127 $195
CARTE TRES CURIEUSE DE LA MER DU SUD, CONTENANT DES REMARQUES NOUVELLES ET TRES UTILES NON SEULEMENT SUR LES PORTS ET ILES DE CETTE MER, MAIS AUSSY SUR LES PRINCIPAUX PAYS DE L'AMERIQUE TANT SEPTENTRIONALE QUE MERIDIONALE ... [1719] 82x141cm (32½x55½") Orig color. [16] £7,597 $11,702
[SAME TITLE] ... [1719] Americas with opposite continental regions; insular California; many vignettes & insets. 81x142cm (32x55½") Color. Fine. [63] £7,661 $11,800
CARTE TRES CURIEUSE DE LA MER DU SUD, CONTENANT DES REMARQUES NOUVELLES ET TRES UTILES NON SEULEMENT SUR LES PORTS ET ILES DE CETTE MER ... [SOUTHERN HALF] [1719] From *Atlas Historique*. Complete map; neatline all around. 40x139cm (16x55") Ref: Schwartz & Ehrenberg pl.85. [33] £1,883 $2,900
DES MERS [c. 1705-1722] In "Historic and Methodic Geographical Atlas". Double globe. 32x56cm (12½x22") Color. [16] £209 $322
MAPPE MONDE OU DESCRIPTION GENERALE DU GLOBE TERRESTRE [1705] Double hemi; insular Calif. 33x44cm (13½x17½") Color. Ref: Phillips (A) 548, v.1. [26] £568 $875
[SAME TITLE] [c. 1732] Double hemi; astronomical diagrams. [same dimen] Later color. Margins bit foxed. Ref: Phillips (A) 548. [28] £351 $540

MAPPE-MONDE POUR CONNOITRE LES PROGRES & LES CONQUESTES LE PLUS REMARQUABLES DES PROVINCES-UNIES, AINSY QUE CELLES DES COMPAGNIES D'ORIENT ET D'OCCIDENT, ET LES PAIS QUELLES POSSEDENT DANS L'UN ET DANS L'AUTRE HEMISPHERE [1705] Double hemi; insular Calif. 34x46cm (13½x18") Color. Ref: Phillips (A) 548, v.2. [26] £601 $925
NOUVELLE CARTE D'ECOSSE ... [1708] 36x33cm (13½x12½") Old color. Fine. [21] £211 $325
NOUVELLE CARTE DE L'AFRIQUE AVEC DES REMARQUES ET DES TABLES POUR TROUVER SANS PEINE LES DIFFERENTS PEUPLES DE CETTE PARTIE DU MONDE ... [1705+] Tables at sides and below. 47x58cm (18½x23") [14] £120 $185
[SAME TITLE] [c. 1730.] [same dimen] Orig full color. Some folds reinforced on verso; minor c'fold darkening. [32] £299 $460
NOUVELLE CARTE POUR CONDUIRE A L'ASTRONOMIE ET A LA GEOGRAPHIE ET POUR FAIRE CONNOITRE LES DIFFERENS SISTEMES DU MONDE AVEC DIVERSES OBSERVATIONS [1705] Double hemi; insular Calif; celestial diagrams below. 51x61cm (20x23½") Color. Ref: Phillips (A) 548, v.1. [26] £503 $775
[SAME TITLE] [1732 - 1739] Double hemi; astronomical diagrams. 51x64cm (20x24½") Old color. Margins bit ragged. Ref: Phillips (A) 579. [28] £422 $650
VUE ET DESCRIPTION DE BETHLEHEM ET DE NAZARETH ET DE PLUSIEURS SINGULARITEZ CURIEUSES ... [1719] 4 views. 38x48cm (15x19") Color. [23] £107 $165

CHILD

ISLAND OF MADERA [1752] From *Universal Traveller*. With "Dragon Tree" depiction & town plans. 22x15cm (8½x6") Color. Exc. [62] £62 $95

CHINESE CARTOGRAPHY

[CHINA: AMOY REGION] [c. 1810] Manuscript map folding into self covers. 55x115cm (21½x45½") Full orig color. Few folds torn; minor loss at tear lower ctr; minor worming; overall clean. [33] £1,071 $1,650

CHIQUET

[ATLAS] LE NOUVEAU ET CURIEUX ATLAS GEOGRAPHIQUE ET HISTORIQUE ... [c. 1719] Paris: Chaveanau. Oblong 8vo, later boards; pp. 3-56; 24 maps, orig OL color except one; 3 globe plates. Lacks engraved title; sm margin wormhole enters some map borders; lt dampstains, browning to last leaves. Ref: Phillips (A) 4279. [28] £1,753 $2,700

CLASON MAP CO.

GUIDE TO COLORADO WITH MAP [1911] Map folds into large 12mo with 30 pp text & index. 43x56cm (17x22") Litho color. Starting to separate at folds; near fine. [6] £49 $75

CLOPPENBURGH

CHINA [1630] 18x25cm (7x9½") Exc. [63] £250 $385
HISPANIAE NOVAE NOVA DESCRIPTIO [1630] 19x25cm (7½x10") Two close margins; strong impression, but weakly printed lf border. [14] £49 $75
IAPONIA. PETRUS KAERIUS COELAVIT [1630] 18x24cm (7x9½") Full col, not orig. Exc. [62] £552 $850
SEPTENTRIONALIUM TERRARUM DESCRIPTIO [1630] 4 arctic islands. 18x25cm (7x10") Exc. [63] £185 $285
VIRGINIA ITEM ET FLORIDAE [1630] 19x26cm (7½x10") Color. Exc. [63] £250 $385

CLUVER

[ATLAS] INTRODUCTION IN UNIVERSAM GEOGRAPHIAM [1697] Amsterdam: J. Wolters. octavo; prelim + 565 pp + index + 43 uncolored maps + plates. Incl double hemi world & America with insular Calif. Rebound in cloth, raised spine bands; some misbinding; maps exc except Ancient Italy with sm missing piece; o/w overall VG. Ref: Phillips (A) 4270. [59] £812 $1,250
AMERICA [1697] Amsterdam: J. Walters. Insular Calif. 21x26cm (8½x10") Color. Ref: Phillips (A) 4270, 46. [22] £250 $385
[SAME TITLE] [1729] Insular California. 21x26cm (8x10") B&W. [47] £292 $450
ASIA [1704] 12x12cm (4½x5") [14] £49 $75
BRITANNICARUM INSULARUM TYPUS [1661] 12x12cm (4½x5") Color. [57] £58 $90
CRETA, CYPRUS ET RHODUS [1701] 13x13cm (4½x5") OL & wash color. [57] £45 $70
DANIA, SVECIA ET NORVEGIA [1701] Incl Finland & Baltics. 13x13cm (4½x5") OL & wash col. [57] £45 $70
EUROPAE NOVA TABULA [1683] 14x20cm (5½x8") Color. [14] £26 $40
HELVETIAE ... [1661] 13x13cm (4½x5") Color. [57] £39 $60
HISPANIAE [1697] 28x33cm (11x13½") B&W. [46] £45 $70

IMPERII SINARUM, NOVA DESCRIPTIO [1661] Incl Japan. 13x13cm (4½x5") Color. [57] £71 $110
NOVA TOTIUS GERMANIAE DESCRIPTIO [1672] 13x13cm (4½x5") Color. Fine. [55] £49 $75
ORBIS TERRARUM TYPUS [1661] 12x23cm (4½x9") Color. Framed. Ref: Shirley (W) 407. [16] £451 $695
[SAME TITLE] [1701] From *Introductionis in Universum Geographiam*. Double hemi; insular Calif. 13x23cm (4½x9") OL color. Fine. [57] £179 $275
ORBIS TERRARUM VETERIBUS COGNITA TYPUS GEOGRAPHICUS [1683] After Mercator. 16x20cm (6x8") [14] £42 $65
TYPUS HISPANIAE VETERIS [1672] Classical Spain. 10x13cm (4x5") Color. Fine. [55] £42 $65
TYPUS ORBIS TERRARUM [1729] 15x30cm (6½x12") Wash color. Exc. Ref: Shirley (W) 586; Phillips (A) 573. [47] £276 $425

COLBY

CITY OF BANGOR [1884] In *Atlas of Maine*. 38x30cm (15x12½") Full color. [36] £29 $45
GEOLOGICAL MAP OF MAINE [1884] From *Atlas of the State of Maine*. According to C.H. Hitchcock. 41x33cm (16x12½") Geology by color. [35] £32 $50
MAP OF LINCOLN COUNTY [ME] [1884] In *Atlas of Maine*. 41x30cm (16x12½") Full color. [36] £39 $60
MAP OF WASHINGTON COUNTY [ME] [1884] In *Atlas of Maine*. 38x33cm (15x12½") Full col. [36] £39 $60

COLLINS, G.

[ENGLAND: BRISTOL CHANNEL] [1693, c.1740] St. Gowans Head to Tintagel; Severn to Chepstow. Robert Southwell dedication. 43x56cm (17x21½") Color. [15] £230 $354
[ENGLAND: CORNWALL] [1693 (1779)] Polkerris to Pencarrah Head. 46x56cm (18x22") Sm repair, no loss. [15] £180 $277
[ENGLAND: CORNWALL & SCILLY ISLANDS] [1686 (1693)] Lizard to Cape Cornwall. 46x58cm (18x22½") Uncolored. Sl offsetting; spotting mainly in margins. [15] £190 $293
[ENGLAND: NORFOLK] [1693, c.1750] Blakeney area. 28x46cm (11x17½") [15] £180 $277
[ENGLAND: SUSSEX, RYE] [1693 (c. 1740)] 46x28cm (17½x11") Color. Sh repaired margin tear to border; no loss. [15] £140 $216
[IRELAND: CARLINGFORD] [1693, c. 1740] 43x33cm (17x12½") Col. One lt fold as usual. [15] £140 $216
[IRELAND: DUBLIN BAY] [1683 (1779)] 45x57cm (17½x22½") Color. [14] £140 $215
[IRISH SEA: ANGLESEY TO MULL OF GALLOWAY WITH ISLE OF MAN] [1781] 46x56cm (18x23") Margins stained. Ref: Phillips (A) 2895-7, 4003, 4005. [28] £175 $270
[SCOTLAND: APPROACHES TO DUNDEE] [1781] Insets: Aberdeen; Montrose. 46x58cm (18x23") Dampstains margins; repaired c'fold margin split. Ref: Phillips (A) 2895-7, 4003, 4005. [28] £195 $300
[SCOTLAND: SHETLAND ISLANDS] [1693 (c. 1740)] Bressay, Noss & opposite mainland. 46x56cm (17½x22") Neat ms title in French, upper margin. Color. Some spotting; generally VG. [15] £110 $169
[SAME TITLE] [1781] H. Moll, sc. 46x58cm (18x22½") Dampmarks margins. Ref: Phillips (A) 2895-7, 4003, 4005. [28] £146 $225
[WALES: CARDIGAN BAY] [1693 (c. 1750)] St. Gowans Head to Beaumaris. 46x56cm (17½x22") Neat ms. title upper margin. [15] £280 $431
MILFORD HAVEN AND THE ISLAND ADJACENT [1693 (1779)] Shows St. Bride's Bay. 44x56cm (17½x22") Faint dampmarking in margins; some sm wormholes. [15] £100 $154
THE CHEIFE HARBOURS IN THE ISLANDS OF ORKNEY ... [1693, c. 1740] 46x56cm (18x22") Color. [15] £150 $231
THE ISLANDS OF SCILLY [1689 (1693)] 45x56cm (17½x22") Few sm wormholes, two brown marks upper margin. [15] £270 $416

COLOM

'T SUYDER-DEEL VAN AMERICA NIEULYX UYTGEGEVEN ... [1663] J. Colom. 40x53cm (15½x21") Uncolored. [53] £450 $693
CUST VAN BARBARIA VAN C. DE GEER TOT VERBY C. VERDE BY IACOB COLOM [1648] From *The Upright Fyrie Colomne*. Pilot book chart. 24x28cm (9½x11") Exc. [62] £276 $425
DE CUSTE VAN NOORWEGEN TUSSCHEN SCHAERSONDT EN SCHUYTENS ... [1648] From *Vijerighe Colom*. 38x53cm (15x21") Uncolored. Good, clean. [15] £280 $431
PASCAARTE VAN HISPANGIEN VAN DE ZUYD SYDE VAN YRLANDT TOT DE STRAET [1658] From *Zee Atlas*. Arnold Colom. 53x64cm (21½x25") Color. [15] £825 $1,271

PASCAARTE VAN NIEU NEDERLANDT ... [c. 1653-54] Boston to Carolina. 56x64cm (21½x25") Early (?) color. Exc. Ref: Koeman IV, p.115; Suarez p.147-48. [38] £11,686 $18,000
PASCAERTE VERTOONENDE DE MONT VANDE TEEMSE EN VOORT DE CUSTE VAN ENGELANDT TOT CRAMMER [1632 (1647)] In *Fierie Sea Columne*. Jacob Aertsz Colom. 38x53cm (15x21") Color. Lt brown dampmarking lower margin; sl chipped narrow side margins. [15] £320 $493

COLTON (Atlas Maps)

[ATLAS] COLTON'S ATLAS OF THE WORLD ... VOL. II EUROPE, ASIA, AFRICA, OCEANICA, ETC. [1856] J.H. Colton & Co. Folio. Quarter-leather covers worn at spine ends & corners; hinges starting. 31 (of 36) colored maps (none U.S.), some double-page. (lacking 3 Germany, Palestine, Australia). Maps bright, clean. [5] £292 $450
ALABAMA [1855] 40x32cm (16x12½") Color. [36] £49 $75
[SAME TITLE] [1855-56] J.H. Colton. 46x38cm (18x15") VG. [61] £36 $55
ARKANSAS [1856] 41x36cm (16x13½") Full color. [45] £39 $60
AUSTRALIA [entered 1855] J.H. Colton. 31x39cm (12½x15") Orig color. Ref: Tooley (Australia) pl.18. [28] £97 $150
BOSTON AND ADJACENT CITIES [1855-56] J.H. Colton. 46x38cm (18x15") Full Col. VG. [61] £42 $65
CALIFORNIA [1855 (1856)] From *Atlas of the World*. 33 counties. 38x31cm (15x12") Orig full color. VG-. Ref: Phillips (A) 816. [59] £97 $150
[SAME TITLE] [1856] 41x36cm (16x13½") Full color. [45] £78 $120
CANADA EAST OR LOWER CANADA [1855-56] J.H. Colton. 33x40cm (13x16") VG. [61] £36 $55
CANADA WEST OR UPPER CANADA [1855-56] J.H. Colton. 33x40cm (13x15½") VG. [61] £36 $55
CHICAGO [ON SHEET WITH] ST. LOUIS [1855-56] J.H. Colton. 46x38cm (18x15") Full Col. VG. [61] £29 $45
CITY OF BALTIMORE [1855-56] J.H. Colton. 32x39cm (12½x15½") VG. [61] £42 $65
CITY OF PHILADELPHIA [1855-56] J.H. Colton. 46x38cm (18x15") [61] £49 $75
CITY OF SAVANNAH, GEORGIA [ON SHEET WITH] CITY OF CHARLESTON, SOUTH CAROLINA [1856] 31x37cm (12x14½") [36] £49 $75
CITY OF ST. LOUIS [ON SHEET WITH] CITY OF CHICAGO [1855] 30x38cm (12x15") [36] £32 $50
COLTON'S CALIFORNIA AND NEVADA [1873] 64x46cm (25x17½") Full color.. [36] £81 $125
COLTON'S DOMINION OF CANADA NO.3 THE PROVINCES OF NEW BRUNSWICK & NOVA SCOTIA AND PRINCE EDWARD ISLAND [1874] 43x66cm (17½x26½") Color. Exc. [29] £58 $90
COLTON'S GEORGETOWN AND THE CITY OF WASHINGTON THE CAPITAL OF THE UNITED STATES OF AMERICA [1888] With Potomac Flats in progress. 33x40cm (13x16") Full color. [56] £42 $65
COLTON'S IRELAND [c. 1855] G.W. & C.B. Colton. 36x28cm (14x11½") Full color. Good. [21] £42 $65
COLTON'S LAKE SUPERIOR AND THE UPPER PENINSULA OF MICHIGAN [1876] 43x66cm (17x25½") [61] £55 $85
COLTON'S NEBRASKA [1884] 43x69cm (16½x26½") Full color. [56] £45 $70
COLTON'S NORTH AMERICA [1855] 40x33cm (15½x13") Full color. [14] £26 $40
COLTON'S PALESTINE [1855] 41x33cm (16x13") Color. [23] £23 $35
COLTON'S TERRITORIES OF NEW MEXICO AND UTAH [1855 (1859)] Provisional Confederate territory bounded at 34° N. 33x39cm (13x15½") Color. Blemish toward edge; bright, clean. [11] £146 $225
COLTON'S UNITED STATES [1862] As in *Rebellion Record*. West to Rockies; dated 1855. 38x43cm (15x17") Color. Repaired tear enters side; a margin trimmed to neat line. Ref: Stephenson (CW) 7.5. [13] £97 $150
COLTON'S WISCONSIN [1873] 41x33cm (16x12½") Color. [36] £32 $50
CONNECTICUT WITH PORTIONS OF NEW YORK & RHODE ISLAND [1855-56] J.H. Colton. 32x40cm (12½x15½") VG. [61] £36 $55
CUBA, JAMAICA & PORTO RICO [1855-56] J.H. Colton. 38x46cm (15x18") Full color. VG. [61] £42 $65
[SAME TITLE] [1855-1862] Puerto Rico inset. 33x41cm (13x16") Color. [25] £42 $65
DAKOTA [1873] Present ND & SD. 39x32cm (15½x12½") Color. [36] £55 $85
DELAWARE AND MARYLAND [1855] 1st ed. DC inset. 32x40cm (12½x16") Color. [36] £49 $75
[SAME TITLE] [1855-56] J.H. Colton. DC inset. 38x46cm (15x18") VG. [61] £36 $55
DR. F.V. HOPKINS' PRELIMINARY GEOLOGICAL MAP OF LOUISIANA [c. 1870] G.W. & C.B. Colton & Co. 30x38cm (12x15") Full coding color. Fine. [20] £97 $150
FLORIDA [1855] 1st ed. 28 counties. 30x38cm (12x15") With text sheet. Orig wash color. [4] £55 $85
[SAME TITLE] [1855 / 1857] Plain border. [same dimen] Orig color. Margin soil; minor age flaws; good. [4] £36 $55

GEORGETOWN AND THE CITY OF WASHINGTON [1857] 3 vignettes. 32x40cm (13x16") Full col. [44] £39 $60
GEORGIA [1855-56] J.H. Colton. 46x38cm (18x15") VG. [61] £29 $45
ILLINOIS [1855-56] J.H. Colton. Chicago inset. 40x32cm (15½x12½") VG. [61] £29 $45
IOWA [1855] 1st ed. 32x41cm (12½x16") Orig full color. [46] £36 $55
J.H. COLTON'S MAP OF NEVADA UTAH AND ARIZONA [1865] From "Octavo Atlas". 28x20cm (11x8") Color. Minor spotting. [13] £62 $95
KENTUCKY AND TENNESSEE [1855-56] 38x46cm (15x18") VG. [61] £36 $55
LAKE SUPERIOR AND THE NORTHERN PART OF MICHIGAN [1855] J.H. Colton. 32x41cm (13x16") [61] £62 $95
LOUISIANA [1854] Early issue. 32x40cm (12½x15½") Faint color. Age toning; VG. [20] £81 $125
[SAME TITLE] [1855-56] J.H. Colton. 46x38cm (18x15") VG. [61] £36 $55
[SAME TITLE] [1856] 30x38cm (12x14½") Full color. Fine. [20] £65 $100
MAINE [1855-56] J.H. Colton. 40x29cm (16x11½") VG. [61] £36 $55
MAP OF NEW YORK AND THE ADJACENT CITIES [1855-56] 41x65cm (16½x25½") [61] £62 $95
MAP OF PORT ROYAL, BEAUFORT AND VICINITY ... [1861] From *Pictorial History of the War of 1861*. G.W. Colton. 38x53cm (15x21") Edge repairs. [13] £65 $100
MASSACHUSETTS AND RHODE ISLAND [1855] 33x41cm (13x16") Color. VG or better. [29] £23 $36
[SAME TITLE] [same date & dimen] Orig pastel color. [46] £39 $60
[SAME TITLE] [1855-56] Inset: Boston area. 38x46cm (15x18") VG. [61] £29 $45
MEXICO [1855-56] J.H. Colton. 32x39cm (12½x15½") VG. [61] £36 $55
MICHIGAN [1855] J.H. Colton. 40x32cm (15½x12½") [61] £55 $85
MINNESOTA [1855] 1st ed. 33x41cm (13x16") One spot; clean. [13] £78 $120
[SAME TITLE] [1857] Border does not follow Big Sioux River. 30x41cm (12x15½") Full col. [56] £65 $100
MISSISSIPPI [1855-56] J.H. Colton. 46x38cm (18x15") VG. [61] £42 $65
MISSOURI [1855-56] J.H. Colton. Inset: St. Louis area. 46x38cm (18x15") VG. [61] £49 $75
NEW MAP OF THE STATE OF TEXAS, COMPILED FROM J. DE CORDOVA'S LARGE MAP [1855] 43x66cm (16½x26") Full orig color. Fine. [46] £185 $285
[SAME TITLE] [1855 / 1857] 41x64cm (15½x25") Full color. [51] £179 $275
[SAME TITLE] [1857] 41x58cm (16x23") Full color. VG. [44] £114 $175
NEW ORLEANS [ON SHEET WITH] LOUISVILLE [1855-56] J.H. Colton. 46x38cm (18x15") [61] £29 $45
NORTH CAROLINA [1855] 32x40cm (12½x15½") Orig pastel color. Minor border tears repaired. [46] £49 $75
[SAME TITLE] [1855-56] J.H. Colton. 38x46cm (15x18") VG. [61] £49 $75
OHIO [1855 / 1857] 30x38cm (12x14½") Color. [51] £81 $125
OREGON, WASHINGTON AND IDAHO [1884] 43x64cm (17½x25½") Full color. [56] £78 $120
PHILADELPHIA [1856] 38x32cm (15x13") Pastel col. Ref: Simonetti 408; Phillips (M) 706. [36] £39 $60
PITTSBURGH [ON SHEET WITH] CINCINNATI [1855-56] J.H. Colton. 46x38cm (18x15") Full Color. VG. [61] £29 $45
SOUTH AMERICA [1855-56] J.H. Colton. 46x38cm (18x15") VG. [61] £29 $45
TERRITORIES OF NEW MEXICO AND UTAH [1855] 1st ed. Territories extend to Calif. 31x40cm (12½x15½") Color. Ref: Wheat (TM) IV frontis, 832. [36] £97 $150
[SAME TITLE] [same date & dimen] Incl present AZ & NV. Full color. [51] £97 $150
THE CITY OF LOUISVILLE KENTUCKY [AND] THE CITY OF NEW ORLEANS LOUISIANA [1855] 36x29cm (14x11") Full color. Fine. [20] £49 $75
THE TERRITORIES OF WASHINGTON AND OREGON [1855 / 1857] East to Rockies. 32x41cm (12½x16") Full color. Margin loss, image unaffected. [51] £81 $125
THE UNITED STATES OF AMERICA [1856] 38x64cm (14½x25") [36] £127 $195
WASHINGTON AND OREGON [1855] 1st ed. East to South Pass. 32x39cm (12½x15½") Col. [36] £65 $100
WASHINGTON AND OREGON [1856] East to Continental Divide. 28x38cm (11x15") With text page. Full color. Edges browned; fine. [19] £81 $125
WEST INDIES [1855-56] J.H. Colton. 32x40cm (12½x15½") VG. [61] £42 $65
WISCONSIN [1855-56] 38x46cm (15x18") Full color. VG. [61] £49 $75
WYOMING, COLORADO AND UTAH [1884] 44x65cm (17½x25½") Color. [56] £81 $125

COLTON (Pocket & Wall Maps)

BURR'S MAP OF THE STATE OF NEW YORK [1840] Folding map; later ed of Colton's 1st imprint acquired from Burr, reengraved by Samuel Stiles. 33x38cm (13x15") Color. Misfolding & minor separations; generally good. [13] £123 $190

COLTON'S DOMINION OF CANADA NO.3. THE PROVINCES OF NEW BRUNSWICK & NOVA SCOTIA AND PRINCE EDWARD ISLAND [1871] G.W. & C.B. Colton. Backed on linen in sections; folds into cloth covers. 46x66cm (18x26½") Sm splits lower edge folds; backstrip chipped, crude tape repair. [28] £146 $225

COLTON'S ILLUSTRATED & EMBELLISHED STEEL PLATE MAP OF THE WORLD ON MERCATOR'S PROJECTION ... EXHIBITING THE RECENT ARCTIC AND ANTARCTIC DISCOVERIES & EXPLORATIONS [Ent. 1848] Wall map on rollers; surround of plans & views. D.Griffing Johnson, sc. 142x201cm (56x79") Orig color. Side margin tears; dampmarks upper portion; lower margin starting to separate from roller. [28] £847 $1,305

COLTON'S MAP OF THE STATES AND TERRITORIES FROM THE MISSISSIPPI RIVER TO THE PACIFIC OCEAN &C, &C. [1874] G.W. & C.B. Colton. Pocket map folds into 8vo boards. 71x104cm (28x41") OL & full color. Map fold separations; clean. Sl rubbed boards split at spine; good. [6] £312 $480

COLTON'S NEW TOWNSHIP MAP OF THE WESTERN COUNTIES OF PENNSYLVANIA [1876] Folds into 6x4" boards. Western third of PA. 97x69cm (37½x26½") Color. Average wear; repairs, no loss. [9] £62 $95

MAP OF IOWA [1852] Folds into orig case. 33x41cm (12½x16") Full color. Previous owners pencil extensions partially erased; VG. [44] £162 $250

MAP OF OHIO [1853] J.H. Colton. Pocket map, folds into 12mo embossed boards. 30x38cm (12x15") OL & full color. Missing only sm corner edge; sl stain front board; clean, nice. [6] £237 $365

MAP SHOWING THE ATCHISON, TOPEKA AND SANTA FE RAILROAD SYSTEM [1885] Issued with 1884 annual report to stockholders. 53x84cm (21x33") OL & RR line color. Cracking at folds, verso repairs, minor loss at fold junctions. Ref: Ristow (Amer M&M) fig.19-11. [10] £179 $275

COMPANY MAPS

CORRECT COUNTY MAP OF THE STATE OF KANSAS [1880] Smith & Keating (implements & carriages), with booklet by Ramsey, Millett and Hudson, lith., K.C. 28x53cm (11x20½") Browning; edge chipping. [11] £97 $150

MAP SHOWING LINES OF THE BELL TELEPHONE COMPANIES IN THE UNITED STATES ... [1906] Folding map. Phone lines in green. 64x97cm (25x38½") Printed color. [58] £42 $65

CONKEY

MAP OF NORTH AMERICA SHOWING ALL ROUTES TO ALASKA AND KLONDIKE COUNTRY [1898] Reverse: Six AK sectional maps. 36x38cm (13½x14½") Full printed color. Fine. [19] £49 $75

CONSTABLE

[ATLAS] CONSTABLE'S HAND ATLAS OF INDIA [1893] J.G. Bartholomew. London: A. Constable. Large 12mo; 60 double-page printed color maps & city plans; 129 pp statistics, ads & index. Ex lib, with marks. Boards & rebound spine soiled, pinched; occas spot, contents tight, maps clean; o/w VG. [7] £62 $95

COOK   Try *Benard, Hogg*

A CHART OF THE NORTH WEST COAST OF AMERICA AND NORTH EAST COAST OF ASIA [c. 1780+] Voyages of 1778-79; by Hogg. 21x35cm (8½x14") B&W. [40] £75 $116

CARTE D'UNE PARTIE DE LA COTE DE LA N'LE GALLES MERID'LE ... [1774] French ed. Passage through Barrier Reef. 30x35cm (12x13½") OL color. Ref: Tooley (Australia) 344; Clancy p.124. [16] £275 $424

CARTE DE L'HEMISPHERE AUSTRAL [1778] 54x55cm (21½x22") OL color. Ref: Tooley (Australia) 75, Antarc 335. [16] £304 $468

CARTE DE L'ISLE DE TAITI PAR LE LIEUTENANT J. COOK 1769 [1780] 23x41cm (9x16") [51] £162 $250

CARTE DE LA N'LE. GALLES MERID'LE ... N'LE HOLLANDE ... [1774] French ed. 1st pub chart of Australian east coast. 36x77cm (14x30") OL color. Ref: Tooley (Australia) 342. [16] £522 $804

ENTREE DE LA RIVIERE ENDEAVOUR DANS LA NLE. GALLES MERID. [ON SHEET WITH] BAYE DE BOTANIQUE DANS LA NLE. GALLES MERIDIONALE [1774] French ed. 14x34cm (5½x13½") Color. Ref: Tooley (Australia) 343 pl.166; Clancy pp 126-7. [16] £180 $278

KAART VAN DE EILANDEN IN DEN OMTREK VAN OTAHITI ... [1773 (1795)] Society & Tuamotu Islands. Allart & Van Cleef after Hawkesworth; Dutch ed 1st voyage. 25x51cm (9½x19½") Lt spotting; margins reduced. [15] £50 $77

KAART VAN DE NOORD-WEST KUST VAN AMERIKA EN DE NOORD-OOST KUST VAN ASIA. OPGENOOMEN IN DE JAAREN 1778 EN 1779 ... [1795] Allart & Van Cleef after Cook & King, Dutch ed of Cook's 3rd voya 38x64cm (15x25½") Damp marking; Fold lines, damage repaired. [15] £170 $262

KAART VAN DEN MOND VAN NORTON, EN VAN DE ENGTE VAN BHERING ... [1798] 26x38cm (10½x15") [14] £49 $75

KAART VAN EEN GEDEELTE VAN DE KUST VAN NIEUW ZUID WALES, VAN KWELLING KAAP TOT DE ENDEAVOUR-STRAAT. DOOR LUIT. J. COOK 1770 [1795] Allart & Van Cleef, Dutch ed of Cook's 1st voyage. York Peninsula, East Coast. 30x33cm (11½x13") Fold lines. [15] £175 $270

NORFOLK ISLE [1777] 2nd voyage. 20x18cm (8x7") Color. [15] £45 $69

PLAN DES COTES DE TERRE NEUVE IIIE. FEUILLE CONTENANT LE PARTIE MERIDIONALE DEPUIS LES ILES DE BURGEO JUSQU'AU CAPE DE RAYE, AVEC L'ENTREE DE GOLFE DE ST. LAURENT ... TIRE DES PLANS ANGLOIS DE J. COOK ET M. LANE ... [1784] 66x97cm (26x38") Sh split lower c'fold. Ref: Tooley (Amer) p.201. [28] £204 $315

SCHETS VAN HET KANAAL VAN NOOTKA [c. 1800] Dutch ed. 26x21cm (10½x8½") [14] £32 $50

SKETCH OF NOOTKA SOUND [c. 1780+] By Hogg. 33x21cm (13x8") B&W. [40] £78 $120

SKETCH OF THE HARBOUR OF SAMGANOODA ON THE ISLAND OONALASKA [c. 1780+] By Hogg. 20x33cm (8x13") B&W. [40] £65 $100

THE PACIFIC OCEAN, THE NEW DISCOVERIES THERE, AND TRACKS OF THE NAVIGATORS [c. 1780-1790] After Cook's South Seas chart. 18x33cm (7x13") OL color. [16] £209 $322

COPLEY

[GLOBE] IMPROVED GLOBE. BOSTON ... [1852 - c.1867] Charles Copley, NY; Gilman Joslin, mfr. 15" hollow metal orb dressed in plaster; steel engraved gores. Color. Nickel time dial & meridian ring; walnut equatorial ring, on iron brackets atop cast iron baluster column on tripod with casters, 42" high. Some repairs, loss at globe surface & paper scales; o/w nice. [17] £8,115 $12,500

CORNELL

UNITED STATES [(1855) c.1870] 32x52cm (12½x20½") Orig color. Very nice. [1] £65 $100

CORONELLI   Try *Nolin*

... GLOBE CELESTE ... [1689-] Depiction of 15 foot globe presented to Louis XIV. 45x62cm (17½x24") Color. [52] £500 $770

[GLOBE GORE: AUSTRALIA] [c. 1688-1699] Probably from 1699 *Libro Dei Globi* reprint. For 110 cm (42") globe. 48x28cm (18½x11") Ref: Shirley (W) 537, pl.376. Tooley (M&M) pl.90; Schilder frontis; Clancy pp.96-7. [16] £1,140 $1,755

[GLOBE GORE: CENTRAL AUSTRALIA] [1688] 47x27cm (18½x11") on uncut sheet. Exc. [62] £1,623 $2,500

[GLOBE GORES: NORTH AMERICA] [c. 1697 - 1701] 5 gores joined & mounted on sheet; hand drawn border. Arctic to Florida, Newfoundland to insular Calif. 48x79cm (19x31") Modern color. Insignificant pinholes; sh tears repaired. [28] £2,110 $3,250

CANADA ORIENTALE NELL'AMERICA SETTENTRIONALI DESCRITTA DAL P. MIO CORONELLI ... [c. 1696] 45x61cm (18x24") Ref: Phillips (A) 521; Portinaro & Knirsch pl.98. [28] £760 $1,170

GLI ARGONAUTI [c. 1691] Navigation & surveying instruments. 39x25cm (15x9½") Color. [52] £280 $431

ISOLA CUBA DESCRITTA DAL P. MRO. CORONELLI LETTORE PUBLICA, E COSMOGRAFO DELLA S.S. REPUBLICA DI VENETIA [1696] 22x29cm (9x11") Separate sheet, wide margins. Exc. [63] £276 $425

ISOLE ANTILI, LA CUBA, E LA SPAGNUOLA DESCRITTO E DEDICATA DAL PADRE MAESTRO CORONELLI [1695-96] From *Atlante Veneto*. 25x43cm (10x17") B&W. Fine. Ref: Phillips (A) 521, 39. [49] £487 $750

ISOLE DI TERRA NUOVA SCOPERTA DA GIO: CABOTA VENETO CO SUO FIGLIUOLO SEBASTIANO L'AN 1596 ... [c. 1690] 23x30cm (9½x12") Lower & lf margin trimmed to plate mark. [28] £351 $540

LA LOUISIANA, PARTE SETTENTRIONALE, SCOPERTA SOTTO LA PROTETTIONE DI LUIGI XIV ... DAL P. COSMOGRAFO CORONELLI ... [1693] Venice. 26x42cm (10½x16½") B&W. Worming in margins; else fine. Ref: Karpinski (MI) XXVII. [55] £1,169 $1,800

[SAME TITLE] [1696] Great Lakes region. [same dimen] Exc. [63] £1,169 $1,800

[SAME TITLE] [c. 1696] [same dimen] Ref: Karpinski (MI) p.117; Phillips (A) 521. [28] £1,169 $1,800

MARE DEL NORD ... [1690] 45x60cm (18x23½") Uncolored. Fine. [30] £1,071 $1,650

MARE DEL SUD, DETTRO ALTRIMENN MARE PACIFICO [1690] 45x60cm (18x23½") Uncolored. VG. Ref: Tooley (Australia) P48, #350. [31] £1,298 $2,000

Mare del Sud, detto Altrimenti Mare Pacifico Auttore il P.M. Coronelli ... [1691 - 1696] Insular Calif. 45x60cm (18x23½") Color. Ref: Tooley (Australia) 350; Clancy, illus. [16] £1,614 $2,487
[Same title] [c. 1692] Insular California. 44x58cm (17½x23") Color. [41] £1,600 $2,464
Planisfero del Mondo Nuovo Descritto dal P. Coronelli Cosmografo Publico Dedicato all'Illustrissimo, et Eccellentissimo Signore Andrea Marcello, Senatore Amplissimo [1695] In *Atlante Veneto*. Circular map with calculations & decor; insular Calif. 46x61cm (18½x24") Exc. Ref: Shirley (W) 548; Phillips (A) 521, 3. [22] £1,298 $2,000
[Same title] [(1695) 1697] From *Atlante Veneto*. Insular California. 38x61cm (15½x24") B&W. Fine. Ref: Shirley (W) pl.383. [1] £1,233 $1,900
Planisfero del Mondo, Vecchio Descritto [in set with] Planisfero del Mondo, Nuovo Descritto [c. 1697] Insular Calif. 2 sheet, each 45x61cm (18x24") Color. Ref: Shirley (W) 548, pl.383 (title citation differs). [16] £3,703 $5,705
Planisfero Settentrionale ... [with] Planisfero Meridionale ... [1692-] Two charts: N & S celestial hemispheres. Each 46x61cm (18x24") Color. [52] £1,600 $2,464
Terre Artiche Descritte dal P.M. Coronelli M.C. Cosmografo della Serenss. Republica di Venetia ... [c. 1696] 46x61cm (18x24") Ref: Phillips (A) 521. [28] £818 $1,260

COVENS & MORTIER

[Title page] Atlas Novus ... [1733] De Hooghe, sc. 48x28cm (19x11") B&W. Fine. Ref: Koeman C&M5, fig.13. [50] £487 $750
Carte de la Louisiane et du Cours du Mississipi Dressee sur un Grand Nombre de Memoires entr'autres sur Ceux de Mr. Le Maire par Guillme. De L'Isle de l'Academie Rle. des Sciences [1730] 44x60cm (17½x23½") Orig OL color. Lt browning at lf; orig off-center fold. Ref: Cumming (SE) 208. Wheat (TM) 17; Martin (TX) pl.17. [46] £1,201 $1,850
[Same title] [same date & dimen] Dutch derivative of De L'Isle. Orig color. [53] £1,200 $1,848
Carte Generale de Toutes les Costes du Monde ... [1733] P. Mortier. Insular California; NW Passage. 2 sheets, each 58x100cm (23x39½") Orig OL col. Good. Ref: Stevens (Evans 1749-55) [14] £1,136 $1,750
Carte Generale de Toutes les Costes du Monde ... Amerique ... [and sheet with] Partie Orientale du Monde ... [c. 1720] Two maps. Insular California; NW Passage. Each 58x51cm (23x19½") Full orig color. [2] £3,571 $5,500
Iudae, sive Terra Sancta ... [1725] From *Atlas Antiquus*. After Sanson. 46x61cm (18x24") + title above. Uncolored. Margins bit soiled; plate residue; bright, clear, o/w clean. Ref: Laor 694; Nebenzahl (Holy Land) p.134-5. [59] £390 $600
Mappa Totius Regni Bohemiae [1740] 51x56cm (19½x21½") OL color. [36] £162 $250
Nouvelle Carte Particuliere de l'Amerique ou Sont Exactement Marquees la Nouvelle Bretagne, le Canada or Nouvelle France ... [c. 1737] 61x56cm (24x21½") Orig OL & border color. Sh margin c'fold tears repaired. Ref: Koeman II C&M 11; Phillips (A) 3448. [28] £701 $1,080
Nova Orbi Tabula ad Usum Serenissimi ... [1733] After De L'Isle, based on De Wit. 50x64cm (19½x25") Orig OL color. Good. [14] £1,006 $1,550
Quebec [c. 1740] City view with key. 13x26cm (5x10") [40] £250 $385
Theatrum Historicum pars Occidentalis [in set with] Theatrum Historicum pars Orientalis [1733] After De L'Isle. Each 48x60cm (19x23½") Orig OL color. [14] £162 $250

COWPERTHWAIT

New Jersey [1847] Pocket map folding into calf binding. 18 counties. 48x33cm (18½x12½") Cover scuffed & sl skewed. Fold line tears, minor loss at 2 junctions. [35] £104 $160

CRAM

[Atlas] Cram's Unrivaled Family Atlas of the World [1883-84] Early or 1st ed. Large quarto. 124 pp; Maps, some double-page, in printed color; some titled, "New Railroad and County Map of ..." Lt damp-stains lower margins, but VG; a good copy. [5] £97 $150
[Same title] [1884] 2nd ed. 115 pp; mainly American atlas of state maps, each with pink/red border & green OL color. (no dims.) Hinges loose; lacks unimportant page; good. [45] £81 $125
[Same title] [1886] G.F. Cram, Chicago; 13th ed. Large quarto; 200 pp, 99 maps (15 double-paged) Printed color. Boards rubbed; torn corners, spine edges; hinge separations; contents VG. [7] £91 $140
Alaska [1902] Insets incl Klondike District. 43x56cm (16½x22½") Full printed color. [51] £62 $95
[Same title] [1905] From *Crams New American Standard Railway Atlas*. 3 gold area insets. 46x64cm (18x25") Much color. [44] £39 $60

ALBERTA, ASSINIBOIA, ATHABASCA & SASKETCHEWAN [1902] 41x56cm (16x21½") OL col. [51] £81 $125
ARIZONA [1885] RR map. 56x41cm (21½x16") Some printed color. [10] £55 $85
[SAME TITLE] [1901] From *Crams New American Standard Railway Atlas*. 64x46cm (25x18") RR's color coded. [44] £52 $80
BRITISH COLUMBIA [1902] 43x56cm (16½x22") OL color. [51] £81 $125
COLORADO [c. 1890] 25x33cm (10x12½") Full color. [36] £39 $60
CRAM'S TOWNSHIP AND RAIL ROAD MAP OF NEW YORK [1889] Folding map with 58 p gazetteer; printed wraps. 43x56cm (16½x22") Wraps spotted; repaired fold split. [11] £55 $85
FLORIDA [1892] From *Cram's Standard American Railway Systems Atlas*. 45 counties; RRs color coded. 56x41cm (22½x16½") With index pages. Printed color. [4] £62 $95
IDAHO [1885] Reverse: part of MT. 28x23cm (11x9") Printed OL color. Fine. [18] £26 $40
[SAME TITLE] [1891] 51x41cm (20x16") [11] £55 $85
[SAME TITLE] [1905] From *Crams New American Standard Railway Atlas*. 64x46cm (25x18") Color. [44] £52 $80
INDIAN TERRITORY [1884] 25x30cm (9½x12") OL color. [36] £42 $65
MAP OF NEW SOUTH WALES [1902] 41x56cm (16x22") Printed color. [51] £62 $95
MAP OF VICTORIA [1902] 41x56cm (16x22") Printed color. [51] £62 $95
MONTANA [1883] 30x48cm (12x18½") OL color. [36] £39 $60
[SAME TITLE] [1885] Reverse: Idaho; Wyoming. 30x46cm (11½x18") Printed OL color. Fine. [18] £45 $70
[SAME TITLE] [1895] 30x46cm (11½x18") Full printed color. Fine. [18] £29 $45
[SAME TITLE] [1905] From *Crams New American Standard Railway Atlas*. 46x64cm (18x25") Color; RR's coded. [44] £52 $80
NEVADA [1895] RR's color coded. 57x41cm (22x16") OL color. [56] £55 $85
NEW HAMPSHIRE AND VERMONT [1890] 56x41cm (22x16") Railroads color coded. [36] £42 $65
NEW MEXICO [1905] From *Crams New American Standard Railway Atlas*. RR's color coded. 64x46cm (25x18") [44] £52 $80
NORTH DAKOTA [1905] From *Crams New American Standard Railway Atlas*. RR's color coded. 46x64cm (18x25") South Dakota offered at same price. [44] £52 $80
NORTH-WEST TERRITORY [1888] 41x56cm (16x22") Printed OL color. [58] £42 $65
PENNSYLVANIA [1889] 41x56cm (16x22½") OL color. [36] £36 $55
POCKET MAP OF VERMONT AND NEW HAMPSHIRE [c. 1896] Folds into 12mo printed wraps, "Compliments of the Lester H Green Co. ..." (Syrup of Tar). 33x25cm (13x10") Color. Lt age-tone wrap; pinhole; near fine. [6] £58 $90
PORTO RICO [1899] 33x56cm (13x21½") Color. [25] £29 $45
SEATTLE, WASHINGTON [c. 1900] Street map. 36x25cm (13½x10") Printed color. [56] £23 $35
TEXAS [1905] From *Crams New American Standard Railway Atlas*. RR's color coded. 46x64cm (18x25") [44] £65 $100
TEXAS, WESTERN PART [c. 1900] 53x33cm (20½x13½") Full color. [46] £81 $125
UTAH [1905] From *Crams New American Standard Railway Atlas*. RR's color coded. 64x46cm (25x18") Exc. [44] £52 $80
WYOMING [1889] 25x30cm (9½x12") Full printed color. Fine. [18] £23 $35
[SAME TITLE] [1893] [same dimen] Full color. [36] £32 $50
[SAME TITLE] [1902] From RR Atlas; routes in color. 41x56cm (16½x22½") Printed OL col. [51] £81 $125
[SAME TITLE] [1905] From *Crams New American Standard Railway Atlas*. RR's color coded. 46x64cm (18x25") [44] £52 $80

CREPY

QUEBEC [c. 1755] 18x22cm (7x8½") Orig color. Protective strip added top margin. [54] £450 $693

CRUCHLEY

MAP OF THE WORLD ON MERCATOR'S PROJECTION SHOWING THE DISCOVERIES AT THE NORTH POLE AND THE NEW SETTLEMENTS IN AUSTRALIA. NEW ZEALAND &C. [Update to 1853] 2 linen backed sheets as issued, with half roan covers, each 94x86cm (37x34") Orig color. Cover spine head chipped & joint starting to crack; some staining & soiling; tear at a crease. [28] £351 $540
SYRIA [1856] 46x36cm (18x14") Color. Ref: Laor 229. [23] £26 $40

CUMMINGS & HILLIARD

[ATLAS] SCHOOL ATLAS [c. 1815] Octavo; 8 double-page maps. U.S. with color, most without. Title page lacking; N. Amer map heavily toned; U.S. soiled; 2 with ink & other stains. [5] £97 $150
NORTH AMERICA [1814] 25x20cm (10½x8") OL color. [57] £65 $100
THE UNITED STATES ... [1817] From *American School Atlas*. 23x28cm (8½x11") Full orig color. Mild soiling. [44] £91 $140
THE WORLD [1817] Double hemi. (no dims.) Later full color. [44] £104 $160

D'ANVILLE

A MAP OF THE WORLD, DRAWN AND ENGRAVED FROM D'ANVILLE'S TWO-SHEET MAP WITH IMPROVEMENTS FOR J. HARRISON [1788] Updated English ed. 40x73cm (15½x28½") Orig OL color. C'fold supported; sl soiled. [14] £143 $220
AMERIQUE MERIDIONALE ... [1748] 3 sheets, each more or less 43x76cm (17x30") Large cartouche. Orig OL color. [28] £321 $495
AMERIQUE SEPTENTRIONALE ... [1746] 2 sheets: north & south, if joined 81x86cm (32x34") Color, not quite matching; different weight paper suggests different editions for each sheet. [13] £438 $675
[SAME TITLE] [1746 / 1761] 5th state. 2 sheets, each 46x89cm (18x34½") Orig OL color. Faint vert creases. Ref: Wagner (NW) 332; Karpinski p.138; Heidenreich & Dahl p.15-6. [28] £760 $1,170
CANADA, LOUISIANE ET TERRES ANGLOISES ... [1755] 4 sheets, each except #3 (St. Lawrence River) about 48x56cm (19x22") Margins foxed; dampmarks upper margin. Ref: Cumming (SE) 296; Karpinski (MI) p.138. [28] £1,052 $1,620
CARTE DE L'INDE DRESSEE POUR LA COMPAGNIE DES INDES PAR LE SR. D'ANVILLE ... [1752] 4 sheets joined to form two, each about 48x104cm (19x41") Crease to one sheet. Ref: cf Gole (India) #54. [28] £204 $315
CARTE DE LA LOUISIANE [1732, 1752] 52x92cm (20½x36") B&W. Fine. Ref: Phillips (A) 571, 35; Lowery 333. [49] £909 $1,400
L'AMERIQUE SEPTENTRIONALE [1746] 2 sheets joined (of 4); present eastern U.S. to Gulf of California. (no dims.) Color. Repaired tear outside printed area. [55] £422 $650
L'ORIENT POUR L'HISTOIRE ANCIENNE DE MR. ROLLIN ... [1740] Middle East. 28x36cm (11x14") Color. [23] £81 $125
THE EAST BY MR. D'ANVILLE ... [1740] E. Bowen, London. 28x36cm (10½x14") Color. [23] £81 $125

D'APRES DE MANNEVILLETTE

CARTE DES ISLES NICOBAR ... [1775] From *Neptune Oriental*. 46x30cm (18x12") Faint browning lower margin. [15] £45 $69
CARTE REDUITE DE L'OCEAN ORIENTAL SEPTENTRIONAL ... [1775] 48x66cm (19x26") Browning on ctr. [15] £50 $77
PLAN DE L'ISLE DE FRANCE ... [1774] 50x72cm (19½x28½") Color. [54] £450 $693
PLAN DE L'ISLE RODRIGUES [1775] In *Neptune Oriental*. 33x49cm (13x19") Lt damp mark upper margin corner. [15] £90 $139
PLAN DE LA RADE D'ACHEM ET DES ISLES CIRCONVOISINES ... [SUMATRA] [1775] From *Neptune Oriental*. 48x33cm (19x13") Faint browning lower edge. [15] £60 $92
PLAN DE SALANGOR ET DE LA COTE DE MALAYE DEPUIS LA POINTE DE CARAN JUSQU'AU MONT PARCELAR [1775] In *Neptune Oriental*. 48x33cm (19x13") [15] £75 $116
VUES DES CAPS D'ADEN, DE ST ANTOINE, ET DE BAB-EL-MANDEB [ON SHEET WITH] VUES DE L'ISLE SOCOTRA [YEMEN] [1775] Views 48x33cm (19x13") [15] £30 $46
VUES DIVERSES DU FORT DE L'AGOUADE PRES DE L'ISLE DE GOA ... [ON SHEET WITH] VUES DIVERSES DE L'ISLE AUX COCHONS [1775] From *Neptune Oriental*. 3 views of Goa; 6 of Sumatra west coast. 43x33cm (17x13") Sl browning. [15] £40 $62

D'ENTRECASTEAUX

CARTE REDUITE DES LA MER DES INDES [1800] From journal of voyage in search of La Perouse. Labillardiere; Barbie du Bocage. 48x71cm (18½x28") OL color. Ref: Tooley (Australia) 139. [16] £665 $1,024

DALRYMPLE

A CHART OF THE STRAIT OF ALLASS CONSTRUCTED FROM OBSERVATIONS MADE IN MARCH 1796 [1798, c. 1828] Hydrographical Office badge. 30x23cm (11½x8½") [15] £100 $154

A MAP OF PART OF BORNEO, AND THE SOOLOO ARCHIPELAGO: LAID DOWN CHIEFLY FROM OBSERVATIONS MADE IN 1761, 2, 3, AND 4 BY A. DALRYMPLE [1769, c.1827] Watermark dated as Admiralty issue. 48x64cm (18½x24½") 1" edge tear; o/w exc. [15] £190 $293

CHART OF PART OF THE ISLANDS OF PORA ... AND POGGYS [1783, c. 1828] Hydrographic Office seal. 30x18cm (11½x7") [15] £70 $108

SKETCH OF THE WEST COAST OF LOMBOCK. FROM A DRAUGHT OF RODDIN TOMOONGOONG COMMUNICATED BY JOHN MARSDEN ESQR ... [1784, c. 1828] Hydrographical Office seal. 28x20cm (11½x7½") Sl reduced margins. [15] £100 $154

THE SOOLOO ARCHIPELAGO, LAID DOWN CHIEFLY FROM OBSERVATIONS IN 1761, 1762, 1763 & 1764, BY A. DALRYMPLE [1771 (c.1827)] Watermark dated Admiralty issue. 46x61cm (18x24") [15] £180 $277

DANCKERTS

ACCURATISSIMA REGNORUM SUECIAE, DANIAE, ET NORVEGIAE. TABULA. PER JUSTINUM DANCKERS ... [c. 1696] 50x59cm (20x23") Orig OL & cartouche color, heightened in gilt. Lt offsetting; sh top margin tears repaired. Ref: Koeman III Dan 1 & 3. [28] £409 $630

AFRICAE NOVISS: CATERES TABULA [c. 1680] Theodore Danckers. 43x53cm (17x20½") Orig OL color; full cartouche color. Lt soiling in margin; o/w exc. [2] £909 $1,400

DE WERELT CAART [1728] Amsterdam: Wetstein & Smith; Leiden: Luchtmans. Double hemi; insular Calif. 38x51cm (14½x20½") Repaired tears below. Ref: cf. Shirley 615; pl.424. [28] £1,694 $2,610

NOVI BELGII NOVAEQUE ANGLIAE NEC NON PENNSYLVANIAE ET PARTIS VIRGINIAE TABULA [1655 / c.1685] With Manhattan view. 46x55cm (18x21½") Orig OL color. 2 tears repaired. Ref: Tooley (Amer) p.285, pl.150. [2] £3,116 $4,800

DAPPER

ARX CAROLINA [1673] From *America*, German ed. View: French Ft. Caroline near present Jacksonville. 28x35cm (11x13½") Minor brown spot; VG. [4] £321 $495

DARTON & HARVEY

A MAP OF NORTH AMERICA, ENGRAVED FOR PRISCILLA WAKEFIELD'S EXCURSION [1806] Fictional travels, Arctic to New Orleans. 36x38cm (14x15") B&W; routes in pink. [46] £29 $45

DASHIELL

EXTRACT FROM A MAP OF THE BRITISH AND FRENCH DOMINIONS IN NORTH AMERICA BY JNO. MITCHELL [1843] Washington; pub in the U.S.-Canada Boundary Commission report. 33x33cm (13x13") Parchment paper. B&W. Ref: Phillips (M) p.384. [46] £45 $70

MAP OF THE NORTHERN PART OF THE STATE OF MAINE AND OF THE ADJACENT BRITISH PROVINCES [1830 (1843)] Washington: pub in the U.S.-Canada Boundary Commission report. 43x38cm (16½x15½") Parchment paper. Orig OL color. Moderate offsetting; trimmed almost to neat lines. Ref: Phillips (M) p.384. [46] £55 $85

DAVIES

SYRIA [1838] London: Fisher & Son. 25x18cm (10x7½") [23] £19 $30

DE AEFFERDEN

[WORLD] [1709] After Jacques Peeters, 1692. 14x27cm (5½x11") Color. [16] £522 $804

GLOBUS TERRESTRIS [1709] Double hemi from Abbreviated Atlas. 16x24cm (6½x9½") Col. [16] £560 $863

LUTZENBURGI [1696] 15x18cm (6x7½") Sm worm hole lower rt. [57] £36 $55

NAMURCI [BELGIUM] [1696] 15x18cm (5½x7") OL color. [57] £36 $55

PLANI-SPHERIUM COELESTE [1709] From *El Atlas Abeviado*. 14x27cm (5½x11") Hemispheres in orig wash. Fine. Ref: Warner, Afferdon 1. [49] £192 $295

DE BELLEFOREST

LA VILLE, CITE, UNIVERSITE, & FAUX-BOURGS DE PARIS [1575] From *La Geographie Universelle* .... Woodblock plan. 42x55cm (16½x21½") Uncolored. Tears restored along orig folds. [54] £800 $1,232

DE BRY

[DISCOVERY OF THE MAGELLAN STRAITS] [1594] Highly allegorical. On page with text. 15x20cm (5½x8") Illuminated initial letter. [14] £243 $375
[DRAKE LANDS IN CALIFORNIA] [1599] Scene of reception by Indians. 13x18cm (5½x7") [14] £114 $175
[RALEIGH AT PORT OF SPAIN] [1599] Text below. 14x18cm (5½x7") [14] £81 $125
[TITLE PAGE] [WORLD] [1599] Oval, with Cavendish circumnavigation; strapwork surround with birds & flora. 9x14cm (3½x5½") Color. [57] £243 $375
AMERICA SIVE NOVUS ORBIS RESPECTU EUROPAEORUM INFERIOR GLOBI TERRESTRIS PARS 1596 [1596] Circular map; 4 corner figures. 33x40cm (13x16") [3] £4,220 $6,500
AMERICA SIVE NOVUS ORBIS RESPECTU EUROPAEORUM INFERIOR GLOBI TERRESTRIS PARS. 1596 [1596] From "Grand Voyages". 33x40cm (13x16") Uncolored. Close top margin; 1 cm bottom image loss replaced in facsimile; old wrinkling & creasing; japan paper backing. [31] £2,337 $3,600
AMERICAE PARS, NUNC VIRGINIA DICTA, PRIMUM AB ANGLIS INVENTA SUMTIBUS DN. WALTERI RALEIGH ... [1590] After John White's Roanoke area map. 30x42cm (12x16½") [3] £5,518 $8,500
AQUAPOLQUE [c. 1630] Acapulco view. 15x19cm (6x7½") Exc. [63] £146 $225
CARTA TRIUM NAVIGATIONUM PER BATAVOS AD SEPTENTRIONALEM PLAGEM [1599] After Barentz, with 1596-7 track. 28x36cm (11x14") Uncolored. [52] £1,200 $1,848
HISPANIAE NOVAE SIVE MAGNAE RECENS ET VERA DESCRIPTIO 1595 [1595] 33x44cm (13x17½") 3 close margins as issued; o/w good. [14] £357 $550
[SAME TITLE] [same date & dimen] Uncolored. Close top margin; o/w VG+. [30] £325 $500
NOVA TABULA INSULARUM IAVAE, SUMATRAE, BORNEONIS ET ALIARUM MALLACAM USQUAE ... NEUWE UND EIGENTICHE FURBILDING, DER INSELN, JAVA, SUMATRA, BORNEO, BIS GEN MALACA ... [1598] From "Petit Voyages", Part II (van Linschoten's voyage). 37x43cm (14½x17") Full later color. Some patched worming; else fine. Ref: TMC 6, p.9-10. [62] £1,818 $2,800
OCCIDENTALIS AMERICAE PARTIS, VELEARUM REGIONUM QUAS CHRISTOPHORUS COLUMBUS PRIMU DETEXIT TABULA CHOROGRAPHICAE MULTORUM AUCTORUM SCRIPTIS, PRAESERTIM VERO EX HIERONYMI BENZONI ... THEODORE DE BRY LEOD. ... [1594] 33x43cm (13x17") Remargined; exc. [62] £3,116 $4,800
TABULA GEOGRA. REGNI CONGO [c. 1605] 31x38cm (12x15") Close margins. [14] £315 $485
TABULA HYDROGRAPHICA MARIS AUSTRALIS VULGO DEL ZUR, DUCTUM NAVIGATIONIS WILHELM SCHOUTEN ET TERRAS AC INSULAS AB EO IBIDEN DETECTAS DEMOSTRANS [1619] From "Grand Voyages", Part XI. 17x41cm (6½x16") Exc. [62] £243 $375
TABULA NAUTICA, QUA REPRAESENTATUR ORAE MARITIMAE MEATUS, AC FRETA, NOVITER A H HUDSON ANGLO AD CAURUM SUPRA NOVAM FRANCIAM INDAGATA ANNO 1612 [1613] As in *Petit Voyages* (Part X). Reduce from Gerritsz. 15x36cm (6½x13½") Creases lower lf margin. Ref: Skelton (Explorer) fig.78; Cumming (Discovery) p.244. [28] £1,169 $1,800

DE FER (Large)

ESTATS DES COURONNES DE DANNEMARK, SUEDE, ET POLOGNE SUR LA MER BALTIQUE [1701 - 1703] 44x70cm (17x27½") Narrow rt margin now supported. [14] £185 $285
INTRODUCTION A LA GEOGRAPHIE DE LA CORRESPONDANCE DU GLOBE TERRESTRE OU MAPPE-MONDE AVEC LA SPHERE CELESTE PAR LES CERCLES, LES LIGNES ET LES POINTS QUI SONT ... [1722] Paris: Danet. Double hemi; insular Calif; 3 armillary globes. 46x69cm (18x27½") Color. [22] £510 $785
LA CALIFORNIE OU NOUVELLE CAROLINE, TEATRO DE LOS TRABAJOS, APOSTOLICOS DE COMPA. E JESUS EN LA AMERICA SEPT. ... A PARIS, DANS L'ISLE DU PALAIS A LA SPHERE ROYALE 1720 [1720] Insular California. 46x65cm (18x25½") OL color. Exc. [63] £4,155 $6,400
LA FRANCE, DANS TOUTE SON ETANDUE ... [1725] Paris: Danet. 48x66cm (19½x26") Orig OL color. Ragged lower margin. Ref: Pastoureau, Fer II C. [28] £175 $270
LE GOUVERNEMENT GENERAL DE NORMANDIE DIVISEE EN HAUTE ET BASSE ... [1710] 48x66cm (18½x26½") Orig OL color. Ref: Pastoureau, Fer II C. [28] £175 $270
LES ETATS DE L'EGLISE ET DE TOSCANE ... [1719] 51x58cm (20½x23") Orig OL color. Lower margin trimmed to border; 2 creases. Ref: Pastoureau, Fer 11 C. [28] £162 $250
LES FRONTIERES D'ESPAGNE ET DE PORTUGAL ... [c. 1705] 55x42cm (21½x16½") Color. [43] £250 $385
MAPPE-MONDE OU CARTE GENERALE DE LA TERRE DIVISEE EN DEUX HEMISPHERES SUIVANT LA PROJECTION LA PLUS COMMUNE OU TOUS LES POINTS PRINCIPAUX ... SUR LES OBSERVATIONS DE MRS. DE L'ACADEMIE ROYALE DES SCIENCES ... AVEC PRIVILEGE DU ROY [1694 - 1717] 4-sheets joined; side panels with text; insular California. 97x146cm (38x57½") Color. Some damage; printed loss reinstated in ms. Ref: Shirley (W) 560, pl.390. [52] £12,497 $19,250

Principaute de Transilvanie Divisee en Cinq Nations Subdivisee en Quartiers et Comtez...1705... [1724] 46x51cm (18x19½") Orig OL col. Impression bit weak; faint vert crease; top edges stained. [28] £204 $315

DE FER (Small) Try *Mortier*

[Solar System: Ptolemy; Copernicus; Descartes; Brahe] [1705] 4 diagrams on sheet. 23x33cm (9½x13") Wash color. [58] £88 $135

[Title page] Introduction a la Geographie [n.d.] Sm double hemi; insular Calif; nothing named. (no dims.) [14] £26 $40

Cette Carte de Californie et du Nouveau Mexique Est Tiree de Celle Qui a Ete Envoyee par un Grande d'Espagne pour Etre Communiquee a Mrs de l'Academie Royale des Sciences [1700] 23x34cm (9x13½") Full old color. Fine. [1] £714 $1,100

[Same title] [same date & dimen] Faint orig color. Fine. [1] £584 $900

[Same title] [1700] From *Atlas Curieux ou le Monde* ... 1st ed. Insular Calif; 314 settlements listed. 25x33cm (10x13½") Color. Ref: Phillips (A) 546. [22] £747 $1,150

Copenhague [1705] View. 13x17cm (5x6½") [14] £45 $70

L'Afrique Dressee selon les Dernieres Relat. et Suivant les Nouvelles Decouvertes ... [1717] 23x32cm (9x12½") Margins trimmed to neat lines as issued. Ref: Tooley (Africa) p.45, pl.33. [14] £114 $175

L'Amerique, Meridionale et Septentrionale ... [1717] Insular Calif. 23x34cm (9x13") Margins trimmed to neat line as issued. [14] £341 $525

L'Asie Suivant les Nouvelles Decouvertes dont les Point Principaux Sont Placez ... [1717] 23x32cm (9x12½") Margins trimmed to neat lines as issued. [14] £114 $175

L'Europe [c. 1700] 14x15cm (5½x6") [14] £19 $30

La Haie Sejour Ordinaire de la Cour Hollandoise [1701-1703] Above, plan of Nieuburg near Riswick. 23x33cm (9x13") Lower margin trimmed to neat line. [14] £97 $150

Le Sund ou Detroit du Sond Passage Ordinaire des Vaisseaux qui Entrent ou qui Sortent de la Mer Baltique ... [1701 - 1703] 33x22cm (13x9") [14] £52 $80

Les Capitaneries Garde-Costes de la Roque de Risle, de Honfleur, Touques ... Caen ... La Grune [1690] From *Les Costes de France* ... 1st ed. 22x33cm (8½x13") [14] £52 $80

Les Isles Philippines et Celles des Larrons ou de Marianes, les Isles Moluques et de la Sonde, avec la Presquisle de l'Inde de la Gange ou Orientale ... [1705] 22x34cm (8½x13") Added OL color. Fine. [59] £195 $300

Les Royaumes de Portugal et d'Algarve ... [c. 1705] 36x25cm (14x10") Col. [43] £225 $347

Lisbonne [c. 1705] Outline city plan & 2 building views. 24x33cm (9½x13") B&W. [43] £240 $370

Mappe-Monde ou Carte Generale de la Terre, Dresse sur les Observations de Mrs. de l'Academie Royale des Sciences ... [1717] Double hemi; insular Calif; medallions of explorers. 23x34cm (9x13") Orig OL color. Margins trimmed to neatline as issued. [14] £276 $425

Partie de la Coste de Bretagne [1690] From *Les Costes de France* ... 1st ed. 22x33cm (8½x13") [14] £52 $80

Partie de la Coste de Provence [same date, source & dimen]. [14] £58 $90

Partie des Capitaineries Garde Costes de Brouage et Bourdeaux [same date, source & dimen]. [14] £62 $95

Quebec, Ville de l'Amerique Septentrionale dans la Nouvelle France ... [1705] Plan of 1670 siege. 21x29cm (8½x11½") Damp stain lower part; vert crease. Ref: Phillips (A) 517a. [28] £263 $405

DE GROOT

De Ommevaart der Middelandsche Zee [1776] 13x18cm (5½x6½") Wash color. [57] £39 $60

DE HERRERA

Descripcion de la Provincia de Chile [1624] Frankfurt: De Bry. 10x25cm (4x9½") [14] £42 $65

Descripcion del Audiencia de los Charcas [same date & source]. [14] £49 $75

Descripcion del Destieto del Audiencia de Lima [same date & source]. 16x23cm (6x9") [14] £55 $85

DE JODE

Primae Partis Asiae Acurata Delineatio ... [1578-1593] 30x51cm (12x20") Uncol. [53] £750 $1,155

Quivirae Regnu, cum Alijs Versus Borea [1593] 36x46cm (14½x18") Full orig color. Minor repairs; o/w superb. [3] £7,790 $12,000

DE L'ISLE   Try *Albrizzi, Buache, Covens & Mortier, Dezauche, Lotter*

ASIE DIVISEE EN SES PRINCIPALS REGIONS ET OU SE PEUVENT VOIR L'ESTENDUE DES EMPIRES MONARCHIES ROYAUMES ET ESTATS [1733] Amsterdam: Covens & Mortier. 47x58cm (18½x23") Orig OL color. [14] £292 $450

CARTE D'AFRIQUE ... [1722] 1st state, 1722 map. 51x64cm (20x25½") Orig OL color. Ref: MCCS 48, p.57. [28] £263 $405

CARTE D'AMERIQUE, DRESSEE POUR L'USAGE DU ROI. PAR GUIL. DELISLE ET PHIL. BUACHE, PREMIERS GEOGRAPHES DU ROI, ET DE L'ACADEMIE DE SCIENCES [1790] Paris: Dezauche; state 11. 48x60cm (19x24") Orig OL color. Minor wrinkling along c'fold; lt age toning; VG. Ref: Tooley (Amer) p.15. [32] £373 $575

CARTE D'AMERIQUE DRESSEE POUR L'USAGE DU ROY PAR GUILLAUME DELISLE ... [1739] Amsterdam: Covens & Mortier. Border title, "America accurate In Imperia, Regna Status & Populos Divisa ..." 51x61cm (20½x24") Orig color. [28] £701 $1,080

CARTE D'AMERIQUE DRESSEE POUR L'USAGE DU ROY PAR GUILLAUME DELISLE PREMIER GEOGRAPHE DE SA MAJESTE ... QUAY DE L'HORLOGE ... [1722] 1st state. Peninsular Calif. 51x64cm (19½x25") Orig OL color. Margin spots; repaired lower margin c'fold split. Ref: Wagner (NW) 523; Portinaro & Knirsch pl.CXIV. [28] £760 $1,170

[SAME TITLE] [1722] 1st ed, State 2; "Quay de l'Horloge". 48x61cm (19x24") Orig OL color. VG. Ref: Tooley (Amer) p.13, #2., pl.1 [59] £519 $800

CARTE DE BRABANT [1730 - 1733] From *Atlas Nouveau*. Amsterdam: Covens & Mortier. 65x64cm (25½x25") Orig OL color; cities highlighted. Sm tear repaired. [14] £153 $235

CARTE DE L'EGYPTE DE LA NUBIE DE L'ABISSINIE &C. ... [1707] 51x64cm (20x25") Orig OL color. Sm stain lower c'fold margin. Ref: Tibbetts 199. [28] £234 $360

CARTE DE L'ISLE DE CEYLON DRESSEE SUR LES OBSERVATIONS DE MRS. DE L'ACADEMIE ROYALE DES SCIENCES [1733] Covens & Mortier. 47x57cm (18½x22½") Orig OL col. Good. [14] £162 $250

CARTE DE L'ISLE ET ROYAUME DE SICILE [1730 - 1733] From *Atlas Nouveau*. Amsterdam: Covens & Mortier. Malta inset. 47x57cm (18½x22½") Orig OL color; cities highlighted. [14] £250 $385

CARTE DE LA BARBARIE DE LA NIGRITIE ET DE LA GUINEE [1734] Amsterdam: Covens & Mortier. 50x61cm (19½x24") Orig OL color. Good. [14] £104 $160

CARTE DE LA GRECE [1730 - 1733] From *Atlas Nouveau*. Amsterdam: Covens & Mortier. 45x59cm (17½x23") Orig OL color. [14] £201 $310

CARTE DE LA LOUISIANE ET DU COURS DU MISSISSIPI DRESSEE SUR UN GRAND NOMBRE DE MEMOIRES ... PAR GUILLAUME DELISLE ... [1718] 1st ed, 1st state. Without New Orleans; 1st to name "Teijas". New York to Rio Grande. 48x65cm (19x25½") [3] £6,167 $9,500

CARTE DE LA LOUISIANE ET DU COURS DU MISSISSIPI ... [1733] Amsterdam: Covens & Mortier. Reissue of 1718 map. 44x60cm (17½x23½") Orig OL color. Fine. [14] £812 $1,250

CARTE DE LA SOUVERAINETE DE NEUCHATEL ET VALLANGIN [1730 - 1733] From *Atlas Nouveau*. Amsterdam: Covens & Mortier. 50x64cm (19½x25") Orig OL color; cities highlighted. [14] £127 $195

CARTE DE LA TERRE FERME DU PEROU, DU BRESIL ET DU PAYS DES AMAZONS ... [1733] Amsterdam: Covens & Mortier. 48x57cm (19x22½") Orig OL color. [14] £162 $250

CARTE DE MOSCOVIE ... [c. 1757] Amsterdam: Covens & Mortier. 53x64cm (20½x25") Orig color. Lower c'fold split repaired. Ref: Bagrow (Russia) p.152. [28] £195 $300

CARTE DE PERSE [1733] Covens & Mortier. 48x61cm (19x24") Orig OL col. Good. [14] £78 $120

CARTE DE TARTARIE [1733] Amsterdam: Covens & Mortier. Moscovy to Korea. 48x61cm (18½x24") Orig OL color. Good. [14] £65 $100

CARTE DE TARTARIE DRESSEE SUR LES RELATIONS DE PLUSIEURS VOYAGEURS DE DIFFERENTES NATIONS ... [c. 1757] Amsterdam: Covens & Mortier. 51x61cm (20x24½") Orig OL color. Sh lower c'fold split; 2 sm wormholes. Ref: Bagrow (Russia) pp.136-8,152; Koeman II C&M 8. [28] £221 $340

CARTE DES ANTILLES FRANCOISES ET DES ISLES VOISINES ... [1717] Guadeloupe to Barbados & Grenada. 64x39cm (25x15") Orig OL color. Margin dampmarks; creases; sm paper flaw near c'fold. [28] £380 $585

[SAME TITLE] [1717 - c.1720] 64x37cm (25x14½") Orig OL color. [52] £340 $524

CARTE DES COTES DE MALABAR ET DE COROMANDEL [1733] Amsterdam: Covens & Mortier. 44x56cm (17½x22") Orig OL color. Good. [14] £97 $150

CARTE DES COURONES DU NORD QUI COMPREND LES ROYAUMES DE DANEMARK, SUEDE, & NORWEGE, &C. [IN SET WITH] SECONDE CARTE DES COURONES DU NORD, QUI COMPREND LE ROYAUME DE DANEMARK &C. [1730 - 1733] From *Atlas Nouveau*. Amsterdam: Covens & Mortier. 2 maps, each 45x60cm (17½x23½") Orig OL color; cities highlighted. [14] £357 $550

CARTE DES INDES ET DE LA CHINE ... [1733] Amsterdam: Covens & Mortier. 61x63cm (24x24½") Orig OL color. A fold joined; o/w good. [14] £243 $375

CARTE DES ISLES DE SAINT DOMINGUE [1733] Amsterdam: Covens & Mortier. 46x61cm (18x24") Orig OL color. Good. [14] £104 $160

CARTE DES PAYS VOISINS DE LA MER CASPIENE ... [1733] Amsterdam: Covens & Mortier. 46x61cm (18x24") Orig OL color. Sh c'fold split joined; good. [14] £78 $120

CARTE DES PROVINCES UNIES DES PAYS BAS [1730 - 1733] Amsterdam: Covens & Mortier. 47x62cm (18½x24½") Orig OL color; cities highlighted. [14] £175 $270

CARTE DU CANADA OU DE LA NOUVELLE FRANCE ... [1703] "Rue des Canettes" imprint. 50x65cm (19½x25½") Old OL color. Lower border trimmed, sl loss; else VG. Ref: Karpinski (MI) XXXI; Tooley (Amer) p.20; Heidenreich & Dahl p.9-12. Skelton (Decorative) pl.79. [55] £2,110 $3,250

[SAME TITLE] [1703 (1718)] Later state, "Quai de L'Horloge". 50x65cm (19½x25½") OL color. Trimmed, laid down on matching contemporary paper; VG. Ref: Karpinski (MI) XXXI; Schwartz & Ehrenberg pl.80. [60] £941 $1,450

[SAME TITLE] [c. 1740] 50x56cm (19½x22") OL color. [40] £980 $1,509

CARTE DU CANADA OU DE LA NOUVELLE FRANCE ET DES DECOUVERTES QUI Y ONT ETE FAITES DRESSEE SUR PLUSIERS OBSERVATIONS ... PAR GUILLAUME DE L'ISLE ... [1703 / 1733] Amsterdam: Covens & Mortier. 49x57cm (19½x22½") Orig OL color. Exc. Ref: Tooley (Amer) p.20. [14] £812 $1,250

CARTE DU CONGO ET DU PAYS DES CAFRES [1733] Amsterdam: Covens & Mortier. 48x61cm (18½x24") Orig OL color. Good. [14] £143 $220

CARTE DU MEXIQUE ET DE LA FLORIDE DES TERRES ANGLOISES ET DES ISLES ANTILLES DU COURS ET DES ENVIRONS DE LA RIVIERE DE MISSISSIPI ... PAR GUILLAUME DE L'ISLE ... [1703 / 1722] Amsterdam: Covens & Mortier. 48x61cm (18½x24") Orig OL color. Good. Ref: Cumming (SE) 137; Lowery 313; Wheat (TM) 84. [47] £812 $1,250

CARTE DU PARAGUAY DU CHILI DU DETROIT DE MAGELLAN &C ... [1733] Amsterdam: Covens & Mortier. 49x58cm (19x22½") Orig OL color. [14] £120 $185

CARTE DU ROYAUME DE DANEMARC [1730 - 1733] From *Atlas Nouveau*. Amsterdam: Covens & Mortier. 48x60cm (19x23½") Orig OL color; cities highlighted. [14] £104 $160

[SAME TITLE] [c. 1757] Covens & Mortier. 48x61cm (19½x24") Orig color Ref: Koeman II C&M 8. [28] £192 $295

CARTE EXACTE DES POSTES ET ROUTES DE L'EMPIRE D'ALLEMAGNE DIVISEE EN SES CERCLES [1730 - 1733] From *Atlas Nouveau*. Amsterdam: Covens & Mortier. 46x59cm (18x23") Orig OL color; cities highlighted. [14] £140 $215

ESTATS DE L'EMPIRE DES TURQS EN EUROPE, DIVISES SUIVANT DE L'ESTENDUE DES BEGLERBEGLICZ, OU GOUVERNEMENTS ... [1730 - 1733] From *Atlas Nouveau*. Amsterdam: Covens & Mortier. Balkans & adjacent. 45x62cm (18x24") Orig OL color. [14] £175 $270

ESTATS DE L'EMPIRE DU GRAND SEIGNEUR DES TURCS, EN EUROPE, EN ASIE, ET EN AFRIQUE DIVISE ... [1730 - 1733] From *Atlas Nouveau*. Amsterdam: Covens & Mortier. 45x61cm (17½x24") Orig OL color. Sm lower c'fold tear repaired. [14] £149 $230

HEMISPHERE SEPTENTRIONAL ... [IN SET WITH] HEMISPHERE MERIDIONAL ... [1714] 1st ed. Each 48x48cm (18½x18½") Orig OL color. [46] £1,039 $1,600

[SAME TITLE] [1733] Amsterdam: Covens & Mortier. 46x46cm (18x18") Orig OL color. [14] £552 $850

HEMISPHERE SEPTENTRIONAL POUR VOIR PLUS DISTINCTEMENT LES TERRES ARCTIQUES [AND SHEET WITH] ... AUSTRALES ... [1714] 1st ed. Two polar projections. Each 46x48cm (18x18½") Orig full color. Good. Ref: Wagner (NW) 450 & 504. [2] £1,136 $1,750

L'AFRIQUE DRESEE SUR LES OBSERVATIONS DE MRS DE L'ACADEMIE ROYAL DES SCIENCES [1733] Amsterdam: Covens & Mortier. 46x57cm (18x22½") Orig OL color. Good. [14] £162 $250

L'AMERIQUE MERIDIONALE ... [1733] Amsterdam: Covens & Mortier. 46x58cm (18x23") Orig OL color. [14] £162 $250

L'AMERIQUE SEPTENTRIONALE DRESSEE SUR LES OBSERVATIONS DE MRS. DE L'ACADEMIE ROYALE DES SCIENCES ... PAR G. DE L'ISLE. A AMSTERDAM CHEZ I. COVENS & C. MORTIER. AVEC PRIVILEGE [1700 (1730)] 46x58cm (17½x23") B&W. Scattered lt foxing; good+. [55] £617 $950

[SAME TITLE] [1730] Covens & Mortier. 48x58cm (18½x23") Orig OL color. Top margin bit foxed at corners. Ref: Tooley (Amer) p.19. Wagner (NW) 459. [28] £760 $1,170

L'ESPAGNE DRESSEE SUR LA DESCRIPTION QUI EN A ETE FAITE PAR RODRIGO MENDEZ SYLVA ... [1730 - 1733] From *Atlas Nouveau*. Amsterdam: Covens & Mortier. 47x60cm (18½x23½") Orig OL color; cities highlighted. [14] £185 $285

L'Europe [1730 - 1733] From *Atlas Nouveau*. Amsterdam: Covens & Mortier. 49x58cm (19½x23") Orig OL color. [14] £127 $195

L'Hemisphere Meridional ... [c. 1740] Shows no continent, one island; French & Dutch text. 48x52cm (18½x20½") Color. [41] £480 $739

L'Hemisphere Septentrionale pour Voir Plus Distinctement les Terres Arctiques [c. 1740] Amsterdam: Covens & Mortier. 46x51cm (18½x20½") Orig OL color. Fine. [49] £357 $550

L'Italie [1730 - 1733] From *Atlas Nouveau*. Amsterdam: Covens & Mortier. 49x60cm (19x23½") Orig OL color. [14] £149 $230

Le Plan de Paris, Ses Faubourgs et Ses Environs [1730 - 1733] From *Atlas Nouveau*. Amsterdam: Covens & Mortier. Title repeated in Dutch. 56x75cm (22x29½") Sm fold tear repaired; lt staining. [14] £325 $500

Les Isles Britanniques ou Sont le Royaumes d'Angleterre ... [1730 - 1733] From *Atlas Nouveau*. Amsterdam: Covens & Mortier. 47x57cm (18½x22½") Orig OL & highlight col. Sm stain. [14] £204 $315

Nouvelle Carte Particuliere de l'Amerique, ou Sont ... la Nouvelle Bretagne, le Canada ou Nouvelle France, la Nouvelle Ecosse, la Nouvelle Angleterre, la Nouvelle York ... [c. 1740] 57x52cm (22½x20½") Color. [40] £750 $1,155

Nova Helvetiae, Foederatarumque cum Ea, Nec Non Subditarum Regionum Tabula ... [1730 - 1733] From *Atlas Nouveau*. Amsterdam: Covens & Mortier. 47x61cm (18½x24") Orig OL color; cities highlighted. [14] £250 $385

Novissima Regni Scotiae Septentrionalis et Meridionalis Tabula Divisee in Ducatus, Comitatus ... [1730 - 1733] From *Atlas Nouveau*. Amsterdam: Covens & Mortier. 50x59cm (19½x23") Orig OL & highlight color. [14] £276 $425

Orbis Veteribus Noti Tabula Nova [c. 1740] Reduction of 1714 De L'Isle map. 38x38cm (15x15") Color. [16] £370 $570

Regni Angliae et Walliae Principatus Tabula, Divisa in LII Regiones, Anglice Shire, Dictas ... [1730 - 1733] From *Atlas Nouveau*. Amsterdam: Covens & Mortier. 50x59cm (20x23½") Orig OL color. Sm repaired tear lower border. [14] £201 $310

DE LA FEUILLE

L'Afrique Selon les Autheurs les Plus Modernes [1710] 14x20cm (5½x8") Orig color. Sl darkening in folds; o/w VG. [32] £62 $95

DE LA HOUVE

Italiae, Illirici, Sardiniae, Corsicae, et Confinium Regionum ... [1605 - c.1680] Folded into sm volume; John Garrett imprint. 39x55cm (15½x21½") Uncolored. [54] £850 $1,309

DE LA RUE

Pinax Geographicus Patriarchatus Hierosolymitani ... [1651] In *La Terre Sainte en Six Cartes Geographiques*. Paris: Mariette. 41x53cm (16x21") Color. Ref: Laor 419. [23] £159 $245

Regnum Salomonicum seu Tabula Digesta ad Libros Judicum Regnum [same date & source]. 38x53cm (15x20½") Color. Ref: Laor 417. [23] £185 $285

Sourie ou Terre Saincte Modern [same date & source] 54x39cm (21½x15½") Color. Ref: Laor 420. [23] £185 $285

Terra Chanaan ad Abrahami Tempora per Populos XI ... [same date & source] Inset: "Abrahae Peregrinatio". 43x56cm (16½x22") Color Ref: Laor 415. [23] £172 $265

Terra Promissa in Sortes seu Tribus XII Distincta seu Tabula ad Librum Iosue [same date & source] Somer, sc. 41x53cm (16x21") Color. Ref: Laor 416. [23] £224 $345

DE LAET

Americae sive Indiae Occidentalis Tabula Generalis [1630] From *Nieuwe Wereldt ofte Beschrijvinghe van West-Indien* .... Map by H. Gerritsz. 28x35cm (11x14") Sm stain; else exc. [37] £487 $750

Chili [same date & source] By H. Gerritsz. 28x36cm (11x14") Exc. [37] £211 $325

Florida et Regiones Vicinae [same date & source] By H. Gerritsz. 28x36cm (11x14") Exc. Ref: Cumming (SE) 34. [37] £1,428 $2,200

Maiores Minoresque Insulae. Hispaniola, Cuba, Lucaiae et Caribes [same date & source] Map by H. Gerritsz. 28x36cm (11x14") Early color. Exc. [37] £308 $475

Nova Anglia Novum Belgium et Virginia [same date & source] 39x51cm (15x20") Exc. [37] £2,921 $4,500

NOVA FRANCIA ET REGIONES ADIACENTES [same date & source] Map by H. Gerritsz. 28x36cm (11x14") Early color. Exc. [37] £974 $1,500
[SAME TITLE] [same date & dimen] Uncolored. Exc. Ref: Phillips (A) 1146, 2. [2] £1,104 $1,700
NOVA HISPANIA, NOVA GALICIA, GUATIMALA [1630] From *Nieuwe Wereldt ofte Beschrijvinghe van West-Indien* .... Map by H. Gerritsz. 28x36cm (11x14") Exc. [37] £292 $450
PARAGUAY, O PROV. DE RIO DE LA PLATA [same date, source & dimen] H. Gerritsz. Exc. [37] £227 $350
PROVINCIA DE BRASIL CUM ADIACENTIBUS [same date, source & dimen] H. Gerritsz. Exc. [37] £292 $450
[SAME TITLE] [same date & dimen] By Hessel Gerritsz. Exc. [63] £341 $525
PROVINCIAE SITAE AD FRETUM MAGALLANIS ITEMQUE FRETUM LE MAIRE [1630] From *Nieuwe Wereldt ofte Beschrijvinghe van West-Indien* .... H. Gerritsz. With Patagonia. 28x36cm (11x14") Exc. [37] £292 $450
TIERRA FIRMA ITEM NUEVO REYNO DE GRANADA [same date, source & dimen] Exc. [37] £195 $300
VENEZUELA, ATQUE OCCIDENTALIS PARS NOVAE ANDALUSIAE [same date, source & dimen] By H. Gerritsz. Exc. [37] £292 $450

DE LAPORTE
CARTE DES ROYAUMES D'IRELANDE [c. 1785] 18x23cm (7x9") OL color. VG. [55] £81 $125

DE LAT
DE NIEUWE EN OUDEN OPPERVLAKKE EN DOORZIGKUNDIGE AARDRYKS BOLLEN ... [1770] Double hemi with sm circles. 18x25cm (7x9½") OL color. [58] £130 $200

DE LETH
CARTE DE LA PETITE TARTARIE ... [c. 1750-1780] Amsterdam: Schenk. 43x48cm (17x19½") Orig OL color. Folds; dampmarking lower margin. [28] £292 $450
MAPPE MONDE OR DESCRIPTION DU GLOBE TERRESTRE VU EN CONCAVE OU CREUX EN DEUX HEMISPHERES ... [1730] Surround of 6 sm spheres. 46x66cm (17½x26") Col. Fine. [26] £1,006 $1,550

DE PRETOT
CARTE NOUVELLE D'AMERIQUE [1787] With "Mer de l'Ouest". 25x38cm (10½x15½") B&W. Fine. Ref: Phillips (A) 663. [47] £315 $485
L'ANGLETERRE ... [dated 1770] Philippe de Pretot. 28x41cm (10½x15½") Full col. [36] £179 $275
LE GLOBE TERRESTRE VU EN CONVEXE PAR LES DEUX POLES ... [1769] Double hemi polar projection. 23x41cm (9x16") Full color. [14] £250 $385

DE VAUGONDY   Try *Delamarche, Diderot*
A NEW MAP OF CANADA, ALSO THE NORTH PARTS OF NEW ENGLAND AND NEW YORK; WITH NOVA SCOTIA AND NEWFOUNDLAND [c. 1760] English version, after Robert de Vaugondy. Inset: Great Lakes region. 20x30cm (8½x11½") B&W. Narrow margins. [46] £49 $75
AMERIQUE MERIDIONALE [1748] 15x20cm (6½x8") Orig color. Narrow rt margin. [46] £32 $50
AMERIQUE MERIDIONALE, DRESSEE, SUR LES MEMOIRES LES PLUS RECENTS ET ASSUJETIE AUX OBSERVATIONS ASTRONOMIQUE. PAR LE SR. ROBERT DE VAUGONDY ... [1766] 51x64cm (19½x24½") Orig OL col. Perimeter dampstained. Ref: Nordenskiold (Col) II,245; cf Phillips (A) 619. [28] £175 $270
AMERIQUE SEPTENTRIONALE DRESSEE SUR LES RELATIONS LES PLUS MODERNES DES VOYAGEURS ET NAVIGATEURS ... 1750 CORRIGEE EN 1775 [1775] From *Atlas Universel* ... 48x59cm (19x23") Sl water mark top margin; sl corner crease; o/w clean, bright. Ref: Pedley 448, state 4. [9] £390 $600
AN ACCURATE MAP OF NORTH AMERICA DRAWN FROM THE SIEUR ROBERT, WITH IMPROVEMENTS [1762] English source; Rollos, sc. 18x30cm (7½x12") OL color. Immaculate. [36] £227 $350
BRITANNICAE, INSULA IN QUIBUS ALBION SEU BRITANNIA MAJOR, ET IVERNIA SEU BRITANNIA MINOR JUXTA PTOLEMAEI MENTEM DIVISAE ... SANSON ... [1750] 51x56cm (19½x22") Orig OL color. Foxing. Ref: Nordenskiold (Col) II,245. [28] £204 $315
CARTE DE L'EGYPTE ANCIENNE ET MODERNE... [1753] Hussard, sc. 66x51cm (26x19½") Orig OL color. Ref: Nordenskiold (Col) II,245. [28] £234 $360
[SAME TITLE] [1753] Nile River. 64x46cm (25x18") OL color. Minor discoloration at c'fold; tape residue, printed area unaffected; else VG. Ref: Pedley 431. [55] £195 $300
CARTE DE LA VIRGINIE ET DU MARYLAND DRESSEE SUR LA GRANDE CARTE ANGLOISE DE MRS. JOSUE FRY ET PIERRE JEFFERSON [1755] 1st state. 48x64cm (19x25½") Orig OL color. [53] £750 $1,155

CARTE DES GRANDES ROUTES D'ANGLETERRE, D'ECOSSE, ET D'IRLANDE. PAR LE SR. ROBERT GEOG. ORDIN. DU ROY. AVEC PRIVILEGE [1757] Gilles Robert de Vaugondy. With roads; large title vignette. 56x58cm (21½x23") OL color. Waterstain top margin; good. [21] £243 $375

CARTE DU DUCHE DE LUXEMBOURG ... [1753] 51x64cm (20x25") Orig OL color. Crease near c'fold; sh tear upper border. Ref: Nordenskiold (Col) II,245. [28] £175 $270

CARTE DU NOUVEAU CONTINENT ... [1749 (1760)] Gilles Robert de Vaugondy. The Americas. 23x18cm (8½x7") Later OL color. [51] £127 $195

COURS DU MISSISSIPI ET LA LOUISIANE ... [1749] Didier Robert de Vaugondy. 21x16cm (8x6") VG. Matted. [20] £250 $385

[SAME TITLE] [1749 -] From *Atlas Portatif, Universel et Militaire* ... 27x20cm (11x8") Orig OL color. [54] £200 $308

ENVIRONS DE PARIS [1753] 51x64cm (19½x25") Orig OL color. Margins bit browned. Ref: Nordenskiold (Col) II,245 [28] £175 $270

ETAT DE L'EGLISE GRANDE DUCHE DE TOSCANE, ET ISLE DE CORSE [1750] 51x64cm (19½x24½") Orig OL color. Deep vert crease near c'fold. [28] £162 $250

ETATS DU GRAND-SEIGNEUR EN ASIE EMPIRE DE PERSE, PAYS DES USBECS, ARABIE ET EGYPTE ... [1753] 48x55cm (18½x21½") OL color. Tape residue in margin; else VG. Ref: Pedley 389. [55] £195 $300

GOUVERNEMENT GENERAL DE L'ISLE DE FRANCE DIVISE PAR PAYS ... [1754] 49x53cm (19½x21") Orig OL color. Margins bit browned. Ref: Nordenskiold (Col) II,245 [28] £162 $250

GUIENNE ET GASCOGNE [1748] From *Petit Atlas*. 15x18cm (6½x7") Orig OL color. Exc. [46] £26 $40

ISLE ET ROYAUME D'IRLANDE, PAR LES SR. ROBERT ... 1748 [1749] 18x18cm (6½x7") Uncolored. VG. [44] £81 $125

ISLES PHILIPPINES ... [1749 -] From *Atlas Portatif, Universel et Militaire* ... 20x27cm (8x11") Orig OL color. Lt staining. [54] £180 $277

JUDEE OU TERRE SAINTE [1760] 25x22cm (9½x8½") Color. [23] £81 $125

L'AFRIQUE ... [1759] 48x64cm (19½x24½") Orig OL color. Ref: Norwich 94; Nordenskiold (Col) II,245. [28] £263 $405

L'AMERIQUE SEPTENTRIONALE ET MERIDIONALE DIVISEE EN SES PRINCIPALES PARTIES PAR LES SRS. SANSON ... [1749] 50x65cm (19½x25½") Dissected into 16 panels laid onto linen as issued. Full orig color. [14] £341 $525

L'ARABIE [1749] 15x18cm (6½x7") Orig OL color. [46] £26 $40

L'EMPIRE DE LA CHINE DRESSE D'APRES LES CARTES DE L'ATLAS CHINOIS [1751] 48x53cm (19x20½") Orig OL color. Good. [14] £162 $250

[SAME TITLE] [1751] 51x56cm (19½x21½") Orig OL col. Ref: Nordenskiold (Col) II,245. [28] £263 $405

L'ISLE ST. DOMINGUE PAR LES SR. ROBERT ... [1749] 18x18cm (7x6½") Uncolored. [45] £49 $75

LA FLORIDE DIVISEE EN FLORIDE ET CAROLINE ... [1749 -] From *Atlas Portatif, Universel et Militaire* ... 27x20cm (11x8") Orig OL color. [54] £220 $339

[SAME TITLE] [1749 / 1766] 18x18cm (6½x7") Orig OL color. [4] £88 $135

LA JUDEE OU TERRE SAINTE, DIVISEE EN SES DOUZE TRIBUS ... [1750] 51x61cm (19½x24") Orig OL color. Margins foxed & browned. Ref: Laor 667. [28] £292 $450

LA PRINCIPAUTE DE LIEGE ET LE DUCHE DE LIMBOURG [1754] 51x48cm (20x18½") Orig OL color. [28] £204 $315

LE CERCLE DE BAVIERE QUI COMPREND LE HAUT PALINAT, LES DUCHES DE HAUTE ET BASSE BAVIERE ET DE NEUBURG, L'ARCHEVECHE DE SALZBURG ... [1751] 53x51cm (20½x19½") Orig OL color. Dampmarks margin edges. Ref: Nordenskiold (Col) II,245. [28] £195 $300

LE ROYAUME D'ANGLETERRE, DIVISE SELON LES SEPT ROYAUMES, OU HEPTARCHIE DES SAXONS, AVEC LA PRINCIPAUTE DE GALLES ... [1753] 51x53cm (19½x21") Orig OL color. Dampstains to margins. Ref: Nordenskiold (Col) II,245. [28] £221 $340

LE ROYAUME DE POLOGNE, DIVISE EN SES DUCHES ET PROVINCES, ET SUBDIVISE EN PALATINATS ... [1752] 51x56cm (19½x22") Orig OL col. Dampmark rt margin. Ref: Buczek p.84. [28] £192 $295

LES INDES ORIENTALES, OU SONT DISTINGUES LES EMPIRES ET ROYAUMES QU'ELLES CONTIENNENT ... [1751] 51x58cm (19½x23") Orig OL col. Ref: Gole (Ganges) 66 2.1; Nordenskiold (Col) II,245. [28] £204 $315

LES ISLES ANTILLES, PAR LE SR. ROBERT DE VAUGONDY FILS ... [1749] 16x18cm (6½x7") Uncolored. [44] £81 $125

LES LACS DU CANADA ET NOUVELLE ANGLETERRE PAR LE SR. ROBERT DE VAUGONDY FILS ... [1749] 16x22cm (6½x9") Orig OL color. Close borders. [44] £179 $275

MAINE, PERCHE, ANJOU, SAUMUROIS, TOURAINE [1748] From *Petit Atlas*. 15x18cm (6½x7") Orig OL color. Exc. [46] £26 $40

MAPPE-MONDE ... [1761] 24x39cm (9½x15½") Color. [16] £228 $351

MAPPE MONDE DRESSEE SUIVANT LES NOUVELLES RELATIONS ET ASSUJETTIE AUX OBSERVATIONS ASTRONOMIQUES [1778] Double hemi. 47x74cm (18½x29") Color. [26] £568 $875

MAPPE-MONDE OU DESCRIPTION DU GLOBE TERRESTRE ... [1757] 1st state. Double hemisphere. 46x70cm (18x27½") Orig OL col. Image fine, overall VG. Ref: Pedley #8; Phillips (A) 619. [59] £649 $1,000

NOUVELLE ANGLETERRE NOUVELLE YORK, NOUVELLE JERSEY, PENSILVANIE MARILAND ET VIRGINIE [1749] 19x16cm (7½x6½") Color. [36] £130 $200

[SAME TITLE]. [1749] Robert de Vaugondy Fils 18x16cm (7x6½") Uncolored. [44] £146 $225

[SAME TITLE] [1749] From *Atlas Portatif, Universel et Militaire* .... dated 1748. 27x20cm (11x8") Orig OL color. [54] £200 $308

NOUVELLE ESPAGNE, NOUVEAU MEXIQUE, ISLES ANTILLES [1762] From *Nouvel Atlas Portatif*. Didier Robert de Vaugondy. Incl present Southwest. 24x31cm (9½x12") [9] £146 $225

ORBIS VETUS IN UTRAQUE CONTINENTE JUXTA MENTEM SANSONIANAM DISTINCTUS, NEC NON OBSERVATIONIBUS ASTRONOMICIS [1752] Double hemi.. 47x71cm (18½x28") Color. [26] £601 $925

[SAME TITLE] [1757] New World as it would have been in ancient times. 47x70cm (18½x27½") Orig OL color. 2" lower c'fold repair; image fine, overall VG. Ref: Pedley #13; Phillips (A) 619,1. [59] £519 $800

ORLEANOIS [1748] From *Petit Atlas*. 15x18cm (6½x7") Orig OL color. Exc. [46] £26 $40

PARTIE DE L'AMERIQUE SEPTENT? QUI COMPREND LA NOUVELLE FRANCE OU LE CANADA ... [1755 (1757)] From *Atlas Universel*. State 1 of 5. Great Lakes inset. 47x61cm (18½x24") Orig OL color. Fine-. Ref: Pedley 459; Karpinski (FC) pp 141-2; Phillips (A) 619,98; Sellers & Van Ee 61; Streeter VI 3775. [59] £519 $800

PARTIE DE L'AMERIQUE SEPTENT QUI COMPREND LA NOUVELLE FRANCE OU LE CANADA ... [1755+] Undated state. Great Lakes inset. 51x61cm (19½x24") Orig OL color. Few spots. Ref: Karpinski (FC) p.141; Phillips (A) 619. [28] £467 $720

PARTIE DU MEXIQUE OU DE LA NOUVELLE ESPAGNE OU SE TROUVE L'AUD'CE DE GUADALAJARA, NOUVELLE MEXIQUE, NOUVELLE NAVARRE, CALIFORNIE &C. PAR LE SR. ROBERT DE VAUGONDY FILS ... [1749] 16x18cm (6½x7") Uncolored. VG. [44] £156 $240

PARTIE DU MEXIQUE OU DE LA NOUVELLE ESPAGNE OU SE TROUVE L'AUDIENCE DU MEXIQUE, PAR LE SR. ROBERT DE VAUGONDY FILS ... [1749] 16x18cm (6½x7") Uncolored. [44] £81 $125

PARTIE DU MEXIQUE OU DE LA NOUVLE. ESPAGNE ... [1749] From *Atlas Portatif* .... 16x20cm (6½x7½") Orig OL color. [53] £280 $431

PARTIE MERIDIONALE DU ROYAUME DE NAPLES ... [1750] With Sicily; Malta & Goze inset. 48x58cm (19x23") OL color. Tape residue verso, printed area not affected; else fine. [55] £162 $250

PARTIE SEPTENTRIONALE DU CERCLE D'AUTRICHE QUI COMPREND L'ARCHIDUCHE D'AUTRICHE, DIVISE EN SES HUIT QUARTIERS ... [1752] Robert de Vaugondy Fils. 51x64cm (19½x25") Orig OL color. Creases; dampmarks; margin tears. Ref: Nordenskiold (Col) II,245. [28] £192 $295

ROYAUME D'IRLANDE ... [1750] Didier Robert de Vaugondy. 49x55cm (19½x21½") OL color. Waterstains at top 1" into map; else good. [21] £162 $250

ROYAUME DE DANEMARCK, QUI COMPREND LE NORT-JUTLAND ... ET LES ISLES DE FIONIE, SELANDE, LALAND &C. ... [1750] 51x58cm (19½x23") Orig OL color. Dampmarks margins. Ref: Nordenskiold (Col) II,245. [28] £175 $270

ROYAUMES D'ESPAGNE [1748] From *Petit Atlas*. 15x18cm (6½x7") Orig OL color. Exc. [46] £32 $50

DE WIT

ACCURATISSIMA TOTIUS ASIAE TABULA RECENS EMENDATA PER FREDERICUM DE WIT AMSTELODAMI [c. 1683 - 1710] Possibly published by Visscher. 48x58cm (19x22½") Orig color. Sh tears upper & lower margins; sm stain; crease near c'fold. [28] £438 $675

BARBARIA [c. 1688] 48x58cm (19½x23") Orig color. Lt foxing to margin. Ref: Koeman III Wit 13. [28] £338 $520

CARTA NOVA ACCURATA DEL PASSAGIO ET STRADA DALLI PAESI BASSI PER VIA DE ALLEMAGNA PER ITALIA ET PER VIA DI PAESI SUIZERI A GENEVA, LIONE ET ROMA ... [1671] N. Italy to Netherlands. 47x55cm (18½x21½") Orig color. Fine. [62] £237 $365

INDIAE ORIENTALIS NEC NON INSULARUM ADIACENTIUM ... PER F. DE WIT [c. 1688] 51x60cm (20x23½") Orig & later color. [16] £926 $1,426

INSULARUM DANICARUM UT ZEE-LANDIAE, FIONIAE LANGELANDIAE, LANANDIAE FALSTRIAE ... [c. 1680] 48x58cm (19x23") Orig OL & cartouche color. Ref: Koeman III Wit 9. [28] £409 $630

NOVA ORBIS TABULA IN LUCEM EDITA, A.F. DE WIT [c. 1670] Double hemi; insular Calif. 48x57cm (19x22½") Orig color & highlights. Ref: Shirley (W) 451, pl.333. [16] £5,128 $7,899
POLI ARCTICI, ET CIRCUMIACENTIUM TERRARUM DESCRIPTIO NOVISSIMA [1675] From *Orbis Maritimus*. 43x49cm (17x19½") Repair, some loss at Greenland; early color weakened paper backed for strength with archival tissue. [15] £490 $755
REGNI POLONIAE ET DUCATUS LITHUANIAE, VOLINIAE, PODOLIAE, PRUSSIAE, LIVONIAE ET CURLANDIAE [c. 1680] 49x56cm (19x22") Orig OL & cartouche col. Ref: MCCS 25, 119; Koeman III Wit 4. [28] £393 $605
TERRA SANCTA SIVE PROMISSIONIS, OLIM PALESTINA RECENS DELINEATA ET IN LUCEM EDITA [1680] 46x56cm (18½x22") Full color. Ref: Laor 860. [23] £315 $485
TURCICUM IMPERIUM [c. 1680] 2nd state. 45x55cm (18x22") Orig OL & cartouche color. Crease upper corner. Ref: Tibbetts 117; Koeman III Wit 3. [28] £454 $700

DELAMARCHE   Try *De Vaugondy*

CONGO CAFRERIE PAR ROBERT DE VAUGONDY ... [1804] Southern Africa. 25x28cm (9½x11") OL color. Lt foxing. [36] £52 $80

DEPOT DE LA MARINE   Try *Bellin*

CARTE DE L'ILE DE FOGO A LA COTE ORIENTALE DE TERRE-NEUVE ... MICHAEL LANE EN 1785 ... [1792] From *Hydrographie Francoise*. 61x91cm (24½x36") Dampmarks; sh margin tears; 2 sm wormholes. Ref: Tooley (Amer) p.201. Phillips (A) 589 & 590. [28] £221 $340
CARTE DE L'ILE DE WIGHT ET DE LA COTE ADJACENTE DE HAMPSHIRE CONTENANT UNE DESCRIPTION PARTICULIERE DES RADES DE STE. HELENE SPITHEAD &C. ... [1803-1804] After William Price and Laurie & Whittle's 1800 chart. 61x91cm (24x35½") Color. Sl margin chipping, verso reinforcement. [15] £290 $447
CARTE DE LA MER DES ANTILLES PARTIE OCCIDENTALE ... [1843] Venezuela to Virgin Islands. 89x60cm (35x23½") C'fold split repaired. Ref: Phillips (A) 795 & 909. [14] £114 $175
CARTE DE LA PARTIE OCCIDENTALE DES ILES ANTILLES ... [1801] Southern Florida & Greater Antilles. 60x91cm (23½x35½") Uncolored. [53] £360 $554
CARTE DES COTES DE L'AMERIQUE MERIDIONALE ... [1800 - 1801] Cabo San Antonio & Conception southward. 91x62cm (36x24½") Fine. [15] £150 $231
CARTE PARTICULIERE DU CANAL DE BRISTOL ... [1797-98] By "Depot des Cartes et Plans de la Marine". 57x89cm (22½x35") Some offsetting, sl browning at c'fold. [15] £160 $246
CARTE REDUITE DE L'ILE ROYALE ... PAR ORDRE DE M. DE SARTINE [ON SHEET WITH] PLAN DU PORT ET DES ILES AU JUSTE AU CORPS [AND] ... CHETECAN [AND] ... MORIENNE [AND] ... BAIE DES ESPAGNOLES [AND] ... D'ASPE [1780] One large & 5 sm plans. 89x61cm (35x24") Faint dampmarks; lt offsetting. Ref: Phillips (A) 1211; Sellers & Van Ee 117. [28] £351 $540
CARTE REDUITE DE L'OCEAN MERIDIONAL ... [1753, c.1770] Depot des Cartes Plans et Journaux de la Marine. Equator to 55° S. 53x86cm (21½x34½") Lt browning; some worming in margins. [15] £140 $216
CARTE REDUITE DES ... MER DU SUD OU MER PACIFIQUE ... [1776] Uncertain joining of Tasmania to Australia. 56x83cm (22x32½") Color. [52] £1,000 $1,540
ENTREE DE LA CASAMANCE ET MOUILLAGE DE CARABANE [1871 (1882)] Vallon, 1862. 48x66cm (18½x25½") Fold line. [15] £20 $31
PLAN D'UNE PARTIE DE L'ILE DE WIGHT ET DE LA COTE DE HAMPSHIRE ... [1823] After 1793 Mackenzie survey and 1808 Admiralty chart. 94x61cm (37x24") Fine. [15] £300 $462
PLAN DE L'ILE DE ST. JEAN AU NORD DE L'ACADIE ... SUIVANT L'ARPENTAGE DU CAPITAINE ANGLOIS HOLLAND ... PAR ORDRE DE M. DE SARTINE ... [1778] 43x61cm (17x24") Faint margin dampmarks. Ref: Sellers & Van Ee 628; Phillips (A) 1211. [28] £279 $430
PLAN DE L'ISTHME DE L'ACADIE COMPRENANT LE BEAU-BASSIN AVEC UNE PARTIE DE LA BAIE VERTE ... PAR ORDRE DE M. DE SARTINE ... [1779] 38x58cm (15½x23") Dampmark; horiz crease. Ref: Phillips (A) 1211; Sellers & Van Ee 402. [28] £195 $300
PLAN DE LA BAIE DE GABARUS SITUEE A LA COTE S.E. DE L'ILE ROYALE ... PAR ORDRE DE M. DE SARTINE ... [ON SHEET WITH] PLAN DE LA BAIE DE NERICHAS, A LA COTE DU SUD DE L'ILE MADAME ... [AND] PLAN DU PORT TOULOUSE, A LA COTE DU SUD DE L'ILE ROYALE ... [1779] 61x89cm (24½x35½") Faint dampmarks; foxing traces. Ref: Phillips (A) 1211; Sellers & Van Ee 348. [28] £351 $540
PLAN DE LA BAIE DE MONTEREY (HAUTE CALIFORNIE) LEVE ET DRESSEE EN 1837, A BORD DE LA VENUS ... [1844] No. 1018. Profile view. 59x88cm (23x34½") Fine. [14] £250 $385
PLAN DE LA RADE DE PIRANO [1820-1821] In *Neptune de la Mediterranee*. Beautemps-Beaupre, 1806. 46x61cm (18x23½") [15] £50 $77

PLAN DE LA VILLE ET DU PORT DE LOUISBOURG LEVE EN 1756. SUIVANT L'ORIGINAL ... PAR ORDRE DE M. DE SARTINE ... [1779] 46x61cm (18x24") Sh margin tears. Ref: Phillips (A) 1211; Sellers & Van Ee 341. [28] £367 $565

PLAN DES ENVIRONS DE RAGUSE [DUBROVNIK] [1820-1821] In *Neptune de la Mediterranee*. Beautemps-Beaupre, 1809. 91x61cm (35½x23½") Offsetting. [15] £120 $185

PLAN DES ENVIRONS DE SEBENICO [same date, source & dimen] Offsetting. [15] £110 $169

PLAN DES PORTS DE MOLONTA [same date, source & dimen] Beautemps-Beaupre, 1809. [15] £70 $108

PLAN DU BASSIN ET DE LA RIVIERE DU PORT ROYAL OU ANNAPOLIS, DANS L'ACADIE SUR LA COTE ORIENTALE DE LA BAIE FRANCOISE ... PAR ORDRE DE M. DE SARTINE ... [1779] 43x61cm (16½x24") Ref: Phillips (A) 1211; Sellers & Van Ee 537. [28] £380 $585

PLAN DU GOLFE DE CATTARO [1820-1821] In *Neptune de la Mediterranee*. Beautemps-Beaupre, 1808. 91x61cm (35½x23½") Browning & offsetting. [15] £80 $123

PLAN DU PORT DAUPHIN, DE LA RADE DE STE. ANNE, DE L'ENTREE DE LABRADOR ET DE LA BAIE DE NIGANICHE ... PAR ORDER DE M. DE SARTINE ... [1778] 46x61cm (17½x24") Faint dampmarks near lower border; 2 sm margin stains. Ref: Phillips (A) 1211; Sellers & Van Ee 331. [28] £204 $315

PLAN DU PORT DE LA RIVIERE ST. JEAN SITUE A LA COTE SEPTENTRIONALE ... [ON SHEET WITH] PLAN DU PORT DE LA HEVE A LA COTE MERIDIONALE DE L'ACADIE [AND] PLAN DU PORT ROCHELOIS A LA COTE MERIDIONALE ... [n.d.] 61x41cm (24½x15½") Dampmark affecting few inches of engraved surface. Ref: Phillips (A) 1211; Sellers & Van Ee 576. [28] £234 $360

PLAN DU PORT DE PARENZO [ON SHEET WITH] PLAN DU PORT D'UMAGO [AND] PLAN DE L'ENTREE DU LEMO [1820-1821] In *Neptune de la Mediterranee*. Beautemps-Beaupre. 46x61cm (18x23½") [15] £70 $108

PLAN DU PORTO-QUIETO [same date, source & dimen] Beautemps-Beaupre, 1806. [15] £50 $77

PLAN DU PRINCIPAL PORT DE L'ILE DE PORTO RICO LEVE ... PAR ORDRE DU MINISTRE DE LA MARINE ET DES COLONIES [1794-1801] San Juan. 41x56cm (16x22") Color. [25] £487 $750

DES BARRES

[MAINE: CASCO BAY] [1776] From *The Atlantic Neptune*. 74x107cm (29½x42") Border in wash color. Sm lower margin fold split; o/w exc. [15] £550 $847

[MAINE: FALMOUTH HARBOR (PORTLAND)] [c. 1777] From *The Atlantic Neptune*. With street plan. 74x53cm (29½x21") Orig wash color. Offsetting; overall VG. [38] £779 $1,200

[MASSACHUSETTS: BOSTON] [1781] As in *The Atlantic Neptune*. Shows town layouts & prominent features. 76x104cm (30x41½") Offered with text sheet of sailing directions, 30½x22". Wash color. Faint offsetting; generally exc. [15] £3,199 $4,928

[MASSACHUSETTS: BOSTON BAY] [1781] 76x104cm (30x41") Full orig color. Sl offsetting; else exc. [38] £2,272 $3,500

[MASSACHUSETTS: MARTHA'S VINEYARD, ELIZABETH ISLANDS, BUZZARDS BAY] [1776] From *The Atlantic Neptune*. 104x74cm (41½x29") Full color. Superb. [38] £3,571 $5,500

[MASSACHUSETTS: PLYMOUTH BAY & TOWN] [1781] From *The Atlantic Neptune*. 66x48cm (26x19") Orig color. Exc. [38] £779 $1,200

[NEW BRUNSWICK AND QUEBEC: BAY OF CHALEUR] [1781] 61x76cm (24x29½") Upper & lower margins trimmed to borders; 2" tear above lower border; browning, lt foxing. Ref: Phillips (A) 1198; Sellers & Van Ee 559. [28] £467 $720

[NEW BRUNSWICK: MIRAMICHI BAY] [1777] 54x75cm (21x29½") Orig wash col. Good. [14] £211 $325

[NOVA SCOTIA: CHART OF SPRY HARBOUR, PORT PALLISSER, PORT NORTH, PORT PARKER, BEAVER HARBOUR AND FLEMING RIVER. ...] [1779] 70x99cm (27½x39") Two Bates paper sheets joined. VF. [14] £373 $575

[PENNSYLVANIA] [1777] 79x104cm (30½x41") Uncolored. Beautiful condition. [2] £4,869 $7,500

[QUEBEC: BAIE DES SEPT-ISLES] [1781] 76x56cm (30x21½") Orig OL & border color. Margins bit chipped. Ref: Sellers & Van Ee 589; cf Phillips (A) 1198. [28] £526 $810

[QUEBEC: GASPE HARBOR & BAY] [1781] 3 sheets joined. 157x79cm (62x30½") Orig OL & border color. Lt offsetting; lower side margin creased. Ref: Sellers & Van Ee 593; Phillips (A) 1198. [28] £876 $1,350

[QUEBEC: HARBOR & BAY OF GASPEE AND MAUL BAY] [1781] Three sheets joined. 157x77cm (62x30") Orig wash color. Sl browned; good. [14] £276 $425

[QUEBEC & NEW BRUNSWICK: BAY OF CHALEURS] [1781] 61x75cm (24x29½") Orig wash color. Good. [14] £211 $325

[QUEBEC: RIVIERE ST. JEAN TO GRAND HERMINE BAY] [1781] 4 sheets joined 79x213cm (31x84") Orig OL & border color. Margins creased & ragged; fold tear; moderate offsetting. Ref: Sellers & Van Ee 585; Phillips (A) 1198. [28] £701 $1,080

[QUEBEC: ST. LAWRENCE RIVER, COOK COVE TO QUEBEC] [1781] 4 sheet joined, 76x246cm (30x97") Orig border color. Ragged side margins; few paper joins separating; some offsetting. Ref: Sellers & Van Ee 244; Phillips (A) 1198. [28] £2,045 $3,150

[U.S. GULF COAST] [c. 1777] Louisiana to Alabama. 74x104cm (29x41") Orig wash color. Lt offsetting; o/w exc. [2] £5,518 $8,500

A CHART OF PORT ROYAL AND KINGSTON HARBOURS, IN THE ISLAND OF JAMAICA ... [1780] From *The Atlantic Neptune*. 74x104cm (29x40½") Early wash color. Fold split & lf margin repaired & backed for strength. [15] £750 $1,155

A PLAN OF THE TOWN OF NEWPORT IN THE PROVINCE OF RHODE ISLAND [1776] Reference keys in lower panel. 74x53cm (28½x20½") Orig wash color. Linen backing; water-stains restored. Ref: Sellers & Van Ee 101. [2] £2,077 $3,200

A VIEW OF NEW CASTLE WITH THE FORT AND LIGHT HOUSE ON THE ENTRANCE OF PISQUATAQUA RIVER [before 1777] From *The Atlantic Neptune*. Early state; lacks stippling in water. 20x30cm (7½x11½") Few sm stains; else exc. Ref: Deak #164. [39] £487 $750

ANNAPOLIS ROYAL. ST. MARY'S BAY [dated 1776] 4th state? 5 ships, Annapolis named. 74x104cm (29x41") Orig OL col. Offsetting; 2" clean tear, no loss. Ref: Phillips (A) 1198; Sellers & Van Ee 535. [28] £701 $1,080

BARRINGTON BAY ... [NOVA SCOTIA] [1776] 2 sheet joined, 76x107cm (29½x41½") Orig OL color. Lt offsetting; fold tear repaired. Ref: Phillips (A) 1198; Sellers & Van Ee 516. [28] £584 $900

BOSTON, SEEN BETWEEN CASTLE WILLIAMS AND GOVERNORS ISLAND ... [ON SHEET WITH] THE ENTRANCE OF BOSTON HARBOR [AND] BOSTON BAY ... [AND] APPEARANCE OF THE HIGH LANDS OF AGAMENTICUS [1777] From *The Atlantic Neptune*. 4 views on sheet 56x79cm (21½x31") Faint stain traces; else fine. [39] £2,597 $4,000

CHARLOTTE BAY. PUBLISHED ACCORDING TO ACT OF PARLIAMENT BY J.F.W. DES BARRES ESQ. FEBY. 11TH 1776 [1776] St. Margaret's Bay. 2 sheet joined, 71x102cm (28x40") Ms error correction. Orig OL color. Lt offsetting; fold & margin tears repaired. Ref: Phillips (A) 1198; Sellers & Van Ee 502. [28] £584 $900

KEPPELL HARBOUR [OWLS HEAD BAY] ... KNOWLES HARBOUR [SHIP HARBOUR] ... TANGIER HARBOUR ... SAUNDER'S HARBOUR [SHOAL BAY] ... DEANE HARBOUR [PORT HARBOUR] ... [NOVA SCOTIA] [c. 1777] 2 views. 2 sheets joined, 74x102cm (28½x40") Orig OL and border color. Lt offsetting; join starting to separate. Ref: Phillips (A) 1198; Sellers & Van Ee 437. [28] £844 $1,300

KING'S BAY AND LUNENBURG [NOVA SCOTIA] [1779] 68x98cm (27x38½") Two Bates paper sheets. Sl soiled. [14] £315 $485

RIVER OF ST. LAWRENCE, FROM CHAUDIERE TO LAKE ST. FRANCIS ... [1781] 6 sheets joined, 79x315cm (30½x124½") Orig color. Fold tears & joins repaired. Ref: Sellers & Van Ee 252; Phillips (A) 1198. [28] £3,214 $4,950

SPRY HARBOUR ... PORT PALLISSER [MUSHABOOK HARBOUR] ... PORT NORTH [SHEET HARBOUR] ... PORT PARKER ... BEAVER HARBOUR ... FLEMING RIVER [QUODDY INLET] [NOVA SCOTIA] [1779] Views. 2 sheet joined, 104x74cm (40½x29") Orig border color. Lt offsetting; sh margin tears, some repaired. Ref: Phillips (A) 1198; Sellers & Van Ee 443. [28] £649 $1,000

THE ENTRANCE OF HAVANNAH, FROM WITHIN THE HARBOUR [ON SHEET WITH] THE HARBOUR AND PART OF THE TOWN OF HAVANNAH [c. 1775-1780] From *The Atlantic Neptune*. 2 aquatint views, each 25x46cm (9½x18") Upper view, B&W; lower sepia ink. Sl staining; overall fine. [39] £1,818 $2,800

THE HARBOURS OF RISHIBUCTO & BUCTASH ON THE WEST SHORE OF THE GULPH OF ST. LAWRENCE [1778] 79x51cm (30½x20½") Orig border color. Sh margin tears. Ref: Phillips (A) 1198; Sellers & Van Ee 568 & 569. [28] £526 $810

THE RIVER ST. JOHN ... [NEW BRUNSWICK] [1776] Cape Spencer to Pt. Charles; inset of Entrance. 53x76cm (21½x30") Orig color. Side margins trimmed beyond borders; edges ragged; horiz creases. Ref: Phillips (A) 1198; Sellers & Van Ee 265. [28] £555 $855

THE SOUTH EAST COAST OF THE ISLAND OF ST. JOHN ... [1781] By Holland et al. 4 sheets joined into two, each 109x89cm (42½x34½") Orig location & border color. Offsetting; margins spotted; joins starting to separate; part of sheet a bit ragged. Ref: Sellers & Van Ee 629; Phillips (A) 1198. [28] £876 $1,350

DESILVER

A NEW MAP OF ALABAMA WITH ITS ROADS AND DISTANCES FROM PLACE TO PLACE ALONG THE STAGE AND STEAM BOAT ROUTES [1856 (1857)] From Mitchell, *New Universal Atlas*. 33x26cm (13x10") Orig full color. image fine, overall VG-. [59] £65 $100

A New Map of Arkansas with Its Counties, Towns, Post Offices, &c. [1856] 39x32cm (15x12½") Color. [58] £65 $100

A New Map of Michigan with Its Canals, Roads & Distances [1856] 38x30cm (15x12") Color. [45] £58 $90

A New Map of South Carolina with Its Roads & Distances from Place to Place, along the Stage & Steam Boat Routes [1856 (1857)] From Mitchell, *New Universal Atlas*. Charleston inset. 26x33cm (10x13") Orig full color. Fine. [59] £81 $125

A New Map of Tennessee with Its Roads and Distances from Place to Place Along the Stage and Steamboat Routes [1856] 30x38cm (12x15") Full color. [45] £58 $90

A New Map of the State of Georgia Exhibiting Its Internal Improvements, Roads, Distances &c. By J.H. Young [1856] 38x30cm (15x12") Color. [45] £58 $90

[Same title] [1856 (1857)] From Mitchell, *New Universal Atlas*. 37x29cm (14½x11½") Orig full color. Fine. [59] £88 $135

A New Map of the State of Iowa [1856] 30x38cm (12x15") Full color. [45] £58 $90

A New Map of the State of Missouri [1856] 30x38cm (12x15") Color. [45] £58 $90

[Same title] [1856] 33x41cm (13x16") [58] £52 $80

New Hampshire and Vermont [1859] 37x31cm (14½x12½") Full color. [35] £42 $65

DESNOS

Amerique Septentrionale [c 1770] 10x10cm (4x4") Wash color. [57] £58 $90

L'Amerique Meridionale et Septentrionale ... [1731-1781] After G. Danet. Ornate border with portraits. 48x69cm (19x27½") Orig color. [53] £1,400 $2,156

DIDEROT

Carte de la Californie et des Pays Nord-Ouest, Separes de l'Asie par le Detroit d'Anian ... [1772] Vaugondy after Visscher 30x36cm (11½x14½") Uncol. Folded; o/w good. Ref: Pedley 473. [9] £146 $225

[Same title] [1772] 30x35cm (11½x14") Uncolored. Narrow lf margin; exc. [29] £114 $175

[Same title] [1777]. 30x35cm (11½x14") OL & wash color. [58] £162 $250

Carte de la Californie Suivant I. La Carte Manuscrite de l'Amerique de Mathieu Neron Pecci Olen Dresses a Florence en 1604, II. Sanson 1656, III. De l'Isle Amerique Sept 1700, IV. Le Pere Kino Jesuite en 1705, V. La Societe des Jesuites en 1767 [1770] From Diderot, *Encyclopedie*. 29x38cm (11½x15") Full color. Fold strengthened on verso with archival tape; sl puckering; o/w very nice. Ref: Leighly 24. [1] £292 $450

Carte des Nouvelles Decouvertes Dressee par Phil. Buache ... Aout 1752 [on sheet with] Extrait d'une Carte Japonaise de l'Univers ... [1772] By Robert de Vaugondy. 28x36cm (11½x14") OL color. Wrinkled; fine. [19] £146 $225

[Same title] [1772 - 1779] From *Encyclopedie*. By Robert de Vaugondy. 29x38cm (11½x15") Uncolored. Top edge splits repaired; c'fold creases; VG. Ref: TMC 12 p.47; Pedley 452; Tooley (Amer) pp 31-7, pl.21; Wagner (NW) I, pp 158-162. [59] £195 $300

Carte Generale des Decouvertes de l'Admiral de Fonte est Autres Navigateurs Espagnols, Anglois et Russes ... par M. De l'Isle ... [1772] By Robert de Vaugondy. 30x38cm (11½x14½") Later color. Folded; generally good. Ref: Pedley 454. [12] £179 $275

[Same title] [same date & dimen] OL color. Fine. [19] £162 $250

[Same title] [1772] From *Encyclopedie*. 38x30cm (**15x11½**") B&W. Ref: Phillips (A) 1195, 7; cf. Wagner (NW) 673; Pedley 455. [36] £146 $225

[Same title] [c. 1780] 29x37cm (11½x14½") Later full color. Sl dampstaining; VG. [30] £227 $350

Carte Generale des Decouvertes de l'Amiral de Fonte Representant la Grande Probabilite d'un Passage au Nord Ouest par T. Jefferys ... [1772] From Diderot & de Lambert. *Encyclopedie*. 29x35cm (11x13½") Later full color. Ref: Portinaro & Knirsch pl.159. [32] £243 $375

Partie de la Carte du Capitaine Cluny ... [1772] By Vaugondy. 30x48cm (11½x19") Later color. Folded; couple spots; else nice, clean. Ref: Pedley 460. [12] £185 $285

DIRECCION DE HIDROGRAFIA

Carta Esferica de la Costa Orientale de China desde el Rio Ngau-Keang hasta el Whang-Ho-Kau segun los Trabajos de los Capitanes Kellett y Collinson de la Marina Real Inglesa [1862] 94x61cm (37x24½") Minor edge tears; generally good, clean. [15] £60 $92

Carta Esferica de las Islas Antillas ... [1802] By Churruca. 91x61cm (35½x23½") Later coastline color. VG. [2] £357 $550

CARTA ESFERICA EN QUATRO HOJAS DE LAS COSTAS DE TERRA FIRMA ... [1816] Trinidad, Margarita & mainland coast. 60x95cm (23½x37"). [14] £812 $1,250
MAPA DE LA ISLA DE LA CULEBRA ... HIDROGRAFIA EN 1878 [1880] 28x41cm (10½x16") Col. [25] £71 $110
MAPA DE LAS ISLAS DEL PASAGE VIRGENES [1880] Sociedad Geografica de Madrid. 25x28cm (10x11") [27] £58 $90
PLANO DEL PTO. DE SAN TOMAS [VIRGIN IS.] [1809] In *Portulano de America*. Madrid: Ministerio de Marina. 18x25cm (7x9½") Exc. Ref: Phillips (A) 1223. [27] £172 $265
PLANO DEL PUERTO PRINCIPAL DE LA TORTOLA [same date, source, dimen & reference] Road Town harbor. [27] £159 $245

DJURBERG   Try *Schraembl*

KARTA OVER POLYNESIEN ... [1780] 1st Swedish map of Australia after Cook's voyages. 48x71cm (18½x28") Orig color. Tears crudely repaired; ms replacement lower rt corner. Ref: Tooley (Australia) #446. [2] £974 $1,500

POLYNESIEN (INSELWELT) ODER DER FUNFTE WELTTHEIL VERFAFST VON HERRN DANIEL DJURBERG NEU HERAUSGEGEBEN VON HERN F.A. SCHRAEMBL ... [1789] Schraembl reissue. Djurberg adopted native name *Ulimaroa* for Australia. 48x72cm (18½x28") Orig OL color. Some margin staining; beautiful. Ref: Tooley (Australia) #447. [2] £974 $1,500

DODSLEY

A NEW AND CORRECT PLAN OF LONDON, WESTMINSTER AND SOUTHWARK WITH SEVERAL ADDITIONAL IMPROVEMENTS, NOT IN ANY FORMER SURVEY [1761] 36x66cm (14x26") Color. Few fold reinforcements; else VG. [39] £438 $675

DONALDSON, T.

MAP OF THE YELLOWSTONE NATIONAL PARK [1881 (1883)] 38x43cm (15½x17½") Printed col. [58] £52 $80

MAP SHOWING INDIAN RESERVATIONS IN THE UNITED STATES, WEST OF THE 84TH MERIDIAN AND NUMBER OF INDIANS BELONGING THERETO [1883] From *The Public Domain*, ... 33x46cm (13x17½") Color keyed. Ref: Howes (US) D417. [58] £52 $80

MAP SHOWING PRIVATE LAND CLAIMS, PATENTED OR UNPATENTED, OR CONFIRMED IN NEW MEXICO, COLORADO AND ARIZONA ... [1883] From *The Public Domain*, ... 33x46cm (12½x17½") Color. Tear repair at rt, near invisible. Ref: Howes (US) D417. [58] £65 $100

DONCKER

'T EYLANDT CYPRUS ... [c. 1670] Inset: Nile delta. 40x52cm (15½x20½") Uncol. [53] £800 $1,232
CORFU EN BY-LEGGENDE PLAATSEN [c. 1670] 40x52cm (15½x20½") Uncolored. [53] £400 $616
PAS-CAERT VAN DE LEVANT ... [c. 1670] 41x51cm (16x20") Uncolored. [53] £600 $924
PAS-CAERTE VAN GROENLANDT, YSLANDT, STRAET DAVIDS EN IAN MAYEN EYLANT; HOEMEN DE SELVIGE VAN HITLANT EN DE NOORDKUSTEN VAN SCHOTLANDT EN YRLANDT ... HENDRICK DONCKER [c. 1660] As in *De Zee-Atlas*. 43x53cm (17x21") Orig OL & cartouche color. Faint foxing; sh lower ctr margin tears repaired. Ref: Koeman IV Don 2. [28] £584 $900
PAS-KAART VAN EUROPA ... 1665 ... [c. 1670] Hendrick Doncker. 42x52cm (16½x20½") Uncolored. [53] £550 $847
PAS KAERT VAN 'T OOSTELYCKE DEEL DER MIDDELANDSCHE ZEE ... [c. 1670] 41x51cm (16x20") Uncolored. [53] £650 $1,001
PASKAERT VAN 'T WESTELYCKE DEEL DER MIDDELANDSCHE ZEE ... [c. 1670] 41x51cm (16x20") Uncolored. [53] £650 $1,001

DOPPELMAYR   Try *Homann*

PHAENOMENA CIRCA QUANITATEM DIERUM ARTIFICIALUM ET SOLARIUM PERPETUO MUTABILEM, EX HYPOTHESI COPERNICANA DEDUCTA ... [c. 1742] Homann Heirs. 51x58cm (20x23½") Orig OL color. [28] £380 $585

PHAENOMENA IN PLANETIS PRIMARIIS QUAE FACIES DIVERSAS, EX ILLORUM PHASIBUS MACULIS ET FASCIIS SEU ZONUS ... [c. 1742] Homann Heirs. 51x58cm (20x23") Orig OL color. Crease near c'fold. [28] £380 $585

PLANISPHAERIUM COELESTE [c.1720 (1742)] Nuremberg: J.B. Homann. Double hemisphere. 48x56cm (19x22½") Wash color. Minor margin repair; good. Ref: Warner, Dopp 1. [49] £1,039 $1,600

THEORIA COMETARUM, IN QUA PRAECIPUAEORUM PHAENOMENA EX RECENTIORUM ASTRONOMORUM OBSERVATIONIBIS SECUNDUM ILL. NEWTONI ET CEL. WHISTONI ... [c. 1740] Homann Heirs. Double hemisphere showing comet paths; text panel. 48x56cm (19x22") Orig OL color. [52] £400 $616
[SAME TITLE] [c. 1742] 51x58cm (19½x22½") Orig OL color. [28] £380 $585

DOWER

NORTH AMERICA [c. 1840-1850] 25x20cm (10x8") Orig OL & wash color. Fine. [59] £81 $125
VAN DIEMAN'S LAND [1831] 34x41cm (13x16½") Orig color. [16] £183 $282
WESTERN HEMISPHERE [c. 1840-50] Diameter 20cm (8") OL & wash color. VG+. [59] £42 $65

DRAKE

THE WORLD, ACCORDING TO THE LATEST DISCOVERIES [1768] From Edward Cavendish Drake, *Travels*, London. 20x38cm (7½x14½") Color. Remargined at rt; fine. [47] £250 $385

DRIPPS

NEW YORK CITY, COUNTY, AND VICINITY [1864] In Valentine's Manual. 66x48cm (26x18½") Full orig color. Narrow margins as issued. [51] £97 $150

DU HALDE

THE KINGDOM OF KOREA [CALLED BY THE CHINESE KAU-LI-QUAE ...] [1741] 51x35cm (20x14") [14] £357 $550

DU VAL

A MAP OF THE HOLY LAND DELINEATED FOR THE BETTER UNDERSTANDING OF THE HISTORY OF IOSEPHUS [1675] Translated from 1668 French ed. 33x43cm (13x17") Color. Ref: Laor 263. [23] £211 $325
CARTE DES INDES ORIENTALES ... [1665] Indian Ocean & adjacent continents. 40x54cm (15½x21½") Color. Ref: Tooley (Australia) pl.129; Schilder 86 p.415; Clancy pp.106-7. [16] £3,229 $4,973
CARTE UNIVERSELLE DU COMMERCE, C'EST A DIRE CARTE HIDROGRAPHIQUE, OU SONT EXACTEMENT DECRITES LES COSTES DES 4 PARTIES DU MONDE AVEC LES ROUTES POUR LA NAVIGATION DE INDES OCCIDENTALES ET ORIENTALES [1677] In *Carte de Geographie*. Insular Calif. 37x53cm (14½x21") Color. Ref: Shirley (W) 465. [22] £617 $950
CARTE UNIVERSELLE DU MONDE ... [SOUTHERN SHEETS: TERRES AUSTRALES; AMERIQUE MERIDIONALE] [1679] Two of 4 untrimmed joinable sheets, each 41x58cm (16x22½") Color. Sl spotting in margins. Ref: Shirley (W) pl.356. [16] £4,273 $6,582
LE CANADA FAICT PAR LE SR. DE CHAMPLAIN, OU SONT LA NOUVELLE FRANCE, LA NOUVELLE ANGLETERRE, LA NOUVELLE HOLLANDE, LA NOUVELLE SUEDE, LA VIRGINIE &C. ... [1616 (1653-64)] Du Val restrike of plate intended for Champlain's 1619 *Les Voyages*. 35x55cm (14x21½") OL color. Sm tear ctr repaired. Ref: Karpinski (MI) XII; Imago Mundi XI (Wroth, "An Unknown Champlain Map of 1616"). [55] £3,571 $5,500
[SAME TITLE] [1616 / 1677] Incl revisions & additions. 36x53cm (13½x21½") Orig OL color. Minor margin mend; else exc. Ref: Schwartz & Ehrenberg, pl.47; Verner-Stubbs, Northpart p.31-3 [38] £4,869 $7,500
[SAME TITLE] [1664] 2nd state. 35x55cm (14x21½") Orig OL color. Fine. Ref: Kershaw (Canada) 77; Schwartz & Ehrenberg p.91. [2] £4,869 $7,500
[SAME TITLE] [same date & dimen] 2nd state; after 1616 map (one known example Orig color. C'fold reinforcement; overall fine. [63] £5,064 $7,800
ORBIS VETUS AUTHORE P. DE VAL [1663] 36x52cm (14x20½") Color. Fine. [26] £276 $425
REGNUM HISPANIAE [1678] 10x12cm (4x4½") Place names underlined in red crayon. [14] £19 $30

DUDLEY

CARTA PARTICOLARE DELL' ISOLE FILLIPINE E DI LUZON [1646] 49x38cm (19½x15") Mint. [63] £1,883 $2,900
CARTA PARTICOLARE DELL' MARE E ISOLE SCOPERTE DAL CAPITNO. IACOMO MAIER OLANDESE NEL 1617 CON PARTE DELLA NUOVA GUINEA ... [1646] 48x75cm (18½x29½") Fine. [15] £675 $1,040
CARTA PARTICOLARE DELL'ISOLE DI ISLANDIA E FRISLANDIA, CON L'ISOLETTE DI FARE [1646-1661] From *Arcano delle Mare* ... Legendary Frisland. 48x75cm (19x29½") Uncol. [53] £1,500 $2,310
CARTA PARTICOLARE DELLA NUOVA BELGIA E PARTE DELLA NUOVA ANGLIA ... [1646 / 1661] In *Arcano del Mare*. Maine to New Jersey. 46x37cm (18x15") Exc. [38] £5,518 $8,500

CARTA PARTICOLARE DELLO ISTRETO E MARE ISCOPERTO DA HEN: HUDSON INGILESE NEL. 1611 ... CARTA LIIII [1646-47] From *Arcano del Mare*. Two sheets joined 71x48cm (28x19") Ref: Phillips (A) 457; Nordenskiold (Col) I,70. [28] £2,103 $3,240

CARTA PARTICULARE DEL MARE DI ETHOPIA CON L'ISOLA DI S. ELENA E PARTE DELLA COSTA ... D'AFFRICA [1646] From *Arcano del Mare*. St. Helena & Ascension. 48x76cm (19x29½") [15] £500 $770

DUFOUR

[ATLAS] ATLAS PHYSIQUE, HISTORIQUE ET POLITIQUE DE GEOGRAPHIE MODERNE ... [c. 1860] Paris: Paulin et Le Chevalier. Large folio; 15 double-page maps, a selection from *Atlas Universel*, world & continents, France (5), etc. Modern quarter morocco. Partial color. Pub blind stamps lower map margins. [28] £730 $1,125

ETATS-UNIS ... [c. 1835] 25x36cm (10x14") OL color. Sl foxing lower margin; exc. [29] £75 $115

L'AMERIQUE DU SUD [1836] From d'Orbigny's *Voyage Pittoresque* ... 51x33cm (19½x13") B&W. Trimmed close at lower lf where bound. [46] £32 $50

MEXIQUE ... [c. 1835] With present Southwest & Calif. 36x25cm (13½x10") OL color. Faint foxing; VG. [29] £75 $115

MEXIQUE, ANTILLES ET CALIFORNIA [1858] Configuration similar to "Mexique ... Etats-Unis" with nearly all U.S. 55x75cm (22x29½") OL color. Edge browning; clear, crisp, bright. [9] £227 $350

DUNN   Try *Laurie & Whittle, Sayer*

A NEW CHART OF THE WORLD ON MERCATOR'S PROJECTION ... [1794] 31x41cm (12x16") OL color. [16] £228 $351

DUPERREY

PLAN DE L'ILE DE L'ASCENSION [1825] 36x51cm (14x19½") [15] £125 $193

DURY

[ATLAS] A NEW, GENERAL AND UNIVERSAL ATLAS CONTAINING FORTY-FIVE MAPS [1761] Printed for and sold by Dury & Sayer. Complete; oblong 8vo; 31 maps by Kitchin & others on 39 leaves, some counted as two in title. Orig OL color. In full orig calf. One map torn; another trimmed to neat line. Ref: Phillips (A) 627. [14] £812 $1,250

EDWARDS

A MAP OF THE WEST INDIES FROM THE BEST AUTHORITIES [1799] Outline map. 25x40cm (9½x15½") Folds; o/w good. [14] £39 $60

MAP OF THE ISLAND ANTIGUA ... [1794] 18x23cm (7x9") Folds. [14] £45 $70

MAP OF THE ISLAND OF BARBADOES ... [1794] 23x18cm (9x7") With 35 pp of text. Folds. [14] £49 $75

MAP OF THE ISLAND OF DOMINICA ... [1794] 23x18cm (9x7") With 22 pp of text. Folds. [14] £23 $35

MAP OF THE ISLAND OF ST. CHRISTOPHER'S ... [1794] Nevis inset. 19x24cm (7½x9½") Folds. [14] £32 $50

MAP OF THE ISLAND OF ST. VINCENT ... [1794] 1773 grant to Caribs noted. 24x18cm (9½x7") Folds. [14] £23 $35

ELLICOTT

PLAN OF THE CITY OF WASHINGTON, IN THE TERRITORY OF COLUMBIA, CEDED BY THE STATES OF VIRGINIA AND MARYLAND TO THE UNITED STATES OF AMERICA, AND BY THEM ESTABLISHED AS THE SEAT OF THEIR GOVERNMENT AFTER THE YEAR 1800 [1795] From Winterbotham, *An Historical View of the United States*. London. Russell, sc. 41x53cm (15½x20½") B&W. Repaired 3" tear; fold reinforced, partly remargined rt; good. Ref: Howes W-581; Phillips (Wash) p.22. [47] £1,428 $2,200

ELWE

GENERALE KAART VAN HET BELOOFDE LAND ... [1792] 51x58cm (20x23½") Old color. Ref: Laor 268. [23] £315 $485

MAPPE MONDE OU DESCRIPTION DU GLOBE TERRESTRE [1792] After Jaillot via Ottens. Double hemi; insular Calif. 47x61cm (18½x24") Orig & later color. Ref: cf. Shirley (W) 561, pl.13. [16] £3,893 $5,997

ENGLISH PILOT   See *Mount & Page, Thornton*

ENSIGN, BRIDGMAN & FANNING

CHARLESTON [SC] [1854] 20x13cm (8x5") Later color. [44] £26 $40

EVANS

A MAP OF THE MIDDLE BRITISH COLONIES IN NORTH AMERICA. FIRST PUBLISHED BY MR. LEWIS EVANS, OF PHILADELPHIA, IN 1755; AND SINCE CORRECTED AND IMPROVED, AS ALSO EXTENDED, WITH THE ADDITION OF NEW ENGLAND, AND BORDERING PARTS OF CANADA ... [1776] Authorized Pownall update. 49x81cm (19x32") Lt browned; rubbing at folds; areas reinforced; good. Ref: Schwartz & Ehrenberg pl.98; Streeter (Evans) pp 17-28. [38] £3,116 $4,800

FADEN

A CHART OF THE ISLE OF TRINIDAD ... [1798] 43x56cm (17x22") Orig OL color. Good. Ref: MCCS 10, Trinidad 4. [2] £974 $1,500

A GENERAL CHART EXHIBITING THE DISCOVERIES MADE BY CAPTAIN JAMES COOK [1799-1800] British & Russian Pacific discoveries color coded. 54x91cm (21½x35½") Orig color. [16] £712 $1,097

A MAP OF BENGAL, BAHAR, OUDE & ALLAHABAD WITH PART OF AGRA AND DELHI EXHIBITING THE COURSE OF THE GANGES FROM HURDWAR TO THE SEA BY JAMES RENNELL, R.F.S. ... [1786] 71x107cm (28x41½") Orig color. Ref: Gole (Ganges) 34.1. [28] £234 $360

A MAP OF ENGLAND, WALES & SCOTLAND. DESCRIBING ALL THE DIRECT AND PRINCIPAL CROSS ROADS IN GREAT BRITAIN, WITH THE DISTANCES ... [1801] To accompany Patterson's Book of the Roads. 76x64cm (29½x24½") Orig color. Lt offsetting. [28] £192 $295

A MAP OF THE INHABITED PART OF CANADA FROM THE FRENCH SURVEYS; WITH THE FRONTIERS OF NEW YORK AND NEW ENGLAND FROM THE LARGE SURVEY BY CLAUDE JOSEPH SAUTHIER. ENGRAVED BY WM. FADEN, 1777. LONDON, PUBLISHED ... FEBY. 25, 1777 BY WM. FADEN ... [1777] 3rd state; Borgoyne dedication. 61x89cm (23½x34½") Orig color. Lt foxing; sh fold tears repaired. Ref: Sellers & Van Ee 152; Nebenzahl (Biblio Amer Rev) 43. [28] £847 $1,305

A MAP OF THE PROVINCE OF NEW YORK, REDUCED FROM THE LARGE DRAWING OF THAT PROVINCE ... [1776] After Sauthier & Ratzer. Lake Champlain to Delaware Bay. 72x58cm (28½x22½") Dissected into 12 panels, laid on linen as issued, Orig OL color. [14] £812 $1,250

A NEW CHART OF THE GULF OF ST. LAWRENCE ... [1790] By Thomas Wright. 4 sheets joined, each 66x53cm (26x21½") Orig border color. Some offsetting. [28] £1,461 $2,250

A NEW MAP OF THE ISLAND OF TOBAGO ... [1779] Attributable to T. Kitchin & J. Rhodes. 43x58cm (17½x23½") Orig OL color. Some foxing; good. Ref: MCCS 10, Tobago #36. [2] £1,136 $1,750

A PLAN OF NEW YORK ISLAND, WITH PART OF LONG ISLAND, STATEN ISLAND, & EAST NEW JERSEY, WITH A PARTICULAR DESCRIPTION OF THE ENGAGEMENT...ON THE 27TH OF AUGUST 1776 ... [1775] 4th issue. 48x43cm (19x17") Some OL color. Exc. Ref: Stevens & Tree 41a; Nebenzahl (Amer Rev) #12 [later state]; Stokes (Manhattan) pl.45b. [2] £2,921 $4,500

A PLAN OF THE ACTION AT BUNKERS HILL, ON THE 17TH OF JUNE 1775, BETWEEN HIS MAJESTY'S TROOPS UNDER THE COMMAND OF MAJOR GENERAL HOWE, AND THE REBEL FORCES. BY LIEUT. PAGE OF THE ENGINEERS, WHO ACTED AS AIDE DE CAMP TO GENERAL HOWE IN THAT ACTION. [n.d.] 50x43cm (19½x17") OL color. Sl discoloring rt margin. Ref: Nebenzahl (Amer Rev) #4. [2] £4,220 $6,500

A TOPOGRAPHICAL CHART OF THE BAY OF NARRAGANSET IN THE PROVINCE OF NEW ENGLAND ... TO WHICH HAVE BEEN ADDED THE SEVERAL WORKS & BATTERIES RAISED BY THE AMERICANS [1777] By C. Blaskowitz. 94x64cm (36½x25") Minor repairs to external areas; else fine. Ref: Schwartz & Ehrenberg pl.126; Nebenzahl (Amer Rev) map 16. [38] £3,895 $6,000

A TOPOGRAPHICAL CHART OF THE ENTRANCE TO THE RIVER TAGUS DESCRIBING THE COAST FROM CAPE ROCA TO SACAVEM WITH THE HARBOUR AND ENVIRONS OF LISBON ... [1810] Chapman, 1806. Handstamped by Hydrographic Office for use on H.M ships. 58x91cm (23½x36") Lower fold split repaired; margins dust soiled, piece missing below not affecting engraving. [15] £220 $339

A TOPOGRAPHICAL MAP OF THE NORTHN. PART OF NEW YORK ISLAND, EXHIBITING THE PLAN OF FORT WASHINGTON, NOW FORT KNYPHAUSEN, WITH THE REBEL LINES TO THE SOUTHWARD WHICH WERE FORCED BY THE TROOPS UNDER THE COMMAND OF THE RT. HONBLE. EARL PERCY ... [1777] After Sauthier. 47x26cm (18½x10½") Some OL color. VG. Ref: Nebenzahl (Amer Rev) #14; Stokes (Manhattan) I:355. [2] £1,169 $1,800

AN ACCOUNT OF THE EXPEDITION OF THE BRITISH FLEET ON LAKE CHAMPLAIN ... [1775] Text panel below. 76x48cm (29½x18½") OL color marks fleet track. Exc. Ref: Stevens & Tree 24a; Nebenzahl (Amer Rev) #10. [2] £3,571 $5,500

BRITISH CAMP AT TRUDRUFFRIN ... [PA] [1776/7] Near Paoli. 25x41cm (10x16") OL color. Exc. Ref: Nebenzahl (Amer Rev) #25. [2] £4,220 $6,500

HIND, HINDOOSTAN, OR INDIA. BY L.S. DE LA ROCHETTE. MDCCLXXXVIII. LONDON. PUBLISHED BY WILLIAM FADEN ... 3D. EDITION WITH CONSIDERABLE IMPROVEMENTS JUNE 1ST 1800 [1800] 71x53cm (28x21") Orig color. Ref: cf Gole (Ganges) 105 1.1. [28] £175 $270
NOUVELLE CARTE DE LA SUISSE ... [1799] 63x85cm (25x33½") Orig OL color. [53] £400 $616
POSITION OF THE DETACHMENT UNDER LIEUT. COL. BAUM, AT WALMSCOCK NEAR BENNINGTON SHEWING THE ATTACKS OF THE ENEMY ON THE 16TH AUGUST 1777 [1780] 27x35cm (11x13½") Positions in orig color. [14] £97 $150
SPHERICAL CHART COMPREHENDING THE WEST COAST OF AMERICA, FROM THE SEVENTH DEGREE OF SOUTH LATITUDE TO THE NINTH DEGREE OF NORTH LATITUDE ... [1805, c.1825] Watermark dated to Admiralty period. After Malaspina, 1791. 86x58cm (34x22½") Some lt brown spotting; o/w exc. [15] £350 $539
THE COURSE OF DELAWARE RIVER FROM PHILADELPHIA TO CHESTER ... [1777 / 1778] 1st state; Fort Island inset. 43x69cm (17½x26½") Orig OL color. Exc. Ref: Stevens & Tree 17a; cf. Nebenzahl (Amer Rev) #29 [2nd state]. [2] £3,571 $5,500
THE NORTH SEA WITH THE KATTEGAT ... [1796] English Coast to Sweden. Attributed to De La Rochette. 66x61cm (26x24") Contemp OL color. Fold lines. [15] £300 $462
THE PROVINCE OF NEW JERSEY, DIVIDED INTO EAST AND WEST, COMMONLY CALLED THE JERSEYS ... [1778] 2nd ed. Based on Ratzer's surveys. 79x56cm (30½x22½") Uncolored. VG. Ref: Schwartz & Ehrenberg pl.120; Snyder p.57-61. [2] £4,382 $6,750
WESTERN HEMISPHERE [1802] 58x58cm (23x23") Orig color. Sh side margin tear; close upper & lower margins. [28] £292 $450

FERGUSON

A MAP OF THE EARTH UPON WHICH ARE MARKED THE HOURS AND MINUTES OF TRUE TIMES OF THE ENTRANCE AND EXIT OF VENUS, IN ITS PASSAGE OVER THE SUN'S DISC, JUNE 6TH, 1761 [1770] James Ferguson, London. Polar double hemi. 20x36cm (8x14") OL & wash color. [58] £97 $150
MAP OF THE PLANTING DISTRICTS OF CEYLON ... [c. 1890] A.M. & J. Ferguson. Pub Columbo; sold by Standidge & Co., London. Mounted on linen; folds into cover. 117x88cm (46x34½") Orig col. [54] £320 $493
THE ORRERY ... [1770] Mechanical solar system illustration. 20x23cm (8x9") Uncolored. [44] £49 $75

FINLEY

ENGLAND AND WALES [1829] 36x25cm (14x10½") Full color. Good. [21] £55 $85
ILLINOIS [1824] 26 counties. 29x22cm (11½x8½") Color. Fine. [11] £107 $165
[SAME TITLE] [1834] Shows MI in Wisconsin Terr. 36x50cm (14x19½") Full color. [61] £114 $175
IRELAND [1829] 36x25cm (14x10½") Full color. Good. [21] £62 $95
KENTUCKY [1831] 22x29cm (8½x11½") Color. Exc. Matted. [51] £179 $275
LOUISIANA [1824] 22x28cm (8½x11") Full color. Fine. [20] £127 $195
[SAME TITLE] [1829] From *New General Atlas.* 25x36cm (10½x14") Full color. Lt browned at margins; fine. [20] £114 $175
MAINE [1825] 9 counties. 29x22cm (11½x8½") Orig color. Immaculate. [35] £88 $135
[SAME TITLE] [1831] From *New General Atlas.* 29x22cm (11x9") Color. [51] £114 $175
MAP OF FLORIDA ACCORDING TO THE LATEST AUTHORITIES [1826] From *New American Atlas.* Includes table of American cities, mountains, etc. 41x25cm (16x9½") Full col. Ref: Phillips (A) 1378, 13. [55] £292 $450
MAP OF THE STATE OF MISSOURI AND TERRITORY OF ARKANSAS COMPILED FROM THE LATEST AUTHORITIES [1826] From *New American Atlas.* 43x55cm (17x21½") Full color. C'fold split repaired; minor foxing; good+. [55] £390 $600
MASSACHUSETTS [1829] 23x29cm (9x11½") Color. [36] £91 $140
MISSISSIPPI [1824] 28x21cm (11x8½") Color. Narrow margins. [36] £88 $135
MISSOURI [1831] 30x23cm (11½x9") Full orig color. [51] £146 $225
[SAME TITLE] [1834] 29 counties. 28x22cm (11x8½") Full color. [61] £114 $175
NEW HAMPSHIRE [1831] From *New General Atlas.* 29x22cm (11x9") Color. [51] £114 $175
NEW JERSEY [1827] 14 counties. 28x22cm (11x8½") Full color. Sm browned area. [36] £91 $140
PALESTINE [1825] Young & Delleker, sc. 30x23cm (11½x9") Color. [23] £26 $40
RHODE ISLAND [1831] From *New General Atlas.* 29x22cm (11x9") Color. [51] £114 $175
SOUTH AMERICA [1831] 28x23cm (11½x9") Full orig color. [51] £114 $175
SOUTH CAROLINA [1831] 22x29cm (8½x11½") Color. Exc. Matted. [51] £179 $275
TENNESSEE [1831] 22x29cm (8½x11½") Color. Exc. Matted. [51] £179 $275

UNITED STATES [1831] 29x22cm (11½x8½") Full orig color. Some staining. [51] £162 $250
VERMONT [1831] From *New General Atlas*. 29x22cm (11x9") Color. [51] £114 $175

FISHER
POLAND [c. 1814] 18x21cm (7x8½") Color. [42] £25 $39

FISHER & SON
STATES OF AMERICA [1838] Shows "Franklinia". 19x22cm (7½x8½") Orig color. [54] £160 $246

FLEISCHMANN
ERSTER ABRISS DER STADT JERUSALEM ... [1708 (?)] In German Bible, reduced version of 1584 Van Adrichom. 38x48cm (14½x19") Uncolored. Ref: Laor 1022. [58] £162 $250

FLEMMING
CALIFORNIEN, OREGON, UTAH UND NEU-MEJICO [1849-1852] 40x35cm (15½x13½") OL color. Trimmed in atlas to side neat lines. [46] £97 $150
MEXICO, MITTEL AMERICA, TEXAS [c. 1850] 33x41cm (13x16") Orig OL color. [46] £107 $165
[SAME TITLE] [1851] Incl Calif. 30x38cm (12x15") OL color. [44] £162 $250
TEXAS [1841 (1846)] Reduced version of Arrowsmith. 40x32cm (15½x12½") Orig OL color. Some spotting. [46] £552 $850

FORES
FORES'S NEW PLAN OF LONDON INCLUDING THE NEW IMPROVEMENTS [1822] N.R. Hewitt, sc. Dissected into 20 panels, linen mounted, folding into wraps; 12mo marbled case. 43x79cm (17x31") Color. Rubbed case; broken sides; map sl soiled & age-toned; o/w VG. [7] £185 $285

FORSTER
CARTE DES NORDENS VON AMERICA, ZUR BEURTHEILUNG DER WAHRSCHEINLICHKEIT EINER NORD=WESTLICHEN DURCHFAHRT; GEZEICHNET VON G. FORSTER ... [1791] 51x65cm (20x25½") Full color. Trace of offsetting; overall VG. [32] £364 $560

FOSTER
THE SEAT OF WAR IN THE WEST INDIES ... [1740] London: George Foster. Illustrates "War of Jenkins' Ear". West Indies map with plans of Spanish ports. 43x47cm (16½x18½") Separate publication. Orig OL color. Orig folds reinforced. [52] £720 $1,109

FOSTER, JOHN
A MAP OF NEW ENGLAND, ... [FACSIMILE] [(1677) 1826] Actual size facsimile of 1st map printed in English America. 30x38cm (12x15") Few tears repaired; else exc. [38] £292 $450

FRANK LESLIE'S ILLUSTRATED NEWSPAPER
MAP OF THE MISSISSIPPI, FROM HELENA TO PORT HUDSON ... [April 25, 1863] G.W. Colton. 23x13cm (9½x5") VG. [20] £91 $140
MAP OF THE MISSISSIPPI RIVER, FROM CAIRO TO THE GULF OF MEXICO, SHOWING THE POSITION OF THE REBEL FORTIFICATIONS AT THE MOUTH OF THE RIVER ... [May 10 1862] G.W. Colton. 3 parallel strip maps, each 51x13cm (20½x5") Reverse: Island No.10. Modern color. Browned; good. [20] £120 $185
[SAME TITLE] [same date] 3 strip maps in complete 16 pp newspaper. 51x38cm (20x14½") [36] £58 $90

FRANKLIN, J.
A CHART OF THE DISCOVERIES & ROUTE OF THE NORTH LAND EXPEDITION, UNDER THE COMMAND OF CAPT. FRANKLIN, R.N. IN THE YEARS 1820 & 21, LAID DOWN UNDER HIS INSPECTION BY THE OFFICERS ASSISTING IN THE EXPEDITION ... [1823] From *Narrative of a Journey to the Shores of the Polar Sea*. 83x49cm (32½x19½") Orig linen backed. 2 sm worm holes. [14] £42 $65
ROUTE OF THE EXPEDITION FROM YORK FACTORY TO CUMBERLAND HOUSE AND THE SUMMER AND WINTER TRACKS FROM THENCE TO ISLE A LA CROSSE IN 1819 & 1820 [1823] From *Narrative of a Journey to the Shores of the Polar Sea*. 25x56cm (9½x22") [14] £29 $45

FREMONT   Try U.S.
MAP OF AN EXPLORING EXPEDITION TO THE ROCKY MOUNTAINS IN THE YEAR 1842 AND TO OREGON & NORTH CALIFORNIA IN THE YEARS 1843-44 [1845] Drawn by Preuss. 130x81cm (51x31½") Some blue water OL, o/w B&W. Minor splitting some folds; minor tear repaired. Ref: Wheat (TM) 497. [46] £487 $750
MAP OF OREGON AND UPPER CALIFORNIA [1850] By Charles Preuss; E. Weber & Co., Balt. 51x43cm (19½x16½") Uncolored. VG. Ref: Wagner-Camp. [19] £292 $450

FRIES Try *Ptolemy (1522-1541 Strassburg)*

[PTOLEMAIC ARABIA] [1522-] From Ptolemy's *Geographia*. 28x46cm (11x18") Uncol. [53] £750 $1,155

[SOUTHEAST ASIA AND EAST INDIES] [1522] From the Strassburg Ptolemy. 1st issue; 1st printed map devoted to region. 30x44cm (11½x17½") Uncolored. [52] £1,500 $2,310

[SOUTHERN ASIA] [1522] From the Strassburg Ptolemy. 1st issue. 2nd map of the region 30x44cm (11½x17½") Uncolored. [52] £950 $1,463

DIEFERT SITUS ORBIS HYDROGRAPHORUM ... [1522 - 1541] From the Strassburg Ptolemy. 31x46cm (12x18") Uncolored. Lt surface browning. Ref: Shirley (W) 49. [52] £3,399 $5,236

TAB. MO. SECUNDAE PARTIS APHRICAE [1522 / 1525] Southern Africa. Waldseemuller's 1513 map re-cut & elaborated. 31x43cm (12x16½") Orig color, map & verso woodcut. Exc. [62] £1,818 $2,800

TABU. NOVA ORBIS [1535] From Ptolemy, *Geographia*, after Waldseemuller. 28x46cm (11x18") Sm holes at c'fold, one affects note letters. Ref: Shirley 49; Phillips (A) 364. Nordenskiold (Col) II,209. [28] £1,899 $2,925

TABU. TERRE SANCTAE [1522 - 1525] After Waldseemuller. 29x42cm (11x16½") Uncol. [54] £850 $1,309

TABULA MODERNA INDIAE [1522 - 1535] In Ptolemy's *Geographia*, Melchoir & Treschel ed. After Waldseemuller. 30x44cm (11½x17½") B&W. [16] £855 $1,316

TABULA NOVA INDIAE ORIENTALIS & MERIDIONALIS [1522/1525] 28x43cm (11x17") Fine. [62] £1,623 $2,500

TABULA NOVA PARTIS AFRICAE [1522 - 1541] After Waldseemuller from the Strassbourg Ptolemy. 30x40cm (11½x16") Orig color. Sm restoration upper c'fold. [54] £520 $801

TABULA SUPERIORIS INDIAE & TARTARIAE MAIORIS [1522 / 1541] 1st printed map focusing on Japan & China. 29x46cm (11½x18") Exc. [62] £1,818 $2,800

TYPUS ORBIS DESCRIPTIONE PTOLEMAEI [(1522) 1541] From the Strassbourg "Ptolemy". 30x46cm (12x18") B&W. Ref: Shirley (W) 47. [16] £2,849 $4,388

FROISETH

MAP OF THE TERRITORY OF UTAH [1870] 3 maps on sheet: also Great Salt Lake Valley; Salt LakeCity plat. Printed NY, with "Osborne's Process". 53x38cm (21x15") Color. Crisp, bright. Ref: Storm (Graff) 1449. [13] £97 $150

FULLARTON

A MAP OF ENGLAND AND WALES [c. 1834] 56x46cm (22x17½") On thin wove paper. Full color. Few fold repairs; good. [21] £55 $85

AUSTRALIA AND NEW ZEALAND [1864] Insets. 41x51cm (16x20") Orig wash color. [14] £29 $45

CENTRAL AMERICA, NAMELY THE [LATE] CONFEDERATED STATES OF CENTRAL AMERICA: THE MEXICAN STATES OF CHIAPAS, TABASCO & YUCATAN; OR BRITISH HONDURAS [1845] J. McNab. 52x41cm (20½x16") Orig wash color. [14] £23 $35

OREGON AND CALIFORNIA [1849] By Swanston. East to Rockies. 23x15cm (9x6") Soft col. [57] £65 $100

TURKEY IN ASIA (BIBLICAL REGIONS) THE HOLY LAND AND ITS BORDERS INCLUDING ANCIENT PHOENICIA, THE HAURAN AND ADJACENT DISTRICTS; SHOWING JEWISH, ROMAN & MODERN DIVISIONS [1858] J.H. Johnson. 53x41cm (21x16") Color. Ref: cf. Laor 377. [23] £32 $50

UNITED STATES OF AMERICA ... THE SOUTH CENTRAL SECTION [1860] 51x41cm (20x16") OL color. [10] £101 $155

FULLER

[HOLY LAND, ARABIAN DESERT AND MESOPOTAMIA] [1650] London: W. Hole. 30x36cm (12x14") Color. [23] £159 $245

A DESCRIPTION OF THE LAND OF GOSEN AND MOSES' PASSAGE THROUGH THE DESERTS [1614] Exodus route. 28x38cm (11x14½") Color. Ref: Laor 337. [23] £169 $260

GALILAEA INFERIOR [ZEBULON] [1650] From *A Pisgah Sight of Palestine*. 28x34cm (11x13½") Uncolored. Lt uniform age tone; VG. Ref: Laor 285 [30] £162 $250

IERUSALEM QUALIS (VT PLURIMUM) EXTITIT AETATE SOLOMONIS [1650] From Thomas Fuller, *A Pisgah-Sight of Palestine* ... Imaginary plan. 28x37cm (11x14½") Uncolored. Old lib stamp on back; VG. Ref: Laor 1024. [59] £65 $100

ISSACHAR [1650] Goddard, sc. 28x33cm (11x13") Color. Ref: Laor 286 [23] £130 $200

NAPTHALI [1650] Cross, sc. 28x33cm (11x13½") Color. Ref: Laor 283. [23] £127 $195

TERRA MORIATH SIVE SOLYMARUM AGER SUBURBANUS [1650] From *A Pisgah Sight of Palestine*. 28x34cm (11x13½") Uncolored. Lt uniform age tone; VG. Ref: Laor 293. [30] £162 $250

FURST
ABBILDUNG DES KONIGREICH UNGARN DURCH TURCKEY BIS NACH ... [c. 1666] Lower Danube regions. 37x85cm (14½x33½") Separately published. Uncolored. Surface staining; VG. [52] £950 $1,463

GALL & INGLIS
GALL & INGLIS'S HANDY MAP & GUIDE TO LONDON, 1876 [c. 1880] Folding map, with index. 48x74cm (19x29") Partial color. Fine. [21] £36 $55
SHEET NUMBER 9. THE 'HALF INCH' MAP OF ENGLAND FOR CYCLISTS, TOURISTS ETC. NORTH DEVON. [c. 1880] Folds into cloth covers. 51x64cm (20x25½") Main roads colored. Some misfolding & fold tears; good. [21] £42 $65

GALLUCI
[ATLAS] THEATRUM MUNDI, ET TEMPORIS ... [1588] Venice: Somasco. 1st ed. 1st celestial atlas with readable coordinates. Quarto; pp.8.l.,478; 144 full-page woodcuts, 51 with volvelle parts, etc. Full calf antique. Lt dampstains; title soiled, old inscriptions; table fold repairs, no loss. Ref: Warner pp.xi,91. [28] £5,843 $9,000

GARNERAY
VUE DE NEW YORK. PRISE DE WEAHAWK / A VIEW OF NEW-YORK, TAKEN FROM VEAHAWK ... [1834] 1st state. Paris: Chez Basset; Himely, sc. 38x46cm (14½x17½") Minor repair; mounted on rice paper; overall fine. Ref: Stokes (Manhattan) III, pl.110; Stokes & Haskell pp.78-79; Deak #433. [39] £4,220 $6,500

GARNIER
ETATS-UNIS DE L'AMERIQUE DU NORD. LIMITES EN 1860 [1862] In *Atlas Spheroidal et Universel*. 36x50cm (14x19½") Orig full color. Fine-. Ref: Phillips (A) 836,50. [59] £114 $175

GASTALDI
[ATLAS] LA GEOGRAPHIA ... AGGIUNTEUI DI MESER IACOPO GASTALDI ... [1548] 26 Ptolemaic & 34 new copper engraved maps incl new world; octavo. 19 c. quarter vellum binding with marbled boards. Ref: Phillips (A) 369. [3] £11,686 $18,000
AFRICA NOVA TABULA [1548] From *Ptolemeo. La Geografia* .... 13x17cm (5½x7") Uncol. [53] £450 $693
ARABIA FELIX NOVA TABULA [1548] From the Ptolemy. 13x18cm (5½x6½") Uncol. [57] £130 $200
CARTA MARINA NOVA TABULA [1548] From *Ptolemeo. La Geografia* .... 13x17cm (5½x7") Uncolored. Ref: Shirley (W) 88. [53] £500 $770
[SAME TITLE] [same date & source] 13x18cm (5x7") Sm wormhole upper lf border; overall VG. Ref: Shirley (W) 88; Suarez 24. [55] £812 $1,250
ISOLA CUBA [1548] From Ptolemy, *Geographia*. 13x17cm (5x6½") Sl weak impression; fine. [62] £390 $600
NUEVA HISPANIA TABULA NOVA [1548] From *Ptolemeo. La Geografia* .... First printed map of New Spain; insular Yucatan. 13x17cm (5½x7") Uncolored. Uneven impression; lower c'fold restoration. Ref: Wagner (NW) 48. [53] £850 $1,309
[SAME TITLE] [1548] 1st printed map of New Spain; insular Yucatan. 13x17cm (5x7") + title above. Uncolored. Faintness at rt; smudges at unevenly printed title; lt show-through lf; o/w bright, clear, clean. Ref: Wagner (NW) I,pp 27-8, II #18; Wheat (TM) #7; MCC 103, pl.1; Nordenskiold pp 25-6; Martin (TX) pl.3. [59] £1,623 $2,500
SICILIA & SARDINIA NOVA TABULA [1548] From the Ptolemy. 13x18cm (5x6½") Uncol. [57] £130 $200
TABULA ASIAE XI [SOUTHEAST ASIA] [1548] After Ptolemy. 13x17cm (5x7") Minor c'fold repair. [57] £146 $225
UNIVERALE NOVO [1548] Ptolemy, *Geographia*. 13x18cm (5x7") Some surface dirt; overall VG. Ref: Shirley (W) 87. [55] £812 $1,250

GAZZETTIERE AMERICANO
CARTA ESATTA RAPPRESENTANTE, L'ISOLA DELLA GUADALUPA [1763] 22x30cm (9x12") [14] £32 $50
CARTA RAPPRESENTANTE IL PORTO DI BOSTON [1763] 21x18cm (8½x7") [14] £127 $195

GENERAL MAGAZINE OF ARTS & SCIENCES
A MAP OF NEW ENGLAND & YE COUNTRY ADJACENT, EXTENDING NORTHWARD TO QUEBEC, & WESTWARD TO NIAGARA, ON LAKE ONTARIO; SHEWING GEN: SHIRLEY AND GEN: IOHNSON'S ROUTS, & MANY PLACES OMITTED IN OTHER ... [1755] W. Owen. 20x18cm (8x7") Uncolored. Ref: Jolly GENMAS-70 [54] £260 $400

GENTLEMAN'S MAGAZINE

[NORTH AMERICA: LOUISIANA, VIRGINIA & CAROLINA]. [1763] Present US: Delaware River to Rio Grande. 18x24cm (7x9½") OL color. Ref: Jolly GENT-169 [56] £143 $220

A MAP OF 100 MILES ROUND BOSTON [1775] 23x25cm (9x9½") Uncolored. Folded; some offsetting. Ref: Jolly GENT-234; Phillips (M) 149. [36] £130 $200

A MAP OF PART OF WEST FLORIDA, FROM PENSACOLA TO THE MOUTH OF THE IBERVILLE RIVER, WITH A VIEW TO SHEW THE PROPER SPOT FOR A SETTLEMENT ON THE MISSISSIPI [1772] Lodge, sc. 19x35cm (7½x13½") Uncolored. Tiny hole rt border; overall VG. Ref: Jolly GENT-217 [4] £114 $175

[SAME TITLE] [same date, source, dimen & reference] Wash color. [46] £81 $125

A MAP OF PHILADELPHIA AND PARTS ADJACENT, BY N. SCULL AND G. HEAP [1777] 34x29cm (13½x11½") Ref: Jolly GENT-256 [14] £338 $520

A MAP OF POLAND WITH ITS APPENDAGES; SHEWING THE LATE PARTITION OF THAT KINGDOM. [1772] 17x21cm (7x8") B&W. Ref: Jolly GENT-222 [46] £19 $30

A MAP OF THAT PART OF AMERICA WHICH WAS THE PRINCIPAL SEAT OF WAR, IN 1756. [1757] 22x33cm (8½x13") Skewed printing, upper rt border off page; o/w nearly fine. Ref: Jolly GENT-102 [35] £127 $195

A MAP OF THE CARIBBEE ISLANDS; SHEWING WHICH BELONG TO ENGLAND, FRANCE, SPAIN, DUTCH & DANES, COLLECTED FROM THE BEST AUTHORITIES; BY THOS. JEFFERYS, GEOGRAPHER TO HIS ROYAL HIGHNESS THE PRINCE OF WALES. [1756] 33x21cm (13x8") Some offsetting; sh tear into map joined. Ref: Jolly GENT-98 [14] £39 $60

A MAP OF THE COUNTRY BETWEEN CROWN POINT AND FORT EDWARD [1759] 19x11cm (7½x4½") With text page. Ref: Jolly GENT-129 [14] £39 $60

A MAP OF THE ISLAND OF TOBAGO, DRAWN FROM AN ACTUAL SURVEY, BY THOS. BOWEN, 1779. [1779] 19x24cm (7½x9½") Fine. Ref: Jolly GENT-262 [14] £81 $125

A MAP OF THE NEW CONTINENT ACCORDING TO ITS GREATEST DIAMETRICAL LENGTH FROM THE RIVER LA PLATA TO BEYOND THE LAKE OF THE ASSINIBOILS. [1758] After De Vaugondy. 21x17cm (8½x7") Uncolored. Offsetting; o/w fine-. Ref: Jolly GENT-122 [59] £81 $125

A MAP OF THE NEW GOVERNMENTS, OF EAST & WEST FLORIDA. [1763] By Gibson. 20x25cm (8x10") Later full color. Ref: Jolly GENT-171 [51] £292 $450

[SAME TITLE] [same date, dimen & reference] With text furnished. Uncol. Sl toned; fine. [4] £179 $275

A MAP OF THE SOUTH POLE, WITH THE TRACK OF HIS MAJESTY'S SLOOP RESOLUTION IN SEARCH OF A SOUTHERN CONTINENT. [1776] 22x21cm (8½x8½") Ref: Jolly GENT-241 [14] £49 $75

A MAP OF THE WORLD, ON MERCATORS PROJECTION. [1755] 18x28cm (7x11") Ref: Jolly GENT-94 [16] £152 $234

A MAP SHEWING THE COMMUNICATION OF THE LAKES AND THE RIVERS BETWEEN LAKE SUPERIOR AND SLAVE LAKE IN NORTH AMERICA [1790] 20x23cm (8x9") With text page. Ref: Jolly GENT-283. [14] £120 $185

A NEW CHART OF THE COAST OF NEW ENGLAND, NOVA SCOTIA NEW FRANCE OR CANADA, WITH THE ISLANDS OF NEWFOUNDLD. CAPE BRETON ST. JOHN'S &C. DONE FROM THE ORIGINAL PUBLISH'D IN 1744. AT PARIS. BY MONSR. N. BELLIN. ... [1746] Jefferys, sc. 34x47cm (13½x18½") Wash color. Occas spotting. Ref: Jolly GENT-40 [14] £227 $350

A PARTICULAR MAP, TO ILLUSTRATE GEN. AMHERSTS, EXPEDITION, TO MONTREAL; WITH A PLAN OF THE TOWN & DRAUGHT OF YE ISLAND. [1760] 18x23cm (7x9") Ref: Jolly GENT-145 [36] £78 $120

A PHYSICAL PLANISPHERE WHEREIN ARE REPRESENTED ALL THE KNOWN LANDS AND SEAS WTH. THE GREAT CHAINS OF MOUNTAINS WCH. TRAVERSE THE GLOBE FROM THE NORTH POLE. ADAPTED TO MONSR: BUACHE'S MEMOIRE READ AT THE R. ACADEMY OF SCIENCES. [1757] 31x29cm (12½x11½") Ref: Jolly GENT-104 [16] £328 $505

A PLAN OF CONSTANTINOPLE, PLACES ADJACENT AND CANAL OF THE BLACK SEA [1770] 17x24cm (6½x9½") Uncolored. Fine. Ref: Jolly GENT-204 [30] £104 $160

[SAME TITLE]. [same date, dimen & reference] Incl Bosphorus. Color. [58] £49 $75

A PLAN OF THE CITY & HARBOUR OF LOUISBURG, SHEWING THAT PART OF GABARUS BAY IN WHICH THE ENGLISH LANDED, ALSO THEIR ENCAMPMENT DURING THE SIEGE IN 1745. [1746] 19x26cm (7½x10") With leaf of text. Ref: Jolly GENT-145 [14] £39 $60

A PLAN OF THE CITY OF PRAGUE, WITH THE FRENCH AND AUSTRIAN CAMPS. [ON PLATE WITH] CITY OF EGRA. DESCRIB'D IN OCTR. MAG. P.530. [AND] SOUTHERN VIEW OF PRAGUE. [AND] MARIA TERESA Q. OF HUNGARY BORN MAY 13TH. 1717. [1742] 29x36cm (11½x14") Uncolored. Ref: Jolly GENT-18 [58] £81 $125

A Plan of the Harbour of Chebucto and Town of Halifax. [1750] 22x27cm (8½x10½") B&W. Remargined rt; good. Ref: Jolly GENT-70 [48] £211 $325

[SAME TITLE] [same date, dimen & reference] With porcupine engraving Uncolored. Orig narrow margins; minor flaws repaired; image VG; good. [59] £162 $250

A Plan of the Town and Chart of the Harbour of Boston Exhibiting a View of the Islands, Castles, Forts and Entrances into the Said Harbour [1775] 26x34cm (10½x13") Some offsetting; folds. Ref: Jolly GENT-232 [14] £78 $120

[SAME TITLE] [same date, dimen] Uncolored. Folded; some offsetting; sh mended tear, faint tape remnant show-through. Ref: Jolly GENT-232; Phillips (M) p.150. [36] £130 $200

A View of the Town and Castle of St. Augustine, and the English Camp before It June 20. 1740. By Thos. Silver [1740] Text below. 30x17cm (11½x6½") Ref: Jolly GENT-12 [14] £211 $325

An Accurate Map of the British Empire in Nth. America As Settled by the Preliminaries in 1762 [1762] Cessions to England shaded. 21x24cm (8½x9½") Color. Ref: Jolly GENT-165 [14] £81 $125

An Accurate Map of the West Indies, with the Adjacent Coast. [1762] By J. Gibson. 18x29cm (7x11½") B&W. Remargining rt; fine. Ref: Jolly GENT-156 [47] £185 $285

An Authentic Plan of the River St. Laurence, from Sillery to the Falls of Montmorency. [1759] Battle of Quebec. Gibson, sc. 11x19cm (4x7½") OL & wash color. Ref: Jolly GENT-137. [57] £58 $90

Chart of the Antarctic Polar Circle, with the Countries Adjoining, According to the New Hypothesis of M. Buache. from the Memoirs of the Royal Accademy at Paris [1763] 20x22cm (7½x8½") B&W. Ref: Jolly GENT-166 [46] £49 $75

[SAME TITLE] [same date, dimen & reference] Uncolored. Fine-. [59] £130 $200

Map of Hudson's River, with the Adjacent Country. [1778] 30x21cm (11½x8½") B&W. Fine. Ref: Jolly GENT-257 [50] £172 $265

Plan of Gibraltar. [1762] By Gibson. 17x45cm (7x17½") Later full color. Ref: Jolly GENT-157 [51] £114 $175

Plan of St Petersburg; with It's Fortifications, Built by Peter the Great in 1703. [ON PLATE WITH] The Harbour of Crownslot River Neva, Canal Made from the Said River to the R. Wolschowa. [1749] 19x24cm (7½x9½") OL & wash color. Ref: Jolly GENT-65 [58] £49 $75

Sketch of the Country Illustrating the Late Engagement in Long Island. [1776] 20x31cm (8x12½") Uncolored. Sl browned; narrow lf margin. Ref: Jolly GENT-248. [36] £130 $200

Spain and Portugal. [ON PLATE WITH] A Map of the Mouth of the River Tagus, or Harbour of the City of Lisbon. [1756] 23x18cm (9x7") B&W. Ref: Jolly GENT-96 [46] £26 $40

The British Governments in Nth. America Laid Down Agreeable to the Proclamation of Octr. 7. 1763. [1763] By Gibson. 20x23cm (8x9") B&W. Remargined top, upper rt neat line affected; o/w good. Ref: Jolly GENT-170; Fite & Freeman pp.218-21. [48] £237 $365

GIBSON

A Map of the Island of Orleans with the Environs of Quebec [c. 1759] 11x19cm (4½x7½") Color. [40] £45 $69

A Plan of the City of Quebec and Its Fortifications [1769] 18 places referenced. 6x11cm (2½x4½") [14] £39 $60

Asia [1798] From *Atlas Minimus*, Phila. Joseph Scott, sc. 8x10cm (2½x4") OL color. Ref: Wheat & Brun 897. [57] £23 $35

GILPIN

Map Illustrating the System of Parcs, and the Domestic Relations of the Great Plains, the North American Andes, and the Pacific Maritime Front [1873] 53x58cm (21x22½") Full color. Narrow margins; smoke stains rt edge; lt waterstain along fold; orig outside fold darkened. [1] £97 $150

GOAD

Area of Fire - Wholesale District - Toronto - Canada ... [1904] FP No.50 (2nd Edition). Scale: 50'/inch. 63x52cm (24½x20½") Color. [14] £32 $50

Castries, St. Lucia, West Indies [1897] Fire insurance map. 62x52cm (24½x20½") Orig litho color. [14] £55 $85

Frederiksted, Santa Cruz or St. Croix, Danish West Indies [1897] Fire insurance map. 62x51cm (24½x20") Full orig color. [14] £97 $150

Insurance Plan of Kingston, Jamaica [1894] Buildings & streets named. 62x53cm (24½x20½") [14] £81 $125

INSURANCE PLAN OF VALPARAISO, CHILE [1909] 55x50cm (21½x19½") Orig. color. [14] £32 $50
MEXICO CITY [1899] Key fire insurance map; 2 sheets, each 62x52cm (24x20½") Orig col. [14] £78 $120
ST. JOHNS, ANTIGUA [1897] Fire insurance map. 62x51cm (24x20") Printed litho col. Fine. [14] £55 $85

GOLDTHWAIT

MAP OF THE TERRITORIES & PACIFIC STATES ... [1865] From S. Bowles, *Across the Continent*. NY: G.W. & C.B. Colton. 36x46cm (13½x18") Full color. VG. [19] £65 $100

GOOS

DE ZEE CUSTEN VAN RUSLANT, LAPLANT, FINMARCKEN, SPITZBERGEN EN NOVA ZEMLA [c. 1660] 44x54cm (17½x21") Full orig color. Weakened area strengthened. [14] £250 $385
[SAME TITLE] [1680] From *Zee Atlas*. Archangel inset. 44x55cm (17½x21½") Early color. Sl dampmarking & paper softness at margins. [15] £300 $462
PAS-CAART VANT CANAAL VERTGONENDE IN 'T GHEHEEL ENGELANDT, SCHOTLANDT, YRLANDT, EN EEN GEDEELTE VAN VRANCRYCK [1669] From *Zee-Atlas*. 45x55cm (17½x21½") Early OL col. [15] £490 $755
PAS CAERTE VAN NIEU NEDERLANDT EN DE ENGELSCHE VIRGINIES VAN CABO COD TOT CABO CANRICK [1666] Pieter Goos. 44x53cm (17½x20½") Early color, gold highlighting; exc. Ref: Deak #48. [38] £3,571 $5,500
PASCAARTE VAN DE MONT VAN DE WITTE ZEE [c. 1660] 26x36cm (10x14") Color. [14] £127 $195
PASKAARTE VAN HET SUYDELIJCKSTE VAN AMERICA VAN RIO DE LA PLATA, TOT CAAP DE HOORN, ENDE INDE ZUYDE ZEE, TOT B. DE KOQUIMBO [1666] Pieter Goos. 44x55cm (17½x21½") Early color. Damp marking top edge; o/w fine. [15] £370 $570
PASKAERTE VAN NOVA GRANADA, EN T'EYLANDT CALIFORNIA [1666] 44x54cm (17½x21½") [63] £4,415 $6,800

GRANT

RAILROAD AND COUNTY MAP OF INDIAN TERRITORY / INDIAN TY. [1886] Area labeled "Unknown Nation". 41x56cm (16x22") Printed OL color. [58] £71 $110
RAILROAD AND COUNTY MAP OF MONTANA [1886] 12 counties. 41x58cm (16½x22½") Printed OL color. [58] £58 $90
RAILROAD & COUNTY MAP OF FLORIDA [1887] From *Grant's Railroad & Business Atlas*. A.A. Grant. 56x41cm (22½x16½") Printed color. [4] £55 $85
TEXAS [c. 1890] A. Grant. With ephemeral Buchel Co. 41x56cm (16x22") Full color. [46] £71 $110

GRATTAN & GILBERT

SYRIA [1820] 28x23cm (11½x9½") Color. [23] £23 $35

GRAY

ALABAMA [1884] 66x41cm (26x16") Full printed color. As if just printed. [46] £32 $50
BRITISH ISLES [1876] Reverse: Europe. 41x33cm (16x13") Full color. VG. [21] £26 $40
CHICAGO [1876] 41x33cm (15½x12½") Color. [36] £49 $75
COLORADO [1878] 31x38cm (12x15") Full color. [45] £58 $90
FLORIDA [1877] S Florida inset. Verso: GA; AL. 43x66cm (16½x26") Orig wash color. [4] £62 $95
GRAY'S ATLAS MAP CALIFORNIA, NEVADA, UTAH, COLORADO, ARIZONA & NEW MEXICO [1873] 41x66cm (16x25½") Color. Edge chipping; repaired margin tear; o/w good. [9] £81 $125
GRAY'S ATLAS MAP OF FLORIDA [1873] 36 counties. Verso: AL. 30x38cm (12x15") Orig wash color. Lt browned edges. [4] £36 $55
GRAY'S ATLAS MAP OF NEW YORK CITY [1875] North to 83rd St., with surrounding cities. 38x30cm (15x12") Full color. [35] £45 $70
GRAY'S IDAHO, MONTANA AND WYOMING [1876] Verso: UT. 30x38cm (12x15") Full col. Fine. [18] £49 $75
GRAY'S NEW MAP OF INDIANA [1884] 64x38cm (25x15½") Full orig color. [51] £62 $95
GRAY'S NEW MAP OF KANSAS [1884] 41x69cm (16x27") Full orig color. [51] £62 $95
GRAY'S NEW MAP OF OHIO [1884] Several insets. 38x64cm (15½x25") Full orig color. [51] £81 $125
GRAY'S NEW MAP OF TEXAS AND THE INDIAN TERRITORY [1876] With "Wegefarth" County. 58x41cm (23½x16½") Color. [58] £114 $175
GRAY'S NEW MAP OF THE WORLD IN HEMISPHERES ... [1884] Frank A. Gray. With mountain heights & river lengths. 43x66cm (16½x26") Full color. [51] £81 $125

Map of the Territory of Alaska [1884] From *National Atlas*. Subtitle: "Russian America". 30x38cm (12x15") Color. [51] £62 $95

Massachusetts and Rhode Island [1874] Verso: Boston. 31x37cm (12x14½") Orig color. Lt, evenly aged. [46] £32 $50

Mexico [1884] 31x38cm (12x15") Pastel color. [46] £26 $40

Nebraska [1877 (1884)] 30x38cm (12x15") OL color. Repaired margin tears at top. [46] £26 $40

[Same title] [1878] 38x46cm (15x18") Color. VG. [45] £49 $75

Palestine [1884] 38x30cm (15x12") Pastel color. [46] £19 $30

San Francisco [1877] 38x30cm (15x12") Full color. [35] £49 $75

United States [1879] 41x69cm (15½x27") Full printed color. As fresh off press. [46] £45 $70

GREENLEAF

Indiana [1832 (cited)] 33x28cm (12½x10½") Color. [61] £81 $125

Map of the Territory of Florida [1840] 16 counties. 33x28cm (13x10½") Orig full wash color. A light spot in water area; o/w VG. [4] £114 $175

New Holland and New Zealand [1842] 28x33cm (10½x13") [36] £114 $175

The United States of Mexico [1842] Independent TX to Nueces. 32x27cm (12½x10½") Orig color. [46] £120 $185

[Same title] [same date & dimen] Orig full color. Fine. Ref: Phillips (A) 748,57. [59] £179 $275

United States [1842] 28x33cm (11x12½") Color. [35] £130 $200

GREGORY

A Chart of the Island Mauritius in the Indian Ocean ... [1779] H. Gregory. Inset & view. 58x75cm (23x29½") Fine. [14] £357 $550

A Plain Chart of the Seychelles, Praslin & Other Adjacent Islands ... [1779] H. Gregory. Tracks of "La Flute", " La Digue" & "Curieuse". 42x55cm (16½x22") Fine. [14] £227 $350

GRIERSON

A New and Correct Large Draught of the Tradeing Part of the West Indies ... [1749 - 1767] From pirate ed *English pilot, The Fourth Book*; Boulter Grierson reissue. 49x82cm (19½x32½") Orig OL color. Orig folds, creasing. [52] £1,400 $2,156

A New Chart of the Bahama Islands and the Windward Passage ... [same date & source] 42x52cm (16½x20½") Uncolored. Orig folds, creasing. [52] £600 $924

A New Map of Germany, Hungary, Transilvania and the Suisse ... [c.1735 - 1757] Dublin piracy of Moll's *Germany*. 59x99cm (23x39") Orig OL color. [53] £420 $647

New England, New York, New Jersey and Pensilvania ... [c. 1735] [same source] From Dublin piracy of Moll's *Atlas Minor*. 20x27cm (8x11") Uncolored. [54] £340 $524

The Coast of New Found Land from Salmon Cove to Cape Bonavista Sold by George Grierson Dublin [1749] From plagiarized *English pilot, The Fourth Book*. 41x49cm (16x19½") Exc. [62] £422 $650

The Island of Barbadoes ... [c. 1735] From Dublin piracy of Moll's *Atlas Minor*. From 1722 Mayo map with "1728" date erased. 28x35cm (11x14") Uncolored. [54] £200 $308

The Island of Jamaica ... [1749 - 1767] From pirate ed *English pilot, The Fourth Book*; Boulter Grierson reissue. 40x51cm (15½x20") Uncolored. Orig folds, creasing. [52] £600 $924

GRIMMEL

Ladozhskiy Kanal Canalis Ladogensis [c. 1741-44] 46x64cm (17½x25½") Mounted; trimmed to borders; creases near rt border; 4" lf border strip restored; margins foxed. Ref: Bagrow (Russia) p.242, 18.4. [28] £292 $450

GRYNAEUS

Typus Cosmographicus Universalis [1532 / c.1537] First in *Novus Orbis Regionum*. Border by Hans Holbein the Younger. 36x56cm (14x22") Exc. Ref: Shirley (World Encompassed) #67; Nordenskiold (Facsimile) pl.XLII. [2] £9,413 $14,500

GUICCIARDINI

Brugae Flandicarum Urbium Decus [1581 / 1625] From *Discrittione di Tutti i Paesi Bassi*. Bird's eye plan. 23x31cm (9x12") [14] £91 $140

Delpium. Urbis Hollandiae [same date, source & dimen] Bird's eye plan. [14] £84 $130

DORDRECHT [same date, source & dimen] Bird's eye plan.	[14]	£75	$115
FLANDRIA [same date, source & dimen]	[14]	£81	$125
FRISIAE OCCIDENTALIS TYPUS [same date, source & dimen]	[14]	£71	$110
GRONIGA OPULETA POPULOSA ... [same date, source & dimen] Bird's eye plan.	[14]	£75	$115
LOVANIUM BRABANTIARUM URBIUM ... [same date, source & dimen] Bird's eye plan.	[14]	£75	$115
SWOLLA [same date, source & dimen] Bird's eye plan.	[14]	£75	$115
TRAIECTUM AD MOSAM [same date, source & dimen] Bird's eye plan.	[14]	£81	$125

GUSSEFELD   Try *Homann*

CHARTE UBER DIE XIII VEREINIGTE STAATEN VON NORD-AMERICA ... [1784] Nuremberg: Homann Heirs. 44x57cm (17½x22") Orig full color. Old folds reinforced on verso; age darkening, spotting, mostly in margins; good+. Ref: Phillips (A) 624, v3,65. [31] £341 $525
[SAME TITLE] [1784] After Homann. 45x58cm (17½x22½") Orig wash & OL color. [46] £487 $750

GUTHRIE

THE BRITISH COLONIES IN NORTH AMERICA ... [c. 1785] 33x33cm (13x13") OL color. [40] £75 $116

GUTHRIE & JONES

IRELAND [1808] 20x23cm (7½x8½") Full orig color. [45] £39 $60
NORTH AMERICA [1808] 20x23cm (7½x8½") Full orig color. [45] £52 $80
SCOTLAND [1808] 20x23cm (7½x8½") Full orig color. [45] £39 $60

HALE

MAP OF THE NEW ENGLAND STATES [1826 / 1853] By Nathan Hale (the nephew). Folding map in orig green boards. RRs indicated. Inset: Maine. 114x94cm (44½x37") Paper backing; good. [2] £552 $850

HALL, S.

MEXICO, CALIFORNIA & TEXAS [1854] Pub Edinburgh. 26x37cm (10½x14½") Color. [51] £179 $275
PALESTINE [1828] London: Longman & Co. 51x41cm (20x16") Color. [23] £32 $50
PALESTINE [1848] 38x25cm (14½x10½") Color. [23] £23 $35

HAMILTON

A MAP OF THE SEA COASTS OF SIAM, CAMBODIA, COUCHIN CHINA AND TONQUIN WITH THE ISLANDS TO THE EASTWARD OF THEM AS FAR AS LUCONIA [WITH] A MAP OF THE EAST COAST OF THE BAY OF BENGALL WITH THE ISLANDS [1727] Accompanied *New Account of East Indies*. Alexander Hamilton of the Merchant East India Company. Robert Mylne, sc. Two sheets: 19x31cm (7½x12") & 19x23cm (7½x9") Exc. [62] £250 $385

HANDTKE

VEREINIGTE STAATEN VON NORD AMERIKA [c. 1848] Glogau: Flemming. 2 sheets joined. 51x69cm (20½x27") Orig OL color. Minor brown spots; rt sheet offset ¼" at top neat line. [46] £143 $220

HARDESTY

MAP OF IDAHO [1884] Chicago: Rand, McNally. 33x51cm (13x20") Full printed color. VG. [18] £45 $70
MAP OF MONTANA [1882] 33x51cm (12½x19½") Printed OL col. Marginal stains; else good. [18] £42 $65
[SAME TITLE] [1884] Chicago: Rand, McNally. 33x51cm (13x20") Full printed color. VG. Ref: Phillips (A) 11041. [18] £49 $75
VICINITY OF LOS ANGELES [1884] With adjacent counties. 25x33cm (9½x12½") Printed col. [56] £42 $65

HARPER

MAP OF THE ROUTES IN NEW YORK, NEW ENGLAND AND PENNSYLVANIA DRAWN FOR THE NORTHERN TRAVELLER [1830] D.S. Throop, sc. 15x14cm (6x5½") Fine. [14] £19 $30

HARPER & BROS.

CENTRAL AMERICA AND THE WEST INDIES ... [1845] Insets. 30x51cm (12x20") Later color. Old creases, not intrusive. [44] £81 $125
MAP OF THE UNITED STATES, AND TEXAS [1844] From *M'Cullochs Universal Gazetteer*. C. Copley, sc. To Rockies. 46x56cm (18x22") Uncolored. [44] £156 $240

HARPER'S WEEKLY

[BOSTON, MASSACHUSETTS & ENVIRONS] [1872] Woodcut bird's eye view. 23x38cm (9x14½") B&W. [36] £32 $50

BIRDS-EYE VIEW OF THE COURSE OF THE MISSISSIPPI, AND THE SEAT OF WAR IN TENNESSEE AND THE VICINITY [1862] Waters & Son (?) South at top. 36x23cm (13½x9") Few spots; good. [20] £88 $135

GENERAL VIEW OF THE MISSISSIPPI RIVER FROM CAIRO, ILLINOIS TO THE MOUTH OF THE RIVER [Jan. 11, 1862] Bird's-eye strip map. 36x23cm (14x9") OL color. Minor marginal foxing; VG. [20] £97 $150

LIBERTY ENLIGHTENING THE WORLD - BARTHOLDI'S COLOSSAL STATUE ON BEDLOW'S ISLAND, NEW YORK HARBOR [Oct. 30, 1886] 18-item landmark key. 36x104cm (13½x41") Color. Rice paper backing; fine. [48] £552 $850

MAP OF THE GOLD REGION WITH ROUTES THERETO [COLORADO] [1859] Black Hills to NM; accompanies article, "How to get to Pike's Peak Gold Mines". 10x20cm (4x7½") B&W. Corner chip, text unaffected. [9] £29 $45

MAP OF THE MISSISSIPPI, FROM HAINES'S BLUFF TO BELOW GRAND GULF, SHOWING THE THEATER OF GEN. GRANT'S AND ADMIRAL FARRAGUT'S OPERATIONS, ETC. [1863] May 23. Waters & Son. 36x23cm (14x9") Full color. Fine. [20] £107 $165

MISSISSIPPI RIVER FROM CAIRO TO MEMPHIS [1862] March 15. Strip map; reverse: Civil War views. 36x5cm (14x2½") Modern color. Dust soiling, stains; good. [20] £81 $125

THE NEW YORK COLUMBIAN CELEBRATION - THE NAVAL REVIEW [Oct. 22, 1892] Drawn by Victor Perard. Lower Manhattan roofs & harbor. 33x107cm (13x42") Color. Rice paper backing; fine. [48] £487 $750

HARRIS   Try *Bowen*

[ADVERTISEMENT] THOMAS HARRIS & SON, OPTICIANS AND GLOBE MAKERS [c. 1830] Letterpress page, show 2 globes, incl. 16" model. 22x12cm (8½x4½") Uncolored. [52] £80 $123

A NEW MAP OF THE WORLD SHEWING THE COURSE OF SR. FRANCIS DRAKE, WILL SCHOUTEN AND CAPT. WILLIAM DAMPIERS VOYAGES ROUND IT [c.1705 - 1740] In *Compleat Collection of Voyages and Travels ...* Double hemispheres; insular Calif. On sheet 38x61cm (15x23½") Recent OL & wash color. VG. [59] £406 $625

HARRISON

A MAP OF AFRICA DRAWN AND ENGRAVED FROM D'ANVILLE'S TWO SHEET MAP [1791] 50x71cm (20x28") Orig OL color. [14] £78 $120

A NEW MAP OF IRELAND DIVIDED INTO PROVINCES AND COUNTIES [1787] By James Haywood; London: J. Harrison. 41x36cm (16½x14½") [24] £120 $185

A NEW MAP OF THE WORLD WITH THE LATEST DISCOVERIES [1788] 28x51cm (11x20") B&W. Rt side remargined. [46] £49 $75

A PARTICULAR MAP OF THE AMERICAN LAKES, RIVERS, ETC. III [1790] After D'Anville. 50x72cm (19½x28") Lower margin trimmed to neat line as issued. [14] £341 $525

ARABIAN GULF OR RED SEA [1788] After D'Anville. 46x33cm (18x13") [14] £55 $85

MAP OF LOUISIANA FROM D'ANVILLE'S ATLAS [1788] 31x49cm (12x19½") Fine. [20] £308 $475

[SAME TITLE] [same date & dimen] [14] £120 $185

PARTICULAR MAP OF THE WESTERN COAST OF AFRICA FROM CAPE BLANCO TO CAPE DE VERGA AND OF THE COURSE OF THE RIVERS SENAGA AND GAMBIA 1788] After D'Anville. 50x35cm (19½x13½") [14] £49 $75

PERSIAN GULF FROM THE ORIGINAL BY D'ANVILLE [1788] 29x43cm (11½x17") [14] £62 $95

SECOND PART OF A MAP OF ASIA, CONTAINING CHINA, PART OF TARTARY AND INDIA BEYOND THE GANGES, WITH THE ISLES OF SUNDA, PHILIPPINES, MOLUCCAS AND JAPON [1791] After D'Anville. 72x50cm (28½x20") Orig OL color. Lower lf margin trimmed to neat line as issued. [14] £114 $175

THE EUPHRATES AND THE TIGRIS [1788] After D'Anville. 33x39cm (13x15½") [14] £39 $60

THE FIRST PART OF ASIA [1791] Arabia to India. 50x72cm (19½x28") Orig OL col. [14] £58 $90

THE RIVER ST. LAWRENCE, ACCURATELY DRAWN FROM D'ANVILLE'S MAP PUBLISH'D UNDER THE PATRONAGE OF THE DUKE OF ORLEANS [c. 1780] 36x48cm (14x18½") Margins soiled, repaired tears; old label remnant on verso. Ref: Sellers & Van Ee 251. [28] £146 $225

[SAME TITLE] [1788] English nomenclature; orig appeared as inset to D'Anville's 4-sheet map. 38x42cm (15x16½") [14] £55 $85

HAVEN

MAP OF THE UNITED STATES AND MEXICO INCLUDING OREGON, TEXAS AND THE CALIFORNIAS [1846] Extended TX, many trails, information side bars & surround of state seals. 38x38cm (14½x15½"). Color. No margin; age spotting; minor separations. Ref: Wheat 513. [12] £552 $850

HAYWARD

THE UNITED STATES FROM THE LATEST AUTHORITIES [1853] From *A Gazetteer of the United States of America* ... 54x100cm (21½x39½") Orig full color. Orig folds & narrow side margins; VG. Ref: Wheat (TM) III #787. [59] £243 $375

HEARNE

A MAP EXHIBITING MR. HEARNE'S TRACKS IN HIS TWO JOURNIES FOR THE DISCOVERY OF THE COPPER MINE RIVER ... [1796] Dublin. 26x37cm (10½x14½") [14] £65 $100
A PLAN OF ALBANY RIVER IN HUDSONS BAY [1796] London. 27x35cm (10½x13½") [14] £42 $65
A PLAN OF MOOS RIVER IN HUDSONS BAY, NORTH AMERICA [1796] 24x44cm (9½x17") [14] £42 $65
A PLAN OF THE COPPER MINE RIVER ... [1796] London, 20x44cm (8x17") [14] £81 $125

HEATHER

[ENGLISH CHANNEL] [1815] Norie revision of 1801 chart. 3 joinable sheets, each 64x79cm (25x31") Exc. [15] £650 $1,001

[ROUTE TO THE EAST] TO THE OFFICERS IN THE HONOURABLE EAST INDIA COMPANY'S SERVICE MOST RESPECTFULLY DEDICATED [1796] Brazil east to Western Pacific. 66x119cm (25½x47") Two joined sheets. Narrow margins; cleaned mark traces; some verso reinforcement. [15] £450 $693

A NEW PLAN OF EGYPT. SHEWING THE ENTRANCES TO THE NILE, ETC. [1801] Stephenson, sc. 41x94cm (15½x37") Edges ragged & bit soiled. [28] £221 $340

HECK

CONSTANTINOPEL [1851] Panoramic view. 20x25cm (8x10") Wash color. [57] £32 $50

HENN, WILLIAMS & CO.

A TOWNSHIP MAP OF THE STATE OF IOWA [1856] Pub to accompany *The Emigrants Handbook of Iowa*. 55x90cm (21½x35½") Orig wash & OL color. Folds; sh tears just affecting a border. [14] £162 $250

HENNEPIN

CARTE DE LA NOUVELLE FRANCE ET DE LA LOUISIANE ... [1683] 1st ed. 30x48cm (12x19") Clean tear upper rt repaired w/out loss; o/w exc. Ref: Fite & Freeman #45; Cumming (Exploration) p.39. [2] £11,686 $18,000

HENRY

CHART OF THE N.W. COAST OF AMERICA AND THE N.E. COAST OF ASIA, EXPLORED IN THE YEARS 1778 AND 1779. PREPARED BY LIEUT. HENY. ROBERTS...LONDON: PUBLISHED BY WM. FADEN...CHARING CROSS JULY 24, 1784. 2D. EDITION. PUBLISHED JANUARY 1ST. 1794 [1794] 43x71cm (17x27½") Orig OL color. Folds. Ref: Tooley (Amer) p.92,64b. cf. Wagner (NW) 700. [28] £484 $745

HERBERT

[GULF OF THAILAND] [1767] From *New Directory for the East Indies*. 53x69cm (21x26½") Pencil mark. [15] £300 $462

HEYDT

WELT CHARTEN, WORAUF DIE REIFE NACH INDIEN [1744] 22x26cm (8½x10") Color. [16] £608 $936

HILDBURGHAUSEN BIBLIOGRAPHISCHES INSTITUT

[AUSTRIA: STEIERMARK] [c. 1850] 26x20cm (10x8") [64] £37 $57
[BELGIUM AND LUXEMBURG] [c. 1850] 20x26cm (8x10") [64] £16 $25
[BRAZIL] [c. 1850] 26x20cm (10x8") [64] £45 $69
[CAUCASUS REGION: DER KAUKASISCHE ISTHMUS] [c. 1850] 20x26cm (8x10") [64] £37 $57
[EAST AFRICA & MADAGASCAR] [c. 1850] 20x26cm (8x10") [64] £33 $50
[FRANCE: PARIS] [c. 1850] 20x26cm (8x10") [64] £20 $31
[GERMANY: BAVARIA & SWABIA: KINGDOM OF BAVARIA, SOUTHERN HALF] [c. 1850] 20x26cm (8x10") Some foxing. [64] £90 $138

[GERMANY: HESSE, ELECTORATE] [c. 1850] Inset: Kassel; Circle of Schaumberg. 26x20cm (10x8") [64] £65 $101
[GERMANY: HESSE, GRAND DUCHY] [c. 1850] Inset: Darmstadt plan. 26x20cm (10x8") [64] £37 $57
[GERMANY: HOLSTEIN WITH LAUENBURG, HAMBURG & LUBECK] [c. 1850] 20x26cm (8x10") [64] £29 $44
[GERMANY: PRINCIPALITIES OF WALDECK, LIPPE-DETMOLD & SCHAUENBERG-LIPPE] [c. 1850] 26x20cm (10x8") [64] £225 $346
[GERMANY: RHEINPROVINZ JULICH - CLEVE - BERG] [c. 1850] 20x26cm (8x10") [64] £69 $107
[GERMANY: SCHLESWIG] [c. 1850] 20x26cm (8x10") [64] £29 $44
[HOLY LAND. PALAESTINA] [c. 1850] With Jerusalem & Solomon's Temple plans. 26x20cm (10x8") Historical map. [64] £90 $138
[ITALY, NORTHERN & CENTRAL: LOMBARDY,. VENETIA, PARMA, MODENA, TOSCANY, LUCCA, ST. MARINO & THE PAPAL STATES] [c. 1850] 26x20cm (10x8") [64] £20 $31
[LONDON: PLAN MIT UMGEBUNG] [c. 1850] 20x26cm (8x10") [64] £24 $38
[NORTH AFRICA. MOROCCO, ALGIER & TUNIS] [c. 1850] 20x26cm (8x10") [64] £16 $25
[NORTH AMERICA: MOUNTAIN CHAINS] [c. 1850] 20x26cm (8x10") [64] £16 $24
[PATAGONIA - TIERRA DEL FUEGO] [c. 1850] 20x26cm (8x10") [64] £41 $63
[POLAND, FORMERLY GERMANY: SILESIA. PROVINZ SCHLESIEN] [c. 1850] 20x26cm (8x10") [64] £69 $107
[POLAND, FORMERLY GERMANY. WEST PRUSSIA] [c. 1850] 20x26cm (8x10") [64] £122 $189
[RUSSIA IN EUROPE] [c. 1850] With adjacent areas. 20x26cm (8x10") [64] £16 $25
[SCANDINAVIA] [c. 1850] 20x26cm (8x10") [64] £29 $44
[SOUTH AFRICA] [c. 1850] Insets: Indian Ocean islands. 20x26cm (8x10") [64] £49 $75
[SOUTH AMERICA: SOUTHERN] [c. 1850] 20x26cm (8x10") [64] £37 $57
[SWITZERLAND] [c. 1850] Panorama of the Alps below. 20x26cm (8x10") [64] £29 $44
[UNITED STATES: NEW YORK, PENNSYLVANIA, MARYLAND, NEW JERSEY, DELAWARE & VIRGINIA] [c. 1850] City plan insets. 26x20cm (10x8") [64] £57 $88
[WEST INDIES & CENTRAL AMERICA] [c. 1850] 20x26cm (8x10") [64] £10 $16
AFRICA [c. 1850] 20x26cm (8x10") [64] £24 $38
AMERICA [c. 1850] 26x20cm (10x8") [64] £20 $31
ASIA [c. 1850] 20x26cm (8x10") [64] £12 $19
ASIATISCHER ARCHIPEL UND NEU HOLLAND [c. 1850] 20x26cm (8x10") [64] £41 $63
BALTIC REGION: RUSSLAND: GOUV. ST. PETERSBURG, ESTHLAND, LIEFLAND, KURLAND [c. 1850] 20x26cm (8x10") [64] £57 $88
BAYERN, WURTEMBERG, BEYDE HOHENZOLLERN UND BADEN [c. 1850] 20x26cm (8x10") [64] £33 $50
BRITISCHES NORD-AMERICA [c. 1850] With Alaska, Greenland & Iceland. 20x26cm (8x10") [64] £49 $75
CHINA PROPRIA ODER DAS EIGENTLICHE CHINA [c. 1850] 26x20cm (10x8") [64] £24 $38
DAS ADRIAMEER MIT SEINEN UFERSTAATEN [c. 1850] Adriatic region. 20x26cm (8x10") [64] £8 $13
DAS CHINESISCHE REICH MIT SEINEN SCHUTZ STAATEN, NEBST DEM JAPANISCHEN INSEL REICH [c. 1850] 20x26cm (8x10") Sl foxing. [64] £57 $88
DAS KONIGREICH HOLLAND [c. 1850] 26x20cm (10x8") [64] £16 $25
DER NECKAR-KREIS VOM KONIGREICH WURTEMBERG [c. 1850] 26x20cm (10x8") [64] £98 $151
DER SCHWARZWALD KREIS VOM KONIGREICH WURTEMBERG [c. 1850] 20x26cm (8x10") [64] £90 $138
DIE EUROP. TURKEI: CROATIEN, HERZEGOVINA, SERBIEN, BOSNIEN UND DAS LAND DER MONTENE-GRINER [c. 1850] 20x26cm (8x10") [64] £8 $13
DIE LAENDER DES PASCHA VON AEGYPTEN. AEGYPTEN, NUBIEN, ARABIEN, DARFUR, CORDOFAN, CANDIA, SYRIEN NEBST DEN DISTRICT ADANA [c. 1850] 26x20cm (10x8") [64] £41 $63
DIE PFALZ ODER RHEIN BAYERN [c. 1850] 20x26cm (8x10") [64] £37 $57
DIE REPUBLIK POLEN NACH IHREM BESTANDE IM JAHRE 1772 UND DAS KONIGREICH POLEN SEIT DEM JAHRE 1815 [c. 1850] 20x26cm (8x10") [64] £41 $63
DIE STAATEN VON ARKANSAS, MISSISSIPPI, LOUISIANA UND ALABAMA [same date & dimen] [64] £45 $69
DIE STAATEN VON MAINE, NEW HAMPSHIRE, MASSACHUSETTS, VERMONT, CONNECTICUT & RHODE I. [c. 1850] 26x20cm (10x8") [64] £49 $75
DIE STAATEN VON MISSOURI, ILLINOIS, INDIANA, OHIO, KENTUCKY & TENNESSEE [c. 1850] 26x20cm (10x8") [64] £53 $82
DIE STAATEN VON N. & S. CAROLINA, GEORGIA & FLORIDA [same date & dimen] 4 insets [64] £90 $138
ERZ-HERZOGTHUM OESTERREICH: UNTER DER ENNS [c. 1850] 20x26cm (8x10") [64] £8 $13

GRAFSCHAFT TYROL [c. 1850] 20x26cm (8x10") [64] £24 $38
GRIECHENLAND DIE JONISCHEN JNSELN UND CANDIA [c. 1850] 26x20cm (10x8") [64] £16 $25
GROSS-HERZOGTHUM SACHSEN-WEIMAR UND EISENACH [c. 1850] 20x26cm (8x10") [64] £49 $75
GROSSHERZOGTHUM BADEN NORDLICHE HALFTE [c. 1850] 20x26cm (8x10") [64] £98 $151
HERZOGTHUM BRAUNSCHWEIG [c. 1850] 20x26cm (8x10") [64] £78 $119
ITALIEN MIT DER DALMAT.-ALBANESISCHEN KUSTE [c. 1850] Insets. 20x26cm (8x10") [64] £16 $25
JRELAND [c. 1850] 26x20cm (10x8") [64] £29 $44
KARTE VON DEM DEUTSCHEN MEERE UND DEN ANGRANZENDEN THEILEN DES ATLANTISCHEN OCEANS ... [c. 1850] 26x20cm (10x8") [64] £33 $50
KRIEGS- UND SPEZIAL KARTE VOM FINNISCHEN MEERBUSEN VON KRONSTADT BIS ST. PETERSBURG [c. 1850] With St. Petersburg & Kronstadt plans. 20x26cm (8x10") [64] £53 $82
PORTUGAL UND DIE AZOREN [c. 1850] 26x20cm (10x8") [64] £20 $31
PROVINZ OST-PREUSSEN [c. 1850] 26x20cm (10x8") [64] £131 $201
RHEINPROVINZ NEIDERRHEIN [c. 1850] 20x26cm (8x10") [64] £45 $69
SUDLICHES NORWEGEN [c. 1850] 26x20cm (10x8") [64] £24 $38
UMRISSE DER PFLANZENGEOGRAPHIE [c. 1850] World map of plants. 20x26cm (8x10") [64] £20 $31
VEREINIGTE STAATEN VON NORD-AMERICA: CALIFORNIEN, TEXAS UND DIE TERRITORIEN NEW MEXICO U. UTAH [c. 1850] 20x26cm (8x10") Some foxing. [64] £98 $151
VERGLEICHENDE UEBERSICHT DER BEDEUTENDSTEN STROMLANGEN [c. 1850] River lengths. 26x20cm (10x8") [64] £8 $13

HINTON

A GEOLOGICAL MAP OF THE UNITED STATES [1832] Hinton, Simpkin & Marshall. 25x39cm (10x15½") Geology by color. [35] £62 $95
[SAME TITLE] [1832] From *The History and Topography of the United States*. Coast to coast; color west to Rockies. 25x39cm (9½x15½") Ref: Howes (US) H512. [56] £88 $135
MAP OF THE STATE OF FLORIDA [c. 1831] Hinton, Simpkin & Marshall. 17 counties. 20x25cm (8x9½") Orig full wash color. Printed low, sl loss lower border. [4] £97 $150
MAP OF THE STATE OF MISSOURI [1832] From *The History and Topography of the United States*. 30 counties. 25x37cm (9½x14½") Full color. No lower margin. [56] £94 $145
MAP OF THE STATES OF ALABAMA AND GEORGIA [1832] From *The History and Topography of the United States*. 25x40cm (10x15½") Full color. Little or no margins. [56] £91 $140
MAP OF THE STATES OF KENTUCKY AND TENNESSEE [1832] From *The History and Topography of the United States*. 25x39cm (9½x15½") Full color. Narrow margins. [56] £88 $135
MAP OF THE STATES OF NORTH & SOUTH CAROLINA [1832] From *The History and Topography of the United States*. 25x38cm (10x15½") Full color. Little margin. Ref: Karpinski (Carolina) 155,156; PLP m 618,8; Fitch 51,275 [56] £88 $135

HOFFMAN

NEUE UNGARARISCH UND TURCKISCHE GROSSE LAND CHARLE NEBENDT ... [c. 1666] Johannes Hoffman; Wilhelm Pfann, sc. Lower Danube regions. 43x71cm (16½x28") Separately published. Uncolored. Superficial restoration; remargined above. [52] £890 $1,371

HOGG   Try *Cook*

[JAPAN: HONSHU, WEST COAST] [1795] Cook's Third Voyage. Intermittent coastline. 30x23cm (12x8½") Color. [15] £25 $39
A CHART AND VIEWS OF PITCAIRNS ISLAND [1790] Carteret's voyage. 20x33cm (8x13") [15] £44 $68
CHRISTMAS ISLAND ... [c. 1790] After Cook & King, for 3rd voyage.. 23x30cm (8½x12") [15] £24 $37

HOLE, W.

[MIDDLE EAST: CYPRUS TO PERSIAN GULF] [1614] From Raleigh, *History of the World*. "Passage of Abram from Charran". 30x35cm (12x14") Ref: Laor 334. [23] £159 $245
[MIDDLE EAST: GREECE TO PERSIA] [1614] From Raleigh, *History of the World*. Tower of Babel at ctr. 31x39cm (12x15") Color. Lower margin restored. Ref: Laor 336. [23] £146 $225

HOMANN & HOMANN HEIRS   Try *Doppelmayr*

[PORTRAIT] IOANNES BAPTISTA HOMANN, SAC. CAES. REGO. CATH. MAJ., GEOGRAPHUS, NEC NON REGINE SCIENTIARUM SOCIETIS BEROLINENSIS MENBRUM ... [1715 - 1724] After J. Kenckel painting; J. Wilhelm Winter, sc. 38x28cm (15x11") Uncolored. Repairs; rebacked. [44] £162 $250

[SAME TITLE] [c. 1730-1747] 34x27cm (13½x10½") Uncolored. [52] £300 $462

ACCURATER GRUNDRISS U: GEGEND ... LONDON ... [c. 1720] J.B. Homann. 5 views. 48x58cm (19½x23") Map in orig wash color; views uncolored. Exc. [39] £617 $950

AMERICA SEPTENTRIONALIS. A DOMINO D'ANVILLE IN GALLIIS EDITA NUNC IN ANGLIA COLONIIS IN INTERIOREM VIRGINIAM DEDUCTIS NEC NON FLUVII OHIO CURSU ... [1756] 46x51cm (18½x20") Orig OL color. Vert crease near c'fold; margins spotted. Ref: Sellers & Van Ee 68. [28] £380 $585

[SAME TITLE] [1756] Extensive German text. 46x51cm (18x20") Full color. [46] £282 $435

AMERICAE MAPPA GENERALIS SECUNDUM LEGITIMAS PROJECTIONIS STEREOGRAPHICAE REGULAS ... MDCCXXXXVI [1746] August Gottlieb. 48x56cm (19x21½") Orig OL & later cartouche color. Foxed margins, dampstains lower margin. Ref: Wagner (NW) 555; Phillips (A) 3499. [28] £409 $630

[SAME TITLE] [1746] Homann Heirs. 46x53cm (18x21") Full color. Clean. [32] £519 $800

AMPLISSIMA REGIONIS MISSISSIPI SEU PROVINCIAE LUDOVICIANAE A R.P. LUDOVICO HENNEPIN FRANCISC MISS IN AMERICA SEPTENTRIONALI ANNO 1687. DETECTAE, NUNC GALLORUM COLONIIS ET ACTIONUM NEGOTIIS TOTO ORBE CELEBERRIMAE ... [c. 1725] J.B Homann. 49x58cm (19x23") Full orig color. Minor staining rt, minor c'fold discoloration; o/w VG+. Ref: Cumming (SE) 170. Goss (N Amer) #49. [31] £714 $1,100

[SAME TITLE] [c. 1730] [same dimen] Full wash color. Sm tear at gutter, image unaffected; sl soiling at margins; VG. [60] £1,136 $1,750

[SAME TITLE] [c. 1735] Homann Heirs. [same dimen] Full orig cor. Bit browned; good. [20] £974 $1,500

AMPLISSIMA REGIONIS MISSISSIPI SEU PROVINCIAE LUDOVICIANAE A R.P. LUDOVICO HENNEPIN FRANCISC MISS IN AMERICA SEPTENTRIONALI ANNO 1687. DETECTAE, NUNC GALLORUM COLONIIS ET ACTIONUM NEGOTIIS TOTO ORBE CELEBERRIMAE ... [c. 1737] De L'Isle derivative. [same dimen] Orig wash col. Exc. [1] £844 $1,300

[SAME TITLE] [c. 1759] Based on De L'Isle. 51x61cm (19½x23½") Orig color. Pinhole upper c'fold. Ref: Sellers & Van Ee 102; Phillips (A) 622. [28] £643 $990

CARTA TOPOGRAPHIQUE DE L'ISLE MINORQUE ... [1757] Homann Heirs. 2 views. 46x53cm (17½x21½") Orig color. Creases; reinforced paper weakness at c'fold on verso. [28] £234 $360

CARTE DES INDES ORIENTALES ... [1748] 51x87cm (20x34½") Orig color. [53] £520 $801

CIRCULUS SAXONIAE INFERIORIS IN OMNES SUOS STATUS ET PRINCIPATUS ... [1720] 48x56cm (18½x21½") Full color. [36] £227 $350

[SAME TITLE] [1730+] Hamburg view. 48x58cm (19x22½") Full orig color. [14] £162 $250

DANUBII FLUMINIS A FONTIBUS PROPE DONESCHINGAM USQ POSONIUM URBEM DESIGNATI PARS SUPERIOR, IN QUA SUEVIA, BAVARIA, AUSTRIA, STIRIA, CARINTHIA ... [c. 1730-1750] J.B. Homann. 53x58cm (21x23") Orig color. Stains at margin & lower part. Ref: Nordenskiold (Col) I,91. [28] £175 $270

DANUBII FLUMINIS (HIC AB URBE BELGRADO ...) PARS INFIMA, IN QUA TRANSYLVANIA, WALACHIA, MOLDAVIA, BULGARIA, SERVIA, ROMANIA ET BESARABIA ... [c. 1730-1750] J.B. Homann. 51x58cm (19½x23") Orig color. Dampmark top; few sm spots. Ref: Nordenskiold (Col) I,91. [28] £175 $270

DOMINIA ANGLORUM IN AMERICA SEPTENTRIONALI. SPECIALIBUS MAPPIS LONDINI PRIMUM A MOLLIO EDITA, NUNC RECUSA AB HOMANNIANIS HERED / DIE GROSS-BRITANNISCHE COLONIE-LAENDER IN NORD-AMERICA [1737] 4 maps after Moll: Newfoundland & Nova Scotia; New England; Virginia & Maryland; Carolinas. 50x55cm (20x22") Orig wash color. Narrow lower margin. Ref: Cumming (SE) 233. [46] £211 $325

[SAME TITLE] [1750] 50x55cm (20x21½") Orig Color. VG. [31] £390 $600

DOMINIA ANGLORUM IN PRAECIPUIS INSULIS AMERICAE UT SUNT INSULA S. CHRISTOPHORI ANTEGOA JAMAICA BARBADOS NEC NON INSULAE BERMUDES VEL SOMMERS DICTAE ... [c. 1781] Homann Heirs. 5 maps on sheet. 51x58cm (20x23½") Orig OL color. Ref: Sellers & Van Ee 1723. [28] £321 $495

DUCATUS LUNEBURGICI ET COMITATUS DANNEBERGENSIS ... [1730+] 48x57cm (19x22½") Full orig color. [14] £185 $285

ELECTORATUS MOGUNTINUS UT ET PALATIN: INFER. HASSIAE & FLUMINIS MOENI ALIQUA ... [c. 1730-1750] J.B. Homann. German border title. 58x51cm (23x20½") Orig color. C'fold tear repaired; few margin tears & stains. Ref: Nordenskiold (Col) I,91. [28] £204 $315

GENERALIS TOTIUS IMPERII MOSCOVITICI NOVISSIMA TABULA MAGNAM ORBIS TERRARUM PARTEM A POLO ARCTICO ... [c. 1710] J.B. Homann. 2nd state. 49x58cm (19½x23") Orig color. Pinhole worming, mainly margins. Ref: Bagrow (Russia) p.78. [28] £204 $315

GUINEA PROPRIA, NEC NON NIGRITIAE VEL TERRAE NIGORUM ... AETHIOPIA INFERIOR ... [1743] By J.M. Haas. Title also in French. 51x58cm (20x23") Orig color. Few sm stains; partial showthrough of ms title on verso; crease near c'fold; repaired 5" tear. Ref: Nordenskiold (Col) I,91. [28] £234 $360

HIBERNIAE REGNUM ENTAM IN PRAECIPIAS ULTONIAE, CONNACIAE, LACEMIAE ET MOMONIAE, QUAM IN MINORES EARUNDEM PROVINCIAS ... [1710 - 1740] 48x56cm (19x22") Orig full color. Image fine, overall VG-. [59] £243 $375

[SAME TITLE] [1730] 58x48cm (22½x18½") Color. Ref: Phillips (A) 4289, 12. [24] £373 $575

ICHNOGRAPHIA URBIS IN TUSCIA PRIMARIAE FLORENTIAE ... [1731] Homann Heirs. Plan & view. 48x58cm (19½x23") Orig & later color. Printer's crease lower rt corner; lower c'fold reinforced; else exc. [39] £617 $950

ICONOGRAFICA RAPPRESENTATIONE DELLA INCLITA CITTA DI VENETIA [1729 (c.1745)] View below. 48x56cm (19x22") Orig wash color. Repaired wormhole; good. [19] £812 $1,250

ITALIA IN SUOS STATUS DIVISA ... [1742] Homann Heirs after De L'Isle. 49x58cm (19½x22½") Orig wash color. Fine. [48] £357 $550

IUDAEA SEU PALAESTINA OB SACRATISSIMA REDEMTORIS VESTIGIA HODIE DICTA TERRA SANCTA PROUT OLIM IN DUODECIM TRIBUS DIVISA SEPARATIS ... [1707] 51x58cm (19½x22½") Old color. Ref: Laor 340. [23] £315 $485

MAGNA BRITANNIA COMPLECTENS ANGLIAE, SCOTIAE ET HIBERNIAE REGNA [c. 1725] J.B. Homann. 2nd plate; Queen Anne portrait. 48x57cm (19x22½") Orig wash color. Fine. [48] £438 $675

MAGNAE BRITANNIAE COMPLECTENS ANGLIAE, SCOTIAE ET HYBERNIAE REGN ... [1710 - 1740] Title above, "A General Map of Great Britain and Ireland ..." 48x56cm (19x22") Orig full color. Image VG, overall good+. [59] £243 $375

MAGNAE BRITANNIAE PARS MERIDIONALIS IN QUA REGNUM ANGLIAE TAM IN SEPTEM ANTIQUA ANGLO-SAXONUM ... [1710 - 1740] 48x56cm (19x22") Orig full col. Image fine, overall good+. [59] £243 $375

MAGNAE BRITANNIAE PARS SEPTENTRIONALIS QUA REGNUM SCOTIAE ... [1710 - 1740] 48x56cm (19x22") Orig full color. Image fine, overall VG-. [59] £243 $375

MAPPA GEOGRAPHICA COMPLECTENS 1. INDIAE OCCIDENTALIS PARTEM MEDIAM CIRCUM ISTHMUS PARAMENSEM ... [1740] Gulf, Caribbean & adjacent; inset maps & view. 58x49cm (23x19½") Orig OL color. Near mint. [14] £276 $425

MAPPA GEOGRAPHICA PROVINCIAE NOVAE EBORACI AB ANGLIS NEW YORK DICTAE EX AMPLIORI DELINEATIONE AD EXACTAS DIMENSIONES CONCINNATA IN ARCTIUS SPATIUM REDACTA CURA CLAUDII JOSEPHI SAUTHIER ... [1778] Reduced from Faden's 6-sheet "Chorographical Map of the Province of New York". Two sheets joined. 71x56cm (28x22") Orig OL col. Support on verso; o/w good. [14] £487 $750

MISSISSIPI SEU PROVINCIAE SEU LUDOVICIANAE ... [c. 1735] The "Buffalo Map". 48x58cm (19x23") Orig wash & OL color; uncolored cartouche. Spotting & browning, mostly in margin; border corner repaired. [46] £649 $1,000

NEUE WELT KARTE ... [1784] Double hemisphere. 48x57cm (19x22") Orig color. [16] £665 $1,024

NOVA ANGLIA SEPTENTRIONALI AMERICAE IMPLANTATA ANGLORUMQUE COLONIIS FLORIENTISSIMA GEOGRAPHICE EXHIBITA ... [c. 1714] J.B. Homann. 48x58cm (19x22½") Orig wash color. Exc. Ref: Portinaro & Knirsch pl.116; Goss (NA) #50 [63] £812 $1,250

[SAME TITLE] [1720] 48x57cm (19x22½") Orig color. Lt staining; else exc. [38] £779 $1,200

[SAME TITLE] [(1730)] 48x57cm (19x22½") Full orig color; uncolored cartouche. Minor darkening at edges; wormhole; o/w fine.. [33] £1,039 $1,600

[SAME TITLE] [c. 1740] 48x58cm (19x22½") Orig full color. All margins trimmed; bright, clear clean. Ref: Van Ermen #26. [59] £941 $1,450

NOVISSIMA ... INSULARUM ... SICILIA, SARDINIA, CORSICA, MALTA ... [1762] Homann Heirs. With African & Italian coasts. 47x57cm (18½x22") Orig full body color; uncolored title-piece. [53] £480 $739

PALAESTINA IN XII TRIBUS DIVISA CUM TERRIS ADIACENTIBUS DENUO REVISA & COPIOSIR REDDITA. STUDIO IOHANNIS CHRISTOPH. HARENBERG ... [1750] Homann Heirs. 48x53cm (19x21") Color. Ref: Laor 325. [23] £224 $345

PARTIE OCCIDENTALE DE LA NOUVELLE FRANCE OU DU CANADA ... [1755] After Bellin. 43x53cm (17x21½") B&W. Ref: MCCS 96 (Tooley) #684. [1] £844 $1,300

PARTIE OCCIDENTALE DE LA NOUVELLE FRANCE OU DU CANADA. PAR MR. BELLIN ... [1755] 43x54cm (16½x21") Orig yellow OL color. Fine. Ref: Phillips (M) p.191; Karpinski (MI) p.138. [2] £974 $1,500

PARTIE ORIENTALE DE LA NOUVELLE FRANCE OU DU CANADA. PAR MR. BELLIN ... [1755] Homann Heirs, after 1745 Bellin map. 45x56cm (18x22") Orig OL color. Ref: Heidenreich & Dahl p.8; Phillips (A) 3498. [28] £409 $630

PLANIGLOBII TERRESTRIS MAPPA UNIVERSALIS ... / MAPPE-MONDE QUI REPRESENTE LES DEUX HEMISPHERES ... DRESSEE PAR G.M. LOWITZ [1746] Double hemi, with other hemispheres & diagrams. 46x55cm (18x21½") Orig wash & OL color. [14] £503 $775

[SAME TITLE] [1746] Homann Heirs. 46x55cm (18x21½") Color. [26] £682 $1,050

PROPRIAE LUGUDUNENSIS GENERALITATIS MAPPA CHOROGRAPHIA INSUAS V. ELECTIONES ... [1762] Homann Heirs: Border title: "La Generalite Proprie Taire de Lyon, Divisee en Ses V. Elections, Scavoir, de Lyon, Roanne, Monbrison, Ville Franche ..." 48x58cm (18½x22½") Orig color. 2 dampmarks; sh margin tears; sm paper flaw lower margin. [28] £162 $250

REGNI DANIAE ... [c. 1720] J.B. Homann. 48x58cm (19½x22½") Orig wash color. Fine. [48] £321 $495

REGNI HUNGARIAE ... [1740] Incl Bosnia, Transylvania, part of Poland. 47x57cm (18½x22½") Color. [36] £243 $375

REGNI & INSULAE SICILIAE TABULA GEOGRAPHICA ... [1747] Homann Heirs. 46x55cm (18x21½") Orig body color. Light cartouche impression. [53] £380 $585

REGNI MEXICANI SEU NOVAE HISPANIAE, LUDOVICIANAE, N. ANGLIAE, CAROLINAE, VIRGINIAE, ET PENSYLVANIAE NEC NON INSULARUM ARCHIPELAGI MEXICANI IN AMERICA SEPTENTRIONALI ACCURATA TABULA ... [1720] 48x57cm (19x22½") Orig color. Sh tear top margin; fine. [30] £844 $1,300

[SAME TITLE] [c. 1730] 48x57cm (19x22") Orig pastel & OL color; uncolored cartouche. Ref: Martin (TX) pl.17. [46] £649 $1,000

REGNI SINAE VEL SINAE PROPRIAE MAPPA ET DESCRIPTIO GEOGRAPHICA ... [1730+] Homann Heirs. 58x52cm (23x20½") Full orig wash & OL color. [14] £179 $275

REGNORUM HUNGARIAE DALMATIAE, CROATIAE, SCLAVONIAE BOSNIAE ET SERVIAE ... [n.d.] 4-sheet map, trimmed & mounted on larger sheet; each sheet at platemark 48x58cm (19x23") Orig color. 1 sm color smudge. [28] £526 $810

REGNUM PORTUGALLIAE ... REGNO ALGARBIAE ... [c. 1736] 59x45cm (23x17½") Col. [43] £320 $493

SCANDINAVIA COMPLECTENS SUECIAE, DANIAE & NORVEGIAE REGNA ... [c. 1790] J.B. Homann. 48x57cm (19x22½") Orig wash color. Fine. [48] £357 $550

TABULA MARCHIONATUS BRANDENBURGICI ET DUCATUS POMERANIAE QUAE SUNT PARS SEPTEN-TRIONALIS CIRCULI SAXONIAE SUPERIORIS ... [c. 1720-1750] 43x56cm (17½x22") Orig color. Vert crease near c'fold. Ref: Nordenskiold (Col) I,91. [28] £175 $270

TABULA SELENOGRAPHICA IN QUA LUNARIUM ... DESCRIPTIO ... [c. 1740] Double moon chart. 49x58cm (19x22½") Orig color. [52] £650 $1,001

TOTIUS AMERICAE SEPTENTRIONALIS ET MERIDIONALIS NOVISSIMA REPRAESENTATIO ... [1710 - 1729] Insular Calif. 49x58cm (19x23") Orig full color. Cleaned, conserved, margins restored; VG+. Ref: Lowery 474; Tooley (Amer) p.129, pl.57; Portinaro & Knirsch pl.CIX. [59] £964 $1,485

[SAME TITLE] [c.1729 - 1750] Peninsular Calif. 49x57cm (19x22") Orig full color. Some restoration; VG+. Ref: McCorkle 45 & 45; cf. Lowery 474; Tooley (Amer) p.129 #79, pl.57. [59] £584 $900

[SAME TITLE] [c. 1750] [same dimen] Orig full color. VG. [31] £617 $950

TYPUS GEOGRAPHICUS CHILI A PARAGUAY, FRETI MAGELLANICI &C. ... [1733] Homann Heirs. 51x58cm (20x22½") Orig color. Sh lower c'fold tear repaired. Ref: Nordenskiold (Col) I,91. [28] £292 $450

UKRANIA QUAE ET TERRA COSACCORUM CUM VICINIS WALACHIAE, MOLDAVIAE, MINORIS TARTARIAE, PROVINCIIS [c. 1720] J.B. Homann. 51x58cm (19½x23") Orig col. Repaired tears. Ref: Bagrow (Russia) p.91. [28] £351 $540

[SAME TITLE] [1730] 48x58cm (18½x22½") Full color. [36] £276 $425

URBIS ROMAE VETERIS AC MODERNAE ACCURATA DELINEATIO ... [c. 1720] J.B. Homann. 48x58cm (19x23") Orig & later color. C'fold reinforced; else exc. [39] £633 $975

VIRGINIA MARYLANDIA ET CAROLINA IN AMERICA SEPTENTRIONALIS ... [1710] 48x58cm (19x22½") Orig color. Minor c'fold wrinkling; overall fine. Ref: Cumming (SE) 156. [32] £909 $1,400

[SAME TITLE] [1714] CT to SC. [same dimen] Orig wash color. Lower c'fold repaired; lt printed rt neatline; good. Ref: Morrison #27. [47] £909 $1,400

[SAME TITLE] [same date & dimen] Orig OL color. 2" repaired tear below, no loss; soft crease lf; sl margin soiling; bright, clear. Ref: Van Ermen #25; Phillips (M) p.982. [59] £941 $1,450

[SAME TITLE] [c. 1714] [same dimen] Orig wash col. Corner repaired, no loss; else fine. [63] £812 $1,250

VORSTELLUNG EINIGER GEGENDEN UND PLAETZE IN NORD-AMERICA UNTER FRANZOESISCH UND ENGLISCHE JURISDICTION GEHOERIG ZU FINDEN BEY DEN HOMAENNISCHEN ERBEN [1756] 4 plans: Quebec, Louisbourg, Halifax, Chebucto harbor. 48x53cm (18½x20½") Orig color. Margins bit soiled & chipped. Ref: Tooley (Amer) p.214, #134. [28] £380 $585
[SAME TITLE] [c. 1756] 43x49cm (17x19½") Color. [40] £350 $539

HONDIUS   Try *Jansson, Mercator*

AFRICAE NOVA TABULA [1631] 38x49cm (15x19½") Orig OL color; full cartouche color. Exc. Ref: Norwich 34; Tooley (Africa) pl.III. [2] £1,071 $1,650
AMERICA [1606] 38x50cm (15x19½") Orig color. Exc. [62] £2,921 $4,500
[SAME TITLE] [same date & dimen] With De Bry vignettes. Later full color. Exc. [63] £2,727 $4,200
[SAME TITLE] [1606 (1607)] 38x51cm (15x20") Color. Fine. Ref: Koeman Me 16. [55] £2,597 $4,000
AMERICA NOVITER DELINEATA [(1641)] Amsterdam: Jansson. 38x50cm (15x19½") Full color. Minor stains at margin corners; overall VG. Ref: Goss (NA) 27. [33] £1,493 $2,300
AMERICA NOVITER DELINEATA AUCT HENRICO HONDIO [1631] 38x51cm (15x19½") Full (unusual) color. Exc. Ref: Tooley (Amer) p.298, pl.172; Goss (NA) #27, p.66. [2] £1,591 $2,450
CHINA [1606] Mercator-Hondius atlas. 34x46cm (13½x18") Full orig color. Exc. [62] £1,428 $2,200
GLOBUS COELESTRIS [1616] Celestial double hemi. 10x15cm (3½x5½") Color. [58] £114 $175
GUINEA NOVA DESCRIPTIO [1606] 35x49cm (13½x19½") Ref: Tooley (Landmarks) p.154. [28] £526 $810
INSULAE INDIAE ORIENTALIS [1607] From *Atlas Minor*. 14x20cm (5½x7½") Orig col. Exc. [63] £224 $345
INSULAE INDIAE ORIENTALIS PRAECIPUAE, IN QUIBUS MOLUCCAE CELEBERRIMAE SUNT [1606] Mercator-Hondius atlas. 35x48cm (13½x19") Orig color. Fine. [62] £1,169 $1,800
MAPPA AESTIVARUM INSULARUM ALIAS BARMUDAS, DICTARUM ... [1629 - c.1650] With attribution to W. Blaeu. 40x53cm (15½x20½") Color. Ref: Palmer, p.10 [53] £1,500 $2,310
[SAME TITLE] [1633] From Jansson's *Novus Atlas*. [same dimen] Orig color. Soft age tone; old mat line discernible; fine. Ref: MCS 19 (Palmer) #8. [1] £974 $1,500
[SAME TITLE] [1633 / 1639] [same dimen] Color. Sl browning at c'fold; good. Ref: Koeman Me 93B, 98; Palmer (Bermuda) 8. [47] £1,104 $1,700
NOVISSIMA ARRAGONIAE ... [1639] 46x56cm (17½x21½") OL color. Thick paper; VG. [55] £162 $250
POLUS ANTARCTICUS HENRICUS HONDIUS EXCUDIT [1639] 1st ed; blank cartouche. 43x49cm (17x19½") Orig color. Ref: Tooley (Australia) pl.124 & 246; Schilder 44; Clancy pp 84-5. [16] £1,401 $2,157
SEPTENTRIONALIUM TERRARUM DESCRIPTIO [1595 / c.1620] Mercator-Hondius. 38x41cm (14½x15½") Orig color. Good. Ref: Nordenskiold (Fac) 57,64,95; Cumming (Discovery); Verner, "The north Part of America", pp.142-87. [2] £1,818 $2,800
TYPUS ORBIS TERRARUM [1621] From Mercator, *Atlas Minor*. Double hemi. 15x23cm (5½x8½") Uncolored. [44] £454 $700
VIRGINIAE ITEM ET FLORIDAE AMERICAE PROVINCIARUM, NOVA DESCRIPTIO [1606] 34x48cm (13½x19") Orig color. Exc. Ref: Cumming (SE) 26; Goss (NA) illus #23. [62] £1,233 $1,900
[SAME TITLE] [same date & dimen] Hondius-Mercator Full later color. Exc. [63] £1,169 $1,800
[SAME TITLE] [1606+] Mercator-Hondius. [same dimen] Early color. Browned, soiled; margins trimmed, loss of some verso text but not map. [14] £487 $750
[SAME TITLE] [same date & dimen] In Mercator atlas. Orig color. Minor soiling; margins trimmed, no loss to map area. Framed. [51] £1,948 $3,000

HOPKINS

COUNTIES OF ESSEX, UNION AND HUDSON [NJ] [1873] 30x41cm (12½x15½") Color. [35] £32 $50
COUNTIES OF MORRIS, PASSAIC AND BERGEN AND VICINITY OF NEWARK [NJ] [1873] 38x33cm (14½x13") Color. [35] £32 $50
TOPOGRAPHICAL MAP OF OCEAN COUNTY [NJ] [1873] 38x30cm (14½x11½") Color. [35] £42 $65

HORSBURGH

[INDONESIA: BANGKA & GASPAR STRAITS] [1826 (1857)] 94x64cm (36½x25") Pencil positions of 1862 voyage. [15] £150 $231
CHINA SEA SHEET II [1823 (1850)] With recommended routes to Canton. 66x99cm (26x39") Penciled navigation marks. Brown marking; upper margin chipped. [15] £280 $431

HOUZE
L'OCEANIE [c. 1849] Key, with island discovery dates. 25x40cm (10x15½") OL color. [41] £45 $69

HOWE
MAP OF NEBRASKA AND KANSAS [1856] Pub in *Historical Collections of the Great West* ... NE & KS to Rockies; NE to Canada. Wood engraving. 15x13cm (5½x4½") OL color. Ref: Howes (US) 721. [57] £29 $45

MAP OF THE GREAT WEST [1856] Pub in *Historical Collections of the Great West* ... Wood engraving, with "Utah or Deseret". (no dims.) OL color. Ref: Howes (US) 721. [57] £32 $50

HULSIUS
INSULAE INDIAE ORIENTALIS ET MOLUCAE [c. 1615] 16x27cm (6½x10½") Uncol. [52] £560 $862

WORLD [IN SET WITH] AFRICA [AND] AMERICA [AND] ASIA [AND] EUROPE [1604] Frankfurt ed. Continents after Ortelius. Each about 8x12cm (3½x5") Later full col. Fine. Ref: Shirley (W) 230. [33] £974 $1,500

HUNTINGTON
UNITED STATES [1835] Nathaniel G. Huntington. To Rockies. Population table. 28x46cm (10½x17½") Orig wash color. Good. [47] £185 $285

ILLUSTRATED LONDON NEWS
BIRDS EYE VIEW OF THE SOUDAN AND SURROUNDING COUNTRIES [1884] Portraits: Gen. Gordon; Col. Stewart. 42x53cm (16½x20½") Orig color. [54] £240 $370

ENVIRONS OF LONDON - WINDSOR CASTLE TO GRAVES HEAD [1851] Vignettes of major features. 58x81cm (23x32") Later color. Sl smudges at edge. [44] £58 $90

MAP OF THE SEAT OF WAR IN VIRGINIA [1863] 36x23cm (14x9") Highlight color. [14] £26 $40

NEW YORK FROM BERGEN HILL: HOBOKEN [1876] Aug. 19 supplement. Bird's-eye view. 46x114cm (17½x45") Color. Rice paper backing; fine. [48] £812 $1,250

PANORAMA OF THE RIVER THAMES IN 1845 [1845] Bird's eye wood engraving; 1st ed; 8 text pages with key. 2 joinable sheets, each 30x120cm (11½x47") Color. [14] £510 $785

THE CITY OF DUBLIN [1846] Bird's eye wood engraving; 8 text pages with key. 36x103cm (14x40½") [14] £204 $315

IMRAY
A CHART OF SOUTHERN AFRICA AND THE ISLANDS OF MADAGASCAR, BOURBON AND MAURITIUS ... [1875 (1878)] Blueback chart. 102x180cm (39½x71½") Repaired tear, no loss; o/w exc for type. [15] £220 $339

A NEW CHART OF THE GULFS OF MEXICO AND FLORIDA ... [1846] Honduras to Florida to Puerto Rico; many insets. 99x183cm (39x72") Blueback; linen bound edges. Several penciled tracks to New Orleans. Soiling, wear; two repaired tears; generally good. [15] £300 $462

CHART OF THE EAST COAST OF NORTH AMERICA ... [1861] Delaware to Cape Canso; Insets: New York; Halifax. 104x183cm (41x72") Blueback, linen bound edges. Colored dots & flares at lights. Penciled positions. Good, clean. [15] £300 $462

EAST INDIA ARCHIPELAGO [EASTERN PASSAGES TO CHINA AND JAPAN] [CHART NO.4] [1866] E. Borneo, Sulawest, W. Mindanao. 127x102cm (50x40") Bluebacked. 2 repaired tears; o/w good. [15] £100 $154

THE STRAIT OF SUNDA [1859] Insets, incl Batavia Roads. 98x103cm (38½x40½") Blue-back. Good, clean. [15] £140 $216

IRVING, W.
SKETCH OF THE ROUTES OF HUNT & STUART [1836] Whole Missouri River to the Pacific 25x46cm (10x17½") VG. [19] £97 $150

JACOBSZ
CUST VAN ENGELANT VAN LEZARD TOT ENGELANDS EYND, DE SORLINGES, ENDE CANAEL VAN BRESTOU ... [1676] From *Lighting Coulumne* or *Sea Mirrour*. Jacob & Caspar Lootsman reengraving of 1644 plates. 43x53cm (16½x21") Color. [15] £370 $570

DE CUST VAN BARBARYEN ... [1644-] A. Jacobsz. In two sections. 43x52cm (17x20½") Uncolored. [53] £280 $431

DE CUST VAN NORMANDIE EN PICARDIE ... [1644, 1676] From Lootsman Brothers, *Lighting Columne or Sea Mirror*. English coast, Dover to Portland. 43x52cm (16½x20½") Color. Brown mark rt edge; o/w VG. [15] £240 $370

DE CUSTEN VAN ENGELANDT TUSSCHEN FIERLEY EN POORTLANT; OOK HOESE VAN ORNAY GELEGEN ZYN [1644, 1676] From Lootsman Brothers *Lighting Columne or Sea Mirror*. 43x53cm (16½x20½") Color. [15] £320 $493
DE CUSTEN VAN NOORWEGEN TUSSCHEN DER NEUS EN SCHUITENES [1668 - 1689] 42x53cm (16½x20½") Color. Repaired tear lower c'fold; top margin trimmed to neat line. [14] £149 $230
DE CUSTEN VAN SCHOTLAND MET DE EYLANDEN VAN ORCANESE; VAN'T EYLAND COKET TOT I. SANDE [1644, 1676] From Lootsman Brothers *Lighting Columne or Sea Mirror*. 43x53cm (17x20½") Color. [15] £280 $431
EYLANDEN VAN HITLANT OFTE SCHETLANT ... [ON SHEET WITH] EYLANDEN VAN HEBRIDES ... [AND] EYLANDEN VAN FERO ... [1644 (1676)] From Lootsman Brothers, *Lighting Columne or Sea Mirror*. 43x53cm (17x20½") Color. Narrow lower margin. [15] £270 $416
PASCAERTE VANDE WEST EN OOST-ZYDE VAN IUTLANDT ... [1644-] A. Jacobsz. 43x72cm (17x28") Uncolored. Protective margins added. [53] £550 $847

JAILLOT

[PORTRAIT] ALEXIUS HUBERTUS IAILLOT ... 1698 [1695 - 1698] From *Atlas Francois*. By Vermeulen, after Culin. 37x30cm (14½x12") Uncolored. [52] £300 $462
AMERIQUE SEPTENTRIONALE [1719] 46x64cm (18x25") OL color. Lt wear; VG Ref: Karpinski (MI) XXI. [60] £1,136 $1,750
AMERIQUE SEPTENTRIONALE DIVISEE EN SES PRINCIPALES PARTIES ... [c. 1694-1700] After Sanson; insular Calif. 46x58cm (18x23") + title. Orig OL color. Fine-. Ref: Leighly #64, #87; Tooley (Amer) p.122, #38; Kaufman (Gt.Lakes) 10. [59] £1,201 $1,850
AMERIQUE SEPTENTRIONALE DIVISEE EN SES PRINCIPALES PARTIES, OU SONT DISTINGUES LES UNS DES AUTRES LES ETATS SUIVANT QU'ILS APPARTIENEMENT PRESENTEMENT AUX FRANCOIS, CASTILLANS, ANGLOIS, SVEDOIS, DANOIS, HOLLANDOIS ... PAR SR. SANSON [(1674) 1692] 56x86cm (22½x34½") Orig old color. Fine. Ref: Tooley (Amer) p.121, #37, pl.44. [1] £1,915 $2,950
CARTE DE L'ENTREE DE LA TAMISE AVEC LES BANCS, PASSES, ISLES ET COSTES COMPRISE ENTRE SANDWICH ET CLAY [1693, c.1750] First in *Neptune Francois*. 46x91cm (18x35½") Uncolored. Good. [15] £150 $231
IUDAEA SIVE TERRA SANCTA IN DUODECUM TRIBUS DIVISA ... [1696] 48x61cm (19x24") Old color. Ref: Laor 368. [23] £357 $550
LA RUSSIE BLANCHE OU MOSCOVIE DIVISEE SUIVANT L'ENTENDUE DES ROYAUMES, DUCHES ... H. JAILLOT PARIS [c. 1741] Amsterdam: Covens & Mortier. Latin border title, "Nova Russiae ..." 51x61cm (20x24") Orig color. Sh tear upper c'fold. [28] £204 $315
LE ROYAUME DE PORTUGAL ET DES ALGARVES ... [1695] 2 sheet map. 77x55cm (30x21½") Orig OL color. [53] £520 $801
LES ISLES BRITANNIQUES; QUI CONTIENNENT LES ROYAUMES D'ANGLETERRE, ECOSSE, ET IRELANDE ... [1719] 58x86cm (22½x34") Full old color. Faint age tone; few sm margin tears; very nice. Ref: Potter illus. p.19. [1] £714 $1,100
[SAME TITLE] [1695] 46x66cm (18x25½") Color. Exc. [29] £276 $425
MAPPE-MONDE GEO-HYDROGRAPHIQUE, OU DESCRIPTION GENERALE DU GLOBE TERRESTRE ET AQUATIQUE, EN DEUX PLANS-HEMISPHERES ... [1706] After Sanson; later state. Insular California; NW passage. 46x64cm (18x25½") Orig OL color. On heavy paper; good. Ref: Shirley (W) 569, pl.392. [2] £1,233 $1,900
PARTIE DU CERCLE D'AUSTRICHE, OU SONT LES DUCHES DE STIRIE, DE CARINTHIE, DE CARNIOLE ET AUTRES ESTATES HEREDITAIRES A LA MAISON D'AUSTRICHE PAR LE SR. SANSON ... [1681] 58x89cm (22½x34½") Lt foxing lower margin. Ref: Pastoureau, Jaillot 1 B. [28] £308 $475

JANSSON   Try *Hondius, Mercator, Valk & Schenk*

ALEXANDRI MAGNI MACEDONIS EXPEDITIO [1658] Classical Greece to India. 38x48cm (14½x18½") Contemporary color. Water stain lower lf; c'fold browning, split repaired; overall good. [55] £162 $250
AMERICA SEPTENTRIONALIS ... [1633-41 & after] Insular Calif. 47x55cm (18½x22") Orig OL color. Sh lower c'fold split restored. [54] £2,200 $3,388
[SAME TITLE] [(1636) 1638] 1st state; blank title cartouche; Hondius attribution. [same dimen] Old color. Fine. Ref: Leighly pl.V. [1] £1,948 $3,000
[SAME TITLE] [1640] State 2. [same dimen] Orig color. Sm repair ctr lower margin. [63] £1,883 $2,900
ANDALUZIA ... [1639] 38x51cm (15x19½") Color. VG. [55] £179 $275
ARCHIEPISCOPATUS TREVIRENSIS DESCRIPTIO NOVA [1647] 41x50cm (16½x19½") OL col. [36] £162 $250

BRITANNIA PROUT DIVISA SUIT TEMPORIBUS ANGLO-SAXONUM, PROESERTIM DURANTE ILLORUM HEPTACHIA [1646] "Heptarchy" map. 42x53cm (16½x20½") Orig color. Lt toned; fine. [63] £974 $1,500

CHINA [1676] From "Nieuwe en Beknopte Uytbeeldinghe en Vertooninge ... Amsterdam: Van Waesberghe; from Cloppenburgh 1630 plates after J. Hondius. About 18x25cm (7x9½") B&W. [54] £320 $493

ERYTHRAEI SIVE RUBRI MARIS PERIPLUS [1658] "Hyperborei" inset. 41x46cm (15½x18½") Contemporary color. Creasing at c'fold; else fine. Ref: Koeman Me 177A. [55] £162 $250

EUROPA EXACTISSIME DESCRIPTA AUCTORE HENRICO HONDIO [1641 (1649)] Mercator-Hondius atlas. 38x51cm (15x20") Orig OL color. C'fold strengthened on back; lt soiling; image VG; overall good. [59] £422 $650

FRETI MAGELLANICI AC NOVI FRETI VULGO LE MAIRE EXACTISSIMA DELINEATIO [1630] 38x49cm (15x19½") Col. Minor wormholes upper c'fold; early repair on verso; o/w fine. Ref: Koeman Me31A [33] £406 $625

GEOGRAPHICA SACRA [c. 1650 (1740)] After Ortelius, with world map inset; attributable to Horn. 36x48cm (14x18½") Orig OL & cartouche color. Tear to neat line repaired; VG. [46] £130 $200

GUINEA [1636] 38x52cm (15x20½") Color. Minor dampstaining margin; o/w fine. [33] £308 $475

HASSIA LANDGRAVIATUS [1636] 44x56cm (17½x22") OL color. All but lower margin trimmed; else VG. [55] £162 $250

HIBERNIA REGNUM VULGO IRELAND. APUD JOANNEM JANSSONIUM [1633] Amsterdam: H. Hondius. 39x50cm (15½x20") Color. Ref: Phillips (A) 5935, 8. [24] £276 $425

INSULAE AMERICANAE IN OCEANO SEPTENTRIONALI, CUM TERRIS ADIACENTIBUS [1636] 38x52cm (15x20½") Orig color. Very nice. Ref: Koeman II, #455. [2] £974 $1,500

INSULARUM BRITANNICARUM ACURATA DELINEATIO EX GEOGRAPHICIS CONATIBUS ABRAHAMI ORTELII [c. 1650] 39x51cm (15½x20") OL color. Fine. [21] £357 $550

INSULARUM HISPANIOLAE ET CUBAE CUM INSULIS CIRCUMJACENTIBUS ACCURATA DELINEATIO [1650] Incl S.Florida, Bahamas & Jamaica. 41x53cm (16x20½") Color. VG. [32] £649 $1,000

ITALIAE ANTIQUAE NOVA DELINEATIO ... [c. 1630] 38x51cm (15x20") OL color. Lower c'fold repaired; else fine. [55] £195 $300

MAGNI DUCATUS FINLANDIAE ... [1658] Jansson Heirs. 44x53cm (17x21") Orig OL col. [54] £750 $1,155

MAPPA AESTIVARUM INSULARUM ALIAS BERMUDAS DICTARUM ... [1676] From "Nieuwe en Beknopte Uytbeeldinghe en Vertooninge ... Amsterdam: Van Waesberghe; from Cloppenburgh 1630 plates after J. Hondius. About 18x25cm (7x9½") B&W. [54] £600 $924

MAR DEL ZUR HISPANIS MARE PACIFICUM [1646 and later] Insular California. 43x54cm (17x21½") OL & wash color. Japan paper backing; restored c'fold tears & at lf, sl lettering loss; sl show-through; restored to VG+. Ref: Leighly pl.VI; Tooley (Amer) pl.30; Lowery 138; Potter p.129; Wagner I p.125 #359; Koeman II ME 164 #657. [59] £1,558 $2,400

[SAME TITLE] [1650] 44x54cm (17½x21½") 1st issue; blank verso. Orig color. Exc. [62] £2,077 $3,200

[SAME TITLE] [1650 - 1657] [same dimen] Orig color. [16] £1,329 $2,048

MAR DI AETHIOPIA VULGO OCEANUS AETHIOPUS [c. 1650] 43x55cm (17x22") Probably orig OL color. VG. [59] £325 $500

MAR DI INDIA [1650] 44x55cm (17x22") Color. Ref: Tooley (Australia) 747 pl.57; Schilder 45 p.333; Clancy pp 82-3. [16] £1,804 $2,779

MOREA OLIM PELOPONNESUS [1639] 34x41cm (13½x16½") OL col. Lt age-toning; else fine. [55] £179 $275

NOVA ANGLIA NOVUM BELGIUM ET VIRGINIA [1636] 1st state. 39x51cm (15½x20") Full orig color. Some toning; good. Ref: Karpinski (MI) pp.36-7; Cumming (Exploration) pp.46,57. [2] £1,298 $2,000

[SAME TITLE] [1636] 1st ed. No dimensions. Orig color. Lt staining; else exc. Ref: Goss (NA) #29; Morrison fig.10; Karpinski (FC) pl.II. [38] £1,298 $2,000

NOVA ANGLIA NOVUM BELGIUM ET VIRGINIA. AMSTELODAMI JOHANNES JANSSONIUS EXCUDIT [c. 1645] 39x51cm (15½x20") Later color. Sh tear lower margin. Ref: Cumming (SE) 39, pl.25; Cumming (Exploration) p.57; Karpinski p.89; Koeman II Me 78. [28] £1,201 $1,850

NOVA BELGICA ET ANGLIA NOVA [1647] Reissue of 1636, with Blaeu's decor. 38x50cm (15x19½") Color. Exc. Ref: Cumming (SE) 43; Morrison fig. 10 (2nd state). [38] £1,169 $1,800

NOVA ET ACCURATA POLI ARCTICI ... [1637] 41x53cm (16x20½") Orig OL color. Exc. Ref: Goss (NA) p.26. [2] £974 $1,500

NOVA HISPANIA ET NOVA GALICIA [1664 or later] 35x48cm (13½x19") Orig partial color. Lt age toned; minor stitch holes in c'fold; overall VG. [31] £250 $385

NOVA TOTIUS TERRARUM ORBIS GEOGRAPHICA AC HYDROGRAPHICA TABULA [1608 / 1626] By Van Den Keere. With rhumb lines; panels all around. 41x53cm (15½x21") Full orig color. Exc. Ref: Shirley (W) 264, pl.207. [2] £6,167 $9,500

NOVA TOTIUS TERRARUM ORBIS GEOGRAPHICA AC HYDROGRAPHICA TABULA [1632] After Dirck Lons, 1622. Panels all around. 46x56cm (18x22") Color. Ref: Shirley (W) 309, pl.9. [16] £8,546 $13,164
[SAME TITLE] [1641] After Hondius. Double hemisphere with decorative surround; with Dutch Australian discoveries; Insular California. 39x54cm (15x21½") Full orig color. Narrow lf margin extended; exc. Ref: Shirley 336, pl.256. [1] £4,220 $6,500
NOVA TOTIUS TERRARUM ORBIS GEOGRAPHICA AC HYDROGRAPHICA TABULA AUCT. HENR. HONDIO [1641] State 2; Jansson name added. Double hemi; insular Calif. 38x54cm (15x21½") Orig color. Ref: Shirley (W) 336, pl.256. Clancy pp 72-3; Schilder 39. [16] £6,172 $9,508
NOVA VIRGINIAE TABULA [1676] From "Nieuwe en Beknopte Uytbeeldinghe en Vertooninge ... Amsterdam: Van Waesberghe; from Cloppenburgh 1630 plates after J. Hondius. About 18x25cm (7x9½") B&W. [54] £550 $847
NOVA ZEMLA, WAYGATS, FRETUM NASSOVICUM, ET TERRA SAMOIEDUM ... [c. 1650] 41x51cm (16x20½") Orig OL & cartouche color. Sh lower c'fold split. Ref: cf. Koeman II Me 164. [28] £380 $585
NOVI BELGICA ET ANGLIA NOVA [1636 / c.1695] Valk & Schenk imprint. 39x49cm (15x19½") Orig wash color. Mint. Ref: Cumming (SE) 43. [62] £1,169 $1,800
NOVISSIMA POLONIAE REGNI DESCRIPTIO [c. 1652] 43x54cm (17x21½") Orig color. Browned; sh margin tears. Ref: MCCS 56, 591; Koeman II Me 110. [28] £192 $295
OLDENBURG COMITATUS [1647] 38x51cm (15x19½") Old color. Minor repaired edge chip; sm hole, faint stain rt margin; faint foxing; VG. [29] £195 $300
ORBIS TERRARUM VETERIBUS COGNITI TYPUS GEOGRAPHICUS [1650] 40x51cm (16x20") Color. Ref: Shirley (W) 385. [16] £617 $951
[SAME TITLE] [c. 1666] 2nd state. [same dimen] Color. [16] £665 $1,024
PASCAART VANT CANAAL TUSSCHEN ENGELANT EN VRANCRYCK, ALSMEDE GEHEEL IERLANT EN SCHOTLANT ... [1650] In *Atlantis Majoris Quinta Pars Orbem Maritimum* ... British Isles. 43x55cm (17x21½") Modern OL color. Repaired margin tears; else VF. Ref: Shirley (BI to 1650) 659, pl.160. [62] £438 $675
POLI ANTARCTICI ... [1676] From "Nieuwe en Beknopte Uytbeeldinghe en Vertooninge ... Amsterdam: Van Waesberghe. 18x25cm (7x9½") B&W. [54] £360 $554
POLUS ANTARCTICUS [1650] 2nd in Hondius-Jansson series; blank cartouche removed. 44x49cm (17x19½") Orig color. Ref: Tooley (Australia) 750; Schilder 78; Clancy pp 84-5. [16] £1,401 $2,157
SABAUDIA DUCATUS. SAVOYE [c. 1644-60] 38x51cm (15x19½") Orig OL & cartouche color. Crease near c'fold. Ref: Koeman II Me 75A. [28] £234 $360
SCOTIA REGNUM [c. 1646] 38x50cm (15x19½") Full orig color. Sl browning; o/w fine. [51] £487 $750
STIRIA. PER GERARDUM MERCATOREM [1638] 30x43cm (12x16½") Ref: Koeman II Me 51A. [28] £175 $270
TERRA FIRMA ET NOVUM REGNUM GRANATENSE ET POPAYAN ... [c. 1647] 38x49cm (15x19½") Orig color. Lt browned; c'fold & top margin tears repaired. Ref: Koeman II Me 59. [28] £234 $360
TYPUS ORBIS TERRARUM [IN SET WITH] AFRICAE NOVA TABULA AUCT. J. HONDIO [AND] AMERICAE NOVITER DELINEATA [AND] ASIA [AND] NOVA EUROPAE DESCRIPTIO [1673 or 1676] 5 maps by pub by Jansson Heirs. World after Cloppenburgh's 1630-36 Mercator-Hondius pocket atlas; engraved by Van den Keere or Hondius. All about 18x26cm (7x10") Recent OL color. VG+. Ref: cf. Shirley (W) 334, pl.252. [59] £1,720 $2,650
VETUS DESCRIPTIO DACIARUM NEC NON MOESIARUM ... [1658] 36x48cm (14½x19") [28] £175 $270
VIRGINIA [1648] 15x19cm (5½x7½") Uncolored. [54] £400 $616
VIRGINIAE ITEM ET FLORIDAE ... [1676] From "Nieuwe en Beknopte Uytbeeldinghe en Vertooninge ... Amsterdam: Van Waesberghe; from Cloppenburgh 1630 plates after J. Hondius. About 18x25cm (7x9½") B&W. [54] £380 $585
VIRGINIAE PARTIS AUSTRALIS, ET FLORIDAE PARTIS ORIENTALIS INTERJACENTIUMQ. REGIONUM NOVA DESCRIPTIO [1641 - 1658] 39x50cm (15x20") Probably orig or early OL color. Surface toning; staining & other flaws; image VG, overall good. Ref: Cumming (SE) #42; Schwartz & Ehrenberg p.108; Lowery 126; Phillips (M) p.978. [59] £844 $1,300

JANVIER

L'AMERIQUE DIVISEE PAR GRANDS ETATS PAR LE SR. JANVIER ... [1783] 30x46cm (12½x18") Orig OL & cartouche color. [28] £279 $430
L'AMERIQUE SEPTENTRIONALE DIVISEE EN SES PRINCIPAUX ETATS [1762] With "West Sea". 31x45cm (12x17½") OL & wash color. [56] £260 $400
[SAME TITLE] [1782] With "West Sea"; *Etats Unis* shown. 30x48cm (12x19") OL color. Minor spots; o/w good, clean. [10] £227 $350

JAPANESE CARTOGRAPHY

BANKOKU YOCHI SANKAI ZUSETSU [c. 1780] Woodblock. 38x48cm (15x19½") Orig col. [2] £1,558 $2,400

CHIKYO ZENZU [c. 1793] Manuscript map of Western Hemisphere on 4 sheets on backing paper. 51x42cm (20x16½") Color. Backing sheet folded, minor fold wear; sm wormhole; good. [33] £519 $800

JEFFERYS Try *Laurie & Whittle, Sayer, Sayer & Bennett*

[ADVERTISEMENT] THOMAS JEFFERYS SELLS ... ALL SORTS OF MAPS ... [c. 1750] Advertisement, cum trade card; examples illustrated. 17x24cm (6½x9½") Uncolored. [52] £520 $801

A GENERAL CHART OF THE ISLAND OF NEWFOUNDLAND WITH THE ROCKS & SOUNDINGS. ... BY JAMES COOK AND MICHAEL LANE SURVEYORS AND OTHERS. ... BY THOMAS JEFFERYS GEOGRAPHER TO THE KING. PRINTED FOR ROB.T SAYER & JN.E BENNET ... [1775] 55x56cm (21½x22") Orig wash color. Close orig margins, sl toning top & bottom; else fine. [62] £536 $825

A MAP OF CANADA AND THE NORTH PART OF LOUISIANA WITH THE ADJACENT COUNTRYS. BY THOS. JEFFERYS, GEOGRAPHER TO HIS ROYAL HIGHNESS THE PRINCE OF WALES [c. 1760] 1st state. 33x53cm (12½x21½") Lt offsetting; fold tear repaired, no loss; pinholes rt border. Ref: Karpinski (MI) p.154; Sellers & Van Ee 95. [28] £497 $765

[SAME TITLE] [1762] State II; to West Coast. 30x76cm (12½x30") OL color. Some transferral; breaks at folds; backed; VG. [19] £325 $500

A MAP OF SOUTH AMERICA CONTAINING TIERRA-FIRMA, GUAYNA, NEW GRANADA, AMAZONIA, BRASIL, PERU ... FROM MR. D'ANVILLE ... [1775] London: Sayer. 4 sheets joined to form two, each 51x119cm (20½x47") Orig OL & old cartouche color. Lt offsetting; pinholes, sm paper flaws; sh margin tears; horiz creases. Ref: Phillips (A) 1165. [28] £409 $630

A MAP OF THE DISCOVERIES MADE BY THE RUSSIANS ON THE NORTH WEST COAST OF AMERICA. PUBLISHED BY THE ROYAL ACADEMY OF SCIENCES AT PETERSBURG [1761] English ed after 2nd state of 1758 Muller map. 48x64cm (19½x24½") Orig OL color. Lt offsetting; lower rt margin restored; several inch tear repaired. Ref: Wagner (NW) 597; Falk 1761-3. [28] £526 $810

A MAP OF THE ISLAND OF ST. JOHN IN THE GULF OF ST. LAURENCE DIVIDED INTO COUNTIES & PARISHES AND THE LOTS AS GRANTED BY GOVERNMENT ... IMPROV'D FROM THE SURVEY OF CAPTAIN HOLLAND [1775] 38x71cm (15x28") Sh margin tears; foxing traces. Ref: Sellers & Van Ee 626; Armstrong 30. [28] £467 $720

A MAP OF THE ISLE OF CUBA, WITH THE BAHAMA ISLANDS ... [1762] From *Description of the Spanish Islands* ... 34x49cm (13½x19") Uncolored. [54] £320 $493

A MAP OF THE MOST INHABITED PART OF NEW ENGLAND, CONTAINING THE PROVINCES OF MASSACHUSETS BAY AND NEW HAMPSHIRE, WITH THE COLONIES OF CONNECTICUT AND RHODE ISLAND, DIVIDED INTO COUNTIES AND TOWNSHIPS ... [Nov. 29, 1774] Two sheets, each about 53x99cm (20½x38½") Orig OL color; early color cartouche. Corner restored, sl loss; else VG. Ref: Goss (NA) 66; Stevens & Tree 33e; Cumming (Colonial Amer) p 45-7; Benes #12. [38] £2,272 $3,500

A NEW AND EXACT PLAN OF CAPE FEAR RIVER FROM THE BAR TO BRUNSWICK, BY EDWARD HYRNE 1749 [1753] 38x33cm (15½x12½") Orig OL color. Linen backing; fine. Ref: Sellers & Van Ee 1502. [2] £779 $1,200

A NEW CHART OF THE WEST INDIES, DRAWN FROM THE BEST SPANISH MAPS ... [1762] From *Description of the Spanish Islands* ... 17x49cm (6½x19½") Orig OL key color. Ref: Sellers & Van Ee 1734. [54] £200 $308

A NEW MAP OF NOVA SCOTIA, AND CAPE BRITAIN, WITH THE ADJACENT PARTS OF NEW ENGLAND AND CANADA ... 1755 PUBLISHED ACCORDING TO ACT OF PARLIAMENT BY THOS. JEFFERYS ... [1755] 2nd state; Nova Scotia-New England boundary at Kennebec. By Braddock Mead (pseudonym John Green). 47x62cm (18½x24½") Ref: Tooley (Amer) p.93; #66. Cumming (Colonial Amer) p.59-60. [28] £584 $900

A PLAN OF THE CITY OF QUEBEC THE CAPITAL OF CANADA. AS IT SURRENDER'D 18 SEPTEMBR. 1759 ... [1760] 2nd state, much revision. 33x48cm (13½x19") Lt offsetting; close top margin. Ref: cf Sellers & Van Ee 608. [28] £584 $900

AN EXACT CHART OF THE RIVER ST. LAURENCE, FROM FORT FRONTENAC TO THE ISLAND OF ANTICOSTI SHEWING THE SOUNDINGS, ROCKS, SHOALS, &C. WITH VIEWS OF THE LANDS AND ALL NECESSARY INSTRUCTIONS FOR NAVIGATING THAT RIVER TO QUEBEC [1757-1775] London: R. Sayer. 59x94cm (23½x37") Orig OL color. Ref: Tooley (Amer) p.98; #76. [54] £320 $493

[SAME TITLE] [1775] 4th state. London: R. Sayer. 5 insets. 60x94cm (23½x37") 2 sheets joined. Orig color. Ragged lower margins; horiz & vert folds, with few creases & tears nearby. Ref: Phillips (A) 1165; Tooley (Amer) p.98, #76d. [28] £497 $765

AN INDEX MAP TO THE FOLLOWING SIXTEEN SHEETS, BEING A COMPLEAT CHART OF THE WEST INDIES [1775] London: Sayer. 38x63cm (15x24½") B&W. [46] £143 $220
CHART CONTAINING THE GREATER PART OF THE SOUTH SEA TO THE SOUTH OF THE LINE, WITH THE ISLANDS DISPERSED THRO' THE SAME [1775] 43x53cm (16½x20½") Linen-backed; some discoloration. [62] £146 $225
IRELAND [1760] 18x20cm (7½x7½") Color. [24] £71 $110
PLAN OF NEW ORLEANS THE CAPITAL OF LOUISIANA; WITH THE DISPOSITION OF ITS QUARTERS AND CANALS ... [ON SHEET WITH] THE COURSE OF THE MISSISSIPPI RIVER ... [AND] THE EAST MOUTH OF THE MISSISSIPI ... [1760] 33x49cm (13x19") Some offsetting; close side margins. Ref: Sellers & Van Ee 1677. [28] £438 $675
PLAN OF THE AGUADA NUEVA DE PUERTO RICO [1768] Mayaguez area. 25x18cm (9½x7") Color. [25] £91 $140
PLAN OF THE HARBOUR AND SETTLEMENT OF PENSACOLA [1762] From *Description of the Spanish Islands* ... 18x26cm (7x10") Uncolored. Archival tissue backing. [54] £240 $370
PLAN OF THE TOWN AND CITIDEL OF FORT ROYAL THE CAPITAL OF MARTINICO. WITH THE BAY OF CUL DE SAC ROYAL. BY MR. DE CAYLUS ... [1760] 30x36cm (12x14") Ref: Sellers & Van Ee 2051. [?8] £204 $315
PLAN OF THE TOWN AND FORTIFICATIONS OF MONTREAL OR VILLE MARIE IN CANADA [1758 - 1760] 33x51cm (13x20") Lt offsetting; close side margin. Ref: Sellers & Van Ee 619; Trudel p.211. [28] £584 $900
PLAN OF THE TOWN AND HARBOUR OF SAN JUAN DE PUERTO RICO [1768] 21x30cm (8x11½") Color. [25] £172 $265
PLAN OF THE TOWN AND HARBOUR OF ST. AUGUSTINE [1762] From *Description of the Spanish Islands* ... 20x29cm (8x11") Uncolored. Archival tissue backing. [54] £200 $308
PLAN OF THE TOWN OF BASSE TERRE THE CAPITAL OF GUADELOUPE FROM AN AUTHENTIC SURVEY [1760] 33x24cm (13x9½") Ref: Sellers & Van Ee 2028. [28] £175 $270
THE BAY OF HONDURAS [1775] 47x62cm (18½x24½") Linen backed. Fine. [62] £146 $225
THE COAST OF WEST FLORIDA AND LOUISIANA ... [1775] 1st issue, from West India Atlas; sheet with U.S. south coast & Gulf. 48x64cm (19x25") Later color. [46] £974 $1,500
THE GEOGRAPHY OF THE GREAT SOLAR ECLIPSE OF JULY, 14. MDCCXLVIII. EXHIBITING AN ACCURATE MAP OF ALL PARTS OF THE EARTH IN WHICH IT WILL BE VISIBLE WITH THE NORTH POLE ACCORDING TO THE LATEST DISCOVERIES. BY G. SMITH ESQR. [1748] Eurasia & E. North America. Jefferys, sc. 30x44cm (12x17") Uncolored. Fold separations repaired; backed. Ref: Jolly GENT-59 [32] £162 $250
THE ISLAND OF HISPANIOLA CALLED BY THE FRENCH ST. DOMINGO. SUBJECT TO FRANCE & SPAIN ... [1760] 36x51cm (13½x19½") Lt offsetting. Ref: Sellers & Van Ee 1853. [28] £263 $405
THE PROVINCES OF NEW YORK, AND NEW JERSEY; WITH PART OF PENSILVANIA AND THE PROVINCE OF QUEBEC [1776] From *The North American Atlas*. 52x133cm (20½x52½") Linen backed; wear at folds, some loss. [62] £454 $700
THE VIRGIN ISLANDS FROM ENGLISH AND DANISH SURVEYS ... [1775] From *West India Atlas*. R. Sayer, pub. 46x61cm (18½x24") Uncolored. Nice. [2] £974 $1,500
THE WINDWARD PASSAGE, WITH THE SEVERAL PASSAGES, FROM THE EAST END OF CUBA, AND THE NORTH PART OF ST. DOMINGO [1775] London: Sayer. 51x66cm (19½x25½") Orig color. Offsetting; few stains; sh tears lower margin. Ref: Sellers & Van Ee 1735; Phillips (A) 2699. [28] £497 $765

JOHNSON

[ATLAS] JOHNSON'S NEW ILLUSTRATED (STEEL PLATE) FAMILY ATLAS [1862] Johnson & Browning. Sm folio. Half leather binding worn at spine ends. 99 pp. Maps in bright color; some not called for in index. Occas lt foxing; generally bright, clean. Better than average. [5] £503 $775
[SAME TITLE] [1864] Johnson & Ward. Sm folio. Half leather binding; worn, hinges starting. 123 pp. Maps in bright color. Lt damp-stain, mostly top margins; OH torn at c'fold, worn; occas foxing & browning. [5] £422 $650
CHINA [1862] Johnson & Ward. 33x38cm (12½x15") Orig wash color. [46] £26 $40
GEORGETOWN AND THE CITY OF WASHINGTON [1861] Johnson & Browning. 32x40cm (12½x15½") Full Color. VG. [61] £29 $45
JOHNSON'S ARKANSAS, MISSISSIPPI AND LOUISIANA [1861] Johnson & Browning. 66x46cm (26x18") Color. Some wear; just VG. [61] £29 $45
[SAME TITLE] [1862] Johnson & Ward. 58x41cm (23x16") Full color. fine. [20] £58 $90
[SAME TITLE] [1864] Johnson & Ward. [same dimen] Full color. Minor fold spotting. [20] £52 $80
[SAME TITLE] [c. 1867] A.J. Johnson. 56x41cm (21½x15½") Full color. Fine. [20] £49 $75

JOHNSON'S CALIFORNIA, ALSO UTAH, NEVADA, COLORADO, NEW MEXICO AND ARIZONA [1866] Johnson & Ward. AZ with western "point". 43x60cm (17x24") Full color. VG. [44] £97 $150

JOHNSON'S CALIFORNIA. TERRITORIES OF NEW MEXICO AND UTAH [(1860)] NM-AZ proposed border at 33°40' as proposed at April 1860 Tucson constitutional convention; early NV formed from extended UT. 43x62cm (17x24") Color. Even age-tone, 2 minor spots; o/w good. [9] £114 $175

JOHNSON'S CALIFORNIA WITH TERRITORIES OF UTAH, NEVADA, COLORADO, NEW MEXICO, AND ARIZONA [1864] Johnson & Ward. 44x60cm (17x24") VG. [61] £62 $95

JOHNSON'S CENTRAL AMERICA [1861] Johnson & Browning. 31x40cm (12x15½") Full col. VG. [61] £29 $45

JOHNSON'S CUBA, JAMAICA & PORTO RICO [1860] Johnson & Browning. Puerto Rico inset. 32x41cm (12½x16½") Color. [25] £36 $55

[SAME TITLE] [1861] Johnson & Browning. 32x41cm (12½x16") Full color. VG. [61] £29 $45

JOHNSON'S DELAWARE AND MARYLAND [1861] 36x46cm (14x18") Full color. VG. [61] £29 $45

JOHNSON'S FLORIDA [1861] Johnson & Browning. 32x39cm (12½x15½") Orig wash color. Minor lt browning; o/w good. [4] £39 $60

[SAME TITLE] [1863 / 1870] A.J. Johnson. 31x39cm (12x15½") Soft horiz crease. [4] £36 $55

[SAME TITLE] [1864] Johnson & Ward. 32x39cm (12½x15½") [4] £42 $65

JOHNSON'S GEORGIA AND ALABAMA [1861] Johnson & Browning. 46x66cm (18x26") Full color. VG. [61] £23 $35

[SAME TITLE] [1863] 40x57cm (15½x22") Full color. [36] £49 $75

JOHNSON'S ILLINOIS [1861] Johnson & Browning. Chicago court house view. 46x36cm (18x14") Full color. VG. [61] £23 $35

JOHNSON'S INDIANA [1864] 58x43cm (23x17") [14] £19 $30

JOHNSON'S IOWA AND NEBRASKA [1861] Johnson & Browning. 36x46cm (14x18") Full col. VG. [61] £26 $40

JOHNSON'S KANSAS AND NEBRASKA [1870] 42x58cm (16½x23") [14] £29 $45

JOHNSON'S KENTUCKY AND TENNESSEE [1861] Johnson & Browning. 46x66cm (18x26") Full color. VG. [61] £29 $45

[SAME TITLE] [1863] 46x61cm (18x24") Color. VG or better. [29] £29 $45

[SAME TITLE] [1865] 2 engravings. 43x59cm (17x23") Color. [36] £49 $75

JOHNSON'S MAINE [1861] Johnson & Browning. 46x36cm (18x14") Full color. VG. [61] £23 $35

[SAME TITLE] [1866] A.J. Johnson. 55x39cm (22x15½") Color. [14] £19 $30

JOHNSON'S MAP OF THE UNITED STATES [1864] 46x66cm (18x26") Wear at c'fold; just VG. [61] £49 $75

JOHNSON'S MAP OF THE WORLD [1864] Johnson & Ward. 46x66cm (18x26") Full col. VG. [61] £42 $65

JOHNSON'S MEXICO [1861] Johnson & Browning. 30x38cm (12x15") Full color. VG. [61] £29 $45

JOHNSON'S MINNESOTA & DAKOTA [1861] Johnson & Browning. 31x38cm (12x15") Full col. VG. [61] £39 $60

[SAME TITLE] [1864] Johnson & Ward. 31x38cm (12x15") VG. [61] £42 $65

JOHNSON'S MISSOURI AND KANSAS [1865] 43x59cm (17x23½") Orig color. [14] £23 $35

JOHNSON'S NEBRASKA AND KANSAS [1861] Johnson & Browning. Nebraska to Rockies & Canada. 32x39cm (12½x15½") Full color. VG. [61] £97 $150

JOHNSON'S NEBRASKA, DAKOTA, COLORADO, IDAHO & KANSAS [1863] 33x41cm (12½x15½") Color. [11] £55 $85

JOHNSON'S NEBRASKA, DAKOTA, COLORADO, & KANSAS [1861] Johnson & Ward. Extended Dakota to divide. 33x41cm (12½x15½") [10] £88 $135

[SAME TITLE] [1862] Johnson & Browning. 33x41cm (13x16") Full color. [45] £91 $140

[SAME TITLE] [1862] NE touches UT. 33x39cm (12½x15½") Full color. [56] £65 $100

JOHNSON'S NEBRASKA, DAKOTA, COLORADO, MONTANA & KANSAS [1864] Johnson & Ward. 46x66cm (18x26") VG. [61] £49 $75

JOHNSON'S NEBRASKA, DAKOTA, IDAHO AND MONTANA [1865] 43x59cm (17x23") Wear & chipping at margins; c'fold separation. [61] £49 $75

JOHNSON'S NEBRASKA, DAKOTA, IDAHO, MONTANA AND WYOMING [1865 (1877-79)] 43x59cm (17x23") Color. Nice, clean. [12] £81 $125

JOHNSON'S NEBRASKA, DAKOTA, MONTANA AND KANSAS [1865] Johnson & Ward. 30x36cm (11½x14½") Partial color. Some browning; good. [18] £65 $100

JOHNSON'S NEW BRUNSWICK, NOVA SCOTIA, NEWFOUNDLAND, AND PRINCE EDWARD ID. [1861] 32x40cm (12½x15½") Full color. VG. [61] £29 $45

JOHNSON'S NEW ENGLAND [1861] Johnson & Browning. 66x46cm (26x18") Full color. VG. [61] £49 $75

JOHNSON'S NEW JERSEY [1867] 21 counties. 40x32cm (16x12½") [35] £39 $60
JOHNSON'S NEW MAP OF THE STATE OF TEXAS [1860-1861] Johnson & Browning; early ed. 43x62cm (17x24") Orig full color. [46] £156 $240
[SAME TITLE] [1862] Johnson & Ward. 41x56cm (16x22") Orig full color. [46] £146 $225
JOHNSON'S NEW MILITARY MAP OF THE UNITED STATES SHOWING THE FORTS, MILITARY POSTS, &C. WITH ENLARGED PLANS OF THE SOUTHERN HARBORS [1861] Johnson & Ward; shows states rather than military departments. 43x60cm (17x24") [61] £81 $125
JOHNSON'S NORTH AMERICA [1860] AZ-NM horizontally divided; NE to Canada. 61x43cm (23½x17") Color. Evenly toned; c'fold repairs; else good. [10] £71 $110
[SAME TITLE] [1864] 56x43cm (22x17") VG. [61] £55 $85
JOHNSON'S NORTH AND SOUTH CAROLINA [1861] Johnson & Browning. 46x66cm (18x26") Full color. VG. [61] £36 $55
JOHNSON'S NORTH CAROLINA AND SOUTH CAROLINA [1865] Inset: Charleston Harbor; 2 engravings. 44x58cm (17½x23") Color. [36] £39 $60
JOHNSON'S OHIO [1866] 43x58cm (17x22½") Full color. [36] £29 $45
JOHNSON'S OREGON AND WASHINGTON [1866] 41x28cm (15½x10½") Full color. VG. [19] £49 $75
JOHNSON'S TEXAS [1866] 43x59cm (17x23") Color. Minor edge browning; else fine. [11] £120 $185
JOHNSON'S WASHINGTON AND OREGON [1861] Johnson & Browning. WA to Continental Divide. 28x38cm (11x15") Full color. Minor margin browning; VG. [19] £71 $110
JOHNSON'S WASHINGTON, OREGON AND IDAHO [1864] Johnson & Ward. Oversize Idaho. 28x36cm (11x14") Full color. Marginal browning; VG. [18] £71 $110
[SAME TITLE] [1864] Dakota & Idaho overlap. [same dimen] Full color. Minor browning & repair; VG. [19] £55 $85
JOHNSON'S WESTERN HEMISPHERE [AND] JOHNSON'S EASTERN HEMISPHERE [1864] NY: Johnson & Ward. 46x66cm (18x26") Full color. VG. [61] £42 $65
MAP OF ARIZONA, CALIFORNIA, COLORADO, NEVADA, NEW MEXICO, AND UTAH [1882] From *Johnson's Encyclopedia*. 23x30cm (8½x12") Color. [44] £58 $90
MAP OF THE VICINITY OF RICHMOND AND PENINSULAR CAMPAIGN [1862] Johnson & Ward. 43x61cm (17x24") Full color. VG. [61] £81 $125
MASSACHUSETTS, CONNECTICUT & RHODE ISLAND [1861] Johnson & Browning. 43x58cm (17x23") Full color. VG. [61] £29 $45
MOUNTAINS AND RIVERS [1863] Johnson & Ward. 43x66cm (17x26") Color. [45] £58 $90
NEW MILITARY MAP OF THE UNITED STATES SHOWING THE FORTS, MILITARY POSTS, &C. WITH ENLARGED PLANS OF SOUTHERN HARBORS ... [1861 (1864)] 44x61cm (17½x24") Orig full col. VG. [59] £114 $175
PALESTINE [1862] Johnson & Ward. 40x32cm (15½x12½") Orig full color. [46] £26 $40
PENNSYLVANIA, VIRGINIA, DELAWARE AND MARYLAND [1863] Johnson & Ward. Vignettes. 43x61cm (17½x24") Wash color. [46] £49 $75
WASHINGTON AND OREGON [1862] Statehood OR; extended WA Terr. 30x41cm (12½x16") Full color. [56] £55 $85
WASHINGTON, OREGON AND IDAHO [1865] With part of MT & Dakota. 31x39cm (12½x15½") Full color. [56] £52 $80

JOHNSTON

[ATLAS] THE ROYAL ATLAS OF MODERN GEOGRAPHY ... [1865] A.K. Johnston; Edinburgh & London: Wm. Blackwood & Sons. Folio. With all 48 double page OL color maps. Contemporary half morocco, rubbed; front cover detached, rear loose, defective spine; contents fine. Ref: cf. Phillips (A) 835. [59] £454 $700
[ATLAS] THE ROYAL ATLAS OF MODERN GEOGRAPHY [1894] Edinburgh: A.K & T.B. Johnston. Imperial folio; 56 double-page maps in mainly OL color, interspersed with indices. Ex lib, with marks. Rebound, boards soiled, endpapers & frontispiece maps loose; o/w VG. [7] £250 $385
[ATLAS] THE STATISTICAL ATLAS OF ENGLAND, SCOTLAND AND IRELAND [1882] G.P. Bevan. Edinburgh: W. & A.K. Johnston. Imperial folio; 45 printed color maps; 75 pp text. Ex lib, with marks. Edge browning; contents clean, tight, complete; overall VG. [7] £159 $245
GEOGRAPHICAL DISTRIBUTION OF PLANTS ACCORDING TO HUMBOLDT'S STATISTICS OF THE PRINCIPAL FAMILIES & GROUPS; SCHOUWS TWENTY FIVE PHYTO-GEOGRAPHIC REGIONS ... [1850] From the *Physical Atlas*. Mountain profiles showing elevation effects. 20x28cm (7½x10½") with text pages. Col. [58] £42 $65

GEOLOGICAL & MINERALOGICAL MAP OF SUTHERLAND [1881] Dissected, linen mounted, folding into cloth covers. 81x97cm (31½x38") Partial color by strata. Fine. [21] £117 $180
ISLANDS IN THE PACIFIC OCEAN [c. 1860] 50x60cm (20x24") OL color. [41] £45 $69
JOHNSTON'S MAP OF RAILWAY SYSTEMS OF SCOTLAND [c. 1880] Dissected, linen-backed, in cloth covers. 84x69cm (33x27½") Routes in color. VG. [21] £97 $150
JOHNSTON'S MAP OF THE COUNTIES OF NAIRN & ELGIN [c. 1860] Sheet 23. Dissected, linen mounted, folding into gilt stamped cover. 74x58cm (28½x22½") OL color. VG. [21] £88 $135
KEITH JOHNSTON'S "TRAVELLING MAP OF SCOTLAND" [c. 1880] From 186286x58cm (34x23") Printed color. VG. [21] £81 $125
MAP OF THE COUNTIES OF PERTH AND CLACKMANNAN WITH THE RAILWAYS [c. 1860] Dissected, linen mounted, folding map; case lacking. 79x91cm (31x36") Uncolored. VG. [21] £97 $150
MAP OF THE COUNTY OF SELKIRK ... [c. 1840] W. & A.K. Johnston. Folds within gilt decorated boards. 69x53cm (27x21") Full color. Fine. [21] £81 $125
MAP OR CHART OF THE CALEDONIAN CANAL ... [1852] 30x117cm (11½x46") [15] £60 $92
NEW ZEALAND [c. 1855] 48x45cm (19x17½") OL color. Exc. [41] £125 $193
NORTH POLAR CHART [1885] Atlas frontis. Pole at ctr; south to Mediterranean. 36x48cm (13½x19") Color. [36] £42 $65
OCEANIA [c. 1870] Australia & N.Z. insets. 44x56cm (17½x22") OL color. [41] £35 $54
PALESTINE [1844] In *National Atlas*. 61x51cm (24x19½") Color. [23] £39 $60
PALESTINE OR THE HOLY LAND [1862] 58x44cm (23x17½") OL color. Ref: Laor 379. [23] £29 $45
VAN DIEMEN'S LAND OR TASMANIA [c. 1855] From *The National Atlas*. 60x49cm (23½x19½") Color. [41] £78 $120

JOSLIN
[GLOBE] JOSLIN'S TERRESTRIAL GLOBE ... [c. 1875] After Smith's new English globe; additions by Annin & Smith; revised by G.W. Boynton. Brass half meridian on walnut stand; 21" high overall. Diameter: 30cm (12") Color. Few sl surface blemishes; base dish repaired. [17] £2,921 $4,500
[GLOBE] JOSLIN'S TERRESTRIAL GLOBE CONTAINING THE LATEST DISCOVERIES [1854] Gilman Joslin, Boston. 6" globe eccentrically mounted on filigree cast-iron base, geared to rotate. Color. Age-toned, crackled; occas rubs, sl loss; 3" crack; good. [7] £747 $1,150

JULIEN, R.
[ATLAS] CARTE DE FRANCE DIVIDEE EN XXXI GOUVERNEMENTS MILITAIRES ... [BOUND WITH 2ND PART] PLANS ET DESCRIPTIONS DES PRINCIPALES PLACES DE GUERRE [1751] 1st part with index map and France on 24 sheets; 2nd part with general map shows fortresses, text, etc. on 9 double pages and 7 pairs of single pages. Quarto. Modern binding. [53] £550 $847

JUTA
JUTA'S MAP OF SOUTH AFRICA FROM THE CAPE TO THE ZAMBESI [c. 1899] Capetown & E. Stanford, London. Dissected, mounted on linen, marbled edges with case. 89x119cm (35x47") Color. Sl rubbed case with library number; sl edge soiling, separating at fold; bright, clean. [7] £146 $225

KAEMPFER
CARTE DU COURS DE LA RIVIERE DE MEINAM DEPUIS JUDIA JUSQU'A SON EMBOUCHURE [1733] From Ayutthaya (former capital) through Bangkok to delta. 31x19cm (12x7½") Exc. [63] £292 $450
URBS NANGASAKI CUM PORTO & AGRO CIRCUMJACENTI. EX IPSIS JAPONUM MAPPIS DESCRIPSIT & E KOEMPFERI OBSERVATIONIBUS ILLUSTRATAM SISTU J.G. SCHEUCHZER [1727] Scheuchzer's map after Kaempfer's sketch. 32x47cm (12½x18½") Exc. Ref: Walter (Japan) p.200. [63] £422 $650

KELLER
CARTE DE LA SUISSE EN 8 FEUILLES ... [1839] German title also. Folding map mounted on linen in sections. 117x175cm (45½x69") Andriveau-Goujon label on verso. Orig OL color. Some faint creases; marbled folder edges worn. [28] £175 $270
H. KELLER'S KEILCHARTE DER SCHWEIS, CARTE ROUTIERE DE LA SUISSE, ROAD MAP OF SWITZERLAND [1834] Dissected into 12 panels, folded into 8vo case. 51x66cm (19½x26") OL color. Case split, sl soiled; Ex lib penciled numbers; "Keller" blind stamp, map near fine. [7] £159 $245

KELLY
BRITISH COLONIES IN NORTH AMERICA [1815] To Rockies. 19x25cm (7½x9½") Uncol. [36] £29 $45

KEUR
ORBIS TERRARUM TABULA RECENS EMENDATA ET IN LUCEM EDITA [1682] Double hemi; insular Calif. Resembles Visscher; astronomical diagrams replace polar circles. 36x47cm (14x18½") Orig color. Ref: Shirley (W) 513. [16] £2,659 $4,096

KIEPERT
AEQUATORIAL-OST-AFRIKA [1892] From *Deutscher Kolonial-Atlas fur den Amtlichen Gebrauch*. 61x78cm (24x30½") Orig OL color. Orig folds visible. [53] £220 $339

KINCAID, A.
PALESTINE OR THE HOLY LAND [1791] J. Fraser, sc. Exodus route. 20x15cm (8½x5½") Col. [23] £26 $40

KINO
UN PASSAGGIO PAR TERRA A CALIFORNIA SCOPERTA DAL P. EUSEBIO KINO [c. 1720] Unidentified Italian copyist. 23x20cm (9x7½") Uncolored. [52] £340 $524

KIRCHER
[MEXICO: MEXICO CITY TO GULF] [1678] From *Mundus Subterraneous*. Lakes with tunnel connectors to Gulf. 14x8cm (5½x3½") Uncolored. Fine. [32] £62 $95

CHOROGRAPHIA ORIGINIS NILI ... [1652] Southern Africa & Nile source notions. 2 out of 3 orig maps on a sheet, each 19x17cm (7½x6½") Exc. Ref: Tooley (Africa) p.64. [62] £146 $225

SYSTEMA IDEALE PYROPHYLACIORUM SUBTERRANEORUM, QUORUM MONTES VULCANII VELUTI SPIRACULA QUEDAM EXISTANT [1678] From ... *Mundus Subterraneus* .... 33x41cm (13x16") Uncolored. Corner margin repair; VG. [30] £260 $400

TABULA QUA HYDROPHYLACIUM ANDIUM EXHIBETUR, QUO UNIVERSA AMERICA AUSTRALIS INNUMERIS FLUVIIS LACUBUS Q. IRRIGATUR [same date & source] 34x20cm (13½x8") Uncol. Fine. [32] £211 $325

TYPUS COMMUNICATIONIS MARIS CASPII, CUM PERSICO ET EUXINO [1678] Show "subterranean channels". 18x15cm (6½x6½") on text sheet. Wash color. [57] £39 $60

KITCHIN Try *London Magazine*

A NEW & ACCURATE MAP OF CHINA ... [c. 1760] 34x41cm (13½x16") [14] £91 $140

A NEW AND CORRECT MAP OF SCOTLAND ... [1783] Attribution uncertain. 28x23cm (11x8½") Old OL color. Deacidified; good. [21] £62 $95

A NEW CHART OF THE RIVER ST. LAWRENCE FROM THE ISLAND OF ANTICOSTI TO LAKE ONTARIO [c. 1760] Insets. 18x25cm (7x10") Color. [40] £75 $116

A NEW MAP OF THE BRITISH DOMINIONS IN NORTH AMERICA WITH THE LIMITS OF THE GOVERNMENTS ANNEXED THERETO BY THE LATE TREATY OF PEACE AND SETTLED BY PROCLAMATION OCT. 7, 1763 [c. 1763] For "History of the War in the Annual Register". 24x31cm (9½x12") Uncolored. Tape repaired fold tear. Ref: Jolly ANNREG-3. [36] £211 $325

A NEW MAP OF THE KINGDOM OF POLAND WITH ITS DISMEMBERED PROVINCES [c. 1789+] 47x64cm (18½x25") OL color. [42] £90 $139

AN ACCURATE CHART OF THE WORLD WITH THE NEW DISCOVERIES [1783] Cook's discoveries; Botany Harbour marked. 31x44cm (12½x17½") Orig color. [16] £522 $804

AN ACCURATE MAP OF THE SEAT OF WAR IN THE KINGDOM OF PRUSSIA AS ALSO IN BOHEMIA, LUSATIA, SILESIA, SAXONY WESTPHALIA &C. BY THO: KITCHIN GEOGR. [1763] (possibly later ed, c. 1790) 20x23cm (8x9") Uncolored. Orig narrow margins; exc. Ref: Jolly ANNREG-1 [29] £23 $36

ASIA DRAWN FROM THE LATEST AND BEST AUTHORITES [c. 1790] 33x36cm (13x14") Uncolored. Repaired chip at lf neat line; half rt margin trimmed close; fold creases & margins reinforced; good. [29] £23 $36

EUROPE DIVIDED INTO ITS EMPIRES, KINGDOMS, STATES REPUBLICS, &C. ... [1795] London: Laurie & Whittle. Joined northern two sections of 4 sheet map. 53x122cm (21x48") Orig OL color. Margin tears; lt offsetting; few color smudges. Ref: Phillips (A) 3529. [28] £234 $360

ISLAND OF ST. HELENA, BELONGING TO YE ENGLISH EAST INDIA COMPANY [1756] 15x10cm (6x3½") OL color. [57] £26 $40

MAP OF THE GULF OF MEXICO, THE ISLANDS AND COUNTRIES ADJACENT [1778] For Robertson's *History of America*. London: Strahan & Cadell. 33x48cm (12½x19") Uncolored. Fold creases; repaired tear to image on rt; third of lower margin trimmed close. [29] £71 $110

Map of the United States in North America with the British, French and Spanish Dominions Adjoining, According to the Treaty of 1783 [1783] From Raynal, *A Philosophical and Political History of the Settlements ... in the East and West Indies*. 41x50cm (16x19½") B&W. Fold breaks repaired; overall VG. [55] £552 $850

Mexico or New Spain, in Which the Motions of Cortes May Be Traced, for the Rev. Dr. Robertson's History of America ... [1795] 29x38cm (11½x15") Uncolored. Folded as issued; exc. [45] £156 $240

North America Drawn from the Best Authorities ... [c. 1785] 20x25cm (8x9½") Old OL color. [45] £78 $120

North Britain or Scotland Divided into Its Counties ... [1773 / 1778] London: Faden. 69x56cm (27x22") Orig color. Sh tears side margins; lt cartouche offsetting. Ref: Royal Scot p.197. [28] £221 $340

KNOX

Map of the Basin of the Firth of Forth [c.1860] Edinburgh: Anderson & Hunter; Chas. Thomson, sc. Linen mounted case map. 66x81cm (25½x31½") Full color. Case fair; map good. [21] £114 $175

LA HONTAN

Ataque de Quebec [1705] 11x17cm (4x6½") [14] £62 $95

Attack of Quebec [1703] English ed. 10x16cm (4x6½") Minor margin restoration. [14] £62 $95

Carte Generale de Canada Dediee au Roy de Denemark par ... Lahontan [1705] East coast to Mississippi, with Great Lakes. 41x55cm (16½x21½") [14] £1,136 $1,750

Carte que les Guacsitares Ont Dessine sur ... Carte de la Riviere Longue et de Quelques Autres [1705] 28x66cm (11x26") Ref: Sabin 38642. [14] £617 $950

LA PEROUSE

Carte des Cotes de l'Amerique et de l'Asie depuis la Californie jusqu' a Macaoe. d'Apres les Decouvertes Faites en 1786-7 par les Fregates Francaises la Boussole et l'Astrolabe en 1786 [1797] From *Atlas du Voyage de la Perouse*. 50x68cm (20x27") Margin dampstains; some offsetting. Ref: Wagner (NW) 839; Phillips (A) 688. [28] £438 $675

Carte du Grand Ocean ou Mer du Sud [1797] 50x69cm (19½x27") Color. Ref: Tooley (Australia) 834. [16] £522 $804

Carte ... Iles Sandwich ... [1797] From *Atlas du Voyage de la Perouse*. Two maps: Cook above; La Perouse's additions below. 48x36cm (19½x14½") Color. Hint of offsetting & waterstain; few margin tears; very nice. [1] £390 $600

[Same Title] [n.d.] Cook version of Hawaii (only upper map of two on sheet). (no dims.) Full color. Lower margin added; fine. [1] £211 $325

Carte Particuliere de la Cote du Nord-Ouest de l'Amerique Reconnue par les Fregates Francaises la Boussole et l'Astrolabe en 1786. 1e Feuille [1797] From *Atlas du Voyage de la Perouse*. Mt. St. Elias to Graham I. 49x69cm (19½x27") Paper flaws below upper border & lower margin. 2nd sheet, Graham I. to Tillamook Head, in same condition, offered at same price. Ref: Wagner (NW) 841; Phillips (A) 688; Falk (AK) 1797-9. [28] £409 $630

Chart of Discoveries Made in 1787, in the Seas of China and Tartary between Manilla and Avatcha ... [1798] Centered on Japan. 50x38cm (19½x15") Exc. Ref: cf Cortazzi pl.62. [62] £227 $350

Chart of Part of the North West Coast of America Explored by the Boussole & Astrolabe Laid Down Conformably to the Situation of the Boussole Every Day at Noon as Determined Astronomically by Mr. Dagelet [1798] Monterey to St. Elias Mountains. 50x38cm (19½x15") Exc. [62] £250 $385

[Same Title] [1798] by Dagelet. 49x38cm (19x15") Little browned. [14] £62 $95

Chart of the Discoveries, Made in 1787, in the Seas of China and Tartary by the Boussole and Astrolabe, from Their Leaving Manilla, to Their Arrival at Kamtschatka. Sheet 1 [1798] Philippines to Taiwan to Sea of Japan. 38x50cm (15x19½") Exc. [63] £185 $285

Chart of the North West Coast of America, Explored by the Boussole & Astrolabe in 1786. 3d Sheet [1798] Monterey to Columbia River. 39x50cm (15x19½") Exc. [62] £276 $425

Part of the Great Pacific Ocean Shewing the Route of the Spanish Frigate La Princesa ... in 1781 [1798] With NE Australia. 25x38cm (9½x15") Exc. [62] £114 $175

Plan de l'Entree du Port de Bucarelli sur la Cote du Nord Ouest de l'Amerique par 55°15' de Latitude Nord ... [1797] From *Atlas du Voyage de la Perouse*. 50x69cm (20x27") Repaired fold tears; sm holes mostly blank areas. Ref: Wagner (NW) 841; Phillips (A) 688; Falk (AK) 1797-12. [28] £351 $540

PLAN DE LA BAIE DE MONTEREY SITUEE DANS LA CALIFORNIE SEPTENTRIONALE ... [1797] 34x49cm (13½x19½") Later color. [51] £308 $475
PLAN OF PORT ST. FRANCISCO IN CALIFORNIA ... [1798] London: G.G. & J. Robinson. 36x24cm (14x9½") [14] £185 $285
PLAN OF PORT ST. FRANCISCO, IN CALIFORNIA / POINT DE REYES IN 37°59' OF LATITUDE NORTH ... [1798] 36x24cm (14x9½") Exc. [62] £302 $465
PLAN OF THE BAY OF MONTEREY SITUATE IN NORTH CALIFORNIA IN 36°38' OF LATITUDE NORTH, ... [1798] Carmel to Santa Cruz. 25x37cm (10x14½") Exc. [62] £227 $350
PLAN OF THE PORT OF S. DIEGO IN CALIFORNIA SITUATE IN 32°39'0" LATITUDE NORTH & 12°4'0" EST O ST. BLAS FROM A SURVEY IN 1782 [ON SHEET WITH] PLAN OF THE PORT & DEPARTMENT OF S. BLAS SITUATE IN 21°30 OF LATITUDE NTH. ... LATITUDE NTH. ... FROM A SURVEY IN NOVEMBER 1777 [1798] La Perouse's voyages; English ed. 36x24cm (14x9½") [14] £88 $135
[SAME TITLE] [same date & dimen] Exc. [62] £227 $350
VIEW OF MACAO IN CHINA [1798] London: G.G. & J. Robinson. 20x30cm (8x12") Good. [14] £65 $100

LAFITAU

CITADELLE DE DIU [INDIA] [1733] Bird's eye view, with scene of Sultan Badur's death. 19x14cm (7½x5½") [14] £32 $50
L'ISLE DE MOSAMBIQUE [ON SHEET WITH] SOFALA [1734] 19x14cm (7½x5½") Folds. [14] £39 $60
L'ISLE ET VILLE DE GOA [1734] 14x19cm (5½x7½") Folds. [14] £39 $60
LA VILLE DE CALICUT [1733] Bird's eye view; Vasca de Gama portrait. 19x14cm (7½x5½") [14] £55 $85
LA VILLE DE COCHIN [ON SHEET WITH] LA VILLE CANANOR [1734] Plan & view. 19x14cm (7½x5½") Folds. [14] £49 $75
LA VILLE DE DAMAN [INDIA] [1733] Bird's eye view; Bragance portrait. 19x14cm (7½x5½") [14] £39 $60
LA VILLE DE MALACA [1733] Bird's eye view; de Castro portrait. 19x14cm (7½x5½") [14] £55 $85
MAPPE-MONDE POUR SERVIR A L'HISTOIRE DES DECOUVERTES ET CONQUESTS DES PORTUGAIS DANS LE NOUVEAU-MONDE [1734] Oval map. 24x45cm (9½x18") [14] £308 $475

LAFRERI SCHOOL   Try *Gastaldi*

... PORTUUM OSTIENSIUM ORTHOGRAPHIA ... [1575 - c.1615] J. De Rubeis. 2-sheet classical Ostia plan. 41x70cm (16x27½") Uncolored. [52] £500 $770

LANGE

BAI SAN FRANCISCO UND VEREINIGUNG DES SACRAMENTO MIT DEM SAN JOAQUIN [1854] Henry Lange. 210x27cm (82½x10½") plus title. [62] £162 $250

LANGENES

ARACAM [1598] 1st state, 1st issue. Burma. 9x13cm (3½x5") Exc. [63] £130 $200
MALACCA [1598] 1st state, 1st issue; lacks longitude marking at top & equator. 9x13cm (3½x5") Exc. [63] £250 $385

LAPIE

CARTE DE L'AMERIQUE SEPTENTRIONALE [1841] Texas Republic in sm form. 55x40cm (21½x15½") Some foxing. [11] £146 $225
CARTE DES ETATS UNIS D'AMERIQUE [1837] Texas Republic in sm form. 39x53cm (15½x21") OL color. Water marks to border. [12] £227 $350
CARTE DES ETATS-UNIS DU MEXIQUE [1829] With present U.S. Southwest & CA; Central America inset. 54x39cm (21½x15½") OL col. Sl browning one edge; publisher's blind stamp; o/w clean. [10] £256 $395
[SAME TITLE] [same date & dimen] OL color. [56] £195 $300
[SAME TITLE] [1841] Texas as republic. [same dimen] OL color. Couple minor spots. [10] £211 $325

LAPORTE

CARTE DU ROYAUME D'IRLANDE [1781] From *Atlas Moderne Portatif*. 18x23cm (7x8½") Color. Ref: Phillips (A) 654. [24] £71 $110

LASO

PENINSULA DEL INDO DE ESTA PARTE DEL GOLFO DEL GANGES [ON SHEET WITH] PENINSULA DEL INDO DE LA OTRA PARTE DEL GOLFO DEL GANGES [1711] From *El Atlas Abreviado*. Madrid. 13x16cm (5½x6") Close upper margin; o/w fine. [14] £29 $45

LATTRE   Try *Bonne, Janvier, Rizzi-Zannoni*

CARTE DE L'ARABIE [1771 - 1783] From *Atlas Moderne* .... Paris: Lattre & Delalain. 30x43cm (12x17") Orig OL color. Ref: Phillips (A) 646. [59] £32 $50

CARTE DE L'EGYPTE ANCIENNE ET MODERNE [same date, source & reference] 43x30cm (17x12") Orig OL color. [59] £32 $50

CARTE DE L'EMPIRE DE PERSE [same date, source & reference] 30x43cm (12x17") Orig OL col. [59] £32 $50

CARTE DE L'EMPIRE DE RUSSIE EN EUROPE ET EN ASIE [same date, source, dimen & reference] Orig OL color. [59] £26 $40

CARTE GENERALE DE FRANCE DIVISEE PAR GOUVERNEMENTS [same date, source, dimen & reference] Orig OL color. [59] £32 $50

CARTE HYDRO-GEO-GRAPHIQUE DES INDIES ORIENTALES ... [1771] By Rigobert Bonne. 4 sheets joined. 57x80cm (22½x31½") Orig OL color. Sl wear along one join. [53] £280 $431

LAURENT

CARTE DU GROENLAND [1770] From David Cranz, *The History of Greenland*, Fr ed. 20x25cm (7½x10") B&W. [46] £23 $35

LAURIE & WHITTLE   Try *D'Anville, Dunn, Jefferys*

[ATLAS] A COMPLETE BODY OF ANCIENT GEOGRAPHY [1804] 13 maps: after D'Anville (10), De L'Isle (2) & Horsley (1); 12 on 28x21" sheets. Colored boarders. Modern paper boards; end papers present; lib stamp title page verso; maps age-toned, clean & sharp. [9] £325 $500

[PHILIPPINES: SORGOSON BAY; BONGO BAY] [1794] 2 plans on one sheet. After van Keulen; 1st pub Sayer & Bennett, 1778. 51x25cm (19½x9½") Sl damp spotting in margin. [15] £80 $123

... NEW & CORRECT CHART OF SPITHEAD, FROM THE EAST END OF HAYLING ISLAND TO STOKES BAY ... [1801] Owen, 1800. 76x61cm (30x24") Offsetting; o/w good. [15] £450 $693

A CHART OF THE CHOPS OF THE CHANNEL TO THE SOUTH OF SCILLY ISLANDS; CONTAINING THE WEST COAST OF CORNWALL, AND SCILLY ISLANDS, CORRECTED FROM THE SURVEY MADE BY ORDER OF THE TRINITY HOUSE 1795 [1795] Lizard to Cape Cornwall; 7 profiles. 51x69cm (20x27") Sl staining at extreme blank corners. [15] £140 $216

A CHART OF THE COAST OF DEVONSHIRE FROM EXMOUTH TO RAME HEAD; CONTAINING TOR BAY, START BAY, PLYMOUTH SOUND, &CA. [1799] William Price. 9 large insets with profiles. Superseded in 1800. 64x79cm (25x31") Lt offsetting; narrow upper & lower margins; o/w VG. [15] £420 $647

A CHART OF THE DOWNS WITH THE FLATS OF THE NORTH AND SOUTH FORELANDS ... FROM THE OBSERVATIONS &C. OF THE TRINITY-HOUSE PILOTS AND SURVEYORS [1796] 1st version, 1779. 53x71cm (20½x27½") [15] £260 $400

A CHART OF THE GULF OF PERSIA FROM BASRA TO CAPE ROSALGATE ... [1794] Based on 1761 Danish expedition & d'Apres de Mannevillette. 48x71cm (18½x27½") Offsetting & browning; o/w good. [15] £280 $431

A CHART OF THE ISLE, ROADS, AND RACE OF PORTLAND WITH THE SHAMBLES &C. [1794] Reissue of 1779 Sayer & Bennett. 51x71cm (20x27½") Offsetting. [15] £85 $131

A CHART OF THE RED SEA FROM MOKA TO GEDDAH ... [1794] Southern part. After d'Apres de Mannevillette; 1st pub by Sayer & Bennett, 1781. 48x66cm (19x25½") [15] £185 $285

A CHART OF THE WEST AND SOUTH WEST COAST OF IRELAND, FROM THE MOUTH OF THE RIVER SHANNON TO WATERFORD HAVEN ON THE SAME SCALE AS THE CHART OF ST. GEORGES CHANNEL BY CAPT. JOS. HUDDART [1795] First pub Sayer & Bennett, 1786. 79x127cm (31x50") Lt offsetting; sm fold tear repair, no loss. [15] £180 $277

A CORRECT CHART OF THE TERRAQUEOUS GLOBE ON WHICH ARE DESCRIBED LINES SHEWING THE VARIATION OF THE MAGNETIC NEEDLE ... BY THE CELEBRATED DR. EDMUND HALLEY; RENEWED BY WILLIAM MOUNTAINE AND JAMES DODSON ... 1756 ... [1794] Mercator projection between 60 degrees N. & S., with isogonic lines; side text panels. 53x142cm (21x55½") [15] £800 $1,232

A NEW AND ACCURATE PLAN OF LONDON ... [1798] Dissected; laid down on linen. 43x58cm (17x23") Partial color. Some staining; good. [21] £71 $110

A NEW AND CORRECT MAP OF SCOTLAND OR NORTH BRITAIN WITH ALL THE POST AND MILITARY ROADS, DIVISIONS ... [1794] After Sayer, 1790; Lt. Robert Campbell. 4 sheets joined to form two, each 64x107cm (25x42") Orig OL color. Folds, nearby creases; dampmarks southern part; sh margin tear; lt offsetting. Ref: Royal Scot p.203 n. [28] £438 $675

A NEW CHART OF THE COAST OF BRAZIL FROM THE BANKS OF ST. ROQUE, TO THE ISLAND OF ST. SEBASTIAN ... [1794] In *East India Pilot*. 86x58cm (34x22½") Browning & offsetting; o/w VG. [15] £180 $277

A NEW CHART OF THE COAST OF DORSETSHIRE AND DEVONSHIRE FROM ST. ALBAN'S HEAD TO SIDMOUTH ... [1799] In later ed *East India Pilot*. William Price. 64x81cm (25x31½") Some offsetting; narrow upper to lower margins due to size. [15] £120 $185

A NEW CHART OF THE ISLANDS OF SCILLY WITH THEIR SOUNDINGS CHANNELS AND SAILING MARKS [1794] 1st pub Sayer & Bennett, 1779. 51x66cm (19½x26½") C'fold creasing; lt surface soiling; extensive tears repaired; replacement just within rt engraved area. [15] £200 $308

A NEW MAP OF THE WORLD WITH CAPT. COOK'S TRACKS, HIS DISCOVERIES AND THOSE OF THE OTHER NAVIGATORS [1800] 48x71cm (19x28") Orig color. [16] £1,424 $2,194

A PLAN OF TABLE BAY, WITH THE ROAD OF THE CAPE OF GOOD HOPE ... [1794] Orig pub by Sayer & Bennett, after van Keulen. 48x56cm (19x21½") Sl browning at edges; generally good. Ref: Tooley (Africa) p.63. [15] £300 $462

AFRICA WITH ALL ITS STATES, KINGDOMS, REPUBLICS, REGIONS, ISLANDS &C. IMPROVED AND INLARGED FROM D'ANVILLE'S MAP: TO WHICH HAVE BEEN ADDED A PARTICULAR CHART OF THE GOLD COAST, WHEREIN ARE DISTINGUISHED ALL THE EUROPEAN FORTS AND FACTORIES [1800] S. Bolton. 4 sheets joined in two pairs. 102x122cm (40x48") Orig OL color. Good. [14] £292 $450

AMERICA DIVIDED INTO NORTH AND SOUTH WITH THEIR SEVERAL SUBDIVISIONS AND THE NEWEST DISCOVERIES [1800] 50x54cm (19½x21") Color. Sl creased. [14] £146 $225

AN ACCURATE CHART OF THE BAY OF BISCAY ... [1794] Sounding lines. 71x99cm (28x39") [15] £140 $216

AN ACTUAL SURVEY OF THE COAST OF KENT FROM DIM CHURCH TO RYE HARBOUR WITH THE NEW SHOAL TO THE WESTWARD OF DUNGENESS [1794] Reissue of Sayer & Bennett, 1787. 48x69cm (19½x27½") [15] £100 $154

AN ACTUAL SURVEY OF VARNE, & RIDGE ... [1793, 1794] Christopher Collins survey at Dover Strait. 51x69cm (20x27") Dampmarking extreme upper corners; o/w VG. [15] £90 $139

AN EYE SKETCH OF THE ENTRANCE OF YEALME RIVER WITH THE DEPTHS OF WATER &C. &C. [1795] Shows tracks of sounding yachts. 48x36cm (18½x14½") [15] £110 $169

AN HYDROGRAPHICAL SURVEY OF THE COAST OF DEVONSHIRE FROM EXMOUTH BAR TO STOKE POINT ... [1794] 1st pub. in Sayer & Bennett, 69x51cm (27x20") Offsetting. [15] £130 $200

CHART OF THE SOUTH CHANNEL FROM PRINCE OF WALES ISLAND TO SEA [1798] In *East India Pilot*. Key to buoys & colors. 61x41cm (24x16") Lt margin damp-marking; a brown mark; overall good. [15] £400 $616

LAURIE AND WHITTLE'S NEW CHART OF THE INDIAN AND PACIFIC OCEANS BETWEEN THE CAPE OF GOOD HOPE, NEW HOLLAND, AND JAPAN ... [1800] Based on Sayer. Numerous printed tracks. 74x109cm (29x43") Mounted on canvas; good, clean. [15] £1,050 $1,617

LAURIE AND WHITTLE'S NEW MAP OF LONDON, WITH ITS ENVIRONS, &C. INCLUDING THE RECENT IMPROVEMENTS [1817] Linen-backed folding map; in self covers. 58x77cm (23x30½") Orig full color. Age toned Ref: Howgego 213(7) [33] £390 $600

PALAESTINA BY MONS. D'ANVILLE OF THE ROYAL ACADEMY ... [1794] Insets. 38x43cm (15½x16½") Color. [23] £81 $125

PLAN OF THE BAYS OF POLKERRIS AND MEVAGIZEY IN CORNWALL [1794] Gribben Head to Gorran Haven. 1st pub, Sayer & Bennett, 1779. 66x47cm (26x18½") Lt dampmarking extreme blank corners; o/w exc. [15] £110 $169

PLAN OF THE ISLAND OF FERNAND DE NORONHA ... [1794] From *East India Pilot*. 48x61cm (19x23½") Offsetting; o/w good. [15] £80 $123

PLAN OF THE PORT OF SUBEC ... SURVEY'D IN THE YEAR 1776 ... [1794] 47x32cm (18½x12½") Sl dampmarking in margin. [15] £80 $123

PLYMOUTH SOUND, HAMOAZE AND CATWATER SURVEYED IN 1797 [1798] Based on Sayer & Bennett, 1779. 71x51cm (28x20½") Some brown offsetting. Ref: Elisabeth Stewart, *Lost Landscapes of Plymouth*. [15] £190 $293

SEVERAL APPEARANCES OF THE AGOADA FORT NEAR THE ISLAND OF GOA ... [1794] In *East India Pilot*. 3 views. 20x33cm (7½x13") [15] £40 $62

THE BAY OF ALGOA ... [ON SHEET WITH] PLAN OF MOSSEL BAY ... [AND] PLAN OF FLESH BAY ... [1794] 3 plans. Orig pub by Sayer & Bennett, after van Keulen. 58x25cm (23x10½") [15] £220 $339

THE BERMUDAS, OR SUMMER'S ISLANDS FROM A SURVEY BY C. LEMPRIERE, REGULATED BY ASTRONOMICAL OBSERVATIONS [1794] 46x61cm (18x24") Pencil sketch of schooner on verso. Sl dust soiling, mainly toward edges; lt fold line. [15] £800 $1,232

THE CAPE VERD ISLANDS ... [1794] After D'Apres de Mannevillette. 53x28cm (21x11½") [15] £45 $69
THE COAST OF INDIA FROM MOUNT DILLY TO PONDICHERRY ... WITH THE ISLAND OF CEYLON [1798] In *East India Pilot*. 58x89cm (23x34½") Offsetting; some browning in margins. [15] £60 $92
THE EMPIRE OF CHINA WITH ITS PRINCIPAL DIVISIONS ... FROM THE MAPS OF M. D'ANVILLE [1794] 48x63cm (19x25") Orig OL color. Exc. [14] £91 $140
THE SOUTH PART OF THE STRAITS OF MALACCA INSCRIBED TO CAPT. G.G. RICHARDSON, BY CAPTN. J. LINDSEY [1798] In *East India Pilot*. Singapore. 46x71cm (17½x27½") Lt browning, mainly in margins; 2 brown marks. [15] £350 $539
THE STRAITS OF SINCAPORE WITH THOSE OF DRION, SABON, MANDOL, &CA AND SOUTH PART OF MALACCA STRAITS. IMPROVED AND CORRECTED FROM THE OBSERVATIONS OF CAPTN. JOHN HALL ... AND OTHER NAVIGATORS [1799] 43x58cm (16½x22½") Brown markings lower ctr. [15] £350 $539
TRACK OF THE CALCUTTA EAST INDIAMAN OVER THE BASSAS DE CHAGAS ... [1794] In *East India Pilot*. 46x56cm (17½x21½") Close lower margin. [15] £90 $139

LAVOISNE

GEOGRAPHICAL AND STATISTICAL MAP OF ITALY [1821] On 17x21" sheet with text surround. 38x33cm (15x13") Color. [45] £52 $80
GEOGRAPHICAL AND STATISTICAL MAP OF SCOTLAND [1821] On 17x21" sheet with text surround. 38x33cm (15x13") Color. [45] £52 $80
GEOGRAPHICAL, HISTORICAL AND STATISTICAL MAP OF AMERICA [1821] From *A Complete Geneological ... and Geographical Atlas* .... 2 maps with surround of text: "North America ...", by E. Paguenaud; "South America ..." by J. Aspin & E. Paguenaud. Printed surface dimensions 46x53cm (17½x21") [61] £81 $125
GEOGRAPHICAL MAP OF THE WORLD ... [1821] Double hemispheres, by C. Gros; text below. 43x53cm (17x21") With world history text pages. Full color. Very nice. [44] £156 $240
[SAME TITLE] [1821] From *A Complete Geneological ... and Geographical Atlas* .... 46x56cm (17½x22") [61] £62 $95

LAW

LOUISIANA BY DE RIVER MISSISIPPI [1720] Accompanied *Het Groote Tafereel der Dwassheid*. Account of "Mississippi Bubble". 19x16cm (7½x6") Mint. [62] £276 $425

LAY

LAY'S MAP OF THE UNITED STATES. COMPILED FROM THE LATEST AND BEST AUTHORITIES AND ACTUAL SURVEYS BY AMOS LAY ... [1828] Wall map; to 100 deg. W. 130x150cm (50½x59") Heavy paper on linen. OL color. Dampstain & mildew at SE; minor cracks & separation near rod; o/w VG. [6] £812 $1,250

LE ROUGE

[ATLAS] PILOTE AMERICAIN 2E PARTIE. TRADUIT DE L'ANGLOIS [1779] 1st French version of Jefferys, *The North American Pilot*. Folio. Uncut in orig boards. Spine chipped, cords strong, corners bumped. Ref: Tooley (M&M) p.114; cf Howes J-84; Sabin 35969. [28] £4,674 $7,200
A MAP OF THE MOST INHABITED PART OF NEW ENGLAND CONTAINING THE PROVINCES OF MASSACHUSETS BAY AND NEW HAMPSHIRE WITH THE COLONIES OF CONECTICUT AND RHODE ISLAND ... AFTER THE ORIGINAL ... 1777 [1777] English ed after Jefferys; also entitled, "La Nouvelle Angleterre en 4 feuilles". Folding map of southern 2 sheets mounted on linen in sections. 51x97cm (20x38") Orig OL color. Rubber stamp upper lf; trace of foxing; faint dampmark upper rt. Ref: Sellers & Van Ee 802. [28] £292 $450
AMERIQUE MERIDIONALE [c. 1750] 21x28cm (8x11") Orig or early full color. Fine. [59] £65 $100
AMERIQUE SUIVANT LE R.P. CHARLEVOIX JTE. MR. DE LA CONDAMINE ... [1746] May be 1st to show Bering's 2nd voyage. 48x64cm (19½x25") Orig OL color. [46] £552 $850
ANTIGUE ... [1748] From *Atlas Nouveau Portatif*. 20x27cm (8x10½") Orig OL color. Exc. [14] £55 $85
ISLE DE LA MARTINIQUE [1748] From *Atlas Nouveau Portatif*. 22x29cm (8½x11½") Orig OL color. Exc. [14] £26 $40
ISLE ST. CHRISTOPHLE UNE DES ANTILLES AUX ANGLOIS. A PARIS. PAR LE SR. LE ROUGE ... [ON SHEET WITH] LA BARBADE UNE DES ANTILLES AUX ANGLOIS DIVISEE PAR PAROISSES [1748] From *Atlas Nouveau Portatif*. 27x20cm (10½x8") Orig OL color. Exc. [14] £97 $150
[SAME TITLE] [1748] 27x20cm (11x8") Orig OL color. [54] £170 $262
ISLES DE LA SONDE [1748] From *Atlas Nouveau Portatif*. East Indies. 22x29cm (8½x11½") Orig OL color. Exc. [14] £81 $125
L'ESPAGNE SUIVANT LES NOUVELLES OBSERVATIONS [1748] 20x26cm (7½x10") Color. [14] £26 $40

L'Irelande [1756] From *Atlas Nouveau*. Paris: Chez Perault. 28x20cm (11x8½") Ref: Phillips (A) 5983, 12. [24] £88 $135

L'Isle de Terre Neuve [1778] After Cook & Lane 1769 surveys. 53x53cm (21x21") C'fold split & 1" tear joined; o/w fine. [14] £552 $850

La Basse Austriche ... [1743] 20x26cm (8x10") Orig OL color. [54] £65 $100

La Guadeloupe ... [1753] 47x54cm (18½x21½") Orig OL color. [52] £300 $462

La Jamaique aux Anglois dans le Golfe du Mexique a Paris. Chez le Sr. Le Rouge 1746 [on sheet with] La Bermude aux Anglois ... [1746] 20x27cm (8x10½") Orig OL col. [54] £420 $647

La Savoye ... [1743] 20x26cm (8x10") Orig OL color. [54] £75 $116

La Scandinavie ou la Suede et Danemark ... [c. 1743-1748] 20x26cm (8x10") Orig OL color. [54] £85 $131

La Suisse ... [1746] 20x26cm (8x10") Orig OL color. [54] £100 $154

Le Cercle d'Austriche ... [1743] 20x26cm (8x10") Orig OL color. [54] £65 $100

[same title] [1748] 20x26cm (8x10½") Orig OL color. [14] £36 $55

Le Royaume de Hongrie ... [1743] 20x26cm (8x10") Orig OL color. [54] £60 $92

Le Tirol [1748] 21x28cm (8½x11") Orig OL color. [14] £29 $45

Les Virges, Levees par les Anglais, et par les Danois Traduit de l'Anglais [1779] After Jefferys. 46x36cm (18x13½") Color. [27] £1,201 $1,850

Mappe-Monde qui Comprend les Nouvelles Decouvertes Faites Jusqua ce Jour [1748] Based on van der Aa. 22x30cm (8½x12") Color. [16] £783 $1,207

Nouvelle Carte des Cotes des Carolines ... du Cap Fear a Sud Edisto [1777] Compiled by N. Pocock; French ed. 41x54cm (16x21") Uncolored. [52] £1,200 $1,848

Partie des Cotes de Labrador depuis le Cap Charles a la Baye de Sandwich ... par M. Lane. Publie a Londres en 1777 [1778] In *Pilote Americain*. After Jefferys. One of pair; complete by itself. 48x56cm (19½x22") Ref: Phillips (A) 1210; cf. Sellers & Van Ee 691. [28] £467 $720

Partie Orientale du Canada Traduitte de l'Anglois de la Carte de Jefferys ... [1755+] 46x60cm (18x23½") Separately printed. Orig OL color. [14] £974 $1,500

Port de Halifax de la Nouvelle Ecosse avec les Recifs, Dangers, Bas Fonds et Sondes ... [1778] As in *Pilote Americain*. French ed of chart by Charles Morris in Jefferys *North American Pilot*. 48x56cm (19½x22½") Ref: Sellers & Van Ee 465; Phillips (A) 1210. [28] £497 $765

Porte de Louisbourg [c. 1758] 51x60cm (20x23½") Some wear at top & bottom margins; creasing near c'fold. [60] £1,136 $1,750

Ruatan or Rattan ... [1779] After Jefferys, 1775. Inset: Providencia Island, Colombia. 46x61cm (18x24") Early OL color. Repaired worming on c'fold; sm margin fold split. [15] £120 $185

LEIGH

Urania's Mirror or a View of the Heavens [c. 1830] S. Leigh. Card set with pin holes showing star positions. Each 14x20cm (5½x8") Orig color. In orig box; lacks orig booklet. [52] £950 $1,463

LEVASSEUR

Amerique Meridional [1847+] Surround of scenes. 28x43cm (11x16½") Orig wash col. [14] £49 $75

Amerique Septentrionale [c. 1840] Pictorial surround. Texas as Republic. 32x45cm (12½x17½") Orig full color on map. Fine. [63] £146 $225

[same title] [c. 1845] Texas as Republic. 30x46cm (12x18") OL color. Exc. [44] £130 $200

[same title] [1849] Texas as Republic. 29x44cm (11½x17") Orig wash color. [14] £97 $150

[same title] [c. 1850] 30x46cm (12x17½") OL color. VG. [61] £179 $275

Oceanie [(1838) 1854] Decorative surround. 28x41cm (11x16½") Color & orig OL color. Ref: Tooley (Australia) 860. [16] £133 $205

LIZARS

Europe [1853] 14x15cm (5½x6") + vignettes. Orig OL color. [14] £19 $30

Map of Part of N.S.W. [and] Map of Van Dieman's Land [(1821) 1824] 2 views. 30x46cm (12x18") Orig OL color. Ref: Tooley (Australia) NSW 37, T 335 pl.213. [16] £199 $307

United States & Texas. With all the Railways & Canals [c. 1840] TX in sm form. 41x52cm (16x20½") Orig OL color. [54] £350 $539

LLOYD

KANSAS AND THE TERRITORIES OF ARIZONA, COLORADO, NEW MEXICO, UTAH AND INDIAN TERRITORY [1872] NY: H.H. Lloyd. 41x64cm (16x25") Orig full color. Image fine; overall good+. Ref: Phillips (A) 2346. Ristow (Amer M&M) pp 429-30. [59] £97 $150

LLOYD'S NEW MAP OF THE UNITED STATES, THE CANADAS AND NEW BRUNSWICK ... SHOWING EVERY RAILROAD & STATION FINISHED TO JUNE 1862 ... [1863] Wall map. J.T. Lloyd & Co., NY. 94x124cm (36½x49") Full color. Stiff paper, spring rolls shut; transparent tape repaired margin tears top & bottom; damp stained above. [6] £185 $285

LLOYD'S TOPOGRAPHICAL RAILWAY MAP OF NORTH-AMERICA OR THE UNITED STATES CONTINENT IN 1900 [1900] Wall map. Copyright J.T. Lloyd, 1866; pub E. Lloyd, 1874. Casual updating. 152x145cm (60x57") Full col. Damp staining, wrinkling, occas surface cracks; separation from upper rod; o/w VG. [6] £211 $325

MAP OF THE PROVINCE OF MANITOBA ... [1878] H.H. Lloyd; D. Laird; London: H.B. Walker. 45x62cm (17½x24½") Close margins top & bottom as issued. [14] £227 $350

PLAN OF THE PART OF THE ISTHMUS OF PANAMA ELIGIBLE FOR EFFECTING A COMMUNICATION BETWEEN THE ATLANTIC & PACIFIC [c. 1840] J.A. Lloyd, London. 45x40cm (17½x15½") [14] £39 $60

LOBINEAU

PLAN DE PARIS ... [1726] D.M. Felibien. Locations referenced at sides. 61x84cm (24x33½") Full color. Some folds reinforced; else exc. [39] £974 $1,500

LOCAL & STATE GOVERNMENT

MAP OF WATER REGION ADJACENT TO CHARLESTOWN & CHELSEA SHOWING ROUTE OF THE CHARLESTOWN WATER WORKS [1865] Boston north suburban area. 56x41cm (22x16") Uncolored. [44] £32 $50

RAILROAD MAP OF NEW MEXICO [1913] Linen mounted, folds into 8x6" printed boards. Depots & distances between. 91x97cm (36x38") Color coded RR's. Minor fold junction separations; generally VG. [9] £373 $575

LOCAL & STATE MAPS - Infrequent Publishers

CASTER'S MAP 70 MILES AROUND PETERBOROUGH [ENGLAND] [c. 1890] Peterborough: Geo. Caster. Folding road map in oil cloth pictorial cover. 69x84cm (27x33½") Partial color. VG. [21] £36 $55

GRANGER'S MAP OF BIRMINGHAM [ENGLAND] [c. 1860] Pocket map folds into wrapper. 38x51cm (15x20") No color. Little dusty; map fine. [21] £49 $75

PLAN DE A FORET DE COMPIEGNE ED DE SES ENVIRONS. [LEVE EN 1772. PAR ORDRES ET AUX FRAIS DE M. PANNELIER D'ANNEL ...] [1820] Paris: J. Goujon. Linen-backed. Royal forest near Oise River. 56x76cm (22x30") Uncolored. [33] £308 $475

PLAN OF THE GROUNDS AND BUILDINGS OF THE CENTENNIAL EXHIBITION, AT PHILADELPHIA [1875] Chromolithograph. Creased, folded; staining on verso; VG. 44x59cm (17x23") With uncolored, 40x30 cm "Reference Map of a Portion of Philadelphia Showing the Principal Points of Interest"; narrow margins, stain on verso. [33] £49 $75

TOPOGRAPHICAL AND DRAINAGE MAP OF NEW ORLEANS AND SURROUNDINGS FROM RECENT SURVEYS AND INVESTIGATIONS [1879] T.S. Hardee; New Orleans: F.S. Hansell, J.A. Greshem. Note on yellow fever epidemic pursuant to "focus of infection" theory. 56x56cm (22x22") Laid down, restored; few sm holes & losses; browned; fair. [20] £487 $750

LOCAL & STATE WALL MAPS - Infrequent Publishers

MAP OF BURLINGTON IN VERMONT [1836] J. Johnson. Burlington: J.H. Hopkins, Jr. Insets: Downtown; Winooski. 61x81cm (24x32") Color. Cleaned, rebacked on acid-free linen, restored, sl loss; o/w VG. Ref: Cobb (VT) 220. [8] £698 $1,075

MAP OF BURLINGTON, VERMONT [1853] Presdee & Edwards, NY. Lots with names or function; views in upper & lower margins. 104x79cm (41x31") Color. Cleaned, rebacked on acid-free linen, restored, sl loss; VG. Ref: Cobb (VT) 275. [8] £448 $690

MAP OF JOHNSON COUNTY IA [1902] Iowa City: The Iowa Citizen. Cadastral map. 122x91cm (48x36") Full color. 2 sm holes; soiling, occas stain at upper rail; clean. [6] £71 $110

MAP OF WINDSOR COUNTY VERMONT FROM ACTUAL SURVEYS [1855] Hosea Doton; Pomfret, VT (only known map). Cadastral map; 29 insets, 10 views. 137x112cm (54x44") OL color. Honey toned; wrinkled; sl margin stain & 1" sq surface loss at bottom. [6] £276 $425

LODGE

An Exact Map of the Province of Quebec with Part of New York & New England from the Latest Surveys [1778] 21x27cm (8½x10½") OL color. [51] £179 $275

The British Channel Including the Coasts of England and France [1786] From John Andrews, *History of the Late War*. 18x30cm (6½x11½") OL color. Transferral; VG. [21] £29 $45

LOGEROT

Paris Illustre et Ses Fortifications [1854] Linen-backed folding map in orig slipcase. 55x72cm (21½x28½") Partial wash & highlight color. VG+. [33] £260 $400

LONDON MAGAZINE

A Map of Bohemia Being the Present Seat of War in Germany. [1756] 17x23cm (6½x9") B&W. Ref: Jolly LOND-110 [46] £16 $25

A Map of the Five Great Lakes with Part of Pensilvania, New York, Canada and Hudsons Bay Territories &c. [1755] 21x26cm (8½x10½") Uncolored. Ref: Jolly LOND-97; Phillips (M) p.575. [36] £179 $275

A Map of the Passage of the Moons Shadow over England, &c. in the Annular Eclipse of the Sun, Which Will Happen April 1t. 1764. [1764] 20x16cm (8x6") Ref: Jolly LOND-234 [58] £49 $75

A Map of the Province of Pensilvania Drawn from the Best Authorities by T. Kitchin Gr. [1756] 15x22cm (5½x8½") Uncolored. Ref: Jolly LOND-112 [56] £146 $225

A Map of the Seat of War in Bavaria and Bohemia. By Thos. Kitchin Senr. Hydrographer to His Majesty. [1778] 24x19cm (9½x7½") OL color. Ref: Jolly LOND-325 [58] £42 $65

A Map of the Seat of War in the Western Part of the Kingdom of Poland. By T. Kitchin Geogr. [1759] 23x18cm (9x7") B&W. Ref: Jolly LOND-171 [46] £16 $25

A Map of the Western Parts of the Colony of Virginia. [1754] 19x12cm (7½x5") Uncolored. Ref: Jolly LOND-85 [54] £200 $308

A New and Accurate Map of East and West Florida Drawn from the Best Authorities. [1765] 18x22cm (7x9") Modern color. Ref: Jolly LOND-243 [35] £162 $250

[Same Title] [same date & dimen] B&W. Exc. [49] £192 $295

A New Chart of the River St. Lawrence from the Island of Anticosti to Lake Ontario by T. Kitchin, Geogr. [1759] 18x26cm (7x10") Uncolored. VG. Ref: Jolly LOND-174 [59] £49 $75

A New Chart of the Vast Atlantic Ocean; Exhibiting the Seat of War, Both in Europe and America, Likewise the Trade Winds & Course of Sailing from One Continent to the Other; with the Banks Shoals and Rocks: Drawn According to the Latest Discoveries ... [1755] E. Bowen, sc. 31x43cm (12x16½") Narrow lf margin; Clean, bright. Ref: Jolly LOND-98 [36] £162 $250

A New Map of the Cherokee Nation with the Names of the Towns & Rivers. They Are Situated on No. Lat. from 34 to 36. [1760] 17x22cm (6½x8½") B&W. Some creasing; else VG. Ref: Jolly LOND-183 [55] £325 $500

A New Map of the Island of Corsica, Divided into Cantons, Called Pieves: by Thos. Kitchin Geogr. [1762] 24x18cm (9½x7") B&W. Ref: Jolly LOND-208 [46] £16 $25

A New Map of the North East Coast of Asia, and North West Coast of America, with the Late Russian Discoveries [1764] 17x23cm (6½x9") B&W. Exc. Ref: Jolly LOND-237; Winsor (NW) VIII, 211. [49] £159 $245

A New Map of the River Mississipi from the Sea to Bayagoulas [1761] 18x24cm (7x9½") Modern color. Fine. Matted. Ref: Jolly LOND-198 [20] £211 $325

A Plan of the City of Berlin [on plate with] A Prospect of the City of Berlin. [1760] 18x24cm (7x9½") B&W. Ref: Jolly LOND-194 [46] £16 $25

A Plan of the River St. Lawrence, from the Falls of Montmorenci to Sillery; with the Operations of the Siege of Quebec. [1759] 18x25cm (7x10") Uncolored. Tear repaired on back; image fine; map good. Ref: Jolly LOND-178 [59] £49 $75

A Plan of the Straits of St. Mary, and Michilimakinac, to Shew the Situation & Importance of the Two Westernmost Settlements of Canada for the Fur Trade [1761] 23x33cm (9x13") Ref: Jolly LOND-197 [44] £179 $275

Berkshire Drawn from the Best Authorities and Regulated by Astronl. Observations by T. Kitchin Geogr. [1751] 17x22cm (6½x8½") OL color. Ref: Jolly LOND-63 [57] £29 $45

Durham Drawn from the Best Authorities and Regulated by Astronl. Observations by T. Kitchin Geographr. [1751] 16x22cm (6½x8½") OL color. Ref: Jolly LOND-68 [57] £29 $45

LOUISIANA, AS FORMERLY CLAIMED BY FRANCE, NOW CONTAINING PART OF BRITISH AMERICA TO THE EAST & SPANISH AMERICA TO THE WEST OF THE MISSISSIPI. FROM THE BEST AUTHORITIES BY T. KITCHIN GEOGR. [1765] 18x23cm (7x9") With text leaf. Modern OL color. Fine. Ref: Jolly LOND-245 [20] £195 $300

NOTTINGHAM SHIRE DRAWN FROM THE BEST AUTHORITIES AND REGULATED BY ASTRONL. OBSERVATIONS BY T. KITCHIN GEOGR. [1751] 22x17cm (8½x6½") OL col. Ref: Jolly LOND-62 [57] £29 $45

PART OF THE COUNTIES OF CHARLOTTE AND ALBANY, IN THE PROVINCE OF NEW YORK; BEING THE SEAT OF WAR BETWEEN THE KING'S FORCES UNDER LIEUT. GEN. BURGOYNE AND THE REBEL ARMY. BY THOS. KITCHIN SENR. HYDROGRAPHER TO HIS MAJESTY. [1778] 25x19cm (10x7½") B&W. Fine. Ref: Jolly LOND-320 [50] £159 $245

STAFFORD SHIRE DRAWN FROM AN ACCURATE SURVEY CORRECTED FROM ASTRONL. OBSERVATNS. BY T. KITCHIN GEOGRAR. [1751] 22x17cm (8½x6½") OL color. Ref: Jolly LOND-61 [57] £29 $45

LONGCHAMPS

CARTE DES POSSESSIONS FRANCOISES ET ANGLOISES DANS LE CANADA, ET PARTIE DE LA LOUISIANE [1756] Inset: present SE U.S. 54x75cm (21½x29½") Minor repairs; margins trimmed to neat lines. [14] £1,461 $2,250

LONGMAN

BATALLA DE AYACUCHO [1829] (Peru, Dec. 1824.) 20x25cm (8x10") Troops in orig color. [14] £32 $50

OXFORDSHIRE [1835] London: Longman, Rees, Orme & Co. Pocket map; dissected, laid down on linen, folded into 16mo cloth covers. 41x33cm (15½x13") OL color. VG. [21] £130 $200

POLAND [c. 1823] 19x23cm (7½x9") OL color. [42] £25 $39

LOTTER

A MAP OF THE PROVINCES OF NEW-YORK AND NEW-JERSEY, WITH A PART OF PENNSYLVANIA AND THE PROVINCE OF QUEBEC. FROM THE TOPOGRAPHICAL OBSERVATIONS OF C.J. SAUTHIER [1777] 2 sheets as issued. 75x56cm (29½x22") Orig color. Lt c'fold age toning; VG. [33] £1,688 $2,600

[SAME TITLE] [same date & dimen] Orig wash & OL color. Ref: Phillips (M) p.505. [46] £974 $1,500

ACCURATER PROSPECT DER HOCH-FURSTL. MARGGAF BAADEN DURLACHISCHEN NEU ERBAUTEN VERWUNDERUNGS WURDIGEN RESIDENZ STADT CARLSRUHE [c. 1760] View of city & palace. 50x58cm (19½x23") Orig color. Sl waterstain lf; no c'fold [64] £1,429 $2,201

AFRICAE PARS MERIDIONALIS CUM PROMONTORIO BONAE SPEI ... [c. 1760] 50x58cm (19½x22½") Orig color. Ref: Norwich 177. [64] £563 $868

AMERICA MERIDIONALIS ... [1772] From *Atlas Novus* ... 45x58cm (18x23") Orig full color. Faint narrow c'fold stain; o/w fine-. Ref: Phillips (A) 3513. [59] £292 $450

AMERICA SEPTENTRIONALIS, CONCINNATA JUXTA OBSERVATIONES DNN ACADEMIAE REGALIS SCIENTIARUM ET NUNNULLORUM ALIORUM, ET JUXTA ANNOTATIONES RECENTISSIMAS, PER G. DE L'ISLE ... [c. 1760] Peninsular Calif. 48x59cm (18½x23") Orig color, incl cartouche. Ref: Tooley (Amer) p.19, #34. [64] £449 $692

AMPLISSIMA UCRANIAE REGIO, PALATINATUS KIOVIENSEM ET BRACLAVIENSEM [c. 1760] 49x58cm (19½x22½") Orig color. [64] £204 $314

ANHALTINUS PRINCIPATUS STIRPIS ASCANIENSIS [c. 1760] After Seutter. 51x59cm (20x23") Orig color. [64] £278 $428

ARCHIEPISCOPATUS ET ELECTORATUS MOGUNTINUS UT ET COMITATUS UTERQ. CATIMELIBOCENS. WERTHEIMENSIS ERPACENS [c.1760] 50x58cm (19½x22½") Orig col. Sh wrinkles at below. [64] £241 $371

BELGICA FOEDERATA COMPLECTENS SEPTEM PROVINCIAS, DUCATUM GELDRIAE, COMITATUS HOLLANDIAE ET ZEELANDIAE DIOEC. TRAJECT. TRANSISUL. GRONINGAM ET FRISIAM [1761] 48x59cm (18½x23") Orig color. Remargined; outer neat line restored. [64] £147 $226

BORUSSIAE REGNUM COMPLECTENS CIRCULOS SAMBIENSEM, NATANGIENSEM ET HOCKERLANDIAE NEC NON BORUSSIA POLONICA EXHIBENS PALATINATUS CULMIENSEM, MARIENBURGENSEM, POMERELLIAE ET VARMIAE [1759] 51x58cm (20x23") Orig color. Trimmed to lower rt neat line. [64] £531 $818

CARTE DE L'OCEAN PACIFIQUE AU NORD DE L'EQUATEUR, ET DES COTES QUI LE BORNENT DES DEUX COTES: D'APRES LES DERNIERES DECOUVERTES FAITES PAR LES ESPAGNOLS, LES RUSSES ET LES ANGLOIS, JUSQU'EN 1780. PUBLIEE PAR TOBIE CONRAD LOTTER A AUGSBOURG [1780/ 1781] Title also in German. Shows Hawaii. 48x51cm (18½x20") Orig wash color to ocean & coastlines. Fine. [2] £1,104 $1,700

[SAME TITLE] [1781] Based on Kitchin. 48x56cm (19x22") Orig color. Old ms notes; margins little discolored & ragged. Ref: Wagner (NW) 672. [28] £584 $900

CARTE GEOGRAPHIQUE DU COMTE DE LA MARCK [c. 1760] 49x58cm (19½x23") Orig col. [64] £604 $931

CARTE NOUVELLE DE L'AMERIQUE ANGLOISE CONTENANT TOUT CE QUE LES ANGLOIS POSSEDENT SUR LE CONTINENT DE L'AMERIQUE SEPTENTRIONALE SAVIOR LE CANADA, LA NOUVELLE ECOSSE OU ACADIE, LES TREIZE PROVINCES UNIES ... AVEC LA FLORIDE ... [before 1763] 60x49cm (23½x19½") Full color except cartouche. Few sm wormholes, mostly in margins; narrow soiled lf margin; overall bright: VG. Ref: Phillips (A) 3517,93. [31] £552 $850

[SAME TITLE] [1775] 60x49cm (23½x19") Full orig col. Good. Ref: Phillips (A) 3517,93. [14] £422 $650

CASTELLUM GIBRALTAR IN ANDALUSIA SITUM, CUM CELEBRI FRETO INTER EUROPAM ET AFRICAM, ANNEXIS CIRCUMJACENTIBUS PORTUBUS ET CASTELIS [c. 1760] Below map a view of the fortress;, key in German & French. 49x59cm (19x23") Orig color. [64] £490 $755

CIRCULUS FRANCONICUS [c. 1760] 50x58cm (19½x23") Orig color. [64] £335 $516

DELINEATIO AC FINITIMA REGIO MAGNAE BRITTANIAE METROPOLEOS LONDONI AD NOVISSIMAM NORMAM. [c. 1760] 50x58cm (19½x23") Orig color. [64] £359 $553

DELINEATIO GEOGRAPHICA COMITATUS MANSFELDENSIS [c. 1750] After Seutter. 50x59cm (19½x23") Orig color. [64] £188 $289

DELINEATIO GEOGRAPHICA SPECIALIS TERRITORII CELSISSIMORUM S.R.I. COMITUM RUTHENORUM DE PLAUIA UTRIUSQUE LINEA SENIORIS ET IUNIORIS PARTEM VOGTLANDIAE [c. 1760] 58x50cm (23x19½") Orig color. Narrow left margin. [64] £229 $352

DOMINIUM VENETUM CUM ADJACENTIBUS MEDIOLAN. MANTUANO, MUTINENSI, MIRANDOLANO, PARMENSI, PLACENTINO DUCATIBUS [1729] After Seutter. 50x58cm (19½x22½") Orig color. [64] £278 $428

DUCATUS IULIACENSIS, CLIVIENSIS ET MONTENSIS, UT ET PRINCIPATUS MEURSIANI ET COMITATUS ZUTPHANIENSIS NOVISSIMA ET ACCURATISSIMA DELINEATIO [c. 1760] 58x50cm (23x19½") Orig color. [64] £449 $692

EPISCOPATUM MONASTERIENSIS ET OSNABRUGENSIS UT ET COMITATUUM BENTHEIM, TECLENBURG, STENFORD, LINGEN, DIEPHOLT, DELMENHORST, RIETBERG ETC. [c. 1760] 58x50cm (22½x19½") Orig color. [64] £727 $1,119

EUROPA REGNORUM [c. 1760] 50x59cm (19½x23") Orig color. Brown spot; some place names underlined. [64] £204 $314

GERMANIAE INFERIORIS SIVE BELGII PARS MERIDIONALIS [c. 1760] 51x59cm (20x23") Orig color. [64] £176 $270

GRUND-RISS DER KAYSERLICHEN UND DES HEIL. ROM. REICHS FREYEN STADT LUBECK [c. 1730] Plan with fortifications; view. 50x59cm (19½x23") Orig color. [64] £1,143 $1,761

HOLSATIAE MAPPA UNIVERSALIS IN SUOS DUCATUS NIMIRUM HOLSATIAM IN SPECIE, DITHMARSIAM, STORMARIAM, WAGRIAM ACCURATE DISTINCTA [c. 1760] 51x59cm (20x23") Orig color. Narrow margin below. [64] £237 $365

L'ISLE DE CORSE [c. 1760] 50x58cm (19½x23") Orig color. [64] £343 $528

LA PRINCIPAUTE D'OST-FRISE, OU LE COMTE D'EMBDEN, AVEC SES PRINCIPALES JURISDICTIONS [c. 1760] 49x59cm (19½x23") Orig color. [64] £939 $1,446

LE LANDGRAVIAT DE HESSE-CASSEL MERIDIONAL ET SEPTENTR. AVEC UNE PARTIE DU LANDGRAVIAT DE HESSE-DARMSTAT ET DE LA VETTERAVIE AVEC AUTRES DEPENDENCES [4 SHEETS] [1761] Each about 54x45cm (21½x17½") Orig color. [64] £776 $1,195

MAGNI DUCATUS FINLANDIAE RUSSIAE PARTIM, PARTIM SUECIAE SUBJECTI, SINUS ITEM BOTHNICI AC FINNICI NOVA ET ACCURATA DELINEATIO [c. 1760] 50x59cm (19½x23") Orig color. [64] £857 $1,321

MAGNUS DUCATUS LITHUANIA IN SUOS PALATINATUS ET CASTELLANIAS DIVISA [c. 1760] 49x58cm (19½x23") Orig color. [64] £229 $352

MAPPA CIRCULI RHENANI SUPERIORIS IN QUO OCULIS SISTUNTUR LANDGRAVIATUS HASSO-CASSELLANUS, DARMSTADIENSIS, RHENOFELDENSIS, ABBATIA FULDENSIS, PRINCIPATUS WALDECKENSIS ET HIRSCHFELT ... URBES IMPERIALES FRANCOFURT. FRIDBERG, WEZLAR ET R ET GELENHAUSEN [c. 1760] 50x58cm (19½x22½") Orig color. Remargined at bottom. [64] £225 $346

MAPPA GEOGRAPHICA, CONTINENS ARCHIEPISCOPATUM ET ELECTORATUM COLONIENSEM, CUM CONTERMINIS DUCATIBUS IULIACENSI ET MONTENSI, NEC NON COMITATU MURSANO [c. 1760] 50x58cm (19½x23") Orig color. Close lower margin; sh wrinkles at rt. [64] £531 $818

MAPPA GEOGRAPHICA EXHIBENS ELECTORATUM BRANDENBURGENSEM, SIVE MARCHIAM VETEREM, MEDIAM ET NOVAM, NEC NON MARCHIAM VKERAM [1758] 50x58cm (19½x23") Orig color. Narrow margin below. [64] £347 $535

MAPPA TOTIUS MUNDI ADORNATA JUXTA OBSERVATIONES DNN. ACADEMIAE REGALIS SCIENTARUM ET NONNULLORUM, SECONDUM ANNOTATIONS RECENTISSIMAS ... [1775] Double hemi, with polar spheres. 45x63cm (18x25") Old color. Fine. [26] £665 $1,025

MAPPE MONDE OU CARTE GENERALE DE L'UNIVERS SUR UNE PROJECTION NOUVELLE D'UNE SPHERE OVALE ... [1782] Show Cook's track. 2 sheet joined. 48x97cm (19½x38") Orig color. Sh tears; dampmarks in margins. [28] £1,285 $1,980
[SAME TITLE] [1800] 47x93cm (18½x36½") Orig color. [16] £1,519 $2,340
NOVA ET ACCURATA DESCRIPTIO DUCATUS BREMAE ET FERDAE CUM MAXIMA PARTE FINITIMI DUCATUS STORMARIENSIS ET COMITATUS OLDENBURGICI, ITEMQUE FLUMINUM ALBIS ET VISURGIS [c. 1760] 50x58cm (19½x23") Orig color. [64] £449 $692
NOVA ET ACCURATA GEOGRAPHICA DELINEATIO DUCATUS TESCHENENSIS IN SILESIA SUPERIORE CUM FINITIMORUM HUNGARIAE ET POLONIAE REGNORUM, UT ET MORAVIAE LIMITIBUS [c. 1760] With view. 50x58cm (19½x23") Orig color. [64] £269 $415
NOVA ET ACCURATISSIMA DUCATUS WURTENBERGICI [c. 1760] 51x58cm (20x23") Orig col. [64] £531 $818
NOVA ET EXACTA MAPPA GEOGRAPHICA EXHIBENS CIRCULUM WESTPHALICUM, IN OMNES SUOS STATUS ET PROVINCIAS ACCURATE DIVISUM [c. 1760] 58x50cm (23x19½") Orig color. [64] £592 $912
NOVA MAPPA MARIS NIGRI ET FRETI CONSTANTINO POLITANI ... [c. 1765] 51x58cm (20x23") Orig color. Sh tear below; lt foxing lower margin. [28] £221 $340
NOVISSIMA ET ACCURATISSIMA DELINEATIO STATUS ECCLESIAE ET MAGNI DUCATUS HETRURIAE [c. 1760] 50x58cm (19½x23") Orig color. [64] £212 $327
NOVISSIMA ET ACCURATISSIMA HELVETIAE, RHAETIAE, VALESIAE, ET PARTIS SABAUDIAE TABULA [c. 1750] 49x58cm (19½x23") Orig color. [64] £449 $692
PARS SUEVIAE BOREALIOR [c. 1760] After De L'Isle. 49x64cm (19x25") Orig color. [64] £327 $503
PENSYLVANIA NOVA JERSEY ET NOVA YORK CUM REGIONIBUS AD FLUVIUM DELAWARE IN AMERICA SITIS ... [c.1744] T.C. Lotter. 58x51cm (23x20") Orig col. C'fold splits; sm stain upper lf margin. [28] £964 $1,485
PLAN VON CONSTANTINOPEL, MIT DER UMLIEGENDEN GEGEND, UND DES CANALS VOM SCHWARZEN MEER [1770] With environs & overall view. 49x58cm (19½x22½") Orig color. [64] £776 $1,195
PLANISPHAERIUM COELESTE [c. 1760] After Eimmart. Double hemisphere, 6 sm spheres. 48x56cm (19½x22½") [52] £1,200 $1,848
REGNUM MOREAE ACCURATISSIME DIVISUM IN PROVINCIAS SACCANIAM, TZACONIAM, CALISCOPIUM ET DUCATUM CLARENSAE; UNA CUM INSULIS CEPHALONIA, ZACYNTHO CYTHERA, AEGINA ET SIDRA [c. 1760] 50x59cm (19½x23") Orig color. Trimmed to upper rt neat line. Ref: Zacharakis 1266 [64] £200 $308
RICHTIGE ANZEIGE WIE WEIT DIE HAUPT-ORTE IN DEUTSCHLAND UND ANDERE BERUHMTE STAEDTE IN EUROPA VON EINANDER ENTLEGEN [c. 1760] Distance table. 47x57cm (18½x22½") Orig color. Lower rt somewhat browned. [64] £171 $264
SPATIOSISSIMUM IMPERIUM RUSSIAE MAGNAE [c. 1760] 50x58cm (19½x23") Orig col. [64] £163 $252
TABULA GEOGRAPHICAE PRINCIPATUS BRANDENBURG. CULMB. SIVE BARUTHINI PARS INFERIOR CUM ADJACENTIBUS REGIONIBUS [c. 1760] 50x58cm (19½x23") Orig color. [64] £367 $566
TABULA PRINCIPATUS BRADENBURGICO-CULMBACENSIS SIVE BARUTHINI PARS SUPERIOR CUM ADJACENTIBUS REGIONIBUS [c. 1760] After Riediger. 58x50cm (23x19½") Orig color. [64] £327 $503
TABULA SYNOPTICA TOTIUS FLUMINIS DANUBII A FONTIBUS USQUE AD OSTIA ... ET PONTUS EUXINUS [SET OF 3 MAPS] [c. 1760] Each 50x58cm (19½x23") Orig color. [64] £449 $692
TERRITORIUM SAC. ROM. IMP. LIB. CIVITATIS FRANCOFURTI AD MOENUM CUM MAGNA PARTE ARCHI-EPISCOPATUS MOGUNTINI, COMITATUS HANOVIENSIS [c. 1760] 51x58cm (20x23") Orig color. [64] £653 $1,006
TIROLIS COMITATUS CONTINENS EPISCOP. TRIDENTINUM ET BRIXIENSEM NEC NON COMIT. BRIGANTINUM, FELDKIRCH SONNEBERG ET PLUDENTIN [1761] 49x59cm (19½x23") Orig color. [64] £449 $692
TOPOGRAPHIA SEDIS IMPERATORIAE MOSCOVITARUM PETROPOLIS ... [1744] Key below in Latin & German. 51x59cm (20x23") Orig color. Without c'fold. [64] £449 $692
ZEELANDIAE COMITATUS [c. 1760] 50x57cm (19½x22½") Orig color. [64] £572 $880

LOWRY

THE LEEWARD OR NORTH CARIBBEE ISLANDS [1852] London: Black & Son. Virgin Is. to Dominica, 25x36cm (10½x13½") Color. [27] £45 $70

LUCAS

ANTIGUA [1823] 22x29cm (8½x11½") Color. VG. [61] £62 $95
BAHAMAS [1823] 25x28cm (10x11½") Color. VG. [61] £114 $175
BARBADOES [1823] 29x23cm (11½x9") Color. VG. [61] £81 $125
BRAZIL [1823] 38x30cm (15x12") Color. VG. [61] £42 $65

CHILI [1823] 38x28cm (15x11") Color. VG.			[61]	£42	$65
COLOMBIA [1823] 38x30cm (15x12") Color. VG.			[61]	£36	$55
DOMINICA [1823] 30x22cm (11½x8½") Color. VG.			[61]	£55	$85
GRENADA [1823] 22x33cm (8½x13") Color. VG.			[61]	£55	$85
GUADELOUPE ETC. [1823] 28x38cm (11x15") Color. VG.			[61]	£55	$85
HAYTI OR SAINT DOMINGO [1823] 38x51cm (15x20") Color. VG.			[61]	£81	$125
JAMAICA [1823] 23x31cm (9x12") Color. VG.			[61]	£81	$125
LOUISIANA. [1823] 28x43cm (11x17½") Full color. Fine.			[20]	£292	$450
LOUISIANA. [1823] 28x43cm (11x17½") Full color. Minor transferral; some foxing; good.			[20]	£227	$350
MARTINICO [1823] 24x31cm (9½x12½") Color. VG.			[61]	£62	$95
MISSISSIPPI [1823] 38x28cm (15x11") Color. VG.			[61]	£62	$95
NEVIS [1823] 25x20cm (10x8") Color. VG.			[61]	£55	$85
NEW JERSEY [1823] From *General Atlas* ... 13 counties. 28x23cm (11½x9") Full pastel col.			[35]	£114	$175
PERU [1823] 38x28cm (15x11") Color. VG.			[61]	£36	$55
PORTO RICO [1823] 22x31cm (8½x12") Color. VG.			[61]	£81	$125
ST. CHRISTOPHERS [1823] 22x31cm (8½x12") Color. VG.			[61]	£62	$95
SOUTH AMERICA [1823] 38x28cm (15x11") Color. VG.			[61]	£42	$65
TOBAGO [1823] 25x29cm (10x11½") Color. VG.			[61]	£55	$85
TRINIDAD [1823] 24x29cm (9½x11½") Color. VG.			[61]	£55	$85
UNITED PROVINCES [1823] 38x28cm (15x11") Color. VG.			[61]	£36	$55
WEST INDIES [1823] 28x38cm (11x15") Color. VG.			[61]	£81	$125

LUTKE

[CAROLINE ISLANDS] [1836] Complete set, 26 charts on 16 sheets. First "Carte Generale de l'Archipel des Carolines" shows archipelago & voyage of Frederic Lutke. Each sheet 65x97cm (25½x38") Some with margin water staining, printing generally unaffected. Ref: Sabin 42738.   [14] £974 $1,500

MacKENZIE

A GENERAL CHART OF THE IRISH CHANNEL [1775] 117x97cm (45½x37½") Dampmark stains down c'fold.   [15] £160 $246

CAERNARVON BAY IN WALES ... [1775] Holyhead to Harlech. 97x104cm (37½x40½") Dampmarking down c'fold.   [15] £130 $200

THE FIRTH OF CLYDE IN SCOTLAND ... [1776] 76x127cm (30x49½") Repaired fold tears; some browning.   [15] £100 $154

THE MOUTH OF THE CLYDE AND LOCH FYNE ... [1776] 71x150cm (28½x59") Sm repaired fold tears; browning, mainly at folds.   [15] £130 $200

THE NORTH PART OF CARDIGAN BAY IN WALES ... [1775] 91x104cm (35½x40½")   [15] £110 $169

THE NORTH-WEST COAST OF ENGLAND FROM WALNEY ISLAND TO ST. BEE'S HEAD ... [1775] 71x102cm (28x40") C'fold repair, sm loss not in engraved area; dampmarking at c'fold.   [15] £100 $154

THE NORTH-WEST COAST OF SCOTLAND, FROM RUREA IN ROSS SHIRE, TO CAPE WRATH IN STRATHNAVER ... [1776] 104x97cm (40½x38") Sm repaired fold split; lt browning near folds.   [15] £110 $169

THE WEST COAST OF SCOTLAND FROM ARDNAMURCHAN TO THE ISLAND SKY ... [1776] 107x102cm (41½x39½") Repaired fold tears; lt brown damp-marking.   [15] £110 $169

MAGINI

[ATLAS] GEOGRAFIA CIOE DESCRITTIONE UNIVERSALE DELLA TERRA ... NUOVAMENTE ... RINCONTRATI, & CORRETTI ... GIO. ANT. MAGINI ... OPERA ... TRADOTTA DAL R.D. LEONARDO CERNOTI ... [1597-98] Venice: Galignani. Sm folio; 2 volumes in one; double-page world hemispheres & 63 half-page maps, 27 Ptolemaic & 37 modern, engraved by G. Porro. Contemporary limp vellum, recased; one margin repair; fine. Ref: Nordenskiold (Col) II,226; Nordenskiold (Fac) p.28; Phillips (A) 405; Stevens (Ptolemy) p.55.   [28] £4,441 $6,840

ASIA [1617] Arnhem: Jansson. 12x17cm (5x6½")		[14]	£49	$75
EUROPA [1621] From Ptolemy's *Geographia*. 13x17cm (5x7") on Italian text page.		[14]	£52	$80
GALLIAE REGNUM [1598] From the Ptolemy. 13x18cm (5x7") Color.		[57]	£55	$85
GRAECIA [same date & source] Porro, sc. 13x17cm (5x6½") on text sheet. Full color.		[57]	£65	$100
MARCA ANCONAE OLIM PICENUM [same date, source & dimen] Color.		[57]	£52	$80

Orbis Terrae Compendiosa Descriptio ... Porro Redact [1597] In *Geographiae ... Ptolemaei*. Reduced from 1587 R. Mercator. 15x24cm (6x9½") Color. Framed. Ref: Shirley (W) 202, pl.166. [16] £926 $1,426
Palaestina sive Totius Terrae Promissionis [1596] From the Ptolemy. Nile to Beirut. 13x18cm (5x7") B&W. Fine. [50] £172 $265
Scandia. Sive Regiones Septentrionales [1621] 2nd ed. Shows Zeno claims. 13x17cm (5x7") on text page. [14] £97 $150
Tabula Aphricae II [1598] Ptolemaic N Africa. 13x18cm (5x7") on text sheet. Color. [57] £49 $75
Tabula Europae VII [1621] Ptolemaic Sicily & Sardinia. Verso: Sarmatia. 13x17cm (5x6½") [14] £49 $75
Tartariae Imperium [1598] From the Ptolemy. Incl NW North America. 13x17cm (5x6½") on text sheet. Wash color. [57] £162 $250
Turcici Imperii Descriptio [same date, source & dimen] Porro, sc. Full color. [57] £97 $150
Tuscia [1597] From the Cologne Ptolemy. Porro, sc. 13x18cm (5x6½") Full color. [58] £81 $125

MAGNELLI
Pianta della Citta di Firenze Rileveta Esattamente nell Anno 1783 [1783] Zocchi, sc. 6 views below. 137x150cm (54x59") Color, gold accent. Mounted on rice paper; exc. Ref: Mori & Boffito, *Piante e Vedute di Firenze*, pp 91-92. [39] £6,167 $9,500

MAGNUS, C.
One Hundred & Fifty Miles Around Richmond [1864] Circular map; 13 sm circular maps. 53x38cm (21x15") 2 printed colors. Water mark, noticeable at corner; edge flaws repaired; o/w nice. Ref: Stephenson (CW) 632.2. [13] £357 $550
Union Military Chart. Complete Map of the Railroads and Water Courses in the United States and Canada [1861] Insets, figures & Capitol view. 58x69cm (22½x27") Orig wash color. Cloth-backed; fine. Ref: Modelski (RR) 44. [47] £315 $485

MALLET
[Armillary Sphere] [c. 1687] German issue. 14x10cm (5½x4") Later full color. Fine. [32] £71 $110
Ancien Continent avec Plusieurs Isles [1683] Separate Australia. 10x15cm (4x5½") Col. [16] £95 $146
Ancienne Jerusalem [c. 1687] From *Histoire de l'Univers*. German ed. Plan & view. 15x10cm (5½x4") Later color. [30] £97 $150
Bergen [Norway] [1683] City view. 15x10cm (5½x4") Full color. [57] £42 $65
Canada ou Nouvelle France [1683] Greenland to Delaware. 14x10cm (5½x4") Wash col. [56] £136 $210
Carte du Monde de Marc Paul [on sheet with] Carte du Monde de Jacques Castaldo [and] Carte du Monde de Miguel Lopez [1683] 14x10cm (5½x4") [14] £29 $45
Columbo [on sheet with] Gale [1683] Views. 14x10cm (5½x4") [14] £19 $30
Constantinople [c. 1687] From *Histoire de l'Univers*. German ed. 14x10cm (5½x3½") Later full color. Close lf margin; o/w fine. [33] £97 $150
Continent Arctique [1683] North polar projection. 15x11cm (6x4") [14] £32 $50
Continent Meridional [c. 1683] Diameter: 10cm (4") Color. [41] £85 $131
Continent Meridional Austral ou Antarctique [1683] 11x15cm (4x6") Color. Ref: Tooley (Australia) Antarc 34. [16] £93 $143
Das Landt Florida Floride [c. 1686] German ed. 15x13cm (6x4½") Uncolored. [4] £88 $135
De Fero, de Scheland Orknay et Hebrides [1683] 18x10cm (6½x4½") Uncolored. VG. [44] £32 $50
Detroit de Waigats [1683] Russian Arctic. 15x10cm (6x4") [57] £26 $40
Dublin [1683] Paris: Thierry. Bird's eye plan. 15x10cm (6x4") Color. Ref: Sabin 44130. [24] £62 $95
Equateur / Carte Generale du Monde [1683] From *Description de l'Univers*. Compilation of spheres. 11x15cm (4x6") Color. [16] £76 $117
Figure 13 [Eastern Hemisphere] [1683] Separate Australia. 10x15cm (4x5½") Color. [16] £57 $88
Figure IV [Armillary Sphere] [1683] Detailed illus. 10x14cm (4x5½") Color. [16] £62 $95
Figure XII [Globes: Terrestrial & Celestial] [1683] 10x15cm (4x5½") Color. [16] £57 $88
Floride [1683] Present Southeast. 15x11cm (6x4½") Full color. [56] £120 $185
[Same Title] [1683 (1686)] From *Description...* German ed. [same dimen] B&W. Fine. [50] £146 $225
Globe Terrestre [1683] Globe on design device in town view. 15x10cm (5½x4") [14] £23 $35
Groenlande [1683] 15x10cm (5½x4") [14] £32 $50
Is de Nio, Nampho Sta. Erini [1683] Incl Santorini, Ios. 15x10cm (6x4") Ref: SHC (Greek Islands) illus. [57] £45 $70

Is de Pelagnisi, Dromi, etc. [1683] Incl Pelagos, Saraquino, Skiathos, Adelphi. 15x10cm (6x4") Full color.	[57]	£45 $70
Isle d'Albion [1683] 18x10cm (6½x4½") Uncolored.	[44]	£39 $60
Isle d'Irlande [1683] Paris: Thierry. 15x10cm (6x4")	[24]	£45 $70
Isles de Ceylan [1683] 15x10cm (6x4")	[14]	£26 $40
Macedoine Thessalie Epire [1683] 15x13cm (6x4½") Color.	[57]	£39 $60
Nouveau Continent avec Plusieurs Isles [1683] Paris: Denys Thierry. Insular Calif. 14x10cm (5½x4") Ref: Sabin 44130.	[22]	£97 $150
[Same Title] [same date & dimen] From *Description de l'Univers*. B&W. Exc.	[47]	£162 $250
[Same Title] [c. 1684] From *Histoire de l'Universe*. German ed. [same dimen] Later full color. Minor printing smudges; overall VG.	[31]	£182 $280
Nouveau Mexique et Californie [1683] Insular Calif. 15x10cm (5½x4")	[14]	£179 $275
[Same Title] [1683 (1686)] From *Description ...* German ed. [same dimen] B&W. Good.	[50]	£211 $325
Nouvelle Guinee et Carpentarie [1683] German ed. 11x15cm (4½x5½") Color.	[16]	£128 $197
[Same Title] [1683] 18x10cm (6½x4½") Uncolored.	[44]	£26 $40
Palerme [Sicily] [c. 1683] City view. 15x10cm (5½x4") Full color.	[57]	£42 $65
Partie Meridionale de l'Ancienne Germany, ou la Vraye Germanie [1683] 18x10cm (6½x4½") Uncolored.	[44]	£39 $60
Partie Septentrionale de l'Ancienne Germanie [1683] Ancient Scandinavia. 18x10cm (6½x4½") Uncolored.	[44]	£32 $50
Pays Bas Catholiques [1683] 18x10cm (6½x4½") Uncolored.	[44]	£39 $60
Planisphere de Turquet [on sheet with] Planisphere de Bertius [and] Planisphere d'Rzael [1683] 14x10cm (5½x4")	[14]	£29 $45
Provinces Unies [1683] The Netherlands. 18x10cm (6½x4½") Uncolored.	[44]	£32 $50
Royaume d'Angleterre [1683] 18x10cm (6½x4½") Uncolored.	[44]	£39 $60
Royaume d'Irlande [1686] Above, "Das Konigreich Irrland". Frankfurt: Zunner. 15x13cm (6½x4½") Color. Ref: Sabin 44130.	[24]	£52 $80
Royaume de Chili [1683] 18x10cm (6½x4½") Uncolored.	[44]	£26 $40
Royaume des Amazones [1686] Figures hold map. German ed. 15x10cm (5½x4") Full col.	[57]	£55 $85
St. Augus de Floride [1683] View. 15x11cm (6x4½")	[4]	£81 $125
[Same Title] [same date & dimen] Full color.	[56]	£81 $125
Vienne [1686] Pub Frankfurt. City view. 14x10cm (5½x4")	[14]	£36 $55
Virginie [1683 (1686)] From *Description de l'Univers*. German ed. 15x10cm (6x4") B&W. Fine.	[50]	£159 $245
[Same Title] [c. 1684] From *Histoire de l'Universe*. German ed. [same dimen] Later col.	[31]	£143 $220
Waradin [1683] Bird's eye view, Hungary. 15x11cm (5½x4")	[14]	£16 $25

MALTE-BRUN

[Atlas] A New General Atlas, Exhibiting the Five Great Divisions of the Globe ... to Illustrate the Universal Geography by M. Malte-Brun [1828] Phila: John Grigg. Quarto; 40 maps in full color, incl 5 U.S. regionals. Orig 3/4 leather covers scuffed. Overall fine. Ref: Phillips (A) 751.	[5]	£584 $900
Perou et Bresil [1810] 23x30cm (8½x12")	[58]	£52 $80

MANUSCRIPT MAPS

[Louisiana: Algiers District with Riverfront on Opposite Bank] [1878] Survey copy; probably court exhibit. Detail incl New Orleans' Vieux Carre. 127x122cm (50x48½") Colored & india ink on silk. Fold repairs; fair.	[20]	£2,435 $3,750
[Louisiana: Central and East Feliciana Parish] [1863] Wall map; Baton Rouge to Port Hudson. Possibly by staff surveyor for Gen. Banks. 185x163cm (73½x64") India & colored inks on surveying silk. Restored; few sm fold losses; VG.	[20]	£5,518 $8,500
[United States Coast Chart: Philadelphia to Florida] [1780] Spanish source. 120 place names; much detail, but unfinished beyond St. Augustine; blank title panel. Publication maybe intended by Spanish Admiralty. 95x59cm (37½x23") Pen & ink on paper watermarked "J. Honig & Zoonem". Fine.	[14]	£1,201 $1,850
A Plan of a Plantation Called Bevon Island ... in ... St. Christopher ... [1810] W. McMahon. Willett family sugar estates. 53x42cm (20½x16½") Ink & OL watercolor. Pencil notes; surface creasing; archival tissue backing.	[54]	£1,200 $1,848

AFRICA DRAWN BY AMANDA M. CHAPIN [c. 1832] 43x56cm (17x21½") Ink & OL color. Sl wrinkled; sm stain near bottom; o/w near fine. [7] £422 $650

CHART OF THE COAST FROM SALINAS TO PARA ... [BRAZIL] [c. 1780] 18 c. style; 1824 ship positions added. 48x61cm (19x24") Pen & ink; color wash. Sl frayed & chipped edges, no margins, border affected. [15] £380 $585

LA SITUATION D'ALGIER [c. 1780] By Rasbech, Algerian native (?). 33x48cm (12½x19½") Orig wash color. Laid down on paper; exc. [2] £487 $750

MAP OF SOUTH AMERICA [1841] Phebe Teed, in S.A. Mitchell style. 38x33cm (14½x13") Ink & OL color. Sl toning & foxing; occas sm stains, damp-stained lower rt; margin tears affecting map, no loss. [7] £276 $425

PLAN OF THE LAST DIVISION OF THE TOWN OF CHESTER [MA] [1849] 2 plans after 1784 Property Book, "... Division of the Commons ..." (no dims.) Lt age-toning; some damp stain; VG. [6] £49 $75

SUITE DU PLAN DE LA COSTE DE MALAYA DEPUIS PLAIRA LISLE DE SANSELAM JUSQUES A QUEDA, ET LES ISLES DES NICOBARS [c. 1770] Depot de la Marine (?), Paris. Centered on Phuket, Nicobar Islands. 50x71cm (19½x28") Pen & Ink with color. Exc. [63] £1,558 $2,400

SWELLY CHANNEL AND APPROACHES [1872] J.H. Kerr. Pen & ink on tracing paper laid down on a card. 41x69cm (16x27") [15] £100 $154

THE WORLD'S INDUSTRIAL AND COTTON CENTENNIAL EXPOSITION NEW ORLEANS [c. 1882] Sam Mullen (?) Now Audubon Park; 96 feet/inch; with various specs. 175x69cm (69x26½") 2 joined sheets on orig silk; backed. Colored inks. Some dust soiling; VG. [20] £4,220 $6,500

MARIETTE

DESCRIPTION DE L'ISLE DE GUADELOUPE HABITEE DES FRANCOIS DESPUIS L'AN 1634 ... [c. 1645] Paris: Boisseau. 37x50cm (14½x19½") Orig color probably by Boisseau, "Enlumineur du Roi pour les cartes geographique". Minor repairs lower margin; o/w VF. [14] £487 $750

NOVA TOTIUS TERRARUM ORBIS GEOGRAPHICA AC HYDPOGRAPHICA [sic] TABULA AUCT: JUD: HONDIO [1642] Double hemi with sm spheres. 38x56cm (15x22") Color. Ref: Shirley (W) 358. [16] £3,798 $5,851

PLANISPHERE DU GLOBE CELESTE [1658] 38x45cm (15x17½") Folds, with binder for bookcase storage. Orig color. Ref: Warner p.172. [52] £1,600 $2,464

MARSHALL

[ATLAS] ATLAS TO MARSHALL'S LIFE OF WASHINGTON [1832] Phila: Crissy. Octavo; 10 double-page maps, 9 with some color; Yeager, sc. Half cloth cover. Occas lt foxing & offsetting; lacks rear endpaper; Ex lib, stamp on title page. Ref: Phillips (A) 1342 [5] £243 $375

A MAP OF PART OF RHODE ISLAND SHEWING THE POSITIONS OF THE AMERICAN AND BRITISH ARMIES AT THE SIEGE OF NEWPORT, AND THE SUBSEQUENT ACTION ON THE 29TH OF AUGUST 1778 [1807] S. Lewis. 42x25cm (16½x10") Fine. [36] £81 $125

A MAP OF THE COUNTRY FROM RARITON RIVER IN EAST JERSEY TO ELK HEAD IN MARYLAND SHEWING THE SEVERAL OPERATIONS OF THE AMERICAN AND BRITISH ARMIES, IN 1776 & 1777 [1807] From *Life of Washington*. 25x39cm (10x15½") Uncolored. Sl age darkening along c'fold; some thinning; overall VG. [33] £104 $160

A PLAN OF THE COUNTRY FROM FROG'S POINT TO CROTON RIVER SHEWING THE POSITIONS OF THE AMERICAN AND BRITISH ARMIES FROM THE 12TH OF OCTOBER 1776 UNTIL THE ENGAGEMENT ON THE WHITE PLAINS ON THE 28TH [1807] From *Life of Washington*. 41x22cm (16½x9") Uncolored. Lt staining near c'fold; VG. [33] £104 $160

[SAME TITLE] [same date & dimen] C.P. Wayne, Phila. Later color. [51] £162 $250

BOSTON AND ITS ENVIRONS [1807] London: R. Phillips. 20x33cm (8x12½") Uncolored. Some offsetting. [51] £162 $250

MAP OF THE NORTHERN PROVINCES OF THE UNITED STATES [1807] From *Life of Washington*. London: R. Phillips. Found in some early editions. 33x51cm (13x19½") Uncolored. Left margin loss; some foxing. [51] £195 $300

MAP OF THE SOUTHERN PROVINCES OF THE UNITED STATES [1807] From *Life of Washington*. London: R. Phillips. 36x51cm (14x20") Uncolored. Some loss at left margin. [51] £195 $300

PLAN OF THE INVESTMENT AND ATTACK OF YORK IN VIRGINIA [1807] From *Life of Washington*. 23x21cm (9x8½") Uncolored. Fine. [33] £78 $120

MARZOLLA

[ATLAS] MARZOLLA / ATLANTE / GEOGRAFICO [SPINE TITLE] [c. 1856] Elephant folio. 49 double-page maps, many of Italy, with marginal text on thick paper; OL & highlight color. Old calf & cloth binding, somewhat worn & scuffed. Sporadic foxing; some maps dampstained at top & side margins. [5] £1,948 $3,000
SETTENTRIONALE INGLESE E RUSSO, GROENLANDIA, ISLAND, TERRE ARTICHE COL PASSAGGIO NORD-OUEST ... [1853] Text below. 43x59cm (17x23½") Orig OL color. [14] £179 $275

MAURO

[FACSIMILE] ABOZZO DE MAPPAMONDO DI F. MAURO CAMALDOLESE [18th c.] Fra Mauro's vanished 1459 world map from contemporary copy. 1st to show Japan. 36x36cm (13½x13½") Minor margin defects. [46] £78 $120

MAYNARD

JERUSALEM [1740] 36x43cm (14x17") Color. [23] £153 $235

MELA

NOVELLAE ETATI AD GEOGRAPHIE UMICULATOS CALLES HUMANO VIRO NECESSARIOS FLORES ASPIRATI VOLUBNMERETI PONTIF [1482] Appeared in *Novellae etate ad geographie*, Venice: E. Ratdolt. 1st Italian woodcut map. 14x19cm (5½x7½") Chip at rt corners repaired. Ref: Shirley (W) 8. [62] £3,376 $5,200

MELISH

NEW ORLEANS AND ADJACENT COUNTRY [1816] Show British HQ. 18x10cm (6½x4") Uncol. [57] £49 $75
ST. LOUIS AND ADJACENT COUNTRY [1816 (1822)] From *Geographical Description of the United States*. 17x10cm (6½x4") B&W. Fine. Ref: Howes (US) M490. [50] £55 $85
UNITED STATES OF AMERICA [1821] From Lavoisne's From Lavoisne's *Genealogical, Historical, Chronological and Geographic Atlas*, 3rd ed. 43x56cm (17x22") With text sheet & U.S. history chart. Full color. VG. [44] £260 $400
VIEW OF THE COUNTRY ROUND THE FALLS OF NIAGARA [1816 (1822)] From *Geographical Description of the United States*. 18x10cm (6½x4") B&W. Sl pale foxing; good. [50] £62 $95

MENTELLE

[BOOK] COSMOGRAPHIE ELEMENTAIRE. DIVISEE EN PARTIES ASTRONOMIQUE ET GEOGRAPHIQUE ... [1785] Paris. Quarto, 399 pp., 14 folding maps (mostly European) on thick pale blue paper with OL color, 3 celestial plates, table. "Comtesse Rzewuska, nee Princesse Lubomerska" bookplate. Contemporary calf scuffed; gold tooled spine with label worn; internally VG+. [55] £292 $450

MERCATOR (Folio)   Try *Hondius, Jansson*

[IRLANDIAE REGNUM, NORTHERN HALF] [1602] 46x36cm (18½x13½") Old color. (May be paired with companion "Irlandiae Regnum" southern half for $875.) Ref: Phillips (A) 5920, 86. [24] £302 $465
ABISSINORUM SIVE PRETIOSI IOANNIS IMPERIU [1623] 34x49cm (13½x19") Full orig color. Lt uniform age toning; c'fold reinforcement verso. [33] £260 $400
AFRICA ... [1607] 38x46cm (15x18") OL color. Fine. Ref: Norwich 21. [55] £974 $1,500
AFRICA EX MAGNA ORBIS TERRE DESCRIPTIONE GERARDI MERCATORIS DESUMPTA, STUDIO & INDUSTRIA G.M. IUNIORIS [1595] 38x47cm (15x18½") Orig color. Discreet c'fold mend. [62] £779 $1,200
[SAME TITLE] [same date & dimen] Full orig color. Lower c'fold mend; else exc. [63] £876 $1,350
ALSATIA INFERIOR [1607] 35x45cm (14x17½") Orig color. Sh tear lower c'fold repaired. [64] £200 $308
ALSATIA SUPERIOR DU SUNTGOIA & BRISGOIA [c. 1623] Mercator-Hondius atlas. 36x48cm (14x18½") Orig OL color. Fine. Ref: Koeman Me27A [59] £185 $285
AMERICA SIVE INDIA NOVA AD MAGNA GERARDI MERCATORIS AVI UNIVERSALIS IMITATIONEM IN COMPENDIUM REDACTA. PER MICHAELEM MERCATOREM DUYSBURGENSEM [1595] 37x46cm (14½x18") Orig color. Exc. Ref: Goss (NA) #19. [62] £3,116 $4,800
[SAME TITLE] [c. 1620] [same dimen] Color. [64] £1,715 $2,641
ANGLESEY [ON SHEET WITH] WIGHT VECTIS OLIM [AND] GARNESAY [AND] JARSAY [1606] 32x43cm (12½x17") Sm stains. Ref: Koeman II Me 15. [28] £325 $500
[SAME TITLE] [1619] 32x43cm (12½x17") Color. [64] £286 $440
ANGLIA REGNUM [(1595) 1623] 33x41cm (13x16") Full orig color. C'fold reinforcement verso; minor abrasion lower c'fold; minor margin staining. Ref: Shirley (BI to 1650) 383. [33] £260 $400
[SAME TITLE] [1607] 36x47cm (14x18½") Orig color; gold highlighted cartouche. Restored tear to ctr; 4x3½ cm hole in North Sea restored. [64] £33 $50

ANGLIA, SCOTIA ET HIBERNIA [(1595) 1623] 33x41cm (13x16") Full orig color. Fold reinforced on verso; minor abrasion lower c'fold; printer's fold into image. Ref: Shirley (BI to 1650) 382. [33] £260 $400
[SAME TITLE] [1619] [same dimen] Color. Ref: Shirley (BI to 1650) 180 [64] £278 $428
AQUITANIA AUSTRALIS REGNU ARELATENSE CUM CONFINIJS [1607] 36x47cm (14x18½") Orig color. [64] £200 $308
ARGOW. IN HAC TABULA LUCERNA, VREN, SWYTZ, UNDERWALD, GLARONA PAGI [c. 1630] Mercator-Hondius. 35x45cm (14x17½") Color. 2 sh tears restored. [64] £212 $327
ARRAGONIA ET CATALONIA [1607] Mercator-Hondius. 35x45cm (14x17½") Orig color; gold highlight. [64] £204 $314
ASIA EX MAGNA ORBIS TERRAE DESCRIPTIONE GERARDI MERCATORIS DESUMPTA, STUDIO ET INDUSTRIA G.M. IUNIORIS [1619] 38x47cm (15x18½") Col. Sm rust spot. Ref: Koeman Me 26, 77. [64] £735 $1,132
AUSTRIA ARCHIDUCATUS [1619] 35x45cm (14x17½") Color. [64] £245 $377
BAVARIA DUCATUS [1607] 37x47cm (14½x18½") Orig color. C'fold restored at bottom. [64] £327 $503
BELGII INFERIORIS DESCRIPTIO EMENDATA CUM CIRCUMIACENTIUM REGIONU CONFINIJS [1619] 35x45cm (14x17½") Color. [64] £245 $377
BERRY DUCATUS [1607] 35x45cm (14x17½") Orig color. Sh tear backed. [64] £94 $145
BOHEMIA [1619] 41x55cm (16½x21½") Color. [64] £196 $302
BOLONIA & GUINES COMITATUS [1619] 45x35cm (17½x14") Color. [64] £78 $119
BRAUNSWYCK & MEYDBURG CUM CETERIS ADIACENTIBUS [1619] 35x45cm (14x17½") Col. [64] £286 $440
BRESCIA EPISCOPATUS MEDIOLANUM DUCTUS ... [1606] 38x48cm (14½x18½") Sh lower c'fold split. Ref: Koeman II Me 15. [28] £175 $270
BURGUNDIA DUCATUS [1607] 35x45cm (14x17½") Orig color. [64] £245 $377
CAMBRIAE TYPUS AUCTORE HUMFREDO LHUYDO, DENBIGIENSE CAMBROBRITANNO, PETRUS KAERIUS CAELA [1607] Mercator-Hondius. 36x49cm (14x19½") Orig color. Lf margin reinforced; c'fold split repaired. [64] £327 $503
CANDIA CUM INSULIS ALIQUOT CIRCA GRAECIAM [1607] Map of Corfu, Zante, Milo, Nicsia, Santorini, Scarpanto 34x48cm (13½x18½") Orig color; gold highlighted cartouche. Some place names underlined in brown ink. Ref: Zacharakis 1420. [64] £318 $491
CASTILIAE VETERIS ET NOVAE DESCRIPTIO [1606] Mercator-Hondius. 35x45cm (14x17½") Orig color; gold highlighted cartouche. [64] £225 $346
CHINA [1606 / 1623] Mercator-Hondius. E-W Japan; insular Korea. 34x46cm (13½x18") Full orig color. Edges lined with paper; good. Ref: Koeman Me 27a; Potter p.122-23. [2] £974 $1,500
CUBA INSULA [ON SHEET WITH] HISPANIOLA INSULA [AND] INSULA IAMAICA [AND] INS. S. IOANNIS [AND] IS. MARGARETA CUM CONFINIIS [c. 1606] 36x50cm (14x19½") Color. [25] £682 $1,050
[SAME TITLE] [1607] [same dimen] Orig color. Sh c'fold tear restored. [64] £376 $579
[SAME TITLE] [1606 - 1637] [same dimen] Full color. Fine-. Ref: MCC 42, #7. [59] £633 $975
DAS WIFLISPURGERGOV [1607] 39x51cm (15x20") Orig color. [64] £171 $264
EBORACUM, LINCOLNIA, DERBIA, STAFFORDIA, NOTINGHAMAIA, LECESTRIA, RUTLANDIA, ET NORFOLCIA [1607] 35x42cm (14x16½") Orig color. [64] £155 $239
EUROPA [1619] R. Mercator. 38x47cm (15x18½") Color. [64] £898 $1,383
FESSAE ET MAROCCHI REGNA ... [1607] Mercator-Hondius. 36x48cm (14x19") Orig col. [64] £327 $503
FIONIA [1619] Denmark. 35x45cm (14x17½") Color. [64] £184 $283
FORUM IULIUM, KARSTIA CARNIOLA, HISTRIA ET WINDORUM MARCHIA [1607] 35x45cm (14x17½") Orig color. Sh lower c'fold tear restored. [64] £155 $239
FRISIA OCCIDENTALIS [1607] 36x46cm (14½x18") Orig color. [64] £367 $566
GELDRIA ET TRANSYSULANA [1607] 35x45cm (14x17½") Orig color. Sh lower c'fold split repaired. [64] £359 $553
GRAECIA [1607] 36x47cm (14x18½") Orig col. Sh c'fold tear repaired. Ref: Zacharakis 1447. [64] £347 $535
HANNONIA. NAUVRCUM COMITATUS [1607] 35x45cm (14x17½") Orig color. Smudges in margin. [64] £102 $157
HASSIA LANDTGRAVIATUS [1607] 35x45cm (14x17½") Orig color. [64] £294 $453
HELVETIA CUM FINITIMIS REGIONIBUS CONFOEDERATIS [1607] 35x47cm (14x18½") Orig color; gold heightened mileage scale. [64] £449 $692
HIBERNIA REGNUM VULGO IRELAND [1636] From atlas of Ireland & Isle of Man. 39x50cm (15x19½") Modern color. Exc. [62] £357 $550

HIBERNIAE III. TABULA. IN QUA MOMONIA ET LAGENIAE RELIQUA [1607] 35x45cm (14x17½") Orig color. [64] £102 $157
HOLLANDT COMITATUS UTRICHT EPISCOP. [1619] 35x45cm (14x17½") Color. [64] £388 $597
HOLSATIA DUCATUS [1619] 35x48cm (14x19") Color. [64] £318 $491
HUNGARIA [1607] 37x44cm (14½x17") Orig color. Browned; lower margin repaired. [64] £225 $346
INS. CEILAN QUAE INCOLIS TENARISIN DICITUR [1619] 35x45cm (14x17½") Color. [64] £367 $566
IRLANDIAE REGNUM [1602] From *Atlas sive Cosmographicae*. Southern half. 36x46cm (13½x18½") Old color. Fine. Ref: Phillips (A) 5920, 85. [24] £302 $465
IRLANDIAE REGNUM [1607] "Hiberniae V. Tabula continens Vdrone Baroniam, partem Comitatus Regniae, ac Dominy Fortonely: In Vdronis medio iacet civitas Laghlyn alys Leighlin" 34x43cm (13x17") Orig color. [64] £135 $208
IUTIA SEPTENTRIONALIS ... [1606] 29x40cm (11½x15½") Upper margin ragged, curled. Ref: Koeman II Me 15. [28] £175 $270
[SAME TITLE] [1619] [same dimen] Color. [64] £155 $239
L'ISLE DE FRANCE. PARISIESIS AGRI DESCRIPTIO [c. 1630] 35x45cm (14x17½") Color. [64] £159 $245
LA SECONDE TABLE D'ECOSSE [c. 1630] 35x45cm (14x17½") Color. C'fold restored. [64] £171 $264
LEODIENSIS DIOECESIS TYPUS [1619] Mercator-Hondius; by Van Doeticbum. 35x45cm (14x17½") Color. [64] £225 $346
LIVONIA [1607] 35x45cm (14x17½") Orig color. C'fold restoration. [64] £306 $472
LOTHARINGIA DUCATUS [1619] 35x45cm (14x17½") Color. [64] £327 $503
MACEDONIA EPIRUS ET ACHAIA [1589 (1639)] 36x43cm (14x17") OL color. VG. [55] £195 $300
[SAME TITLE] [1607] [same dimen] Orig color. Ref: Zacharakis 1448. [64] £147 $226
MORAVIA [1607] 35x45cm (14x17½") Orig color. [64] £143 $220
MURS COMITATUS [ON SHEET WITH] REGIONUM URBIUM ET FLUMINUM QUE POTISSIMU COMITATUM MURS AMBIUNT BREUIS DESCRIPTIO [1607] 2 maps on sheet, each 36x24cm (14x9½") Orig col. [64] £898 $1,383
NORTHUMBRIA, CUMBERLANDIA, ET DUNELMENSIS EPISCOPATUS [c. 1630] 35x47cm (14x18½") Color. [64] £118 $182
ORBIS TERRAE COMPENDIOSA DESCRIPTIO ... [1587] From Strabo, *Geographia*. 1st ed. 36x51cm (14x20½") including text below. Later color. Exc. Ref: Koeman Me 12 [74]; Shirley (W) 157, pl.129; Wagner (NW) 146. [2] £4,220 $6,500
[SAME TITLE] [1595] Double hemispheres, with text below. 29x53cm (11x20½") plus text panel. Full orig color. Mend lower c'fold; exc. [63] £3,765 $5,800
PALATINATUS RHENI [1607] 35x45cm (14x17½") Orig color. Wrinkle at rt; repaired tear [64] £490 $755
PEDEMONTANA REGIO CUM GENVENSIUM TERRITORIO & MONTISFERRATI MARCHIONATU [1607] 35x45cm (14x17½") Orig color. Sh wrinkle ctr; sm margin tear restored. [64] £163 $252
POLONIA ET SILESIA [1619] 34x46cm (13½x18") Color. [64] £204 $314
PRUSSIA [1607] 35x45cm (14x17½") Orig col; gold heightened cartouche. C'fold restored. [64] £572 $880
PUGLIA PIANA, TERRA DI BARRI, TERRA DI OTRANTO, CALABRIA ET BASILICATA ... [1606] 36x46cm (13½x18") Ref: Koeman II Me 15. [28] £221 $340
QUERCY CADURCIUM [1619] 38x50cm (15x19½") Color. [64] £90 $138
SALTZBURG ARCHIEPISCOPATUS CUM DUCATU CARINTHIAE [1619] 35x45cm (14x17½") Col. [64] £282 $434
SAXONIA INFERIOR ET MEKLENBORG DUC. [1619] 35x45cm (14x17½") Color. [64] £265 $409
SCLAVONIA, CROATIA, BOSNIA CUM DALMATIAE PARTE [1619] 35x45cm (14x17½") Orig col. [64] £171 $264
SCOTIA REGNUM [1607] 35x40cm (14x16") Orig color. C'fold split restored; upper margin repaired with other paper, sl image loss. [64] £53 $82
SEPTENTRIONALIUM TERRARUM DESCRIPTIO. PER GERARDUM MERCATOREM CUM PRIVILEGIO [c. 1613] From *Atlas sive Cosmographicae*. 2nd state; Mercator-Hondius. 37x39cm (14½x15½") Margins foxed with few tears. Ref: Wagner (NW) 177; Skelton (Explorer) p.100-1; Koeman II Me 22; Nordenskiold (Fac) p.95 (1st state). [28] £1,022 $1,575
TABULA ISLANDIAE AUCTORE GEORGIO CAROLO FLANDRO ... [1630 - 1650] Mercator-Hondius atlas. 38x49cm (15x19½") Orig OL color. VG-. [59] £390 $600
TAURICA CHERSONESUS NOSTRA AETATE PRZECOPSCA ET GAZARA DICITUR [1595 - 1638] Pub by Jansson. 31x40cm (12½x16") Orig color. [14] £88 $135
[SAME TITLE] [1607] 32x41cm (12½x16") Orig color. Tissue repair of complete c'fold split; surface abrasions with color loss at c'fold; browned. [64] £24 $38

TERRA SANCTA QUAE IN SACRIS TERRA PROMISSIONIS OL: PALESTINA [1619] 36x50cm (14x20") Old color. Minor fold & margin repairs. [23] £357 $550
TOTIUS LEMOVICI ET CONFINIUM PROVINCIARUM QUANTUM AD DIOCESIN LEMOVICENSEN SPECTANT. NOVISSIMA ET FIDISSIMA DESCRIPTIO [1607] Mercator-Hondius; by Van den Keere, after Jean du Fayen. 35x45cm (14x17½") Orig color. [64] £118 $182
TRIER ET LUTZENBURG [1607] 35x45cm (14x17½") Orig color. Surface abrasion with some color loss at ctr; margins reinforced; c'fold splits lined full length. [64] £122 $189
TUSCIA [1607] 35x45cm (14x17½") Orig color; gold heightened cartouche. [64] £237 $365
UDRONE IRLANDIAE IN CATHERLAGH BARONIA [1619] 45x35cm (17½x14") Color. [64] £90 $138
ULTONIAE ORIENTALIS PARS [1619] 35x45cm (14x17½") Color. [64] £102 $157
ULTONIAE ORIENTALIS PARS PER GERARDIUM MERCATOREM CUM PRIVILEGIO [1602] From *Atlas sive Cosmographicae*. NE Ireland. 36x38cm (14x15") Old color. Ref: Phillips (A) 5920, 88. [24] £250 $385
VIRGINIAE ITEM ET FLORIDAE AMERICAE PROVINCIARUM NOVA DESCRIPTIO [1606 (1638)] 34x49cm (13½x19") Color. C'fold repair; good. Ref: Cumming (SE) # 26; Koeman Me 20A. [48] £1,266 $1,950
VVESTFALIAE SECUNDA TABULA [c. 1600] 35x45cm (14x17½") Orig color. Rust spot. [64] £531 $818
WESTMORLANDIA, LANCASTRIA, CESTRIA, CAERNARVAN, DENBIGH, FLINT, MERIONIDH, MONTGOMERY, SALOPIA CUM INSULIS MANIA ET ANGLESEY [1607] 36x42cm (14x16½") Orig color; gold highlights on cartouche. Sh c'fold tear restored. [64] £143 $220
ZELANDIA COMITATUS [1607] 34x49cm (13½x19½") Orig color; gold heightened cartouche. Mended c'fold split. [64] £531 $818
ZURICHGOVV, ET BASILIENSIS PROVINCIA [1607] 36x47cm (14x18½") Orig color. [64] £490 $755

MERCATOR (Small)

AFRICAE DESCRIPTIO [1628] Abraham Goos, sc. 13x20cm (5x8") Color. [58] £107 $165
ALSATIA SUPERIOR ... [1628] 15x20cm (5½x7½") Color. [57] £52 $80
AMERICAE DESCRIP. [1621] Arnhem: Jansson. Spherical projection. 15x20cm (6x7½") [14] £192 $295
[SAME TITLE] [c. 1635] same dimen] Later full color. Margin corner repair; printer's crease rt, 5 mm separated in image; o/w VG. [32] £260 $400
CUBA INSUL [ON SHEET WITH] HISPANIOLA [AND] HAVANA PORTUS [AND] I.IAMAICA [AND] I.S. IOANNIS [AND] I.MARGARETA [c. 1630] Mercator-Hondius. 15x18cm (6x7½") Color. Ref: cf. Phillips (A) 450. [25] £179 $275
DANIAE REGNUM [1628] Incl N. Germany & S. Sweden. 16x20cm (6x8") Color. [57] £55 $85
DESIGNATIO ORBIS CHRISTIANI [1621] Arnhem: Jansson. 15x19cm (6x7½") [14] £146 $225
HISPANIAE NOVAE NOVA DESCRIPTIO [(1630)] Amsterdam: Hondius/Jansson. 19x26cm (7½x10") Blank verso. Fine. [33] £195 $300
INDIA ORIENTALIS [1621] Arnhem: Jansson. 36x51cm (14x19½") Ref: Phillips (A) 435. [14] £120 $185
INSULAE INDIAE ORIENTALIS [1621] Arnhem: Jansson. 14x20cm (5½x7½") Poor impression in parts. Ref: Phillips (A) 435, p.639. [14] £146 $225
[SAME TITLE] [1628] [same dimen] Color. [57] £107 $165
JAPAN I. [1621] Arnhem: Jansson. 13x17cm (5x6½") Ref: Phillips (A) 435. [14] £211 $325
LOTHARINGIA SEPTENTRIONAL [AND] LOTHARINGIA MERIDIONALIS [c. 1630] 2 maps; each 13x15cm (5½x6") Full color. [57] £97 $150
NOVA VIRGINIAE TABULA ... [(1637)] Van den Keere, sc. 18x25cm (7x10") Uncol. Fine. [33] £292 $450
PALATINATUS RHENI [1628] 15x20cm (5½x8") Color. [57] £58 $90
POLUS ARCTICUS CUM VICINIS REGIONIBUS [1621] Arnhem: Jansson. 13x19cm (5x7½") [14] £146 $225
PROVINCIA, LA PROVENCE [c. 1630] 13x20cm (5½x7½") Color. [57] £58 $90
SALTZBURG ET CARINTHIE [1628] 13x18cm (5½x7") Color. [57] £55 $85
SAXONIA INFERIOR ET MEKLENBORG [1628] 15x20cm (5½x8") [57] £49 $75
SCOTIA MERIDIONALIS [AND] SCOTIA SEPTENTRIONALIS [1628] 2 maps, each 13x20cm (5½x7½") Full color. [57] £107 $165
TAURICA CHERSONESUS [1647] 38x50cm (15x19½") Color. [57] £52 $80
THE YLANDES OF THE WEST INDIES [1635] From *Historia Mundi*. English ed, printed for Michael Sparke, London. Text verso. 17x23cm (6½x9½") B&W. Fine. [47] £162 $250
[SAME TITLE] [same date & dimen] Added to English ed by M. Sparke. Uncolored. [53] £180 $277
VALENTIA, MURCIA CUM INSULIS MAJORCA, MINORCA ET YVICA [1628] E Spain & Balearics. 15x20cm (5½x8") Color. [57] £58 $90

MERIAN

[POLAND: ELBING] [c. 1640+] Bird's eye view. 23x31cm (9x12") B&W. [42] £95 $146
AMERICA NOVITER DELINEATA [1630] After Hondius. 36x45cm (14x17½") Minor restoration. Ref: Tooley (Amer) p.299. [14] £552 $850
[SAME TITLE] [c. 1640] Based on Hondius. Inset: Greenland, but not Antarctica. 28x36cm (11x14") Washed; backed on archival tissue. Ref: Wagner (NW) 329. [28] £584 $900
ANTWERPIA [c. 1645] From *Theatrum Europaeum*. Bird's eye plan. 27x36cm (10½x14") [14] £120 $185
BURGOS [c. 1640] City view. 19x31cm (7½x12½") Sm printer's crease [14] £175 $270
HISPANIA REGNUM [1646+] 26x36cm (10½x14") Lf margin damage to neat line now replaced. [14] £110 $170
LONDON [c. 1670] View from south before Great Fire; key below. 20x71cm (8½x27½") B&W; Some creasing; else fine. [55] £876 $1,350
NOVA TOTIUS TERRARUM ORBIS GEOGRAPHICA AC HYDROGRAPHICA TABULA [1638] Mercator projection, polar insets. 26x36cm (10½x14") Blank verso. B&W. Lf margin at plate line; fine. Ref: Shirley (W) 345, pl.262. [1] £714 $1,100
[SAME TITLE] [1646] 27x36cm (11x14") Color. Fine [26] £714 $1,100

MEYER

DIE STAATEN DIE MISSOURI ILLINOIS, INDIANA, OHIO, KENTUCKY & TENNESSEE [1850] Hildberghausen. Includes MI. 28x20cm (11x8") Color. VG. Ref: Karpinski (MI) 158. [61] £62 $95
FLORIDA ... [1845] From *Meyer's Handatlas*. 3 insets. 38x30cm (14½x12") Orig OL color. Good. [49] £185 $285
NEUESTE KARTE VIRGINIA [1845] From *Hand Atlas*. 30x38cm (12½x14½") OL color. [35] £81 $125
VEREINIGTE STAATEN VON NORD-AMERICA: CALIFORNIEN, TEXAS UND DIE TERRITORIEN NEW MEXICO U. UTAH ... [1852] From Joseph Meyer, *Neuester Zeitungs-Atlas*. 23x28cm (9x11") Orig full color. VG. [59] £120 $185

MICHELOT

NOUVELLE CARTE GENERALE DE LA MER MEDITERRANEE [1718] Western part. 48x70cm (18½x27½") Mounted on paper as issued; lt toned; else exc. [63] £357 $550

MIDDLETON

A PERSPECTIVE VIEW OF THE CHURCH OF THE HOLY SEPULCHRE AT JERUSALEM ... [1778] Bird's eye view; nearby buildings keyed. 18x28cm (7½x10½") Color. [23] £62 $95
NEW & COMPLETE MERCATOR CHART OF THE WORLD [1794] 18x28cm (7x11") [14] £49 $75
THE TERMS AND PRINCIPLES OF GEOGRAPHY WITH THEIR ASTRONOMICAL CONNECTIONS [c. 1780] Images of orrery, exemplary map, earth & solar diagrams. 28x18cm (11½x7") Color. Fine. [50] £81 $125

MILITARY MAPS - Infrequent Publishers

[RUSSIAN TITLE, FIRST] ... PLAN DE L'EXPEDITION DE M. 'LE GENERAL-MAJOR DE VEISMANN DE L'AUTRE COTE DU DANUBE, SUR LES CAMPS ENNEMIS PRES DE SOMOW, TULTSCHA, ISAKTSCHI & SUR LA CAMP DU GRAND-VISIR ... 1771 ... [THEN GERMAN TITLE] [c. 1771] Done in the field for Lt. Col. de Stricker. 2 sheets joined. 91x64cm (35½x25") With 4 pp explication. 2 tears, one sl through margin. [28] £292 $450
BATTLEFIELDS IN FRONT OF NASHVILLE WHERE THE UNITED STATES FORCES COMMANDED BY MAJOR GENERAL GEO. H. THOMAS DEFEATED AND ROUTED THE REBEL ARMY UNDER GENERAL HOOD [1865] By M. Peseux; Bowen & Co., Lith., Phila. With narrative. 33x38cm (13x15") Highlight color. [51] £97 $150
CHAMPION HILL [ON SHEET WITH] BIG BLACK RIVER BRDGE [AND] PORT HUDSON [1876] From *Comte de Paris* Civil War atlas. Vorzet; Wuhrer; Calman Levy, Paris. 25x56cm (9½x22") Printed color. VG. [20] £65 $100
CHARTE DER KRIEGS OPERATIONEN AM DONN UND DNIEPER ... AO 1736 GESTOCHEN BEY DER KEYSERL: ACAD. DER WISSENSCH IN ST. PETERSB. [c. 1736] 41x46cm (16x18½") B&W. Wormholes at c'fold; lower corners soiled; margin tears repaired. [28] £263 $405
MISSISSIPPI RIVER FROM CAIRO TO MEMPHIS [1863] From E.G. Storke, 25x10cm (9½x4½") 3 colors. Good. [20] £114 $175
PORT HUDSON AND ITS DEFENCES [c. 1863] To illustrate *The War with the South*, 1st ed. C.W. Sholl. NY: Virtue, Yorston & Co. 20x18cm (8½x6½") Partial color. Fair. [20] £23 $35

MINING MAPS - Infrequent Publishers

MAP OF THE LOWER COMSTOCK AND EMIGRANT CONSOLIDATED MINING CO.S MINES [1870] Claims under Silver City, NV street plan. 20x41cm (7½x15½") Folded as issued. [10] £81 $125

THE LEADVILLE MINING DISTRICT COMPILED FROM OFFICIAL RECORDS ... BY CHAS. F. SAUNDERS ... [1901] Denver Litho Co. 117x79cm (46x31") Hand color. Rolled, never folded; minor edge repairs on verso. [45] £179 $275

MITCHELL, S.A. (Atlas Maps 1859 & Earlier)
Try *Desilver, Tanner, Thomas Cowperthwait*

A NEW MAP OF ARKANSAS [1848] 41x33cm (16x13") Color. [45] £45 $70

A NEW MAP OF INDIANA WITH ITS ROADS & DISTANCES [1846] From Mitchell, *New Universal Atlas*. Phila: Burroughs. 32x26cm (12½x10") Orig full color. Image VG, overall good. [59] £49 $75

CONNECTICUT [1846] 31x37cm (12½x14½") Color. [36] £81 $125

FLORIDA [1848] 3 insets. 38x30cm (14½x11½") Full orig color. Edges browned; exc. [4] £88 $135

[SAME TITLE] [1849] 3 insets. [same dimen] Full color. [36] £94 $145

MAP OF MISSOURI [1847] 41x36cm (16x13½") Full color. [61] £81 $125

MAP OF TEXAS FROM THE MOST RECENT AUTHORITIES [1845] Probably 1st issue by Williams, Young. Incl Santa Fe, ephemeral Spring Creek Co. 30x38cm (12x15") Orig pastel color. [46] £390 $600

[SAME TITLE] [c. 1845] Williams mentioned, not Young. Without Spring Creek Co. [same dimen] Orig pastel color. [46] £325 $500

NORTH AMERICA [1847] TX is part of US. 41x33cm (15½x12½") Orig full color. Ref: Wheat (TM) 549. [46] £91 $140

OREGON & UPPER CALIFORNIA [1845 (1847)] 41x33cm (15½x12½") Orig full color. Lower margin sl chipped. [46] £179 $275

PALESTINE & ADJACENT COUNTRIES [1846] 41x33cm (16x13") Color. [23] £29 $45

MITCHELL, S.A. (Atlas Maps 1860 & Later)   Try *Bradley*

[ATLAS] MITCHELL'S NEW GENERAL ATLAS ... EMBRACED IN SIXTY-THREE QUARTO MAPS AND PLANS ... [1871] Sm folio. Half leather covers; tape over leather. Color. Maps bright, clean; occas lt foxing. [5] £649 $1,000

[ATLAS] MITCHELL'S NEW GENERAL ATLAS ... EMBRACING FORTY-SEVEN QUARTO MAPS, FORMING A SERIES OF SEVENTY-SIX MAPS AND PLANS [1860] 1st ed. Sm folio. Half leather covers worn, nearly detached. Maps in bright color; occas lt foxing & damp-staining top margin; few margin tears. Ref: Phillips (A) 831. [5] £649 $1,000

ARIZONA AND NEW MEXICO [1867 (1871)] 29x36cm (11½x14½") Full color. [36] £42 $65

CANADA EAST IN COUNTIES [1860] 32x39cm (12½x15") Full color. VG. [61] £29 $45

CANADA WEST IN COUNTIES [1860] 32x39cm (12½x15") Full color. VG. [61] £29 $45

COUNTY AND TOWNSHIP MAP OF OREGON AND WASHINGTON [1889] 51x37cm (20x14½") Color. [11] £81 $125

COUNTY MAP OF CALIFORNIA [1860] From *New General Atlas*. 33 counties. 34x27cm (13½x10½") Full orig color. VG. Ref: Phillips (A) 831. [59] £75 $115

[SAME TITLE] [same date & dimen] Color. [9] £55 $85

[SAME TITLE] [1883] 53x36cm (21x14") Color. [10] £65 $100

COUNTY MAP OF COLORADO, WYOMING, DAKOTA, MONTANA [1877] 50x36cm (20x14½") Color. [10] £78 $120

COUNTY MAP OF DAKOTA, WYOMING, KANSAS, NEBRASKA AND COLORADO [1871-72] 50x35cm (19½x13½") Orig litho color. [14] £32 $50

COUNTY MAP OF FLORIDA [1870 / 1871] 27x34cm (10½x13½") Orig wash color. 1873, 1878 & 1880 editions offered at same price. [4] £26 $40

COUNTY MAP OF ILLINOIS [1861 (1864)] Chicago inset. 34x27cm (13½x10½") Full col. VG. [61] £16 $25

COUNTY MAP OF IOWA AND MISSOURI [1861 (1864)] 36x29cm (14x11½") Full color. VG. [61] £32 $50

COUNTY MAP OF KENTUCKY & TENNESSEE [1872] 28x36cm (11x14") Color. VG or better. [29] £23 $35

COUNTY MAP OF MASSACHUSETTS, CONNECTICUT AND RHODE ISLAND [1861 (1864)] 30x38cm (12x15") Full color. VG. [61] £23 $35

COUNTY MAP OF MICHIGAN AND WISCONSIN [1863] 29x35cm (11½x14") Color. [14] £16 $25

[SAME TITLE] [same date & dimen] OL & Full color. [61] £49 $75

County Map of Minnesota [1861 (1864)] 36x30cm (14x11½") Full color. VG. [61] £32 $50
County Map of Ohio and Indiana [1861 (1864)] 28x35cm (11x13½") Full color. VG. [61] £39 $60
County Map of Oregon and Washington [1881] School atlas map. Phila: Wm. Bradley & Bros. 28x20cm (11x8") Full color. VG. [19] £32 $50
County Map of Texas [1861 (1864)] 27x34cm (10½x13½") Full color. VG. [61] £49 $75
[Same Title] [1871] [same dimen] Full color. [51] £97 $150
[Same Title] [1872] 28x35cm (11x13½") Orig full color. [46] £101 $155
County Map of the State of Illinois [1863] Chicago inset. 38x30cm (15x12") Full col. [45] £49 $75
County Map of the State of Maine [1861 (1864)] 34x27cm (13½x10½") Full col. VG. [61] £23 $35
[Same Title] [1867] 36x28cm (14x10½") Color. [35] £32 $50
County Map of the State of Texas, Showing Also Portions of the Adjoining States and Territories [1879] 36x54cm (14x21½") Orig full color. [46] £88 $135
County Map of the States of New York, New Hampshire, Vermont, Massachusetts, Rhode Id. and Connecticut [1860] 38x66cm (15x26") Full color. VG. [61] £29 $45
County Map of Virginia and North Carolina [1860] 28x33cm (11x13½") Color. [35] £39 $60
[Same Title] [dated 1860] 27x33cm (11x13") Color. [36] £42 $65
County Map of Virginia and West Virginia [1861 (1864)] 30x38cm (12x15") Full col. VG. [61] £29 $45
Map of Kansas, Nebraska and Colorado. Showing Also the Eastern Portion of Idaho [1861 (1864)] 27x33cm (11x13") Full color. VG. [61] £42 $65
Map of Kansas, Nebraska and Colorado Showing Also the Southern Portion of Dacotah [1867] 29x36cm (11½x14½") Color. [36] £58 $90
Map of Mexico, Central America and the West Indies [1860] 34x54cm (13½x21½") Color. Exc. [29] £39 $60
Map of Oregon, Washington and Part of Idaho [1861 (1864)] 27x34cm (10½x13½") Full color. VG. [61] £49 $75
[Same Title] [1863] Extended rectangular ID. 26x34cm (10x13½") Color. [58] £58 $90
Map of Oregon, Washington, Idaho, and Part of Montana [1874] 25x31cm (9½x12") Full color. Margins browned; VG. [18] £49 $75
Minnesota and Dacotah [1860] 1st ed. 28x33cm (11x13") Strong color. [10] £62 $95
North Carolina [on sheet with] South Carolina [and] Florida [1860] 36x30cm (14x12") Color. VG or better. [29] £23 $35
Northwestern America Showing the Territory Ceded by Russia to the United States [1867] 30x36cm (11½x14") Color. [11] £55 $85
Nova Scotia, New Brunswick, Cape Breton [1860] 38x33cm (15x12½") Full color. VG. [61] £29 $45
Plan of Baltimore [1860 (1864)] 25x29cm (10x11½") Full color. VG. [61] £29 $45
Plan of Boston [1860 (1864)] 38x29cm (15x11½") Full Color. VG. [61] £29 $45
Plan of Cincinnati and Vicinity [1860 (1864)] 28x29cm (11x11½") Full Color. VG. [61] £29 $45
Plan of New Orleans [1860] 20x23cm (7½x9½") Full color. Bright, fine. [20] £39 $60
[Same Title] [1860] 25x29cm (9½x11") Color. [36] £39 $60
[Same Title] [1860 (1864)] 25x30cm (10x11½") Full color. [61] £36 $55
[Same Title] [1867] 20x25cm (7½x9½") Full color. Fine. [20] £42 $65
[Same Title] [1884] 20x25cm (8x9½") Full color. Bright; fine. [20] £32 $50
Plan of New York ... [1860 (1864)] 33x27cm (13x10½") [61] £36 $55
Territory of Idaho [1880] Phila: Wm M. Bradley. 36x23cm (14x9") Full color. Fine. [18] £36 $55
Territory of Montana [1880] 27x36cm (10½x14") Full color. VG. [18] £26 $40

MITCHELL, S.A. (Pocket, School & Wall Maps)

A New Map of Texas Oregon and California ... [1846] Originally issued as wall map inset; identical to folding map, but without ornate border; distance chart starts at Independence, MO; extended Texas. 53x48cm (21x19") Clear orig varnish, minor mottling. Ref: Wheat (TM) 520; Martin 36. [12] £2,435 $3,750
Map of Louisiana, Mississippi and Alabama Constructed from the Latest Authorities [1832] Pocket map. 43x56cm (16½x22") Full color. Cover lacking; backed; VG. [20] £617 $950
Map of Michigan and Wisconsin [1844] 23x28cm (9x11") Color. VG. [61] £39 $60

MAP OF OREGON AND UPPER CALIFORNIA [c. 1846] "No. 15", engraved to illustrate the School and Family Geography. 1st state, with border to 54°40'. Also, "No. 16, Map of the Columbia River..." 27x20cm (10½x8") Full color. Fair. [19] £65 $100

[SAME TITLE] [c.1846 / 1848] "No. 15" ... School and Family Geography. Shows post-1846 Treaty boundary. Also, "No. 16 ... Columbia River..." [same timen] Full color. VG. [19] £65 $100

MAP OF THE NEW ENGLAND OR EASTERN STATES [1852] From *Mitchell's School & Family Geography*. 46x28cm (18x11") Color. Wear & age-toning. [61] £26 $40

MAP OF THE STATE OF TEXAS ... [1846 (1850)] From *School and Family Geography*. Statehood; northern extension before 1850 borders. 27x21cm (10½x8") Orig full color. Ref: Day (TX) #128. [59] £97 $150

[SAME TITLE] [1848] Pre-1850 borders; 1st map to include Dallas. [same dimen] Color. [44] £78 $120

[SAME TITLE] [1852] From *School and Family Geography*. Present border; 2 insets. 20x28cm (8½x10½") Orig full color. Fine. Ref: Day (TX) #51. [59] £65 $100

MAP OF THE UNITED STATES [1844] Wall Map; last ed of Mitchell's first. By J.H. Young; sold by T.& E.H. Ensign, NY. Several insets. 109x89cm (43x34½") OL & full color. 3" missing strip, upper margin; 1" hole; dark varnish; wrinkled/rubbed; margin damp-stained; restorable; fair. [6] £211 $325

MAP OF THE UNITED STATES [1852 (1855)] Extended NE, NM, UT Territories; Calif Gold Region inset. 28x43cm (11x17") Orig wash color. Good. [50] £185 $285

MAP OF THE UNITED STATES AND TEXAS [1839] Pub Hartford. Independent Texas to Nueces; Mexico inset. 25x41cm (10½x16½") Orig wash color. Minimal foxing; good. [50] £224 $345

MAP OF THE UNITED STATES OF AMERICA ENGRAVED TO ILLUSTRATE MITCHELL'S SCHOOL AND FAMILY GEOGRAPHY [1858] 1858 28x43cm (10½x16½") Color. [36] £81 $125

MAP OF THE WESTERN STATES [1839] Hartford. OH, IN, IL, MI, WI. 28x46cm (11x18") Color. VG. [61] £42 $65

MEXICO, CENTRAL AMERICA, WEST INDIES [1852] 23x30cm (9x12") Color. Sl wear. [61] £26 $40

MITCHELL'S MILITARY MAP OF THE UNITED STATES ... [1861] Wall map showing a set of maps. 61x64cm (23½x25") Linen mounted; old replacement of roller & rail. Color. Lt age-toning; few wrinkles & margin stains; VG. [6] £422 $650

MITCHELL'S TRAVELERS GUIDE THROUGH THE UNITED STATES. A MAP OF THE ROADS, DISTANCES, STEAMBOAT & CANAL ROUTES &C. BY J.H. YOUNG [1847] West to MO; 8 inset city plans. 45x56cm (18x22") Color. Rebacked; sl discolored. [45] £195 $300

MOLL (Large)

... ASIA ... [c. 1710] 58x97cm (23x38") Orig OL color. Fold splits repaired; stains in Indian Ocean; else fine. [55] £487 $750

A MAP OF THE EAST INDIES AND THE ADJACENT COUNTRIES WITH THE SETTLEMENTS, FACTORIES AND TERRITORIES EXPLAINING WHAT BELONGS TO ENGLAND, SPAIN, FRANCE, HOLLAND, DENMARK PORTUGAL ETC. ... [1709 (c. 1719+)] From *The World Described* .... 61x100cm (24x39½") OL color. Sl wear; o/w fine. [60] £633 $975

A MAP OF THE WEST INDIES OR THE ISLANDS OF AMERICA IN YE NORTH SEA WITH YE ADJACENT COUNTRIES EXPLAINING WHAT BELONGS TO SPAIN, ENGLAND FRANCE HOLLAND, ETC. AND ALSO YE TRADE WINDS AND ... SEVERAL TRACTS MADE BY YE GALLEONS AND FLOTA ... [1715 (c. 1719+)] [same source] Mexico City view; 5 insets. 59x100cm (23x39") OL color. Sl wear at folds; tear 1 cm into image; o/w fine. [60] £1,623 $2,500

A NEW AND CORRECT MAP OF THE WORLD, LAID DOWN ACCORDING TO THE NEWEST DISCOVERIES ... [1709] Double hemispheres; insular California; celestial diagrams. Prince George of Denmark dedication. 57x97cm (22x38½") Old OL color. Age-toned; creasing at folds, rt fold discolored; split lower lf fold, sm facsimile replacement at Saturn diagram; strong impression. [55] £974 $1,500

[SAME TITLE] [1709 (c. 1719+)] From *The World Described* ... 56x96cm (22x37½") OL color. Worn at c'fold & rt fold; chipping & sl discoloration and sl loss at lower rt fold. [60] £812 $1,250

[SAME TITLE] [1732+] George II dedication. 57x97cm (22x38½") Old color; modern in cartouche. Fold reinforcements; old repair to 3½" tear; mat burn in margin. [55] £1,623 $2,500

A NEW AND EXACT MAP OF FRANCE DIVIDED INTO ALL ITS PROVINCES AND ACQUISITIONS ACCORDING TO THE NEWEST OBSERVATIONS AND THAT ACCURATE SURVEY MADE BY THE KING'S COMMAND BY MR. PICAR AND DE LA HIRE ... [c. 1711] 64x99cm (24½x38½") Old OL color. Fold splits repaired; ink stain in ocean; else VG. [55] £325 $500

[SAME TITLE] [c.1711-1719+] From *The World Described* .... 61x97cm (24x38") Sl wear & discoloration at rt fold; o/w VG. [60] £321 $495

A New and Exact Map of Spain and Portugal Divided into Its Kingdoms and Principalities ... 1711 ... [(c. 1719+)] From *The World Described* .... 61x97cm (24x38½") OL color. Sl wear at folds; o/w fine. [60] £438 $675

A New and Exact Map of the Coast Countries and Islands within ye Limits of ye South Sea Company ... to ye North Part of California etc ... According to ye Newest Observations ... [1720] [same source] Insular California. Several insets. 65x49cm (26x19") OL color. Sl wear lower lf fold; o/w fine. [60] £568 $875

A New and Exact Map of the Dominions of the King of Great Britain on Ye Continent of North America ... [1715 / 1731] The "Beaver Map". 101x60cm (40x23½") Uncolored. Good, clean. Ref: Schwartz & Ehrenberg pl. 78; Stevens & Tree 55c. [2] £3,571 $5,500

A New and Exact Map of the Electorate of Brunswick-Lunenburg and ye Rest of ye King's Dominion in Germany Much Improved by ye Kind Assistance of Several Curious Gentleman Natives of Those Countries ... [(c. 1719+)] From *The World Described* .... 60x100cm (23½x39½") OL color. Sl wear at c'fold; else fine. [60] £308 $475

A New and Exact Map of the United Provinces or Netherlands, etc. ... [1719 or earlier] [same source] 61x101cm (24x40") Sl wear; creases at folds; o/w fine. [60] £568 $875

A New & Correct Map of the Whole World Shewing ye Situation of its Principal Parts ... with the Most Remarkable Tracks of the Bold Attempts which Have Been Made to Find Out the Northeast and Northwest Passages ... 1719 [1719] From *The World Described* .... 69x119cm (27x46½") OL color. 6 folds; sl wear at c'fold; o/w fine [60] £2,921 $4,500

A New Map of Denmark and Sweden ... By H. Moll Geographer [1708 (c. 1719+)] From *The World Described* .... 5 inset views of Lapland life. 60x101cm (23½x39½") Sl fold wear; o/w fine. [60] £487 $750

A New Map of Germany, Hungary, Transilvania and the Suisse Cantons with Many Remarks Not Extant on Any Other Map ... 1712 [(c. 1719+)] From *The World Described* .... 61x97cm (24x38") OL color. Worn at side folds, some loss, 3 cm at upper rt fold; creased c'fold; needs restoration. [60] £195 $300

A New Map of Great Britain ... 1717 [(c. 1719+)] From *The World Described* .... 100x61cm (39½x24") OL color. Minor wear at c'fold; fine. Ref: Shirley (BI 1650-1750) Moll 7.3. [60] £438 $675

[Same title] [c. 1730.] 102x62cm (40x24½") Orig OL color. Sh tears side margins; top & bottom margins bit curled. Ref: Phillips (A) 3469. [28] £338 $520

[Same title] [1732] [same dimen] Orig OL color. Narrow side margins. [14] £227 $350

A New Map of Ireland Divided into its Counties, Provinces and Baronies Wherein are Distinguished the Bishopricks, Burroughs, Barracks, Bogs, Passes, Bridges, etc., with the Principal Roads and Common Reputed Miles ... [1714 (c. 1719+)] From *The World Described* .... 100x61cm (39½x24") OL color. Heavy wear upper fold, 1x4 cm loss; needs restoration. [60] £243 $375

A New Map of Italy Distinguishing All the Sovereignties in It, Whether States, Kingdoms, Principalities ... etc. ... with the Post Roads Extant ... 1714 [(c. 1719+)] From *The World Described* .... 61x101cm (24x39½") OL color. Wear at lf fold, sl surface loss. [60] £308 $475

An Historical Map of the Roman Empire and the Neighboring Barbarous Nations the Year of Our Lord 400 When the Empire Began to be Rent with Foreign Invasions By Monsieur William De Lisle ... 1709 ... [same date & source] 48x112cm (19x44") Wear; creasing at folds; o/w VG. [60] £308 $475

Les Provinces des Pays Bas Catholiques ... A Most Exact Map of Flanders or Austrian Netherlands, etc. ... [1709 (c. 1719+)] From *The World Described* .... 61x99cm (24x39") Sl wear; creasing at folds; o/w fine. [60] £321 $495

The North Part of Great Britain Called Scotland with Considerable Improvements ... 1714 [(c. 1719+)] From *The World Described* .... Views at sides. 61x100cm (24x39½") OL color. Sl wear at folds; fine. Ref: Potter p.96; Shirley (BI) p.88. [60] £487 $750

[Same title] [1714 / 1730-40] Views at sides. [same dimen] OL color; old yellow outlining. Laid down on foam board, shrinkwrapped; VG. [21] £617 $950

The South Part of Great Britain, Called England and Wales Containing All ye Cities, Market Towns, Boroughs and Whatever Places Have ye Election of Members of Parliament ... A.D.1710... [1710] 61x98cm (24x38½") Orig OL color. [14] £250 $385

[Same title] [(c. 1719+)] 61x96cm (24x38") OL color. Lower c'fold separation; o/w VG. [60] £390 $600

The Turkish Empire in Europe Asia and Africa Divided into All Its Governments with the Other Territories that are Tributary to It ... and Also ye Dominions of the Emperor of Morocco ... [1715 (c. 1719+)] From *The World Described* .... 61x101cm (24x39½") OL color. Tear lower lf, sl loss; lower rt fold split 3 cm into image. [60] £812 $1,250

[Same title] [1715 - c.1730] 61x101cm (24x40") Orig OL color. [54] £1,200 $1,848

To Her Most Sacred Majesty Ann Queen of Great Britain France and Ireland ... This Map of Europe ... Is Most Humbly Dedicated ... [1708 (c. 1719+)] From *The World Described* .... 58x95cm (22½x37½") Wear at folds; VG. [60] £192 $295

To His Most Serene and August Majesty Peter ... Absolute Lord of Russia, Etc. ... This Map of Moscovy, Poland, Little Tartary and ye Black Sea is Most Humbly Dedicated ... [(c. 1719+)] From *The World Described* .... 61x94cm (24x37") Heavy wear; creasing & surface loss at lf fold; rest very good; restoration needed. [60] £256 $395

To the Right Honorable Charles Earl of Peterborow ... This Map of Africa is Most Humbly Dedicated ... [1710 - c.1735] 59x97cm (23x38") Color. [54] £800 $1,232

[Same Title] [1714 (c. 1719+)] From *The World Described* .... 5 insets. 58x95cm (23x37½") OL color. Sl wear at c'fold & side folds; rt fold separation into engraving. Ref: Tooley (M&M) p.99. [60] £487 $750

To the Right Honorable Charles Earl of Sunderland and Baron Spencer of Wormleighton ... This Map of South America According to the Newest and Most Exact Observations Is Most Humbly Dedicated ... [1710 (c. 1719+)] From *The World Described* .... Potosi inset. 57x95cm (22½x37½") OL color. Fine. [60] £568 $875

[Same Title] [c. 1720] 59x97cm (23x38½") Full later color. Side margins replaced; top & bottom repaired; folds strengthened on verso; clean, bright. [32] £617 $950

To the Right Honourable John Lord Sommers ... This Map of North America According to Ye Newest and Most Exact Observations Is Most Humbly Dedicated by ... Herman Moll Geographer [1720] From *The World Described* .... The "Cod Fish" map. Insular California. 10 insets. 57x96cm (22½x38") OL color. Separation at lf fold .5 cm into image. Ref: Schwartz & Ehrenberg; Karpinski (MI) pp.40-8; Tooley (Amer) #82; Wheat (TM) 105; Wagner (NW) 514. [60] £2,921 $4,500

To the Right Honourable William Lord Cowper Lord High Chancellor of Great Britain This Map of Asia According to Ye Newest and Most Exact Observations Is Most Humbly Dedicated ... [1705 (c. 1719+)] From *The World Described* .... 58x95cm (22½x37½") OL color. Sl wear at folds; lf fold split 9 cm into image; sm hole at blank area. [60] £422 $650

MOLL (Small)

A Chart of the Sea Coast of Naples, Sicily, Greece and the Archipelago Islands &C [c. 1745] 28x43cm (11½x16½") OL color. [58] £81 $125

A Draught of the City of Jerusalem As It Is Now, Taken from the South East ... By Corneille Le Bruyn [1737] 13x23cm (5x9") [23] £49 $75

A Map of America According to ye Newest and Most Exact Observations ... [1716] London: C. Bowles. Insular Calif. 26x17cm (10x7") Color. Ref: Phillips (A) 3477, 24. [22] £260 $400

A Map of ... Gibraltar [On Sheet With] An Exact Plan of Part of Gibraltar [And a Map of the Western Mediterranean Region and 2 Views of Gibraltar] [1739] 23x61cm (9x24") [58] £81 $125

A Map of New France Containing Canada, Louisiana &C. in Nth. America According to the Patent Granted by the King of France to Monsieur Crozat Dated 14th Sep. 1712 N.S. and Registered in the Parliament of Paris the 24th of Same Month [1739] To Rio Grande. 18x25cm (7x10") OL color. [56] £237 $365

A Map of the North Pole with All the Territories That Lye Near It Known to Us &C. According to the Latest Discoveries and Most Exact Observations Agreeable to Modern History [c. 1729] London: T. & J. Bowles. 20x28cm (8x11") Old OL color. Sh margin tears repaired, one to image; good. [49] £146 $225

A Map of the Seven Provinces of the United Netherlands [1723] 20x20cm (7½x7½") on 12x7½" sheet with text. Uncolored. [45] £49 $75

A New Map of New Found Land, New Scotland, the Isles of Breton, Anticoste, St. John's &C. [1741] 18x26cm (7x10") [14] £97 $150

A New Map of North America According to the Newest Observations [1716] For J. Nicholson. Insular Calif. 18x25cm (7x10") Color. Ref: Phillips (A) 3477, 35. [22] £325 $500

A New Map of the Whole World with the Trade Winds According to Ye Latest and Most Exact Observations by H. Moll Geographer [1739] From Salmon's *Modern History*. Insular Calif; many figures below. 20x26cm (8x10") Sl stain top margin; o/w VG. [30] £276 $425

A Plan of Fort St. George, and the City of Madras [1739] From Salmon's *Modern History*. 20x19cm (8x7½") Uncolored. Fine. [30] £65 $100

A View of ye General & Coasting Trade Winds, Monsoons or ye Shifting Trade Winds Through ye World, Variations &C. [1725] For I. Salmons. Insular Calif. 18x53cm (7½x20½") Color. [22] £159 $245

AMERICA [1723] Insular Calif. Bold lettering "... America ..." above. 20x20cm (7½x8") B&W.
[45] £276 $425
[SAME TITLE] [c. 1736] Insular Calif. 25x20cm (10½x8") Later OL color. Fine. Framed. Ref: Leighly 167, pl.XVIII.
[59] £292 $450
ASIA [c. 1730] 20x28cm (8x10½") B&W. Close lower margin.
[46] £26 $40
CANAAN, PALESTINE OR THE HOLY LAND &C. DIVIDED INTO THE TWELVE TRIBES OF ISRAEL [1701] 23x18cm (8½x7") OL color.
[57] £65 $100
EUROPE [1701] 18x18cm (6½x7½") on text sheet. OL color.
[57] £65 $100
[SAME TITLE] [c. 1710] 18x20cm (6½x7½") with text on 13x8½" sheet. B&W. Close irregular trim lf.
[46] £32 $50
FLORIDA CALLED BY YE FRENCH LOUISIANA &C. [1728 (c.1736)] 20x28cm (8x11") Orig OL color. 2 tears repaired in title; good. Ref: Cumming (SE) 201; Martin (TX) p.25.
[49] £315 $485
[SAME TITLE] [c. 1729] [same dimen] OL color. Deacidified; encapsulated; blind stamp; fine.
[20] £243 $375
GREAT BRITAIN [c. 1710] 18x20cm (7x7½") with text on 14x8" sheet. B&W. Trimmed close lf.
[46] £32 $50
GREAT OR ASIATICK TARTARY ... [1739] 20x25cm (8x10½")
[58] £65 $100
ISLAND OF ST. CHRISTOPHERS [c. 1729] With sm map of "Antego" & Caribbean. . 18x25cm (7x10") B&W.
[46] £45 $70
ITALY [1701] In *A System of Geography.* 18x18cm (7x7") on text sheet. OL color.
[57] £49 $75
[SAME TITLE] [1723] 20x20cm (7½x7½") on 12x7½" sheet with text. Uncolored.
[45] £49 $75
MEXICO, OR NEW SPAIN. DIVIDED INTO THE AUDIANCE OF GUADALAYARA, MEXICO, AND GUATIMALA FLORIDA [1701] 16x18cm (6½x7½") on text sheet.
[57] £172 $265
[SAME TITLE] [1723] 20x20cm (7½x7½") on 12x7½" sheet with text. Uncolored. VG.
[45] £211 $325
NEW ENGLAND, NEW YORK, NEW JERSEY, AND PENSILVANIA &C. [1708 - c.1780] Engraved for Oldmixon's *British Empire in America* .... Carington Bowles reissue. 18x26cm (7x10") Orig OL color.
[53] £300 $462
[SAME TITLE] [c. 1715] 20x28cm (8x11") Orig OL color. Exc.
[38] £162 $250
[SAME TITLE] [1729 - c.1740] From *Atlas Minor.* With "Account of ye Post on ye Continent of Nth America ..." 20x27cm (8x11")
[53] £330 $508
NORTH-BRITAIN: OR SCOTLAND [c. 1710] 18x18cm (7½x7") with text on 10x8½" sheet. B&W.
[46] £26 $40
[SAME TITLE] [1723] 20x20cm (7½x7½") with text on 12x7½" sheet. Uncolored.
[45] £49 $75
PERSIA [1723] 23x20cm (9x7½") on 12x7½" sheet with text. Uncolored.
[45] £39 $60
POLAND [1723] Incl Lithuania. 20x20cm (7½x7½") on 12x7½" sheet with text. Uncolored.
[45] £49 $75
PORTUGAL ... [c. 1720] 25x19cm (10x7½") OL color.
[43] £95 $146
SWEDEN AND NORWAY [1723] Incl Finland & Baltic states. 20x20cm (7½x7½") on 12x7½" sheet with text. Uncolored.
[45] £49 $75
[SAME TITLE] [1739] Incl Finland, Denmark & Baltics. 20x25cm (7½x10½") OL color.
[58] £65 $100
THE CASPIAN SEA DRAWN BY THE CZAR'S SPECIAL COMMAND BY CARL VAN VERDEN IN THE YEAR 1719, 1720 AND 1721 [1732] 25x20cm (10½x8") OL color.
[58] £58 $90
THE EMPIRE OF CHINA AND ISLAND OF JAPAN ... [1739] 25x25cm (10x10") OL color.
[58] £107 $165
THE ENGLISH EMPIRE IN AMERICA, NEWFOUND-LAND, CANADA, HUDSONS BAY &C IN PLANO, HERMAN MOLL [1723] As in *Compleat Geographer.* On 12x7½" sheet with text 22x18cm (9x7") B&W.
[45] £227 $350
THE ISLAND OF CELEBES OR MACASSAR [1741] 20x26cm (8x10")
[14] £49 $75
THE ISLAND OF CELEBES, OR MACASSAR WITH THE ISLANDS OF BANDA, AMBOYNA AND THE MOLUCCAS [1739] 20x25cm (8x10") OL color.
[58] £65 $100
THE ISLE OF CALIFORNIA. NEW MEXICO. LOUISIANE. THE RIVER MISISIPI AND THE LAKE'S OF CANADA ... [1723] Insular Calif. 20x20cm (7½x7½") on 12x7½" sheet with text. Uncolored.
[45] £373 $575
THE PRINCIPAL ISLANDS OF THE EAST INDIES [1723] 23x20cm (9x7½") on 12x7½" sheet with text. Uncolored.
[45] £49 $75
THE WORLD IN PLANISPHERE [1723] As in *Compleat Geographer.* Above in bold, "Geography or a Particular Description of all the Known parts of the Earth". Double hemi; insular Calif. On 12x7½" sheet with text 18x20cm (7x8") Uncolored. Close side margin.
[45] £211 $325

MONATH

TYPUS ORBIS TERRARUM [c. 1717] Updating of 1714 Van der Aa double hemi, with Antarctic land; insular Calif. 25x29cm (10x11½") Color.
[16] £1,401 $2,157

MONTANUS   Try *Ogilby*

DE STADT OSACCO [JAPAN] [1669] 1st state. Largely fanciful view. 26x69cm (10x27") Sh margin tear fixed; else exc. Ref: cf. Cortazzi pl.73. [62] £552 $850
HAVANA [1671] Ogilby-Montanus. 29x35cm (11½x13½") Lt toning along c'fold; else exc. [39] £487 $750
NOVUM AMSTERODAMUM [1671-1673] O. Dapper. NYC view. 13x17cm (5x6½") Uncol. [52] £400 $616
PAGUS HISPANORUM IN FLORIDA [1671] St. Augustine view. 27x35cm (10½x14") Exc. Ref: Deak #50. [63] £422 $650
[SAME TITLE] [same date, dimen & reference] Ogilby-Montanus. Exc. [39] £552 $850
PORTO RICO [1671] City view. 28x36cm (11½x14") Color. [25] £406 $625

MONTRESOR

A MAP OF THE PROVINCE OF NEW YORK WITH PART OF PENSILVANIA, AND NEW ENGLAND, FROM AN ACTUAL SURVEY... [1775 / 1777] 135x92cm (53x36½") Orig OL color. Exc. Ref: Stevens & Tree 42d; Schwartz & Ehrenberg p.181-2; Guthorn (Amer Rev) pp.34-6. [2] £6,167 $9,500
MAP OF NOVA SCOTIA, OR ACADIA; WITH THE ISLANDS OF CAPE BRETON AND ST. JOHN'S ... BY CAPTN. MONTRESOR, ENGIR. 1768 [c. 1775] London: A. Dury. P.E.I. updated. 8 sheets joined into four, each 46x48cm (18x18½") Orig color. Some offsetting; sh margin tears; a sheet with vert crease near c'fold. Ref: Sellers & Van Ee 312; Phillips (A) 1207. [28] £1,753 $2,700

MORDEN

A MAP OF FLORIDA AND YE GREAT LAKES OF CANADA BY ROBT. MORDEN [1688] From *Geography Rectified*. Eastern North America & U.S. 13x13cm (5x5") OL & wash color. [56] £162 $250
[SAME TITLE] [same date & dimen]. Color. Exc. Ref: Cumming (SE) p.165; Karpinski (MI) p.111. [62] £224 $345
A NEW MAP OF CAROLINA ... [1688] Differs from 1687 version; printed as "Page 74". 13x13cm (5x5") Orig OL color. [14] £162 $250
A NEW MAP OF NEW ENGLAND AND NEW YORK BY ROBERT MORDEN [1688] 13x15cm (5x6") Color. Verso text bleeding. [62] £211 $325
A NEW MAP OF NEW JARSEY AND PENSILVANIA BY ROBT. MORDEN [1688] 15x12cm (5½x4½") Color. Exc. [62] £237 $365
A NEW MAP OF SCLAVONIA, CROATIA, DALMATIA, BOSNIA ET REPUR, RAGUSA [1700] Former Yugoslavia. 13x15cm (5x5½") on text sheet. Color. [57] £45 $70
A NEW MAP OF YE WORLD [1680] Insular Calif. 9x16cm (3½x6") Color. [16] £560 $863
A NEW MAP OF YE WORLD BY ROBT. MORDEN [1711] Double hemi; insular Calif. 9x16cm (3½x6") [14] £185 $285
AFRICA [1711] 11x13cm (4½x5") [14] £55 $85
AMERICA BY R. MORDEN [1711] Insular Calif. "Page 333". 11x13cm (4½x5") Good. [14] £162 $250
ASIA. A NEW DESCRIPTION [1688] 11x13cm (4½x5") on text sheet. OL & wash color. [58] £58 $90
EMPIRE DE MOGOL BY ROBT. MORDEN [1688] Afghanistan to Bhutan. 10x13cm (4½x5") on text sheet. Color. [58] £49 $75
ENGLAND [c. 1695] 36x43cm (14½x16½") OL color. Minor creasing; else VG. [55] £97 $150
IRELAND [1688] 13x13cm (5½x5") on text sheet. OL & wash color. [57] £58 $90
[SAME TITLE] [1711] From *Geography Rectified*. 13x12cm (5½x5") [14] £52 $80
JAPONAE AC TERRAE IESSONIS NOVISSIMA DESCRIPTIO ROBT. MORDEN [1700] From *Geography Rectified*. 11x13cm (4½x5") Uncolored. Fine. [32] £146 $225
JAPONIAE AC TERRAE IESSONIS NOVISSIMA DESCRIPTIO [c. 1700] 1st English map of Japan. State III. 11x13cm (4½x5") Exc. Ref: Walter (Japan) 44. [63] £276 $425
KENT [1695] From Camden, *Britannia*. 36x64cm (13½x25") OL color. Age-toning; else VG. [55] £130 $200
POLAND BY ROBT. MORDEN [1688] Incl Lithuania, Belorus & Ukraine. 11x13cm (4x5") on text sheet. OL & wash color. [57] £45 $70
SCOTIAE NOVA DESCRIPTIO PER ROBERT MORDEN [1711] From *Geography Rectified*. 14x12cm (5½x5") [14] £52 $80
TARTARIA IN EUROPE 1700] Black Sea region. 10x13cm (4½x5") On text sheet. OL & wash col. [57] £42 $65
TERRA MAGELLANICA [1680] 13x11cm (5x4½") Text below. Fine. [14] £32 $50
[SAME TITLE] [1700] [samd dimen] on text sheet. OL & wash color. [57] £55 $85
THE COAST OF ZANGUEBAR AND AIEN ... [1700] 12x10cm (5x4") on text sheet. [57] £42 $65

The County Palantine of Lancaster by Robt. Morden [1695] Swale & Churchill. 43x38cm (17x14½") Old color. Creases; ragged margins. Ref: Chubb CXIII. [28] £146 $225

The Kingdom of Ireland [c. 1695] 41x35cm (16x13½") Later color. Margins trimmed but ample. Framed. [51] £812 $1,250

[SAME TITLE] [c. 1695] In *Britannia* ... 41x34cm (16x13") Orig OL color. Repaired tear; good. Ref: MCC 49 p.198 #117. [59] £179 $275

The Kingdom of Ireland by Robt. Morden [1695] 41x35cm (16½x13½") Color. [24] £227 $350

The Philipine Isles [1688] 10x13cm (4x5") on text sheet. OL & wash color. [57] £58 $90

MORRIS

A Plan of Milford Haven ... [1748, 1800] From *Plans of Harbours ... in St. George's Channel*. Lewis Morris; his son William's edition. 18x23cm (7x9") Col. Upper rt corner repaired, sl loss engraved area. [15] £15 $23

Goldtop Road in St. Brides Bay ... [1748, 1800] From *Plans of Harbours ... in St. George's Channel*. Lewis Morris; son William's edition. 18x23cm (7x9") Color. [15] £34 $52

Newport Bay & Harbour ... [1748, 1800] From *Plans of Harbours ... in St. George's Channel*. Lewis Morris; son William's edition. 18x23cm (7x9") Color. Lacks blank margin corner. [15] £34 $52

MORSE, J.   Try *Stockdale*

A Chart of the Nth. West Coast of America, & the Nth. East Coast of Asia Showing Discoveries that Have Been Lately Made in Those Parts [1802] Boston: Thomas & Andrews. Gridley, sc. 20x30cm (7½x11½") Uncolored. [44] £78 $120

[SAME TITLE] [1804] 18x30cm (7x11½") Transferral; spotting; good. [19] £97 $150

A Map of Georgia Also the Two Floridas, from the Best Authorities [1796] From *The American Universal Geography*, 3rd ed. Boston: Thomas & Andrews. Doolittle, sc. 19x31cm (7½x12") Uncolored. Ref: Wheat & Brun 614 [4] £114 $175

[SAME TITLE] [same date & dimen] [58] £162 $250

A Map of Massachusetts from the Best Authorities by A. Adams [1802] Gridley, sc. 20x30cm (8x12") Uncolored. Repaired fold separations, insignificant loss. [44] £78 $120

A Map of Massachusetts from the Best Authorities by J. Denison [1796] W. Mass. inset. 18x24cm (7½x9½") Separated vertical folds rejoined; else fine. Ref: Wheat & Brun 218. [63] £107 $165

[SAME TITLE] [1796] 20x25cm (8x10") B&W. VG. [45] £58 $90

A Map of the District of Maine with New Brunswick & Nova Scotia [1796] 18x23cm (7x9") Exc. Ref: Wheat & Brun 175. [63] £107 $165

A Map of the North Western Territory [1796] 19x24cm (7½x9½") B&W. VG. [45] £146 $225

A Map of the State of Kentucky and the Tennessee Government Compiled from the Best Authorities by Cyrus Harris [1796] 19x29cm (7½x11½") Uncolored. Ref: Wheat & Brun 645. [58] £146 $225

[SAME TITLE] [1796] 20x28cm (7½x11") Splitting fold mended; overall fine. [63] £159 $245

A Map of the States of New Hampshire and Vermont by J. Denison [1802] 20x24cm (8x9½") B&W. Fold repairs, minor loss. [44] £58 $90

Map of North and South Carolina by J. Denison [1796] Engraved by Doolittle. 19x23cm (7½x9") B&W. Two close margins. Ref: Wheat & Brun 585 [46] £65 $100

[SAME TITLE] [same date & dimen] Uncolored. [58] £81 $125

Map of the Southern Parts of the United States of America ... [1802] By Abraham Bradley, "corrected by the Author". 20x39cm (8x15½") Fold repairs; edge chips. [44] £130 $200

Map of the State of New York [1796] 20x25cm (8x10") B&W. Incidental discolorations; VG. [45] £58 $90

Map of the States of Maryland and Delaware by J. Denison [1796] 20x25cm (8x10") B&W. [45] £58 $90

New Jersey [1796] From *American Universal Geography*. 19x15cm (7½x5½") B&W. Ref: Wheat & Brun 417; Phillips (M) p.489. [36] £71 $110

[SAME TITLE] [1796] 20x15cm (8x6") B&W. Incidental discoloration. [45] £65 $100

Rhode-Island and Connecticut [1796] 20x33cm (8x13½") B&W. [45] £58 $90

United States [1822] From *A Report ... Comprising a Narrative of a Tour ... 1820*. New Haven. By A. Daggett. 25x41cm (10½x16½") Orig OL & wash color. Sm margin repairs; fine. [50] £256 $395

Virginia [1796] 15x20cm (6x7½") B&W. [45] £81 $125

MORSE, S.

[BOOK] SYSTEM OF GEOGRAPHY FOR THE USE OF SCHOOLS [1845] NY: Harper & Bros. Large quarto; 72 pp; 54 partial & full page cerographic maps. B&W & mono-color. Boards soiled, sl water-stained, warped; text shaken; even age-tone, lt foxing; edges ragged; good. [7] £146 $225

LOUISIANA, MISSISSIPPI AND ARKANSAS [1846] NY: Harper & Bros., 1st school atlas with printed color. Reverse: GA & AL. 23x15cm (9x6½") Green cerographic color. Browned; fair. [20] £32 $50

UNITED STATES [1826] From *Pocket Gazetteer*. 28x43cm (10½x17") Color. [44] £130 $200

MORSE & BREESE

A MAP OF THE INDIAN TERRITORY, NORTHERN TEXAS AND NEW MEXICO SHOWING THE GREAT WESTERN PRAIRIES BY JOSIAH GREGG [1845] Platte River to El Paso. 38x30cm (14½x11½") Soft green color. [44] £211 $325

INDIANA [1843] Cerograph; see Schwartz & Ehrenberg, p.266. 36x28cm (14x11") Fine. [61] £65 $100

IOWA AND WISCONSIN CHIEFLY FROM THE MAP OF J.N. NICOLLET [1845] Extended territorial forms. 30x38cm (12x15") Uncolored. [45] £146 $225

LOUISIANA [1842] 29x36cm (11½x14") Full printed color. Minor marginal browning; VG. [20] £65 $100

MAP OF THE CALIFORNIAS BY T.J. FARNHAM [1845] 38x30cm (14½x11½") Soft green col. [44] £211 $325

MAP OF THE JOURNEYINGS OF THE ISRAELITES IN THE DESERT CHIEFLY FROM THE MAP OF ROBINSON AND SMITH [1843] Sinai inset. 30x38cm (12½x15½") [23] £19 $30

TEXAS [1844 (1846)] Cerographic printing process. 37x30cm (15x12") Green overprinting. [46] £227 $350

[SAME TITLE] [1845] 38x30cm (15x12") Uncolored. [45] £308 $475

MORSE & GASTON

[ATLAS] THE DIAMOND ATLAS. WITH DESCRIPTIONS OF ALL COUNTRIES ... [1857] Charles Colby; NY: S.N. Gaston. Small quarto. Pp: vi + 7-239(1). 54 full & double page cerographic maps of American states, countries & territories. Most with color. Full leather gold embossed boards & spine; gilt edges. Minor occas spotting; endpapers stained; overall VG+. [34] £224 $345

MORTIER

[PILOS, GREECE] [c. 1705] From *Les Forces de l'Europe* ... View with ships in foreground. 11x15cm (4x6") [64] £57 $88

ANVERS ANTWERPEN EN FLAMAND [same date & source] After De Fer. 20x28cm (8x11") [64] £61 $94

ARRAS. VILLE FORTE CAPITALE DU COMTE D'ARTOIS [same date & source] Fortification plan. 21x27cm (8x10½") [64] £20 $31

ATH, VILLE FORTE DES PAIS BAS, DANS LE COMTE DE [same date & source] By De Fer. Fortification plan. 20x28cm (8x11") [64] £33 $50

AUGSBOURG VILLE IMPERIALE D'ALLEMAGNE TRES CONSIDERABLE DU CERCLE DE SOUABE [same date & source] Fortification plan. 20x29cm (8x11½") [64] £61 $94

BASLE VILLE CAPITALE DU CANTON DU MEME NOM [same date & source] Bird's-eye view. 21x24cm (8x9½") [64] £347 $535

BONNE, OU BONN [same date & source] By De Fer. Fortifications. 21x29cm (8x11") [64] £241 $371

BRISACH VILLE FORTE SUR LE RHEIN CAPITALE DE LA PROVINCE DE BRISCOW [same date & source] Fortification plan. 20x27cm (8x10½") [64] £90 $138

BRUXELLES VILLE CONSIDERABLE DES PAIS BAS. CAPITALE DU DUCHE DE BRABANT [[same date & source] Fortification plan. 22x28cm (8½x11") [64] £102 $157

CARTE DE LA TERRE SAINTE DIVISEE SELON LES DOUZE TRIBUS D'ISRAEL OU SONT ... JESUS CHRIST ... [1705] 41x48cm (16x18½") Color. [23] £179 $275

CARTE GENERAL DE LA CAROLINE DESSE SUR LES MEMOIRES LE PLUS NOUVEAUX [1696] Based on Thornton-Morden-Lea. 57x47cm (22½x18½") Orig wash color. Mint. [62] £1,428 $2,200

CARTE PARTICULIERE DE L'AMERIQUE SEPTENTRIONALE, OU SONT COMPRIS LE DETROIT DE DAVIDS, LE DETROIT DE HUDSON, &C. ... [c. 1696-1708] 2 sheets joined 58x84cm (23x32½") Orig OL color. Faint partially washed out rubber stamp top border. Ref: Koeman III Mor 1. [28] £584 $900

[SAME TITLE] [c. 1700] Incl Greenland & Iceland. [same dimen] Early color. Sl discoloration; color weakened paper strengthened on reverse. [15] £580 $893

CARTE PARTICULIERE DE LA CAROLINE DRESSE SUR LES MEMOIRES LE PLUS NOUVEAU [1700] 48x60cm (19x23½") Orig OL color. 2 clean tears repaired; no loss. Ref: Cumming (SE) 121. [2] £1,039 $1,600

[SAME TITLE] [c. 1696] [same dimen] Orig OL color. Framed. [51] £2,077 $3,200

COBLENTZ [1693] From *Les Forces de l'Europe* ... 16x14cm (6½x5½") [64] £82 $126
COLLONGE [c. 1705] From *Les Forces de l'Europe* ... With fortifications. 21x29cm (8x11") [64] £225 $346
COPENHAGUE [same date & source] Fortification plan. 22x32cm (8½x12½") [64] £73 $113
DENDERMONDE VILLE FORTE DES PAIS BAS, DU COMTE DE FLANDRES [same date & source] By De Fer. Fortification plan. 22x27cm (8½x10½") [64] £24 $38
DONQUERQUE DUYNKERK EN FLAMAND [same date & source] By De Fer. Fortification plan. 20x28cm (8x11") [64] £29 $44
F. D'ASSO [same date & source] Fortification plan; Assos, Asia Minor. 11x15cm (4x6") [64] £33 $50
FORTERESSE DE CERIGO [same date & source] Ionian Islands. 11x15cm (4x6") [64] £37 $57
FORTERESSE DE VOLO [same date & source] Greece. Fortifications. 11x15cm (4x6") [64] £29 $44
FORTERESSE DE ZANTE [same date & source] Greece. 11x15cm (4x6") [64] £37 $57
FRIBOURG EST UNE VILLE FORTE CAPITAL DE BRISGAW [same date & source] Fortification plan. 21x29cm (8½x11½") [64] £122 $189
GOTHEBOURG [same date & source] Fortification plan. 19x28cm (7½x11") [64] £37 $57
HAMBORG, VILLE IMPERIALE D'ALLEMAGNE ... [same date & source] Fortification plan. 22x30cm (8½x11½") [64] £163 $252
HEIDELBERG [same date & source] View by De Fer. 21x24cm (8x9½") Sm rust spot in sky. [64] £363 $560
HOMBOURG [same date & source] View of palace. 11x15cm (4x6") [64] £188 $289
HUY PETITE VILLE DU PAIS DE LIEGE [same date & source] Fortification plan. 22x29cm (8½x11½") [64] £24 $38
INDIA VETUS INTRA EXTRA GAGEM ... [c. 1700] N India. 21x28cm (8½x11") Orig OL col. [14] £39 $60
LA HAIE SEJOUR ORDINAIRE DE LA COUR HOLLANDOISE [c. 1705] From *Les Forces de l'Europe* ... 24x29cm (9½x11½") [64] £82 $126
LA VILLE D'ATHENES [same date & source] View of Acropolis & walls. 11x15cm (4x6") [64] £65 $101
LE PORT D'ALGER [same date & source] 22x29cm (8½x11½") [64] £37 $57
LE SAS DE GAND [same date & source] On Ghent-Terneuzen canal; fortifications. 20x26cm (8x10") [64] £33 $50
LEPANTHE [c. 1705] From *Les Forces de l'Europe* ... View; Naupaktos, Greece with harbor. 11x15cm (4½x6") [64] £53 $82
LES ENVIRONS DE FRANCFORT [same date & source] 19x25cm (7½x10") [64] £159 $245
LUXEMBOURG VILLE FORTE, CAPITALE DU DUCHE DE MEME NOM ... [same date & source] By De Fer. Fortification plan. 20x27cm (8x10½") [64] £327 $503
MAESTRICHT VILLE DU BRABANT HOLLANDOIS [same date & source] By De Fer. Fortification plan. 20x28cm (8x11") [64] £49 $75
MONS [same date & source] Fortification plan. 20x27cm (8x10½") [64] £33 $50
NAMUR [same date & source] View. 11x16cm (4x6") [64] £16 $25
NEGROPONT [same date & source] Chalkis view. 11x16cm (4x6") [64] £73 $113
OSTENDE [same date & source] After De Fer. Fortification plan. 20x25cm (8x10") [64] £16 $25
PHALSBOURG [same date & source] Lorraine. After De Fer. 21x30cm (8½x11½") [64] £29 $44
PLAN DE LA CITIDELLE DE NANCY [same date & source] 11x15cm (4x6") [64] £8 $13
PLAN DE LA VILLE D'AXEL [same date & source] Fortification plan. 11x15cm (4x6") [64] £16 $25
PLAN DE LA VILLE D'IPRE [same date & source] Ypres. Fortifications. 11x15cm (4x6") [64] £12 $19
PLAN DE LA VILLE DE BURICK [same date & source] Buderich fortifications. 11x15cm (4½x6") [64] £49 $75
PLAN DE LA VILLE DE CHARLEROI [same date & source] Fortifications. 11x15cm (4½x6") [64] £8 $13
PLAN DE LA VILLE DE GUERMSHEIM [same date & source] Fortifications & Rhine. 11x15cm (4x6") [64] £163 $252
PLAN DE LA VILLE DE KAISERSWERT same date & source] Fortifications. 11x16cm (4x6") [64] £118 $182
PLAN DE LA VILLE DE SPIRE [same date & source] Fortification plan. 11x16cm (4½x6") [64] £49 $75
PLAN DE LA VILLE DE TREUES [same date & source] Trier fortification plan. 11x15cm (4x6") [64] £184 $283
PLAN DE LA VILLE DE VALENCIENNES [same date & source] Fortifications. 11x15cm (4x6") [64] £8 $13
PLAN DE LA VILLE DE WESEL [same date & source] Fortification plan. 11x15cm (4½x6") [64] £78 $119
PLAN DE LA VILLE ET CHASTEAU DE BOUILLON [same date & source] Belgium. Fortification plan. 11x16cm (4½x6") [64] £33 $50
PLAN DE LA VILLE ET CITADELLE DE NUISS [same date & source] 11x16cm (4x6") [64] £131 $201
PLAN DE LA VILLE ET CITIDELLE DE TOURNAY [same date & source] 11x15cm (4½x6") [64] £8 $13

PLAN DE LA VILLE ET DU FORT DE REES [c. 1705] From *Les Forces de l'Europe* ... Germany. Fortifications. 11x15cm (4½x6") [64] £82 $126

PLAN DE STRASBOURG [same date & source] Fortification plan. 23x33cm (9x13") [64] £114 $176

PLAN DE TRIPOLY EN BARBARIE [same date & source] Fortifications & harbor. 23x29cm (9x11½") [64] £159 $245

PLAN DES VILLES, ET CHASTEAU DE CREUTZHNAC AU PALATINAT DU RHIN [same date & source] Fortification plan. 11x15cm (4x6") [64] £188 $289

PLAN DU FORT DE SKENK [same date & source] 11x15cm (4½x6") [64] £49 $75

QUEBEC, VILLE DE L'AMERIQUE SEPTENTRIONALE DANS LA NOUVELLE FRANCE [same date & source] English fleet positions in 1670, fortifications & surroundings. 21x29cm (8x11½") [64] £196 $302

REGNUM SALOMONICUM ... [1705 - 1725] From *Atlas Antiquus*. After Phillipe de La Rue, 1651. 39x53cm (15x20½") Uncolored. Fine. Ref: Laor 417. [59] £250 $385

RHEINFELS [ST. GOAR, GERMANY] [c. 1705] From *Les Forces de l'Europe* ... Castle plan & surroundings. 21x26cm (8x10") [64] £82 $126

TERRA CHANAAN AD ABRAHAMI TEMPORA ... [1705] 41x56cm (16½x21½") OL color. [23] £159 $245

WISMAR [c. 1705] From *Les Forces de l'Europe* ... Fortification plan. 20x26cm (8x10") [64] £49 $75

MOUNT & PAGE

A CHART OF THE COASTS OF IRELAND AND PART OF ENGLAND [1745] 43x56cm (17½x22") Color. Minor repairs. [24] £120 $185

A CHART OF THE ISLAND OF HISPANIOLA WITH THE WINDWARD PASSAGE FROM IAMAICA BETWENE YE EAST END OF CUBA & THE WEST END OF HISPANIOLA [1713] Bahamas to Great Exuma. 43x53cm (16½x20½") Uncolored. [15] £300 $462

A CHART SHEWING PART OF THE SEA COAST OF NEWFOUNDLAND FROM YE BAY OF BULLS TO LITTLE PLACENTIA EXACTLY AND CAREFULLY LAYD DOWN BY JOHN GAUDY [c.1715 - 1780] 46x56cm (18x22") Ref: Phillips (A) 1157 [8]. Phillips (M) p.475; Sellers & Van Ee 666. [28] £497 $765

A LARGE DRAUGHT FROM BENJAR ON THE ISLAND OF BORNEO TO MACASSER ON THE ISLAND OF CELEBES SHEWING THE STREIGHTS OF BALLY ... [c. 1750] From *The English Pilot, Third Book*. 44x54cm (17½x21") Exc. [63] £438 $675

A LARGE DRAUGHT OF THE COAST OF IAVA FROM BANTAM POINT TO BATAVIA [c. 1750] 44x104cm (17½x41") Exc. [63] £552 $850

A NEW AND CORRECT CHART OF CUBA, STRAIGHTS OF BAHAMA, WINDWARD PASSAGE, THE CURRENT THROUGH THE GULF OF FLORIDA ... [1789] From *English Pilot IV Book*. 46x65cm (18x25½") Some sm faint stains. [14] £422 $650

A NEW AND CORRECT CHART OF THE COAST OF NEW FOUNDLAND FROM CAPE RAZE TO CAPE BONAVISTA, WITH CHEBUCTO HARBOUR IN NOVA SCOTIA [c. 1755] Two sheets joined, 42x102cm (16½x40") Old Ol color. Lf margin dampstained; sm holes repaired, blank area affected; sh upper c'fold split. Ref: Sellers & Van Ee 748; Phillips (A) 3652. [28] £555 $855

A NEW AND CORRECT CHART OF THE ISLAND OF JAMAICA WITH THE BAYS, HARBOURS, ROCKS, SOUNDINGS &C. [1768] From *English Pilot IV Book*. 46x69cm (18x27") Sl repair to fold; o/w nice. [14] £325 $500

A NEW AND CORRECT CHART OF THE NORTH PART OF AMERICA FROM NEW FOUND LAND TO HUDSON'S BAY [c. 1755] From *English Pilot Fourth Book*. 43x55cm (17x22") Orig color. Sh tears lower margin repaired; pinhole in blank area. Ref: Phillips (A) 3562; Sellers & Van Ee 198. [28] £380 $585

A NEW & CORRECT CHART OF CUBA, STREIGHTS OF BAHAMA, WINDWARD PASSAGE, THE CURRENT THROUGH THE GULF OF FLORIDA, ... [1767] From *The English Pilot*. 47x65cm (18½x25½") Faint dampstaining upper rt; minor wear at fold; overall fine. [62] £552 $850

A NEW SURVEY OF THE HARBOUR OF BOSTON IN NEW ENGLAND ... [1706] From *The English Pilot, Book IV*. 43x56cm (16½x21½") Some staining; else exc. Ref: Mercator Soc. 1, Map 19. [38] £2,499 $3,850

A SEA CHART OF THE GULPH OF VENICE ... [c. 1770] As in *The English Pilot*. 41x51cm (16x20½") [15] £290 $447

BARBADOS [1789] From *English Pilot IV Book*. 29x26cm (11½x10") plus text. [14] £114 $175

BERMUDA [1784] [same source] Sailing directions below & verso. 29x22cm (11½x9") Sl brown stain at corner. [14] £552 $850

LARGE DRAUGHT OF THE COAST OF CHINA FROM AMOY TO CHUSAN WITH YE HARBOUR OF AMOYE AT LARGE ... [c. 1750] In *The English Pilot*, 1st in 1703. 53x43cm (21x17") [15] £340 $524

Map of the Coast of New England from Staten Island to the Island of Breton As It Was Actualy Survey'd by Capt. Cyprian Southack ... [1789] From *English Pilot IV Book*. New York to Nova Scotia; Insets: Boston; North Atlantic. 60x79cm (23½x31") Some discoloration; tissue support; fine. [14] £2,272 $3,500

The Harbour of Casco Bay and Islands Adjacent [1789] From *English Pilot IV Book*. 43x54cm (17x21") Some discoloration & support. [14] £357 $550

Virginia, Maryland, Pennsylvania, East & West New Jersey [1789] From *English Pilot IV Book*. 51x80cm (20x31½") Sl discoloration & support to verso. [14] £2,272 $3,500

MOUZON

An Accurate Map of North and South Carolina with Their Indian Frontiers ... [1775] Printed for Sayer & Bennett. 102x142cm (39½x55½") Pocket map in 32 panels, each 10x7", on linen edged with green cloth, with orig slipcase. Full orig color. Ref: Cumming (SE) #450. [51] £5,518 $8,500

MOXON

Canaan or the Land of Promise, Possessed by the Children of Israel and Travelled Through by Our Saviour Jesus Christ; and His Apostles. Translated by Joseph Moxon ... [1671] Amsterdam: Visscher. 31x46cm (12½x18½") Color. Ref: Laor 521. [23] £282 $435

Israels Perigrination, or the Forty Years Travels of the Children of Israel out of Egypt through the Red Sea ... into Canaan ... [1671] Amsterdam: Visscher. 32x46cm (12½x18½") Full color. Ref: Laor 519. [23] £308 $475

The Travels of St. Paul and Other Apostles or a Geographical Description of Those Lands and Countries Where in the Gospel of Christ Was First Propagated ... [1671] Amsterdam: Visscher. Vignettes top & bottom. 33x48cm (12½x18½") Color. Ref: Laor 523. [23] £276 $425

Totius Orbis Terrarum Tabula ... per J. Moxon [c. 1671] 21x33cm (8½x13") Color. Ref: Shirley (W) 458. [16] £465 $717

MULLER

[United States: Southeast] [c. 1700] Johan Ulrich Muller. A reduced version of Sanson; without text below map. 8x8cm (2½x3") B&W. Fine. Ref: Cumming (SE) 112; Phillips (A) 512, 91. [55] £227 $350

Nouvelle Carte des Decouvertes Faites par des Vaisseaux Russiens aux Cotes Inconnues de l'Amerique Septentrionale ... [1773] 48x65cm (19x25½") Orig color. Sh tears lower margin; lf margin soiled; trace of foxing. Ref: Bagrow (Russia) 163; Fite & Freeman 51; Wagner (NW) 591; Falk (AK) 1773-1; Tooley (Landmarks) p.131. [28] £876 $1,350

[Same Title] [1773] Von Stahlin modifications. 46x64cm (18x25") Orig OL color. Sl frayed margins; old shorthand notes. Ref: Wagner (NW) 633; Streeter 3466; Imago Mundi III (Breitfuss) p.95. [46] £487 $750

MUNSTER

[Palestine] [1575] 17x26cm (6½x10½") Uncolored. Fine. Ref: cf. Laor 528. [33] £136 $210

Africa XXV. Nova Tabula [1545] Ptolemy's *Geographia*. Entire continent. 28x36cm (10½x13½") Color. Exc. Ref: Norwich #2; MCCS 29, #6. [37] £617 $950

Aphrica mit Seinen Befundern Lendern [c. 1550] From *Cosmographia*. 13x16cm (5x6½") on full text sheet. [63] £62 $95

Aphricae Tabula I [1545] Ptolemy's *Geographia*. Ptolemaic N.W. Africa. 26x33cm (10½x13") Color. Exc. [37] £195 $300

Aphricae Tabula II [same date, source & dimen] Ptolemaic North Africa. Col. Exc. [37] £260 $400

Aphricae Tabula III [same date, source & dimen] Ptolemaic Egypt. Color. Exc. [37] £227 $350

Behemer Funigreich [sic] mit Bergen und Walden Geringo unb Beschossen [c. 1550] 26x35cm (10x13½") Exc. [63] £227 $350

Civitas Florentina [c. 1560] View. 22x36cm (8½x14") Exc. [63] £276 $425

Das Erst General Inhaltend die Beschreibung und den Circkel des Gantzen Erdtrichs ... [1550] From same woodblock as "Typus Universalis" with German title. 26x38cm (10½x15") Color. Exc. [37] £1,623 $2,500

[Same Title] [1553] Decorative surround; David Kandel initials lower lf. [same dimen] Uncolored. No show-through; margin repair; nice. Ref: Shirley (W) 92. [26] £747 $1,150

Das Heilig Landt mit Ausztheilung der Zwolff Geschlechter [1588] 32x36cm (12½x14½") Color. Ref: Laor 532. [23] £211 $325

DER STATT ROM [c. 1560] Aerial view. 21x23cm (8½x9") Exc. [63] £81 $125
DESCRIPTION NOUVELLE DU PAIS D'ESPAIGNE [1540 / 1555] 25x35cm (10x13½") Exc. [62] £227 $350
DEUSCHLAND MIT SEINEM GENGEN BEGRIFF UND EINGSCHLOSZNEN LANDSCHAFFTEN [c. 1550] South at top. 26x35cm (10x13½") Exc. [63] £227 $350
DIE ENDEGNOSCHAFFE ODER SCHWENZERLAND MIT DEN ANSTOSSENDEN LANDERN [c. 1550] 26x35cm (10x13½") Exc. [63] £227 $350
DIE ERST GENERAL TAFEL / DIR BESCHREIBUNG UND DEN CIRCKEL DES GANTZEN ERDTRICHS UND MEERS INNHALTENDE [1588] Basel: Petrie. From later editions of *Cosmographia*. 31x36cm (12x14½") Color. Ref: Shirley (W) 163, pl.134. [16] £1,329 $2,048
[SAME TITLE] [c. 1588] [same dimen] Later full color. Uniform age toning; sl marginal chipping; wrinkling; good. [31] £812 $1,250
DIE LANDER ASIE NACH IRER GELEGENHEIT BISS IN INDIA WERDEN IN DISER TAFEL VERZEICHNET [1540 - 1567] 27x35cm (10½x13½") Uncolored. Lt impression along c'fold. [54] £800 $1,232
DIE LANGER AIE ... [1540 (c.1550)] Asia. 26x35cm (10x13½") Some early (?) color. Margin tears mended; generally VF. [63] £487 $750
DIE NEUWEN INSELN ... [1540+] With "Verrazano Sea". 26x34cm (10x13½") + title. Exc. Illustrated in Danforth, *The Land of Nurembega*. [62] £1,883 $2,900
[SAME TITLE] [1540 (1572)] With "Verrazano Sea". 25x36cm (10x13½") B&W. Fine. Ref: Schwartz & Ehrenberg pl.18; Johnson (Amer Expl) 67; Kershaw (Canada) 12a. [55] £2,110 $3,250
DIE NEUWE INSELN SO ZU UNSERN ZEITEN DURCH DIE KUNIG VON HISPANIA IM GROSSEN OZEANO GEFUNDEN SINDT [1546] With "Verrazano Sea". 28x36cm (10½x13½") B&W. Fine. Ref: Schwartz & Ehrenberg pp.43-45; Wagner (NW) XXXI; Wolff 108. [1] £1,948 $3,000
DIE NEUWEN INSELN / SO HINDER HISPANEN GEGEN ORIENT / BEY DEM LANDT INDIE GELEGEN [1540 - c.1562] Narrow "Verrazano Isthmus" at Carolina. 27x34cm (10½x13½") Uncolored. [54] £2,200 $3,388
[SAME TITLE] [1574 or 1578] Probably from *Cosmographey oder Beschreibung Aller Lander ...* Narrow "Verrazano Isthmus". 25x34cm (10x13½") Full later color. Strengthened on verso; sm lower c'fold margin repair. Ref: Kershaw (Canada) state 12; Schwartz & Ehrenberg 18. [31] £1,623 $2,500
DIE STATT AUGSPURG [c. 1560] View. 26x35cm (10x14") Exc. [63] £211 $325
DIE STATT BASELL [c. 1560] View. 26x35cm (10x14") + title. Exc. [63] £276 $425
DIE STATT BERN [c. 1560] View. 21x30cm (8½x12") Exc. [63] £276 $425
DIE STATT CHUR [c. 1560] Switzerland. View. 14x35cm (5½x13½") + title. Exc. [63] £162 $250
DIE STATT COLMAR [c. 1560] View. 23x35cm (9x13½") Exc. [63] £114 $175
DIE STATT EGER [c. 1560] Cheb, Bohemia. View. 23x34cm (9x13½") + title. Exc. [63] £97 $150
DIE STATT ERDFURT [c. 1560] Two views on sheet. 21x37cm (8½x14½") Fine. [63] £81 $125
DIE STATT FRANKFURT [c. 1560] View. 25x38cm (10x15") + title. Side margins trimmed; else fine. [63] £292 $450
DIE STATT FREISINGEN [c. 1560] View. 13x36cm (5x14") Exc. [63] £120 $185
DIE STATT LANDAW [(1547) c.1560] Date next to woodcutter's initials. View. 17x38cm (6½x15") [63] £185 $285
DIE STATT LINDAW [c. 1560] View 27x36cm (10½x14") + title. Exc. [63] £211 $325
DIE STATT NORDELINGEN. MDXLIX [c. 1560] View. 23x34cm (9x13½") + title. Exc. [63] £114 $175
DIE STATT PARIS [c. 1560] Plan view. 25x36cm (10x14") Full color. C'fold repaired; lower lf corner repaired; else good. [63] £292 $450
DIE STATT SCHLETSTAT [c. 1560] View. In Alsace. 20x33cm (8x13") + title. Exc. [63] £114 $175
DIE STATT SITTEN [c. 1560] View of Sion, Switzerland. 26x36cm (10x14") Exc. [63] £185 $285
DIE STATT SOLOTHURN [c. 1560] Switzerland. View. 23x30cm (9x12") Exc. [63] £120 $185
DIE STATT SPEIER [c. 1560] View. 17x38cm (6½x15") Tight side margins. [63] £146 $225
DIE STATT WUSSENBURG [c. 1560] View. In Alsace. 27x38cm (10½x15") Close margins. [63] £114 $175
DISCRIZZION DELL'ISOLA DELLA SICILIA, & DI TUTTO 'L REGNO DI QUELLA SECONDO UARII RISPETTI DI QUELLA [1575] 21x15cm (8½x5½") Uncolored. Fine. [33] £123 $190
EGRANA CIVITAS OLIM DE IMPERIO ROMANORUM, HODIE VERO REGNO BOHEMIAE SUBIECTA [c. 1550] Wood cut bird's eye view of Eger. 23x34cm (9x13½") [14] £81 $125
FIGURA DEL MONDO UNIVERSALE [1550 - c.1558] Munster's 2nd modern map of world, with "Verrazano Sea". 26x38cm (10x15") Uncolored. Ref: Shirley (W) 92. [53] £2,000 $3,080

FIRENZE CITTA NOBILISSIMA DELLA TOSCANA SECONDO I NOSTRI TEMPI DISEGNATA [1575] Bird's eye view. 22x35cm (8½x14") Sm pinhole lower margin; upper lf neatline did not print; VG. [33] £195 $300

FRANCKFURT AN DER ODER ANNO DMI 1548 [c. 1560] View from east. 20x29cm (8x11½") + title & key. Exc. [63] £114 $175

FRIBURG IM BRISGEW 1549 [c. 1560] View. 20x36cm (7½x14") Exc. [63] £292 $450

HERBIPOLIS WURTZPURG [c. 1560] View. 28x38cm (11x15") [63] £162 $250

HISPANIA III. NOVA TABULA [1545] Ptolemy's *Geographia*. Ptolemaic Iberia. 25x33cm (10½x13½") Color. Exc. [37] £260 $400

HISPANIA NACH AFFER SEINER GELEGENHEIT IN BERGEN WASSERNIFSTATTEN VOLKERN UND INSELN [c. 1550] 26x35cm (10x13½") Filled hole; else fine. [63] £227 $350

INDIA EXTREMA XIX NOVA TABULA [1540] From Ptolemy's *Geographia*. 26x35cm (10x13½") Exc. Ref: Potter p.13. [62] £552 $850

INDIA EXTREMA XXIIII. NOVA TABULA [1540] 25x34cm (10x13½") Orig color. Ref: Clancy pp 42-3. [16] £1,329 $2,048

[SAME TITLE] [1552] With border grids. 30x38cm (11½x14½") Minor mend; else exc. [37] £649 $1,000

ITALIA XIX. NOVA TABULA [1545] Ptolemy's *Geographia*. 25x33cm (10½x13½") Col. Exc. [37] £292 $450

LA SECONDE TABLE GENERALE SELON PTOL. [1540 / 1555] 25x34cm (10x13½") Ref: Shirley (W) 76. [62] £357 $550

LA TABLE DES ISLES NEUFUES, LESQUELLES ON APPELLE ISLES D'OCCIDENT & D'INDIE POUR DIVERS REGARDZ [c. 1550] Americas with "Verrazano Sea". 28x36cm (11x13½") Superb. Ref: Kershaw p.8, 4d; Skelton (Decorative) p.40, pl.7; cf. Schwartz & Ehrenberg pl.18. [2] £1,883 $2,900

LANDTAFEL DES UNGERLANDS, POLANDS, REUSSEN, LITTAW, WALACHEY UND BULGAREY [c. 1550] 26x35cm (10x13½") + title. [63] £243 $375

LES MARINS MONSTRES & TERRESTRES, LESQUELZ ON TROUVE EN BEAUCOUP DE LIEUX ES PARTIES SEPTENTRIONALES [1580] From *Cosmographia*. 20 monsters. 26x34cm (10x13½") French text verso. Uncolored. Lt age-darkening; minor show-through; sm wormholes near c'fold; sh separation lower c'fold; VG. [31] £487 $750

LONDINUM FERACIS ANG. MET. [c. 1560] Earliest obtainable "true" view. 23x36cm (9x14") Full color. Exc. [63] £552 $850

LUNENBURG [c. 1560] Panorama. 9x38cm (3½x15") Side margins shaved; else fine. [63] £94 $145

MEERVANDER UND SELCZAME THIER WIE DIE IN DEN MITNACH-CIGEN LANDERN MEER UND AUFF DEM LANDT GEFUNDEN WERDEN [c. 1561] From *Cosmographica*. "Sea wonder and strange animals as they are in the Western Countries, as they are found on land and sea." By Martin Hoffmann & Hans Rudolfe Manue. 28x36cm (11x13½") B&W. Thin paper; a natural crease; nice. Ref: Cumming (Discovery) illus p.44. [1] £584 $900

MODERNA DISCRISSION DELLA HELVEZIA [1575] 26x34cm (10x13½") Uncolored. Lt age toned; fine. [33] £390 $600

NEW EUROPA [c. 1550] South at top. 26x34cm (10x13½") Replaced 1x2 cm chip, lower rt; else good. [63] £292 $450

NEW GRIECHEN LAND [c. 1550] 25x34cm (10x13½") Exc. [63] £292 $450

NOU GRECIA SECONDO TUTTE LE REGIONI, & PROVINCIE DI QUELLA DI QUA & DI LA DAL HELLESPONTO [1575] 26x35cm (10x13½") Uncolored. VG. [33] £390 $600

NOVAE INSULAE XVII NOVA TABULA [1540] 1st ed. 26x34cm (10x13½") Uncol. [52] £2,499 $3,850

NOVAE INSULAE XXVI. NOVA TABULA [1545] Ptolemy's *Geographia*. 1st state; with "Verrazano Sea". 30x38cm (11½x14½") Minor mend; else exc. Ref: Schwartz & Ehrenberg pp.43,45,50; Tooley (M&M) pl.80; Cortazzi pl.12. [37] £2,402 $3,700

OBER BADEN [c. 1560] Switzerland. View. 26x35cm (10x14") Exc. [63] £120 $185

PRAGA ... [1582] Bird's eye view on text page. 12x15cm (5x6") [14] £36 $55

PTOLEMAISCH GENERAL TAFEL [1541-1552] From *Geographia* ... With hairline crack in plate. 25x34cm (10x13½") B&W. Ref: Shirley (W) 76. [16] £570 $878

PTOLEMEISCH GENERAL TAFEL / DIE HALBE KUGEL DER WELTBEGREIFFENDE [1588] Basel: Petri. Oval; clouds, 12 windheads. 33x36cm (12½x14") Color. No see-through; fine. Ref: Shirley (W) 162. [26] £487 $750

RUBEAQUUM RUFACH [c. 1560] View. In Alsace. 24x35cm (9½x14") + title. Exc. [63] £114 $175

SCHWABEN UND BAIERLAND DAR BEN AUCH BEGRIFFEN WERDEN SCHWARZWALD OCENWALD UND NORDGOW [c. 1550] 26x35cm (10x14") Exc. [63] £292 $450

SITO & FIGURA DI FRANCOFORDIA CITTA, COME E NEL 1546 [1575] City view. 25x40cm (10x15½") Uncolored. A wormhole top margin; VG+. [33] £292 $450

SUMATRA EIN GROSSE INSEL ... [1544 - 1578] 25x33cm (9½x13") + title above. Uncolored. Few flaws; VG-. Ref: Tooley (Landmarks) p.104; Karrow (16c) #58/100 p.423. [59] £292 $450
[SAME TITLE] [1588] From *Cosmographia*. Petri revision. Elephant illustration. 31x36cm (12x14") Exc. [63] £422 $650
TABULA ASIAE II [1545] Ptolemy's *Geographia*. Ptolemaic Sarmatia (Crimea-Caucasus region). 25x33cm (10x13") Color. Close top margin; else exc. [37] £195 $300
TABULA ASIAE IIII [1545] Ptolemy's *Geographia*. Ptolemaic Middle East. 25x34cm (10x13") Color. Lt toning; else VG. Ref: Laor 615A. [37] £292 $450
TABULA ASIAE V [same date & source] Persia. 26x34cm (10½x13½") Color. Exc. [37] £195 $300
TABULA ASIAE VI [same date & source] Arabia. 26x34cm (10x13½") Color. Exc. [37] £292 $450
TABULA ASIAE IX [1571] 25x34cm (10x13") Old color. Lt foxing to margins. Ref: Nordenskiold (Col) II,287. [28] £234 $360
TABULA ASIAE X [1545] Ptolemy's *Geographia*. India & environs. 25x33cm (10½x13½") Color. Exc. [37] £227 $350
TABULA ASIAE XI [same date & source] Far East. 25x34cm (10x13½") Color. Exc. [37] £292 $450
TABULA ASIAE XII [same date & source] Ptolemaic Taprobana; with elephant. 26x34cm (10x13½") Color. Exc. [37] £292 $450
TABULA EUROPAE V [same date & source] Croatia, Serbia, Albania, etc. 28x33cm (10½x13") Color. Some creasing; close lower margin; else VG. [37] £195 $300
TABULA EUROPAE VII [same date & source] Sicily & Sardinia. 25x33cm (10½x13½") Color. Lower border extended, very sl loss; else exc. [37] £243 $375
TABULA EUROPAE X [same date & source] Greece. 25x33cm (10½x12½") Color. Exc. Ref: Zacharakis 1834. [37] £243 $375
TABULA NOVARUM INSULARUM, QUAS DIVERSIS RESPECTIBUS OCCIDENTALES & INDIANAS VOCANT [1550] With "Verrazano Sea". 27x34cm (10½x13½") B&W. Fine. [1] £1,948 $3,000
TERRA SANCTA XVI NOVA TABULA [1540] 26x34cm (10x13½") Exc. Ref: Laor 616 [62] £357 $550
[SAME TITLE] [1545] From Ptolemy, *Geographia*. Basel: Petri. [same dimen] B&W. [50] £357 $550
TERRA SANCTA XXIII. NOVA TABULA [same date & source] 25x36cm (10½x13½") Color. Lower border extended, very sl loss; else exc. Ref: Loar 617. [37] £422 $650
TRANSSYLVANIA XXI. NOVA TABULA [c. 1550] 25x34cm (10x13½") Lt browning in c'fold; o/w good. [14] £75 $115
TREVERIS TRIER [c. 1560] View. 23x38cm (9x15") Fine. [63] £146 $225
TYPUS COSMOGRAPHICUS UNIVERSALIS [1532] Border decor attributed to Holbein the Younger. 38x56cm (15x22") Mend at separated fold; else exc. Ref: Shirley (W) 67; Harley (Encounter) p.84-6; Suarez 21. [38] £9,413 $14,500
TYPUS ORBIS PTOL. DESCRIPTUS [1549 - 1550] 26x34cm (10½x13½") B&W. Fine. [1] £552 $850
TYPUS ORBIS UNIVERSALIS [c. 1550] David Kandel woodcut, with Verrazano Sea; oval projection; 12 wind cherubs 25x38cm (10½x15") Ref: Shirley (W) 92, pl.78. [46] £1,461 $2,250
TYPUS ORBIS UNIVERSALIS [c. 1550]. 26x38cm (10x15") Exc [62] £1,493 $2,300
TYPUS UNIVERSALIS [1540] As in *Geographia* & *Cosmographia*. 1st ed. 28x36cm (11x14") Exc. Ref: Shirley (W) 77, pl.67; Nordenskiold (Fac) p.23,24,90, pl.XLIV; Imago Mundi XVI, p.89,93. [2] £1,883 $2,900
[SAME TITLE] [1545] Ptolemy's *Geographia*. With "Verrazano Sea". 28x38cm (11x15") Fine. Ref: Shirley 92. [37] £1,623 $2,500
VALESIAE ALTERA ET VII. NOVA TABULA [1545] 1st issue. Switzerland with St. Moritz. 28x33cm (10½x13") Color. Exc. [37] £292 $450
VALESIAE CHARTA PRIOR ET VI. NOVA TABULA [1545] 1st issue. Switzerland with Bern. 25x33cm (10½x13") Color. Exc. [37] £243 $375
VON DEN BRITANNISCHEN INSULN [1578 or later] 25x17cm (10x6½") Uncolored. Pinhole; lt wrinkling; overall VG. Ref: Shirley (BI to 1650) 122. [33] £130 $200

MURRAY, J.
SURVEY OF PORT BOWEN 1819 [1821] J. Walker. Canadian Arctic. 10x17cm (4x6½") [14] £16 $25
SURVEY OF WINTER HARBOUR, MELVILLE ISLAND, JUNE 1820 [1821] 25x17cm (10x7") [14] £19 $30

MYRITIUS
UNIVERSALIS ORBIS DESCRIPTIO [1590] 27x39cm (10½x15½") Color. Ref: Shirley (W) 175, pl.142. [16] £3,703 $5,705

NATIONAL PUBLISHING CO.
NEW RAILROAD, POST OFFICE, TOWNSHIP, AND COUNTY MAP OF NEW YORK [1902] Folding map; lined; printed boards. 102x112cm (40x44") Printed color. Sl wear at folds & intersections; generally VG. [9] £42 $65

NATIONAL SOC. FOR PROMOTING EDUC. OF THE POOR
MAP SHOWING THE DISTRIBUTION OF THE CHIEF MINERAL PRODUCTIONS OF ENGLAND & WALES WITH PART OF SCOTLAND [1848] By W. Hughes. 51x36cm (20½x14½") Full printed color. VG. [21] £81 $125

PHYSICAL MAP OF ENGLAND AND WALES WITH PART OF SCOTLAND [1848] 53x36cm (20½x14½") OL color. Dust soiled; mended; fair. [21] £49 $75

NAVAL CHRONICLE
CHART OF THE SUPPOSED COURSE OF THE FLORIDA STREAM [1804] 16x39cm (6x15½") B&W. Fine. Ref: Jolly NAV-8 [49] £94 $145

NEELE
CANADA [1813] Nova Scotia to Lake of the Woods. 23x30cm (9x11½") Color. Lt even browning. [11] £114 $175

NELSON
NORTH AMERICA. BRITISH PROVINCES OF NEW BRUNSWICK, NOVA SCOTIA, & PART OF CANADA ... [c. 1840] London: V.H. Nelson. Mounted on linen in sections as issued; roan cover. 48x69cm (19x26½") Orig color. Front cover detached; tie wanting. [28] £204 $315

NEW YORK HERALD
FORT WRIGHT ON THE MISSISSIPPI [1862] Headline with map. 23x13cm (9x5") Fine. [20] £97 $150

THE MISSISSIPPI AND ITS REBEL FORTIFICATIONS, FROM COLUMBUS, KY. TO MEMPHIS, TN. [Dec. 4, 1861] Waters & Son. 12 pp triple sheet with 5 front page maps. (no dims.) Disbound; good. [20] £114 $175

NEW YORK STATE DOCUMENTARY HISTORY
MAP OF THE HEAD WATERS OF THE RIVERS SUSQUEHANNA & DELAWARE EMBRACING THE EARLY PATENTS ON THE SOUTH SIDE OF THE MOHAWK FROM THE ORIGINAL, DRAWN ABOUT THE YEAR 1790, BY SIMEON DE WITT ... [c. 1850] Facsimile. 51x53cm (20x21") Uncolored. Folded as issued. [44] £32 $50

NEW YORK TRIBUNE
THE SEAT OF WAR IN THE SOUTH-WEST [1863] April 22. G.W. Colton. 8 pp, with illustrations. 33x23cm (13½x9½") Disbound; good. [20] £114 $175

NICHOLSON
A DRAUGHT OF THE GREAT BAY, BACK BAY AND HARBOUR OF TRINCOMALAY, ON THE ISLAND OF ZELOAN ... [1762] Wm. Nichelson (alternate spelling). 4 sheets joined as issued. 91x98cm (35½x38½") Separate publication. Few sm worm holes; ctr folding point tear repaired; o/w fine. [14] £357 $550

NICOL
[CHINA: SHANTUNG PENINSULA] [1769] Chefoo eastward. 69x51cm (26½x19½") [15] £90 $139

NICOLOSI
ITALIA SECUNDUM DOMINATUS ... [1660] 41x46cm (16x18") Lt foxing; c'fold bit browned. [28] £192 $295

NOLIN
LE NOUVEAU MEXIQUE APPELE AUSSI NOUVELLE GRENADE ET MARATA. AVEC PARTIE DE CALIFORNIE [1688-89 (1742)] 45x59cm (17½x23") Orig OL color. Exc. [63] £5,583 $8,600

MAPPE MONDE CARTE UNIVERSELLES DU LA TERRE [1755] Double hemi with celestial charts. 48x65cm (19x25½") Color. [16] £4,653 $7,167

PARTIE OCCIDENTALE DU CANADA OU DE LA NOUVELLE FRANCE ... [1688] Paris. By Coronelli. 45x60cm (17½x23½") OL color. Fine. Ref: Karpinski (MI) XXIV. [55] £3,895 $6,000

PARTIE ORIENTALE DU CANADA OU DE LA NOUVELLE FRANCE ... AVEC LA NOUVELLE ANGLETERRE, LA NOUVELLE ECOSSE, LA NOUVELLE YORCK, ET LA VIRGINIE ... PAR LE P. CORONELLI ... A PARIS ... CHEZ I.B. NOLIN ... 1688 [1689] 45x59cm (17½x23") Orig OL color. VG. [38] £1,818 $2,800

[SAME TITLE] [same date & dimen] OL color. Old c'fold repair; some offsetting; sl wear at margin. [60] £1,623 $2,500

NORIE

A New Chart of the Andaman and Nicobar Islands with the Adjacent Continent ... [1817 (1831)] After Heather. 64x94cm (25½x36½") Fold lines; sh repaired fold & margin splits. [15] £90 $139

NUREMBERG CHRONICLE   See *Schedel*

OAKLEY

A Plan of Quebec ... by E. Oakley & Sold by J. Roque [1759] 2nd state with St. Lawrence inset. 33x53cm (13½x20½") Modern color. Sm nick rt margin & border. Ref: Tooley (Amer) p.215, #135; Sellers & Van Ee 603. [28]   £964 $1,485

OGILBY   Try *Montanus*

Brasilia ... [1671] From *America*. 29x36cm (11½x14") Color. [53] £280 $431

Cusco [same date, source & dimen] View. 29x36cm (11½x14") Uncolored. [53] £220 $339

Guiana ... [same date & source] 29x36cm (11½x14") Color [53] £160 $246

Insulae Americanae in Oceano Septentrionali, cum Terris Adiacentibus [same date & source] 29x36cm (11x14½") Uncolored. [53] £600 $924

Mappa Aestivarium Insularum ... [same date & source] 29x36cm (11½x14") Uncol. [53] £1,400 $2,156

Nova Hispania Nova Galicia Guatimala [same date & source] 29x36cm (11½x14") Col. [53] £260 $400

Nova Virginiae Tabula [same date & source] 29x36cm (11½x14") Uncolored. [53] £750 $1,155

Novi Belgii, Quod Nunc Novi Yorck Vocatur ... [same date & source] Derivative of Jansson-Visscher series. 29x36cm (11½x14½") Color. [53] £1,400 $2,156

Novissima et Accuratissima Barbados. Descriptio per Johannem Ogilvium. Cosmographum Regium [same date & source] 29x36cm (11½x14") Uncol. Ref: MCS 21 (Campbell) #3, pl.II. [53] £480 $739

Novissima et Accuratissima Jamaicae Descriptio per Johannem Ogilvium. Cosmographum Regium [same date & source] Earliest English map of colony. 43x54cm (17x21") Uncolored. [53] £500 $770

Novissima et Accuratissima Totius Americae Descriptio ... [same date & source] 43x54cm (17x21") Uncolored. [53] £1,500 $2,310

Pagus Hispanorum in Florida [1671] St. Augustine view. 27x36cm (10½x14") Exc. Ref: Deak 50. [62] £480 $740

Paraguaria ... [1671] From *America*. 29x36cm (11½x14") Color. [53] £200 $308

Porte Rico [1670] San Juan view. 28x35cm (11x13½") Wash color. [14] £276 $425

Porto Rico [1671] San Juan view. 28x35cm (11x13½") Exc. Ref: See Deak. [62] £292 $450

Tabula Magellanica [1671] From *America*. 29x36cm (11½x14") Color. [53] £350 $539

Terra Firma et Novum Regnum Granatense et Popayan [1671] From *America*. 29x36cm (11½x14") Color. [53] £320 $493

The Road from Chelmsford ... to ... Saffron Walde [1676] From *Britannia*, ... 33x43cm (13x17") Color. VG. Ref: Chubb C,94. [55] £179 $275

The Road from Huntington to Ipswich [same date & source] 33x46cm (13x18½") Color. VG. Ref: Chubb C,75. [55] £179 $275

The Road from London to Barwick [1675] Strip map. 33x46cm (13x17½") Full orig color. VG. Ref: Chubb p.85, #6. [2] £308 $475

The Road from London to Darby ... [1676] From *Britannia*, ... 33x43cm (12½x17") Color. VG. Ref: Chubb C,42. [55] £179 $275

The Road from Maldon ... to ... Gravesend [same date, source & dimen] Color. VG. Ref: Chubb C,95. [55] £195 $300

The Road from Monmouth to Llanbeder [same date & source] 33x43cm (13x17") Color. VG. Ref: Chubb C,79. [55] £179 $275

The Road from Nottingham to Grimsley [same date, source & dimen] Color. VG. Ref: Chubb C,80. [55] £179 $275

The Road from Oxford to Salisbury [1698] Strip map. 36x46cm (14½x18") Full orig color. Exc. Ref: Chubb p.86, #85. [2] £308 $475

The Roads from Exeter ... Devon to Dorchester and from Plimouth to Dartmouth ... [1675] From *Britannia*. 32x46cm (12½x18") Orig color. Lt creasing lower c'fold. [14] £149 $230

Venezuela cum Parte Australi Novae Andalusiae [1671] From *America*. 29x36cm (11½x14") Color [53] £300 $462

VIRGINIAE PARTIS AUSTRALIS ET FLORIDAE PARTIS ORIENTALIS ... [1671] From *America*. 29x36cm (11½x14") Uncolored. [53] £750 $1,155
YUCATAN CONVENTUS IURIDICI HISPANIA NOVAE PARS OCCIDENTALIS ET GUATIMALA CONVENTUS [1671] From *America*. 29x36cm (11½x14") Color. [53] £260 $400

OLMSTED
A MAP OF THE COTTON KINGDOM AND ITS DEPENDENCIES IN AMERICA [1861] In book of same name by Frederick Law Olmsted. Color coding. 25x43cm (10x17") Mild misfolding. [44] £146 $225

OLNEY
MAP OF THE SOUTH WESTERN AND PART OF THE WESTERN STATES [1858] School geography. Sherman & Smith; NY: Pratt, Oakley & Co. 46x28cm (18x11") Full color. Good. [20] £39 $60
MAP OF THE UNITED STATES [1844 (1850)] Extended NM & UT Terr. 28x46cm (11x18") Color. Some age spotting. [9] £62 $95
WESTERN TERRITORIES OF THE UNITED STATES [1847 (1856)] 28x46cm (11x18") Full color. Brown (ink?) spots; good. [45] £58 $90
[SAME TITLE] [1858] Sherman & Smith; Pratt, Oakley & Co., NY. 28x46cm (10½x18") Full color. Good. [19] £81 $125

ORR & SMITH
EASTERN HEMISPHERE [IN SET WITH] WESTERN HEMISPHERE [c. 1836] Each diameter 23cm (8½") Full color. [36] £107 $165
PACIFIC OCEAN [c. 1836] 20x25cm (8½x10½") [36] £45 $70

ORTELIUS (Folio)
[PORTRAIT] ABRAHAM ORTELIUS [1592 - c.1603] C. Plantin; Philip Galle, sc. 21x32cm (8½x12½") Color. [52] £240 $370
[TITLE PAGE] PARERGON ... [1581 - c.1590] 38x25cm (15x10") Color. [53] £240 $370
[TITLE PAGE] THEATRUM ORBIS TERRARUM [1603] 42x24cm (16½x9½") Color. [53] £220 $339
ABRAHAMAE PATRIARCHATUS PEREGRINATIO ... [1589-] From *Theatrum* ... 32x45cm (12½x17½") Color. [53] £850 $1,309
ABRAHAMI PATRIARCHAE PEREGRINATIO ET VITA [1586] From the *Paregon*. Inset of travels; 22 vignettes. 35x46cm (13½x18") Later full color. Exc. [63] £1,428 $2,200
ACORES INSULAE [1584-1592] From *Theatrum* ... 33x47cm (13x18½") Orig color. [53] £350 $539
AEGYPTUS ANTIQUA [1584] 2 sheets forming vertical map, each 40x49cm (15½x19") Color. Exc. [63] £552 $850
AEVI VETERIS, TYPUS GEOGRAPHICUS [1590] In 4th *Additamentum*. Old world only, on part of global oval; 4 continents in corner rondels. 31x44cm (12½x17½") Color. Framed. Ref: Shirley (W) 176, pl.143. [16] £1,140 $1,755
[SAME TITLE] [same date & dimen] Full color. VG+. [33] £454 $700
AFRICA TABULA NOVA [1574] 37x50cm (14½x19½") Color. [54] £1,000 $1,540
ALEXANDRI MAGNI MACEDONIS EXPEDITIO [1595] 36x46cm (14x18") Uncolored. [54] £450 $693
AMERICAE SIVE NOVI ORBIS, NOVA DESCRIPTIO [1570] 37x51cm (14½x20") Full color, not orig. Exc. Ref: Goss (NA) #11. [62] £2,921 $4,500
[SAME TITLE] [1570 / 1573] [same dimen] Orig & later color. Framed. [51] £3,051 $4,700
[SAME TITLE] [1570 - 1574] [same dimen] Color. [54] £2,999 $4,620
[SAME TITLE] [1579] Potato shaped S. Amer. 36x49cm (14x19") Orig full color. Narrow side margins. Ref: Wheat (TM) 15; Tooley (Amer) p.320; Martin (TX) pl.4. [46] £2,110 $3,250
[SAME TITLE] [1587] 2nd version (4th state). [same dimen] Full modern color. Mint. [62] £2,986 $4,600
[SAME TITLE] [1587 (1592)] [same dimen] Latin text verso. Color. C'fold split lower margin; else fine. Ref: Tooley (Amer) 320; Johnson (Amer Expl) 140-41. [55] £2,921 $4,500
ANGLIAE ET HIBERNIAE ACCURATA DESCRIPTIO VETERIBUS ET RECENTIORIBUS [1605 -] From *Theatrum* .... Added & pub by Vrients. 44x58cm (17x22½") Col. Ref: Shirley (BI to 1650) 275, pl.57. [54] £1,500 $2,310
ANGLIAE REGNI FLORENTISSIMI NOVA DESCRIPTIO, AUCTORE HUMFREDO LHUYD DENBYGIENSE [1574] 38x47cm (15x18½") Color. 2 sm splits near lower c'fold. [54] £500 $770
ANGLIAE, SCOTIAE, ET HIBERNIAE, SIVE BRITANNICAR: INSULARUM DESCRIPTIO [1574] 35x50cm (14x19½") Color. [54] £480 $739

ASIAE NOVA DESCRIPTIO [1570] 37x48cm (14½x19") Full orig color. Exc. Ref: Cortazzi p.20-21, pl.19. [62] £1,169 $1,800
[SAME TITLE] [same date & dimen] Later full color. Fine. [63] £974 $1,500
[SAME TITLE] [1574] 37x49cm (14½x19½") Color. [54] £1,000 $1,540
AUSTRIAE DESCRIP ... [1602] From *Theatrum Orbis Terrarum*. Italian ed. By Wolfgang Lazio. 35x48cm (14x19") Full orig color. [51] £487 $750
AUSTRIAE DUCATUS CHOROGRAPHIA, WOLFGANGO LAZIO AUCTORE [1574] 35x48cm (14x19") Color. [54] £400 $616
BAVARIAE OLIM VINDELICIAE, DELINEATIONIS COMPENDIUM EX TABULA PHILIPPI APIANI MATH. [1573 / 1602] From *Theatrum*. 39x49cm (15x19½") Full orig color. Exc. [62] £438 $675
BRITANNICARUM INSULARUM VETUS DESCRIPTIO [1590 -] 2-sheet Roman British Isles, 49x35cm (19½x14") Uncolored. [54] £1,400 $2,156
BURGUNDIAE DUCATUS [ON SHEET WITH] BURGUNDIAE COMITATUS [1602] 36x51cm (14x20") Full orig color. [51] £487 $750
CALETENSIUM ET BONONIENSIUM ... [ON SHEET WITH] VEROMANDUORUM EORUM QUE CONFINIUM ... [1584] 33x48cm (13½x19") Foxing, mainly in margins. Ref: Koeman III Ort 21. [28] £204 $315
CAMBRIAE TYPUS AUCTORE HUMFREDO LHUYDO DENBIGIENSE ... [1574] 37x49cm (14½x19½") Color. [54] £380 $585
CARINTHIAE DUCATUS, ET GORITIAE ... [ON SHEET WITH] HISTRIAE ... [AND] ZARAE, ET SEBENICI ... [1574] From *Theatrum* ... 33x48cm (13x19") Uncolored. [53] £240 $370
[SAME TITLE] [c. 1578] [same dimen] Ref: Koeman III Ort 32. [28] £192 $295
CHINAE, OLIM SINARUM REGIONIS, NOVA DESCRIPTIO. AUCTORE LUDOVICO GEORGIO [1584] 37x47cm (14½x18½") Full orig color. Exc. [63] £1,818 $2,800
[SAME TITLE] [1584 / 1603] [same dimen] Later col. Good. Ref: Tooley (M&M) pl.78. [2] £1,883 $2,900
CRETA IOVIS MAGNI, ... [ON SHEET WITH] CORSICA [AND] INSULAE MARIS IONIAE [AND] SARDINIA [1574] From *Theatrum* ... 33x48cm (13½x19½") Color. [53] £340 $524
CYPRI INSULAE NOVA DESCRIPT. 1573 [1574] 35x50cm (14x19½") Color. Lt worming. [54] £600 $924
DANIAE REGNI TYPUS [1574] 30x41cm (12½x16½") Color. [54] £500 $770
DAPHNE [1595] Suburb of Antioch in Asia Minor. 37x49cm (14½x19½") Full orig col. Exc. [63] £357 $550
DESCRIPTIO GERMANIAE INFERIORIS [1574] From *Theatrum* ... 38x50cm (15x20") Color. [53] £400 $616
ERYN. HIBERNIAE, BRITANNICAE INSULAE, NOVA DESCRIPTIO. IRLANDT [1570] 36x48cm (14x19") Later color. Beautiful. Ref: Shirley (BI to 1650) #86. [2] £779 $1,200
EUROPAE [1570 (1588)] From *Theatrum*. 1st Spanish ed. 34x46cm (13½x18") Later full color. Minor repair; else exc. [62] £373 $575
GALLIAE REGNI POTENTISS. NOVA DESCRIPTIO, IOANNE IOLIVETO AUCTORE [1574] 35x50cm (13½x20") Color. Sh split lower c'fold. [54] £450 $693
GEOGRAPHIA SACRA [1603] Oval world inset. 36x48cm (14x19") Pristine. Ref: cf. Laor 549. [23] £250 $385
GERMANIA [1574] From *Theatrum* ... 36x50cm (14½x20") Color. [53] £450 $693
GRAECIAE UNIVERSAE SECUNDUM HODIERNUM SITUM NEOTERICA DESCRIPTIO [1570 - c.1595] From *Theatrum* ... 36x51cm (14½x20") Uncolored. Sm printers crease. [53] £450 $693
HASSIAE ... / HOLSATIAE DESCRIP [1574] From *Theatrum* ... 34x49cm (13x19½") Orig col. [53] £280 $431
HIBERNIAE, BRITANNICAE INSULAE, NOVA DESCRIPTIO [1574] 35x48cm (14x19") Col. [54] £550 $847
HOLLANDIAE ... [1574] From *Theatrum* ... 35x48cm (14x19") Color. [53] £420 $647
HUNGARIAE DESCRIPTIO ... [1574] From *Theatrum* ... 35x50cm (14x19½") Color. [53] £340 $524
INDIAE ORIENTALIS INSULARUMQUE ADIACIENTIUM TYPUS [1570] From *Typus Orbis Terrarum*. 35x50cm (13½x19½") Orig color. Ref: Tooley (Australia) 937; Clancy pp 44-5. [16] £1,875 $2,889
[SAME TITLE] [same date & dimen] Full orig color. Sm rubbed area; o/w exc. [62] £974 $1,500
[SAME TITLE] [(1570) 1580] [same dimen] Orig color. Fine. Ref: Humphreys illus p.68. Cortazzi pl.17. [1] £1,169 $1,800
[SAME TITLE] [1570 - 1612] [same dimen] + extended margins. Recent full color. Cleaned, conserved; VG. Ref: Karrow (16c) #1/68; MCC 79 #937; Walter (Japan) #11D. [59] £1,169 $1,800
[SAME TITLE] [1574] [same dimen] Color. [54] £1,500 $2,310
INSULARUM ALIQUOT MARIS MEDITERRANEI DESCRIPTIO [1574] From *Theatrum* ... 5 maps: Sardinia, Sicily, Corfu, Zerbi, Elba & Malta. 36x48cm (14x19") Color. [53] £320 $493
ITALIAE NOVISSIMA DESCRIPTIO ... [1574] 37x50cm (14½x19½") Color. [54] £500 $770

L'ISLE DE FRANCE. PARISIENSIS AGRI DESCRIP. [1598 / 1602] 34x46cm (13½x18") Full orig color. Exc. [62] £292 $450

LA FLORIDA [ON SHEET WITH] PERUVIAE AURIFERAE REGIONIS TYPUS [AND] GUASTECAN REG. [1584 / 1595] Spain's New World empire on 3 maps; 1st separate map of Florida. 33x48cm (13x18½") Full orig color. Good. Ref: Cumming (SE) #5; Schwartz & Ehrenberg 73; Portinaro & Knirsch p.210. [2] £1,104 $1,700

[SAME TITLE] [after 1584] 34x46cm (13x18") Full later color. Margins chipped, some browning; verso restorations. [30] £714 $1,100

[SAME TITLE] [1584 (1602)] [same dimen] Orig color. Fine. Ref: Goss (NA) 13; Potter p.142-43. [62] £1,039 $1,600

MANSFELDIAE COMITATUS DESCRIPTIO ... [1584] 37x43cm (14½x17") Lt foxing c'fold & margins. Ref: Koeman III Ort 21. [28] £192 $295

MARIS PACIFICI (QUOD VULGO MAR DEL ZUR) CUM REGIONIBUS CIRCUMIACENTIBUS, INSULISQUE IN CODEM PASSIM SPARSIS, NOVISSIMA DESCRIPTIO [1589] 35x50cm (13½x19½") Orig color. Framed. Ref: Campbell (Early) pl.9; Tooley (Landmarks) p.200. [16] £5,935 $9,142

[SAME TITLE] [same date & dimen] Full orig color. Exc. [63] £3,376 $5,200

[SAME TITLE] [1589 (1591)] 2nd issue. From German text *Additamentum*. [same dimen] Full color. Fine. Ref: Campbell (Early) 26-28; Cortazzi pl.21; Suarez #35; Wagner (NW) 73. [55] £3,116 $4,800

NAMURCUM COMITATUS. JOES. SURHON DESCRIB. 1579 [1584] 39x51cm (15½x20") Sm hole ctr margin; margins bit foxed. Ref: Koeman III Ort 21. [28] £234 $360

OOST ENDE WEST VRIESLANDTS BESCHRYUINGHE UTRIVSQUE FRISIORUM REGIONIS NOVISS: DESCRIPTIO. 1568 [1602] 34x51cm (13½x20") Full orig color. Exc. [62] £438 $675

PALAESTINAE SIVE TOTIUS TERRAE PROMISSIONIS NOVA DESCRIPTIO AUCTORE TILEMANNO STELLA SIGENENSI [1570 / 1579] 34x46cm (13½x18") Later color. Exc. Ref: Laor 540b; Nebenzahl (Holy Land) pp.84-5. [2] £779 $1,200

PALATINATUS BAVARIAE DESCRIPTIO, ERHARDO REYCH TIROLENSE AUCTORE [ON SHEET WITH] ARGENTORATENSIS AGRI DESCRIPTIO [1584] 30x49cm (12x19½") Tear lower margin; verso & margins bit foxed. Ref: Koeman III Ort 21. [28] £192 $295

PALESTINAE SIVE TOTIUS TERRAE PROMISSIONIS NOVA DESCRIPTIO AUCTORE TILEMANNO STELLA SIGENENS [1570] From *Theatrum*. 1st state. 35x47cm (13½x18½") Full modern color. Exc. Ref: Nebenzahl (Holy Land) pl.30. [62] £714 $1,100

[SAME TITLE] [1584] 34x46cm (13½x18") Color. Fine. Ref: Laor 540B. [23] £568 $875

PEREGRINATIONIS DIVI PAULI TYPUS COROGRAPHICUS ... [1579 - 1612] 34x50cm (13½x19½") OL & wash color. Fine. Ref: Laor 545; Karrow (16c) #1/129; Phillips (A) 396. [59] £747 $1,150

PERSICI SIVE SOPHORUM REGNI TYPUS [1570 (1587)] 35x50cm (14x19½") Color. Fine. Ref: Koeman Ort 22. [55] £179 $275

POICTOU. PICTONUM VICINARUM ... 1579 [c. 1592] 36x50cm (14x19½") Orig color. [28] £263 $405

POLONIAE ... [1574] From *Theatrum* ... 37x49cm (14½x19") Color. [53] £350 $539

[SAME TITLE] [c. 1574] [same dimen] Color. [42] £300 $462

POMERANIAE, WANDALICAE REGIONIS [ON SHEET WITH] TYP. LIVONIAE ... [AND] DUCATUS OSWIECZENSIS, ET ZATORIENSIS ... [1573 - c.1600] From *Theatrum* ... 39x50cm (15x19½") Uncolored. [53] £220 $339

[SAME TITLE] [1584] (no dims.) Orig color. Sh margin tears, c'fold, sm hole repaired. Ref: Koeman III Ort 21. [28] £263 $405

PORTUGALLIAE ... [1574] From *Theatrum* ... 34x51cm (13½x20") Color. [53] £400 $616

PRESBITERI IOHANNIS, SIVE, ABISSINORUM IMPERII DESCRIPTIO [1598] 37x44cm (14½x17½") Full color. Minor repairs lower c'fold verso; VG. [30] £390 $600

PRESBITERI JOHANNIS, SIVE, ABISSINORUM IMPERII DESCRIPTIO [1574] 38x47cm (15x18½") Color. [54] £550 $847

REGNI BOHEMIAE DESCRIPTIO [1570-] From *Theatrum* ... 34x50cm (13½x19½") Color. [53] £300 $462

[SAME TITLE] [1570 (1573)] 33x50cm (13x20") Full orig color. [14] £153 $235

ROMANI IMPERII IMAGO [1584] Gibraltar to Caspian. 36x48cm (13½x19½") OL color. Some surface dirt; else fine. [55] £325 $500

RUSSIAE, MOSCOVIAE ET TARTARIAE DESCRIPTIO. AUCTORE ANTONIO IENKENSONO ANGLO, EDITA LONDINI ANNO 1562 ... [1570] 35x44cm (13½x17½") Later color. Exc. [2] £406 $625

[SAME TITLE] [c. 1570] [same dimen] Orig col. Fine. Ref: Tooley (Landmarks) illus p.120. [1] £422 $650

[SAME TITLE] [1574] [same dimen] Color. [54] £480 $739

SALISBURGENSIS JURISDICTIONIS ... [1574] 34x44cm (13½x17") Color. [54] £400 $616

SAXONIAE, MISNIAE, THURINGIAE ... [1584] 35x50cm (13½x19½") Orig color. Lower c'fold tear. Ref: Koeman III Ort 21. [28] £221 $340
SCOTIAE TABULA [1574] 36x48cm (14x19") Color. [54] £500 $770
SENENSIS DITIONIS ... / CORSICA / MARCHA ANCONA ... [1574] From *Theatrum* ... 33x49cm (13x19") Uncolored. [53] £240 $370
SEPTENTRIONALIUM REGIONUM DESCRIP. [1574] 36x49cm (14x19½") Color. [54] £1,200 $1,848
SILESIAE TYPUS DESCRIPTUS ET EDITUS A MARTINO HEILWIG ... 1561 [c. 1572] 28x38cm (11x15") Color. [42] £250 $385
TARTARIAE SIVE MAGNI CHAMI REGNI TYPUS [1570] With N. Pacific, N. Amer. & Japan. 35x47cm (14x18½") Orig wash color. Mild browning at fold. Ref: Wheat (TM) 16; Wagner (NW) 81. [46] £714 $1,100
[SAME TITLE] [1570 / 1598] [same dimen] Sh tears lower margin; old tape stains verso. Ref: Skelton (Decorative) pl.16; Koeman III Ort 32. [28] £876 $1,350
[SAME TITLE] [same date & dimen] From *Theatrum* .... Color. [53] £900 $1,386
[SAME TITLE] [1573] [same dimen] Orig color. Sm foxing spot; sm worm hole; very nice [1] £812 $1,250
TERRA SANCTA A PETRO LAICSTAIN PERLUSTRATA, ET AB EIUS ORE ET SCHEDIS A CHRISTIANO SCHROT IN TABULAM REDACTA [1584] 37x50cm (14½x19½") Later color. Exc. Ref: Laor 543; Nebenzahl (Holy Land) #31. [2] £714 $1,100
[SAME TITLE] [same date & dimen] Ref: cf. Laor 543. [23] £536 $825
[SAME TITLE] [same date & dimen] Old highlight color. Dampmarks upper corners; lower c'fold tear repaired. Ref: Koeman III Ort 21. [28] £701 $1,080
[SAME TITLE] [same date & dimen] Orig color. Exc. [62] £909 $1,400
THUSCIAE DESCRIPTIO ... [1574] From *Theatrum* ... 32x49cm (12½x19½") Uncolored. [53] £300 $462
TURCICI IMPERII DESCRIPTIO [1574] 37x50cm (14½x19½") Color. [54] £700 $1,078
TYPUS ORBIS TERRARUM [1584] Unrecorded edition, "1584" engraved after engraver's name. 34x49cm (13x19½") Orig color. Ref: Shirley (W) 122, pl.104 (1st state). [16] £6,077 $9,361
[SAME TITLE] [1587 (1588)] 3rd plate. French ed. 35x50cm (14x19½") Wash color. C'fold repaired; fine. Ref: Shirley (W) 158; Koeman Ort32(1); Wagner (NW) p.69-71. [50] £3,571 $5,500
VALENTIA REGNUM [n.d.] 36x48cm (14x19") Later full color. [51] £292 $450

ORTELIUS (Miniature)

AUSTRIAE DESCRIPTIO [1589] 8x11cm (3x4½") Full color. [57] £45 $70
CANDIA OLIM CRETA [1612] From *Epitome Theatri Orbis Terrarum*, Antwerp: Coignet. 8x13cm (3½x4½") Color. [58] £52 $80
CORFU [same date & source] 8x13cm (3½x4½") Color. [58] £55 $85
HIBERNIA [1602] 8x13cm (3½x4½") B&W. Lt age-toning; else fine. [55] £97 $150
IAPONIA INSULA [1612] From *Epitome* ..., Antwerp. 8x12cm (3½x4½") Full color. [58] £211 $325
INDIA ORIENT [1595+] With NW America. 8x11cm (3x4") [14] £81 $125
INDIAE ORIENTALIS INSULARUM UMQUE ADIACIENTIUM TYPUS [VERSO] TARTARIAE SIVE MAGNI CHAMI REGNI TYPUS [1585] Favolium ed of Ortelius-Galle miniature atlas. Each 8x11cm (3x4½") on full text sheet. [63] £211 $325
ISCHIA INSULA [1612] From *Epitome* ..., Antwerp: Coignet. 8x13cm (3½x4½") Color. [58] £42 $65
ISLANDIA [1612] From *Epitome*. 8x13cm (3½x4½") Full color. [58] £58 $90
LAC LEMANI ... [1609] Pub by Vrients. Lake Geneva. 8x13cm (3½x5") Color. [57] £45 $70
LIVONIAE NOVA DESCRIPTIO JOANNE PORTANTIO AUCTORE [1583] From *Epitome*. Incl Estonia. 8x10cm (3x4½") Full color [57] £58 $90
MALTA OLIM MELITA [1612] From *Epitome* ..., Antwerp: Coignet. 8x13cm (3½x4½") Col. [58] £52 $80
PORTUGALLIA [c. 1602] 8x10cm (3x4") Color. [43] £125 $193
SARDINIA [1612] From *Epitome* ..., Antwerp: Coignet. 8x12cm (3½x4½") Color. [58] £49 $75
TERCERA [same date & source] 8x10cm (3½x4½") Full color. [58] £42 $65
WESTFALIA [1601] Pub by Vrients. 8x13cm (3½x5") Full color. [57] £49 $75

OTTENS

[LESSER ANTILLES] [c. 1750] Puerto Rico to Venezuela. 41x53cm (16x21") Orig wash color. Tiny burn hole in sea; fine. [47] £357 $550
[TITLE PAGE] ATLAS [1725 - 1750] Frontispiece; Atlas holds globe in seaport scene. 46x30cm (17½x11½") Lt soiled. Ref: Goss (Art) p.327. [12] £81 $125

Carte de la Nouvelle France ou Se Voit le Cours des Grandes Rivieres de S. Laurens & de Mississipi Aujour d'Hui S. Louis, aux Environs des Quelles ... [c. 1730] 50x55cm (19½x21½") Orig color. Narrow margins top & bottom; c'fold damage at FL; framed with linen mat. [51] £1,493 $2,300

Nette Aftekening der Stad Oran &c. Giegen in Barbaryen Opgedragen aan den Ed. Heer Cornelis Schryver ... [1732] Inset coastal view. 43x56cm (16½x22") Full orig color. [28] £204 $315

Nova ac Verissima Maris Caspii ... ac Regionum Adjacentium Delineatio ... [c. 1723] 2nd state. (no dims.) Orig color. Vert crease; minute splits. Ref: Bagrow (Russia) p.111 & 127. [28] £234 $360

Nova & Accuratissima ... Tabula Nautica [1702 / c.1730] Edmond Halley map; 1st world maps with isogones (Halleyan lines). 3 sheets joined 53x142cm (20½x56") Full orig color. [3] £7,141 $11,000

OVERTON

A New and Correct Map of Ye World ... [c. 1720] Double hemisphere; insular California. Border of scientific diagrams & data. 59x95cm (23x37½") Separately issued. Orig OL color. Restored; lower corners reattached without loss. [52] £2,799 $4,312

A New Mapp of Lincoln Shire with the Post & Cross Roads ... Printed & sold by Henry Overton ... [1712] 39x49cm (15½x19½") Orig color. Overall fine. [62] £373 $575

PAGE

A Hand Map of the Island of Newfoundland [1859] Frederick R. Page. Mounted on linen in sections; cloth covers. 56x48cm (22x18½") Orig color. Cable & wire routes added in ms. Map bit spotted; covers frayed. [28] £250 $385

Map of Texas ... [1887] Chicago: H.R. Page & Co. 66x43cm (26x16½") Full color. [58] £94 $145

Page's Map of New Mexico [1887] 66x41cm (26x16½") Full color. [58] £81 $125

PALLAS

Carte Generale de l'Empire de Russie, 1787 [1793] From *Voyage du Professeur Pallas, dans ... l'Empire de Russie* Paris: Maradan. 2 sheets joined. Poland to Alaska. 56x117cm (21½x46") Sl stain along c'fold; pinholes; clean. [7] £185 $285

PAYNE

North Carolina ... [1800 (c.1806-8)] NY: J. Low. 20x36cm (8x13½") Uncolored. [44] £81 $125

Rhode Island [1799] From *A New and Complete Universal Geography*. 24x19cm (9½x7½") Uncolored. Exc. Ref: Wheat & Brun 255. [35] £71 $110

[Same Title] [same date & dimen] Uncolored. [56] £78 $120

The Province of Maine ... [1799] 28x18cm (10½x7½") Uncol. Ref: Wheat & Brun 178 [56] £91 $140

The State of New Hampshire Compiled Chiefly from Actual Surveys [1799] 29x19cm (11½x7½") Uncolored. [56] £78 $120

The State of Pennsylvania from the Latest Surveys [1810] NY: Low. 18x26cm (7x10½") Uncolored. Exc. [56] £71 $110

The States of Maryland and Delaware from the Latest Surveys [1799] Payne's Geography, pub by Low, NY; possibly 1808 ed. 19x24cm (7½x9½") Uncolored. Normal age toning. [44] £78 $120

[Same Title] [same date & dimen] By Anderson. Uncolored. [56] £78 $120

PEETERS

[Hemisphere on Mobile Set Up] [1692 - c.1709] From De Afferden republication of pocket geography book. 14x15cm (5½x5½") Color. [16] £123 $190

PENNANT

Map for Mr. Pennant's Outline of the Globe [1800] 50x59cm (19½x23") Color. [16] £712 $1,097

PENNSYLVANIA MAGAZINE

A Map of the Present Seat of War on the Border of Canada [1775] Lake George to St. Lawrence River. Robert Aitken, sc. 16x36cm (6x14") October issue, partially disbound; sm part of last leaf torn off. Map rt border & lf 7 cm clipped, facsimile replacement; map poor. Ref: Jolly (Amer) 269; Wheat & Brun 89. [62] £584 $900

A New Plan of Boston Harbour from an Actual Survey [1775] By Robert Aitken. First depiction of Bunker Hill Battle. 25x18cm (10½x7½") June issue, partially disbound. Map reinforced, one tear repaired. Ref: Jolly (Amer) 266; Wheat & Brun 239. [62] £974 $1,500

EXACT PLAN OF GENERAL GAGE'S LINES ON BOSTON NECK IN AMERICA [1775] Phila: Robert Aitken. 30x23cm (11½x9") August issue, partially disbound. Map lightly cleaned. Ref: Jolly (Amer) 268. Wheat & Brun 237. [62] £974 $1,500

PEOPLE'S ATLAS
OKLAHOMA AND INDIAN TERRITORY [1900] "I" is only remaining lettered county. 25x33cm (10x13") Printed color. Clean. [11] £26 $40

PERROT
AMERIQUE SEPTENTRIONALE [1824] 20x25cm (8x9½") Color. Bright, crisp. [9] £39 $60

PERRY
AN OUTLINE MAP OF THE SETTLEMENTS IN NEW SOUTH WALES [c.1819] 36x78cm (14x30½") Early lithograph map. [41] £150 $231

PETERMANN   Try *Stieler*
AUSTRALIAN ... [1864] Gotha: Perthes. 38x46cm (15x18") Orig OL color. Sh tears lower margin; lt foxing. Ref: Tooley (Australia) 953. [28] £97 $150
DIE FRANZOSOSCHEN MILITAR-EXPEDITION IN MAROKKO 1866 & 1870 [1872] From Geographic Annual, Gotha. 25x33cm (10x13") Some color. [44] £39 $60
G.W. HAYWARD'S REISE LEH NACH KASCHGAR, 1868/9 [1871] After Royal Geographic Society map. 33x28cm (13x10½") Full color. [45] £29 $45
GEOLOGISCHE KARTE DER VEREINIGTEN STAATEN UND BRITISCHEN PROVINZEN VON NORD-AMERIKA [1855] By Jules Marcou. 25x41cm (9½x15½") Full color. Surface yellowed. [58] £120 $185
KARTE DES ARKTISCHEN ARCHIPEL'S DER PARRY-INSELN [1855] 2 views. 25x57cm (9½x22") Two rust spots. [14] £52 $80
NEUER SEEWIG VON EUROPA NAC SIBERIEN, NORDENSKOLDS EXPEDITION VON TROMSO ZUM JENISSEI, JUNI-SEPT. 1875 [1875] From Geographic Annual, Gotha. 25x33cm (10x13") Some color. [44] £39 $60
ORIGINALKARTE DER CALIFORNISCHEN HALBINSEL ... FUR DIE LOWER CALIFORNIA COMPANY ... [1868] In Petermann's Geographical Magazine. 33x23cm (13x9") Wash color. Ref: Phillips (M) 378. [58] £81 $125
ORIGINALKARTE DER PORTUCIESISCHEN REISEN IN INNER-AFRIKA SEIT 1798 NACH DEN PORTUCIESISCHEN QUELLENWERKEN ZUSAMMENGESTELLT NEBST SKISSE VON LIVINGSTONES REISE 1866-1869 [1870] From Geographic Annual, Gotha. Livingston's trip incomplete. 25x33cm (10x13") Some color. [44] £39 $60
ORIGINALKARTE VON RUSSISCH LAPPLAND VON J.A. FRIIS [1870] 33x28cm (13x10½") Color [45] £23 $35
SPECIALKARTE VON ARMENIEN, ZUR UBERSICHT DES NACH DEM FRIEDEN VON S. STEFANO, 3 MARZ, 1878 ZU RUSSLAND GEKOMENNAN GEBIETES [1878] From Geographic Annual, Gotha. (no dims.) [44] £39 $60
UBERSICHT VON GERHARD ROHLFS REISEN IN AFRICA 1861-1867 [1867] From Geographic Annual, Gotha. Sahara region. 6 explorations 1825-67. 25x33cm (10x13") Some color. [44] £39 $60
VEREINIGTEN STAATEN VON NORD-AMERIKA IN 6 BLATTERN, BL. 1 [1872] Published in Stieler's Atlas. Northwestern U.S. 33x41cm (13x16") OL color. Fair. [19] £49 $75

PHILIP
CHART OF THE NORTH WEST PASSAGE BETWEEN ASIA AND AMERICA [c. 1856] Richardson & Franklin discoveries. 49x57cm (19½x22½") Color. [40] £48 $74
NEW ZEALAND [c. 1860] 59x49cm (23x19½") OL color. [41] £78 $120

PHILIP, G.
PERTHSHIRE [c. 1850] London: George Philips & Son. 15x18cm (6x6½") Full color. Good. [21] £36 $55
PHILIP'S NEW PLAN OF LONDON ... [1880] Folding paper plan in cloth folder; 19 pp city guide. 53x79cm (21x30½") Partial color. Damp damage; fold tears, loose from cover; fair. [21] £32 $50
SHEET 1, WESTERN STATES, UNITED STATES [c. 1856] Large OR, NM, UT configurations. 51x61cm (20x24") Broad OL color. Little or no margin top & bottom, nicks; overall good. [56] £146 $225
SOUTHERN HEMISPHERE, PROJECTED ON THE PLANE OF THE HORIZON OF LONDON [1856] Diameter 51cm (20") Full orig wash color. [14] £19 $30

PIGAFETTA
TABULAM HANC AEGYPTI, SI AEQUUS AC DILIGENS LECTOR, CUM ALYS, QUAE HACTENUS PRODICUT ... [1597] From de Bry's *Voyages*. All Africa except bulge. 2 sheets joined, 55x40cm (21½x15½") Full color, not orig. Ref: TMC 9, p.8-10. [62] £1,558 $2,400

PINKERTON

AFRICA [1814] 71x51cm (27½x20") Orig OL color. Ref: Phillips (A) 724; cf Norwich 122. [28] £162 $250
AUSTRALASIA [1813] 51x71cm (20x27½") Orig OL color. Ref: cf Tooley (Australia) 979. [28] £351 $540
[SAME TITLE] [c. 1813] Incl New Zealand. 44x69cm (17½x27") OL color. [41] £250 $385
BRITISH POSSESSIONS IN NORTH AMERICA ... [1814] 51x69cm (20x27½") Orig OL color. Ref: Phillips (A) 724. [28] £409 $630
CHILI [1809] 71x51cm (28x20") Orig OL color. lt offsetting. Ref: Phillips (A) 724. [28] £175 $270
EAST INDIA ISLES [1813] 51x69cm (20x27") Orig OL color. Ref: Phillips (A) 724. [28] £263 $405
ENGLAND NORTHERN PART [IN SET WITH] ... SOUTHERN PART [1811] 2 sheets, each 51x71cm (20x28") Orig OL color. Tears, chips lower margins. Ref: Phillips (A) 724. [28] £292 $450
NORTH AMERICA [1812] In *Modern Atlas*. 51x70cm (20x27½") Orig OL color. Ref: Phillips (A) 724. [28] £292 $450
[SAME TITLE] [same date, source & dimen] [53] £220 $339
POLYNESIA [1813] Incl NE Australia. 51x71cm (20x27½") Orig OL color. Soil marks top margin; lower margin bit ragged. Ref: Phillips (A) 724. [28] £263 $405
[SAME TITLE] [c. 1813+] 51x70cm (20½x27½") OL color. [41] £95 $146
SOUTHERN AFRICA [1809] 50x69cm (20x27½") Orig OL color. Lt offsetting. Ref: Phillips (A) 724; cf Norwich 186. [28] £175 $270
SOUTHERN HEMISPHERE [c. 1812] Incl Australia & N.Z. Diameter 49cm (19½") Color. [41] £98 $151
SPANISH DOMINIONS IN NORTH AMERICA, MIDDLE PART [1811] Southern Mexico & Yucatan. . 51x71cm (20x27½") Orig OL color. Ref: Phillips (A) 724. [28] £204 $315
[SAME TITLE] [1812] From *Modern Atlas*. 50x70cm (19½x27½") [53] £140 $216
SPANISH DOMINIONS IN NORTH AMERICA. NORTHERN PART [1811] In *Modern Atlas*. Incl Spanish Southwest. 51x70cm (20x27½") Orig OL color. Ref: Phillips (A) 724. [28] £321 $495
[SAME TITLE] [1812] [same source] 50x70cm (19½x27½") [53] £400 $616
SPANISH DOMINIONS IN NORTH AMERICA SOUTHERN PART [1812] From *Modern Atlas*. Central America. 50x70cm (19½x27½") [53] £100 $154
SWISSERLAND [1809] 51x71cm (19½x28") Orig OL color. Ref: Phillips (A) 724. [28] £204 $315
THE WORLD ON MERCATOR'S PROJECTION - WESTERN PART [WITH ANOTHER SHEET] EASTERN PART [1812] From *Modern Atlas*. Each 69x51cm (27½x20½") Orig OL color. Sh tear rt margin; lt offsetting. Ref: Phillips (A) 727. [28] £351 $540
UNITED STATES OF AMERICA NORTHERN PART [1810] 51x70cm (20x27½") OL color. Minor c'fold discoloration; repaired margin tears; o/w very nice. [9] £127 $195
[SAME TITLE] [same date & dimen] Orig OL col. Sh tears lower margin. Ref: Phillips (A) 724. [28] £292 $450
UNITED STATES OF AMERICA SOUTHERN PART [1809] 51x70cm (20x28") Orig OL color. Pinhole paper flaw. Ref: Phillips (A) 724. [28] £234 $360

PIQUET

POLE ARTIQUE [c. 1785] 18x20cm (7x8") B&W. [46] £29 $45

PITT

LALANDIAE ET FALSTRIAE ACCURATA DESCRIPTIO. APUD JANSSONIO WAESBERGIOS, ET MOSEM PITT [1680-83] 41x53cm (16x21") Orig OL & cartouche color; red-ruled borders. Pinholes lower margin. [28] £292 $450
MAGNI DUCATUS LITHUANIAE ... SUMPTIB. JANSSONIO WAESBERGIAR [1680-83] 44x54cm (17x21½") Blank verso. Orig OL & cartouche color; red ruled borders. Backed to reinforce color burned areas. [28] £351 $540
NOVA TOTIUS TERRARUM ORBIS GEOGRAPHICA AC HYDROGRAPHICA TABULA [1680] After 1608 Van Den Keere plate. Surround of panels. 40x54cm (15½x21") Full color. Lower margin c'fold repair on verso; minor margin spotting; overall fine. Ref: Shirley (W) 504. [33] £4,480 $6,900
PALATINATUS POSNANIENSIS, IN MAIORI POLONIA PRIMARII NOVA DELINEATIO PER G.F.M. [1680-83] 46x53cm (18x21") Blank verso. Orig OL & cartouche color; red ruled borders. Backed to reinforce color burned areas. [28] £292 $450

PLANCIUS

CEILAN ... [early 17th c.] 36x51cm (13½x19½") Col. Lt age color & soiling; generally good. [13] £243 $375
EUROPAM AB ASIA ET AFRICA SEGREGANT MARE MEDITERRANEUM ... [1594-1605] 39x54cm (15½x21½") Uncolored. Orig folds restored. [53] £2,200 $3,388

ORBIS TERRARUM TYPUS DE INTEGRO MULTIS IN LOCIS EMENDATUS AUCTORE PETRO PLANCIO [1594] Double hemi; pictorial surround. 41x58cm (16x22½") Exc. Ref: Shirley (W) 187, pl.152. [62] £5,518 $8,500
[SAME TITLE] [1594] 40x58cm (16x23") Orig color. Framed. [16] £8,784 $13,530

PLON
[AUSTRALIA] [1872] 25x36cm (10x14") Full color. [45] £39 $60
MALAISIE ET INDOCHINE CARTE SPECIALE POUR JAVA, SIAM ET CANTON VOYAGE AUTOUR DU MONDE PAR LE COMTE DE BEAUVOIR [1872] 25x36cm (10x14") Full color. [45] £39 $60

POIRSON
CARTE DE LA PARTIE DE LA COTE NORD OUEST DE L'AMERIQUE [c. 1820] 43x34cm (17x13½") OL color. [40] £125 $193
PARTIE SEPTENTRIONALE DE L'OCEAN PACIFIQUE OU L'ON A MARQUE LES DESCOUVERTES ET LES ROUTES DE MRS. DE LA PEROUSE ET COOK. PAR J.B. POIRSON INGENIEUR GEOGRAPHE [c. 1820] 35x46cm (14x18") OL color. [40] £95 $146
[SAME TITLE] [c. 1824] 39x50cm (15½x19½") Orig color. Sh tears upper margin. [28] £234 $360

POLITICAL MAGAZINE
A MAP OF EAST AND WEST FLORIDA, GEORGIA AND LOUISIANA, WITH THE ISLANDS OF CUBA, BAHAMA, AND THE COUNTRIES SURROUNDING THE GULF OF MEXICO, WITH THE TRACT OF THE SPANISH GALLEONS, AND OF OUR FLEETS THRO' THE STRAITS OF FLORIDA ... ...[1781] 27x37cm (11x14½") Uncolored. Old glycine tape repair rt margin; o/w VG. Ref: Jolly POL-27 [4] £179 $275
NEW AND ACCURATE CHART OF HUDSON'S BAY, IN NORTH AMERICA. [1782] 18x23cm (7x9") Trimmed close. Ref: Jolly POL-64 [14] £26 $40

PONTANUS
AMSTELODAMUM EMPORIUM [1611] 25x36cm (10½x13½") Sh split upper c'fold. [28] £292 $450
TABULA GEOGR. IN QUA ADMIRANDA NAVIGATIONIS CURSUS ET RECURSUS DESIGNATUR [1611] From *Rerum et Urbis Amstelodamensium Historia*. Polar map. 28x36cm (10½x14½") Repaired c'fold tear; some offsetting. [28] £701 $1,080

POPPLE
[A MAP OF THE BRITISH EMPIRE IN AMERICA. SHEET 5] [c. 1733] Middle West: Present IL, IA, MO, NE & SD. 51x69cm (20x27") C'fold split; tears to margins & engraving repaired; dampmark top margin. Ref: Cumming 217; Tooley (Amer) p.315-6; Schwartz & Ehrenberg p.151; Johnson (Amer Expl) p.176-7. [28] £1,022 $1,575
[A MAP OF THE BRITISH EMPIRE IN AMERICA. SHEET 9] [c. 1733] Present TX & LA. 51x69cm (20x27") C'fold & margin tears repaired; dampmark top margin. Ref: Cumming 217; Tooley (Amer) p.315-6; Schwartz & Ehrenberg p.151; Johnson (Amer Expl) p.176-7. [28] £1,022 $1,575
A MAP OF THE BRITISH EMPIRE IN AMERICA WITH THE FRENCH AND SPANISH SETTLEMENTS ADJACENT THERETO. BY HENRY POPPLE [c. 1740] Amsterdam: Covens & Mortier after 21 folio sheet map. French title above. 112x102cm (44x40") Full color. Side margins extended, no loss; sm wormholes mended; else exc. Framed. [38] £4,869 $7,500

PORCACCHI
[WORLD] [after 1572] 11x14cm (4x5½") on page with text. Later full color. Pale impression; VG. Ref: cf. Shirley (W) 128 & 155. [31] £227 $350
[SAME TITLE] [(1590)] [same dimen] Uncolored. Ref: Shirley (W) 128. [32] £292 $450
CUBA [1572] From *Le Isole Piu Famoso del Mondo*. Porro, sc. 10x14cm (4x5½") Cut from text page. Exc. [63] £162 $250
DESCRITTIONE DEL MAPPAMONDO [1572 - 1620] 11x15cm (4x6") Modern color. [14] £143 $220
DESCRITTIONE DI COSTANTINOPOLI [1572] From *Le Isole Piu Famoso del Mondo*. Bird's-eye view. 11x14cm (4x5½") on text sheet. Partially restored margin top & rt; else fine. [63] £81 $125
S. GIOVANNI [1576+] From *Isolario*. Puerto Rico. Porro, sc. 10x14cm (4x5½") on text sheet. Modern color. Margin worming repaired; VG. [62] £237 $365

POWELL, J.W.
LINGUISTIC STOCK OF AMERICAN INDIANS NORTH OF MEXICO [1890] From *7th Annual Report of the Bureau of Ethnology*. Chromolithograph by Sackett & Wilhelm. 53x46cm (20½x17½") Some browning; fold repairs; else VG. Ref: Schwarz & Ehrenberg pl.198. [11] £146 $225

PROBST

AFRICA ... [1788] After Schreiber. 17x20cm (6½x8") Orig color. Lt staining removed. [54] £140 $216
AMERICA ... [same date, dimen, color & condition] After Schreiber. [54] £350 $539
AMERICA SEPTENTRIONALIS COLONIIS IN ENTERIOREM ... [1782] After Schreiber. 1760's geography. [same dimen, color & condition] [54] £300 $462
CHARTE DAS RUSSISCHE REICH ... [1788] After Schreiber. [same dimen, color & condition] [54] £100 $154
DAS KONIGREICH PREUSSEN NEBST DEM POLISCHEN ANTHEIL ... [1787] After Schreiber. [same dimen, color & condition] [54] £80 $123
DER SCHWABISCHE CREIS ... [same date, dimen, color & condition] After Schreiber. [54] £70 $108
DIE OESTEREICHISCHE NIEDERLANDE ... [1785] After Schreiber. [same dimen, color & condition] [54] £60 $92
DIE PHILIPPINISCHE INSELEN ... [1782] After Schreiber. [same dimen, color & condition] [54] £320 $493
EUROPE ... [1788] After Schreiber. [same dimen, color & condition]. [54] £100 $154
GLOBUS TERRESTREIS ... [1786] After Schreiber. 17x24cm (6½x9½") [same color & condition] [54] £300 $462
GROS BRITAN ODER ENGELLAND SCHOT = U IRRLA ... [1785] After Schreiber. 17x20cm (6½x8") Orig color. Lt staining removed. [54] £140 $216
HELVETIA FOEDERATA ... [1788] After Schreiber. 17x20cm (6½x8") Orig color. Lt staining removed. [54] £120 $185
NOVA ET ACCURATA TARTARIAE EUROPAEAE SEU MINORIS ET IN SPECIE CRIMEAE ... CUM OMNIBUS CIRCA PONTIUM EUXINUM [c. 1750] After Seutter. 50x59cm (19½x23") Orig col. Sl browning. [64] £122 $189
PALESTINA IN XII TRIBUS DIVISA ... [1788] After Schreiber. 17x20cm (6½x8") Orig color. Lt staining removed. [54] £120 $185
REISE CHARTE DURCH DEUTSCHLAND ... [same date, dimen, color & condition] After Schreiber. [54] £80 $123
SCANDINAVIA ... [same date, dimen, color & condition] After Schreiber. [54] £140 $216
SYSTEMA SOLARE ET PLANETARIUM EX HYPOTHESI COPERNICANA [1782-88] After Schreiber [same dimen, color & condition] [54] £50 $77
VII. PROVINTIA SEU BELGIU FOEDERATUM ... [1782] After Schreiber. [same date, dimen, color & condition] [54] £120 $185

PTOLEMY (1478-1508 Rome)

NONA ASIAE TABULA [1478 (1507-8)] Ptolemaic Pakistan & India. 36x30cm (14½x11½") on sheet 17x22". B&W. Surface dirt; else fine. [55] £308 $475
SECUNDA ASIAE TABULA [1478 (1507-8)] Sarmatia; present Crimea, Caucasus & Caspian region. 41x36cm (16x14") on sheet 17x22". B&W. Surface dirt; else fine. [55] £308 $475
SEPTIMA ASIAE TABULA [1507] From *Geographia*. 30x53cm (11½x21") C'fold join repaired; ms numbers recto & verso. [28] £234 $360

PTOLEMY (1482 Florence)

CAELESTEM HIC TERRAM INSPICIAS TERRESTRE QB CAELUM [c. 1480] Francesco Berlinghieri's *Geographia*. (no dims.) Tears fixed; badly tattered side margins, side windheads reinstated in facsimile. [63] £20,774 $32,000
TABULA TERTIA D ASIA [1482] F. Berlinghieri. 35x46cm (13½x18") Uncolored. Sl restoration to blank gutter along c'fold; o/w good. [52] £800 $1,232

PTOLEMY (1513-1520, Strassburg)   Try *Waldseemuller*

PTOLEMY (1522-1541, Strassburg)   Try *Fries*

[ATLAS] GEOGRAPHICAE ENARRATIONIS LIBRI OCTO ... [1535] 1st Servetus ed; Lyon: Trechsel. Folio; 3 parts in one; 50 woodcut maps; 27 Ptolemaic, 23 modern from Laurent Fries blocks adapted from Waldseemuller; diagrams incl sphere by Durer. Old full morocco rebinding in antique style for Henry Stevens. Trifle rubbed; bookplate & title page blind stamp; minor flaws & repairs, 2 Asia maps, sl loss verso text; overall fine. Ref: Nordenskiold (Col) II,209; Nordenskiold (Fac) pp.22-3; Phillips (A) 364; Stevens (Ptolemy) 48. [28] £20,450 $31,500
[PTOLEMAIC CEYLON] [1522 - 1541] Laurent Fries. 28x46cm (11x18") Uncolored. [52] £480 $739
[PTOLEMAIC NORTH AFRICA] [1522 - 1541] Laurent Fries. 30x45cm (11½x17½") Uncol. [52] £400 $616

[PTOLEMAIC PERSIA] [1522 - 1541] Laurent Fries. 30x46cm (12x18") Uncolored. [52] £320 $493
ASIAE TABULA DECIMA CONTINET INDIAM INTRA GANGEM [VERSO TITLE] [1541] From *Geographia*. 30x48cm (11½x19") Foxed; sh c'fold splits. Ref: Nordenskiold (Col) II,211. [28] £175 $270
ASIAE TABULA SECUNDA CONTINET [1541] After Waldseemuller; Vienne. Russia. 30x40cm (12x15½") [14] £227 $350
TABULA OCTAVA ASIAE CONTINET SCYTHIAM EXTRA IMAUM MONTEM, ET SERICAM [1541] After Waldseemuller; Vienne. N Russia. 30x39cm (12x15½") [14] £195 $300
[SAME TITLE] [1541] From *Geographica*. Lyon-Vienna ed. 30x35cm (12x14") Browning c'fold; foxing. Ref: Nordenskiold (Col) II, 211. [28] £162 $250
TABULA SEPTIMA ASIAE [1541] After Waldseemuller; Vienne. Text panels on verso. 28x46cm (11x18") Sm worm holes in margin; o/w near mint. [14] £227 $350
TABULA TERTIA APHRICAE CONTINET CYRENICA, QUAE ET PENTAPOLIS, MARMARICAM, LIBYAM, AEGYPTUM, ET THEBAIDEM [1541] From *Geographia*. Lyon-Vienna ed. Verso: "Libyae Interioris pars". 28x43cm (11x17½") Old color. Sm c'fold hole repaired. Ref: Nordenskiold (Col) II,211. [28] £234 $360
TABULA TERTIA ASIA [1541] After Waldseemuller; Vienne. Text panels on verso. 30x42cm (12x16½") Sm worm holes in margin; o/w near mint. [14] £162 $250
TYPUS ORBIS DESCRIPTIONE PTOLEMAEI [1541] Laurent Fries. 30x46cm (12x18") Fine. [14] £1,558 $2,400
[SAME TITLE] [1541] By Fries. Michael Servetus ed. 33x46cm (12½x18") Blank verso; missing top border piece. B&W. Fine. Ref: Shirley (W) 47, pl.46. [1] £1,363 $2,100

PTOLEMY (1540-1552, Basle) See *Munster*

PTOLEMY (1548, Venice) See *Gastaldi*

PTOLEMY (1561-1599, Venice) See *Ruscelli*

PTOLEMY (1596-1621, Magini) See *Magini*

PURCHAS

FRETUM MAGELLANI [1625] By Hondius, after Mercator. Text below. 13x17cm (5x6½") [14] £55 $85
POLUS ARTICUS CUM VICINIS REGIONIBUS / HONDIUS HIS MAP OF THE ARCTIKE POLE, OR NORTHERNE WORLD [1625] From *Purchas His Pilgrimes*. 13x18cm (5½x7½") Uncolored. Printed to rt edge of page; offsetting; VG. [36] £127 $195
THE MAP OF CHINA [same date & source] 30x37cm (11½x14½") Uncolored. Bright, clean. [36] £227 $350
[SAME TITLE] [same date & dimen] Based on Ricci. Mint. [62] £941 $1,450

PUTTER

ANCIEN PLAN DE L'ISLE DE MALTE ... [1729] A. de Putter. Time of St. Paul's shipwreck; modern fortifications. 31x43cm (12x17") Color. [53] £400 $616

QUAD

[ATLAS] FASCICULUS GEOGRAPHICUS COMPLECTENS PRAECIPUARUM TOTIUS ORBIS REGIONUM TABULAS CIRCITER CENTUM ... [1608] Cologne: Bussemacher. 1st Latin ed (orig with German text, 1600). Quarto. 87 double-page maps. Early vellum. Title soiled & backed; some leaves browned; tear repaired, no loss; margin tears & repairs; worming lower margin 2nd half. Ref: Nordenskiold (Col) II,240; Nordenskiold (Fac) p.125n; Phillips (A) 4253a; Sabin 66893. [28] £15,776 $24,300
ASIA PARTIU ORBIS MAXIMA MDXCVIII [1598 / 1600] 21x30cm (8½x11½") Exc. [62] £357 $550
BARBAIA AFRICANA, ET BILEDULGERID [1603 (1608)] 23x30cm (9x12") Uncolored. [58] £120 $185
BELGIUM [1608] 2 portraits. 23x30cm (9x12") Uncolored. [58] £120 $185
BOHEMIA [1608] 18x26cm (7½x10½") Uncolored. [58] £120 $185
BURGUNDIAE INFERIORIS QUAE DUCATUS NOMINE CENSETUR DESC. [1592 (1608)] 18x25cm (7½x10½") Uncolored. [58] £114 $175
CHICA SIVE PATAGONICA ET AUSTRALIS TERRA M.DC [1600] 2 maps: partial polar circle; Strait of Magellan. 22x28cm (8½x11") Color. [16] £997 $1,536
DUCATUS OSWIECZENSIS & ZATORIENSIS DESCRIPTIO [1592 / 1608] Southern Poland. 19x27cm (7½x10½") [14] £91 $140
HISPANIAE NOVAE SIVE MAGNAE VERA DESCRIPTIO [1600] 21x29cm (8x11½") Fine. [63] £292 $450
ISLANDIA [1600] King Christian IV portrait. Bussemacher, sc. 23x29cm (9x11½") Full color. Exc. [62] £584 $900

MORAVIA [c.1592 / 1608] From *Fasciculus Geographicus*. 21x30cm (8x12") Some orig OL color.
[14] £101 $155

NOVI ORBIS PARS BOREALIS, AMERICA SCILICET, COMPLECTENS FLORIDAM, BACCALAON, CANADAM, TERRAM CORTERIALEM, VIRGINIAM, NOROMBECAM, PLURESQUE ALIAS PROVINCIAS [1600] 23x30cm (9x11½") Lower margin c'fold mended; else exc. Ref: Goss (NA) 22. [62] £1,883 $2,900

[SAME TITLE] [same date & dimen] Uses De Jode model. Uncolored. Exc. [63] £2,077 $3,200

[SAME TITLE] [(1608)] From *Geographische Handtbuch*. [same dimen] Full color, presumed later. VG. Ref: Schwartz & Ehrenberg p.83. [31] £2,142 $3,300

PERUVIA ID EST, NOVI ORBIS PARS MERIDIONALIS A PRAESTANTISSIMA EIUS IN OCCIDETEM REGIONE SIC APPELLATA. 1598 [1600] 21x28cm (8x11") Full later color. Exc. [62] £422 $650

[SAME TITLE] [(1608)] From *Geographische Handtbuch*. [same dimen] Uncolored. Lt age toned; VG.
[31] £779 $1,200

TRIER [1608] 20x30cm (8x12") Uncolored. [58] £120 $185

RADEFELD   Try *Hildburghausen Blbliographishes Institut*

BRITISCHES NORD-AMERICA [1847] 20x25cm (8½x10½") OL col. Narrow margins as pub; exc.
[29] £36 $55

RAILROAD COMPANY MAPS   Try *Colton, Rand McNally*

[NEW ENGLAND: TROLLEY ROUTES] [1905] A Trolley Wayfinder; bird's eye view, pub by New England Street Railway Club. 51x36cm (20x14") Full color; street RR routes in red. [36] £55 $85

[SOUTHERN NEW ENGLAND: INTERURBAN TROLLEY LINES] [1905] Bird's eye view; pub by Metropolitan News Co. 36x53cm (14x20½") [36] £55 $85

A GEOGRAPHICALLY CORRECT MAP OF THE STATE OF TEXAS [1876 (1878)] Texas and Pacific Railway Co. Folding map. Verso: time tables & promotionals. 46x51cm (18x20") Ticket agent's stamp. Minor fold separations; generally fine. [13] £243 $375

CHICAGO AND NORTHWESTERN RAILWAY [1893] Chicago to Pacific; with timetables. 18x36cm (7x13½") Chipping; loss on cover; fair to good. [10] £36 $55

CLIMATIC MAP OF CALIFORNIA [1897] Southern Pacific Company. H.S. Crocker, S.Fran. lith. 71x23cm (28x9") Mean temperatures color keyed. Some wear; folds repaired. [11] £49 $75

MAP OF BOSTON AND MAINE RAILROAD [1890] New Brunswick to Chicago. Folds into 9x6" leather covered boards. Insets. 64x109cm (25x43") Spine rubbed. Generally VG. [12] £55 $85

MAP OF NEBRASKA AND EASTERN COLORADO [1887] Burlington Route. Folds into 9x6" wraps with 14 page pamphlet. 58x99cm (22½x38½") Printed color. Wraps have lt soil, spot & minor chip; map has fold separations. [12] £250 $385

MAP OF THE ARKANSAS LAND GRANT [1880] St. Louis, Iron Mountain and Southern RR. Folding map. Checkerboard of grants along RR shown. Double sided, each around   71x23cm (28x9")   Minor separations; lt soil & spotting. [12] £179 $275

MAP OF THE NORTHERN PACIFIC RAIL ROAD [1886] Duluth to Pacific; shows land grants. Inset: NE U.S. 38x79cm (15x31") Color. Some separations & repaired tears; else good. [10] £88 $135

MAP OF THE NORTHERN PACIFIC RAILROAD AND TRIBUTARY COUNTRY. [1872] Wall map. Jay Cooke land sale promotional; Phila: National Railway Publication. 53x84cm (21½x33") Full color. Rods lacking; top margin needing sm repair; fair. [19] £487 $750

MAP OF THE SOUTHERN CONTINENTAL R.R. WITH CONNECTIONS FROM KANSAS CITY MO., FORT SMITH ARK., AND SHREVEPORT LA. GIVING A GENERAL VIEW OF THE RECENT SURVEYS OF THE KANSAS PACIFIC RAILWAY CO. ... UNDER THE DIRECTION OF GEN. WM. J. PALMER ... [1867-68 (1869)] From *Palmer's Survey's across the Continent*. 76x97cm (30x38") RR routes in color. Orig folded; rebacked, sl loss at corners. Ref: Wheat (TM) 1206. [45] £325 $500

MAP OF THE TEXAS AND PACIFIC RAILWAY AND CONNECTIONS [1897] With annual report. Covers St. Louis & New Orleans to El Paso. 46x58cm (18x23") Fine. [10] £94 $145

MAP OF THE YELLOWSTONE NATIONAL PARK [1882] Northern Pacific Railroad. Inset of rail spur from Livingston, MT. Verso: text & photos. Folds into wraps. 61x46cm (24x18") Printed color. Couple spots; fold repair; o/w good. [11] £120 $185

MAP SHOWING THE UNION PACIFIC RAILWAY AND CONNECTING RAILROADS [1881] In *Report to the Stockholders of the Union Pacific* ... NY: Rufus Adams. On thin paper in 22 pp booklet. 43x75cm (17x29½") Orig OL color; RR routes color highlighted. Crease at bottom; sm splits; fold separations repaired; bright, clear, clean; Booklet has 2 rubber stamps; VG. Ref: cf. Wheat V, 1156. [59] £195 $300

MAPS OF THE NEW AND POPULAR ST. LOUIS AND TEXAS SHORT LINE [1878] St. Louis, Iron Mountain and Southern Railway. 2 maps: Eastern US; MO-AR-TX (region of the RR). Verso: Timetable; promotional material. 46x79cm (18x31") Printed color. Minor paper loss at fold, maps unaffected. [10] £185 $285

PANORAMIC VIEWS ALONG THE LINE OF THE DENVER & RIO GRANDE RAILROAD [1890 - 1893] Knight, Leonard & Co., Chicago. 12mo folding brochure; 2-color cerographed route map; 9 views on verso. Lt age-toning; uneven folding; VG. [6] £55 $85

SKELETON MAP OF THE ST. LOUIS & SAN FRANCISCO RAILWAY AND CONNECTIONS [1880] Herald Printing Co., Springfield, MO. Double sided broadside, with route map on reverse. 18x53cm (6½x20½") Browned; some creasing & soiling; no loss. [13] £321 $495

RAMSAY

CAROLINE MERIDIONALE ... [1787] First in *History of the Revolution* ..., London, 1785. 37x42cm (14½x16½") [14] £243 $375

RAMUSIO

[MEXICO] [1565] From *Delle Navigationi e Viaggi*. "Tenochtitlan". 28x18cm (10½x7") Uncol. [54] £300 $462

[NORTHEASTERN NORTH AMERICA: CANADA & NEW ENGLAND] [1556 / 1606] After Gastaldi 28x38cm (10½x14½") Exc. Ref: Goss (NA) 8; Danforth (Nuremberga) 57. [38] £1,623 $2,500

LA NUOVA FRANCIA [1565] From *Navigationi*. After Gastaldi, 1548. 27x37cm (10½x14½") Uncolored. Ref: Danforth (Nurumbega) p.44; cf. Kershaw (Canada) #15a, pl.8. [2] £1,266 $1,950

[SAME TITLE] [after 1556] As in *Delle Navigationi et Viaggi*. Gastaldi. 2nd state (with willow trees; recut after fire). [same dimen] Ref: Cumming (Discovery) p.90; Johnson (Amer Expl) p.52. [28] £1,344 $2,070

[SAME TITLE] [1556 / 1565] From *Navigationi*, vol.3. State 2. Attributed to Gastaldi [same dimen] Exc. Ref: Potter, illus p.141. [62] £1,623 $2,500

LA TERRA DE HOCHELEGA NELLA NOVA FRANCIA [after 1556] 2nd state, incl weeping willow trees. 28x38cm (11x15") Ref: Schwartz & Ehrenberg p.64; Johnson (Amer Expl) p.55; Tooley (Amer) p.211; Tooley (Landmarks) p.221. [28] £1,256 $1,935

PRIMA TAVOLA [AFRICA] [1550 (c.1580)] State 2, copperplate; possible Gastaldi attribution. South at top. 28x38cm (11x15") Sl clipping at c'fold where pinched in binding; else exc. [63] £633 $975

UNIVERSALE DELLA PARTE DEL MONDO NUOVAMENTE RITROVATA [1556 / 1565] State II. 1st map showing Coronado expedition & Sierra Nevada. 26x26cm (10x10") Minor c'fold mend; else exc. [62] £1,623 $2,500

RAND, McNALLY & CO. (Atlas Maps)

[ATLAS] RAND, MCNALLY & CO.'S BUSINESS ATLAS, CONTAINING LARGE SCALE MAPS OF EACH STATE AND TERRITORY ... [1877] Company's 2nd atlas. Folio. Orig half-leather covers scuffed, but sound. 212 pp; 45 maps with printed OL color, 3 fold-outs on linen. Maps & contents tight & VG. Ref: Phillips (A) 1399; Le Gear (US) L63. [5] £454 $700

[ATLAS] RAND, MCNALLY & CO.'S NEW DOLLAR ATLAS OF THE UNITED STATES AND DOMINION OF CANADA, CONTAINING NEW COLORED MAPS OF EACH STATE AND TERRITORY [1884] Sm quarto. Quarter-cloth & printed boards worn. 128 pp; some colored maps double page. Ex lib; contents VG. Ref: Le Gear (US) L75. [5] £26 $40

ALASKA [1887] From *Atlas of the World*. 20x28cm (7½x10½") Uncolored. [36] £29 $45

FLORIDA [1887] From ... *New Indexed Atlas of the World* ... 33x48cm (13x19") With text pages. Printed color. [4] £29 $45

[SAME TITLE] [1892] From *Indexed Atlas of the World*. 48x66cm (19x26") Col. VG or better. [29] £19 $30

IDAHO [1888] [same source] 17 counties 48x30cm (19x12") Full printed color. Fine. [18] £36 $55

MAP OF FLORIDA [1892] Insets. 51x66cm (20x26") OL color. Lt water mark at inset side. [45] £49 $75

MICHIGAN CENTRAL [c. 1880] RR map. 36x48cm (13½x19") Black & yellow. [44] £58 $90

MONTANA [1883] In *New Indexed Atlas of the World*. With 2 page index. 32x50cm (13x20") Full printed color. VG. [18] £49 $75

NEW MEXICO [1888] 48x33cm (19x13") [13] £52 $80

PUERTO RICO [1899] 4 insets. 23x30cm (9x12") Color. [25] £23 $35

RAILROAD MAP OF ILLINOIS ... [1881] For report of Railroad & Warehouse Commissioners. RR's color coded. 71x43cm (28x17") [44] £65 $100

RAND, MCNALLY & CO.'S ARIZONA [1888] 51x33cm (20x13") OL color. Faint water mark upper lf. [45] £39 $60

[SAME TITLE] [1896] 33x51cm (13x20") Full color. [45] £49 $75

RAND MCNALLY & CO.'S CALIFORNIA [1892] 2 insets. 66x51cm (26x20") Full color. [45] £49 $75

Rand McNally & Co.'s Florida [1881] *Rand McNally's Business Atlas & Shippers Guide.* 39 counties. 51x33cm (19½x13") Printed color. [4] £29 $45

Rand McNally & Co.'s Indian Territory and Oklahoma [1892 / 1897] Panhandle inset; County "D" remains. 33x51cm (13x20") Full color. [45] £49 $75

Rand McNally & Co.'s Kansas [1888] 51x66cm (20x26") OL color. [45] £49 $75

Rand McNally & Co.'s Montana [1893] 33x51cm (13x20") OL color. [45] £39 $60

[Same title] [1895] 33x51cm (13x20") Full color. [45] £49 $75

Rand McNally & Co.'s Nebraska [1895] 51x66cm (20x26") Full color. [45] £49 $75

Rand McNally & Co.'s New Mexico [1888] Mining districts color coded. 51x33cm (20x13") OL color. [45] £39 $60

[Same title] [1896] 33x51cm (13x20") Full color. [45] £49 $75

Rand McNally & Co.'s Texas [1892] 51x66cm (20x26") OL col. Faint water mark at edge. [45] £49 $75

Rand McNally & Co.'s Washington [1895] 51x66cm (20x26") Full color. [45] £49 $75

Rand McNally & Co.'s Wyoming [1891] 33x51cm (13x20") OL color. [45] £39 $60

[Same title] [1895] 33x51cm (13x20") Full color. [45] £49 $75

Texas [1895] Greer Co. uncertain. 43x66cm (17x26") Full color. [46] £97 $150

[Same title] [1898] From *Indexed Atlas* ... 51x66cm (20x26") Color. [9] £62 $95

Texas, Eastern Section [and] Western Section [1896] Each half 66x48cm (26x19") Full color. [46] £114 $175

Wyoming [1891] 13 counties. 33x43cm (12½x17") Printed color. [13] £49 $75

[Same title] [1898] 13 counties. 33x48cm (12½x19") Printed color. [9] £32 $50

RAND, McNALLY & CO. (Pocket & Wall Maps; Globes)

[Globe] Rand, McNally & Co.s New Three Inch Terrestrial Globe [c. 1891-1900] Coated paper gores over solid paper mache orb. Simplified geography; not a toy. Paperweight base. Color. [17] £617 $950

[Globe] Rand, McNally & Co.s New Twelve Inch Terrestrial Globe [c. 1891] Dull finish paper gores over cork on cast iron; nickel plated table mount. Cast one-sided meridian ring moves in wood horizon ring on iron brackets. On tripod stand 21" high. Color. Some metal corrosion with flaking; some restorable horizon paper scale loss. [17] £1,461 $2,250

[Same title] [c. 1909] Coated paper gores over metal & plaster. Time dials at poles. Axis pivoting without meridian from bracket on ball & claw tripod; 20½" high overall. Color. A few surface abrasions. [17] £1,136 $1,750

Chicago and North Western R'w. [c. 1885] RR wall map; linen backed, 2 rods. Surround of promotional material. 61x81cm (24x32") Color. Separating from upper rod; chipping & minor loss above; o/w VG. [6] £146 $225

Map of Alaska including the Klondike District and Adjacent Gold Fields [1897] Pocket map, folds into 12mo boards 61x91cm (24x36") Litho color. Sm fold separation; sl spotted cover; o/w near fine. [6] £146 $225

Map of Louisiana. Showing the Tensas Delta District [c. 1895] In land sale promotional booklet "The Tensas District of Louisiana ... James D. Lacey & Co. Chicago / New Orleans"; illustrations. 28x36cm (11x14") Printed color; district overprinted in red. VG. [20] £65 $100

Map of the Atchison, Topeka and Santa Fe Railroad ... [1880] Railroads of whole U.S. Back panel promotionals and 8x7" map of Colorado mining camps. 61x94cm (24x37") Fold repairs, no significant loss. [11] £130 $200

Map Showing Routes of the Pacific Coast Steamship Company [1887] Pocket map. Reverse: travel information. 69x33cm (27x12½") Full printed color. VG. [19] £81 $125

Rand, McNally & Co.'s Indexed County and Township Pocket Map and Shippers' Guide of Missouri [1893] Folding map with 62 pp text. (no dims.) Text with mild soiling; map VG. [44] £39 $60

Rand, McNally & Co.'s Indexed Map of Louisiana [1878] Folds into 3½x6" hard cloth covers; 12 pp index. 23x30cm (9x12") Printed OL color. VG. [20] £97 $150

Rand McNally & Co.'s Indexed Map of Mexico [1899] Folding map & 62 p gazetteer in 7x4" hard boards. 48x66cm (19x25½") Printed color. one repaired fold split; else VG. [11] £58 $90

Rand, McNally & Co's New Indexed Large Scale County and Township Map of Montana [1884] Folds into 7x4" gilt labeled hard boards. 14 counties. 56x89cm (21½x35") Hand & printed color. Minor bumping; near pristine. [9] £146 $225

The Rand McNally Indexed County and Township Pocket Map and Shippers Guide to Colorado [1904] Stiff wrappers; 62 pp text. 58x71cm (23x28") [45] £52 $80
The Rand McNally Indexed Township and County Pocket Map and Shippers Guide of Kansas [1885] Stiff wrappers; 34 pp text. 33x51cm (13x20"). Color. Map loose; map & case exc. [45] £114 $175

RAPIN   Try *Tindal*

Ghent [1743-47] Bird's-eye view. 38x48cm (15½x19") B&W. [1] £162 $250
Menin A Very Strong Town in the Earldom of Flanders Taken by ye Allies in the Year 1776 and Retaken by ye French in 1744 [n.d.] For Tindal's Continuation of Rapin's *History of England*. 38x48cm (15x19") Uncolored. [36] £97 $150
Plan of the City of Bouchain Situated upon the Rivers Sensette and Scheld in the County of Hainault [n.d.] For Tindal's Continuation of Rapin's *History of England*. 38x48cm (14½x18½") Uncolored. [36] £97 $150

RAPKIN   Try *Tallis*

West India Islands [1860] Similar to Tallis; lacks vignettes. 26x33cm (10x13") Color. [36] £91 $140

RASPE

Plan des Hafens und Festung Louisbourg auf der Insul Cap Breton ... [1757 - 1764] 23x38cm (9x15") Orig color. Ref: Phillips (A) 2825. [28] £234 $360

RATHBONE

[Title page] The Surveyor in Foure Bookes ... [1616] With terrestrial & celestial globes, figures of Arithmetica & Geometrica. 25x16cm (9½x6") Uncolored. Trimmed close. [52] £280 $431

REAL ESTATE & PROMOTIONAL MAPS - Infrequent Publishers

[Scotland: Blair Athole, Perthshire] [c. 1880] A 44,847 acre tract. Dissected, linen mounted, folded into limp morocco cover with marbled lining. 107x152cm (41½x60") No color. Cover rubbed; map fine. [21] £65 $100
Canada Lands The Haslam Land and Investment Co. [(1905)] Winnepeg to Rockies, incl whole Assiniboia District. 36x76cm (14x29½") Company lands in red. Fold separations; else VG. [9] £49 $75
F.G. Conley & Co.'s Map of the East End Complements of F.C. Bell, F.G. Conley, Real Estate Brokers ... [c. 1900] Squirrel Hill area. 46x43cm (18x17") Full color. Corner tack holes; separation at corners, lower lf missing, minor loss; sl misfolded. [45] £39 $60
Map Illustrating the Position of Duluth in the United States [1885] Northern U.S. & Canada. M.H. Traubel, lith, Phila; possibly for Northern Pacific. 53x74cm (21x29") Color. Issued folded; border damage, map unaffected. [11] £179 $275
N.O. Brashier City, Paris of St. Mary, La. [1871] Barnes; H. Lewis. 312 lots for sale; six 5-cent LA law stamps. 46x56cm (18½x21½") Good. [20] £179 $275

REICHARD

Nordlicher Theil der Vereinigten Staaten [1817] ME to VA to Lake Michigan. 28x34cm (11x13") Orig OL color. Borders soiled; map fine. [46] £42 $65

RENARD

[Frontispiece] Planisphere Representant Tout l'Etendue du Monde ... [1715-] Reissue from 42x27cm (16½x10½") Color. [52] £450 $693
Magnum Mare del Zur cum Insula California [1715] After De Wit, c.1680. 49x57cm (19½x22½") Orig color. [16] £2,303 $3,547
Orientaliora Indiarum Orientalium ... [1715] After De Wit. 44x54cm (17½x21½") Orig color. [16] £2,303 $3,547

RIZZI-ZANNONI

[Frontispiece] [1762] From sm atlas; cherub & figure pointing to glove. 10x5cm (4x2½") Col. [57] £26 $40
Carte Geo-Hydrographique du Golfe du Mexique et de Ses Isles [1770] Paris: Lattre. 31x45cm (12x17½") Full color. Fine. [32] £162 $250
[Same title] [1771] 30x46cm (12½x17½") Orig full OL color. Lt sm stain upper lf. [46] £260 $400
Mapa Dos Reynos de Portugal e Algarve ... [c. 1770] OL color. [43] £125 $193

ROBERT DE VAUGONDY   See *De Vaugondy*

ROBERTS
GOGLEDD-BARTH AMERICA [1815] North America in Welsh. "Cyhoedded yn Nghaergybi Mehefin 4, 1815, gan R. Roberts." Woodthorpe, sc. 19x22cm (7½x8½") Orig OL color. [54] £150 $231

ROBINSON
CHART OF PART OF THE NORTH WEST COAST OF AMERICA ... [c. 1798] San Francisco to Mt. St. Elias. 38x49cm (15x19½") B&W. [40] £75 $116

PLAN OF THE ENTRANCE OF THE PORT OF BUCARELLI ON THE NORTH WEST COAST OF AMERICA ... [c. 1798] 38x48cm (15x19") B&W. [40] £95 $146

ROCQUE
A MAP OF THE KINGSOM OF IRELAND ... [1790] From Sayer, *General Atlas*. Detailed 4-sheet map 64x99cm (25½x39½") OL color. Needs sm repairs; fine. [21] £487 $750

ENGLAND AND WALES DRAWN FROM THE MOST ACCURATE SURVEYS [1790] From Sayer, *General Atlas*. Detailed 4-sheet map 124x102cm (49x40½") OL color. Lower sheet needs sm repair; fine. [21] £487 $750

ROMANUS
[ATLAS] **PARVUM THEATRUM URBIUM SIVE URBIUM PRAECIPUARUM TOTIUS ORBIS BREVIS ET METHODICA DESCRIPTIO** [1595] Frankfurt: 1st ed. Sm quarto; 67 woodcuts in text, mostly European town views, 2 full-pages. (no dims.) Ownership inscription, 1606. Contemporary calf; worn, oxidized, joints cracked, hinges repaired; internally VG. Ref: Phillips (A) 65. Sabin 73000. [28] £3,798 $5,850

ROSACCIO   Try *Ruscelli*
FIGURA DELLA SPAGNA [1596] Woodcut on 2 joined sheets. 13x18cm (5x7") Lower lf margin repaired. [57] £97 $150

ORBIS TERRAE COMPENDIOSA DESCRIPTIO [(1598) 1713] From Lasor a Varea, *Universus Terrarum Orbis Scriptorum*. Recognizable by addition of "T.2.pag.284." 17x25cm (7x10") Uncolored. C'fold reinforced on verso; minor show-through; VG Ref: cf. Shirley (W) 217 [31] £390 $600

UNIVERSALE ECC.TE DESCRITTIONE DI TUTTO IL MONDO DEL GIOSEPPE ROSACCIO [c. 1610] State II, with bearded Cosimo II de Medici portrait. 27x32cm (10½x12½") Wear at folds, sm loss; else good. Ref: Shirley (W) 268. [62] £2,467 $3,800

ROSE
JOHN BULL AND HIS FRIENDS A SERIO-COMIC MAP OF EUROPE ... [1900] Human personifications of nations. 49x69cm (19x27") Orig color. Folded originally; paper covers detached. [52] £400 $616

ROSSI
L'ISOLE BRITANNICHE OVERO L'INGHILTERRA ... LA SCOTIA ... L'IRLANDA ... [dated 1697] G.G. Rossi, after Sanson; 2nd state. 41x53cm (16½x20½") Ref: Shirley (BI 1650-1750) pp.120-1. [28] £292 $450

LE POSTE CON LE SUE STRADE PRINCIPALI DELL'ALTA E BASSA GERMANIA E DE PAESI ADIACENTI ... [1711] Domenico De Rossi. 46x58cm (18½x22½") Horiz fold; lower margin trimmed to border; border tears repaired, one affecting engraving. [28] £175 $270

LE POSTE DELLA FRANCIA CON LE SUE STRADE PRINCIPALI [1697] Domenico de Rossi. 2 sheets joined, 66x53cm (26x21½") Folds; stains; crease; sh margin tear. [28] £263 $405

LEGATIONE DEL DUCATO D'URBINO CON LA DIOCESI, E GOVERNO DI CITTA DI CASTELLO EL ALTRI GOVERNI, E STATI CONFINANTI ... [1697] Domenico de Rossi. 43x56cm (17x21½") Close upper margin. [28] £175 $270

LEGAZIONE DI BOLOGNA DESCRITTA DA ... MAGINI [1710] Domenico de Rossi. 56x43cm (21½x17½") [28] £204 $315

MAPPA MONDO O VERO CARTA GENERALE DEL GLOBO TERESTRE RAPRESENTATO IN DUE PLANISFERI ... [Dated 1684] Rome: G. de Rossi. 2nd state; 1692-1714. Italian ed of Sanson; insular Calif. On sheet 44x59cm (17½x23½") Orig or early wash & OL color. Verso repair lower c'fold separation, minor loss; o/w VG+. Ref: cf. Shirley (W) 419, pl.310; Phillips (A) 516. [59] £633 $975

PROVINCIE MERIDIONALI DE PAESI BASSI, INTESE SOTTO NOME DI FLANDRA, OVERO LI PAESI BASSI CATTOLICI, CON LI CONFINI DI FRANCIA, DI ALLEMAGNA, ET DI HOLLANDA ... [1692] Rome: G.G. Rossi. 38x51cm (14½x20½") Sm stains. [28] £221 $340

REGNO DI DANIMARCA DIVISO NELLE SUE DUE JUTLANDIE CIOE SETTENTRIONALE IN QUATTRO DIOCESI ET AUSTRALE ... [1697] After Sanson. 41x53cm (16x20½") Sm spot. [28] £175 $270

ROUX
BARUT [LEBANON] [1764] Harbor chart. 13x18cm (5x7½") Wash color. [57] £39 $60

ROYAL GEOGRAPHIC JOURNAL
MAP OF PART OF NIPON ISLAND TO ACCOMPANY MR. ADAMS REPORT ON THE SILK DISTRICT OF JAPAN [1871] 20x23cm (7½x8½") Some color. [44] £39 $60

ROYAL GEOGRAPHICAL SOCIETY
MAP OF EASTERN AUSTRALIA ON WHICH ARE DELINEATED THE ROUTES OF MESSRS. BURKE & WILLS, MCKINLAY, LANDSBOROUGH & WALTER &C. [1863] London: J. Murray; compiled by J. Arrowsmith. 46x31cm (18x12") Laid on linen as published, folds. [14] £146 $225
MAP OF THE PROVINCES OF CANTERBURY AND OTAGO (NEW ZEALAND) [1864] 29x35cm (11½x14") Printed on thin paper; folds. [14] £49 $75
MAP OF THE ROUTE IN EASTERN AFRICA BETWEEN ZANZIBAR, THE GREAT LAKES AND THE NILE, EXPLORED AND SURVEYED BY CAPTN. J H SPEKE 1857-1863 [1864] London: J. Murray. 75x59cm (29½x23½") Orig OL color. On thin paper laid on tissue as issued; folds. [14] £162 $250
MAP OF THE SOUTH EAST PORTION OF AUSTRALIA ... [1837] J. Arrowsmith, sc. 33x42cm (13x16½") Orig wash color; routes in red. Printed on thin paper; folds. [14] £97 $150
MAP OF VANCOUVER ISLAND TO ILLUSTRATE THE PAPER OF DR. C. FORBES, RN [1864] London: J. Murray. 26x37cm (10½x14½") Orig wash color. On thin paper; folds. [14] £39 $60
MAP TO COMPLETE DIARIES OF EXPLORATION ACROSS AUSTRALIA (FROM SOUTH TO NORTH) BY ... STUART ESQ. 1861 & 1862 [1863] J. Arrowsmith; London: J. Murray. 20x12cm (8x4½") Routes in color. Laid down on linen as issued. [14] £39 $60
MAP TO ILLUSTRATE DIARIES OF EXPLORATION OF CENTRAL AUSTRALIA BY ... STUART ESQ. 1860 & 1861 [1861] J. Arrowsmith; London: J. Murray. 37x20cm (14½x8") Orig OL color. Printed on thin paper; folds. [14] £78 $120
MELVILLE & BATHURST ISLAND WITH COBURG PENINSULA, NORTHERN AUSTRALIA [1834] London: J. Murray. 18x44cm (7x17½") Orig wash color. Printed on thin paper; folds. [14] £45 $70
PART OF BRITISH COLUMBIA TO ILLUSTRATE THE PAPERS OF MR. JUSTICE BEGBIE, COMR. MAYNE...PALMER & DOWIE [1861] J. Arrowsmith; London: J. Murray. Gold field area. 21x31cm (8x12") Orig col. [14] £49 $75
UPPER CALIFORNIA TO ILLUSTRATE THE PAPER BY DR. COULTER [1835] 25x13cm (10x4½") B&W. [45] £32 $50

ROYAL MAGAZINE
A NEW AND ACCURATE MAP OF THE PRESENT SEAT OF WAR IN NORTH AMERICA. [1759] New York to Cape Cod to Quebec. 16x22cm (6½x8½") Full color. Ref: Jolly ROYMAG-5 [36] £146 $225

RUSCELLI
ASIA [1599] 18x25cm (7x9½") Uncolored. Sm wormholes lower margin; o/w fine. [33] £234 $360
CARTA MARINA NUOVA TAVOLA [1562] Venice: Valgrisi. Many rhumb lines. 18x25cm (7½x10") Ref: Shirley 111. [26] £419 $645
DI HUNGARIA ET TRANSILVANIA. TAVOLA NOVISSIMA [1599] From the Ptolemy. 15x20cm (6x8") Color. [57] £81 $125
EUROPA [1599] 18x25cm (7x9½") Uncolored. Sm wormholes lf margin; o/w fine. [33] £260 $400
INDIA TERCERA NUOVA TAVOLA [1574] In *Geographica*. After Gastaldi. 18x24cm (7x9½") Color. [16] £560 $863
ISOLA CUBA NOVA [1561] From Ptolemy, *Geographia*. 1st ed. 18x25cm (7½x9½") Later full color. Age toning to c'fold; o/w VG+. [31] £143 $220
NUEVA HISPANIA TABULA NOVA [1561] 18x25cm (7x9½") B&W. Fine. Ref: Wagner (NW) 48; Martin (TX) 3. [49] £487 $750
[SAME TITLE] [1561-1598] From the Ptolemy *Geographia*.. Peninsular Yucatan. 18x25cm (7½x10") Uncolored. [53] £450 $693
[SAME TITLE] [same date, source & dimen] Rosaccio reissue. "Calmifor" (California) & Sierra Nevada. Exc. [62] £422 $650
ORBIS DESCRIPTIO [1561] Venice: Valgrisi. 20x25cm (7½x10") Nice. Ref: Shirley (W) 110. [26] £438 $675
[SAME TITLE] [1562 (c.1598)] From Ptolemy's *Geographiae*. Double hemi. 18x26cm (7x10") B&W. Framed. Ref: Shirley (W) 202, pl.166. [16] £712 $1,097

PERSIA NUOVA TAVOLA [1561] 18x25cm (7x9½") Color. Exc. [29] £58 $90

SEPTENTRIONALIUM PERTIUM NOVA TABULA [1561 / 1599] From Ptolemy, *Geographia*. North Atlantic lands; the "Zeno" map. 19x24cm (7½x9½") Exc. [62] £292 $450

SORIA ET TERRA SANTA NUOVA TAVOLA [1561] From Ptolemy's *Geographia*. 19x24cm (7½x9½") Exc. Ref: Nebenzahl (Holy Land) pl.27. [62] £211 $325

[SAME TITLE] [1561 (1574)] [same source]. 18x24cm (7x9½") B&W. Ref: Laor 621A [50] £185 $285

TABULA APHRICA IIII [NORTHERN AFRICA] [1561] From Ptolemy's *Geographia*. 1st ed; Valgrisi; Italian text verso. 20x28cm (8x11") Uncolored. [44] £130 $200

TABULA ASIA V [PERSIA] [same date, source & dimen] Italian text verso. Uncolored. [44] £49 $75

TABULA ASIAE I [ASIA MINOR] [1599] 19x25cm (7½x10") Uncolored. Fine. [33] £71 $110

TABULA ASIAE VI [ARABIA] [1561] From Ptolemy, *Geographia*. 1st ed; Valgrisi; Italian text verso. 20x28cm (8x11") Uncolored. [44] £143 $220

TABULA EUROPA VI [ITALY] [same date, source & dimen] Italian text verso. Uncolored. [44] £78 $120

TABULA EUROPAE II [SPAIN & PORTUGAL] [same date, source & dimen] Italian text verso Uncolored. Benign edge discoloration. [44] £91 $140

TIERRA NUEVA [1561] From Ptolemy, *Geographia*. 1st state 18x25cm (7½x9½") Uncolored. Weak impression lower lf; overall good. Ref: Kershaw (Canada) 18a. [33] £487 $750

[SAME TITLE] [1561] From the "Ptolemy"; 2nd ed. 18x25cm (7½x10") OL color, possibly orig. Ref: Nordenskiold (Fac) p.26, #30; Phillips (A) 371, #32. [46] £390 $600

[SAME TITLE] [1599] From Ptolemy, *Geographia*. Decorative ships added; 2 cracks visible in plate. 18x25cm (7x9½") Strong impression. [33] £487 $750

RUSSELL

A GENERAL MAP OF SOUTH AMERICA DRAWN FROM THE BEST SURVEYS [1794] 36x45cm (14½x17½") Uncolored. Top half rt margin trimmed to border; exc. [29] £26 $40

MAP OF THE NORTHERN. OR, NEW ENGLAND STATES OF AMERICA, COMPREHENDING VERMONT, NEW HAMPSHIRE, DISTRICT OF MAIN, MASSACHUSETTS, RHODE ISLAND, AND CONNECTICUT. BY J. RUSSELL [1795] 37x46cm (14½x18") Exc. [63] £179 $275

MAP OF THE SOUTHERN STATES OF AMERICA, COMPREHENDING MARYLAND, VIRGINIA, KENTUCKY, TERRITORY STH OF THE OHIO, NORTH CAROLINA, TENNESSEE GOVERNMT. SOUTH CAROLINA, & GEORGIA [1795] 37x50cm (14½x20") Exc. [63] £211 $325

RUSSIAN GOVERNMENT

DOROZHNAIA KARTA KAVKAZSKAGO KRAIA. TIFLIS: SOSTAVLENA I LITOGRAFIROVANA V VOENNO-TOPOGRAFICHESKOM OTDELE KAVKAZKAGO VOENNAGO OKRUGA ... [1870-1887] Compiled by Military-Topographical Dept. Road map of Caucasus region. Folding map mounted on linen in sections in quarter cloth cover. 130x150cm (51x58½") Colored litho. Dampstaining outer side. [28] £234 $360

KARTA ZHELEZNYKH SHOSEINYKH I VNUTRENNIKH VODNYKH PUTEI SOOBSHCHENIIA ROSSIJKOI IMPERII ... [1887] Communications Ministry. Russian Empire rail, highways & waterways. Folding map mounted on linen in sections. 165x132cm (64½x52") Colored litho. Punched holes upper corners.
[28] £292 $450

S.D.U.K.   See *Society for the Diffusion of Useful Knowledge*

SALMON

A DRAUGHT OF THE CITY OF JERUSALEM AS IT IS NOW, TAKEN FROM THE SOUTH EAST BY CORNEILLE LE BRUYN [1739] From *Modern History*. View; text below. 13x23cm (5x9") Uncolored. [30] £65 $100

A PLAN OF FORT ST. GEORGE AND THE CITY OF MADRAS [1747] 20x20cm (8x7½") [14] £39 $60

AMSTERDAM [ON SHEET WITH] ROTTERDAM [1739] Amsterdam view over Rotterdam plan. Henry Burgh, sc. 15x20cm (6x7½") Uncolored. [57] £36 $55

THE PLAN OF CONSTANTINOPLE [1739] From *Modern History*. View by Herman Moll. 17x29cm (6½x11") Uncolored. [30] £97 $150

VIENNA [1739] City view. 20x30cm (8½x11½") Uncolored. [58] £55 $85

SANSON (Folio)   Try *Jaillot*

AFRIQUE [1650] 41x56cm (15½x22½") Orig OL color. Vert creases; minor spots, color smudges. Ref: MCCS 48, p.84. [28] £584 $900

AMERIQUE SEPTENTRIONALE PAR N. SANSON D'ABBEVILLE ... [1650] 1st issue. Insular California; Five Great Lakes. 39x55cm (15½x22") Orig OL color. Good. Ref: Schwartz & Ehrenberg pl.61; Leighly 7; Tooley (Amer) p.114, #7, pl.29; Wheat (NY) 47. [2] £3,571 $5,500
[SAME TITLE] [same date & dimen] Orig OL color. Exc. [63] £2,272 $3,500
[SAME TITLE] [1669] Insular Calif. [same dimen] Old OL col. Somewhat light impression. [9] £974 $1,500
BRITANNICAE INSULAE ... [1641] J.B. Tavernier; Paris: Mariette. 41x53cm (16x21") Old color. Fine. [21] £325 $500
CARTE DE LISLE DE SAINCT CHRISTOPHLE. SCITUEE A 17 DEGREZ 30 MINUTES DE LAT. SEPTENTRIONALE [1650] 31x43cm (12½x17") Orig color throughout. Dotted line of grease marks lf margin, little affect. Ref: MCC 81, pl.1. [14] £292 $450
ERTZ-HERZOGTHUMB OESTERREICH / ARCHIDUCHE D'AUSTRICHE [1659] 30x51cm (12x20") OL color. [36] £195 $300
GEOGRAPHIAE SACRAE EX VETERI, ET NOVO TESTAMENTO DESUMPTAE TABULA SECUNDA IN QUA TERRA PROMISSA, SIVE IUDAEA IN SUAS TRIBUS PARTESQ. DISTINCTA ... [1662] 40x50cm (15½x19½") Color. Ref: Laor 688. [23] £162 $250
HARMONIE OR CORRESPONDANCE DU GLOBE ... LA SPHERE PAR LES POINTS, LIGNES, CERCLES &C. QUI DESCRIVENT EN LA SURFACE DES GLOBES TERRESTRES ... [1659] Double hemi, outlining the continents; insular Calif. J. Somer, sc. 41x53cm (15½x21") Almost mint. Ref: Shirley 408. [26] £276 $425
[SAME TITLE] [c. 1663 - 1670] Double hemi; continent only outlined. 43x53cm (16½x21½") Orig color. Ref: Phillips (A) 3436. [28] £454 $700
IESU CHRISTI SALVATORIS NOSTRI ET APOSTOLORUM PETRI, ET PAULI MANSIONES, ITINERA PEREGRINATIONES &C. ... [1665] Paris: Mariette. 38x56cm (14½x22") Color. Ref: Laor 697. [23] £179 $275
IRLANDE ROYAUME DIVISE EN SES QUATRE PROVINCES, ET CES PROVCES EN LEURS COUNTES ... [1665] Paris: Mariette. 41x51cm (16½x20½") Orig OL color. Worm tracks & dampmarks upper margin. Ref: Pastoureau, Sanson V B. [28] £292 $450
ISLE ET ROYAUME DE SICILE ... [1663] Paris: Mariette. 41x58cm (15½x23") Orig OL col. [28] £234 $360
L'HYDROGRAPHIE OU DESCRIPTION DE L'EAU C'EST A DIRE DES MERS, GOLFES, LACS, DESTROITS ET RIVIERES PRINCIPALES ... DU GLOBE TERRESTRE [1652] Double hemi; insular Calif. 41x53cm (15½x21") Color. Ref: Shirley (W) 394. [22] £519 $800
LE CANADA OU NOUVELLE FRANCE... [1656] 1st ed. 5 Great Lakes. 41x56cm (16x21½") Full orig color. Ref: Schwartz & Ehrenberg pl.62; Cumming (SE) #48; Cumming (Exploration) p.47. [2] £2,921 $4,500
[SAME TITLE] [1656] 40x54cm (15½x21½") Orig OL color. Exc. Ref: Karpinski (MI) pp.31, 90; Kaufman (GL) #3, p.25-6. [38] £3,149 $4,850
[SAME TITLE] [same date & dimen] OL color. Trimmed & laid down on matching contemporary paper; VG. [60] £2,240 $3,450
LE NOUVEAU MEXIQUE, ET LA FLORIDE; TIREE DE DIVERSE CARTES, ET RELATIONS ... [1656] 1st ed. Insular California. 33x56cm (12½x21½") Orig OL color. Exc. Ref: Tooley (Amer) #14; Leighly 27; Wheat (TM) pp.39-40. [2] £3,116 $4,800
[SAME TITLE] [1656 - 1679] 31x55cm (12x21½") Orig OL color. Inlaid on old paper. [54] £2,499 $3,850
LE ROYAUME DE HONGRIE, ET LES ESTATS QUI EN ONT ESTE SUJETS, ET QUI FONT PRESENTEMENT LA PARTIE SEPTENTRIONALE DE LA TURQUIE EN EUROPE ... [1696] 2 sheets joined 58x89cm (23½x35") Orig OL color. Bit browned; offsetting traces. [28] £308 $475
LES DEUX POLES ARCTICQUE OU SEPTENTRIONAL, ET ANTARCTICQUE OU MERIDIONAL, OU DESCRIPTION DES TERRES ARCTICQUES ET ANTARCTICQUES; ET DES PAYS CIRCOMVOISINS JUSQUES AUX 45 DEGRES DE LATITUDE [1657] Jean Somer Pruthenus, sc. 38x53cm (15x21") Color. Ref: See note Shirley (W) 408. [32] £617 $950
LES ISLES ANTILLES &C. ENTRE LESQUELLES SONT LES LUCAYES, ET LES CARIBES. PAR N SANSON D'ABBEVILLE ... [1656] Paris: Mariette. 38x56cm (15½x22") OL color. 1" repaired break near c'fold; fine. [50] £568 $875
MAPPE MONDE OU CARTE GENERALE DU MONDE. DESIGNEE EN DEUX PLANS HEMISPHERES PAR LE SR. SANSON [1651] C. Riviere, sc. Insular Calif; Great Lakes distinguished. 41x53cm (15½x21") Color. Ref: Shirley (W) 390. [22] £584 $900
MAPPEMONDE OU CARTE MARINE UNIVERSELLE REDUITE ... [1695] Pierre Moullard-Sanson. Mercator projection, 46x48cm (18x19") Separately issued. Orig OL color. Trimmed to border & laid on contemporary paper for composite atlas; minor surface wear; o/w good. Ref: Shirley (W) 573. [52] £720 $1,109

Orbis Vetus, et Orbis Veteris, Utraque Continens, Terrarumq Tractus Arcticus, et Antarcticus ex Platone, Theopompo sive Aehano, Manilio, &c. [1657] Paris: P. Mariette; J. Somer, sc. Double hemi; insular Calif. 38x54cm (15x21½") Col. Ref: Shirley (W) 400. [26] £471 $725
Stato del Gran Turco Diviso ne Suoi Beglierbati, o Gouverni...da Guglielmo Sansone...e di Nuovo Dissegnata ... [c. 1692 - 1714] Rome: G.G. Rossi. 43x58cm (17½x23") Minor spots. [28] £221 $340
Terra Sancta sive Promissionis olim Palestina in Duo Divisa Regna Israel et Juda ... [1679] Rome: G. Rossi. 43x56cm (16½x21½") OL color. Ref: Laor 682. [23] £292 $450
Tribocci Evesche de Strasbourg [dated 1659] 41x51cm (16x20") Uncolored. [36] £130 $200

SANSON (Small)

Audiencia de Guadalajara, Nova Mexico, California, &c. [c. 1657] 20x24cm (8x9½") B&W. Ref: Tooley (Amer) p.116, #15 cf. Wheat (TM) 50. [46] £373 $575
Canada or Niew Vrankryk ... [c. 1680] Amsterdam; reduce derivative of 1650 map, updated, but omitting Hudson Bay. 21x31cm (8x12") [14] £315 $485
Destroit de Magellan, Terre et Isles Magellanicques, &c. [1683] 19x24cm (7½x9½") Mint. [14] £49 $75
La Floride [1657 (c.1700)] 18x25cm (7x10") B&W. Ref: Cumming (SE) 53 & 97. [46] £227 $350

SANTINI

Nouvelle Mappe Monde [c. 1790] Double hemi with Cook's discoveries. 38x65cm (15x25½") Orig color. [16] £1,994 $3,072

SARTINE

Carte Reduite des Cotes Orientales de l'Amerique Septentrionale ... [1778] From *Neptune Americo-Septentrionale*. 58x89cm (23½x34½") Orig wash color. [46] £974 $1,500
Plan de la Baie de Narraganset ... [1780] After Blaskowitz model. 58x41cm (23x16") Exc. [38] £1,298 $2,000
Plan de la Baie et du Havre de Casco et des Iles Adjacentes Par le Cap. Cyprian Southack ... [1779 / 1780] Cape Elizabeth to Small Point. 41x58cm (16x23") Faint waterstain; else exc. [38] £357 $550
Plan de la Riviere du Cap Fear depuis la Barre jusques a Brunswick [1778] Panel of sailing directions. 58x43cm (23x16½") Later full color. [51] £812 $1,250

SAUER

Carte du Detroit qui Separe l'Asie de l'Amerique, avec la Cote des Tschoutskis, Tracee d'Apres les Observations Faites dans la Mer Glaciale depuis 1786 jusqu'en 1794 [c. 1802] From French ed of *An Account of a Geographical Expedition to the Northern Parts of Russia* ... led by Commodore Billings, R.N. 40x61cm (15½x24") Uncolored. Lt toning, scattered margin staining; VG. Ref: Howes S117. [59] £325 $500

SAUTHIER

A Map of the Province of New-York, Reduc'd from the Large Drawing of that Province, Compiled ... by Order of ... William Tryon, by Claude Joseph Sauthier; to which Is Added New Jersey, from Topographical Observations of C.J. Sauthier & B. Ratzer [1776 (1777)] From Faden, *North American Atlas*. 2nd or 3rd English ed . 72x57cm (28½x22½") Orig full color. Thin paper backing; repaired fold separation; VG. Ref: Nebenzahl (Amer Rev) #37; Sellers & Van Ee 1047; Phillips (M) p.503; Streeter II #878. [59] £1,159 $1,785

SAVERY

Geographische Beschryvinge van t'Beloofde - Landt Canaan ... Iesu Christo Weffens Syne Apostelen ... [1648] 33x48cm (12½x19") Color. [23] £276 $425

SAXTON

Lecestriae Comitatus [1607 (1637)] By Kip. 28x36cm (11x14½") Early color. [14] £175 $270

SAYER   Try *Jefferys*

A New and Correct Map of Scotland ... [1790] From *General Atlas*. Lt. Archibald Campbell. 132x109cm (52x43") OL color. Sm fold tears; good. [21] £487 $750
A New Map of North America ... According to the Definitive Treaty, Concluded at Paris ... [1763] 58x96cm (23x37½") 2 sheet map; separately issued. Orig OL color. Restoration at old folds; o/w good. [53] £1,800 $2,772

A NEW MAP OF NORTH AMERICA, WITH THE WEST INDIA ISLANDS, DIVIDED ACCORDING TO THE PRELIMINARY ARTICLES OF PEACE, SIGNED AT VERSAILLES, 20 JAN. 1783, WHEREIN ARE PARTICULARLY DISTINGUISHED THE UNITED STATES ... [1786] 4 sheets joined to make two, each about 51x118cm (20x46½") Later full color. Minor margin chipping; clean, bright. Ref: Stevens & Tree 1786(j). [32] £1,233 $1,900

A NEW MAP OF THE WHOLE CONTINENT OF AMERICA, DIVIDED INTO NORTH AND SOUTH AND WEST INDIES WHEREIN ARE EXACTLY DESCRIBED THE UNITED STATES OF NORTH AMERICA ... ACCORDING TO THE PRELIMINARIES OF PEACE ... JAN. 20, 1783 ... LONDON: 15TH AUGUST 1786 [1786] John Gibson, after D'Anville. 4 sheets joined to form two, each 53x119cm (21x47") Orig OL color. Faint offsetting. [28] £1,052 $1,620

COURSE OF THE RIVER MISSISSIPPI, FROM THE BALISE TO FORT CHARTRES; TAKEN ON AN EXPEDITION TO THE ILLINOIS, IN THE LATTER END OF THE YEAR 1765 ... PRINTED FOR ROBT. SAYER, NO 53 IN FLEET STREET PUBLISHD AS THE ACT DIRECTS. 1 JUNE 1775 [1775] By Lieut. John Ross; 3rd ed. 112x34cm (44x13½") Color. Margin stains; paper backing; rolled; VG. [20] £1,266 $1,950

[SAME TITLE] [same date & dimen]] 2nd state. By Lt. John Ross. Orig OL color. [54] £850 $1,309

PLAN OF THE STRAITS OF BANCA [1791] In *East India Pilot*. After d'Apres de Mannevillette. 48x33cm (18½x13") [15] £75 $116

SAYER & BENNETT Try *Jefferys*

A CHART OF NORTH AND SOUTH AMERICA, INCLUDING THE ATLANTIC AND PACIFIC OCEANS, WITH THE NEAREST COASTS OF EUROPE, AFRICA, AND ASIA. PUBLISHED ACCORDING TO ACT OF PARLIAMENT 10 JUNE 1775, BY ROB. SAYER & J. BENNETT [c. 1775] By John Green, updated by Jefferys. 6 sheets joined to form 3, each 46x112cm (18½x44") Orig OL color. Sh margin tears repaired; some folds strengthened; erased verso stamps; sl offsetting. Ref: Phillips (A) 1165-1166; Wagner (NW) 649. [28] £1,753 $2,700

A CHART OF THE BANKS OF NEWFOUNDLAND, DRAWN FROM A GREAT NUMBER OF HYDROGRAPHICAL SURVEYS, CHIEFLY FROM THOSE OF CHABERT, COOK AND FLEURIEU ... [1775] 50x68cm (20x27") Orig OL color. Sh margin tears & dampmarks; verso rubber stamp erased. [28] £308 $475

A CHART OF THE RED SEA FROM GEDDAH TO SUEZ ... [1781] Northern part. After d'Apres de Mannevillette. Insets, profiles. 49x69cm (19½x27") [15] £185 $285

A CHART OF THE STRAITS OF SUNDA FROM THE MANUSCRIPT DRAUGHT OF THE DUTCH EAST INDIA COMPANY [1778] 61x88cm (24x34½") Minor margin chipping; generally VG. [15] £180 $277

A CHART TO SAIL FROM THE STRAITS OF SUNDA OR BATAVIA, TO THE STRAITS OF BANCA, BY MR. D'APRES DE MANNEVILLETTE [1778] 66x48cm (26x19") Exc. [63] £438 $675

A GENERAL MAP OF THE NORTHERN BRITISH COLONIES IN AMERICA, WHICH COMPREHENDS THE PROVINCE OF QUEBEC, THE GOVERNMENT OF NEWFOUNDLAND, NOVA-SCOTIA, NEW-ENGLAND AND NEW-YORK [1776] After Thomas Pownall. 1st pub in 48x66cm (19x26") Orig OL color. VG. Ref: Nebenzahl (Amer Rev) pp.11-13. [2] £779 $1,200

[SAME TITLE] [same date & dimen] Title above, "The Seat of war, in the Northern Colonies, ..." Separate publication of "Holster Atlas" map. Orig OL color. Lt toning; margin mends; top c'fold reinforced; else VG. Ref: Tooley (Amer) p.92, #65a. [38] £1,298 $2,000

A NEW MAP OF IRELAND DIVIDED INTO PROVINCES, COUNTIES &C. [1777] By Kitchin. 64x56cm (25x22½") Full orig color. [24] £250 $385

A SURVEY OF LAKE CHAMPLAIN INCLUDING LAKE GEORGE, CROWN POINT AND ST. JOHN. SURVEYED BY ORDER OF HIS EXCELLENCY MAJOR GENERAL SR. JEFFERY AMHERST ... BY WILLIAM BRASSIER ... [1776] 2nd state with Battle of Valcour. 66x48cm (26x19") Orig wash col. Lt toned; sl fold reinforcement; else exc. Ref: Tooley (Amer) p.65, #24b; Nebenzahl (Amer Rev) p.61-3, #9; Nebenzahl (Biblio) #46. [38] £2,402 $3,700

PLAN OF THE ISLAND RODRIGUEZ. COMMONLY CALLED DIEGO RAYS ISLAND ... [1778] In *East India Pilot*. Based on d'Apres de Mannevillette. 33x48cm (13x19") [15] £90 $139

PLAN OF THE RIVER & SOUND OF DAWFOSKEE IN SOUTH CAROLINA [1776] After John Gascoigne. Hilton Head. 64x46cm (25½x18") Uncolored. Exc. Ref: Sellers & Van Ee 1525; Cumming (Colonial Amer) pp.47-8. [2] £1,233 $1,900

THE COAST OF INDIA AND CHINA FROM THE POINT AND RIVER OF CAMBOJA TO CANTON COMPREHENDING THE COASTS OF TSIOMPA AND COCHINCHINA WITH THE COAST OF TONKIN AND THE COAST OF KOEN-TON WITH THE ISLE OF HAI-NAN [1780] In *East India Pilot*. 60x45cm (23½x17½") Sm repaired edge tear. [15] £300 $462

SCHAUS

THE SEAT OF WAR. BIRDS EYE VIEW OF VIRGINIA, MARYLAND ... [1861] Inset: Eastern N. Amer. 57x75cm (22x29½") Orig color. Thick, stiff paper with restored margin splits. [52] £600 $924

SCHEDEL

[WORLD] [1493] From *Nuremburg Chronicle*. Pre-Columbian, Ptolemaic configuration. 37x52cm (14½x20½") Ref: Shirley 19; Potter p.33. [62] £5,648 $8,700

[SAME TITLE] [same date & source (German ed)]. 43x60cm (16½x23½") Full color, partly early. Restoration at ctr; two replacements affecting side vignette & text, not map. [63] £3,571 $5,500

ALEXANDRIA [1493] From *Liber Chronicarum* (Nuremberg Chronicle). 15x23cm (5½x9") on 15x9" printed surface. Full color. Exc. [39] £292 $450

ANGLIE PROVINCIA [same date & source] Composite sketch of fanciful England. 23x23cm (9½x9") on 14½x9" printed surface. Full color. Exc. [39] £292 $450

[SAME TITLE] [same date & source] 24x22cm (9½x8½") plus text. Exc. Ref: Shirley (BI to 1650) p.ix. [62] £250 $385

BAMBERGA [same date & source] 23x53cm (9x21") on 14½x21" printed surface. Full col Exc. [39] £552 $850

BASILEA [same date & source] 25x53cm (10x21") on 15x21" printed surface. Full color. C'fold repair; else VG. [39] £974 $1,500

BAVARIA [same date & source] Composite, fictionalized view of structures. 23x23cm (9x9") on 14x9" printed surface. Full color. Exc. [39] £357 $550

BRESSLA [same date & source] Wroclaw, Poland. 23x53cm (9½x20½") on 14x21" printed surface. Color. C'fold reinforced; else exc. [39] £552 $850

CARTHAGO [same date & source] 18x13cm (6½x5") on 15x9" printed surface. Full col. Exc. [39] £243 $375

COLONIA [same date & source] Cologne. 20x53cm (7½x21") on 14x21" printed surface. Full color. Exc. [39] £779 $1,200

CONSTANTINOPOLIS ... [same date & source] 23x23cm (9x9") on 15x9" printed surface. Full color. Exc. [39] £487 $750

CRACOVIA [same date & source] 25x53cm (10x20½") on 15x20½" printed surface. Full color. C'fold repair; else exc. [39] £779 $1,200

DESTRUCCIO IHEROSOLIME [same date & source] Synopsis of 6 previous destructions. 28x51cm (11x20") on 15x21" printed surface. Full color. Threadhole repairs; exc. [39] £1,298 $2,000

ELECTORUM IMPERII INSTITUTIO [same date & source] Composite of elector's territories. 24x53cm (9½x21") on 14x21" printed surface. Full color. Reinforced c'fold, lower margin repair; overall exc. [39] £974 $1,500

FOLIUM CCXXX-CCXXI [PRAGUE] [same date & source] 43x61cm (17x24") Side margins stained. [28] £552 $850

FRANCIA [same date & source] Composite view to give sense of country. 23x23cm (9x9") on 15x9" printed surface. Full color. Exc. [39] £227 $350

GEBENNA [same date & source] Honnom (Gehenna); Jerusalem's city dump. 15x23cm (6x9") on 13x9" printed surface. Full color. Exc. [39] £292 $450

HIERICHO [same date & source] Imagined Jericho destruction. 2 images, each about 13x23cm (5x8½") on 14½x9" printed surface. Full color. Exc. Ref: Laor 1126. [39] £308 $475

HIEROSOLIMA [1493] Largely imaginary. 20x23cm (7½x9") Soiling; stains, most in margin. Ref: Laor 1123. [28] £584 $900

[SAME TITLE] [1493] From *Liber Chronicarum* (Nuremberg Chronicle). Largely imaginary. 20x23cm (7½x9") on 15x9" printed surface. Full color. Exc. Ref: Laor 1123. [39] £487 $750

LACEDEMONIA [same date & source] Sparta; with tableau & portraits. 15x23cm (5½x9") on 15x9" printed surface. Full color. Exc. [39] £357 $550

MACEDONIA [same date & source] Collage. 20x23cm (7½x9") on 14x9" printed surface. Full color. Exc. [39] £227 $350

MANTUA [same date & source] 20x23cm (7½x9") on 14x9" printed surface. Full color. Exc. [39] £308 $475

MEDIOLANUM [same date & source] 15x23cm (5½x9") on 14x9" printed surface. Full col. Exc. [39] £422 $650

NINEVE [same date & source] 15x20cm (5½x8½") on 14½x9" printed surface. Full col. Exc. [39] £243 $375

PAPIA [same date & source] Pavia. 15x23cm (5½x9") on 13x9" printed surface. Full col. Exc. [39] £227 $350

PARISIUS [same date & source] 20x23cm (7½x9") on 14x9" printed surface. Full color. Exc. [39] £552 $850

PATAVIA [same date & source] 20x53cm (8x20½") on 14x20½" printed surface. Full color. Exc. [39] £779 $1,200

PERUSIA [same date & source] Perugia; Solomon's Temple on verso. 20x23cm (7½x9") on 14x9" printed surface. Full color. Exc. [39] £292 $450

PISA [same date & source] 23x23cm (9x9") on 14x9" printed surface. Full color. Exc. [39] £292 $450

ROMA [c. 1580] [same source] Verso: Genoa. 23x53cm (9x21") on 15x21" printed surface. Full color. Reinforced c'fold; overall exc. [39] £1,428 $2,200

SALCZBURGA [1493] [same source] 25x53cm (9½x21") on 15x21" printed surface. Full color. C'fold repair; overall VG. [39] £1,071 $1,650

SENA [same date & source] Siena. 20x23cm (7½x9") on 14x9" printed surface. Full col. Exc. [39] £292 $450

TYBERIAS ALS TYBERIADIS [same date & source] 15x23cm (5½x9") on 13x9" printed surface. Full color. Exc. [39] £292 $450

ULMA [same date & source] 20x53cm (8x20½") on 14x21" printed surface. Full color. C'fold repair; overall exc. [39] £779 $1,200

VENECIE [same date & source] Verso: Padua view; portraits. 20x53cm (7½x21") on 14x21" printed surface. Full color both sides. Lt toning; threadhole repairs; else exc. [39] £1,818 $2,800

VERONA [same date & source] 20x23cm (7½x9") on 14x9" printed surface. Full color. Exc. [39] £292 $450

SCHEDLER

[GLOBE] SCHEDLER'S TERRESTRIAL GLOBE [c. 1875] 20" hollow metal orb dressed in plaster with dull paper gores. Offset metal bracket from wood baluster on iron legs; 40" high. Old surface restorations; bubbling. [17] £6,167 $9,500

SCHENK

ACCURATE GEOGRAPHISCHE DELINEATION DE HOCHF: SACHSS: AMMES WEISSENFELS NEBST ALLEN DARZU GEHORIGEN STADTEN FLECKEN DORFFSCHAFFTEN WIE AUCH ETLICHEN AGRAENT ZENDEN ORTEN [c. 1708] 2 column index. 51x58cm (19½x23") Orig color. Margins ragged; old label verso. Ref: Koeman III Sche 17. [28] £175 $270

ALEXANDRIA ... [c. 1690] 21x26cm (8½x10") Full color. Exc. [63] £120 $185

ALGIERS ... [c. 1690] View. 21x26cm (8½x10") Full color. Exc. [63] £120 $185

ALKAIRO / MEMPHIS ... [c. 1690] Cairo, Egypt. 21x26cm (8½x10") Full color. Exc. [63] £146 $225

AMERICA SEPTENTRIONALIS NOVISSIMA [AND 2ND CARTOUCHE] AMERICA MERIDIONALIS ACCURATISSIMA [1695] Insular California. 48x56cm (19x22") Full orig color. VG. Ref: Tooley (Amer) p.125, #56; Leighly 102. [2] £1,623 $2,500

[SAME TITLE] [1700] 48x57cm (19x22½") Orig old color. Fine [1] £1,623 $2,500

GALLIAE REGNUM IN OMNES SUAS PROVINCIAS ACCURATE DIVISUM [1709] 48x58cm (19x23") Color; cartouche uncolored. Pinholes; minor chips lower margin. Exc. [29] £114 $175

HAVANA INSULAE CUBAE IMO TOTIUS OCCIDENTIS NOTISSIMG PORTUS [c. 1690] View. 21x26cm (8½x10") Exc. [63] £308 $475

TABULA MOSCOVIAE NUNC ACCURATIUS ... PER G. DE L'ISLE ... [c. 1720] 2 sheets joined, 99x64cm (38½x24½") Orig OL color. Sh tears lf margin. Ref: Koeman II p.120. [28] £321 $495

TANGER ... [c. 1690] 21x26cm (8½x10") Full color. Exc. [63] £120 $185

SCHERER

DELINEATIO NOVA ET VERA PARTIS AUSTRALIS NOVI MEXICI CUM AUSTRALI PARTE INSULAE CALIFORNIAE [c. 1700] 24x35cm (9½x14") Uncolored. [52] £320 $493

EUROPA [1703 - 1710] Polar projections above. 11x18cm (4½x7") [14] £26 $40

REGIONUM CIRCUMPOLARIUM LAPPONIAE ISLANDIAE ET GROENLANDIAE NOVA ET VETERIS DESCRIPTIO GEOGRAPHICA 1701 [c. 1700] NE America, NW Eurasia; rich decor. 23x35cm (9x13½") Mint. [14] £487 $750

REPRAESENTATIO TOTIUS ORBIS TERRAQUEI ... CATHOLICA [c. 1700] Christian territories. N polar projection; insular California. 23x35cm (9x13½") Color. Ref: Shirley (W) 628. [52] £650 $1,001

REPRESENTATIO TOTIUS AFRICAE ... [1702 - 1737] 23x36cm (9x13½") Uncolored. Fine. Ref: Norwich #68. [59] £250 $385

SCHILLER

CONSTELLATIO XLV [1621] From *Coelum Stellatum Christianum* ... "S. Israeli seu Jacob Patriache" (Lupus). 25x30cm (9½x12½") Modern color, heightened in gilt. Lt foxing; few sh margin tears. Ref: Warner p.229-32; Brown (Astron) p.31-2. [28] £263 $405

CONSTELLATIO XXII [same date, source, dimen, color & condition] Saint Petro" (Aries). Ref: Warner p.229-32. [28] £279 $430

CONSTELLATIO XXIII [same date, source, dimen, color, condition & reference] "S. Andrae" (Taurus). [28] £279 $430

SCHRAEMBL

[NORTH AMERICA: CENTRAL UNITED STATES & CANADA] [1800] Inset: N.E. Canada. 51x59cm (20x23") Full color. Fine. [33] £357 $550

KARTE VON DEN N.W. AMERIKANISCHEN UND N.OE. ASIATISCHEN KUSTEN ... [1788] 39x68cm (15½x26½") Ol color. Fine. [32] £146 $225

POLYNESIEN (INSELWELT) ODER DER FUNFTE WELTTHEIL VERFAFST VON HERRN DANIEL DJUBERG NEU HERAUSGEGEBEN VON HERN F.A. SCHRAEMBL ... [1789] Austrian issue of 1780 Djuberg map; which 1st used *Ulimaroa* for Australia. 47x71cm (18½x28") Color. [16] £940 $1,448

SCHREIBER

AFRICA ... [1744] Side bar key. 18x28cm (7x11") Full early color. [44] £130 $200

AMERICA VERFERTIGET VON ... SCHREIBEM IN LEIPZIG [same date, dimen & color] Insular Calif. Side bar key. [44] £308 $475

ASIA VERFERLIGET VON JOH. GEORGE SCHREIBEM IN LEIPZIG [same date, dimen & color] Unusual Japan. [44] £156 $240

DAS GANTZE RUSSISCHE KAYSERTHUM MIT ALLEN SEINEN LAENDERN ... [same date, dimen & color] [44] £91 $140

DAS GELOBTE LAND SAMML DER 40 IAHRIGEN REISE DER KINDER ISRAEL AUS EGYPTEN [same date, dimen & color] Mild margin soiling. [44] £156 $240

DAS KONIGREICH DANNEMARCK NEBST DENEN ANGRANTZENDEN LENDEM ... [same date, dimen & color] Side bar key. Sm ink spot in Sweden. [44] £78 $120

DAS KONIGREICH SCHWEGEN UND NORWEGEN ... [same date, dimen & color] Incl Finland, much of Russia. [44] £104 $160

DAS KONIGREICH UNGARN NEBST DEN ANGRANTZENDEN KEYSERLICHEN LANDEM ... [same date, dimen & color] Side bar key. [44] £104 $160

DE REPUBLIC SCHWEITZ MIT IHREN UNTERTHANEN UND BUNDSGENOSSEN ... [same date, dimen & color] Side bar key [44] £91 $140

DER KONIGREICH PREUSSEN NEBST DEM POLNISCHEN ANTHEIL... [same date, dimen & color] [44] £78 $120

DIE EUROPEASCHE ODER KLEINE TARTARY NEBST DEN ANGRANTZENDEN LANDEM ... [same date, dimen & color] Black Sea lands; side bar key. [44] £78 $120

DIE GEGEND UM DIA HAUFT STADT PRAG IM KONIGREICH BOHMEN ... [same date, dimen & color] Prague area. [44] £91 $140

DIE REPUBLIC HOLLAND ODER DIE VEREINIGLE NIEDERLANDE ... [same date, dimen & color] Insets of colonies, incl New York-New England! Side bar key. [44] £97 $150

EUROPA VERFERLIGET VON J.G. SCHEIBERN IN LEIPZIG [same date, dimen & color] [44] £117 $180

GLOBUS TERRESTRIS [same date, dimen & color] Double hemi . Sl edge soiling. [44] £373 $575

GROS BRITANNE ODER ENGLELAND SCHOTTLAND UND IRRLAND ... [same date, dimen & color][44] £117 $180

ITALIEN IN SEIN UNTERSCHEIDE NE LANDER ... [same date, dimen & color] [44] £130 $200

REISE CHARTE DURCH DAS KONIGREICH BOHMEN HERTTZOGTHUM SCHLESI EN MARGGRAFTHUM MAEHREN UND LAUSITZ ... [same date, dimen & color] [44] £91 $140

REISE CHARTE DURCH DEUTSCHLAND ... [same date, dimen & color] Side bar key. [44] £91 $140

REISE CHARTE DURCH FRANKREICH IN SEINE 12 PROVINTZIEN... [same date, dimen & color] [44] £91 $140

REISE CHARTE DURCH OESTERREICH ... [same date, dimen & color] Side bar key. [44] £91 $140

SCOTS MAGAZINE

A MAP OF THE COUNTRY ROUND PHILADELPHIA INCLUDING PART OF NEW JERSEY NEW YORK STATEN ISLAND & LONG ISLAND. [1776] Chesapeake Bay to L.I. Sound. 17x22cm (7x8½") B&W. Ref: Jolly SCOT-45; Phillips (M) 699. [36] £123 $190

A PLAN OF THE OPERATIONS AT THE TAKING OF QUEBEC AND THE BATTLE FOUGHT NEAR THAT CITY, SEPTR: 13. 1759. [1759] 11x19cm (4½x7½") Lower & lf margins trimmed into neat lines. Ref: Jolly SCOT-25 [14] £39 $60

AN ACCURATE MAP OF THE WEST INDIES. ENGRAVED BY A. BELL. [1762] 17x24cm (6½x9½") B&W. Exc. Ref: Jolly SCOT-32 [47] £159 $245

SEALE

A MAP OF NORTH AMERICA [c. 1744] From *Tindal's Continuation of Rapin's History of England* . Insular California. 37x46cm (14½x18") Recent color. Fine. Ref: Leighly pl.XXIII. [1] £649 $1,000

A MAP OF NORTH AMERICA WITH THE EUROPEAN SETTLEMENTS & WHATEVER ELSE IS REMARKABLE IN YE WEST INDIES ... [1744 - 1747] Insular Calif. 38x48cm (15x18½") Lt offsetting. Ref: cf. Sellers & Van Ee 195. [28] £409 $630
A MAP OF THE KINGDOM OF IRELAND FROM YE LATEST & BEST OBSERVATIONS [1732] Rapin's History. 48x38cm (19½x15½") Color. Margin restored. Ref: Phillips (A) 8019. [24] £179 $275
AN ACCURATE MAP OF EUROPE WITH ITS EMPIRES, KINGDOMS ... [c.1750 - c.1755] John Marshall imprint, Dicey's successor. 61x105cm (24x41") Two sheets joined. Orig OL col. [53] £1,000 $1,540
CORRECT CHART OF ST. GEORGE'S CHANNEL AND THE IRISH SEA, INCLUDING ALL THE COAST OF IRELAND, AND YE WEST COAST OF GREAT BRITAIN ... FOR MR. TINDAL'S CONTINUATION OF MR. RAPIN'S HISTORY [1732] London: Knapton. 48x38cm (18½x15") Color. [24] £130 $200

SEILE

AMERICAE NOVA DESCRIPTIO IMPENSIS ANE SEILE 1663 [1663] Vaughn, sc. Insular Calif. 33x43cm (13½x16½") Color. Ref: Tooley (Amer) Calif #12. [22] £779 $1,200

SELLER

[TITLE PAGE] PRACTICAL NAVIGATION ... [c. 1680] Mariners & instruments. 17x12cm (6½x4½") Uncolored. Trimmed to border. [52] £380 $585
A CHART OF THE SEA COASTS OF NEW ENGLAND NEW JERSEY VIRGINIA MARYLAND AND CAROLINA FROM C. COD TO C. HATTERAS ... [1675] 43x56cm (17½x21½") Orig color. Few stains, else exc. Framed. [38] £12,659 $19,500
A MAPP OF THE CITIE AND PORT OF TRIPOLI IN BARBARY [1675 -] Plan and W. Hollar view. Later issue; imprints erased. 41x52cm (16x20½") Orig color. [54] £600 $924
IRELAND [1685] 13x15cm (5x5½") Ref: Phillips (A) 3450. [24] £52 $80
NOVISSIMA TOTIUS TERRARUM ORBIS TABULA [1708] Double hemi with sm circles incl moon surface. 44x54cm (17½x21½") Orig color. Ref: Shirley (W) 460. [16] £4,463 $6,875

SELLER and PRICE

BAHAMA'S AND WINDWARD PASSAGE BY JER. SELLER & CHA. PRICE AT THE HERMITAGE STAIRES LONDON [c. 1700] Separately published. 43x54cm (17x21½") Orig linen backing as issued; toned overall; c'fold wear, some loss. [62] £2,077 $3,200

SENEX

... THIS MAP OF NORTH AMERICA (CORRECTED FROM THE LATEST DISCOVERIES AND OBSERVATIONS) ... [c. 1715] Geo. Wildey commercial decor. 97x66cm (37½x25½") Early color; Fold reinforcements; overall VG. [38] £2,921 $4,500
A MAP OF LOUISIANA AND OF THE RIVER MISSISSIPI BY IOHN SENEX [1719] 49x58cm (19x23") Orig OL color. Fine. Ref: Cumming (SE) 182; Lowery 297; Wheat (TM) 100. [47] £1,136 $1,750
A NEW AND CORRECT MAP OF THE WORLD ... [c. 1737] Double hemispheres; insular Calif. 15x29cm (6x11½") Added full color. Fine. [59] £325 $500
A NEW MAP OF AMERICA FROM THE LATEST OBSERVATIONS REVIS'D BY I. SENEX [1719-1721] Insular Calif. 49x56cm (19x22") Orig OL color. Lt narrow stain & repair at c'fold; overall VG-. Ref: Leighly 155; Wagner (NW) II, #520; Tooley (Amer) p.130, #81; see TMC 57 (Cain). [59] £1,266 $1,950
[SAME TITLE] [1721] London: D. Brown. Insular Calif; Sea of the West. 49x56cm (19x22") Old color. Ref: Phillips (A) 563, 29. [22] £1,169 $1,800
A NEW MAP OF FRANCE, SHEWING THE ROADS AND POST STAGES THRO'OUT THAT KINGDOM ... [1720] 51x58cm (20x23") Orig OL color. Narrow margins. [14] £84 $130
A NEW MAP OF VIRGINIA, MARYLAND AND THE IMPROVED PARTS OF PENNSYLVANIA AND NEW JERSEY [1719] 3rd & final state of C. Browne's 1685 map. 49x56cm (19½x22") Orig OL color. Lt crease lower lf; fine. Ref: Phillips (M) p.980; Morrison 24; Stevens & Tree 86c. [47] £1,720 $2,650
MOSCOVEY IN EUROPE ... [1721] 59x50cm (23x19½") Orig OL color. Sh tears; margins browned. Ref: Bagrow (Russia) p.152. [28] £204 $315
NORTH AMERICA CORRECTED FROM THE OBSERVATIONS COMMUNICATED TO THE ROYAL SOCIETY AT LONDON, AND THE ROYAL ACADEMY AT PARIS [1710 (c.1750)] 97x64cm (37½x25") Old OL color. Folds repaired; sm filled loss at cartouche; good. Ref: Wheat (TM) 92; Wagner (NW) 495; Lowery 273; Phillips (A) 550; Stevens & Tree 61(d). [50] £1,818 $2,800
POLAND ... [c.1708-1712] Joined sheets, 66x97cm (26x38") Orig OL col. Top margin reinforced. [28] £308 $475
THE SPANISH NETHERLANDS COMMONLY CALLED FLANDERS ... 1719 [1721] 41x53cm (16x21½") Orig OL color. Margins foxed; sh lower margin tears repaired. [28] £234 $360

SEUTTER

ACCURATA DELINEATIO CELEBERRIMAE REGIONIS LUDOVICIANAE VEL GALLICE LOUISIANAE OL. CANADAE ET FLORIDAE ADPELLATIONE IN SEPTEMTRIONALI AMERICA DESCRIPAE QUOE HODI NOMINE FLUMINIS MISSIPPI ... [1730] 49x57cm (19½x22") Orig wash color. Fine. [62] £1,169 $1,800

ACCURATA DELINEATIO CELEBERRIMAE REGIONIS LUDOVICIANAE, VEL GALLICE LOUISIANE OT CANADAE ET FLORIDAE ADPELLATIONE IN SEPTEMTRIONALE AMERICA DESCRIPTAE QUOE HODIE NOMINE FLUMINIS MISSIPPI VEL ST. LOUIS ... MATTHAEI SEUTTERI, CHALCOG. AUGUSTON [1740] 49x57cm (19½x22") Full color. Early verso repair sm tear 5 mm into image; o/w VG+. Ref: Portinaro & Knirsch 117. [33] £1,428 $2,200

[SAME TITLE] [c. 1740] After Chatelain without Quebec view. 49x56cm (19½x22") Orig color. Sl ragged margins. Ref: Phillips (A) 583. [28] £1,123 $1,730

AFRICA JUXTA NAVIGATIONES ET OBSERVATIONES RECENTISSIMA AUCTA CORRECTA ET IN SUA REGNA ET STATUS DIVISA, IN LUCEM EDITA A MATTTHAEO SEUTTER ... [(1735)] 50x58cm (19½x22½") Full color. Minor margin chipping; narrow lower margin; lt soiling lower rt corner; o/w VG. Ref: Tooley (Africa) pl.80. [32] £308 $475

AUGSPURG DIE HAUPT STADT UND ZIERDE DES SCHWAEBISCHEN CRAISES SAMT DER UMLIGENDEN GEGEND IN DIE BREITE AUF 3 UND IN DIE LANGE AUF 1« STUND GERECHNET [c. 1730] 51x59cm (20x23") Orig color. Narrow margins. [64] £408 $629

BAVARIAE PARS INFERIOR [c. 1730] 50x58cm (19½x22½") Orig col. Fold restored. [64] £306 $472

CIRCULUS SUEVICUS IN QUO DUCATUS WIRTENBERGENSIS [c. 1730] 50x58cm (19½x22½") Orig color. [64] £408 $629

DELINEATIO AC FINITIMA REGIO MAGNAE BRITANNIAE METROPOLEOS LONDINI ... [c. 1734] 51x58cm (20x23") Orig color. Margins bit foxed; 8" remargined below; ms date. [28] £409 $630

DUCATUS MAGDEBURGENSIS ET HALENSIS [c. 1730] 50x58cm (19½x23") Orig color. Upper part browned & some at ctr; narrow top margin; sm holes repaired. [64] £225 $346

DUCATUS WESTPHALIA [c. 1730] 50x58cm (19½x23") Orig color. Remargined below; lower neat line restored. [64] £257 $396

ELECTORATUS HANOVERANI [c. 1730] 58x50cm (23x19½) Orig color. [64] £604 $931

EPISCOPATUS HILDESIENSIS [c. 1730] 49x56cm (19x22") Orig color. [64] £490 $755

IERUSALEM, CUM SUBURBIIS, PROUT TEMPORE CHRISTI FLORUIT ... [c. 1730] 50x57cm (19½x22½") Color. [54] £750 $1,155

IMPERII MAGNI MOGOLIS SIVE INDICI PADSCHACH ... [c. 1750] 50x58cm (19½x22½") Full color. Margins trimmed to neat lines; browning at ctr seam & sl loss top ¾" into image; VG. [29] £234 $360

IMPERII MOSCOVITICI PARS AUSTRALIS IN LUCEM, EDITA PAR G. DE L'ISLE [c. 1730] 51x59cm (20x23") Orig color. [64] £143 $220

[SAME TITLE] [c. 1750] 51x58cm (20x23") Orig color. [28] £204 $315

L'EVECHE ET L'ETAT DE LIEGE [c. 1730] After T.C. Lotter. 50x58cm (19½x22½") Orig col. [64] £196 $302

MARCHIONATUS BRANDENBURGENSIS DUCATUS POMERANIAE ET DUCATUS MECKLENBURGICUS [c. 1730] 50x59cm (19½x23") Orig color. Narrow lower margin. [64] £449 $692

MARCHIONATUS ONOLDINI COMITATUS OETTINGENSIS PRAEPOSITURAE ELEVACENSIS ET PAPPENHEIMENSIS [c. 1730] 59x51cm (23x20") Orig color. [64] £408 $629

MORAVIA MARCHIONATUS IN SEX CIRCULOS DIVISUS [c. 1730] With Brno view. 50x59cm (19½x23") Orig color. [64] £176 $270

NOVA ORBIS SIVE AMERICA SEPTENTRIONALIS, DIVISA PER SUA REGNA PROVINC: ET INSUL: CURA ET OPERA MATTH: SEUTTER ... [(1744)] From *Atlas Minor*. Exaggerated North-South dimension; insular Calif. 20x26cm (7½x10") Orig color. Lt soiled & age toned; overall VG. [31] £552 $850

OPULENTISSIMUM SINARUM IMPERIUM [c. 1730] 49x57cm (19½x22½") Color. [54] £480 $739

PRAGA CELEBERRIMA ET MAXIMA TOTIUS BOHEMIAE METROPOLIS ET UNIVERSITATIS FLORENTISSIMA AD MULDAM FL ... [c. 1720] German title also. View. 48x58cm (19½x23") Orig col to plan. [28] £438 $675

RECENS EDITA TOTIUS NOVI BELGII, IN AMERICA SEPTENTRIONALI SITI, DELINEATIO CURA ET SUMTIBUS MATTHAEI SEUTTERI [1730] With "Restitutio" view of New York. 49x58cm (19x22½") Orig color. Rubbing along horiz fold; minor repair; else VG. Ref: Tooley (Amer) p.291, #25. [38] £1,948 $3,000

[SAME TITLE] [1730] 2nd state. 50x57cm (19½x22½") Full orig wash color. Exc. Ref: Tooley (Amer) Campbell 25. [63] £2,077 $3,200

[SAME TITLE] [c. 1730] With NY view. [same dimen] Color. [54] £2,000 $3,080

RECENS ET ACCURATA DESIGNATIO EPISCOPATUS PADERBORNENSIS [c. 1740] After T.C. Lotter. View at top. 50x55cm (19½x21½") OL color. Sh wrinkle at bottom. [64] £1,511 $2,327

REGIO CANAAN SEU TERRA PROMISSIONIS POSTEA IUDAEA VEL PALESTINA NOMINATA HODIE TERRA SANCTA VOCATA [1725] 50x58cm (19½x22½") Full color. Ref: Laor 720. [23] £292 $450

[SAME TITLE] [c. 1725] [same dimen] Orig col. Fold restored. Ref: Nebenzahl (Holy Land) 55. [64] £400 $616

[SAME TITLE] [c. 1730] [same dimen] Color. Good. [50] £487 $750

REGNUM HIBERNIAE, TAM SECUNDUM IV PROVINCIAS PRINCIPALES ULTONIAM, CONNACIAM, LAGENIAM, MOMONICAM ... [1745] 58x51cm (23x19½") Color. Ref: Phillips (A) 5977, 29. [24] £422 $650

SILESIAE DUCATUS TAM SUPERIOR QUAM INFERIOR ... [c. 1730] 50x58cm (19½x23") Orig color. Fold tears repaired. [64] £359 $553

[SAME TITLE] [c. 1740] 53x58cm (20½x23") Orig color. Lower margin bit ragged, sm stain; faint creases near c'fold. [28] £221 $340

SYNOPSIS CIRCULI RHENANI INFERIORIS SIVE ELECTORUM RHENI, EXHIBENS ARCHI-EPISCOPATUM MOGUNTINUM, COLONIENSEM, TREVIRENSEM ET PALATINATUM RHENI, COMITATUS BEILSTEIN, NEWENAER, ISENBURG INFER. ET REIFFERSCHEID [c. 1730] 50x58cm (19½x22½") Orig color. Upper c'fold & sm margin tears repaired. [64] £241 $371

TABULA ICHNOGRAPHICA ACCURATISSIMA BRUNSUIGAE ... ACCURATE ICHNOGRAPHISCHE VORSTELLUNG DER HAUPT-STADT UND VESTUNG BRAUNSCHWEIG NEBST DER UM DIESELBE LIEGENDEN GEGEND [c. 1730] 50x58cm (19½x23") Orig color. Sh lower c'fold tear repaired; lined. [64] £653 $1,006

TRAIECTI AD RHENUM [c. 1730] Plan above; view below, German & Latin key. 50x58cm (19½x23") Orig color. Without c'fold. Wrinkle top & bottom. [64] £388 $597

SHARP

MAP OF THE COUNTIES OF FIFE AND KINROSS [1828] Thomas Sharp; London: Sharp, Greenwood & Fowler; Dower, sc. Dissected, linen mounted, folds into orig cloth case. 89x117cm (35x46") No color. Fine. [21] £227 $350

SHARP'S CORRESPONDING MAPS NO.6. ENGLAND AND WALES RAILWAY MAP [c. 1855] J.W. Lowry, sc; London: Chapman & Hall. Linen mounted; folds into 12mo cloth cover with chipped label. 66x46cm (26½x18") Full color. Good. [21] £62 $95

SHERMAN & SMITH

WESTERN TERRITORIES OF THE UNITED STATES [1847] By D.F. Robinson, Hartford. 28x46cm (10½x17½") Full color. VG. [19] £146 $225

SHERWOOD, NEELY & JONES

NORTH AMERICA [1821] Attributed to Neely. 25x20cm (9½x7½") Color. [12] £32 $50

SMITH, GEORGE

PLAN OF BOSTON COMPRISING A PART OF CHARLESTOWN AND CAMBRIDGE [1835] Wall map. 53x53cm (21x21") OL & full color. Dull, lt fly-specking; margin surface worm damage & 2 wormholes; good. [6] £341 $525

SMITH, JOHN

VIRGINIA [1612 / 1625] Samuel Purchas, *Pilgrimes*. State: Verner 10 or Hind 8 or Church 9. 32x41cm (12½x16") Top margin shaved at neatline as originally bound; page number reinstated in orig ms; else exc. Ref: Schwartz & Ehrenberg p.95; Fite & Freeman #32; Morrison p.11-12. [62] £5,973 $9,200

SMITH, ROSWELL C.

MAP NO.1 EASTERN STATES [1843] From *Smith's Geography for Schools*. VT, NH, ME. 23x28cm (9x11") Color. Some wear & age-toning. [61] £23 $35

MAP NO.2 EASTERN STATES [same date, source, dimen, color & condition] MA, CT, RI. [61] £23 $35

MAP OF THE SOUTHERN STATES [same date, source, color & condition] 28x46cm (11x18") [61] £29 $45

MAP OF THE WESTERN STATES [1839] [same source] Published Hartford. OH, IN, IL, MI, WI. 28x46cm (11x18") Color. VG. [61] £42 $65

SNOW & CO.

MAP OF RAILWAYS IN NEW ENGLAND AND PART OF NEW YORK [1849] Folds into 89 pp *Pathfinder Railway Guide* ..., 16mo. Map lt foxed. Stiff wrap, rear missing; lt age-toning; VG. [6] £94 $145

SOCIETY FOR THE DIFFUSION OF USEFUL KNOWLEDGE

[ADVERTISEMENT] GLOBES OF THE SOCIETY FOR THE DIFFUSION OF USEFUL KNOWLEDGE ... [c. 1850] Show 8 globes by Messrs Malby & Co. 36x22cm (14x8½") [52] £100 $154

ANCIENT BRITAIN I [1834] Baldwin & Cradock. Roman period. 38x28cm (14½x11½") OL color. Browned; good. [21] £32 $50

ANCIENT BRITAIN II [1834] Baldwin & Cradock. 36x28cm (13½x11") OL col. Browned; fair. [21] £32 $50

ANCIENT SYRIA [1843] Wm. Hughes; Chapman & Hall. 41x33cm (16x12½") OL color. [23] £19 $30

ANTILLES OR WEST INDIA ISLANDS [1852] 36x43cm (14x17") Color. VG. [61] £36 $55

AUSTRALIA IN 1839 [1840] 31x40cm (12½x15½") Blind lib stamp in corner. [14] £19 $30

[SAME TITLE] [1840] 32x40cm (12½x15½") Orig OL color. [51] £146 $225

BRITISH ISLANDS IN THE WEST INDIES [1852] 32x39cm (12½x15½") Color. VG. [61] £42 $65

BRITISH NORTH AMERICA [1834] London: Baldwin & Cradock. 31x39cm (12½x15½") OL color. Close orig margins; minor marginal browning; VG. [19] £81 $125

[SAME TITLE] [1852] [same dimen] Color. VG. [61] £49 $75

CENTRAL AMERICA II. INCLUDING TEXAS, CALIFORNIA AND THE NORTHERN STATES OF MEXICO [1842] With Texas Republic, large form. 31x39cm (12x15½") Some browning; close margins as issued; else VG. [13] £179 $275

[SAME TITLE] [same date & dimen] Orig OL color. Blind lib stamp in corner. [14] £39 $60

EMPIRE OF JAPAN [1835] 39x32cm (15½x12½") OL color. [36] £97 $150

ENGLAND I [1831] North. 38x33cm (15x13") OL col. Sl stain upper lf; margins browned; good. [21] £39 $60

ENGLAND II [1831] Southwest; includes Wales. 30x38cm (12x14½") OL color. Corner stained, margins spotted; 2 sm margin tears; fair. [21] £39 $60

ENGLAND III [1830] Baldwin & Cradock. Northeast. 28x36cm (11x14") OL color. Lt browned; good. [21] £39 $60

ENGLAND IV [same date & publisher] Southwest. 25x38cm (10½x15") OL col. Lt browned; good. [21] £39 $60

ENGLAND V [same date & publisher]. Southeast. 28x36cm (10½x14½") OL color. Lt browned; margins damped; good. [21] £39 $60

ENGLAND WITH ITS CANALS AND RAILWAYS [1837] Baldwin & Cradock. 38x30cm (15½x12") Red & yellow OL color. Good. [21] £49 $75

GEOLOGICAL MAP OF ENGLAND AND WALES [1843] 38x31cm (15x12") Full color. VG. [21] £97 $150

IRELAND [1838] List of round towers. 60x47cm (23½x18½") OL color. Margins browned; good. [21] £107 $165

[SAME TITLE] [1842] 41x30cm (15½x12½") OL color. Lt browned margins; good. [21] £49 $75

IRELAND [IN SET WITH] IRELAND NORTH SHEET [1838] 30x46cm (12½x18½") OL col. VG. [21] £62 $95

LONDON 1843. DRAWN & ENGRAVED FROM AUTHENTIC & PERSONAL OBSERVATION. BY B.R. DAVIES ... [1843] Chapman & Hall. True folio strike; not joined sheets. 40x64cm (15½x25") Partial color. Good. [21] £162 $250

[SAME TITLE] [same date & dimen] Color. Tear to lower neat line; else fine. [55] £162 $250

MILAN [1832] 33x38cm (12½x15") OL color. Fine. [55] £42 $65

NAPLES [c. 1840] 36x38cm (13½x15") [51] £62 $95

NEW SOUTH WALES [1833] 34x40cm (13x16") OL color. [36] £97 $150

[SAME TITLE] [1833 / 1840] Baldwin & Cradock. Sydney inset. 41x33cm (15½x13") OL col. [51] £114 $175

NORTH AMERICA - CANADA & THE UNITED STATES [1852] 36x43cm (14x17") Color. VG. [61] £62 $95

NORTH AMERICA SHEET II LOWER CANADA AND NEW BRUNSWICK WITH PART OF NEW YORK, VERMONT AND MAINE [1852] 31x39cm (12½x15½") Color. VG. [61] £36 $55

NORTH AMERICA SHEET III UPPER CANADA WITH PARTS OF NEW YORK, PENNSYLVANIA AND MICHIGAN [1832] 35x43cm (14x17") Uncolored. VG. [61] £81 $125

NORTH AMERICA SHEET IV LAKE SUPERIOR REDUCED FROM THE ADMIRALTY SURVEY [1852] 30x39cm (12x15") Color. VG. [61] £114 $175

NORTH AMERICA SHEET V THE NORTHWEST AND MICHIGAN TERRITORIES [1833] London: Baldwin & Cradock. 33x38cm (12½x15") OL color. [51] £97 $150

NORTH AMERICA SHEET VI NEW-YORK, VERMONT, MAINE, NEW-HAMPSHIRE, MASSACHUSETTS, CONNECTICUT, RHODE-ISLAND, AND NEW-JERSEY [1852] 43x36cm (17x14") Color. VG. [61] £23 $35

NORTH AMERICA SHEET VIII OHIO, WITH PARTS OF KENTUCKY, VIRGINIA AND INDIANA [1852] 31x35cm (12x14") Color. VG. [61] £49 $75

NORTH AMERICA SHEET IX PARTS OF MISSOURI, ILLINOIS, IOWA AND INDIANA [1852] 30x37cm (12x14½") [14] £16 $25
[SAME TITLE] [1852] 36x43cm (14x17") Color. VG. [61] £16 $25
NORTH AMERICA SHEET X PARTS OF MISSOURI, ILLINOIS, KENTUCKY, TENNESSEE, ALABAMA, MISSISSIPPI AND ARKANSAS [1833] 31x39cm (12½x15") Orig OL color. Blind lib stamp in corner. [14] £16 $25
[SAME TITLE] [1852] 36x43cm (14x17") Color. VG. [61] £16 $25
NORTH AMERICA SHEET XI PARTS OF NORTH AND SOUTH CAROLINA [1852] 43x36cm (17x14") Color. VG. [61] £36 $55
NORTH AMERICA SHEET XII GEORGIA WITH PARTS OF NORTH & SOUTH CAROLINA, TENNESSEE, ALABAMA & FLORIDA [1852] 43x36cm (17x14") Color. VG. [61] £36 $55
NORTH AMERICA SHEET XIII PARTS OF LOUISIANA, ARKANSAS, MISSISSIPPI, ALABAMA & FLORIDA [1833] 31x39cm (12½x15½") Orig OL color. Blind lib stamp in corner. [14] £16 $25
[SAME TITLE] [1833] London: Baldwin & Cradock. 31x40cm (12½x16") OL color. Fine. [20] £65 $100
[SAME TITLE] [1852] 43x36cm (17x14") Color. VG. [61] £29 $45
[SAME TITLE] [1860] London: E. Stanford. 30x41cm (12x15½") OL color. Fine. [20] £65 $100
NORTH AMERICA SHEET XIV FLORIDA [1834] Panhandle inset. 40x31cm (15½x12") Orig OL color. Blind lib stamp in corner. [14] £26 $40
[SAME TITLE] [1834/1844] [same dimen] Orig OL color. Narrow orig upper & lower margins. [4] £81 $125
OPORTO [c. 1833] 31x38cm (12x15") Color. [43] £75 $116
PALESTINE WITH THE HAURAN AND THE ADJACENT DISTRICTS [1843] Wm. Hughes. 41x30cm (15½x12½") Color. Ref: Laor 362 [23] £26 $40
PARIS [c. 1840] Two sheets joined. 39x53cm (15x21") Color. Lt age-toning; else VG. [55] £162 $250
PHILADELPHIA [1852] 38x30cm (15x12") Color. [61] £49 $75
SCOTLAND [1841] 41x30cm (15½x12½") OL color. Good. [21] £49 $75
SCOTLAND I ... [1834] Baldwin & Cradock. Southern part. 28x38cm (10½x15") OL color. Margins browned & dry; good. [21] £42 $65
SCOTLAND II ... [1834] Baldwin & Cradock. Northern part. 33x41cm (13x15½") OL color. Margins browned & dry; fair. [21] £42 $65
SCOTLAND III ORKNEYS, SHETLANDS AND HEBRIDES ... [1834] Baldwin & Cradock. 2 charts on sheet. 36x33cm (14x12½") OL color. Margins browned; good. [21] £39 $60
SOUTH AFRICA ... [1834] By Baldwin & Cradock. 36x41cm (13½x16") Orig OL color. Sh tear lower margin. Ref: MCCS #48 p.95 & #61 256. [28] £75 $115
SOUTH AMERICA [1852] 43x36cm (17x14") Color. VG. [61] £29 $45
SOUTH AMERICA [SET OF 6 MAPS] [1852] 43x36cm (17x14") Color. VG. [61] £81 $125
SYRIA [1843] Wm. Hughes; Chapman & Hall. 41x33cm (16x12½") OL color. [23] £23 $35
THE BRITISH ISLANDS IN THE WEST INDIES [1835] Baldwin & Cradock. Jamaica and 14 sm island maps. 32x39cm (13x15½") Color. [27] £62 $95
[SAME TITLE] [1835 (1840)] Baldwin & Cradock. [same dimen] Orig OL color. [51] £81 $125
THE BRITISH ISLES [1842] Chapman & Hall. 41x33cm (15½x13") OL color. Good. [21] £42 $65
THE ENVIRONS OF DUBLIN [1837] Baldwin & Cradock. 31x39cm (12x15½") OL color. VG. [21] £42 $65
[SAME TITLE] [1837] Baldwin & Cradock. 32x39cm (13x15½") Color. [24] £55 $85
[SAME TITLE] [1837] 32x39cm (12½x15½") OL color. Fine. [55] £49 $75
THE ENVIRONS OF EDINBURGH [1938] Chapman & Hall. 30x39cm (12x15½") OL col. VG. [21] £58 $90
THE ENVIRONS OF LONDON [1832] Baldwin & Cradock. 30x41cm (12x15½") Partial color. Browned, margins chipped; fair. [21] £55 $85
THE ISLANDS OF NEW ZEALAND [1833 / 1840] 39x31cm (15½x12½") Orig OL color. [51] £114 $175
[SAME TITLE] [1838] 40x31cm (15½x12") Orig OL color. Blind lib stamp in corner. [14] £19 $30
[SAME TITLE] [c. 1844] 39x31cm (15x12½") OL color. [41] £95 $146
VENICE [1853] In *General Atlas* of the Society. George Cox. 2 joined sheets. 38x58cm (15x23") Color. Fine. Ref: Phillips (A) 811. [49] £185 $285
WESTERN AUSTRALIA [ON SHEET WITH] VAN DIEMEN ISLAND [1833] 31x39cm (12½x15½") Blind lib stamp in corner. [14] £19 $30
[SAME TITLE] [c. 1864] 32x39cm (12½x15½") Color. [41] £95 $146
WESTERN HEMISPHERE [c. 1840] J. & C. Walker, London. 36x36cm (14½x14") Orig OL col. [51] £81 $125

SPEED Try *Van den Keere*

A MAP OF JAMAICA ... [ON SHEET WITH] **BARBADOS** [1676] From *A Prospect of the Most Famous Parts of the World.* 38x51cm (15x19½") Color. Exc. [37] £487 $750

A MAP OF NEW ENGLAND AND NEW YORK [1676] Bassett & Chiswell, pub. 38x50cm (15x20") Uncolored. Exc. Ref: Tooley (Amer) pp.290-1, #23. [2] £2,272 $3,500

[SAME TITLE] [same date & dimen] From *A Prospect of the Most Famous Parts of the World* Color. A repair, few stains; overall VG. [37] £2,077 $3,200

A MAP OF RUSSIA [1676] From *A Prospect of the Most Famous Parts of the World.* Carte a figures. 40x51cm (15½x20") Color. Exc. [37] £779 $1,200

A MAP OF VIRGINIA AND MARYLAND [1676] From *A Prospect of the Most Famous Parts of the World.* 1st state. 38x50cm (15x19½") Faint c'fold discoloration; else mint. Ref: Tooley (Amer) Verner, p.170, pl.78. [37] £2,402 $3,700

[SAME TITLE] [same date, source & dimen] Uncol. Lower c'fold restoration; o/w good. [54] £2,000 $3,080

[SAME TITLE] [same date & dimen] 1st of 3 states. OL color. Fine. [63] £2,077 $3,200

A MAPP OF THE SOMMER ILANDS ONCE CALLED THE BERMUDAS ... [1631] From *A Prospect of the Most Famous Parts of the World.* 2nd state; Humble imprint. 41x53cm (16x21") Color. Lt toning; side margin extended, sl loss; else VG. Ref: MCCS 19 (Palmer #2) [37] £1,298 $2,000

[SAME TITLE] [1676] [same source & dimen] Color. Exc. [37] £1,623 $2,500

A NEW AND ACCURAT MAP OF THE WORLD DRAWNE ACCORDING TO YE TRUEST DESCRIPTIONS, LATEST DISCOVERIES & BEST OBSERVATIONS YT HAVE BEEN MADE BY ENGLISH OR STRANGERS [1676] From *A Prospect of the Most Famous Parts of the World.* Carte a figures; double hemispheres; insular California. 41x53cm (15½x20½") Color. Exc. Ref: Shirley (W) 317. [37] £4,869 $7,500

[SAME TITLE] [1626 (1676)]. 42x56cm (16½x22") Later color. Mint. [63] £4,869 $7,500

A NEW DESCRIPTION OF CAROLINA ... [1676] From *A Prospect of the Most Famous Parts of the World.* 38x51cm (14½x19½") Strong impression; faint c'fold discoloration; else mint. Ref: Cumming (SE) #77; Goss (NA) #41. [37] £2,110 $3,250

[SAME TITLE] [same date, source & dimen] Color. Exc. [37] £1,948 $3,000

[SAME TITLE] [same date, source & dimen] Uncol. Lower c'fold restoration; o/w good. [54] £1,600 $2,464

[SAME TITLE] [same date & dimen] Later color. Ctr repaired & restored; margins reinforced; clean. Framed. [51] £1,753 $2,700

A NEW MAPE OF YE XVII PROVINCES OF LOW GERMANIE ... [1676] From *A Prospect of the Most Famous Parts of the World.* Carte a figures. 41x53cm (16x21") Color. Exc. [37] £974 $1,500

A NEW MAPPE OF THE ROMANE EMPIRE NEWLY DESCRIBED BY JOHN SPEEDE [1626] In *Prospect ....* Carte a figures. London: G. Humble. 39x51cm (15½x20") Orig color. Hint of tape residue top edge; image fine. Framed. [1] £649 $1,000

[SAME TITLE] [1676] From *A Prospect of the Most Famous Parts of the World.* Carte a figures. 38x48cm (15½x19") Color. Top margin extended, no loss; else exc. [37] £633 $975

A NEWE MAPE OF GERMANY [1676] From *A Prospect of the Most Famous Parts of the World.* Carte a figures. 40x52cm (16x20½") Color. Top margin extended, very sl loss; else exc. [37] £909 $1,400

A NEWE MAPE OF TARTARY [1676] Panels top & sides. 39x51cm (15½x20") Orig col. Paper a little brittle; mended long, obtuse tear from top ctr; rough margin sections. Ref: Gohm (Antique) illus p.67. [1] £325 $500

[SAME TITLE] [same date & dimen Color. Exc. [37] £633 $975

AFRICAE, DESCRIBED, THE MANNERS OF THEIR HABITS, AND BUILDINGE: ... [1676] From *A Prospect of the Most Famous Parts of the World.* Carte a figures. 38x51cm (15½x20½") Color. Top margin extended, no loss; exc. Ref: Norwich 30. [37] £1,623 $2,500

AMERICA WITH THOSE KNOWN PARTS IN THAT UNKNOWNE WORLD ... [1626 / 1676] From *A Prospect of the Most Famous Parts of the World.* Carte a figures. Insular California. 39x51cm (15½x20") Color. Lt c'fold discoloration; else exc. Ref: Tooley (Amer) #5, p.113; Leighly #6, pl.IV. [37] £3,376 $5,200

ASIA WITH THE ISLANDS ADIOYNING DESCRIBED ... [1676] From *A Prospect of the Most Famous Parts of the World.* Panels at top and sides. 41x51cm (15½x20½") Color. Exc. [37] £2,272 $3,500

BEDFORDSHIRE [1662] 38x51cm (15x19½") Color. Some transference; else VG. [55] £422 $650

BOHEMIA NEWLY DESCRIBED ... [1676] From *A Prospect of the Most Famous Parts of the World.* Top & side panels. 41x53cm (16½x20½") Color. Exc. [37] £487 $750

BUCKINGHAMSHIRE [1676] 38x51cm (15x19½") Col. Good impression on thick paper; fine. [55] £552 $850

CANAAN [1676] From *A Prospect of the Most Famous Parts of the World.* 38x52cm (15x20½") Color. Exc. Ref: Laor 737; Nebenzahl (Holy Land) 39. [37] £1,428 $2,200

EUROP, AND THE CHEIFE CITIES CONTAYNED THEREIN ... [1676] From *A Prospect of the Most Famous Parts of the World*. Top and side panels. 38x51cm (15½x20"). Color. Exc. [37] £1,818 $2,800

FRANCE REVISED AND AUGMENTED ... [1676] From *A Prospect of the Most Famous Parts of the World*. Carte a figures. 41x56cm (16x21½") Color. Exc. [37] £617 $950

GREECE [1676] From *A Prospect of the Most Famous Parts of the World*. 39x50cm (15½x20") Color. Exc. Ref: Zacharakis 2243. [37] £617 $950

ITALIA NEWLY AUGMENTED ... [1676] From *A Prospect of the Most Famous Parts of the World*. Carte a figures. 39x51cm (15½x20") Color. Exc. [37] £1,169 $1,800

MAPPA AESTIVARUM INSULARUM ALIAS BERMUDAS ... A MAPP OF THE SOMMER ISLANDS [1676] Sold by Bassett & Chiswell; A. Goos, engr. 40x53cm (15½x20½") Blank verso. Modern color. Browned, creased, soiled. Ref: cf. Palmer *Printed Maps of Bermuda*, Pl.XXV. [14] £487 $750

MONTGOMERYSHIRE [1611 (1627)] 38x51cm (15x20") Color. Fine. Framed. Ref: Skelton (County) 16. [55] £325 $500

NEW ENGLAND AND NEW YORK [1676] Miniature; 8x12cm (3½x5") Weak impression at top neat lines. [14] £208 $320

[SAME TITLE] [c. 1680] 9x13cm (3½x5") Exc. [63] £224 $345

NORTHAMPTONSHIRE [1672] 38x51cm (15x20") Color. Lower c'fold repaired; sm top margin; else VG. [55] £325 $500

OXFORDSHIRE DESCRIBED, WITH YE CITIE AND THE ARMES OF THE COLLEDGES OF YE FAMOUS UNIVERSITY [1610 (1627)] From *The Theatre of the Empire of Great Britaine*. Dated 1605. 38x52cm (15x20½") Color; gold highlights. [14] £682 $1,050

POLONIA [c. 1676] 9x12cm (3½x4½") B&W. [42] £56 $86

SOMERSET-SHIRE [1610] 1st ed. 38x51cm (15x20") Old color. Narrow margins with some waterstain; faint age tone; image fine. [1] £584 $900

SPAINE NEWLY DESCRIBED ... [1676] From *A Prospect of the Most Famous Parts of the World*. Carte a figures. 42x53cm (16½x21") Color. Top margin extended, very sl loss; else exc. [37] £779 $1,200

THE COUNTIE OF LEINSTER WITH THE CITIE OF DUBLIN DESCRIBED [1610 / 1614] 38x51cm (15x20") Full color. C'fold reinforced with sl rubbing; else exc. [39] £617 $950

THE KINGDOME OF CHINA ... [1676] From *A Prospect of the Most Famous Parts of the World*. Carte a figures. 39x51cm (15½x20") Color. Exc. Ref: Cortazzi p.94, pl.29. [37] £2,499 $3,850

THE KINGDOME OF DENMARKE ... [same date & source] Carte a figures. 40x50cm (15½x20") Color. Exc. [37] £617 $950

THE KINGDOME OF ENGLAND [1610 - 1616] Costume side panels. 38x51cm (15x20") Uncolored. [54] £1,200 $1,848

THE KINGDOME OF PERSIA ... [1676] From *A Prospect of the Most Famous Parts of the World*. Carte a figures. 40x51cm (15½x20") Color. Exc. [37] £633 $975

THE TURKISH EMPIRE [1626] Carte a figures. London: G. Humble. 39x51cm (15½x20") Orig col. Lower c'fold ¼x3" gusset replacement of image; 3 tiny worm holes; very nice. Ref: Potter illus p.119. [1] £812 $1,250

VIRGINIA AND MARYLAND [1676] From miniature atlas after folio. 8x13cm (3½x5") B&W. Fine. [50] £302 $465

WALES [1610 (1713)] Roads added by Overton. 38x51cm (15x20") Early color. [14] £649 $1,000

WILTSHIRE [1662] 38x51cm (15x19½") Color. Sl darkening at c'fold; repaired edge tear ¼" into lower border. [55] £552 $850

STACKHOUSE

A MAP OF CANAAN DIVIDED AMONG YE XII TRIBES [1744] 30x20cm (11½x8") Color. Ref: Laor 742. [23] £88 $135

JUDEA OR THE HOLY LAND [1798] 38x38cm (15x14½") Old color. Ref: Laor 747. [23] £88 $135

MAP OF IRELAND [1796] 41x38cm (16½x14½") Old color. [24] £114 $175

NORTH AMERICA IN ITS PRESENT DIVISIONS ... [1783] 38x36cm (15x14") Orig col. VG. [2] £779 $1,200

STANFORD

ENGLAND AND WALES [c. 1885] Dissected, linen mounted, in cloth folder. 69x58cm (26½x22½") Full color. VG. [21] £55 $85

ETHNOLOGICAL MAP OF THE BRITISH ISLES [c, 1880] Edward Stanford; reproduced from S.D.U.K., with linguistic definition. 38x36cm (15x13½") Yellow & blue. VG. [21] £49 $75

MAP OF THE SEAT OF WAR IN AMERICA [1862] London: Davies & Co. Linen-backed folding map; in self covers. 55x75cm (21½x29½") Orig OL color. Sm ex lib stamp inside cover; blind stamp on map; overall VG+. [33] £568 $875

STANFORD'S MAP OF METROPOLITAN RAILWAYS, TRAMWAYS AND OTHER IMPROVEMENTS, WITHIN THE COUNTY OF LONDON [1897] Pocket map, dissected into 32 panels, linen mounted & folded into 12mo boards. 61x97cm (24x38") Color. Lt soiled boards & linen, front separated, lacks spine; map clean; VG to near fine. [7] £81 $125

STANFORD'S POPULAR MAP OF THE SEAT OF MILITARY OPERATIONS IN THE SUDAN [1885] Pocket map, folded into 8vo wraps. 38x71cm (15x28") Color. Wraps soiled; map clean; VG. [7] £62 $95

THE LEEWARD ISLANDS [1868] 48x61cm (19x24") Color. [27] £49 $75

STARLING

ASIA [1831] 9x13cm (3½x5½") With index. Full color. [57] £23 $35

MAP OF ENGLAND & WALES DIVIDED INTO COUNTIES SHEWING THE PRINCIPAL ROADS, RAILWAYS, CANALS & RIVERS AS FAR AS THEY ARE NAVIGABLE [1842] For *Lewis's Topographical Dictionary*. 48x38cm (18½x15") OL color. VG. [21] £49 $75

STEDMAN

SKETCH OF GENERAL GRANTS POSITION ON LONG ISLAND ... [1794] From 36x28cm (14x11") Uncolored. [44] £114 $175

STEINBERGER

TAB.I GEOGRAPHIA ET ASTRONOMIA [1680] L. Steinberger, Augsburg. Double hemi & 7 sm globes; insular Calif; much decor. 20x23cm (7½x9") Color. [26] £172 $265

STIELER   Try *Petermann, Von Stulpnagel*

[ATLAS] HAND-ATLAS UBER ALLE THEILE DER ERDE NACH DEM DEUESTEN ZUSTANDE UND UBER DAS WELTGEBAUDE. [c. 1851] Gotha: Justus Perthes. Oblong folio; title vignette map & 51 maps on 82 sheets, most in OL color; separate Africa bound in. Orig cloth; rubbed, extremities worn & frayed. Frontis soiled & margin tears; some foxing throughout; early leaves creased. Ref: Phillips (A) 819. [28] £643 $990

[UNITED STATES: NORTHERN PLAINS] [1873] MN & IA, west to Denver. 33x41cm (13x16") OL color. [56] £58 $90

MEXICO UND CENTRO-AMERICA [1828] By von Stulpnagel. 30x36cm (11½x14") OL & wash color. Margin foxing, map unaffected. [58] £114 $175

POLAR-KARTE ... [1840's] Incl northern continental lands. 33x38cm (12½x14½") Color. Minor foxing; overall very nice. [58] £49 $75

STOCKDALE   Try *Morse*

A NEW MAP OF UPPER & LOWER CANADA [1798] Centered on Great Lakes. 18x23cm (7x9") OL & wash color. [56] £81 $125

SKETCH OF SYDNEY COVE, PORT JACKSON IN THE COUNTY OF CUMBERLAND, NEW SOUTH WALES, JULY 1788 [1789] In *Voyage of Governor Phillip to Botany Bay*. 45x45cm (17½x17½") Color. Ref: McCormick #2. [16] £855 $1,316

STONE

A CORRECT MAP OF THE CITY OF WASHINGTON. CAPITAL OF THE UNITED STATES OF AMERICA [1820] 1st ed. W.J. Stone, sc. Pub by Peter Force, 41x53cm (16x21½") B&W. Repaired 7" tear; lt stain; rice paper backing, sl loss at folds; fair. Ref: Phillips (M) p.1010; Phillips (Wash) p.29. [47] £1,233 $1,900

STOOPENDAAL

HET BELOOFDE LANDT CANAAN DOORWANDELT VAN ONSEN SALICHMAECKER IESU CHRISTO ... [1702] 35x46cm (14x18") Color. Ref: Laor 809. [23] £276 $425

JERUSALEM [c. 1730] From Dutch Bible. After Vallapando's imaginary city plan. Border illustrations. 30x46cm (12x18") Vert folds. sh margin tears; tear 2" into engraving. Ref: cf Laor 1151 (sl size difference). [28] £292 $450

ORBIS TERRARUM TABULA RECENS EMENDATA ET IN LUCEM EDITA [1680] Rotterdam: Keur. 35x45cm (14x18") Color. Ref: Shirley (W) 498. [22] £1,087 $1,675

STRADA

DE BELLO BELGICO DE CADES DUAE AUCTORES ET CORRECTIORES ... [1651] Leo Belgicus. 18x14cm (7x5½") Exc. Ref: MCCS 7, #29, pl.IX. [62] £438 $675

SUDLOW

THE WORLD WITH THE LATEST DISCOVERIES [c. 1795] Botany Bay noted as convict destination. 25x50cm (10x19½") OL color. Narrow top margin. [46] £55 $85

SWANSTON

UNITED STATES, NORTH AMERICA [1845] London: A. Fullarton. 41x52cm (16x20½") Orig OL color. [14] £29 $45

UNITED STATES NORTH AMERICA ACCORDING TO CALVIN SMITH & TANNER ... THE NORTH CENTRAL SECTION, COMPRISING MICHIGAN, ILLINOIS, WISCONSIN, IOWA, INDIANA, NEBRASKA, MINNESOTA, AND PART OF MISSOURI AND KENTUCKY [c. 1854] Edinburgh, London & Dublin. 40x51cm (15½x20") Orig printed color. Mint. Ref: Phillips (A) 838,57. [14] £16 $25

UNITED STATES OF NORTH AMERICA [c. 1856] Edinburgh: Fullarton. Pre-Gadsden Purchase border. 41x53cm (16½x21") Printed color. Ref: Wheat (TM) 903. [46] £75 $115

TALLIS

[TITLE PAGE] THE ILLUSTRATED ATLAS AND MODERN HISTORY OF THE WORLD [1851] R. Montgomery Martin, ed. 30x23cm (12x9") Color. Good. Ref: Phillips (A) 804. [50] £81 $125

ANCIENT PALESTINE [1851] 5 vignettes. 34x24cm (13½x9½") Color. Ref: Laor 634. [23] £71 $110

ASIA MINOR [1851] With Cyprus & Syria. 25x33cm (9½x13") Orig OL color. [14] £29 $45

AUSTRALIA [1851] 24x32cm (9½x13") Orig OL color. Ref: Tooley (Australia) 1217. [16] £214 $329

[SAME TITLE] [c. 1851] Vignettes. 25x32cm (10x13") OL color. No c'fold. [41] £195 $300

[SAME TITLE] [c. 1860] London Publishing Co. ed; no vignettes. 24x32cm (9½x13") Color. [16] £147 $227

AUSTRALIA [IN SET WITH] NEW SOUTH WALES [AND] VICTORIA OR PORT PHILLIP [AND] SOUTH AUSTRALIA [AND] TASMANIA [AND] WESTERN AUSTRALIA [1851] Complete 6 map Australian set. Orig OL color. [16] £950 $1,463

BRITISH AMERICA [1850] 1st state, 1st issue; with "Boston City" view. 26x33cm (10x13") Orig OL color. [14] £55 $85

[SAME TITLE] [same date & dimen] 2nd state, 1st issue; Montreal view replaces Boston; "Oregon" appears in U.S. Orig OL color. [14] £52 $80

[SAME TITLE] [c. 1850] 20x30cm (8x12") OL color. VG. [19] £97 $150

[SAME TITLE] [c. 1850] Several vignettes, incl Boston. 26x32cm (10x12½") OL color. [40] £98 $151

[SAME TITLE] [1851] 6 vignettes, incl Montreal. 26x33cm (10x13") OL color. Reinforced ctr seam; exc. [29] £62 $95

[SAME TITLE] [same date & dimen] Orig OL color. [51] £114 $175

[SAME TITLE] [c. 1865] Montreal vignette replaces Boston. 23x33cm (9x13") OL col. Fine. [19] £114 $175

CENTRAL AMERICA [c. 1850] 26x32cm (10x12½") Orig OL color. Upper & lower margins trimmed; image fine, overall good. Ref: MCC 103 pl.25; MCC 106 p.45 #175; Phillips (A) 804. [59] £55 $85

EAST CANADA AND NEW BRUNSWICK [1850] 1st state, 1st issue. 26x34cm (10x13½") Orig OL color. [14] £55 $85

[SAME TITLE] [c. 1850] [same dimen] OL color. Reinforced ctr seam, filled binding thread holes; VG. [29] £31 $48

[SAME TITLE] [c. 1861] Vignettes; foliate border. [same dimen] OL col. Some foxing. [40] £49 $75

EUROPE [c. 1850] 25x32cm (10x13") OL color. Reinforced ctr seam; sl edge chipping; exc. [29] £49 $75

HUNGARY [1851] 25x32cm (9½x12½") [14] £39 $60

ISTHMUS OF PANAMA [c. 1850] 26x33cm (10x13") Orig OL color; RR & canal routes highlighted. Lower margins trimmed; overall VG. Ref: MCC 73 p.30 #116; Phillips (A) 804. [59] £81 $125

[SAME TITLE] [c. 1851] 25x33cm (9½x13") Orig OL color. [46] £49 $75

MEXICO, CALIFORNIA AND TEXAS [1850] 25x33cm (10x13") Orig OL color. [46] £175 $270

[SAME TITLE] [1851] [same dimen] Gold region highlighted. Browning at c'fold. [36] £127 $195

[SAME TITLE] [1851] Vignettes; gold districts in yellow. 28x33cm (11x13½") Orig OL col. [51] £179 $275

[SAME TITLE] [1851] 25x33cm (10x13") Orig OL color. Very narrow stain down c'fold; o/w VG+. Ref: Goss (NA) #80; Phillips (A) 804. [59] £195 $300

[SAME TITLE] [1857] 3 vignettes. 28x38cm (11x15") OL color. C'fold as issued. [45] £179 $275

MODERN PALESTINE [1851] 4 vignettes. 34x25cm (13½x10") Color. Ref: Laor 635. [23] £71 $110

NEW SOUTH WALES [1851] 33x25cm (13x10") Orig OL color. [16] £183 $282

[SAME TITLE] [c. 1851] With gold diggings; vignettes. 34x25cm (13½x10") Color. [41] £150 $231

NORTH AMERICA [c. 1850] Several vignettes. 32x24cm (13x9½") OL color. [40] £125 $193
[SAME TITLE] [1851] Vignettes; bizarre boundaries. 36x24cm (14x9½") Orig OL color. [51] £146 $225
[SAME TITLE] [same date & dimen] Some soiling; o/w nice. [11] £97 $150
[SAME TITLE] [c. 1851] 9 vignettes. 33x25cm (13x9½") [36] £114 $175
PART OF SOUTH AUSTRALIA [1851] 34x25cm (13½x9½") Orig OL & later cartouche color. Pencil notes. Ref: Tooley (Australia) 1231. [28] £204 $315
[SAME TITLE] [c. 1861] Vignettes of Adelaide, etc. 34x24cm (13½x9½") Color. [41] £115 $177
POLYNESIA, OR ISLANDS IN THE PACIFIC OCEAN [1851] 25x36cm (9½x13½") With text sheet. Lt orig wash & OL color. [46] £26 $40
SCOTLAND [c. 1865] 3rd state. 6 vignettes. 30x23cm (12x8½") OL color. Fine. [21] £97 $150
SOUTH AMERICA [1851] 35x25cm (14x9½") Orig OL color. [51] £114 $175
SYRIA [1851] 3 vignettes. 34x25cm (13½x10") Color. [23] £71 $110
THE BRITISH ISLES [c. 1865] 3rd state; 1st issue. London, Dublin, Edinburgh vignettes. 30x23cm (12x9") OL color. Fine. [21] £78 $120
THE WORLD ON MERCATOR'S PROJECTION [1851] Show Cook's 3 voyages. 26x35cm (10x13½") Orig OL color. [16] £180 $278
[SAME TITLE] [1851] 26x35cm (10x14") OL color. Narrow margins as pub; exc. [29] £49 $75
TURKEY IN ASIA [1851] 24x32cm (9½x12½") Orig OL color. [14] £29 $45
UNITED STATES [1851] Vignettes. 25x34cm (10x13½") [10] £97 $150
[SAME TITLE] [same date & dimen] From *Illustrated Atlas*. Color. [36] £130 $200
VICTORIA OR PORT PHILIP [1851] 25x33cm (10x13") Orig OL color. Ref: Tooley (Australia) 1234. [16] £123 $190
[SAME TITLE] [same date & dimen] Orig OL & later cartouche color. Pencil notes. [28] £221 $340
[SAME TITLE] [c. 1861] 25x34cm (10x13") Color. [41] £115 $177
WEST CANADA [1850] 1st state, 1st issue. 25x33cm (10x13") Orig OL col; vignettes colored. [14] £81 $125
[SAME TITLE] [c. 1851] Vignettes. 25x34cm (10x13") OL color. [40] £125 $193
WEST INDIA ISLANDS [1850-1851] Vignettes. 26x33cm (10x13") OL color. [36] £110 $170
[SAME TITLE] [c. 1850] [same dimen] OL color. Reinforced ctr seam, binding thread holes filled; chips lf margin; good. [29] £23 $36
[SAME TITLE] [same date & dimen] Orig OL color. Image VG, overall good. Ref: Phillips (A) 804. [59] £58 $90
WESTERN AUSTRALIA, SWAN RIVER [c. 1851] Vignettes. 34x24cm (13½x9½") Color. [41] £195 $300
WESTERN HEMISPHERE [IN SET WITH] EASTERN HEMISPHERE [1850-1851] Each 25x34cm (9½x13½") Orig OL color. [16] £266 $410

TANNER

A MAP OF THE ROADS LEADING TO THE TOWN OF BRITANIA IN THE BRITISH SETTLEMENT SUSQUEHANNA COUNTY PENNA. [c. 1820] Adapted from 1819 British Emigrant Society broadside map. 20x18cm (8x6½") B&W. Remargined lf; good. [50] £107 $165
A NEW MAP OF ARKANSAS [1836] 36 counties. 35x28cm (13½x11") Color. Minor browning; else good. [10] £78 $120
A NEW MAP OF LOUISIANA WITH ITS CANALS, ROADS AND DISTANCES FROM PLACE TO PLACE ALONG THE STAGE & STEAMBOAT ROUTES [1846] Phila: Carey & Hart. 27x35cm (11x13½") Full color. Bright, fine. [20] £120 $185
A NEW MAP OF MARYLAND AND DELAWARE WITH THEIR CANALS, ROADS & DISTANCES [1844] Phila: Carey & Hart. 28x35cm (11x14") Color. [58] £65 $100
A NEW MAP OF MICHIGAN WITH ITS CANALS, ROADS & DISTANCES [1841] 38x30cm (14½x11½") Sl wear. [61] £114 $175
A NEW MAP OF MISSISSIPPI WITH ITS ROADS AND DISTANCES [1836 (1845)] 34x27cm (13½x11") Full color. [58] £65 $100
A NEW MAP OF PENNSYLVANIA WITH ITS CANALS, RAIL-ROADS & DISTANCES FROM PLACE TO PLACE ALONG THE STAGE ROADS [ent 1840] Philadelphia: Carey & Hart. 25x36cm (10x14") Color. VG or better. [29] £42 $65
A NEW MAP OF VIRGINIA WITH ITS CANALS, ROADS AND DISTANCES FROM PLACE TO PLACE ALONG THE STAGE AND STEAMBOAT ROUTES [1833] 28x36cm (10½x14") [36] £104 $160
CONNECTICUT [1839] 30x36cm (12x14") Full color. [51] £179 $275

LOUISIANA AND MISSISSIPPI [1823] From *New American Atlas*. 69x56cm (27x21½") Full color. Rough upper & lower margins; minor browning at repaired c'fold; bright, VG. [20] £568 $875

MEXICO & GUATEMALA [1834 (1844)] TX independence period. 33x41cm (13x16") Full col. [45] £104 $160

[SAME TITLE] [1834 (1846)] Mitchell / Burroughs. 29x37cm (11½x14½") Orig wash col. [46] £179 $275

NEW JERSEY REDUCED FROM T. GORDON'S MAP [1841] 18 counties. 41x33cm (15½x12½") Color. Bright. [35] £101 $155

[SAME TITLE] [1843] 18 counties. [same dimen] Full color age darkened. [36] £88 $135

PHILADELPHIA [ent. 1836] Phila: Carey & Hart. (no dims.) Color. VG or better. [29] £36 $55

TERRA FILIORUM ISRAELIS ... COM TERRA PHILISTAEORUM, PARTE PHOENICES [1806] D. Macpherson, Historical Geography, Phila. Inset. 28x41cm (10½x15½") [23] £23 $35

UNITED STATES [(1839) 1846] 38x31cm (15x12") Color. VG. [61] £81 $125

TARDIEU

A MAP OF LOUISIANA AND MEXICO / CARTE DE LA LOUISIANE ET DU MEXIQUE [1820] Shows Adams-Onis 1819 boundary. 15 panels on linen folding to 7x11". 107x79cm (42x31½") Full orig OL color. Mild splitting at few folds; virtually flawless. [46] £1,623 $2,500

CARTE DU MEXIQUE [1821] To 42° N. 41x25cm (15½x10") Some soiling; else strong. [13] £114 $175

LONDRES... [c.1790] 33x46cm (12½x17½") Col. Minor creasing, wormholes filled; else VG. [55] £162 $250

TASSO

AMERICA SETTENTRIONALE DISEGNATA DOPI I VIAGGI DI LEWIS, CLARKE, PARRY E FRANKLIN E DALL'ATL. DI BUCHON ... [1832] 36x48cm (14x19½") Orig color. [28] £380 $585

TAVERNIER

CARTE FAITE SUR LES LIEUX PAR DANIEL TAVERNIER EN PLUSIEURS VOIAGES QUIL A FAIT AU TONQUIN [1679] In Jean-Baptiste Tavernier, *Recueil de Plusieurs Relations...* Vietnam & S. China. 49x40cm (19½x15½") Exc. [62] £617 $950

PATRIARCHATUS ANTIOCHENI GEOGRAPHICA DESCRIPTIO TABULARUM GEOGRAPHICARUM HYDROGRAPHICARUM [1640] Cyprus to Persian Gulf. 38x51cm (14½x20") Full color. Ref: Laor 768. [23] £130 $200

TAYLOR

NEW TRAVELLING AND COMMERCIAL MAP OF THE CANADAS, FROM THE SAULT OF ST. MARIE TO THE RIVER SAGUENAY; AND A LARGE SECTION OF THE UNITED STATES OF AMERICA [1834] David Taylor. Folding map; roan covers, gilt stamped title; 2 sheets, each 79x61cm (31x24") Orig OL color. Fold tears repaired, some lettering affected; lt foxing; spine chipped. [28] £876 $1,350

PLAN EXPLANATORY OF THE PASSAGE OF THE RED-SEA, BY THE ISRAELITES [1797] C. Taylor. 20x33cm (8x13½") Color. [23] £52 $80

TAYLOR & SKINNER

[ATLAS] MAPS OF THE ROADS OF IRELAND, SURVEYED 1777 [1778] 288 strip maps. 26x16cm (10x6½") Spine ineptly repaired but adequate. [14] £195 $300

TEESDALE

CANADA, NEW BRUNSWICK AND NOVA SCOTIA [1831] 34x41cm (13½x16½") Full color. [61] £62 $95

IRELAND [1828] 64x53cm (25½x20½") Color. Margin repair. [24] £55 $85

UNITED STATES [(1782) c.1830] 34x41cm (13x16") OL color. Fine. [1] £97 $150

THERBU

ATTAQUES DU FORT WILLIAM-HENRI EN AMERIQUE PAR LES TROUPES FRANCAISES AUX ORDRES DU MARQUIS DE MONTCALM. PRISE DE CE FORT LE 7 AOUT 1757 ... [1793] Frankfurt; Coentgen, sc. 43x28cm (16½x11") Positions in color. Dampmarks top margin & title area. Ref: Phillips (A) 3979,[8]. [28] £292 $450

THEVENOT

[EAST AFRICA] [1649 (1663)] After Teixeira portolan chart. 69x51cm (27x20") Uncolored. Orig folds. [54] £1,450 $2,233

IMPERII SINARUM NOVA DESCRIPTIO [1663] As in Blaeu, *Atlas Sinensis*. 45x64cm (18x25") Uncolored. C'fold restoration. [54] £650 $1,001

THOMAS, COWPERTHWAIT & CO.
Try *Mitchell (Atlas Maps 1859 or Earlier)*

A NEW MAP OF GEORGIA WITH ITS ROADS AND DISTANCES [1850 / 1854] 36x30cm (14x11½") Full orig color. [51] £162 $250
A NEW MAP OF LOUISIANA WITH ITS CANALS, ROADS AND DISTANCES FROM PLACE TO PLACE ALONG THE STAGE AND STEAMBOAT ROUTES [1851] 29x37cm (11½x14½") Full col. Fine. [20] £91 $140
A NEW MAP OF MAINE [1850] 38x31cm (15x12") Color. VG or better. [29] £23 $36
A NEW MAP OF MARYLAND AND DELAWARE AND THEIR CANALS, ROADS AND DISTANCES [1850] 30x38cm (12x15") Color. VG or better. [29] £23 $36
A NEW MAP OF MICHIGAN WITH ITS CANALS, ROADS, AND DISTANCES [1850 (1854)] From Mitchell, *New Universal Atlas*. 38x31cm (15x12") Orig full color. Good. Ref: Karpinski (MI) #161. [59] £49 $75
A NEW MAP OF THE STATE OF WISCONSIN [1850] 41x34cm (16x13") Color. VG. [61] £55 $85
A NEW MAP OF THE UNITED STATES OF AMERICA [1850] Insets: DC; CA gold region. 40x67cm (16x26½") Full color. [36] £211 $325
[SAME TITLE] [1850 / 1854] 40x67cm (16x26") Color. [51] £195 $300
CANADA EAST FORMERLY LOWER CANADA [1850] 33x41cm (13x16") Col. VG or better. [29] £29 $45
CHINA [1854] 29x36cm (11½x14") Color. [14] £16 $25
CITY OF WASHINGTON [1852] 31x39cm (12x15½") Color. [58] £52 $80
MAP OF FLORIDA [1850 / 1854] 38x30cm (14½x12") Orig wash color. Bright. [4] £75 $115
[SAME TITLE] [same date & dimen] Full orig color. [51] £179 $275
MAP OF MASSACHUSETTS AND RHODE ISLAND [1850] 30x38cm (12x15") Color. VG or better. [29] £23 $36
MAP OF MINNESOTA TERRITORY [1850 /1854] Incl eastern Dakotas. 33x41cm (13x16") Full orig color. [51] £162 $250
MAP OF NEW HAMPSHIRE & VERMONT [1850] 38x31cm (15x12") Color. VG or better. [29] £23 $36
MAP OF NEW JERSEY [1850 / 1854] 39x32cm (15x12½") Full color. [51] £146 $225
MAP OF NORTH AMERICA [1850] 41x33cm (16x13") Color. VG or better. [29] £29 $45
[SAME TITLE] [1850 / 1854] 39x32cm (15½x12½") Full orig color. [51] £130 $200
MAP OF TEXAS FROM THE MOST RECENT AUTHORITIES [1845 (1850)] By Williams. Inset of new Panhandle configuration. 31x38cm (12x15") Color. [46] £292 $450
MAP OF THE STATE OF NEW YORK ... [c. 1850] 41x66cm (16x26") Color. VG or better. [29] £39 $60
MEXICO & GUATEMALA [1852] Extended NM & UT. 31x38cm (12x15") Color (not US part). [58] £78 $120
PHILADELPHIA [1846] 41x33cm (16x13") Color. VG or better. [29] £23 $36
SCOTLAND [1850] 31x25cm (12x10") Full color. VG. [21] £49 $75

THOMPSON

A NEW MAP OF THE WORLD. WITH ALL THE NEW DISCOVERIES ... [1798] G. Thompson. Separately issued double hemisphere. 64x95cm (25x37½") Orig OL color. Restored; protective margins added. [53] £2,749 $4,235

THOMSON

A CHART OF NEW SOUTH WALES, VAN DIEMEN'S LAND &C [1820] Insets: Tasmania; Port Jackson; Australia. 51x58cm (19½x23") OL color. A little wrinkled. [58] £114 $175
A CHART OF THE DISCOVERIES OF CAPTAINS ROSS, PARRY & FRANKLIN IN THE ARCTIC REGIONS IN THE YEARS 1818, 1819, 1820, 1821 & 1822 [c. 1827] Aspin, del; Hewitt, sc. 49x59cm (19½x23") Orig OL color. Some offsetting; sh tears lower margin. Ref: Phillips (A) 750,76. [28] £292 $450
AMERICA [1814] 48x56cm (19x22") Orig color. C'fold split repaired. Ref: Phillips (A) 731. [28] £204 $315
ATLANTIC OR WESTERN OCEAN [1820] Shows Gulf Stream. 51x64cm (19½x24½") Color. Lt offsetting. [58] £114 $175
BRITISH INDIA, NORTHERN PART [IN SET WITH] BRITISH INDIA, SOUTHERN PART [1817] From 1st ed. Each about 50x60cm (19½x23½") Orig full color. Fine. [30] £130 $200
CANADA AND NOVA SCOTIA [c. 1817] 53x66cm (21x25½") Orig color. Creases; a margin stain. Ref: Phillips (A) 731. [28] £292 $450
CHART OF THE NORTHERN PASSAGE BETWEEN ASIA & AMERICA [1816] 50x59cm (19½x23") Orig color. Margins foxed; lt offsetting. Ref: Phillips (A) 731. [28] £292 $450
[SAME TITLE] [1820] [same dimen] Broad OL color. [58] £146 $225

COREA AND JAPAN [1815] 47x61cm (18½x24") Color. Rt top margin browned & wrinkled; faint offsetting; o/w VG. Ref: Walter (Japan) #128; Phillips (A) 731. [59] £227 $350

DENMARK [1814] For *New General Atlas*. 53x64cm (21x24½") Orig color. Sh tear lower margin; lt browning upper c'fold. Ref: Phillips (A) 731. [28] £133 $205

GRENADA [ON SHEET WITH] TOBAGO [AND] CURACAO [AND] TRINIDAD [1820] 51x58cm (19½x23½") [58] £97 $150

HYDROGRAPHICAL CHART OF THE WORLD ON WRIGHT OR MERCATOR'S PROJECTION WITH TRACKS OF THE LAST CIRCUMNAVIGATORS [c. 1817] 51x56cm (20x22") Orig OL color. Some foxing, offsetting; sh tear to lower border. Ref: Phillips (A) 731. [28] £221 $340

IRELAND [1815] For "General Atlas" by Neele. Dissected, laid down on linen. 60x50cm (23½x20") Full color. Fold repairs on reverse; browned; good. [21] £65 $100

[SAME TITLE] [same date & dimen] Old color. Minor repair. [24] £88 $135

MAP OF THE ISLANDS IN THE PACIFIC OCEAN [1817] From *New General Atlas*. Insets: 2 of Hawaii; 2 of Tahiti. 53x64cm (21x25") Orig color. Ref: Phillips (A) 731. [28] £204 $315

NEW HOLLAND AND ASIATIC ISLES [c. 1814] [same source] 50x61cm (19½x24") OL color. [41] £280 $431

NORTH AMERICA ... [1814] 53x64cm (21x25") Orig OL color. Sh tear lower border repaired. Ref: Phillips (A) 731. [28] £234 $360

NORTHERN HEMISPHERE [1815] Diameter: 50cm (19½") Full orig color. [14] £39 $60

NORTHERN PART OF IRELAND [IN SET WITH] SOUTHERN PART ... [1817] 2 sheets, each 53x64cm (21x24½") Orig color. Lt offsetting; repaired lower c'fold split on one sheet. Ref: Phillips (A) 731. [28] £292 $450

NORTHERN PART OF SCOTLAND [IN SET WITH] SOUTHERN PART ... [c. 1821] 2 sheets, each 53x61cm (20½x24½") Orig color. Lt offsetting; sm hole blank area. Ref: Royal Scot p.221. [28] £325 $500

NORTHERN PROVINCES OF THE UNITED STATES ... [1817] Niagara view. 53x64cm (21x24½") Orig color. Lt offsetting. Ref: Phillips (A) 731. [28] £204 $315

PORTO RICO AND VIRGIN ISLES [1817] 25x61cm (9½x24") Color. Ref: Phillips (A) 731. [25] £130 $200

PORTO RICO AND VIRGIN ISLES [ON SHEET WITH] HAITI, HISPANIOLA OR ST. DOMINGO ... [1815] As in *New General Atlas*. 53x66cm (21x25½") Orig OL color. Ref: Phillips (A) 731. [28] £204 $315

REMOTE BRITISH ISLANDS [CHANNEL ISLANDS, SCILLY ISLANDS, WIGHT, MANN] [1817] 2 views. 53x61cm (20½x24½") Orig OL color. Ref: Phillips (A) 731. [28] £175 $270

SOUTHERN PROVINCES OF THE UNITED STATES ... [1817] 53x64cm (20½x25") Orig OL color. Repaired 2" tear to engraved surface; lt offsetting. Ref: Phillips (A) 731. [28] £250 $385

THE BRITISH CHANNEL [1814] 51x58cm (20x23") Orig Ol color. Lt offsetting. Ref: Phillips (A) 731. [28] £117 $180

UNITED STATES AND ADDITIONS [1820] 50x60cm (19½x23½") Color. [58] £195 $300

WESTERN HEMISPHERE [1815] 58x53cm (23x21") Orig OL color. Close side margins as usual. Ref: Phillips (A) 731. [28] £195 $300

THORNTON   Try *Mount & Page*

PART OF NEW ENGLAND ... [1689 / 1706] In *The English Pilot, The Fourth Book*; First 3 editions only. 43x48cm (17x18½") Lt toning; else exc. Ref: Verner, ... *Coast Pilot* ..., facsimile ed, #14, pp.v-xx. [38] £9,089 $14,000

TILLOTSON

ZULULAND. THE SEAT OF THE WAR WITH THE ZULU KING ... [1879] In Supplement to *Bolton Weekly Journal*. Tillotson & Son. 54x41cm (21x16") Uncolored. [54] £280 $431

TINDAL   Try *Rapin*

A VIEW OF CASAL, A VERY STRONG CITY AND CASTLE IN ITALY ... [1744-47] Basire; Rapin's History. 36x48cm (14x19") Margins trimmed to plate marks [28] £175 $270

ATTACK OF THE REBELS UPON FORT PENOBSCOT IN THE PROVINCE OF NEW ENGLAND IN WHICH THEIR FLEET WAS TOTALLY DESTROYED AND THEIR ARMY DISPERSED THE 14TH AUGUST 1779 [1785] 36x38cm (14x15") Few creases. [14] £97 $150

PLAN OF THE CITY AND CITIDEL OF ANTWERP ... [1744-47] Basire, sc. 38x48cm (15x19") Margins trimmed to plate marks; lt offsetting. [28] £175 $270

PLAN OF THE TOWN AND FORTIFICATIONS OF GIBRALTAR ... [1744-47] Basire, sc. 38x61cm (15x23½") Vert folds; top & rt margins trimmed to platemarks. [28] £234 $360

PLAN OF TURIN AS BESIEGED IN 1706 ... [1744-47] 36x48cm (14½x19") Margins trimmed to plate marks. [28] £175 $270

TIRION

ALGEMEENE KAART VAN DE WESTINDISCHE EILANDEN. TE AMSTERDAM BY ISAAK TIRION [1744 - 1769] From *Nieuwe en Beknopte Hand-Atlas*. 35x46cm (13½x18") Orig color. Fine. [47] £315 $485
CARTA ACCURATA DELL'IMPERIO DEL GIAPPONE ... [c. 1738] Italian version. 25x32cm (9½x12½") Color. Ref: Campbell (Japan) #57. [52] £800 $1,232
DE HOOFDSTADT EN HAVEN, VAN'T EILAND PORTO RICO, IN DE WESTINDIEN [1769] From *Hedendaagsche Historie*. San Juan. 18x26cm (7x10½") Color. [25] £169 $260
GRONDVLAKTE VAN NIEUW ORLEANS, DE HOOFDSTAD VAN LOUISIANA [ON SHEET WITH] **DE UITLOOP VAN DE RIVIER MISSISIPPI** [AND] **DE OOSTELYKE INGANG VAN DE MISSISIPPI, MET EEN PLAN VAN HET FORT, 'T WELK HET KANAAL BEHEERSCHT** [c. 1765] 33x45cm (13x17½") Uncolored. [53] £300 $462
[SAME TITLE] [c. 1769] [same dimen] Later full color. VG. [30] £422 $650
HET WESTINDISCH EILAND MARTENIQUE VOLGENS DE NIEUWSTE WAARNEEMINGEN IN KAART GEBRAGT. 'T AMSTERDAM BY I. TIRION [1769] After Jefferys. 31x36cm (12x14½") Cut into rt margin. [14] £49 $75
KAART VAN HET WESTELYK GEDEELTE VAN NIEUW MEXICO EN VAN CALIFORNIA VOLGENS DE LAATSTE ONTDEKKINGEN DER JESUITEN EN ANDEREN. TE AMSTERDAM BY ISAAK TIRION, MDCCLXV [1765] 33x36cm (13x14") Orig wash col. Flawless. Ref: Wagner (NW) 608; Wheat (TM) 148. [46] £390 $600
[SAME TITLE] [1765-1767] 32x34cm (13x13½") Uncolored. Traces of orig folds. [53] £300 $462
NIEUWE KAART VAN DE GROOTBRITTANNISCHE VOLKPLANTINGEN IN NOORD AMERICA ... [1755] 36x45cm (14½x18") Full color. Pale edge darkening; o/w fine. [30] £325 $500
NIEUWE KAART VAN HET OOSTELYKSTE DEEL DER WEERELD [1753] 32x36cm (12½x14") Orig color. [16] £361 $556
NIEUWE KAART VAN HET WESTELYKSTE DEEL DER WEERELD ... [1754] Americas. 34x36cm (13x14") OL & wash color. [58] £195 $300
NIEUWE KAART VAN KANADA DE LANDEN AAN DE HUDSONS-BAAY EN DE NOORDWESTELYKE DEELEN VAN NOORD-AMERIKA. TE AMSTERDAM BY ISAAK TIRION [1769] 33x46cm (12½x17½") Ref: Phillips (A) 600. [28] £175 $270
[SAME TITLE] [1769] 31x44cm (12x17") OL & wash color. [58] £179 $275
NIEUWE KAART VAN'T KEIZERRYK JAPAN ... [1735] 27x32cm (10½x12½") Orig color. Ref: Campbell (Japan) #54. [52] £1,200 $1,848
NIEUWE WERELD KAART WAAR IN DE REIZEN VAN DEN HR. ANSON RONDSOM DE WERELD MET EEN GESTIPTE LINIE WORDEN AANGEWEZEN [1754] 23x40cm (9x16") Old color. Ref: Sabin 1641 [22] £292 $450
NUOVA CARTA DELLE ISOLE DI SUNDA, COME BORNEO, SUMATRA, IAVA GRANDE &C. FATTA IN AMSTERDAM PER ISAAC TIRION [c. 1770] Italian ed. 27x36cm (10½x14") Wash color. Exc. [63] £172 $265
QUEBEK, DE HOOFDSTAD VAN KANADA AAN DE RIVIER VAN ST. LAURENS: DOOR DE ENGELSCHEN BELEGERD EN BY VERDRAG BEMAGTIGD, IN'T JAAR 1759... [1769] Siege plan; reference key. 33x43cm (13x17") Rt margin cut as issued. [14] £120 $185
[SAME TITLE] [c. 1769] Based on Jefferys. [same dimen] Later color. Ref: Koeman III Tir 4. [28] £308 $475

TORNIELLO

SITUS PARTIUM PRAECIPUARUM TOTIUS ORBIS TERRARUM [1609] From *Annales Sacri et Profani ...* 19x37cm (7½x14½") Uncolored. Sl printer's crease lf; o/w fine. Ref: Shirley (W) 267, pl.210 [32] £1,266 $1,950
[SAME TITLE] [same date & dimen] State 1. Color.. [16] £1,875 $2,889
[SAME TITLE] [1610] State 2; "Nova Guinea" named. 20x38cm (7½x15") B&W. [16] £1,614 $2,487
[SAME TITLE] [1620] Dal Re, sc; Antwerp. 14x28cm (5½x11") Color. [16] £423 $651

TUNISON

TUNISON'S FLORIDA [c. 1883] Inset: Mouths of Mississippi. 25x30cm (10x12½") Color. [4] £29 $45

U.S.   Try *Freemont & other U.S. categories*

[ATLAS] **ATLAS OF THE PHILIPPINE ISLANDS** [1900] Jose Algue. 1st ed. Lithographed title, "Atlas de Filipinas. Coleccion de 30 Mapas. Trabajados por Delineantes Filipinos ... 1899" Washington: GPO. Folio; 30 colored maps. Orig cloth scuffed, frayed. [28] £438 $675
[ATLAS] **STATISTICAL ATLAS OF THE UNITED STATES BASED UPON RESULTS OF THE ELEVENTH CENSUS** [1898] Henry Gannett. Based on 1890 population data. Folio; 67 pp; 409 maps & diagrams. Ex lib. Clean [45] £97 $150

[BOOK] MAPS AND VIEWS TO ACCOMPANY MESSAGE AND DOCUMENTS [FROM THE PRESIDENT OF THE UNITED STATES] 1855-6. [1856] Quarto. 35 maps & views, many folding, relating to AR, CA, FL, IA, KS, MI, MN, NE, NM, NY, OH, OR, WA, WI, Red River & San Francisco. Several maps have internal tears; only good. [55] £162 $250

A MAP OF THE EXTREMITY OF CAPE COD INCLUDING THE TOWNSHIPS OF PROVINCETOWN & TRURO: WITH A CHART OF THEIR SEA COAST AND OF CAPE COD HARBOUR, STATE OF MASSACHUSETTS ... 1833, 34, 35 [1836] 4 joinable sheets, each about 73x88cm (28½x34½") Uncolored. Tears & chips, some into image, no significant loss; repairs on verso. [31] £584 $900

CHART OF THE HARBOR OF SAN JUAN, PUERTO RICO [1902] U.S. Congress. 18x23cm (7½x9") [25] £19 $30

CONSOLIDATED MAP OF INDIAN AND SETTLER'S LANDS IN BITTER ROOT VALLEY, STATE OF MONTANA [1890] H.B. Carrington, DOI. Shows "Indian lands in 40 acre tracts" and "Lands taken by Settlers". 36x18cm (14x7½") Fine. [18] £23 $35

EAST CENTRAL LOUISIANA [1860] Amer. State Papers. 25x30cm (10x12") OL color. Fine. [20] £49 $75

MAP ILLUSTRATING THE PLAN OF THE DEFENCES OF THE WESTERN & NORTH WESTERN FRONTIER, AS PROPOSED BY CHARLES GRATIOT ... [1837 (1861)] After Hood. 54x38cm (21x15") Orig OL color. Ref: Wheat (TM) 426. [46] £162 $250

MAP NO.2. SHOWING A CONTINUATION OF DETAILS OF FORT SMITH AND SANTA FE ROUTE ... [1849] Oklahoma section of 4-sheet map. 28x51cm (11x20") B&W. Ref: Variation on Wheat (TM) 640. [46] £65 $100

MAP OF ISLAND OF PORTO-RICO SHOWING ROADS, RAIL ROADS AND LIGHT HOUSES [1900] Dept. of Interior. 20x36cm (8x14") Later color. [44] £49 $75

MAP OF OREGON AND UPPER CALIFORNIA FROM THE SURVEY'S OF JOHN CHARLES FREMONT AND OTHER AUTHORITIES [1850] 2nd ed. 66x51cm (26x20") B&W. Folded as issued; VG. Ref: Wheat 613. [44] £162 $250

MAP OF PORTIONS OF LOWER CLEAR CREEK AND GILPIN COUNTIES SHOWING MINING CLAIMS IN THE VICINITY OF IDAHO SPRINGS COLORADO ... BY JAMES UNDERHILL ... U.S. DEP. MIN. SURVEYOR ... [c. 1906] 91x102cm (36x40") Red key color. On weak paper; repaired tears on side. [44] £179 $275

MAP OF PUBLIC LANDS OF PORTO RICO [1905] DOI; Norris Peters, Wash. 328 areas delineated. 36x18cm (14x7½") [25] £26 $40

MAP OF THE DES MOINES RAPIDS OF THE MISSISSIPPI [1866] N.B. Buford, H.M. Shreve; in American State Papers. 15x25cm (6x10½") Channels in red. VG. [20] £32 $50

MAP OF THE GREAT SALT LAKE AND ADJACENT COUNTRY IN THE TERRITORY OF UTAH. SURVEYED IN 1849 AND 1850 ... [IN SET WITH] MAP OF A RECONNOISSANCE BETWEEN FORTH LEAVENWORTH ON THE MISSOURI RIVER, AND THE GREAT SALT LAKE IN THE TERRITORY OF UTAH ... [1853] Maps by Gunnison & Preuss in volume accompanying report of Stansbury's Expedition. Dimensions: 112x76 cm (44½x30½") and 72x175cm (28½x69"). Cloth boards worn & lacking spine; maps VG to fine. Ref: Howes S884; Wheat (TM) III #764 & 765. [59] £179 $275

MAP OF THE ISLAND OF PORTO-RICO [1903] J.F. Callejo, Public Works Bureau; Wash: Norris Peters. 30x58cm (12x22½") [25] £23 $35

MAP OF THE MINING CLAIMS ADJOINING LEADVILLE [c. 1880] Source uncertain. 18x20cm (7x8") [13] £49 $75

MAP OF THE ROCK RIVER RAPIDS OF THE MISSISSIPPI [1866] N.B. Buford, H.M. Shreve; in American State Papers. 15x25cm (6x10") Channels in red. Good. [20] £23 $35

MAP SHOWING INDIAN RESERVATIONS IN THE UNITED STATES WEST OF THE 84TH MERIDIAN AND THE NUMBER OF INDIANS BELONGING THERETO 1881 [1881] DOI. 38x48cm (14½x18½") Color. Issued folded. [45] £52 $80

MAP SHOWING THE DIFFERENT ROUTES TRAVELLED OVER BY ... THE OVERLAND COMMAND IN THE SPRING OF 1855 FROM SALT LAKE CITY, UTAH, TO THE BAY OF SAN FRANCISCO [1855] Lts. Mowry & Steptoe. 56x51cm (22x20") B&W. Folded; fresh paper; good. [44] £58 $90

MAP SHOWING THE LANDS ASSIGNED TO THE EMIGRANT INDIANS ... [1836] After Lt. Hood's ms map. 48x46cm (18½x17½") B&W. Ref: Wheat (TM) 418. [46] £179 $275

MAP SHOWING THE PROPORTION OF DEATHS FROM CONSUMPTION TO DEATHS FROM ALL CAUSES ... [n.d.] From atlas accompanying the 9th census of the U.S. (1870). Eastern half of U.S. 48x38cm (19x15") Red shades indicates incidence. Also offered at same price: "... Deaths from Intestinal Diseases", "... Deaths from Enteric, Cerebro-Spinal and Typhus Fevers" and "... Deaths from Malarial Diseases". [56] £29 $45

MAP SHOWING THE SYSTEM OF REBEL FORTIFICATIONS ON THE MISSISSIPPI RIVER AT ISLAND NO.10 AND NEW MADRID, ALSO THE OPERATIONS OF THE U.S. FORCES UNDER GENERAL JOHN POPE AGAINST THESE POSITIONS [1866] Capt. Wm. Hoelcke. Joint Committee on the Conduct of the War; Senate Report No.142, 38th Cong., 2d Sess., Vol.2. 56x48cm (22x19") Good. Sl repair. Ref: Stephenson (CW) 299.8. [20] £292 $450

PARTS OF EASTERN AND SOUTHEASTERN ARIZONA, WESTERN AND SOUTHWESTERN NEW MEXICO ... [n.d.] Wheeler Survey Atlas Sheet No.83. 41x51cm (16x20") Issued folded. Tan & black. [44] £58 $90

PLAN OF THE FRONT PART OF THE CITY OF NEW ORLEANS IN 1818 [1860] Philie. Amer. State Papers. 18x56cm (7½x22") VG. [20] £32 $50

ROAD & RAILROAD MAP OF PORTO RICO [1906] U.S. Senate; Norris Peters, Wash. With 27 pp report. 33x64cm (13x24½") [25] £26 $40

SAN JUAN PORTO-RICO. LIMITS OF LANDS TO BE RETAINED BY THE NAVY DEPT. IN SAN JUAN [1901] M. Parks; Norris Peters, Wash. Detailed street plan. 36x51cm (14x19½") OL color. [25] £29 $45

SKETCH OF A DAYS TRAVEL [NEW MEXICO] [1845] Pub in Abert's *Through the Country of the Comanche Indians*. Raton Pass area. 20x13cm (7½x5") Ref: Howes (US) A10. [56] £39 $60

SKETCH OF GENERAL RILEY'S ROUTE THROUGH THE MINING DISTRICTS JULY AND AUG. 1849 [1850] By Lt. George H. Derby. Doc. 17, 31st Cong. 1st Sess. 53x51cm (21½x20") Color. Thin paper, orig folds strengthened; rt margin replaced, bottom redrawn; image very nice. Ref: Wheat, Gold Region, 79. [1] £325 $500

[SAME TITLE] [1850] 71x61cm (28x24") B&W. Folded as issued; exc. [44] £211 $325

SKETCH OF PART OF LOUISIANA ACCOMPANYING A REPORT OF THE COMMISSIONER OF THE GEN'L LAND OFFICE OF THE 12TH OF JANUARY 1829 [1860] Amer. State Papers. With diagrams. 58x48cm (22½x18½") OL color. Minor transferral & taping; VG. [20] £81 $125

SOIL MAP - PORTO RICO, ARECIBO SHEET [1902] C.W. Dorsey. Ponce to Arecibo in detail. 99x51cm (39x20") 36 colors. [25] £23 $35

THE SACRAMENTO VALLEY FROM THE AMERICAN RIVER TO BUTTE CREEK, SURVEYED AND DRAWN BY ORDER OF GEN. RILEY ... [1849 (1850)] Tyson; Derby. 54x45cm (21x18") B&W. Outer edge loss affecting 2" of border; o/w exc. Ref: Wheat (TM) 149. [44] £211 $325

U.S. COAST & GEODETIC SURVEY

COAST CHART NO.162 FROM CAPE CANAVERAL SOUTHWARD TO LATITUDE 27°41' [FL] [1892] Canvas-backed for use. 81x109cm (32x43") Trimmed into top neat line; lt smudged, mild offsetting; VG. [46] £243 $375

COAST CHART NO.164 JUPITER INLET TO HILLSBORO INLET [FL] [1897] Canvas-backed for use. 84x104cm (32½x41") Lt smudged, mild offsetting; VG. [46] £227 $350

COAST CHART NO.167 FLORIDA REEFS, FROM THE ELBOW TO LOWER MATECUMBE KEY [FL] [1878] Canvas-backed for use. 76x99cm (30x39") Lt smudged, mild offsetting; VG. [46] £227 $350

COAST CHART NO.170 FLORIDA REEFS, KEY WEST TO REBECCA SHOAL [FL] [1892] Canvas-backed for use. 84x104cm (32½x41") Lt smudged, mild offsetting; VG. [46] £260 $400

COAST CHART NO.171 FLORIDA REEFS, REBECCA SHOAL TO DRY TORTUGAS [FL] [1882] Canvas-backed. 84x104cm (32½x41") Lt smudged, mild offsetting; 3 side trimmed to neat line; VG. [46] £227 $350

COAST CHART NO.174 BIG MARCO PASS TO SAN CARLOS BAY [FL] [1890] Canvas-backed for use. 102x81cm (39½x32") Lt smudged, mild offsetting; VG. [46] £227 $350

COAST CHART NO.201 WEST END OF PECAN ISLAND TO THE MERMENTAU RIVER [LA] [1894] Canvas-backed for use. 84x94cm (32½x37") Lt smudged, mild offsetting; VG. [46] £227 $350

COAST CHART NO.202 CALCASIEU PASS TO SABINE LIGHT [LA] [1892] Canvas-backed for use. 84x109cm (32½x42½") Trimmed into lower lf neat line; lt smudged, mild offsetting; VG. [46] £227 $350

ENTRANCE TO TAMPA BAY [1895] Canvas-backed for use. 69x97cm (26½x37½") Lt smudged, mild offsetting; VG. [46] £282 $435

RECONNAISSANCE OF THE WESTERN COAST OF THE UNITED STATES LOWER SHEET FROM SAN FRANCISCO TO SAN DIEGO ... [IN SET WITH] MIDDLE SHEET FROM SAN FRANCISCO TO UMPQUAH RIVER ... [AND] NORTHERN SHEET FROM UMPQUAH RIVER TO THE BOUNDARY ... [1854-56 (1865)] 3 chart set; 9 to 17 views. Each about 59x57cm (23x22") Uncolored. Few spots; minimal or no fold browning; few repaired separations; VG to fine. Ref: cf. Schwartz & Ehrenberg, pl.174. [59] £243 $375

U.S. COAST SURVEY

A CHART EXHIBITING THE NORMAL COURSE & VELOCITY OF THE TIDAL CURRENT AT EBB IN BOSTON HARBOR [1848] 20x23cm (7½x9") [35] £26 $40

APPROACHES TO GRAND GULF MISS. [1864] F.H. Gerdes. Separately published, with ms note. 56x38cm (22x14½") Orig linen backing in contemporary paper folder. Somewhat browned; VG. [20] £162 $250

BOSTON HARBOR, MASSACHUSETTS [1857] 71x91cm (28x36") Uncolored. Folded; some browning, few fold junction tears. [36] £62 $95

BURLINGTON VERMONT [1872] Street plan, topography & buildings. 58x51cm (23x20") Uncol. [44] £39 $60

COAST FROM PEMAQUID POINT TO SEGUIN ISLAND [ME] [1879] 53x33cm (21x13") Uncolored. Folded. [36] £29 $45

DAMARISCOTTA AND MEDOMAK RIVERS [ME] [1872] 97x64cm (38x25½") Uncol. Folded. [36] £39 $60

GLOUCESTER HARBOR [MA] [1879] 46x33cm (17½x13½") Uncolored. Folded. [36] £36 $55

HARBOR OF NEW HAVEN [1872] 84x61cm (33x24") Uncolored. [44] £39 $60

HARBOR OF NEW LONDON [1849] 51x41cm (19½x16") On sturdy paper. [35] £42 $65

HELL GATE AND ITS APPROACHES [1849] 76x91cm (30x36") On sturdy paper. [35] £81 $125

HUNTINGTON BAY [1849] 36x43cm (14x17½") On sturdy paper. [35] £42 $65

LYNN HARBOR, MASSACHUSETTS [1864] 44x37cm (17x14½") Uncolored. Folded. [36] £39 $60

MAP ILLUSTRATING THE OPERATIONS OF THE U.S. FORCES AGAINST VICKSBURG [1863] J.W. Maedel. Fourth of 5 states; shows "Hard Times", not "Coffee Point". 43x41cm (17½x16½") Partial color. Dissected, laid down on cotton. Fabric fragile, torn at folds; good. Ref: Stephenson (CW) 289.5. [20] £649 $1,000

MAP OF A PART OF LOUISIANA AND MISSISSIPPI [1863] H. Lindenkohl. One of 3 issues, omitting "Molitor" as lithographer; below, "Line of marsh [sic] of Gen. Banks corps d'armee ..." 66x71cm (25½x28½") March in red; water in blue. Dissected, laid down on linen; VG. Ref: Stephenson (CW) 231.5. [20] £1,623 $2,500

MOUTH OF THE COLUMBIA RIVER [1851] With view. 43x69cm (17x27") Fold repair; VG. [19] £94 $145

OYSTER BAY TO MATAGORDA BAY, TEXAS COAST CHART NO.107 [1858] 51x102cm (19½x39½") OL color. Fine. [46] £110 $170

OYSTER OR SYOSSET BAY [1849] 46x36cm (17½x14") On sturdy paper. [35] £42 $65

PLAN OF FORT JACKSON, SHOWING THE EFFECT OF THE BOMBARDMENT BY THE U.S. MORTAR FLOTILLA AND GUNBOATS, APRIL 18TH TO 24TH 1862 [c. 1865] E. Hergesheimer. 33x48cm (12½x18½") Waterstained, browned; fold tears, margin chips; fair. [20] £81 $125

PORTSMOUTH HARBOR NEW HAMPSHIRE [1866 (1878)] 48x66cm (18½x26") Linen backed chart for use. Lt soiled, even age-tone; sl linen separation at corners; good. [6] £123 $190

PRELIMINARY CHART OF HUDSON RIVER FROM TELLER'S POINT TO THE MOUTH [1855] Little land detail. 97x38cm (38x15") Minor browning; a fold split. [36] £29 $45

PUERTO RICO ... [1899] From Spanish, British & U.S. surveys; improved from 1898 ed; scale 1/400,000. 56x84cm (21½x33½") OL color. [25] £55 $85

PUGET SOUND [1867] 71x43cm (28x17") Later col. Fold splits & sh tear repaired; generally VG. [13] £292 $450

RECONNAISSANCE OF THE WESTERN COAST OF THE UNITED STATES FROM GRAY'S HARBOR TO THE ENTRANCE OF ADMIRALTY INLET [1853] 4 views. 37x44cm (14½x17½") Fine. [19] £97 $150

RECONNAISSANCE OF THE WESTERN COAST OF THE UNITED STATES FROM SAN FRANCISCO TO SAN DIEGO [1852] 58x58cm (23x23") Uncolored. VG. [45] £97 $150

SAN FRANCISCO PENINSULA [1869] Much land detail. 74x43cm (28½x17") Later color. Fold repairs; o/w fine. [13] £292 $450

SAN JUAN HARBOR PUERTO RICO [1900] Much detail; scale: 1/10,000. 84x99cm (32½x39½") OL color. [25] £97 $150

SHEET NO.1. MISSISSIPPI RIVER, RODNEY, ST. JOSEPH, BRUINSBURG. RECONNAISSANCE FOR THE USE OF THE MISSISSIPPI SQUADRON ... [1864] F.H. Gerdes. 30x43cm (12x16½") Modern OL color. Fold browning; good. [20] £97 $150

SHEET NO.2. MISSISSIPPI RIVER GRAND GULF, TURNER'S PT., NEW CARTHAGE. RECONNAISSANCE FOR THE USE OF THE MISSISSIPPI SQUADRON [1864] F.H. Gerdes. Incl a Jefferson Davis plantation. 53x41cm (20½x16½") Modern color. Lt fold browning; good. [20] £97 $150

SKETCH F SECTION VI COAST OF FLORIDA 1848-61 [1862] Whole peninsula; insets: St. Johns River, Charlotte Harbor, Indian River. 64x41cm (25½x16½") Uncolored. Orig folds; VG. [4] £42 $65

SKETCH F SECTION VI WESTERN COAST OF FLORIDA 1848-51 [c. 1851] Peninsula west coast; 2 sailing direction sets. 58x41cm (23x16½") Uncolored. Orig folds; lf margin trimmed below binding tab; o/w VG. [4] £29 $45

SKETCH II SHOWING THE PROGRESS OF THE SURVEY IN SECTION NO.8 [1855] AL & LA. 38x84cm (14½x33½") Minor fold repairs; VG. [20] £55 $85
SKETCH II SHOWING THE PROGRESS OF THE SURVEY IN SECTION NO. VIII FROM 1846 TO 1862 ... [ON SHEET WITH] PLAN OF FORT JACKSON SHOWING THE EFFECT OF THE BOMBARDMENT [AND] RECONNAISSANCE OF THE MISSISSIPPI RIVER BELOW FORTS JACKSON AND ST. PHILIP ... [1862] F.H. Gerdes et al. 48x84cm (19½x33") Fold browning; good. [20] £130 $200
SKETCH J. NO. 3 SHOWING THE PROGRESS OF THE SURVEY OF WASHINGTON SOUND AND VICINITY [1855] Shows triangulation. 41x36cm (16x13½") Fold browning & repair; VG. [19] £36 $55
SKETCH OF THE SOUTH WEST PASS AT AND NEAR THE GULF OF MEXICO [1857] Scale: 6½"/mile. 94x69cm (36½x26½") Good. [20] £65 $100
SOUTHWEST HARBOR AND SOMES SOUND, MAINE [1872] 56x38cm (21½x15") Uncol. Folded. [36] £26 $40
THE PROGRESSIVE CHANGES IN SANDY HOOK FROM 1779-1851 [1851] 38x30cm (14½x11½") [36] £32 $50

U.S. EXPLORING EXPEDITION

CHART OF THE ANTARCTIC CONTINENT SHEWING THE ICY BARRIER ATTACHED TO IT. ... [1840 (1844)] Wilkes. Lithographed chart from accompanying atlas. 105 to 165° West. 61x86cm (23½x34") Fold lines. [15] £90 $139
MAP OF THE OREGON TERRITORY ... [1849] 23x33cm (8½x13") VG. [19] £97 $150

U.S. GEOLOGICAL SURVEY

[COLORADO: PANORAMIC VIEWS] [1877] From *Atlas of Colorado*. F.V Hayden. 3 panels: Pikes Peak Group; Sawatch Range; Elk Mountains. 76x94cm (30x37") Wash color. Sl water mark top edge. Another, with views of Mesa Verde, Quartzite Group, La Plata Mountains offered at same price. [44] £104 $160
ASPEN SPECIAL MAP [CO] [1898] Street & mine plan; identical to Aspen Monograph map, but separately issued. 43x38cm (17x15") [45] £58 $90
BITTERROOT FOREST RESERVE SHOWING LAND CLASSIFICATION [1898] J.B. Leiberg. 66x61cm (26x24") Full color. [45] £39 $60
DRAINAGE MAP OF COLORADO [1877] From *Atlas of Colorado*. F.V. Hayden. 76x94cm (30x37") Some color. [44] £97 $150
ECONOMIC MAP OF COLORADO [same date, source & dimen] Color coding. [44] £97 $150
[SAME TITLE] [1878] Color keyed. 64x89cm (25½x35") Browning at folds; o/w good. [13] £91 $140
GENERAL GEOLOGICAL MAP OF COLORADO [1877] From *Atlas of Colorado*. F.V. Hayden. 76x94cm (30x37") Substantial color coding. [44] £97 $150
INDIAN TERRITORY [1898] South & east Oklahoma. 51x46cm (20x18") Uncolored. Folded as issued; minor browning; o/w good. [12] £81 $125
MAP OF ALASKA ... [1903 (1907)] By E.C. Berhard under direction of R.U. Goode. 43x53cm (17x21") Tinted. [45] £49 $75
MAP OF THE ELK MOUNTAINS COLORADO FROM SURVEY BY G.B. CHITTENDEN IN 1874 WITH GEOLOGY BY F.V. HAYDEN AND W.H. HOLMES [1876] Hayden Survey. 48x25cm (19x10") Color. [44] £49 $75
NORTHERN CENTRAL COLORADO [1877] From *Atlas of Colorado*. F.V. Hayden. Geological map; one of 6 in series. 76x94cm (30x37") Full color coding. [44] £81 $125
PARTS OF WESTERN WYOMING AND SOUTHEASTERN IDAHO [c. 1879] G.R. Bechler, F.A. Clark. NY: Bien & Co. 58x58cm (23x23½") Minor stain top margin; VG. [18] £97 $150
PRELIMINARY MAP OF CENTRAL COLORADO SHOWING THE REGION SURVEYED IN 1873 AND 1874 ... [1876] Hayden Survey. 64x57cm (25x22") Uncolored. [44] £58 $90
RECONNAISSANCE MAP OF MT. MCKINLEY REGION ALASKA [1904] 46x30cm (18x12") Some color. [45] £49 $75
TETON FOREST RESERVE AND SOUTHERN PART OF YELLOWSTONE PARK FOREST RESERVE SHOWING LAND CLASSIFICATION AND WOODED AREAS [1898] T.S Brandagee. Jackson Hole region. 51x38cm (20x15") Color. [45] £39 $60
THE COAL AND GOLD FIELDS OF ALASKA TOGETHER WITH THE PRINCIPAL STEAMER ROUTES AND TRAILS [1898] Bright chromolithograph. 61x71cm (24x28") With descriptive documents. VG. [45] £143 $220
TOPOGRAPHY OF THE DENVER BASIN COLORADO [1888] Boulder to Parker. 56x53cm (22x21") Minor color. [45] £49 $75
YELLOWSTONE NATIONAL PARK AND PORTION OF YELLOWSTONE FOREST PRESERVE [1904] 46x61cm (18x23½") Color keyed geology. Waterstain outside printed area. [58] £32 $50

U.S. HYDROGRAPHIC OFFICE
ANEGADA PASSAGE WITH ADJACENT ISLANDS [1886] Corrected to 1894. Virgin Is., Saba & St. Barts. 58x102cm (23x39½") Color. [27] £146 $225

U.S. PACIFIC R.R. SURVEY
FROM GREAT SALT LAKE TO THE HUMBOLDT MTS. ... [1853] 53x46cm (20½x18") Browning along folds; edge chipping. [12] £49 $75
MAP NO.1 FROM SAN FRANCISCO BAY TO THE PLAINS OF LOS ANGELES ... BY LIEUT. JOHN G. PARKE ... 1854 & 55 [1858] 74x89cm (29x35") Uncolored. Folded as issued; minor browns at folds. [45] £78 $120
MAP NO.2 FROM THE NORTHERN BOUNDARY OF CALIFORNIA TO THE COLUMBIA RIVER ... BY LIEUT. R.S. WILLIAMSON ... 1855 [1858] 71x61cm (28x24") Uncolored. Folded as issued. [45] £78 $120
PRELIMINARY SKETCH OF THE NORTHERN PACIFIC RAIL ROAD EXPLORATION AND SURVEY FROM RIVIERE DES LACS TO THE ROCKY MOUNTAINS MADE IN 1853 BY I.I. STEVENS, GOVERNOR OF WASHINGTON TERRITORY [1853] 58x86cm (23x34") Uncolored. Fragile, browned at folds; repaired on reverse, sm loss; encapsulated; fair. [19] £179 $275
ROUTE NEAR THE 47TH AND 49TH PARALLELS. MAP NO. 3. ROCKY MOUNTAINS TO PUGET SOUND ... [1854] I.I. Stevens. 62x92cm (24x36") Fold repair & browning; sm hole in vert fold; VG. [19] £127 $195
ROUTES IN OREGON AND CALIFORNIA. MAP NO. 2. FROM THE NORTHERN BOUNDARY OF CALIFORNIA TO THE COLUMBIA RIVER ... [1855] Lt. H.L. Abbott. 69x58cm (27½x23½") Fold repairs; VG. [19] £97 $150

U.S. STATE SURVEYS
A PLAT EXHIBITING THE STATE OF THE SURVEYS IN THE STATE OF FLORIDA WITH REFERENCES [1854] 61x61cm (24x24") Later color. Issued folded. [45] £65 $100
[SAME TITLE] [1855] [same dimen] Uncolored. Folded as issued; clean. [44] £49 $75
INDIAN TERRITORY [1885] GLO: 1887. 61x81cm (24x32") Chromolithograph; tribes color coded. Fine. [44] £195 $300
[SAME TITLE] [1887] Compiled to accompany Catlin's *Indian Gallery*, by Donaldson. 62x82cm (24x32½") Full orig OL & wash color. [14] £65 $100
MAP OF A PART OF THE WASHINGTON TERRITORY TO ACCOMPANY THE REPORT OF THE SURVEYOR GENERAL [1855] 38x51cm (15x20") Uncolored. VG. [44] £52 $80
[SAME TITLE] [1855] 38x48cm (14½x19") Uncolored. Fine. [56] £58 $90
MAP OF A PART OF WASHINGTON TERRITORY EAST OF THE CASCADE MTS. SHOWING TOPOGRAPHY OF THE MINES REGION &C. TO ACCOMPANY THE REPORT OF E. GIDDINGS [1862] Grand Coulee to Rockies; much of ID. 46x58cm (18x23") Uncolored. Issued folded; mild browning on fold. [45] £58 $90
MAP OF INDIAN TERRITORY AND OKLAHOMA [1890] Folding map; 13 RRs listed. 57x75cm (22½x29½") Full color coding. [14] £162 $250
MAP OF LOUISIANA REPRESENTING THE SEVERAL LAND DISTRICTS ... [1849] 39x43cm (15½x16½") Fine. [20] £55 $85
MAP OF OREGON TERRITORY WEST OF THE CASCADE MOUNTAINS [1855] 46x28cm (18x11") Uncolored. [44] £49 $75
MAP OF PART OF LOUISIANA NORTH OF THE BASE LINE [c. 1828] 28x30cm (11x12") OL color. Minor transferral; VG. [20] £49 $75
MAP OF PUBLIC SURVEYS IN COLORADO TERRITORY [1863] 41x56cm (16½x22") [58] £146 $225
MAP OF PUBLIC SURVEYS IN THE TERRITORY OF WASHINGTON ... [1862] Incl present ID. 41x81cm (16x32") Uncolored. Folded. [45] £58 $90
MAP OF THAT PART OF WASHINGTON TERRITORY LYING WEST OF THE CASCADE MOUNTS. [1856] 38x25cm (15x10") VG. [19] £65 $100
[SAME TITLE] [1857] [same dimen] Uncolored. [56] £52 $80
MAP OF THE COLORADO TERRITORY [1862] 41x56cm (16½x22") Uncolored. [58] £146 $225
MAP OF THE DISTRICT NORTH OF RED RIVER LOUISIANA [1839] 26th Cong., 1st Sess. W.J. Stone. 25x28cm (9½x11½") OL color. Margin stains, else clean; fine. [20] £26 $40
MAP OF THE OREGON TERRITORY WEST OF THE CASCADE MOUNTAINS [1855] 46x25cm (17½x10½") [56] £52 $80
MAP OF THE SOUTH WESTERN DISTRICT LOUISIANA [1837] 25th Cong., 2nd Sess., Doc.11, No.7. 33x25cm (13x10") OL color. Fine. [20] £32 $50
MAP OF THE TERRITORY OF HAWAII [1904] GLO. 56x84cm (22x33") 3 colors. [9] £23 $35

MAP SHOWING THE EXTENT OF SURVEYS IN THE TERRITORY OF UTAH [1856] Utah Lake to ID. 84x41cm (32½x15½") Uncolored. [56] £65 $100

MAP SHOWING THE PROGRESS OF THE PUBLIC SURVEYS IN KANSAS AND NEBRASKA ... [1862] Coverage to western parts. 62x49cm (24x19") Uncolored. Exc. [45] £52 $80

OKLAHOMA TERRITORY [1906] North & west Oklahoma; Guthrie is capital. 36x56cm (13½x22") Printed color. Folded as issued; some browning; o/w fine. [12] £55 $85

SKETCH OF PUBLIC SURVEYS IN NEW MEXICO & ARIZONA [1866] GLO. Exploration routes, wagon roads, topo. Mineral areas in col. 53x71cm (21x28") Browning on folds; splits repaired, minor loss. [12] £250 $385

SKETCH OF THE PUBLIC SURVEYS IN KANSAS AND NEBRASKA [1855] 51x30cm (20x11½") Folded; clean, crisp. 1856 edition, with differences, offered at same price. [56] £39 $60

SKETCH OF THE PUBLIC SURVEYS IN WISCONSIN AND TERRITORY OF MINNESOTA [1855] GLO. 46x53cm (17½x21") Later color. Fold repairs; else good. [12] £39 $60

SOUTH EASTERN DISTRICT LOUISIANA [1837] 25th Cong., 2nd Sess., Doc.11, No.9. 23x28cm (9x11") OL color. Fine. [20] £32 $50

[SAME TITLE] [1839] 26th Cong., 1st Sess. W.J. Stone. 23x28cm (9½x11½") OL col. Fine. [20] £26 $40

STATE OF IOWA [1878] From *Atlas of the States and Territories over which Land Surveys Have Been Extended*. Much detail. 74x64cm (29x25") Color. Minor discoloration lower c'fold; o/w VG. [45] £91 $140

STATE OF KANSAS [1879] GLO. 56x76cm (21½x30") OL & full color. Lt age-toning; sm tear across neat line where attached; near fine. [6] £156 $240

STATE OF LOUISIANA [1879] GLO. Topo & demographic map. 86x69cm (34x27") Full printed color. Fine. [20] £130 $200

STATE OF MONTANA [1897] GLO. Friedenwald Co., Baltimore. 84x124cm (32½x49") OL & full color. Folded; sl tears at margin; near fine. [6] £182 $280

TERRITORY OF ARIZONA [1896] Earliest ed. 53x43cm (21x17") Full color. [45] £52 $80

TERRITORY OF IDAHO [1879] C. Roeser; NY: Bien & Co. Orig linen backing. 84x56cm (33x22") Printed OL color. Minor stains; VG. [18] £114 $175

TERRITORY OF IDAHO [1879] 56x33cm (22x13") Later color. VG. [45] £52 $80

WASHINGTON TERRITORY [1884] 56x71cm (22x28") Color. Folds. [45] £81 $125

U.S. UNION & CONFEDERATE ARMIES ATLAS

BATTLE-FIELD OF WINCHESTER VA. SEPT 19, 1864 ... [ON SHEET WITH] BATTLE-FIELDS OF FISHER'S HILL AND CEDAR CREEK, VIRGINIA ... [1891-1895] 43x71cm (17x28") Color. Perforations at edge, maps unaffected. [44] £39 $60

GENERAL TOPOGRAPHICAL MAP SHEET XVIII [MISSOURI & TENNESSEE] [1893] Plate CLIII. 43x71cm (16½x27½") Partial printed color. VG. [20] £71 $110

GENERAL TOPOGRAPHICAL MAP SHEET XX [MISSISSIPPI & LOUISIANA] [1893] Plate CLV. Vicksburg at ctr. 43x69cm (16½x27½") Printed OL color. Fine. [20] £81 $125

GENERAL TOPOGRAPHICAL MAP SHEET XXI [LOUISIANA] [1896] Gulf Coast to Red River. 43x71cm (16½x27½") Printed OL color. Laid down on linen. Little browned; good. [20] £65 $100

GENERAL TOPOGRAPHICAL MAP SHEET XXIII [N.E. TEXAS; N.W. LOUISIANA] [1893] Plate CLVIII. 46x74cm (18½x29") Partly printed color. Fine. [20] £97 $150

[SAME TITLE] [1894] 43x71cm (16½x27½") Printed OL color. Close side margins as issued. [46] £81 $125

MAP OF NORTHEASTERN VIRGINIA AND VICINITY OF WASHINGTON [1891-95] Plate VII. 41x69cm (16½x27") Chromolithograph. Minor margin flaws; good. [50] £192 $295

MAP OF TEXAS AND PART OF NEW MEXICO ... [1891-95] Dated 1857. 2 unrelated maps at rt. 42x69cm (16½x27") [13] £114 $175

[SAME TITLE] ... [1891-95] 43x71cm (17x28") Some color. VG. [45] £114 $175

MAP OF THE BATTLE-FIELDS OF HARPER'S FERRY AND SHARPSBURG [ON SHEET WITH] ANTIETAM [1891-95] Plate XXIX. 41x69cm (16½x27") Chromolithograph. Fine. [50] £185 $285

MAP OF THE BATTLE OF ANTIETAM FOUGHT ON THE 16TH AND 17TH OF SEPTEMBER, 1862 ... [1891-95] Plate XXVIII. With 5 other maps of battle. 43x71cm (17x28") Color. [44] £39 $60

[SAME TITLE] [1891-95] 41x69cm (16½x27") Chromolithograph. Fine. [50] £185 $285

PLAN OF THE BATTLE-FIELD AT BULL RUN, JULY 21ST 1861 [ON SHEET WITH] MAP OF THE BATTLE-FIELDS OF MANASSAS, AND THE SURROUNDING REGION [1891-95] Plate III. 41x69cm (16x27") Chromolithograph. Sm marginal loss; fine. [50] £185 $285

U.S. WAR DEPARTMENT

ANTIETAM, PREPARED BY BVT. BRIG. GENL. N. MICHLER ... [1867 (c.1872)] 58x71cm (23x28") Little color. Ref: Stephenson (CW) 245.85. [45] £146 $225

APPOMATTOX COURT HOUSE ... [1867 (c.1872)] From *Military Maps ... Armies of the Potomac and James*. 76x58cm (30x23") Uncolored. VG. Ref: Stephenson (CW) 525.3. [45] £91 $140

BATTLEFIELD IN FRONT OF FRANKLIN, TENN. ... NOVEMBER 30TH, 1864 [1874] 71x46cm (28x18") Some color. Ref: Stephenson (CW) 423, no lithographer given. [45] £179 $275

BATTLEFIELD IN FRONT OF NASHVILLE ... DEC. 15TH AND 16TH, 1864 [1866] Bowen, Phila. 33x38cm (13x15") Positions in color. Unfolded offprint on heavy stock; VG. Ref: Consistent with Stephenson (CW) 432. [45] £91 $140

BERMUDA HUNDRED ... [VA] [1867 (c.1872)] From *Military Maps ... Armies of the Potomac and James*. 51x74cm (20x29") Some color. Ref: Stephenson (CW) 525b.3. [45] £91 $140

CHANCELLORVILLE, PREPARED BY BVT. BRIG. GENL. N. MICHLER ... [1867 (c.1872)] From *Military Maps ... Armies of the Potomac and James*. 56x64cm (22x25") Uncolored. VG. Ref: Stephenson (CW) 528.3. [45] £97 $150

ECONOMIC FEATURES OF CENTRAL COLORADO [1876] From Wheeler, 43x51cm (17x20") Tan & black. Fold discoloration outside image. Ref: Phillips (a) 1281. [44] £58 $90

ECONOMIC FEATURES OF PARTS OF NORTH CENTRAL NEW MEXICO, ATLAS SHEET 70 (C) [1877] From Wheeler, 41x51cm (16x20") Full color. Issued folded; minor discoloration at edge. [44] £58 $90

ECONOMIC FEATURES OF PARTS OF SOUTH'N COLORADO AND NORTH'N NEW MEXICO, ATLAS SHEET 70 (A) [1877] From Wheeler, 41x51cm (16x20") Full color. Issued folded; fold repairs verso, a sm loss outside image. [44] £52 $80

ECONOMICAL FEATURES OF S.W. COLORADO, SAN JUAN MINING REGION, ATLAS SHEET NO. 61 (C) [1877-78] From Wheeler, 43x51cm (17x20") Full soft color. Issued folded. Ref: Phillips (a) 1281. [44] £78 $120

FREDERICKSBURG, PREPARED BY BVT. BRIG. GENL. N. MICHLER ... [1867 (c.1872)] From *Military Maps ... Armies of the Potomac and James*. 71x58cm (28x23") Uncolored. VG. Ref: Stephenson (CW) 553.7. [45] £114 $175

HARPERS FERRY, PREPARED BY BVT. BRIG. GENL. N. MICHLER ... [same date & source] 58x71cm (23x28") Uncolored. VG. Ref: Stephenson (CW) 697.6. [45] £97 $150

MAP ILLUSTRATING THE MILITARY OPERATIONS IN FRONT OF ATLANTA, GA. FROM THE PASSAGE OF PEACH TREE CREEK, JULY 19TH 1864 ... [1875] NY: Graphic Co. 71x79cm (28x31") Some color. Consistent toning. Ref: Stephenson (CW) 143. [45] £156 $240

MAP ILLUSTRATING THE PLAN OF THE DEFENSES OF THE WESTERN FRONTIER, AS PROPOSED BY MAJ. GEN. GAINES, IN HIS PLAN DATED FEB 28TH, 1838 [1838] From Gaines report, *The Defense of the Western Frontier* .... By D. Burr; litho by P. Haas. 61x38cm (23½x14½") Color. Soft aging of very thin paper; archival tape tear repair. Ref: Wheat (TM) vol.2, #432. [1] £130 $200

MAP OF MILITARY RECONNAISSANCE FROM FORT TAYLOR TO THE COEUR D'ALENE MISSION, WASHINGTON TERRITORY ... [1858] Under direction of Capt. Humphreys by Lt. Mullan. 56x53cm (22x21") Uncolored. [44] £65 $100

MAP OF PORT HUDSON AND VICINITY [1875] Civil War topo & position map. 86x64cm (34x24½") Printed OL color. Rough margins; 2 long tears repaired; VG. Ref: Stephenson (CW) #238. [20] £195 $300

MAP OF THE BATTLEFIELD OF BIG BLACK WATER BRIDGE MISSISSIPPI ... MAY 17TH, 1863 ... [1875] 48x46cm (19x18") Some color. Sl loss to corner, image unaffected; 2 sm tears repaired. Ref: Stephenson (CW) 264. [45] £179 $275

MAP OF THE BATTLEFIELD OF CHATTANOOGA ... 1864 [1875] 74x69cm (29x27") Some color. Lt paper; loss at lf, image unaffected. Ref: Consistent with Stephenson (CW) 405 & 406 but no lithographer given. [45] £130 $200

MAP OF THE BATTLEFIELD OF GETTYSBURG JULY 1ST, 2ND, 3RD 1863. ... [SET OF 3 MAPS:] FIRST DAY'S BATTLE [WITH] SECOND DAY'S BATTLE [AND] THIRD DAY'S BATTLE [1876] Boston: John B. Bachelder; engr by Bien. Chromolithographic color. 3 maps, each 89x71cm (35x28") Exc. Ref: Stephenson (CW) 325. [45] £876 $1,350

MAP OF THE BATTLEFIELD OF ROANOKE ID., FEB. 8TH 1862. DRAWN BY LT. ANDREWS ... [1870's] 2 maps: battlefield; island. 41x64cm (16x25") Some color. VG. Ref: Stephenson (CW) 317. [45] £162 $250

MAP OF THE DEPARTMENT OF THE COLUMBIA ... [1881] Lt. T. Symons. 79x104cm (31x40½") Printed OL color. Minor fold repair; browning; orange ms cross; fine. [19] £114 $175

MAP OF THE FIELD OF SHILOH, NEAR PITTSBURGH LANDING, TENN. SHEWING THE POSITIONS OF THE U.S. FORCES UNDER THE COMMAND OF MAJ. GENL. U.S. GRANT, U.S. VOL. ON THE 6TH AND 7TH OF APRIL, 1862 ... [1866] J. Bien, NY. 46x64cm (18x25") Positions in color. Wear at edge, image unaffected. Ref: Stephenson (CW) 437. [45] £211 $325

MAP OF THE HARBOR OF ST. LOUIS MISSISSIPPI RIVER [1837] Surveyed by Lt. R.E. Lee. 33x102cm (13x40") Uncolored. [44] £114 $175

MAP OF THE MISSOURI RIVER IN THE VICINITY OF OMAHA ... [1878] With part of Omaha incl UP shops. 23x30cm (8½x11½") Later color. [44] £49 $75

MAP OF THE REGION BETWEEN GETTYSBURG PA. AND APPOMATTOX COURT HOUSE, VA. EXHIBITING THE CONNECTION BETWEEN THE CAMPAIGN AND BATTLEFIELD MAPS PREPARED BY ... MICHLER ... [AND WEYSS, THOMPSON & DE LA CAMP] [c. 1869] 2 joined sheets 107x69cm (42x27") Some color. Ref: Phillips (A) 3688,1. [45] £130 $200

MAP OF THE SIEGE OF VICKSBURG, MISS. BY U.S. FORCES UNDER ... MAJ. GENL. U.S. GRANT ... AUG. 20TH 1863. ENGR. ON STONE BY J. SCHEDLER., N.Y. [c. 1863-64] Confederate forces in red. 74x69cm (29x27") VG. Ref: Stephenson (CW) 285. [45] £179 $275

MAP OF THE TERRITORY OF MINNESOTA, EXHIBITING THE ROUTE OF THE EXPEDITION TO THE RED RIVER OF THE NORTH, IN THE SUMMER OF 1849, BY CAPTN. JOHN POPE [1849] From *Report of an Exploration of the Territory of Minnesota.* 63x72cm (25x28") B&W. Rice paper backing; repaired 2" tear; fine. Ref: Phillips (M) p.432. [48] £357 $550

MAP OF THE TERRITORY OF NEW MEXICO [1846-1847] Rio Grand valley. Accompanied by J.W. Abert narrative. 64x51cm (25x19½") Folded. Ref: Howes (US) A11. [11] £192 $295

MAP OF THE UNITED STATES TERRITORY OF OREGON WEST OF THE ROCKY MOUNTAINS, EXHIBITING THE VARIOUS TRADING DEPOTS OR FORTS OCCUPIED BY THE BRITISH HUDSON BAY COMPANY. ... [1838] Under direction of Col. Abert, compiled by Capt. Hood; drawn by Stansbury. 44x52cm (17½x20½") Uncolored. Exc. [56] £227 $350

MAP OF THE UPPER END OF MEMPHIS HARBOR [1891] G.W. Roessler. 30x25cm (12x10") Fine. [20] £55 $85

MAP[S] ILLUSTRATING THE MILITARY OPERATIONS OF THE ATLANTA CAMPAIGN ... 1864 [SET OF 5 MAPS] [1874-1877] Tennessee River to Oostanaula River; Resaca to Ackworth; Rome to Marietta; Kennesaw Mountain to Atlanta; Chattahoochie River to Jonesboro. Dimensions vary around 60x75cm (24x30"). Some color. Exc. Ref: Stephenson (CW) 131 [45] £876 $1,350

MAP SHOWING THE SYSTEM OF CONFEDERATE FORTIFICATIONS ON THE MISSISSIPPI RIVER AT ISLAND NO.10 AND NEW MADRID ALSO THE OPERATIONS OF THE UNITED STATES FORCES UNDER GENERAL JOHN POPE AGAINST THESE POSITIONS [c. 1866] Capt. Wm. Hoelcke. Joint Committee on the Conduct of the War; Senate Report No.142, 38th Cong., 2d Sess., Vol.2. 53x46cm (21x18") Some color. Ref: Stephenson (CW) 300. [45] £162 $250

MILITARY MAP SHOWING THE MARCHES OF THE UNITED STATES FORCES UNDER COMMAND OF MAJ. GENL. W.T. SHERMAN, U.S.A. DURING THE YEARS 1863, 1864, 1865. COMPILED BY ORDER OF MAJ. GENL. W.T. SHERMAN ... MILITARY DIVISION OF THE MISSISSIPPI ... [c. 1865] Memphis to Savannah to Virginia. 66x91cm (26x36") Minor discoloration below; overall exc. Ref: Stephenson (CW) 73. [45] £227 $350

MISSISSIPPI RIVER SHEET NO.3 [AND] SHEET NO.4 [c. 1863] From Cairo to St. Louis survey. 58x38cm (22½x15") Fold browning; VG. [20] £97 $150

NEW MAP OF TENNESSEE BY CAPT. MICHLER ... [1863] Civil War map. 56x81cm (22x32") Uncolored. Folded as issued. Ref: Stephenson (CW) 394. [45] £81 $125

NORTH ANNA, PREPARED BY BVT. BRIG. GENL. N. MICHLER ... [VA] [1867 (c.1872)] From *Military Maps ... Armies of the Potomac and James.* 41x48cm (16x19") Positions in color. VG. Ref: Stephenson (CW) 590.1. [45] £65 $100

OFFICIAL COPY OF A MAP ACCOMPANYING THE REPORT OF MAJ. D. FERGUSON ... ON THE ROUTES FROM TUCSON TO LIBERTAD AND LOBOS BAY ... [1863] Rio Grand to Los Angeles. 18x36cm (7x14") Uncolored. [45] £81 $125

OUTLINE MAP OF PUERTO RICO ... ADJUTANT GENERAL'S OFFICE [1899] Norris Peters, Wash. Detailed; 2½ miles/inch. 71x127cm (28x50") OL color. [25] £81 $125

PART OF CENTRAL COLORADO. ATLAS SHEET NO. 53(C) [1877] From Wheeler, 43x51cm (17x20") Tan & black. Fold discoloration outside image. Ref: Phillips (a) 1281,68. [44] £58 $90

PART OF SOUTHWESTERN COLORADO ATLAS SHEET NO. 61(D) [1878] From Wheeler, 43x51cm (17x20") Issue folded. Ref: Phillips (a) 1281. [44] £52 $80

PETERSBURG AND FIVE FORKS ... [1867 (c.1872)] From *Military Maps ... Armies of the Potomac and James*. 56x79cm (22x31") Some color. Ref: Stephenson (CW) 607.9. [45] £91 $140

PLAN OF FORT HENRY AND ITS OUTWORKS ... [TN] [1875] 38x43cm (15x17") Some color. VG. Ref: Stephenson (CW) 413 [45] £146 $225

PLAN OF THE ROUTE OF THE EXPEDITION OF MAJOR BEALL ... FOR THE RELIEF OF THE WAGONS OF MR. F.X. AUBREY AGAINST THE APACHE INDIANS ... [1850] Bent's Fort to Santa Fe. 20x13cm (8x5") B&W. [44] £32 $50

PROGRESS MAP OF THE U.S. GEOGRAPHICAL SURVEYS WEST OF THE 100TH MERIDIAN [1879] Lt. G.M. Wheeler; routes marked in red. 41x56cm (16x22") Exc. [29] £58 $90

REBEL LINE OF WORKS AT BLAKELY CAPTURED BY THE ARMY OF WEST MISS., APRIL 9, 1865 ... [c. 1865] Alabama Civil War map. 25x38cm (10x15") Positions in color. Ref: Stephenson (CW) 104. [45] £39 $60

RECONNOISSANCES IN THE DAKOTA COUNTRY BY G.K. WARREN ... [1856] MO to Ft. Laramie. 91x152cm (36x60") Uncolored. Folded as issued; verso corner reinforcement; exc. [45] £211 $325

RICHMOND ... [1867 (c.1872)] From *Military Maps ... Armies of the Potomac and James*. 58x79cm (23x31") Some color. Ref: Stephenson (CW) 632.8. [45] £91 $140

RIO COLORADO OF THE WEST, MAP NO.1 ... [1858 (1861)] Pub in Lt. Ives report; by Egloffstein. Lower Colorado River in 4 sections. 39x89cm (15x35") B&W. Some fold splits; repaired 6" tear. Ref: Wheat (TM) 947. [46] £49 $75

SKETCH ACCOMPANYING COL. PRICE DESPATCH [1848] Taos Pueblo, NM. 24x29cm (9½x11½") Later color. Age spotting; generally good. [13] £62 $95

SKETCH OF PART OF THE MARCH & WAGON ROAD OF LT. COLONEL COOKE FROM SANTA FE TO THE PACIFIC OCEAN, 1846-7 ... [1847] 30x58cm (11½x23") With Cooke's text. [10] £81 $125

[SAME TITLE] [1848] 30x56cm (12x22") Uncolored. Folded as issued; VG. [45] £81 $125

SKETCH OF THE COUNTRY BETWEEN SOUTH PASS & THE GREAT SALT LAKE [1860] 45x56cm (18x22") Uncolored. Folded. [45] £58 $90

SKETCH OF THE PASSAGE OF THE RIO SAN GABRIEL, UPPER CALIFORNIA BY THE AMERICANS DISCOMFITTING THE OPPOSING MEXICAN FORCES, JANUARY 8, 1847 [1848] 13x21cm (5x8") Uncol. VG. [44] £23 $35

SKETCH OF THE VICINITY OF FORT FISHER ... BY OTTO JULIAN SCHULTZE, PRIVATE, 15TH N.Y.V. [NC] [(1865)] 36x25cm (14x10") Uncolored. Ref: Stephenson (CW) 314. [45] £49 $75

SOUTH MOUNTAIN SHOWING THE POSITIONS OF THE FORCES OF THE UNITED STATES AND THE ENEMY DURING THE BATTLE FOUGHT BY THE ARMY OF THE POTOMAC UNDER ... GENERAL G.B. MCCLELLAN, SEPT. 14TH 1862 [MD] [1872] NY: Am. Photolithographic Co. 79x53cm (31½x21½") Uncolored. Ref: Stephenson (CW) 259. [45] £156 $240

SOUTHWESTERN COLORADO ATLAS SHEET NO. 61 (C) [1877-78] From Wheeler,43x51cm (17x20") Black on tan. Ref: Phillips (a) 1281. [44] £52 $80

SPOTSYLVANIA COURTHOUSE, PREPARED BY BVT. BRIG. GENL. N. MICHLER ... [1867 (c.1872)] From *Military Maps ... Armies of the Potomac and James*. 53x79cm (21x31") Positions in color. VG. Ref: Stephenson (CW) 658.2. [45] £114 $175

THE WILDERNESS, PREPARED BY BVT. BRIG. GENL. N. MICHLER ... [VA] [1867 (c.1872)] From *Military Maps ... Armies of the Potomac and James*. 53x51cm (21x20") Positions in color. VG. Ref: Stephenson (CW) 665.9. [45] £114 $175

TOPOGRAPHICAL MAP OF THE APPROACHES AND DEFENCES OF KNOXVILLE, E. TENNESSEE, SHEWING THE POSITIONS OCCUPIED BY THE UNITED STATES AND CONFEDERATE FORCES DURING THE SIEGE ... [c. 1863-64] The Graphic Co., NY. 66x76cm (26x30") Some color. VG. Ref: Stephenson (CW) 427. [45] £146 $225

TOPOGRAPHICAL SKETCH OF THE BATTLEFIELD OF STONE'S RIVER NEAR MURPHREESBORO, TENNESSEE DECEMBER 31, 1862 TO JANUARY 3RD, 1863 [1863] In gov't report. 51x58cm (20x23") Uncolored. Folds; VG. Ref: Stephenson (CW) 441. [45] £81 $125

TOTOPOTOMOY ... [VA] [1867 (c.1872)] From *Military Maps ... Armies of the Potomac and James*. 56x79cm (22x31") Positions in color. VG. Ref: Stephenson (CW) 663.3. [45] £81 $125

UNIVERSAL MAGAZINE

A NEW AND ACCURATE MAP OF CONNECTICUT AND RHODE ISLAND, FROM THE BEST AUTHORITIES. [1780] 26x34cm (10x13½") Uncolored. Ref: Jolly UNIV-189 [56] £195 $300

A NEW AND ACCURATE MAP OF NORTH CAROLINA, IN NORTH AMERICA. [1779] 27x36cm (10½x14") B&W. Minor fold reinforcement; fine. Ref: Jolly UNIV-182 [48] £321 $495

A New and Accurate Map of the Present Seat of War in North America, Comprehending New Jersey, Philadelphia, Pensylvania, New-York &c. [1777] 36x29cm (14x11½") Uncolored. Ref: Jolly UNIV-178 [56] £227 $350
A New and Accurate Map of the Province of Pennsylvania in North America, from the Best Authorities. [1780] 27x33cm (10½x13") B&W. Fine. Ref: Jolly UNIV-185 [48] £302 $465
A New and Accurate Map of the Province of South Carolina in North America [1779] London: Hinton. 33x28cm (13x11") B&W. Lt offsetting. Ref: Jolly UNIV-180; Phillips (M) p.820. [46] £117 $180
[Same Title] [same date & dimen] B&W. Minor fold reinforcement; fine. [48] £321 $495
A New Map of the Province of Maryland in North America. [1780] 28x33cm (11x13") B&W. Minor fold reinforcement; fine. Ref: Jolly UNIV-184; Papenfuse & Coale fig.49. [48] £357 $550
An Accurate Map of the Present Seat of War Between Great Britain and Her Colonies in North America. [1776] 26x35cm (10½x13½") Orig color. Ref: Jolly UNIV-176 [56] £260 $400
Chart of New Holland with the Adjacent Countries and New Discover'd Islands. 1787 [1787] 16x26cm (6x10½") Color. Ref: Jolly UNIV-200 [16] £280 $431
Plan of the Town and Fortifications of Montreal or Ville Marie in Canada [1759] 24x36cm (9½x14½") Ref: Jolly UNIV-83 [14] £243 $375

VADIANUS
Typus Cosmographicus Universalis [1534] 1st ed. Woodblock. 30x41cm (11½x16") Superb. Ref: Shirley (W) 70; Sabin 98279; Nordenskiold (Fac) p.106. [2] £4,869 $7,500

VALENTYN
[Philippines: Northern Islands] [1724] Chart: 31x39cm (12x15½") Exc. [63] £445 $685
Kaart van het Eyland Mauritius [1724] From *Oud en Niew Oost-Indien*. 43x54cm (17x21½") Exc. [63] £552 $850

VALK
America Aurea Pars Altera Mundi ... [c. 1706] Insular Calif. 48x59cm (19x23") Orig full color. Ref: Leighley 134, pl.XIX. [46] £1,169 $1,800
Novus Planiglobii Terrestris per Utrumque Polum Conspectus [c.1672 (c.1695)] Polar projection by Joan Blaeu; only Blaeu with insular California. 41x54cm (16x21") Full color. C'fold splits repaired; old hand notations, many placenames underlined Ref: Shirley (W) 459. [55] £1,623 $2,500

VALK & SCHENK
Aethiopia Superior vel Interior Vulgo Abissinorum sive Presbiteri Ioannis Imperium [(1708)] 38x49cm (15x19") Verso blank. Orig full wash color. C'fold margin end splits, old verso repair; VG+. [33] £373 $575
Herefordia Comitatus Vernacule Heretfordshire [c. 1683-1724] Reissue of Jansson. 38x50cm (15x19½") Orig color. Sm old mount discolorations verso. Ref: Koeman III p.111. [28] £292 $450

VAN ADRICHEM
Chorographia Terrae Sanctae in Angustiorem Formam ... [c. 1620] E. Belling reissue of 1590 map. Jerusalem inset. 2 plates on one sheet, 33x86cm (12½x33½") Uncolored. VG. Ref: Not in Laor. [2] £584 $900
Dimidia Tribus Manasse Hoc Est, Ea Terrae Sanctae Pars ... [1590] 23x46cm (9x18") Color. Ref: Laor 14. [23] £130 $200

VAN AELST
Explicatio Aliquot Locorum Quae Puteolis Spectantur [c. 1560] Pozzuoli woodcut bird's eye view. 38x51cm (15x19½") Sm stains; margin tears & c'fold restored; minute holes. [28] £526 $810

VAN CAMPEN
De Grondt en Vloor de Groote Burger Sael [1661] Vennekool's drawing of Amsterdam City Hall entrance floor plan with 6 meter diameter inlaid hemispheres (2 terrestrial, 1 celestial), not extant. 43x75cm (17x29½") B&W. Ref: Shirley (W) 423. Schilder 66. [16] £1,187 $1,828

VAN DEN KEERE
Africa [1646] From *A Prospect of the Most Famous Parts of the World*. The "Miniature Speed atlas". 8x13cm (3½x5") Full color. Ref: Norwich illus. [57] £94 $145
America [same date, source & dimen] Insular Calif. Wash color. Exc. [57] £211 $325

ASIA [same date, source & dimen] Full color. [57] £97 $150
GALLIA [same date, source & dimen] Color. [57] £42 $65
HISPANIAE VETERIS DES. [c. 1595] 15x20cm (6x8") Even gray tone. [46] £71 $110
ITALIAE VETERIS SPECIMEN [c. 1595] 15x20cm (6x8") Even gray tone. [46] £71 $110
NOVA TOTIUS TERRARUM ORBIS GEOGRAPHICA AC HYDROGRAPHICA TABULA [1608, c.1630-31] Amsterdam: Jansson. Panels all around. 40x54cm (16x21"). Color. Pristine. Framed. Ref: Shirley (W) 264. [38] £4,869 $7,500
REGNI BOHEMIAE NOVA DESCRIPTIO [1618] 39x51cm (15x20") Separately issued. Color. Sl c'fold wear. [53] £1,000 $1,540
THE ROMANE EMPIRE [1646] From *A Prospect of the Most Famous Parts of the World*. The "Miniature Speed atlas". 8x13cm (3½x5") Wash color. [57] £42 $65

VAN DER AA

'T KONINKRYK VAN CHINA ... [1706+] From *Cartes des Itineraires et Voyages Modernes*. 15x22cm (6x8½") Uncolored. Light age-toning. [53] £180 $277
AMERIKA OF DE NIEUWE WEERLD ... [1706+] From *Cartes des Itineraires et Voyages Modernes*. 15x22cm (6x8½") Uncolored. Light age-toning. [53] £400 $616
ARX CAROLINA CHARLES FORT SUR FLORIDA [c. 1710] Conjectural view of Ft. Caroline on St. Johns River. 28x35cm (11x14") [14] £292 $450
CARTE D'UN TRES GRAND PAYS ENTRE LE NOUVEAU MEXIQUE ... [1698 / 1704] All of North America. Based on Hennepin. 43x51cm (17x20½") Japan paper backing; staining at top; strong impression. Ref: MCCS 38, #59; Leighly 104; cf. Cumming (Exploration) pp.36-41; Schwartz & Ehrenberg p.130. [2] £1,623 $2,500
CUBA EN IAMAICA ... [1706+] From *Cartes des Itineraires et Voyages Modernes*. 15x22cm (6x8½") Uncolored. Light age-toning. [53] £150 $231
DE MOLUCCOS, OF SPECERI-DRAGENDE EILANDEN ... [1706+] From *Cartes des Itineraires et Voyages Modernes*. 15x22cm (6x8½") Uncolored. Light age-toning. [53] £85 $131
DE ROODE ZEE IN VEN ZEADE SCHEEPSTOGT DER ENGELZE MAATSCHAPPIE ONDER H. MIDDLETON TOT SAN MOCHA [1707] Arabian peninsula. 15x23cm (6x9") OL & wash color. [57] £97 $150
DE VASTE KUST VAN CHERIBICHI ... [1706+] From *Cartes des Itineraires et Voyages Modernes*. Venezuela. 15x22cm (6x8½") Uncolored. Light age-toning. [53] £100 $154
DE VASTE KUSTE VAN CHICORA TUSSEN FLORIDA EN VIRGINIE ... HISPANIOLA ... [1706+] From *Cartes des Itineraires et Voyages Modernes*. 15x22cm (6x8½") Uncolored. Light age-toning. [53] £260 $400
DE VOOR EYLANDEN VAN AMERICA TEGENS DE VASTE KUSTEN VAN FLORIDA, MEXICO, NIEUW SPANJE, CARTAGENA, IUCATAN EN DARIEN MET DE GRENZEN AANDE ZUYD ZEE GELEGEN [1706+] From *Cartes des Itineraires et Voyages Modernes*. 15x22cm (6x8½") Uncolored. Light age-toning. [53] £200 $308
HET EILAND SUMATRA; HOE TEN AANSIEN VAN MALACCA ... [1706+] From *Cartes des Itineraires et Voyages Modernes*. 15x22cm (6x8½") Uncolored. Light age-toning. [53] £250 $385
HIBERNIA [1706] East at top. 13x15cm (5x6½") [24] £71 $110
IUKATAN EN VASTE KUSTEN VAN NIEUW SPANJE ... [1706+] From *Cartes des Itineraires et Voyages Modernes*. 15x22cm (6x8½") Uncolored. Light age-toning. [53] £240 $370
JONATHAN DICKENSON RAMSPOEDIGE ... VAN JAMAICA NA PENSYLVANIA ... [1707-] From *Cartes des Itineraires et Voyages Modernes*. Engraved mock-frame border. 22x29cm (8½x11") Uncolored. Light age-toning. [53] £760 $1,170
KEYSERLYNK GEZANDSCHAP UYT AETHIOPIEN ... [1706+] From *Cartes des Itineraires et Voyages Modernes*. 15x22cm (6x8½") Uncolored. Light age-toning. [53] £150 $231
L'AMERIQUE SELON LES NOUVELLES OBSERVATIONS DE MESSRS, DE L'ACADEMIE DES SCIENCE, ETC. ... [1700] Insular California. 46x66cm (18½x25½") B&W. Exc. Ref: Tooley (Amer) p.129 #71, pl.54. [48] £2,532 $3,900
L'AMERIQUE SEPTENTRIONALE ... [1706+] From *Cartes des Itineraires et Voyages Modernes*. 22x30cm (9x12") Uncolored. Light age-toning. [53] £420 $647
LAND TOGTEN DOOR FERDINAND CORTES ... [1706+] From *Cartes des Itineraires et Voyages Modernes*. Mexico. 15x22cm (6x8½") Uncolored. Light age-toning. [53] £160 $246
LE PORTUGAL SUIVANT LES NOUVELLES OBSERVATIONS ... [c.1720] 23x23cm (9x9") B&W. [43] £250 $385
LES COTES DE LA VIRGINIE LES DETROITS DE FORBISHER ET DE HUDSON [1706+] From *Cartes des Itineraires et Voyages Modernes*. North Atlantic. 15x22cm (6x8½") Uncolored. Light age-toning. [53] £150 $231
NAAUKEURIGE KAART VAN TARTARYEN ... [1706+] From *Cartes des Itineraires et Voyages Modernes*. 15x22cm (6x8½") Uncolored. Light age-toning. [53] £120 $185

NICARAGUA ... [1706+] From *Cartes des Itineraires et Voyages Modernes.* 15x22cm (6x8½") Uncolored. Light age-toning. [53] £150 $231

NIEUW ENGELAND IN TWEE SCHEEP TOGTEA DOOR KAPITEIN JOHAN SMITH INDE IAREN 1614 ER 1615 BESTEREND [1707] In *Atlas Nouveau et Curieux* ... Elaborate printed border. 23x30cm (8½x11½") OL color. Margin waterstain, image unaffected. [36] £487 $750

NIEUW SPAANJE ... [1706+] From *Cartes des Itineraires et Voyages Modernes.* 15x22cm (6x8½") Uncolored. Light age-toning. [53] £150 $231

NOVA DELINEATIO TOTIUS ORBIS TERRARUM PER PETRUM VANDER AA [1703] In cartouche,"Nouveau Carte du Monde"; surround of vignettes. 26x34cm (10x13½") Col. Ref: cf. Shirley (W) pl.295. [26] £812 $1,250

PLAN DE VILLE ET DU CHATEAU DE BATAVIA EN L'ISLE DE IAVA [c. 1714] With view. 27x36cm (10½x14") Full color. Exc. [63] £250 $385

SCHEEPS-TOGT DOOR FERDINAND MAGELLAAN [1706+] From *Cartes des Itineraires et Voyages Modernes.* The Americas. 15x22cm (6x8½") Uncolored. Light age-toning. [53] £360 $554

SCHEEPS TOGT VAN IAMAICA GEDAAN NA PANUCO EN RIO DE LAS PALMAS ... [1706+] From *Cartes des Itineraires et Voyages Modernes.* Entire Gulf Coast & Cuba. 15x22cm (6x8½") Uncolored. Light age-toning. [53] £260 $400

T NOORDER DEEL VAN AMERIKA DOOR C. KOLUMBUS IN ZYN EERSTE TOGT ONTDEKT EN DESSELS KUSTEN EN VOOR-EYLANDEN [1700] Insular Calif. 20x30cm (8x12") Color. [22] £503 $775

T VASTE LAND VAN DARIEN ... [1706+] From *Cartes des Itineraires et Voyages Modernes.* 15x22cm (6x8½") Uncolored. Light age-toning. [53] £220 $339

VAN DER SCHLEY

CARTE DE L'ISLE D'HAYTI AUJOURD'HUI L'ESPAGNOL OU L'ISLE DE ST. DOMINGUE AVEC PAR M. BELLIN [c. 1771] Hispaniola, Jamaica & Puerto Rico. 23x33cm (9½x13") Color. [25] £107 $165

VAN KEULEN

[NEWFOUNDLAND COAST IN 8 SECTIONS] [1734] G. Van Keulen. Composite sheet. 51x58cm (20x23") Uncolored. [52] £550 $847

A NEW AND ACCURATE CHART OF THE MOUTH OF THE THAMES, AND ITS ENTRANCES, VIZ; THE KINGS AND QUEENS AND SOUTH CHANNELS & HARWICH FROM NORTH FORELAND THE NORE TO ORFORDNESS [1798] Title repeated in Dutch. 65x99cm (25½x39") [14] £292 $450

CARTE DE LA NOUVELLE FRANCE OU SE VOIT LE COURS DES GRANDES RIVIERES DE S. LAURENS & DE MISSISSIPI AUJOUR D'HUI S. LOUIS, AUX ENVIRONS DES QUELLES SE TROUVENT LES ETATS PAIS NATIONS PEUPLES &C. DE LA FLORIDE, DE LA LOUISIANE, DE LA VIRGINIE ... [c. 1720] 58x97cm (22½x38½") Full orig color. Sm repairs at fold & lower margin; facsimile title block replacement; overall VG. [20] £6,492 $10,000

NIEUWE EN ALDEREERSTE AFTEEKENING VAN 'T EYLAND ST. THOMAS. MET ALL DESSELFS HAVENEN, ANKER PLAATSE ... [1719] Gerard van Keulen. 58x87cm (23x34½") Later wash color. Exc. [62] £2,921 $4,500

NIEUWE LAND IN ZEE KAART VAN DE EYLANDEN GUADALOUPE EN MARIEGALANDE, &C. [1720] Gerard van Keulen. 49x57cm (19½x22½") + title. Exc. [63] £552 $850

NIEUWE PASCAERT VAN ALLE DE VLAEMSE EYLANDEN ... [1681] 51x59cm (20x23") Orig color. [28] £380 $585

NIEUWE PASCAERT VAN DE OOST CUST VAN SCHOTLANDT BEGINNENDE VAN BARWYCK TOT AEN DE ORCADES YLANDEN ... [1681] From *Zee Fakkel.* 53x58cm (20½x23") Color. [15] £280 $431

NIEUWE PLATTE PASKAART VAN DE STRAAT DAVIS, VAN 67 GRAADE TOT 73 GRAAEDE NOORDER BREETON, OF VAN DE ZUYD BAY TOT VERBY DE VROUWE EYLANDEN ... [c. 1727] As in *Zee-Fakkel.* Gerard Van Keulen. 61x102cm (23½x39½") Orig color. Sh tear lower c'fold, sl loss; old fold repairs, no loss. Ref: Koeman IV Keu 44. [28] £701 $1,080

NOUVELLE CARTE DE LA RIVIERE DE CANADA OU ST. LAURENS DE L'ILE DE ANTICOSTE JUSQUA QUEBEC. DANS LA PARTIE D'AMERIQUE LA PLUS SEPTENTRIONALE [c. 1728] In *Zee-Fakkel.* Gerard van Keulen. Chart in sections. 53x61cm (20½x24") Close top margin. Ref: Koeman IV 113B, p.375-6. [28] £1,052 $1,620

NOUVELLE CARTE MARINE DU GRAND BANQ DE TERRA NEUFF A GRAND POINT POINT SUR LA QUELLE OUTES LES PROFOUNDEURS PAR BRASSES SONT MARQUEES [c. 1680] 51x57cm (20x22½") [14] £357 $550

[SAME TITLE] [c. 1734] In *Zee-Fakkell.* Gerard Van Keulen. 53x58cm (20½x23") Sm spot near c'fold; Institutional marking (?) obliterated on verso. [28] £584 $900

PAS-KAART VAN DE GRAND BANQ BY TERRA NEUFF MET ALLE SYN DIEPTEN OP VAADEMEN DOOR J.C. VOOGHT GEOMETRA [c. 1684] In *Zee-Fakkell.* Johannes Van Keulen. 53x61cm (20½x23½") Old color. Sh tears lower margin; pinholes. Ref: Koeman IV p.381. [28] £555 $855

PAS KAART VAN RIO ORONOQUE GOLFO DE PARIA MET D'EYLANDEN TRINIDAD, GRANADA, GRANADILLOS, EN BEQUIA [1683] Tobago inset. 52x59cm (20½x23") Orig color.   [14]   £422 $650

PAS-KAART VANDE ZEE KUSTEN VAN NIEW NEDERLAND ANDERS GENAAMT NIEW YORK TUSSCHEN RENSELAARS HOEK EN DE STAATEN HOEK ... [1685] Hudson River detail. 51x56cm (20½x22") Color. Exc. Ref: Stokes (Manhattan) II, p158-9; Deak #68.   [38]   £3,246 $5,000

PASCAARTE VANDE NOORDER ZEE CUSTEN VAN AMERICA, VANDE WEST-HOECK VAN ISLAND DOORDE STRAET DAVIS EN HUDSON, TOT AEN TERRA NEUF [c. 1683] Joannes Van Keulen. 51x58cm (20x23") C'fold split lower margin; unobtrusive spots. Ref: Phillips (A) 3453; Koeman IV Keu 8.   [28]   £876 $1,350

PASCAERT, VANDE WESTKUST VAN SCHOTLANT, ALS MEDE EEN GEDEELTE VANDE LEWYS EYLANDEN ... [1681 (1704)] From *Zee Fakkel*. 51x58cm (20x23") Color.   [15]   £270 $416

PASKAART VAN DE BOGHT VAN FLORIDA MET DE CANAAL TUSSCHEN FLORIDA EN CUBA ... [c. 1680] 51x58cm (20½x23") Orig color. Some restoration; overall good.   [4]   £1,785 $2,750

PASKAART VANDE NOORD CUST VAN SCHOTLAND ALS MEDE DE EYLANDEN VAN HITLANDT EN FERO ... [1681] 51x58cm (20x23") Color.   [15]   £300 $462

PASKAERTE VANDE ARCHIPEL ... [1680] Aegean Sea. 51x58cm (19½x23") Full orig color. Exc.   [2]   £617 $950

VAN LINSCHOTEN

A CIDADE DE ANGRA NA ILHA DE IESU XPO DA TERCERA ... [1595 / 1599] Azores. Latin ed; 2nd use of plate. 48x81cm (18½x32½") Few folds reinforced, one repair; else exc.   [37]   £974 $1,500

DELINEATIO ORARUM MARITIMARUM, TERRAE VULGO INDIGETATAE TERRA DO NATAL, ITEM SOFALAE, MOZAMBICAE, & MELINDAE ... [1599] Latin ed; 2nd use of plate. 38x53cm (15x21") Color. Fold intersections reinforced; else exc. Ref: Norwich 236b; MCCS 29 (Tooley #168). Tooley (Landmarks) ill. pp. 168-9.   [37]   £1,753 $2,700

DELINIANTUR IN HAC TABULA, ORAE MARITIMAE ABEXIAE, FRETI MECANI: AL MARIS RUBRI: ARABIAE, ORMI, PERSIAE, SUPRA SINDAM USQUE ... [1599] Near & Middle East. Latin ed; 2nd use of plate. 38x53cm (15x20½") Color. Fold intersections reinforced; else exc. Ref: Tibbetts p.23, #46.   [37]   £1,623 $2,500

DESCRIPTIO HYDROGRAPHICA ACCOMMADATA AD BATTAVORUM NAVIGATIONE IN JAVAM INSULAM ... [1599] Dutch route to Java. 2nd use of plate. 36x66cm (13½x26") Color. Some repair with loss.   [37]   £617 $950

INSULA D. HELENAE SACRA COELI CLEMENTIA ET AEQUABILITATE ... [1589 / 1599] 36x51cm (14½x19½") Fold reinforcement; else exc.   [37]   £357 $550

TYPUS ORARUM MARITIMARUM GUINEAE, MANICONGO, & ANGOLAE ULTRAP PROMONTORIUM BONAE SPEI ... [1599] Latin ed; 2nd use of plate. Ascension & St. Helena views. 38x51cm (15x20½") Color. On heavy paper; exc. Ref: Norwich 236a; MCCS 29 (Tooley #167).   [37]   £1,948 $3,000

VERA EFFIGIES ET DELINEATIO INSULA SANCTAE HELENAE, QUA ORTUM OCCASUM, ET SEPTENTRIONEM SPECTAT, SITAE IN ALTITUDINE 16 GRADUUM AD AUSTRUM LINEA AEQUINOCTIALIS ... [1598] 3 views. 31x48cm (12x18½") Narrow lf margin.   [15]   £300 $462

VERA EFFIGIES ET DELINEATIO INSULAE ASCENSIO ... [1598] From *Itinerario*. 3 profile views. 28x36cm (10½x13½") Color.   [15]   £300 $462

VERA EFFIGIES ET DELINEATIO INSULAE SANCTAE HELENAE ... [1599] Profile views. 31x48cm (12x18½") Exc.   [37]   £292 $450

VAN LOON

PAS-CAERTE VANT IN COMEN VAN DE CANAEL ... [1661 (1666)] From *Zee-Atlas*. Western approaches to English Channel. 43x53cm (17x21") Color.   [15]   £260 $400

PASCAERTE VAN'T WESTELYCKSTE DEEL VANDE MIDDELANDSCHE ZEE ... [1660] 31x46cm (12x18") Orig OL color.   [52]   £800 $1,232

VAN MEURS

PEKING [c. 1650] 20x33cm (8x12½") B&W. Unobtrusive foxing; else fine.   [55]   £97 $150

VAN SCHAGEN

THEATER DES OORLOGS IN HONGARYE ... [c. 1680] 45x59cm (17½x23") Uncolored.   [54]   £300 $462

VANCOUVER

COTE NORD-OUEST DE L'AMERIQUE ... 2E. PARTIE ... [1800] French atlas ed. Bodega Bay to Tillamook. 75x61cm (29½x24") Uncol. Fine-. Ref: Howes (US) V23; Johnson (Amer Expl) p.194.   [59]   £380 $585

COTE NORD-OUEST DE L'AMERIQUE RECONNUE PAR LE CAPE. VANCOUVER. VE. PARTIE DEPUIS 57°7'30"... [c.1800] 3 insets. 79x66cm (31x25½") Lt foxing trace. Ref: Falk (AK) 1799-5; cf. Wagner (NW) 859.   [28]   £454 $700

VANDERMAELEN

[ATLAS] ATLAS UNIVERSEL ..., VOL. IV, AMERIQUE SEPTENTRIONALE [1827] Large folio; 76 maps, 2 key maps. Henry Ode, sc. 1st lithographed atlas; 1st on uniform scale. Orig OL col. Contents tight; half-leather covers worn but serviceable; title page stained & spotted. Few browned or spotted maps; VG to exc. [46] £3,246 $5,000

[ATLAS] ATLAS UNIVERSEL ..., ; 44 maps & key map. Henry Ode, sc. 1st lithographed atlas; 1st on uniform scale. Orig OL color. Contents tight; half-leather covers worn but serviceable. Few browned or spotted maps; VG to exc. [46] £1,623 $2,500

[CATALOGUE] ETABLISSEMENT GEOGRAPHIQUE DE BRUXELLES ... CATALOGUE [1841] 16 pp. octavo, with atlas, map & globe prices. [52] £300 $462

AMER. SEP. NO.47 PARTIE DU MEXIQUE [1827] Present Utah. 46x56cm (18½x22") Partial color. Fine. Ref: Wheat (TM) 378. Moffat 3. [10] £179 $275

AMER. SEP. NO.55 PARTIE DES ETATS UNIS [1827] TX 46x51cm (18x20") Orig OL col. [46] £325 $500

AMER. SEP. NO.69 PORTO-RICO [1825] 2 plans: Puerto Rico, Virgin Islands & Anguilla; Humboldt's route from La Guayra to Caracas. 46x53cm (18x21") Color. [25] £97 $150

PARTIE DES ETATS UNIS [TEXAS & OKLAHOMA] [1827] From *Atlas Universel*. 48x51cm (18½x20") Minor age browning; edge chips, 1 to printed surface. [13] £276 $425

VARIN

PLAN GEOMETRAL DE LA VILLE & DU PORT DE MALTE [1784] With key to buildings. 28x35cm (11x13½") Uncolored. [53] £260 $400

VAUGONDY   See *De Vaugondy*

VIELE

THE TRANSVAL OF THE CITY OF NEW YORK [1880] Folding map. Development plan north of 130th St. 33x132cm (13x52") In orig gold-stamped binding. Orig printed color. Superb. [2] £438 $675

VIRTUE

AUSTRALIA [1840] 20x24cm (7½x9½") Orig OL color. Ref: Tooley 1299 pl.96. [16] £71 $110

VISSCHER

AFBEELDINGE VAN DE VEERTICH-JAARIGE REYSE DER KINDEREN ISRAELS. UYT EGYPTEN DOOR DE ROODE ZEE END DE WOESTYNE ... [1728] From Dutch Bible. Amsterdam: Wetstein & Smith; Leiden: Luchtmans. 36x53cm (14½x20½") Vert folds; 3" lower c'fold tear repaired; lt stains. [28] £250 $385

DE BESCHRYVINGH VAN DE REYSEN PAULI, EN VAN DE ANDERE APOSTELEN ... [1730] From Dutch Bible. Stoopendaal, fec. 30x46cm (12½x18½") Vert folds; sh tear lower c'fold & lower border. Ref: Laor 812. [28] £292 $450

DE GELEGENTHEYT VAN'T PARADYS EN'T LANDT CANAAN, MITSGADERS D'EERST BEWOONDE LANDEN DER PATRIARCHEN ... [1645 - 1728] From Dutch Bible. Amsterdam: Wetstein & Smith; Leiden: Luchtmans. 36x51cm (14x20½") Vert folds; margins bit stained with sh tears. [28] £263 $405

DE GELEGENTHEYT VAN'T PARADYS EN'T LANDT CANAAN, MITSGADERS D'EERST BEWOOUDE LANDEN DER PATRIARCHEN ... DOOR HENDRIK JACOB EN PIETER KEUR ... [1645 / c.1702] From Dutch Bible. Stoopendaal, fec. 30x46cm (12½x18") Ref: cf Laor 805. [28] £279 $430

DE GELEGENTHEYT VAN'T PARADYS ENDE T'LANDT CANAAN, MITSGADERS DE EERST BEWOONDE LANDEN ... [1660] 30x48cm (12½x18½") Color. Ref: Laor 794 [23] £211 $325

[SAME TITLE] [1665] 32x47cm (12½x18½") Ref: Laor 794. [14] £211 $325

DE HEYLIGE EN WYTVERMAERDE STADT IERUSALEM EERST GENAEMT SALEM ... [1643] 33x43cm (13½x16½") Color. Ref: Laor 1155. [23] £237 $365

[SAME TITLE] [c. 1643-1645] From Dutch Bible. 33x48cm (12½x18½") Vert folds; sh margin tears. [28] £325 $500

[SAME TITLE] [1665] Bird's eye view. 32x48cm (12½x19") [14] £292 $450

DIE GEGEND DES IRDISCHEN PARADIESES UND DES LANDES CANAAN ... [1736] From *Bibla*, by Martin Luther, Nurnberg. 38x51cm (15x20½") Color. Ref: Laor 814. [23] £302 $465

HANC TABULAM CONTINENS LAETAM PHARNAMBUCI VICTORIAM ... [c. 1630] Pernambuco area. 36x69cm (14x27") Extra sheet extends map to north. Uncolored. Ref: Differs from MCS 46, #67, pl.23. [54] £500 $770

HET BELOOFDE LANDT CANAAN DOOR WANDELT VAN ONSEN SALICHMAECKER IESU CHRISTO ... [1682] Stoopendaal, sc. 51x46cm (20x18") Color. Ref: Laor 809. [23] £289 $445

HET BELOOFDE LANDT CANAAN DOOR WANDELT VAN ONSEN SALICHMAECKER JESU CHRISTO NEFFENS SIJNE APOSTOLEN [1665] 32x48cm (12½x18½") Ref: Laor 791. [14] £243 $375

HET BELOOFDE LANDT CANAAN, DOOR WANDELT VAN ONSEN SALISCHMAKKER JESUS CHRISTUS NEFFENS SYNE APOSTELEN [c. 1730] From Dutch Bible. Stoopendaal, fec. 30x46cm (12½x18") Vert folds; paper flaws top margin; lf margin ragged; sm stains lower c'fold. Ref: cf Laor 809. [28] £279 $430

INDIAE ORIENTALIS NEC NON INSULARUM ADIACENTIUM NOVA DESCRIPTIO [c. 1680] 47x57cm (18½x22½") Old OL color. 1¼" tear & c'fold repairs; good. Ref: Koeman Vi 183. [48] £714 $1,100

INDIAE ORIENTALIS NEC NON INSULARUM ADIACENTIUM NOVA DESCRIPTIO PER NICOLAUM VISSCHER [1730] Schenk reissue. 46x56cm (18x22") Color. Ref: Fell pl.4. [16] £1,329 $2,048

MAGNAE BRITANNIAE TABULA, ANGLIAM, SCOTIAM, ET HIBERNIAM ... [c. 1700] 48x56cm (18½x22½") Full color. VG. [21] £779 $1,200

NOUVELLE CARTE GEOGRAPHIQUE DE LA MER D'ASOF OU DE ZEBACHE; & DES PALUS MEOTIDES [c. 1717] Based on Ruggel. 48x58cm (19½x23") Orig color. Sh tear lower c'fold. Ref: Bagrow (Russia) p.123. [28] £221 $340

NOVA TABULA GEOGRAPHICA COMPLECTENS BOREALIOREM AMERICAE PARTEM: IN QUA EXACTE DELINEATAE SUNT CANADA SIVE NOVA FRANCIA, NOVA SCOTIA, NOVA ANGLIA, NOVUM BELGIUM, PENSYLVANIA, VIR- GINIA, CAROLINA ET TERRA NOVA, ... [c.1685 / 1695] 2 sheets joined. 61x91cm (23½x35½") Orig OL color. Exc. Ref: Phillips (A) 3478, 125-6; Koeman III, p.179, #93; Morrison p.45, fig.28. [2] £1,850 $2,850

NOVI BELGII NOVAEQUE ANGLIAE NEC NON PARTIS VIRGINIAE TABULA MULTIS IN LOCIS EMENDATA A NICOLAO JOANNIS VISSCHERO [c. 1655 - 1680] With view of New York. 46x55cm (18½x21½") Color. Exc. Ref: Tooley (Amer) p.284-5, #5, 2nd state. [38] £4,220 $6,500

[SAME TITLE] [1655 (c.1680)] State IV. With view of New York. 47x56cm (18½x22") Orig color. Exc. Ref: Tooley (Amer) Campbell. [63] £3,116 $4,800

[SAME TITLE] [c. 1680- 1685] With view of New York; Philadelphia appears. 46x55cm (18½x21½") Full orig color. Exc. Ref: Tooley (Amer) p.285, #6, 4th state. [38] £3,895 $6,000

NOVISSIMA ET ACCURATISSIMA TOTIUS AMERICAE DESCRIPTIO PER N. VISSCHER [1670] 1st issue. Insular California. 43x54cm (17x21½") Blank verso. Orig color. Soft age tone; Lower c'fold margin split; old repair; lower margin verso strengthened; very nice. Ref: Tooley (Amer) p.119, #29, pl.41. Leighly 56, pl.XI. [1] £1,104 $1,700

ORBIS TERRARUM NOVA ET ACCURATISSIMA TABULA ... [1658] Double hemispheres; insular California. 46x56cm (18½x22") Full color. Fine. Ref: Shirley (W) 406; Leighly 32; Wagner (NW) 314. [55] £3,571 $5,500

[SAME TITLE] [1658 - 1680] [same dimen] Full color, probably orig, perhaps recolored. Cleaned, c'fold & margin restoration; thin paper backing; bright, clear. Ref: Wagner (NW) II #379. [59] £3,765 $5,800

ORBIS TERRARUM TABULA RECENS EMENDATA ET IN LUCEM EDITA PER N. VISSCHER [1663] Double hemi; no Great Lakes. 31x47cm (12x18½") Color. Ref: Shirley (W) 431. [26] £1,136 $1,750

ORBIS TERRARUM TYPUS DE INTEGRO ILLUSTRATUS 1657 [1657] 1st Visscher Dutch Bible map. 31x48cm (12x18½") Orig color. Ref: Shirley (W) 401, pl.300. Schilder 77. [16] £2,754 $4,242

PERIGRINATIE OFTE VEERTICH-IARIGE REYSE DER KINDEREN ISRAELS UYT EGYPTEN DOOR DE ROODE-ZEE ... [1648] 30x48cm (12x19") Color. Ref: Laor 785. [23] £302 $465

[SAME TITLE] [same date & dimen] Dampmarks lower margins; 2" crease near top. [28] £308 $475

[SAME TITLE] [1665] [same dimen] Ref: Laor 795. [14] £227 $350

VIVIEN

CARTE GENERALE DE LA TURQUIE D'ASIE [1824] 48x58cm (18½x22½") OL color. [58] £65 $100

CARTE GENERALE DES ETATS UNIS DE L'AMERIQUE SEPTENTRIONALE [1834] 31x41cm (12x16") OL color. [9] £114 $175

CARTE GENERALE DU MEXIQUE ... [1834] 30x41cm (12x16") [9] £104 $160

VOLKAMER

[WORLD] [1708] Map rendered on columns of a portico in book on citrus fruit. 26x41cm (10x16") Color. [16] £209 $322

VON BREYDENBACH

RHODIS [1486] From Reuwich woodcuts. 25x79cm (10x30½") Margin repair sl into printed surface; else VG. Ref: cf. Nebenzahl (Holy Land) p.63. [39] £2,272 $3,500

VON EULER
TABULA GEOGRAPHICA PARTIS SEPTENTRIONALIS MARIS PACIFICI CUM ADJACENTIBUS REGIONIBUS SUPERIME TAM A RUSSIS ORIENTEM ... [1753 (1756/60)] Incl most of North America; reduced from 1752 De L'Isle / Buache. 33x38cm (13x15") Orig OL & wash color. VG-. Ref: Moreland & Bannister pp 237-8; Phillips (A) 625. [59] £454 $700
[SAME TITLE] [1760]. [same dimen] Color. Rubber stamp near lower border. [28] £584 $900

VON REILLY
KARTE VON AMERIKA NACH D'ANVILLE UND POWNALL ... [1795] 61x81cm (24x31½") Orig OL colors. Dampmarked near borders. Ref: Phillips (A) 686. [28] £701 $1,080
KARTE VON DEM KOENIGREICHE SCHWEDEN ... [1796] 56x74cm (22½x29½") OL color. C'fold split repaired; few sm wax stains in margin to border; sm ink blot in blank map area; else VG. [55] £292 $450
KARTE VON FRANKREICH [1796] 56x69cm (21½x27") Old color. Minor spotting; surface dirt lower margin; else fine. [55] £195 $300

VON STULPNAGEL   Try *Stieler*
NORD AMERICA [1847] Large TX configuration. 30x38cm (12x15½") OL color. [56] £78 $120
VEREIN-STAATEN VON NORD-AMERICA, MEXICO, YUCATAN [1880] 33x41cm (13x16") Margin inscription; clean. [9] £52 $80

VUILLEMIN
NOUVELLE CARTE ILLUSTREE DE L'AMERIQUE DU NORD ... [1860] Pictorial side-panels. 62x85cm (24x33½") Orig OL color. [53] £300 $462

WAGHENAER
ORGANUM URANICUM SIVE COMPASSUS MOBILIS AUSTRIFERUS ... [1583 - 1586] Celestial hemisphere with volvelle & paper scale bar; functional diagram. 33x26cm (13x10") Orig color. [52] £850 $1,309

WAITE
PALESTINE [1894] 36x28cm (13½x10½") Color. [23] £10 $15

WALCH
[L'AMERIQUE SELON L'ENTENDUE DE SES PRINCIPALES PARTIES ...] [c. 1785] One untitled sheet of pair; Arctic to Venezuela. 48x61cm (19x24") Orig col. Corners reinforced; c'fold ends repaired, no loss. [28] £438 $675

WALDSEEMULLER
GENERALE PTHOLEMEI [1513] Ptolemy, *Geographia*. 46x61cm (17½x24½") Strong impression; exc. Ref: Shirley (W) 34, pl.37. [2] £5,518 $8,500
OCTAVA EUROPE TABULA [1513] From Ptolemy's *Geographia*. Russia & Ukraine. 39x59cm (15½x23") Uncolored. [53] £800 $1,232
ORBIS TYPUS UNIVERSALIS IUXTA HYDROGRAPHORUM TRADITIONEM [1513] "The Admiral's Map". Shows South America, some of the Greater Antilles, and a North American land. 43x58cm (17x22½") [3] £14,282 $22,000
TABULA MODERNA INDIAE [1513] 1st "modern" map of Asia. 40x51cm (16x20") + title & longitude extensions. Lower c'fold mend; else exc. [63] £2,921 $4,500

WALKER
MAP OF THE CITY OF MONTREAL AND VICINITY [1878] H.B. Walker. 41x62cm (16x24") [14] £49 $75
MAP OF THE CITY OF QUEBEC [1878] H.B. Walker. 32x38cm (12½x15") [14] £29 $45

WALKER, G.
[MASSACHUSETTS, CHARLES RIVER BASIN] [c. 1895] Walker Lith. & Pub. Co., Boston. 48x69cm (19x27") Chromolithograph. Exc. [48] £192 $295
NANTUCKET [1891] 46x66cm (18x26") Lt color. Rolled, never folded. [45] £58 $90

WALKER, J. & C.
EAST RIDING OF YORKSHIRE [1845] London: Longman, Rees, Orme, Brown & Co. Pocket map; dissected, laid down on linen, folding into 16mo cloth covers. Similar to S.D.U.K. map. 33x41cm (12½x15½") OL color. VG. [21] £114 $175
KENT [c. 1830] London: Letts & Son. 33x38cm (12½x15") Full color. VG. [21] £36 $55
[SAME TITLE] [c. 1845] London: Letts & Son. 38x48cm (14½x18½") OL color. Fine. [21] £65 $100

WALLING

MAP OF ADDISON COUNTY, VERMONT [1857] Boston; NY: W.E. Baker & Co. Wall map; 15 insets; directories, etc. 135x137cm (53x54") OL & full color. Detached from upper rail; torn, stained & holes upper border; stain lf margin, tears lower margin; wrinkled, age-toning; Fair-good. Ref: Cobb (VT) 306. [8] £211 $325

MAP OF CHITTENDEN COUNTY, VERMONT [1857] NY: Baker, Tilden & Co. Wall map; 18 insets; 17 views, directories, etc. 135x130cm (53x51") OL & full color. Detaching from rails; staining, wrinkling, frayed edges, holes at top, sl loss; needs restoration; fair. Ref: Cobb (VT) 308. [8] £169 $260

MAP OF ORANGE COUNTY, VERMONT [1858] NY: Baker & Tilden. Wall map; 30 insets; 4 views, directories, etc. 135x137cm (53x54") OL & full color. VG. Ref: Cobb (VT) 313. [8] £341 $525

MAP OF THE COUNTIES OF ORLEANS, LAMOILLE, AND ESSEX, VERMONT [1859] NY: Loomis & Way. Wall map: 45 insets, etc. 135x137cm (53x54") OL & full color. Top fifth stained, wrinkled, 2 holes at rail; rest almost new, occas lt foxing; margin tape detaching. Ref: Cobb (VT) 318. [8] £536 $825

MAP OF THE STATE OF VERMONT [1859] NY: Johnson & Browning. Wall map; 31 town insets; geological map. 63x59cm (24½x23") Color. Frayed borders, cracked, stained top & bottom edges, occas sm holes; detaching from rods; good. Ref: Cobb (VT) 322; Phillips (M) p.974. [8] £250 $385

[SAME TITLE] [1860] Wall map; 45 town insets; geological map. 160x150cm (62½x58½") Color. Peripheral staining & wrinkling; good. Ref: Cobb (VT) 329. [8] £471 $725

MAP OF WASHINGTON COUNTY, VERMONT [1858] NY: Baker & Tilden. Wall map; 26 insets, 4 views, directory, etc. 135x137cm (53x54") OL & full color. Lt age-toning; staining at top rail; 2 sm rips at bottom; overall VG. Ref: Cobb (VT) 314. [8] £315 $485

WALLING & GRAY

MAP OF NEW ENGLAND WITH ADJACENT PORTIONS OF NEW YORK & CANADA [1871] 56x38cm (22x15½") Color. Exc. [29] £39 $60

MASSACHUSETTS [1871] 38x61cm (15x24") Color. VG or better. [29] £26 $40

WALTON

A NEW AND ACCURATE MAP OF THE WORLD [1646] From Speed miniature atlas. 10x13cm (3½x5") Orig color. Ref: Shirley (W) 397, pl.297. [16] £4,748 $7,313

WARE

IERUSALEM ... SOLD BY RICHD. WARE AND WILL. TAYLOR ... [1725] 36x43cm (14x16½") Color. Ref: Laor 1158. [23] £224 $345

WARNER & BEERS

COLORADO, UTAH, NEW MEXICO AND ARIZONA [1872] 41x38cm (16x14½") Full color. Crayon marks verso; else exc. [56] £114 $175

COUNTY MAP OF COLORADO, UTAH, NEW MEXICO AND ARIZONA [1873] 41x36cm (16x14") Lt spotting; else good. [12] £81 $125

COUNTY MAP OF IDAHO, MONTANA AND WYOMING [1872] 33x41cm (13x16") Color. [56] £58 $90

[SAME TITLE] [1873] 36x43cm (14x16½") Color. Lt soil; else VG. [12] £65 $100

COUNTY MAP OF KANSAS, NEBRASKA, DAKOTA AND MINNESOTA [1873] 46x36cm (17½x14") Color. Soil & lt stain at side. [12] £62 $95

COUNTY MAP OF OREGON, WASHINGTON [ON SHEET WITH] TERRITORY OF ALASKA [1873] By H.H. Lloyd & Co. 38x43cm (14½x17") Color. [12] £55 $85

COUNTY MAP OF TEXAS AND INDIAN TERRITORY [1873] 43x37cm (17x14½") Color. Lt soil, minor spotting; else good. [12] £88 $135

WARNER, B.

UNITED STATES OF AMERICA [1820] 43x66cm (17x25½") On banknote paper. Color. Fine. [6] £471 $725

WATERS & SON

[ENGLISH CHANNEL OFF CHERBOURG SHOWING COURSE AND SINKING OF CONFEDERATE SHIP ALABAMA] [1864] Proof map on newsprint sheet, probably for *New York Herald*. 30x23cm (12x9") Scattered browning; VG. [21] £260 $400

[LOUISIANA & MISSISSIPPI: DELTA TO VICKSBURG] [c. 1863] Proof map on newsprint. 28x23cm (10½x9") Old fold repair, some loss; minor browning; VG. [20] £276 $425

[MISSISSIPPI RIVER FROM NEW CARTHAGE PAST GRAND GULF] [1862] Proof map on newsprint. 28x23cm (11½x9") Lt browning; VG. [20] £260 $400

WATSON

[ATLAS] NEW INDEXED FAMILY ATLAS OF THE UNITED STATES, WITH MAPS OF THE WORLD ... SHOWING IN DETAIL THE RAILWAY SYSTEM AND POST ROUTES ... [1882] Gaylord Watson; Chicago: Tenney & Weaver. Sm folio. Cloth covers worn at edges & corners. 112 pp; printed col maps; contents fair to VG. [5] £97 $150
TEXAS [1886] Greer Co. in TX. Verso: AR; Indian Terr. 30x43cm (11½x17") OL color. [46] £49 $75
WATSON'S NEW COUNTY, RAILROAD AND DISTANCE MAP OF DAKOTA AND NEBRASKA [1875] 43x33cm (16½x13") Color. Fine. [9] £49 $75

WEEKLY DISPATCH Try *Weller*

CALIFORNIA, UTAH, LR. CALIFORNIA AND NEW MEXICO [1858-63] Theodor Ettling. 43x30cm (17x12") Orig full color. Fine. [59] £120 $185
MAP OF GREAT BRITAIN SHOWING ALL THE RAILWAYS, & RAILWAY STATIONS THE CANALS, NAVIGABLE RIVERS, & PRINCIPAL ROADS [c. 1860] Edward Weller. 4 sheet map. 132x94cm (52x36½") Partial color. VG. [21] £114 $175
SEAT OF WAR IN VIRGINIA AND MARYLAND, SHEET 1 [1861] Fredericksburg to Gettysburg. 46x33cm (18x13") Some color. [45] £78 $120
SEAT OF WAR IN VIRGINIA AND MARYLAND. SHEET 1 [IN SET WITH] ... SHEET 2 [AND] ... SHEET 3 [1863] E. Weller. Covers Baltimore to Richmond. Each about 31x46cm (12x18") Orig OL color. [14] £162 $250
SEAT OF WAR IN VIRGINIA, SHEET 2 [1861] 46x33cm (18x13") Some color. [45] £78 $120
THE "LANDMARKS" OF LONDON [1860] Edward Weller. 43x64cm (17x24½") Date seal. No color. Misfolded; few sm spots; good. [21] £39 $60
THE PACIFIC OCEAN [1858 - 1863] E. Weller. 45x65cm (17½x25½") Orig OL color. [16] £190 $293
UNITED STATES OF NORTH AMERICA [1858-1863] Theodor Ettling. U.S. to Rockies; 6 sheets, each 43x31cm (16½x12") Orig OL color. VG. [59] £227 $350
UNITED STATES WESTERN SHEET [1862] T. Ettling. One of 2 joinable sheets. 46x33cm (18x13") Some color. Minor repairs verso. [45] £78 $120

WEIGEL

FACIES POLI ARCTICI ADIACENTIUMQUE EX RECENTISSIMIS ITINERARIIS DELINEATA ... [c. 1730] 33x36cm (12½x14") Orig color. [28] £292 $450
GLOBI COELESTIS IN SEX TABULAS PLANAS REDACTI DESCRIPTIO [c. 1720] Ignatio Pardies (a Burritt precursor?) Complete set of 6 charts, each about 35x36cm (13½x14") with 2 text pages. Uncolored, VG+. [32] £1,233 $1,900
HELVETIA [c. 1724] 28x33cm (11½x13") B&W. [46] £45 $70
NOVI ORBIS SIVE TOTIUS AMERICAE CUM ADIACENTIBUS INSULIS NOVA EXHIBITIO [c. 1712] Insular Calif. 27x34cm (11x13½") Full color. C'fold reinforced on verso; VG+. [31] £390 $600
[SAME TITLE] [c.1720] 28x34cm (11x13½") Wash col. Fine. Ref: Tooley (Amer) p.132 #90. [48] £552 $850
PLANIGLOBIUM TERRESTRE MINUS [c. 1730] Based on Homann. Insular Calif. 28x35cm (11x14") Part orig color. [16] £1,130 $1,741
SAXONIA INFERIOR [1720] 33x38cm (13x15½") Full color. [36] £146 $225
SAXONIA SUPERIOR [1720] 33x38cm (13x15") Full color. [36] £146 $225

WEILAND

AMERICA [1846] 64x46cm (24½x17½") Color. Edges chipped, print unaffected. [12] £81 $125
DAS AUSTRAL CONTINENT ODER NEU HOLLAND [c. 1862] Insets. 46x57cm (18x22½") OL col. [41] £180 $277

WEIMAR GEOGRAPHISCHES INSTITUT

DER NOERDLICHE THEIL DES GROSSEN WELT MEERES NACH DEN NEUESTEN BESTIMMUNGEN UND ENTDECKUNGEN ... [1820] By Reichard. North Pacific regions. 53x71cm (21½x28") Orig OL col. [28] £351 $540
GENERAL CHARTE VON AUSTRALIEN [1804] 45x62cm (17½x24½") OL color. Ref: Tooley (Australia) 999, pl.148. [16] £617 $951
SUDLICHE UND NOERDLICH HALBKUGEL DER ERDE ... [1817] Polar hemispheres. 47x60cm (18½x23½") Orig OL color. [14] £208 $320
VEREINIGTEN STAATEN V. NORD-AMERICA [1846 (1847)] TX Republic outlined; German, French, Irish & Sutter's colonies noted. 48x64cm (19½x25") Orig OL color. [46] £292 $450

WELD, I.
PART OF THE UNITED STATES OF NORTH AMERICA [1800] In *Travels Through ... North America ... 1795-1797*. Northeastern U.S. 41x46cm (16x18") Some wash color. Ref: Howes (US) W235 [56] £146 $225

WELLER   Try *Weekly Dispatch*
PALESTINE [1853] 30x23cm (12½x9") Color. [23] £16 $25

PART OF THE UNITED STATES AND CANADA [1884] From Henry Barneby, *Life and Labour in the Far, Far West*. 53x69cm (21½x27") Full printed color. VG. [19] £97 $150

THE ARCTIC REGIONS OF NORTH AMERICA [c. 1859] London: Cassell, Pelter & Galpin. 31x43cm (12x17") Orig OL color. [14] £32 $50

WELLS
A NEW MAP OF SOUTH AMERICA, SHEWING ITS GENERAL DIVISIONS, CHIEF CITIES & TOWNS; RIVERS, MOUNTAINS &C. ... [c. 1701 - 1719] 38x48cm (14½x19½") [28] £175 $270

A NEW MAP OF THE BRITISH ISLES, SHEWING THEIR PRESENT GENL. DIVISIONS, CITIES ... [c. 1701-1719] 38x51cm (15½x20") Ref: Shirley (BI 1650-1750) pp.149-150. [28] £192 $295

A NEW MAP OF THE LAND OF CANAAN AND PARTS ADJOINING SHEWING THE DIVISION THEREOF AMONG THE TWELVE TRIBES OF ISRAEL ... [c. 1719-22] 38x48cm (15x19½") Ref: Laor 835. [28] £162 $250

[SAME TITLE] [1722] Sutton Nichols, sc. 36x48cm (14x19") Ref: Laor 835. [23] £114 $175

A NEW MAP OF THE SO. & MID. PARTS OF ANTIENT GREECE VIZ. EPIRUS, HELLAS, OR GRAECIA PROPRIA, AND PELOPONNESUS, TOGETHER WITH THE ADJOYNING ISLANDS ... [1710-38] Nicholls, sc. 38x51cm (15x19½") Modern OL & cartouche color. Ref: Zacharakis 2127. [28] £146 $225

A NEW MAP OF THE TERRAQUEOUS GLOBE ACCORDING TO THE ANCIENT DISCOVERIES AND MOST GENERAL DIVISIONS OF IT INTO CONTINENTS AND OCEANS [1700] Double hemi; insular Calif. 38x51cm (14½x20½") Color. Minor repairs. Ref: Shirley (W) 608. [26] £552 $850

A NEW MAP SHEWING ALL THE SEVERALL COUNTRIES, CITIES, TOWNS AND OTHER PLACES MENTIONED IN THE NEW TESTAMENT ... [1722] 3 maps on sheet: Holy Land; Eastern Mediterranean; entire Mediterranean. 36x48cm (14x19") Color. Ref: Laor 836. [23] £120 $185

A NEW MAP SHEWING THE TRAVELS OF THE PATRIARCHS. AS ALSO OF THE CHILDREN OF ISRAEL FROM EGYPT THROUGH THE WILDERNESS TO THE LAND OF CANAAN [1722] 36x50cm (14½x19½") Color. Ref: Laor 834. [23] £114 $175

ANTIQUAE GRAECIAE TABULA [1709] 10x15cm (4x6") Color. [57] £42 $65

THE TERRAQUEOUS GLOBE ACCORDING TO THE LATEST DISCOVERIES [1701] From *A New Sett of Maps both of Ancient and Present Geography* E. Wells. Double hemisphere; insular California. 36x51cm (14½x20") Full color. Fine. Ref: Shirley (W) pl.420. [1] £974 $1,500

WERNER
GEBIET MISSOURI, GEBIET OREGAN [1830] Leipzig. Western territories. 20x28cm (8x10½") Orig OL color. [46] £49 $75

WESCOATT
MAP OF GOLD HILL FRONT LODES ON THE COMSTOCK RANGE N.T. [1864] Boston: Oakley & Thomson. 30x56cm (12x22") B&W. Lt scattered foxing; ragged edges. [6] £97 $150

WHITE
MAP OF NEW HAMPSHIRE [1853] Geo. White; Greenbush, VT. Wall map. 16 miles/inch. 33x20cm (12½x8½") 2 rails. OL & full color. Dark, fly-specked; cracked surface, no loss; margin binding loose; good. [6] £341 $525

WHITE, W.
WHITE'S PLANE SPHERICAL GLOBE [1839] W. White, Sheffield, England. Not a globe; hemispheric maps mounted beneath brass meridian rules within quarto, folding half morocco game board. With Texas Republic; peripheral diagrams. OL color. Fine. [17] £487 $750

WILKES
1. ARMILLARY SPHERE 2. TERRSTRIAL GLOBE 3. CELESTIAL GLOBE [1807] London: J. Wilkes; J. Pass, sc. 23x20cm (9x7½") Orig wash color. Fine. [49] £120 $185

MAP OF THE HAWAIIAN GROUP OR SANDWICH ISLANDS BY THE U.S. EX. EX. [1844 (1845)] 21x28cm (8½x11") Uncol. Thin paper as issued; overall VG. Ref: Fitzpatrick (HI) pp.68-9, 141. [59] £120 $185

MAP OF THE OREGON TERRITORY FROM THE BEST AUTHORITIES [1849] From Charles Wilkes, *Western America* ... Reduced version, near identical to 1841 U.S. Ex. Ex. map. 21x33cm (8½x13") Uncol. Half lf margin extended, rt margin corner repaired; bright, clear, clean. Ref: Howes (US) W416; Wheat III, #655. [59] £162 $250

WILKIE

AFRICA DRAWN AND ENGRAVED FROM THE BEST MAPS AND CHARTS [1786] 34x37cm (13½x14½") Orig OL color. [14] £45 $70

MAP OF THE SOUTHERN EXTREMITY OF THE CONTINENT OF AFRICA, COMPREHENDING THE CAPE OF GOOD HOPE, THE DUTCH COLONIES AND THE HOTTENTOT SETTLEMENTS [1786] 23x42cm (9x16½") Orig OL color. [14] £97 $150

WILKINSON

A MAP OF THE CIRCLE OF AUSTRIA DRAWN FROM THE BEST AUTHORITIES [Dated 1794] 20x25cm (7½x10") Full color. [35] £36 $55

A MAP OF THE DUCHY OF SILESIA, DRAWN FROM THE BEST AUTHORITIES [Dated 1794] Formerly Germany. 23x20cm (9x8½") OL color. [35] £36 $55

A NEW AND ACCURATE MAP OF NEW SOUTH WALES, ALSO NORFOLK AND LORD HOWE ISLANDS [1792] 1st ed. 23x27cm (9x10½") Orig color. Ref: Tooley (Australia) 1357. [16] £183 $282

AN ACCURATE MAP OF THE ISLANDS AND CHANNELS BETWEEN CHINA AND NEW HOLLAND [Dated 1794] In *General Atlas*. East Indies. 23x28cm (9x11") Orig OL color. [35] £42 $65

BAVARIA DIVIDED INTO ITS RESPECTIVE SOVEREIGN STATES [Dated 1806] 23x28cm (9x11") Full color. [35] £42 $65

BOHEMIA INCLUDING MORAVIA AUSTRIAN SILESIA EGER & GLATZ [Dated 1800] 23x30cm (9x11½") Color. [35] £39 $60

CANAAN FROM THE TIME OF JOSHUA TO THE BABYLONISH CAPTIVITY [1798] From *Atlas Classica*. Palmer, sc. 44x28cm (17x11") Color. Ref: Laor 853. [23] £32 $50

CANAAN OR THE LAND OF PROMISE TO ABRAHAM AND HIS POSTERITY [same date & source] Baker, sc. 28x23cm (11½x8½") Color. Ref: Laor 851. [23] £29 $45

HUNGARY AND TRANSILVANIA DRAWN FROM THE LATEST AUTHORITIES [Dated 1806] 23x28cm (9x11") Color. [35] £42 $65

LOWER AND UPPER RHINE WITH FRANCONIA [Dated 1802] 22x28cm (9x11") Full color. [35] £42 $65

MAP OF THE BRITISH PROVINCE OF NEW BRUNSWICK FROM THE BEST EXISTING MATERIALS; ... WITH ADJACENT PARTS OF CANADA, NOVA SCOTIA & MAINE [1859] Mounted on linen in sections. 124x130cm (49½x50½") Orig color. [28] £292 $450

PRUSSIA [Dated 1808] Royal Prussia, Polish Prussia, Great Poland & Kingdom of Prussia. 23x28cm (9x11") Full color. [35] £39 $60

SWABIA [Dated 1802] 23x28cm (9x11") Color. [35] £39 $60

THE NETHERLANDS INCLUDING LIEGE [Dated 1809] Benelux. 23x30cm (9x11½") Full color. [35] £36 $55

THE PURVEYORSHIPS IN THE REIGN OF SOLOMON ... [1798] From *Atlas Classica*. 28x22cm (11x8½") Color. Ref: Laor 855. [23] £29 $45

THE UNITED STATES OF AMERICA ... [1812] 24x29cm (9½x11") Orig color. [54] £250 $385

THE UNITED STATES OF AMERICA CONFIRMED BY TREATY. 1783 [1806] State of "Franklinia" appears in Western NC and listing. 25x28cm (10x11") Orig color. [54] £350 $539

WILL

KRIEGS SCHAUPLATZ ... [1770] Balkans; concentric circles on Belgrade. 52x59cm (20½x23") Full orig color. VG+. [30] £276 $425

WILLARD

[ATLAS] ANCIENT ATLAS TO ACCOMPANY THE UNIVERSAL GEOGRAPHY BY WM. C. WOODBRIDGE AND E. WILLARD [1827] Hartford: Oliver D. Cooke. 1st ed. Quarto; 4 single-page, 2 double-page maps. OL & full color. Much used, soiled, ink-scarred; ragged edges. [7] £146 $225

WILLIAMS

TERRA SANCTA VEL REGIO MARITIMA A LIBANO AD HALAKUM USQUE MONTEM ... [1841] E.P. Williams. 30x23cm (12½x9") Color. [23] £23 $35

WILLIAMS, W.

MAP OF THE MISSISSIPPI RIV. [1849] 4 maps on 2 sheets. 18x13cm (7x5") River in blue; cities in red. VG. [20] £71 $110

WILMORE

MAP OF MONTANA [1885] 13x20cm (5x8") Full printed color. Good. [18] £13 $20

WILSON

A GENERAL CHART OF THE INDIAN AND PART OF THE PACIFIC OCEANS, SHEWING THE VARIOUS PASSAGES TO & FROM CHINA, AUSTRALIA, NEW ZEALAND, &C. ... [1850 (1856)] Charles Wilson. 114x198cm (44½x78") Bluebacked, linen bound edges. MS ship tracks with names & dates. Soiling & wear; above average for chart long used at sea. [15] £400 $616

WINTERBOTHAM

A GENERAL MAP OF SOUTH AMERICA DRAWN FROM THE BEST SURVEYS [1794] 37x45cm (14½x18") [14] £32 $50

PLAN OF THE CITY OF WASHINGTON IN THE TERRITORY OF COLUMBIA ... [1795] London. After 1792 Ellicott plan with additions. 40x53cm (16x21") [14] £974 $1,500

WOLFE, J.

THE DESCRIPTION OF THE WHOLE COAST LYING IN THE SOUTH SEAS OF AMERICAE CALLED PERU, BEGINNING AT RIO DE PLATA ... TO THE CAPE OF FLORIDA ... IMPRINTED AT LONDON BY IOHN WOLFE AND GRAVEN BY ROBERT BECKIT [1598] South America with Florida. 38x55cm (15x21½") Paper backing, sm engraved area at lf border supplied from another copy; orig & complete. [62] £2,337 $3,600

WOODBRIDGE

POLITICAL MAP OF THE UNITED STATES ... [1845] School atlas map; incl Mexico. Insets: DC; rail & canals. 28x46cm (11x17½") Lt soil; c'fold repair; o/w good. [11] £88 $135

WOOLMAN & ROSE

[ATLAS] HISTORICAL AND BIOGRAPHICAL ATLAS OF THE NEW JERSEY COAST [1878] Folio; 372 pp; 45 town maps in Monmouth, Ocean, Atlantic & Cape May Counties; 65 pictorial plates. Orig binding scuffed, but tight. 3 foldout maps loose, 5 with browning & tears, rest fine. Ref: Phillips (A) 2141; Le Gear (US) 2307. [35] £1,071 $1,650

WYLD

[CATALOGUE] A CATALOGUE OF ATLASES, MAPS, PLANS ... [1851] Incl Amer. Revolutionary War maps from Faden's stock acquired by Wyld in 1823. Sm quarto. [52] £300 $462

A NEW MAP OF THE PROVINCE OF LOWER CANADA, DESCRIBING ALL THE SEIGNEURIES, TOWNSHIPS, GRANTS OF LAND, &C. ... SAMUEL HOLLAND ... TO WHICH IS ADDED A PLAN OF THE RIVERS SCOUDIAC AND MAGAGUADAVIC, SURVEYED IN 1796, 97, AND 98 ... 98 ... PUBLISHED BY JAMES WYLD [1838] 2nd ed. Folding map mounted on linen in sections. 58x88cm (22½x34½") Orig OL color. Lt browned; holes to margins & below borders, some loss at corners. Ref: Tooley (Amer) p.67, #28d. [28] £221 $340

CAPE DISTRICT CAPE OF GOOD HOPE [1792-1838] Late issue of Faden map by De La Rochette. 51x33cm (20x13") Orig OL color. [53] £280 $431

EAST INDIA ISLES AND AUSTRALIA [1824] 23x30cm (9x11½") Orig OL color. Ref: Tooley (Australia) 1558 pl.120. [16] £71 $110

MAP OF AMERICA [1835] 53x61cm (21½x24") Orig OL color. Ragged lower margin; Lower c'fold split. [28] £195 $300

MAP OF NORTH AMERICA, EXHIBITING THE RECENT DISCOVERIES. GEOGRAPHICAL & NAUTICAL ... [c. 1870] Later state. 47x36cm (18½x14") Orig OL color. Margins trimmed to border. [14] £49 $75

MAP OF SOUTH AUSTRALIA, NEW SOUTH WALES, VAN DIEMEN'S LAND [1841-1852] 93x61cm (36½x24") Orig OL color. Ref: Tooley (Australia) p.362, #530. [53] £340 $524

MAP OF THE UNITED KINGDOM OF GREAT BRITAIN AND IRELAND ... [c. 1755] Wyld the Younger. Dissected, linen mounted, folds into cloth slipcase. 53x41cm (21x16½") OL color. Fine. [21] £162 $250

MAP OF THE WEST INDIA & BAHAMA ISLANDS WITH THE ADJACENT COASTS OF YUCATAN, HONDURAS, CARACAS &C. [1825] Linen backed folding map, marbled self-backs & slipcase. 53x78cm (21x30½") Orig full wash color. Orig intact slipcase worn; map VG+. [33] £422 $650

[SAME TITLE] [1841] 53x77cm (21x30½") Wash OL color. [14] £120 $185

PLAN OF LONDON AND WESTMINSTER [1835] Reduced from 40-sheet plan. Dissected, linen mounted. 58x107cm (22½x41½") Full color. VG. [21] £114 $175

SKETCH OF THE NORTH EASTERN BOUNDARY BETWEEN GREAT BRITAIN AND THE UNITED STATES AS SETTLED BY TREATY AUGT. 1842. PUBLISHED. SEPT. 29TH. 1842. BY JAS. WYLD ... [1842] Mounted on linen in sections; orig cloth cover. 24x33cm (9½x13") Orig OL color. [28] £234 $360

THE BASIN OF THE PACIFIC [1847] 57x84cm (22x33") Orig OL color. Minor offset stains in blank fold area; lower portion cut & joined with tape as issued. [14] £55 $85

THE PROVINCE OF CANADA BY JAMES WYLD ... [c. 1855-61] Folding map. 61x97cm (24x38") Orig OL color. Remounted on new linen in sections; orig cloth cover & ad slip. [28] £204 $315
THE UNITED STATES OF NORTH AMERICA WITH THE BRITISH TERRITORIES [1805] 56x66cm (21½x25½") Orig color. Corner torn from lower margin; sh tears to margin affecting ¼" of border. [28] £234 $360
[SAME TITLE] [1838] 54x64cm (21½x25") OL color. Generally bright, clean. [10] £243 $375
WYLD'S ROAD DIRECTOR THROUGH ENGLAND AND WALES ... [c. 1836] Dissected, linen mounted folding into case. 69x51cm (26½x20") OL color. VG. [21] £81 $125

WYTFLIET

[ATLAS] HISTOIRE UNIVERSELLE DES INDES OCCIDENTALES ET ORIENTALES, ET DE LA CONVERSION DES INDIENS, DIVISEE EN TROIS PARTIES ... [1611] Douai: Francois Fabri; 3rd French ed. Folio; 23 maps (19 double page); 4 sm East Asia maps on 2 leaves. Old mottled calf, rebacked; 1st title trimmed to platemark & mounted, sl loss. Ref: cf Schwartz & Ehrenberg pl.40, 41. Tooley (M&M) p.112; Nordenskiold (Col) II,309-10; cf Nordenskiold (Fac) p.133-4, pl.LI. [28] £9,349 $14,400
CASTILIA AURIFERA CUM VICINIS PROVINCIIS [1597 / 1605] 23x29cm (9x11½") Uncol. Fine. [2] £227 $350
CHICA SIVE PATAGONI CAET AUSTRALIS TERRA [1597 / 1605] 23x30cm (9x11½") Uncolored. Fine. Ref: Tooley (Australia) #1430. [2] £909 $1,400
CONIBAS REGIO CUM VICINIS GENTIBUS [1597] 23x28cm (9x10½") Uncolored. Fine. [2] £909 $1,400
CUBA INSULA ET IAMAICA [1597] 23x29cm (9x11½") Exc. [62] £552 $850
ESTOTILANDIA ET LABORATORIS TERRA [c. 1605] 23x28cm (8½x10½") Lower c'fold tear repaired; sm wormholes lower margin. Ref: Trudel p.65; Koeman III Wyt 1A; Nordenskiold (Fac) Pl.LI. [28] £876 $1,350
NORUMBEGA ET VIRGINIA [1597 / ?] 23x30cm (9x11½") Exc. Ref: Schwartz & Ehrenberg pl.40; Morrison fig.4; Danforth #49; Benes #1. [38] £1,623 $2,500
PERUANI REGNI DESCRIPTIO [1597 / 1605] From *Descriptionis Ptolemaicae Augmentum*. State 2 (date removed). 23x29cm (9x11½") Exc. Ref: Nordenskiold (Fac) pl.LI. [62] £146 $225
UTRIUSQUE HEMISPHERII DELINEATO [1597 / 1605] Woodblock. 23x28cm (9x11½") VG. Ref: Shirley (W) 207; Nordenskiold (Fac) pp.29,133-34; Wagner (NW) 191. [2] £779 $1,200

ZATTA

[FRONTISPIECE] ATLANTE NOVISSIMO TOMO I [1779] 32x43cm (12½x17") Full later color. Wormhole lower margin; fine. [32] £130 $200
EMISFERO TERRESTRE MERIDIONALE [1779] 30x30cm (11½x11½") OL color. [16] £404 $622
[SAME TITLE] [c. 1785] From *Atlante Novissimo*. [same dimen] Orig OL color. [53] £300 $462
IL MAPPA MONDO O SIA DESCRIZIONE GENERALE DEL GLOBO RIDOTTO IN QUADRO ... [dated 1774] From *Atlante Novissimo*, 1779-1788. 27x39cm (10½x15") Orig OL color to coasts, cartouche, side borders. Fine. Ref: Phillips (A) 650,6. [59] £250 $385
[SAME TITLE] [c. 1785] From *Atlante Novissimo*. 27x40cm (11x15½") Orig OL col. [53] £550 $847
IL MARYLAND, IL JERSEY MERIDIONALE, LA DELAWARE, E LA PARTE ORIENTALE DELLA VIRGINIA, E CAROLINA SETTENTRIONALE [1778] 33x43cm (12½x16½") OL color. Ref: Portinaro & Knirsch pl.151. [36] £243 $375
IL PAESE DE CHERACHESI CON LA PARTE OCCIDENTALE DELLA CAROLINA SETTENTRIONALE E DELLA VIRGINIA [c. 1780] Includes present IN, KY, TN and middle Mississippi River. 32x42cm (13x16½") Orig OL color. Superb. Matted. [51] £325 $500
IL PAESE DE'SELVAGGI OUTAGAMIANI, MASCOUTENSI, ILLINESI, E PARTE DELLA VI NAZIONI [1778] 33x43cm (13x17½") Orig OL color. Ref: Phillips (A) 650; Portinaro & Knirsch 147. [28] £292 $450
IL PAESE DE'SELVAGGI OUTAUACESI E KILISTINESI INTORNO AL LAGO SUPERIORE [1778] Florida inset. 33x43cm (13x17½") Orig OL color. Ref: Phillips (A) 650; Portinaro & Knirsch 144. [28] £308 $475
[SAME TITLE] [1778] 36x46cm (13½x17½") Orig OL color. VG. [45] £227 $350
[SAME TITLE] [1778] 32x42cm (12½x16½") B&W. [46] £143 $220
IMPERIUM ALEXANDRI MAGNI PER EUROPAM ASIAM, ET AFRICAM ... [1785] From *Atlante Novissimo*. 33x44cm (13x17½") Orig OL color. [53] £120 $185
ISOLE FILIPPINE [c. 1785] From *Atlante Novissimo*. 40x31cm (16x12") Orig OL color. [53] £400 $616
L'ACADIA, LE PROVINCIE DI SAGADAHOOK E MAIN, LA NUOVA HAMPSHIRE, LA RHODE ISLAND, E PARTE DI MASSACHUSSET E CONNECTICUT [1778] 32x42cm (12½x16½") Orig color. Ref: Phillips (A) 650; Portinaro & Knirsch 149. [28] £234 $360
[SAME TITLE] [c. 1785] From *Atlante Novissimo*. 33x43cm (13x16½") Orig OL color. [53] £200 $308

L'AMERICA DIVISA NE SUOI PRINCIPALI STATI DI NUOVA PROJEZIONE ... [1776] 31x40cm (12x16")
Orig OL & cartouche color. Lt browning at c'fold. [28] £325 $500
[SAME TITLE] [same date & dimen] From *Atlante Novissimo*, 1779-1788. Vestigial NW passage Some
orig OL color. Fine. Ref: Lowery 586; Phillips (A) 650,14; Wheat (TM) 168. [59] £315 $485
[SAME TITLE] [1776 - c.1785] [same source & dimen] Orig OL color. [53] £260 $400
L'ELVEZIA ... [c. 1785] From *Atlante Novissimo*. 32x41cm (12½x16") Orig OL color. [53] £240 $370
L'ESTREMADURA DI PORTOGALLO ... [c. 1775] 31x31cm (12x12") OL color. [43] £98 $151
L'IMPERO DEL GIAPON DIVISO IN SETTE PRINCIPALI PARTI... [c. 1785] From *Atlante Novissimo*.
32x40cm (12½x15½") Orig OL color. [53] £1,200 $1,848
L'ISOLA D'ISLANDA [c. 1785] From *Atlante Novissimo*. 31x41cm (12x16") Orig OL color. [53] £200 $308
LA BAJA D'HUDSON TERRA DI LABRADOR E GROENLANDIA CON LE ISOLE ADIACENTI ... [c. 1785] From
Atlante Novissimo. 30x41cm (12x16") Orig OL color. [53] £200 $308
LA NUOVA ZELANDA TRASCORSA NEL 1769 E 1770 DAL COOK ... [1778] From *Atlante Novissimo*. 1st
atlas map of New Zealand. 45x36cm (17½x14") Orig OL color. [52] £750 $1,155
LA PALATINATI DI MAZOVIA ... [POLAND] [c. 1781] 31x40cm (12x15½") Color. [42] £75 $116
LA PALATINATI DI NOWOGRODEK ... [POLAND] [c. 1785] 31x40cm (12x15½") Color. [42] £75 $116
LA PARTE OCCIDENTALE DELLA NUOVA FRANCIA O CANADA [1778] 33x46cm (13½x17½") Orig color.
Ref: Portinaro & Knirsch pl.145; Phillips (A) 650. [28] £234 $360
LA PENSILVANIA, LA NUOVA YORK, IL JERSEY SETTENTRIOLE, CON LA PARTE OCCIDENTALE DEL
CONNECTICUT, MASSACHUSSET-S-BAY E L'IROCHESIA. FOGL. V. [1778] 33x46cm (13½x17½") Orig
color. Sm wormhole ctr margin. Ref: Phillips (A) 650; Portinaro & Knirsch 148. [28] £292 $450
LE COLONIE UNITE DELLA AMERICA SETTENTR.LE ... [c. 1785] From *Atlante Novissimo*. 12-sheet map
after John Mitchell. Each sheet about 30x40cm (12x15½") Orig OL col. [53] £2,499 $3,850
LE ISOLE DI TERRA NUOVA E CAPO BRETON ... [1778] From *Atlante Novissimo*. 46x33cm (17½x13½")
Orig OL & cartouche color. Sh paper crease. Ref: Phillips (A) 650. [28] £351 $540
[SAME TITLE] [c. 1785] From *Atlante Novissimo*. 42x32cm (16½x12½") Orig OL color. [53] £300 $462
MARE DEL SUD [c. 1776] Incl eastern Australia & N.Z. 30x41cm (12x16") Color. [41] £890 $1,371
MESSICO OUVERO NUOVA SPAGNA CHE CONTIENE IL NUOVO MESSICO, LA CALIFORNIA, CON UNA PARTE DE'
PAESI ADJACENT ... [c. 1785] From *Atlante Novissimo*. 31x40cm (12x16") Orig OL col. [53] £220 $339
NUOVE SCOPERTE DE RUSSI AL NORD DEL MARE DEL SUD SI NELL'ASIA, CHE NELL'AMERICA [1776]
31x40cm (12x15½") Orig full color. Lt browned fold. Ref: Wheat (TM) 167. [46] £325 $500
NUOVE SCOPERTE FATTE NEL 1765, 67, E 69 NEL MARE DEL SUD [1776] 30x41cm (12x16½") Orig
color. Ref: Tooley (Australia) 1431. [16] £855 $1,316
PARTE DEL REGNO D'IRLANDA CIOE LE PROVINCIE DE CONNAUGHT E MUNSTER DI NUOVA PROJEZIONE
[1778] Western part. 43x30cm (16½x12½") Old color. [24] £195 $300
PARTE OCCIDENTALE DELL'ELVEZIA ... [c. 1785] From *Atlante Novissimo*. 41x31cm (16x12") Orig OL color.
[53] £180 $277
PARTE ORIENTALE DEL CANADA, NUOVA SCOZIA SETTENTRIONALE, E PARTE DI LABRADOR [1778]
33x43cm (13½x17½") Orig OL color. Ref: Phillips (A) 650. [28] £234 $360
[SAME TITLE] [c. 1780] 30x42cm (12x16½") OL color. [40] £140 $216
PARTE ORIENTALE DELL'ELVEZIA ... [c. 1785] From *Atlante Novissimo*. 41x31cm (16x12") Orig OL
color. [53] £180 $277
PARTE ORIENTALE DELLA FLORIDA, DELLA GIORGIA, E CAROLINA MERIDIONALE [1778] 33x43cm (13½x17½")
Orig OL color. C'fold bit browned. Ref: Phillips (A) 650; Portinaro & Knirsch pl.153. [28] £234 $360
[SAME TITLE] [same date & dimen] Orig wash color. [46] £162 $250
PLANISFERIO CELESTE SETTENTRIONALE ... [WITH] ... MERIDIONALE ... [1777] Two charts, each
32x40cm (12½x15½") Orig color. [52] £520 $801

ZURNER

PLANISPHAERIUM TERRESTRE CUM UTROQUE COELESTI HAEMISPHAERIO ... [c. 1700] Engraved for
Pieter Schenk. Double hemisphere; insular California. Decor of scientific & natural phenomena. 51x58cm
(20x22½") Separate index leaf. Full orig color. Fine. Ref: Shirley 639, pl.440. [2] £2,272 $3,500

References Cited

The references listed below have been cited by dealers in their catalogues and reported in the *Price Listing*. If an author is cited more than once, an identifying word or phrase appears in parentheses. Note is made in square brackets if a comment appears in the *Recommended References* section above. If reviewed in this or other volumes of the *Price Record* the date is given in square brackets.

Armstrong, J.C.W., *From Sea unto Sea: Art & Discovery Maps of Canada*. 1982

Bagrow, L., (Russia) *The History of the Cartography of Russia up to 1600*. 1975 [reviewed in 1990]

— *The History of Cartography*. [see "General References"]

Benes, P., ed. *New England Prospect: Maps, Place Names, and Hisorical Landscape*. 1982

Buczek, K. *The History of Polish Cartography* ... 1981. [reviewed in 1985]

Campbell, T. (Earliest) *The Earliest Printed maps 1472-1500* [reviewed in 1989]

— (Early).. *Early Maps*. 1981 [reviewed in 1985]

— (Japan) *Japan, European Printed Maps to 1800*.

Chapin, H., *Contributions to Rhode Island Bibliography No. V. Checklist of Maps of Rhode Island*. 1928.

Chubb, T., *Printed Maps in the Atlases of Great Britain and Ireland: 1579-1870*. 1970.

Clancy, R. & A. Richardson. *So They Came South*.

Clark, D., *Index to Maps of the American Revolution in Books and Periodicals*. 1974.

Cobb, D.A. (NH) *New Hampshire Maps to 1900: An annotated checklist*. [reviewed in 1989]

— (VT) "Vermont Maps Prior to 1900: An Annotated Cartobibliography" in *Vermont History*, Vol. XXXIX, Nos 3 & 4. 1971.

Cortazzi, H. (Japan) *Isles of Gold; Antique Maps of Japan*. 1983.

Cumming, W.P. (Colonial Amer) *British Maps of Colonial America*. 1974

— (Discovery) *The Discovery of North America*. 1972

— (SE) *The Southeast in Early Maps*. 1957.

Cumming, W.P. et al, (Exploration) *The Exploration of North America 1630-1776*. 1974.

Day, J.M., compiler, *Maps of Texas 1527-1900*. 1964.

Danforth, S. *The Land of Nurembega*.

Deak, G.G., *Picturing America: 1497-1899*. 1988.

Falk, M.W. (AK) *Alaskan Maps: A Cartobibliography to 1900*. 1983. [reviewed in 1987]

Fell, R.T. *Early Maps of South-East Asia*. 1991. [reviewed in 1993]

Fite, E.D. & A. Freeman, *A Book of Old Maps Delineating American History from the Earliest Days Down to the Close of the Revolutionary War*. 1926.

Fitzpatrick, G.L. (HI) *The Early Mapping of Hawai'i*. 1987

Gole, S. *Early Maps of India*. 1978

Goss. J. (Grand Atlas) *Blaeu's The Grand Atlas of the 17th-century World*. 1990. [reviewed in 1992]

— (Euro Cities) *The City Maps of Europe; 16th Century Town Plans* ... 1992

— (Art) *The Mapmaker's Art: An Illustrated History of Cartography*. 1993. [reviewed in 1994]

— (NA) *The Mapping of North America: Three Centuries of Map-Making 1500-1860*. 1990.

Guthorn, P. (Amer.Rev.) *British Maps of the American Revolution*.

— (Charts) *United States Coastal Charts, 1783-1861*. 1984.

Harley, J.B. (Encounter) Maps of the Columbian Encounter; An Interpretive Guide ... 1990

Haskell, D.C., "Manhattan Maps - A Co-operative List" in *Bulletin of the New York Public Library*, April - October 1930.

Heidenreich & Dahl. *French Mapping of North America*.

Howes, W., *U.S.Iana (1650-1950)*. 1962.

Howgego, J., *Printed Maps of London circa 1553-1850*. 1978.

Howse, D. & M. Sanderson, *Sea Chart, The: An Historical Survey ...* 1973.

Humphreys, A.L., *Antique Maps and Charts*. 1989.

Jolly, D.C., *Maps in British Periodicals: Part I* and *Part II*. [reviewed in 1990, 1991]

Johnson, Adrian. *American Explored*. 1974

Kapp, K.S. (Panama) *Early Maps of Panama up to 1865*. 1971.

— (Jamaica) *The Printed Maps of Jamaica up to 1825*. 1968.

Karpinski, L.C. (MI) *Bibliography of the Printed Maps of Michigan, 1804-1880*. 1931.

— (Carolina) *Early Maps of Carolina and Adjoining Regions*. 1937.

— (FC) *Maps of Famous Cartographers Depicting North America. An Historical Atlas of the Great Lakes and Michigan ...* 1977. 2nd edition of Karpinski (MI) above.

Karrow, R.W., Jr., ed. *Checklist of Printed Maps of the Middle West to 1900*. 1981.

— (16c) *Mapmakers of the Sixteenth Century and Their Maps: Bio-Bibliographies*. 1993. [reviewed in 1994]

Kaufman, K. (Gt. Lakes) *The Mapping of the Great Lakes in the Seventeenth Century*. 1989 [reviewed in 1994]

Kershaw, K.A. *Early Printed Maps of Canada*. 1993. [reviewed in 1994]

Koeman, I.C., *Atlantes Neerlandici: Bibliography of terrestrial, Maritime and celestial atlases and pilot books, published in the Netherlands up to 1880*, 5 vols. 1967-71. [see "General References"]

Laor, E., *Maps of the Holy Land: Cartobibliography of Printed Maps, 1475-1900*. [reviewed in 1988]

Lawson, S. & W.J. Faupel, *A Foothold in Florida; The Eye-Witness Account of Four Voyages made by the French to that Region and their attempt at Colonisation 1562-1568*. [reviewed in 1994]

Le Gear, C.E., compiler (US) *United States Atlases: A List of National, State, County, City, and Regional Atlases in the Library of Congress*. 1950.

Leighly, J., *California as an Island*. 1972.

Lowery, W., *A Descriptive List of Maps of the Spanish Possessions within the Present Limits of the United States 1502-1820*. 1912.

Map Collector, The. Tring, England: Map Collector Publications. Quarterly since Dec. 1977 [see "General References"]

Map Collectors' Series, London: The Map Collectors' Circle. 110 numbered issues in 11 volumes, 1964-1974. [see "General References"]

Martin, J.C. & R.S. Martin, *Maps of Texas and the Southwest, 1513-1900*. [reviewed in 1987]

McCorkle, B.B. *America Emergent; An Exhibition of Maps and Atlases ...* 1985

McCormick, T. *First Views of Australia 1788-1825*

Mickwitz, A. (Nordenskiold Col) *The A.E. Nordenskiold Collection ...* 1979- [reviewed in 1986]

Modelski, A.M., *Railroad Maps of the United States: A selective annotated bibliography of original 19th-century maps in the Geography and Map Division of the Library of Congress*. [see "Specialized References"]

Moreland, C. & D. Bannister, *Antique Maps: A collector's handbook*. [reviewed in 1985, 1987]

Morrison, Russell, et al, *On the Map*. 1983.

Nebenzahl, K. (Biblio Amer Rev) *A Bibliography of Printed Battle Plans of the American Revolution.* 1975

— (Amer Rev) *Atlas of the American Revolution.* 1975.

— (Holy Land) *Maps of the Holy Land: Images of Terra Sancta through two millennia* [reviewed in 1988]

Nordenskiöld, A.E., *Facsimile-Atlas: To the Early History of Cartography with Reproductions of ... Maps Printed in the XV and XVI Centuries.* 1973.

(Nordenskiold Col) see Mickwitz.

Norwich, O.I., *Maps of Africa: An illustrated carto-bibliography* [reviewed in 1986]

Palmer, M. (Bermuda) *Printed Maps of Bermuda.*

Papenfuse, E.C. & J.M. Coale III, *The Hammond-Harwood House Atlas of Historical Maps of Maryland, 1608-1908.* 1982.

Pastourçau, M. *Les Atlas Français XVIe-XVIIe Siecles: Repertoire Bibliographique et Etude.* 1984

Pedley, M. S., *BEL ET UTILE: The work of the Robert De Vaugondy Family of mapmakers.* [reviewed in 1993]

Phillips, P.L. (A) *A List of Geographical Atlases in the Library of Congress*, Vols. I-IV, continued by Clara Egli LeGear, Vols. 5-8. [see "General References"]

— (M) *A List of Maps of America in the Library of Congress Preceded by a List of Works Relating to Cartography.* [see "Specialized References"]

— (Wash) *Maps & Views of Washington.*

Portinaro, P. & F. Knirsch, *The Cartography of North America 1500-1800.* [rev. 1990]

Potter, J., *Country Life Book of Antique Maps: An introduction to the history of maps and how to appreciate them.* [reviewed in 1990]

Quirino, C., *Philippine Cartography, 1320-1899.* 1963.

Reps, J.W., *Views & Viewmakers of Urban America: Lithographs of towns and cities in the United States and Canada, notes on the artists and publishers, and a union catalog of their work, 1825-1925.* [see "Specialized References"; reviewed in 1985]

Ristow, W.W., compiler, *A la Carte: Selected Papers on Maps and Atlases.* 1972.

Royal Scottish Geographical Society. *The Early Maps of Scotland to 1850* 1973.

Sabin, J. *Bibliotheca Americana. A Dictionary of Books Relating to America ...* reprinted 1962.

Schilder, G. *Australia Unveiled.*

Schwartz, S.I., & R.E. Ehrenberg, *The Mapping of America.* 1980. [see "Specialized References"]

Sellers, J.R. & P.M. van Ee, *Maps and Charts of North America and the West Indies 1750-1789: A guide to the collections in the Library of Congress.* 1981. [see "Specialized References"]

Shirley, R.W., (BI to 1650) *Early Printed Maps of the British Isles 1477-1650.* [reviewed in 1994]

— (BI 1650-1750) *Printed Maps of the British Isles 1650-1750.* 1988.

— (W) *The Mapping of the World: Early printed world maps 1472-1700* [see "Specialized References"; reviewed in 1985]

Simonetti, M.L., *Descriptive List of the Map Collection in the Pennsylvania State Archives.* 1976.

Skelton, R.A., (County) "County Atlase of the British Isles, 1579-1850." Map Col. Series, 1964-

— *Decorative Printed Maps of the 15th to 18th Centuries.* [see "General References"]

Snyder, J.P. (NJ) *The Mapping of New Jersey.* 1973.

Society for Hellenistic Cartography. *Cartography of the Shores and Islands of Greece.* 1989

Stephenson, R.W. (CW) *Civil War Maps; An Annotated List.* 1961.

Stevens, H.N. (Evans 1749-55) *A Comparative Account of the Original Editions of Lewis Evans' Maps pf 1749 and 1755 and their Derivatives.* 1926

— (Ptolemy) *Ptolemy's Geography; A Brief Account of All the Printed Editions ...* 1908 (1972)

Stevens, H. & R.Tree, *Comparative Cartography Exemplified in an Analytical & Bibliographical Description of Nearly One Hundred Maps and Charts of the American Continent Published in Great Britain during the Years 1600 to 1850,* Map Collectors' Circle, No.39, 1967 (Revised 2nd ed.). Revised 3rd ed. appeared as Chapter 2 of R.V. Tooley, *The Mapping of America,* 1980.

Stokes, I.N.P. (Manhattan) *The Iconography of Manhattan Island.* 1967.

Stokes, I.N.P. & Haskell, *American Historical Prints; Early Views of American Cities, ...* 1933.

(Streeter) *The Celebrated Collection of Americana Formed by the Late Thomas Winthrop Streeter.* Parke-Bernet, 1966-69.

Suarez, T., *Shedding the Veil: Mapping the European discovery of America and the world ... 1434-1865* [reviewed in 1992]

Thompson, Edmund (CT) *Maps of Connecticut for the Years of the Industrial Revolution, 1801-1860.* 1942.

Tibbetts, G.R. *Arabia in Early Maps.* 1978.

Tooley, R.V., (Africa) *Collector's Guide to Maps of the African Continent and Southern Africa.* 1969.

— (Amer.) *The Mapping of America.* 1979.

— (Australia) *The Mapping of Australia and Antarctica.*

— (M&M) *Maps and Map-Maker.* [see "General References"]

Tooley, R.V., C. Bricker, & G.R. Crone (Landmarks) *Landmarks of Mapmaking.* [see "General References"]

Trudel, M. *Atlas de la Nouvelle-France. An Atlas of New France.* 1968.

Van Ermen, E. *The United States in Old Maps & Prints.* 1990. [reviewed in 1992]

Verner, C. & B. Stuart-Stubbs. *The North Part of America.* 1979

Wagner, H.R. (NW) *Cartography of the Northwest Coast of America to the Year 1800.* 1937.

Walter, L. *Japan A Cartographic Vision: European Printed Maps ...* 1994. [reviewed in 1995]

Warner, D.J., *The Sky Explored: Celestial cartography, 1500-1800* [see "Specialized References"; reviewed in 1986]

Winearls, J. *Mapping Upper Canada 1780-1867; An Annotated Bibliography ...* 1991

Wheat, Carl I. (TM) *Mapping the Transmississippi West 1540-1861,* Vols. 1-5. [see "Specialized References"]

Wheat, James C. & Christian F. Brun, *Maps and Charts Published in America before 1800: A bibliography.* [see "Specialized References"]

Wolff, H., ed. *America: Early Maps of the World.* 1992.

Zacharakis, C., *A Catalogue of Printed Maps of Greece.*

Abbreviations Used

B&W – black & white	*engr* – engraver	*occas* - occasional	*sl* – slight, slighly
cf (latin) – compare	*esp* –especially	*orig* – original	*sm* – small
c'fold – centerfold	*exc, excel* - excellent	*o/w* – otherwise	*uncol* – uncolored
col – color	*horiz* – horizontal	*pub* – published	*vert* – vertical
ctr – center	*lf* - left	*Ref:* – reference	*VF* – very fine
dims – dimensions	*litho* – lithograph (ic)	*rev* – reverse	*VG* – very good
deriv – derivative	*lt* – light, lightly	*rt* - right	
ed – edition	*ms* – manuscript	*sh* – short	

TITLE INDEX

ATLASES and BOOKS WITH MAPS:

Title	Author	Size
A Complete Body of Ancient Geography	LAURIE & WHITTLE	Folio
A Comprehensive Atlas Geographical, Historical & Commercial	BRADFORD	Sm folio
A New, General and Universal Atlas Containing Forty-five Maps	DURY	Oblong octavo
A New General Atlas, Exhibiting the Five Great Divisions of the Globe .	MALTE-BRUN	Quarto
Ancient Atlas to Accompany the Universal Geography by Wm. C. Woodbridge	WILLARD	Quarto
Atlas of the Philippine Islands	U.S.	Folio
Atlas Physique, Historique et Politique de Geographie Moderne ...	DUFOUR	Lg folio
Atlas to Marshall's Life of Washington	MARSHALL	Octavo
Atlas Universel ..., Vol. IV, Amerique Septentrionale	VANDERMAELEN	Lg folio
Atlas Universel ..., Vol. V, Amerique Meridionale	VANDERMAELEN	Lg folio
Berghaus' Physikalischer Atlas	BERGHAUS	Folio
Black's General Atlas: A Series of Fifty-Four Maps ... by Sydney Hall	BLACK	Folio
Bradley's Atlas of the World for Commercial and Library Reference	BRADLEY	Folio
Carte de France Dividee en XXXI Gouvernements Militaires [with]	JULIEN, R.	Quarto
Civitates Orbis Terrarum [Facsimile Atlas]	BRAUN & HOGENBERG	Folio
Colton's Atlas of the World ... Vol. II Europe, Asia, Africa, Oceanica	COLTON (Atlas Maps)	Folio
Constable's Hand Atlas of India	CONSTABLE	Lg 12mo
Cosmographie Elementaire. Divisee en Parties Astronomique et Geographique	MENTELLE	Quarto
Cram's Unrivaled Family Atlas of the World	CRAM	Lg quarto
Cyclone Tracks in the South Indian Ocean	BRITISH GOVERNMENT	Oblong folio
Doctrina De Ponderibus	ANGELOCRATOR	28x53cm
Fasciculus Geographicus Complectens Praecipuarum Totius Orbis Regionum	QUAD	Quarto
Geografia Cioe Descrittione Universale della Terra ... Nuovamente ...	MAGINI	Sm folio
Geographicae Enarrationis Libri Octo ...	PTOLEMY (1522-1541)	Folio
Hand-Atlas uber Alle Theile der Erde nach dem Deuesten Zustande ...	STIELER	Oblong folio
Histoire Universelle des Indes Occidentales et Orientales, ...	WYTFLIET	Folio
Historical and Biographical Atlas of the New Jersey Coast	WOOLMAN & ROSE	Folio
Introduction in Universam Geographiam	CLUVER	Octavo
Johnson's New Illustrated (Steel Plate) Family Atlas	JOHNSON	Sm folio
La Geographia ... Aggiunteui di Meser Iacopo Gastaldi ...	GASTALDI	Octavo
Le Nouveau et Curieux Atlas Geographique et Historique ...	CHIQUET	Oblong octavo
Library Reference Atlas of the World	BARTHOLOMEW	Sm folio
Maps and Views to Accompany Message and Documents [from President]	U.S.	Quarto
Maps of the Roads of Ireland, Surveyed 1777	TAYLOR & SKINNER	26x16cm
Marzolla / Atlante / Geografico [spine title]	MARZOLLA	Elephant folio
Mitchell's New General Atlas ... Embracing Forty-Seven Quarto Maps ...	MITCHELL, S.A. (1860+)	Sm folio
Mitchell's New General Atlas ... Embraced in Sixty-Three Quarto Maps ...	MITCHELL, S.A. (1860+)	Sm folio
New Indexed Family Atlas of the United States, with Maps of the World	WATSON	Sm folio
Parvum Theatrum Urbium sive Urbium Praecipuarum Totius Orbis ...	ROMANUS	Sm quarto
Pilot Charts for Atlantic Ocean	BRITISH ADMIRALTY	94x65cm
Pilote Americain 2e partie. Traduit de l'Anglois	LE ROUGE	Folio
Quarterly Current Charts for the Pacific Ocean	BRITISH ADMIRALTY	Lg folio
Rand, McNally & Co.'s Business Atlas, Containing Large Scale Maps ...	RAND, McNALLY (Atlas Maps)	Folio
Rand, McNally & Co.'s New Dollar Atlas of the United States and ...	RAND, McNALLY (Atlas Maps)	Sm quarto
School Atlas	CUMMINGS & HILLIARD	Octavo
Statistical Atlas of the United States Based upon Results of ...	U.S.	Folio
System of Geography for the Use of Schools	MORSE, S.	Lg quarto
The Diamond Atlas. With Descriptions of All Countries ...	MORSE & GASTON	Sm quarto
The Royal Atlas of Modern Geography ...	JOHNSTON	Folio
The Scribner-Black Atlas of the World	BLACK	Imp folio
The Statistical Atlas of England, Scotland and Ireland	JOHNSTON	Imp folio
Theatrum Mundi, et Temporis ...	GALLUCI	Quarto
Wind and Current Charts for the Pacific, Atlantic and Indian Oceans	BRITISH ADMIRALTY	Lg folio

ADVERTISEMENTS and CATALOGUES:

Title	Author	Size
A Catalogue of Atlases, Maps, Plans ...	WYLD	Sm quarto
Etablissement Geographique de Bruxelles ... Catalogue	VANDERMAELEN	Octavo
Globes of the Society for the Diffusion of Useful Knowledge [Advertisement]	S.D.U.K.	36x22cm
New Globes, Celestial and Terrestrial ... [Advertisement]	CARY	14x9cm
Thomas Harris & Son, Opticians and Globe Makers [Advertisement]	HARRIS	22x12cm
Thomas Jefferys Sells ... All Sorts of Maps ... [Advertisement]	JEFFERYS	17x24cm

The dimensions given may not always exactly match those given for multiple entries in the *Price Listing*

GLOBES, GLOBE GORES and CARTOGRAPHIC DEVICES:

Title	Author	Size
[Globe Gore: Australia]	CORONELLI	48x28cm
[Globe Gore: Central Australia]	CORONELLI	47x27cm
[Globe Gores: North America]	CORONELLI	48x79cm
[Hemisphere on mobile set up]	PEETERS	14x15cm
Andrews' 18 Inch Terrestrial Globe	ANDREWS	Diam 46cm
Betts Portable Terrestrial Globe Compiled from the Latest and Best Authorities	BETTS	Diam 36cm
Cary's New Terrestrial ... [and] Celestial Globe ...	CARY	Diam 30cm
Improved Globe. Boston ...	COPLEY	Diam 38cm
Joslin's Terrestrial Globe ...	JOSLIN	Diam 30cm
Joslin's Terrestrial Globe Containing the Latest Discoveries	JOSLIN	Diam 15cm
Rand, McNally & Co.s New Three Inch Terrestrial Globe	RAND, McNALLY (Pocket, etc)	Diam 8cm
Rand, McNally & Co.s New Twelve Inch Terrestrial Globe	RAND, McNALLY (Pocket, etc)	Diam 30cm
Schedler's Terrestrial Globe	SCHEDLER	Diam 51cm
White's Plane Spherical Globe	WHITE, W.	No dimen

PORTRAITS:

Title	Author	Size
Abraham Ortelius	ORTELIUS (Folio)	21x32cm
Alexius Hubertus Iaillot ... 1698	JAILLOT	37x30cm
Ioannes Baptista Homann, Sac. Caes. Rego. Cath. Maj ...	HOMANN	38x28cm

TITLE PAGES and FRONTISPIECES:

Title	Author	Size
[Frontispiece]	RIZZI-ZANNONI	10x6cm
[World]	DE BRY	9x14cm
Atlante Novissimo Tomo I [Frontispiece]	ZATTA	32x43cm
Atlas	OTTENS	44x29cm
Atlas Novus ...	COVENS & MORTIER	48x27cm
Civitates Orbis Terrarum	BRAUN & HOGENBERG	36x22cm
Introduction a la Geographie	DE FER (Small)	No dimen
Le Theatre du Monde ou Nouvel Atlas Contenant les Chartes et Descr	BLAEU	39x23cm
Parergon ...	ORTELIUS (Folio)	38x25cm
Planisphere Representant Tout l'Etendue du Monde ... [Frontispiece]	RENARD	42x27cm
Practical Navigation ...	SELLER	17x12cm
The Illustrated Atlas and Modern History of the World	TALLIS	30x23cm
The Surveyor in Foure Bookes ...	RATHBONE	25x16cm
Theatrum Orbis Terrarum	ORTELIUS (Folio)	42x24cm

UNTITLED MAPS:

Title	Author	Size
[A Map of the British Empire in America. Sheet 5]	POPPLE	51x69cm
[A Map of the British Empire in America. Sheet 9]	POPPLE	51x69cm
[Aquarius, Capricorn]	BODE	58x79cm
[Arctic Regions]	BRITISH ADMIRALTY	61x61cm
[Armillary Sphere]	MALLET	14x10cm
[Australia]	PLON	25x36cm
[Austria: Steiermark]	HILDBURGHAUSEN BIBLIO.	26x20cm
[Belgium and Luxemburg]	HILDBURGHAUSEN BIBLIO.	20x26cm
[Brazil]	HILDBURGHAUSEN BIBLIO.	26x20cm
[Canada: St. Lawrence River. Point des Monts to Quebec on set of 7 sheets]	BRITISH ADMIRALTY	46x62cm
[Caribbean Sea]	BLUNT	91x206cm
[Caroline Islands]	LUTKE	65x97cm
[Caucasus Region: Der Kaukasische Isthmus]	HILDBURGHAUSEN BIBLIO.	20x26cm
[Cetus Monstrum Marium, Apparatus Chemicus]	BODE	58x79cm
[China: Amoy region]	CHINESE CARTOGRAPHY	55x115cm
[China: Shantung Peninsula]	NICOL	67x50cm
[Colorado: Panoramic views]	U.S. GEOLOGICAL SURV.	76x94cm
[Crete]	BORDONE	16x34cm
[Cyprus]	BORDONE	25x33cm
[Discovery of the Magellan Straits]	DE BRY	15x20cm
[Drake Lands in California]	DE BRY	13x18cm
[East Africa & Madagascar]	HILDBURGHAUSEN BIBLIO.	20x26cm
[East Africa]	THEVENOT	69x51cm
[England: Bristol Channel]	COLLINS, G.	43x55cm
[England: Cornwall & Scilly Islands]	COLLINS, G.	46x57cm
[England: Cornwall]	COLLINS, G.	46x56cm
[England: Norfolk]	COLLINS, G.	28x44cm
[England: Sussex, Rye]	COLLINS, G.	44x28cm
[English Channel]	HEATHER	64x79cm
[Europe]	BORDONE	28x38cm
[France: Paris]	HILDBURGHAUSEN BIBLIO.	20x26cm
[Germany: Bavaria & Swabia: Kingdom of Bavaria, Southern Half]	HILDBURGHAUSEN BIBLIO.	20x26cm

[Germany: Hesse, Electorate]	HILDBURGHAUSEN BIBLIO.	26x20cm
[Germany: Hesse, Grand Duchy]	HILDBURGHAUSEN BIBLIO.	26x20cm
[Germany: Holstein with Lauenburg, Hamburg & Lubeck]	HILDBURGHAUSEN BIBLIO.	20x26cm
[Germany: Principalities of Waldeck, Lippe-Detmold & Schauenberg-Lippe]	HILDBURGHAUSEN BIBLIO.	26x20cm
[Germany: Rheinprovinz Julich - Cleve - Berg]	HILDBURGHAUSEN BIBLIO.	20x26cm
[Germany: Schleswig]	HILDBURGHAUSEN BIBLIO.	20x26cm
[Gulf of Thailand]	HERBERT	53x67cm
[Holy Land, Arabian Desert and Mesopotamia]	FULLER	30x36cm
[Holy Land. Palaestina]	HILDBURGHAUSEN BIBLIO.	26x20cm
[Indonesia: Bangka & Gaspar Straits]	HORSBURGH	93x63cm
[Ireland: Carlingford]	COLLINS, G.	43x32cm
[Ireland: Dublin Bay]	COLLINS, G.	45x57cm
[Irish Sea: Anglesey to Mull of Galloway with Isle of Man]	COLLINS, G.	45x58cm
[Irlandiae Regnum, northern half]	MERCATOR (Folio)	46x34cm
[Italy, Northern & Central: Lombardy, Venetia, Parma, Modena, Toscany ...]	HILDBURGHAUSEN BIBLIO.	26x20cm
[Japan: Honshu, West Coast]	HOGG	30x22cm
[L'Amerique selon l'Entendue de Ses Principales Parties ...]	WALCH	48x61cm
[Leo, Cancer, Sentous Uraniae]	BODE	58x79cm
[Lesser Antilles]	OTTENS	41x53cm
[Libra, Virgo]	BODE	58x79cm
[London: Plan mit Umgebung]	HILDBURGHAUSEN BIBLIO.	20x26cm
[Louisiana & Mississippi: Delta to Vicksburg]	WATERS & SON	27x22cm
[Louisiana: Algiers District with Riverfront on Opposite Bank]	MANUSCRIPT MAPS	127x123cm
[Louisiana: Central and East Feliciana Parish]	MANUSCRIPT MAPS	186x162cm
[Maine: Casco Bay]	DES BARRES	74x106cm
[Maine: Falmouth Harbor (Portland)]	DES BARRES	74x54cm
[Massachusetts: Boston & environs]	HARPER'S WEEKLY	23x37cm
[Massachusetts: Boston Bay]	DES BARRES	76x104cm
[Massachusetts: Boston]	DES BARRES	76x105cm
[Massachusetts: Charles River Basin]	WALKER, G.	48x68cm
[Massachusetts: Martha's Vineyard, Elizabeth Islands, Buzzards Bay]	DES BARRES	105x74cm
[Massachusetts: Plymouth Bay & Town]	DES BARRES	66x48cm
[Mexico: Mexico City to Gulf]	KIRCHER	14x8cm
[Mexico]	RAMUSIO	27x17cm
[Middle East: Cyprus to Persian Gulf]	HOLE, W.	30x35cm
[Middle East: Greece to Persia]	HOLE, W.	31x39cm
[Milky Way - Cygnus, Vultur et Lyra, Hercules]	BODE	58x79cm
[Milky Way - Perseus, Andromeda]	BODE	58x79cm
[Mississippi River from New Carthage past Grand Gulf]	WATERS & SON	29x23cm
[New Brunswick and Quebec: Bay of Chaleur]	DES BARRES	60x75cm
[New Brunswick: Miramichi Bay]	DES BARRES	54x75cm
[New England: Trolley Routes]	RAILROAD CO. MAPS	51x36cm
[Newfoundland Coast in 8 sections]	VAN KEULEN	51x58cm
[North Africa. Morocco, Algier & Tunis]	HILDBURGHAUSEN BIBLIO.	20x26cm
[North America: Central United States & Canada]	SCHRAEMBL	51x59cm
[North America: Louisiana, Virginia & Carolina].	GENTLEMAN'S MAG.	18x24cm
[North America: Mountain chains]	HILDBURGHAUSEN BIBLIO.	20x26cm
[Northeastern North America: Canada & New England]	ALEXANDER	25x35cm
[Northeastern North America: Canada & New England]	RAMUSIO	27x37cm
[Nova Scotia: Chart of Spry Harbour, Port Palliser, Port North, ...]	DES BARRES	70x99cm
[Palestine]	MUNSTER	17x26cm
[Patagonia - Tierra del Fuego]	HILDBURGHAUSEN BIBLIO.	20x26cm
[Pennsylvania]	DES BARRES	77x104cm
[Philippines: Northern islands]	VALENTYN	31x39cm
[Philippines: Sorgoson Bay; Bongo Bay]	LAURIE & WHITTLE	50x24cm
[Pilos, Greece]	MORTIER	11x15cm
[Poland, formerly Germany. West Prussia]	HILDBURGHAUSEN BIBLIO.	20x26cm
[Poland, formerly Germany: Silesia. Provinz Schlesien]	HILDBURGHAUSEN BIBLIO.	20x26cm
[Poland: Elbing]	MERIAN	23x31cm
[Pole Star - Draco, Cepheus, Ursa Minor]	BODE	58x79cm
[Proof Map of English Channel off Cherbourg Showing Course and Sinking ...]	WATERS & SON	30x23cm
[Ptolemaic Arabia]	FRIES	28x46cm
[Ptolemaic Ceylon]	PTOLEMY (1522-1541)	28x46cm
[Ptolemaic North Africa]	PTOLEMY (1522-1541)	30x45cm
[Ptolemaic Persia]	PTOLEMY (1522-1541)	30x46cm
[Quebec & New Brunswick: Bay of Chaleurs]	DES BARRES	61x75cm
[Quebec: Baie des Sept-Isles]	DES BARRES	76x55cm
[Quebec: Gaspe Harbor & Bay]	DES BARRES	157x77cm

[Quebec: Harbor & Bay of Gaspee and Maul Bay]	DES BARRES	157x77cm
[Quebec: Riviere St. Jean to Grand Hermine Bay]	DES BARRES	79x213cm
[Quebec: St. Lawrence River, Cook Cove to Quebec]	DES BARRES	76x246cm
[Raleigh at Port of Spain]	DE BRY	14x18cm
[Route to the East] To the Officers in the Honourable East India Company's...	HEATHER	65x119cm
[Russia in Europe]	HILDBURGHAUSEN BIBLIO.	20x26cm
[Russian title] ... Plan de l'Expedition de M. 'le General-Major de Veismann	MILITARY MAPS	90x64cm
[Sagittarius, Scorpio]	BODE	58x79cm
[Scandinavia]	HILDBURGHAUSEN BIBLIO.	20x26cm
[Scotland: Approaches to Dundee]	COLLINS, G.	45x58cm
[Scotland: Blair Athole, Perthshire]	REAL ESTATE MAPS	105x152cm
[Scotland: Shetland Islands]	COLLINS, G.	46x57cm
[Solar System: Ptolemy; Copernicus; Descartes; Brahe]	DE FER (Small)	23x33cm
[South Africa]	HILDBURGHAUSEN BIBLIO.	20x26cm
[South America: Southern]	HILDBURGHAUSEN BIBLIO.	20x26cm
[South Pole Star - Indus, Argo Navis]	BODE	58x79cm
[Southeast Asia and East Indies]	FRIES	30x44cm
[Southern Asia]	FRIES	30x44cm
[Southern New England: Interurban Trolley Lines]	RAILROAD CO. MAPS	35x52cm
[Switzerland]	HILDBURGHAUSEN BIBLIO.	20x26cm
[The Great Bear, Ursa Major, Leo Minor]	BODE	58x79cm
[United States Coast Chart: Philadelphia to Florida]	MANUSCRIPT MAPS	95x59cm
[United States. Gulf Coast]	DES BARRES	74x104cm
[United States: New York, Pennsylvania, Maryland, New Jersey, Delaware...]	HILDBURGHAUSEN BIBLIO.	26x20cm
[United States: Northern Plains]	STIELER	33x41cm
[United States: Southeast]	MULLER	6x8cm
[Wales: Cardigan Bay]	COLLINS, G.	44x56cm
[West Indies & Central America]	HILDBURGHAUSEN BIBLIO.	20x26cm
[West Indies: St. Croix & Antiqua to Dominica]	BORDONE	10x15cm
[Western United States]	BORGHI	22x29cm
[World: Medieval]	ANONYMOUS	Diam 30cm
[World]	DE AEFFERDEN	14x27cm
[World]	PORCACCHI	11x14cm
[World]	SCHEDEL	37x52cm
[World]	SCHEDEL	43x60cm
[World]	VOLKAMER	26x41cm

TITLED MAPS:

... Asia ...	MOLL (Large)	58x97cm
... Chinese Tartary ... [set of 12 sheets]	BOWEN, E.	29x47cm
... Globe Celeste ...	CORONELLI	45x62cm
... New & Correct Chart of Spithead, from the East End of Hayling Island ...	LAURIE & WHITTLE	76x61cm
... Plan of the Harbour of Fowey Laid Down from Actual Survey ...	BRITISH ADMIRALTY	76x58cm
... Portuum Ostiensium Orthographia ...	LAFRERI SCHOOL	41x70cm
... This Map of North America (Corrected from the Latest Discoveries ...	SENEX	96x65cm
... ye Map of Tibet ... [set of 9 sheets]	BOWEN, E.	45x30cm
1. Armillary Sphere 2. Terrstrial Globe 3. Celestial Globe	WILKES	22x19cm
8eme Carte Particuliere des Costes de Bretagne ...	BELLIN (Large)	61x83cm
A Chart and Views of Pitcairns Island	HOGG	20x33cm
A Chart Exhibiting the Normal Course & Velocity of the Tidal Current ...	U.S. COAST SURVEY	19x23cm
A Chart of Baffin's Bay, with Davis & Barrow Straits; by Captn. Ross ...	BRITISH ADMIRALTY	61x46cm
A Chart of New South Wales, Van Diemen's Land &c	THOMSON	50x58cm
A Chart of North and South America, Including the Atlantic and Pacific...	SAYER & BENNETT	46x111cm
A Chart of Part of Scotland from Berwick Upon Tweed to Skateraw Harbour	AINSLIE	57x52cm
A Chart of Part of the Coast of Devonshire ...	BRITISH ADMIRALTY	58x78cm
A Chart of Port Royal and Kingston Harbours, in the Island of Jamaica ...	DES BARRES	74x104cm
A Chart of Rio de la Plata	BOUGAINVILLE	31x49cm
A Chart of Southern Africa and the Islands of Madagascar, Bourbon ...	IMRAY	100x181cm
A Chart of the Banks of Newfoundland, Drawn from a Great Number ...	SAYER & BENNETT	50x68cm
A Chart of the Chops of the Channel to the South of Scilly Islands; ...	LAURIE & WHITTLE	51x69cm
A Chart of the Coast of Devonshire from Exmouth to Rame Head; ...	LAURIE & WHITTLE	64x79cm
A Chart of the Coasts of Ireland and Part of England	MOUNT & PAGE	44x56cm
A Chart of the Discoveries & Route of the North Land Expedition, ...	FRANKLIN, J.	83x49cm
A Chart of the Discoveries of Captains Ross, Parry & Franklin in the Arctic ...	THOMSON	49x59cm
A Chart of the Downs with the Flats of the North and South Forelands ...	LAURIE & WHITTLE	52x70cm
A Chart of the Gulf of Persia from Basra to Cape Rosalgate ...	LAURIE & WHITTLE	47x70cm
A Chart of the Island Mauritius in the Indian Ocean ...	GREGORY	58x75cm
A Chart of the Island of Hispaniola with the Windward Passage from Jamaica	MOUNT & PAGE	42x52cm

Title	Publisher	Size
A Chart of the Isle of Trinidad ...	FADEN	43x55cm
A Chart of the Isle, Roads, and Race of Portland with the Shambles &c.	LAURIE & WHITTLE	51x70cm
A Chart of the North West Coast of America and North East Coast of Asia	COOK	21x35cm
A Chart of the Nth. West Coast of America, & the Nth. East Coast of Asia	MORSE, J.	19x29cm
A Chart of the Red Sea from Geddah to Suez ...	SAYER & BENNETT	49x69cm
A Chart of the Red Sea from Moka to Geddah ...	LAURIE & WHITTLE	48x65cm
A Chart of the Sea Coast of Naples, Sicily, Greece and the Archipelago...	MOLL (Small)	29x42cm
A Chart of the Sea Coasts of New England New Jersey Virginia Maryland	SELLER	44x55cm
A Chart of the Strait of Allass Constructed from Observations made in ...	DALRYMPLE	29x22cm
A Chart of the Straits of Sunda from the Manuscript Draught of the Dutch ...	SAYER & BENNETT	61x88cm
A Chart of the West and South West Coast of Ireland, from the Mouth ...	LAURIE & WHITTLE	79x127cm
A Chart Shewing Part of the Sea Coast of Newfoundland from Ye Bay ...	MOUNT & PAGE	46x56cm
A Chart to Sail from the Straits of Sunda or Batavia, to the Straits ...	SAYER & BENNETT	66x48cm
A Cidade de Angra na Ilha de Iesu Xpo da Tercera ...	VAN LINSCHOTEN	47x82cm
A Complete Map of the Southern Continent Survey'd by Capt. Abel Tasman	BOWEN, E.	37x48cm
A Correct Chart of the Terraqueous Globe on which Are Described Lines ...	LAURIE & WHITTLE	53x141cm
A Correct Map of the City of Washington. Capital of the United States ...	STONE	40x54cm
A Correct Map of the Countries Surrounding the Garden of Eden or Paradise	BOWEN, T.	20x17cm
A Correct Map of the United States of North America, Including the British ...	BOWEN, T.	29x42cm
A Description of East India Conteyning the Empire of the Great Mogoll	BAFFIN	36x28cm
A Description of the Land of Gosen and Moses' Passage through the Deserts	FULLER	28x37cm
A Draught of Falklands Islands ...	BOWLES	45x69cm
A Draught of the City of Jerusalem As It Is Now, Taken from the South East	MOLL (Small)	13x23cm
A Draught of the City of Jerusalem as It Is Now, Taken from the South East	SALMON	13x23cm
A Draught of the Great Bay, Back Bay and Harbour of Trincomalay, ...	NICHOLSON	91x98cm
A General Chart Exhibiting the Discoveries Made by Captain James Cook	FADEN	54x91cm
A General Chart of the Indian and Part of the Pacific Oceans, ...	WILSON	113x198cm
A General Chart of the Irish Channel	MacKENZIE	116x95cm
A General Chart of the Island of Newfoundland with the Rocks & Soundings	JEFFERYS	55x56cm
A General Map of Eastern and Western Tartary, Commonly Called Tartary ...	CAVE	38x54cm
A General Map of South America Drawn from the Best Surveys	RUSSELL	36x45cm
A General Map of South America Drawn from the Best Surveys	WINTERBOTHAM	37x45cm
A General Map of the Northern British Colonies in America, ...	SAYER & BENNETT	48x66cm
A Geographically Correct Map of the State of Texas	RAILROAD CO. MAPS	46x51cm
A Geological Map of the United States	HINTON	25x39cm
A Hand Map of the Island of Newfoundland	PAGE	56x47cm
A Large Draught from Benjar on the Island of Borneo to Macasser ...	MOUNT & PAGE	44x54cm
A large Draught of the Coast of Iava from Bantam Point to Batavia	MOUNT & PAGE	44x104cm
A Map Exhibiting Mr. Hearne's Tracks in His Two Journies for the Discovery...	HEARNE	26x37cm
A Map of ... Gibraltar [on sheet with] An Exact Plan of Part of Gibraltar	MOLL (Small)	23x61cm
A Map of 100 Miles Round Boston	GENTLEMAN'S MAG.	23x25cm
A Map of Africa Drawn and Engraved from D'Anville's Two Sheet Map	HARRISON	50x71cm
A Map of America According to ye Newest and Most Exact Observations ...	MOLL (Small)	26x17cm
A Map of Bengal, Bahar, Oude & Allahabad with Part of Agra and Delhi ...	FADEN	71x105cm
A Map of Bohemia Being the Present Seat of War in Germany.	LONDON MAGAZINE	17x23cm
A Map of Canaan Divided Among ye XII Tribes	STACKHOUSE	30x20cm
A Map of Canada and the North Part of Louisiana with the Adjacent Countrys	JEFFERYS	31x76cm
A Map of East and West Florida, Georgia and Louisiana, with the Islands ...	POLITICAL MAGAZINE	27x37cm
A Map of England and Wales	FULLARTON	56x44cm
A Map of England, Wales & Scotland. Describing All the Direct and Principal...	FADEN	75x62cm
A Map of Florida and Ye Great Lakes of Canada by Robt. Morden	MORDEN	13x13cm
A Map of Georgia Also the Two Floridas, from the Best Authorities	MORSE, J.	19x31cm
A Map of Georgia, Also the Two Floridas, from the Best Authorities	MORSE, J.	19x31cm
A Map of Hennepin County [MN]	ANDREAS	39x33cm
A Map of Jamaica ... [on sheet with] Barbados	SPEED	38x50cm
A Map of Louisiana and Mexico / Carte de la Louisiane et du Mexique	TARDIEU	107x79cm
A Map of Louisiana and of the River Mississipi by Iohn Senex	SENEX	49x58cm
A Map of Massachusetts from the Best Authorities by A. Adams	MORSE, J.	20x30cm
A Map of Massachusetts, from the Best Authorities by J. Denison	MORSE, J.	20x25cm
A Map of New England & Ye Country Adjacent, Extending Northward ...	GEN. MAG. OF ARTS & SCI.	20x18cm
A Map of New England and New York	SPEED	38x50cm
A Map of New England, ... [Facsimile]	FOSTER, JOHN	30x38cm
A Map of New France Containing Canada, Louisiana &c. in Nth. America	MOLL (Small)	18x25cm
A Map of North America	SEALE	37x46cm
A Map of North America with the European Settlements & Whatever Else ...	SEALE	38x47cm
A Map of North America, Engraved for Priscilla Wakefield's Excursion	DARTON & HARVEY	36x38cm
A Map of Part of Borneo, and the Sooloo Archipelago: Laid Down ...	DALRYMPLE	47x62cm
A Map of Part of Rhode Island Shewing the Positions of the American ...	MARSHALL	42x25cm

A Map of Part of West Florida, from Pensacola to the Mouth of the Iberville ...	GENTLEMAN'S MAG.	19x35cm
A Map of Philadelphia and Parts Adjacent, by N. Scull and G. Heap	GENTLEMAN'S MAG.	34x29cm
A Map of Poland with Its Appendages; Shewing the Late Partition ...	GENTLEMAN'S MAG.	17x21cm
A Map of Royal Island or Cape Breton ... [on sheet with] The Town ...	BOWLES	50x31cm
A Map of Russia	SPEED	40x51cm
A Map of South America Containing Tierra-Firma, Guayna, New Granada ...	JEFFERYS	51x119cm
A Map of That Part of America Which Was the Principal Seat of War ...	GENTLEMAN'S MAG.	22x33cm
A Map of the British Empire in America with the French and Spanish ...	POPPLE	111x102cm
A Map of the Caribbee Islands; Shewing Which Belong to England, France ...	GENTLEMAN'S MAG.	33x21cm
A Map of the Circle of Austria Drawn from the Best Authorities	WILKINSON	19x25cm
A Map of the Cotton Kingdom and Its Dependencies in America	OLMSTED	25x43cm
A Map of the Countries Situate about the North Pole as Far as the 50th Deg	CAREY, M.	26x25cm
A Map of the Country Between Crown Point and Fort Edward	GENTLEMAN'S MAG.	19x11cm
A Map of the Country from Rariton River in East Jersey to Elk Head ...	MARSHALL	25x39cm
A Map of the Country round Philadelphia Including Part of New Jersey ...	SCOTS MAGAZINE	17x22cm
A Map of the Discoveries Made by Capts. Cook & Clarke in the Years ...	CAREY, M.	18x29cm
A Map of the Discoveries Made by the Russians on the North West Coast ...	JEFFERYS	49x62cm
A Map of the District of Maine with New Brunswick & Nova Scotia	MORSE, J.	18x23cm
A Map of the Divisions & Situations of the Tribes of the Canaanites, ...	BOWEN, E.	28x28cm
A Map of the Duchy of Silesia, Drawn from the Best Authorities	WILKINSON	22x21cm
A Map of the Earth upon which Are Marked the Hours and Minutes ...	FERGUSON	20x36cm
A Map of the East Indies and the Adjacent Countries with the Settlements ...	MOLL (Large)	61x100cm
A Map of the Extremity of Cape Cod Including the Townships of Provincetown	U.S.	73x88cm
A Map of the Five Great Lakes with Part of Pensilvania, New York, ...	LONDON MAGAZINE	21x26cm
A Map of the Holy Land Delineated for the Better Understanding ...	DU VAL	33x43cm
A Map of the Indian Territory, Northern Texas and New Mexico ...	MORSE & BREESE	37x29cm
A Map of the Inhabited Part of Canada from the French Surveys; ...	FADEN	60x88cm
A Map of the Island of Orleans with the Environs of Quebec	GIBSON	11x19cm
A Map of the Island of St. John in the Gulf of St. Laurence Divided ...	JEFFERYS	38x71cm
A Map of the Island of Tobago, Drawn from an Actual Survey, by Thos. Bowen	GENTLEMAN'S MAG.	19x24cm
A Map of the Isle of Cuba, with the Bahama Islands ...	JEFFERYS	34x49cm
A Map of the Journey in the Wilderness, and of the Conquest and Partition ...	BOWEN, E.	30x26cm
A Map of the Kingdom of Ireland from ye Latest & Best Observations	SEALE	49x39cm
A Map of the Kingsom of Ireland ...	ROCQUE	64x100cm
A Map of the Middle British Colonies in North America. First Published ...	EVANS	49x81cm
A Map of the Most Inhabited Part of New England Containing the Provinces	LE ROUGE	51x97cm
A Map of the Most Inhabited Part of New England, Containing the Provinces	JEFFERYS	52x98cm
A Map of the New Continent According to Its Greatest Diametrical Length ...	GENTLEMAN'S MAG.	21x17cm
A Map of the New Governments, of East & West Florida.	GENTLEMAN'S MAG.	20x25cm
A Map of the North Pole with All the Territories That Lye Near It ...	MOLL (Small)	20x28cm
A Map of the North Western Territory	MORSE, J.	19x24cm
A Map of the Passage of the Moons Shadow over England ... Annular Eclips	LONDON MAGAZINE	20x16cm
A Map of the Present Seat of War on the Border of Canada	PENNSYLVANIA MAG.	16x36cm
A Map of the Province of New York with Part of Pensilvania, and New Eng. ...	MONTRESOR	135x92cm
A Map of the Province of New York, Reduced from the Large Drawing ...	FADEN	72x58cm
A Map of the Province of New-York, Reduc'd from the Large Drawing ...	SAUTHIER	72x57cm
A Map of the Province of Pensilvania Drawn from the Best Authorities ...	LONDON MAGAZINE	15x22cm
A Map of the Provinces of New-York and New-Jersey, with a Part of Penn.	LOTTER	75x56cm
A Map of the Roads leading to the Town of Britania in the British Settlement	TANNER	20x17cm
A Map of the Sea Coasts of Siam, Cambodia, Couchin China and Tonquin ...	HAMILTON	19x23cm
A Map of the Seat of War in Bavaria and Bohemia. By Thos. Kitchin ...	LONDON MAGAZINE	24x19cm
A Map of the Seat of War in the Western Part of the Kingdom of Poland. ...	LONDON MAGAZINE	23x18cm
A Map of the Seven Provinces of the United Netherlands	MOLL (Small)	19x19cm
A Map of the Sources of the Colorado & Big Salt Lake, Platte, Yellow-Stone ...	BONNEVILLE	44x41cm
A Map of the South Pole, with the Track of His Majesty's Sloop Resolution ...	GENTLEMAN'S MAG.	22x21cm
A Map of the State of Kentucky and the Tennessee Government ...	MORSE, J.	19x29cm
A Map of the States of New Hampshire and Vermont by J. Denison	MORSE, J.	20x24cm
A Map of the West Indies from the Best Authorities	EDWARDS	25x40cm
A Map of the West Indies or the Islands of America in ye North Sea ...	MOLL (Large)	59x100cm
A Map of the Western Parts of the Colony of Virginia.	LONDON MAGAZINE	19x12cm
A Map of the World, Drawn and Engraved from d'Anville's Two-Sheet Map ...	D'ANVILLE	40x73cm
A Map of the World, on Mercators Projection.	GENTLEMAN'S MAG.	18x28cm
A Map of Virginia and Maryland ...	SPEED	38x49cm
A Map Shewing the Communication of the Lakes and the Rivers ...	GENTLEMAN'S MAG.	20x23cm
A Mapp of the Citie and Port of Tripoli in Barbary	SELLER	41x52cm
A Mapp of the Kingdome of Ireland by Ric. Blome ...	BLOME	37x39cm
A Mapp of the Sommer Ilands Once Called the Bermudas ...	SPEED	40x53cm
A Mapp of the Travels and Voyages of the Apostles in Their Mission ...	BLOME	29x46cm

Title	Author/Publisher	Size
A Mapp of ye County of Essex; With Its Hundreds ...	BLOME	26x32cm
A Mapp or Generall Carte of the World Designed in Two Plaine Hemisphers ...	BLOME	39x52cm
A New & Accurate Map of Asia. Drawn from Actual Surveys ... by ...	BOWEN, E.	35x43cm
A New & Accurate Map of China ...	KITCHIN	34x41cm
A New & Accurate Map of China, Drawn from Surveys Made by Jesuit ...	BOWEN, E.	34x42cm
A New & Accurate Map of the Province of North & South Carolina, Georgia...	BOWEN, E.	35x43cm
A New & Correct Chart of Cuba, Streights of Bahama, Windward Passage, ...	MOUNT & PAGE	47x65cm
A New & Correct Map of the Whole World Shewing ye Situation ...	MOLL (Large)	69x119cm
A New & Correct Map of Thirty Miles round London Showing all the Towns...	BOWLES	64x94cm
A New and Accurat Map of the World Drawne According to ye Truest ...	SPEED	42x56cm
A New and Accurate Chart of the Mouth of the Thames, and Its Entrances ...	VAN KEULEN	65x99cm
A New and Accurate Map of Connecticut and Rhode Island, from the Best ...	UNIVERSAL MAGAZINE	26x34cm
A New and Accurate Map of East and West Florida, Drawn from the Best ...	LONDON MAGAZINE	18x22cm
A New and Accurate Map of New South Wales, also Norfolk ...	WILKINSON	23x27cm
A New and Accurate Map of North Carolina, in North America.	UNIVERSAL MAGAZINE	27x36cm
A New and Accurate Map of the Present Seat of War in North America ...	UNIVERSAL MAGAZINE	36x29cm
A New and Accurate Map of the Present Seat of War in North America.	ROYAL MAGAZINE	16x22cm
A New and Accurate Map of the Province of Pennsylvania in North Amer. ...	UNIVERSAL MAGAZINE	27x33cm
A New and Accurate Map of the Province of South Carolina in North Amer.	UNIVERSAL MAGAZINE	33x28cm
A New and Accurate Map of the World	WALTON	9x13cm
A New and Accurate Plan of London ...	LAURIE & WHITTLE	43x58cm
A New and Correct Chart of Cuba, Straights of Bahama, Windward Passage	MOUNT & PAGE	46x65cm
A New and Correct Chart of the Coast of New Foundland from Cape Raze ...	MOUNT & PAGE	42x102cm
A New and Correct Chart of the Island of Jamaica with the Bays, ...	MOUNT & PAGE	46x69cm
A New and Correct Chart of the North Part of America from New Found Land	MOUNT & PAGE	43x55cm
A New and Correct Large Draught of the Tradeing Part of the West Indies ...	GRIERSON	49x82cm
A New and Correct Map of Africa ...	BOWEN, E.	37x45cm
A New and Correct Map of Scotland ...	KITCHIN	28x22cm
A New and Correct Map of Scotland ...	SAYER	132x109cm
A New and Correct Map of Scotland or North Britain with All the Post ...	LAURIE & WHITTLE	64x107cm
A New and Correct Map of the Coast of Africa from Cape Blanco ...	BOLTON	38x48cm
A New and Correct Map of the World ...	SENEX	15x29cm
A New and Correct Map of the World Laid Down according to the Newest ...	MOLL (Large)	56x96cm
A New and Correct Map of Ye World ...	OVERTON	59x95cm
A New and Correct Plan of London, Westminster and Southwark ...	DODSLEY	35x66cm
A New and Exact Map of Asia	BOWEN, E.	36x45cm
A New and Exact Map of France Divided into All Its Provinces ...	MOLL (Large)	61x97cm
A New and Exact Map of Spain and Portugal Divided into Its Kingdoms ...	MOLL (Large)	61x97cm
A New and Exact Map of the Coast Countries and Islands within ye Limits ...	MOLL (Large)	65x49cm
A New and Exact Map of the Dominions of the King of Great Britain ...	MOLL (Large)	101x60cm
A New and Exact Map of the Electorate of Brunswick-Lunenburg ...	MOLL (Large)	60x100cm
A New and Exact Map of the United Provinces or Netherlands, etc. ...	MOLL (Large)	61x101cm
A New and Exact Plan of Cape Fear River from the Bar to Brunswick, ...	JEFFERYS, T.	39x32cm
A New Chart of the Andaman and Nicobar Islands with the Adjacent ...	NORIE	64x93cm
A New Chart of the Bahama Islands and the Windward Passage ...	GRIERSON	42x52cm
A New Chart of the Coast of Brazil from the Banks of St. Roque, ...	LAURIE & WHITTLE	86x57cm
A New Chart of the Coast of Dorsetshire and Devonshire from St. Alban's ...	LAURIE & WHITTLE	64x80cm
A New Chart of the Coast of New England, Nova Scotia New France ...	GENTLEMAN'S MAG.	34x47cm
A New Chart of the Gulf of St. Lawrence ...	FADEN	66x54cm
A New Chart of the Gulfs of Mexico and Florida ...	IMRAY	99x183cm
A New Chart of the Islands of Scilly with Their Soundings Channels ...	LAURIE & WHITTLE	50x67cm
A New Chart of the River St. Lawrence from the Island of Anticosti to ...	KITCHIN	18x25cm
A New Chart of the River St. Lawrence from the Island of Anticosti to ...	LONDON MAGAZINE	18x26cm
A New Chart of the Vast Atlantic Ocean; Exhibiting the Seat of War, ...	LONDON MAGAZINE	31x43cm
A New Chart of the West Indies, Drawn from the Best Spanish Maps ...	JEFFERYS	17x49cm
A New Chart of the World on Mercator's Projection ...	DUNN	31x41cm
A New Chart of the World, on Mercator's Projection ...	CARY	46x52cm
A New Description of Carolina ...	SPEED	37x50cm
A New Map of Alabama with Its Roads and Distances from Place to Place ...	DESILVER	33x26cm
A New Map of America from the Latest Observations Revis'd by ...	SENEX	49x56cm
A New Map of Arkansas	MITCHELL, S.A. (to 1859)	41x33cm
A New Map of Arkansas	TANNER	35x28cm
A New Map of Arkansas with Its Counties, Towns, Post Offices, &c.	DESILVER	39x32cm
A New Map of Berkshire ...	CARY	51x57cm
A New Map of Canada, Also the North Parts of New England and New York...	DE VAUGONDY	21x29cm
A New Map of Carolina ...	MORDEN	13x13cm
A New Map of Chinese & Independent Tartary from the Latest Authorities	CARY	52x60cm
A New Map of Denmark and Sweden ... By H. Moll Geographer	MOLL (Large)	60x101cm

Title	Author	Size
A New Map of Egypt ...	CARY	51x59cm
A New Map of England ...	CARY	51x60cm
A New Map of France, Shewing the Roads and Post Stages ...	SENEX	51x58cm
A New Map of Georgia with Its Roads and Distances	THOMAS, COWPERTHWAIT	36x29cm
A New Map of Germany, Hungary, Transilvania and the Suisse ...	GRIERSON	59x99cm
A New Map of Germany, Hungary, Transilvania and the Suisse Cantons ...	MOLL (Large)	61x97cm
A New Map of Great Britain ... 1717	MOLL (Large)	100x61cm
A New Map of Indiana with Its Roads & Distances	MITCHELL, S.A. (to 1859)	32x26cm
A New Map of Ireland Divided into its Counties, Provinces and Baronies ...	MOLL (Large)	100x61cm
A New Map of Ireland Divided into Provinces and Counties	HARRISON	41x36cm
A New Map of Ireland Divided into Provinces, Counties &c.	SAYER & BENNETT	64x57cm
A New Map of Italy Distinguishing All the Sovereignties in It, ...	MOLL (Large)	61x101cm
A New Map of Louisiana with Its Canals, Roads and Distances ...	TANNER	27x35cm
A New Map of Louisiana with Its Canals, Roads and Distances ...	THOMAS, COWPERTHWAIT	29x37cm
A New Map of Maine	THOMAS, COWPERTHWAIT	38x31cm
A New Map of Maryland and Delaware and Their Canals, Roads and ...	THOMAS, COWPERTHWAIT	30x38cm
A New Map of Maryland and Delaware with Their Canals, Roads & ...	TANNER	28x35cm
A New Map of Michigan with Its Canals, Roads & Distances	DESILVER	38x30cm
A New Map of Michigan with Its Canals, Roads & Distances	TANNER	37x29cm
A New Map of Michigan with Its Canals, Roads, and Distances	THOMAS, COWPERTHWAIT	38x31cm
A New Map of Mississippi with Its Roads and Distances	TANNER	34x27cm
A New Map of New England and New York by Robert Morden	MORDEN	13x15cm
A New Map of New Found Land, New Scotland, the Isles of Breton, ...	MOLL (Small)	18x26cm
A New Map of New Jarsey and Pensilvania by Robt. Morden	MORDEN	15x12cm
A New Map of North America ...	CARY	46x52cm
A New Map of North America ... According to the Definitive Treaty, ...	SAYER	58x96cm
A New Map of North America According to the Newest Observations	MOLL (Small)	18x25cm
A New Map of North America, with the West India Islands, Divided ...	SAYER	51x118cm
A New Map of Nova Scotia, and Cape Britain, with the Adjacent Parts ...	JEFFERYS	47x62cm
A New Map of Nova Scotia, Newfoundland &c. from the Latest Authorities	CARY	46x52cm
A New Map of Part of the United States ..., Containing New York ...	CARY	46x52cm
A New Map of Part of the United States ..., Containing the Carolina ...	CARY	46x52cm
A New Map of Part of the United States ..., Exhibiting the Western ...	CARY	46x52cm
A New Map of Pennsylvania with Its Canals, Rail-Roads & Distances ...	TANNER	25x36cm
A New Map of Poland and the Grand Duchy of Lithuania Shewing ...	CARY	45x46cm
A New Map of Sclavonia, Croatia, Dalmatia, Bosnia et Repur, Ragusa	MORDEN	13x14cm
A New Map of Scotland from the Latest Authorities ...	CARY	54x107cm
A New Map of South America from the Latest Authorities	CARY	52x41cm
A New Map of South America, Shewing Its General Divisions, Chief Cities ...	WELLS	37x49cm
A New Map of South Carolina with Its Roads & Distances ...	DESILVER	26x33cm
A New Map of Tennessee with Its Roads and Distances ...	DESILVER	30x38cm
A New Map of Texas Oregon and California ...	MITCHELL, S.A. (Pocket, etc)	53x48cm
A New Map of the British Dominions in North America with the Limits ...	KITCHIN	24x31cm
A New Map of the British Isles ...	CARY	51x59cm
A New Map of the British Isles, Shewing Their Present Genl. Divisions, ...	WELLS	39x50cm
A New Map of the Cherokee Nation with the Names of the Towns ...	LONDON MAGAZINE	17x22cm
A New Map of the Circle of Austria ...	CARY	50x56cm
A New Map of the East India Isles ...	CARY	46x52cm
A New Map of the Island of Corsica, Divided into Cantons, Called Pieves: ...	LONDON MAGAZINE	24x18cm
A New Map of the Island of Tobago ...	FADEN	44x59cm
A New Map of the Kingdom of Poland with Its Dismembered Provinces	KITCHIN	47x64cm
A New Map of the Kingdom of Portugal	CARY	48x50cm
A New Map of the Land of Canaan and Parts Adjoining Shewing ...	WELLS	36x48cm
A New Map of the North East Coast of Asia, and North West Coast ...	LONDON MAGAZINE	17x23cm
A New Map of the Province of Lower Canada, Describing All the Seigneuries...	WYLD	58x88cm
A New Map of the Province of Maryland in North America.	UNIVERSAL MAGAZINE	28x33cm
A New Map of the River Mississipi from the Sea to Bayagoulas	LONDON MAGAZINE	18x24cm
A New Map of the So. & Mid. Parts of Antient Greece viz. Epirus, Hellas, ...	WELLS	37x50cm
A New Map of the State of Georgia Exhibiting Its Internal Improvements ...	DESILVER	37x29cm
A New Map of the State of Iowa	DESILVER	30x38cm
A New Map of the State of Missouri	DESILVER	30x38cm
A New Map of the State of Wisconsin	THOMAS, COWPERTHWAIT	41x34cm
A New Map of the Terraqueous Globe According to the Ancient Discoveries ...	WELLS	37x51cm
A New Map of the United States of America	THOMAS, COWPERTHWAIT	40x67cm
A New Map of the United States of America ...	CARY	46x52cm
A New Map of the United States of ... Containing Those of New York, ...	CARY	46x52cm
A New Map of the West India Isles ...	CARY	46x52cm
A New Map of the Whole Continent of America, Divided into North and South	SAYER	53x119cm

A New Map of the Whole World with the Trade Winds According to Ye Latest	MOLL (Small)	20x26cm
A New Map of the World Shewing the Course of Sr. Francis Drake, ...	HARRIS	38x60cm
A New Map of the World with Capt. Cook's Tracks, His Discoveries ...	LAURIE & WHITTLE	48x71cm
A New Map of the World with the Latest Discoveries	HARRISON	28x51cm
A New Map of the World. with All the New Discoveries ...	THOMPSON	64x95cm
A New Map of Upper & Lower Canada	STOCKDALE	18x23cm
A New Map of Upper and Lower Canada from the Latest Authorities by ...	CARY	52x60cm
A New Map of Virginia with Its Canals, Roads and Distances ...	TANNER	27x36cm
A New Map of Virginia, Maryland and the Improved Parts of Pennsylvania ...	SENEX	49x56cm
A New Map of Ye World	MORDEN	9x16cm
A New Map of ye World by Robt. Morden	MORDEN	9x16cm
A New Map Shewing All the Severall Countries, Cities, Towns and ...	WELLS	36x48cm
A New Map Shewing the Travels of the Patriarchs. As Also of the Children ...	WELLS	36x50cm
A New Mape of Ye XVII Provinces of Low Germanie ...	SPEED	41x53cm
A New Mapp of Lincoln Shire with the Post & Cross Roads ...	OVERTON	39x49cm
A New Mappe of the Romane Empire Newly Described by John Speede	SPEED	39x51cm
A New Plan of Boston Harbour from an Actual Survey	PENNSYLVANIA MAG.	26x18cm
A New Plan of Egypt. Shewing the Entrances to the Nile, etc.	HEATHER	39x93cm
A New Plan of London Westminster and Southwark ...	ASHBY	42x69cm
A New Survey of the Harbour of Boston in New England ...	MOUNT & PAGE	42x55cm
A Newe Mape of Germany	SPEED	40x52cm
A Newe Mape of Tartary	SPEED	39x51cm
A Particular Map of the American Lakes, Rivers, etc. III	HARRISON	50x72cm
A Particular Map, to Illustrate Gen. Amhersts, Expedition, to Montreal; ...	GENTLEMAN'S MAG.	18x23cm
A Perspective View of the Church of the Holy Sepulchre at Jerusalem ...	MIDDLETON	18x27cm
A Perspective View of the City of Dublin from Phoenix Park	BANKES	20x33cm
A Physical Planisphere Wherein Are Represented All the Known Lands ...	GENTLEMAN'S MAG.	31x29cm
A Plain Chart of the Seychelles, Praslin & Other Adjacent Islands ...	GREGORY	42x55cm
A Plan of a Plantation Called Bevon Island ... in ... St. Christopher ...	MANUSCRIPT MAPS	53x42cm
A Plan of Albany River in Hudsons Bay	HEARNE	27x35cm
A Plan of Captain Carver's Travels in the Interior Parts of North America ...	CARVER	26x34cm
A Plan of Constantinople, Places Adjacent and Canal of the Black Sea	GENTLEMAN'S MAG.	17x24cm
A Plan of Fort St. George and the City of Madras	SALMON	20x20cm
A Plan of Fort St. George, and the City of Madras	MOLL (Small)	20x19cm
A Plan of Milford Haven ...	MORRIS	18x23cm
A Plan of Moos River in Hudsons Bay, North America	HEARNE	24x44cm
A Plan of New York Island, with Part of Long Island, Staten Island, & ...	FADEN	48x43cm
A Plan of Quebec ... by E. Oakley & Sold by J. Roque	OAKLEY	34x52cm
A Plan of Table Bay, with the Road of the Cape of Good Hope ...	LAURIE & WHITTLE	48x55cm
A Plan of the Action at Bunkers Hill, on the 17th of June 1775, ...	FADEN	50x43cm
A Plan of the City & Harbour of Louisburg, Shewing That Part of Gabarus ...	GENTLEMAN'S MAG.	19x26cm
A Plan of the City and Harbour of Macao, a Colony of the Portugueze ...	BAKER	69x53cm
A Plan of the City of Berlin [on plate with] A Prospect of the City of Berlin.	LONDON MAGAZINE	18x24cm
A Plan of the City of Jerusalem According to the Description in the Books ...	BOWEN, E.	40x41cm
A Plan of the City of Prague, with the French and Austrian Camps. ...	GENTLEMAN'S MAG.	29x36cm
A Plan of the City of Quebec The Capital of Canada. as It surrender'd ...	JEFFERYS	34x48cm
A Plan of the City of Quebec and Its Fortifications	GIBSON	6x11cm
A Plan of the Copper Mine River ...	HEARNE	20x44cm
A Plan of the Country from Frog's Point to Croton River Shewing ...	MARSHALL	41x22cm
A Plan of the Establishment of Clarence in the Island of Fernando Po ...	BRITISH ADMIRALTY	61x94cm
A Plan of the Harbour of Chebucto and Town of Halifax.	GENTLEMAN'S MAG.	22x27cm
A Plan of the Operations at the Taking of Quebec and the Battle ...	SCOTS MAGAZINE	11x19cm
A Plan of the Port and Bay in the Island of Mahe ... [Seychelles]	BRITISH ADMIRALTY	44x59cm
A Plan of the River St. Lawrence, from the Falls of Montmorenci to Sillery ...	LONDON MAGAZINE	18x25cm
A Plan of the Straits of St. Mary, and Michilimakinac, to Shew the Situation...	LONDON MAGAZINE	23x33cm
A Plan of the Town and Chart of the Harbour of Boston Exhibiting a View ...	GENTLEMAN'S MAG.	26x34cm
A Plan of the Town of Newport in the Province of Rhode Island	DES BARRES	72x52cm
A Plat Exhibiting the State of the Surveys in the State of Florida ...	U.S. STATE SURVEYS	61x61cm
A Prospect of the City of Dublin from the North	BROOKING	19x88cm
A Sea Chart of the Gulph of Venice ...	MOUNT & PAGE	40x51cm
A Survey of Lake Champlain Including Lake George, Crown Point ...	SAYER & BENNETT	66x48cm
A Survey of Port El Roque, Coast of Terra Firma ...	BRITISH ADMIRALTY	28x41cm
A Survey of the Keys and Shoals in the Mira-Por-Vos Passage ...	BRITISH ADMIRALTY	30x46cm
A Topographical Chart of the Bay of Narraganset in the Province of ...	FADEN	93x63cm
A Topographical Chart of the Entrance to the River Tagus Describing ...	FADEN	59x91cm
A Topographical Map of the Northn. Part of New York Island, Exhibiting ...	FADEN	47x26cm
A Township Map of the State of Iowa	HENN, WILLIAMS & CO.	55x90cm
A View of Casal, a Very Strong City and Castle in Italy ...	TINDAL	36x48cm

Title	Author	Size
A View of New Castle with the Fort and Light House on the ... Pisquataqua	DES BARRES	19x29cm
A View of the Town and Castle of St. Augustine, and the English Camp ...	GENTLEMAN'S MAG.	30x17cm
A View of ye General & Coasting Trade Winds, Monsoons or ye Shifting ...	MOLL (Small)	18x52cm
Abbildung des Konigreich Ungarn durch Turckey bis nach ...	FURST	37x85cm
Aberdeen Harbour	BRITISH ADMIRALTY	48x61cm
Abissinorum sive Pretiosi Ioannis Imperiu	MERCATOR (Folio)	34x49cm
Abozzo de Mappamondo di F. Mauro Camaldolese [Facsimile]	MAURO	34x34cm
Abrahamae Patriarchatus Peregrinatio ...	ORTELIUS (Folio)	32x45cm
Abrahami Patriarchae Peregrinatio et Vita	ORTELIUS (Folio)	35x46cm
Accurata Delineatio Celeberrimae Regionis Ludovicianae vel Gallice Louisianae	SEUTTER	49x57cm
Accurate Geographische Delineation de Hochf: Sachss: Ammes Weissenfels...	SCHENK	50x58cm
Accurater Grundriss u: Gegend ... London ...	HOMANN	49x58cm
Accurater Prospect der Hoch-Furstl. Marggaf Baaden Durlachischen ...	LOTTER	50x58cm
Accuratissima Regnorum Sueciae, Daniae, et Norvegiae. Tabula. Per ...	DANCKERTS	50x59cm
Accuratissima Totius Asiae Tabula Recens Emendata per Fredericum de Wit	DE WIT	48x58cm
Acores Insulae	ORTELIUS (Folio)	33x47cm
Aegyptus Antiqua	ORTELIUS (Folio)	40x49cm
Aequatorial-Ost-Afrika	KIEPERT	61x78cm
Aethiopia Inferior, vel Exterior	BLAEU	38x50cm
Aethiopia Superior vel Interior Vulgo Abissinorum sive Presbiteri Ioannis ...	VALK & SCHENK	38x49cm
Aethiopia Superior vel Interior; Vulgo Abissinorum sive Presbiteriioannis ...	BLAEU	38x49cm
Aevi Veteris Typus Geographicus	ORTELIUS (Folio)	31x44cm
Afbeelding van 't Land van Israel, naar Deszelts ...	BACHIENE	48x38cm
Afbeelding van Egypte, de Woestyne der Schelf-Zee en 't Land Kanaan ...	BACHIENE	49x39cm
Afbeelding van t' Joodsche Land Toen het aan de Heerschappy der Romeinen	BACHIENE	38x47cm
Afbeeldinge van de Veertich-Jaarige Reyse der Kinderen Israels. Uyt Egypten ...	VISSCHER	36x52cm
Afbeeldinge van't Zeer Vermaarde Eiland Geks-Kop. ...	ANONYMOUS	15x23cm
Africa	HILDBURGHAUSEN BIBLIO.	20x26cm
Africa	MORDEN	11x13cm
Africa	PINKERTON	70x50cm
Africa	VAN DEN KEERE	8x13cm
Africa with All Its States, Kingdoms, Republics, Regions, Islands &c. ...	LAURIE & WHITTLE	102x122cm
Africa ...	MERCATOR (Folio)	37x46cm
Africa ...	PROBST	17x20cm
Africa ...	SCHREIBER	18x28cm
Africa Drawn and Engraved from the Best Maps and Charts	WILKIE	34x37cm
Africa Drawn by Amanda M. Chapin	MANUSCRIPT MAPS	43x55cm
Africa ex Magna Orbis Terre Descriptione Gerardi Mercatoris Desumpta, ...	MERCATOR (Folio)	38x47cm
Africa juxta Navigationes et Observationes Recentissima Aucta Correcta ...	SEUTTER	50x58cm
Africa Nova Tabula	GASTALDI	13x17cm
Africa Tabula Nova	ORTELIUS (Folio)	37x50cm
Africa Tertia Pars Terrae	BUNTING	26x34cm
Africa XXV. Nova Tabula	MUNSTER	27x34cm
Africae Descriptio	MERCATOR (Small)	13x20cm
Africae Nova Descriptio	BLAEU	41x55cm
Africae Nova Tabula	HONDIUS	38x49cm
Africae Noviss: Cateres Tabula	DANCKERTS	43x52cm
Africae Pars Meridionalis cum Promontorio Bonae Spei ...	LOTTER	50x58cm
Africae, Described, the Manners of their Habits, and Buildinge: ...	SPEED	39x51cm
Afrique	SANSON (Folio)	39x57cm
Agricultural Map of the County of Edinburgh by Ralph Richardson, ...	BLACK	34x48cm
Ajaccio [Corsica]	BELLIN (Small)	22x18cm
Alabama	BRADFORD	36x29cm
Alabama	COLTON (Atlas Maps)	46x38cm
Alabama	GRAY	66x41cm
Alaska	CRAM	42x57cm
Alaska	RAND, McNALLY (Atlas Maps)	19x27cm
Alberta, Assiniboia, Athabasca & Sasketchewan	CRAM	41x55cm
Alemannia sive Suevia Superior	BLAEU	38x50cm
Alexandri Magni Macedonis Expeditio	JANSSON	37x47cm
Alexandri Magni Macedonis Expeditio	ORTELIUS (Folio)	36x46cm
Alexandria	BRAUN & HOGENBERG	36x48cm
Alexandria	SCHEDEL	14x23cm
Alexandria ...	SCHENK	21x26cm
Algemeene Kaart van de Westindische Eilanden. Te Amsterdam by ..	TIRION	35x46cm
Algerii ...	BRAUN & HOGENBERG	Folio
Algiers ...	SCHENK	21x26cm
Alkairo / Memphis ...	SCHENK	21x26cm

Alsatia Inferior	MERCATOR (Folio)	35x45cm
Alsatia Superior ...	MERCATOR (Small)	15x20cm
Alsatia Superior du Suntgoia & Brisgoia	MERCATOR (Folio)	36x48cm
Amer. Sep. No.47 Partie du Mexique	VANDERMAELEN	46x56cm
Amer. Sep. No.55 Partie des Etats Unis	VANDERMAELEN	46x51cm
Amer. Sep. No.69 Porto-Rico	VANDERMAELEN	46x53cm
America	BEER	10x13cm
America	CLUVER	21x26cm
America	HILDBURGHAUSEN BIBLIO.	26x20cm
America	HONDIUS	38x51cm
America	MOLL (Small)	19x20cm
America	MOLL (Small)	26x20cm
America	PROBST	17x20cm
America	THOMSON	48x56cm
America	VAN DEN KEERE	8x12cm
America	WEILAND	62x44cm
America By R. Morden	MORDEN	11x13cm
America Aurea Pars Altera Mundi ...	VALK	48x59cm
America Divided into North and South with Their Several Subdivisions ...	LAURIE & WHITTLE	50x54cm
America Meridionalis ...	LOTTER	45x58cm
America Noviter Delineata	HONDIUS	38x50cm
America Noviter Delineata	MERIAN	27x36cm
America Noviter Delineata Auct Henrico Hondio	HONDIUS	37x50cm
America Septentrionalis	JANSSON	47x55cm
America Septentrionalis. a Domino D'Anville in Gallis Edita Nunc in Anglia ...	HOMANN	46x51cm
America Septentrionalis Coloniis in Enteriorem ...	PROBST	17x20cm
America Septentrionalis Novissima ...	SCHENK	48x57cm
America Septentrionalis Novissima [& 2nd Cartouche] America Meridionalis...	SCHENK	48x56cm
America Septentrionalis, Concinnata juxta Observationes Dnn Academiae ...	LOTTER	48x59cm
America Settentrionale Disegnata Dopi i Viaggi di Lewis, Clarke, Parry e ...	TASSO	36x49cm
America sive India Nova ad Magna Gerardi Mercatoris Avi Universalis ...	MERCATOR (Folio)	37x46cm
America sive Novus Orbis Respectu Europaeorum Inferior Globi Terrestris ...	DE BRY	33x40cm
America Verfertiget von ... Schreibem in Leipzig	SCHREIBER	18x28cm
America with Those Known Parts in that Unknowne World ...	SPEED	39x51cm
Americae Descrip.	MERCATOR (Small)	15x20cm
Americae Mappa Generalis Secundum Legitimas Projectionis Stereographicae	HOMANN	46x53cm
Americae Nova Descriptio Impensis Ane Seile 1663	SEILE	34x42cm
Americae Nova Tabula	BLAEU	41x56cm
Americae Pars, Nunc Virginia Dicta, Primum ab Anglis Inventa Sumtibus ...	DE BRY	30x42cm
Americae sive Indiae Occidentalis Tabula Generalis	DE LAET	28x35cm
Americae sive Novi Orbis, Nova Descriptio	ORTELIUS (Folio)	36x49cm
Amerika of de Nieuwe Weerld ...	VAN DER AA	15x22cm
Amerique Meridional	LEVASSEUR	28x43cm
Amerique Meridionale	CHAMOUIN	29x22cm
Amerique Meridionale	DE VAUGONDY	16x20cm
Amerique Meridionale	LE ROUGE	21x28cm
Amerique Meridionale ...	D'ANVILLE	43x76cm
Amerique Meridionale, Dressee, sur les Memoires les Plus Recents et ...	DE VAUGONDY	50x63cm
Amerique Septentrionale	DESNOS	10x10cm
Amerique Septentrionale	JAILLOT	46x64cm
Amerique Septentrionale	LEVASSEUR	30x44cm
Amerique Septentrionale	PERROT	20x24cm
Amerique Septentrionale ...	D'ANVILLE	46x88cm
Amerique Septentrionale ...	D'ANVILLE	81x86cm
Amerique Septentrionale ...	SANSON (Folio)	39x55cm
Amerique Septentrionale Divisee en Ses Principales Parties, ou Sont ...	BRION DE LA TOUR	45x64cm
Amerique Septentrionale Divisee en Ses Principales Parties, ou Sont ...	JAILLOT	57x87cm
Amerique Septentrionale Dressee sur les Relations les Plus Modernes ...	DE VAUGONDY	48x59cm
Amerique Septentrionale par N. Sanson d'Abbeville ...	SANSON (Folio)	39x55cm
Amerique Suivant le R.P. Charlevoix Jte. Mr. de la Condamine ...	LE ROUGE	49x64cm
Amplissima Regionis Mississipi seu Provinciae Ludovicianae a ...	HOMANN	49x58cm
Amplissima Ucraniae Regio, Palatinatus Kioviensem et Braclaviensem	LOTTER	49x58cm
Amplissimae Regionis Mississipi seu Provinciae Ludovicianae ...	HOMANN	49x58cm
Amstelodamum Emporium	PONTANUS	26x34cm
Amsterdam [on sheet with] Rotterdam	SALMON	15x19cm
An Account of the Expedition of the British Fleet on Lake Champlain ...	FADEN	75x47cm
An Accurate Chart of the Bay of Biscay ...	LAURIE & WHITTLE	71x99cm
An Accurate Chart of the World with the New Discoveries	KITCHIN	31x44cm

Title	Publisher/Author	Size
An Accurate Map of Europe with Its Empires, Kingdoms ...	SEALE	61x105cm
An Accurate Map of North America Drawn from the Sieur Robert, ...	DE VAUGONDY	18x30cm
An Accurate Map of North and South Carolina with Their Indian Frontiers	MOUZON	100x141cm
An Accurate Map of the British Empire in Nth. America As Settled by ...	GENTLEMAN'S MAG.	21x24cm
An Accurate Map of the East Indies Exhibiting the Course of the European ...	BOWEN, E.	37x45cm
An Accurate Map of the Holy Land with the Adjacent Countries	BOWEN, T.	29x18cm
An Accurate Map of the Islands and Channels between China and ...	WILKINSON	23x28cm
An Accurate Map of the Present Seat of War Between Great Britain ...	UNIVERSAL MAGAZINE	26x35cm
An Accurate Map of the Seat of War in the Kingdom of Prussia As Also ...	KITCHIN	20x23cm
An Accurate Map of the West Indies, with the Adjacent Coast.	GENTLEMAN'S MAG.	18x29cm
An Accurate Map of the West Indies. Engraved by A. Bell.	SCOTS MAGAZINE	17x24cm
An Actual Survey of the Coast of Kent from Dim Church to Rye Harbour ...	LAURIE & WHITTLE	49x69cm
An Actual Survey of Varne, & Ridge ...	LAURIE & WHITTLE	51x69cm
An Authentic Plan of the River St. Laurence, from Sillery to the Falls ...	GENTLEMAN'S MAG.	11x19cm
An Exact Chart of the River St. Laurence, from Fort Frontenac to the Island ...	JEFFERYS	59x94cm
An Exact Map of the Province of Quebec with Part of New York & ...	LODGE	21x27cm
An Eye Sketch of the Entrance of Yealme River with the Depths of Water ...	LAURIE & WHITTLE	47x36cm
An Historical Map of the Roman Empire and the Neighboring Barbarous ...	MOLL (Large)	48x112cm
An Hydrographical Survey of the Coast of Devonshire from Exmouth Bar ...	LAURIE & WHITTLE	69x51cm
An Index Map to the Following Sixteen Sheets, Being a Compleat Chart ...	JEFFERYS	38x63cm
An Outline Map of the Settlements in New South Wales	PERRY	36x78cm
Anchorages in the New Hebrides	BRITISH ADMIRALTY	46x66cm
Anchorages on the East Coast of Jura	BRITISH ADMIRALTY	43x36cm
Ancien Continent avec Plusieurs Isles	MALLET	10x15cm
Ancien Plan de l'Isle de Malte ...	PUTTER	31x43cm
Ancienne Jerusalem	MALLET	15x10cm
Ancient Britain I	S.D.U.K.	37x29cm
Ancient Britain II	S.D.U.K.	34x28cm
Ancient Palestine	TALLIS	34x24cm
Ancient Syria	S.D.U.K.	40x32cm
Ancona Civitas Piceni Celeberrima ad Mare Adriaticum Posita ...	BRAUN & HOGENBERG	34x48cm
Andaluzia	BERTIUS	9x13cm
Andaluzia ...	JANSSON	38x50cm
Anegada Passage with Adjacent Islands	U.S. HYDROGRAPHIC	58x100cm
Anglesey [on sheet with] Wight Vectis [and] Garnesay [and] Iarsay	MERCATOR (Folio)	32x43cm
Anglia	BEER	10x13cm
Anglia Regnum	MERCATOR (Folio)	36x47cm
Anglia, Scotia et Hibernia	MERCATOR (Folio)	33x41cm
Angliae et Hiberniae Accurata Descriptio Veteribus et Recentioribus	ORTELIUS (Folio)	44x58cm
Angliae Regni Florentissimi Nova Descriptio, Auctore Humfredo Lhuyd ...	ORTELIUS (Folio)	38x47cm
Angliae, Scotiae, et Hiberniae, sive Britannicar: Insularum Descriptio	ORTELIUS (Folio)	35x50cm
Anglie Provincia	SCHEDEL	23x23cm
Anhaltinus Principatus Stirpis Ascaniensis	LOTTER	51x59cm
Annapolis Royal. St. Mary's Bay	DES BARRES	73x104cm
Antietam, Prepared by Bvt. Brig. Genl. N. Michler ...	U.S. WAR DEPARTMENT	58x71cm
Antigua	LUCAS	22x29cm
Antigue ...	LE ROUGE	20x27cm
Antilles or West India Islands	S.D.U.K.	36x43cm
Antiquae Graeciae Tabula	WELLS	10x15cm
Antiquae Urbis Romae Imago Accuratiss:	BRAUN & HOGENBERG	2 folio
Antwerpia	MERIAN	27x36cm
Anverpia	BRAUN & HOGENBERG	34x48cm
Anvers Antwerpen en Flamand	MORTIER	20x28cm
Aphrica mit Seinen Befundern Lendern	MUNSTER	13x16cm
Aphricae Tabula I	MUNSTER	26x33cm
Aphricae Tabula II	MUNSTER	26x33cm
Aphricae Tabula III	MUNSTER	26x33cm
Appleton's Map of the Seat of War No.2	APPLETON	32x51cm
Appletons Railway Map of the United States and Canada ... by G.F. Thomas	APPLETON	64x71cm
Appomattox Court House ...	U.S. WAR DEPARTMENT	76x58cm
Approaches to Grand Gulf Miss.	U.S. COAST SURVEY	56x37cm
Aquapolque	DE BRY	15x19cm
Aquitania Australis Regnu Arelatense cum Confinijs	MERCATOR (Folio)	36x47cm
Arabia	BEER	10x13cm
Arabia	BERTIUS	9x12cm
Arabia Felix Nova Tabula	GASTALDI	13x17cm
Arabian Gulf or Red Sea	HARRISON	46x33cm
Aracam	LANGENES	9x13cm

Arbroath	BRITISH ADMIRALTY	37x48cm
Archiepiscopatus et Electoratus Moguntinus ut et Comitatus Uterq. ...	LOTTER	50x58cm
Archiepiscopatus Trevirensis Descriptio Nova	JANSSON	41x50cm
Arctic Regions and British America Containing All Discoveries in Arctic Seas ...	BARTHOLOMEW	42x56cm
Area of Fire - Wholesale District - Toronto - Canada ...	GOAD	63x52cm
Argentoratum Strasburg ...	BRAUN & HOGENBERG	34x43cm
Argow. In hac Tabula Lucerna, Vren, Swytz, Underwald, Glarona Pagi	MERCATOR (Folio)	35x45cm
Arizona	CRAM	55x41cm
Arizona and New Mexico	BRADLEY	36x56cm
Arizona and New Mexico	MITCHELL, S.A. (1860+)	29x36cm
Arkansas	COLTON (Atlas Maps)	41x34cm
Arkansas and Portion of Indian Territory	ASHER & ADAMS	41x57cm
Arragonia et Catalonia	MERCATOR (Folio)	35x45cm
Arras. Ville Forte Capitale du Comte d'Artois	MORTIER	21x27cm
Arx Carolina	DAPPER	28x35cm
Arx Carolina Charles Fort sur Florida	VAN DER AA	28x35cm
Asher & Adams' Arizona	ASHER & ADAMS	58x42cm
Asher & Adams' California & Nevada Northern Portion [in set with] ...	ASHER & ADAMS	42x60cm
Asher & Adams' Dakota	ASHER & ADAMS	58x41cm
Asher & Adams' Utah	ASHER & ADAMS	42x57cm
Asia	BEER	10x13cm
Asia	CLUVER	12x12cm
Asia	GIBSON	6x10cm
Asia	HILDBURGHAUSEN BIBLIO.	20x26cm
Asia	MAGINI	12x17cm
Asia	MOLL (Small)	20x27cm
Asia	RUSCELLI	18x25cm
Asia	STARLING	9x13cm
Asia	VAN DEN KEERE	9x13cm
Asia Drawn from the Latest and Best Authorites	KITCHIN	33x36cm
Asia ex Magna Orbis Terrae Descriptione Gerardi Mercatoris ...	MERCATOR (Folio)	38x47cm
Asia Minor	TALLIS	25x33cm
Asia Partiu Orbis Maxima MDXCVIII	QUAD	21x30cm
Asia Secunda Pars Terrae in Forma Pegasi	BUNTING	25x35cm
Asia Secunda Pars Terre in Forma Pegasir	BUNTING	25x35cm
Asia Verferliget von Joh. George Schreibem in Leipzig	SCHREIBER	18x28cm
Asia with the Islands Adioyning Described ...	SPEED	39x51cm
Asia. A New Description	MORDEN	11x13cm
Asiae Nova Descriptio	ORTELIUS (Folio)	37x49cm
Asiae Tabula Decima Continet Indiam intra Gangem [verso title]	PTOLEMY (1522-1541)	29x48cm
Asiae Tabula Secunda Continet	PTOLEMY (1522-1541)	30x40cm
Asiatischer Archipel und Neu Holland	HILDBURGHAUSEN BIBLIO.	20x26cm
Asie Divisee en Ses Principals Regions et ou se Peuvent Voir l'Estendue ...	DE L'ISLE	47x58cm
Aspen Special Map [CO]	U.S. GEOLOGICAL SURV.	43x38cm
Aspins Familiar Treatise on Astronomy to Accompany ... Urania's Mirror	ASPIN	14x20cm
Ataque de Quebec	LA HONTAN	11x17cm
Ath, Ville Forte des Pais Bas, dans le Comte de Hainaut	MORTIER	20x28cm
Atlantic [NJ: Monmouth Co.]	BEERS	32x34cm
Atlantic or Western Ocean	THOMSON	50x62cm
Attack of Quebec	LA HONTAN	10x16cm
Attack of the Rebels Upon Fort Penobscot in the Province of New England ...	TINDAL	36x38cm
Attaques du Fort William-Henri en Amerique par les Troupes Francaises ...	THERBU	42x27cm
Audiencia de Guadalajara, Nova Mexico, California, &c.	SANSON (Small)	20x24cm
Augsbourg Ville Imperiale d'Allemagne ... du Cercle de Souabe	MORTIER	20x29cm
Augspurg die Haupt-Stadt und Zierde des Schwaebischen Craises ...	SEUTTER	51x59cm
Australasia	PINKERTON	44x69cm
Australia	COLTON (Atlas Maps)	31x39cm
Australia	TALLIS	25x32cm
Australia	VIRTUE	20x24cm
Australia [in set with] New South Wales [and] Victoria or Port Phillip ...	TALLIS	No dimen
Australia and New Zealand	FULLARTON	41x51cm
Australia in 1839	S.D.U.K.	31x40cm
Australian ...	PETERMANN	37x45cm
Austria Archiducatus	MERCATOR (Folio)	35x45cm
Austriae Descrip ...	ORTELIUS (Folio)	35x48cm
Austriae Descriptio	ORTELIUS (Miniature)	8x11cm
Austriae Ducatus Chorograph, Wolfgango Lazio Auctore	ORTELIUS (Folio)	35x48cm
Avignon	BRAUN & HOGENBERG	31x47cm

Bacon's Gem Pocket Map of London and Suburbs	BACON	46x60cm
Bacon's New Large Print Map of China	BACON	61x71cm
Bacon's New Large Print Map of London	BACON	67x93cm
Bacon's New Map of London and Stranger's Guide ...	BACON	57x89cm
Bahama's and Windward Passage by Jer. Seller & Cha. Price ...	SELLER and PRICE	43x54cm
Bahamas	LUCAS	25x29cm
Bai San Francisco und Vereinigung des Sacramento mit dem San Joaquin	LANGE	210x27cm
Baltic region: Russland: Gouv. St. Petersburg, Esthland, Liefland, ...	HILDBURGHAUSEN BIBLIO.	20x26cm
Bamberga	SCHEDEL	23x53cm
Bankoku Yochi Sankai Zusetsu	JAPANESE CARTOGRAPHY	37x49cm
Barbadoes	LUCAS	29x23cm
Barbados	MOUNT & PAGE	29x26cm
Barbaia Africana, et Biledulgerid	QUAD	23x30cm
Barbaria	DE WIT	49x58cm
Barcelona, Barcino, que vulgo Barcelona Dicitur [on sheet with] Ecija	BRAUN & HOGENBERG	44x47cm
Baronia Udrone in Comitatu Catherloughae	BLAEU	38x25cm
Barrington Bay ... [Nova Scotia]	DES BARRES	75x105cm
Bartholomew's New Pocket Map of Environs of Edinburgh Reduced from ...	BARTHOLOMEW	44x58cm
Barut [Lebanon]	ROUX	13x18cm
Basilea	SCHEDEL	25x53cm
Basle Ville Capitale du Canton du Meme Nom	MORTIER	21x24cm
Bass Strait	BRITISH ADMIRALTY	97x65cm
Batalla de Ayacucho	LONGMAN	20x25cm
Battle-field of Winchester Va. Sept 19, 1864 ... [on sheet with] ...	U.S. UNION & CONFED.	43x71cm
Battlefield in Front of Franklin, Tenn. ... November 30th, 1864	U.S. WAR DEPARTMENT	71x46cm
Battlefield in Front of Nashville ... Dec. 15th and 16th, 1864	U.S. WAR DEPARTMENT	33x38cm
Battlefields in Front of Nashville where the United States Forces ...	MILITARY MAPS	33x38cm
Bavaria	SCHEDEL	23x23cm
Bavaria Divided into Its Respective Sovereign States	WILKINSON	23x28cm
Bavaria Ducatus	MERCATOR (Folio)	37x47cm
Bavariae olim Vindeliciae, Delineationis Compendium ex Tabula ...	ORTELIUS (Folio)	39x49cm
Bavariae Pars Inferior	SEUTTER	50x58cm
Bay Bulls [Newfoundland]	BRITISH ADMIRALTY	46x66cm
Bay of the Seven Islands	BRITISH ADMIRALTY	46x60cm
Bayern, Wurtemberg, beyde Hohenzollern und Baden	HILDBURGHAUSEN BIBLIO.	20x26cm
Bedford Comitatus ...	CAMDEN	27x33cm
Bedfordshire	SPEED	38x50cm
Behemer Funigkeich [sic] mit Bergen und Walden Geringo unb ...	MUNSTER	26x35cm
Belgica Foederata Complectens Septem Provincias, Ducatum Geldriae ...	LOTTER	48x59cm
Belgii Inferioris Descriptio Emendata cum Circumiacentium Regionu Confinijs	MERCATOR (Folio)	35x45cm
Belgium	QUAD	23x30cm
Benedict Arias Montanus Sacrae Geographiae Tabulum ex Antiquissimorum	ARIAS MONTANUS	31x53cm
Bergen [Norway]	MALLET	14x10cm
Bergen Op Zoom	BRAUN & HOGENBERG	38x34cm
Berkshire Drawn from the Best Authorities and Regulated by Astronl. ...	LONDON MAGAZINE	17x22cm
Bermuda	MOUNT & PAGE	29x22cm
Bermuda Hundred ... [VA]	U.S. WAR DEPARTMENT	51x74cm
Berry Ducatus	MERCATOR (Folio)	35x45cm
Bird's Eye View of Louisiana, Mississippi, Alabama and part of Florida	BACHMANN	47x71cm
Bird's Eye View of North and South Carolina and part of Georgia	BACHMANN	46x70cm
Bird's Eye View of Texas and part of Mexico	BACHMANN	47x70cm
Birds Eye View of the Soudan and Surrounding Countries	ILLUS. LONDON NEWS	42x53cm
Birds-eye View of the Course of the Mississippi, and the Seat of War in Tenn.	HARPER'S WEEKLY	35x23cm
Bitterroot Forest Reserve Showing Land Classification	U.S. GEOLOGICAL SURV.	66x61cm
Black's Road & Railway Travelling Map of Scotland	BLACK	85x62cm
Blairstown [NJ: Warren Co.]	BEERS	37x29cm
Bloys [France]	BRAUN & HOGENBERG	Folio
Bohemia	MERCATOR (Folio)	41x55cm
Bohemia	QUAD	18x26cm
Bohemia Including Moravia Austrian Silesia Eger & Glatz	WILKINSON	23x29cm
Bohemia Newly Described ...	SPEED	41x52cm
Bolonia & Guines Comitatus	MERCATOR (Folio)	45x35cm
Bonne, ou Bonn	MORTIER	21x29cm
Boon Point to Pelican Point [Antigua]	BRITISH ADMIRALTY	62x94cm
Borussiae Regnum Complectens Circulos Sambiensem, Natangiensem ...	LOTTER	51x58cm
Boston	BRADFORD	30x36cm
Boston and Adjacent Cities	COLTON (Atlas Maps)	46x38cm
Boston and Its Environs	MARSHALL	20x32cm

Boston Harbor, Massachusetts	U.S. COAST SURVEY	71x91cm
Boston, Seen between Castle Williams and Governors Island ...	DES BARRES	55x79cm
Bowles's Reduced New Pocket Atlas of the Cities of London and Westminster	BOWLES	38x54cm
Bradore Bay [Quebec]	BRITISH ADMIRALTY	46x66cm
Bradshaw's Map of Great Britain Showing the Railways	BRADSHAW	88x66cm
Bradshaw's Map of the Rhine	BRADSHAW	52x31cm
Brasilia ...	OGILBY	29x36cm
Brasilien	BELLIN (Small)	24x32cm
Braunswyck & Meydburg cum Ceteris Adiacentibus	MERCATOR (Folio)	35x45cm
Brazil	BURR	38x30cm
Brazil	LUCAS	38x30cm
Brescia Episcopatus Mediolanum Ductus ...	MERCATOR (Folio)	37x47cm
Bressla	SCHEDEL	23x52cm
Brightstowe	BRAUN & HOGENBERG	33x44cm
Brisach Ville Forte sur le Rhein Capitale de la Province de Briscow	MORTIER	20x27cm
Britannia Prout Divisa Fuit Temporibus Anglo-Saxonum Praesertim ...	BLAEU	41x52cm
Britannia Prout Divisa suit Temporibus Anglo-Saxonum, Proesertim ...	JANSSON	42x53cm
Britannicae Insulae ...	SANSON (Folio)	41x53cm
Britannicae, Insula in Quibus Albion seu Britannia Major, et Ivernia seu Britann	DE VAUGONDY	50x56cm
Britannicarum Insularum Typus	CLUVER	12x12cm
Britannicarum Insularum Vetus Descriptio	ORTELIUS (Folio)	49x35cm
Britisches Nord-America	HILDBURGHAUSEN BIBLIO.	20x26cm
Britisches Nord-America	RADEFELD	21x26cm
British America	TALLIS	26x32cm
British Camp at Trudruffrin ... [PA]	FADEN	25x40cm
British Colonies in North America	KELLY	19x25cm
British Columbia	CRAM	42x56cm
British India, Northern Part [in set with] British India, Southern Part	THOMSON	50x60cm
British Islands in the West Indies	S.D.U.K.	32x39cm
British Isles	GRAY	41x33cm
British North America	S.D.U.K.	31x39cm
British Possessions in America	ARROWSMITH & LEWIS	20x24cm
British Possessions in North America	CAREY & LEA	44x56cm
British Possessions in North America ...	PINKERTON	51x69cm
Brugae Flandicarum Urbium Decus	GUICCIARDINI	23x31cm
Brusxella, Urbs Aulicorum Frequentia, Fontium Copia, Magnificentia ...	BRAUN & HOGENBERG	34x48cm
Bruxelles Ville Considerable des Pais Bas. Capitale du Duche de Brabant	MORTIER	22x28cm
Buckinghamshire	SPEED	37x50cm
Buda, Vulgo Ofen, Prima et Regia Ungarici Regni Civitas, ad Danubium Sita ...	BRAUN & HOGENBERG	15x47cm
Burgos	MERIAN	19x31cm
Burgundia Ducatus	MERCATOR (Folio)	35x45cm
Burgundiae Ducatus [on sheet with] Burgundiae Comitatus	ORTELIUS (Folio)	36x50cm
Burgundiae Inferioris quae Ducatus Nomine Censetur Desc.	QUAD	18x26cm
Burlington Vermont	U.S. COAST SURVEY	58x51cm
Burr's Map of the State of New York	COLTON (Pocket & Wall)	33x38cm
Byzantium, nunc Constantino	ANONYMOUS	13x43cm
Byzantium, nunc Constantinopolis	BRAUN & HOGENBERG	Folio
Cadiz nach Malaga durch die Straasse oder Meer-Enge von Gibraltar ...	BODENEHR	17x51cm
Caelestem Hic Terram Inspicias Terrestre Ob Caelum	PTOLEMY (1482 Florence)	No dimen
Caernarvon Bay in Wales ...	MacKENZIE	95x103cm
Cairus, quae olim Babylon; Aegypti Maxima Urbs	BRAUN & HOGENBERG	33x48cm
Calechut Celeberrimum Indiae Emporium [on sheet with] Ormus [and] ...	BRAUN & HOGENBERG	34x48cm
Caletensium et Bononiensium ... [on sheet with] Veromanduorum ...	ORTELIUS (Folio)	34x48cm
California	BRADLEY	56x41cm
California	COLTON (Atlas Maps)	38x31cm
California, Utah, Lr. California and New Mexico	WEEKLY DISPATCH	43x30cm
Californien, Oregon, Utah und Neu-Mejico	FLEMMING	40x35cm
Cambriae Typus Auctore Humfredo Lhuydo Denbigiense ...	ORTELIUS (Folio)	37x49cm
Cambriae Typus Auctore Humfredo Lhuydo, Denbigiense Cambrobritanno ...	MERCATOR (Folio)	36x49cm
Campbelton Loch	BRITISH ADMIRALTY	46x64cm
Canaan	SPEED	38x52cm
Canaan Commonly Called the Holy Land or the Land of Promise ...	BLOME	27x46cm
Canaan from the Time of Joshua to the Babylonish Captivity	WILKINSON	44x28cm
Canaan or the Land of Promise to Abraham and His Posterity	WILKINSON	29x22cm
Canaan or the Land of Promise, Possessed by the Children of Israel ...	MOXON	31x46cm
Canaan, Palestine or the Holy Land &c. Divided into the Twelve Tribes ...	MOLL (Small)	22x18cm
Canada	BEER	10x13cm
Canada	BONNE	25x36cm

Title	Author	Size
Canada	NEELE	23x29cm
Canada and Nova Scotia	THOMSON	53x65cm
Canada East Formerly Lower Canada	THOMAS, COWPERTHWAIT	33x41cm
Canada East in Counties	MITCHELL, S.A. (1860+)	32x39cm
Canada East or Lower Canada	COLTON (Atlas Maps)	33x40cm
Canada Lands The Haslam Land and Investment Co.	REAL ESTATE MAPS	36x75cm
Canada or Niew Vrankryk ...	SANSON (Small)	21x31cm
Canada Orientale nell'America Settentrionali Descritta dal P. Mio ...	CORONELLI	45x61cm
Canada ou Nouvelle France	MALLET	14x10cm
Canada West in Counties	MITCHELL, S.A. (1860+)	32x39cm
Canada West or Upper Canada	COLTON (Atlas Maps)	33x40cm
Canada, Louisiane et Terres Angloises ...	D'ANVILLE	48x56cm
Canada, New Brunswick and Nova Scotia	TEESDALE	34x41cm
Candia	BEER	10x13cm
Candia [on sheet with] La Cita de Corphu	BRAUN & HOGENBERG	37x49cm
Candia cum Insulis Aliquot Circa Graeciam	MERCATOR (Folio)	34x48cm
Candia olim Creta	ORTELIUS (Miniature)	8x11cm
Cantebrigia, Opulentissimi Anglie Regni ...	BRAUN & HOGENBERG	33x45cm
Cantium quod nunc Kent	CAMDEN	25x37cm
Cape District Cape of Good Hope	WYLD	51x33cm
Cape Ferrat to Cape Carbon [Algeria]	BRITISH ADMIRALTY	47x62cm
Cape Poge and Adjacent Shoals [MA]	BLUNT	11x18cm
Cardigan Comitatus pars olim Dimetarium	CAMDEN	27x31cm
Carinthiae Ducatus, et Goritiae ... [on sheet with] Histriae ... [and] Zarae	ORTELIUS (Folio)	33x48cm
Carlisle Bay to St. John's Harbour [Antigua]	BRITISH ADMIRALTY	62x94cm
Caroline Meridionale ...	RAMSAY	37x42cm
Carta Accurata dell'Imperio del Giappone ...	TIRION	25x32cm
Carta dell' Isole Filippine di Mr. Bellin Ingegnere della Marina Foglio 1.mo	BELLIN (Small)	21x16cm
Carta Esatta Rappresentante, l'Isola della Guadalupa	GAZZETTIERE AMERICANO	22x30cm
Carta Esferica de la Costa Orientale de China desde el Rio Ngau-Keang ...	DIRECCION DE HIDRO.	94x62cm
Carta Esferica de las Islas Antillas ...	DIRECCION DE HIDRO.	90x60cm
Carta Esferica en Quatro Hojas de las Costas de Terra Firma ...	DIRECCION DE HIDRO.	60x95cm
Carta Geografica del Messico o Sia della Nuova Spagna	ALBRIZZI	33x43cm
Carta Hydrographica oder Algemeine Welf	BODENEHR	15x23cm
Carta Marina Nova Tabula	GASTALDI	13x18cm
Carta Marina Nuova Tavola	RUSCELLI	18x25cm
Carta Nova Accurata del Passagio et Strada dalli Paesi Bassi per Via ...	DE WIT	47x55cm
Carta Particolare dell' Isole Fillipine e di Luzon	DUDLEY	49x38cm
Carta Particolare dell' Mare e Isole Scoperte dal Capitno. Iacomo Maier ...	DUDLEY	48x75cm
Carta Particolare dell'Isole di Islandia e Frislandia, con l'Isolette di Fare	DUDLEY	48x75cm
Carta Particolare della Nuova Belgia e Parte della Nuova Anglia ...	DUDLEY	46x37cm
Carta Particolare Dello Istreto e Mare Iscoperto da Hen: Hudson Ingilese ...	DUDLEY	71x48cm
Carta Particulare del Mare di Ethopia con l'Isola di S. Elena e Parte ...	DUDLEY	48x75cm
Carta Rappresentante il Porto di Boston	GAZZETTIERE AMERICANO	21x18cm
Carta Topographique de l'Isle Minorque ...	HOMANN	44x54cm
Carta Trium Navigationum per Batavos ad Septentrionalem Plagem	DE BRY	28x36cm
Carte ... Berri, Nivernois, La Marche, Bourbonnis, Limosin et l'Auvergne	BONNE	30x43cm
Carte ... Dauphine et de Provence	BONNE	43x30cm
Carte ... Iles Sandwich ...	LA PEROUSE	49x36cm
Carte ... Normandie avec celui Maine et Perche	BONNE	30x43cm
Carte Contenant le Royaume du Mexique et la Floride, Dressez sur les ...	CHATELAIN	40x52cm
Carte d'Afrique ...	DE L'ISLE	50x64cm
Carte d'Amerique Dressee pour l'Usage du Roy par Guillaume ...	DE L'ISLE	51x61cm
Carte d'Amerique, Dressee pour l'Usage du Roi. Par Guil. Delisle et Phil. ...	DE L'ISLE	48x60cm
Carte d'un Tres Grand Pays entre le Nouveau Mexique ...	VAN DER AA	43x51cm
Carte d'une partie de la Cote de la N'le Galles Merid'le ...	COOK	30x35cm
Carte dans laquelle on Voit la Route que le Centurion A Tenu dans la Voiage ...	ANSON	23x40cm
Carte de Brabant	DE L'ISLE	65x64cm
Carte de l'Accadie Dressee sur les Manuscrits du Depost des Cartes ...	BELLIN (Small)	21x32cm
Carte de l'Amerique Meridionale	BRUE	51x37cm
Carte de l'Amerique Septentrionale	LAPIE	55x40cm
Carte de l'Arabie	LATTRE	30x43cm
Carte de l'Egypte Ancienne et Moderne	LATTRE	43x30cm
Carte de l'Egypte Ancienne et Moderne...	DE VAUGONDY	66x50cm
Carte de l'Egypte de la Nubie de l'Abissinie &c. ...	DE L'ISLE	50x63cm
Carte de l'Empire de Perse	LATTRE	30x43cm
Carte de l'Empire de Russie en Europe et en Asie	LATTRE	30x43cm
Carte de l'Empire du Japon pour Servir a l'Histoire Generale des Voyages	BELLIN (Small)	22x32cm

Carte de l'Entree de la Tamise avec les Bancs, Passes, Isles et Costes ...	JAILLOT	46x90cm
Carte de l'Entree de Norton et du Detroit de Bhering ...	BONNE	24x35cm
Carte de l'Hemisphere Austral	COOK	54x55cm
Carte de l'Hemisphere Austral Montrant les Routes des Navigateurs ...	BELLIN (Small)	53x53cm
Carte de l'Hemisphere Austral Montrant les Routes des Navigateurs ...	BENARD	54x52cm
Carte de l'Ile de Fogo a la Cote Orientale de Terre-Neuve ... Michael Lane ...	DEPOT DE LA MARINE	62x91cm
Carte de l'Ile de Wight et de la Cote Adjacente de Hampshire ...	DEPOT DE LA MARINE	61x90cm
Carte de l'Inde Dressee pour la Compagnie des Indes par le Sr. ...	D'ANVILLE	48x104cm
Carte de l'Islande ...	BELLIN (Small)	32x39cm
Carte de l'Isle d'Hayti Aujourd'hui l'Espagnol ou l'Isle de St. Domingue ...	VAN DER SCHLEY	23x33cm
Carte de l'Isle d'Orleans et du Passage de la Traverse dans le Fleuve ...	BELLIN (Small)	19x28cm
Carte de l'Isle de Ceylon Dressee sur les Observations de Mrs. de l'Academie	DE L'ISLE	47x57cm
Carte de l'Isle de France ... M.DCC.LXIII	BELLIN (Large)	57x88cm
Carte de l'Isle de la Barbade pour Servir a l'Histoire Generale des Voyages	BELLIN (Small)	20x15cm
Carte de l'Isle de la Grenade ...	BELLIN (Small)	21x17cm
Carte de l'Isle de la Guadeloupe, pour Servir a l'Histoire Generale ...	BELLIN (Small)	21x32cm
Carte de l'Isle de la Jamaique ... 1758	BELLIN (Small)	22x33cm
Carte de l'Isle de la Martinique ...	BONNE	31x20cm
Carte de l'Isle de Portsey, et Havre de Portsmouth	BELLIN (Small)	21x15cm
Carte de l'Isle de Sainte Lucie, pour Servir a l'Histoire Generale ...	BELLIN (Small)	22x33cm
Carte de l'Isle de Taiti par le Lieutenant J. Cook 1769	COOK	23x41cm
Carte de l'Isle et Royaume de Sicile	DE L'ISLE	47x57cm
Carte de l'Isle Saint Pierre Dressee au Depot des Cartes et Plans ...	BELLIN (Large)	59x90cm
Carte de l'Isle St. Christophe, pour Servir a l'Histoire Generale ...	BELLIN (Small)	22x33cm
Carte de l'Ocean Pacifique au Nord de l'Equateur, et des Cotes Qui le Bornent	LOTTER	47x51cm
Carte de la Barbarie de la Nigritie et de la Guinee	DE L'ISLE	50x61cm
Carte de la Baye de Chesapeak et Pays Voisins	BELLIN (Small)	28x38cm
Carte de la Baye de Hudson ...	BELLIN (Small)	22x30cm
Carte de la Baye de l'Oristan	BELLIN (Small)	22x17cm
Carte de la Californie et des Pays Nord-Ouest, Separes de l'Asie par le Detroit	DIDEROT	30x35cm
Carte de la Californie Suivant I. La Carte Manuscrite de l'Amerique ...	DIDEROT	29x38cm
Carte de la Caroline et Georgie	BELLIN (Small)	19x28cm
Carte de la Cote N.O. de l'Amerique et de la Cote N.E. de l'Asie ...	BONNE	24x35cm
Carte de la Floride, de la Louisiane et Pays Voisins ...	BELLIN (Small)	25x33cm
Carte de la Grece	DE L'ISLE	45x59cm
Carte de la Inde au-dela du Gange Comprenant les Royaumes de Siam ...	BELLIN (Small)	28x28cm
Carte de la Louisiane	D'ANVILLE	52x92cm
Carte de la Louisiane et du Cours du Mississipi ...	COVENS & MORTIER	44x60cm
Carte de la Louisiane et du Cours du Mississipi ...	DE L'ISLE	44x60cm
Carte de la Louisiane, et de la Floride	BONNE	32x21cm
Carte de la Mer des Antilles Partie Occidentale ...	DEPOT DE LA MARINE	89x60cm
Carte de la N.le. Galles Merid'le ... N'le Hollande ...	COOK	36x77cm
Carte de la Nouvelle Angleterre ...	BELLIN (Small)	20x30cm
Carte de la Nouvelle Angleterre, Nouvelle Yorck et Pensilvanie	BELLIN (Small)	20x29cm
Carte de la Nouvelle Angleterre, Nouvelle York, Nouvelle Jersey, et Penn...	BERTHOLON	18x22cm
Carte de la Nouvelle France et de la Louisiane ...	HENNEPIN	30x48cm
Carte de la Nouvelle France ou Se Voit le Cours des Grandes Rivieres ...	CHATELAIN	42x48cm
Carte de la Nouvelle France ou Se Voit le Cours des Grandes Rivieres ...	OTTENS	50x55cm
Carte de la Nouvelle France ou Se Voit le Cours des Grandes Rivieres ...	VAN KEULEN	58x97cm
Carte de la Partie de la Cote Nord Ouest de l'Amerique	POIRSON	43x34cm
Carte de la Partie Occidentale des Iles Antilles ...	DEPOT DE LA MARINE	60x91cm
Carte de la Petite Tartarie ...	DE LETH	43x49cm
Carte de la Souverainete de Neuchatel et Vallangin	DE L'ISLE	50x64cm
Carte de la Suisse en 8 Feuilles ...	KELLER	116x175cm
Carte de la Terre Ferme du Perou, du Bresil et du Pays des Amazons ...	DE L'ISLE	48x57cm
Carte de la Terre Sainte Divisee selon les Douze Tribus d'Israel ou Sont ...	MORTIER	40x47cm
Carte de la Virginie et du Maryland Dressee sur la Grande Carte Angloise ...	DE VAUGONDY	48x64cm
Carte de Lisle de Sainct Christophle. Scituee a 17 Degrez 30 Minutes ...	SANSON (Folio)	31x43cm
Carte de Moscovie ...	DE L'ISLE	52x63cm
Carte de Perse ...	DE L'ISLE	48x61cm
Carte de Tartarie ...	DE L'ISLE	48x61cm
Carte de Tartarie Dressee sur les Relations de Plusiers Voyageurs ...	DE L'ISLE	50x62cm
Carte des Antilles Francoises et des Isles Voisines ...	DE L'ISLE	64x39cm
Carte des Bayes, Rades et Port de Plaisance dans l'Isle de Terre Neuve...	BELLIN (Small)	21x30cm
Carte des Cotes de l'Amerique et de l'Asie depuis la Californie jusqu' a ...	LA PEROUSE	50x68cm
Carte des Cotes de l'Amerique Meridionale ...	DEPOT DE LA MARINE	91x62cm
Carte des Cotes de Malabar et de Coromandel	DE L'ISLE	44x56cm
Carte des Courones du Nord qui Comprend les Royaumes de Danemark ...	DE L'ISLE	45x60cm

Title	Author	Size
Carte des Declinaisons et Inclinaisons de l'Aiguille Aimantee ... l'Anne	BUFFON	42x54cm
Carte des Douze Tribus d'Israel ...	BONNE	31x44cm
Carte des Entrees de la Tamise ...	BELLIN (Large)	58x87cm
Carte des Etats Unis d'Amerique	LAPIE	39x53cm
Carte des Etats-Unis du Mexique	LAPIE	54x39cm
Carte des Grandes Routes d'Angleterre, d'Ecosse, et d'Irlande. par ...	DE VAUGONDY	55x58cm
Carte des Indes en deca et au dela du Gange ...	BONNE	33x22cm
Carte des Indes et de la Chine ...	DE L'ISLE	61x63cm
Carte des Indes Orientales ...	DU VAL	40x54cm
Carte des Indes Orientales ...	HOMANN	51x87cm
Carte des Isles de Java, Sumatra, Borneo &c. les Detroits de la Sonde ...	BELLIN (Small)	26x29cm
Carte des Isles de la Sonde et des Isles Moluques	BONNE	21x31cm
Carte des Isles de Saint Domingue	DE L'ISLE	46x61cm
Carte des Isles de St. Dominque et de Porto-Rico	BONNE	22x32cm
Carte des Isles Nicobar ...	D'APRES DE MANNEVILLETTE	46x30cm
Carte des Isles Philippines ... 1re Feuille ...	BELLIN (Small)	23x17cm
Carte des Isles Philippines ... 2e. Feuille ...	BELLIN (Small)	22x30cm
Carte des Isles Sandwich ...	BONNE	23x34cm
Carte des Isles Situees au Nord de St. Domingue avec les Passages ...	BELLIN (Small)	23x38cm
Carte des Lacs du Canada Dressee sur les Manuscrits du Depost des Cartes ...	BELLIN (Small)	30x46cm
Carte des Nordens von America, zur Beurtheilung der Wahrscheinlichkeit ...	FORSTER	51x65cm
Carte des Nouvelles Decouvertes au Nord de la Mer du Sud, ...	BUACHE	47x67cm
Carte des Nouvelles Decouvertes Dressee par Phil. Buache ... Aout 1752	DIDEROT	29x35cm
Carte des Pays Voisins de la Mer Caspiene ...	DE L'ISLE	46x61cm
Carte des Possessions Francoises et Angloises dans le Canada, ...	LONGCHAMPS	54x75cm
Carte des Provinces de Caracas, Comana, et Paria ...	BELLIN (Small)	19x29cm
Carte des Provinces de Tabasco, Chiapa, Verapaz, Guatimala, Honduras ...	BELLIN (Small)	20x34cm
Carte des Provinces Unies des Pays Bas	DE L'ISLE	47x62cm
Carte des Regions et des Lieux Dont Il Est Parle dans le Nouveau Testament	BONNE	30x44cm
Carte des Royaumes d'Irelande	DE LAPORTE	17x22cm
Carte du Canada ou de la Nouvelle France ...	DE L'ISLE	50x56cm
Carte du Canada ou de la Nouvelle France, & des Decouvertes Qui Y Ont ...	CHATELAIN	40x52cm
Carte du Comte de Kent et du Pas de Calais ...	BELLIN (Large)	58x86cm
Carte du Congo et du Pays des Cafres	DE L'ISLE	48x61cm
Carte du Cours de la Riviere de Meinam depuis Judia jusqu'a son Embouchure	KAEMPFER	31x19cm
Carte du Cours du Fleuve de Saint Laurent depuis la Mer jusqu'a Quebec ...	BELLIN (Large)	60x90cm
Carte du Cours du Fleuve de Saint Laurent depuis Quebec jusqu'a la Mer ...	BELLIN (Large)	57x85cm
Carte du Detroit qui Separe l'Asie de l'Amerique, avec la Cote ...	SAUER	40x61cm
Carte du Duche de Luxembourg ...	DE VAUGONDY	51x63cm
Carte du Golphe du Mexique et des Isles de l'Amerique	BELLIN (Small)	27x38cm
Carte du Gouvernment de l'Isle de France et de celui de l'Orleanois ...	BONNE	43x30cm
Carte du Grand Ocean ou Mer du Sud	LA PEROUSE	50x69cm
Carte du Groenland	LAURENT	19x25cm
Carte du Lac de Mexico et de Ses Environs Lors de la Conqueste ...	BELLIN (Small)	21x15cm
Carte du Mexique	TARDIEU	39x25cm
Carte du Mexique et de la Floride des Terres Angloises et des Isles Antilles ...	DE L'ISLE	47x61cm
Carte du Monde de Marc Paul [on sheet with] Carte du Monde ... Castaldo	MALLET	14x10cm
Carte du Nouveau Continent ...	DE VAUGONDY	22x18cm
Carte du Paraguay du Chili du Detroit de Magellan &c ...	DE L'ISLE	49x58cm
Carte du Royaume d'Irlande	LAPORTE	18x22cm
Carte du Royaume de Congo du Monomotapa et de la Cafrerie ...	CHATELAIN	41x52cm
Carte du Royaume de Danemarc	DE L'ISLE	48x60cm
Carte du Territoire d'Arkansas et des Autres Territoires des Etats-Unis	BUCHON	37x38cm
Carte Exacte des Postes et Routes de l'Empire d'Allemagne Divisee ...	DE L'ISLE	46x59cm
Carte Faite sur les Lieux par Daniel Tavernier en Plusieurs Voiages ...	TAVERNIER	49x40cm
Carte General de la Caroline Desse sur les Memoires le Plus Nouveaux	MORTIER	57x47cm
Carte Generale de Canada Dediee au Roy de Denemark par ... Lahontan	LA HONTAN	41x55cm
Carte Generale de France Divisee par Gouvernements	LATTRE	30x43cm
Carte Generale de l'Empire de Russie, 1787	PALLAS	55x117cm
Carte Generale de la Turquie d'Asie	VIVIEN	47x57cm
Carte Generale de Toutes les Costes du Monde ...	COVENS & MORTIER	58x100cm
Carte Generale de Toutes les Costes du Monde ... [and sheet with]	COVENS & MORTIER	58x50cm
Carte Generale des Decouvertes de l'Admiral de Fonte est autres Navigateurs	DIDEROT	29x37cm
Carte Generale des Decouvertes de l'Amiral de Fonte Representant la Grande	DIDEROT	29x35cm
Carte Generale des Etats Unis de l'Amerique Septentrionale	VIVIEN	31x41cm
Carte Generale du Mexique ...	VIVIEN	31x40cm
Carte Geo-Hydrographique du Golfe du Mexique et de Ses Isles	RIZZI-ZANNONI	31x45cm
Carte Geographique du Comte de la Marck	LOTTER	49x58cm

Title	Author	Size
Carte Geographique, Statistique et Historique de la Floride	BUCHON	29x24cm
Carte Geographique, Statistique et Historique de Porto Rico	BUCHON	25x42cm
Carte Geographique, Statistique et Historique des Possessions Russes	BUCHON	37x43cm
Carte Geographique, Statistique et Historique du Mexique	BUCHON	32x38cm
Carte Geographique, Statistique et Historique du Territoire d'Arkansas ...	BUCHON	46x61cm
Carte Hydro-Geo-Graphique des Indies Orientales ...	LATTRE	57x80cm
Carte Magnetique des Deux Hemispheres	ANONYMOUS	57x99cm
Carte Nouvelle d'Amerique	DE PRETOT	26x39cm
Carte Nouvelle de l'Amerique Angloise Contenant Tout Ce Que les Anglois ...	LOTTER	60x49cm
Carte Particuliere de l'Amerique Septentrionale, ou Sont Compris le Destroit...	MORTIER	58x83cm
Carte Particuliere de la Caroline Dresse sur les Memoires le Plus Nouveau	MORTIER	48x60cm
Carte Particuliere de la Cote du Nord-Ouest de l'Amerique Reconnue par ...	LA PEROUSE	49x69cm
Carte Particuliere du Canal de Bristol ...	DEPOT DE LA MARINE	57x89cm
Carte Physique de la Mer des Indes	BUACHE	30x35cm
Carte que les Guacsitares Ont Dessine sur ... Carte de la Riviere Longue...	LA HONTAN	28x66cm
Carte Reduite de l'Ile Royale ... par Ordre de M. De Sartine	DEPOT DE LA MARINE	89x61cm
Carte Reduite de l'Isle de Saint Christophe ... M.DCC.LVIII	BELLIN (Large)	59x88cm
Carte Reduite de l'Ocean Meridional ...	DEPOT DE LA MARINE	54x87cm
Carte Reduite de l'Ocean Oriental Septentrional ...	D'APRES DE MANNEVILLETTE	48x66cm
Carte Reduite de l'Ocean Septentrionale Compris Entre l'Asie et l'Amerique	BELLIN (Large)	56x85cm
Carte Reduite de la Mer du Sud ...	BELLIN (Small)	21x35cm
Carte Reduite de la Partie Septentrionale de l'Isle de Terre Neuve ...	BELLIN (Large)	62x81cm
Carte Reduite de la Rade des Dunes ...	BELLIN (Large)	58x42cm
Carte Reduite des ... Mer du Sud ou Mer Pacifique ...	DEPOT DE LA MARINE	56x83cm
Carte Reduite des Costes Occidentales d'Afrique ...	BELLIN (Large)	89x55cm
Carte Reduite des Cotes Orientales de l'Amerique Septentrionale ...	SARTINE	59x88cm
Carte Reduite des Debouquemens de St. Domingue Dressee pour le Service...	BELLIN (Large)	58x90cm
Carte Reduite des la Mer des Indes	D'ENTRECASTEAUX	48x71cm
Carte Reduite des Mers du Nord	BELLIN (Large)	54x87cm
Carte Reduite des Mers du Nord	BELLIN (Small)	33x45cm
Carte Reduite des Mers du Nord pour Servir a l'Histoire Generale ...	BELLIN (Small)	33x44cm
Carte Reduite des Parties Connues du Globe Terrestre ...	BELLIN (Large)	54x82cm
Carte Reduite des Parties Septentrionales du Globe, Situees Entre l'Asie et ...	BELLIN (Small)	21x34cm
Carte Reduite des Terres Australes	BELLIN (Small)	20x28cm
Carte Reduite du Globe Terrestre	BELLIN (Small)	22x34cm
Carte Tres Curieuse de la Mer du Sud Contenant des Remarques Nouvelles ...	CHATELAIN	81x142cm
Carte Universelle du Commerce, c'est a Dire Carte Hidrographique, ...	DU VAL	37x53cm
Carte Universelle du Monde ... [southern sheets: Terres Australes; ...]	DU VAL	41x58cm
Carthago	SCHEDEL	17x12cm
Cary's Reduction of His Large Map of England and Wales, with Part of ...	CARY	91x65cm
Castellum Gibraltar in Andalusia Situm, cum Celebri Freto inter Europam ...	LOTTER	49x59cm
Caster's Map 70 Miles Around Peterborough [England]	LOCAL & STATE MAPS	69x84cm
Castilia Aurifera cum Vicinis Provinciis	WYTFLIET	23x29cm
Castiliae Veteris et Novae Descriptio	MERCATOR (Folio)	35x45cm
Castleton, VT	BURLEIGH	42x64cm
Castries, St. Lucia, West Indies	GOAD	62x52cm
Ceilan ...	PLANCIUS	34x50cm
Central America	TALLIS	26x32cm
Central America and the West Indies ...	HARPER & BROS.	30x51cm
Central America II Including Texas, California and the Northern States ...	S.D.U.K.	31x39cm
Central America, Namely the [Late] Confederated States of Central America	FULLARTON	52x41cm
Cerro de Potosi	BERTIUS	8x13cm
Cestria (Vulgo Chester) Angliae Civitas	BRAUN & HOGENBERG	33x43cm
Cette Carte de Californie et du Nouveau Mexique Est Tiree de Celle ...	DE FER (Small)	25x34cm
Chala Point to Kwyhoo Bay [Kenya]	BRITISH ADMIRALTY	63x48cm
Champion Hill [on sheet with] Big Black River Brdge [and] Port Hudson	MILITARY MAPS	24x55cm
Chancellorville, Prepared by Bvt. Brig. Genl. N. Michler ...	U.S. WAR DEPARTMENT	56x64cm
Chang Tau Harbour and Approaches	BRITISH ADMIRALTY	49x65cm
Charleston [SC]	ENSIGN, BRIDGMAN & FANNING	20x13cm
Charlotte Bay. Published According to Act of Parliament by	DES BARRES	71x102cm
Chart Containing the Greater Part of the South Sea to the South of the Line ...	JEFFERYS	43x53cm
Chart of Discoveries Made in 1787, in the Seas of China and Tartary ...	LA PEROUSE	50x38cm
Chart of Long Island Sound	BLUNT	18x43cm
Chart of New Holland with the Adjacent Countries and New Discover'd ...	UNIVERSAL MAGAZINE	16x26cm
Chart of Part of the Islands of Pora ... and Poggys	DALRYMPLE	29x18cm
Chart of Part of the North West Coast of America ...	ROBINSON	38x49cm
Chart of Part of the North West Coast of America Explored by the Boussole	LA PEROUSE	50x38cm
Chart of the Antarctic Continent Shewing the Icy Barrier Attached to It.	U.S. EXPLORING EXPED.	60x86cm

Chart of the Antarctic Polar Circle, with the Countries Adjoining, ...	GENTLEMAN'S MAG.	20x22cm
Chart of the Coast from Salinas to Para ... [Brazil]	MANUSCRIPT MAPS	48x61cm
Chart of the Coast of France from Banduff to Riou Isle	BRITISH ADMIRALTY	44x60cm
Chart of the Discoveries, Made in 1787, in the Seas of China and Tartary ...	LA PEROUSE	38x50cm
Chart of the East Coast of North America ...	IMRAY	104x183cm
Chart of the Harbor of San Juan, Puerto Rico	U.S.	18x22cm
Chart of the N.W. Coast of America and the N.E. Coast of Asia, ...	HENRY	43x70cm
Chart of the North West Coast of America, Explored by the Boussole ...	LA PEROUSE	39x50cm
Chart of the North West Passage Between Asia and America	PHILIP	49x57cm
Chart of the Northern Passage between Asia & America	THOMSON	50x59cm
Chart of the Seychelle Islands by the Officers of H.M. Ships Leven & ...	BRITISH ADMIRALTY	46x62cm
Chart of the South Channel from Prince of Wales Island to Sea	LAURIE & WHITTLE	61x41cm
Chart of the Supposed Course of the Florida Stream	NAVAL CHRONICLE	16x39cm
Chart of the Track and Discoveries of the East India Company's Cruizers ...	BRITISH ADMIRALTY	30x50cm
Chart of the West Indies and Spanish Dominions in North America	ARROWSMITH	61x189cm
Charta Cosmographica, cum Ventorum Propia Natura et Operatione	APIANUS	19x28cm
Charte das Russische Reich ...	PROBST	17x20cm
Charte der Kriegs Operationen am Donn und Dnieper ... Ao 1736 ...	MILITARY MAPS	40x46cm
Charte uber die XIII Vereinigte Staaten von Nord-America ...	GUSSEFELD	44x57cm
Chateau Bay [Labrador]	BRITISH ADMIRALTY	46x66cm
Chester, Mass.	BURLEIGH	37x58cm
Chica sive Patagoni caet Australis Terra	WYTFLIET	23x29cm
Chica sive Patagonica et Australis Terra M.DC	QUAD	22x28cm
Chicago	GRAY	39x32cm
Chicago [on sheet with] St. Louis	COLTON (Atlas Maps)	46x38cm
Chicago and North Western R'w.	RAND, McNALLY (Pocket, etc)	61x81cm
Chicago and Northwestern Railway	RAILROAD CO. MAPS	18x34cm
Chikyo Zenzu	JAPANESE CARTOGRAPHY	51x42cm
Chile and Patagonia	BURR	38x30cm
Chili	BLAEU	36x48cm
Chili	DE LAET	28x35cm
Chili	LUCAS	38x28cm
Chili	PINKERTON	70x50cm
China	BEER	10x13cm
China	CLOPPENBURGH	18x25cm
China	HONDIUS	34x46cm
China	JANSSON	18x25cm
China	JOHNSON	32x38cm
China	MERCATOR (Folio)	34x46cm
China	THOMAS, COWPERTHWAIT	29x36cm
China Sheet I South Coast from Hainan Id. to Macao [in set with] China ...	BRITISH ADMIRALTY	46x61cm
China Propria oder das Eigentliche China	HILDBURGHAUSEN BIBLIO.	26x20cm
China Sea Sheet II	HORSBURGH	66x99cm
Chinae, Olim Sinarum Regionis, Nova Descriptio. Auctore Ludovico Georgio	ORTELIUS (Folio)	37x47cm
Chorographia Originis Nili ...	KIRCHER	19x17cm
Chorographia Terrae Sanctae in Angustiorem Formam ...	VAN ADRICHEM	32x85cm
Christmas Island ...	HOGG	22x30cm
Circulus Franconicus	LOTTER	50x58cm
Circulus Saxoniae Inferioris ...	HOMANN	47x55cm
Circulus Suevicus in quo Ducatus Wirtenbergensis	SEUTTER	50x58cm
Citadelle de Diu [India]	LAFITAU	19x14cm
City of Baltimore	COLTON (Atlas Maps)	32x39cm
City of Bangor	COLBY	38x31cm
City of Paterson [NJ]	BEERS	22x36cm
City of Philadelphia	COLTON (Atlas Maps)	46x38cm
City of Savannah, Georgia [on sheet with] City of Charleston ...	COLTON (Atlas Maps)	31x37cm
City of St. Louis [on sheet with] City of Chicago	COLTON (Atlas Maps)	30x38cm
City of Washington	THOMAS, COWPERTHWAIT	31x39cm
Civitas Acon sive Ptolomayda	BONGARS	15x20cm
Civitas Exoniae (vulgo Excester)	BRAUN & HOGENBERG	Folio
Civitas Florentina	MUNSTER	22x36cm
Clayoquot Sound, Vancouver Island	BRITISH ADMIRALTY	64x97cm
Climatic Map of California	RAILROAD CO. MAPS	71x23cm
Coast Chart No.162 From Cape Canaveral Southward to Latitude 27° 41'	U.S. COAST & GEODETIC	81x109cm
Coast Chart No.164 Jupiter Inlet to Hillsboro Inlet [FL]	U.S. COAST & GEODETIC	83x104cm
Coast Chart No.167 Florida Reefs, From the Elbow to Lower Matecumbe ...	U.S. COAST & GEODETIC	76x99cm
Coast Chart No.170 Florida Reefs, Key West to Rebecca Shoal [FL]	U.S. COAST & GEODETIC	83x104cm
Coast Chart No.171 Florida Reefs, Rebecca Shoal to Dry Tortugas [FL]	U.S. COAST & GEODETIC	83x104cm

Coast Chart No.174 Big Marco Pass to San Carlos Bay [FL]	U.S. COAST & GEODETIC	100x81cm
Coast Chart No.201 West End of Pecan Island to the Mermentau River	U.S. COAST & GEODETIC	83x94cm
Coast Chart No.202 Calcasieu Pass to Sabine Light [LA]	U.S. COAST & GEODETIC	83x108cm
Coast from Pemaquid Point to Seguin Island [ME]	U.S. COAST SURVEY	53x33cm
Coblentz	MORTIER	16x14cm
Coelum Stellatum Hemisphaerium Arietis ... [with] Coelum Stellatum ...	BODE	58x79cm
Collonge	MORTIER	21x29cm
Colombia	BURR	38x30cm
Colombia	LUCAS	38x30cm
Colonia	SCHEDEL	19x53cm
Coloniae Agrippina	BRAUN & HOGENBERG	34x48cm
Colorado	BRADLEY	42x57cm
Colorado	CRAM	25x32cm
Colorado	GRAY	31x38cm
Colorado, Utah, New Mexico and Arizona	WARNER & BEERS	41x37cm
Colton's California and Nevada	COLTON (Atlas Maps)	64x44cm
Colton's Dominion of Canada No.3 The Provinces of New Brunswick ...	COLTON (Atlas Maps)	44x67cm
Colton's Dominion of Canada No.3. The Provinces of New Brunswick ...	COLTON (Pocket & Wall)	46x67cm
Colton's Georgetown and the City of Washington the Capital ...	COLTON (Atlas Maps)	33x40cm
Colton's Illustrated & Embellished Steel Plate Map of the World on Mercator's	COLTON (Pocket & Wall)	142x201cm
Colton's Ireland	COLTON (Atlas Maps)	36x29cm
Colton's Lake Superior and the Upper Peninsula of Michigan	COLTON (Atlas Maps)	44x65cm
Colton's Map of the States and Territories from the Mississippi River ...	COLTON (Pocket & Wall)	71x104cm
Colton's Nebraska	COLTON (Atlas Maps)	42x67cm
Colton's New Township Map of the Western Counties of Pennsylvania	COLTON (Pocket & Wall)	95x67cm
Colton's North America	COLTON (Atlas Maps)	40x33cm
Colton's Palestine	COLTON (Atlas Maps)	41x33cm
Colton's Territories of New Mexico and Utah	COLTON (Atlas Maps)	33x39cm
Colton's United States	COLTON (Atlas Maps)	38x43cm
Colton's Wisconsin	COLTON (Atlas Maps)	40x32cm
Colts Neck [on sheet with] Edinburg [and] ... [NJ: Monmouth Co.]	BEERS	32x27cm
Columbo [on sheet with] Gale	MALLET	14x10cm
Congo Cafrerie par Robert de Vaugondy ...	DELAMARCHE	24x28cm
Conibas Regio cum Vicinis Gentibus	WYTFLIET	22x27cm
Connatia	BERTIUS	12x14cm
Connecticut	ARROWSMITH & LEWIS	22x27cm
Connecticut	MITCHELL, S.A. (to 1859)	31x37cm
Connecticut	TANNER	30x35cm
Connecticut from the Best Authorities	CAREY, M.	31x39cm
Connecticut with Portions of New York & Rhode Island	COLTON (Atlas Maps)	32x40cm
Consolidated Map of Indian and Settler's Lands in Bitter Root Valley, ...	U.S.	36x19cm
Constantinopel	HECK	20x25cm
Constantinople	MALLET	14x10cm
Constantinopolis ...	SCHEDEL	23x23cm
Constellatio XLV	SCHILLER	24x31cm
Constellatio XXII	SCHILLER	24x31cm
Constellatio XXIII	SCHILLER	24x31cm
Contado di Molise et Principato Ultra	BLAEU	38x50cm
Continent Arctique	MALLET	15x11cm
Continent Meridional	MALLET	Diam 10 cm
Continent Meridional Austral ou Antarctique	MALLET	11x15cm
Copenhague	DE FER (Small)	13x17cm
Copenhague	MORTIER	22x32cm
Corea and Japan	THOMSON	47x61cm
Corfu	ORTELIUS (Miniature)	8x11cm
Corfu en By-Leggende Plaatsen	DONCKER	40x52cm
Correct Chart of St. George's Channel and the Irish Sea, Including All ...	SEALE	47x37cm
Correct County Map of the State of Kansas	COMPANY MAPS	28x52cm
Corsica	BERTIUS	8x13cm
Cote Nord-Ouest de l'Amerique ... 2e. Partie ...	VANCOUVER	75x61cm
Cote Nord-Ouest de l'Amerique Reconnue par le Cape. Vancouver. Ve. Partie	VANCOUVER	78x65cm
Counties of Essex, Union and Hudson [NJ]	HOPKINS	31x39cm
Counties of Morris, Passaic and Bergen and Vicinity of Newark [NJ]	HOPKINS	37x33cm
Country around Sandhurst	BRITISH ORDNANCE	66x96cm
County and Township Map of Montana Idaho and Wyoming	BRADLEY	37x54cm
County and Township Map of Oregon and Washington	MITCHELL, S.A. (1860+)	51x37cm
County Map of California	MITCHELL, S.A. (1860+)	34x27cm
County Map of California	MITCHELL, S.A. (1860+)	53x36cm

Title	Author	Size
County Map of Colorado, Utah, New Mexico and Arizona	WARNER & BEERS	41x36cm
County Map of Colorado, Wyoming, Dakota, Montana	MITCHELL, S.A. (1860+)	50x36cm
County Map of Dakota, Wyoming, Kansas, Nebraska and Colorado	MITCHELL, S.A. (1860+)	50x35cm
County Map of Florida	BRADLEY	28x37cm
County Map of Florida	MITCHELL, S.A. (1860+)	27x34cm
County Map of Idaho, Montana and Wyoming	WARNER & BEERS	33x41cm
County Map of Illinois	MITCHELL, S.A. (1860+)	34x27cm
County Map of Iowa and Missouri	MITCHELL, S.A. (1860+)	36x29cm
County Map of Kansas, Nebraska, Dakota and Minnesota	WARNER & BEERS	44x36cm
County Map of Kentucky & Tennessee	MITCHELL, S.A. (1860+)	28x36cm
County Map of Massachusetts, Connecticut and Rhode Island	MITCHELL, S.A. (1860+)	30x38cm
County Map of Michigan and Wisconsin	MITCHELL, S.A. (1860+)	29x35cm
County Map of Minnesota	MITCHELL, S.A. (1860+)	36x30cm
County Map of Ohio and Indiana	MITCHELL, S.A. (1860+)	28x35cm
County Map of Oregon and Washington	MITCHELL, S.A. (1860+)	28x20cm
County Map of Oregon, Washington [on sheet with] Territory of Alaska	WARNER & BEERS	37x43cm
County Map of Texas	MITCHELL, S.A. (1860+)	27x34cm
County Map of Texas and Indian Territory	WARNER & BEERS	43x37cm
County Map of the State of Illinois	MITCHELL, S.A. (1860+)	38x30cm
County Map of the State of Maine	MITCHELL, S.A. (1860+)	36x27cm
County Map of the State of Texas, Showing Also Portions of the Adjoining ...	MITCHELL, S.A. (1860+)	36x54cm
County Map of the States of New York, New Hampshire, Vermont, ...	MITCHELL, S.A. (1860+)	38x66cm
County Map of Virginia and North Carolina	MITCHELL, S.A. (1860+)	28x34cm
County Map of Virginia and West Virginia	MITCHELL, S.A. (1860+)	30x38cm
Cours du Mississipi et la Louisiane	DE VAUGONDY	21x16cm
Course of the River Mississippi, from the Balise to Fort Chartres; ...	SAYER	112x34cm
Cracovia	SCHEDEL	25x52cm
Cram's Township and Rail Road Map of new York	CRAM	42x56cm
Creta Iovis Magni, ... [on sheet with] Corsica [and] Insulae Maris Ioniae	ORTELIUS (Folio)	34x49cm
Creta, Cyprus et Rhodus	CLUVER	11x13cm
Cuba	PORCACCHI	10x14cm
Cuba en Iamaica ...	VAN DER AA	15x22cm
Cuba Insul [on sheet with] Hispaniola [and] Havana Portus [and] ...	MERCATOR (Small)	15x18cm
Cuba Insula [on sheet with] Hispaniola Insula [and] Insula Iamaica [and]	MERCATOR (Folio)	36x50cm
Cuba Insula et Iamaica	WYTFLIET	23x29cm
Cuba, Jamaica & Porto Rico	COLTON (Atlas Maps)	32x40cm
Cusco	OGILBY	29x36cm
Cust van Barbaria van C. de Geer tot verby C. Verde By Iacob Colom	COLOM	24x28cm
Cust van Engelant van Lezard tot Engelands Eynd, de Sorlinges, ...	JACOBSZ	43x53cm
Cypri Insulae Nova Descript. 1573	ORTELIUS (Folio)	35x50cm
Dakota	ASHER & ADAMS	58x41cm
Dakota	COLTON (Atlas Maps)	39x32cm
Dalmatia Maritima Occidentale e Dalmatia Maritime Orientale Descritta	CANTELLI DA VIGNOLA	57x43cm
Damariscotta and Medomak Rivers [ME]	U.S. COAST SURVEY	97x64cm
Dania, Svecia et Norvegia	CLUVER	11x13cm
Daniae Regni Typus	ORTELIUS (Folio)	31x41cm
Daniae Regnum	MERCATOR (Small)	16x20cm
Danubii Fluminis a Fontibus Prope Doneschingam usq Posonium Urbem ...	HOMANN	53x58cm
Danubii Fluminis (hic ab Urbe Belgrado ...) Pars Infima, in qua Transylvania ...	HOMANN	50x58cm
Daphne	ORTELIUS (Folio)	37x49cm
Das Adriameer mit seinen Uferstaaten	HILDBURGHAUSEN BIBLIO.	20x26cm
Das Austral Continent oder Neu Holland	WEILAND	46x57cm
Das Chinesische Reich mit Seinen Schutz Staaten, nebst dem Japanischen ...	HILDBURGHAUSEN BIBLIO.	20x26cm
Das Erst General Inhaltend die Beschreibung und den Circkel des Gantzen ...	MUNSTER	26x38cm
Das Gantze Russische Kayserthum mit Allen Seinen Laendern ...	SCHREIBER	18x28cm
Das Gelobte Land Samml der 40 Iahrigen Reise der Kinder Israel aus Egypten	SCHREIBER	18x28cm
Das Heilig Landt mit Ausztheilung der Zwolff Geschlechter	MUNSTER	32x36cm
Das Konigreich Dannemarck nebst denen Angrantzenden Lendem ...	SCHREIBER	18x28cm
Das Konigreich Holland	HILDBURGHAUSEN BIBLIO.	26x20cm
Das Konigreich Preussen nebst dem Polischen Antheil ...	PROBST	17x20cm
Das Konigreich Schwegen und Norwegen ...	SCHREIBER	18x28cm
Das Konigreich Ungarn nebst den Angrantzenden Keyserlichen Landem ...	SCHREIBER	18x28cm
Das Landt Florida Floride	MALLET	15x11cm
Das Wiflispurgergov	MERCATOR (Folio)	39x51cm
De Bello Belgico de Cades Duae Auctores et Correctiores ...	STRADA	18x14cm
De Beschryvingh van de Reysen Pauli, en van de Andere Apostelen ...	VISSCHER	31x46cm
De Cust van Barbaryen ...	JACOBSZ	43x52cm
De Cust van Engelandt tusschen de Singels en de Drooghten van Weembrugh	BLAEU	26x36cm

Title	Author	Size
De Cust van Normandie en Picardie ...	JACOBSZ	43x52cm
De Custe van Noorwegen tusschen Schaersondt en Schuytens ...	COLOM	38x53cm
De Custen van Engelandt tusschen Fierley en Poortlant; Ook Hoese van ...	JACOBSZ	42x52cm
De Custen van Noorwegen tusschen der Neus en Schuitenes	JACOBSZ	42x53cm
De Custen van Schotland met de Eylanden van Orcanese; van't Eyland Coket	JACOBSZ	43x52cm
De Fero, de Scheland Orknay et Hebrides	MALLET	17x11cm
De Gelegentheyt van't Paradys en't Landt Canaan, Mitsgaders d'Eerst ...	VISSCHER	31x46cm
De Gelegentheyt van't Paradys ende t'Landt Canaan, Mitsgaders de Eerst ...	VISSCHER	31x47cm
De Grondt en Vloor de Groote Burger Sael	VAN CAMPEN	43x75cm
De Haven en Straat van Gibralter ...	ALLARD	50x59cm
De Heylige en Wytvermaerde Stadt Jerusalem ...	VISSCHER	32x48cm
De Heylige en Wytvermaerde Stadt Ierusalem Eerst Genaemt Salem	VISSCHER	34x42cm
De Hoofdstad en Haven, van't Eiland Porto Rico, in de Westindien	TIRION	18x26cm
De Moluccos, of Speceri-Dragende Eilanden ...	VAN DER AA	15x22cm
De Nieuwe en Ouden Oppervlakke en Doorzigkundige Aardryks Bollen ...	DE LAT	18x24cm
De Ommevaart der Middelandsche Zee	DE GROOT	13x17cm
De Republic Schweitz mit Ihren Unterthanen und Bundsgenossen ...	SCHREIBER	18x28cm
De Roode Zee in ven Zeade Scheepstogt der Engelze Maatschappie ...	VAN DER AA	15x23cm
De Stadt Osacco [Japan]	MONTANUS	26x69cm
De Vaste Kust van Cheribichi ...	VAN DER AA	15x22cm
De Vaste Kuste van Chicora tussen Florida en Virginie ... Hispaniola ...	VAN DER AA	15x22cm
De Voor Eylanden van America Tegens de Vaste Kusten van Florida, ...	VAN DER AA	15x22cm
De Werelt Caart	DANCKERTS	37x51cm
De Zee Custen van Ruslant, Laplant, Finmarcken, Spitzbergen en Nova Zemla	GOOS	44x54cm
Delaware	ARROWSMITH & LEWIS	27x22cm
Delaware	CAREY, M.	19x15cm
Delaware and Maryland	BURR	33x40cm
Delaware and Maryland	COLTON (Atlas Maps)	32x40cm
Delineatio ac Finitima Regio Magnae Britanniae Metropoleos Londini ...	SEUTTER	50x58cm
Delineatio ac Finitima Regio Magnae Brittaniae Metropoleos Londoni ...	LOTTER	50x58cm
Delineatio Geographica Comitatus Mansfeldensis	LOTTER	50x59cm
Delineatio Geographica Specialis Territorii Celsissimorum S.R.I. Comitum ...	LOTTER	58x50cm
Delineatio Nova et Vera Partis Australis Novi Mexici cum Australi Parte ...	SCHERER	24x35cm
Delineatio Orarum Maritimarum, Terrae Vulgo Indigetatae Terra do Natal ...	VAN LINSCHOTEN	38x54cm
Deliniantur in Hac Tabula, Orae Maritimae Abexiae, Freti Mecani: al Maris Rubri	VAN LINSCHOTEN	38x52cm
Delpium. Urbis Hollandiae	GUICCIARDINI	23x31cm
Dendermonde Ville Forte des Pais Bas, du Comte de Flandres	MORTIER	22x27cm
Denmark	THOMSON	53x62cm
Der Alte Welt Begriff ... Africa, Europa, Asia ...	BODENEHR	15x13cm
Der Gantze Welt Kress in Seinen Zwey Grossen Begrissen als dem Neuren ...	BODENEHR	13x15cm
Der Konigreich Preussen nebst dem Polnischen Antheil ...	SCHREIBER	18x28cm
Der Neckar-Kreis vom Konigreich Wurtemberg	HILDBURGHAUSEN BIBLIO.	26x20cm
Der Noerdliche Theil des Grossen Welt Meeres nach den Neuesten ...	WEIMAR GEOG. INSTITUT	54x70cm
Der Schwabische Creis ...	PROBST	17x20cm
Der Schwarzwald Kreis vom Konigreich Wurtemberg	HILDBURGHAUSEN BIBLIO.	20x26cm
Der Statt Rom	MUNSTER	21x23cm
Des Mers	CHATELAIN	32x56cm
Des Spheres Artificielles	CHANLAIRE	43x56cm
Descripcion de la Provincia de Chile	DE HERRERA	10x25cm
Descripcion del Audiencia de los Charcas	DE HERRERA	15x17cm
Descripcion del Destieto del Audiencia de Lima	DE HERRERA	16x23cm
Descriptio Germaniae Inferioris	ORTELIUS (Folio)	38x50cm
Descriptio Hydrographica Accommadata ad Battavorum Navigatione in Javam	VAN LINSCHOTEN	34x65cm
Description de l'Ancienne Jerusalem selon Villalpand	CALMET	31x43cm
Description de l'Isle de Guadeloupe Habitee des Francois despuis l'An ...	MARIETTE	37x50cm
Description Nouvelle du Pais d'Espaigne	MUNSTER	25x35cm
Descrittione del Mappamondo	PORCACCHI	11x15cm
Descrittione di Costantinopoli	PORCACCHI	11x14cm
Designatio Orbis Christiani	MERCATOR (Small)	15x19cm
Destroit de Magellan, Terre et Isles Magellanicques, &c.	SANSON (Small)	19x24cm
Destruccio Iherosolime	SCHEDEL	28x51cm
Detroit de Magellan	BELLIN (Small)	19x34cm
Detroit de Waigats	MALLET	15x10cm
Detroit du Magellan	BERNARD	42x51cm
Deuschland mit Seinem Gengen Begriff und Eingschlosznen Landschafften	MUNSTER	26x35cm
Di Hungaria et Transilvania. Tavola Novissima	RUSCELLI	15x20cm
Die Eigentliche und Warhafftige Gestalt der Erden und des Meers. ...	BUNTING	27x36cm
Die Endegnoschaffe oder Schwenzerland mit den Anstossenden Landern	MUNSTER	26x35cm

Die Erst General Tafel / Die Beschreibung und den Circkel des Gantzen ...	MUNSTER	31x36cm
Die Europ. Turkei: Croatien, Herzegovina, Serbien, Bosnien und ...	HILDBURGHAUSEN BIBLIO.	20x26cm
Die Europeasche oder Kleine Tartary nebst den Angrantzenden Landem ...	SCHREIBER	18x28cm
Die Franzososchen Militar-Expedition in Marokko 1866 & 1870	PETERMANN	25x33cm
Die Gegend des Irdischen Paradieses und des Landes Canaan ...	VISSCHER	38x51cm
Die Gegend um Dia Haufft Stadt Prag im Konigreich Bohmen ...	SCHREIBER	18x28cm
Die Laender des Pascha von Aegypten. Aegypten, Nubien, Arabien, ...	HILDBURGHAUSEN BIBLIO.	26x20cm
Die Lander Asie nach Irer Gelegenheit Biss in India Werden in diser Tafel ...	MUNSTER	27x35cm
Die Langer Aie ...	MUNSTER	26x35cm
Die Neuwen Inseln ...	MUNSTER	25x34cm
Die Neuwen Inseln / So Hinder Hispanen gegen Orient / Bey dem Landt Indie	MUNSTER	27x34cm
Die Oestereichische Niederlande ...	PROBST	17x20cm
Die Pfalz oder Rhein Bayern	HILDBURGHAUSEN BIBLIO.	20x26cm
Die Philippinische Inselen ...	PROBST	17x20cm
Die Republic Holland oder die Vereinigle Niederlande ...	SCHREIBER	18x28cm
Die Republik Polen nach ihrem Bestande im Jahre 1772 und ...	HILDBURGHAUSEN BIBLIO.	20x26cm
Die Staat Wussenburg	MUNSTER	27x38cm
Die Staaten die Missouri Illinois, Indiana, Ohio, Kentucky & Tennessee	MEYER	28x20cm
Die Staaten von Arkansas, Mississippi, Louisiana und Alabama	HILDBURGHAUSEN BIBLIO.	20x26cm
Die Staaten von Maine, New Hampshire, Massachusetts, Vermont, ...	HILDBURGHAUSEN BIBLIO.	26x20cm
Die Staaten von Missouri, Illinois, Indiana, Ohio, Kentucky & Tennessee	HILDBURGHAUSEN BIBLIO.	26x20cm
Die Staaten von N. & S. Carolina, Georgia & Florida	HILDBURGHAUSEN BIBLIO.	26x20cm
Die Statt Augspurg	MUNSTER	26x35cm
Die Statt Basell	MUNSTER	26x35cm
Die Statt Bern	MUNSTER	21x30cm
Die Statt Chur	MUNSTER	14x35cm
Die Statt Colmar	MUNSTER	23x35cm
Die Statt Eger	MUNSTER	23x34cm
Die Statt Erdfurt	MUNSTER	21x37cm
Die Statt Frankfurt	MUNSTER	25x38cm
Die Statt Freisingen	MUNSTER	13x36cm
Die Statt Landaw	MUNSTER	17x38cm
Die Statt Lindaw	MUNSTER	27x36cm
Die Statt Nordelingen. MDXLIX	MUNSTER	23x34cm
Die Statt Paris	MUNSTER	25x36cm
Die Statt Schletstat	MUNSTER	20x33cm
Die Statt Sitten	MUNSTER	26x36cm
Die Statt Solothurn	MUNSTER	23x30cm
Die Statt Speier	MUNSTER	17x38cm
Diefert Situs Orbis Hydrographorum ...	FRIES	31x46cm
Dimidia Tribus Manasse Hoc Est, Ea Terrae Sanctae Pars ...	VAN ADRICHEM	23x45cm
Dioecesis Stavangerensis, & Partes Aliquot Vicinae ...	BLAEU	41x50cm
Dioecesis Trundhemiensis pars Australis	BLAEU	42x53cm
Discrizzion dell'Isola della Sicilia, & di Tutto 'l Regno di Quella Secondo ...	MUNSTER	21x15cm
District of Columbia	BRADFORD	25x19cm
Diversite des Ombres	CHANLAIRE	No dimen
Dominia Anglorum in America Septentrionali Specialibus Mappis ...	HOMANN	50x55cm
Dominia Anglorum in Praecipuis Insulis Americae ut Sunt Insula ...	HOMANN	50x59cm
Dominica	LUCAS	30x22cm
Dominium Venetum cum Adjacentibus Mediolan. Mantuano, Mutinensi ...	LOTTER	50x58cm
Donquerque Duynkerk en Flamand	MORTIER	20x28cm
Dordrecht	GUICCIARDINI	23x31cm
Doro Channel to Gulf of Saloniki	BRITISH ADMIRALTY	64x97cm
Dorozhnaia Karta Kavkazskago Kraia. Tiflis: Sostavlena i Litografirovana ...	RUSSIAN GOVERNMENT	130x149cm
Douay Duacum Catuacorum Urbs ...	BRAUN & HOGENBERG	33x40cm
Dr. F.V. Hopkins' Preliminary Geological Map of Louisiana	COLTON (Atlas Maps)	30x38cm
Drainage Map of Colorado	U.S. GEOLOGICAL SURV.	76x94cm
Dublin	MALLET	15x10cm
Ducatus Iuliacensis, Cliviensis et Montensis, ut et Principatus Meursiani ...	LOTTER	58x50cm
Ducatus Luneburgici et Comitatus Dannebergensis ...	HOMANN	48x57cm
Ducatus Magdeburgensis et Halensis	SEUTTER	50x58cm
Ducatus Oswieczensis & Zatoriensis Descriptio	QUAD	19x27cm
Ducatus Uplandia	BLAEU	38x50cm
Ducatus Westphalia	SEUTTER	50x58cm
Durham Drawn from the Best Authorities and Regulated by Astronl. ...	LONDON MAGAZINE	16x22cm
East Canada and New Brunswick	TALLIS	25x34cm
East Central Louisiana	U.S.	25x30cm
East India Archipelago [Eastern Passages to China and Japan] [Chart No.4]	IMRAY	127x102cm

Title	Author	Size
East India Isles	PINKERTON	50x69cm
East India Isles and Australia	WYLD	23x30cm
East Riding of Yorkshire	WALKER, J. & C.	32x40cm
Eastern Hemisphere [in set with] Western Hemisphere	ORR & SMITH	Each diam 23cm
Eatontown [NJ: Monmouth Co.]	BEERS	36x52cm
Eboracum, Lincolnia, Derbia, Staffordia, Notinghamaia, Lecestria, ...	MERCATOR (Folio)	35x42cm
Economic Features of Central Colorado	U.S. WAR DEPARTMENT	43x51cm
Economic Features of Parts of North Central New Mexico, Atlas Sheet ...	U.S. WAR DEPARTMENT	41x51cm
Economic Features of Parts of South'n Colorado and North'n New Mexico ...	U.S. WAR DEPARTMENT	41x51cm
Economic Map of Colorado	U.S. GEOLOGICAL SURV.	64x89cm
Economical Features of S.W. Colorado, San Juan Mining Region, ...	U.S. WAR DEPARTMENT	43x51cm
Edenburgum, Scotiae Metropolis	BRAUN & HOGENBERG	34x45cm
Egrana Civitas olim de Imperio Romanorum, hodie Vero Regno Bohemiae ...	MUNSTER	23x34cm
Election Map of Midlothian ...	BARTHOLOMEW	34x47cm
Electoratus Hanoverani	SEUTTER	58x50cm
Electoratus Moguntinus ut et Palatin: Infer. Hassiae & Fluminis Moeni ...	HOMANN	58x51cm
Electorum Imperii Institutio	SCHEDEL	4x53cm
Ellis Bay in the Island of Anticosti	BRITISH ADMIRALTY	27x22cm
Emisfero Terrestre Meridionale	ZATTA	30x30cm
Empire de Mogol by Robt. Morden	MORDEN	11x13cm
Empire of Japan	S.D.U.K.	39x32cm
England	MORDEN	36x42cm
England and Wales	FINLEY	35x26cm
England and Wales	STANFORD	68x57cm
England and Wales Drawn from the Most Accurate Surveys	ROCQUE	124x102cm
England I	S.D.U.K.	37x33cm
England II	S.D.U.K.	30x37cm
England III	S.D.U.K.	27x35cm
England IV	S.D.U.K.	26x38cm
England V	S.D.U.K.	27x36cm
England Northern Part [in set with] ... Southern Part	PINKERTON	50x71cm
England with Its Canals and Railways	S.D.U.K.	39x30cm
Entrance to Sierra Leone River	BRITISH ADMIRALTY	66x99cm
Entrance to Tampa Bay	U.S. COAST & GEODETIC	67x95cm
Entrance to the Chou-Kiang or Canton River from the Outer Islands ...	BRITISH ADMIRALTY	47x62cm
Entrances to the Salm and Joombas Rivers on the West Coast of Africa	BRITISH ADMIRALTY	29x29cm
Entree de la Casamance et Mouillage de Carabane	DEPOT DE LA MARINE	47x65cm
Entree de la Riviere Endeavour dans la Nle. Galles Merid. [on sheet with] ...	COOK	14x34cm
Environs de Paris	DE VAUGONDY	50x63cm
Environs of London - Windsor Castle to Graves Head	ILLUS. LONDON NEWS	58x81cm
Episcopatum Monasteriensis et Osnabrugensis Ut et Comitatuum Bentheim ...	LOTTER	58x50cm
Episcopatus Hildesiensis	SEUTTER	49x56cm
Epping (Great Dunmow) and Chelmsford (Braintree)	BRITISH ORDNANCE	72x102cm
Equateur / Carte Generale du Monde	MALLET	11x15cm
Erster Abriss der Stadt Jerusalem ...	FLEISCHMANN	37x48cm
Ertz-Herzogthumb Oesterreich / Archiduche d'Austriche	SANSON (Folio)	30x51cm
Eryn. Hiberniae, Britannicae Insulae, Nova Descriptio. Irlandt	ORTELIUS (Folio)	36x48cm
Erythraei sive Rubri Maris Periplus	JANSSON	39x46cm
Erz-Herzogthum Oesterreich: Unter der Enns	HILDBURGHAUSEN BIBLIO.	20x26cm
Esquisse des Operations du Siege de Charleston, Capitale de la Caroline ...	BARTRAM	35x28cm
Essay d'une Carte Reduite Contenant les Parties Connuees du Globe ...	BELLIN (Large)	52x70cm
Estats de l'Empire des Turqs en Europe, Divises Suivant l'Estendue ...	DE L'ISLE	45x62cm
Estats de l'Empire du Grand Seigneur des Turcs, en Europe, en Asie, et ...	DE L'ISLE	45x61cm
Estats des Couronnes de Dannemark, Suede, et Pologne sur la Mer Baltique	DE FER (Large)	44x70cm
Estotilandia et Laboratoris Terra	WYTFLIET	22x27cm
Etat de l'Eglise Grande Duche de Toscane, et Isle de Corse	DE VAUGONDY	50x62cm
Etats du Grand-Seigneur en Asie Empire de Perse, Pays des Usbecs, Arabie ...	DE VAUGONDY	48x55cm
Etats Unis	BRUE	37x51cm
Etats-Unis ...	DUFOUR	25x35cm
Etats-Unis d'Amerique	BUCHON	42x53cm
Etats-Unis de l'Amerique du Nord. Limites en 1860	GARNIER	36x50cm
Etats Unis et Grandes Antilles	CHAMOUIN	30x22cm
Ethnological Map of the British Isles	STANFORD	38x34cm
Europ, and the Cheife Cities Contayned Therein ...	SPEED	39x51cm
Europa	MAGINI	13x17cm
Europa	MERCATOR (Folio)	38x47cm
Europa	RUSCELLI	18x25cm
Europa	SCHERER	11x18cm

Title	Author	Size
Europa Exactissime Descripta Auctore Henrico Hondio	JANSSON	38x51cm
Europa Recens Descripta ...	BLAEU	41x54cm
Europa Regnorum	LOTTER	50x59cm
Europa Verferliget von J.G. Scheibern in Leipzig	SCHREIBER	18x28cm
Europae	ORTELIUS (Folio)	34x46cm
Europae Nova Tabula	CLUVER	14x20cm
Europam Ab Asia et Africa Segregant Mare Mediterraneum ...	PLANCIUS	39x54cm
Europe	BOWEN, E.	33x42cm
Europe	LIZARS	14x15cm
Europe	MOLL (Small)	17x18cm
Europe	TALLIS	25x32cm
Europe ...	PROBST	17x20cm
Europe Divided into Its Empires, Kingdoms, States Republics, &c. ...	KITCHIN	53x122cm
Exact Plan of General Gage's Lines on Boston Neck in America	PENNSYLVANIA MAG.	29x22cm
Explicatio Aliquot Locorum quae Puteolis Spectantur	VAN AELST	38x50cm
Extract from a Map of the British and French Dominions in North America	DASHIELL	33x33cm
Extrema Americae versus Boream, ubi Terra Nova Francia Adjacentiaq.	BLAEU	45x56cm
Eylanden van Hitlant ofte Schetlant ... [on sheet with] Eylanden van Hebrides	JACOBSZ	43x52cm
F. d'Asso	MORTIER	11x15cm
F.G. Conley & Co.'s Map of the East End Complements of F.C. Bell ...	REAL ESTATE MAPS	46x43cm
Facies Poli Arctici Adiacentiumque ex Recentisimis Itinerariis Delineata ...	WEIGEL	32x36cm
Fair Haven [on sheet with] Navesink [and] Oceanic ... [NJ: Monmouth Co.]	BEERS	28x36cm
Falmouth and English Harbours [Antigua]	BRITISH ADMIRALTY	62x46cm
Fessae et Marocchi Regna ...	MERCATOR (Folio)	36x48cm
Fezzae et Marocchi Regna Africae Celeberrima ...	BLAEU	38x50cm
Field Map of Lothians Hunt	BARTHOLOMEW	33x55cm
Figura della Spagna	ROSACCIO	13x18cm
Figura del Mondo Universale	MUNSTER	26x38cm
Figure 13 [Eastern Hemisphere]	MALLET	10x15cm
Figure IV [Armillary Sphere]	MALLET	10x14cm
Figure XII [Globes: Terrestrial & Celestial]	MALLET	10x15cm
Fionia	MERCATOR (Folio)	35x45cm
Fionia Vulgo Funen	BLAEU	38x50cm
Firenze Citta Nobilissima della Toscana Secondo i Nostri Tempi Disegnata	MUNSTER	22x35cm
Flandria	GUICCIARDINI	23x31cm
Florida	BALCH	32x23cm
Florida	BEER	10x13cm
Florida	BRADFORD	26x20cm
Florida	BRADFORD	36x31cm
Florida	COLTON (Atlas Maps)	30x37cm
Florida	CRAM	57x41cm
Florida	GRAY	42x66cm
Florida	MEYER	37x30cm
Florida	MITCHELL, S.A. (to 1859)	37x30cm
Florida	RAND, McNALLY (Atlas Maps)	33x49cm
Florida	RAND, McNALLY (Atlas Maps)	48x66cm
Florida Called by ye French Louisiana &c.	MOLL (Small)	20x28cm
Florida et Regiones Vicinae	DE LAET	28x36cm
Floride	MALLET	15x11cm
Flusse de la Plata	BELLIN (Small)	18x28cm
Folium CCXXX-CCXXXI [Prague]	SCHEDEL	43x61cm
Fores's New Plan of London Including the New Improvements	FORES	43x79cm
Fort Wright on the Mississippi	NEW YORK HERALD	23x12cm
Forteresse de Cerigo	MORTIER	11x15cm
Forteresse de Volo	MORTIER	11x15cm
Forteresse de Zante	MORTIER	11x15cm
Fortsetzung der Karte von Jandostan ...	BELLIN (Small)	22x24cm
Forum Iulium, Karstia Carniola, Histria et Windorum Marchia	MERCATOR (Folio)	35x45cm
France Revised and Augmented ...	SPEED	40x55cm
Francia	SCHEDEL	23x23cm
Franckfurt an der Oder Anno Dmi 1548	MUNSTER	20x29cm
Fredericksburg, Prepared by Bvt. Brig. Genl. N. Michler ...	U.S. WAR DEPARTMENT	71x58cm
Frederiksted, Santa Cruz or St. Croix, Danish West Indies	GOAD	62x51cm
Freehold [NJ: Monmouth Co.]	BEERS	53x34cm
Frelinghuysen [NJ: Warren Co.]	BEERS	37x30cm
Freti Magellanici ac Novi Freti Vulgo le Maire Exactissima Delineatio	JANSSON	38x49cm
Fretum Magellani	PURCHAS	13x17cm
Fribergum Misinae	BRAUN & HOGENBERG	33x46cm

Title	Author	Size
Fribourg Est une Ville Forte Capital de Brisgaw	MORTIER	21x29cm
Friburg im Brisgew 1549	MUNSTER	20x36cm
Frisia Occidentalis	MERCATOR (Folio)	36x46cm
Frisiae Occidentalis Typus	GUICCIARDINI	23x31cm
From Great Salt Lake to the Humboldt Mts. ...	U.S. PACIFIC R.R. SURV.	52x46cm
Frugiferi ac Amaeni Herefordiae Comitatus ...	CAMDEN	27x33cm
G.W. Hayward's Reise Leh nach Kaschgar, 1868/9	PETERMANN	33x27cm
Gades ab Occiduis Insulae Partibus Anno 1564	BRAUN & HOGENBERG	37x49cm
Galilaea Inferior [Zebulon]	FULLER	28x34cm
Gall & Inglis's Handy Map & Guide to London, 1876	GALL & INGLIS	48x74cm
Gallia	VAN DEN KEERE	8x13cm
Gallia Narbonensis Lugdunensis et Aquitaina	BOWEN, E.	20x30cm
Galliae Regni Potentiss. Nova Descriptio, Ioanne Ioliveto Auctore	ORTELIUS (Folio)	35x50cm
Galliae Regnum	MAGINI	13x18cm
Galliae Regnum in Omnes Suas Provincias Accurate Divisum	SCHENK	48x58cm
Galloflandria	BLAEU	38x50cm
Gaspar Strait Chiefly from Surveys Published by the Netherlands ...	BRITISH ADMIRALTY	97x64cm
Gaspe and Mal Bays	BRITISH ADMIRALTY	59x46cm
Gebenna	SCHEDEL	15x23cm
Gebiet Missouri, Gebiet Oregan	WERNER	20x27cm
Geldria et Transysulana	MERCATOR (Folio)	35x45cm
General Chart of the Colony of the Cape of Good Hope Constructed ...	BARROW	32x46cm
General Charte von Australien	WEIMAR GEOG. INSTITUT	45x62cm
General Geological Map of Colorado	U.S. GEOLOGICAL SURV.	76x94cm
General Map of the United States	BLACK	41x55cm
General Topographical Map Sheet XVIII [Missouri & Tennessee]	U.S. UNION & CONFED.	42x70cm
General Topographical Map Sheet XX [Mississippi & Louisiana]	U.S. UNION & CONFED.	42x70cm
General Topographical Map Sheet XXI [Louisiana]	U.S. UNION & CONFED.	42x70cm
General Topographical Map Sheet XXIII [N.E. Texas; N.W. Louisiana]	U.S. UNION & CONFED.	42x70cm
General Topographical Map Sheet XXIII [N.E. Texas; N.W. Louisiana]	U.S. UNION & CONFED.	46x74cm
General View of the Mississippi River from Cairo, Illinois to the Mouth ...	HARPER'S WEEKLY	36x23cm
Generale Kaart van het Beloofde Land ...	ELWE	50x59cm
Generale Ptholemei	WALDSEEMULLER	44x62cm
Generalis Totius Imperii Moscovitici Novissima Tabula Magnam Orbis ...	HOMANN	49x58cm
Genua [on sheet with] Florentia Urbs Est Insignis Hetruariae, ...	BRAUN & HOGENBERG	32x48cm
Geographia Sacra	ORTELIUS (Folio)	36x48cm
Geographiae Sacrae ex Veteri, et Novo Testamento Desumptae Tabula ...	SANSON (Folio)	40x50cm
Geographica Sacra	JANSSON	36x48cm
Geographical and Statistical Map of Italy	LAVOISNE	38x33cm
Geographical and Statistical Map of Scotland	LAVOISNE	38x33cm
Geographical Distribution of Plants According to Humboldt's Statistics ...	JOHNSTON	19x27cm
Geographical Map of the World ...	LAVOISNE	43x53cm
Geographical, Historical and Statistical Map of America	CAREY & LEA	44x53cm
Geographical, Historical and Statistical Map of America	LAVOISNE	44x53cm
Geographical, Statistical, and Historical Map of Arkansa Territory ...	CAREY & LEA	37x40cm
Geographical, Statistical and Historical Map of Brazil	CAREY & LEA	44x56cm
Geographical, Statistical and Historical Map of Chili	CAREY & LEA	44x56cm
Geographical, Statistical and Historical Map of Connecticut	CAREY & LEA	24x29cm
Geographical, Statistical and Historical Map of Cuba and the Bahama ...	CAREY & LEA	44x56cm
Geographical, Statistical and Historical Map of Florida	CAREY & LEA	29x24cm
Geographical, Statistical and Historical Map of Jamaica	CAREY & LEA	44x56cm
Geographical, Statistical, and Historical Map of Louisiana	CAREY & LEA	42x52cm
Geographical, Statistical and Historical Map of Mexico	CAREY & LEA	41x37cm
Geographical, Statistical, and Historical Map of Michigan Territory	CAREY & LEA	37x27cm
Geographical, Statistical and Historical Map of New Jersey	CAREY & LEA	28x23cm
Geographical, Statistical and Historical Map of North America	CAREY & LEA	37x33cm
Geographical, Statistical and Historical Map of Pennsylvania	CAREY & LEA	30x45cm
Geographical, Statistical and Historical Map of Peru	CAREY & LEA	35x32cm
Geographical, Statistical, and Historical Map of Porto Rico and the Virgin ...	CAREY & LEA	44x56cm
Geographical, Statistical and Historical Map of Porto Rico and Virgin ...	CAREY & LEA	42x53cm
Geographical, Statistical and Historical Map of St. Domingo	CAREY & LEA	44x56cm
Geographical, Statistical and Historical Map of the Leeward Islands	CAREY & LEA	44x56cm
Geographical, Statistical and Historical Map of the United Provinces ...	CAREY & LEA	41x31cm
Geographical, Statistical and Historical Map of the West Indies	CAREY & LEA	44x56cm
Geographical, Statistical, and Historical Map of the Windward Islands	CAREY & LEA	42x52cm
Geographical, Statistical and Historical Map of Upper and Lower Canada ...	CAREY & LEA	42x52cm
Geographical, Statistical and Historical Map of Virginia	CAREY & LEA	33x47cm
Geographische Beschryvinge van t'Beloofde - Landt Canaan ... Iesu Christo ...	SAVERY	32x48cm

Title	Author	Size
Geography [World]	BLOME	38x24cm
Geological & Mineralogical Map of Sutherland	JOHNSTON	80x97cm
Geological Map of England and Wales	S.D.U.K.	38x31cm
Geological Map of Maine	COLBY	41x32cm
Geological Survey of Great Britain. Ordnance Survey of Scotland. Sheet 32	BRITISH ORDNANCE	48x62cm
Geologische Karte der Vereinigten Staaten und Britischen Provinzen ...	PETERMANN	24x39cm
Georgetown and the City of Washington	COLTON (Atlas Maps)	32x40cm
Georgetown and the City of Washington	JOHNSON	32x40cm
Georgia	COLTON (Atlas Maps)	46x38cm
Georgia & Florida	BLACK	37x27cm
Germania	ORTELIUS (Folio)	36x50cm
Germaniae Inferioris sive Belgii Pars Meridionalis	LOTTER	51x59cm
Ghent	RAPIN	39x48cm
Ghubbet Soghra	BRITISH ADMIRALTY	48x65cm
Gli Argonauti	CORONELLI	39x25cm
Globe Terrestre	MALLET	15x10cm
Globi Coelestis in Sex Tabulas Planas Redacti Descriptio	WEIGEL	35x36cm
Globus Coelestris	HONDIUS	9x14cm
Globus Terrestreis ...	PROBST	17x24cm
Globus Terrestris	DE AEFFERDEN	16x24cm
Globus Terrestris	SCHREIBER	18x28cm
Gloucester Harbor [MA]	U.S. COAST SURVEY	44x34cm
Goa Fortissima Indiae Urbs in Christianorum Potestatem Anno Salutis 1509	BRAUN & HOGENBERG	34x47cm
Gogledd-Barth America	ROBERTS	19x22cm
Goldtop Road in St. Brides Bay ...	MORRIS	18x23cm
Gothebourg	MORTIER	19x28cm
Gouvernement General de l'Isle de France Divise par Pays ...	DE VAUGONDY	49x53cm
Graecia	MAGINI	13x17cm
Graecia	MERCATOR (Folio)	36x47cm
Graeciae Universae Secundum Hodiernum Situm Neoterica Descriptio	ORTELIUS (Folio)	36x51cm
Grafschaft Tyrol	HILDBURGHAUSEN BIBLIO.	20x26cm
Granada 1563	BRAUN & HOGENBERG	33x51cm
Granata	BRAUN & HOGENBERG	37x50cm
Granger's Map of Birmingham [England]	LOCAL & STATE MAPS	38x51cm
Gray's Atlas Map California, Nevada, Utah, Colorado, Arizona & New Mexico	GRAY	41x65cm
Gray's Atlas Map of Florida	GRAY	30x37cm
Gray's Atlas Map of New York City	GRAY	38x30cm
Gray's Idaho, Montana and Wyoming	GRAY	30x38cm
Gray's New Map of Indiana	GRAY	64x39cm
Gray's New Map of Kansas	GRAY	40x69cm
Gray's New Map of Ohio	GRAY	39x64cm
Gray's New Map of Texas and the Indian Territory	GRAY	59x41cm
Gray's New Map of the World in Hemispheres ...	GRAY	42x66cm
Great Britain	MOLL (Small)	18x19cm
Great or Asiatick Tartary ...	MOLL (Small)	20x26cm
Greece	SPEED	39x50cm
Grenada	LUCAS	22x33cm
Grenada [on sheet with] Tobago [and] Curacao [and] Trinidad	THOMSON	50x59cm
Griechenland die Jonischen Jnseln und Candia	HILDBURGHAUSEN BIBLIO.	26x20cm
Groenlande	MALLET	15x10cm
Grondvlakte van Nieuw Orleans, de Hoofdstad van Louisiana ...	TIRION	33x45cm
Groniga Opuleta Populosa ...	GUICCIARDINI	23x31cm
Gros Britan oder Engelland Schot = u Irrla ...	PROBST	17x20cm
Gros Britanne oder Engeland Schottland und Irrland ...	SCHREIBER	18x28cm
Gross-Herzogthum Sachsen-Weimar und Eisenach	HILDBURGHAUSEN BIBLIO.	20x26cm
Grossherzogthum Baden Nordliche Halfte	HILDBURGHAUSEN BIBLIO.	20x26cm
Grund-Riss der Kayserlichen und des Heil. Rom. Reichs Freyen Stadt Lubeck	LOTTER	50x59cm
Guadeloupe Etc.	LUCAS	28x38cm
Guasopa Harbour, Kiriwina Islands	BRITISH ADMIRALTY	46x66cm
Guayane Terre Ferme, Isles Antilles et Nlle. Espagne	BRION DE LA TOUR	28x48cm
Guiana ...	OGILBY	29x36cm
Guide to Colorado with Map	CLASON MAP CO.	43x56cm
Guienne et Gascogne	DE VAUGONDY	16x18cm
Guinea	JANSSON	38x52cm
Guinea Nova Descriptio	HONDIUS	35x49cm
Guinea Propria, nec non Nigritiae vel Terrae Nigorum ... Aethiopia Inferior ...	HOMANN	51x59cm
Guyana	BELLIN (Small)	20x31cm
Gynfelin Patches, Aberystwith and New-Quay	BRITISH ADMIRALTY	46x62cm

Title	Author	Size
H. Keller's Keilcharte der Schweis, Carte Routiere de la Suisse, Road Map ...	KELLER	50x66cm
Haec Est Nobilis, & Florens Illa Neapolis ...	BRAUN & HOGENBERG	33x48cm
Hamborg, Ville Imperiale d'Allemagne ...	MORTIER	22x30cm
Hanc Tabulam Continens Laetam Pharnambuci Victoriam ...	VISSCHER	36x69cm
Hannonia. Nauvrcum Comitatus	MERCATOR (Folio)	35x45cm
Harbor of New Haven	U.S. COAST SURVEY	84x61cm
Harbor of New London	U.S. COAST SURVEY	50x41cm
Harmonie or Correspondance du Globe ... la Sphere par les Points, Lignes ...	SANSON (Folio)	39x53cm
Harmony [NJ: Warren Co.]	BEERS	29x37cm
Harpers Ferry, Prepared by Bvt. Brig. Genl. N. Michler ...	U.S. WAR DEPARTMENT	58x71cm
Hartlepool Bay	BRITISH ADMIRALTY	91x61cm
Hassia Landgraviatus	JANSSON	44x56cm
Hassia Landtgraviatus	MERCATOR (Folio)	35x45cm
Hassiae ... / Holsatiae Descrip	ORTELIUS (Folio)	34x49cm
Havana	MONTANUS	29x35cm
Havana Insulae Cubae Imo Totius Occidentis Notissimg Portus	SCHENK	21x26cm
Hayti or Saint Domingo	LUCAS	38x51cm
Head of the Gulf of Nauplia	BRITISH ADMIRALTY	46x66cm
Heidelberg	MORTIER	21x24cm
Helgoland	BRITISH ADMIRALTY	95x62cm
Hell Gate and Its Approaches	U.S. COAST SURVEY	76x91cm
Helvetia	WEIGEL	29x33cm
Helvetia cum Finitimis Regionibus Confoederatis	MERCATOR (Folio)	35x47cm
Helvetia Foederata ...	PROBST	17x20cm
Helvetiae ...	CLUVER	11x13cm
Hemisphere Septentrional ... [in set with] Hemisphere Meridional ...	DE L'ISLE	47x47cm
Hemisphere Septentrional pour Voir Plus Distinctement les Terres Arctiques	DE L'ISLE	46x47cm
Herbipolis Wurtzpurg	MUNSTER	28x38cm
Herefordia Comitatus Vernacule Heretfordshire	VALK & SCHENK	38x50cm
Heresfeldensis	BLAEU	38x50cm
Herzogthum Braunschweig	HILDBURGHAUSEN BIBLIO.	20x26cm
Het Beloofde Landt Canaan door Wandelt van Onsen Salichmaecker Iesu ...	VISSCHER	50x46cm
Het Beloofde Landt Canaan door Wandelt van Onsen Salichmaecker Jesu ...	VISSCHER	32x48cm
Het Beloofde Landt Canaan doorwandelt van Onsen Salichmaecker Iesu ...	STOOPENDAAL	35x46cm
Het Eiland Sumatra; Hoe ten Aansien van Malacca ...	VAN DER AA	15x22cm
Het Westindisch Eiland Martenique Volgens de Nieuwste Waarneemingen ...	TIRION	31x36cm
Hibernia	ORTELIUS (Miniature)	8x11cm
Hibernia	VAN DER AA	13x16cm
Hibernia Regnum vulgo Ireland	MERCATOR (Folio)	39x50cm
Hibernia Regnum Vulgo Ireland. Apud Joannem Janssonium	JANSSON	39x50cm
Hiberniae III. Tabula. In qua Momonia et Lageniae Reliqua	MERCATOR (Folio)	35x45cm
Hiberniae Ireland, Anglis Yverdon Britannis Erin-Incolis. Iema Orpheo & Arist.	CAMDEN	27x33cm
Hiberniae Regnum Entam in Praecipias Ultoniae, Connaciae, Lacemiae ...	HOMANN	58x48cm
Hiberniae, Britannicae Insulae, Nova Descriptio	ORTELIUS (Folio)	35x48cm
Hiericho	SCHEDEL	13x22cm
Hierosolima	SCHEDEL	19x23cm
Hierosolyma, Clarissima Totius Orientis Civitas Iudaee Metropolis	BRAUN & HOGENBERG	34x48cm
Hind, Hindoostan, or India. By L.S. de la Rochette. MDCCLXXXVIII. ...	FADEN	71x53cm
Hispania III. Nova Tabula	MUNSTER	26x34cm
Hispania nach Affer Seiner Gelegenheit in Bergen Wassernifstatten ...	MUNSTER	26x35cm
Hispania Regnum	MERIAN	26x36cm
Hispaniae	CLUVER	28x34cm
Hispaniae Novae Nova Descriptio	CLOPPENBURGH	19x25cm
Hispaniae Novae Nova Descriptio	MERCATOR (Small)	19x26cm
Hispaniae Novae sive Magnae Recens et Vera Descriptio 1595	DE BRY	33x44cm
Hispaniae Novae sive Magnae Vera Descriptio	QUAD	21x29cm
Hispaniae Veteris Des.	VAN DEN KEERE	15x20cm
Hollandiae ...	ORTELIUS (Folio)	35x48cm
Hollandt Comitatus Utricht Episcop.	MERCATOR (Folio)	35x45cm
Holsatia Ducatus	MERCATOR (Folio)	35x48cm
Holsatiae Mappa Universalis in suos Ducatus Nimirum Holsatiam in Specie ...	LOTTER	51x59cm
Hope [NJ: Warren Co.]	BEERS	37x29cm
Hope [on sheet with] Townsbury [and] Marksboro ... [NJ: Warren Co.]	BEERS	37x29cm
Hombourg	MORTIER	11x15cm
Hungaria	MERCATOR (Folio)	37x44cm
Hungariae Descriptio ...	ORTELIUS (Folio)	35x50cm
Hungary	TALLIS	25x32cm
Hungary and Transilvania Drawn from the Latest Authorities	WILKINSON	23x28cm

Huntington Bay	U.S. COAST SURVEY	36x44cm
Huntington Comitatus ...	CAMDEN	27x33cm
Huy Petite Ville du Pais de Liege	MORTIER	22x29cm
Hyberniae ...	ALLARD	58x50cm
Hyberniae Regni in Provincias Ultoniam, Connachian, Lageniam, Momoniamq	ALLARD	59x51cm
Hydrographical Chart of the World on Wright or Mercator's Projection ...	THOMSON	51x55cm
Iaponia	BEER	10x13cm
Iaponia Insula	ORTELIUS (Miniature)	8x12cm
Iaponia Regnum	BLAEU	42x57cm
Iaponia. Petrus Kaerius Coelavit	CLOPPENBURGH	18x24cm
Iava Minore	BORDONE	8x15cm
Ichnographia Urbis in Tuscia Primariae Florentiae ...	HOMANN	49x58cm
Iconografica Rappresentatione della Inclita Citta di Venetia	HOMANN	48x55cm
Idaho	CRAM	28x23cm
Idaho	CRAM	51x41cm
Idaho	RAND, McNALLY (Atlas Maps)	48x30cm
Ierusalem ... sold by Richd. Ware and Will. Taylor ...	WARE	36x42cm
Ierusalem Qualis (vt Plurimum) Extitit Aetate Solomonis	FULLER	28x37cm
Ierusalem, Cum Suburbiis, Prout Tempore Christi Floruit ...	SEUTTER	50x57cm
Ierusalem, et Suburbia Eius, Sicut Tempore Christi Floruit, Cu Locis ...	BRAUN & HOGENBERG	36x48cm
Iesu Christi Salvatoris Nostri et Apostolorum Petri, et Pauli Mansiones ...	SANSON (Folio)	37x56cm
Il Corso del Fiume Reno dalle Sue Fonti sino al Mare con Tutti li Fiumi ...	CANTELLI DA VIGNOLA	44x57cm
Il Mappa Mondo o Sia Descrizione Generale del Globo Ridotto in Quadro ...	ZATTA	27x39cm
Il Maryland, il Jersey Meridionale, la Delaware, e la Parte Orientale ...	ZATTA	32x42cm
Il Paese de Cherachesi con la Parte Occidentale della Carolina Settentrionale	ZATTA	32x42cm
Il Paese de' Selvaggi Outauacesi, e Kilistinesi Intorno al Lago Superiore	ZATTA	32x42cm
Il Paese de' Selvaggi Outagamiani, Mascoutensi, Illinesi, e Parte della ...	ZATTA	33x44cm
Il Regno della Servia detta Altrimenti Rascia ...	CANTELLI DA VIGNOLA	41x55cm
Il Regno di Aragona Descritto da D. Nicolo Cantelli Geografo ...	CANTELLI DA VIGNOLA	42x55cm
Il Regno di Castiglia Vecchia Descritto da Giacomo Cantelli da Viga ...	CANTELLI DA VIGNOLA	43x55cm
Il Regno di Galicia Descritta da Giacomo da Vignola Geografo ...	CANTELLI DA VIGNOLA	42x55cm
Ilfracombe Harbour	BRITISH ADMIRALTY	25x22cm
Illinois	ASHER & ADAMS	57x40cm
Illinois	COLTON (Atlas Maps)	40x32cm
Illinois	FINLEY	29x22cm
Imperii Magni Mogolis sive Indici Padschach ...	SEUTTER	50x58cm
Imperii Moscovitici Pars Australis in Lucem, Edita par G. De L'Isle	SEUTTER	51x59cm
Imperii Sinarum Nova Descriptio	BLAEU	46x59cm
Imperii Sinarum Nova Descriptio	BUNO	21x26cm
Imperii Sinarum Nova Descriptio	THEVENOT	45x64cm
Imperii Sinarum, Nova Descriptio	CLUVER	11x13cm
Imperium Alexandri Magni per Europam Asiam, et Africam ...	ZATTA	33x44cm
Index to the Charts of the Coast of China	BRITISH ADMIRALTY	64x48cm
India Extra Gangem	BEER	10x13cm
India Extrema XIX Nova Tabula	MUNSTER	26x35cm
India Extrema XXIIII. Nova Tabula	MUNSTER	29x37cm
India Orien.	BERTIUS	9x12cm
India Orient	ORTELIUS (Miniature)	8x11cm
India Orientalis	MERCATOR (Small)	36x50cm
India quae Orientalis Dicitur, et Insulae Adiacentes	BLAEU	28x41cm
India Tercera Nuova Tavola	RUSCELLI	18x24cm
India Vetus intra extra Gagem ...	MORTIER	21x28cm
Indiae Orientalis Insularum umque Adiacientium Typus [verso] Tartariae ...	ORTELIUS (Miniature)	8x11cm
Indiae Orientalis Insularumque Adiacientium Typus	ORTELIUS (Folio)	35x50cm
Indiae Orientalis nec non Insularum Adiacentium ... per F. De Wit	DE WIT	51x60cm
Indiae Orientalis nec non Insularum Adiacentium Nova Descriptio	VISSCHER	47x57cm
Indiae Orientalis, Insularumque Adiacentibus Typus	ORTELIUS (Folio)	35x50cm
Indian Territory	ARBUCKLE BROS.	8x13cm
Indian Territory	CRAM	24x30cm
Indian Territory	U.S. GEOLOGICAL SURV.	51x46cm
Indian Territory	U.S. STATE SURVEYS	61x81cm
Indiana	GREENLEAF	32x27cm
Indiana	MORSE & BREESE	36x28cm
Ins. Ceilan quae Incolis Tenarisin Dicitur	MERCATOR (Folio)	35x45cm
Insula Ceilon	BEER	10x13cm
Insula D. Helenae Sacra Coeli Clementia et Aequabilitate ...	VAN LINSCHOTEN	36x50cm
Insula Gaditana, vulgo Isla de Cadiz ...	BLAEU	38x50cm
Insula Islandia	BEER	10x13cm

Insulae Americanae in Oceano Septentrionali, cum Terris Adiacentibus	BLAEU	38x53cm
Insulae Americanae in Oceano Septentrionali, cum Terris Adiacentibus	JANSSON	38x52cm
Insulae Americanae in Oceano Septentrionali, cum Terris Adiacentibus	OGILBY	29x36cm
Insulae Antilles	BEER	10x13cm
Insulae Balearides et Pytiusae	BLAEU	38x49cm
Insulae Britanniae	BEER	10x13cm
Insulae Capitis Viridis	BERTIUS	9x13cm
Insulae Divi Martini ...	BLAEU	38x53cm
Insulae Indiae Orientalis	HONDIUS	14x20cm
Insulae Indiae Orientalis	MERCATOR (Small)	14x20cm
Insulae Indiae Orientalis et Molucae	HULSIUS	16x27cm
Insulae Indiae Orientalis Praecipuae, in Quibus Moluccae Celeberrimae Sunt	HONDIUS	35x48cm
Insulae Moluccae	BEER	10x13cm
Insulae Philippinae	BEER	10x13cm
Insulae Sindae	BEER	10x13cm
Insulae Tercerae alias Acores	BEER	10x13cm
Insularum Aliquot Maris Mediterranei Descriptio	ORTELIUS (Folio)	36x48cm
Insularum Britannicarum Acurata Delineatio ex Geographicis Conatibus ...	JANSSON	39x51cm
Insularum Danicarum ut Zee-Landiae, Fioniae Langelandiae, Lanandiae ...	DE WIT	49x58cm
Insularum Hispaniolae et Cubae cum Insulis Circumjacentibus ...	JANSSON	41x53cm
Insurance Plan of Kingston, Jamaica	GOAD	62x53cm
Insurance Plan of Valparaiso, Chile	GOAD	55x50cm
Introduction a la Geographie de la Correspondance du Globe Terrestre ...	DE FER (Large)	46x69cm
Iowa	COLTON (Atlas Maps)	32x41cm
Iowa and Wisconsin	BRADFORD	36x29cm
Iowa and Wisconsin Chiefly from the Map of J.N. Nicollet	MORSE & BREESE	30x38cm
Ireland	ARROWSMITH	39x24cm
Ireland	BARTHOLOMEW	41x30cm
Ireland	FINLEY	35x26cm
Ireland	GUTHRIE & JONES	19x22cm
Ireland	JEFFERYS	18x19cm
Ireland	MORDEN	13x12cm
Ireland	SELLER	12x14cm
Ireland	S.D.U.K.	39x31cm
Ireland	S.D.U.K.	60x47cm
Ireland	TEESDALE	64x52cm
Ireland	THOMSON	60x50cm
Ireland [in set with] Ireland North Sheet	S.D.U.K.	31x46cm
Irlande Royaume Divise en Ses Quatre Provinces, et Ces Provces ...	SANSON (Folio)	41x51cm
Irlandia	BEER	10x13cm
Irlandiae Regnum	MERCATOR (Folio)	34x46cm
Is de Nio, Nampho Sta. Erini	MALLET	15x10cm
Is de Pelagnisi, Dromi, etc.	MALLET	15x10cm
Ischia Insula	ORTELIUS (Miniature)	8x11cm
Island of Madera	CHILD	22x15cm
Island of St. Christophers	MOLL (Small)	18x25cm
Island of St. Helena, Belonging to ye English East India Company	KITCHIN	15x9cm
Islandia	ORTELIUS (Miniature)	8x11cm
Islandia	QUAD	23x29cm
Islands in the Pacific Ocean	JOHNSTON	50x60cm
Isle d'Albion	MALLET	17x11cm
Isle d'Irlande	MALLET	15x10cm
Isle de France oder Gegend um Paris	ANONYMOUS	33x41cm
Isle de la Martinique	LE ROUGE	22x29cm
Isle et Banc de Terre Neuve, Isle Royale et Isle St. Jean; avec l'Acadie ...	BONNE	23x34cm
Isle et Royaume d'Irlande, par les Sr. Robert ... 1748	DE VAUGONDY	17x18cm
Isle et Royaume de Sicile ...	SANSON (Folio)	39x58cm
Isle Formosa	BELLIN (Small)	24x29cm
Isle St. Christophe ... [on sheet with] La Barbade ...	LE ROUGE	27x20cm
Isle St. Christophle une des Antilles aux Anglois. A Paris. Par le Sr.	LE ROUGE	27x20cm
Isles Antilles ou du Vent avec les Isles sous le Vent	BONNE	32x22cm
Isles de Ceylan	MALLET	15x10cm
Isles de la Sonde	LE ROUGE	22x29cm
Isles Philippines ...	DE VAUGONDY	20x27cm
Isola Cuba	GASTALDI	13x17cm
Isola Cuba Descritta dal P. Mro. Coronelli Lettore Publica, e Cosmografo ...	CORONELLI	22x29cm
Isola Cuba Nova	RUSCELLI	18x25cm
Isole Antili, la Cuba, e la Spagnuola Descritto e Dedicata dal Padre ...	CORONELLI	25x43cm

Title	Author	Size
Isole dell' India Cioe le Molucche le Filippine e della Sonda ...	CANTELLI DA VIGNOLA	45x58cm
Isole di Terra Nuova Scoperta da Gio: Cabota Veneto co suo Figliuolo ...	CORONELLI	23x30cm
Isole Filippine	ZATTA	40x31cm
Israels Perigrination, or the Forty Years Travels of the Children of Israel ...	MOXON	32x46cm
Issachar	FULLER	28x33cm
Isthmus of Panama	TALLIS	25x33cm
Italia in Suos Status Divisa ...	HOMANN	49x58cm
Italia Newly Augmented ...	SPEED	39x51cm
Italia Secundum Dominatus ...	NICOLOSI	40x46cm
Italia XIX. Nova Tabula	MUNSTER	26x34cm
Italiae Antiquae Nova Delineatio ...	JANSSON	38x51cm
Italiae Novissima Descriptio ...	ORTELIUS (Folio)	37x50cm
Italiae Tabula	BEER	10x13cm
Italiae Veteris Specimen	VAN DEN KEERE	15x20cm
Italiae, Illirici, Sardiniae, Corsicae, et Confinium Regionum ...	DE LA HOUVE	39x55cm
Italien in Sein Unterscheide ne Lander ...	SCHREIBER	18x28cm
Italien mit der Dalmat.-Albanesischen Kuste	HILDBURGHAUSEN BIBLIO.	20x26cm
Italy	MOLL (Small)	19x19cm
Iudae, sive Terra Sancta ...	COVENS & MORTIER	46x61cm
Iudaea seu Palaestina ob Sacratissima Redemtoris Vestigia Hodie Dicta ...	HOMANN	50x57cm
Iudaea sive Terra Sancta in Duodecum Tribus Divisa ...	JAILLOT	48x61cm
Iukatan en Vaste Kusten van Nieuw Spanje ...	VAN DER AA	15x22cm
Iutia Septentrionalis	MERCATOR (Folio)	29x40cm
J.H. Colton's Map of Nevada Utah and Arizona	COLTON (Atlas Maps)	28x20cm
Jamaica	LUCAS	23x31cm
Japan I.	MERCATOR (Small)	13x17cm
Japoniae ac Terrae Iessonis Novissima Descriptio	MORDEN	11x13cm
Jerusalem	MAYNARD	35x43cm
Jerusalem	STOOPENDAAL	30x46cm
Jerusalem, et Suburbia Eius Sicut Tempore Christi Floruit, cum Locis ...	BRAUN & HOGENBERG	35x48cm
John Bull and His Friends A Serio-Comic Map of Europe ...	ROSE	49x69cm
Johnson's Arkansas, Mississippi and Louisiana	JOHNSON	57x40cm
Johnson's California with Territories of Utah, Nevada, Colorado, New Mexico	JOHNSON	44x60cm
Johnson's California, also Utah, Nevada, Colorado, New Mexico and Arizona	JOHNSON	43x60cm
Johnson's California. Territories of New Mexico and Utah	JOHNSON	43x62cm
Johnson's Central America	JOHNSON	31x40cm
Johnson's Cuba, Jamaica & Porto Rico	JOHNSON	32x41cm
Johnson's Delaware and Maryland	JOHNSON	36x46cm
Johnson's Florida	JOHNSON	32x39cm
Johnson's Georgia and Alabama	JOHNSON	40x57cm
Johnson's Illinois	JOHNSON	46x36cm
Johnson's Indiana	JOHNSON	58x43cm
Johnson's Iowa and Nebraska	JOHNSON	36x46cm
Johnson's Kansas and Nebraska	JOHNSON	42x58cm
Johnson's Kentucky and Tennessee	JOHNSON	46x61cm
Johnson's Maine	JOHNSON	46x36cm
Johnson's Map of the United States	JOHNSON	46x66cm
Johnson's Map of the World	JOHNSON	46x66cm
Johnson's Mexico	JOHNSON	30x38cm
Johnson's Minnesota & Dakota	JOHNSON	31x38cm
Johnson's Missouri and Kansas	JOHNSON	43x59cm
Johnson's Nebraska and Kansas	JOHNSON	32x39cm
Johnson's Nebraska, Dakota, Colorado & Kansas	JOHNSON	32x39cm
Johnson's Nebraska, Dakota, Colorado, Idaho & Kansas	JOHNSON	32x39cm
Johnson's Nebraska, Dakota, Colorado, Montana & Kansas	JOHNSON	46x66cm
Johnson's Nebraska, Dakota, Idaho and Montana	JOHNSON	43x59cm
Johnson's Nebraska, Dakota, Idaho, Montana and Wyoming	JOHNSON	43x59cm
Johnson's Nebraska, Dakota, Montana and Kansas	JOHNSON	29x36cm
Johnson's New Brunswick, Nova Scotia, Newfoundland, and Prince Edward...	JOHNSON	32x40cm
Johnson's New England	JOHNSON	66x46cm
Johnson's New Jersey	JOHNSON	40x32cm
Johnson's New Map of the State of Texas	JOHNSON	41x56cm
Johnson's New Military Map of the United States Showing the Forts, ...	JOHNSON	43x60cm
Johnson's North America	JOHNSON	56x43cm
Johnson's North and South Carolina	JOHNSON	46x66cm
Johnson's North Carolina and South Carolina	JOHNSON	44x58cm
Johnson's Ohio	JOHNSON	43x58cm
Johnson's Oregon and Washington	JOHNSON	39x27cm

Title	Author	Size
Johnson's Texas	JOHNSON	43x59cm
Johnson's Washington and Oregon	JOHNSON	28x38cm
Johnson's Washington, Oregon, and Idaho	JOHNSON	29x36cm
Johnson's Western Hemisphere [and] Johnson's Eastern Hemisphere	JOHNSON	46x66cm
Johnston's Map of Railway Systems of Scotland	JOHNSTON	84x70cm
Johnston's Map of the Counties of Nairn & Elgin	JOHNSTON	72x57cm
Jonathan Dickenson Ramspoedige ... van Jamaica na Pensylvania ...	VAN DER AA	22x29cm
Jreland	HILDBURGHAUSEN BIBLIO.	26x20cm
Judah & Israel: Illustrating the Books of Kings	ARROWSMITH	25x20cm
Judea or the Holy Land	STACKHOUSE	37x37cm
Judee ou Terre Sainte	DE VAUGONDY	25x22cm
Juta's Map of South Africa from the Cape to the Zambesi	JUTA	89x119cm
Kaart van de Eilanden in den Omtrek van Otahiti ...	COOK	24x50cm
Kaart van de Noord-West Kust van Amerika en de Noord-Oost Kust van Asia	COOK	38x64cm
Kaart van den Mond van Norton, en van de Engte van Bhering ...	COOK	26x38cm
Kaart van een Gedeelte van de Kust van Nieuw Zuid Wales, van Kwelling ...	COOK	29x32cm
Kaart van het Eyland Mauritius	VALENTYN	43x54cm
Kaart van het Kanaal in de Filippynsche Eilanden Waar door het Galjoen ...	ANSON	53x42cm
Kaart van het Westelyk Gedeelte van Nieuw Mexico en van California	TIRION	32x34cm
Kansas and the Territories of Arizona, Colorado, New Mexico, Utah ...	LLOYD	41x64cm
Karta over Polynesien ...	DJURBERG	47x71cm
Karta Zheleznykh Shoseinykh I Vnutrennikh Vodnykh Putei Soobshcheniia ...	RUSSIAN GOVERNMENT	164x132cm
Karte des Arktischen Archipel's der Parry-Inseln	PETERMANN	25x57cm
Karte von Amerika nach D'Anville und Pownall ...	VON REILLY	61x80cm
Karte von dem Deutschen Meere und den Angranzenden Theilen des ...	HILDBURGHAUSEN BIBLIO.	26x20cm
Karte von dem Flusse Richelieu und oem See Champlain ...	BELLIN (Small)	30x14cm
Karte von dem Koenigreiche Schweden ...	VON REILLY	57x74cm
Karte von den Eylanden von Japon und der Halbinsel Corea	BELLIN (Small)	20x28cm
Karte von den Kusten des Franzosischen Florida	BELLIN (Small)	20x14cm
Karte von den Kusten von Persien, Guzaratte und Malabar	BELLIN (Small)	24x20cm
Karte von den N.W. Amerikanischen und N.OE. Asiatischen Kusten ...	SCHRAEMBL	39x68cm
Karte von Frankreich	VON REILLY	55x69cm
Keith Johnston's "Travelling Map of Scotland"	JOHNSTON	87x58cm
Kent	MORDEN	34x64cm
Kent	WALKER, J. & C.	32x39cm
Kentucky	FINLEY	22x29cm
Kentucky & Tennessee	ASHER & ADAMS	41x59cm
Kentucky and Tennessee	BURR	30x38cm
Kentucky and Tennessee	COLTON (Atlas Maps)	38x46cm
Keppell Harbour [Owls Head Bay] ... Knowles Harbour [Ship harbour] ...	DES BARRES	72x102cm
Keyserlynk Gezandschap Uyt Aethiopien ...	VAN DER AA	15x22cm
King's Bay and Lunenburg [Nova Scotia]	DES BARRES	68x98cm
Kingstown Harbour	BRITISH ADMIRALTY	61x47cm
Klyn Loretten in Noord-America / Petit Lorette Etats Unis de Lamerique / ...	ANONYMOUS	27x33cm
Kriegs Schauplatz ...	WILL	52x59cm
Kriegs- und Spezial Karte vom Finnischen Meerbusen von Kronstadt bis ...	HILDBURGHAUSEN BIBLIO.	20x26cm
L'Acadia, le Provincie di Sagadahook e Main, la Nouva Hampshire, ...	ZATTA	33x43cm
L'Afrique ...	DE VAUGONDY	49x62cm
L'Afrique Dresee sur les Observations de Mrs de l'Academie Royal ...	DE L'ISLE	46x57cm
L'Afrique Dressee selon les Dernieres Relat. et Suivant les Nouvelles ...	DE FER (Small)	23x32cm
L'Afrique Selon les Autheurs les Plus Modernes	DE LA FEUILLE	14x20cm
L'America Divisa ne Suoi Principali Stati ...	ZATTA	31x40cm
L'Amerique Divisee par Grands Etats par le Sr. Janvier ...	JANVIER	31x45cm
L'Amerique du Sud	DUFOUR	50x32cm
L'Amerique Meridionale	BENARD	44x33cm
L'Amerique Meridionale ...	DE L'ISLE	46x58cm
L'Amerique Meridionale et Septentrionale ...	DE FER (Small)	23x34cm
L'Amerique Meridionale et Septentrionale ...	DESNOS	48x69cm
L'Amerique Selon les Nouvelles Observations de Messrs. de l'Academie ...	VAN DER AA	47x65cm
L'Amerique Septentrionale	D'ANVILLE	No dimen
L'Amerique Septentrionale Dressee sur les Observations ...	DE L'ISLE	47x58cm
L'Amerique Septentrionale ...	VAN DER AA	22x30cm
L'Amerique Septentrionale Divisee en Ses Principaux Etats	JANVIER	30x48cm
L'Amerique Septentrionale Dressee sur les Observations ...	DE L'ISLE	44x58cm
L'Amerique Septentrionale et Meridionale Divisee en Ses Principales Parties	DE VAUGONDY	50x65cm
L'Ancien et le Nouveau Mexique, avec la Floride et la Basse Lousiane	BONNE	36x23cm
L'Ancien Monde et le Nouveau en Deux Hemispheres	BONNE	21x41cm
L'Angleterre ...	DE PRETOT	27x39cm

Title	Author	Size
L'Arabie	DE VAUGONDY	16x18cm
L'Asie Suivant les Nouvelles Decouvertes dont les Point Principaux ...	DE FER (Small)	23x32cm
L'Elvezia ...	ZATTA	32x41cm
L'Empire de la Chine Dresse d'apres les Cartes de l'Atlas Chinois	DE VAUGONDY	48x53cm
L'Espagne Dressee sur la Description qui en A Ete Faite par ...	DE L'ISLE	47x60cm
L'Espagne Suivant les Nouvelles Observations	LE ROUGE	20x26cm
L'Estremadura di Portogallo ...	ZATTA	31x31cm
L'Europe	DE FER (Small)	14x15cm
L'Europe	DE L'ISLE	49x58cm
L'Eveche et L'Etat de Liege	SEUTTER	50x58cm
L'Hemisphere Meridional ...	DE L'ISLE	48x52cm
L'Hemisphere Septentrionale pour Voir Plus Distinctement les Terres Arctiques	DE L'ISLE	46x51cm
L'Hydrographie ou Description de l'Eau c'est a Dire des Mers, Golfes, ...	SANSON (Folio)	39x53cm
L'Impero del Giapon Diviso in Sette Principali Parti...	ZATTA	32x40cm
L'India di qua e di la dal Gange Oue Sono li Stati del G. Mogol ...	CANTELLI DA VIGNOLA	42x52cm
L'Irelande	LE ROUGE	28x21cm
L'Irlande Divisee par Provinces Civiles et Ecclesiastiques	BRION DE LA TOUR	48x29cm
L'Isle de Corse	LOTTER	50x58cm
L'Isle de France. Parisiensis Agri Descrip.	ORTELIUS (Folio)	34x46cm
L'Isle de France. Parisiesis Agri Descriptio	MERCATOR (Folio)	35x45cm
L'Isle de Mosambique [on sheet with] Sofala	LAFITAU	19x14cm
L'Isle de Terre Neuve	LE ROUGE	53x53cm
L'Isle de Terre-Neuve, l'Acadie ou la Nouvelle Ecosse, l'Isle St Jean ...	BONNE	21x32cm
L'Isle et Ville de Goa	LAFITAU	14x19cm
L'Isle St. Domingue par les Sr. Robert ...	DE VAUGONDY	18x17cm
L'Isola d'Islanda	ZATTA	31x41cm
L'Isole Britanniche overo L'Inghilterra ... la Scotia ... l'Irlanda ...	ROSSI	41x52cm
L'Italie	DE L'ISLE	49x60cm
L'Oceanie	HOUZE	25x40cm
L'Orient pour l'Histoire Ancienne de Mr. Rollin ...	D'ANVILLE	27x36cm
La Baja d'Hudson Terra di Labrador e Groenlandia con le Isole Adiacenti ...	ZATTA	30x41cm
La Basse Austriche ...	LE ROUGE	20x26cm
La Bataille de Zornsdorf Donne sur le 25.eme d'Aout ... [Copper printing plate]	ANONYMOUS	41x54cm
La Californie ou Nouvelle Caroline, Teatro de los Trabajos, Apostolicos ...	DE FER (Large)	46x65cm
La Division de LOcean du Nouveau Monde	BRIET	19x14cm
La Florida [on sheet with] Peruviae Auriferae Regionis Typus [and] ...	ORTELIUS (Folio)	34x46cm
La Floride	SANSON (Small)	18x25cm
La Floride Divisee en Floride et Caroline	DE VAUGONDY	17x17cm
La Floride Divisee en Floride et Caroline ...	DE VAUGONDY	27x20cm
La France, dans Toute Son Etandue ...	DE FER (Large)	49x65cm
La Guadeloupe ...	LE ROUGE	47x54cm
La Haie Sejour Ordinaire de la Cour Hollandoise	DE FER (Small)	23x33cm
La Haie Sejour Ordinaire de la Cour Hollandoise	MORTIER	24x29cm
La Jamaique aux Anglois dans le Golfe du Mexique a Paris. Chez le Sr.	LE ROUGE	20x27cm
La Judee ou Palestine Dressee pour l'Intelligence de l'Histoire Sainte	BRION DE LA TOUR	27x30cm
La Judee ou Terre Sainte, Divisee en Ses Douze Tribus ...	DE VAUGONDY	50x60cm
La Louisiana, Parte Settentrionale, Scoperta Sotto la Protettione di Luigi XIV	CORONELLI	27x43cm
La Nuova Francia	RAMUSIO	27x37cm
La Nuova Zelanda Trascorsa nel 1769 e 1770 dal Cook ...	ZATTA	45x36cm
La Palatinati di Mazovia ... [Poland]	ZATTA	31x40cm
La Palatinati di Nowogrodek ... [Poland]	ZATTA	31x40cm
La Parte Occidentale della Nuova Francia o Canada	ZATTA	34x44cm
La Pensilvania, la Nuova York, il Jersey Settentriole, con la Parte Occidentale	ZATTA	34x44cm
La Principaute d'Orange et Comtat de Venaissin, par Jaques de Chieze ...	BLAEU	38x50cm
La Principaute d'Ost-Frise, ou le Comte d'Embden, avec Ses Principales ...	LOTTER	49x59cm
La Principaute de Liege et le Duche de Limbourg	DE VAUGONDY	51x47cm
La Prussia Divisa in Reale che Appartiene al Re di Polonia et in Ducale ...	CANTELLI DA VIGNOLA	43x58cm
La Russie Blanche ou Moscovie Divisee Suivant l'Entendue des Royaumes ...	JAILLOT	51x60cm
La Savoye ...	LE ROUGE	20x26cm
La Scandinavie ou la Suede et Danemark ...	LE ROUGE	20x26cm
La Seconde Table d'Ecosse	MERCATOR (Folio)	35x45cm
La Seconde Table Generale selon Ptol.	MUNSTER	25x34cm
La Situation d'Algier	MANUSCRIPT MAPS	32x49cm
La Suisse ...	LE ROUGE	20x26cm
La Table des Isles Neufues, lesquelles on Appelle Isles d'Occident & d'Indie ...	MUNSTER	28x34cm
La Terra de Hochelega nella Nova Francia	RAMUSIO	28x38cm
La Ville d'Athenes	MORTIER	11x15cm
La Ville de Calicut	LAFITAU	19x14cm

La Ville de Cochin [on sheet with] La Ville Cananor	LAFITAU	19x14cm
La Ville de Daman [India]	LAFITAU	19x14cm
La Ville de Malaca	LAFITAU	19x14cm
La Ville, Cite, Universite, & Faux-bourgs de Paris	DE BELLEFOREST	42x55cm
Lac Lemani ...	ORTELIUS (Miniature)	8x13cm
Lacedemonia	SCHEDEL	14x23cm
Ladozhskiy Kanal Canalis Ladogensis	GRIMMEL	44x64cm
Lake Erie	BRITISH ADMIRALTY	64x93cm
Lake Huron	BRITISH ADMIRALTY	98x66cm
Lake Nyasa	BRITISH ADMIRALTY	114x66cm
Lake Ontario and the Back Communication with Lake Huron	BRITISH ADMIRALTY	60x93cm
Lake Superior and the Northern Part of Michigan	COLTON (Atlas Maps)	32x41cm
Lalandia Falstria et Mona Insulae ...	BLAEU	39x52cm
Lalandiae et Falstriae Accurata Descriptio. Apud Janssonio Waesbergios ...	PITT	41x53cm
Land Togten door Ferdinand Cortes ...	VAN DER AA	15x22cm
Landtafel des Ungerlands, Polands, Reussen, Littaw, Walachey und ...	MUNSTER	26x35cm
Large Draught of the Coast of China from Amoy to Chusan with ...	MOUNT & PAGE	53x43cm
Laurie and Whittle's New Chart of the Indian and Pacific Oceans ...	LAURIE & WHITTLE	74x109cm
Laurie and Whittle's New Map of London, with its Environs. &c. ...	LAURIE & WHITTLE	58x77cm
Lay's Map of the United States. Compiled from the Latest and Best ...	LAY	128x150cm
Le Brixa [on sheet with] Settenil [Spain}	BRAUN & HOGENBERG	Folio
Le Canada Faict par le Sr. de Champlain, ou Sont la Nouvelle France ...	DU VAL	35x54cm
Le Canada ou Nouvelle France	SANSON (Folio)	40x54cm
Le Cercle d'Austriche ...	LE ROUGE	20x26cm
Le Cercle de Baviere qui Comprend le Haut Palinat, les Duches de Haute ...	DE VAUGONDY	52x50cm
Le Colonie Unite della America Settentr.le ...	ZATTA	30x40cm
Le Globe Terrestre Vu en Convexe par les Deux Poles ...	DE PRETOT	23x41cm
Le Gouvernement General de Normandie Divisee en Haute et Basse ...	DE FER (Large)	47x67cm
Le Isole di Terra Nuova e Capo Breton ...	ZATTA	44x34cm
Le Landgraviat de Hesse-Cassel Meridional et Septentr. avec une Partie ...	LOTTER	54x45cm
Le Nouveau Mexique Appele Aussi Nouvelle Grenade et Marata. Avec ...	NOLIN	45x59cm
Le Nouveau Mexique, avec la Partie Septentrionale de l'Ancien, ou de ...	BONNE	21x32cm
Le Nouveau Mexique, et la Floride; Tiree de Diverse Cartes, et Relations ...	SANSON (Folio)	32x55cm
Le Pays des Hottentots aux Environs du Cap de Bonne Esperance	BELLIN (Small)	24x34cm
Le Plan de Paris, Ses Faubourgs et Ses Environs	DE L'ISLE	56x75cm
Le Port d'Alger	MORTIER	22x29cm
Le Portugal Suivant les Nouvelles Observations ...	VAN DER AA	23x23cm
Le Poste con le Sue Strade Principali dell'Alta e Bassa Germania e de ...	ROSSI	46x57cm
Le Poste della Francia con le Sue Strade Principali	ROSSI	66x54cm
Le Royaume d'Angleterre, Divise Selon les Sept Royaumes, ou Heptarchie ...	DE VAUGONDY	50x53cm
Le Royaume de Hongrie ...	LE ROUGE	20x26cm
Le Royaume de Hongrie, et les Estats qui en Ont Este Sujets, et qui ...	SANSON (Folio)	59x89cm
Le Royaume de Pologne, Divise en Ses Duches et Provinces, et Subdivise ...	DE VAUGONDY	50x56cm
Le Royaume de Portugal et des Algarves ...	JAILLOT	77x55cm
Le Sas de Gand	MORTIER	20x26cm
Le Sund ou Detroit du Sond Passage Ordinaire des Vaisseaux qui Entrent ...	DE FER (Small)	33x22cm
Le Tirol	LE ROUGE	21x28cm
Lebrixa [on sheet with] Settenil	BRAUN & HOGENBERG	32x41cm
Lecestriae Comitatus	SAXTON	28x36cm
Legatione del Ducato d'Urbino con la Diocesi, e Governo di Citta di Castello ...	ROSSI	43x55cm
Legazione di Bologna Descritta da ... Magini	ROSSI	55x44cm
Leodiensis Dioecesis Typus	MERCATOR (Folio)	35x45cm
Lepanthe	MORTIER	11x15cm
Les Capitaneries Garde-Costes de la Roque de Risle, de Honfleur, Touques ...	DE FER (Small)	22x33cm
Les Cotes de la Virginie Les Detroits de Forbisher et de Hudson	VAN DER AA	15x22cm
Les Deux Poles Arcticque ou Septentrional, et Antarcticque ou Meridional ...	SANSON (Folio)	38x53cm
Les Environs de Francfort	MORTIER	19x25cm
Les Etats de l'Eglise et de Toscane ...	DE FER (Large)	51x58cm
Les Etats Unis de l'Amerique Septentrionale ...	BONNE	32x22cm
Les Etats Unis de l'Amerique Septentrionale Contenant en Outre les Isles ...	BONNE	32x22cm
Les Etats Unis de l'Amerique Septentrionale, Partie Occidentale ...	BONNE	34x23cm
Les Etats Unis de l'Amerique Septentrionale, Partie Orientale Par M. ...	BONNE	36x25cm
Les Frontieres d'Espagne et de Portugal ...	DE FER (Large)	55x42cm
Les Indes Orientales, ou Sont Distingues les Empires et Royaumes ...	DE VAUGONDY	50x58cm
Les Isles Antilles &c. Entre Lesquelles Sont les Lucayes, et les Caribes ...	SANSON (Folio)	39x55cm
Les Isles Antilles, par le Sr. Robert de Vaugondy Fils ...	DE VAUGONDY	16x18cm
Les Isles Britanniques ou Sont le Royaumes d'Angleterre ...	DE L'ISLE	47x57cm
Les Isles Britanniques Qui Contiennent les Royaumes d'Angleterre, Ecosse ...	JAILLOT	45x65cm

Title	Cartographer	Size
Les Isles Philippines et Celles des Larrons ou de Marianes, les Isles Moluques	DE FER (Small)	22x34cm
Les Isles Philippines, Celle de Formose, le Sud de la Chine, les Royaumes ...	BONNE	21x31cm
Les Lacs du Canada et Nouvelle Angleterre par le Sr. Robert ...	DE VAUGONDY	16x22cm
Les Marins Monstres & Terrestres, lesquelz on Trouve en Beaucoup ...	MUNSTER	26x34cm
Les Provinces des Pays Bas Catholiques ... A Most Exact Map of Flanders ...	MOLL (Large)	61x99cm
Les Royaumes de Portugal et d'Algarve ...	DE FER (Small)	36x25cm
Les Virges, Levees par les Anglais, et par les Danois Traduit de l'Anglais	LE ROUGE	46x34cm
Liberty Enlightening the World - Bartholdi's Colossal Statue on Bedlow's ...	HARPER'S WEEKLY	34x104cm
Linguistic Stock of American Indians North of Mexico	POWELL, J.W.	52x44cm
Lisbonne	DE FER (Small)	24x33cm
Livonia	MERCATOR (Folio)	35x45cm
Livoniae Nova Descriptio Joanne Portantio Auctore	ORTELIUS (Miniature)	8x11cm
Lloyd's New Map of the United States, the Canadas and New Brunswick ...	LLOYD	93x124cm
Lloyd's Topographical Railway Map of North-America or the United States ...	LLOYD	152x145cm
Londinum Feracis Ang. Met.	MUNSTER	23x36cm
Londinum Feracissimi Angliae Regni Metropolis	BRAUN & HOGENBERG	34x49cm
London	MERIAN	21x70cm
London 1843. Drawn & Engraved from Authentic & Personal Observation. ...	S.D.U.K.	40x64cm
Londres ...	TARDIEU	32x44cm
Loop van de Maragon of de Groote Rivier der Amazones	BELLIN (Small)	16x38cm
Lotharingia Ducatus	MERCATOR (Folio)	35x45cm
Lotharingia Septentrional [and] Lotharingia Meridionalis	MERCATOR (Small)	13x15cm
Lough Ree on the River Shannon	BRITISH ADMIRALTY	89x56cm
Louisiana	BRADLEY	53x44cm
Louisiana	CAREY, M.	19x15cm
Louisiana	CAREY, M.	39x44cm
Louisiana	COLTON (Atlas Maps)	32x40cm
Louisiana	FINLEY	22x28cm
Louisiana	LUCAS	28x44cm
Louisiana	MORSE & BREESE	29x36cm
Louisiana and Mississippi	TANNER	69x55cm
Louisiana and Part of Arkansas	BRADFORD	26x20cm
Louisiana by de River Mississippi	LAW	19x16cm
Louisiana, As Formerly Claimed by France, Now Containing Part of British ...	LONDON MAGAZINE	18x23cm
Louisiana, Mississippi and Arkansas	MORSE, S.	23x16cm
Lovanium Brabantiarum Urbium ...	GUICCIARDINI	23x31cm
Lower and Upper Rhine with Franconia	WILKINSON	22x28cm
Lundy Island	BRITISH ADMIRALTY	48x64cm
Lunenburg	MUNSTER	9x38cm
Lutetia Vulgari Nomine Paris, Urbs Galliae Maxima, Sequana Navigabili ...	BRAUN & HOGENBERG	34x48cm
Lutzenburgi	DE AEFFERDEN	15x18cm
Luxembourg Ville Forte, Capitale du Duche de Meme Nom ...	MORTIER	20x27cm
Lynn Harbor, Massachusetts	U.S. COAST SURVEY	44x37cm
Macedoine Thessalie Epire	MALLET	15x11cm
Macedonia	SCHEDEL	19x23cm
Macedonia Epirus et Achaia	MERCATOR (Folio)	36x43cm
Macquarie Harbour [Tasmania]	BRITISH ADMIRALTY	47x61cm
Maestricht Ville du Brabant Hollandois	MORTIER	20x28cm
Magna Britannia Complectens Angliae, Scotiae et Hiberniae Regna	HOMANN	48x57cm
Magnae Britanniae Complectens Angliae, Scotiae et Hyberniae Regn ...	HOMANN	48x56cm
Magnae Britanniae Pars Meridionalis in qua Regnum Angliae tam in ...	HOMANN	48x56cm
Magnae Britanniae Pars Septentrionalis qua Regnum Scotiae ...	HOMANN	48x56cm
Magnae Britanniae Tabula, Angliam, Scotiam, et Hiberniam ...	VISSCHER	47x57cm
Magni Ducatus Finlandiae ...	JANSSON	44x53cm
Magni Ducatus Finlandiae Russiae Partim, Partim Sueciae Subjecti, ...	LOTTER	50x59cm
Magni Ducatus Lithuaniae ...	BLAEU	44x53cm
Magni Ducatus Lithuaniae ... Sumptib. Janssonio Waesbergiar	PITT	44x54cm
Magnifica Illa Civitas Verona [on sheet with] Colonia Augusta Verona ...	BRAUN & HOGENBERG	36x47cm
Magnum Mare del Zur cum Insula California	RENARD	49x57cm
Magnus Ducatus Lithuania in suos Palatinatus et Castellanias Divisa	LOTTER	49x58cm
Maine	ARROWSMITH & LEWIS	22x27cm
Maine	BRADFORD	25x19cm
Maine	BRADFORD	37x29cm
Maine	BURR	33x27cm
Maine	COLTON (Atlas Maps)	40x29cm
Maine	FINLEY	29x22cm
Maine, Perche, Anjou, Saumurois, Touraine	DE VAUGONDY	16x18cm
Maiores Minoresque Insulae. Hispaniola, Cuba, Lucaiae et Caribes	DE LAET	28x36cm

Malacca	LANGENES	9x13cm
Malaisie et Indochine Carte Speciale pour Java, Siam et Canton ...	PLON	25x36cm
Malta olim Melita	ORTELIUS (Miniature)	8x11cm
Maltha	BEER	10x13cm
Mansfeldia	BLAEU	38x50cm
Mansfeldiae Comitatus Descriptio ...	ORTELIUS (Folio)	37x43cm
Mantua	BRAUN & HOGENBERG	Folio
Mantua	SCHEDEL	19x22cm
Map for Mr. Pennant's Outline of the Globe	PENNANT	50x59cm
Map Illustrating the Military Operations in Front of Atlanta, Ga. ...	U.S. WAR DEPARTMENT	71x79cm
Map Illustrating the Operations of the U.S. Forces against Vicksburg	U.S. COAST SURVEY	44x41cm
Map Illustrating the Plan of the Defences of the Western & North Western ...	U.S.	54x38cm
Map Illustrating the Plan of the Defenses of the Western Frontier, as ...	U.S. WAR DEPARTMENT	60x37cm
Map Illustrating the Position of Duluth in the United States	REAL ESTATE MAPS	53x74cm
Map Illustrating the System of Parcs, and the Domestic Relations of the ...	GILPIN	53x57cm
Map No.1 Eastern States	SMITH, ROSWELL C.	23x28cm
Map No.1 From San Francisco Bay to the Plains of Los Angeles ...	U.S. PACIFIC R.R. SURV.	74x89cm
Map No.2 Eastern States	SMITH, ROSWELL C.	23x28cm
Map No.2 From the Northern Boundary of California to the Columbia River ...	U.S. PACIFIC R.R. SURV.	71x61cm
Map No.2. Showing a Continuation of Details of Fort Smith and Santa Fe ...	U.S.	28x51cm
Map of a Part of Louisiana and Mississippi	U.S. COAST SURVEY	65x72cm
Map of a Part of the Washington Territory	U.S. STATE SURVEYS	37x48cm
Map of a Part of the Washington Territory to Accompany the Report ...	U.S. STATE SURVEYS	38x51cm
Map of a Part of Washington Territory East of the Cascade Mts. ...	U.S. STATE SURVEYS	46x58cm
Map of Addison County, Vermont	WALLING	135x137cm
Map of Alaska ...	U.S. GEOLOGICAL SURV.	43x53cm
Map of Alaska including the Klondike District and Adjacent Gold Fields	RAND, McNALLY (Pocket, etc)	61x91cm
Map of America	WYLD	54x60cm
Map of an Exploring Expedition to the Rocky Mountains in the Year 1842 ...	FREMONT	130x80cm
Map of Arizona, California, Colorado, Nevada, New Mexico, and Utah	JOHNSON	22x30cm
Map of Boston and Maine Railroad	RAILROAD CO. MAPS	64x109cm
Map of Burlington, Vermont	LOCAL & STATE WALL	104x79cm
Map of Burlington in Vermont	LOCAL & STATE WALL	61x81cm
Map of Chittenden County, Vermont	WALLING	135x130cm
Map of Eastern Australia on which Are Delineated the Routes of ...	ROYAL GEOG. SOCIETY	46x31cm
Map of England & Wales Divided into Counties Shewing the Principal Roads ...	STARLING	47x38cm
Map of Florida	APPLETON	30x24cm
Map of Florida	RAND, McNALLY (Atlas Maps)	51x66cm
Map of Florida	THOMAS, COWPERTHWAIT	36x30cm
Map of Florida according to the Latest Authorities	FINLEY	41x24cm
Map of Gold Hill Front Lodes on the Comstock Range N.T.	WESCOATT	30x56cm
Map of Great Britain Showing All the Railways, & Railway Stations ...	WEEKLY DISPATCH	132x93cm
Map of Hudson's River, with the Adjacent Country.	GENTLEMAN'S MAG.	30x21cm
Map of Idaho	HARDESTY	33x50cm
Map of Indian Territory and Oklahoma	U.S. STATE SURVEYS	57x75cm
Map of Iowa	COLTON (Pocket & Wall)	32x41cm
Map of Ireland	STACKHOUSE	41x37cm
Map of Island of Porto-Rico Showing Roads, Rail Roads and Light Houses ...	U.S.	20x36cm
Map of Johnson County IA	LOCAL & STATE WALL	122x91cm
Map of Kansas, Nebraska and Colorado Showing Also the Southern ...	MITCHELL, S.A. (1860+)	29x36cm
Map of Kansas, Nebraska and Colorado. Showing Also the Eastern ...	MITCHELL, S.A. (1860+)	27x33cm
Map of Lincoln County [ME]	COLBY	41x31cm
Map of Louisiana from D'Anville's Atlas	HARRISON	31x49cm
Map of Louisiana Representing the Several Land Districts ...	U.S. STATE SURVEYS	39x43cm
Map of Louisiana, Mississippi and Alabama Constructed from the Latest ...	MITCHELL, S.A. (Pocket, etc)	42x55cm
Map of Louisiana. Showing the Tensas Delta District	RAND, McNALLY (Pocket, etc)	28x36cm
Map of Massachusetts and Rhode Island	THOMAS, COWPERTHWAIT	30x38cm
Map of Mexico, Central America and the West Indies	MITCHELL, S.A. (1860+)	34x54cm
Map of Michigan and Wisconsin	MITCHELL, S.A. (Pocket, etc)	23x28cm
Map of Military Reconnaissance from Fort Taylor to the Coeur D'Alene ...	U.S. WAR DEPARTMENT	56x53cm
Map of Minnesota Territory	THOMAS, COWPERTHWAIT	33x41cm
Map of Missouri	MITCHELL, S.A. (to 1859)	40x34cm
Map of Montana	HARDESTY	33x50cm
Map of Montana	WILMORE	12x20cm
Map of Nebraska and Eastern Colorado	RAILROAD CO. MAPS	57x98cm
Map of Nebraska and Kansas	HOWE	14x11cm
Map of New England with Adjacent Portions of New York & Canada	WALLING & GRAY	56x39cm
Map of New Hampshire	WHITE	32x21cm

Map of New Hampshire & Vermont	THOMAS, COWPERTHWAIT	38x31cm
Map of New Jersey	THOMAS, COWPERTHWAIT	39x32cm
Map of New South Wales	CRAM	41x56cm
Map of New York and the Adjacent Cities	COLTON (Atlas Maps)	41x65cm
Map of North America	THOMAS, COWPERTHWAIT	39x32cm
Map of North America Showing All Routes to Alaska and Klondike Country	CONKEY	34x37cm
Map of North America, Exhibiting the Recent Discoveries. Geographical ...	WYLD	47x36cm
Map of North and South Carolina by J. Denison	MORSE, J.	19x23cm
Map of Northeastern Virginia and Vicinity of Washington	U.S. UNION & CONFED.	42x69cm
Map of Nova Scotia, or Acadia; with the Islands of Cape Breton ...	MONTRESOR	45x47cm
Map of Ohio	COLTON (Pocket & Wall)	30x38cm
Map of Orange County, Vermont	WALLING	135x137cm
Map of Oregon and Upper California	FREMONT	50x42cm
Map of Oregon and Upper California	MITCHELL, S.A. (Pocket, etc)	26x20cm
Map of Oregon and Upper California from the Survey's of ... Fremont ...	U.S.	66x51cm
Map of Oregon Territory West of the Cascade Mountains	U.S. STATE SURVEYS	46x28cm
Map of Oregon, Washington and Part of Idaho	MITCHELL, S.A. (1860+)	26x34cm
Map of Oregon, Washington, Idaho, and Part of Montana	MITCHELL, S.A. (1860+)	25x31cm
Map of Part of Louisiana North of the Base Line	U.S. STATE SURVEYS	28x30cm
Map of Part of N.S.W. [and] Map of Van Dieman's Land	LIZARS	30x46cm
Map of Part of Nipon Island to Accompany Mr. Adams Report on the Silk ...	ROYAL GEOG. JOURNAL	19x22cm
Map of Port Hudson and Vicinity	U.S. WAR DEPARTMENT	86x62cm
Map of Port Royal, Beaufort and Vicinity ...	COLTON (Atlas Maps)	38x53cm
Map of Portions of Lower Clear Creek and Gilpin Counties Showing Mining ...	U.S.	91x102cm
Map of Public Lands of Porto Rico	U.S.	36x18cm
Map of Public Surveys in Colorado Territory	U.S. STATE SURVEYS	41x56cm
Map of Public Surveys in the Territory of Washington ...	U.S. STATE SURVEYS	41x81cm
Map of Railways in New England and Part of New York	SNOW & CO.	16mo
Map of South America	MANUSCRIPT MAPS	37x33cm
Map of South Australia, New South Wales, Van Diemen's Land	WYLD	93x61cm
Map of Texas ...	PAGE	66x42cm
Map of Texas and Part of New Mexico ...	U.S. UNION & CONFED.	42x69cm
Map of Texas from the Most Recent Authorities	MITCHELL, S.A. (to 1859)	30x38cm
Map of Texas from the Most Recent Authorities	THOMAS, COWPERTHWAIT	31x38cm
Map of That Part of Washington Territory Lying West of the Cascade ...	U.S. STATE SURVEYS	38x25cm
Map of the Arkansas Land Grant	RAILROAD CO. MAPS	71x23cm
Map of the Atchison, Topeka and Santa Fe Railroad ...	RAND, McNALLY (Pocket, etc)	61x94cm
Map of the Basin of the Firth of Forth	KNOX	65x81cm
Map of the Battle of the Antietam ...	U.S. UNION & CONFED.	41x69cm
Map of the Battle-Fields of Harper's Ferry and Sharpsburg ...	U.S. UNION & CONFED.	41x69cm
Map of the Battlefield of Big Black Water Bridge Mississippi ... May 17th ...	U.S. WAR DEPARTMENT	48x46cm
Map of the Battlefield of Chattanooga ... 1864	U.S. WAR DEPARTMENT	74x69cm
Map of the Battlefield of Gettysburg July 1st, 2nd, 3rd 1863. ...	U.S. WAR DEPARTMENT	89x71cm
Map of the Battlefield of Roanoke Id., Feb. 8th 1862. ...	U.S. WAR DEPARTMENT	41x64cm
Map of the British Province of New Brunswick from the Best Existing ...	WILKINSON	125x128cm
Map of the Californias by T.J. Farnham	MORSE & BREESE	37x29cm
Map of the City of Montreal and Vicinity	WALKER	41x62cm
Map of the City of Quebec	WALKER	32x38cm
Map of the Coast of New England from Staten Island to the Island of Breton	MOUNT & PAGE	60x79cm
Map of the Colorado Territory	U.S. STATE SURVEYS	41x56cm
Map of the Counties of Fife and Kinross	SHARP	89x117cm
Map of the Counties of Orleans, Lamoille, and Essex, Vermont	WALLING	135x137cm
Map of the Counties of Perth and Clackmannan with the Railways	JOHNSTON	79x91cm
Map of the County of Selkirk ...	JOHNSTON	69x53cm
Map of the Department of the Columbia ...	U.S. WAR DEPARTMENT	78x103cm
Map of the Des Moines Rapids of the Mississippi	U.S.	15x26cm
Map of the District North of Red River Louisiana	U.S. STATE SURVEYS	24x29cm
Map of the Eastern Townships of Lower Canada, Drawn Principally from ...	ARROWSMITH	64x54cm
Map of the Elk Mountains Colorado from Survey by G.B. Chittenden ...	U.S. GEOLOGICAL SURV.	48x25cm
Map of the Field of Shiloh, near Pittsburgh Landing, Tenn. Shewing ...	U.S. WAR DEPARTMENT	46x64cm
Map of the Gold Region with Routes Thereto [Colorado]	HARPER'S WEEKLY	10x19cm
Map of the Great Salt Lake and Adjacent Country in the Territory of Utah ...	U.S.	72x175cm
Map of the Great West	HOWE	No dimen
Map of the Gulf of Mexico, the Islands and Countries Adjacent	KITCHIN	32x49cm
Map of the Harbor of St. Louis Mississippi River	U.S. WAR DEPARTMENT	33x102cm
Map of the Hawaiian Group or Sandwich Islands by the U.S. Ex. Ex.	WILKES	21x28cm
Map of the Head Waters of the Rivers Susquehanna & Delaware ...	NEW YORK STATE DOC.	51x53cm
Map of the Island Antigua ...	EDWARDS	18x23cm

325

Map of the Island of Barbadoes ...	EDWARDS	23x18cm
Map of the Island of Dominica ...	EDWARDS	23x18cm
Map of the Island of Elba	BOWYER	34x22cm
Map of the Island of Porto-Rico	U.S.	30x57cm
Map of the Island of St. Christopher's ...	EDWARDS	19x24cm
Map of the Island of St. Vincent ...	EDWARDS	24x18cm
Map of the Islands in the Pacific Ocean	THOMSON	53x64cm
Map of the Journeyings of the Israelites in the Desert ...	MORSE & BREESE	31x39cm
Map of the Lower Comstock and Emigrant Consolidated Mining Co.s ...	MINING MAPS	19x39cm
Map of the Mining Claims Adjoining Leadville	U.S.	18x20cm
Map of the Mississippi Riv.	WILLIAMS, W.	18x13cm
Map of the Mississippi River, from Cairo to the Gulf of Mexico ...	FRANK LESLIE'S ILLUS.	51x12cm
Map of the Mississippi, from Haines's Bluff to below Grand Gulf, ...	HARPER'S WEEKLY	36x23cm
Map of the Mississippi, from Helena to Port Hudson ...	FRANK LESLIE'S ILLUS.	24x12cm
Map of the Missouri River in the Vicinity of Omaha ...	U.S. WAR DEPARTMENT	22x29cm
Map of the New England or Eastern States	MITCHELL, S.A. (Pocket, etc)	46x28cm
Map of the New England States	HALE	113x94cm
Map of the Northern Pacific Rail Road	RAILROAD CO. MAPS	38x79cm
Map of the Northern Pacific Railroad and Tributary Country.	RAILROAD CO. MAPS	54x83cm
Map of the Northern Part of the State of Maine and of the Adjacent British ...	DASHIELL	42x39cm
Map of the Northern Provinces of the United States	MARSHALL	33x50cm
Map of the Northern, or, New England States of America, Comprehending ...	RUSSELL	37x46cm
Map of the Oregon Territory ...	U.S. EXPLORING EXPED.	22x33cm
Map of the Oregon Territory from the Best Authorities	WILKES	21x33cm
Map of the Oregon Territory West of the Cascade Mountains	U.S. STATE SURVEYS	44x26cm
Map of the Planting Districts of Ceylon ...	FERGUSON	117x88cm
Map of the Province of Manitoba ...	LLOYD	45x62cm
Map of the Provinces of Canterbury and Otago (New Zealand)	ROYAL GEOG. SOCIETY	29x35cm
Map of the Region between Gettysburg Pa. and Appomattox Court House ...	U.S. WAR DEPARTMENT	107x69cm
Map of the Rock River Rapids of the Mississippi	U.S.	15x25cm
Map of the Route in Eastern Africa between Zanzibar, the Great Lakes ...	ROYAL GEOG. SOCIETY	75x59cm
Map of the Routes in New York, New England and Pennsylvania ...	HARPER	15x14cm
Map of the Seat of War in America	STANFORD	55x75cm
Map of the Seat of War in Virginia	ILLUS. LONDON NEWS	36x23cm
Map of the Siege of Vicksburg, Miss. by U.S. Forces under ... Maj. Genl. ...	U.S. WAR DEPARTMENT	74x69cm
Map of the South East Portion of Australia ...	ROYAL GEOG. SOCIETY	33x42cm
Map of the South Western and Part of the Western States	OLNEY	46x27cm
Map of the South Western District Louisiana	U.S. STATE SURVEYS	33x25cm
Map of the South-Western Portion of the United States and of Sonora ...	BELL	33x37cm
Map of the Southern Continental R.R. with Connections from Kansas City ...	RAILROAD CO. MAPS	76x97cm
Map of the Southern Extremity of the Continent of Africa, Comprehending ...	WILKIE	23x42cm
Map of the Southern Parts of the United States of America ...	MORSE, J.	20x39cm
Map of the Southern Provinces of the United States	MARSHALL	35x51cm
Map of the Southern States	SMITH, ROSWELL C.	27x46cm
Map of the Southern States of America, Comprehending Maryland, ...	RUSSELL	37x50cm
Map of the State of Florida	HINTON	20x25cm
Map of the State of Missouri	HINTON	25x37cm
Map of the State of Missouri and Territory of Arkansas Compiled from ...	FINLEY	43x55cm
Map of the State of New York	MORSE, J.	20x25cm
Map of the State of New York ...	THOMAS, COWPERTHWAIT	41x66cm
Map of the State of Texas ...	MITCHELL, S.A. (Pocket, etc)	21x27cm
Map of the State of Texas ...	MITCHELL, S.A. (Pocket, etc)	27x21cm
Map of the State of Vermont	WALLING	159x149cm
Map of the State of Vermont	WALLING	63x59cm
Map of the States of Alabama and Georgia	HINTON	25x40cm
Map of the States of Kentucky and Tennessee	HINTON	25x39cm
Map of the States of Maryland and Delaware by J. Denison	MORSE, J.	20x25cm
Map of the States of North & South Carolina	HINTON	25x39cm
Map of the Territories & Pacific States ...	GOLDTHWAIT	34x46cm
Map of the Territory of Alaska	GRAY	30x37cm
Map of the Territory of Florida	GREENLEAF	33x27cm
Map of the Territory of Hawaii	U.S. STATE SURVEYS	56x84cm
Map of the Territory of Minnesota, Exhibiting the Route of the Expedition ...	U.S. WAR DEPARTMENT	63x72cm
Map of the Territory of New Mexico	U.S. WAR DEPARTMENT	64x50cm
Map of the Territory of Utah	FROISETH	53x38cm
Map of the Territory West of the Rocky Mountains	BONNEVILLE	44x41cm
Map of the Texas and Pacific Railway and Connections	RAILROAD CO. MAPS	46x58cm
Map of the United Kingdom of Great Britain and Ireland ...	WYLD	53x41cm

Title	Publisher/Author	Size
Map of the United States	BURR	80x124cm
Map of the United States	MITCHELL, S.A. (Pocket, etc)	109x88cm
Map of the United States	MITCHELL, S.A. (Pocket, etc)	28x43cm
Map of the United States	OLNEY	28x46cm
Map of the United States and Mexico Including Oregon, Texas and the ...	HAVEN	37x39cm
Map of the United States and Texas	MITCHELL, S.A. (Pocket, etc)	26x42cm
Map of the United States in North America with the British, French and ...	KITCHIN	41x50cm
Map of the United States of America Engraved to Illustrate Mitchell's ...	MITCHELL, S.A. (Pocket, etc)	27x42cm
Map of the United States Territory of Oregon West of the Rocky ...	U.S. WAR DEPARTMENT	44x52cm
Map of the United States, and Texas	HARPER & BROS.	46x56cm
Map of the Upper End of Memphis Harbor	U.S. WAR DEPARTMENT	30x25cm
Map of the Vicinity of Richmond and Peninsular Campaign	JOHNSON	43x61cm
Map of the West India & Bahama Islands with the Adjacent Coasts of ...	WYLD	53x78cm
Map of the Western States	MITCHELL, S.A. (Pocket, etc)	28x46cm
Map of the Western States	SMITH, ROSWELL C.	28x46cm
Map of the World on Mercator's Projection Showing the Discoveries at ...	CRUCHLEY	94x86cm
Map of the Yellowstone National Park	DONALDSON, T.	39x44cm
Map of the Yellowstone National Park	RAILROAD CO. MAPS	61x46cm
Map of Vancouver Island to Illustrate the Paper of Dr. C. Forbes, RN	ROYAL GEOG. SOCIETY	26x37cm
Map of Victoria	CRAM	41x56cm
Map of Washington County [ME]	COLBY	38x32cm
Map of Washington County, Vermont	WALLING	135x137cm
Map of Water Region Adjacent to Charlestown & Chelsea Showing ...	LOCAL & STATE GOV'T	56x41cm
Map of Windsor County Vermont from Actual Surveys	LOCAL & STATE WALL	137x112cm
Map or Chart of the Caledonian Canal ...	JOHNSTON	29x117cm
Map Showing Indian Reservations in the United States West of the 84th ...	U.S.	37x47cm
Map Showing Indian Reservations in the United States, West of the 84th ...	DONALDSON, T.	33x44cm
Map Showing Lines of the Bell Telephone Companies in the United States ...	COMPANY MAPS	64x97cm
Map Showing Private Land Claims, Patented or ... in New Mexico ...	DONALDSON, T.	32x44cm
Map Showing Routes of the Pacific Coast Steamship Company	RAND, McNALLY (Pocket, etc)	69x32cm
Map Showing the Atchison, Topeka and Santa Fe Railroad System	COLTON (Pocket & Wall)	53x84cm
Map Showing the Different Routes Travelled over by ... the Overland ...	U.S.	56x51cm
Map Showing the Distribution of the Chief Mineral Productions of England ...	NAT'L SOC. FOR PROMOTING	51x37cm
Map Showing the Extent of Surveys in the Territory of Utah	U.S. STATE SURVEYS	83x39cm
Map Showing the Lands Assigned to the Emigrant Indians ...	U.S.	47x44cm
Map Showing the Progress of the Public Surveys in Kansas and Nebraska ...	U.S. STATE SURVEYS	62x49cm
Map Showing the Proportion of Deaths from Consumption to Deaths ...	U.S.	48x38cm
Map Showing the System of Confederate Fortifications on the Mississippi ...	U.S. WAR DEPARTMENT	53x46cm
Map Showing the System of Rebel Fortifications on the Mississippi River ...	U.S.	56x48cm
Map Showing the Union Pacific Railway and Connecting Railroads	RAILROAD CO. MAPS	43x75cm
Map to Complete Diaries of Exploration Across Australia (from South to North)	ROYAL GEOG. SOCIETY	20x12cm
Map to Illustrate Diaries of Exploration of Central Australia by ...	ROYAL GEOG. SOCIETY	37x20cm
Map[s] Illustrating the Military Operations of the Atlanta Campaign ...	U.S. WAR DEPARTMENT	c.60x75cm
Mapa de la Isla de la Culebra ... Hidrografia en 1878	DIRECCION DE HIDRO.	27x41cm
Mapa de las Islas del Pasage Virgenes	DIRECCION DE HIDRO.	25x27cm
Mapa Dos Reynos de Portugal e Algarve ...	RIZZI-ZANNONI	No dimen
Mappa Aestivarium Insularum ...	OGILBY	29x36cm
Mappa Aestivarum Insularum Alias Barmudas ...	HONDIUS	40x53cm
Mappa Aestivarum Insularum alias Bermudas ... A Mapp of the Sommer ...	SPEED	40x53cm
Mappa Aestivarum Insularum Alias Barmudas Dictarum ...	JANSSON	18x25cm
Mappa Aestivarum Insularum, Alias Barmudas Dictarum ...	BLAEU	40x53cm
Mappa Circuli Rhenani Superioris in quo Oculis Sistuntur Landgraviatus ...	LOTTER	50x58cm
Mappa Geographica Complectens 1. Indiae Occidentalis Partem Mediam ...	HOMANN	58x49cm
Mappa Geographica Exhibens Electoratum Brandenburgensem, sive ...	LOTTER	50x58cm
Mappa Geographica Provinciae Novae Eboraci ab Anglis New York ...	HOMANN	71x56cm
Mappa Geographica, Continens Archiepiscopatum et Electoratum ...	LOTTER	50x58cm
Mappa Mondo o Vero Carta Generale del Globo Terestre Rapresentato ...	ROSSI	44x59cm
Mappa Totius Mundi Adornata juxta Observationes Dnn. Academiae ...	LOTTER	45x63cm
Mappa Totius Regni Bohemiae	COVENS & MORTIER	50x55cm
Mappe-Monde ...	DE VAUGONDY	24x39cm
Mappe Monde Carte Universelles du la Terre	NOLIN	48x65cm
Mappe Monde Dressee Suivant les Nouvelles Relations et Assujettie ...	DE VAUGONDY	47x74cm
Mappe Monde l'Usage du Roy Par Guillaume Delisle ... 1720. ...	BUACHE	44x67cm
Mappe Monde or Description du Globe Terrestre Vu en Concave ou ...	DE LETH	44x66cm
Mappe Monde ou Carte Generale de l'Univers ...	LOTTER	47x93cm
Mappe Monde ou Carte Generale du Monde. Designee en Deux Plans ...	SANSON (Folio)	39x53cm
Mappe Monde ou Description du Globe Terrestre	ELWE	47x61cm
Mappe Monde ou Description Generale du Globe Terrestre	CHATELAIN	34x44cm

Mappe Monde sur le Plan d'un Meridien Hemisphere Oriental	BONNE	23x34cm
Mappe Monde sur le Plan de l'Equateur Hemisphere Meridionale	BONNE	24x35cm
Mappe Monde sur un Plan Horisontal ... Hemisphere Oriental [in set with]	BONNE	25x36cm
Mappe-Monde Dresse pour l'Etude de la Geographie ...	BRION DE LA TOUR	23x27cm
Mappe-Monde en Deux Hemispheres, l'Oriental et l'Occidental	BONNE	22x33cm
Mappe-Monde Geo-Hydrographique, ou Description Generale du Globe ...	JAILLOT	45x64cm
Mappe-Monde ou Carte Generale de la Terre Divisee en Deux Hemispheres ...	DE FER (Large)	97x146cm
Mappe-Monde ou Carte Generale de la Terre, Dresse sur les Observations ...	DE FER (Small)	23x34cm
Mappe-Monde ou Description du Globe Terrestre ...	DE VAUGONDY	46x70cm
Mappe-Monde pour Connoitre les Progres & les Conquestes le Plus ...	CHATELAIN	34x46cm
Mappe-Monde pour Servir a l'Histoire des Decouvertes et Conquests des ...	LAFITAU	24x45cm
Mappe-Monde qui Comprend les Nouvelles Decouvertes Faites jusqua ...	LE ROUGE	22x30cm
Mappemonde ou Carte Marine Universelle Reduite ...	SANSON (Folio)	46x48cm
Maps of the New and Popular St. Louis and Texas Short Line	RAILROAD CO. MAPS	46x79cm
Mar del Zur Hispanis Mare Pacificum	JANSSON	43x54cm
Mar di Aethiopia vulgo Oceanus Aethiopus	JANSSON	43x55cm
Mar di India	JANSSON	44x55cm
Marca Anconae olim Picenum	MAGINI	13x17cm
Marchionatus Brandenburgensis Ducatus Pomeraniae et Ducatus ...	SEUTTER	50x59cm
Marchionatus Onoldini Comitatus Oettingensis Praepositurae Elevacensis ...	SEUTTER	59x51cm
Mare del Nord ...	CORONELLI	45x60cm
Mare del Sud	ZATTA	30x41cm
Mare del Sud, dettro Altrimenn Mare Pacifico ...	CORONELLI	45x60cm
Maris Pacifici (Quod Vulgo Mar del Zur), cum Regionibus Circumiacentibus ...	ORTELIUS (Folio)	35x50cm
Marlboro [NJ: Monmouth Co.]	BEERS	34x29cm
Marseille	BRAUN & HOGENBERG	Folio
Martinico	LUCAS	24x31cm
Maryland	ARROWSMITH & LEWIS	22x27cm
Massachusetts	ARROWSMITH & LEWIS	22x27cm
Massachusetts	BRADFORD	29x36cm
Massachusetts	FINLEY	23x29cm
Massachusetts	WALLING & GRAY	38x61cm
Massachusetts and Rhode Island	COLTON (Atlas Maps)	33x41cm
Massachusetts and Rhode Island	GRAY	31x37cm
Massachusetts, Connecticut & Rhode Island	JOHNSON	43x58cm
Massachusetts, Rhode Island and Connecticut	BURR	27x32cm
Mediolanum	SCHEDEL	14x22cm
Meervander und Selczame Thier Wie die in den Mitnach-cigen Landern ...	MUNSTER	28x34cm
Melville & Bathurst Island with Coburg Peninsula, Northern Australia	ROYAL GEOG. SOCIETY	18x44cm
Menin A Very Strong Town in the Earldom of Flanders Taken by ye Allies ...	RAPIN	38x48cm
Messico Ouvero Nuova Spagna che Contiene il Nuovo Messico, la California ...	ZATTA	31x40cm
Mexicana	BERTIUS	9x12cm
Mexico	BLACK	25x37cm
Mexico	COLTON (Atlas Maps)	32x39cm
Mexico	GRAY	31x38cm
Mexico ... [on sheet with] Cusco ...	BRAUN & HOGENBERG	27x47cm
Mexico & Guatemala	TANNER	29x37cm
Mexico & Guatemala	THOMAS, COWPERTHWAIT	31x38cm
Mexico & Texas	ARCHER	23x29cm
Mexico, California & Texas	HALL, S.	26x37cm
Mexico, California and Texas	TALLIS	27x34cm
Mexico, Central America, West Indies	MITCHELL, S.A. (Pocket, etc)	23x30cm
Mexico City	GOAD	62x52cm
Mexico, Guatemala and the West Indies	BRADFORD	20x25cm
Mexico, Mittel America, Texas	FLEMMING	30x38cm
Mexico or New Spain	CAREY, M.	44x39cm
Mexico or New Spain Divided into the Audiance of Guadalayara, Mexico ...	MOLL (Small)	19x19cm
Mexico or New Spain, in Which the Motions of Cortes May Be Traced ...	KITCHIN	29x38cm
Mexico, Regia et Celebris Hispaniae Novae Civitas... [on sheet with] Cusco ...	BRAUN & HOGENBERG	27x47cm
Mexico sive N. Hispania	BEER	10x13cm
Mexico und Centro-America	STIELER	30x36cm
Mexique ...	DUFOUR	34x26cm
Mexique, Antilles et California	DUFOUR	55x75cm
Michigan	ASHER & ADAMS	58x41cm
Michigan	BRADFORD	36x29cm
Michigan	COLTON (Atlas Maps)	40x32cm
Michigan and the Great Lakes	BRADFORD	20x25cm
Michigan Central	RAND, McNALLY (Atlas Maps)	34x48cm

Title	Publisher	Size
Milan	S.D.U.K.	32x38cm
Milford Haven	BRITISH ADMIRALTY	48x62cm
Milford Haven and the Island Adjacent	COLLINS, G.	44x56cm
Military Map Showing the Marches of the United States Forces under ...	WAR DEPARTMENT	66x91cm
Millburn and Springfield [NJ]	BEERS	48x38cm
Minnesota	COLTON (Atlas Maps)	30x39cm
Minnesota and Dacotah	MITCHELL, S.A. (1860+)	28x33cm
Misena, Hermunduroum Urbs	BRAUN & HOGENBERG	33x48cm
Missionary Map of China Embracing Chiefly the Eighteen Provinces ...	BIDWELL	168x213cm
Mississipi seu Provinciae seu Ludovicianae ...	HOMANN	48x58cm
Mississippi	COLTON (Atlas Maps)	46x38cm
Mississippi	FINLEY	28x21cm
Mississippi	LUCAS	38x28cm
Mississippi & Alabama	BRADFORD	20x26cm
Mississippi River Sheet No.3 [and] Sheet No.4	U.S. WAR DEPARTMENT	57x38cm
Mississippi River from Cairo to Memphis	HARPER'S WEEKLY	35x6cm
Mississippi River from Cairo to Memphis	MILITARY MAPS	24x11cm
Mississippi Territory and Georgia	CAREY, M.	15x19cm
Missouri	ASHER & ADAMS	41x57cm
Missouri	COLTON (Atlas Maps)	46x38cm
Missouri	FINLEY	29x22cm
Missouri, Illinois and Iowa	BRADFORD	25x20cm
Mitchell's Military Map of the United States ...	MITCHELL, S.A. (Pocket, etc)	60x64cm
Mitchell's Travelers Guide Through the United States. A Map of the Roads ...	MITCHELL, S.A. (Pocket, etc)	45x56cm
Mittaegliches America	BELLIN (Small)	19x14cm
Modern Palestine	TALLIS	34x25cm
Moderna Discrission della Helvezia	MUNSTER	26x34cm
Momonia Hibernice Moun et Woun; Anglise Mounster	BLAEU	42x52cm
Mons	MORTIER	20x27cm
Montana	CENTURY ATLAS	27x38cm
Montana	CRAM	30x47cm
Montana	RAND, McNALLY (Atlas Maps)	32x50cm
Montana, Eastern Portion	ASHER & ADAMS	40x57cm
Montgomeria Comitatus et Comitatus Mervinia	BLAEU	38x50cm
Montgomeryshire	SPEED	38x51cm
Moravia	MERCATOR (Folio)	35x45cm
Moravia	QUAD	21x30cm
Moravia Marchionatus in Sex Circulos Divisus	SEUTTER	50x59cm
Morea ... Greece ... and Islands	BOWEN, E.	22x32cm
Morea olim Peloponnesus	JANSSON	34x41cm
Moscavw	BRAUN & HOGENBERG	35x49cm
Moscovey in Europe ...	SENEX	59x50cm
Mountains and Rivers	JOHNSON	43x66cm
Mouth of the Columbia River	U.S. COAST SURVEY	43x69cm
Murs Comitatus [on sheet with] Regionum Urbium et Fluminum ...	MERCATOR (Folio)	36x24cm
N.O. Brashier City, Paris of St. Mary, La.	REAL ESTATE MAPS	46x55cm
Naaukeurige Kaart van Tartaryen ...	VAN DER AA	15x22cm
Namur	MORTIER	11x16cm
Namurci [Belgium]	DE AEFFERDEN	14x18cm
Namurcum Comitatus. Joes. Surhon Describ. 1579	ORTELIUS (Folio)	39x51cm
Nantucket	WALKER, G.	46x66cm
Naples	S.D.U.K.	34x38cm
Napthali	FULLER	28x34cm
Neapolis	BRAUN & HOGENBERG	Folio
Nebraska	BRADLEY	42x57cm
Nebraska	GRAY	30x37cm
Negropont	MORTIER	11x16cm
Nette Aftekening der Stad Oran &c. Giegen in Barbaryen Opgedragen ...	OTTENS	42x55cm
Neue Ungararisch und Turckische Grosse Land Charle Nebendt ...	HOFFMAN	43x71cm
Neue Welt Karte ...	HOMANN	48x57cm
Neuer Seewig von Europa nac Siberien, Nordenskolds Expedition ...	PETERMANN	25x33cm
Neueste Karte Virginia	MEYER	31x37cm
Nevada	CRAM	57x41cm
Nevis	LUCAS	25x20cm
New & Complete Mercator Chart of the World	MIDDLETON	18x28cm
New and Accurate Chart of Hudson's Bay, in North America.	POLITICAL MAGAZINE	18x23cm
New England and New York	SPEED	9x13cm
New England, New York, New Jersey and Pensilvania ...	GRIERSON	20x27cm

New England, New York, New Jersey and Pensilvania ...	MOLL (Small)	20x27cm
New Europa	MUNSTER	26x34cm
New Griechen Land	MUNSTER	25x34cm
New Hampshire	ARROWSMITH & LEWIS	27x22cm
New Hampshire	FINLEY	29x22cm
New Hampshire and Vermont	BRADFORD	25x20cm
New Hampshire and Vermont	CRAM	56x41cm
New Hampshire and Vermont	DESILVER	37x31cm
New Hampshire, Vermont, Massachusetts, Rhode Island & Connecticut	ASHER & ADAMS	41x56cm
New Holland and Asiatic Isles	THOMSON	50x61cm
New Holland and New Zealand	GREENLEAF	27x32cm
New Jersey	COWPERTHWAIT	47x32cm
New Jersey	FINLEY	28x22cm
New Jersey	LUCAS	29x23cm
New Jersey	MORSE, J.	20x15cm
New Jersey Reduced from T. Gordon's Map	TANNER	39x32cm
New Map of Tennessee by Capt. Michler ...	U.S. WAR DEPARTMENT	56x81cm
New Map of the State of Texas	COLTON (Atlas Maps)	39x63cm
New Map of the State of Texas Compiled from J. Decordova's Large Map	COLTON (Atlas Maps)	41x58cm
New Mexico	ASHER & ADAMS	42x57cm
New Mexico	CRAM	64x46cm
New Mexico	RAND, McNALLY (Atlas Maps)	48x33cm
New Military Map of the United States Showing the Forts, Military Posts ...	JOHNSON	44x61cm
New Orleans [on sheet with] Louisville	COLTON (Atlas Maps)	46x38cm
New Orleans and Adjacent Country	MELISH	17x10cm
New Railroad, Post Office, Township, and County Map of New York	NATIONAL PUBLISHING	102x112cm
New South Wales	S.D.U.K.	39x33cm
New South Wales	TALLIS	34x25cm
New Travelling and Commercial Map of the Canadas, from the Sault ...	TAYLOR	78x60cm
New York	CAREY, M.	15x19cm
New York and Pensilvania	BOWEN & GIBSON	6x10cm
New York City, County, and Vicinity	DRIPPS	66x47cm
New York from Bergen Hill: Hoboken	ILLUS. LONDON NEWS	44x115cm
New Zealand	JOHNSTON	48x45cm
New Zealand	PHILIP	59x49cm
Newport Bay & Harbour ...	MORRIS	18x23cm
Nicaragua ...	VAN DER AA	15x22cm
Nieuw Engeland in Twee Scheep Togtea door Kapitein Johan Smith ...	VAN DER AA	22x29cm
Nieuw Spaanje ...	VAN DER AA	15x22cm
Nieuwe en Aldereerste Afteekening van 't Eyland St. Thomas. ...	VAN KEULEN	58x87cm
Nieuwe en Naukeurige Kaart des Geheelen Aardbolems, Opgemaakt ...	BACHIENE	36x44cm
Nieuwe Kaart van de Grootbrittannische Volkplantingen in Noord America ...	TIRION	36x45cm
Nieuwe Kaart van het Oostelykste Deel de Weereld	TIRION	32x36cm
Nieuwe Kaart van het Westelykste Deel der Weereld ...	TIRION	34x36cm
Nieuwe Kaart van Kanada de Landen aan de Hudsons-Baay en de ...	TIRION	32x44cm
Nieuwe Kaart van't Keizerryk Japan ...	TIRION	27x32cm
Nieuwe Land in Zee Kaart van de Eylanden Guadaloupe en Mariegalande ...	VAN KEULEN	49x57cm
Nieuwe Pascaert van Alle de Vlaemse Eylanden ...	VAN KEULEN	51x59cm
Nieuwe Pascaert van de Oost Cust van Schotlandt beginnende van Barwyck	VAN KEULEN	52x58cm
Nieuwe Platte Paskaart van de Straat Davis, van 67 Graade tot 73 ...	VAN KEULEN	60x100cm
Nieuwe Wereld Kaart Waar in de Reizen van den Hr. Anson ...	TIRION	23x40cm
Ninety Miles Beach to Otago [New Zealand]	BRITISH ADMIRALTY	93x62cm
Nineve	SCHEDEL	14x21cm
Nitidissimae Civitatis Mechlineensis ...	BRAUN & HOGENBERG	33x46cm
Nona Asiae Tabula	PTOLEMY (1478-1508)	36x29cm
Nord America	VON STULPNAGEL	31x39cm
Nordlicher Theil der Vereinigten Staaten	REICHARD	28x34cm
Nordovicum Angliae Civitas	BRAUN & HOGENBERG	29x42cm
Norfolk Isle	COOK	20x18cm
North America	BELL	28x33cm
North America	CUMMINGS & HILLIARD	26x20cm
North America	DOWER	25x20cm
North America	GUTHRIE & JONES	19x22cm
North America	MITCHELL, S.A. (to 1859)	39x32cm
North America	PINKERTON	50x70cm
North America	SHERWOOD, NEELY & JONES	24x19cm
North America	TALLIS	33x24cm
North America ...	THOMSON	53x63cm

North America. British Provinces of New Brunswick, Nova Scotia, & ...	NELSON	48x67cm
North America - Canada & the United States	S.D.U.K.	36x43cm
North America Corrected from the Observations Communicated to ...	SENEX	95x64cm
North America Drawn from the Best Authorities ...	KITCHIN	20x24cm
North America in Its Present Divisions ...	STACKHOUSE	37x36cm
North America. Performed under the Patronage of Louis Duke of Orleans ...	BOLTON	46x60cm
North America Sheet II Lower Canada and New Brunswick with Part ...	S.D.U.K.	31x39cm
North America Sheet III Upper Canada with Parts of New York, Penn ...	S.D.U.K.	35x43cm
North America Sheet IV Lake Superior Reduced from the Admiralty Survey	S.D.U.K.	30x39cm
North America Sheet V The Northwest and Michigan Territories	S.D.U.K.	32x38cm
North America Sheet VI New-York, Vermont, Maine, New-Hampshire ...	S.D.U.K.	43x36cm
North America Sheet VIII Ohio, with Parts of Kentucky, Virginia and ...	S.D.U.K.	31x35cm
North America Sheet IX Parts of Missouri, Illinois, and Indiana	S.D.U.K.	36x43cm
North America Sheet IX Parts of Missouri, Illinois, Iowa & Indiana	S.D.U.K.	30x37cm
North America Sheet X Parts of Missouri, Illinois, Kentucky, Tennessee ...	S.D.U.K.	31x39cm
North America Sheet XI Parts of North and South Carolina	S.D.U.K.	43x36cm
North America Sheet XII Georgia with Parts of North & South Carolina ...	S.D.U.K.	43x36cm
North America Sheet XIII Parts of Louisiana, Arkansas, Mississippi, ...	S.D.U.K.	31x40cm
North America Sheet XIV Florida	S.D.U.K.	40x31cm
North and South America for the Elucidation of the Abbe Gaultier's ...	ASPIN	36x43cm
North and South Carolina	BURR	30x38cm
North Anna, Prepared by Bvt. Brig. Genl. N. Michler ... [VA]	U.S. WAR DEPARTMENT	41x48cm
North Britain or Scotland Divided into Its Counties ...	KITCHIN	68x55cm
North Carolina	BRADFORD	28x36cm
North Carolina	CAREY, M.	15x19cm
North Carolina	COLTON (Atlas Maps)	32x40cm
North Carolina [on a sheet with] South Carolina [and] Florida	MITCHELL, S.A. (1860+)	36x30cm
North Carolina ...	PAYNE	20x34cm
North Dakota	CRAM	46x64cm
North Polar Chart	JOHNSTON	34x48cm
North Sunderland Harbour	BRITISH ADMIRALTY	62x47cm
North-Britain: Or Scotland	MOLL (Small)	18x18cm
North-West Africa	ARROWSMITH	48x60cm
North-West Territory	CRAM	41x56cm
Northamptonshire	SPEED	38x50cm
Northern Central Colorado	U.S. GEOLOGICAL SURV.	76x94cm
Northern Hemisphere	THOMSON	Diam 50cm
Northern Part of Ireland [in set with] Southern Part ...	THOMSON	53x62cm
Northern Part of Scotland [in set with] Southern Part ...	THOMSON	52x62cm
Northern Provinces of the United States ...	THOMSON	53x62cm
Northumberland	BARTHOLOMEW	47x34cm
Northumbria, Cumberlandia, et Dunelmensis Episcopatus	MERCATOR (Folio)	35x47cm
Northwestern America Showing the Territory Ceded by Russia to the ...	BRADLEY	29x36cm
Northwestern America Showing the Territory Ceded by Russia to the ...	MITCHELL, S.A. (1860+)	29x36cm
Norumbega et Virginia	WYTFLIET	23x30cm
Nottingham Shire Drawn from the Best Authorities and Regulated by ...	LONDON MAGAZINE	22x17cm
Nou Grecia Secondo Tutte le Regioni, & Provincie di quella di qua ...	MUNSTER	26x35cm
Nouveau Continent avec Plusieurs Isles	MALLET	14x10cm
Nouveau Mexique et Californie	MALLET	15x10cm
Nouvelle Angleterre Nlle. York Nlle. Jersey Pensilvanie Mariland et Virginie	DE VAUGONDY	27x20cm
Nouvelle Angleterre Nouvelle York, Nouvelle Jersey, Pensilvanie Mariland ...	DE VAUGONDY	19x16cm
Nouvelle Carte d'Ecosse ...	CHATELAIN	34x32cm
Nouvelle Carte de l'Afrique avec des Remarques et des Tables pour Trouver...	CHATELAIN	47x58cm
Nouvelle Carte de la Riviere de Canada ou St. Laurens de l'Ile de Anticoste ...	VAN KEULEN	52x60cm
Nouvelle Carte de la Suisse ...	FADEN	63x85cm
Nouvelle Carte des Cotes des Carolines ... du Cap Fear a Sud Edisto	LE ROUGE	41x54cm
Nouvelle Carte des Decouvertes Faites par des Vaisseaux Russiens ...	MULLER	48x65cm
Nouvelle Carte Generale de la Mer Mediterranee	MICHELOT	48x70cm
Nouvelle Carte Geographique de la Mer d'Asof ou de Zebache; & des Palus ...	VISSCHER	49x58cm
Nouvelle Carte Illustree de l'Amerique du Nord ...	VUILLEMIN	62x85cm
Nouvelle Carte Marine du Grand Banq de Terra Neuff a Grand Point ...	VAN KEULEN	51x57cm
Nouvelle Carte Particuliere de l'Amerique ou Sont Exactement Marquees ...	COVENS & MORTIER	61x55cm
Nouvelle Carte Particuliere de l'Amerique ou Sont...la Nouvelle Bretagne ...	DE L'ISLE	57x52cm
Nouvelle Carte pour Conduire a l'Astronomie et a la Geographie et pour ...	CHATELAIN	51x60cm
Nouvelle Espagne, Nouveau Mexique, Isles Antilles	DE VAUGONDY	24x31cm
Nouvelle Guinee et Carpentarie	MALLET	17x11cm
Nouvelle Mappe Monde	SANTINI	38x65cm
Nova & Accuratissima ... Tabula Nautica	OTTENS	52x142cm

Nova ac Verissima Maris Caspii ... ac Regionum Adjacentium Delineatio ...	OTTENS	No dimen
Nova Anglia Novum Belgium et Virginia ...	DE LAET	39x51cm
Nova Anglia Novum Belgium et Virginia ...	JANSSON	39x51cm
Nova Anglia Septentrionali Americae Implantata Anglorumque Coloniis ...	HOMANN	48x57cm
Nova Belgica et Anglia Nova	BLAEU	39x50cm
Nova Belgica et Anglia Nova	JANSSON	38x50cm
Nova Delineatio Totius Orbis Terrarum per Petrum Vander Aa	VAN DER AA	26x34cm
Nova et Accurata Descriptio Ducatus Bremae et Ferdae cum Maxima Parte ...	LOTTER	50x58cm
Nova et Accurata Geographica Delineatio Ducatus Teschenensis in Silesia ...	LOTTER	50x58cm
Nova et Accurata Poli Arctici ...	JANSSON	41x53cm
Nova et Accurata Tartariae Europaeae seu Minoris et in Specie Crimeae ...	PROBST	50x59cm
Nova et Accuratissima Ducatus Wurtenbergici	LOTTER	51x58cm
Nova et Exacta Mappa Geographica Exhibens Circulum Westphalicum ...	LOTTER	58x50cm
Nova Francia et Regiones Adiacentes	DE LAET	28x36cm
Nova Helvetiae, Foederatarumque cum ea, nec non Subditarum Regionum ...	DE L'ISLE	47x61cm
Nova Hispania	BERTIUS	10x13cm
Nova Hispania Nova Galicia Guatimala	OGILBY	29x36cm
Nova Hispania et Nova Galicia ...	BLAEU	38x50cm
Nova Hispania et Nova Galicia	JANSSON	35x48cm
Nova Hispania, Nova Galicia, Guatimala	DE LAET	28x35cm
Nova Mappa Maris Nigri et Freti Constantino Politani ...	LOTTER	50x58cm
Nova Mexico	BEER	10x13cm
Nova Orbi Tabula ad Usum Serenissimi ...	COVENS & MORTIER	50x64cm
Nova Orbis sive America Septentrionalis, Divisa per sua Regna Provinc ...	SEUTTER	20x26cm
Nova Orbis Tabula in Lucem Edita, A.F. de Wit	DE WIT	48x57cm
Nova Scotia, New Brunswick, Cape Breton	MITCHELL, S.A. (1860+)	38x32cm
Nova Tabula America	ANONYMOUS	27x34cm
Nova Tabula Geographica Complectens Borealiorem Americae Partem ...	VISSCHER	60x90cm
Nova Tabula Insularum Iavae, Sumatrae, Borneonis et Aliarum Mallacam ...	DE BRY	37x43cm
Nova Totius Germaniae Descriptio	CLUVER	12x13cm
Nova Totius Terrarum Orbis Geographica ac Hydpographica [sic] Tabula ...	MARIETTE	38x56cm
Nova Totius Terrarum Orbis Geographica ac Hydrographica Tabula	BLAEU	41x54cm
Nova Totius Terrarum Orbis Geographica ac Hydrographica Tabula	JANSSON	39x53cm
Nova Totius Terrarum Orbis Geographica ac Hydrographica Tabula	MERIAN	26x36cm
Nova Totius Terrarum Orbis Geographica ac Hydrographica Tabula	PITT	40x54cm
Nova Totius Terrarum Orbis Geographica ac Hydrographica Tabula	VAN DEN KEERE	40x54cm
Nova Virginiae Tabula	JANSSON	18x25cm
Nova Virginiae Tabula	OGILBY	29x36cm
Nova Virginiae Tabula ...	MERCATOR (Small)	18x25cm
Nova Zemla, Waygats, Fretum Nassovicum, et Terra Samoiedum ...	JANSSON	41x51cm
Novae Insulae XVII Nova Tabula	MUNSTER	26x34cm
Novae Insulae XXVI. Nova Tabula	MUNSTER	29x37cm
Novellae Etati ad Geographie Umiculatos Calles Humano Viro Necessarios ...	MELA	14x19cm
Novi Belgica et Anglia Nova	JANSSON	39x49cm
Novi Belgii Novaeque Angliae nec non Partis Virginiae Tabula Multis in Locis ...	VISSCHER	46x55cm
Novi Belgii Novaeque Angliae nec non Pennsylvaniae et Partis Virginiae ...	DANCKERTS	46x55cm
Novi Belgii, Quod Nunc Novi Yorck Vocatur ...	OGILBY	29x36cm
Novi Orbis Pars Borealis, America Scilicet, Complectens Floridam, ...	QUAD	23x30cm
Novi Orbis sive Totius Americae cum Adiacentibus Insulis Nova Exhibitio	WEIGEL	27x34cm
Novissima ... Insularum ... Sicilia, Sardinia, Corsica, Malta ...	HOMANN	47x57cm
Novissima Arragoniae ...	HONDIUS	44x55cm
Novissima et Accuratissima Barbados. Descriptio per Johannem Ogilvium ...	OGILBY	29x36cm
Novissima et Accuratissima Delineatio Status Ecclesiae et Magni Ducatus ...	LOTTER	50x58cm
Novissima et Accuratissima Helvetiae, Rhaetiae, Valesiae, et Partis ...	LOTTER	49x58cm
Novissima et Accuratissima Jamaicae Descriptio per Johannem Ogilvium ...	OGILBY	43x54cm
Novissima et Accuratissima Totius Americae Descriptio ...	OGILBY	43x54cm
Novissima et Accuratissima Totius Americae Descriptio per N. Visscher	VISSCHER	43x54cm
Novissima Poloniae Regni Descriptio	JANSSON	43x54cm
Novissima Regni Scotiae Septentrionalis et Meridionalis Tabula Divisee ...	DE L'ISLE	50x59cm
Novissima Totius Terrarum Orbis Tabula	SELLER	44x54cm
Novum Amsterodamum	MONTANUS	13x17cm
Novus Planiglobii Terrestris per Utrumque Polum Conspectus	VALK	41x54cm
Nubie et Abissinie	BONNE	29x41cm
Nueva Hispania Tabula Nova	GASTALDI	13x17cm
Nueva Hispania Tabula Nova	RUSCELLI	18x25cm
Nullus in Orbe Locus Baiis Praelucet Amoenis	BRAUN & HOGENBERG	34x48cm
Nuova Carta delle Isole di Sunda, come Borneo, Sumatra, Iava Grande ...	TIRION	27x36cm
Nuove Scoperte de Russi al Nord del Mare del Sud Si nell'Asia, ...	ZATTA	31x40cm

Title	Author	Size
Nuove Scoperte Fatte nel 1765, 67, e 69 nel Mare del Sud	ZATTA	30x41cm
Ober Baden	MUNSTER	26x35cm
Occidentalis Americae Partis, Velearum Regionum Quas Christophorus ...	DE BRY	33x43cm
Oceania	JOHNSTON	44x56cm
Oceanie	LEVASSEUR	28x41cm
Octava Europe Tabula	WALDSEEMULLER	39x59cm
Oenipons, sive Enipontius vulgo Insspruck, Tirolensis Comitatus Urbs ...	BRAUN & HOGENBERG	34x44cm
Official Copy of a Map Accompanying the Report of Maj. D. Ferguson ...	U.S. WAR DEPARTMENT	18x36cm
Ohio	COLTON (Atlas Maps)	30x37cm
Ohio and N.W. Territory	CAREY, M.	18x15cm
Oklahoma and Indian Territory	PEOPLE'S ATLAS	25x33cm
Oklahoma Territory	U.S. STATE SURVEYS	34x56cm
Old Jerusalem	BURDER	35x43cm
Oldenburg Comitatus	JANSSON	38x50cm
One Hundred & Fifty Miles Around Richmond	MAGNUS, C.	53x38cm
Ontario	ASHER & ADAMS	40x59cm
Oost Ende West Vrieslandts Beschryuinghe Utrivsque Frisiorum Regionis ...	ORTELIUS (Folio)	34x51cm
Oporto	S.D.U.K.	31x38cm
Opulentissimum Sinarum Imperium	SEUTTER	49x57cm
Orbis Descriptio	RUSCELLI	18x26cm
Orbis Terrae Compendiosa Descriptio	MERCATOR (Folio)	29x53cm
Orbis Terrae Compendiosa Descriptio	ROSACCIO	17x25cm
Orbis Terrae Compendiosa Descriptio ... Porro Redact	MAGINI	15x24cm
Orbis Terrarum Nova et Accuratissima Tabula ...	VISSCHER	46x55cm
Orbis Terrarum Tabula Recens Emendata et in Lucem Edita	KEUR	36x47cm
Orbis Terrarum Tabula Recens Emendata et in Lucem Edita	STOOPENDAAL	35x45cm
Orbis Terrarum Tabula Recens Emendata et in Lucem Edita per N. ...	VISSCHER	31x47cm
Orbis Terrarum Typus	CLUVER	12x23cm
Orbis Terrarum Typus de Integro Illustratus 1657	VISSCHER	31x48cm
Orbis Terrarum Typus de Integro Multis in Locis Emendatus ...	PLANCIUS	40x58cm
Orbis Terrarum Veteribus Cognita Typus Geographicus	CLUVER	16x20cm
Orbis Terrarum Veteribus Cogniti Typus Geographicus	JANSSON	40x51cm
Orbis Typus Universalis Iuxta Hydrographorum Traditionem	WALDSEEMULLER	44x57cm
Orbis Veteribus Noti Tabula Nova	DE L'ISLE	38x38cm
Orbis Vetus Authore P. de Val	DU VAL	36x52cm
Orbis Vetus in Utraque Continente juxta Mentem Sansonianam Distinctus ...	DE VAUGONDY	47x71cm
Orbis Vetus, et Orbis Veteris, Utraque Continens, Terrarumq Tractus ...	SANSON (Folio)	38x54cm
Ordnance Survey of Scotland. Geological Survey of Great Britain. Sheet 33.	BRITISH ORDNANCE	53x69cm
Ordnance Survey of Scotland, Geological Survey of Scotland, Sheet 81 ...	BRITISH ORDNANCE	52x65cm
Ordnance Survey of Scotland. Sheet 16. St. Mary's Lock. Ettrick	BRITISH ORDNANCE	53x70cm
Ordnance Survey of Scotland. Sheet 21. Island of Arran. Buteshire.	BRITISH ORDNANCE	53x70cm
Ordnance Survey of Scotland. Sheet 25. Berwickshire	BRITISH ORDNANCE	53x70cm
Oregon & Upper California	MITCHELL, S.A. (to 1859)	39x32cm
Oregon and California	FULLARTON	23x15cm
Oregon, Washington and Idaho	COLTON (Atlas Maps)	44x64cm
Organum Uranicum sive Compassus Mobilis Austriferus ...	WAGHENAER	33x26cm
Orientaliora Indiarum Orientalium ...	RENARD	44x54cm
Originalkarte der Californischen Halbinsel ... Fur die Lower California Company	PETERMANN	34x23cm
Originalkarte der Portuciesischen Reisen in Inner-Afrika Seit 1798 ...	PETERMANN	25x33cm
Originalkarte von Russisch Lappland von J.A. Friis	PETERMANN	33x27cm
Orleanois	DE VAUGONDY	16x18cm
Orleans [on sheet with] Bourges	BRAUN & HOGENBERG	Folio
Ostende	MORTIER	20x25cm
Ostia [Italy]	BRAUN & HOGENBERG	Folio
Outline Map of Puerto Rico ... Adjutant General's Office	U.S. WAR DEPARTMENT	71x127cm
Oxford [NJ: Warren Co.]	BEERS	37x29cm
Oxford Furnace [NJ: Warren Co.]	BEERS	36x81cm
Oxfordshire	LONGMAN	39x33cm
Oxfordshire Described, with ye Citie and the Armes of the Colledges ...	SPEED	38x52cm
Oxonium Nobile Anglie Oppidum [on sheet with] Vindesorium ...	BRAUN & HOGENBERG	36x49cm
Oyster Bay to Matagorda Bay, Texas Coast Chart No.107	U.S. COAST SURVEY	50x100cm
Oyster or Syosset Bay	U.S. COAST SURVEY	44x36cm
Pacific Ocean	ORR & SMITH	21x26cm
Page's Map of New Mexico	PAGE	66x41cm
Pagus Hispanorum in Florida	MONTANUS	27x35cm
Pagus Hispanorum in Florida	OGILBY	27x36cm
Palaestina	CADELL & DAVIES	21x26cm

Palaestina by Mons. D'Anville of the Royal Academy ...	LAURIE & WHITTLE	39x42cm
Palaestina in XII Tribus Divisa cum Terris Adiacentibus Denuo Revisa ...	HOMANN	48x53cm
Palaestina sive Totius Terrae Promissionis	MAGINI	13x17cm
Palaestinae sive Terrae Promissionis in Duodecim Tribus Partitae ...	BLAIR	42x57cm
Palaestinae sive Totius Terrae Promissionis Nova Descriptio Auctore ...	ORTELIUS (Folio)	34x46cm
Palatinatus Bavariae Descriptio, Erhardo Reych Tirolense Auctore ...	ORTELIUS (Folio)	30x49cm
Palatinatus Posnaniensis, in Maiori Polonia Primarii Nova Delineatio per ...	PITT	46x53cm
Palatinatus Rheni	MERCATOR (Folio)	35x45cm
Palatinatus Rheni	MERCATOR (Small)	15x20cm
Palerme [Sicily]	MALLET	14x10cm
Palermo	BRAUN & HOGENBERG	Folio
Palestina in XII Tribus Divisa ...	PROBST	17x20cm
Palestinae sive Totius Terrae Promissionis Nova Descriptio Auctore ...	ORTELIUS (Folio)	35x47cm
Palestine	FINLEY	30x23cm
Palestine	GRAY	37x30cm
Palestine	HALL, S.	37x26cm
Palestine	HALL, S.	51x41cm
Palestine	JOHNSON	40x32cm
Palestine	JOHNSTON	61x50cm
Palestine	WAITE	34x27cm
Palestine	WELLER	31x23cm
Palestine & Adjacent Countries	MITCHELL, S.A. (to 1859)	41x33cm
Palestine According to Its Ancient Divisions	BLACK	37x25cm
Palestine or the Holy Land	JOHNSTON	58x44cm
Palestine or the Holy Land	KINCAID, A.	21x14cm
Palestine or the Holy land or the Land of Canaan	BURR	32x27cm
Palestine with the Hauran and the Adjacent Districts	S.D.U.K.	39x31cm
Panorama of the River Thames in 1845	ILLUS. LONDON NEWS	30x120cm
Panoramic Views along the Line of the Denver & Rio Grande Railroad	RAILROAD CO. MAPS	12mo
Papia	SCHEDEL	14x23cm
Paraguaria ...	OGILBY	29x36cm
Paraguay	BELLIN (Small)	20x29cm
Paraguay, O Prov. de Rio de la Plata	DE LAET	28x35cm
Paris	S.D.U.K.	39x53cm
Paris Illustre et Ses Fortifications	LOGEROT	55x72cm
Parisius	SCHEDEL	19x23cm
Pars Sueviae Borealior	LOTTER	49x64cm
Part of British Columbia to Illustrate the Papers of Mr. Justice Begbie ...	ROYAL GEOG. SOCIETY	21x31cm
Part of Central Colorado. Atlas Sheet No. 53(C)	U.S. WAR DEPARTMENT	43x51cm
Part of New England ...	THORNTON	43x47cm
Part of Phillipsburgh [NJ: Warren Co.]	BEERS	37x79cm
Part of South Australia	TALLIS	34x25cm
Part of Southwestern Colorado Atlas Sheet No. 61(D)	U.S. WAR DEPARTMENT	43x51cm
Part of the Channel between the Isle of Wight and Hampshire ...	BRITISH ADMIRALTY	64x95cm
Part of the Counties of Charlotte and Albany, in the Province of New York ...	LONDON MAGAZINE	25x19cm
Part of the Great Pacific Ocean Shewing the Route of the Spanish Frigate ...	LA PEROUSE	25x38cm
Part of the North East Coast of Africa, in the Gulph of Aden, from Cape ...	BRITISH ADMIRALTY	22x28cm
Part of the United States and Canada	WELLER	54x68cm
Part of the United States of North America	WELD, I.	41x46cm
Parte del Regno d'Irlanda cioe le Provincie di Connaught e Munster ...	ZATTA	42x31cm
Parte Meridionale delle Coste della Francia, che Sono Poste sul Grande ...	CANTELLI DA VIGNOLA	43x58cm
Parte Occidentale del Governo Generale d'Orleans nella quale Sono ...	CANTELLI DA VIGNOLA	57x43cm
Parte Occidentale dell'Elvezia ...	ZATTA	41x31cm
Parte Orientale del Canada, Nuova Scozia Settentrionale, e Parte di Labrador	ZATTA	30x42cm
Parte Orientale dell'Elvezia ...	ZATTA	41x31cm
Parte Orientale della Florida, della Giorgia, e Carolina Meridionale	ZATTA	32x42cm
Particular Map of the Western Coast of Africa from Cape Blanco to ...	HARRISON	50x35cm
Partie de l'Amerique Septent qui Comprend la Nouvelle France ou le Canada ...	DE VAUGONDY	50x60cm
Partie de la Carte du Capitaine Cluny ...	DIDEROT	29x48cm
Partie de la Coste de Bretagne	DE FER (Small)	22x33cm
Partie de la Coste de Provence	DE FER (Small)	22x33cm
Partie des Capitaineries Garde Costes de Brouage et Bourdeaux	DE FER (Small)	22x33cm
Partie des Cotes de Labrador depuis le Cap Charles a la Baye de Sandwich ...	LE ROUGE	49x56cm
Partie des Etats Unis [Texas & Oklahoma]	VANDERMAELEN	47x51cm
Partie du Cercle d'Austriche, ou Sont les Duches de Stirie, de Carinthie ...	JAILLOT	57x88cm
Partie du Mexique ou de la Nouvle. Espagne ...	DE VAUGONDY	16x20cm
Partie du Mexique ou de la Nouvelle Espagne ou Se Trouve l'Aud'ce de ...	DE VAUGONDY	16x18cm
Partie du Mexique ou de la Nouvelle Espagne ou Se Trouve l'Audience du ...	DE VAUGONDY	16x18cm

Title	Author	Size
Partie Meridionale de l'Ancien Mexique ...	BONNE	22x33cm
Partie Meridionale de l'Ancienne Germany, ou la Vraye Germanie	MALLET	17x11cm
Partie Meridionale du Royaume de Naples ...	DE VAUGONDY	48x58cm
Partie Occidentale de la Nouvelle France ou du Canada ...	BELLIN (Large)	48x60cm
Partie Occidentale de la Nouvelle France ou du Canada ...	HOMANN	43x54cm
Partie Occidentale de la Nouvelle France ou du Canada par Mr. Bellin ...	BELLIN (Large)	44x55cm
Partie Occidentale du Canada ou de la Nouvelle France ...	NOLIN	45x60cm
Partie Orientale ... Nouvelle France	BELLIN (Large)	48x62cm
Partie Orientale de la Nouvelle France ou du Canada. Par Mr. Bellin ...	HOMANN	45x56cm
Partie Orientale du Canada ou de la Nouvelle France ... Avec la Nouvelle ...	NOLIN	45x59cm
Partie Orientale du Canada Traduitte de l'Anglois de la Carte de Jefferys ...	LE ROUGE	46x60cm
Partie Septentrionale de l'Ancienne Germanie	MALLET	17x11cm
Partie Septentrionale de l'Ocean Pacifique ou l'On A Marque les ...	POIRSON	35x46cm
Partie Septentrionale du Cercle d'Autriche qui Comprend l'Archiduche ...	DE VAUGONDY	50x63cm
Parts of Eastern and Southeastern Arizona, Western and Southwestern ...	U.S.	41x51cm
Parts of Western Wyoming and Southeastern Idaho	U.S. GEOLOGICAL SURV.	58x59cm
Pas-Caart Vant Canaal Vertgonende in 't Gheheel Engelandt, Schotlandt ...	GOOS	45x55cm
Pas-Caert van de Levant ...	DONCKER	41x51cm
Pas-caerte van Groenlandt, Yslandt, Straet Davids en Ian Mayen Eylant ...	DONCKER	43x53cm
Pas Caerte van Nieu Nederlandt en de Engelsche Virginies van Cabo Cod ...	GOOS	44x53cm
Pas-caerte vant in Comen van de Canael ...	VAN LOON	43x53cm
Pas Kaart van Rio Oronoque Golfo de Paria met d'Eylanden Trinidad ...	VAN KEULEN	52x59cm
Pas-Kaart van de Grand Banq by Terra Neuff met Alle Syn Diepten ...	VAN KEULEN	52x60cm
Pas-Kaart van Europa ... 1665 ...	DONCKER	42x52cm
Pas-Kaart vande Zee Kusten van Niew Nederland Anders Genaamt ...	VAN KEULEN	51x56cm
Pas Kaert van 'T Oostelycke Deel der Middelandsche Zee ...	DONCKER	41x51cm
Pascaart Vant Canaal tusschen Engelant en Vrancryck, alsmede geheel ...	JANSSON	43x55cm
Pascaarte van de Mont van de Witte Zee	GOOS	26x36cm
Pascaarte van Hispangien van de Zuyd Syde van Yrlandt tot de Straet	COLOM	54x64cm
Pascaarte van Nieu Nederlandt ...	COLOM	55x64cm
Pascaarte vande Noorder Zee Custen van America, vande West-hoeck ...	VAN KEULEN	50x58cm
Pascaarte Verrthoonende de Mont vande Teemse de Rivier van Londen ...	BLAEU	25x36cm
Pascaert, vande Westkust van Schotlant, als Mede een Gedeelte ...	VAN KEULEN	51x58cm
Pascaert van't Westelyckste Deel vande Middelandsche Zee ...	VAN LOON	31x46cm
Pascaerte vande West en Oost-Zyde van Iutlandt ...	JACOBSZ	43x72cm
Pascaerte Vertoonende de Mont vande Teemse en Voort de Custe ...	COLOM	38x53cm
Paskaart van de Boght van Florida met de Canaal Tusschen Florida ...	VAN KEULEN	52x59cm
Paskaart vande Noord Cust van Schotland als Mede de Eylanden ...	VAN KEULEN	51x58cm
Paskaart van het Suydelijckste van America van Rio de la Plata ...	GOOS	44x55cm
Paskaert van 'T Westelycke Deel der Middelandsche Zee ...	DONCKER	41x51cm
Paskaerte van Nova Granada, en t'Eylandt California	GOOS	44x54cm
Paskaerte vande Archipel ...	VAN KEULEN	50x58cm
Patavia	SCHEDEL	20x52cm
Patriarchatus Antiocheni Geographica Descriptio Tabularum Geographicarum ...	TAVERNIER	37x50cm
Pays Bas Catholiques	MALLET	17x11cm
Pedemontana Regio cum Genvensium Territorio & Montisferrati ...	MERCATOR (Folio)	35x45cm
Peking	VAN MEURS	20x32cm
Pekoa Channel and Wawa Channel, Espiritu Santo Is., New Hebrides	BRITISH ADMIRALTY	64x97cm
Penang or Prince of Wales Island	BRITISH ADMIRALTY	62x47cm
Peninsula del Indo de Esta Parte del Golfo del Ganges [on sheet with] ...	LASO	13x16cm
Pennsylvania	ARROWSMITH & LEWIS	22x27cm
Pennsylvania	CRAM	41x57cm
Pennsylvania & New Jersey	ASHER & ADAMS	41x57cm
Pennsylvania, Virginia, Delaware and Maryland	JOHNSON	44x60cm
Pensacola Harbour Reduced from the Surveys of Maj. Kearney	BLUNT	25x20cm
Pensylvania Nova Jersey et Nova York cum Regionibus ad Fluvium ...	LOTTER	58x50cm
Peregrinationis Divi Pauli Typus Corographicus ...	ORTELIUS (Folio)	34x50cm
Perigrinatie ofte Veertich-Iarige Reyse der Kinderen Israels uyt Egypten ...	VISSCHER	30x48cm
Perou et Bresil	MALTE-BRUN	22x30cm
Persia	BEER	10x13cm
Persia	MOLL (Small)	23x19cm
Persia Nuova Tavola	RUSCELLI	18x25cm
Persian Gulf from the Original by D'Anville	HARRISON	29x43cm
Persici sive Sophorum Regni Typus	ORTELIUS (Folio)	35x50cm
Perthshire	PHILIP, G.	15x17cm
Peru	BLAEU	38x49cm
Peru	LUCAS	38x28cm
Peru and Bolivia	BURR	38x30cm

Title	Author	Size
Peruani Regni Descriptio	WYTFLIET	23x29cm
Perusia	SCHEDEL	19x22cm
Peruvia id Est Novi Orbis Pars Meridionalis a Praestantissima Eius in ...	QUAD	21x28cm
Petersburg and Five Forks ...	U.S. WAR DEPARTMENT	56x79cm
Petites Antilles ou Isles du Vent	BELLIN (Small)	23x32cm
Phaenomena circa Quanitatem Dierum Artificialum et Solarium Perpetuo ...	DOPPELMAYR	51x59cm
Phaenomena in Planetis Primariis quae Facies Diversas, ex Illorum Phasibus ...	DOPPELMAYR	51x58cm
Phalsbourg	MORTIER	21x30cm
Philadelphia	COLTON (Atlas Maps)	38x32cm
Philadelphia	S.D.U.K.	36x30cm
Philadelphia	TANNER	No dimen
Philadelphia	THOMAS, COWPERTHWAIT	41x33cm
Philip's New Plan of London ...	PHILIP, G.	53x77cm
Physical Map of England and Wales with Part of Scotland	NAT'L SOC. FOR PROMOTING	52x37cm
Pianta della Citta di Firenze Rileveta Esattamente nell Anno 1783	MAGNELLI	137x150cm
Pinax Geographicus Patriarchatus Hierosolymitani ...	DE LA RUE	41x53cm
Pisa	SCHEDEL	22x22cm
Pittsburgh [on sheet with] Cincinnati	COLTON (Atlas Maps)	46x38cm
Plan and View of the Island Fernando Noronha ...	BRITISH ADMIRALTY	29x33cm
Plan d'une Partie de l'Ile de Wight et de la Cote de Hampshire ...	DEPOT DE LA MARINE	94x61cm
Plan de a Foret de Compiegne ed de Ses Environs. [Leve en 1772. ...	LOCAL & STATE MAPS	56x76cm
Plan de l'Entree du Port de Bucarelli sur la Cote du Nord Ouest de ...	LA PEROUSE	50x69cm
Plan de l'Ile de l'Ascension	DUPERREY	36x50cm
Plan de l'Ile de St. Jean au Nord de l'Acadie ... Suivant l'Arpentage ...	DEPOT DE LA MARINE	43x60cm
Plan de l'Isle de France ...	D'APRES DE MANNEVILLETTE	50x72cm
Plan de l'Isle Rodrigues	D'APRES DE MANNEVILLETTE	33x49cm
Plan de l'Isthme de l'Acadie Comprenant le Beau-Bassin avec une Partie ...	DEPOT DE LA MARINE	39x58cm
Plan de la Baie de Gabarus Situee a la Cote S.E. de l'Ile Royale ...	DEPOT DE LA MARINE	62x90cm
Plan de la Baie de Monterey (Haute Californie) Leve et Dressee en 1837 ...	DEPOT DE LA MARINE	59x88cm
Plan de la Baie de Monterey Situee dans la Californie Septentrionale ...	LA PEROUSE	34x49cm
Plan de la Baie de Narraganset ...	SARTINE	58x41cm
Plan de la Baie et du Havre de Casco et des Iles Adjacentes Par le Cap. ...	SARTINE	41x58cm
Plan de la Baye de Chibouctou Nommee par les Anglois Halifax 1763	BELLIN (Small)	24x37cm
Plan de la Baye de Pensacola	BELLIN (Small)	19x17cm
Plan de la Citidelle de Nancy	MORTIER	11x15cm
Plan de la Nouvelle Orleans	BELLIN (Small)	20x29cm
Plan de la Rade d'Achem et des Isles Circonvoisines ... [Sumatra]	D'APRES DE MANNEVILLETTE	48x33cm
Plan de la Rade de Pirano	DEPOT DE LA MARINE	46x60cm
Plan de la Riviere du Cap Fear depuis la Barre jusques a Brunswick	SARTINE	58x42cm
Plan de la Ville d'Axel	MORTIER	11x15cm
Plan de la Ville d'Ipre	MORTIER	11x15cm
Plan de la Ville de Burick	MORTIER	11x15cm
Plan de la Ville de Charleroi	MORTIER	11x15cm
Plan de la Ville de Guermsheim	MORTIER	11x15cm
Plan de la Ville de Jerusalem telle qu'elle Est Descrite dans les Livres ...	ANONYMOUS	34x40cm
Plan de la Ville de Kaiserswert	MORTIER	11x16cm
Plan de la Ville de Louisbourg dans l'Isle Royale	BELLIN (Small)	23x37cm
Plan de la Ville de Quebec	BELLIN (Small)	19x28cm
Plan de la Ville de Spire	MORTIER	11x16cm
Plan de la Ville de Treues	MORTIER	11x15cm
Plan de la Ville de Valenciennes	MORTIER	11x15cm
Plan de la Ville de Wesel	MORTIER	11x15cm
Plan de la Ville et Chasteau de Bouillon	MORTIER	11x16cm
Plan de la Ville et Citadelle de Nuiss	MORTIER	11x16cm
Plan de la Ville et Citidelle de Tournay	MORTIER	11x15cm
Plan de la Ville et du Fort de Rees	MORTIER	11x15cm
Plan de la Ville et du Port de Louisbourg leve en 1756. Suivant l'Original ...	DEPOT DE LA MARINE	46x61cm
Plan de Paris ...	LOBINEAU	61x85cm
Plan de Paris ... Dessine et Grave sous les Ordres de Michel Etienne ...	BRETEZ	No dimen
Plan de Salangor et de la Cote de Malaye depuis la Pointe de Caran ...	D'APRES DE MANNEVILLETTE	48x33cm
Plan de Strasbourg	MORTIER	23x33cm
Plan de Tripoly en Barbarie	MORTIER	23x29cm
Plan de Ville et du Chateau de Batavia en l'Isle de Iava	VAN DER AA	27x36cm
Plan des Cotes de Terre Neuve IIIe. Feuille Contenant le Partie Meridionale ...	COOK	66x96cm
Plan des Environs de Raguse [Dubrovnik]	DEPOT DE LA MARINE	90x60cm
Plan des Environs de Sebenico	DEPOT DE LA MARINE	90x60cm
Plan des Hafens und Festung Louisbourg auf der Insul Cap Breton ...	RASPE	23x37cm
Plan des Ports de Molonta	DEPOT DE LA MARINE	46x60cm

Plan des Villes, et Chasteau de Creutzhnac au Palatinat du Rhin	MORTIER	11x15cm
Plan du Bassin et de la Riviere du Port Royal ou Annapolis, dans l'Acadie ...	DEPOT DE LA MARINE	42x61cm
Plan du Fort de Skenk	MORTIER	11x15cm
Plan du Golfe de Cattaro	DEPOT DE LA MARINE	90x60cm
Plan du Port Dauphin, de la Rade de Ste. Anne, de l'Entree de Labrador ...	DEPOT DE LA MARINE	44x61cm
Plan du Port de la Riviere St. Jean Situe a la Cote Septentrionale ...	DEPOT DE LA MARINE	62x39cm
Plan du Port de Parenzo [on sheet with] Plan du Port d'Umago [and] ...	DEPOT DE LA MARINE	46x60cm
Plan du Port et du Carenage de Cariacoua Situe dans Paris	BELLIN (Small)	17x22cm
Plan du Port et Ville de Civita-Vecchia	BELLIN (Small)	22x17cm
Plan du Porto-Quieto	DEPOT DE LA MARINE	46x60cm
Plan du Principal Port de l'Ile de Porto Rico Leve ... par Ordre du Ministre ...	DEPOT DE LA MARINE	40x56cm
Plan et Distribution de la Terre de Chanaan Suivant le Vision d'Ezechiel ...	CALMET	32x44cm
Plan Explanatory of the Passage of the Red-Sea, by the Israelites	TAYLOR	20x34cm
Plan Geometral de la Ville & du Port de Malte	VARIN	28x35cm
Plan of Baltimore	MITCHELL, S.A. (1860+)	25x29cm
Plan of Boston	MITCHELL, S.A. (1860+)	38x29cm
Plan of Boston Comprising a Part of Charlestown and Cambridge	SMITH, GEORGE	53x53cm
Plan of Cincinnati and Vicinity	MITCHELL, S.A. (1860+)	28x29cm
Plan of Fort Henry and Its Outworks ... [TN]	U.S. WAR DEPARTMENT	38x43cm
Plan of Fort Jackson, Showing the Effect of the Bombardment by the U.S....	U.S. COAST SURVEY	32x47cm
Plan of Gibraltar.	GENTLEMAN'S MAG.	17x45cm
Plan of London and Westminster	WYLD	57x105cm
Plan of New Orleans	BRADLEY	20x24cm
Plan of New Orleans	MITCHELL, S.A. (1860+)	20x24cm
Plan of New Orleans the Capital of Louisiana; with the Disposition of ...	JEFFERYS	33x49cm
Plan of New York ...	MITCHELL, S.A. (1860+)	33x27cm
Plan of Port St. Francisco in California ...	LA PEROUSE	36x24cm
Plan of Port St. Francisco, in California / Point de Reyes in 37°59' ...	LA PEROUSE	36x24cm
Plan of Portland Harbour [ME]	BLUNT	18x10cm
Plan of Spencer's Bay on the West Coast of Africa	BRITISH ADMIRALTY	29x15cm
Plan of St Petersburg; with It's Fortifications, Built by Peter the Great ...	GENTLEMAN'S MAG.	19x24cm
Plan of the African Islands from the Observations of Lieut Campbell ...	BRITISH ADMIRALTY	29x22cm
Plan of the Aguada Nueva de Puerto Rico	JEFFERYS	24x18cm
Plan of the Battle-Field at Bull Run, July 21st 1861 [on sheet with] ...	U.S. UNION & CONFED.	41x69cm
Plan of the Bay of Monterey Situate in North California in 36°38' ...	LA PEROUSE	25x37cm
Plan of the Bays of Polkerris and Mevagizey in Cornwall	LAURIE & WHITTLE	66x47cm
Plan of the City and Citidel of Antwerp ...	TINDAL	38x48cm
Plan of the City of Aberdeen	BRITISH GOVERNMENT	44x56cm
Plan of the City of Bouchain Situated upon the Rivers Sensette and Scheld ...	RAPIN	37x47cm
Plan of the City of St. Paul and Vicinity	ANDREAS	41x67cm
Plan of the City of Washington	ANONYMOUS	22x25cm
Plan of the City of Washington in the Territory of Columbia ...	WINTERBOTHAM	40x53cm
Plan of the City of Washington, in the Territory of Columbia, Ceded by ...	ELLICOTT	40x52cm
Plan of the Entrance of the Port of Bucarelli on the North West Coast ...	ROBINSON	38x48cm
Plan of the Front Part of the City of New Orleans in 1818	U.S.	19x55cm
Plan of the Grounds and Buildings of the Centennial Exhibition, at Phila ...	LOCAL & STATE MAPS	44x59cm
Plan of the Harbour and Settlement of Pensacola	JEFFERYS	18x26cm
Plan of the Inlets of Ferrol Coruna and Betanzos ...	BRITISH ADMIRALTY	44x57cm
Plan of the Investment and Attack of York in Virginia	MARSHALL	23x21cm
Plan of the Island of Fernand de Noronha ...	LAURIE & WHITTLE	48x60cm
Plan of the Island Rodriguez. Commonly called Diego Rays Island ...	SAYER & BENNETT	33x48cm
Plan of the Last Division of the Town of Chester [MA]	MANUSCRIPT MAPS	No dimen
Plan of the Part of the Isthmus of Panama Eligible for Effecting a ...	LLOYD	45x40cm
Plan of the Port of S. Diego in California Situate in 32°39'0" Latitude ...	LA PEROUSE	36x24cm
Plan of the Port of Subec ... Survey'd in the Year 1776 ...	LAURIE & WHITTLE	47x32cm
Plan of the Port of Tchesme in the Strait of Scio ...	BRITISH ADMIRALTY	29x27cm
Plan of the River & Sound of Dawfoskee in South Carolina	SAYER & BENNETT	64x45cm
Plan of the Route of the Expedition of Major Beall ... for the Relief of ...	U.S. WAR DEPARTMENT	20x13cm
Plan of the Straits of Banca	SAYER	47x33cm
Plan of the Town and Citidel of Fort Royal the Capital of Martinico. ...	JEFFERYS	30x36cm
Plan of the Town and Fortifications of Gibraltar ...	TINDAL	38x60cm
Plan of the Town and Fortifications of Montreal or Ville Marie in Canada	JEFFERYS	33x51cm
Plan of the Town and Fortifications of Montreal or Ville Marie in Canada	UNIVERSAL MAGAZINE	24x36cm
Plan of the Town and Harbour of San Juan de Puerto Rico	JEFFERYS	21x30cm
Plan of the Town and Harbour of St. Augustine	JEFFERYS	20x29cm
Plan of the Town of Basse Terre the Capital of Guadeloupe from an ...	JEFFERYS	33x24cm
Plan of Turin as Besieged in 1706 ...	TINDAL	36x48cm
Plan von Constantinopel, mit der Umliegenden Gegend, und des Canals ...	LOTTER	49x58cm

Title	Author	Size
Plani-Spherium Coeleste	DE AEFFERDEN	14x27cm
Planiglobii Terrestris Mappa Universalis ... / Mappe-Monde Qui Represente ...	HOMANN	46x55cm
Planiglobium Terrestre Minus	WEIGEL	28x35cm
Planisferio Celeste Settentrionale ... [with] ... Meridionale ...	ZATTA	32x40cm
Planisfero del Mondo Nuovo Descritto dal P. Coronelli Cosmografo ...	CORONELLI	46x61cm
Planisfero del Mondo, Vecchio Descritto [in set with] Planisfero del Mondo ...	CORONELLI	45x61cm
Planisfero Settentrionale ... [with] Planisfero Meridionale ...	CORONELLI	46x61cm
Planisphaerium Coeleste	DOPPELMAYR	49x57cm
Planisphaerium Coeleste	LOTTER	49x57cm
Planisphaerium Terrestre cum Utroque Coelesti Haemisphaerio ...	ZURNER	51x58cm
Planisphere de Turquet [on sheet with] Planisphere de Bertius [and] ...	MALLET	14x10cm
Planisphere du Globe Celeste	MARIETTE	38x45cm
Planisphere Suivant la Projection de Mercator	BONNE	21x32cm
Plano del Pto. de San Tomas [Virgin Is.]	DIRECCION DE HIDRO.	18x24cm
Plano del Puerto Principal de la Tortola	DIRECCION DE HIDRO.	18x24cm
Plans of Anchorages in the Grecian Archipelago (Psara Island, ...)	BRITISH ADMIRALTY	46x66cm
Plans of Ports in Wales ...	BRITISH ADMIRALTY	47x61cm
Plymouth Sound, Hamoaze and Catwater Surveyed in 1797	LAURIE & WHITTLE	70x51cm
Pocket Map of Vermont and New Hampshire	CRAM	33x25cm
Poictou. Pictonum Vicinarum ... 1579	ORTELIUS (Folio)	36x50cm
Poland	FISHER	18x21cm
Poland	LONGMAN	19x23cm
Poland	MOLL (Small)	19x19cm
Poland ...	SENEX	66x96cm
Poland by Robt. Morden	MORDEN	11x13cm
Polar-Karte ...	STIELER	32x37cm
Pole Artique	PIQUET	18x20cm
Poli Antarctici ...	JANSSON	18x25cm
Poli Arctici, et Circumiacentium Terrarum Descriptio Novissima	DE WIT	43x49cm
Political Map of the United States ...	WOODBRIDGE	28x44cm
Polonia	SPEED	9x12cm
Polonia et Silesia	MERCATOR (Folio)	34x46cm
Poloniae ...	ORTELIUS (Folio)	37x49cm
Polus Antarcticus Henricus Hondius Excudit	HONDIUS	43x49cm
Polus Antarticus	JANSSON	44x49cm
Polus Arcticus cum Vicinis Regionibus	MERCATOR (Small)	13x19cm
Polus Articus cum Vicinis Regionibus / Hondius His Map of the Arctike Pole ...	PURCHAS	13x18cm
Polynesia	PINKERTON	50x70cm
Polynesia, or Islands in the Pacific Ocean	TALLIS	24x34cm
Polynesien (Inselwelt) oder der Funfte Welttheil Verfafst von Herrn ...	SCHRAEMBL	47x71cm
Polynesien (Inselwelt) oder der Funfte Welttheil Verfafst von Herrn ...	DJURBERG	48x72cm
Pomeraniae, Wandalicae Regionis [on sheet with] Typ. Livoniae ... [and] ...	ORTELIUS (Folio)	39x50cm
Port au Port [Newfoundland]	BRITISH ADMIRALTY	64x97cm
Port de Halifax de la Nouvelle Ecosse avec les Recifs, Dangers, ...	LE ROUGE	49x57cm
Port et Ville de Porto-Rico dans l'Isle de ce Nom	BELLIN (Small)	22x32cm
Port Hudson and Its Defences	MILITARY MAPS	21x17cm
Porte de Louisbourg	LE ROUGE	51x60cm
Porte Rico	OGILBY	28x35cm
Portions of Shrewsbury and Ocean Twps. [NJ: Monmouth Co.]	BEERS	32x53cm
Porto Rico	CRAM	33x55cm
Porto Rico	LUCAS	22x31cm
Porto Rico	MONTANUS	29x35cm
Porto Rico	OGILBY	28x35cm
Porto Rico and Virgin Isles	THOMSON	24x61cm
Porto Rico and Virgin Isles [on sheet with] Haiti, Hispaniola or St. Domingo	THOMSON	53x65cm
Porto Vecchio [Corsica]	BELLIN (Small)	22x18cm
Ports Ibrahim and Thewfik [Suez]	BRITISH ADMIRALTY	65x48cm
Portsmouth Harbor New Hampshire	U.S. COAST SURVEY	47x66cm
Portugal ...	MOLL (Small)	25x19cm
Portugal und die Azoren	HILDBURGHAUSEN BIBLIO.	26x20cm
Portugallia	ORTELIUS (Miniature)	8x10cm
Portugalliae ...	ORTELIUS (Folio)	34x51cm
Position of the Detachment under Lieut. Col. Baum, at Walmscock Near ...	FADEN	27x35cm
Pourtraict et Description de la Grande Cite de Temistitan, ou, Tenuctutlan ...	ANONYMOUS	13x16cm
Praga ...	MUNSTER	12x15cm
Praga Celeberrima et Maxima Totius Bohemiae Metropolis et Universitatis ...	SEUTTER	49x58cm
Preliminary Chart of Hudson River from Teller's Point to the Mouth	U.S. COAST SURVEY	97x38cm
Preliminary Map of Central Colorado Showing the Region Surveyed in ...	U.S. GEOLOGICAL SURV.	64x57cm

Title	Author	Size
Preliminary Sketch of the Northern Pacific Rail Road Exploration and ...	U.S. PACIFIC R.R. SURV.	58x86cm
Premiere Partie de l'Hemisphere Celeste Septentrional ... [with] ...	ANONYMOUS	29x29cm
Presbiteri Iohannis, Sive, Abissinorum Imperii Descriptio	ORTELIUS (Folio)	37x44cm
Presbiteri Johannis, Sive, Abissinorum Imperii Descriptio	ORTELIUS (Folio)	38x47cm
Prima Tavola [Africa]	RAMUSIO	28x38cm
Primae Partis Asiae Acurata Delineatio ...	DE JODE	30x51cm
Principaute de Transilvenie Divisee en Cinq Nations Subdivisee en ...	DE FER (Large)	45x50cm
Progress Map of the U.S. Geographical Surveys West of the 100th Meridian	U.S. WAR DEPARTMENT	41x56cm
Propriae Lugudunensis Generalitatis Mappa Chorographia Insuas V. ...	HOMANN	47x57cm
Province of Canada	BLACKWOOD	44x56cm
Provinces Unies	MALLET	17x11cm
Provincia de Brasil cum Adiacentibus Provinciis	DE LAET	29x36cm
Provincia, La Provence	MERCATOR (Small)	13x19cm
Provinciae Sitae ad Fretum Magallanis itemque Fretum le Maire	DE LAET	28x36cm
Provincie Meridionali de Paesi Bassi, Intese Sotto Nome di Flandra, ...	ROSSI	37x51cm
Provinz Ost-Preussen	HILDBURGHAUSEN BIBLIO.	26x20cm
Prussia	MERCATOR (Folio)	35x45cm
Prussia	WILKINSON	22x28cm
Ptolemaisch General Tafel	MUNSTER	25x34cm
Ptolemeisch General Tafel / Die Halbe Kugel der Weltbegreiffende	MUNSTER	32x36cm
Puerto Rico	RAND, McNALLY (Atlas Maps)	22x30cm
Puerto Rico ...	U.S. COAST SURVEY	55x84cm
Puget Sound	U.S. COAST SURVEY	71x43cm
Puglia Piana, Terra di Barri, Terra di Otranto, Calabria et Basilicata ...	MERCATOR (Folio)	34x46cm
Quebec	COVENS & MORTIER	13x26cm
Quebec	CREPY	18x22cm
Quebec, Ville de l'Amerique Septentrionale dans la Nouvelle France ...	DE FER (Small)	21x29cm
Quebec, Ville de l'Amerique Septentrionale dans la Nouvelle France	MORTIER	21x29cm
Quebek, de Hoofdstad van Kanada; aan de Rivier van St. Laurens: ...	TIRION	33x43cm
Quercy Cadurcium	MERCATOR (Folio)	38x50cm
Quivirae Regnu, cum Alijs versus Borea	DE JODE	37x45cm
Railroad & County Map of Florida	GRANT	57x41cm
Railroad and County Map of Indian Territory / Indian Ty.	GRANT	41x56cm
Railroad and County Map of Montana	GRANT	41x57cm
Railroad Map of Illinois ...	RAND, McNALLY (Atlas Maps)	71x43cm
Railroad Map of New Mexico	LOCAL & STATE GOV'T	91x97cm
Rand, McNally & Co.'s Arizona	RAND, McNALLY (Atlas Maps)	33x51cm
Rand McNally & Co.'s California	RAND, McNALLY (Atlas Maps)	66x51cm
Rand McNally & Co.'s Florida	RAND, McNALLY (Atlas Maps)	50x32cm
Rand, McNally & Co.'s Indexed County and Township Pocket Map ...	RAND, McNALLY (Pocket, etc)	No dimen
Rand McNally & Co.'s Indexed Map of Louisiana	RAND, McNALLY (Pocket, etc)	23x30cm
Rand McNally & Co.'s Indexed Map of Mexico	RAND, McNALLY (Pocket, etc)	48x65cm
Rand McNally & Co.'s Indian Territory and Oklahoma	RAND, McNALLY (Atlas Maps)	33x51cm
Rand McNally & Co.'s Kansas	RAND, McNALLY (Atlas Maps)	51x66cm
Rand McNally & Co.'s Montana	RAND, McNALLY (Atlas Maps)	33x51cm
Rand McNally & Co.'s Nebraska	RAND, McNALLY (Atlas Maps)	51x66cm
Rand, McNally & Co.'s New Indexed Large Scale County ... of Montana	RAND, McNALLY (Pocket, etc)	55x89cm
Rand McNally & Co.'s New Mexico	RAND, McNALLY (Atlas Maps)	51x33cm
Rand McNally & Co.'s Texas	RAND, McNALLY (Atlas Maps)	51x66cm
Rand McNally & Co.'s Washington	RAND, McNALLY (Atlas Maps)	51x66cm
Rand McNally & Co.'s Wyoming	RAND, McNALLY (Atlas Maps)	33x51cm
Raritan [NJ: Monmouth Co.]	BEERS	29x39cm
Rebel Line of Works at Blakely Captured by the Army of West Miss., ...	U.S. WAR DEPARTMENT	25x38cm
Recens Edita Totius Novi Belgii, in America Septentrionali Siti, Delineatio ...	SEUTTER	50x57cm
Recens et Accurata Designatio Episcopatus Paderbornensis	SEUTTER	50x55cm
Recentissima Novi Orbis sive Americae Septentrionalis et Meridionalis ...	ALLARD	50x58cm
Reconnaissance Map of Mt. McKinley Region Alaska	U.S. GEOLOGICAL SURV.	46x30cm
Reconnaissance of the Western Coast of the United States Lower Sheet ...	U.S. COAST & GEODETIC	59x57cm
Reconnaissance of the Western Coast of the United States from Gray's ...	U.S. COAST SURVEY	37x44cm
Reconnaissance of the Western Coast of the United States from San Fran ...	U.S. COAST SURVEY	58x58cm
Reconnoissances in the Dakota Country by G.K. Warren ...	U.S. WAR DEPARTMENT	91x152cm
Red Bank [NJ: Monmouth Co.]	BEERS	53x61cm
Regio Canaan seu Terra Promissionis Postea Iudaea vel Palestina Nominata ...	SEUTTER	50x58cm
Regiones Sub Polo Arctico ...	BLAEU	41x53cm
Regionum Circumpolarium Lapponiae Islandiae et Groenlandiae Nova et ...	SCHERER	23x35cm
Regni & Insulae Siciliae Tabula Geographica ...	HOMANN	46x55cm
Regni Angliae et Walliae Principatus Tabula, Divisa in LII Regiones, ...	DE L'ISLE	50x59cm

Title	Author	Size
Regni Bohemiae Descriptio	ORTELIUS (Folio)	34x50cm
Regni Bohemiae Nova Descriptio	VAN DEN KEERE	39x51cm
Regni Daniae ...	HOMANN	49x57cm
Regni Hungariae ...	HOMANN	47x57cm
Regni Mexicani seu Novae Hispaniae Ludovicianae, N. Angliae, Carolinae ...	HOMANN	48x57cm
Regni Poloniae et Ducatus Lithuaniae, Voliniae, Podoliae, Prussiae, ...	DE WIT	49x56cm
Regni Sinae vel Sinae Propriae Mappa et Descriptio Geographica ...	HOMANN	58x52cm
Regno di Danimarca Diviso nelle Sue Due Jutlandie Cioe Settentrionale ...	ROSSI	41x52cm
Regnorum Hungariae Dalmatiae, Croatiae, Sclavoniae Bosniae et Serviae ...	HOMANN	48x58cm
Regnum Chinae	BOTERO	16x21cm
Regnum Hiberniae, Tam Secundum IV Provincias Principales Ultoniam, ...	SEUTTER	58x50cm
Regnum Hispaniae	DU VAL	10x12cm
Regnum Moreae Accuratissime Divisum in Provincias Saccaniam ...	LOTTER	50x59cm
Regnum Portugalliae ... Regno Algarbiae ...	HOMANN	59x45cm
Regnum Salomonicum ...	MORTIER	39x53cm
Regnum Salomonicum seu Tabula Digesta ad Libros Judicum Regnum	DE LA RUE	39x53cm
Reise Charte durch das Konigreich Bohmen Hertzzogthum Schlesi en ...	SCHREIBER	18x28cm
Reise Charte durch Deutschland ...	PROBST	17x20cm
Reise Charte durch Deutschland ...	SCHREIBER	18x28cm
Reise Charte durch Frankreich in Seine 12 Provintzion ...	SCHREIBER	18x20cm
Reise Charte durch Oesterreich ...	SCHREIBER	18x28cm
Reisen der Kinder von Israel aus Egypten	BUNTING	26x36cm
Remote British Islands [Channel Islands, Scilly Islands, Wight, Mann]	THOMSON	52x62cm
Repraesentatio Totius Orbis Terraquei ... Catholica	SCHERER	23x35cm
Representatio Totius Africae ...	SCHERER	22x34cm
Rheinfels [St. Goar, Germany]	MORTIER	21x26cm
Rheinprovinz Neiderrhein	HILDBURGHAUSEN BIBLIO.	20x26cm
Rhode Island	FINLEY	29x22cm
Rhode Island	PAYNE	24x19cm
Rhode-Island and Connecticut	MORSE, J.	20x34cm
Rhodis	VON BREYDENBACH	25x77cm
Richmond ...	U.S. WAR DEPARTMENT	58x79cm
Richtige Anzeige Wie Weit die Haupt-Orte in Deutschland und Andere ...	LOTTER	47x57cm
Rio Colorado of the West, Map No.1 ...	U.S. WAR DEPARTMENT	39x89cm
Rio de Janeiro Harbour	BRITISH ADMIRALTY	95x62cm
River Dulce in Guatemala	BRITISH ADMIRALTY	47x61cm
River Gaboon	BRITISH ADMIRALTY	64x97cm
River of St. Lawrence, from Chaudiere to Lake St. Francis ...	DES BARRES	77x316cm
Road & Railroad Map of Porto Rico	U.S.	33x62cm
Roma	BRAUN & HOGENBERG	33x48cm
Roma	SCHEDEL	23x53cm
Romani Imperii Imago	ORTELIUS (Folio)	34x49cm
Route Near the 47th and 49th Parallels. Map No. 3. Rocky Mountains to ...	U.S. PACIFIC R.R. SURV.	62x92cm
Route of the Expedition from York Factory to Cumberland House and ...	FRANKLIN, J.	25x56cm
Routes in Oregon and California. Map No. 2. From the Northern Boundary ...	U.S. PACIFIC R.R. SURV.	69x59cm
Royaume d'Angleterre	MALLET	17x11cm
Royaume d'Irlande	MALLET	16x11cm
Royaume d'Irlande ...	DE VAUGONDY	49x55cm
Royaume de Chili	MALLET	17x11cm
Royaume de Danemarck, qui Comprend le Nort-Jutland ... et les Isles ...	DE VAUGONDY	50x58cm
Royaume des Amazones	MALLET	15x10cm
Royaumes d'Espagne	DE VAUGONDY	16x18cm
Ru Ruag to Gruinard Bay Including Loch Ewe and Gairloch	BRITISH ADMIRALTY	95x62cm
Ruatan or Rattan ...	LE ROUGE	46x60cm
Rubeaquum Rufach	MUNSTER	24x35cm
Rugia Insula ...	BLAEU	38x50cm
Russiae, Moscoviae et Tartariae Descriptio. Auctore Antonio Ienkensono...	ORTELIUS (Folio)	35x44cm
S. Giovanni	PORCACCHI	10x14cm
Sabaudia Ducatus. Savoye	JANSSON	38x50cm
Sabaudiae	BEER	10x13cm
St. Augus de Floride	MALLET	15x11cm
St. Christophers	LUCAS	22x31cm
St. Helena Island	BRITISH ADMIRALTY	45x61cm
St. John's Harbour to Boon Point [Antigua]	BRITISH ADMIRALTY	62x94cm
St. Johns, Antigua	GOAD	62x51cm
St. Louis and Adjacent Country	MELISH	17x10cm
St. Mary's Pool	BRITISH ADMIRALTY	34x27cm
Salczburga	SCHEDEL	24x53cm

Title	Author	Size
Salisburgensis Jurisdictionis ...	ORTELIUS (Folio)	34x44cm
Saltzburg Archiepiscopatus cum Ducatu Carinthiae	MERCATOR (Folio)	35x45cm
Saltzburg et Carinthie	MERCATOR (Small)	13x18cm
San Francisco	GRAY	38x30cm
San Francisco Peninsula	U.S. COAST SURVEY	72x43cm
San Juan Porto-Rico. Limits of Lands to Be Retained by the Navy Dept. ...	U.S.	35x50cm
San Juan Harbor Puerto Rico	U.S. COAST SURVEY	83x100cm
Santander	BRAUN & HOGENBERG	32x36cm
Sardinia	ORTELIUS (Miniature)	8x12cm
Saxonia Inferior	WEIGEL	33x39cm
Saxonia Inferior et Meklenborg	MERCATOR (Small)	14x20cm
Saxonia Inferior et Meklenborg Duc.	MERCATOR (Folio)	35x45cm
Saxonia Superior	WEIGEL	33x38cm
Saxoniae, Misniae, Thuringiae ...	ORTELIUS (Folio)	35x50cm
Scandia. Sive Regiones Septentrionales	MAGINI	13x17cm
Scandinavia ...	PROBST	17x20cm
Scandinavia Complectens Sueciae, Daniae & Norvegiae Regna ...	HOMANN	48x57cm
Scheeps Togt van Iamaica Gedaan na Panuco en Rio De Las Palmas ...	VAN DER AA	15x22cm
Scheeps-Togt door Ferdinand Magellaan	VAN DER AA	15x22cm
Schets van het Kanaal van Nootka	COOK	26x21cm
Schwaben und Baierland Dar Ben auch Begriffen Werden Schwarzwald ...	MUNSTER	26x35cm
Sclavonia, Croatia, Bosnia cum Dalmatiae Parte	MERCATOR (Folio)	35x45cm
Scotia	BEER	10x13cm
Scotia Meridionalis [and] Scotia Septentrionalis	MERCATOR (Small)	13x19cm
Scotia Regnum	JANSSON	38x50cm
Scotia Regnum	MERCATOR (Folio)	35x40cm
Scotiae Nova Descriptio per Robert Morden	MORDEN	14x12cm
Scotiae Tabula	ORTELIUS (Folio)	36x48cm
Scotland	GUTHRIE & JONES	19x22cm
Scotland	S.D.U.K.	40x31cm
Scotland	TALLIS	30x22cm
Scotland	THOMAS, COWPERTHWAIT	31x25cm
Scotland I ...	S.D.U.K.	27x38cm
Scotland II ...	S.D.U.K.	33x40cm
Scotland III Orkneys, Shetlands and Hebrides ...	S.D.U.K.	35x32cm
Scotland with the Principal Roads from the Best Authorities	CAREY, M.	36x28cm
Seabright & Monmouth Beach Property [NJ: Monmouth Co.]	BEERS	39x29cm
Seat of War in Virginia and Maryland, Sheet 1	WEEKLY DISPATCH	46x33cm
Seat of War in Virginia and Maryland. Sheet 1 [in set with] ... Sheet 2 ...	WEEKLY DISPATCH	31x46cm
Seat of War in Virginia, Sheet 2	WEEKLY DISPATCH	46x33cm
Seattle, Washington	CRAM	34x25cm
Second Part of a Map of Asia, Containing China, Part of Tartary and India ...	HARRISON	72x50cm
Secunda Asiae Tabula	PTOLEMY (1478-1508)	40x35cm
Sena	SCHEDEL	19x22cm
Senensis Ditionis ... / Corsica / Marcha Ancona ...	ORTELIUS (Folio)	33x49cm
Septentrionalium Pertium Nova Tabula	RUSCELLI	19x24cm
Septentrionalium Regionum Descrip.	ORTELIUS (Folio)	36x49cm
Septentrionalium Terrarum Descriptio	CLOPPENBURGH	18x25cm
Septentrionalium Terrarum Descriptio	HONDIUS	37x39cm
Septentrionalium Terrarum Descriptio. Per Gerardum Mercatorem ...	MERCATOR (Folio)	37x39cm
Septima Asiae Tabula	PTOLEMY (1478-1508)	29x53cm
Settentrionale Inglese e Russo, Groenlandia, Island, Terre Artiche ...	MARZOLLA	43x59cm
Several Appearances of the Agoada Fort near the Island of Goa ...	LAURIE & WHITTLE	19x32cm
Sevilla	BRAUN & HOGENBERG	36x48cm
Sevilla Hispalis	BRAUN & HOGENBERG	38x50cm
Sharp's Corresponding Maps No.6. England and Wales Railway Map	SHARP	67x46cm
Sheet 1 Point de Monts to Bersimis River [St. Lawrence River]	BRITISH ADMIRALTY	46x64cm
Sheet 1, Western States, United States	PHILIP, G.	51x61cm
Sheet 3 Green Island to the Pilgrims [St. Lawrence River]	BRITISH ADMIRALTY	46x64cm
Sheet No.1. Mississippi River, Rodney, St. Joseph, Bruinsburg. ...	U.S. COAST SURVEY	30x42cm
Sheet No.2. Mississippi River Grand Gulf, Turner's Pt., New Carthage ...	U.S. COAST SURVEY	52x41cm
Sheet Number 9. The 'Half Inch' Map of England for Cyclists, Tourists. .	GALL & INGLIS	51x64cm
Sicilia	BEER	10x13cm
Sicilia & Sardinia Nova Tabula	GASTALDI	13x17cm
Silesiae Ducatus tam Superior quam Inferior ...	SEUTTER	52x58cm
Silesiae Typus Descriptus et Editus a Martino Heilwig ... 1561	ORTELIUS (Folio)	28x38cm
Sito & Figura di Francofordia Citta, Come E nel 1546	MUNSTER	25x40cm
Situs Partium Praecipuarum Totius Orbis Terrarum	TORNIELLO	19x37cm

Skeleton Map of the St. Louis & San Francisco Railway and Connections	RAILROAD CO. MAPS	17x52cm
Sketch 11 Showing the Progress of the Survey in Section No.8	U.S. COAST SURVEY	37x85cm
Sketch Accompanying Col. Price Despatch	U.S. WAR DEPARTMENT	24x29cm
Sketch F Section VI Coast of Florida 1848-61	U.S. COAST SURVEY	64x42cm
Sketch F Section VI Western Coast of Florida 1848-51	U.S. COAST SURVEY	58x41cm
Sketch II showing the Progress of the Survey in Section No. VIII ...	U.S. COAST SURVEY	49x84cm
Sketch J. No. 3 Showing the Progress of the Survey of Washington Sound ...	U.S. COAST SURVEY	41x34cm
Sketch of a Days Travel [New Mexico]	U.S.	19x13cm
Sketch of General Grants Position on Long Island ...	STEDMAN	36x28cm
Sketch of General Riley's Route Through the Mining Districts ... 1849	U.S.	54x50cm
Sketch of Nootka Sound	COOK	33x21cm
Sketch of Part of Louisiana Accompanying a Report of the Commissioner ...	U.S.	57x47cm
Sketch of Part of the March & Wagon Road of Lt. Colonel Cooke from ...	U.S. WAR DEPARTMENT	30x56cm
Sketch of Public Surveys in New Mexico & Arizona	U.S. STATE SURVEYS	53x71cm
Sketch of Sydney Cove, Port Jackson in the County of Cumberland, ...	STOCKDALE	45x45cm
Sketch of the Country Between South Pass & the Great Salt Lake	U.S. WAR DEPARTMENT	45x56cm
Sketch of the Country Illustrating the Late Engagement in Long Island.	GENTLEMAN'S MAG.	20x31cm
Sketch of the Harbour of Samganooda on the Island Oonalaska	COOK	20x33cm
Sketch of the North Eastern Boundary Between Great Britain and ...	WYLD	24x33cm
Sketch of the Passage of the Rio San Gabriel, Upper California by the ...	U.S. WAR DEPARTMENT	13x21cm
Sketch of the Public Surveys in Kansas and Nebraska	U.S. STATE SURVEYS	51x29cm
Sketch of the Public Surveys in Wisconsin and Territory of Minnesota	U.S. STATE SURVEYS	44x53cm
Sketch of the Routes of Hunt & Stuart	IRVING, W.	25x44cm
Sketch of the South West Pass at and near the Gulf of Mexico	U.S. COAST SURVEY	93x67cm
Sketch of the Vicinity of Fort Fisher ... by Otto Julian Schultze, ...	U.S. WAR DEPARTMENT	36x25cm
Sketch of the West Coast of Lombock. From a Draught of Roddin ...	DALRYMPLE	29x19cm
Slusa, Teutonicae Flandriae Opp. Admodum Elegans.	BRAUN & HOGENBERG	29x41cm
Sneecha, vulgo Sneek Frisiae Occidentalis ... Sloten. Doccum. Yista.	BRAUN & HOGENBERG	35x41cm
Soil map - Porto Rico, Arecibo Sheet	U.S.	99x51cm
Somerset-shire	SPEED	37x51cm
Soria et Terra Santa Nuova Tavola	RUSCELLI	19x24cm
Sound of Barra	BRITISH ADMIRALTY	98x66cm
Sound of Islay	BRITISH ADMIRALTY	97x64cm
Sourie ou Terre Saincte Modern	DE LA RUE	54x39cm
South Africa ...	S.D.U.K.	34x40cm
South America	BURR	38x30cm
South America	COLTON (Atlas Maps)	46x38cm
South America	FINLEY	29x22cm
South America	LUCAS	38x28cm
South America	S.D.U.K.	43x36cm
South America	TALLIS	35x25cm
South America [set of 6 maps]	S.D.U.K.	43x36cm
South America West Coast Sheet XIV	BRITISH ADMIRALTY	63x47cm
South Carolina	FINLEY	22x29cm
South Eastern District Louisiana	U.S. STATE SURVEYS	24x29cm
South Mountain Showing the Positions of the Forces of the United States ...	U.S. WAR DEPARTMENT	79x54cm
Southern Africa	PINKERTON	50x69cm
Southern Hemisphere	PINKERTON	Diam 49cm
Southern Hemisphere, Projected on the Plane of the Horizon of London	PHILIP, G.	Diam 51cm
Southern Provinces of the United States ...	THOMSON	52x63cm
Southwest Harbor and Somes Sound, Maine	U.S. COAST SURVEY	55x38cm
Southwestern Colorado Atlas Sheet No. 61 (C)	U.S. WAR DEPARTMENT	43x51cm
Spain and Portugal. [on plate with] A Map of the Mouth of the River ...	GENTLEMAN'S MAG.	23x18cm
Spaine Newly Described ...	SPEED	42x53cm
Spanish Dominions in North America Middle Part	PINKERTON	50x70cm
Spanish Dominions in North America Northern Part	PINKERTON	50x70cm
Spanish Dominions in North America Southern Part	PINKERTON	50x70cm
Spatiosissimum Imperium Russiae Magnae	LOTTER	50x58cm
Specialkarte von Armenien, zur Ubersicht des nach dem Frieden ...	PETERMANN	No dimen
Spezial Karte vom Himalaya in Kumaon, Gurhwal, Sirmur &c.&c.	BERGHAUS	60x84cm
Spherical Chart Comprehending the West Coast of America, from ...	FADEN	86x57cm
Spotsylvania Courthouse, Prepared by Bvt. Brig. Genl. N. Michler ...	U.S. WAR DEPARTMENT	53x79cm
Spry Harbour ... Port Palliser [Mushabook Harbour] ... Port North ...	DES BARRES	103x73cm
Stafford Shire Drawn from an Accurate Survey Corrected from Astronl. ...	LONDON MAGAZINE	22x17cm
Stanford's Map of Metropolitan Railways, Tramways and Other ...	STANFORD	61x97cm
Stanford's Popular Map of the Seat of Military Operations in the Sudan	STANFORD	38x71cm
State of Iowa	U.S. STATE SURVEYS	74x64cm
State of Kansas	U.S. STATE SURVEYS	55x76cm

Title	Cartographer	Size
State of Louisiana	U.S. STATE SURVEYS	86x69cm
State of Montana	U.S. STATE SURVEYS	83x124cm
States of America	FISHER & SON	19x22cm
Stato del Gran Turco Diviso ne Suoi Beglierbati, o Gouverni ...	SANSON (Folio)	44x58cm
Stiria. Per Gerardum Mercatorem	JANSSON	30x42cm
Stockholm / Stocholm	BRAUN & HOGENBERG	32x47cm
Strait of Singapore Sheet II	BRITISH ADMIRALTY	49x64cm
Stromgebiete der Neuen Welt	BERGHAUS	33x42cm
Sudliche und Noerdlich Halbkugel der Erde ...	WEIMAR GEOG. INSTITUT	47x60cm
Sudliches Norwegen	HILDBURGHAUSEN BIBLIO.	26x20cm
Suite du Cours de Fleuve de St. Laurent depuis Quebec jusqu'au Lac Ontario...	BELLIN (Small)	23x34cm
Suite du Plan de la Coste de Malaya depuis Plaira Lisle de Sanselam ...	MANUSCRIPT MAPS	50x71cm
Sumatra	BOHN	47x57cm
Sumatra Ein Grosse Insel ...	MUNSTER	25x33cm
Sumatra West Coast Sheet II Chingkuk Bay to the Strait of Sunda	BRITISH ADMIRALTY	64x100cm
Summaria Descriptio Germaniae Inferioris Antiquae cis & ultra Rhenum ...	ALTING	32x42cm
Supplement pour les Isles Antilles Extrait des Cartes Angloises	BONNE	32x21cm
Surrey	BRITISH ORDNANCE	64x95cm
Survey of Falmouth Harbour and the Coast to The Manacles with Helford ...	BRITISH ADMIRALTY	64x95cm
Survey of Lake Superior. By Lieut. Henry W. Bayfield, R.N. assisted by...	BRITISH ADMIRALTY	90x62cm
Survey of Port Bowen 1819	MURRAY, J.	10x17cm
Survey of Southampton River The Brambles and Cowes Road with ...	BRITISH ADMIRALTY	95x64cm
Survey of Winter Harbour, Melville Island, June 1820	MURRAY, J.	25x17cm
Swabia	WILKINSON	23x28cm
Swansea and Neath	BRITISH ADMIRALTY	29x43cm
Sweden and Norway	MOLL (Small)	19x26cm
Swelly Channel and Approaches	MANUSCRIPT MAPS	41x68cm
Swisserland	PINKERTON	50x70cm
Swolla	GUICCIARDINI	23x31cm
Synopsis Circuli Rhenani Inferioris sive Electorum Rheni, Exhibens ...	SEUTTER	50x58cm
Syria	ARROWSMITH	25x20cm
Syria	CRUCHLEY	46x36cm
Syria	DAVIES	25x18cm
Syria	GRATTAN & GILBERT	29x23cm
Syria	S.D.U.K.	41x32cm
Syria	TALLIS	34x25cm
Systema Ideale Pyrophylaciorum Subterraneorum, Quorum Montes Vulcanii ...	KIRCHER	33x41cm
Systema Solare et Planetarium ex Hypothesi Copernicana	PROBST	17x20cm
'T Eylandt Cyprus ...	DONCKER	40x52cm
'T Koninkryk van China ...	VAN DER AA	15x22cm
T Noorder Deel van Amerika door C. Kolumbus in Zyn Eerste Togt Ontdekt ...	VAN DER AA	20x30cm
'T Suyder-Deel van America Nieulyx Uytgegeven ...	COLOM	40x53cm
T Vaste Land van Darien ...	VAN DER AA	15x22cm
Tab. Mo. Secundae Partis Aphricae	FRIES	31x43cm
Tab.I Geographia et Astronomia	STEINBERGER	19x23cm
Tabu. Nova Orbis	FRIES	28x45cm
Tabu. Terre Sanctae	FRIES	29x42cm
Tabula Aphrica IIII [Northern Africa]	RUSCELLI	20x28cm
Tabula Aphricae II	MAGINI	13x18cm
Tabula Asia V [Persia]	RUSCELLI	20x28cm
Tabula Asiae I [Asia Minor]	RUSCELLI	19x25cm
Tabula Asiae II	MUNSTER	25x33cm
Tabula Asiae IIII	MUNSTER	25x34cm
Tabula Asiae V	MUNSTER	26x34cm
Tabula Asiae VI	MUNSTER	26x34cm
Tabula Asiae VI [Arabia]	RUSCELLI	20x28cm
Tabula Asiae IX	MUNSTER	25x34cm
Tabula Asiae X	MUNSTER	26x34cm
Tabula Asiae XI	MUNSTER	25x34cm
Tabula Asiae XI [Southeast Asia]	GASTALDI	13x17cm
Tabula Asiae XII	MUNSTER	26x34cm
Tabula Europa VI [Italy]	RUSCELLI	20x28cm
Tabula Europae II [Spain & Portugal]	RUSCELLI	20x28cm
Tabula Europae V	MUNSTER	27x33cm
Tabula Europae VII	MAGINI	13x17cm
Tabula Europae VII	MUNSTER	26x34cm
Tabula Europae X	MUNSTER	26x32cm
Tabula Geogr. in qua Admiranda Navigationis Cursus et Recursus Designatur	PONTANUS	27x36cm

Tabula Geogra. Regni Congo	DE BRY	31x38cm
Tabula Geographica Partis Septentrionalis Maris Pacifici cum Adjacentibus ...	VON EULER	33x38cm
Tabula Geographicae Principatus Brandenburg. Culmb. sive Baruthini ...	LOTTER	50x58cm
Tabula Hydrographica Maris Australis Vulgo del Zur, Ductum Navigationis ...	DE BRY	17x41cm
Tabula Ichnographica Accuratissima Brunsuigae...Accurate Ichnographische ...	SEUTTER	50x58cm
Tabula Islandiae Auctore Georgio Carolo Flandro ...	MERCATOR (Folio)	38x49cm
Tabula Magellanica	OGILBY	29x36cm
Tabula Marchionatus Brandenburgici et Ducatus Pomeraniae quae Sunt ...	HOMANN	44x56cm
Tabula Moderna Indiae	FRIES	30x44cm
Tabula Moderna Indiae	WALDSEEMULLER	40x51cm
Tabula Moscoviae nunc Accuratius ... per G. De L'Isle ...	SCHENK	98x62cm
Tabula Nautica, qua Repraesentatur Orae Maritimae Meatus, ac Freta ...	DE BRY	16x34cm
Tabula Nova Indiae Orientalis & Meridionalis	FRIES	28x43cm
Tabula Nova Partis Africae	FRIES	30x40cm
Tabula Novarum Insularum, quas Diversis Respectibus Occidentales & ...	MUNSTER	27x34cm
Tabula Octava Asiae Continet Scythiam Extra Imaum Montem, et Sericam	PTOLEMY (1522-1541)	12x14cm
Tabula Principatus Bradenburgico-Culmbacensis sive Baruthini Pars Superior ...	LOTTER	58x50cm
Tabula qua Hydrophylacium Andium Exhibetur, quo Universa America ...	KIRCHER	34x20cm
Tabula Selenographica in qua Lunarium ... Descriptio ...	HOMANN	49x58cm
Tabula Septima Asiae	PTOLEMY (1522-1541)	28x46cm
Tabula Superioris Indiae & Tartariae Maioris	FRIES	29x46cm
Tabula Synoptica Totius Fluminis Danubii a Fontibus Usque ad Ostia ...	LOTTER	50x58cm
Tabula Terrae Promissae ab Auctore Commentarii Josue Delineata et ...	CALMET	46x23cm
Tabula Tertia Aphricae Continet Cyrenica, quae et Pentapolis, Marmaricam ...	PTOLEMY (1522-1541)	28x44cm
Tabula Tertia Asia	PTOLEMY (1522-1541)	30x42cm
Tabula Tertia D Asia	PTOLEMY (1482 Florence)	35x46cm
Tabulam hanc Aegypti, si Aequus ac Diligens Lector, cum Alys, ...	PIGAFETTA	55x40cm
Tanger ...	SCHENK	21x26cm
Tartaria in Europe	MORDEN	11x13cm
Tartariae Imperium	MAGINI	13x17cm
Tartariae sive Magni Chami Regni Typus	ORTELIUS (Folio)	35x47cm
Taurica Chersonesus	MERCATOR (Small)	38x50cm
Taurica Chersonesus. Nostra Aetate Przecopsca et Gazara Dicitur	BLAEU	38x50cm
Taurica Chersonesus. Nostra Aetate Przecopsca et Gazara Dicitur	MERCATOR (Folio)	32x41cm
Tavola Secondo Moderni [on verso] Tavola Secondo Tolomeo	BORDONE	23x16cm
Tennessee	FINLEY	22x29cm
Tercera	ORTELIUS (Miniature)	8x11cm
Terra Antarctica	BEER	10x13cm
Terra Arctica	BEER	10x13cm
Terra Chanaan ad Abrahami Tempora ...	MORTIER	41x55cm
Terra Chanaan ad Abrahami Tempora per Populos XI ...	DE LA RUE	42x56cm
Terra Filiorum Israelis ... com Terra Philistaeorum, Parte Phoenices	TANNER	27x39cm
Terra Firma et Novum Regnum Granatense et Popayan	OGILBY	29x36cm
Terra Firma et Novum Regnum Granatense et Popayan ...	JANSSON	38x49cm
Terra Magellanica	MORDEN	13x11cm
Terra Moriath sive Solymarum Ager Suburbanus	FULLER	28x34cm
Terra Promissa in Sortes seu Tribus XII Distincta seu Tabula ad Librum ...	DE LA RUE	41x53cm
Terra Sancta a Petro Laicstain Perlustrata, et ab Eius Ore et Schedis ...	ORTELIUS (Folio)	37x50cm
Terra Sancta quae in Sacris Terra Promissionis OI: Palestina	MERCATOR (Folio)	36x50cm
Terra Sancta sive Promissionis olim Palestina in Duo Divisa Regna Israel ...	SANSON (Folio)	42x55cm
Terra Sancta sive Promissionis, Olim Palestina Recens Delineata et ...	DE WIT	46x56cm
Terra Sancta vel Regio Maritima a Libano ad Halakum usque Montem ...	WILLIAMS	31x22cm
Terra Sancta XVI Nova Tabula	MUNSTER	26x34cm
Terra Sancta XXIII. Nova Tabula	MUNSTER	26x34cm
Terre Artiche Descritte dal P.M. Coronelli M.C. Cosmografo della ...	CORONELLI	46x61cm
Territories of New Mexico and Utah	COLTON (Atlas Maps)	31x40cm
Territorium Sac. Rom. Imp. Lib. Civitatis Francofurti ad Moenum cum ...	LOTTER	51x58cm
Territory of Arizona	U.S. STATE SURVEYS	53x43cm
Territory of Idaho	MITCHELL, S.A. (1860+)	35x23cm
Territory of Idaho	U.S. STATE SURVEYS	56x33cm
Territory of Idaho	U.S. STATE SURVEYS	83x55cm
Territory of Montana	MITCHELL, S.A. (1860+)	27x36cm
Teton Forest Reserve and Southern Part of Yellowstone Park Forest Reserve	U.S. GEOLOGICAL SURV.	51x38cm
Texas	BRADFORD	36x29cm
Texas	CRAM	46x64cm
Texas	FLEMMING	40x32cm
Texas	GRANT	41x56cm
Texas	MORSE & BREESE	38x30cm

Title	Author/Publisher	Size
Texas	RAND, McNALLY (Atlas Maps)	51x66cm
Texas	WATSON	29x43cm
Texas, Eastern Section [and] Western Section	RAND, McNALLY (Atlas Maps)	66x48cm
Texas Western Portion	ASHER & ADAMS	57x40cm
Texas, Western Part	CRAM	52x34cm
The Absent-Minded Beggar [South Africa: Transvaal / Orange Free State]	ANONYMOUS	44x46cm
The Arctic Regions of North America	WELLER	31x43cm
The Basin of the Pacific	WYLD	57x84cm
The Bay of Algoa ... [on sheet with] Plan of Mossel Bay ... [and] ...	LAURIE & WHITTLE	58x26cm
The Bay of Honduras	JEFFERYS	47x62cm
The Bermudas, or Summer's Islands from a Survey by C. Lempriere, ...	LAURIE & WHITTLE	46x61cm
The British Channel	THOMSON	50x58cm
The British Channel Including the Coasts of England and France	LODGE	17x30cm
The British Colonies in North America ...	GUTHRIE	33x33cm
The British Governments in Nth. America Laid Down Agreeable to ...	GENTLEMAN'S MAG.	20x23cm
The British Islands in the West Indies	S.D.U.K.	32x39cm
The British Isles	S.D.U.K.	39x32cm
The British Isles	TALLIS	30x23cm
The Cape Verd Islands ...	LAURIE & WHITTLE	53x29cm
The Caspian Sea Drawn by the Czar's Special Command by Carl ...	MOLL (Small)	26x20cm
The Cheife Harbours in the Islands of Orkney ...	COLLINS, G.	46x56cm
The City of Dublin	ILLUS. LONDON NEWS	36x103cm
The City of Louisville Kentucky [and] the City of New Orleans Louisiana	COLTON (Atlas Maps)	36x29cm
The Coal and Gold Fields of Alaska Together with the Principal Steamer ...	U.S. GEOLOGICAL SURV.	61x71cm
The Coast of India and China from the Point and River of Camboja to ...	SAYER & BENNETT	60x45cm
The Coast of India from Mount Dilly to Pondicherry ... with the Island ...	LAURIE & WHITTLE	58x88cm
The Coast of New Found Land from Salmon Cove to Cape Bonavista ...	GRIERSON	41x49cm
The Coast of West Florida and Louisiana ...	JEFFERYS	48x63cm
The Coast of Zanguebar and Aien ...	MORDEN	12x10cm
The Countie of Leinster with the Citie of Dublin Described	SPEED	38x51cm
The County Palantine of Lancaster by Robt. Morden	MORDEN	43x37cm
The Course of Delaware River from Philadelphia to Chester ...	FADEN	44x67cm
The Description of the Whole Coast Lying in the South Seas of Americae ...	WOLFE, J.	38x55cm
The East by Mr. D'Anville ...	D'ANVILLE	27x35cm
The Eastern States with Part of Canada	BROOKES	20x25cm
The Empire of China and Island of Japan ...	MOLL (Small)	25x25cm
The Empire of China with Its Principal Divisions ... From the Maps of ...	LAURIE & WHITTLE	48x63cm
The English Empire in America, Newfound-Land, Canada, Hudsons Bay ...	MOLL (Small)	22x18cm
The Entrance of Havannah, from within the Harbour [on sheet with] ...	DES BARRES	24x45cm
The Entrance to the River Min	BRITISH ADMIRALTY	46x61cm
The Environs of Dublin	S.D.U.K.	32x39cm
The Environs of Edinburgh	S.D.U.K.	30x39cm
The Environs of London	S.D.U.K.	30x39cm
The Euphrates and the Tigris	HARRISON	33x39cm
The Falkland Islands	BRITISH ADMIRALTY	91x64cm
The First Part of Asia	HARRISON	50x72cm
The Firth of Clyde in Scotland ...	MacKENZIE	76x126cm
The Gallapagos Islands Discovered and Discribed by Capt. Cowley ...	BOWEN, E.	32x20cm
The Geography of the Great Solar Eclipse of July, 14. MDCCXLVIII ...	JEFFERYS	30x44cm
The Glenan Isles and Penmark Rocks with the Adjacent Coast of France ...	BRITISH ADMIRALTY	62x94cm
The Harbour and Road of Pernambuco ...	BRITISH ADMIRALTY	27x22cm
The Harbour of Casco Bay and Islands Adjacent	MOUNT & PAGE	43x54cm
The Harbour of Santa Marta ... [Colombia]	BRITISH ADMIRALTY	38x30cm
The Harbours of Rishibucto & Buctash on the West Shore of the Gulph ...	DES BARRES	77x51cm
The Historical War Map	ASHER & CO.	61x61cm
"The Hub" Cycling Map of England and Wales	BARTHOLOMEW	86x70cm
The Island of Barbadoes ...	GRIERSON	28x35cm
The Island of Celebes or Macassar	MOLL (Small)	20x26cm
The Island of Celebes, or Macassar with the Islands of Banda, Amboyna ...	MOLL (Small)	20x25cm
The Island of Hispaniola Called by the French St. Domingo. Subject to ...	JEFFERYS	34x50cm
The Island of Jamaica ...	GRIERSON	40x51cm
The Islands of New Zealand	S.D.U.K.	39x31cm
The Islands of Scilly	COLLINS, G.	45x56cm
The Isle of California. New Mexico. Louisiane. The River Misisipi and ...	MOLL (Small)	19x19cm
The Kaiser Wilhelm Canal	BRITISH ADMIRALTY	28x99cm
The Kingdom of Ireland	MORDEN	41x34cm
The Kingdom of Ireland by Robt. Morden	MORDEN	41x35cm
The Kingdom of Korea [called by the Chinese Kau-Li-Quae ...]	DU HALDE	51x35cm

The Kingdome of China ...	SPEED	39x51cm
The Kingdome of Denmarke ...	SPEED	40x50cm
The Kingdome of England	SPEED	38x51cm
The Kingdome of Persia ...	SPEED	40x51cm
The "Landmarks" of London	WEEKLY DISPATCH	44x62cm
The Leadville Mining District Compiled from Official Records ...	MINING MAPS	117x79cm
The Leeward Islands	STANFORD	48x61cm
The Leeward or North Caribbee Islands	LOWRY	26x34cm
The Map of China	PURCHAS	30x37cm
The Middle States and Western Territories of the United States ...	BROOKES	20x25cm
The Mississippi and Its Rebel Fortifications, from Columbus, Ky. to ...	NEW YORK HERALD	No dimen
The Mouth of the Clyde and Loch Fyne ...	MacKENZIE	72x150cm
The Netherlands including Liege	WILKINSON	22x29cm
The New York Columbian Celebration - The Naval Review	HARPER'S WEEKLY	32x107cm
The North Part of Cardigan Bay in Wales ...	MacKENZIE	90x103cm
The North Part of Great Britain Called Scotland with Considerable ...	MOLL (Large)	61x100cm
The North Sea with the Kattegat ...	FADEN	66x61cm
The North-West Coast of England from Walney Island to St. Bee's Head ...	MacKENZIE	71x102cm
The North-West Coast of Scotland, from Rurea in Ross Shire, to Cape ...	MacKENZIE	103x97cm
The Northwestern Territories of the United States	BROOKES	20x25cm
The Orrery ...	FERGUSON	20x23cm
The Pacific Ocean	WEEKLY DISPATCH	45x65cm
The Pacific Ocean, the New Discoveries There, and Tracks of the Navigators	COOK	18x33cm
The Peninsula of Korea	BRITISH ADMIRALTY	62x46cm
The Philipine Isles	MORDEN	10x13cm
The Plan of Constantinople	SALMON	17x29cm
The Port of Veracruz, and Anchorage of Anton Lizardo ...	BRITISH ADMIRALTY	60x79cm
The Principal Islands of the East Indies	MOLL (Small)	23x19cm
The Progressive Changes in Sandy Hook from 1779-1851 [NJ]	U.S. COAST SURVEY	37x29cm
The Province of Canada by James Wyld ...	WYLD	61x97cm
The Province of Maine ...	PAYNE	27x18cm
The Province of Maine from the Best Authorities by Samuel Lewis 1794	CAREY, M.	38x25cm
The Province of New Jersey, Divided into East and West, Commonly ...	FADEN	78x57cm
The Provinces of New York, and New Jersey; with Part of Pensilvania ...	JEFFERYS	52x133cm
The Purveyorships in the Reign of Solomon ...	WILKINSON	28x22cm
The Rand McNally Indexed County and Township Pocket Map and Shippers ...	RAND, McNALLY (Pocket, etc)	58x71cm
The River Congo ...	BRITISH ADMIRALTY	30x46cm
The River St. John ... [New Brunswick]	DES BARRES	54x76cm
The River St. Lawrence, Accurately Drawn from D'Anville's Map ...	HARRISON	36x47cm
The Road from Chelmsford ... to ... Saffron Walde	OGILBY	33x43cm
The Road from Huntington to Ipswich	OGILBY	32x46cm
The Road from London to Barwick	OGILBY	33x44cm
The Road from London to Darby ...	OGILBY	32x43cm
The Road from Maldon ... to ... Gravesend	OGILBY	33x43cm
The Road from Monmouth to Llanbeder	OGILBY	33x43cm
The Road from Nottingham to Grimsley	OGILBY	32x43cm
The Road from Oxford to Salisbury	OGILBY	36x46cm
The Roads from Exeter ... Devon to Dorchester and from Plimouth to ...	OGILBY	32x46cm
The Romane Empire	VAN DEN KEERE	8x13cm
The Sacramento Valley from the American River to Butte Creek, ...	U.S.	54x45cm
The Scilly Isles	BRITISH ADMIRALTY	65x98cm
The Seat of War in the South-West	NEW YORK TRIBUNE	34x24cm
The Seat of War in the West Indies ...	FOSTER	43x47cm
The Seat of War. Birds Eye View of Virginia, Maryland ...	SCHAUS	57x75cm
The Sooloo Archipelago, Laid Down Chiefly from Observations in 1761 ...	DALRYMPLE	46x61cm
The South East Coast of the Island of St. John ...	DES BARRES	108x88cm
The South Part of Great Britain Called England and Wales Containing ...	MOLL (Large)	61x96cm
The South Part of the Straits of Malacca Inscribed to Capt. G.G. Richardson...	LAURIE & WHITTLE	44x70cm
The Spanish Netherlands Commonly Called Flanders ... 1719	SENEX	41x54cm
The State of New Hampshire Compiled Chiefly from Actual Surveys	PAYNE	29x19cm
The State of New Hampshire Compiled Chiefly from Actual Surveys ...	CAREY, M.	46x30cm
The State of Pennsylvania from the Latest Surveys	PAYNE	18x26cm
The State of Pennsylvania. Reduced with Permission from Reading Howells	CAREY, M.	31x47cm
The State of Rhode-Island Compiled from the Surveys and Observations ...	CAREY, M.	35x24cm
The States of Maryland and Delaware from the Latest Surveys	PAYNE	19x24cm
The Strait of Sunda	IMRAY	98x103cm
The Straits of Sincapore with Those of Drion, Sabon, Mandol, &ca ...	LAURIE & WHITTLE	42x57cm
The Terms and Principles of Geography with Their Astronomical ...	MIDDLETON	29x18cm

Title	Author	Size
The Terraqueous Globe According to the Latest Discoveries	WELLS	36x51cm
The Territories of Washington and Oregon	COLTON (Atlas Maps)	32x41cm
The Transval of the City of New York	VIELE	33x131cm
The Travels of St. Paul and Other Apostles or a Geographical Description ...	MOXON	32x47cm
The Turkish Empire	SPEED	39x51cm
The Turkish Empire in Europe Asia and Africa Divided into All Its ...	MOLL (Large)	61x101cm
The United States ...	CUMMINGS & HILLIARD	22x28cm
The United States from the Latest Authorities	HAYWARD	54x100cm
The United States of America	COLTON (Atlas Maps)	37x64cm
The United States of America ...	WILKINSON	24x29cm
The United States of America Confirmed by Treaty. 1783	WILKINSON	25x28cm
The United States of Mexico	GREENLEAF	31x27cm
The United States of North America with the British Territories	WYLD	55x65cm
The United States of North America, Pacific States	BLACKIE & SON	36x27cm
The Virgin Islands from English and Danish Surveys ...	JEFFERYS, T.	46x61cm
The West Coast of Scotland from Ardnamurchan to the Island Sky ...	MacKENZIE	105x100cm
The Wilderness, Prepared by Bvt. Brig. Genl. N. Michler ... [VA]	U.S. WAR DEPARTMENT	53x51cm
The Windward Passage, with the Several Passages, from the East End ...	JEFFERYS	50x65cm
The World	CUMMINGS & HILLIARD	No dimen
The World in Planisphere	MOLL (Small)	18x20cm
The World on Mercator's Projection	TALLIS	26x35cm
The World on Mercator's Projection - Western Part [with another sheet] ...	PINKERTON	69x51cm
The World with the Latest Discoveries	SUDLOW	25x50cm
The World's Industrial and Cotton Centennial Exposition New Orleans	MANUSCRIPT MAPS	175x67cm
The World, According to the Latest Discoveries	DRAKE	19x37cm
The Ylandes of the West Indies	MERCATOR (Small)	17x23cm
Theater des Oorlogs in Hongarye ...	VAN SCHAGEN	45x59cm
Theatrum Historicum pars Occidentalis [in set with] Theatrum Historicum ...	COVENS & MORTIER	48x60cm
Theoria Cometarum in qua Praecipuaeorum Phaenomena ex Recentiorum ...	DOPPELMAYR	50x57cm
Theoriatrum Superiorum Planetarum	CELLARIUS	43x51cm
Thusciae Descriptio ...	ORTELIUS (Folio)	32x49cm
Tiburtum volgo Tivoli	BRAUN & HOGENBERG	Folio
Tierra Firma item Nuevo Reyno de Granada	DE LAET	28x35cm
Tierra Nueva	RUSCELLI	18x25cm
Timor and Some Neighbouring Islands ...	BRITISH ADMIRALTY	46x64cm
Tirolis Comitatus Continens Episcop. Tridentinum et Brixiensem nec non ...	LOTTER	49x59cm
To Her Most Sacred Majesty Ann Queen of Great Britain France ...	MOLL (Large)	58x95cm
To His Most Excellent Majesty King William IVth This Map of the Provinces ...	BOUCHETTE	99x191cm
To His Most Serene and August Majesty Peter ... Absolute Lord of Russia ...	MOLL (Large)	61x94cm
To the Right Honorable Charles Earl of Peterborow ... This Map of Africa ...	MOLL (Large)	58x95cm
To the Right Honorable Charles Earl of Sunderland ... Map of South America	MOLL (Large)	57x95cm
To the Right Honourable John Lord Sommers ... Map of North America ...	MOLL (Large)	57x96cm
To the Right Honourable William Lord Cowper Lord High Chancellor of ...	MOLL (Large)	58x95cm
Tobago	LUCAS	25x29cm
Tobermory Harbour	BRITISH ADMIRALTY	61x47cm
Toletum	BRAUN & HOGENBERG	37x50cm
Topographia Insulae Huenae	BRAUN & HOGENBERG	34x48cm
Topographia Sedis Imperatoriae Moscovitarum Petropolis ...	LOTTER	51x59cm
Topographical and Drainage Map of New Orleans and Surroundings ...	LOCAL & STATE MAPS	55x56cm
Topographical Map of Monmouth County [NJ: Monmouth Co.]	BEERS	36x55cm
Topographical Map of Morris County [NJ: Morris Co.]	BEERS	36x56cm
Topographical Map of Ocean County [NJ]	HOPKINS	37x29cm
Topographical Map of the Approaches and Defences of Knoxville, E. Tenn ...	U.S. WAR DEPARTMENT	66x76cm
Topographical Sketch of the Battlefield of Stone's River near Murphreesboro...	U.S. WAR DEPARTMENT	51x58cm
Topography of the Denver Basin Colorado	U.S. GEOLOGICAL SURV.	56x53cm
Totius Americae Septentrionalis et Meridionalis Novissima Repraesentatio ...	HOMANN	49x57cm
Totius Lemovici et Confinium Provinciarum Quantum ad Diocesin ...	MERCATOR (Folio)	35x45cm
Totius Orbis Terrarum Tabula ... per J. Moxon	MOXON	21x33cm
Totopotomoy ... [VA]	U.S. WAR DEPARTMENT	56x79cm
Toulon and the Adjacent Coast	BRITISH ADMIRALTY	46x60cm
Toulon bis Marsilien, und S: Tropez	BODENEHR	17x31cm
Town of Freehold [NJ: Monmouth Co.]	BEERS	55x48cm
Track of the Calcutta East Indiaman over the Bassas de Chagas ...	LAURIE & WHITTLE	44x55cm
Traiecti ad Rhenum	SEUTTER	50x58cm
Traiectum ad Mosam	GUICCIARDINI	23x31cm
Transsylvania XXI. Nova Tabula	MUNSTER	25x34cm
Treveris Trier	MUNSTER	23x38cm
Tribocci Evesche de Strasbourg	SANSON (Folio)	41x51cm

Title	Author	Size
Trier	QUAD	20x30cm
Trier et Lutzenburg	MERCATOR (Folio)	35x45cm
Trinidad	LUCAS	24x29cm
Tubuai Island [on sheet with] Anchorages North Coast Tubuai Island	BRITISH ADMIRALTY	46x66cm
Tunison's Florida	TUNISON	25x31cm
Turcici Imperii Descriptio	MAGINI	13x17cm
Turcici Imperii Descriptio	ORTELIUS (Folio)	37x50cm
Turcicum Imperium	DE WIT	45x55cm
Turkey [on sheet with] Fairfield [and] West Farms [NJ: Monmouth Co.]	BEERS	36x27cm
Turkey in Asia	TALLIS	24x32cm
Turkey in Asia (Biblical Regions) The Holy Land and Its Borders ...	FULLARTON	53x41cm
Tuscia	MAGINI	13x17cm
Tuscia	MERCATOR (Folio)	35x45cm
Tyberias als Tyberiadis	SCHEDEL	14x23cm
Typus Communicationis Maris Caspii, cum Persico et Euxino	KIRCHER	17x16cm
Typus Cosmographicus Universalis	GRYNAEUS	36x56cm
Typus Cosmographicus Universalis	MUNSTER	37x56cm
Typus Cosmographicus Universalis	VADIANUS	29x40cm
Typus Geographicus Chili a Paraguay, Freti Magellanici &c. ...	HOMANN	50x57cm
Typus Hispaniae Veteris	CLUVER	10x12cm
Typus Orarum Maritimarum Guineae, Manicongo, & Angolae Ultrap ...	VAN LINSCHOTEN	38x52cm
Typus Orbis Descriptione Ptolemaei	FRIES	30x46cm
Typus Orbis Descriptione Ptolemaei	PTOLEMY (1522-1541)	30x46cm
Typus Orbis Ptol. Descriptus	MUNSTER	26x34cm
Typus Orbis Terrarum	BEER	10x13cm
Typus Orbis Terrarum	CLUVER	16x30cm
Typus Orbis Terrarum	HONDIUS	14x22cm
Typus Orbis Terrarum	MONATH	25x29cm
Typus Orbis Terrarum	ORTELIUS (Folio)	35x50cm
Typus Orbis Terrarum [in set with] Africae Nova Tabula Auct. J. Hondio ...	JANSSON	18x26cm
Typus Orbis Universalis	MUNSTER	26x38cm
Typus Universalis	MUNSTER	28x35cm
Ubersicht von Gerhard Rohlfs Reisen in Africa 1861-1867	PETERMANN	25x33cm
Udrone Irlandiae in Catherlagh Baronia	MERCATOR (Folio)	45x35cm
Ukrania quae et Terra Cosaccorum cum Vicinis Walachiae, Moldaviae, ...	HOMANN	50x59cm
Ulma	SCHEDEL	20x52cm
Ultoniae Orientalis Pars	MERCATOR (Folio)	35x45cm
Ultoniae Orientalis Pars Per Gerardium Mercatorem cum Privilegio	MERCATOR (Folio)	35x38cm
Umrisse der Pflanzengeographie	HILDBURGHAUSEN BIBLIO.	20x26cm
Un Passaggio par Terra a California Scoperta dal P. Eusebio Kino	KINO	23x20cm
Union Military Chart. Complete Map of the Railroads and Water Courses ...	MAGNUS, C.	57x68cm
United Provinces	LUCAS	38x28cm
United States ...	BURR	27x32cm
United States	CORNELL	32x52cm
United States	FINLEY	29x22cm
United States	GRAY	39x69cm
United States	GREENLEAF	27x32cm
United States	HUNTINGTON	27x45cm
United States	MORSE, J.	26x42cm
United States	MORSE, S.	27x43cm
United States	TALLIS	25x34cm
United States	TANNER	38x31cm
United States	TEESDALE	34x41cm
United States Western Sheet	WEEKLY DISPATCH	46x33cm
United States & Texas. With All the Railways & Canals	LIZARS	41x52cm
United States and Additions	THOMSON	50x60cm
United States North America According to Calvin Smith & Tanner ...	SWANSTON	40x51cm
United States of America	MELISH	43x56cm
United States of America	WARNER, B.	43x65cm
United States of America Northern Part	PINKERTON	51x70cm
United States of America Southern Part	PINKERTON	51x70cm
United States of America ... The South Central Section	FULLARTON	51x41cm
United States of North America	SWANSTON	41x53cm
United States of North America	WEEKLY DISPATCH	43x31cm
United States of North America. North West Sheet [Idaho, Dakota, ...]	CASSELL, PETER & GALPIN	43x30cm
United States, Western States - California, Oregon, Utah, Washington, ...	BLACK	41x56cm
Univerale Novo	GASTALDI	13x18cm
Universale della Parte del Mondo Nuovamente Ritrovata	RAMUSIO	26x26cm

Title	Author	Size
Universale Ecc.te Descrittione di Tutto il Mondo del Giuseppe Rosaccio	ROSACCIO	27x32cm
Universalis Orbis Descriptio	MYRITIUS	27x39cm
Upper California to Illustrate the Paper by Dr. Coulter	ROYAL GEOG. SOCIETY	25x11cm
Upper Canada &c.	ARROWSMITH	64x53cm
Upper Canada &c. [upper title]; Lower Canada, New Brunswick ...	ARROWSMITH	64x102cm
Upper Freehold [NJ: Monmouth Co.]	BEERS	36x30cm
Urania's Mirror or a View of the Heavens	LEIGH	14x20cm
Urbis Romae Veteris ac Modernae Accurata Delineatio ...	HOMANN	48x58cm
Urbs Nangasaki cum Porto & Agro Circumjacenti. Ex Ipsis Japonum ...	KAEMPFER	32x47cm
Utah	CRAM	64x46cm
Utriusque Hemispherii Delineato	WYTFLIET	23x29cm
Valentia Regnum	ORTELIUS (Folio)	36x48cm
Valentia, Murcia cum Insulis Majorca, Minorca et Yvica	MERCATOR (Small)	14x20cm
Valesiae Altera et VII. Nova Tabula	MUNSTER	27x33cm
Valesiae Charta Prior et VI. Nova Tabula	MUNSTER	26x33cm
Van Dieman's Land	DOWER	34x41cm
Van Dieman's Land or Tasmania	JOHNSTON	60x49cm
Vancouver Island, Harbours in Discovery Passage, Broughton Strait ...	BRITISH ADMIRALTY	48x60cm
Venecie	SCHEDEL	19x53cm
Venetia	BRAUN & HOGENBERG	34x48cm
Venezuela, atque Occidentalis Pars Novae Andalusiae	DE LAET	28x36cm
Venezuela cum Parte Australi Novae Andalusiae	OGILBY	29x36cm
Venezuela, cum Parti Australi Novae Andalusiae	BLAEU	37x47cm
Venice	S.D.U.K.	38x58cm
Vera Effigies et Delineatio Insula Sanctae Helenae, qua Ortum Occasum ...	VAN LINSCHOTEN	31x48cm
Vera Effigies et Delineatio Insulae Ascensio ...	VAN LINSCHOTEN	27x34cm
Vera Effigies et Delineatio Insulae Sanctae Helenae ...	VAN LINSCHOTEN	31x48cm
Verein-Staaten von Nord-America, Mexico, Yucatan	VON STULPNAGEL	33x41cm
Vereinigte Staaten von Nord Amerika	HANDTKE	51x69cm
Vereinigte Staaten von Nord-America: Californien, Texas und die ...	HILDBURGHAUSEN BIBLIO.	20x26cm
Vereinigte Staaten von Nord-America: Californien, Texas und die ...	MEYER	23x28cm
Vereinigten Staaten v. Nord-America	WEIMAR GEOG. INSTITUT	49x64cm
Vereinigte Staaten von Nord-Amerika in 6 Blattern, Bl. 1	PETERMANN	33x41cm
Vergleichende Uebersicht der Bedeutendsten Stromlangen	HILDBURGHAUSEN BIBLIO.	26x26cm
Vermont	FINLEY	29x22cm
Verona	SCHEDEL	19x22cm
Vetus Descriptio Daciarum nec non Moesiarum ...	JANSSON	36x48cm
Vicinity of Los Angeles	HARDESTY	24x32cm
Victoria or Port Phillip	TALLIS	25x34cm
Vienna	SALMON	21x29cm
Vienna Austria Metropolis, Urbs toto orbe Notissima Celebratissimaq ...	BRAUN & HOGENBERG	15x47cm
Vienne	MALLET	14x10cm
View of Bale Principal City of Bale, One of the Cantons of Switzerland	BANKES	11x18cm
View of Macao in China	LA PEROUSE	20x30cm
View of the Country Round the Falls of Niagara	MELISH	17x10cm
View of Zurich Principal City of Zurich, One of the Cantons of Switzerland	BANKES	11x18cm
VII. Provintia seu Belgiu Foederatum ...	PROBST	17x20cm
Virgin Gorda [on sheet with] Dead Chest [and] Peter Is. [and] ...	ANDREWS	20x25cm
Virgin Islands [on sheet with] Ginger Is. [and] Round Is. Passage ...	ANDREWS	20x29cm
Virgin Islands. Tortola, Virgin Gorda, Ginger Island ... Normans I.	BLUNT	13x20cm
Virginia	ARROWSMITH & LEWIS	22x27cm
Virginia	BEER	10x13cm
Virginia	BRADFORD	29x38cm
Virginia	JANSSON	15x19cm
Virginia	MORSE, J.	15x19cm
Virginia	SMITH, JOHN	32x41cm
Virginia Marylandia et Carolina in America Septentrionalis ...	HOMANN	48x58cm
Virginia and Maryland	SPEED	9x13cm
Virginia et Nova Francia	BERTIUS	10x14cm
Virginia Item et Floridae	CLOPPENBURGH	19x26cm
Virginia, Maryland, Pennsylvania, East & West New Jersey	MOUNT & PAGE	51x80cm
Virginia, Marylandia et Carolina in America Septentrionali ...	HOMANN	48x58cm
Virginiae Item et Floridae ...	JANSSON	18x25cm
Virginiae Item et Floridae Americae Provinciarum, Nova Descriptio	HONDIUS	34x48cm
Virginiae Item et Floridae Americae Provinciarum Nova Descriptio	MERCATOR (Folio)	34x49cm
Virginiae Partis Australis et Floridae Partis Orientalis ...	OGILBY	29x36cm
Virginiae Partis Australis et Floridae Partis Orientalis Interjacentiumque ...	BLAEU	38x51cm
Virginiae Partis Australis, et Floridae Partis Orientalis Interjacentiumq ...	JANSSON	39x50cm

Title	Cartographer	Size
Virginie	MALLET	15x10cm
Von den Britannischen Insuln	MUNSTER	25x17cm
Vorstellung Einiger Gegenden und Plaetze in Nord-America unter Franzoesisch	HOMANN	43x49cm
Vue de New York. Prise de Weahawk / A View of New-York ...	GARNERAY	37x45cm
Vue et Description de Bethlehem et de Nazareth et de Plusieurs ...	CHATELAIN	37x48cm
Vues des Caps d'Aden, de St Antoine, et de Bab-El-Mandeb ...	D'APRES DE MANNEVILLETTE	48x33cm
Vues Diverses du Fort de l'Agouade pres de l'Isle de Goa ...	D'APRES DE MANNEVILLETTE	43x33cm
Vvestfaliae Secunda Tabula	MERCATOR (Folio)	35x45cm
Wales	SPEED	38x51cm
Waradin	MALLET	15x11cm
Warnbro Sound [on sheet with] Peel Harbour	BRITISH ADMIRALTY	34x21cm
Warren County [NJ: Warren Co.]	BEERS	36x55cm
Washington	ASHER & ADAMS	40x57cm
Washington [on sheet with] Cincinnati [and] Louisville [and] New Orleans	BRADFORD	29x36cm
Washington and Oregon	COLTON (Atlas Maps)	28x38cm
Washington and Oregon	JOHNSON	31x41cm
Washington Territory	U.S. STATE SURVEYS	56x71cm
Washington, Oregon and Idaho	JOHNSON	31x39cm
Watagheistic Sound, Mary Islands &c. [Canada]	BRITISH ADMIRALTY	61x45cm
Watson's New County, Railroad and Distance Map of Dakota and Nebraska	WATSON	42x33cm
Welt Charten, Worauf die Reife nach Indien	HEYDT	22x26cm
Wembury Bay and Yealm River	BRITISH ADMIRALTY	48x65cm
West Canada	TALLIS	25x34cm
West Coast of Africa Sheet I [through] Sheet XX	BRITISH ADMIRALTY	47x64cm
West India Islands	RAPKIN	26x33cm
West India Islands	TALLIS	26x33cm
West Indies	BURR	28x32cm
West Indies	COLTON (Atlas Maps)	32x40cm
West Indies	LUCAS	28x38cm
West Indies, Anguilla to Puerto Rico Shewing the Approaches to the Virgin ...	BRITISH ADMIRALTY	66x102cm
West Indies Sheet XI From Cayos Ratones to San Juan de Nicaragua	BRITISH ADMIRALTY	48x62cm
West Indies Sheet XIV From Belize to Cape Catoche ...	BRITISH ADMIRALTY	62x47cm
Western Australia [on sheet with] Van Diemen Island	S.D.U.K.	32x39cm
Western Australia, Swan River	TALLIS	34x24cm
Western Hemisphere	DOWER	Diam 20cm
Western Hemisphere	FADEN	58x58cm
Western Hemisphere	S.D.U.K.	36x36cm
Western Hemisphere	THOMSON	58x53cm
Western Hemisphere [in set with] Eastern Hemisphere	TALLIS	25x34cm
Western Territories of the United States	OLNEY	27x46cm
Western Territories of the United States	SHERMAN & SMITH	27x44cm
Westfalia	ORTELIUS (Miniature)	8x13cm
Westmorlandia, Lancastria, Cestria, Caernarvan, Denbigh, Flint, ...	MERCATOR (Folio)	36x42cm
Wiltshire	SPEED	38x50cm
Wisconsin	ASHER & ADAMS	41x57cm
Wisconsin	COLTON (Atlas Maps)	38x46cm
Wismar	MORTIER	20x26cm
World [in set with] Africa [and] America [and] Asia [and] Europe	HULSIUS	8x12cm
Wreck Chart of the British Isles for 1855	BRITISH GOVERNMENT	47x34cm
Wyld's Road Director through England and Wales ...	WYLD	68x51cm
Wyoming	CRAM	24x30cm
Wyoming	CRAM	46x64cm
Wyoming	RAND, McNALLY (Atlas Maps)	32x43cm
Wyoming, Colorado and Utah	COLTON (Atlas Maps)	44x65cm
Yang-Tse-Kiang River	BRITISH ADMIRALTY	61x94cm
Yarmouth and Lowestoft Roads	BRITISH ADMIRALTY	107x66cm
Yellowstone National Park and Portion of Yellowstone Forest Preserve	U.S. GEOLOGICAL SURV.	46x60cm
Yucatan Conventus Iuridici Hispania Novae Pars Occidentalis et Guatimala ...	OGILBY	29x36cm
Zeekaarte van Yerlandt	BLAEU	26x36cm
Zeelandiae Comitatus	LOTTER	50x57cm
Zelandia Comitatus	MERCATOR (Folio)	34x49cm
Zululand. The Seat of the War with the Zulu King ...	TILLOTSON	54x41cm
Zurichgovv, et Basiliensis Provincia	MERCATOR (Folio)	36x47cm
Zurych. Tigarum sive Turegum, Caesari, ut Plerique Existimant, Tigurinus ...	BRAUN & HOGENBERG	37x48cm

GEOGRAPHICAL INDEX

The world has been divided into hemispheres, continents, polar, oceans, and a few miscellaneous categories. Each item is listed in only one location. Where there is more than one item by a particular map-maker, the number of items is indicated in square brackets [ ].

The embracing concept of the Geographical Index is to start with the *general* and end with the *particular.* Accordingly, the first heading is the **World**. Next comes **Hemispheres**; then the **Continents** in alphabetical order, and within North America there is further subdivision into Canada, Mexico and Central America, the United States, and the West Indies; followed by **Polar** regions. The **Oceans** are next, in alphabetical order. And finally, **Celestial** and **Miscellaneous**.

Maps of regions of what is now the United States are listed under the main heading of *North America* if before about 1770, and under *United States* if after about 1770. An exception is in the case of a single colony which became a state -- Pennsylvania, for example -- which would appear under *United States*. Generally when a U.S. map shows two or three states, it is listed under the one occurring first alphabetically. Maps of the Americas -- North and South America together -- are listed in the *Hemisphere* section under *The Americas; Western Hemisphere.* Many maps showing the northwest coast of North America are listed under *Pacific Ocean, North.* Major geographical features such as Chesapeake Bay or the Gulf of Mexico may be under *North America* rather than *United States*. North American cities are listed under their respective countries and states, regardless of age, rather than under North America.

To help locate items, the order of the major headings is listed below:

WORLD: World & continents, sets of continents, sets of globe gores, globes
HEMISPHERES of the WORLD: includes two Americas
AFRICA
ASIA: includes the Holy Land, Persian Gulf, and the East Indies
AUSTRALIA
EUROPE: includes the Mediterranean
NORTH AMERICA: The whole continent and U.S. regions before Independence
    CANADA
    MEXICO and CENTRAL AMERICA
    UNITED STATES: Cities from all periods
    WEST INDIES
SOUTH AMERICA
POLAR
OCEANS:
    ATLANTIC
    INDIAN includes Red Sea
    PACIFIC includes the Philippines
CELESTIAL & MISCELLANEOUS: includes allegorical, oddities, portraits, title pages, etc.

WORLD

ANCIENT: Cluver; Covens & Mortier; Jansson [2]; Mauro; Ortelius (Folio) [2]
- **(ATLASES):** Laurie & Whittle; Willard

GLOBES: TERRESTRIAL: Andrews; Betts; Copley; Joslin [2]; Rand, McNally & Co. (Pocket & Wall Maps) [3]; Schedler
- **TERRESTRIAL & CELESTIAL PAIR:** Cary

GLOBE DEPICTIONS: Mallet

GLOBE GORES, TERRESTRIAL: Coronelli [3]

MODERN: Angelocrator; Anonymous or Unknown [2]; Anson; Apianus [3]; Arias Montanus; Bachiene; Beer; Bellin (Large) [2]; Bellin (Small); Blaeu; Blome [2]; Bodenehr [3]; Bonne [3]; Brion De La Tour; Buache; Cary; Chanlaire; Chatelain [6]; Cluver [3]; Colton (Pocket & Wall Maps); Covens & Mortier [3]; Cruchley; Cummings & Hilliard; D'anville; Danckerts; De Aefferden [2]; De Bry; De Fer (Large) [2]; De Fer (Small); De Lat; De Leth; De Vaugondy [5]; De Wit; Drake; Du Val; Dunn; Elwe; Faden; Ferguson; Fries [2]; Gastaldi [3]; Gentleman's Magazine [2]; Gray; Grynaeus; Harris; Harrison; Heydt; Hildburghausen Bibliographisches Institut; Homann & Homann Heirs [3]; Hondius; Jaillot; Jansson [4]; Japanese Cartography; Johnson [2]; Johnston; Keur; Kircher; Kitchin; Lafitau; Laurie & Whittle [2]; Lavoisne [2]; Le Rouge; Lotter [3]; Magini; Mallet [3]; Mariette; Mercator (Folio) [2]; Mercator (Small); Merian [2]; Middleton; Moll (Large) [4]; Moll (Small) [3]; Monath; Morden [2]; Moxon; Munster [10]; Myritius; Nolin; Ortelius (Folio) [2]; Ottens; Overton; Pennant; Pinkerton; Pitt; Plancius [2]; Porcacchi [3]; Probst; Rosaccio [2]; Rossi; Ruscelli [3]; Sanson (Folio) [7]; Santini; Scherer; Schreiber; Seller; Senex; Speed [2]; Steinberger; Stoopendaal; Sudlow; Tallis [2]; Thompson; Thomson; Tirion; Torniello [4]; Vadianus; Valk; Van Den Keere; Van Der Aa; Visscher [4]; Volkamer; Waldseemuller; Walton; Weigel; Wells [2]; Wytfliet; Zatta [2]; Zurner
- **(ATLASES):** Bartholomew; Berghaus; Black [2]; Bradford; Bradley; Braun & Hogenberg; British Admiralty; Chiquet; Cluver; Colton (Atlas Maps); Cram [2]; Cummings & Hilliard; Dufour; Dury; Gastaldi; Johnson [2]; Johnston; Malte-Brun; Marzolla; Mitchell, S.A. (Atlas Maps 1860 & Later) [2]; Morse, S.; Quad; Stieler; Watson

PTOLEMAIC: Fries; Mela; Munster [4]; Ptolemy (1482 Florence); Ptolemy (1522-1541 Strassburg) [2]; Schedel [2]; Waldseemuller
- **(ATLASES):** Magini; Ptolemy (1522-1541 Strassburg)

SET OF 2 HEMISPHERES: Bodenehr; Bonne; Coronelli; De L'Isle [3]; De Pretot; Orr & Smith; Tallis; Van Campen; Weimar Geographisches Institut; White, W.

WORLD & 4 CONTINENTS: Hulsius; Jansson

HEMISHPERES of the WORLD

The AMERICAS; WESTERN HEMISPHERE: Allard [2]; Anonymous or Unknown; Aspin; Beer; Berghaus; Blaeu; Briet; Carey & Lea; Chatelain [2]; Cluver [2]; Coronelli [2]; De Bry [2]; De Fer (Small); De L'Isle [4]; De Laet; De Pretot; De Vaugondy [2]; Desnos; Dower; Faden; Gentleman's Magazine; Hildburghausen Bibliographisches Institut; Homann & Homann Heirs [5]; Hondius [5]; Janvier; Japanese Cartography; Laurie & Whittle; Lavoisne; Le Rouge; Mallet [3]; Mercator (Folio) [2]; Mercator (Small) [2]; Merian [2]; Moll (Large); Moll (Small) [3]; Morden; Munster [9]; Ogilby; Ortelius (Folio) [6]; Probst; Ramusio; Sayer; Sayer & Bennett; Schenk [2]; Schreiber; Senex [2]; S.D.U.K.; Speed; Thomson [2]; Tirion; Valk; Van Den Keere; Van Der Aa [3]; Visscher; Von Reilly; Weigel [2]; Weiland; Wyld; Zatta [3]
- **(ATLASES)** Morse & Gaston; Wytfliet

EASTERN: Bonne; Bunting; De L'Isle; Du Val; Heather; Mallet [2]; Plancius; Tirion; Van Linschoten

NORTHERN: De L'Isle; Jefferys; Johnston; Stieler; Thomson

SOUTHERN: Bellin (Small); Benard; Bonne; Cook; De L'Isle; Du Val; Gentleman's Magazine; Mallet [2]; Philip, G.; Pinkerton; Wytfliet; Zatta [2]

AFRICA

AFRICA (ALL): Blaeu; Bowen, E.; Bunting; Chatelain [2]; Danckerts; De Fer (Small); De L'Isle [3]; De La Feuille; De Vaugondy; Harrison; Hildburghausen Bibliographisches Institut; Hondius; Laurie & Whittle; Manuscript Maps; Mercator (Folio) [3]; Mercator (Small); Moll (Large) [2]; Morden; Munster [2]; Ortelius (Folio); Pigafetta; Pinkerton; Probst; Ramusio; Sanson (Folio); Scherer; Schreiber; Seutter; Speed; Van Den Keere; Wilkie
- **(CENTRAL):** Blaeu; Kiepert; Petermann; Valk & Schenk

- **(CENTRAL - PRESTER JOHN)**: Blaeu; Mercator (Folio); Ortelius (Folio) [2]
- **(EAST)**: Hildburghausen Bibliographisches Institut; Illustrated London News; Morden; Royal Geographical Society; Thevenot
- **(NORTH)**: Fries; Hildburghausen Bibliographisches Institut; Magini; Munster; Petermann; Ptolemy (1522-1541 Strassburg); Quad; Ruscelli
- **(NORTHEAST)**: Bonne; De L'Isle; Munster; Ptolemy (1522-1541 Strassburg); Stanford
- **(NORTHWEST)**: Munster
- **(SOUTH)**: Blaeu; Chatelain; De L'Isle; Delamarche; Fries; Gastaldi; Imray; Kircher; Pinkerton
- **(SOUTHEAST)**: Van Linschoten
- **(SOUTHWEST)**: Bolton; Van Linschoten
- **(WEST)**: Arrowsmith; Bellin (Large); British Admiralty; Colom; De L'Isle; [1]; Harrison

ALGERIA: British Admiralty; Ottens
- **ALGIERS**: Braun & Hogenberg; Manuscript Maps; Mortier; Schenk

BARBARY: De Wit; Jacobsz

CONGO: De Bry

EGYPT: Bonne; British Admiralty; Cary; De Vaugondy; Heather; Hildburghausen Bibliographisches Institut; Lattre; Ortelius (Folio); Schedel; Schenk [2]
- **(CITIES)**: Braun & Hogenberg [3]

ETHIOPIA: British Admiralty; Van Der Aa

GABON: British Admiralty

GUINEA: British Admiralty; Homann & Homann Heirs; Hondius; Jansson

KENYA: British Admiralty

LIBYA: Mortier; Seller

MALAWI: British Admiralty

MOROCCO: Blaeu; Mercator (Folio); Petermann

MOZAMBIQUE: Lafitau

NAMIBIA: British Admiralty

NILE RIVER: De Vaugondy

SENEGAL: British Admiralty; Depot De La Marine

SIERRA LEONE: British Admiralty

SOMOLIA: British Admiralty

SOUTH AFRICA: Anonymous or Unknown; Barrow; Bellin (Small); Hildburghausen Bibliographisches Institut; Juta; Laurie & Whittle [2]; Lotter; S.D.U.K.; Tillotson; Wilkie; Wyld

TANGIER: Schenk

TUNISIA, CARTHAGE: Schedel

ZAIRE: British Admiralty

ASIA

ASIA (ALL): Beer; Bowen, E. [2]; Cluver; De Fer (Small); De L'Isle; De Wit; Gibson; Hildburghausen Bibliographisches Institut; Kitchin; Magini; Mercator (Folio); Moll (Large) [2]; Moll (Small); Morden; Munster [5]; Ortelius (Folio) [3]; Quad; Ruscelli; Schreiber; Speed; Starling; Van Den Keere
- **(CENTRAL)**: Berghaus; Moll (Small); Ptolemy (1478-1508 Rome); Ptolemy (1522-1541 Strassburg) [2]; Visscher
- **(EAST)**: Harrison
- **(MIDDLE EAST)**: Arrowsmith; Bachiene; Bonne; D'anville [2]; De La Rue; Fullarton; Grattan & Gilbert; Hole, W. [2]; Morse & Breese; Moxon [2]; Munster; Ortelius (Folio); Tavernier; Visscher [2]
- **(SOUTH)**: Fries; Jansson; Munster; Ptolemy (1522-1541 Strassburg); Waldseemuller
- **(SOUTHEAST & EAST INDIES)**: Blaeu; Bonne; De Fer (Small); De L'Isle; De Wit; Fries; Hamilton; Homann & Homann Heirs; Lattre; Mercator (Small); Moll (Large); Ortelius (Folio) [3]; Plon; Renard; Visscher [2]
- **(SOUTHEAST)**: Beer; Bellin (Small); Bertius; Fries; Gastaldi; Jansson; Munster; Ruscelli; Sayer & Bennett
- **(SOUTHWEST)**: Bellin (Small); De Jode; Harrison; Van Linschoten

ARABIA: Beer; Bertius; De Vaugondy; Fries; Gastaldi; Lattre; Munster; Ruscelli; Van Der Aa

ARMENIA: Petermann; Ptolemy (1482 Florence); Ptolemy (1522-1541 Strassburg)

ASIA MINOR: Mortier; Ortelius (Folio); Sanson (Folio); Visscher

BLACK SEA: Morden; Schreiber
- **(& CRIMEA)**: Mercator (Small)

BURMA: Langenes
CASPIAN SEA: Lotter; Moll (Small); Ottens
CAUCASUS REGION: De L'Isle; Hildburghausen Bibliographisches Institut; Kircher; Ptolemy (1478-1508 Rome); Russian Government
CEYLON: Beer; De L'Isle; Ferguson; Mallet [2]; Mercator (Folio); Munster; Nicholson; Plancius; Ptolemy (1522-1541 Strassburg)
CHINA: Beer; Bidwell; Blaeu; Botero; Bowen, E.; De Vaugondy; Hildburghausen Bibliographisches Institut; Homann & Homann Heirs; Jansson; Johnson; Mercator (Folio); Ortelius (Folio) [2]; Purchas [2]; Seutter; Thevenot; Van Der Aa
- (PROVINCES): Chinese Cartography
- FORMOSA: Bellin (Small)
- MACAO: Baker; La Perouse
- (OTHER CITIES): Van Meurs
- (MISCELLANEOUS): British Admiralty [6]; Direccion De Hidrografia; Mount & Page; Nicol
CHINA & JAPAN: Bacon; Cluver; Fries; Hildburghausen Bibliographisches Institut; Moll (Small); Speed
CHINA, JAPAN & KOREA: Buno; Cloppenburgh; Hondius
CHINA & KOREA: Bowen, E.; Cave; De Vaugondy; Kitchin; Laurie & Whittle; Thomas, Cowperthwait & Co.
CYPRUS: Bordone; Doncker; Ortelius (Folio)
EAST INDIES (ALL): Bellin (Small); Bowen, E.; Buache; Cantelli Da Vignola; Cary; D'entrecasteaux; Hondius [2]; Mercator (Small) [2]; Moll (Small); Ortelius (Folio) [2]; Ortelius (Miniature) [2]; Pinkerton; Wilkinson
- BANCA STRAIT: Horsburgh; Sayer
- BANDA SEA: British Admiralty
- CELEBES: Moll (Small)
- MACASSAR STRAIT: Mount & Page
- MALACCA STRAIT: Lafitau; Laurie & Whittle
- MOLUCCAS: Beer; Bonne; Van Der Aa
- NEW GUINEA: Mallet [2]
- SUNDA STRAIT: Beer; Imray; Sayer & Bennett [2]
- (MISCELLANEOUS): Dalrymple; Herbert; Imray
- (OTHER ISLANDS): British Admiralty; Cook
HOLY LAND: Arrowsmith; Bachiene [2]; Black; Blair; Blome; Bonne; Bowen, E. [2]; Bowen, T.; Brion De La Tour; Bunting; Burr; Cadell & Davies; Calmet [2]; Chatelain; Colton (Atlas Maps); Covens & Mortier; Cruchley; Davies; De La Rue [4]; De Vaugondy [2]; De Wit; Du Val; Elwe; Finley; Fries; Fuller [5]; Gray; Hall, S. [2]; Hildburghausen Bibliographisches Institut; Homann & Homann Heirs [2]; Jaillot; Johnson; Johnston [2]; Kincaid, A.; Laurie & Whittle; Magini; Mercator (Folio); Mitchell, S.A. (Atlas Maps 1859 & Earlier); Moll (Small); Mortier [3]; Moxon; Munster [5]; Ortelius (Folio) [9]; Probst; Ruscelli [2]; Sanson (Folio) [3]; Savery; Schreiber; Seutter [3]; S.D.U.K.; Speed; Stackhouse [2]; Stoopendaal [2]; Tallis [2]; Tanner; Van Adrichem [2]; Visscher [10]; Waite; Weller; Wells [3]; Wilkinson [3]; Williams
- JERUSALEM: Anonymous or Unknown; Bowen, E.; Braun & Hogenberg [5]; Burder; Calmet; Fleischmann; Fuller [2]; Mallet; Maynard; Middleton; Moll (Small); Salmon; Schedel [4]; Seutter; Visscher [3]; Ware
- (OTHER CITIES): Schedel [2]
INDIA: Baffin; Cantelli Da Vignola; D'anville; De L'Isle; De Vaugondy; Faden [2]; Fries; Laso; Morden; Mortier; Seutter; Thomson
- (ATLASES): Constable; Johnston
- GOA: Braun & Hogenberg; D'apres De Mannevillette; Lafitau; Laurie & Whittle
- (OTHER CITIES): Braun & Hogenberg; Lafitau [4]; Moll (Small); Salmon
INDIA & SRI LANKA: Bellin (Small); Laurie & Whittle
INDONESIA: De Bry; Hulsius; Tirion
- JAVA: Mount & Page; Van Der Aa
- SUMATRA: Bohn; Bordone; British Admiralty; D'apres De Mannevillette; Dalrymple; Munster [2]; Van Der Aa
- (OTHER ISLANDS): Dalrymple [2]; Le Rouge; Moll (Small)
IRAQ: Harrison
JAPAN: Beer; Bellin (Small) [2]; Blaeu; Hogg; Mercator (Small); Montanus; Morden [2]; Ortelius (Miniature); Royal Geographic Journal; S.D.U.K.; Tirion [2]; Zatta
- (CITIES): Kaempfer
JAPAN & KOREA: Bellin (Small); Cloppenburgh; Thomson
KOREA: British Admiralty; Du Halde

LEBANON: Roux
MALAYSIA: British Admiralty; D'apres De Mannevillette; Laurie & Whittle
MESOPOTAMIA: Schedel
OTTOMAN EMPIRE: De L'Isle; De Vaugondy; De Wit; Magini; Moll (Large) [2]; Ortelius (Folio); Speed
PAKISTAN: Munster; Ptolemy (1478-1508 Rome)
PERSIA: Beer; De L'Isle; Lattre; Moll (Small); Munster; Ortelius (Folio); Ptolemy (1522-1541 Strassburg); Ruscelli [2]; Speed
PERSIAN GULF: Harrison; Laurie & Whittle
RUSSIA (ASIA & EUROPE): Lattre; Lotter; Moll (Large); Ortelius (Folio) [3]; Pallas; Russian Government; Schreiber
- **(ASIA, MISCELLANEOUS):** Homann & Homann Heirs
- **NOVAYA ZEMLYA:** Jansson; Mallet
SINGAPORE: British Admiralty; Langenes; Laurie & Whittle
SYRIA: Bongars; S.D.U.K. [2]; Tallis
TARTARY: Cary; De L'Isle [2]; Magini; Ortelius (Folio) [4]; Ptolemy (1522-1541 Strassburg); Speed [2]; Van Der Aa
THAILAND: Kaempfer
TIBET: Bowen, E.; Petermann
TURKEY: British Admiralty; Ruscelli; Tallis [2]; Vivien
VIETNAM: Tavernier
YEMEN: D'apres De Mannevillette

AUSTRALIA

AUSTRALIA (ALL): Bellin (Small); Bowen, E.; Colton (Atlas Maps); Hildburghausen Bibliographisches Institut; Petermann; Plon; Schraembl; S.D.U.K. [3]; Tallis [4]; Thomson; Universal Magazine; Virtue; Weiland; Weimar Geographisches Institut
- **NEW SOUTH WALES:** Cook [2]; Cram; Perry; Royal Geographical Society; S.D.U.K. [2]; Stockdale; Tallis [2]; Wilkinson; Wyld
- **SOUTH AUSTRALIA:** Tallis
- **TASMANIA:** British Admiralty; Dower; Johnston
- **VICTORIA:** Cram; Tallis [3]
- **WESTERN AUSTRALIA:** S.D.U.K.; Tallis
- **(REGIONS):** Cook; Lizars; Royal Geographical Society [4]; Tallis; Thomson
- **(MISCELLANEOUS):** British Admiralty [2]; Cook
AUSTRALIA & EAST INDIES: Wyld
AUSTRALIA & NEW ZEALAND: Buffon; Fullarton; Greenleaf; Pinkerton [2]; Zatta

EUROPE

EUROPE (ALL): Blaeu; Bordone; Bowen, E.; Cluver; De Fer (Small); De L'Isle; Doncker; Jansson; Lizars; Lotter; Magini; Mercator (Folio); Moll (Large); Moll (Small) [2]; Munster; Ortelius (Folio); Probst; Rose; Ruscelli; Scherer; Schreiber; Seale; Speed; Tallis
- **(ATLASES):** Mentelle; Romanus
- **(CENTRAL):** De L'Isle; De Wit; Grierson; Kitchin; Moll (Large)
- **(EAST):** Waldseemuller
- **(NORTH):** Goos [2]; Kitchin; Petermann
- **(WEST):** Cantelli Da Vignola; Colom
ADRIATIC SEA & COAST: Cantelli Da Vignola; Depot De La Marine [7]; Hildburghausen Bibliographisches Institut; Mercator (Folio); Mount & Page
AEGEAN SEA: Van Keulen
AUSTRIA: Cary; De Vaugondy; Jaillot; Le Rouge [2]; Mercator (Folio); Ortelius (Folio) [2]; Ortelius (Miniature); Sanson (Folio); Schreiber; Wilkinson
- **TIROL:** Hildburghausen Bibliographisches Institut; Le Rouge; Lotter
- **VIENNA:** Braun & Hogenberg; Mallet; Salmon
- **(OTHER CITIES):** Braun & Hogenberg; Schedel
- **(OTHER PROVINCES):** Hildburghausen Bibliographisches Institut [2]; Jansson; Le Rouge; Mercator (Folio); Mercator (Small); Ortelius (Folio) [3]
BALKANS: Cantelli Da Vignola; De L'Isle; Furst; Hildburghausen Bibliographisches Institut; Hoffman; Mercator (Folio); Morden; Munster [2]; Schedel; Will

BALTIC COUNTRIES: Hildburghausen Bibliographisches Institut; Ortelius (Folio) [2]; Ortelius (Miniature)
BELGIUM (ALL): Guicciardini; Hildburghausen Bibliographisches Institut; Lotter; Mallet; Moll (Large); Probst; Quad; Rossi
- **ANTWERP:** Braun & Hogenberg [2]; Merian; Mortier; Tindal
- **BRABANT:** De L'Isle
- **BRUSSELS:** Braun & Hogenberg; Mortier
- **FLANDERS:** Guicciardini; Senex
- **HAINAUT:** Mercator (Folio); Mortier
- **LIEGE:** De Vaugondy; Mercator (Folio); Seutter
- **NAMUR:** De Aefferden; Mortier; Ortelius (Folio)
- **(OTHER CITIES):** Braun & Hogenberg; Guicciardini; Mortier [7]; Rapin [3]

BOHEMIA: Covens & Mortier; London Magazine; Mercator (Folio); Munster [3]; Ortelius (Folio) [2]; Quad; Schreiber; Speed; Van Den Keere; Wilkinson

BRITISH ISLES (ALL): Beer; Bradshaw; British Government; Cary; Cluver; De L'Isle; De Vaugondy [2]; Goos; Gray; Homann & Homann Heirs [2]; Jaillot [2]; Jansson [2]; Mercator (Folio) [2]; Moll (Large); Ortelius (Folio) [3]; Probst; Rossi; Sanson (Folio); Schreiber; S.D.U.K.; Stanford; Tallis; Visscher; Wells; Wyld
- **(ATLASES):** Johnston

CZECH REPUBLIC, PRAGUE: Gentleman's Magazine; Munster; Schedel; Schreiber; Seutter

DANUBE RIVER: Homann & Homann Heirs [2]; Lotter

DENMARK: Blaeu; Braun & Hogenberg; De Fer (Small); De L'Isle [2]; De Vaugondy; De Wit; Homann & Homann Heirs; Mercator (Small); Ortelius (Folio); Pitt; Rossi; Schreiber; Speed; Thomson
- **COPENHAGEN:** De Fer (Small); Mortier
- **FUNEN:** Blaeu; Mercator (Folio)
- **JUTLAND:** Jacobsz; Mercator (Folio) [2]

ENGLAND (ALL): Beer; Bordone; Cary; Homann & Homann Heirs; London Magazine; Mercator (Folio) [2]; Morden; Ortelius (Folio); Pinkerton; Schedel; S.D.U.K.; Speed
- **(ISLANDS):** Thomson
- **(NORTH):** Mercator (Folio) [3]; S.D.U.K. [2]
- **(ROADS):** Ogilby [8]
- **(SOUTHEAST):** Bellin (Large); S.D.U.K.
- **(SOUTHWEST):** S.D.U.K.
- **BEDFORDSHIRE:** Camden; Speed
- **BERKSHIRE:** British Ordnance Survey; Cary; London Magazine
- **BRISTOL CHANNEL:** Collins, G.; Depot De La Marine; Jacobsz
- **BUCKINGHAMSHIRE:** Speed
- **CAMBRIDGESHIRE:** Braun & Hogenberg [3]
- **CHANNEL ISLANDS:** Mercator (Folio) [2]
- **CHESHIRE:** Braun & Hogenberg
- **CORNWALL:** British Admiralty [3]; Collins, G. [2]; Laurie & Whittle [2]
- **DEVONSHIRE:** British Admiralty [4]; Gall & Inglis; Laurie & Whittle [4]
- **DORSETSHIRE:** Laurie & Whittle [2]
- **DURHAM:** British Admiralty; London Magazine
- **ESSEX:** Blome; British Ordnance Survey
- **HAMPSHIRE:** Bellin (Small); British Admiralty [2]; Laurie & Whittle
- **HEREFORDSHIRE:** Camden; Valk & Schenk
- **HUNTINGDONSHIRE:** Camden
- **ISLE OF WIGHT:** Depot De La Marine [2]
- **KENT:** Bellin (Large); Camden; Laurie & Whittle [3]; Morden; Walker, J. & C. [2]
- **LANCASHIRE:** Mackenzie; Morden
- **LEICESTERSHIRE:** Saxton
- **LINCOLNSHIRE:** Overton
- **LONDON:** Ashby; Bacon [3]; Bowles [2]; Braun & Hogenberg; Dodsley; Fores; Gall & Inglis; Hildburghausen Bibliographisches Institut; Homann & Homann Heirs; Illustrated London News [2]; Laurie & Whittle [2]; Lotter; Merian; Munster; Philip, G.; Seutter; S.D.U.K. [3]; Stanford; Tardieu; Weekly Dispatch; Wyld
- **NORFOLK:** Braun & Hogenberg; British Admiralty; Collins, G.
- **NORTHAMPTONSHIRE:** Local & State Maps; Speed
- **NORTHUMBERLAND:** Bartholomew; British Admiralty
- **NOTTINGHAMSHIRE:** London Magazine

- **OXFORDSHIRE:** Braun & Hogenberg; Longman; Speed
- **SCILLY ISLANDS:** British Admiralty; Collins, G.; Laurie & Whittle
- **SOMERSETSHIRE:** Speed
- **STAFFORDSHIRE:** London Magazine
- **SURREY:** British Ordnance Survey
- **SUSSEX:** Blaeu; Collins, G.
- **THAMES RIVER:** Blaeu; Colom; Jaillot; Van Keulen
- **WILTSHIRE:** Speed
- **YORKSHIRE:** Walker, J. & C.
- **(OTHER CITIES):** Braun & Hogenberg [4]; Local & State Maps
- **(MISCELLANEOUS):** Schedel

ENGLAND & WALES: Bartholomew; Cary; De L'Isle; De Pretot; De Vaugondy; Finley; Fullarton; Mallet; Moll (Large) [2]; National Soc. for Promoting Educ. of the Poor [2]; Rocque; Sharp; S.D.U.K. [4]; Stanford; Starling; Wyld

ENGLISH CHANNEL: Bellin (Large); Heather; Jacobsz [2]; Lodge; Thomson; Van Loon; Waters & Son

FINLAND: Jansson; Lotter

FRANCE (ALL): De Fer (Large); Julien, R.; Lattre; Magini; Moll (Large) [2]; Ortelius (Folio); Rossi; Schenk; Schreiber; Senex; Speed; Van Den Keere; Von Reilly
- **(CENTRAL):** Bonne; Mercator (Folio) [2]
- **(MISCELLANEOUS):** Local & State Maps; Schedel
- **(NAUTICAL CHARTS):** Bellin (Large); British Admiralty [2]; Laurie & Whittle
- **(NORTH):** Blaeu; Mercator (Folio); Ortelius (Folio)
- **(OTHER CITIES):** Braun & Hogenberg [6]; Mortier [6]; Munster [4]
- **(SOUTH):** Blaeu; Bodenehr; Bowen, E.; Mercator (Folio)
- **(SOUTHWEST):** Cantelli Da Vignola; De Vaugondy; Mercator (Folio)
- **(WEST):** Blaeu; De Vaugondy
- **ALSACE:** Mercator (Folio); Mercator (Small); Sanson (Folio)
- **ARTOIS:** Mortier
- **BORDEAUX:** De Fer (Small)
- **BRITTANY:** De Fer (Small)
- **BURGUNDY:** Mercator (Folio); Ortelius (Folio); Quad
- **CORSICA:** Bellin (Small) [2]; Bertius; London Magazine; Lotter
- **ISLE DE FRANCE:** Anonymous or Unknown; Bonne; De Vaugondy; Mercator (Folio); Ortelius (Folio)
- **LORRAINE:** Mercator (Folio); Mercator (Small)
- **LYONS:** Homann & Homann Heirs
- **NORMANDY:** Bonne; De Fer (Large); De Fer (Small)
- **ORLEANS:** Braun & Hogenberg; Cantelli Da Vignola; De Vaugondy
- **PARIS:** Braun & Hogenberg [3]; Bretez; De Belleforest; De L'Isle; De Vaugondy; Hildburghausen Bibliographisches Institut; Lobineau; Logerot; Munster; Schedel; S.D.U.K.
- **POITOU:** Ortelius (Folio)
- **PROVENCE:** Bonne; De Fer (Small); Mercator (Small)
- **SAVOY:** Jansson
- **TOULON:** British Admiralty

GERMANY (ALL): Cluver; Mallet; Munster; Ortelius (Folio); Probst; Rossi; Schreiber; Speed
- **(NORTH):** Mercator (Small)
- **(SOUTH):** Hildburghausen Bibliographisches Institut [2]; Munster
- **ANHALT:** Blaeu; Lotter [2]; Ortelius (Folio); Seutter
- **BADEN-WURTTEMBURG:** Hildburghausen Bibliographisches Institut [2]; Lotter [2]; Mortier [3]; Munster
  - **(CITIES):** Schedel
- **BAVARIA:** De Vaugondy; London Magazine; Lotter; Mercator (Folio); Mortier; Munster [6]; Ortelius (Folio) [2]; Seutter [2]; Wilkinson
  - **(CITIES):** Schedel
- **BERLIN:** London Magazine
- **BRANDENBURG:** Homann & Homann Heirs; Lotter; Munster; Seutter
- **BREMEN:** Lotter
- **BRUNSWICK:** Hildburghausen Bibliographisches Institut; Moll (Large); Seutter
- **COBLENZ:** Mortier
- **COLOGNE:** Braun & Hogenberg; Lotter; Mortier; Schedel
- **EAST FRISIA:** Lotter

- **EAST PRUSSIA:** Hildburghausen Bibliographisches Institut; Lotter; Schreiber
- **FRANCONIA:** Homann & Homann Heirs; Lotter [2]; Seutter
- **FRANKFORT:** Lotter; Mortier; Munster [2]
- **HAMBURG:** Mortier
- **HANOVER:** Seutter
- **HELIGOLAND:** British Admiralty
- **HESSE:** Blaeu; Hildburghausen Bibliographisches Institut [2]; Jansson; Lotter [2]; Mercator (Folio)
- **LOWER SAXONY:** Homann & Homann Heirs [2]; Jansson; Mercator (Folio) [2]; Munster; Seutter; Weigel
- **MECKLENBURG:** Mortier
- **PRUSSIA:** Cantelli Da Vignola; Mercator (Folio); Wilkinson
- **RHEINLAND-PFALZ:** Hildburghausen Bibliographisches Institut; Jansson; Lotter; Mercator (Folio); Mercator (Small); Mortier [5]; Munster [2]; Quad
- **RUGEN:** Blaeu
- **SAARLAND:** Mortier
- **SAXONY:** Homann & Homann Heirs; Lotter; Ortelius (Folio); Schenk; Weigel
  –**(CITIES):** Braun & Hogenberg
- **SCHLESWIG-HOLSTEIN:** Hildburghausen Bibliographisches Institut [2]; Lotter [2]; Mercator (Folio); Ortelius (Folio)
- **SWABIA:** Blaeu; Lotter; Probst; Wilkinson
- **THURINGEN:** Hildburghausen Bibliographisches Institut; Munster
- **WESTPHALIA:** Hildburghausen Bibliographisches Institut [2]; Lotter [4]; Mercator (Folio) [2]; Mortier [7]; Ortelius (Miniature); Seutter [2]
- **WURTTEMBERG:** Hildburghausen Bibliographisches Institut; Seutter
- **(OTHER CITIES):** Braun & Hogenberg
- **(MISCELLANEOUS):** British Admiralty; Schedel [2]

GIBRALTAR: Allard; Gentleman's Magazine; Lotter; Moll (Small); Tindal
GIBRALTAR, STRAIT OF: Bodenehr
GREAT BRITAIN (ALL): Blaeu; Faden; Jansson; Mallet; Moll (Large) [2]; Moll (Small); Munster; Weekly Dispatch
GREECE: Bowen, E.; British Admiralty [2]; De L'Isle; Hildburghausen Bibliographisches Institut; Magini; Mercator (Folio) [2]; Munster [3]; Ortelius (Folio); Speed; Wells [2]
- **(PROVINCES):** Jansson; Lotter; Mallet; Mercator (Folio)
- **AEGEAN ISLANDS:** British Admiralty; Mallet [2]; Von Breydenbach
- **ATHENS:** Mortier
- **CORFU:** Doncker; Ortelius (Miniature)
- **CRETE:** Beer; Bordone; Braun & Hogenberg [2]; Mercator (Folio); Ortelius (Miniature)
- **IONIAN ISLANDS:** Mortier
- **(OTHER CITIES):** Mortier [5]; Schedel

HUNGARY: Braun & Hogenberg; Homann & Homann Heirs; Le Rouge; Mallet; Mercator (Folio); Ortelius (Folio); Ruscelli; Schreiber; Tallis; Van Schagen
HUNGARY & BALKANS: Homann & Homann Heirs; Sanson (Folio); Wilkinson
IRELAND (ALL): Allard [2]; Arrowsmith; Bartholomew; Beer; Blaeu; Blome; Brion De La Tour; Camden; Colton (Atlas Maps); De Laporte; De Vaugondy [2]; Finley; Guthrie & Jones; Harrison; Hildburghausen Bibliographisches Institut; Homann & Homann Heirs [2]; Jansson; Jefferys; Laporte; Le Rouge; Mallet [2]; Mercator (Folio); Moll (Large); Morden [5]; Mount & Page; Ortelius (Folio) [2]; Ortelius (Miniature); Rocque; Sanson (Folio); Sayer & Bennett; Seale; Seller; Seutter; S.D.U.K. [3]; Stackhouse; Teesdale; Thomson [3]; Van Der Aa
- **(ATLASES):** Taylor & Skinner
- **(COUNTIES):** Mercator (Folio)
- **(NAUTICAL CHARTS):** British Admiralty [2]; Collins, G. [2]; Laurie & Whittle
- **(REGIONS):** Blaeu; Mercator (Folio) [4]; Zatta
- **CONNAUGHT:** Bertius
- **DUBLIN:** Bankes; Brooking; Illustrated London News; Mallet; S.D.U.K. [3]
- **LEINSTER:** Blaeu; Speed
- **ULSTER:** Mercator (Folio) [2]

IRISH SEA: Collins, G.; Mackenzie; Seale
ITALY (ALL): Beer; De L'Isle; De La Houve; Hildburghausen Bibliographisches Institut; Homann & Homann Heirs; Jansson; Lavoisne; Moll (Large); Moll (Small) [2]; Munster; Nicolosi; Ortelius (Folio); Ruscelli; Schreiber; Speed; Van Den Keere

- **(CENTRAL):** De Fer (Large); De Vaugondy; Lotter; Rossi [2]
- **(NORTHERN):** Hildburghausen Bibliographisches Institut; Lotter
- **(SOUTHERN):** Blaeu; De Vaugondy; Mercator (Folio)
- **ELBA:** Bowyer [2]
- **FLORENCE:** Braun & Hogenberg [2]; Homann & Homann Heirs; Magnelli; Munster [2]
- **LOMBARDY:** Mercator (Folio)
- **MANTUA:** Braun & Hogenberg; Schedel
- **MILAN:** Schedel; S.D.U.K.
- **NAPLES:** Braun & Hogenberg [3]; S.D.U.K.
- **PIEDMONT:** Mercator (Folio)
- **ROME:** Braun & Hogenberg [5]; Homann & Homann Heirs; Munster; Schedel
- **SARDINIA:** Bellin (Small); Ortelius (Miniature)
- **SAVOY:** Beer; Le Rouge
- **SICILY:** Beer; Braun & Hogenberg; De L'Isle; Homann & Homann Heirs; Magini; Mallet; Munster; Sanson (Folio)
- **SICILY & SARDINIA:** Gastaldi; Munster
- **TURIN:** Tindal
- **TUSCANY:** Magini; Mercator (Folio); Ortelius (Folio)
- **VENICE:** Braun & Hogenberg [2]; Homann & Homann Heirs; Schedel; S.D.U.K.
- **(OTHER CITIES):** Braun & Hogenberg [4]; Lafreri School; Schedel [6]; Tindal; Van Aelst
- **(OTHER PROVINCES):** Magini
- **(MISCELLANEOUS):** Bellin (Small); Ortelius (Folio); Ortelius (Miniature)

LITHUANIA: Blaeu; Lotter; Pitt
LIVONIA: Mercator (Folio)
LOW COUNTRIES: Alting
- **LEO BELGICUS:** Strada

LUXEMBURG: De Aefferden; De Vaugondy; Mercator (Folio); Mortier
MALTA: Beer; Ortelius (Miniature); Putter; Varin
MEDITERANEAN SEA (ALL): De Groot; Wells
- **(EAST):** Blome; Doncker [2]; Jansson; Moll (Small); Ortelius (Folio)
- **(ISLANDS):** Cluver
- **(WEST):** Doncker; Homann & Homann Heirs; Michelot; Van Loon
- **(MISCELLANEOUS):** Ortelius (Folio) [2]

MORAVIA: Mercator (Folio); Quad; Seutter
NETHERLANDS (ALL): De L'Isle; Lotter; Mallet; Moll (Large); Moll (Small); Probst; Schreiber
- **AMSTERDAM:** Pontanus; Salmon
- **FRISIA:** Ortelius (Folio)
- **GELDERLAND:** Mercator (Folio)
- **GRONINGEN:** Guicciardini
- **HOLLAND:** Hildburghausen Bibliographisches Institut; Mercator (Folio); Ortelius (Folio)
- **UTRECHT:** Seutter
- **WEST FRISIA:** Guicciardini; Mercator (Folio)
- **ZEELAND:** Lotter; Mercator (Folio); Mortier [2]
- **(OTHER CITIES):** Braun & Hogenberg [3]; De Fer (Small); Guicciardini [4]; Mortier [2]

NETHERLANDS & BELGIUM: Ortelius (Folio)
NETHERLANDS, BELGIUM & LUXEMBOURG: Mercator (Folio); Speed; Wilkinson
NORTH SEA: Faden; Hildburghausen Bibliographisches Institut
NORWAY: Blaeu [2]; Colom; Hildburghausen Bibliographisches Institut; Jacobsz; Mallet
POLAND: Cary; De Vaugondy; Fisher; Gentleman's Magazine; Hildburghausen Bibliographisches Institut; Jansson; Kitchin; London Magazine; Longman; Mercator (Folio); Merian; Morden; Ortelius (Folio) [2]; Pitt; Probst; Quad; Speed; Zatta [2]
- **(CITIES):** Schedel [2]
- **SILESIA:** Hildburghausen Bibliographisches Institut; Lotter; Ortelius (Folio); Seutter [2]; Wilkinson
- **WEST PRUSSIA:** Hildburghausen Bibliographisches Institut

POLAND & LITHUANIA: Cary; De Wit; Moll (Small); Senex
PORTUGAL: Cary; De Fer (Small); Hildburghausen Bibliographisches Institut; Homann & Homann Heirs; Jaillot; Moll (Small); Ortelius (Folio); Ortelius (Miniature); Rizzi-Zannoni; S.D.U.K.; Van Der Aa; Zatta
- **LISBON:** De Fer (Small); Faden

RHINE RIVER: Bradshaw; Hildburghausen Bibliographisches Institut; Mercator (Folio); Seutter; Wilkinson

ROMAN EMPIRE: Moll (Large); Ortelius (Folio); Speed [2]; Van Den Keere
ROMANIA: Jansson; Military Maps
RUSSIA (EUROPEAN): De L'Isle; Hildburghausen Bibliographisches Institut; Jaillot; Probst; Schenk; Senex; Seutter [2]; Speed
- **(PROVINCES):** Goos; Grimmel; Petermann
- **(SOUTHERN):** Mercator (Folio); Munster
- **CRIMEA:** Probst; Ptolemy (1522-1541 Strassburg)
- **MOSCOW:** Braun & Hogenberg
- **ST. PETERSBURG:** Gentleman's Magazine; Hildburghausen Bibliographisches Institut; Lotter

SCANDINAVIA (ALL): Cluver; Danckerts; De Fer (Large); De L'Isle; Hildburghausen Bibliographisches Institut; Homann & Homann Heirs; Le Rouge; Mallet; Moll (Large); Moll (Small) [2]; Probst; Schreiber; Von Reilly

SCOTLAND (ALL): Beer; Black; Carey, M.; Cary; Chatelain; De L'Isle; Guthrie & Jones; Homann & Homann Heirs; Jacobsz; Jansson; Johnston [2]; Kitchin [2]; Laurie & Whittle; Lavoisne; Mercator (Small); Moll (Large) [2]; Moll (Small) [2]; Morden; Ortelius (Folio); Sayer; S.D.U.K.; Tallis; Thomas, Cowperthwait & Co.; Thomson
- **(ISLANDS):** British Ordnance Survey; Mallet; S.D.U.K.
- **(NAUTICAL CHARTS):** Ainslie; British Admiralty [8]; Collins, G. [2]; Jacobsz; Johnston; Mackenzie [4]; Van Keulen [3]
- **(REGIONS):** British Ordnance Survey; Knox; Mercator (Folio) [2]; S.D.U.K. [2]
- **ABERDEEN SHIRE:** British Government
- **BERWICKSHIRE:** British Ordnance Survey
- **EDINBURGH:** Braun & Hogenberg [2]
- **EDINBURGHSHIRE:** Bartholomew [2]; Black; British Ordnance Survey; S.D.U.K.
- **FIFE SHIRE:** Sharp
- **NAIRN SHIRE:** Johnston
- **PERTHSHIRE:** Johnston; Philip, G.; Real Estate & Promotional Maps
- **SELKIRKSHIRE:** British Ordnance Survey; Johnston
- **SHETLAND ISLANDS:** Collins, G. [2]
- **SUTHERLANDSHIRE:** Johnston
- **(OTHER COUNTIES):** Bartholomew; British Ordnance Survey

SPAIN (ALL): Cluver [2]; De Vaugondy; Gentleman's Magazine; Munster; Van Den Keere
- **ANDALUSIA:** Bertius; Jansson
- **ARAGON:** Cantelli Da Vignola; Hondius; Mercator (Folio)
- **BALEARIC ISLANDS:** Blaeu; Homann & Homann Heirs
- **CASTILLE:** Cantelli Da Vignola; Mercator (Folio)
- **GALICIA:** Cantelli Da Vignola
- **GRANADA:** Braun & Hogenberg
- **VALENCIA:** Mercator (Small); Ortelius (Folio)
- **(OTHER CITIES):** Blaeu; Braun & Hogenberg [10]; Merian
- **(MISCELLANEOUS):** British Admiralty

SPAIN & PORTUGAL: De Fer (Large); De L'Isle; Du Val; Le Rouge; Merian; Moll (Large); Munster [2]; Rosaccio; Ruscelli; Speed

SWEDEN: Blaeu
- **STOCKHOLM:** Braun & Hogenberg [2]
- **(OTHER CITIES):** Mortier

SWITZERLAND: Cluver; De L'Isle; Faden; Hildburghausen Bibliographisches Institut; Keller [2]; Le Rouge; Mercator (Folio) [2]; Munster [4]; Pinkerton; Probst; Schreiber; Weigel; Zatta [3]
- **(CANTONS):** De L'Isle; Lotter; Mercator (Folio) [2]; Ortelius (Miniature)
- **BASEL:** Bankes; Mortier; Munster; Schedel
- **(OTHER CITIES):** Bankes; Braun & Hogenberg; Munster [5]

TRANSYLVANIA: De Fer (Large); Munster

TURKEY, CONSTANTINOPLE: Anonymous or Unknown; Braun & Hogenberg; Gentleman's Magazine [2]; Heck; Lotter; Mallet; Porcacchi; Salmon; Schedel

UKRAINE: Blaeu; De Leth; Homann & Homann Heirs [2]; Lotter; Mercator (Folio); Military Maps

WALES (ALL): Mercator (Folio); Ortelius (Folio); Speed
- **(COUNTIES):** Blaeu; Camden; Speed
- **(NAUTICAL CHARTS):** British Admiralty [5]; Collins, G. [2]; Mackenzie [2]; Manuscript Maps; Morris [3]
- **(MISCELLANEOUS):** Ogilby

NORTH AMERICA: General & Pre-Independence U.S. Regions

NORTH AMERICA (ALL): Bell; Bolton; Brion De La Tour; Carey & Lea; Cary [2]; Colton (Atlas Maps); Conkey; Cummings & Hilliard; D'anville [2]; Darton & Harvey; De L'Isle; De Vaugondy [2]; Desnos; Dower; Guthrie & Jones; Hennepin; Homann & Homann Heirs; Jaillot [3]; Jansson [3]; Janvier [2]; Johnson [2]; Kitchin; Lapie; Levasseur [4]; Lloyd; Lotter; Mitchell, S.A. (Atlas Maps 1859 & Earlier); Moll (Large); Moll (Small); Perrot; Pinkerton [2]; Powell, J.W.; Probst; Quad [3]; Roberts; Sanson (Folio) [3]; Sayer [2]; Seale [2]; Seile; Senex [2]; Seutter; Sherwood, Neely & Jones; S.D.U.K.; Stackhouse; Tallis [4]; Tasso; Thomas, Cowperthwait & Co. [2]; Thomson; Van Der Aa [3]; Von Stulpnagel; Vuillemin; Walch; Wyld
- **(ATLASES):** Vandermaelen
- **(CENTRAL):** Bellin (Small) [2]; D'anville; De Vaugondy [2]; Homann & Homann Heirs [4]; La Hontan; Popple [2]; Schraembl; Seutter [2]
- **(EAST):** Bertius; Bonne; Chatelain [4]; Covens & Mortier; D'anville; Dashiell; De Vaugondy [4]; Du Val [2]; Faden; Gentleman's Magazine [2]; Harrison; Homann & Homann Heirs [4]; Jansson; Kitchin; La Hontan; Longchamps; Lotter [2]; Moll (Large); Moll (Small) [2]; Morden [2]; Nolin [2]; Ottens; Popple; Seutter; Tirion; Van Keulen; Wyld [2]; Wytfliet
- **(EAST COAST):** Colom; Dudley; Goos; Imray; Mount & Page; Sartine; Seller; Van Der Aa
- **(NORTH AMERICA & WEST INDIES):** Homann & Homann Heirs [2]
- **(NORTH):** Diderot; Franklin, J.; Marzolla
- **(NORTHEAST):** Alexander; De L'Isle; Du Val [2]; General Magazine of Arts & Sciences; Gentleman's Magazine; Jansson; Mallet; Ogilby; Ramusio; Ruscelli [3]; Sayer & Bennett; Visscher
- **(NORTHWEST):** Cook; De Jode; Diderot [4]; Forster; La Perouse [4]; Poirson; Robinson [2]; Vancouver
- **(SOUTH):** Bonne; Moll (Small) [2]
- **(SOUTHEAST):** De L'Isle; Mallet; Muller; Van Der Aa [2]
- **(UNITED STATES, PRESENT):** Gentleman's Magazine; Senex
- **(WEST):** Moll (Small)
- **(WEST COAST):** La Perouse
- **(MISCELLANEOUS):** Hildburghausen Bibliographisches Institut

ARCTIC: Dudley; Van Keulen [2]
BRITISH COLONIES, MIDDLE: Evans; Lotter [2]; Senex
BRITISH COLONIES, NORTHERN: Bellin (Small) [2]; Danckerts; Faden; Gentleman's Magazine; Grierson; Homann & Homann Heirs [4]; Jansson [2]; Jefferys; Moll (Small) [3]; Royal Magazine; Sayer & Bennett; Seutter [3]; Speed [4]; Van Keulen; Visscher [3]
BRITISH COLONIES, SOUTHERN: Homann & Homann Heirs; Speed [2]
CALIFORNIA: De Fer (Small); Diderot; Goos; Kino; Royal Geographical Society; Sanson (Small)
CALIFORNIA & NEW MEXICO: Beer; De Fer (Large); De Fer (Small) [2]; Mallet [2]; Nolin; Scherer; Tirion
CAROLINA: Morden; Mortier [3]; Mouzon; Speed [2]
CAROLINA & FLORIDA: Bellin (Small); De Vaugondy [2]
CAROLINA & GEORGIA: Bellin (Small) [3]; Bowen, E.
CAROLINA, MARYLAND & VIRGINIA: Homann & Homann Heirs [3]
CHEROKEE NATION: London Magazine
FLORIDA: Beer; Bellin (Small); De Laet; Gentleman's Magazine [2]; London Magazine [2]; Mallet [2]; Moll (Small); Ortelius (Folio) [2]; Sanson (Small); Van Keulen
FLORIDA & LOUISIANA: Gentleman's Magazine; Moll (Small)
FLORIDA & MEXICO: Chatelain; De L'Isle; Ortelius (Folio)
FLORIDA & VIRGINIA: Blaeu [3]; Cloppenburgh; Hondius [4]; Jansson [2]; Mercator (Folio); Ogilby
GREAT LAKES: Bellin (Large); Bellin (Small); British Admiralty [3]; Coronelli [3]; De Vaugondy; Homann & Homann Heirs [2]; London Magazine [2]; Nolin; S.D.U.K.; Zatta [4]
GULF COAST: Gentleman's Magazine
GULF OF MEXICO: Rizzi-Zannoni [2]
LOUISIANA: Covens & Mortier [2]; D'anville; De L'Isle; Homann & Homann Heirs; Law; London Magazine
LOUISIANA REGION: Tirion
MARYLAND & VIRGINIA: Bellin (Small); De Vaugondy; Mallet; Speed [4]
MISSISSIPPI RIVER: Sayer [2]
NEW ENGLAND: Bellin (Small); Blaeu [3]; De Laet; Foster, John; Gentleman's Magazine; Hale; Jefferys; Mitchell, S.A.; Morden; S.D.U.K.; Thornton; Van Der Aa; Zatta

NEW ENGLAND & VIRGINIA: Jansson
NEW FRANCE: Bellin (Large); Chatelain [3]; De L'Isle [2]; De Laet [2]; De Vaugondy; Ramusio [3]; Sanson (Folio) [3]; Sanson (Small)
NEW JERSEY & PENNSYLVANIA: Morden
NEW YORK & PENNSYLVANIA: Bowen & Gibson
NIAGARA RIVER: Melish
SOUTHWESTERN USA & MEXICO: Archer; Greenleaf; Sanson (Folio) [2]; Tallis [2]
VIRGINIA: Beer; De Bry; Jansson; London Magazine; Mallet; Mercator (Small); Ogilby; Smith, John

NORTH AMERICA: CANADA

CANADA (ALL): Arrowsmith & Lewis; Beer; Blackwood; Bonne; Carey & Lea [2]; De L'Isle; Hildburghausen Bibliographisches Institut; Jefferys [2]; Kelly; Pinkerton; Radefeld; S.D.U.K. [2]; Tallis [7]; Teesdale; Tirion; Wyld
- **(ATLASES):** Le Rouge
- **(CENTRAL):** Bellin (Large); Cary; Stockdale; Tirion; Wytfliet
- **(EAST):** Arrowsmith [2]; Blaeu; Bonne; Bouchette; Coronelli; De L'Isle; De Vaugondy; Guthrie; Homann & Homann Heirs; Le Rouge; Neele; Nelson; Tallis [3]; Taylor; Thomas, Cowperthwait & Co.; Thomson; Wyld; Wytfliet; Zatta [2]
- **(NORTH):** Bartholomew; De Bry; Franklin, J.; Hearne [2]; Mortier [2]; Mount & Page; Murray, J. [2]; Petermann; Thomson; Weller; Zatta
- **(NORTHWEST):** Cram
- **(WEST):** Cram; Gentleman's Magazine; Real Estate & Promotional Maps
- **(MISCELLANEOUS):** Homann & Homann Heirs [2]

BAFFIN BAY: British Admiralty
BRITISH COLUMBIA: British Admiralty [2]; Cook [2]; Cram; Royal Geographical Society [2]
CAPE BRETON ISLAND: Bowles; Depot De La Marine [3]
- **LOUISBOURG:** Bellin (Small); Depot De La Marine; Gentleman's Magazine; Le Rouge; Raspe

HUDSON BAY: Bellin (Small) [2]; Hearne [2]; Political Magazine
LABRADOR: British Admiralty; Le Rouge
MANITOBA: Lloyd
MARITIME PROVINCES: Blaeu; Bonne [2]; Cary [2]; Colton (Atlas Maps); Colton (Pocket & Wall Maps); Depot De La Marine; Gentleman's Magazine; Johnson; Mitchell, S.A. (Atlas Maps 1860 & Later); Moll (Small); Zatta [2]
NEW BRUNSWICK: Des Barres [4]; S.D.U.K.; Wilkinson
NEWFOUNDLAND: Bellin (Large); Bellin (Small); British Admiralty [2]; Cook; Coronelli; Depot De La Marine; Grierson; Jefferys; Le Rouge; Mount & Page [2]; Page; Sayer & Bennett; Van Keulen [4]
NOVA SCOTIA: Bellin (Small); Depot De La Marine [2]; Des Barres [7]; Jefferys; Montresor
- **HALIFAX:** Bellin (Small); Gentleman's Magazine [2]; Le Rouge

ONTARIO: Arrowsmith; Asher & Adams; British Admiralty; Colton (Atlas Maps); Mitchell, S.A. (Atlas Maps 1860 & Later); S.D.U.K.; Tallis [2]
- **TORONTO:** Goad

PRINCE EDWARD ISLAND: Depot De La Marine; Des Barres; Jefferys
QUEBEC: British Admiralty; Colton (Atlas Maps); Des Barres; Gibson [2]; Lodge; Mitchell, S.A. (Atlas Maps 1860 & Later)
- **MONTREAL:** Jefferys; Ramusio; Universal Magazine; Walker
- **QUEBEC CITY:** Bellin (Small) [2]; Covens & Mortier; Crepy; De Fer (Small); Jefferys; La Hontan [2]; London Magazine; Mortier; Oakley; Scots Magazine; Tirion [2]; Walker

ST. LAWRENCE GULF: British Admiralty; Des Barres [2]; Faden; Zatta
ST. LAWRENCE RIVER: Bellin (Large) [2]; Bellin (Small) [2]; British Admiralty [6]; Des Barres [4]; Gentleman's Magazine; Harrison [2]; Jefferys [2]; Kitchin; London Magazine; Van Keulen
ST. PIERRE & MIQUELON: Bellin (Large)

NORTH AMERICA: MEXICO and CENTRAL AMERICA

BELIZE: British Admiralty
CENTRAL AMERICA (ALL): Bellin (Small); British Admiralty; Fullarton; Johnson; Pinkerton; Tallis; Van Der Aa
- **(MISCELLANEOUS):** Ferguson

GUATEMALA: British Admiralty

HONDURAS: Jefferys; Le Rouge
MEXICO: Albrizzi; Beer; Bertius [2]; Blaeu [2]; Cloppenburgh; Colton (Atlas Maps); De Bry [2]; De Vaugondy; Gastaldi; Gray; Greenleaf; Jansson; Johnson; Mercator (Small); Ogilby; Pinkerton [2]; Quad; Rand, McNally & Co. (Pocket & Wall Maps); Ruscelli; Van Der Aa [2]
- **(REGIONS):** Kircher; Petermann
- **MEXICO CITY:** Anonymous or Unknown; Bellin (Small); Braun & Hogenberg [2]; Goad; Ramusio
- **VERA CRUZ:** British Admiralty
- **(OTHER CITIES):** De Bry

MEXICO & CENTRAL AMERICA: Bonne; De Laet; Ogilby; Van Der Aa
MEXICO & GUATEMALA: Bellin (Small)
MEXICO & PRESENT U.S. SOUTHWEST: Black [2]; Bonne [2]; Bradford; Buchon; Carey & Lea; Carey, M.; De Vaugondy [2]; Dufour; Flemming; Gastaldi; Kitchin; Lapie [3]; Pinkerton; Ruscelli [2]; Stieler; Tallis [2]; Tanner [2]; Tardieu; Thomas, Cowperthwait & Co.; Tirion; Vivien; Zatta
MEXICO & WEST INDIES: Brion De La Tour; De Vaugondy; Mitchell, S.A.; Mitchell, S.A. (Atlas Maps 1860 & Later)
PANAMA: Lloyd; Tallis [2]

NORTH AMERICA: UNITED STATES

UNITED STATES (ALL): Black; Brue; Buchon; Burr [2]; Colton (Atlas Maps); Company Maps; Cornell; Dufour; Garnier; Gray; Greenleaf; Gussefeld; Handtke; Harper & Bros.; Hayward; Hinton [2]; Huntington; Johnson [3]; Lapie; Lizars; Melish; Mitchell, S.A. [2]; Mitchell, S.A. (Atlas Maps 1859 & Earlier); Morse, J.; Morse, S.; Olney; Petermann; Rand, McNally & Co. (Pocket & Wall Maps) [2]; Swanston [2]; Tallis [2]; Thomas, Cowperthwait & Co. [2]; Thomson; Vivien; Warner, B.; Weekly Dispatch; Weimar Geographisches Institut
UNITED STATES & CANADA: Railroad Company Maps; Real Estate & Promotional Maps
UNITED STATES & MEXICO: Dufour; Haven; Mitchell, S.A.; Tardieu; Von Stulpnagel; Woodbridge
- **(ATLASES):** Cram; Marshall; Rand, McNally & Co. (Atlas Maps) [2]; U.S.
- **(CENTRAL):** Bonne; Buchon; Harrison; Olney; S.D.U.K. [2]; U.S. [2]; Weekly Dispatch; Zatta
- **(EAST COAST):** Manuscript Maps
- **(EAST):** Bonne
- **(EASTERN PORTION):** Appleton; Bonne; Bowen, T.; Cary; Chamouin; Colton (Atlas Maps); Cummings & Hilliard; Finley; Fisher & Son; Gussefeld; Kitchin; Lay; Lloyd; Magnus, C.; Mitchell, S.A.; Tanner; Teesdale; U.S.; Universal Magazine; Wilkinson [2]; Zatta [2]
- **(GREAT PLAINS):** Borghi; Buchon; Carey & Lea [2]; Cassell, Peter & Galpin; Howe; Johnson [9]; Mitchell, S.A. (Atlas Maps 1860 & Later) [4]; Morse & Breese; Railroad Company Maps; Stieler; U.S.; U.S. Pacific R.R. Survey; U.S. War Department; Warner & Beers [2]; Watson
- **(GULF COAST):** Des Barres; Harrison; Jefferys; U.S. Coast Survey
- **(MIDDLE ATLANTIC):** Hildburghausen Bibliographisches Institut; Johnson; Mount & Page; Scots Magazine; U.S. War Department; Universal Magazine; Zatta
- **(MIDWEST):** Bradford; Brookes; Carey, M.; Carver; Cary; Hildburghausen Bibliographisches Institut; Meyer; Mitchell, S.A.; Morse, J.; Smith, Roswell C.; S.D.U.K. [2]; Swanston
- **(MOUNTAIN WEST):** Bonneville [2]; Colton (Atlas Maps); Gray; U.S.; U.S. Geological Survey; U.S. War Department
- **(NEW ENGLAND & NEW YORK):** Gentleman's Magazine; Mitchell, S.A. (Atlas Maps 1860 & Later)
- **(NEW ENGLAND):** Asher & Adams; Johnson; Hildburghausen Bibliographisches Institut; Le Rouge; Railroad Company Maps [2]; Russell; Snow & Co.; Walling & Gray
- **(NORTH):** Railroad Company Maps [2]
- **(NORTHEAST):** Bertholon; Brookes [2]; Cary [2]; Harper; Lotter; Marshall; Pinkerton [2]; Railroad Company Maps; Reichard; Thomson; Weld, I.; Zatta
- **(NORTHWEST):** Johnson; Mitchell, S.A. (Atlas Maps 1860 & Later) [2]; Petermann; U.S. State Surveys
- **(SOUTH):** Appleton; Bachmann; Fullarton; Harper's Weekly; Hildburghausen Bibliographisches Institut; Johnson [3]; Mitchell, S.A.; Morse, J.; New York Tribune; Railroad Company Maps [2]; S.D.U.K. [4]; U.S. War Department
- **(SOUTHEAST):** Asher & Co.; Bonne; Cary; Hildburghausen Bibliographisches Institut; Marshall; Morse, J. [3]; Olmsted; Pinkerton; Political Magazine; Russell; Smith, Roswell C.; Stanford; Thomson; Zatta [2]
- **(SOUTHWEST):** Colton (Atlas Maps); Donaldson, T.; Lloyd; U.S. War Department [3]; Warner & Beers [2]

363

- **(SOUTHWEST & CALIFORNIA):** Gray; Hildburghausen Bibliographisches Institut; Johnson [4]
- **(SOUTHWEST & MEXICO):** Bell; Black; Flemming; Hall, S.; Meyer; Pinkerton; S.D.U.K. [2]; Tallis; Weekly Dispatch
- **(WEST COAST):** Rand, McNally & Co. (Pocket & Wall Maps); U.S. Coast & Geodetic Survey; Vancouver
- **(WEST):** Black; Blackie & Son; Bonneville; Carey, M.; Colton (Pocket & Wall Maps) [2]; Donaldson, T.; Flemming; Fremont; Fullarton; Gilpin; Goldthwait; Howe; Irving, W.; Mitchell, S.A.; Mitchell, S.A. (Atlas Maps 1859 & Earlier); Olney [2]; Philip, G.; Railroad Company Maps [3]; Sherman & Smith; U.S. [2]; U.S. War Department; Weller; Werner
- **(OTHER CITIES):** Bradford; Colton (Atlas Maps)
- **(MISCELLANEOUS):** Hildburghausen Bibliographisches Institut; Mitchell, S.A.; U.S.

ALABAMA: Bradford; Colton (Atlas Maps) [2]; Desilver; Gray; U.S. War Department
ALABAMA & GEORGIA: Hinton; Johnson [2]
ALABAMA & MISSISSIPPI: Bradford
ALASKA: Bonne; Bradley; Buchon; Cook; Cram [2]; Gray; La Perouse; Mitchell, S.A. (Atlas Maps 1860 & Later); Rand, McNally & Co. (Atlas Maps); Rand, McNally & Co. (Pocket & Wall Maps); U.S. Geological Survey [3]
ARIZONA: Asher & Adams; Cram [2]; Rand, McNally & Co. (Atlas Maps) [?]; U.S. State Surveys; U.S. War Department
ARIZONA & NEW MEXICO: Bradley; Mitchell, S.A. (Atlas Maps 1860 & Later); U.S.; U.S. State Surveys
ARKANSAS: Asher & Adams; Colton (Atlas Maps); Desilver; Mitchell, S.A. (Atlas Maps 1859 & Earlier); Railroad Company Maps; Tanner
ARKANSAS & MISSOURI: Finley
ARKANSAS, LOUISIANA & MISSISSIPPI: Johnson
CALIFORNIA: Bradley; Colton (Atlas Maps) [2]; De Bry; Depot De La Marine; La Perouse [4]; Mitchell, S.A. (Atlas Maps 1860 & Later) [3]; Morse & Breese; Railroad Company Maps; Rand, McNally & Co. (Atlas Maps); U.S. [3]; U.S. Coast Survey; U.S. Pacific R.R. Survey; U.S. War Department
- **LOS ANGELES:** Hardesty
- **SAN FRANCISCO:** Gray; La Perouse [2]; Lange; U.S. Coast Survey

CALIFORNIA & NEVADA: Asher & Adams; Colton (Atlas Maps)
CALIFORNIA & OREGON: Fremont; Mitchell, S.A. [2]
COLORADO: Bradley; Clason Map Co.; Cram; Gray; Harper's Weekly; Mining Maps; Railroad Company Maps; Rand, McNally & Co. (Pocket & Wall Maps); U.S. [2]; U.S. Geological Survey [10]; U.S. State Surveys [2]; U.S. War Department [5]
COLORADO & NEW MEXICO: U.S. War Department
CONNECTICUT: Arrowsmith & Lewis; Carey & Lea; Carey, M.; Colton (Atlas Maps); Mitchell, S.A. (Atlas Maps 1859 & Earlier); Tanner; U.S. Coast Survey [2]
CONNECTICUT & RHODE ISLAND: Morse, J.; Universal Magazine
DAKOTA TERRITORY: Asher & Adams [2]; Colton (Atlas Maps)
DAKOTA TERRITORY & MINNESOTA: Johnson [2]; Mitchell, S.A. (Atlas Maps 1860 & Later)
DELAWARE: Arrowsmith & Lewis; Carey, M.
DELAWARE & MARYLAND: Burr; Colton (Atlas Maps) [2]; Johnson; Morse, J.; Payne [2]; Tanner; Thomas, Cowperthwait & Co.
DISTRICT OF COLUMBIA: Anonymous or Unknown; Bradford; Colton (Atlas Maps) [2]; Ellicott; Johnson; Stone; Thomas, Cowperthwait & Co.; Winterbotham
FLORIDA: Appleton; Balch; Bradford [4]; Bradley; Buchon [2]; Carey & Lea [3]; Colton (Atlas Maps) [2]; Cram; Dapper; Finley; Grant; Gray [2]; Greenleaf; Hinton; Johnson [3]; Meyer; Mitchell, S.A. (Atlas Maps 1859 & Earlier) [2]; Mitchell, S.A. (Atlas Maps 1860 & Later); Rand, McNally & Co. (Atlas Maps) [4]; S.D.U.K. [2]; Thomas, Cowperthwait & Co. [2]; Tunison; U.S. Coast & Geodetic Survey [7]; U.S. Coast Survey [2]; U.S. State Surveys [2]; Van Der Aa
- **PENSACOLA:** Bellin (Small); Blunt; Jefferys
- **ST. AUGUSTINE:** Gentleman's Magazine; Jefferys; Mallet [2]; Montanus [2]; Ogilby

FLORIDA & GEORGIA: Black
GEORGIA: Colton (Atlas Maps); Desilver [2]; S.D.U.K.; Thomas, Cowperthwait & Co.; U.S. War Department [2]
GEORGIA, WITH WESTERN TERRITORY: Carey, M.
HAWAII: Bonne; La Perouse [2]; U.S. State Surveys; Wilkes
IDAHO: Cram [3]; Hardesty; Mitchell, S.A. (Atlas Maps 1860 & Later); Rand, McNally & Co. (Atlas Maps); U.S. Geological Survey; U.S. State Surveys [2]; U.S. War Department
IDAHO, MONTANA & WYOMING: Bradley [3]; Warner & Beers

ILLINOIS: Asher & Adams; Colton (Atlas Maps); Finley [2]; Johnson; Mitchell, S.A. (Atlas Maps 1860 & Later) [2]; Rand, McNally & Co. (Atlas Maps)
- **CHICAGO:** Colton (Atlas Maps) [2]; Gray

INDIANA: Gray; Greenleaf; Johnson; Mitchell, S.A. (Atlas Maps 1859 & Earlier); Morse & Breese

INDIANA & OHIO: Mitchell, S.A. (Atlas Maps 1860 & Later)

IOWA: Colton (Atlas Maps); Colton (Pocket & Wall Maps); Desilver; Henn, Williams & Co.; Local & State Wall Maps; U.S. State Surveys

IOWA & MISSOURI: Mitchell, S.A. (Atlas Maps 1860 & Later)

IOWA & NEBRASKA: Johnson

IOWA & WISCONSIN: Bradford; Morse & Breese

KANSAS: Company Maps; Gray; Rand, McNally & Co. (Atlas Maps); Rand, McNally & Co. (Pocket & Wall Maps); U.S. State Surveys

KANSAS & MISSOURI: Johnson

KANSAS & NEBRASKA: Johnson; U.S. State Surveys [2]

KENTUCKY: Anonymous or Unknown; Finley

KENTUCKY & TENNESSEE: Asher & Adams; Burr; Colton (Atlas Maps); Hinton; Johnson [3]; Mitchell, S.A. (Atlas Maps 1860 & Later); Morse, J. [2]

LOUISIANA: Bradford; Bradley; Carey & Lea; Carey, M.; Colton (Atlas Maps) [4]; Finley [2]; Lucas [2]; Manuscript Maps; Morse & Breese; Rand, McNally & Co. (Pocket & Wall Maps) [2]; Tanner; Thomas, Cowperthwait & Co.; U.S. [2]; U.S. Coast & Geodetic Survey [2]; U.S. Coast Survey [2]; U.S. State Surveys [7]; U.S. Union & Confederate Armies Atlas; U.S. War Department
- **NEW ORLEANS:** Bellin (Small) [2]; Bradley; Colton (Atlas Maps); Jefferys; Local & State Maps; London Magazine; Manuscript Maps [2]; Melish; Mitchell, S.A. (Atlas Maps 1860 & Later) [5]; Real Estate & Promotional Maps; Tirion; U.S.

LOUISIANA & MISSISSIPPI: Military Maps; Tanner; U.S. Coast Survey; U.S. Union & Confederate Armies Atlas; Waters & Son

MAINE: Arrowsmith & Lewis; Blunt; Bradford [2]; Burr; Carey, M.; Colby [4]; Colton (Atlas Maps); Dashiell; Des Barres [2]; Finley [2]; Johnson [2]; Mitchell, S.A. (Atlas Maps 1860 & Later) [2]; Morse, J.; Mount & Page; Payne; Sartine; Thomas, Cowperthwait & Co.; Tindal; U.S. Coast Survey [3]; Wyld

MARYLAND: Arrowsmith & Lewis; U.S. Union & Confederate Armies Atlas; [3]; U.S. War Department [2]; Universal Magazine
- **BALTIMORE:** Colton (Atlas Maps); Mitchell, S.A. (Atlas Maps 1860 & Later)

MARYLAND & VIRGINIA: Schaus; Weekly Dispatch [2]

MASSACHUSETTS: Arrowsmith & Lewis; Blunt; Bradford; Burleigh; Des Barres [2]; Finley; Manuscript Maps; Morse, J. [3]; U.S.; U.S. Coast Survey [2]; Walker, G. [2]; Walling & Gray
- **BOSTON:** Bradford; Colton (Atlas Maps); Des Barres [3]; Faden; Gazzettiere Americano; Gentleman's Magazine [2]; Harper's Weekly; Local & State Government; Marshall; Mitchell, S.A. (Atlas Maps 1860 & Later); Mount & Page; Pennsylvania Magazine [2]; Smith, George; U.S. Coast Survey [2]

MASSACHUSETTS & RHODE ISLAND: Colton (Atlas Maps) [3]; Gray; Thomas, Cowperthwait & Co.

MASSACHUSETTS, CONNECTICUT & RHODE ISLAND: Burr; Johnson; Mitchell, S.A. (Atlas Maps 1860 & Later); Smith, Roswell C.

MICHIGAN: Asher & Adams; Bradford [3]; Carey & Lea; Colton (Atlas Maps) [3]; Desilver; Rand, McNally & Co. (Atlas Maps); Tanner; Thomas, Cowperthwait & Co.

MICHIGAN & NORTHWEST TERRITORY: S.D.U.K.

MICHIGAN & WISCONSIN: Mitchell, S.A.; Mitchell, S.A. (Atlas Maps 1860 & Later) [2]

MINNESOTA: Andreas [2]; Colton (Atlas Maps) [2]; Mitchell, S.A. (Atlas Maps 1860 & Later) [2]; Thomas, Cowperthwait & Co.; U.S. War Department

MINNESOTA & WISCONSIN: U.S. State Surveys

MISSISSIPPI: Colton (Atlas Maps); Finley; Lucas; Military Maps; Tanner; U.S. Coast Survey [3]; U.S. War Department [2]

MISSISSIPPI RIVER: Frank Leslie's Illustrated Newspaper [3]; Harper's Weekly [3]; Military Maps; New York Herald; U.S. [3]; U.S. Coast Survey [2]; U.S. War Department [3]; Waters & Son; Williams, W.

MISSOURI: Asher & Adams; Colton (Atlas Maps); Desilver [2]; Finley [2]; Hinton; Mitchell, S.A. (Atlas Maps 1859 & Earlier); Rand, McNally & Co. (Pocket & Wall Maps)
- **ST. LOUIS:** Melish; U.S. War Department

MONTANA: Asher & Adams; Century Atlas; Cram [4]; Grant; Hardesty [2]; Mitchell, S.A. (Atlas Maps 1860 & Later); Rand, McNally & Co. (Atlas Maps) [3]; Rand, McNally & Co. (Pocket & Wall Maps); U.S.; U.S. State Surveys; Wilmore

NEBRASKA: Bradley; Colton (Atlas Maps); Gray [2]; Rand, McNally & Co. (Atlas Maps); U.S. War Department
NEVADA: Cram; Mining Maps; Wescoatt
NEVADA & UTAH: U.S. Pacific R.R. Survey; Vandermaelen
NEW HAMPSHIRE: Arrowsmith & Lewis; Carey, M.; Des Barres; Finley; Payne; U.S. Coast Survey; White
NEW HAMPSHIRE & VERMONT: Bradford; Cram [2]; Desilver; Morse, J.; Thomas, Cowperthwait & Co.
NEW HAMPSHIRE, VERMONT & MAINE: Smith, Roswell C.
NEW JERSEY: Beers [26]; Carey & Lea; Cowperthwait; Faden; Finley; Hopkins [3]; Johnson; Lucas; Marshall; Morse, J. [2]; Tanner [2]; Thomas, Cowperthwait & Co.; U.S. Coast Survey; Woolman & Rose
NEW JERSEY & PENNSYLVANIA: Asher & Adams
NEW MEXICO: Asher & Adams; Cram; Local & State Government; Page; Rand, McNally & Co. (Atlas Maps) [3]; U.S.; U.S. War Department [4]
NEW MEXICO & UTAH: Colton (Atlas Maps) [3]
NEW YORK: Blunt; Carey, M.; Colton (Pocket & Wall Maps); Cram; Gentleman's Magazine [2]; Homann & Homann Heirs; London Magazine; Marshall [2]; Montresor; Morse, J.; National Publishing Co.; New York State Documentary History; Sauthier; Therbu; Thomas, Cowperthwait & Co.; U.S. Coast Survey [3]
- **LAKE CHAMPLAIN:** Bellin (Small); Faden; Pennsylvania Magazine; Sayer & Bennett
- **NEW YORK CITY:** Colton (Atlas Maps); Dripps; Faden [2]; Garneray; Gray; Harper's Weekly [2]; Illustrated London News; Mitchell, S.A. (Atlas Maps 1860 & Later); Montanus; Stedman; U.S. Coast Survey; Viele
NORTH CAROLINA: Bradford; Carey, M.; Colton (Atlas Maps) [2]; Jefferys, T.; Payne; U.S. War Department [2]; Universal Magazine
NORTH CAROLINA & SOUTH CAROLINA: Bachmann; Burr; Hinton; Johnson [2]; Mitchell, S.A. (Atlas Maps 1860 & Later); Morse, J. [2]; Ramsay; S.D.U.K.
NORTH CAROLINA & VIRGINIA: Mitchell, S.A. (Atlas Maps 1860 & Later) [2]
NORTH DAKOTA: Cram
OHIO: Colton (Atlas Maps); Colton (Pocket & Wall Maps); Gray; Johnson; S.D.U.K.
- **CINCINNATI:** Colton (Atlas Maps); Mitchell, S.A. (Atlas Maps 1860 & Later)
OKLAHOMA: Arbuckle Bros.; Cram; Grant; People's Atlas; Rand, McNally & Co. (Atlas Maps); U.S.; U.S. Geological Survey; U.S. State Surveys [4]
OKLAHOMA & TEXAS: Warner & Beers
OREGON: U.S. Pacific R.R. Survey [2]; U.S. State Surveys [2]
OREGON & WASHINGTON: Colton (Atlas Maps) [3]; Johnson [4]; Mitchell, S.A. (Atlas Maps 1860 & Later) [2]; U.S. Coast Survey; U.S. War Department; Warner & Beers
OREGON TERRITORY: U.S. Exploring Expedition; U.S. War Department; Wilkes
OREGON, WASHINGTON & IDAHO: Colton (Atlas Maps); Johnson; Mitchell, S.A. (Atlas Maps 1860 & Later)
PENNSYLVANIA: Arrowsmith & Lewis; Carey & Lea; Carey, M.; Colton (Pocket & Wall Maps); Cram; Des Barres; Faden; London Magazine; Payne; Real Estate & Promotional Maps; Tanner [2]; U.S. War Department; Universal Magazine
- **PHILADELPHIA:** Colton (Atlas Maps) [2]; Faden; Gentleman's Magazine; Local & State Maps; S.D.U.K.; Tanner; Thomas, Cowperthwait & Co.
RHODE ISLAND: Carey, M. [2]; Des Barres; Faden; Finley; Marshall; Payne [2]; Sartine
SOUTH CAROLINA: Colton (Atlas Maps); Desilver; Finley; Le Rouge; Sartine; Sayer & Bennett; Universal Magazine [2]
- **CHARLESTON:** Bartram; Colton (Atlas Maps); Ensign, Bridgman & Fanning
TENNESSEE: Desilver; Finley; Military Maps; New York Herald; U.S. Union & Confederate Armies Atlas; U.S. War Department [9]
TEXAS: Asher & Adams; Bachmann; Bradford; Colton (Atlas Maps) [3]; Cram [2]; Flemming; Grant; Gray; Johnson [3]; Mitchell, S.A. [3]; Mitchell, S.A. (Atlas Maps 1859 & Earlier) [2]; Mitchell, S.A. (Atlas Maps 1860 & Later) [4]; Morse & Breese [2]; Page; Railroad Company Maps; Rand, McNally & Co. (Atlas Maps) [4]; Thomas, Cowperthwait & Co.; U.S. Coast Survey; U.S. Union & Confederate Armies Atlas [4]; Vandermaelen; Watson
TEXAS & OKLAHOMA: Vandermaelen
UTAH: Asher & Adams; Cram; Froiseth; U.S. State Surveys
VERMONT: Burleigh; Faden; Finley; Local & State Wall Maps [3]; U.S. Coast Survey; Walling [7]
VIRGINIA: Arrowsmith & Lewis; Bradford; Carey & Lea; Illustrated London News; Jansson; Johnson; Magnus, C.; Marshall; Meyer; Morse, J.; Tanner; U.S. Union & Confederate Armies Atlas [3]; U.S. War Department [10]; Weekly Dispatch

VIRGINIA & WEST VIRGINIA: Mitchell, S.A. (Atlas Maps 1860 & Later)
WASHINGTON: Asher & Adams; Cram; Rand, McNally & Co. (Atlas Maps); U.S. Coast Survey [3]; U.S. Pacific R.R. Survey; U.S. State Surveys [6]
WEST VIRGINIA: U.S. War Department
WISCONSIN: Asher & Adams [2]; Colton (Atlas Maps) [2]; Thomas, Cowperthwait & Co.
WYOMING: Cram [4]; Donaldson, T.; Railroad Company Maps; Rand, McNally & Co. (Atlas Maps) [4]; U.S. Geological Survey [2]

NORTH AMERICA: WEST INDIES

WEST INDIES (ALL): Arrowsmith; Beer; Bellin (Small) [2]; Blaeu; Burr; Carey & Lea; Cary; Colton (Atlas Maps); Coronelli; De Bry; De Laet; De Vaugondy; Depot De La Marine; Edwards; Foster; Gentleman's Magazine; Grierson; Harper & Bros.; Hildburghausen Bibliographisches Institut; Homann & Homann Heirs; Imray; Jansson; Jefferys [2]; Kitchin; Lucas; Mercator (Small) [2]; Moll (Large); Ogilby; Rapkin; Sanson (Folio); Scots Magazine; S.D.U.K. [3]; Tallis [3]; Tirion; Van Der Aa; Wyld [2]
– **(ISLANDS):** Homann & Homann Heirs; Mercator (Folio) [2]; Thomson
– **(MISCELLANEOUS):** S.D.U.K.
ANTIGUA: British Admiralty [4]; Edwards; Goad; Le Rouge; Lucas
BAHAMAS: British Admiralty; Lucas
BARBADOS: Bellin (Small) [2]; Edwards; Grierson; Le Rouge [2]; Lucas; Mount & Page; Ogilby; Speed
CARIBBEAN SEA: Blunt
CUBA: Carey & Lea; Coronelli; Gastaldi; Jefferys; Porcacchi; Ruscelli
– **HAVANA:** Des Barres; Montanus; Schenk
CUBA, BAHAMAS & FLORIDA: Grierson; Mount & Page [2]; Seller And Price
CUBA & JAMAICA: Colton (Atlas Maps) [2]; Johnson [2]; Wytfliet
DOMINICA: Edwards; Lucas
GREATER ANTILLES: Depot De La Marine; Jansson; Jefferys; Mercator (Folio); Mercator (Small); Thomson; Van Der Aa
GRENADA: Bellin (Small) [3]; Lucas
GUADELOUPE: Bellin (Small); Gazzettiere Americano; Jefferys; Le Rouge; Lucas; Mariette; Van Keulen
HISPANIOLA: Bellin (Large); Bonne; Carey & Lea; De L'Isle; De Vaugondy; Jefferys; Lucas; Mount & Page; Van Der Schley
JAMAICA: Bellin (Small); Carey & Lea; Des Barres; Grierson; Lucas; Mount & Page; Ogilby
– **KINGSTON:** Goad
LEEWARD ISLANDS: Andrews; Bellin (Small); Bordone; Carey & Lea; Lowry; Stanford; U.S. Hydrographic Office
LESSER ANTILLES: Bonne [2]; De L'Isle [2]; Direccion De Hidrografia; Gentleman's Magazine; Ottens
MARTINIQUE: Bellin (Small); Bonne; Jefferys; Le Rouge; Lucas; Tirion
NEVIS: Lucas
PUERTO RICO: Bellin (Small); Buchon; Carey & Lea [2]; Cram; Depot De La Marine; Direccion De Hidrografia; Jefferys [2]; Lucas; Montanus; Ogilby [2]; Porcacchi; Rand, McNally & Co. (Atlas Maps); Thomson; Tirion; U.S. [7]; U.S. Coast Survey [2]; U.S. War Department; Vandermaelen
ST. KITTS: Bellin (Large); Bellin (Small); Edwards; Lucas; Manuscript Maps; Moll (Small); Sanson (Folio)
ST. LUCIA: Bellin (Small); Goad
ST. VINCENT: Edwards
TOBAGO: Faden; Gentleman's Magazine; Lucas
TRINIDAD: De Bry; Faden; Lucas
TURKS & CAICOS ISLANDS: Bellin (Small)
VIRGIN ISLANDS: Andrews; Blunt; British Admiralty; Direccion De Hidrografia [3]; Goad; Jefferys, T.; Le Rouge; Van Keulen
WINDWARD ISLANDS: Carey & Lea; Van Keulen

SOUTH AMERICA

SOUTH AMERICA (ALL): Benard; Brue; Burr; Cary [2]; Chamouin; Chatelain; Colton (Atlas Maps); D'anville; De L'Isle; De Vaugondy [2]; Dufour; Finley; Jefferys; Kircher; Le Rouge; Levasseur; Lotter; Lucas; Manuscript Maps; Moll (Large) [2]; Quad [2]; Russell; S.D.U.K. [2]; Tallis; Wells; Winterbotham; Wolfe, J.
– **(ATLASES):** Vandermaelen;

- **(CENTRAL):** Colom; Malte-Brun
- **(NORTH):** De L'Isle
- **(SOUTH):** De L'Isle; Depot De La Marine; Goos; Hildburghausen Bibliographisches Institut [2]; Homann & Homann Heirs; Morden
- **(WEST):** Faden

AMAZON BASIN & RIVER: Bellin (Small); Mallet
ARGENTINA: Bellin (Small); Bougainville; Carey & Lea; Lucas
BOLIVIA: Bertius; De Herrera
BOLIVIA & PERU: Burr
BRAZIL: Bellin (Small); British Admiralty [3]; Burr; Carey & Lea; De Laet [2]; Hildburghausen Bibliographisches Institut; Laurie & Whittle [2]; Lucas; Manuscript Maps; Ogilby; Visscher
CHILE: Blaeu [2]; Burr; Carey & Lea; De Herrera; De Laet; Goad; Lucas; Mallet; Pinkerton
COLOMBIA: British Admiralty; Burr; De Laet; Jansson; Lucas; Ogilby; Van Der Aa; Wytfliet
FALKLAND ISLANDS: Bowles; British Admiralty
GUIANA: Bellin (Small); Ogilby
LA PLATA BASIN & RIVER: De Laet
MAGELLAN STRAITS & TIERRA DEL FUEGO: Bellin (Small); Bernard; De Bry; De Laet; Jansson; Morden; Ogilby; Purchas; Sanson (Small)
PARAGUAY: Bellin (Small); Ogilby
PERU: Blaeu; British Admiralty; Carey & Lea; De Herrera; Longman; Lucas; Wytfliet
- **CUZCO:** Ogilby

VENEZUELA: Bellin (Small); Blaeu; British Admiralty; De Laet; Direccion De Hidrografia; Ogilby; Van Der Aa

POLAR

ANTARCTICA: Beer; Gentleman's Magazine [2]; Hondius; Jansson; Quad; U.S. Exploring Expedition
ARCTIC REGIONS: Beer; Bellin (Small); Blaeu [2]; British Admiralty; Carey, M.; Cloppenburgh; Coronelli; De Bry; De Wit; Hondius; Jansson [2]; Mallet; Mercator (Folio); Mercator (Small); Moll (Small); Piquet; Pontanus; Purchas; Scherer; Weigel

OCEANS: ATLANTIC

ATLANTIC OCEAN (ALL): British Admiralty; Coronelli; London Magazine
- **(NORTH):** Bellin (Large); Bellin (Small) [3]; Doncker; Dudley; Magini; Ortelius (Folio); Ruscelli; Thomson; Van Der Aa
- **(NORTHERN):** Naval Chronicle
- **(SOUTH):** Depot De La Marine; Jansson

ASCENSION ISLAND: Duperrey; Van Linschoten
AZORES: Beer; Ortelius (Folio); Ortelius (Miniature); Van Keulen; Van Linschoten
BERMUDA: Blaeu; Hondius [3]; Jansson; Laurie & Whittle; Le Rouge; Mount & Page; Ogilby; Speed [3]
CAPE VERDE ISLANDS: Bertius; Laurie & Whittle
GREENLAND: Laurent; Mallet
ICELAND: Beer; Bellin (Small) [2]; Mercator (Folio); Ortelius (Miniature); Quad; Zatta
MADEIRA ISLANDS: Child
ST. HELENA: British Admiralty; Dudley; Kitchin; Van Linschoten [3]

OCEANS: INDIAN

INDIAN OCEAN (ALL): British Government; D'apres De Mannevillette; Du Val; Jansson; Laurie & Whittle; Wilson
- **(ISLANDS):** British Admiralty; Laurie & Whittle; Norie

MAURITIUS: Bellin (Large); D'apres De Mannevillette; Gregory; Valentyn
NICOBAR ISLANDS: D'apres De Mannevillette; Manuscript Maps
RED SEA: Harrison; Laurie & Whittle; Sayer & Bennett; Taylor
RODRIGUES ISLAND: D'apres De Mannevillette; Sayer & Bennett
SEYCHELLES: British Admiralty [2]; Gregory

OCEANS: PACIFIC

PACIFIC OCEAN (ALL): Bellin (Small) [2]; British Admiralty; Cook; Coronelli [3]; Depot De La Marine; Jansson [3]; La Perouse; Orr & Smith; Ortelius (Folio) [3]; Renard; Thomson; Weekly Dispatch; Wyld
- **(ISLANDS):** British Admiralty [4]; Johnston
- **(NORTH):** Bellin (Large); Bonne; Buache; Carey, M.; Cook; Diderot [6]; Henry; Jefferys; London Magazine; Lotter [2]; Morse, J. [2]; Muller [2]; Philip; Poirson [2]; Sauer; Schraembl; Thomson [2]; Von Euler [2]; Weimar Geographisches Institut; Zatta
- **(SOUTH):** De Bry; Dudley; Jefferys; La Perouse; Zatta
- **(WEST):** La Perouse [2]

BHERING STRAIT: Bonne; Cook
CAROLINE ISLANDS: Lutke
CHINA SEA: British Admiralty; Horsburgh
CHRISTMAS ISLAND: Hogg
GALAPAGOS ISLANDS: Bowen, E.
NEW ZEALAND: British Admiralty; Johnston; Philip; Royal Geographical Society; S.D.U.K. [3]; Zatta
OCEANIA: Houze; Johnston; Levasseur
PHILIPPINES: Anson; Beer; Bellin (Small) [3]; Bonne; Dalrymple; De Vaugondy; Dudley; Laurie & Whittle [2]; Morden; Probst; Valentyn; Zatta
- **(ATLASES):** U.S.

PITCAIRN ISLAND: Hogg
POLYNESIA: Djurberg [2]; Pinkerton [2]; Tallis
SOCIETY ISLANDS: Cook
TAHITI: Cook

CELESTIAL

ARMILLARY SPHERE: Mallet
ASTRONOMICAL DIAGRAMS: Aspin; De Fer (Small); Leigh
CELESTIAL CHARTS: Anonymous or Unknown; Bode [11]; Cellarius; Coronelli; De Aefferden; Doppelmayr [5]; Homann & Homann Heirs; Hondius; Lotter; Mariette; Probst; Schiller [3]; Waghenaer; Weigel; Zatta
- **(ATLASES):** Galluci

GLOBE DEPICTIONS: Coronelli

MISCELLANEOUS

ADVERTISEMENTS: Cary; Harris; Jefferys; S.D.U.K.
BIBLICAL & CLASSICAL: Ortelius (Folio); Zatta
CARTOONS: Anonymous or Unknown
MAPSELLERS' CATALOGS: Vandermaelen; Wyld
MOUNTAINS & RIVERS: Johnson
ODDITIES: Bunting [2]
PARADISE: Bowen, T.
PORTRAITS: Homann & Homann Heirs [2]; Jaillot; Ortelius (Folio)
RIVERS: Hildburghausen Bibliographisches Institut
SPHERES: Chanlaire; Mallet [2]; Wilkes
TITLE PAGES: Blaeu; Braun & Hogenberg; Covens & Mortier; De Fer (Small); Ortelius (Folio) [2]; Ottens; Rathbone; Renard; Rizzi-Zannoni; Seller; Tallis; Zatta
UNCLASSIFIED: Anonymous or Unknown; Coronelli; Lotter; Middleton; Munster [2]; Peeters

ORDERING INFORMATION

The *Price Record* and the books described on the next page may be ordered directly from Kimmel Publications. A single copy of the *Price Record* is **$40.00**, plus shipping. Libraries and non-profit institutions may deduct ten percent on *prepaid* orders only. Checks from foreign customers should be payable in U.S. Dollars and drawn on a U.S. bank. Postal money orders in U.S. Dollars are acceptable. Massachusetts residents should add 5% to the merchandise total for Sales Tax.

Price Record Quantity Discount Schedule

2 copies, 10% discount; **3 or 4 copies,** 25% discount; **5 or more copies,** 30%.

Purchasers placing a new standing order will receive a 10% discount. New subscribers should pay in advance. Thereafter an invoice will accompany each annual shipment. Payment must be made within 30 days of receipt to maintain a standing order.

Price Record Shipping Charges

	Book Post/Surface Mail		First Class/Air Mail	
	First copy	Each additional copy	First copy	Each additional copy
U.S.	$2.25	$0.75	$3.50	$2.00
Canada	3.00	1.75	5.00	3.00
Western Hemisphere	3.00	2.00	8.00	5.00
Europe	3.00	2.00	12.00	10.00
Asia, Africa & Pacific Rim	3.00	2.00	16.00	14.00

Alternative carriage may be arranged at the cost of shipping and handling, with a minimum charge of $6.00.

Available Volumes of *Antique Map Price Record & Handbook*

Volumes 1 through 10, (1983) through (1992), are all o*ut of print*

Volume 11 (1993) ISBN 0-9638100-0-6	$36.00
Volume 12 (1994) ISBN 0-9638100-1-4	$36.00
Volume 13 (1995) ISBN..0-9638100-2-2 *(Current Volume)*	$40.00

Order from: **KIMMEL PUBLICATIONS, P.O Box 12, Amherst, MA 01004, USA**
For inquiries: Telephone **(413) 256-8900**, Fax **(413) 256-6291**

Payment should accompany order. Make check payable to *Kimmel Publications*. Massachusetts residents must include 5% sales tax. Foreign customers should pay by check drawn on a U.S. bank and payable in U.S. Dollars, or by postal money order in U.S. dollars.

For the convenience of customers, payment by VISA or MasterCard for *single copies of the current edition at the list price of $40.00 each, plus tax and shipping*, may be made through Amherst Antiquarian Maps, P.O. Box 12, Amherst, MA 01004, USA; Fax (413) 256-6291.

(advertisement)

David Jolly's Carto-Bibliographies are Available
MAPS IN BRITISH PERIODICALS: *PART I* and *PART II*

Together, they are the definitive collation of maps published in British Periodicals from 1669 to 1800. These are the magazines that kept literate English society informed of global events, especially during the tumultuous Eighteenth Century.

> *Part I* describes all 1100 maps in the major monthlies, including *Gentleman's Magazine, London Magazine, Political Magazine, Scots Magazine* and *Universal Magazine.* Part II is a continuation of the first book, covering over 1100 maps from more than 50 different annuals & magazines, mostly before 1800, such as *Annual Register, British Magazine, General Magazine of Arts & Sciences, Gentleman's and London Magazine* or *Exshaw's Magazine, Grand Magazine of Magazines, Royal Magazine, Imperial Magazine, Naval Chronicle,* and many others.

A complete bibliographical description is given with each entry, including full title, dimensions, publisher's imprint, engraver's signature, and other reference works in which the map is mentioned. Entries are arranged chronologically for each periodical with the widely accepted "Jolly" reference number. Each entry is fully indexed by title, geographical region, engraver, personal name, and reference cited.

> Part I. ISBN 0-911775-51-X   1990   6 x 9 inches   1 illus.   256 pages.
> Part II. ISBN 0-911775-52-8   1991   6 x 9 inches   1 illus.   320 pages.

Part I is available only as a pair with Part II for $85.00
Part II may be purchased separately for $35.00

Carriage additional:
Book Rate postage: U.S.A. $2.50; All other countries: $4.00
First Class Mail or Airmail at cost.

MAILING LISTS AVAILABLE

Mailing lists are available from the publisher. These lists do *not* include the names of individuals who have written to order this book. Those names are treated as confidential to protect the privacy of individual customers. The lists are furnished for *one time use* on laser printed, self-adhesive labels. They are updated as soon as we receive any information suggesting additions, changes or deletions. In this regard, the list of North American dealers is more current. The U.S. entries are zip-sorted; Canada is on a separate sheet. Overseas entries are sorted by country.

> List 1. *North American Map Dealers.* About 300 U.S. and Canadian dealers. **$45**
> List 2. *Overseas Map Dealers.* About 400 dealers in the rest of the world. **$45**
> Lists 1 & 2, **World-wide Dealers.** About 700 names. **$85**

Prices include first class postage to the U.S. and Canada. Please add $5.00 for airmail elsewhere.

CUMULATIVE ERRATA

In the 1984 edition:

Cassini, *l'Amerique* ... , $2200 should read *l'America* ... , $220.
Gentleman's Magazine, *A Map of the British and French Settlements in North America* ... should have been listed under General Magazine of Arts & Sciences.

In the 1985 edition:

de Fer, *Le Detroit de Magellan* ... , $855 should be $85.

In the 1989 edition:

Ellis, *North America* should be *United States*.
The Monthly Intelligence item should appear under Grand Magazine of Magazines.

Before 1992:

London Gazette items should be listed under Gentleman's Magazine.
Monthly Chronologer & Monthly Intelligencer items should be listed under London Magazine.

In the 1993 edition:

Dealer [15] *Capt. K.S. Kapp. Catalogue XXVII* ... should be ...*Catalogue XXVIII*

In the interests of uniformity, some names have been changed.

Old Name	New Name	Date Changed			
Reilly	von Reilly	1984	Schley	van der Schley	1987
Linschoten	van Linschoten	1986	Staehlin	von Staehlin	1987
Chabert	de Chabert	1987	Stulpnagel	von Stulpnagel	1987
Charlevoix	de Charlevoix	1987	Herrera	de Herrera	1988
Condamine	de la Condamine	1987	Admiralty	British Admiralty	1994
Crevecoeur	de Crevecoeur	1987	Lewis & Arrowsmith	Arrowsmith & Lewis	1994
Freycinet	de Freycinet	1987			
Humboldt	von Humboldt	1987	Ordnance Survey	British Ordnance Survey	1994

If errors are noted in any edition, especially in prices, please contact the publisher:

Kimmel Publications, P.O. Box 12, Amherst, MA 01004, USA
Tel. (413) 256-8900   Fax. (413) 256-6291

WARNING!

Users of this work are warned that typographical errors may be present, and that prices for some items may not reflect the price that would be set by a majority of dealers. The publisher disclaims responsibility for any consequences of such errors and anomalies. Price information is given as an approximate guide to market values, and should be used with caution. An expert should always be consulted before making purchases or sales.

CURRENCY CONVERSION TABLE

These exchange rates were in effect at **mid-year 1994**, and were used in the compilation of the price listing.

Country (Unit)	Value in U.S. Dollars	Number per U.S. Dollar	Percent change since mid-1993
Argentina *(Peso)*	1.010	0.9901	0.0
Australia *(Dollar)*	0.7314	1.368	9.7
Austria *(Schilling)*	0.0894	11.18	7.1
Belgium *(Franc)*	0.0304	32.92	5.7
Canada *(Dollar)*	0.7236	1.382	- 7.0
Denmark *(Krone)*	0.1593	6.278	3.5
European Currency Unit *(ECU)*	1.206	0.8290	4.5
Finland *(Mark)*	0.1886	5.300	6.9
France *(Franc)*	0.1834	5.452	5.2
Germany *(Mark)*	0.6288	1.591	7.0
Great Britain *(Pound)*	1.540	0.6492	2.6
Greece *(Drachma)*	0.004171	239.8	- 3.4
Hong Kong *(Dollar)*	0.1294	7.729	0.0
Hungary *(Forint)*	0.00985	101.6	- 10.5
Ireland *(Punt)*	1.523	0.6568	6.3
Israel *(Shekel)*	0.3277	3.052	- 9.8
Italy *(Lira)*	0.000629	1589.6	- 2.9
Japan *(Yen)*	0.01014	98.58	9.0
Mexico *(Peso)*	0.2949	3.390	- 8.0
Netherlands *(Guilder)*	0.5578	1.793	6.0
New Zealand *(Dollar)*	0.5961	1.677	10.7
Norway *(Krone)*	0.1433	6.979	2.7
Poland *(Zloty)*	0.0000445	22456.0	- 24.6
Portugal *(Escudo)*	0.006092	164.1	- 1.2
Saudi Arabia *(Riyal)*	0.2667	3.750	0.0
Singapore *(Dollar)*	0.6567	1.524	6.6
Spain *(Peseta)*	0.007619	131.3	0.0
Sweden *(Krona)*	0.1292	7.738	0.0
Switzerland *(Franc)*	0.7499	1.334	13.4
Venezuela *(Bolivar)*	0.0054	186.0	- 51.5

Source: *New York Times*, July 2, 1994.

CATALOGUE CODES

The numbers below in square brackets correspond to the dealer codes in the main "Price Listing". See "Directory of Dealers" for a general listing of antiquarian map dealers. For an explanation of the information in parentheses, see endnotes.

Acquitania Gallery, 158 Carl Street, San Francisco, CA 94117
   [1]   Catalogue #7   (41/78; 18pp; some illustrations)

Richard B. Arkway, Inc., 59 E. 54th St., Suite 62, New York, NY 10022
   [2]   Catalog 43 - Fine Antique Maps   (81/83; 26 pp; near fully illustrated)
   [3]   Antique Maps, Atlases & Globes   (35/42; 11 pp; some illustrations, most in color)

Phyllis Y. Brown, Antique Prints, Maps & Books, 6325 Ellenwood, St Louis, MO 63105
   [4]   50 Maps of Florida   (40/54; 4 pp; no illustrations; good condition unless noted)

Camelot Books, 2403 Hillhouse Road, Baltimore, MD 21207
   [5]   Atlases - January, 1994   (15/81; 11pp; no illustrations)

Cartographics of Vermont, P.O. Box 145, East Middlebury, VT 05740
   [6]   Occasional List No. 16. Americana   (24/46; 8 pp; no illustrations)
   [7]   Occasional List No. 17. Miscellany   (25/70; 8 pp; no illustrations)
   [8]   Occasional List No. 18. Wall Maps of Vermont   (9/12; 2 pp; no illustrations)

André Dumont Maps and Books, Rare Americana, P.O. Box 10117, Santa Fe, NM 87504
   [9]   Catalogue #20 - February, 1994   (30/125; 11 pp; many maps illustrated)
   [10]   Catalogue #21; April, 1994   (26/127; 11 pp; maps near fully illustrated)
   [11]   Catalogue #22; June, 1994   (25/122; 11 pp; maps near fully illustrated)
   [12]   Catalogue #23; August 1994   (27/125; 11 pp; maps near fully illustrated)
   [13]   Catalogue #25 - November 1994   (26/125; 11 pp; maps near fully illustrated)

W.J. Faupel, 3 Halsford Lane, East Grinstead, West Sussex RH19 1NY, England
   [14]   Catalogue 106   (392/562; 32 pp; some illustrations)

Susanna Fisher, Early Sea Charts, 'Spencer', Upham, Southampton, Hampshire SO32 1JD, England
   [15]   List No. 67   (267/351+; 89pp; no illustrations; prices in sterling)

Gowrie Galleries, 316 Oxford St., Woollahra, 2025, Australia
   [16]   The Printed World; An Exhibition of Antique Maps of Australia, South East Asia & the World   (122/142; 18 pp; some illustrations, over 50% in color; prices converted from Australian dollars.) Exhibition mounted with Ely Gallery, 8A Post Office St., Pymble 2073

Murray Hudson Antiquarian Books & Maps, 109 S. Church St., P.O.Box 163, Halls, TN 38040
   [17]   February 1994 - Globes   (and Supplementary Lists - June and July 1994) (10/335 with some repetition, no post-1909 items included; 40 pp; not illustrated)
   [18]   February 1994 - Maps of Montana and Idaho   (23/42; 6 pp; not illustrated)
   [19]   February 1994 - Maps of the Northwest   (36/50; 8 pp; not illustrated)
   [20]   April 1994 - Maps of Louisiana and the Mississippi River   (90/160; 24 pp; not illustrated)
   [21]   Summer 1994 - Maps of Ireland, Scotland and/or England   (98/175; 24 pp; not illustrated)

Capt. K. S. Kapp, Antiquarian Maps, P.O. Box 64, Osprey, FL 34229
- [22] California as an Island - Summer 1994 (17/26; 3 pp; many illustrated)
- [23] Holy Land; Maps & Prints - Summer 1994 (103/110; 7 pp; some illustrations)
- [24] Ireland; Maps & Views - Summer 1994 (32/37; 3 pp; some illustrations)
- [25] Puerto Rico Maps & Views - Summer 1994 (27/34; 2 pp; some illustrations)
- [26] Select World Maps - Summer 1994 (22/22; 2 pp; some illustrations)
- [27] Virgin Islands; Maps & Prints - Summer 1994 (14/32; 3 pp; some illustrations)

D & E Lake Ltd., 239 King Street East, Toronto, Ontario M5A 1J9, Canada
- [28] Cartography No. 11 - Selection of Antique Maps (397/502; 90 pp; few illustrations; all items in very good condition unless otherwise stated, major defects noted)

Don Leeper, 3645 NW Glenridge Drive, Corvallis, OR 97330
- [29] Catalogue 11/30/94 (49/56; 5pp; no illustrations)

G.B. Manasek, Inc., P. O. Box 1204, Norwich VT, 05055-1204
- [30] Mappings, 34; Antique Map Catalogue (20/23; 12 pp; fully illustrated)
- [31] Mappings, 35; Antique Map Catalogue (24/26; 16 pp; fully illustrated)
- [32] Mappings, 36; Antique Map Catalogue (26/29; 16 pp; fully illustrated)
- [33] Mappings, 37; Antique Map Catalogue (44/49; 28 pp; fully illustrated)
- [34] Books: An addendum to Mappings 37 (2/11; 2 pp; no illustrations)

Maps of Antiquity, Lynn Vigeant, P.O. Box 569, Montclair, NJ 07042.
- [35] Catalog No. 7 (66/130; 8 pp; some illustrations; minor defects due to age may be present, significant defects are noted)
- [36] Catalog No. 8 (108/133; 21 pp; some illustrations; condition fine except as noted)

Martayan Lan, 48 East 57th Street, New York, NY 10022
- [37] Catalogue 13; Four Crucial Mapmakers (68/69; 16 pp; many illustrations, some in color)
- [38] Catalogue 14; A Special Selection Focusing on the Cartography of the Northeast (39/41; 16 pp; near fully illustrated, some in color)
- [39] Catalogue 16; Early City Views & Plans 1486-1857 (63/66; 20 pp; many illustrations, some in color)

Avril Noble, 2 Southampton St., Strand, Covent Garden, London WC2E 7HA, England
- [40] Canada (27/39; 2 pp; many illustrations; prices in sterling)
- [41] Pacific with Australia / New Zealand (23/34; 2 pp; some illustrations; prices in sterling)
- [42] Poland (10/12; 2 pp; near fully illustrated; prices in sterling)
- [43] Portugallia (11/12; 2 pp; many illustrations; prices in sterling)

The Old Map Gallery, Paul F. Mahoney, 1746 Blake Street, Denver, CO 80202
- [44] Catalogue #12, Antique Maps and Books, July 1994 (146/211; 50 pp; many illustrations)
- [45] Catalogue #13, Antique Maps and Books, October 1994 (160/269; 62 pp; many illustrations)

Old Maps and Prints, P.O. Box 2234, Forth Worth, TX 76113
- [46] Catalog 8; Winter 1994-95 (150/188; 17 pp; no illustrations; defects not normal for age are noted)

The Old Print Gallery, 1220 31st St. N.W., Washington, DC 20007. (issued in serial; all cartographic items fully illustrated; VG to fine, major faults and restorations noted)
- [47] Showcase; Vol. XXI, Number 1; April 1994 (23/98; 24 pp)
- [48] Showcase; Vol. XXI, Number 2; July 1994 (21/78; 24 pp)
- [49] Showcase; Vol. XXI, Number 3; September 1994 (17/67; 24 pp)
- [50] Showcase; Vol. XXI, Number 4; December 1994 (27/69; 24 pp)

Ridler Page Rare Maps, 205 King Street, Suite 102, Charleston, SC 29401
- [51] Summer 1994 Catalog (93/102; ii, 28 pp; some illustrations; maps good for their age with defects noted)

Jonathan Potter Ltd., 125 New Bond Street, London W1Y 9AF, England
- [52] Choice Items from Stock - 6 (117/124; 8 pp; some illustrations; prices in sterling)
- [53] Choice Items from Stock - 7 (142/148; 8 pp; few illustrations; prices in sterling)
- [54] Choice Items from Stock - 8 (105/115; 8 pp; some illustrations; prices in sterling)

George Ritzlin, Maps & Books, 469 Roger Williams Avenue, Highland Park, IL 60035
- [55] Catalog 13 (84/106; 32+ pp; some illustrations)

G. Robinson Old Prints and Maps, 124-D Bent St., Taos, NM 87571
- [56] Catalogue #58; Winter, 1993-'94; The Old '48' (62/100; 16 pp; fully illustrated; faults described)
- [57] Catalogue #59 - 1994; Small and Miniature Maps (98/100; 16 pp; fully illustrated; most excellent, flaws described)
- [58] Catalogue #61 - Fall, 1994 (86/101; 16 pp; fully illustrated)

Robert Ross & Co., P.O. Box 8362, Calabasas, CA 91372
- [59] Catalogue IX. Antique Maps, Views & Books Depicting the World. (108/171; 58 pp; some illustrations. Most matted or encapsulated)

K.A. Sheets Rare Books, P.O. Box 7024, Ann Arbor, MI 48107
- [60] List 194 - Advance copy The World Described 1703-1719 (32/32; 7pp; no illustrations; defects are noted)
- [61] List 494 - Nineteenth Century Maps of the Americas Mainly by American Commercial Cartographers (165/193; 12pp; few illustrations; very good or better unless otherwise noted; sheet size given frequently)

Thomas & Ahngsana Suarez, 181 Sherman Avenue, Hawthorne, NY 10532
- [62] A Selection of fine Maps, Atlases, and City Views 1482-1854 (131/159; 50 pp; few illustrations)
- [63] Early Maps and Views, Autumn 1994 (126/140 with addendum; 26 + 2 pp; some illustrations)

H.TH. Wenner, Buch- und Kunstantiquariat, Heger Str. 2-3, 49074 Osnabrück, Germany
- [64] Karten und Ansichten - 397 (259/1065; 50 pp.; few illustrations; dimensions sometimes from publishers information; prices converted from Deutsche Mark)

The first number after the parentheses refers to the number of items from the catalogue which are represented in the price listing. The number after the slash (/) is the total number of items in the catalogue (which may vary according to enumeration method).

Illustration quantification is as follows: *fully*, 100%; *near fully*, over 90%; *many*, more than 50% but less than 90%; *some*, more than 20% but less than 50%; *few*, less than 20%; *not illustrated*, none. In some cases only cartographic items are counted.

Where "blanket" condition statements are provided, note is made here rather than in the "Price listing".